ENCYCLOPEDIA LATINA

History, Culture, and Society In the United States

ENCYCLOPEDIA
LATINA

History, Culture, and Society in the United States

Ilan Stavans
Editor in Chief

Harold Augenbraum
Associate Editor

3

Literature, Latin American

—

Race

Grolier Academic Reference, an imprint of
Scholastic Library Publishing, Inc.
Danbury, Connecticut

Published by Grolier Academic Reference, an imprint of Scholastic Library Publishing, Inc.
Danbury, Connecticut

© 2005 by Scholastic Library Publishing, Inc.

Cover image: by Margaret García: 12 Portraits of Latinos: *Adriana, Alma Cervantes, Jose Luis Lopez, Juan Rodriguez, Marian Elena Gaitan, Bill Martinez, Saint Leo, Glenna Avila, Ernie Sanchez, Kay Reiko Torres, Elias Nahmias,* and *Cindy Ramirez.*

Library of Congress Cataloging-in-Publication Data

Encyclopedia Latina: History, Culture, and Society in the United States/Ilan Stavans, editor in chief;
p. cm.
Includes bibliographical references and indexes.
ISBN 0-7172-5815-7 (set)
1. Hispanic Americans--History--Encyclopedias.
2. Hispanic Americans--Intellectual life----Encyclopedias.
3. Hispanic Americans--Social conditions--Encyclopedias.
4. United States--Ethnic relations--Encyclopedias.
5. United States--Civilization--Hispanic influences--Encyclopedias.
6. Civilization, Hispanic--Encyclopedias.
I. Stavans, Ilan. II. Augenbraum, Harold.
E184.S75E587 2005
973'.0468'003--dc

2004023603

Printed and Manufactured in the United States of America.

1   3   5   4   2

♾ The paper used in this publication meets the minimum requirements of the American National Standard for Information Sciences—Permanence of Paper for Printed Library Materials, ANSI Z39.48-1984.

ENCYCLOPEDIA LATINA

History, Culture, and Society In the United States

L

(CONTINUED)

LITERATURE, LATIN AMERICAN

The literature of Latin America is one born and evolved out of cultural contact: the New World encountered and brought back to the Old World by some of its earliest writers, such as Fray Bartolomé de las Casas, Bernal Díaz del Castillo, and Hernando Ruiz de Alarcón. Later the *modernistas* and so-called "boom" writers massively extended this cross-pollinating legacy. Today it can safely be declared that Latin American literature has transformed the cartography of world literature. One cannot talk of writers such as Federico García Lorca, William Faulkner, Salman Rushdie, John Barth, Angela Carter, Ben Okri, Michael Ondaatje, Alejo Carpentier, Zulfikar Ghose, to name a few, without considering the mammoth impact on their work by luminaries such as Pablo Neruda, Jorge Luis Borges, Julio Cortázar, Gabriel García Márquez, and Mario Vargas Llosa.

The impact of Latin American letters on the rest of the world's writers (and readers) became apparent during the *modernismo* period (c. 1870–1920). Though not a geographically unified body of authors following a prescribed style or generic method (unlike, say, surrealism, symbolism, futurism, and so on), the writers did share a common goal and sensibility: to permanently fix Latin America on the world literary map by capturing and creatively expressing its own unique voice and worldview. In poetry, prose, and fiction, writers across Latin America—Peru's José María Eguren, Argentina's Leopoldo Lugones, Cuba's José Martí, and Mexico's Manuel Gutiérrez Nájera, for example—explored different forms for conveying a unique worldview and cultural identity. Perhaps the best known and one of the more influential *modernistas* was Nicaragua's Ruben Darío, especially after the 1888 publication of a collection of his poetry, *Azul*. The radically modern form of his experimental poetry, expressing a Latin American sensibility in opposition to a modernized and imperial North America, was a huge influence on the Spanish poet Lorca (especially in his writing of the *Poet of New York*) as well as on Darío's French avant-garde peers. That Darío traveled to Europe also helped the spread of the *modernistas*. And like Darío celebrating *mestizaje* (ethnic mixture) in his collection *Prosas profanas* (1896), so, too, did his contemporary Martí write idiosyncratic poetry and prose (for example, *Las ruinas indias*) that made visible a unique Latin American cultural sensibility.

This "regionalist" impulse was picked up by the hugely influential Cuban writer and *pensadore* (thinker) Carpentier along with the Guatemalan Miguel Angel Asturias, especially in their 1940s writings and their formulation of the storytelling form identified as *lo real maravilloso* (the truly marvelous), which conveyed a unique Latin American knowledge and subjectivity. Carpentier and Asturias influenced other writers in Latin America, including García Márquez, who later internationalized a variation of Asturias and Carpentier's term *magical realism* with Gregory Rabassa's English translation of *Cien años de soledad* (1967; *One Hundred Years of Solitude*).

During the late 1940s and especially the 1950s, the circulation of Latin American writing within Latin America and other Spanish-speaking parts of the world increased significantly. English (and French) translations of Latin American short stories, novels, and poetry were being published at a steady clip. Meanwhile, the 1947 translation of Mexican writer Agustín Yáñez's historical novel *Al filo del agua* (*The Edge of the Storm*), which dissolved historical time and fragmented narrative space, began what would become the massive internationalization of Latin American letters. This was furthered by the translations of Borges's *Ficciones* and *El Aleph* (both in 1949), which brought him (and other Latin American writers, such as Neruda, especially with his *Canto General*) to the attention of such writers as William Faulkner, Alain Robbe-Grillet, Henry Miller, and Jean Genet. There were many other very influential writers' works during this period, including the 1969 translation by Ruth Simms of *Los recuerdos del porvenir* (*Recollections of Things to Come*) by Mexican novelist Elena Garro and Irene Nicholson's translation in 1963 of Rosario Castellanos's *indiginista* novel *The Nine Guardians*.

It was the tremendous production, near instant translation, and global diffusion of the "boom" generation authors (1960–1970) that had the most impact globally. Writer Carlos Fuentes concludes of this period: "The so-called 'boom' is actually the result of a literature which has at least four hundred years of existence and which felt a definitive urgency at a moment in our history to update, modernize and put in order many lessons of the past." That many Latin American writers were consistently named for international awards such as the Nobel Prize (Neruda, García Márquez, Octavio Paz, Manuel Puig, Severo Sarduy, and Reinaldo Arenas, for example) during this time and stretching into the 1980s also helped identify Latin America as a massive literary force.

The boom authors certainly solidified Latin America's place on the world literary map. As a result, it not only continued to influence new generations of Latin American writers (Rosario Ferre, Arenas, Ricardo Piglia, Olga Orozco, Tomas Eloy Martinez, Alfredo Bryce Echenique, Antonio Skármeta) but also identified postcolonial writers from India and Africa, for example, as well as U.S. Latino writers; and many Chicano and Chicana authors turned from their arguably more proximate Anglo literary environs to engage with and reform Latin American letters with a commitment to a political and aesthetic sensibility. Pioneers of contemporary Mexican American literature—Rudolfo Anaya, Antonio Villarreal, Estella Portillo Trambley, and the poet known as Alurista, among others—textured an American Indian worldview (much like that of *modernistas* Carpentier, Alurista, and Martí, for example) as a way to give creative voice to the Chicano experience and symbolically reclaim lost territories, including the Southwest, or Aztlán.

With writer Victor Villaseñor, one sees more direct influences of Yáñez and Fuentes in his deforming of historical time in *Macho!* And Borges's writing style and aesthetic structure is redeployed in Aristeo Brito's *El Diablo en Texas* (1976), translated as *Devil in Texas* (1990) by David William Foster, and Ron Arias's borderland picaresque *The Road to Tamazunchale* (1975). García Márquez's trademark magical realism is parodically transformed by writers such as Ana Castillo in *So Far from God* (1993) and Cecile Pineda in *Love Queen of the Amazon* (1992). The experimental vision of Julio Cortázar's *Rayuela* (1963; *Hopscotch*) is given a Chicana feminist twist in Castillo's epistolary novel *The Mixquiahuala Letters* (1986) and a gay, biracial inflection with John Rechy's pastiche novel *The Sexual Outlaw* (1977).

Poet Jimmy Santiago Baca was drawn to Neruda and Paz's seemingly compatible identities as political agents and creative writers. And the first openly gay Chicano poet, Francisco X. Alarcón, found refuge in the work of gay Mexican author Elías Nandino. For novelists such as Alfredo Véa (*La Maravilla*, 1993) and Arturo Islas (*The Rain God*, 1984), Latin American writers provided not only new generic containers that could be re-formed but also a necessary road map for transforming the specifics of the Chicano cultural and social experience into larger, more universal concerns.

Latin American literature's impact has paved the way for what many today identify as a literature of the Americas: North and South, East and West, Argentine, Ottawan, Chicano, Cuban émigré, Nuyorican, Puerto Rican, and so on. Moreover, the production and influence of Latin American literature worldwide has helped refigure yesteryear's near exclusive focus on Euro-Anglo and Iberian Peninsular Spanish letters. Its influence has helped writers from around the world (postcolonial, of the Americas, and otherwise) to determine a more broadly inclusive aesthetic and to diversify the shape and direction of future literary expressions.

RELATED ARTICLES

Arenas, Reinaldo; Dorfman, Ariel; Literature, Children's; Literature, Cuban American; Literature, Dominican American; Literature, Gay and Lesbian; Literature, Latinos in Anglo-American; Literature, Mexican American; Literature, Puerto Rican on the Mainland; Literature of Exile; Martí, José; Neruda, Pablo; Paz, Octavio.

FURTHER READING

Foster, David William. *Handbook of Latin American Literature.* 2d ed. New York: Garland, 1992.

González Echevarría, Roberto, and Enrique Pupo-Walker, eds. *The Cambridge History of Latin American Literature Volume 2: The Twentieth Century.* Cambridge: Cambridge Univ. Press, 1996.

Jrade, Cathy L. *Modernismo, Modernity, and the Development of Spanish American Literature.* Austin: Univ. of Tex. Press, 1998.

FREDERICK LUIS ALDAMA

LITERATURE, LATINOS IN ANGLO-AMERICAN

This article provides a survey of Latino representation in literature by non-Latino authors. A vast swath of what is now the United States—including California, Arizona, Colorado, New Mexico, Texas, and Florida—was once controlled by Spain, and substantial numbers of Mexicans, Puerto Ricans, Cubans, Dominicans, and other Spanish-speakers have also settled elsewhere in the United States, so that by the beginning of the 21st century, Latinos were the largest minority in the nation. Yet with a few notable exceptions, figures bearing Hispanic surnames have been the invisible men and women of major American literature.

Except for ruthless Mexican soldiers slaughtering prisoners from the Alamo, Walt Whitman's all-inclusive "Song of Myself" makes no explicit reference to Latinos. Nor do Latinos figure into the demographics of William Faulkner's microcosmic Yoknapatawpha County. Even *Invisible Man* (1952), Ralph Ellison's quintessential account of an American life blighted by bigotry, is devoid of Latino characters; the Harlem that his narrator inhabits is not Spanish Harlem. Though the confrontation of Old World with New is a recurring theme for Henry James, his representative American is a Protestant of English stock encountering a Catholic European, often from France or Italy, not even Spain, too infirm an empire to be challenging to James.

But Washington Irving, the first American author to achieve international renown, was enamored of Spain. Though best known for tales of early New York, Irving, who served as minister to Madrid, published several books with Iberian settings, including *A Chronicle of the Conquest of Granada* (1829) and *The Legends of the Alhambra* (1832), but had little interest in the Spanish speakers of North America, few of whom could yet be found within the boundaries of the United States. William H. Prescott, another Hispanophile, turned to Spain and Latin America for colorful drama in *The History of the Reign of Ferdinand and Isabella the Catholic* (1838), *The History of the Conquest of Mexico* (1843), and *History of the Conquest of Peru (1847).* As a result of the 1848 Treaty of Guadalupe Hidalgo, which concluded the war with Mexico, a large Latino population suddenly found itself living within the borders of the United States and awaiting representation within its literature. Yet 19th-century literature of the United States focused on areas—New England, New York, the Midwest, and the South—without a significant Latino presence. Huckleberry Finn goes rafting with a man named Jim, not Jaime, and the letter *A* that Nathaniel Hawthorne places on wayward Hester Prynne is scarlet, not *escarlata.*

However, as Anglo-Americans discovered and inhabited the Southwest, their contacts widened. In the early records of those encounters, in journals, military memoirs, travel chronicles, and dime novels, Latinos tend to be depicted as stereotypes—the greasers, harlots, and buffoons who persisted in popular movies and television a century later. The Mexican trappers and traders whom Francis Parkman observes during his western travels in *The California and Oregon Trail* (1849) are described as brutish specimens of inferior humanity. Another persistent figure is the effete, pretentious *hidalgo,* like the Californios with whom New England traders in Richard Henry Dana's *Two Years Before the Mast* (1840) must do business. Imbued with a Protestant belief in progress and an ethic of self-assertion, authors projected onto Catholic strangers their own mistrust of sloth and fatalism. They portrayed the "Other" as a compound of cowardice, cruelty, and sensuality, a foil to Yankee reason, restraint, and pragmatism.

Idealization, like demonization, is a form of stereotyping. And when some writers romanticize Latinos of the Southwest as swarthy noble savages or urbane, light-skinned aristocrats, they, too, are denying the human complexities of their characters. Helen Hunt Jackson's popular *Ramona* (1884) offers a nostalgic evocation of Spanish California as a feudal idyll in which European gentility and indigenous peasantry live in harmony, until invaded by rapacious Yankees. In her novel *The Californians* (1898) and her story collection *The Splendid Idle Forties* (1902), Gertrude Atherton also laments the loss of elegance and grace that occurred when American intruders displaced California's Spanish culture. Both Joaquín Miller, in his poetry, and Mark Twain, in *Roughing It* (1899), extol the magnificent horsemanship of the *vaquero* (cowboy), who seems to them to possess a special splendor. Bret Harte, too, mythologizes vanished Spanish California, through Enríquez Saltillo, a courtly Castilian *caballero* (horseman) who recurs in several of the short stories he published at the end of the 19th century. Harte sometimes distinguishes between refined patricians and crude mestizos, a dichotomy that represents the polarity of Latino stereotypes.

Several authors active in the late 19th and early 20th centuries, including Twain and Ambrose Bierce, criticized their country's aggressive expansion into the Spanish Caribbean and appropriation of Cuba and Puerto Rico. Several were fascinated by Mexico as a robust alternative to the dehumanized society north of the Rio Bravo. In *Insurgent Mexico* (1914), John Reed celebrates the revolution into which Bierce disappeared. It was on his way back from Mexico that Hart Crane, frustrated by his inability to compose an ambitious sequence about Montezuma, committed suicide, in 1932, the same year that Archibald MacLeish published *Conquistador,* a dark epic about the subjugation of Mexico. In "The Mexican," a 1911 short story by Jack London, a valiant refugee named Felipe Rivera uses prizefighting to fund the revolution back home. A cult of the primitive—mocked in Katherine Anne Porter's *Flowering Judas* (1932) and *Pale Horse, Pale Rider* (1939)—drew many to visit and write about Mexico. But portraits of Mexican Americans became rare because of political tensions between underdeveloped Mexico and its powerful northern neighbor. An exception is Hamlin Garland, who, after producing the midwestern fiction on which his reputation is based, turned his attention to New Mexico, publishing stories in

which Latinos are presented sympathetically, as victims of social injustice.

Among the many characters in Frank Norris's *McTeague* (1899) is Maria Macapa, a Mexican American charwoman whose throat gets cut. Latinos are associated with violence in another Norris novel, *The Octopus* (1901), in which Mexican Americans enjoy a deadly ritual of clubbing rabbits, and Father Sarria, an otherwise gentle priest, is an aficionado of cockfights. But though best known for recounting the experiences of European immigrants on the midwestern prairie, in *O Pioneers!* (1913) and *My Antonia* (1918), Willa Cather was also able to imagine the lives of Latinos in sustained, nuanced narratives. In *The Song of the Lark* (1915) the inspiration that Thea Kronborg receives from creative Mexican friends, including Johnny Tellamantez, a lively musician, in her Colorado town estranges her from her bigoted family but also propels her toward success as an opera diva. In *Death Comes for the Archbishop* (1927), an account of how Jean Latour is dispatched from Europe to New Mexico, spending the rest of his life administering its newly created Catholic diocese, Cather offers her most fully realized Latino figures. Though Latour, an austere French intellectual, clashes in style and substance with his local clergy and parishioners, the Nuevo Mexicanos and their foreign bishop develop mutual respect and affection.

John Steinbeck grew up among Mexican Americans in Salinas, California, and, more than any other major American author, was drawn to Latino characters throughout his career. An episode in an early book, *The Pastures of Heaven* (1932), plays off the familiar whore-with-a-heart-of-gold in its depiction of sisters María and Rosa Lopez, who offer their bodies along with the enchiladas in the family restaurant outside which they have posted the sign, Spanish Cookings. The Spanish fare is even more piquant in *Tortilla Flat* (1935), set in a barrio of Monterey, California. It recounts the boisterous adventures of Danny, Pilon, and other *paisanos* (countrymen) who, though far from saintly, are holy innocents, living intensely, untainted by materialistic motives. In "The Red Pony," a novella included in the collection *The Long Valley* (1938), which dramatizes the passing of Spanish California, old Gitano shows up at Carl Tiflin's ranch contending that the land belongs to him; rebuffed, Gitano steals an aged horse and rides off to the mountains and his death. In his nonfictional *Travels with Charley* (1962), Steinbeck revisits Johnny

García's bar in Monterey and is moved by the unaffected exuberance of Pilón, Jesús María Corcoran, Joe Portagee, and other regulars. In both *The Forgotten Village* (1941) and *The Pearl* (1947), Steinbeck used Mexican—though not Mexican American—settings and characters to present morality tales.

Ernest Hemingway, who lived for extended periods in Spain and Cuba, depicted Spanish-speaking toreadors, guerrillas, and fishermen as exemplars of his ideal of grace under pressure. In "The Gambler, the Nun and the Radio," a story in *Winner Take Nothing* (1933), a card shark named Cayetano Ruiz dies with virile stoicism in a Montana hospital. But though they embody similar themes, the Spanish speakers of *The Sun Also Rises* (1926), *Death in the Afternoon* (1932), *The Fifth Column* (1938), *For Whom the Bell Tolls* (1940), and *The Old Man and the Sea* (1952) enact their dramas outside the United States.

In works as varied as Tennessee Williams's *The Night of the Iguana* (1962) and Harriet Doerr's *Stones for Ibarra* (1984) and *Consider This, Señora* (1993), Mexico continued to promise release and renewal for jaded city folk from north of the border. It is where, in Jack Kerouac's *On the Road* (1951), Sal Paradise, after a brief, ecstatic romance with Mexican American Teresa, whom he meets on a bus from Bakersfield, and after being revivified by holy madness in the barrios of Fresno, Denver, and San Antonio, goes to purge himself of materialism and puritanism. In Cormac McCarthy's Border Trilogy, which includes of *All the Pretty Horses* (1992), *The Crossing* (1994), and *Cities of the Plain* (1999), Mexico is where Spanish-speaking young Anglos go to come of age. In *The Adventures of Augie March* (1955), when Saul Bellow's title character, who has been initiated into stealing and selling books in his native Chicago by a mathematical genius named Manny Padilla, journeys to Mexico, he is fascinated by the country's cult of death.

But Norman Mailer sets *The Naked and the Dead* (1948) on the Pacific island of Anopopei, and he includes a poor Latino from San Antonio, Julio Martinez, as one of thirteen members of the motley platoon who are the protagonists of his World War II novel. Sergeant Martinez is frustrated in his hope that the army will be the meritocracy missing from civilian life. Edna Ferber sets *Giant* (1952) in Texas, in a town, run by cattle baron Jordan Benedict, where ethnic prejudice prevents war hero Angel

Obregon from receiving a proper funeral and coyote (smuggler) Fidel Gomez preys on the misery of his own people. Sympathetic accounts of Nuevo Mexicano culture include John Nichols's *The Milagro Beanfield War* (1974) and Barbara Kingsolver's *Animal Dreams* (1990). William Goyen's *In a Farther Country* (1955) tells the story of a *puertoriqueña* in New York, while in Louis Begley's *About Schmidt* (1996), a Puerto Rican waitress named Carrie is a throwback to the Latina vamp, except that in addition to seducing and fleecing the wealthy, widowed, WASP patrician Albert Schmidt, she also rejuvenates him.

Two novels that attempt to portray Latino life from the inside remain oddities in American literature. *Famous All Over Town* (1983) won a prestigious award from the American Academy and Institute of Arts and Letters for its detailed depiction of a troubled boyhood in the barrio of East Los Angeles. When it was discovered that the novel's author was not, as claimed, a street-smart newcomer named Danny Santiago but rather Daniel James, an older Anglo with experience as a social worker in the community he writes about, many felt betrayed, and questions were raised about authority and ethnic authenticity. For *Los Gusanos* (1991), a densely textured novel about Cuban exiles in Florida, John Sayles, whose screenplays for *Lone Star* (1996) and *Hombres armados* (1997) include strong Latino roles, taught himself Spanish in order to create credible dialogue for his characters. If *Los Gusanos,* with its panoply of revolutionaries and reactionaries, old and young, men and women, had been written by a Cubano, it would doubtless have been greeted with greater respect—perhaps because by the end of the 20th century, Latino authors were increasingly able to make their own voices heard. But then all fiction, regardless of the ethnicity of its authors and characters, is an attempt to imagine the experience of others.

RELATED ARTICLES

Literature; Southwestern United States, Anglo Immigration to; Stereotypes and Stereotyping.

FURTHER READING

Berg, Charles Ramírez. *Latino Images in Film: Stereotypes, Subversion, & Resistance.* Austin: Univ. of Tex. Press, 2002.
Pettit, Arthur G. *Images of the Mexican American in Fiction and Film.* College Station: Tex. A&M Univ. Press, 2002.

Portales, Marco. *Crowding Out Latinos: Mexican Americans in the Public Consciousness.* Philadelphia: Temple Univ. Press, 2000.

Robinson, Cecil. *Mexico and the Hispanic Southwest in American Literature.* Tucson: Univ. of Ariz. Press, 1977.

Rocard, Marcienne. *The Children of the Sun: Mexican-Americans in the Literature of the United States.* Tr. by Edward G. Brown, Jr. Tucson: Univ. of Ariz. Press, 1989.

Teague, David W. *The Southwest in American Literature and Art: The Rise of a Desert Aesthetic.* Tucson: Univ. of Ariz. Press, 1997.

STEVEN KELLMAN

LITERATURE, MEXICAN AMERICAN

A long and multifaceted tradition that began almost two centuries ago, Mexican American literature has gone from a peripheral collection of vignettes about life on the frontier to a full-grown self-exploration of ethnic life in the United States. Many years, however, were to pass after the Mexican War for Independence (1810–1821), and still more after the signing of the Treaty of Guadalupe Hidalgo in 1849, before the new American citizens of Mexican origin began to produce literature in English.

Origins

In the early 19th century the inhabitants of the northern provinces, owing to the neglect by Mexico's central government, had attained a high degree of self-sufficiency, and therefore the sentiment for the establishment of an independent political entity was prevalent. Some decades later, several Mexicans, among them the writer Lorenzo Zavala (1788–1836), favored the independence of Texas, an idea that, after a short war—famous for the battle at the Alamo—became a reality on March 22, 1836. Zavala was elected vice president of the newly created Texan republic.

The story of this struggle at the Alamo has been told by participant John N. Seguín in his *Personal Memoirs* (1858), covering the years 1834–1842; his autobiography is one of the early documents in the Mexican American literary tradition. Having become disillusioned with the American treatment of Mexicans, Seguín went to Mexico. However, since he had been born in San Antonio, Texas, and with his family in residence there, he finally decided to reintegrate into Texas culture. The duties of a father, he said, won over those of a citizen.

Rivalries between independent Texas and neighboring Mexican territories were frequent. This is

> ## CHICANO
>
> The locomotive roared out of the narrow stone canyon and for a few moments quickly gathered speed as the tracks dropped sharply to meet the level terrain of the valley of desert stretching ahead. The men in the cab strained their eyes and briefly, just before the tracks leveled to the valley floor, they caught a glimpse of the engine and two flatcars carrying the protective troop detachment far ahead. Then, in the valley, the shimmering heat waves cut vision to a few miles, although the tracks stretched out in an arrow-straight path for many miles.
>
> Excerpt from *Chicano* by Richard Vasquez (1970).

reflected in the play *Los tejanos,* an anonymous New Mexican folk drama—and a cornerstone in the early stages of the literary tradition—written soon after 1841, the year General Hugh McLeod tried to expand Texas territory into New Mexico but was defeated by General Manuel Armijo. Of interest in this play is the presence of an Indian, who Aurelio M. Esponosa, the discoverer of the text, said is a dramatic character worthy of the play of a master.

Although General McLeod had not been able to conquer New Mexico for Texas, not many years were to pass before Mexico, as a result of the Mexican War with the United States (1846–1848), lost not only this territory but also Arizona, California, and parts of Colorado. According to the Treaty of Guadalupe Hidalgo, Mexicans in the ceded territories could remain and become full American citizens in a year or go south to Mexico. Most of them decided to stay, thus creating an ethnic group whose writings constitute the body of what today is known as Mexican American or Chicano literature.

In the second half of the 19th century, as part of the resistance to acculturation of the native population in the area of the present-day Southwest, the use of Spanish and of Mexican popular literary forms was commonplace among Mexican Americans. Their contributions (poems, essays, and short stories) appeared in the numerous Spanish-language newspapers published throughout the southwestern United States. Two of the earliest writers fostering the tradition were Francisco P. Ramírez, who in Los Angeles edited the important newspaper *El Clamor Público* (1855–1859), in which he published his own poetry, and Padre Martínez of New Mexico, who was the author of one of the first Mexican American autobiographies.

It was not until the last decades of the 19th century that literary works written in English began to appear. María Amparo Ruíz de Burton (1832?–1895), born in Baja California, married an American officer and became an American citizen. She published two novels, *Who Would Have Thought* (1872; reprinted 1995), and *The Squatter and the Don* (1885; reprinted 1992), the first anonymously and the second under the name C. Loyal. The second novel contains an exposé of the way in which the Californios lost their lands to the American squatters.

In New Mexico, however, writers resisted integration and continued publishing in Spanish. Eusebio Chacón (1870–1948), the author of *Hijo de la tempestad* (Son of the Storm) and *Tras la tormenta la calma* (Calm after the Storm), both published in 1892, claimed to be the first to write original novels in the territory. Manuel C. de Baca, with the novel *Vicente Silva y sus cuarenta bandidos* (1896; Vicente Silva and His Forty Thieves), was the first to treat the theme of the *bandidos,* although a translation of John R. Ridge's *The Life and Adventures of Joaquín Murrieta, the Celebrated California Bandit* (1854) had appeared in 1881 in the *Gaceta* newspaper of Santa Barbara, California. It was also during this period that Manuel M. Salazar (1854–1900) and Felipe Maximiliano Chacón (born 1873) gave expression, in prose and poetry, to the problems of the Nuevomexicanos (New Mexicans). There was also a large amount of popular literature, such as *corridos* (ballads), *pastorelas,* (pastoral plays), romances, and *décimas* (verses with ten octosyllabic lines).

The dilemmas facing Mexican American authors at the time centered on provincial life. The ethnic community had yet to acquire a sense of self-definition. Its entertainment came from border ballads, epic stories of conquest, and nativity plays. The colonialism under which Spanish-language people lived in the Southwest was ignored by Mexico. In fact, Mexican literature still nurtured the northern communities through pamphlets, traveling theater, and so on.

The transition to English came at a price. As the Mexican American community began to assimilate into Anglo culture, not only the language of communication changed but also the parameters of the ethnic culture. By writing in English, Mexican American authors attracted an audience that was no longer exclusively Mexican. Anglo readers became interested, and thus the attempt to re-create for them the inner and outer lives of Mexican Americans became a priority.

From the Early 20th Century to World War II

Mexican American literature in English was brought to New York City by María Cristina Chambers (née Mena, 1892–1965), who in 1913 began publishing short stories in *The Century Illustrated Monthly Magazine, The American Magazine,* and *Cosmopolitan.* Her audience was predominantly non-Mexican. Most of the stories and the five novels she published later are set in Mexico and deal with Mexican subject matter, for the purpose of acquainting the young English-speaking reader with Mexico's culture. Two of her most successful novels were *The Water-Carrier's Secrets* (1942) and *The Bullfighter's Son* (1944).

By the end of the 19th century, the Spanish language in the Southwest, and Mexican culture in general, suffered a decline, but they did not disappear—events during the first two decades of the 20th century changing the course of history. The Mexican Revolution of 1910–1920, the agricultural and industrial expansion of the Southwest, and World War I resulted in a massive emigration from Mexico, which brought not only the needed farmhands and industrial workers but also new blood to the Mexican community and a revitalization of the culture of the barrios (Mexican neighborhoods). This period was dominated by a group of expatriate writers called El México de Afuera (the Mexico Outside), who established important newspapers in which they published poems, stories, and novels in Spanish. These exiled writers (Ignacio Lozano, Ricardo Flores Magón, José Vasconcelos, Martín Luis Guzmán, Jorge Ulica [Julio G. Arce], and Daniel Venegas) gave impetus to the rebirth of the Spanish language. Some of their works, such as Ulica's *Crónicas diabólicas* (1916–1918) and Venegas's novel *Las aventuras de Don Chipote* (1928; The Adventures of Don Chipote), have recently been recovered. This group of writers left permanent imprints, with some of their newspapers, such as *La Opinión* of Los Angeles, still being published.

The period in the history of the Mexican Americans that begins in the early thirties with the Great Depression—when thousands of Mexicans were deported—is characterized by the preference for English of writers born in the United States and well integrated into mainstream American society. Typical of this trend are the works of Fray Angélico Chávez of New Mexico (1910–1996), author of several volumes of poetry and short stories and a historical novel, *Our Lady of Our Conquest* (1949), in which the narrator is the Virgin herself. Characteristic of his writings are religious imagery, magical realism, and an interest in New Mexico's colonial history.

Josephina Niggli (1911–1945), born in Mexico and educated in the United States, followed in the steps of Chambers (Mena), having published the collection of poems *Mexican Silhouettes* in 1931, *Mexican Folk Plays* in 1938, and novels *Mexican Village* (1945) and *Step Down, Big Brother* (1948 [published posthumously]), all of them dealing with Mexican subject matter.

During the 1940s Mario Suárez of Tucson, Arizona, published several short stories in the *Arizona Quarterly,* in which he portrays the people of the Tucson barrios. Having a keen understanding of the psychology of the Chicano and Mexicano peoples, he was able to create such memorable characters as Señor Garza (1947), a barber whose personality is revealed through his conversations with the barrio people who visit his shop. Suárez was the first to use the word Chicano in a literary work, the short story *El Hoyo* (1947), and the first to write a story in which a *pachuco* (a member of a group of young Chicano rebels) is the protagonist (*Kid Zopilote,* 1947).

During the decade of the 1950s, authors continued the trend established in the 1940s of using English in the writing of creative literature and interpretative studies of the Chicano experience. Two works stand out during this period, Américo Paredes's seminal study *With His Pistol in His Hand* (1958) and José Antonio Villarreal's novel *Pocho* (1959). Paredes reconstructed the legends that the people of the border have created about Gregorio Cortez, the folk hero of the lower Rio Grande. Villarreal's novel, often considered to be the first modern Chicano novel, is characterized by the nature of the young hero, Richard, who finds himself torn between two cultures—that of his father, a Mexican revolutionary who finds refuge in the United States after the defeat of the Villistas (the followers of Francisco "Pancho" Villa), and that of his American friends. In view of his decision at the end of the novel to join the marines, it is assumed that he has resolved his problem of identity by opting for American culture.

Chicano Literature

During the middle 1960s, as a result of the black civil rights movement, student protests, efforts on the part of César Chávez to organize the *campesinos* (farmworkers), and other causes, Chicanos for the first time in their history were able to unite under the banner of La Causa, a powerful nationalistic movement (also called El Movimiento) that affected all social classes in all regions of the nation. As a result of this new social consciousness, a new type of literature emerged, animated by a rebellious spirit. Characteristic of this writing was the search for native roots in the Indian past of Mexico, as well as the use of both English and Spanish in the same work and employment of a discourse directed to the Chicano population. Representative of the period are the works of Luis Valdez, the founder of the Teatro Campesino (Farmworkers Theatre) and author of the collection of one-act plays *Actos* (1971). These plays were presented out in the open fields where the *campesinos* worked, oftentimes in the midst of a *huelga* (strike). His topics were first inspired by the problems faced by the farmworkers; later he began to make use of historical subject matter, such as the conquest of Mexico by the Spaniards, to show the farmworkers the necessity to organize in order to act as a united front. Two of his most successful *actos* were *Los vendidos* (1967; The Sellouts) and *Soldado razo* [*sic*] (1971; Private), both designed to arouse the social consciousness of the audience, since they deal with topics of great interest to the people in the barrio.

From the *acto* Valdez went on to create the *mito,* a play in which mythical elements—taken mostly from Aztec and Mayan sources—are essential to the development of the plot. One of his best-known *mitos* is *La gran carpa de los Rasquachis* (1973; The Great Tent of the Rasquachis Family), dealing with the life of Jesús Pelado Rasquachi, a Mexican national who has brought his family to the United States in search of the promised land only to find discrimination and misery. With his play and film *Zoot Suit* (1978), Valdez was able to attract national attention.

In 1969 El Teatro Campesino filmed, with great success, Rodolfo "Corky" Gonzáles's *I Am Joaquín* (1967), an epic poem about the complex identity of the Chicano, which the author traces back to the conquest of Mexico, and even before. Joaquín, the hero of the poem, became a symbol of the Chicano, for he identifies himself with the last Aztec emperor and the Spanish conqueror, as well as with Mexican and Chicano popular heroes: Juárez, Villa, Zapata, Murrieta.

The influence of El Teatro Campesino is present in most of the works published during the late 1960s and the 1970s. Among the poetic compositions, Sergio Elizondós's *Perros y antiperos,* published in 1972 with an English translation by Gustavo Segade, closely follows Gonzáles's poem in its structure, tone, and social philosophy.

According to the Nahuatl myth, the Aztecs (whose name is derived from Aztlán) were the last remaining tribe of seven, and they were advised by their god Huitzilopochtli to leave Aztlán in search of the promised land, which they would know by an eagle sitting on a cactus devouring a serpent. They found it, and there they built Tenochtitlán, today Mexico City. Later the Aztecs remembered the region of their origin as an earthly paradise. With few exceptions the topic of mythical Aztlán was forgotten until the 1960s, when the rebirth of the myth flourished in Chicano thought. The cultural nationalists—one of the most important branches of the Chicano movement—appropriated the term to establish the indigenous nature of their culture, a characteristic central to their philosophy. The adoption of the myth took place during the Crusade for Justice Youth Conference, held in Denver in March 1969. It was there that for the first time the myth of Aztlán was mentioned in a Chicano document, *El Plan Espiritual de Aztlán.*

El Plan, which owes its creation to the poet Alurista (Alberto Urista), became the cultural nationalists' manifesto. First, it establishes the unique nature of Chicano culture, since La Raza (the bronze race) has an Aztec origin. Second, it identifies Aztlán as the Mexican territory ceded to the United States in 1848. Third, following one of the basic ideas of the Mexican Revolution, it recognizes that the land belongs to those who work it; and finally, it identifies the Chicano nation with Aztlán.

Aztlán became the symbol most used by Chicano and Chicana activists as well as by authors writing about the history, culture, or destiny of their people. During spring 1970 the first number of the journal *Aztlán* (still in existence) was published, and in it the Plan was reproduced in both English and Spanish. The prologue consists of a piece by Alurista, "Poem in Lieu of Preface," in which he unites the mythical Aztec past with the present.

It was during the 1970s also that Chicanos introduced a style of writing in which both English and Spanish are used in the same sentence, a literary technique that became one of the distinguishing features of their literature. Representative of this trend are the books *Florycanto en Aztlán* (1971; Flower and Song in Aztlán), *Nationchild Plumaroja* (1972; Nationchild Redfeather), and *Timespace Huracán* (1976) by Alurista; *Canto y grito mi liberación* (1971; I Sing and Shout about My Liberation) and *Hechizospells* (1976; Witchcraft Spells) by Ricardo Sánchez; *Restless Serpents* (1976) by Bernice Zamora; *Rebozos of Love . . .* (1974) by Juan Felipe Herrera; *Crazy Gypsy* (1970) by Luis Omar Salinas; *Arise, Chicano* (1975) and *Chicano Poems for the Barrio* (1975) by Angela de Hoyos; and *Hay otra voz* (1972; There Is Another Voice) by Tino Villanueva.

Also influenced by the ideology of the Chicano movement is the poetry of José Montoya, collected under the title *El sol y los de abajo* (1972; The Sun and the Underdogs), and *In Formation* (1992). His famous poem *El Louie* is the elegy of a pachuco, a member of the important group of young Chicano rebels whose psychology and social meaning in American life were first analyzed by Octavio Paz in his essay *The Pachuco and Other Extremes,* which originally appeared in 1950 in his book *The Labyrinth of Solitude.*

In 1970 a Berkeley, California, publishing house established the Premio Quinto Sol, an award that led to the discovery of four important writers. Tomás Rivera (1935–1984) was awarded the first prize that year for his novel *. . . y no se lo tragó la tierra/ . . . and the Earth Did Not Part* (1971). In a sequence of 12 episodes, preceded by a short prose introduction, "The Lost Year," and followed by a final chapter, "Under the House," the novel depicts life among migrant Chicano and Mexicano workers from Texas, as interpreted by a young boy who tells the story in the first person. *Tierra* has been praised for its innovative narrative technique, for its terse style, and for the true-to-life descriptions of the hardships and tribulations of the migrant workers.

The second Premio Quinto Sol (1972) was awarded to Rudolfo Anaya for *Bless Me, Ultima* (1972), a novel written in English and dealing with life in rural New Mexico. In its tone *Ultima* is not too far removed from the magical realism of such Latin American writers as Juan Rulfo, Gabriel Gárcia Márquez, and Isabel Allende. Other fictional work by Anaya includes the collection of short stories *The Silence of the Llano* (1982).

The third winner of the Premio, Rolando Hinojosa-Smith, is the author of *Klail City Death Trip,* a series of novels depicting the daily life and adventures of people living in fictitious Belken County, supposedly located in the lower Rio Grande Valley area. The first of these novels, *Estampas del valle y otras obras* (Sketches of the Valley and Other Works), winner of the 1973 Premio, was published the following year in a bilingual edition. The second one, *Klail City y sus alrededores* (Klail City and Its Surroundings), was the recipient of Cuba's Premio Casa de las Américas in 1976. Hinojosa-Smith, a Chicano writer, has been able to create in fictional settings a most complete panorama of the life and culture of the Chicano people living along the U.S.- Mexico border.

Estela Portillo Trambley was awarded the fourth and last Premio Quinto Sol for her book *Rain of Scorpions and Other Writings* (1975), a collection of stories considered to be the first major contribution by a Chicana to contemporary literature. The author was already well known for her play *The Day of the Swallows* (1971).

The novels *Peregrinos de Aztlán* (1974; Pilgrims from Aztlán) by Miguel Méndez M. and *El Diablo en Texas* (1976; tr. in 1989 as *The Devil in Texas*) by Aristeo Brito can be classified as border novels, since the events depicted in them take place along the frontier between Mexico and the United States. Méndez's book deals with the destiny of the Yaqui people, who were driven from their homeland in northern Mexico and forced to lead a pariahlike life in the border cities or work like peons in the cotton fields of Arizona and California. Brito's novel also deals with the social and political forces that make life in a border town, Presidio, Texas, unbearable for people of Mexican origin.

The subject of Alejandro Morales's *Caras viejas y vino nuevo* (1975; tr. in 1981 as *Old Faces and New Wine*) is the way of life led by Chicanos living in East Los Angeles, an area of the city that has become a metaphor for life in a barrio. Morales describes in high relief those problems that confront young Chicanos living there and the consequences that result from their inability to cope with the environment.

In his only novel, *The Road to Tamazunchale* (1975), Ron Arias presents the action from the perspective of a quixotic character, Don Fausto Tejeda, who, in order to escape death from old age, undertakes a most extraordinary journey through the city of Los Angeles in the company of several bizarre characters. The protagonist also dedicates some of his time to the task of helping undocumented workers cross the border.

The End of the 20th Century

During the late 1970s and early 1980s, Chicano literature underwent a rapid transformation. Its focus went from predominantly realistic descriptions of the daily life experiences of people in the fields or urban centers and the use of nationalistic symbols drawn from the Indian cultures of Mexico, or the revolutionary struggle of 1910–1920, to the appearance of more universal topics, such as gender conflicts, problems of identity, alternative ways of life, and especially

---

LOOKING FOR WORK

One July, while killing ants on the kitchen sink with a rolled newspaper, I had a nine-year-old's vision of wealth that would save us from ourselves. For weeks I had drunk Kool-Aid and watched morning reruns of *Father Knows Best,* whose family was so uncomplicated in its routine that I very much wanted to imitate it. The first step was to get my brother and sister to wear shoes at dinner.

"Come on, Rick—come on, Deb," I whined. But Rick mimicked me and the same day that I asked him to wear shoes he came to the dinner table in only his swim trunks. My mother didn't notice, nor did my sister, as we sat to eat our beans and tortillas in the stifling heat of our kitchen. We all gleamed like cellophane, wiping the sweat from our brows with the backs of our hands as we talked about the day.

Excerpt from "Looking for Work" in *Living Up the Street* by Gary Soto (1985).

the emphasis given to the personal problems of urban Chicanos. No less important is the fact that writers in the 1980s, with few exceptions, gave almost exclusive preference to English rather than Spanish as the language in which they could best express themselves and, at the same time, reach the mainstream reader. Not that it was a choice—many of them, from Richard Rodriguez to Sandra Cisneros, were no longer fluent in their ancestral tongue.

The above transformation can best be observed in the poetry of Gary Soto, the author of the prizewinning *The Elements of San Joaquín* (1977) and several other collections. In these poems the strident protest tone of some of the earlier poets has given way to the desire to express other human emotions. In addition, the prose of Richard Rodriguez, whose autobiography, *Hunger of Memory* (1982), written in a polished English style, introduced topics and attitudes not found in previous Chicano writers. His criticism of the social and political issues defended by most Chicano writers—bilingual education, affirmative action, the use of the Spanish language in public, and so on—initiated a controversy that lasted for several years. He opposed bilingual education and affirmative action, which are sensitive issues in the Mexican American community. In that first book he also hinted at a gay identity, a subject he later developed in *Days of Obligation* (1992). And the issue of race became the topic of his third book, *Brown* (2002).

It was during this period, as well, that women writers, for the first time in large numbers, began to contribute extensively to the fields of poetry and fiction. For the first time also, literary works were being produced by Chicano writers living outside the Southwest, principally in the Midwest, in, for example, Chicago, among other large urban communities.

In poetry as in nonfiction the author's identity struggle became a sine qua non. Writers used their own circumstances to explore relevant topics such as religion, race, and sexuality. The autobiography of Luis J. Rodriguez, *Always Running* (1993), about gang life in Los Angeles, took a reverse approach to that of Richard Rodriguez; it made the Mexican ghetto, with its domestic abuse and street violence, a topic of conversation for Latinos and Anglos alike. But it was through fiction that Mexican American literature achieved most of its visibility. The novels of Gina Valdez (*There Are No Madmen Here,* 1981),

Laurence Gonzales (*El vago,* 1983; The Vagrant), Sandra Cisneros (*The House on Mango Street,* 1983), Arturo Islas (*The Rain God,* 1984), Margarita Cota-Cárdenas (*Puppet,* 1985), Ana Castillo (*The Mixquiahuala Letters,* 1986), Cecilia Pineda (*Face,* 1986), and Denise Chávez (*The Last of the Menu Girls,* 1987) reveal a rich variety of subjects and themes. These novels introduce not only a new vision of Chicano society but also innovative structures. The diverse approaches to reality and treatment of materials found in them have given Chicano fiction a new dimension, a fact that has not passed unobserved by critics and the reading public.

With few exceptions the trends that appeared during the previous decade continued. Contributors to fiction writing are Arturo Islas with *Migrant Souls* (1990; a sequel to *The Rain God,* 1984), and Luis Alberto Urrea with *In Search of Snow* (1994). However, works by women predominate: *Spirits of the Ordinary* (1997) by Kathleen Alcalá, *Face of an Angel* (1994) by Denise Chávez, *The Days of the Moon* (1999) by Graciela Limón, *Mother Tongue* (1994) by Demetria Martínez, and *Under the Feet of Jesus* (1994) by Helena María Viramontes are some of the most important. Lucha Corpi, who began writing poetry in Spanish, changed to writing detective stories in English (*Delia's Song,* 1989; *Cactus Blood,* 1995). Norma Cantú with *Canícula* (1995) and Alicia Gaspar de Alba with *The Mystery of Survival and Other Stories* (1992) contributed to Chicano short fiction. A new trend in poetry in which Indian motifs reappear was initiated during the decade of the 1990s by Alfred Arteaga with his *Cantos* (1991), and with Francisco X. Alarcón's *Snake Poems* (1992) continuing this theme.

The New Millennium

In the early years of the new century, there were no outstanding changes in the trends that appeared during the 1990s. Works that have contributed to the enrichment of Chicana and Chicano literature are the novels of Sandra Cisneros (*Caramelo,* 2002) and Denise Chávez (*Loving Pedro Infante,* 2002), both dealing with relations between Mexican and Chicano life and culture; Alma Luz Villanueva's *Luna's California Poppie* (2002), concerning the harsh life of a young girl whose story is told in the form of a diary; the short stories of Dagoberto Gilb (*Woodcuts of Women,* 2001); and Ron Arias's *Moving Target: A Memoir of Pursuit* (2002). The poet Jimmy Santiago

Baca enriched the field of autobiography with his own, *A Place to Stand* (2001).

But the arrival of the new millennium also ushered in more diverse themes. Sergio Troncoso's *The Nature of Blood* (2003) deals with Chicanos and the Nazi Holocaust. There was also a return to the farmworker novel with Rigoberto González's *Crossing Vines* (2003). And Manuel Muñoz's *Zigzagger* (2003), mixing gay topics and the life of Mexican Americans in California's Central Valley, was hailed as a promising debut. Further, the genre of autobiography acquired a more cosmopolitan taste. John Philip Santos's *Places Left Unfinished at the Time of Creation* (1999) dealt with San Antonio from a transgenerational perspective. And Ilan Stavans's *On Borrowed Words* (2001) explored language as a ticket to identity and centered on Jewish Latino life north and south of the Rio Grande. These volumes brought the Mexican American literary tradition even nearer to the mainstream.

Observations

As Latino literature is increasingly recognized as the agglomeration of the literatures of various ethnic subgroups all tied under a single rubric, Mexican American authors have seen the need to respond to new artistic and marketing choices. For one thing, a new direction has developed: the publication by mainstream editorial houses of books in simultaneous editions in both English and Spanish. Obviously, the audience of these editions is not limited to Mexican American readers; Cuban Americans, Dominican Americans, Puerto Ricans on the mainland, and others are now, for the first time, fully engaged in reading one another. Moreover, non-Latinos make up a major portion—maybe even the majority—of the readership of this literature. This means that topics considered of interest only to Mexican Americans are displaced in favor of more universal, or at least pan-Latino, material. Conversely, Mexican American authors have responded to this widening of interest in their literature by stressing the particular in order to become more universal. They emphasize what makes them distinct in the larger context of Latino literature.

Smaller publishers such as Arte Público Press and Bilingual Press continue to publish material deemed less appealing to a mainstream audience. And university presses—among them, Ohio, Northwestern, and Wisconsin—have launched literary series focusing on Latino motifs. Many of the books they release are by Mexican Americans. There is also a growth of subgenres within the tradition: Mexican American mystery and science fiction, for instance. Denver attorney Manuel Ramos, with his fictional detective Luis Montez, is one of the scores of practitioners in these areas.

Interestingly, one area not developed yet in the Mexican American literary tradition is biography. The work of luminaries, including politicians, militants, and intellectuals, is the subject of academic studies, but not of full-size biographies. Why this wing of the tradition has not caught up with the rest is open to speculation.

RELATED ARTICLES

Acosta, Oscar; Anaya, Rudolfo; Anzaldúa, Gloria; Aztlán; Chacon Family; Cisneros, Sandra; Gonzales, Rodolfo; Hinojosa-Smith, Rolando; Jaramillo, Cleofas; Leal, Luis; Literature; Mexican Americans; Paz, Octavio; Rivera, Tomás; Rodríguez, Richard; Ruíz de Burton, María Amparo; Valdez, Luis; Villarreal, José Antonio.

FURTHER READING

Baker, Houston A., Jr. *Three American Literatures*. New York: Modern Language Assn. of Am., 1982 [contains the articles "Chicano Literature: An Overview" by Luis Leal and Pepe Barrón and "The Evolution of Chicano Literature" by Raymund Paredes].

Bruce-Novoa, John. *Chicano Authors: Inquiry by Interview*. Austin: Univ. of Tex. Press, 1980.

Bruce-Novoa, John. *Chicano Poetry: A Response to Chaos*. Austin: Univ. of Tex. Press, 1982.

Egger, Ernestina N. *A Bibliography of Criticism of Contemporary Chicano Literature*. Berkeley: Univ. of Calif., Chicano Studies Lib. Pubn., 1980.

Empringham, Toni, ed. *Fiesta in Aztlán: An Anthology of Chicano Poetry*. Santa Barbara, Calif.: Capra Press, 1982.

Gonzales-Berry, Erlinda, and Chuck Tatum, eds. *Recovering the U.S. Hispanic Literary Heritage*. Vol. 2. Houston, Tex.: Arte Público Press, 1996.

Hernández, Guillermo. *Chicano Satire: A Study in Literary Culture*. Austin: Univ. of Tex. Press, 1991.

Herrera-Sobek, María. *Beyond Stereotypes: A Critical Analysis of Chicano Literature*. Binghamton, N.Y.: Bilingual Press/Editorial Bilingüe, 1985.

Kanellos, Nicolás, ed. *Mexican-American Theater: Then and Now*. Houston: Arte Público Press, 1983.

Leal, Luis. *No Longer Voiceless*. San Diego, Calif.: Marín Publications, 1995.

Lomelí, Francisco A., and Carl R. Shirley, eds. *Dictionary of Literary Biography: Chicano Writers*. Detroit: Bruccoli Clark Layman, 1999 [bibliography by Donaldo W. Urioste].

Padilla, Genaro. *My History, Not Yours: The Formation of Mexican-American Autobiography*. Madison: Univ. of Wis. Press, 1993.

Tatum, Charles M. *Chicano Literature*. Boston: Twayne, 1982.

LUIS LEAL

LITERATURE, PUERTO RICAN ON THE MAINLAND

Puerto Rican literature written on the United States mainland can be divided into five periods, each representing a particular sociohistorical context. These loosely chronological groupings of literary trends are late-19th-century political exile, early-20th-century immigrant, post–World War II immigrant, Nuyorican and civil rights era, and contemporary diaspoRican or AmeRícan literature. Historical events have done much to shape the contours of this rich literary tradition. However, it would be reductive to impose a rigidly chronological development. Consequently, the five categories outlined here are not intended as a definitive schema but, rather, as a tool for highlighting significant trends and concerns addressed in U.S. Puerto Rican poetry, plays, essays, novels, and other works of both fiction and nonfiction.

When necessary, the following discussion will address the extent to which elements of continuity and transition as well as rupture mark the relationships among the five periods. Within the framework of an introduction to the key writers and major texts in the specific context of Puerto Rican mainland literature, each section briefly situates this tradition within the broader context of Puerto Rican literature and its particular significance in the United States, as well.

19th-Century Political Exiles

Although the major periods of Puerto Rican immigration to the United States occurred after the U.S. annexation of the island in 1898, relations between Puerto Rico and the United States began much earlier. Predominantly commercial relations were maintained in the 18th and the early 19th century, but Puerto Rican struggles to gain independence from Spain amplified politically motivated relations in the latter 19th century. Consequently, migration to the United States increased significantly following the Puerto Rican declaration of war against Spain, known as the Grito de Lares, on September 23, 1868. Cuban independence fighters also began to assemble in New York City and worked closely with Puerto Rican exiles during this period.

While Cuban writer José María Heredia's famous poem *Oda al Niágara* (Ode to Niagara) as well as other reflections on his 1823–1825 stay in the United States represented in *Cartas sobre los Estados Unidos* (1826; Letters on the United States) are noteworthy precursors to later Puerto Rican and other U.S.-based Latino Caribbean literary production, the first cohesive group of Puerto Rican writers in the United States consisted of late-19th-century political exiles. Foremost among these elite proindependence intellectuals living in exile were Eugenio María de Hostos, Ramón Emeterio Betances, Francisco Gonzalo "Pachín" Marín, Soto Figueroa, and Lola Rodriguez de Tió.

These writers, having temporarily left the island for New York City to promote the efforts for independence from Spain, focused most of their attention on the political struggles of the island community rather than those of the mainland community and worked closely with Cuban political exiles such as José Martí. Although these writers did not remain in New York, they did produce written accounts of their experiences in the United States. While working toward goals of political reform, Caribbean unity, and social justice, the writers were particularly prolific in the essayistic and poetic genres, as evidenced by the numerous newspaper articles, personal journals, and letters they wrote during their brief time in the United States. An example of these accounts is Marín's *Nueva York por dentro: Una faz de su vida bohemia* (1892; Inside New York: A Side of its Bohemian Life).

Early 20th Century

During the Spanish-American War in 1898, the United States Army's occupation of Puerto Rico resulted in the ceding of the island from Spain to the United States in 1899. The passage of Puerto Rico from Spanish to U.S. political control set the stage for the first large-scale immigration of Puerto Ricans to the mainland. Subsequently, in 1917 the Jones Act, the act of Congress that both granted and imposed U.S. citizenship on Puerto Ricans, facilitated the continued growth of Puerto Rican immigrant communities on the mainland. In contrast to the elite, patriotic orientation of the late-19th-century political exiles, these early-20th-century immigrants belonged primarily to the working class. The literature of this period is mostly autobiographical and journalistic.

The two best-known chroniclers of this period are Jesús Colón and Bernardo Vega. Colón, a black Puerto Rican who came to New York at the age of 16, is the author of a collection of autobiographical essays entitled *A Puerto Rican in New York and Other Sketches* (1961). Describing the racial and cultural discrimination he was confronted with in New York, he also wrote about his dedication to socialism and the interests of the working class. The author of *Memorias de Bernardo Vega* (1977; Memoirs of Bernardo Vega, 1984), Vega in the 1940s wrote this chronicle of his life in New York, beginning with his arrival in 1916 at the age of 30. The memoirs were edited and published by Puerto Rican novelist, journalist, and playwright César Andreu Iglesias (1915–1976). A tobacco worker and newspaperman, Vega, like Colón, emphasized the importance of socialism in the struggle for Puerto Rican independence.

Another important, though less well-known, figure of this period is the working-class activist and writer Luisa Capetillo (1879–1922). In 1912 Capetillo came to the United States, where she wrote the majority of her fourth and final published volume *Influencias de las ideas modernas* (1916; "Influences of Modern Ideas"). As an anarcho-feminist, she wrote fiction and nonfiction that analyzed the oppression of women and transgressed generic borders. Pura Teresa Belpré (1902–1982), a children's librarian for the New York Public Library System, also is a lesser-known figure whose essays and stories emphasized the value of Caribbean folklore, cultural history, and oral traditions. Her first book, the animal fable *Perez and Martina* (1932), includes bilingual passages and was followed by the publication of many other stories and essays promoting bilingual and bicultural education.

Arturo Alfonso Schomburg (1874–1938), another librarian, immigrated to New York City and settled in Brooklyn, where he became a prominent essayist and archivist on the African diaspora in the Americas. He was also a cofounder of the Negro Society for Historical Research, established in 1911. Schomburg's collection of literature and art was the first major archive of inter-American Africana. Donated to the New York Public Library in 1926, his collection now belongs to the Schomburg Center for Research in Black Culture, which is located in Harlem and is currently the largest archive of documents

on the African diaspora. Although he is more often associated with the Harlem Renaissance than with the Puerto Rican community, Schomburg publicly asserted his Puerto Rican heritage and had an explicitly transnational and multilingual approach to studying the African diaspora.

William Carlos Williams (1888–1963) is also a writer who is not always discussed in the context of U.S. Puerto Rican literature. Williams, who was a modernist poet primarily associated with the mainstream U.S. literary canon, has recently been reclaimed by scholars such as Julio Marzán, author of *The Spanish American Roots of William Carlos Williams* (1994), as a writer of the Puerto Rican diaspora on the U.S. mainland. While Williams was born in the United States, his mother was born into a middle-class family in Puerto Rico and his father was raised primarily in the Dominican Republic. The poet wrote about his family history and bicultural upbringing in his *Autobiography* (1951) and *Yes, Mrs. Williams* (1959).

Post World War II: 1945–1965

The post–World War II period saw the reformulation of the relationship between the United States and Puerto Rico with the rise to power of the Puerto Rican Popular Democratic party founded by Luis Muñoz Marin. Along with the island's redefinition as a commonwealth, or Estado Libre Asociado (Free Associated State), came a program of rapid industrialization, referred to as Operation Bootstrap. As a result, agricultural patterns on the island were severely altered and many people in rural areas moved to the cities of Puerto Rico as well as to the mainland, particularly to New York City, in what is often called the Great Migration.

A number of celebrated island-based writers spent time on the mainland and wrote about the experiences of these immigrant communities during this period. One such writer was René Marqués (1919–1979), author of *La carreta* (1952; *The Oxcart,* 1969), a play that explores the topic of migration from rural to urban centers in a gloomy light imparted by the play's tragic outcome. José Luis González, Enrique Laguerre, and Emilio Diaz Valcárcel also wrote as observers of life on the mainland during this period and employed a range of literary techniques and genres that extended beyond the mostly autobiographical and testimonial literature of earlier periods.

The most celebrated Puerto Rican poet of the 20th century, Julia Constancia Burgos García (1914–1953), known as Julia de Burgos, was a member of the New York Puerto Rican community in the last years of her life and died in poverty in a Harlem hospital in 1953. She produced three collections of poetry, *Poemas en veinte surcos* (1938; Poems in Twenty Furrows), *Canción de la verdad sencilla* (1939; Song of the Simple Truth), and the posthumously published *El mar y tú, otros poemas* (1954; The Sea and You, Other Poems), of which only the third collection contains poems written in New York City. Although most of her writing was done in Spanish, she wrote two poems in English during her stay at the Goldwater Memorial Hospital on Welfare Island (now known as Roosevelt Island) shortly before her death. "Farewell in Welfare Island" and "The Sun in Welfare Island" are included in the bilingual anthology *Song of the Simple Truth: The Complete Poems of Julia de Burgos* (1997), edited and translated by Jack Agüeros. While life on the mainland was not a major theme in the poetry of de Burgos, her poems—along with those of other island-born poets who also wrote primarily in Spanish while living in New York City, such as Juan Avilés, Jorge Brandon, Pedro Carrasquillo, José Davila Semprít, Emilio Delgado, and Clemente Soto Vélez—have nevertheless influenced the development of Puerto Rican mainland poetry to some extent.

Pedro Juan Soto (b. 1928) is another well-known writer whose influence is felt in both mainland and island literature. Soto is a prolific writer whose numerous short stories, novels, and plays take up themes related to life both on the U.S. mainland as well as on the island of Puerto Rico. His celebrated short story collection *Spiks* (1956; *Spiks,* 1973) provides an unsentimental portrayal of the difficult and degrading circumstances faced by many Puerto Rican immigrants in New York City.

The shift from production of literature written primarily by island-based authors about the mainland community to literature written by the mainland community itself began to solidify with the publication of the novel *Trópico en Manhattan* (1960) by Guillermo Cotto-Thorner as well as the bilingual poem "Neorican Jet" by painter and writer Jaime Carrero. Carrero's *Jet Neorriqueño: Neo-Rican Jetliner* (1964) contains what may be the first written use of the neologism *Neo-Rican*. This term along with the variation *Nuyorican,* popularized by Miguel Piñero

and Miguel Algarín, achieved resonance and became popular during the civil rights era.

The Civil Rights Era

The civil rights era in the United States witnessed the artistic development of many Puerto Rican writers who either were born on the mainland or immigrated as young children. Many of these authors were raised in New York City in the 1940s and 1950s and wrote mainly, if not exclusively, in English. The switch from Spanish to English and Spanglish as languages of literary expression coincided with a growing appreciation of the mainland Puerto Rican community's identity as distinct from that of the island.

The major literary forms of this time were poetry, drama, and the novel. Also characteristic of the literature of this period were concerns with social justice; political engagement; the issue of Puerto Rico's political status, known as "the national question"; and the strengthening of connections to African American groups. The concurrent establishment of both black studies and Puerto Rican studies in 1969 marked the beginning of ethnic studies in U.S. universities.

Piri Thomas (b. 1928) is the U.S.-born author of the highly acclaimed autobiography—often identified as the first major work of Nuyorican literature—*Down These Mean Streets* (1967), in which Thomas recounts his adolescence, incarceration, and search for identity as a man of African and Puerto Rican descent living in the Spanish Harlem of the 1930s and 1940s. Thomas's subsequent publications include *Seven Long Times* and *Savior, Savior, Hold My Hand,* both works continuing his story through the beginning of the 1960s.

Another pioneer of Nuyorican literature is Nicholasa Mohr (b. 1938). Born and raised in New York City, Mohr writes prolifically about the experiences of Puerto Ricans in New York for both children and adults. Her work includes the groundbreaking novel *Nilda* (1973), which includes illustrations by the author and narrates in clear and compelling prose the life of a young girl growing up in East Harlem against the historical background of the New Deal era and the beginning of World War II. She is also the author of many other books, including *El Bronx Remembered* (1975), *In Nueva York* (1977), *Felita* (1979), *Rituals of Survival: A Woman's Portfolio* (1985), *Going Home* (1986), *Growing Up inside the*

> ### SILENT DANCING
>
> My memories of life in Paterson during those first few years are in shades of gray. Maybe I was too young to absorb vivid colors and details, or to discriminate between the slate blue of the winter sky and the darker hues of the snow-bearing clouds, but the single color washes over the whole period. The building we lived in was gray, the streets were gray with slush the first few months of my life there, the coat my father had bought for me was dark in color and too big. It sat heavily on my thin frame.
>
> Excerpt from *Silent Dancing* by Judith Otíz-Cofer (1991).

Sanctuary of My Imagination (1994), and *All for the Better: A Story of El Barrio* (1995).

The most significant playwright of this time is Miguel Piñero (1946–1988), author of *The Sun Always Shines for the Cool* (1979) and the collection of poetry entitled *La Bodega Sold Dreams* (1980). Piñero is best known for *Short Eyes* (1975), his Obie Award–winning play about prison life, which was also made into a film in 1976. In 2000 Leon Ichaso directed a film about his life—*Piñero*. In 1975 Piñero, along with poet and professor of literature Miguel Algarín (b. 1941), popularized the term *Nuyorican*. Piñero and Algarín edited the landmark anthology *Nuyorican Poetry: An Anthology of Puerto Rican Words and Feelings* (1975) and established the Nuyorican Poets Cafe at East Sixth Street. Currently located at 236 East Third Street in Manhattan, the café continues to stage plays and hold poetry readings as well as competitions called slams.

In the 1980s playwright Reinaldo Povod became active in the Nuyorican movement and is best known for his play *Cuba and His Teddy Bear* and his trilogy *La Puta Vida—This Bitch of a Life*. Willie Perdomo is a poet and performer who has remained lively in the Nuyorican movement and has published volumes of his poetry, including *Where a Nickel Costs a Dime* (1996), *Smoking Lovely* (2003), and the illustrated poem in honor of Langston Hughes, *Visiting Langston* (2002). Another founder of the Nuyorican poetry movement is poet and playwright Pedro Pietri (1943). Born in Ponce, Puerto Rico, Pietri came to New York City as a young child and has spent most of his life there. A prolific writer and talented performer, he was influenced by the oral poetry of Jorge Brandon (1905–1995), whom many consider the predecessor of the Nuyorican poetry movement. Pietri writes primarily in English while incorporating Spanglish as an important part of his artistic expression. He is most famous as the author of the widely translated poetry collection *Puerto Rican Obituary* (1973).

Louis Reyes Rivera (b. 1945), poet and founder of the small publishing house Shamal Books, was raised in Brooklyn and identifies as Afro–Puerto Rican. While his grandmother came from Ponce, his mother was born in New York City in the 1920s. He is the author of *Who Pays the Cost* (1977), *This One's for You* (1983), and, his most recent book, *Scattered Scripture* (1996). Jack Agüeros (b. 1934) is also a New York–based poet and has written for the stage as well as television. He was the director of the Museo del Barrio (Neighborhood Museum) in East Harlem for many years and has authored *Correspondence between Stonehaulers* (1991), *Dominoes & Other Stories from the Puerto Rican* (1993), *Sonnets from the Puerto Rican* (1996), and *Lord, Is This a Psalm?* (2002).

Sandra María Esteves (b. 1948) is a poet who was born to a Puerto Rican father and a Dominican mother in the South Bronx. Esteves was director and producer of the African Caribbean Poetry Theater from 1983 to 1988. One of the first Puerto Rican women to write in English, she has had published collections of her poetry, including *Yerba Buena: Dibujos y Poemas/Tropical Rains: A Bilingual Downpour* (1984) and *Bluestown Mockingbird Mambo* (1990), both of which showcase her continuing interest in female identity and experimentation with language. Luz María Umpierre-Herrera, author of several books including *The Margarita Poems* (1987), also exemplifies a poet shaped by the mainland environment and the women's movement. She has engaged Esteves in dialogue with the poem *My Name Is Maria Christina,* to which Esteves responded in a poem entitled *So Your Name Isn't María Cristina.*

Journalist Pablo "Yoruba" Guzmán was one of the founders of the Young Lords Party (YLP), a grassroots community education group modeled on the Black Panthers. The group began as a branch of the Chicago-based Young Lords Organization, from which it eventually broke off in order to reformulate itself as a party. The YLP published the *Palante* newspaper and *Palante: Young Lords Party* (1971), containing their political platform and essays as well as the first published version of Pedro Pietri's poem "Puerto Rican Obituary." The group concerned itself with the question of Puerto Rico's political status and with problems of institutional and internalized racism. Other members of the group, including Denise Oliver and Iris Morales, also dealt specifically with issues of sexism and the importance of the women's liberation movement for the Puerto Rican community. Emmy Award–winning journalist and cofounder of the Young Lords Party, Felipe Luciano was, as well, a founding member of the mainly African American group the Last Poets. Luciano's poetry has been recorded on film in *Right On! Poetry on Film* (1968) and on the audio recordings *Right On! The Original Last Poets* (1969) and *Recorded Live at Sing Sing*, recorded by the artists Eddie Palmieri and Harlem River Drive (1972).

Another important figure of the New York Puerto Rican community who has highlighted cultural connections with the black community in his writing is the bilingual poet and playwright Tato Laviera (b. 1951). Born Jesús Laviera Sánchez in Santurce, Puerto Rico, he is the author of the well-received poetry collection *La Carreta Made a U-Turn* (1979), which satirizes René Marqués's aforementioned midcentury play *La carreta* (The Oxcart). He has also written many plays and published several poetry collections, including *Mainstream Ethics (Ética corriente)* (1989) and *AmeRícan* (1985), which introduced the term *AmeRícan* to describe the Puerto Rican mainland diaspora.

DiaspoRican Literature

While mainland Puerto Rican communities outside of New York City are not a new phenomenon, the recent increase in the literature created both by and about the wider diasporic community has begun to raise consciousness concerning the incapacity of the term *Nuyorican* to describe all Puerto Rican literature on the mainland. The specific connotations of this term do not easily allow it to incorporate the wide variety of experiences and literary styles characteristic of the many Puerto Rican writers on the mainland—thus the coinage of new terms, such as the neologism AmeRícan introduced by Laviera. Lisa Sánchez González has also described this broader concept of Puerto Rican American literature as Bo-

ricua literature, in reference to the indigenous Taino name for the island of Puerto Rico, Borinquen.

An additional trend in the most recent period of literary production is the initiation of further dialogue between island and mainland literary traditions. A major step toward the creation of this space for dialogue can be traced to the publication of *Herejes y mitificadores: Muestra de poesía puertorriqueña en los Estados Unidos* (1980; "Heretics and Mythologizers: Sample of Puerto Rican Poetry in the United States"), an anthology edited by Efraín Barradas and Rafael Rodríguez. This ongoing dialogue can also be seen in the work of island-based writers such as Luis Rafael Sánchez (b. 1936), the renowned playwright, essayist, novelist, and short story writer, whose story "La guagua aerea" (The Flying Bus) deals with the connection between the island and the mainland reinforced by air travel.

The poet Victor Hernández Cruz (b. 1949) moved to the Lower East Side of Manhattan, referred to by the Spanglish name Loisaida, as a young child, then relocated to the West Coast in 1968 and later returned to Puerto Rico, in 1989. Hernández Cruz's poetry reflects his interest in jazz and the relationship between poetry and music. His publications include *Papo Got His Gun* (1966), *Snaps* (1969), *Mainland* (1973), *By Lingual Wholes* (1982), *Red Beans* (1991), *Panoramas* (1997), and *Maraca: New and Selected Poems 1966–2000* (2001).

Julio Marzán, author of a study on William Carlos Williams's Puerto Rican roots as well as *The Numinous Site: The Poetry of Luis Pales Matos* (1995), is also a poet in his own right and author of the collection *Translations without Originals* (1986). Another author who was raised in New York City, but who does not identify as part of the Nuyorican literary movement, is New York Supreme Court judge Edwin Torres (b. 1931). Born in Harlem, Torres began writing later in life and is the author of three detective novels: *Carlito's Way* (1975), *Q&A* (1977), and *After Hours* (1979). *Q&A* inspired the eponymous 1990 film directed by Sidney Lumet, while *Carlito's Way* was made into a film directed by Brian de Palma in 1993.

Aurora Levins Morales (b. 1954) is a Jewish Puerto Rican mainland poet, historian, and activist who coauthored *Getting Home Alive* (1986) with her mother, poet Rosario Morales. Identity as multiple and complementary rather than restrictive and binding is an important theme in the work of these two poets as can be seen in the much anthologized "Ending Poem," the final piece in *Getting Home Alive*. Levins Morales is also the author of *Medicine Stories: History, Culture and the Politics of Integrity* (1998) and *Remedios: Stories of Earth and Iron from the History of Puertorriqueñas* (2001).

Judith Ortiz Cofer (b. 1952) is a professor, poet, essayist, and novelist based in Georgia. Her publications include the novel *The Line of the Sun* (1989), the memoir *Silent Dancing: A Partial Remembrance of a Puerto Rican Childhood* (1990), *The Latin Deli: Prose and Poetry* (1993), the short story collection *An Island Like You: Stories of the Barrio* (1995), and the novel *The Meaning of Consuelo* (2003), set in a suburb of San Juan, Puerto Rico, in the 1950s. In *Cantando bajito / Singing Softly* (1989), the author Carmen de Monteflores (b. 1933) traces the lives of three generations of Puerto Rican women, Pilar, Luisa, and Meli. The novel focuses on the development of the granddaughter, Meli, who ultimately leaves the island in order to attend art school and relocates to the U.S. mainland in self-imposed exile, against the wishes of her family.

Esmeralda Santiago (b. 1948) was born in Santurce and moved to the mainland at age 13. Residing in New York state, she has written screenplays and co-owns the film production company Cantomedia. Her memoir, *When I Was Puerto Rican* (1994), was a resounding success, and she has since published a sequel, *Almost a Woman* (1999), which was made into a motion picture for ExxonMobil Masterpiece Theatre in 2002. Santiago has also published a novel, *America's Dream* (1996), about América González, a young woman from the Puerto Rican island of Vieques who comes to the mainland as a maid and is forced to confront feelings of isolation.

Abraham Rodríguez, Jr. (b. 1961), is the author of the short story collection *The Boy Without a Flag: Tales of the South Bronx* (1992), the American Book Award–winning novel *Spidertown* (1993), and the novel *The Buddha Book* (2001). He is one of the younger writers to have achieved recognition, though his work shows clear connections to the themes dealt with by Nuyorican writers such as Piri Thomas. Another active writer, Edgardo Vega Yunqué (b. 1936), also known as Ed Vega in English, is the author of the novel *The Comeback* (1985), two collections of short stories, and *No Matter How Much You Promise . . . : A Symphonic Novel* (2003). Director of the Clemente Soto Vélez Cultural and Educational Cen-

ter for Latino culture in New York City, he advocates the idea that although Puerto Rican literature is written in two languages, it is not productive to focus exclusively on the divisions between island and mainland literature.

RELATED ARTICLES

Colón, Jesús; de Burgos, Julia; Ferré, Rosario; Laviera, Jesus; Literature; Mohr, Nicholasa; Nuyorican Poets' Cafe; Puerto Ricans on the Mainland; Schomburg, Arthur; Theater; Thomas, Piri; Vega, Bernardo; Williams, William Carlos.

FURTHER READING

Barradas, Efraín. *Partes de un todo: Ensayos sobre literatura puertorriqueña en Los Estados Unidos.* (Parts of a Whole: Essays on Puerto Rican Literature in the United States). San Juan: Universidad de Puerto Rico, 1998.

De Jesús, Joy L., ed. *Growing up Puerto Rican: An Anthology.* New York: Morrow, 1997.

Flores, Juan. "Puerto Rican Literature in the United States: Stages and Perspectives." In *Divided Borders: Essays on Puerto Rican Identity.* Houston, Tex.: Arte Público Press, 1993.

Luis, William. *Dance Between Two Cultures: Latino Caribbean Literature Written in the United States.* Nashville, Tenn.: Vanderbilt, 1997.

Mohr, Eugene V. *The Nuyorican Experience: Literature of the Puerto Rican Minority.* Westport, Conn.: Greenwood Press, 1982.

Rivera, Carmen S. *Kissing the Mango Tree: Puerto Rican Women Rewriting American Literature.* Houston, Tex.: Arte Público Press, 2002.

Sánchez González, Lisa. *Boricua Literature: A Literary History of the Puerto Rican Diaspora.* New York: N.Y. Univ. Press, 2001.

Santiago, Roberto, ed. *Boricuas: Influential Puerto Rican Writings.* New York: Ballantine Bks., 1995.

Turner, Faythe. *Puerto Rican Writers at Home in the U.S.A.: An Anthology.* Seattle: Open Hand Pubs., 1991.

SARA ARMENGOT

LITERATURE OF EXILE

This entry discusses exile as a condition and motif in literature by Spanish, Mexican, South American, and Caribbean writers traveling to and living in the United States.

Pushed out of their homelands, exile writers live and write in limbo. To survive, they live in a milieu that might be alien in multiple ways: linguistically, culturally, and politically, for example. Once the situation at home changes, some stay in their adopted homeland and others return, but the return is often as painful and disorienting as the years in exiles.

Although exile itself is a generic term encompassing a wide range of political displacements, there are inherent historical differences making each case separate. In fact, the differences might be more important than the similarities.

SPAIN

Throughout much of the history of Spain there has been an evident intolerance of diverse points of view. This inflexibility was the cause of the expulsion of the Jews in late 1492 and the Moriscos (Moors who had converted to Christianity) afterward. During the following centuries there seemed to be a feeling of conformity, an adherence to the idea of Spain's greatness or the nation's defiance in the face of its European enemies, so that few needed to go into exile. This situation, however, changed in the Iberian Peninsula in the 19th century, when liberals and conservatives alternatively took power and forced their enemies to exit the political scene.

The great exodus of Spanish people occurred as a result of the bloody Spanish Civil War (1936–1939). Francisco Franco became dictator, remaining so until his death in 1975, and condemned several generations of Spaniards either to live abroad or to exist within Spain deprived of the most essential liberties. Two Spaniards whose exile journey brought them to the United States were Francisco Ayala and Ramón J. Sender. Born in Granada in 1906, Ayala studied law at the University of Madrid and, while a student, completed his first novel, which was very well received by critics and the public. He joined the group of young people who gravitated around the famous philosopher José Ortega y Gasset, collaborating with him on *Revista de Occidente.* Such an impressive literary career was, however, interrupted in 1930 as his studies became more demanding. In 1931 Ayala completed his doctorate in law and traveled to Germany to continue his studies in sociology. He obtained, in 1933, the chair in political law at the University of Madrid. During the Spanish Civil War he represented his country in Czechoslovakia, afterward settling in Argentina, where he taught philosophy and sociology and published extensively. After 1949 he taught at several American institutions, including Princeton, Rutgers, Bryn Mawr, New York University, and the University of Chicago. Ayala's first short story written in exile, *The Bewitched,* was critically praised. Ayala became an influential figure in Spanish departments in American universities.

Sender, from Chalamera de Cinca, a village in the province of Huesca, was born in 1902, and at a very early age he became editor in chief of the daily *La Tierra* in the city of Huesca. Drafted into the army, he fought in the war in Morocco, which inspired him to write a novel, earning him the beginnings of a literary reputation. Sender was awarded the National Literature Prize in 1936 for his book *Mr. Witt in the Canton.* At the outbreak of the war, he sent his wife and their two children to Zamora, Mexico, thinking that they would be safe there. However, his wife was executed by the Nationalist forces. Sender made his way to Mexico, stopping in New York City, where he left his two children in the care of some friends, who eventually adopted them. Having already developed an interest in American topics, previously publishing *The Religious Problem in Mexico* and *America before Columbus,* he appears to have found life in Mexico agreeable. In 1942 he moved to the United States, where he taught Spanish. He continued to write articles on American themes, but from 1957 his narratives returned to his native land. He published *Ariadna's Five Books* and *Mosén Millán,* although probably his best narrative is *Requiem for a Spanish Peasant.* Sender's later literary works tend to be more contemplative and philosophical, less preoccupied with political issues. He did not publish much in his last years, and what he did disappointed many a critic—*Nancy's Thesis* for example. Sender died in San Diego in 1982.

Another Spanish writer exiled in the United States is the celebrated poet Jorge Guillén, best known for his volume *Cántico,* selections of which were translated into English in 1965. Also, Juan Ramón Jiménez, author of *Platero and I* and a Nobel Prize winner, lived in Puerto Rico.

Mexico and South America

Dictatorships in Latin America have confronted the Latin American writers with unique problems, not least among which are the practical absence of a critical reading public—up to 80 percent illiteracy in most of the region—and the gigantic gulf that has existed between the elite and the masses. In the 19th and 20th centuries, literature was understood not only as an instrument of social protest but also as a way to model the national conscience. Much of the great titles in Latin American literature of the 19th century were developed and written in exile, overcoming the physical distance and keeping the memory of the homeland close to heart. Such writers appeared to strive to carry out the political struggle from a distance. Some even titled their novels after women, to allude to emerging nations, as was the case with José Mármol's *Amalia,* Cirilo Villaverde's *Cecilia Valdés,* and Jorge Isaac's *María.*

Authors from countries as diverse as Mexico, Chile, and Argentina arrived in the United States as exiles. Several entered academia as faculty and for years taught language and literature courses. Among the least known of exile writers in the United States were the editors and journalists who were forced from Mexico during the Porfirio Díaz dictatorship in the mid- to late-19th century and who migrated to the U.S. Southwest. There they established and edited dozens of newspapers (or were hired by local entrepreneurs) and authored poetry, short stories, and literary essays.

Throughout a generous portion of the 20th century, Argentines lived under various dictatorships, led by figures such as Juan Domingo Perón or by military juntas. Several of the country's writers went into exile to escape persecution at home, among them Manuel Puig, who lived for a while in New York City, where he wrote—in English—his book *Eternal Curse to the Reader of These Pages* (1982). Luisa Valenzuela, whose novels, among them *The Lizard's Tail* and *He Who Searches,* are part of the so-called Latin American literary boom of the 1970s, also lived in the United States. The writer and academic Sylvia Molloy, who teaches at New York University, is also part of this group.

As for Chile, during the second half of the 20th century young writers such as Poli Délano, Antonio Skármeta (though he was mainly stationed in Germany), Ariel Dorfman, and Carlos Olivares, to name only a few, began to experiment and developed a new rhythm, a revitalization in Chilean literature in which everything was expressed in a more uninhibited language. The young writers wanted to present their opposition to the former generation, offering as a contrast their dreams of freedom and solidarity. They embarked on a self-directed exploration of a new aesthetic language that appeared as the logical consequence of exploring the possibilities of living and dreaming in a different world.

The coup of September 11, 1973, that overthrew the legitimate government of Salvador Allende in Chile with the financial and logistic help of the U.S. authorities and the Central Intelligence Agency (CIA) caused thousands of its citizens to seek refuge precisely in the country responsible for the fall of their government. It also put into question the Chilean writers' promising literary movement as these authors sought refuge in various countries. Some overcame the obstacle, though, as in the case of Dorfman. Born in Buenos Aires and educated in the United States—he is bilingual in Spanish and English—he went back to Chile and was involved with Allende's Socialist government in the early 1970s until General Augusto Pinochet's coup. Dorfman went into exile in Europe and eventually settled in Durham, North Carolina, teaching at Duke University and became a successful playwright, essayist, and novelist whose books include *Konfidenz* (Confidence) and his memoir about language and exile, *Heading South, Looking North.*

Influential writer Isabel Allende settled in the United States in the 1980s. Born in Lima, Peru, in 1942, she is the niece of Salvador Allende, the democratically elected president of Chile. After her parents divorced, at the age of three, Allende returned to Chile where she was raised in her mother's family home. Her writing career began in exile; when the political climate in Chile worsened, she fled to Venezuela with her husband Miguel Frías and their two children. In Caracas she worked in a variety of jobs until her nostalgia for her lost country led her to write. In 1982 she published *The House of the Spirits*—adapted for the screen by the Danish director Bille August and released in the United States in 1994—and two years later *Of Love and Shadows,* both gaining her a considerable reputation in the literary world. *The House of the Spirits* was based on her memories of her family and the political upheaval in her native country. Set in an undetermined Latin American country, the novel narrates the personal and political conflicts in the lives of various generations of a family. Writing, Allende has stated, is her desperate attempt to preserve memories from her life: "I write in order not to be defeated by oblivion and to nurture the naked roots that now I have exposed to the air."

In the following years a number of Allende's other books came to print, among them *Aphrodite, Daughter of Fortune,* and *The City of the Beasts.* Her works move between the personal and the political, between realism and fantasy, merging several stories. Many of her writings present a feminine perspective that the author herself has acknowledged. Allende's upbringing in her native Chile offered her the opportunity to observe the different moral standards between men and women and how society had traditionally placed women in a disadvantageous position, owing, among other things, to prevalent machismo and the influence of the Catholic Church. Another hallmark of a number of her books is their "magic realism," a literary form associated with Latin America as well as with its exiled authors. Allende's *House of the Spirits* has been compared to García Márquez's *One Hundred Years of Solitude*.

During the Mexican Revolution (1910–1921), a number of journalists and writers from Mexico sought refuge in the United States, José Vasconcelos, Mariano Azuela, and the Flores Magón brothers among them. Others like José Escobar, Daniel Venegas, and Julio Arce brought with them sensibilities based on Mexican literature, especially the *Modernista* movement, daily chronicles, and satire, and facilitated a south-of-the border influence in Southwestern newspapers.

RELATED ARTICLES

Dorfman, Ariel; Exile; Literature.

FURTHER READING

Kaminsky, Amy K. *After Exile: Writing The Latin American Diaspora*. Minneapolis: Univ. of Minn. Press, 1999.

Lloréns, Vicente. *Liberales y románticos: Una emigración española en Inglaterra, 1823–1834* (Liberals and Romantics: The Spanish Immigration to England, 1823–1834). Madrid: Castalia, 1968.

Partnoy, Alicia, ed. *You Can't Drown the Fire: Latin American Women Writing in Exile*. Pittsburgh, Penn.: Cleis, 1988.

Pfeiffer, Erna, ed. *Exiliadas, Emigrantes, Viajeras. Encuentros con Diez Escritoras Latinoamericanas* (Exiles, Emigrants, Travelers: Encounters with Ten Latin American Women Writers). Frankfurt, Germany: Vervuert Verlag, 1995).

Rodden, John, ed. *Conversations with Isabel Allende*. 2d ed. Austin: Univ. of Tex. Press, 2004.

Stavans, Ilan. "Life in Translation: Ariel Dorfman." In *Word of Mouth*. Tucson: Univ. of Ariz. Press, 2005.

Winn, Peter. *Americas: The Changing Face of Latin America*. Berkeley: Univ. of Calif. Press, 1999.

LUIS LARIOS VENDRELL

THE SPANISH CARIBBEAN

The history of exiles from the Spanish Caribbean can be traced to the early to mid-19th century, when writers who opposed Spain's colonialism in Cuba and Puerto Rico (its last two colonies), sought asylum in the United States. These early authors included cleric, philosopher, and patriot Félix Valera, poet José María Heredia, and novelist Cirilo Villaverde. After the Ten Years' War (1868–1878), they were joined by others, such as José Martí, Cuba's most famous and prolific exile, who wrote most of his works in the United States. Martí and other writers lived in such cities as New York, Philadelphia, Tampa, and Key West, where they continued their political activities (Martí, for example, founded the Partido Revolucionario Cubano in 1892), and also contributed to the literature of their country of provenance. They wrote in Spanish within a new cultural context, which inadvertently influenced their perspectives and set the groundwork for a Cuban transnational literature.

Cuban writers were joined in the United States by their Puerto Rican counterparts, who shared the same struggle against Spanish colonialism. Eugenio María de Hostos, Emeterio Betances, and Francisco Gonzalo (Pachín) Marín, among other authors, contributed to the cause of freedom through participation in various organizations, as well as with their writings in newspapers, magazines, and books. Some gave their lives to the cause; Marín, for example, died fighting the Spanish colonial forces in Cuba. After the Spanish-American War (1898), Julio J. Henna and Manuel Zeno Gandía, not alone in writing about their opposition to U.S. annexation, published *The Case of Porto Rico* [*sic*] (1899), a document in defense of Puerto Rican independence. These and other writers, such as Afro–Puerto Rican's Arturo Alfonso Schomburg and Jesús Colón, have not been considered "exile" writers; although they opposed the U.S. occupation of Puerto Rico for political reasons, the U.S. government recognizes Puerto Ricans as immigrant citizens and not exiles. Puerto Rico's political status, as a Free Associated State, allows Puerto Ricans to travel to and from the mainland without restrictions.

Though the Dominican Republic had already become independent of Spain, and in fact fought a second war of independence against Haiti as well as a second annexation from Spain, some notable Dominicans joined their Caribbean neighbors to oust Spain from the region. Preeminent among them was General Máximo Gómez, who, with Martí signed the Proclamation of Montecriti (1895) in the Dominican Republic, a document outlining a plan for the independence struggle.

In the 20th century there were other political situations that forced writers from the Spanish Caribbean to abandon their homes. The dictatorship in Cuba of General Gerardo Machado (1927–1933) produced some outstanding exile authors, such as Alejo Carpentier who immigrated to France. General Fulgencio Batista's dictatorship (1952–59) led to a few self-imposed exile writers, as, for example, Edmundo Desnoes and Pablo Armando Fernández, who moved to the United States. Desnoes was the editor of *Visión* from 1956 to 1960; and Fernández's second book of poems, *Nuevos poemas* (1956), with an introduction by Eugenio Florit, was published in New York. Florit, a distinguished poet in his own right, arrived in New York in 1940 to work for the Cuban Consulate, and in 1945 he joined the faculty at Barnard College of Columbia University. Florit promoted Spanish American literature with anthologies and works of scholarship and with his own poetry, which he wrote but did not publish in the United States. One of his best poems, "Los poetas solos de Manhattan," is dedicated to New York.

General Rafael Leónidas Trujillo's fierce control of the Dominican Republic (1930–1961) also forced some to seek asylum in the United States. Among them was Spanish writer Jesús Galíndez, who left for New York, where he wrote against the Trujillo dictatorship and was assassinated by the dictator's henchmen. Pedro Enríquez Ureña and his sister Salomé Camila Ureña refused to collaborate with their country's ruler and spent part of their exile years in the United States. Pedro Enríquez held a visiting position at Harvard, and Salomé Camila was on the faculty of Vassar College.

The Trujillo dictatorship created another type of exile and writer, represented by Julia Alvarez. Her father conspired against the "Benefactor" and with his family fled the Dominican Republic. Alvarez was raised and educated in the United States, and as a Latina, she writes about her parents' country of origin. Though she composes in English, Alvarez has become the most important Dominican writer of the contemporary period.

The Castro revolution of 1959 produced the largest and most significant number of Caribbean exiles to the United States. This occurred in different periods: from 1959 to 1962, 1965 to 1972, 1980 (the Mariel boat lift), and 1989 to 1994. The last group, known as *balseros* (rafters), continue into the present. The first exiles were from well-to-do families, and the latter groups included the children for whom the revolutionaries came to power. By the early period Lino Novás Calvo and Lydia Cabrera had already established themselves as major writers in Cuba. Novás Calvo had written a historical novel,

El negrero (1933), and two collections of short stories, *La luna nona y otros cuentos* (1942) and *Cayo canas* (1946). Cabrera gained recognition with her work on Afro-Cuban religions in works such as *El monte* (1954). In the United States Novás Calvo published *Maneras de contar* (1970), and Cabrera, *Ayapa, cuentos de jicotea* (1971) and *Yemayá y Ochún* (1974), but their writings never achieved the same level of acclaim as that of earlier works published on the island. Novás Calvo also held a teaching position at Syracuse University.

More significant was the group of writers who abandoned the island in 1980. The poet Heberto Padilla had come to the attention of the Castro government as a collaborator on the literary supplement *Lunes de Revolución* and of *Revolución,* the official newspaper of the 26th of July Movement, which brought Castro to power. Later, Padilla was accused of providing information to enemies of the revolution. He was arrested in April 1971, set free, and forced to confess his sins at a gathering of writers and artists. Speaking of his opposition to the government, he named other conspirators, such as his wife, Belkis Cuza Malé, and friends. The Padilla affair led to an international condemnation of Castro's dictatorship and split the intellectual community into two groups: those who supported Castro and those who opposed him. Though Padilla had written *Fuera del juego,* a controversial collection of poetry that won the National Writers Union prize in 1968, the book was published with a dissenting letter from the government. However, by 1971 the political climate had changed. The year before, Castro failed to deliver the much publicized 10-million-ton sugar harvest. Castro lashed out at his enemies, and Padilla became a prime target. In exile in the United States, Padilla founded and edited *Linden Lane Magazine,* and published *Heroes Are Grazing in My Garden* (1981), a novel written in and smuggled out of Cuba, and *Self-Portrait of the Other: A Memoir* (1989), a testimonial about the events surrounding the Padilla affair. Padilla also held a teaching position at New York University.

Of the exile writers, Reinaldo Arenas was the most prolific, and his works have placed him among the leading narrators of contemporary Latin American literature. While in Cuba he wrote *Celestino antes de alba* (1967; *Singing From the Well),* providing him with work at the Biblioteca Nacional José Martí, and other, literary agencies. Because of his sexual orientation, Arenas became an enemy of a government that associated homosexual activity with bourgeois culture. His second novel, *Hallucinations: Or, the Ill-Fated Peregrinations of Fray Servando* (1969), was smuggled out of Cuba and published in France. He fled the island for the United States during the Mariel boat lift, and discovered much to his surprise that he was a well-known writer there. Continuing his literary activities, he founded the magazine and publishing house, *Mariel*, and published *Farewell to the Sea: A Novel of Cuba* (1982), a manuscript he was forced to revise many times in Cuba. Arenas was outspoken about his political beliefs and sexual orientation. As an exile, he wrote about Cuba, but he also wrote about his adopted country. The latter is visible in *The Doorman* (1989) and in his autobiography *Before Night Falls* (published posthumously, 1992), which he dictated from his sickbed in New York. Infected with the AIDS virus, Arenas committed suicide in 1990.

Antonio Benítez Rojo is the other major Cuban writer to seek sanctuary in the United States, and he holds a teaching position at Amherst College, Massachusetts. Known in Cuba as a short story writer—*Tute de Reyes* (1967) and *El escudo de hojas secas* (1969)—and a novelist—*Sea of Lentils* (1979)—in the United States he wrote the scholarly *The Repeating Island* (1989), about the plantation system in the Caribbean. His works of fiction include the collection of short stories *Paso de los vientos* (1999) and, most recently, the novel *Mujer en traje de batalla* (2001), about Henriette Faber, who fought as a man in the Napoleonic Wars.

There is a second generation of exile authors, those who were born or raised and educated in the United States and who, although occasionally using their mother tongue in their works, write mainly in English. A separate voice emerged with the magazine *Areito,* whose pages revealed that the exile community was not homogeneous. *Areito* contains some of the first writings of this next generation, and its members fostered a dialogue between Cubans at home and those in exile. Meanwhile Cuban American writing, in English, and its readership continues to grow. Authors such as Cristina García, Ana Meléndez, Ricardo Pau Llosa, Gustavo Pérez Firmat, Achy Obejas, Roberto Fernández, and Virgil Suárez, among many others, touch on their experiences as Cubans in the United States.

RELATED ARTICLES

Alvarez, Julia; Arenas, Reinaldo; Colón, Jesús; Cuban Americans; Dominican Americans; Henriquez Ureña Family; Literature, Cuban American; Literature, Dominican American; Literature, Puerto Rican on the Mainland; Mariel Boat Lift; Martí, José; Schomburg, Arthur.

FURTHER READING

Alvarez Borland, Isabel. *Cuban-American Literature of Exile: From Person to Persona.* Charlottesville: Univ. Press of Va., 1998.

Bardach, Ann Louise. *Cuba Confidential: Love and Vengeance in Miami and Havana.* New York: Random House, 2002.

Calvo, Hernando, and Katlijn Declercq. *The Cuban Exile Movement: Dissidents or Mercenaries?* Tr. by Mary Todd. Melbourne, Australia: Ocean, 2000.

Casal, Lourdes. *El caso Padilla* (The Padilla Affair). Miami: Ediciones Universal, 1971.

De la Torre, Migue A. *La lucha for Cuba: Religion and Politics on the Streets of Miami.* Berkeley: Univ. of Calif. Press, 2003.

Jonson, Scott, ed. *The Case of the Cuban Poet Heberto Padilla.* New York: Gordon Press, 1977.

Luis, William. *Dance Between Two Cultures: Latino Caribbean Literature Written in the United States.* Nashville, Tenn.: Vanderbilt Univ. Press, 1997.

Pérez Firmat, Gustavo. *Life on the Hyphen: The Cuban American Way.* Austin: Univ. of Tex. Press, 1994.

Thomas, Hugh. *Cuba: The Pursuit of Freedom.* New York: Harper & Row, 1971.

WILLIAM LUIS

LITTLE HAVANA

In Florida, Little Havana is one of Miami-Dade County's most ethnically diverse, historically important neighborhoods. A modern-day Ellis Island, Little Havana is home to tens of thousands of residents who have fled to the United States in recent times from the Caribbean and Latin America. The heart of Little Havana lies within an area stretching from the Miami River and Southwest 2d Avenue on the east to Southwest/Northwest 27th Avenue on the west, although a strong case can be made for placing the western boundary 1 mile (1.6 km) west to 37th Avenue; its north-south parameters are Southwest 11th Street on the south to the same meandering river on the north. This quarter represents one of the most densely populated neighborhoods in the state of Florida. It is a neighborhood with pockets of poverty, but it also contains a solid middle-class population. A sizable number of residents, especially the elderly, rarely leave the "enclave," since most of their needs, from medical care to spiritual nourishment, can be taken care of in the neighborhood; for

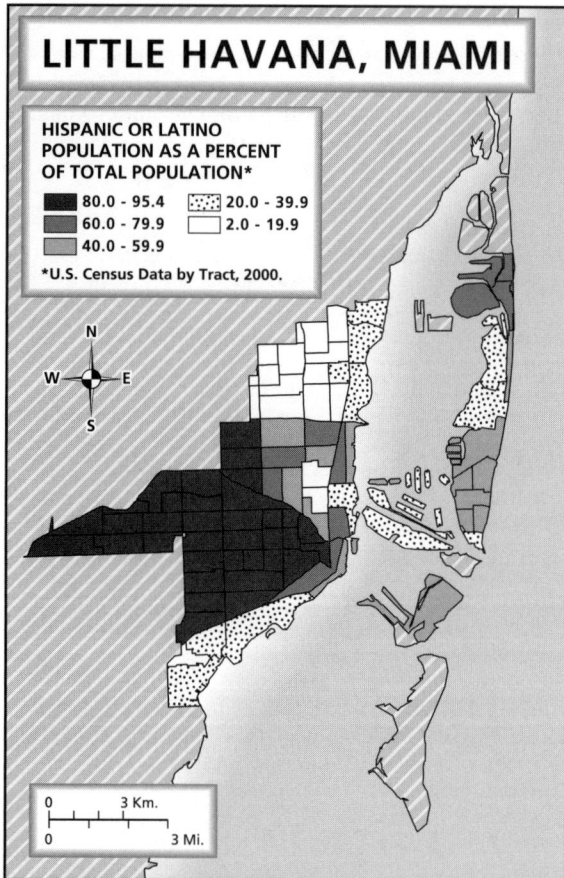

LITTLE HAVANA, MIAMI

HISPANIC OR LATINO
POPULATION AS A PERCENT
OF TOTAL POPULATION*

- 80.0 - 95.4
- 60.0 - 79.9
- 40.0 - 59.9
- 20.0 - 39.9
- 2.0 - 19.9

*U.S. Census Data by Tract, 2000.

century. Earlier the area was dotted with homesteads, pineapple orchards, and dairy farms. During Greater Miami's real estate boom of the 1920s numerous attractive Mediterranean-revival-style homes arose in Shenandoah as it emerged as one of the most attractive neighborhoods in Dade County.

Initially the residents of Riverside and Shenandoah were white, middle-class southerners. By the 1930s, however, increasing numbers of Jews had moved in. Their businesses, professional offices, and institutions followed. The Jewish presence in these neighborhoods remained strong until the late 1950s, when another era of prosperity and population growth brought a new construction boom to Greater Miami, prompting the migration of many residents of its older neighborhoods to move to new suburban developments outside of the city.

This urban exodus took place just as large numbers of Cubans, fleeing the political turbulence of their homeland, came to Miami. (The city welcomed its first Cuban, Eduardo Luis Gonzalez, a cigar manufacturer, in 1896; a Cuban family, the Encinosas, was the first known Hispanic family in today's Little Havana, residing in the quarter as early as 1922). Sizable numbers of Cubans began coming to Greater Miami as early as the 1920s, with exile enclaves emerging in Miami Beach and downtown Miami. A generation later, many refugees from the dictatorship of Cuban strongman Fulgencio Batista had fled the island for Miami. A large number of them settled in the Shenandoah and Riverside neighborhoods. One historian has observed that more than 30,000 Cuban refugees were living in Dade County before Fidel Castro came to power in Cuba in 1959, with many living in the aforementioned neighborhoods. Therefore, it was not surprising when a huge influx of Cuban refugees began pouring into this area with the onset of the Castro regime, leading to its rapid transformation into Little Havana, a name that gained wide currency in the 1960s.

In later decades thousands of Nicaraguans, Hondurans, Salvadorans, Puerto Ricans, Colombians, and other refugees and immigrants from Spanish-speaking countries in the hemisphere entered the neighborhood, bringing with them their institutions, businesses, and traditions. One can observe within a small area of Little Havana a bustling Nicaraguan bakery; Honduran, Mexican, and Salvadoran restaurants; a large Cuban cigar factory; and Protestant storefront churches. The marked transformation of the neigh-

many, primarily the elderly, Spanish is their only language.

While the United States Census report for the year 2000 does not contain population information specifically for Little Havana, it does indicate that the quarter's host city, Miami, contains more than 362,000 residents, with 66 percent of them, or 238,357, Hispanic. Most of the latter reside in Little Havana. For its part, Miami-Dade County, with a population in excess of 2.3 million, claims about 800,000 Cuban Americans and boasts a Hispanic majority of 57 percent; Miami has the largest Spanish-speaking majority of any major American city.

Little Havana emerged from the earlier neighborhoods of Riverside and Shenandoah. One of Miami's first "suburbs," Riverside began developing on the west bank of the Miami River at the outset of the 1900s. Carved out of the piney woods, it stretched from the Miami River west to 17th Avenue, and from Southwest 8th Street north to the edges of the stream. Shenandoah emerged as a residential community in the second and third decade of the 20th borhood is especially notable when one observes that a Honduran eatery standing near a busy Little Havana intersection occupies a former Burger King restaurant, which, in the early 1960s, was among the busiest in the chain.

The "salad bowl" that is Little Havana bustles with a pedestrian life found in few other places in Greater Miami. This is especially true of Calle Ocho, or Southwest 8th Street, the quarter's most famous thoroughfare. What sets Little Havana apart are the human scale of its old structures, a wide variety of architectural styles, a rising artist colony, ubiquitous "mom and pop" businesses, glitzy ethnic restaurants with their surfeit of blinking lights and heaping plates of low-priced food, and outdoor coffee counters where mostly men, fueled with pungently sweet cups, or "thimbles," of *cafecito* (or Cuban espresso coffee), discuss the latest events and conditions in the homeland. Little Havana is an area of political activism, parades and protest marches, shrines and museums, and vendors selling produce, flowers, and rich fruit drinks. Even though the number of non-Cuban Hispanics has risen significantly in recent decades, the neighborhood is dominated politically, economically, and numerically by Cuban Americans whose astounding achievements are the stuff of immigrant dreams. Little Havana's parks, many named for famous Cuban and other Hispanic heroes, are popular gathering places for *viejos* (elderly men) who play dominoes, as well as for young mothers pushing babies in strollers and baseball-crazy youngsters hoping to become the next Hispanic superstar.

Hundreds of thousands of tourists and residents look to Little Havana annually for events such as the gigantic Calle Ocho Open House, held each year on the second Sunday of March. This bustling street fair, the largest Hispanic festival in the United States, typically attracts more than 1 million persons, many from Hispanic countries in the hemisphere, who gather along the street for more than 20 blocks to mingle, dance, eat, enjoy the sounds of salsa, and catch a glimpse of famed entertainers. Others enjoy the annual parade celebrating the Feast of the Three Kings, or the school children who celebrate in parade fashion the birthday of José Martí, the 19th-century poet-activist and apostle of Cuban

© BERNARD BOUTRIT/WOODFIN CAMP & ASSOCIATES

Playing dominoes in Little Havana's Máximo Gómez Park.

independence. Viernes Culturales (Cultural Friday) is a smaller but popular event that takes place the last Friday of each month. On this day artists display their wares, restaurants place tables outside for dining, a historian conducts popular tours of the neighborhood, and live music wafts through a three-block area along Calle Ocho in the center of the Latin Quarter. This quarter is a small historical area in the center of Little Havana, which—with its brick sidewalks, red barrel-tile roofs, sidewalk cafés, and walkway of Hispanic stars (entertainers)—is especially lively and attractive to tourists.

Political passions and patriotic sentiments remain strong here, especially among Cuban Americans. Stirring monuments, partly related to this passion, abound in the quarter, particularly along Cuban Memorial Boulevard (Southwest Thirteenth Avenue); municipios, clubs for exiles from the same city or province, and museums focusing on different elements of Cuban culture and life are other important venues of the area.

Little Havana is exotic, flamboyant, historical, and ever evolving, since additional people continue to pour into the new Ellis Island. The area has helped transform Miami into an international city, as well as the "City of the Future" in the estimation of some observers who note that America is gaining new Hispanic residents at a frenzied pace, with many cities looking to Miami and its Little Havana neighborhood for direction. For millions of other Hispanics in the hemisphere, Miami continues to hold out the hope of a better life, one with greater economic opportunities and more political freedoms.

RELATED ARTICLES

Barrio, El; Calle Ocho; Cuban Americans; Florida; Miami-Dade County.

FURTHER READING

Garcia, Maria Cristina. *Havana USA: Cuban Exiles and Cuban Americans in South Florida, 1959–1994.* Berkeley: Univ. of Calif. Press, 1996.

George, Paul S. *The Dr. Paul George Walking Tour of East Little Havana.* Miami: Hist. Assoc. of Southern Fla., 1991.

George, Paul S. "Little Havana: A Flamboyant, Ever-Evolving 'Ellis Island.'" *Forum* 25 (Spring 2002): 22–28.

Gernand, Renee, and Sandra Stotsky. *The Cuban Americans.* New York: Twayne, 1995.

Sicius, Francis. "The Miami-Havana Connection: The First Seventy-Five Years." *Tequesta* 58 (1998): 5–45.

PAUL S. GEORGE

LLORONA, LA

The three principal female myths in Mexican culture are La Virgen de Guadalupe, La Malinche (Doña Marina, a slave of Aztec ancestry who became translator and mistress to Hernán Cortés), and La Llorona (The Weeping Woman). They are also important in U.S. Latino communities, particularly among Mexican Americans.

The legend of La Llorona is related to the Medea myth, the 15th-century German tale of "Die weisse Frau," (The Wise Woman) and other European sources, which it combines with indigenous elements into a syncretic narrative. There are numerous versions of this legend, some closely follow Amerindian accounts (which occasionally equate the figure of a weeping woman with that of La Malinche); others contain European elements; many are a combination. The indigenous account is based on a legend cycle about a supernatural woman who seduces male travelers or men working in the fields, often killing them. Examples of such figures are the Zapotec mestizo Matlaziwa, a wailing spirit-being, and the "Chanecas," siren women reported to live in the forests of the Mexican state of Veracruz. This siren motif is combined with the legend of the Aztec goddess Ciucoatl (or Cihuacóatl), who is said to appear in the night crying out for dead children. European elements that have been incorporated into the myth are that the woman has children; that she was betrayed by an unfaithful lover or husband, their father; that she (stabbed and) drowned her children to take revenge; and that she repents the infanticide, weeping in anguish for her dead children and (in many versions) drowning herself. Because of the location of the infanticide, it is said that the weeping of La Llorona can especially be heard near rivers and lakes.

Variants of the myth's plot include the following: the woman—usually called María—is of a lower social class, while her lover is of high social standing and therefore cannot marry her; the woman is proud and beautiful, and her tragedy is the just punishment for her haughtiness; the dashing lover frequents brothels and has several girlfriends; the man rejects María and their children when he gets married to a wealthy lady; the woman is of indigenous origin, the man of Spanish ancestry; after her rejection, the woman (dressed in white) takes revenge on the Spanish conquistadores and/or asks her people to forgive her; María is denied access to heaven: her soul cannot rest in peace until she has found her dead children, which is why she keeps looking for them along bodies of water while wailing in distress; La Llorona is out to punish wayward men and disobedient children; as an angel of death, she is dressed in black and her face is blank. In Mexican American folklore the figure appears either as a grieving woman, as a siren, or as a woman who is dangerous to children. While details of the myth vary greatly, the two plot elements that are to be found in all versions are the betrayal of La Llorona by a wayward lover/husband and the killing of her children, followed by regret and weeping.

Patriarchal interpretations have presented La Llorona as a woman who suffers as a result of not complying with the role expectations of marriage and motherhood. Feminist views, by contrast, use her as an illustration of male oppression and female resistance to it, as a refusal to comply with male expectations of motherhood or to endure abuse. In José E. Limón's opinion, La Llorona constitutes a denial of the Mexican conceptualization of women as either madonnas (modeled on La Virgen) or whores (modeled on La Malinche) because the figure challenges the basis of patriarchy, namely the family:

> The infanticide is not the articulation of a repressed resentment against child caring . . . , but rather the humanly understandable, if extreme and morally incorrect, reaction of a woman to sexual and familial betrayal by a man in a Mexican cultural context where such betrayal was a common and recurrent experience for women. In this act La Llorona is violating patriarchal norms, but not in any obvious superficial way which would make her a "moral" example to women. She kills because she is also living out the most extreme articulation of the everyday social and psychological contradictions created by those norms for Mexican women. To this extent, it is here that the legend poses a more fundamental oppositional threat to men because by her act she symbolically destroys the familial basis for patriarchy.

The myth of La Llorona can therefore be interpreted as an instance of painful female empowerment, although, more traditionally, it has been used as a "lesson" for women to stay in their social class, not to think too highly of themselves, and not to fall for the gallantries of an unattainable man. It also serves as a "scarecrow" for disobedient children. The popularity of the Llorona myth in Mexican American culture has been explained as a consequence of a marginalized population identifying with a marginalized figure, seeking redemption with and through her, and of using the folklore of Greater Mexico as a means of cultural self-definition.

Examples of the incorporation of La Llorona into Latin American and U.S. Latino cultural life abound. At least three Mexican horror films are based on the myth (La Llorona by María Luisa Zea et al., 1933; La Llorona by María Elena Márques et al., 1959; and La Maledición de la Llorona [The Curse of La Llorona] by Rosita Arenas et al., 1961). A later documentary is Trina López's short La Llorona (1999). In Guatemala the short stories of Alcina Lubitch Domecq (Intoxicada, 1986) deal with the female mythical character. In Mexican literature the novel Los siete hijos de la Llorona (The Seven Sons of La Llorona, 1986) by Justo S. Alarcón takes up the myth. References to La Llorona are especially frequent in Mexican American writing. Examples include Alurista's poem "Must Be the Season of the Witch" (1971), Alejandro Morales's Caras viejas y vino nuevo (Old Faces and New Wine, 1975), and Rudolfo Anaya's Bless Me, Ultima (1972), as well as The Legend of La Llorona (1984) and his play The Season of La Llorona (1987). More recently, Helena María Viramontes, in her story "The Cariboo Café" (1985), and Sandra Cisneros, in "Woman Hollering Creek" (1991), have modeled heroines of maternal resistance on La Llorona, rather than presenting her as a destructive force.

La Llorona remains a powerful cultural icon. As political, social, and economic conditions continue to change, both inside and outside the Mexican American community north of the Rio Grande, her myth undergoes revisions and reinterpretations. She symbolizes the endurance of a civilization whose history has forced it to internalize female suffering.

RELATED ARTICLES

Family; Feminism; Folklore, Mexican American; Malinche, La; Mexican Americans; Quetzalcóatl; Superstitions; Virgen de Guadalupe.

FURTHER READING

Figueredo, María L. "The Legend of La Llorona: Excavating and (Re)Interpreting the Archetype of the Creative/Fertile Feminine Force." In Latin American Narratives and Cultural Identity: Selected Readings. Ed. by Irene Blayer and Mark Cronlund Anderson. New York: Peter Lang, 2004.

Limón, José E. "La Llorona, the Third Legend of Greater Mexico: Cultural Symbols, Women, and the Political Unconscious." Vol. 2. Renato Rosaldo Lecture Series Monograph. Ed. by Ignacio M. García. Tucson, Ariz.: Mexican Am. Studies & Research Ctr., 1986.

Pérez, Domino Renee. "Crossing Mythological Borders: Revisioning La Llorona in Contemporary Fiction." *Proteus: A Journal of Ideas* 16, no. 1 (Spring 1999): 49–54.

Pérez, Domino Renee. "Caminando con La Llorona: Traditional and Contemporary Narratives." In *Chicana Traditions: Continuity and Change.* Ed. by Norma E. Cantú and Olga Nájera-Ramírez. Urbana: Univ. of Ill. Press, 2002.

Ramírez, Arturo. "La Llorona: Structure and Archetype." In *Chicano Border: Culture and Folklore.* Ed. by José Villarino and Arturo Ramírez. San Diego, Calif: Marin, 1992.

West, John O. "The Weeping Woman: *La Llorona.*" In *Legendary Ladies of Texas.* Ed. by Francis Edward Abernethy. 1981 Reprint. Denton: Univ. of N.Tex. Press, 1994.

JOSEF RAAB

LOISAIDA

The Spanglish term synonymous with the historically Puerto Rican Lower East Side of Manhattan in New York City, *Loisaida* was coined in the early 1970s by poet-activists Chino Garcia and Bimbo Rivas to refer to the area east of Avenue A bounded by 14th Street, Houston Street, and the East River. Mass migration, urban decline, community activism, cultural renaissance, and gentrification are among the factors that have shaped the development of this historic lower Manhattan neighborhood during the latter half of the 20th century and into the 21st. Also including the Alphabet City and the East Village neighborhoods, the Lower East Side has still more monikers, which reflect its diverse ethnic and socioeconomic composition as well as the contested physical, economic, and cultural borders demarcating these communities that edge one another.

Originally home to eastern European and Jewish immigrants arriving during the 1880s, the Lower East Side housed large poor and working-class immigrant populations in substandard and overcrowded conditions that were famously documented by Jacob Riis in *How the Other Half Lives.* Initially, the prevalence of high-density tenement-style housing made it enormously profitable for developers and landlords to house the constant flow of immigrants from eastern Europe, and this population peaked during the 1920s. However, in the decades leading up to World War II, many of the original immigrant families began to leave the neighborhood for the city's outer boroughs and suburbs, and the area saw a steady population decline until the postwar period, when Puerto Ricans began arriving in large numbers.

Puerto Rican migration to New York City increased early in the 20th century, shortly after the U.S. military invaded and annexed the island in 1898 as a result of the Spanish-American War. In 1917 the Jones Act made Puerto Ricans U.S. citizens, and a generation later Operation Bootstrap, a controversial development strategy for the island, would catalyze a great migration to the U.S. mainland, primarily to New York City, where Puerto Ricans established enclaves in East Harlem, North Brooklyn, the South Bronx, and the Lower East Side.

Like their European predecessors, the new immigrants encountered poor housing conditions on the Lower East Side; in addition, they were confronted by a transitioning and ever-more unwelcoming metropolitan economy. Whereas low-skilled manufacturing jobs were a staple for prior generations of immigrants, the erosion of the city's industrial base, poor educational opportunities for the children of Puerto Rican migrants, and exploitative real estate practices contributed to the maintenance of a low-income community on the Lower East Side. The convergence of these forces was devastating for the community, which increasingly became associated with persistent poverty, crime, and drugs—factors that accelerated the widespread abandonment of housing by landlords during the 1960s and 1970s. During this period many property owners neglected routine maintenance and payment of property taxes while raising rents and harassing tenants. A particularly pernicious practice was "torching," or the burning of scores of buildings by landlords or their employees in order to collect insurance payments. These practices had the result of displacing thousands of long-term Puerto Rican residents, and Loisaida saw an overall 40 percent population decline in the decade between 1970 and 1980.

Influenced by the social movements of the 1960s, a new generation of Puerto Ricans, many born or raised, or both, in New York responded to the adverse state of the Lower East Side by establishing organizations to reclaim their communities and assert their political and cultural power. Reflecting this broader Puerto Rican movement, organizations such as Pueblo Nuevo and the Real Great Society/Charas, Inc., were founded to reclaim and redevelop abandoned buildings and vacant land and make them available for the use of community residents. Charas, Inc., for example, with its motto of "Doing More With Less," used its ties to inventor and engineer Buckminster Fuller to build geodesic domes (his invention) and established alternative, low-cost, and autonomous forms of housing. This new architectural form demonstrated the Nuyorican spirit of creativity and innovation in addressing the pressing housing needs of the Loisaida community through the use of alternative technology, such as solar heating and windmills. La Plaza Cultural, comprising an urban garden and amphitheater, and a strong muralist movement were other examples of Charas's commitments to transform deteriorated urban spaces for the benefit of long-term residents.

Urban homesteading and sweat-equity initiatives were also strategies by which residents addressed disinvestment and displacement. Organizations such as Interfaith Adopt-a-Building, Lower East Side Social Action Committee (LESAC), the Urban Homesteading Assistance Board (UHAB), and the Housing Development Institute (HDI) provided support to residents as they gained control of properties from the city, learned building skills, and then renovated and managed those properties. Community land trusts were also established as the result of contentious deliberations between city officials and community activists. Despite the success of these efforts, dramatically rising housing costs during the 1980s made it difficult for lower income residents to maintain Loisaida as a Puerto Rican space. (For example, housing prices doubled in the five-year period between 1979–1984.) Lending institutions, developers, and real estate agents exploited the neighborhood's proximity to Wall Street, and forces of gentrification would continue to transform the Lower East Side during the 1990s, markedly altering the socioeconomic and ethnic composition of its population.

In the 1960s and 1970s, as organizations attempted to reconstruct the physical condition of the community, cultural organizations—among them, the New Rican Village and the Nuyorican Poets Cafe—responded to the hippie counterculture of the East Village and sought to "Ricanstruct" a psychological and cultural identity through their newly invented genre—Nuyorican poetry. Influenced by the Last Poets and the Young Lords, poets such as Miguel Algarín, Tato Laviera, Miguel Piñero, Lucky Cienfuegos, Sandra Maria Esteves, and Bimbo Rivas perfected their craft and created (1975) the Nuyorican Poets Cafe, a performance space that remains a landmark of importance on the Lower East Side and beyond.

Loisaida as a neighborhood continues to be influenced by an array of economic and real estate forces. However, more broadly it symbolizes the hybrid responses to spatial and cultural collisions Puerto Ricans and other Latinos experienced as they arrived and evolved in, specifically, New York City and, generally, the United States.

RELATED ARTICLES

Barrio, El; New York City; Nuyorican Poets Cafe; Washington Heights.

FURTHER READING

Hassell, Malve von. *Homesteading in New York City, 1978–1993: The Divided Heart of Loisaida.* Westport, Conn.: Bergin & Garvey, 1996.

Mele, Christopher. *Selling the Lower East Side: Culture, Real Estate, and Resistance in New York City.* Minneapolis: Univ. of Minn. Press, 2000.

Moore, Alan, and Marc Miller, eds. *ABC No Rio Dinero: The Story of a Lower East Side Art Gallery.* New York: ABC No Rio with Collaborative Projects, 1985.

Riis, Jacob. *How the Other Half Lives.* New York: Scribner, 1890.

Sevcenko, L. "Making Loisaida: Placing Puertoriqueñidad in Lower Manhattan." In *Mambo Montage: The Latinization of New York.* Ed. by Agustín Laó-Montes and Arlene Dávila. New York: Columbia Univ. Press, 2001.

Sites, William. *Remaking New York: Primitive Globalization and the Politics of Urban Community.* Minneapolis: Univ. of Minn. Press, 2003.

ANTHONY DE JESÚS

LÓPEZ, NANCY

Born: January 6, 1957; Torrance, California

A professional golfer, Nancy López is a three-time winner of the Ladies Professional Golf Association (LPGA) Championship, compiling 48 tournament wins overall. She grew up in Roswell, New Mexico, the daughter of parents, Domingo and Marina López, who enjoyed golf, playing at the Roswell Golf Course, a municipal course. When she was eight years old, her father handed her one of her mother's golf clubs and began teaching her the game. She quickly took to the sport and at nine won the pee-wee tournament. The following year she won the state championship. At age 12 she won the New Mexico Women's Amateur and successfully defended her title for the next two years.

In 1970 López enrolled at Roswell Goddard High, where a golf team for girls was not offered, so she played on the boys' team and helped them win the state championship in 1971. She won the United States Golf Association (USGA) Junior Girls' Championship in 1972 and 1974 and the Mexican Amateur in 1975.

Entering the U.S. Women's Open as an amateur in 1975, López finished in a tie for second. The next year she claimed the Association of Intercollegiate Athletics for Women (AIAW) National Championship and was a member of the U.S. Curtis Cup and World Amateur teams. In her first year at the University of Tulsa, Oklahoma, she was named 1976 All-American and the university's Female Athlete of the Year.

López left college after her sophomore year to pursue a professional golf career. During her official rookie season as a pro golfer (1978) she had nine wins, finishing second in her first three tournaments and setting a record by winning five consecutive tournaments including the LPGA Championship— her first major tournament victory. She was the highest money-winner in 1978, 1979, and 1985, and she won the LPGA Championship again in 1985 and 1989.

Despite all her accomplishments she encountered prejudice. Her parents could not join the Roswell Country Club, where she played and practiced her game. She also faced discrimination as a female in golf and was not allowed to play certain courses or could play on some courses only after certain times.

López won Player of the Year honors four times (1978, 1979, 1985, 1988) and was Vare Trophy winner three times, for best scoring average by a player on the LPGA Tour (1978, 1979, 1985); her stroke average in 1985 was 70.73—an LPGA record. With 35 tour victories by the age of 30, she was inducted into the LPGA Hall of Fame in 1987. In 2000, during the LPGA's 50th Anniversary, López was recognized as one of the LPGA's top 50 players and teachers. She retired from the LPGA Tour as a full-time player at the end of 2002. López married former baseball major leaguer Ray Knight; they have three daughters.

RELATED ARTICLES

Golf; Sports in Latino Life.

FURTHER READING

"Who's Who in Golf." *An A-Z Guide to the Leading Professional Golfers*. Great Britain: Hamlyn, 2001.

SELECTED WEB SITE

Golf for Women Magazine. www.golfforwomen.com
Latino Legends in Sports. www.latinosportslegends.com

MERCEDES MARRERO

LÓPEZ, TRINIDAD

Born: May 15, 1937; Dallas, Texas

For almost two years beginning in late 1963, Trini López, the son of Mexican immigrants, was one of the most successful popular music artists in the world.

Trinidad "Trini" López III was born to Trinidad López and Petra Gonzalez, who had immigrated to the United States from Moroleón, Guanajuato, seeking work. His father secured a job at Southern Methodist University, while his mother cared for the growing family, taking in washing to make ends meet. With six children money was always tight.

When López was about 12, his father bought him a cheap guitar and taught him how to play traditional Mexican songs. López learned quickly, adding American popular tunes to his repertoire. As a teenager, he helped support the family by playing music on street corners and in Dallas restaurants. He dropped out of high school after the 11th grade to perform full-time.

His first single, "The Right to Rock," in 1958 led to a contract with rhythm and blues (R&B) impresario Syd Nathan's King Records, where he joined acts such as The Platters and James Brown. King released several R&B and bluegrass songs with López backed by the label's studio musicians. As the only Latino performer for a mostly black record company, López did not fit in. He soon moved to Los Angeles.

After playing for a year in Los Angeles, López landed a regular engagement at PJ's, a popular nightclub. Record producer Don Costa saw the act and recommended him to Frank Sinatra, who signed López to an eight-year contract with Reprise Records. The first album, *Trini López at PJ's,* was recorded live in 1963. The set included Lopez's signature blend of folk, blues, gospel, and traditional Mexican songs, performed with an up-tempo, danceable beat.

The album quickly rose on the charts on the strength of a jaunty cover of Pete Seeger's *If I Had a Hammer,* which rose to number three on the charts, becoming a hit single. Seeger's metaphorical lyrics evoke both the creative and destructive potential of the hammer ("I'd hammer out danger / I'd hammer out a warning"). López reinterprets the song, emphasizing the chorus, "I'd hammer out love between my brothers and my sisters / all over this land." No longer a labor song, his version became a celebration of unity. His unrelentingly optimistic vocals and lively guitar playing made the song a hit in the United States, Europe, and South America. Perhaps the most remarkable aspect of the song's success is its simplicity. It was recorded during a weeknight set, when López did not use a bass player, an expense indulged in only on the weekends. Just two people, López and his drummer, perform the single.

Reprise quickly produced another album, *More Trini López at PJ's,* and another hit, *Kansas City.* Outside the United States, López charted with songs such as *La Bamba, This Land Is Your Land,* and *Amer-i-ca.* He never shied away from his Mexican American heritage, incorporating pop covers of songs such as *Cielito Lindo* and *Corazón de Melon* into his live act. Reprise released many of these Spanish-language standards as singles in Latin America and Spain.

By early 1964 López was a worldwide sensation. He performed for 18 days in Paris, sharing top billing with The Beatles. He appeared on Dick Clark's popular television show *American Bandstand,* and the Gibson guitar company released two "Trini López" signature models. He had one other hit, *Lemon Tree,* in 1965 and a year later his song, *I'm Coming Home, Cindy* made a brief chart appearance. As the 1960s wore on and the mood of the country darkened, López's happy versions of Mexican and American folk songs lost their appeal. He tried acting, appearing in television shows and several movies, including *The Dirty Dozen.* López continues to record albums and perform. In 1998 he toured Europe to promote an album made for a German record label.

RELATED ARTICLES

Music, Popular; Vocalists, Popular.

FURTHER READING

Carter, Walter. "Latin Rock Pioneer Trini Lopez: Still Playing His Signature Gibson." *Gibson and Baldwin Player* 1, no. 1 (September 2002).
Unterberger, Richie. "Liner Notes." *Trini Lopez at PJ's.* CD rerelease. Itasca, Ill.: Collectors Choice Music, 2001.
Unterberger, Richie. "Liner Notes." *More Trini Lopez at PJ's.* CD rerelease. Itasca, Ill.: Collectors Choice Music, 2001.

SELECTED WEB SITE

Official Trini López Web Site. www.trinilopez.com

P. SCOTT BROWN

LÓPEZ, YOLANDA M.

Born: November 1, 1942; San Diego, California

Yolanda López is one of the foremost and best-known Mexican American artists of her generation. She rose to national fame in 1978, when her seminal oil painting *Portrait of the Artist as the Virgin of Guadalupe* was first exhibited. Her paintings, lithographs, drawings, posters, collages, mixed-media installations, and videos reflect her experiences as a woman and as a member of the Mexican American community, as well as her desire to question common images and perceptions. Toward this end she often evokes traditional icons (used in American Indian mythology, Catholic iconography, comic books, advertising, and so on) in order to challenge them through distortions, unusual combinations, or the addition of unexpected elements. Her artistic materials range from found objects to clothes, photos, and magazine clippings, and her media, from charcoal to oil. López's work is shown in major American museums and has also been exhibited in Puerto Rico, Mexico, and Germany.

Growing up speaking English with her mother and Spanish with her grandparents, López studied art at the College of Marin in Kentfield, California, and at San Francisco State University before completing her B.A. in painting and drawing at California State University, San Diego, in 1975 and her M.F.A. in visual arts at the University of California, La Jolla, in 1978. Her political activism was sparked in 1968 while working with the group Los Siete de la Raza in San Francisco's Mission District. She has since used her art to promote political and social change.

López's provocative depictions often rely on well-known public images whose implications and ideologies she questions. Critics have therefore spoken of the "intertextual dialogues" of her work. In the late 1970s López created the "Serie Guadalupe," a number of paintings that revise the traditional Virgin of Guadalupe representation into renderings of, among others, her grandmother, her mother at the sewing machine, a nursing mother, and an indigenous woman carrying her child in a blanket. Angie Chabram-Dernersesian, professor of Chicana-Chicano studies, writes that López discards "the artificial, statuesque portrait of the Chicana/Mexicana Virgen" as a viable image "for contemporary Chicanas and Mexicanas, and she invites the reformulation and displacement of this reified female icon by new images, inspired in everyday work and play. Liberation from further subjection is inscribed in many forms."

The most memorable work in this series is *Portrait of the Artist as the Virgin of Guadalupe*. This reinterpretation shows a self-confident, active young woman; her hair and dress are short; traditional attributes like crown, rose, and visible heart are missing; and the conventional star-covered cloak is transformed into a blanket with blotches. Most strikingly, Juan Diego, the angel figure, is trampled upon, and the depicted woman holds a snake in her right hand. These changes add up to a new conceptualization of the artist herself as well as of Mexican American women in general; instead of the stoic passivity of the Virgin, López propagates self-assuredness and action. As the artist, writer, scholar, and curator Amalia Mesa-Bains has pointed out, her revisions of the traditional depiction are "both satire and provocation, while retaining the transfigurative liberation of the icon. . . . The art in this series does not simply reflect an existing ideology; it actively constructs a new one. It attests to the critique of traditional Mexican women's roles and religious oppression in a self-fashioning of new identities."

In 1978 López's drawing *Who's the Illegal Alien, Pilgrim?* was first shown. It depicts an angry Aztec warrior who defiantly asks this question while crumpling a document entitled "Immigration Plans." Widely distributed as a poster, this image was given a high profile by the Chicano movement. Since the 1990s López has increasingly worked on mixed-media installations; her series Cactus Hearts/Barbed Wire Dreams explores ethnic identity, assimilation, and cultural change, while "Women's Work Is Never Done" questions gender roles, and "Things I Never Told My Son about Being a Mexican" takes on stereotypes.

López has taught at universities and colleges in California and in the Southwest. She has written on art as a means of combating sexism and racism; the University of California at Santa Barbara collects and houses her papers. Her art remains intent on revising conventional public images and demystifying stereotypes. López maintains, "It is crucial that we systematically explore the cultural mis-definition of Mexicans and Latin Americans that is presented in the media."

RELATED ARTICLES
Art Criticism; Art, Mexican American and Chicano; Chicano Movement

FURTHER READING
Chabram Dernersesian, Angie. "And, Yes . . . The Earth Did Part: On the Splitting of Chicana/o Subjectivity." In *Building with Our Hands: New Directions in Chicana Studies*. Ed. by Adela de la Torre and Beatríz M. Pesquera. Berkeley: Univ. of Calif. Press, 1993.
López, Yolanda M., and Moira Roth. "Social Protest: Racism and Sexism." In *The Power of Feminist Art: The American Movement of the 1970s—History and Impact*. New York: Abrams, 1999.
Martínez, Elizabeth. "Artist Provocateur: An Interview with Yolanda López." *Crossroads* (May 1993): 14–18.

JOSEF RAAB

LOS ANGELES

One of the more complex urban centers in the United States, Los Angeles, California, has been home to Latinos since colonial times. As the city has changed, so has its Spanish-speaking population. But that population is still underrepresented in political terms and economically marginalized. This two-part entry first approaches the role of Latinos in Los Angeles as a whole, then focuses on East Los Angeles.

LOS ANGELES

Research across a variety of disciplines shows that the past, present, and future of Los Angeles, California, belong to Latinos. A distant outpost of the Spanish empire, a haven for Mexican bandits and revolutionaries, a terminus for generations of immigrants from Mexico and Central America, and the birthplace of the Chicano movement, Los Angeles now shelters the nation's largest Spanish-speaking barrio and holds a special place in the history of Latinos in the United States. Although that history is buried under layers of myth about valiant conquistadores, benevolent padres, ostentatious dons, and "primitive" Indians, the history of Los Angeles reveals the development of a regionally distinct Mexican American or Chicano identity that draws on a vital commingling of Indian, Spanish, Mexican, as well as modern American cultures.

Like all histories of Latin America, the history of Latino Los Angeles begins with the indigenous inhabitants of Southern California, whose history cannot be understood without some comprehension of the natural environment. The natural environment not only delineated the contours of settlement among indigenous peoples but also shaped subsequent encounters with newcomers to the region. The relationship between Southern California's indigenous peoples and the natural environment was not a passive one, as has been commonly assumed, but rather reflected an acute awareness of the landscape and the optimal utilization of its resources. Southern California's natural environment, distinguished by its plains, streams, rivers, coastline, and mountains, determined indigenous patterns of social organization and culture. The availability of food resources and raw materials, for example, shaped the location, size, and distribution of indigenous settlements and also influenced religious beliefs. The other striking characteristic of Southern California's indigenous population was its diversity, which reflected the overall diversity of California's Indian population. Chumash, Luiseno, Juaneno, Gabrielino, Tataviam, and Kameyaay established scattered settlements throughout the Southern California areas, and their presence and knowledge of the natural environment shaped the subsequent interactions among Indian, Spanish, and Mexican peoples.

The arrival of the Spanish brought sudden and drastic changes for the indigenous peoples of Southern California. Spanish colonization of the California coast began in 1542 with the arrival of Juan Rodriguez de Cabrillo. His expedition marked the final stages of Spain's policy of defensive expansion, which sought to protect Spanish territory from rival imperial powers, France and England in particular. The settlement of Los Angeles began with the establishment of El Pueblo de Nuestra Señora La Reina de Los Angeles de Porciuncula, which was located close to Yang-na, the largest settlement of Gabrielinos in the region. In addition to the pueblo, the mission also played a vital role in the undertaking of Spanish colonization. Its primary function was to maintain a stable pool of Indian converts to Christianity, whose labor sustained Spanish occupation of newly acquired territories. In Los Angeles the Mission San Gabriel, considered the "queen of the missions," housed Alta California's largest neophyte population and maintained vast tracts of cultivated land. On several occasions, however, mission Indians attempted to revolt against their enforced servitude by Spanish padres. In 1781 the neophyte Toypurina, who claimed to have had a vision of Indian liberation from Spanish rule, led an insurrection at the Mission San Gabriel.

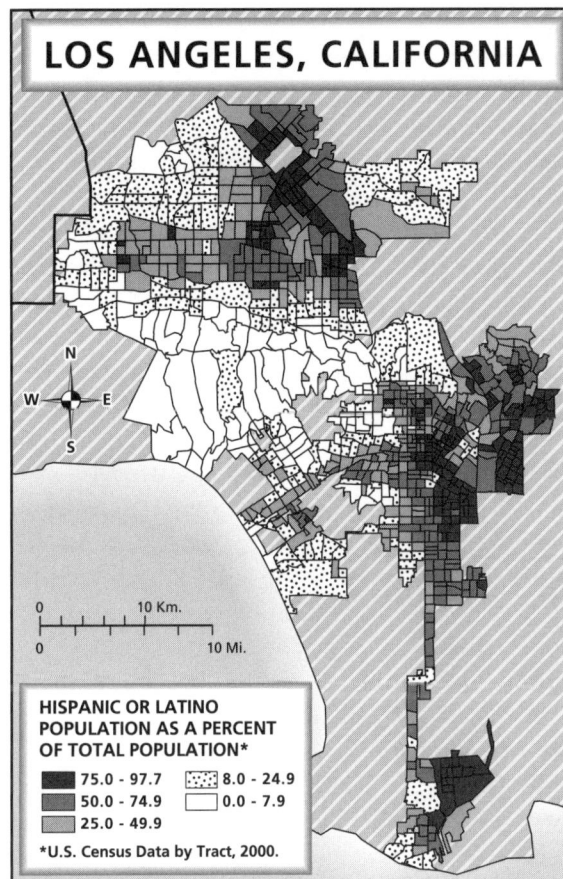

LOS ANGELES, CALIFORNIA

HISPANIC OR LATINO POPULATION AS A PERCENT OF TOTAL POPULATION*

75.0 - 97.7   8.0 - 24.9
50.0 - 74.9   0.0 - 7.9
25.0 - 49.9

*U.S. Census Data by Tract, 2000.

Although Toypurina was eventually captured by Spanish soldiers, she symbolized indigenous resistance against Spanish domination.

The Spanish era of Los Angeles history lasted until 1821, when Mexico declared its independence from Spain under the Plan of Iguala. Under Mexican rule the pueblo of Los Angeles grew slowly but remained a hub of Southern California's social and cultural life. In 1830 the Mexican population of Los Angeles totaled 1,180 persons, 770 of whom lived within the pueblo proper and the remainder on surrounding ranchos and in the missions. The Indian population was then estimated at slightly less than 2,500. The *pobladores* who settled within the parameters of the pueblo occupied a middling position within an emerging socioeconomic hierarchy determined by the massive redistribution of former mission land. The Mexican republic repudiated the union of church and state under Spanish imperial policy, and in California military and political elites resented the padres' ownership of California's richest land. Such resentment provided an underlying basis for the secularization of mission lands, in which Mexican authorities undertook a massive transfer of land from religious to secular authorities.

Under their plan for secularization, Mexican officials envisioned Indian ownership of former mission lands, but these lands ultimately fell into the hands of military and civic elites, who constituted a new elite class. The Californios established sprawling *ranchos* on their newfound land holdings, which displaced the missions as the primary economic institution of Mexican California. Like the missions, the ranchos were self-sustaining economic units, which sheltered not only the don and his family but also his mestizo and Indian labor force. Between 1836 and 1848, over 50 land grants in the vicinity of the Los Angeles pueblo were issued by the Mexican government. The historian Douglas Monroy uses the term *seigneurialism* to describe the basic pattern of social relations on the rancho, in which the don ruled firmly, yet benevolently, over his family and Indian workforce. The Sureños, or the most prominent dons of Southern California—Pio Pico, Jose Antonio Carrillo, Juan Bandini, Juan Sepulveda, Abel Stearns—dominated the political affairs of Mexican Los Angeles and rivaled their northern counterparts, the Arribeños, in terms of wealth and political influence.

The Mexican period of Los Angeles history lasted but a brief 27 years. In 1846 American forces, energized by the ideology of Manifest Destiny, charged into California and seized Mexican property. Californio resistance against the American invasion was strongest in the south, where a series of insignificant and inconclusive skirmishes persisted over the course of the year. Finally, in January 1847 American forces under the command of Commodore Robert Stockton captured Los Angeles in a decisive battle, leading to the conclusion of the Mexican-American War with the signing of the Treaty of Guadalupe Hidalgo in 1848. Under the terms of the treaty, the United States offered Mexico the sum of $15 million for possession of what is now the state of California and the vast expanse of territory north of the Rio Grande River, a sum historians estimate at a mere fraction of the land's actual worth.

The decades following the American conquest of California marked the end of the intricate social distinctions that had characterized Californio society and ushered in a period of intense racial conflict. While the military conquest of Mexican California spanned only a few years, the 1850s and 1860s witnessed a prolonged "race war" in Los Angeles that solidified the political and economic subordination of former Mexican citizens in the new American republic. Although the Treaty of Guadalupe Hidalgo granted the full rights of American citizenship to former Mexican citizens who opted to remain in the United States, the sudden confrontation between an ethnically diverse population of European Americans and former Mexican citizens, who had differentiated themselves according to caste and class, produced a racially polarized climate between "white" Americans and Mexican "greasers." Such tension was particularly pronounced in Los Angeles, where Mexican culture and identity retained its salience, more so than in the northern portion of California. This aroused the resentment of many white Americans, who targeted Mexicans for a similar kind of racial violence faced by African Americans in the South during the Reconstruction years. The historian Carey McWilliams characterized the lynching of Mexicans in Los Angeles as an "outdoor sport," as vigilante groups such as the El Monte Boys, a West Coast derivative of the Texas Rangers, persecuted Mexicans in their enforcement of white supremacy. Such violence galvanized a new brand of oppositional consciousness among this first generation of Mexican Americans, who rallied around the banditry of men such as Joaquin Murieta and Tiburcio Vasquez, who became local symbols of Mexican resistance against the American conquest.

Such racial violence accompanied the massive transfer of land from Mexican to Anglo-American hands. The Californios found themselves at a severe disadvantage in American courts of law, which demanded proof of land ownership under the California Land Act of 1851. Lacking written documentation of property ownership, less fluent in the English language, and wholly dependent on unscrupulous and land-hungry Anglo-American lawyers, the Californios relinquished much, if not all, of their land holdings. Legal manipulations, however, were not the only means by which the Californios saw their vast land holdings disappear. The institution of marriage marked another avenue by which Californio land fell into Anglo-American hands. In the decades following the Mexican-American War, the intermarriage between Anglo-American men and the daughters of elite Californio families became increasingly commonplace, often at the encouragement of the dons, who sought to bring the business acumen of Anglo-American entrepreneurs into their families. Endowed with generous gifts of land from their fathers, the daughters of the most prominent Californio families became attractive prospects for wealth among unattached Anglo-American men. Through this practice the Californios unwittingly forfeited their economic security, as their land holdings substantially diminished at the altar of marriage. Accordingly, toward the end of the 19th century, Californio society had all but faded into the past. The fate of Pio Pico illustrated most poignantly the demise of the Californios and their world. Once the wealthiest and most influential man in Mexican California, Pico was buried in a pauper's grave outside Los Angeles in 1894.

Despite the disappearance of the Californios' wealth and prominence, a community of Mexicans in Los Angeles continued to grow around the city's central plaza district. Many Mexican immigrants, for example, who were denied access to the gold mines of northern California, returned to the southern portion of the state and settled in Sonoratown, where they found an established Spanish-speaking community that retained many of the familiar influences and practices of Mexican culture. The long, low, whitewashed adobes north of the Old Plaza Church, which served as the cultural anchor of Sonoratown, provided space for commerce and residence for recent arrivals from Mexico, many from the state of Sonora. Generally recognized as the city's first barrio, Sonoratown remained the center of Mexican life in Los Angeles during the second half of the 19th century.

Sonoratown sustained the development of a more salient Mexican American identity, which found expression in cultural forms that burgeoned in urban America during the late 19th century. Newspapers, for example, catered to particular readerships within diverse urban populations, and in Los Angeles, Mexicans and Mexican Americans constituted one segment of an expanding urban population that provided an immediate market for Spanish print media. Newspapers such as *La Cronica* and *Las Dos Republicas* generally reflected the views and opinions of what remained of the old Californio elite, while other papers, such as *La Voz de Justicia* and *El Eco Mexicano,* reflected more populist points of view, addressing the concerns of Los Angeles's Spanish-speaking, working-class readers. *El Clamor Publico,* established by Francisco P. Ramirez in 1855, was the city's third-largest newspaper by the turn of the 19th century, reporting the interests of Los Angeles's Spanish-speaking population. Rife with such terms as *nuestra gente, nuestra raza,* and *la raza Latina,* Los Angeles's Spanish-language newspapers recorded the development of a self-conscious Mexican American identity, forged in the context of racial discrimination and economic subordination.

This identity, however, remained hidden behind the concerted development of a regional mythology that drew on elements of the city's Spanish and Mexican past. The arrival of the transcontinental Southern Pacific Railroad in Los Angeles in 1877 provided the basis for rapid growth in Southern California and sparked an elaborate promotional campaign to advertise the allure of the region, and especially its climate. Seeking ways to entice tourists and prospective settlers to the region, local boosters seized on the decaying remnants of the Spanish and Mexican past to create an exotic fantasy about Los Angeles. The wild popularity of Helen Hunt Jackson's 1887 novel *Ramona* drew national attention to an idyllic rendering of benevolent padres and docile Indians, while Charles Fletcher Lummis, Southern California's most fervent booster, established the Landmarks Club in 1895 to renovate California's decaying missions for tourist consumption. "The missions," Lummis wrote, "next to our climate, are the best capital Southern California has." He also organized the Los Angeles Fiesta, an annual pageant designed to commemorate a mythologized and deeply nostalgic version of Mexican Los Angeles. The sum of these cultural renderings, generally known as the Spanish Fantasy Past, presented not only a promotional vehicle by which to induce growth and development in Southern California but also the opportunity to obscure the region's unsightly history of Indian exploitation, military conquest, and racial violence.

If the second half of the 19th century marked an elaborate effort to eradicate the Mexican influence on Los Angeles and its cultural landscape, the course of events at the outset of the next century severely undermined those efforts. In Mexico the misguided pursuit of modernization under the regime of Porfirio Diaz wrought economic deprivation and political turmoil on the Mexican people, while the subsequent Mexican Revolution brought further chaos and instability. These convulsive events sparked a mass migration northward to the United States of Mexicans seeking relief from the pandemics of poverty and war. Diaz's implementation of a national railroad network, moreover, provided easier access to the southwestern United States, while the rapid development of industry and agriculture in cities like Los Angeles generated employment opportunities for a growing pool of mobile and jobless Mexican workers. In the years following the Mexican Revolution, the Mexican population of Los Angeles expanded rapidly, and the confrontation between this generation of immigrants and a quickly modernizing Los Angeles provided the basis for the development of a new, syncretic Chicano identity.

For progressive reformers in Los Angeles, who maintained a strong hold on municipal government in the early decades of the 20th century, the dramatic expansion of the city's Mexican community brought an "immigrant problem" that required an institutional response. Pursuing a vision of a social order rooted in the hegemony of white Anglo-Saxon Protestant (WASP) culture, progressive reformers in Los Angeles collaborated with state officials to establish a series of programs designed to inculcate the

© REED SAXON/AP/WIDE WORLD PHOTOS

Santa Ana Pines, a development of new homes in the Watts district, South-Central Los Angeles, 1999.

cultural norms and values of the dominant society within Mexican immigrant families in Los Angeles. The Commission of Immigration and Housing undertook the responsibility for sponsoring the Americanization programs, which aimed for a thorough transformation of various aspects of Mexican culture, including language, religion, diet, child rearing, and family planning. Social reformers aimed their efforts at Mexican women in particular, who could transmit the dominant values of WASP culture to their children. Ultimately, however, the ebb and flow of Mexican immigration to Southern California, as well as the efforts of the Mexican consulate in Los Angeles to preserve cultural and national allegiance to Mexico, countered the effectiveness of Americanization programs and to some degree ensured the retention of traditional Mexican values.

Los Angeles's Mexican population, however, remained susceptible to other Americanizing influences, particularly the seductive appeal of American mass culture. By the 1920s, with the rise of Hollywood and the film industry, Los Angeles emerged as a national center of mass cultural production, and the city's Mexican population easily accessed this culture, as did other social groups. The debut of radio broadcasts in Spanish during the 1920s, for example, reflected a growing cognizance of a Spanish-language consumer market in Los Angeles, as did the increasing popularity of movies from both Hollywood and Mexico City. Spanish-language newspapers such as La Opinion also debuted during this decade, targeting a Mexican readership interested in current events in both the United States and Mexico, and relying on the sponsorship of advertisers who marketed their products to an expanding Spanish-language readership. The increasing availability of radio programs, movies, and newspapers within Los Angeles's Mexican community during the 1920s reflected not only a growing engagement with modern American consumer culture but also the ability of that culture to cater to the particular tastes and preferences of a growing community of Mexican consumers.

If American popular culture exerted an Americanizing influence on Mexican immigrants and their children in Los Angeles, so too did wage labor. Up through the 1920s the predominance of agriculture within the regional economy offered a means of steady work for Mexican immigrants to Southern California, and the presence of an extensive network of interurban trolley cars allowed for agricultural workers to reside near the city center while commuting to distant agricultural fields. The 1920s, however, also marked an intensive phase of industrialization in Los Angeles that extended into the following decade, providing job opportunities beyond the traditional source, namely farm labor. Mexican women, for example, particularly the daughters of Mexican immigrants, found access to jobs within the burgeoning cannery and food processing industry of Southern California, and their growing presence within the regional labor market brought significant changes to the dynamics of immigrant family life. The historian Vicki Ruiz has shown how these changes brought a newfound sense of independence to young Mexican women as workers and consumers, and heightened demands for union representation through the organized efforts of labor activists in Los Angeles, such as Luisa Moreno and Rose Pesotta.

The 1930s marked a paradoxical moment in the history of Chicano Los Angeles. While the entry of Mexican men and women into the regional labor force reflected their growing participation in the larger society, the Great Depression reignited racial hostility toward Mexicans among the white citizenry. In particular, the sight of Mexicans applying for state and federal relief at the outset of the Depression piqued the resentment of local whites, who held fast to a conviction of white entitlement to government-sponsored assistance. Such resentment provided a basis for the implementation of an official effort to rid Los Angeles of its Mexican population, either through a scare campaign intended to incite Mexicans to voluntarily repatriate back to Mexico or through the attempt to forcibly remove Mexicans from Los Angeles outright. Between 1931 and 1933, the Los Angeles Police Department, sanctioned by officials in city government, conducted random sweeps of barrio neighborhoods, herding Mexicans onto trains headed for the U.S.-Mexico border. In several instances families were separated, sometimes to reunite after prolonged absence. The Mexican government issued its protest of this practice, which eventually ceased by the middle of the decade. Still, the deportation campaigns of the early 1930s demonstrated the persistence of white racism toward Mexicans in Los Angeles and heightened the ambivalence of Los Angeles's Mexican community toward the dominant American society.

The early 1940s, however, brought sudden and drastic changes to Los Angeles and its Mexican community. World War II triggered a massive infusion of federal investment in Southern California's defense industries and saw the establishment of military bases throughout the region. The development of a sprawling military-industrial complex in Southern California triggered a job explosion, prompting the arrival of a stream of migrants and immigrants to Los Angeles ready to work. Such economic and demographic upheaval put severe strains on the regional infrastructure, initiating a concerted effort to accommodate the convulsive expansion of the city and its population. A housing shortage afflicted Los Angeles during the mid-1940s, sparking public demand for new housing. Traffic congestion dramatized the imperative to build new highways, anticipating a massive state project that materialized in the following decades. World War II wrought an unprecedented phase of modernization on Los Angeles and Southern California, which had profound consequences for the pattern of social relations that took shape in the following decades.

Attorney Carey McWilliams, for example, presciently recognized how World War II unleashed a "racial revolution" on Southern California, as the sudden confrontation of racially and ethnically diverse people brought new episodes of racial conflict. In particular, a second "great migration" of African Americans from the rural South brought a stream of black migrants in search of work to American cities, including Los Angeles. The sudden and dramatic expansion of Southern California's black community was most apparent in Watts and its surrounding locale. One of the few neighborhoods in the region open to black residents, Watts sustained an influx of poor black Southerners in the years following the conclusion of World War II. The streaming of African Americans into the south-central portion of Los Angeles reinforced a burgeoning "white" racial consciousness among Southern California's suburban population, particularly within such proximate communities as South Gate and Huntington Park, where a Dust Bowl generation of poor southern whites had settled a decade or so earlier. The 1940s thus witnessed a series of turf wars in which white homeowners sought to enforce their distance from black newcomers to Southern California.

Mexican Americans, particularly young Chicano men, also found themselves the targets of white racism during the war years. While many Mexican American men demonstrated their loyalty to the

United States by their willingness to enlist in military service, the Sleepy Lagoon murder case of 1942 and the Zoot Suit Riots of 1943 demonstrated the paradox of Chicano identity in midcentury Los Angeles. In the summer of 1942, the body of Jose Diaz was found in a hangout spot known among local youth as the Sleepy Lagoon. Although no evidence pointed to any one culprit, the Los Angeles police used the incident to conduct a massive sweep of city streets, arresting over 300 young Chicano men. The arrests ultimately led to a highly sensationalized murder trial in which 12 young Chicano men were falsely convicted of murder without due process of law. The Sleepy Lagoon Defense Committee, led by Carey McWilliams and with the vocal support of such celebrities as Dolores Del Rio, Orson Welles, and Anthony Quinn, labored for two years to successfully overturn the convictions. In June of 1943, the Zoot Suit Riots exploded, in which white sailors stationed near downtown Los Angeles lashed out against the conspicuous presence of Chicano "zoot suits," who sported the tailored suits and feathered hats that were fashionable among black and Chicano youth in American cities during the early 1940s. Over the course of seven days, young Chicano men were subjected to random attacks by white sailors, who left their victims naked and wounded on the streets. The police, instead of arresting the attackers, blamed the Zoot Suits for disturbing the peace. Finally, city officials called on the National Guard to enforce civil order. Both the Sleepy Lagoon incident and the Zoot Suit Riots demonstrated a widespread perception of Chicano youth, one sustained by local media, as criminal and inherently violent.

The racial frictions that surfaced during the war years shaped the racial geography of post–World War II Los Angeles. The decades following the war's conclusion witnessed the development of a Spanish-speaking barrio in East Los Angeles, which took shape through an interrelated set of events and processes linked not by causality but rather by coincidence. Although Boyle Heights had once sheltered a thriving working-class community diverse in RACE and ethnicity, it emerged by the late 1940s as the heart of the Los Angeles barrio. The internment of Japanese Americans during the war dislodged the historic presence of a Japanese American community from Boyle Heights, while the simultaneous departure of Jews for the newer suburban communities of West Los Angeles paralleled a larger pattern of "white flight" that afflicted American cities during the postwar period. Such demographic shifts depleted Boyle Heights of its historic diversity and left East Los Angeles vulnerable to the expansion of a concentration of Chicano poverty.

Urban renewal, another dimension of the transformation of the postwar American city, also precipitated the development of a barrio in East Los Angeles. The most infamous example, one that lingers in contemporary Chicano consciousness in Los Angeles, is the debacle of the Chavez Ravine, once a Mexican American community located approximately one mile north of downtown. In 1948 the City Housing Authority, charged with the responsibility of identifying sites for the construction of public housing, designated the Chavez Ravine community as "blighted" and invoked the authority of eminent domain to clear most of the residents from their properties. Before the plans for public housing could be implemented, however, a powerful bloc of downtown real estate interests rallied behind the election of Mayor Norris Poulson in 1953, who invoked Cold War hysteria to decry the plans for public housing in the Chavez Ravine as "socialistic," and immediately canceled the project when he entered City Hall. Ultimately, through an intense media campaign and the mayor's sly modification of the wording of the city's deed to the Chavez Ravine, some 350 acres (142 ha) of the Ravine fell into the hands of Walter O'Malley, owner and president of the Brooklyn Dodgers, who sought a new home for his franchise. Before O'Malley could begin construction of his new stadium, however, one family who stubbornly defied the will of the City Housing Authority remained in the Ravine. The Arechiga family had settled there during the early 1920s, and when county sheriffs appeared at their door with a second eviction notice on May 8, 1958, the Arechigas once again refused to leave. The confrontation drew the attention of local television stations, who broadcast images of sheriffs dragging Avrana Arechiga out of her home while her children cried in horror as bulldozers razed their home to rubble. Such images incited a national uproar over the city's treatment of the Arechiga family and especially aroused intense opposition among Los Angeles's Chicano community, who remembered the Arechiga evictions as another episode in a larger history of land displacement and dispossession.

Meanwhile, the imposition of freeways on Chicano neighborhoods further diminished the quality of life in the barrio. Highway construction, like urban renewal, transformed the nature and experience of urban life in the United States after World War II, and in Los Angeles the Eastside bore the brunt of that invasive process. The construction of the East Los Angeles Interchange, the largest freeway interchange in the world, depleted Boyle Heights of approximately one-tenth of its housing stock and forced the residents of that community to contend with the noise and pollution from increasing traffic. Between the years of 1950 and 1970, five major freeways sliced through East Los Angeles, wreaking havoc on the communal life of its neighborhoods. Residents organized themselves to fight the imposition of the freeway, but to little avail. While the residents of Beverly Hills successfully defeated plans for the construction of a Beverly Hills Freeway, lower property values in East Los Angeles, the result of decades of neglect and disinvestment, made that community a cost-efficient target for highway construction. The freeway has even found representation in the Chicano art and literature of Los Angeles, which provides a vivid record of the postwar trauma of highway construction and documents how the freeway has insinuated its way into Chicano culture and consciousness in Los Angeles.

The combined effects of highway construction, urban renewal, and police brutality precipitated the explosion of the Chicano movement in Los Angeles during the 1960s, which, to a certain extent, paralleled the civil rights struggles of African Americans. The movement had regional variations, but Los Angeles witnessed some of the most intense confrontations between Chicano activists and government officials. In 1968, for example, over 1,000 Chicano students in five of the city's most severely affected high schools staged the "blowouts," walking out of class to protest the inferior quality of public education in the barrio. The event led to the suspension of Sal Castro, a teacher at Garfield High School who had lent his support to the striking students. School administrators eventually reinstated Castro after community activists occupied the meeting chamber of the board of superintendents. To support the students, the Brown Berets established itself along the lines of a paramilitary organization similar to the Black Panthers. The aggressive posture of the Brown Berets incited the harassment of local police officials, as well as the Federal Bureau of Investigation (FBI), whose Counter Intelligence Program, or COINTEL-

PRO, surveilled the activities and members of the organization. The Los Angeles Chicano movement also maintained close ties to mounting opposition to the Vietnam War. Chicano activists in Los Angeles, like their African American counterparts, decried the disproportionate number of minority inductions into military service, and in August 1970 the Chicano Moratorium staged a demonstration of some 20,000 protesters in Laguna Park. Using batons and tear gas against an otherwise peaceful gathering, local officials incited a panic among demonstrators, provoking mass arrests. On the same day as the Moratorium, outspoken journalist Rubén Salazar, who was completing an investigation of internal corruption within the Los Angeles police department, was killed by sheriffs, who fired a tear gas canister into a bar where Salazar was sitting. The acquittal of the sheriff who killed Salazar raised lingering doubts within the community about the allegedly accidental nature of the reporter's death.

The Chicano movement in Los Angeles also included a cultural dimension, in which Chicano artists and writers used various cultural forms to express a distinct vision of Chicana and Chicano identity. Oscar Zeta Acosta published *Revolt of the Cockroach People* in 1973, which recorded the struggles within the Chicano movement. Patssi Valdez, Willie Herron, Gronk, and Harry Gamboa, Jr., established themselves as an art collective known as ASCO ("nausea" in Spanish) and staged various "happenings" throughout Los Angeles, including a performance in which Valdez taped herself to the walls of the Los Angeles County Museum of Art to dramatize the museum's exclusion of Chicano art. Self-Help Graphics opened in Boyle Heights in 1974, a community resource for cultivating Chicano art and culture in Los Angeles. Chicano musicians also figured prominently in the burgeoning rock scene of Los Angeles. Inheriting the appeal of singers like Ritchie Valens, a Mexican American rock star who died tragically at age 17 in a 1959 plane crash, groups such as The Midnighters, Cannibal and the Headhunters, El Chicano, and Tierra cultivated a distinctly Chicano sound that combined elements of traditional Mexican folk music with modern American rock. Not unlike the Harlem Renaissance of 1920s New York, Los Angeles during and after the Chicano movement witnessed a vital proliferation of Chicano cultural expression, which posited a distinct vision of a syncretic urban identity rooted in collective memory and experience.

Since the 1970s changes in U.S. immigration policy have replenished the stream of immigrants coming to Los Angeles from Mexico and Central America, who are radically reshaping the cultural profile of the city and its environs. While Mexican immigrants and Mexican Americans constitute the majority of Spanish speakers in Southern California, immigrants from Guatemala, Honduras, and El Salvador bring their own cultural markings to the city. The Pico Union neighborhood, immediately west of downtown Los Angeles, is now the nation's largest Central American barrio, and the hegemony of Chicano culture and identity in Los Angeles has given way to a broader Latino identity, diverse by class, region, ethnicity, religion, gender, and sexuality. Spanish-language advertisements proliferate in neighborhoods once identified as white or black; *vendederos* sell oranges, tacos, and flowers at freeway off-ramps, while *jornaleros* sell their labor on street corners; a Chicano middle class retreats from expanding immigrant barrios in the neighborhoods of Montebello and Pico Rivera; Salvadoran and Mexican immigrants who have abandoned traditional Catholic moorings stage fundamentalist revivals in storefront churches; Chicano punk musicians enjoy a current revival in the Los Angeles club scene; and gay Latinos now claim their space in the nightlife of the city.

The Latino influence on Los Angeles and its environs remains apparent within Southern California's physical and cultural landscape. Spanish remains the dominant language used by Southern Californians to identify their towns and streets. The architecture of the Spanish and Mexican periods retains its prominence within the urban and suburban environment, as red-tiled roofs continue to distinguish the region's unique architectural heritage. And Latinos have also exerted a profound influence on the culinary tastes of Southern Californians, as Mexican and Central American foods retain their popularity among the city's global array of restaurants and cuisines.

These cultural influences, however, have yet to translate into political and economic empowerment

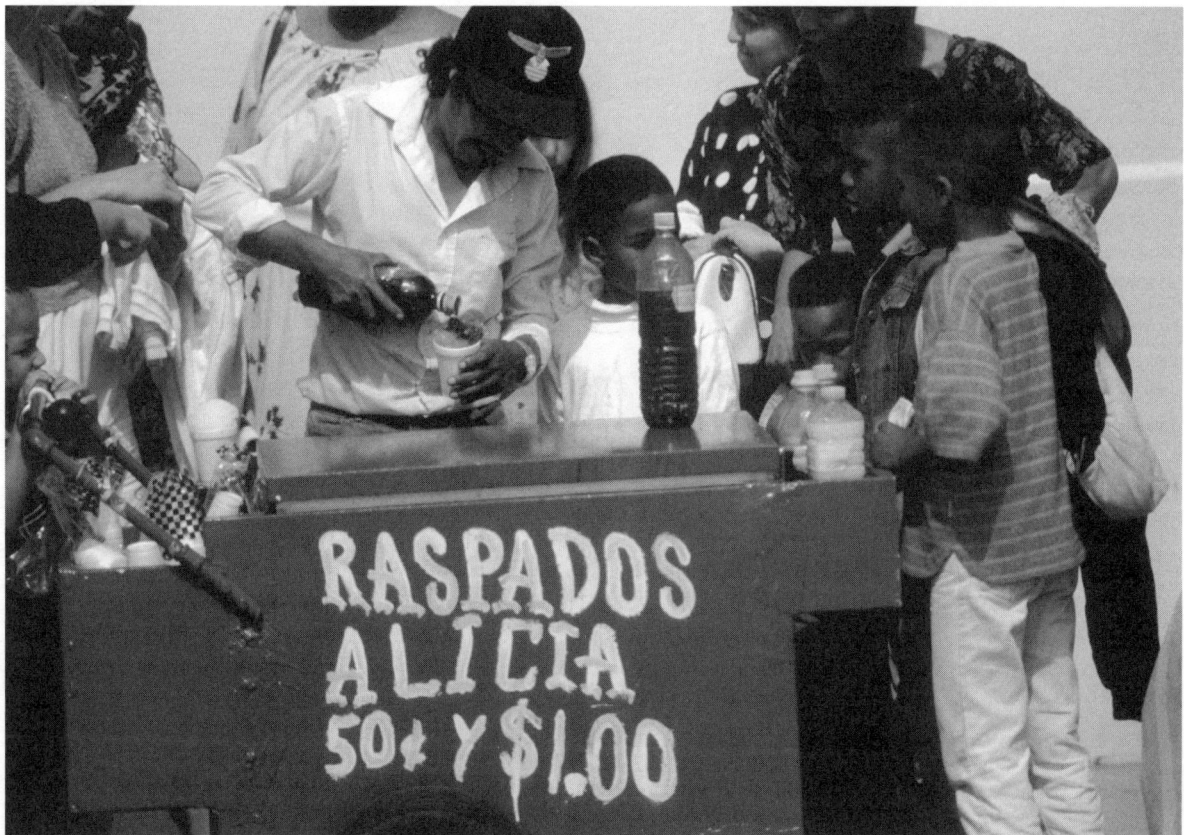

© HALLENBACH/DAS FOTOARCHIV/PETER ARNOLD INC.

Latino man selling shaved ice from a cart, South Los Angeles.

for Southern California's Latino populations. A backlash against Mexican immigrants and Mexican Americans surfaced in California during the 1990s, when white Californians passed a series of propositions that drastically reduced public assistance to immigrants, ended bilingual education, and terminated affirmative action programs. In 1992 Chicano students at the University of California at Los Angeles, inspired by the legacy of the Chicano movement, staged a hunger strike on campus, demanding the establishment of a Chicano studies department. After nine days of fasting, students won a landmark concession from campus administrators, and the César E. Chávez Center for Chicana and Chicano Studies opened its doors in 1993. Yet in a city with a recent Latino majority, to date no Latino has served as mayor and the question of Latino political empowerment remains more pressing than ever. Despite the uncertain forecast for Latino politics in Los Angeles and California, however, it appears that Los Angeles is becoming a Mexican city once again.

RELATED ARTICLES

Barrio, El; Californios; Chicano Movement; Cuisine, California; East Los Angeles School Walkout; Missions; National Chicano Moratorium of Vietnam; Proposition 187; Sleepy Lagoon Case; Zoot Suit Riots.

FURTHER READING

Avila, Eric. *Popular Culture in the Age of White Flight: Fear and Fantasy in Suburban Los Angeles.* Berkeley: Univ. of Calif. Press, 2004.

Davis, Mike. *Magical Urbanism: Latinos Reinvent the U.S. Big City.* London: Verso Press, 2001.

McWilliams, Carey. *North From Mexico: The Spanish-Speaking Peoples of the United States.* Ed. by Matt S. Meier. New York: Praeger, 1990.

Monroy, Douglas. *Thrown Among Strangers: The Making of Mexican Culture in Frontier California.* Berkeley: Univ. of Calif. Press, 1990.

Monroy, Douglas. *Rebirth: Mexican Los Angeles From the Great Migration to the Great Depression.* Berkeley: Univ. of Calif. Press, 1999.

Pardo, Mary. *Mexican American Women Activists: Identity and Resistance in Two Los Angeles Communities.* Philadelphia: Temple Univ. Press, 1998.

Ruíz, Vicki. *Cannery Women, Cannery Lives: Mexican Women, Unionization, and the California Food Processing Industry.* Albuquerque: Univ. of N.Mex. Press, 1987.

Sánchez, George. *Becoming Mexican American: Ethnicity, Identity, and Culture in Chicano Los Angeles.* New York: Oxford Univ. Press, 1992.

ERIC AVILA

EAST LOS ANGELES

Mexicans have been a part of the Los Angeles landscape for centuries, but they have not always been welcome. After the signing of the Treaty of Guadalupe Hidalgo, Mexicans lost their political clout, which substantially limited their ability to protect their interests and create laws to improve their socioeconomic situation. A lack of political power, media bias, and discriminatory laws have all had a dramatic impact contributing to the marginalization of the Mexican community in Los Angeles.

The area now known as East Los Angeles (East L.A.) did not begin as the center of Mexican culture that it is today. Mexicans initially settled in the city's center. Having established a thriving center where Olvera St. and La Plazita are currently located, they were driven east of the Los Angeles River in the 1920s at a time of increased racial tension, civic center development, competition for industrial space, and a need for more housing as Mexican immigrants streamed into the area. Unable to compete with outside influences, Mexicans moved east into neighborhoods that had been abandoned by upwardly mobile Jews, Italians, and Russians. Thus was born East L.A., a cluster of neighborhoods including Belvedere, Maravilla, Boyle Heights, and City Terrace, though today East L.A. has come to include any Latino neighborhood east of the Los Angeles River.

One of the best-known Chicano and Mexican barrios outside of Mexico, East Los Angeles has been vilified as a gang-infested neighborhood. Historically, the neighborhood has been marred by racism, segregation, negative media portrayals, and police harassment. It nonetheless remains a symbol of Chicano and Mexican resistance and a testament to the accomplishments of Mexicans in spite of insurmountable obstacles.

In the early 1900s Mexicans were able to persevere because of employers who had become increasingly addicted to the cheap labor Mexicans offered, especially during World Wars I and II, when there was a lack of American laborers and Mexicans were shipped in through the Bracero program. The Bracero program, however, later backfired as Americans balked at the specter of "racial degeneration," fueling an anti-immigrant movement spearheaded by a nativist movement that eventually lead to the mass deportation of millions of Mexicans during Operation Wetback in the early to mid-1950s, displacing over 3 million Mexicans (many of whom were U.S. citizens). The anti-Mexican sentiment was especially strong during the Great Depression, when immigrants were scapegoated for financial woes of the day. But while laws such as the Literacy Act of 1917 were introduced to put a stranglehold on increased immigration, Congress—pressured by railroad companies, farmers, and ranchers—exempted Mexicans, underscoring the city's dependence on Mexican labor.

By the 1940s Chicanos, feeling considerably excluded by the establishment and under attack by police, began to rebel against the status quo and formed gangs, giving birth to the infamous gangs that continue to plague East L.A. In spring 1942 several minor events served as fodder for newspapers. Over a period of six months, the newspapers played up the "Mexican" gang problem even though at the time less than 3 percent of the 30,000 school-age Mexicans in Los Angeles belonged to a gang. The stories prominently pointed out the Mexican character of those involved, as if the race element made these crimes any different from ordinary crime. In this way the press served as a catalyst for an all-out siege against the Mexican community.

The boiling point came when the body of José Díaz was found at a water-filled gravel pit on the east side of town nicknamed the Sleepy Lagoon. The police arrested 22 suspects, all members of the 38th Street Gang, who were seen at the Sleepy Lagoon the night of the murder. Promptly sensationalizing the case, the media depicted the defendants as bloodthirsty hoodlums. The mass trial that ensued was unprecedented and attracted national attention, and the proceedings resembled more of a witch hunt than a trial, with the civil rights of the defendants routinely ignored. For example, defendants were not allowed to sit with their attorney, nor were they permitted to bathe, change clothes, or shave, giving them the appearance of unkempt vagabonds, which was then used against them during the trial as proof of guilt. The trial ended on January 13, 1943, with 12 defendants convicted of murder, 5 found guilty of assault, and 5 others acquitted. The community set up the Sleepy Lagoon Defense Committee, and the verdicts were reversed when the trial judge was found to be biased against the defendants. The case was the first organized victory for a community that had been tormented by police and the press for decades. But the victory would be short-lived.

Further biased and irresponsible media coverage fostered hysteria about Mexican gang activity. Coupled with an unfriendly police force and an otherwise bored group of servicemen stationed in Chavez Ravine who took their cue from sensationalized newspaper stories about Mexican gangs, the stage was set for the Zoot Suit Riots of June 1943, in which hordes of sailors took the law into their own hands when the police failed to arrest a "gang" of Mexicans who had allegedly attacked a group of sailors. Meeting little or no police resistance, 20 cabs filled with sailors roamed the streets of East L.A. brutally beating any Mexican they encountered on the street. If any of their targets happened to be wearing zoot suits, they were stripped and left naked and bloody in the streets. Remarkably, hundreds of Mexicans were arrested during the riots, while only 17 of the 200 sailors who participated in the rampage were arrested. The riots, which lasted a week and set off several other similar outbreaks countrywide, shed a harsh light on the fractured relationship between the Mexican American community and the Los Angeles Police Department (LAPD) and left a long-lasting feeling of hatred and resentment toward the police, which exists even today.

Around this time of turmoil, Chicanos returning from the World War II came back to a significantly changed barrio. The atrocities of the Sleepy Lagoon case had scarred the community, and the Zoot Suit Riots were still fresh in the minds of the people. These events were in stark contrast to the vets' achievements in the war: many had come back as local heroes, and Chicanos were the war's most decorated ethnic group. It was not long before vets formed the Community Service Organization; challenged Jim Crow laws; demanded local representation, metropolitan services, and community improvements; and fought for equality in the judiciary system.

Though vets set the groundwork for a more politically aware Mexican community, the sixties were by far the most progressive years for Latinos in East Los Angeles. The Civil Rights Act of 1964 had been signed, but by then Latino youth had become increasingly disenchanted with the poor quality of education. Fueled by the anti–Vietnam War atmosphere of the era, Chicanos formed several organizations to fight for their own causes, in particular improved education, relevant social science courses for Chicanos, Mexican American studies, equal representation, and programs to encourage Chicanos to graduate from high school and attend college.

Virtually overnight dozens of such groups as the Brown Berets and the Mexican-American Student Association (MASA) were born. Students began to make demands and organize mass walkouts. In March 1968 almost 10,000 students walked out of five Los Angeles high schools. Police met the walkouts with excessive force, at one point macing participants. The walkouts produced drawn-out trials against 13 defendants, including Sal Castro, a teacher who was one of several walkout organizers. The trials ended two years later, when the felony charges were found to be a violation of the 1st Amendment. As a result of this political activism came improvements such as the hiring of Latino teachers and staff to reflect the student body, policy reforms, and curricular reforms.

The Chicano Moratorium on August 29, 1970, was the pinnacle of the protests. Between 20,000 and 30,000 people participated in the anti–Vietnam War moratorium at Laguna Park (now Rubén Salazar Park). The peaceful protest quickly spiraled out of control when police, wielding clubs and firing tear gas, attacked the protesters in response to a minor disturbance half a block away. Three protesters were killed, including Rubén Salazar, a respected Latino journalist who was killed when a police officer fired a high-velocity tear gas projectile into a restaurant where Salazar and others had gathered. The police officer was never tried, further justifying Chicano's lack of trust in the judicial system.

Though progress has been made, similar challenges from decades ago still confront Latinos in East Los Angeles, as illustrated by Proposition 187, an anti-immigration initiative introduced in 1994 that was voted into law but was later found to be unconstitutional. Like the Literacy Act before it, Proposition 187 targeted immigrants at a time of economic ills. Similar antiminority propositions followed—for example, the antiaffirmative action measure Proposition 209 and the antibilingual education initiative Proposition 227, both of which were passed into law in California and have had significant effects on the East L.A. population.

The relationship between police and Latinos has not improved much, either, as was made clear by the police corruption scandal in 2000 involving an antigang task force implemented by the LAPD, Community Resources Against Street Hoodlums (CRASH). The team, operating out of the Rampart Division, which serves a largely working-class and heavily immigrant area of Los Angeles, was found to have participated in a host of illegal dealings, including planting evidence, routine beatings, witness intimidation, illegal shootings, and frame-ups.

Regardless of, or perhaps because of, the challenges that the East L.A. community have overcome, the barrio has become a tight community. And it continues to be a launching pad for thousands of immigrants looking for a better life and a hub for Mexican culture in the United States.

RELATED ARTICLES

Barrio, El; Brown Berets; Chicano Movement; Gangs; Mexican Americans; Pachuco; Proposition 187; Sleepy Lagoon Case; Zoot Suit Riots.

FURTHER READING

Acuña, Rodolfo F. *A Community under Siege: A Chronicle of Chicanos East of the Los Angeles River 1945–1975.* Los Angeles: Chicano Studies Res. Ctr. Pubns., Univ. of Calif., 1984.

Acuña, Rodolfo F. *Anything but Mexican: Chicanos in Contemporary Los Angeles.* Haymarket Series. New York: Verso Bks., 1996.

Escobar, Edward J. *Race, Police, and the Making of a Political Identity: Mexican Americans and the Los Angeles Police Department, 1900–1945.* Berkeley: Univ. of Calif. Press, 1999.

McWilliams, Carey. *North from Mexico: The Spanish-Speaking People of the United States.* New ed., updated by Matt S. Meier. Westport, Conn.: Praeger, 1990.

Romo, Richard. *East Los Angeles, History of a Barrio.* Austin: Univ. of Tex. Press, 1998.

Sánchez, George J. *Becoming Mexican American: Ethnicity, Culture and Identity in Chicano Los Angeles, 1900–1945.* Ed. by Ricardo Penaranda and Charles Bergquist. 1993. Reprint. Oxford, England: Oxford Univ. Press, 1995.

LUZ MARÍA CASTELLANOS

LOUISIANA

According to the 2000 U.S. Census, 2.4 percent of Louisiana's population, about 108,000 people, are Latinos: 32,267 identify themselves as Mexican, 7,670 as Puerto Rican, 8,448 as Cuban, and 59,353 as "other"—likely belonging to a large Honduran population in New Orleans. While many of the Latinos in the state have immigrated to the state over the past century, Hispanics have lived and worked in the area since the 19th century, along with Native Americans and French, Spanish, and English settlers.

It is quite possible that the first Europeans to see the land encompassed by the present state of Louisiana were those who skirted the area in small boats as part of the Cabeza de Vaca–Pánfilo de Narváez Expedition of the 1530s. It was Robert de La Salle, however, who, journeying in 1682 from Canada to the Gulf of Mexico, gave this area the name Louisiana, in honor of Louis XIV of France, for whom La Salle claimed the entire Mississippi River basin. He dreamed of building an empire there, but when he attempted to return and establish a colony, he missed the mouth of the river and landed at Matagorda Bay on the Texas coast. La Salle's dream was taken up by the two brothers Pierre Le Moyne, sieur d'Iberville, and Jean Le Moyne, sieur de Bienville, in 1699, who established a settlement at Biloxi (in present-day Mississippi). The latter became governor of this small settlement in 1701, and in 1718 he founded the city of New Orleans. However, the colony struggled and was put under direct crown control in 1733, with Bienville remaining as governor.

In an attempt to foster a more stable economy, Bienville introduced cotton and sugarcane to Louisiana around 1750, a transition that altered traditional farming practices and enhanced the region's reliance on slave labor. Increasingly, Louisiana became connected to the Caribbean and parts of Central America through the slave trade, opening the area to an ingression of Latin American people and culture. With the culmination of the French and Indian War in 1763, England acquired much of the French lands west of the Mississippi River. However, before the war ended, France and Spain had secretly established an agreement known as the Treaty of Fontainebleau; instead of passing over to England, French Louisiana west of the Mississippi, including the Isle of Orleans, became Spanish territory. Spanish rule linked the region with Spain's Latin American colonies, bringing increased prosperity as well as a new era of Latin American influence to Louisiana. Spanish and mestizo soldiers from Latin America joined with the French and Native American core populations in the northern regions along the Red River, where together they developed small multicultural communities that were later incorporated into two separate

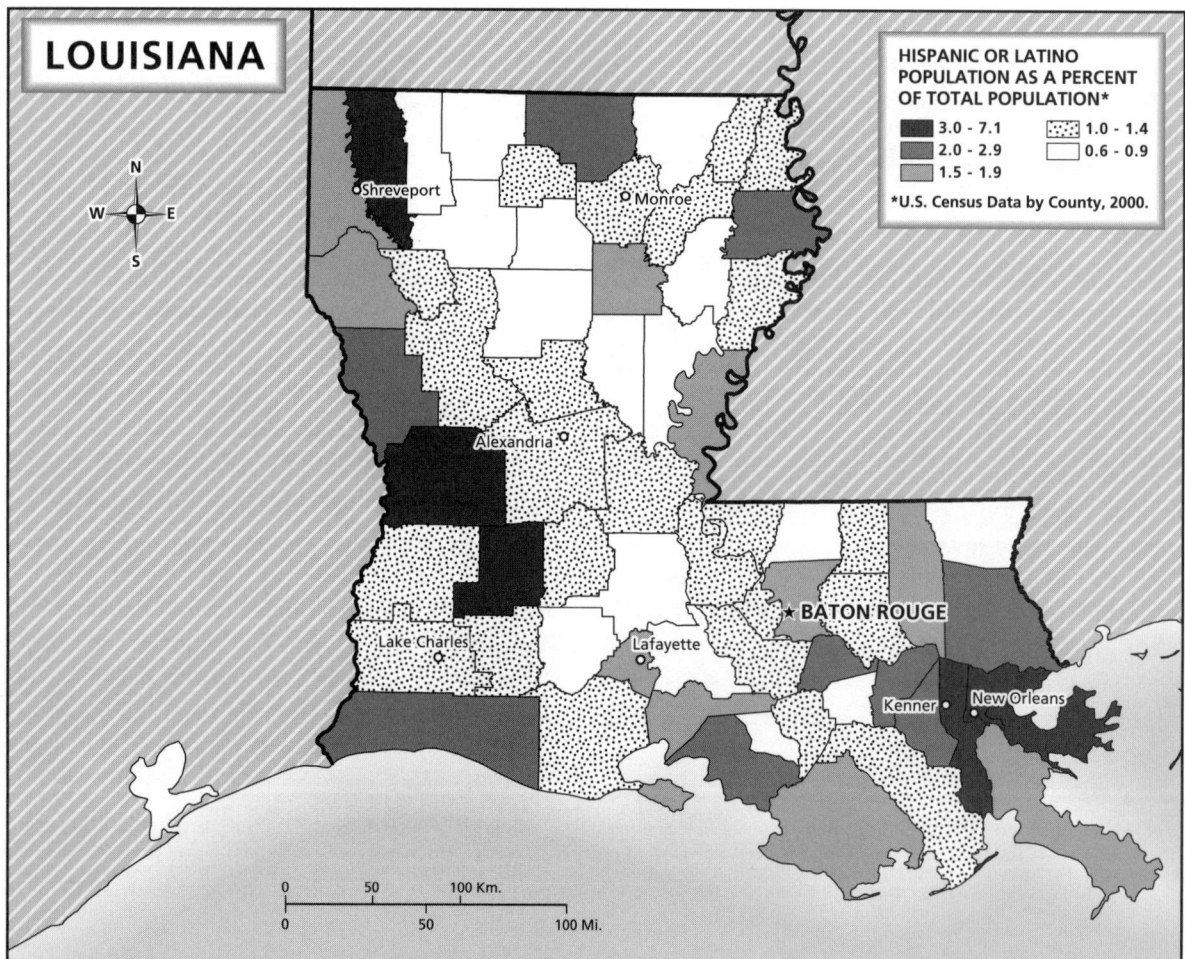

LOUISIANA

HISPANIC OR LATINO POPULATION AS A PERCENT OF TOTAL POPULATION*

3.0 - 7.1   1.0 - 1.4
2.0 - 2.9   0.6 - 0.9
1.5 - 1.9

*U.S. Census Data by County, 2000.

Shreveport
Monroe
Alexandria
Lake Charles
Lafayette
★ BATON ROUGE
Kenner   New Orleans

0   50   100 Km.
0   50   100 Mi.

municipal areas, the Sabine Parish and the Natchitoches Parish. While several of these communities dissolved around 1773, when inhabitants relocated to San Antonio, Texas, others survived; for instance, the Natchitoches Parish is still recognized today as having strong Spanish, Indo-Spanish, and Latino traditions.

Under the Spanish governor Bernardo de Gálvez, Louisiana played an active and important military role on behalf of the United States during the American Revolution. Gálvez led his army of Spanish regulars, mestizos, Indians, Creoles, and freed slaves in numerous battles against the British. If not for his crucial and timely victories at Manchac, Baton Rouge, Natchez, Mobile, and Pensacola, the British capital of West Florida, the United States may well not have won its independence and freedom until the following century. After the war Gálvez was appointed viceroy to New Spain (Mexico), where he endeared himself to the population by dedicating himself, including his own personal resources, to the construction of the Cathedral of Mexico, the largest cathedral in the Western Hemisphere. While technically a full-blooded Spaniard, Gálvez is today considered by many to be a Latino hero and a revered figure in Louisianan Hispanic heritage.

As governor of Louisiana, Gálvez initiated a colonization program beginning in 1778 that engendered a stream of settlers from the Spanish Canary Islands. These immigrants settled in six small communities in the delta areas approximately 35 miles (56 km) southeast of New Orleans. The inhabitants became known as Isleños, and despite the fact that they lived in relative isolation for some 200 years, many aspects of their Canarian culture have blended with French, Anglo, Caribbean, and Mexican influences. Linguistically, Isleños have developed a distinctive "Louisiana Spanish," which borrows a substantial vocabulary from American Spanish, and their *décimas,* or satirical narrative poems, reflect the influences both of traditional Spanish ballad meter and of the *corridos,* or ballads, of Mexico, Central America, and the U.S. Southwest. Because of their Spanish ancestry and the way their Canarian culture has merged with American Hispanic culture, Isleños are often considered a Latino ethnic group.

In present-day Louisiana, Latinos and Latino culture permeate countless areas of the social milieu. Owing to the high volume of trade between Louisiana and Mexico's Yucatán Peninsula, Hispanics hold a variety of professional positions that require them to serve as linguistic and cultural liaisons between Louisianan and Mexican businesses and economic interests. Latinos also participate in a variety of organizations that represent the broad range of Hispanic cultures and groups in the region. These organizations include community groups such as the Casa Argentina and the New Orleans Hispanic Heritage Foundation, a club founded in 1990 to unite and strengthen the Latino community and to provide scholarships to promising Hispanic high school graduates. In addition, Latinos benefit from societies that facilitate networking, thereby enhancing their economic opportunities; among these are the Hispanic Lawyers Association of Louisiana and the Hispanic Chamber of Commerce of Louisiana. The state's Spanish-language radio stations KGLA "Gretna" and WFNO "Norco" as well as television networks such as Univisión represent a long-established Latino media presence that has helped to proliferate Hispanic heritages. Also, many Latinos operate restaurants offering Mexican, Central American, South American, and Caribbean dishes, along with unique Louisianan Latino specialties that mix traditional Hispanic recipes with French and African American infusions.

In February 2003 Latino politics rose to the forefront of media attention for the first time in Louisiana history. Controversy arose when Democratic U.S. senator Mary Landrieu initially pledged, over Spanish radio, support for President Bush's judicial nominee Hispanic lawyer Miguel Estrada; later, however, Landrieu rescinded and participated in a filibuster of Estrada's nomination. She claimed her initial pledge of support was a misunderstanding, but many Latinos in Louisiana felt deceived and betrayed by her decision to oppose Estrada's nomination and questioned the Democratic Party's support of minority candidates. Other Louisianan Hispanics applauded the move, claiming that Estrada's conservative tendencies and Republican backing put him out of touch with the less affluent Latino population. Overall, the controversy in Louisiana raised important questions about Hispanics and political partisanship that will become increasingly relevant as the Latino vote evolves into an even more critical factor in upcoming state and national elections.

RELATED ARTICLES

Immigration, Latino; Politics, Latino; Spain.

FURTHER READING

Churchill, Charles Robert. *Bernardo de Gálvez' Services to the American Revolution.* Baton Rouge: La. Society, Sons of the American Revolution, 1925.

Ferling, John. *Struggle for a Continent.* Arlington Heights, Va.: Harlan Davidson, 1993.

Rosengarten, J. G. *French Colonists and Exiles in the United States.* 1907. Reprint. Westminster, Md.: Heritage Bks. 1989.

ARTHUR E. CHAPMAN

LOUISIANA PURCHASE

The Louisiana Purchase of the Orleans and Louisiana territories by the United States from France in 1803 is one of the most important events in U.S. history. These territories not only doubled the U.S. landmass but also led to the creation of 13 new states, beginning with the admission of Louisiana in 1812 and ending with the annexation of Oklahoma in 1907. For early U.S. statesmen such as Alexander Hamilton, the acquisition of these territories provided a welcome precedent for the eventual conquest of all Spanish territories in the Americas. This early im-

perialist vision would eventually be known as a form of Manifest Destiny. In addition, the purchase extended navigation and commercial rights to U.S. merchants using the Mississippi River.

By the mid-1500s, within three decades of Juan Ponce de León's first explorations of the Florida territories, Spanish conquistadores had traveled through, and laid claim to, most of the territories between present-day Florida and Oregon. By the late 1600s, however, the French had begun to build settlements in the Orleans territory, presently known as Louisiana. Owing to the complex relationship between the Castilian and French monarchies, the Castilian crown did not protest the French incursions into the Louisiana territories.

Throughout the 18th century the Castilian crown negotiated its claims to the Louisiana territories, and by 1800 it had signed the Treaty of San Ildefonso. Under the tenets of this secret treaty, the Spanish crown agreed to cede the Louisiana territories to France with the express condition that France would not sell or cede these territories to the United States.

NORTH WIND PICTURE ARCHIVES

Map of the United States in 1803 showing the area of the Louisiana Purchase.

In signing the treaty, Spain had intended to create a "buffer zone" that would separate the gold-rich territories of New Mexico and Texas from the aggressive United States. However, on April 30, 1803, Napoleon Bonaparte sold the Orleans and Louisiana territories to the United States for approximately $15 million.

The U.S. Constitution is silent on the question of whether the United States can acquire new territories and expand beyond its original compact. Spurring one of the earliest constitutional crises, the Louisiana Purchase meant the eventual admission of new states, which threatened to unbalance the tenuous congressional balance, and the inclusion into the United States of "foreign," or "alien," inhabitants—the Orleans territory being populated with a disproportionate number of people of Spanish, French, and Dominican heritage. Despite this concern, Article III of the treaty provided for the naturalization of the inhabitants of the territory "as soon as possible." This provision would be in place in every treaty of annexation in which the United States was a party until the Treaty of Paris of 1898.

Yet perhaps the most important legacy of this purchase was the development of a territorial policy that would treat the territories as states in the making. American citizens residing in the territory, however, did not have any political rights. Even if Spanish Americans were naturalized, they were disenfranchised. They could not even consent to be governed by the federal government, because the Constitution recognized only states, not territories or provinces. This territorial policy remained in effect until the acquisition of Puerto Rico and the ensuing debates over the status of the island's inhabitants within the United States.

RELATED ARTICLES

Louisiana; Spain.

FURTHER READING

Brown, Everett S. *The Constitutional History of the Louisiana Purchase, 1803–1812.* Washington, D.C.: Beard Bks., 2000.

"Hamilton on the Louisiana Purchase: A Newly Identified Editorial from the New-York Evening Post." *William and Mary Quarterly* 12, no 2 (April 1955): 268–281.

Weber, David J. *The Spanish Frontier in North America.* New Haven, Conn.: Yale Univ. Press, 1992.

SELECTED WEB SITES

Avalon Project. www.yale.edu/lawweb/avalon

Our Documents. www.ourdocuments.gov

CHARLES R. VENATOR SANTIAGO

LOVE

Love and Latino culture are inextricably linked in the popular imagination with the symbol of the Latino Lover—the hypersexualized, overly eroticized individual ruled by violent passions, lacking in rationality, incapable of controlling his or her emotions, and well-endowed with a primitive sensuality and fire. This portrayal cuts across the axis of gender and has enjoyed a long dominance in U.S. popular culture. It is personified by entertainers such as Desi Arnaz in the 1950s and Charo in the 1970s, as well as by contemporary figures such as Jennifer Lopez and Ricky Martin. This problematic image presents a balancing act: negotiating a border between the popular representations of love within Latino society—close family networks, ties of kinship, the eroticization of the Latina and Latino body, and passionate disposition—which are then transformed into caricatures of themselves, and the actual expressions of love within the culture.

On the surface Latinos do generally exhibit a greater range of public expression of affection than do Anglo-Americans. Greeting friends, family, lovers, and even strangers with a kiss on the cheek is a practice that immediately erodes personal boundaries in public spaces. Same-sex physicality, which is not an indication of homosexuality, is commonplace, as is adding affectionate terminology such as "love," "kisses," and "hugs" when signing correspondence, even when the recipient is not an intimate friend or partner. Yet the cultural expressions of Latino love have a complex basis. *Love* in English and *amor* in Spanish are terms that overlap rather than coincide, as can be seen by the various ways in which love is manifested in U.S. Latino culture. Most commonly associated with love is romance, and popular references give the impression that a sentimental and sexual connection is the ultimate expression of love for Latinos. Yet love is clearly and strongly manifested in other significant ways, such as through spirituality, friendships, family, and political and cultural identity.

Spirituality

The history of Latinos in the United States is part of a history that encompasses both Spain and Latin America. Looking at models of family, faith, erotic love, and friendship that have crossed borders and survived over time and exist in the present-day United States allows for a brief sketch of the kinds of practices that gave rise to the popular image of the overly passionate Latino. The early colonial period in Spain coincided with a religiosity that was embodied both in the personal passions of individuals and the structural apparatus of the Catholic Church and the Spanish crown. After the Reconquista of Spain in 1492, a violent Catholicism took hold, which resulted in the expulsion, conversion, or extermination of non-Catholics. The social climate of the period demanded overt expressions of religious practice. It also produced a religiosity that was wed to two different kinds of love—a highly individualized love that bordered on the passionate and ecstatic (which might be described by the Greek term *eros*) and a socially concerned love (which might be described as *agape*). Teresa de Avila, also known as Teresa de Jesus (1515–1582), was noted for her religious ecstasies and her personal writings on religious experience. Her spiritual autobiography elucidates her relationship with God, which was passionate almost to the point of erotic. In her writings she used metaphors of union, marriage, and sexual coupling to describe the penetration of God into her heart and soul, linking sexual ecstasy to spiritual ecstasy.

Socially concerned love is exemplified by Bartolomé de las Casas (1484–1566), the first ordained priest in the New World. Concerned with the violence that characterized the Spanish treatment of indigenous peoples, he advocated the eventual cessation of indigenous slave labor, arguing instead for African labor. His activism led to the widespread use of African slave labor in the New World for the next three centuries (which resulted in the racial triad that characterizes contemporary Latin America and, by extension, Latinos in the United States). De las Casas's actions laid the groundwork for liberation theology, which calls for people to be liberated from the evils of sin and which seeks to liberate people of the Third World from poverty because of social, moral, and theological concerns. In its most radical form liberation theology calls for social reconstruction, but its basis in *agape* remains, as can be seen when Ernesto "Ché" Guevara, the revolutionary icon whose image continues to saturate popular culture worldwide, said, "At the risk of seeming ridiculous, let me say that the true revolutionary is guided by a great feeling of love."

Spiritual practices of U.S. Latinos include the offering of prayers and sacrifices to patron saints (of Spanish, African, and indigenous origin), the celebration of an individual saint's birthday (the saint after whom an individual is named), and an overall reverence and love for God, Jesus, the Virgin(s), and the orishas (in Santería). Latino Catholicism tends to be an embodied and sensual version of the faith. In one representation, for example, the Virgin Mary holds Jesus Christ's broken body and licks his wounds. The Day of the Dead ritual in Mexican culture, which is also celebrated in regions of the United States, involves the construction of an altar to ancestors and deceased loved ones. In an act of everlasting love, deceased friends and family are briefly conjured back to earth and invited to share food, music, and company with those they left behind.

Politics and Love of *la Patria*

The tumultuous political climate of Latin America, from the independence wars in the 19th century to the revolutions, dictatorships, and caudillos of the 20th century, resulted in rebel movements and underground activism intended to liberate the masses from the economic, political, and personal oppression they suffered under puppet governments, American imperialism, dependence economies, and dictatorships. Selfless love motivated some in guerrilla movements, while José Martí's love for *la patria* (the homeland) galvanized others. For the Dominican Republic's Mirabal sisters, known as Las Mariposas (The Butterflies), who worked to overthrow Rafael Trujillo's government, the combination of love for their nation and their families was the motivation for the activism that led to their deaths. In protests and acts that support farmworkers, immigrants, and the Spanish speaking, Latino activists in the United States are guided by a love for social justice.

Considering that political systems in their homelands are often among the reasons for their migration to the States, Latinos are involved with their countries of origin to various degrees. They may exhibit a strong love for their native land by speaking Spanish, displaying the national flag, attending independence day celebrations, participating in local economies that feature their native foods and music, visiting their countries and staying connected to relatives still living there, and staying abreast of contemporary news and involving themselves in political thought and action related to their homelands, as exemplified by Cuban American activism pertaining to the U.S. embargo. Love of the motherland is a significant reality for immigrants who leave their family and native roots behind to forge a new life in the United States. In a great expression of love, Latino immigrants make significant sacrifices and take on menial and low-paying jobs to send money to their loved ones in their homelands. For those who intended to return but were not able to for any number of reasons, the yearning for home is lifelong, and some never find a true "home" in the United States.

Family and Friends

The family unit in Latino culture is known for being extremely close and tight-knit. Familial love is the tie that binds most Latinos together and keeps tradi-

tions strong; family name and family honor are powerful concepts within the Latino world, where the family is a society unto itself. Extended kinship alliances are formed and become the basis of a supportive survival network that is essential for immigrants and generally beneficial for all Latinos who are connected. Unity is emphasized, and rituals such as the tradition of making tamales serve to reinforce the family's closeness. The Latino family structure consists of blood relations, extended family, and friends and lovers of family members. When a family member is dating, the prospective lover is scrutinized by the entire family. For gay, lesbian, and bisexual Latinos, having their partners (and thus, their homosexuality) integrated within the family structure is the ultimate seal of approval (and expression of love). Particularly strong friendships warrant the special status and recognition of *comadre* (for females) and *compadre* (for males). Similar to the concept of godparents in Anglo-American culture, *comadres* and *compadres* transcend friendship and are akin to fam-

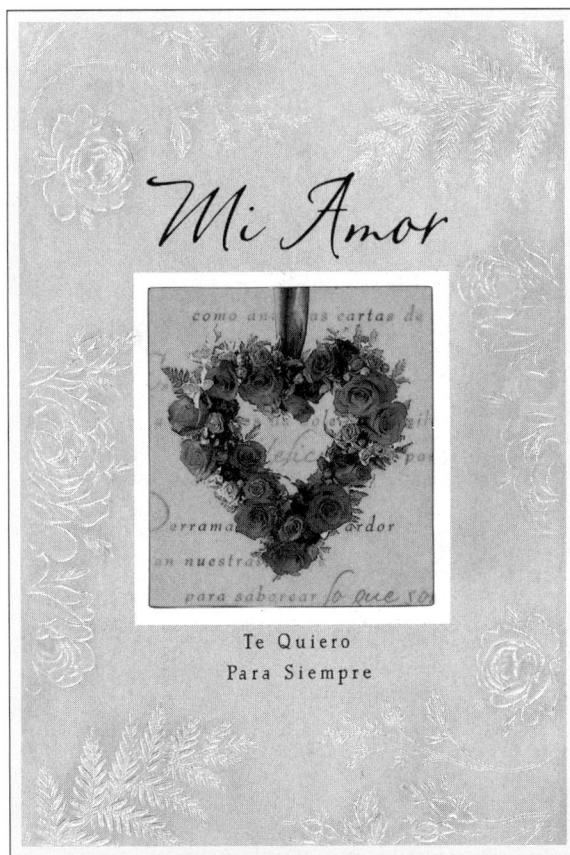

Two love-themed Spanish greeting cards.

ily. As Chicana writer Denise Chavez once said, to bring someone into the family is to love them deeply.

Romance

A human heart pierced by an arrow with a drop of blood at its tip is the only body part represented in the images of the traditional bingo-style Mexican *lotería* card. The saying associated with this card reads: *"No me extrañes corazón que regreso en el camión"* (Don't miss me my dear, I'll soon be near). Romantic love in a Latino context is wrought with the possibility of pain. Popular *telenovelas* (soap operas) feature overly dramatic love stories, often with a (poor) suffering female protagonist who must, against all odds, unite with the man of her life. A huge hit in 2000 in the United States for the music group Son By Four was their love song *A Puro Dolor* (Purest of Pain). The group Los Lobos exemplifies the concept of suffering love with one of its title songs, *La pistola y el corazón* (The Gun and the Heart). In the Aztec love story of La Malinche and Hernan Cortés, La Malinche, who was Cortés's lover and translator, gives birth to the modern Mexican "race," but she is ultimately defamed as a whore and a sellout who aided the enemy in the destruction of her people. This joining of an erotic love defined by vicious conquest to imperatives of cultural loyalty and betrayal is a unique and haunting tendency that is still present within modern Latino culture.

Despite such dramatic associations, erotic love is easily the most celebrated and yearned for Latino love of all, often based on models from Spain and Latin America. It is prominent in cultural expressions, from the 17th-century legend of Tirso de Molina's seductive Don Juan and the love and mystic poetry of Sor Juana Inés de la Cruz to the contemporary poetry of Pablo Neruda, Federico Garcia Lorca, and Gabriela Mistral. It is personified in legendary performances by film stars Pedro Infante and Maria Félix, and it is interpreted anew in the films of Pedro Almodóvar and Alejandro González Iñárritu. It is dramatized on Broadway by John Leguizamo. It is given a queer bent on stage by writers such as Ricardo Bracho, Luis Alfaro, Guillermo Reyes, Susana Cook, and Mónica Palacios. It is brought to Hollywood in films such as *The Mambo Kings Play Songs of Love,* based on Oscar Hijuelos's novel. It is at the center of writings by lesbians such as Cherríe Moraga and Achy Obejas and in anthologies of queer Latino love such as *Bésame Mucho* and *Virgins, Guerrillas, and Locas.*

Love, with its hope and pain, is showcased in music most of all—in ballads, *vallenatos, bachatas,* boleros, *rancheras, son, guarachas, cumbias,* merengues, rock, and salsa—and listened to on radio stations, in cars, in living rooms, and at clubs throughout the United States. Romantic vintage boleros, composed by the likes of Agustín Lara, Consuelo Velázquez, and Alvaro Carrillo, have endured through changing times. While interpreted by contemporary singers such as Luis Miguel and Lila Downs, recordings of some of the classic singers, including Olga Guillot, Lucho Gatica, Daniel Santos, Blanca Rosa Gil, and Los Panchos, are still favored. Romantic love has been a constant strand in the culture of Latinos, who, along with the rest of the country, are now turning to cyberspace in search of love.

RELATED ARTICLES

Family; Feminism; Homosexuality, Female; Homosexuality, Male; Literature; Machismo; Malinche, La; Marriage; Music, Popular; Parenting; Spirituality.

FURTHER READING

Alvarez, Julia. *In the Time of the Butterflies.* Chapel Hill, N.C.: Algonquin Bks., 1994.
Ávila, Teresa. *The Complete Works of St. Teresa of Jesus.* Tr. and ed. by E. Allison Peers. London: Sheed & Ward, 1946.
Chávez, Denise. *Loving Pedro Infante: A Novel.* New York: Farrar, Strauss, 2001.
Cortez, Jaime, ed. *Virgins, Guerrillas and Locas: Gay Latinos Writing on Love.* San Francisco: Cleis Press, 1999.
Deutschmann, David, ed. *Ché Guevara Reader: Writings by Ernesto Ché Guevara on Guerrilla Strategy, Politics, & Revolution.* 2d expanded ed. New York: Ocean Press, 2003.
Manrique, Jaime, ed. *Bésame Mucho.* New York: Painted Leaf Press, 1999.
Martí, José. *José Martí: Selected Writings.* Ed. and tr. by Esther Allen. New York: Penguin, 2002.

LORNA PÉREZ
TATIANA DE LA TIERRA

LOWER EAST SIDE. *See* LOISAIDA.

LOW RIDERS

Mexican American, or Chicano, youth have long expressed a regionally distinctive cultural identity and pride through art, dance, clothing, music, and related forms of social and cultural expression. One particularly unique "vehicle" for Chicana and Chicano cultural communication is that of the lowrider automobile originating with Mexican, Chicano, and African American youth in the U.S. Southwest and borderlands. Today this uniquely Chicano and Chicana rite of passage, an artistic and sociocultural form of expression has been elevated to the status of American pop-culture icon among American youth more generally. For the purposes of distinguishing the customized automobile from the automobile enthusiast or aficionado, here the term *lowrider* is used to identify the low-slung custom cruiser or automobile as opposed to the "Low Rider," or "Lowrider," car club member and/or aficionado.

Despite its early and original association with the Chicano counterculture of the zoot-suit era of the 1930s and 1940s, lowriders and lowriding have evolved from the countercultural expression identified primarily with urban barrio youth and street cliques to one boasting a corporate, media-based international following spanning the Americas, Europe, and Asia. Unlike their predecessors of yesteryear, today's lowriders draw on the inspiration of a tradition revitalized by the introduction of hydraulic lifts in the 1960s and 1970s. Hydraulics ushered in a new era in custom car devotion and popularity, and as a consequence, the tradition was radically redefined in custom car circles and beyond. Today lowriders and lowriding represent but one facet of an expressive form that has grown into an international pop culture and commercial phenomenon with multinational dimensions and appeal.

Briefly defined, Low Riders are those automobile enthusiasts who maintain and customize their low-profile vehicles in such a way that the chassis is lowered through the removal or modification of the suspension system that anchors the chassis to the wheelbase; a toggle-switch-activated hydraulic lift system, "lifters," or "stems," are often installed in lieu of the stock suspension system noted. The "lowrider" is that low-profile vehicle modified accordingly, and with the artistic and cultural embellishments that attend such custom retrofitting. "Lowriding," in turn, is the act of cruising—"lowly" and slowly—along the boulevards and byways of one's community in a low-slung automobile. Cruising, which constitutes the primary ritualized activity of the lowrider tradition, includes the formation of car club caravans, or convoys, that can include from 5 to 50 of these custom cruisers proceeding slowly in formation. Features of such caravans, or of solo cruising, are undercarriage and cockpit light shows and music, as well as radical automobile maneuvers set in motion by way of lowrider hydraulic systems, which pump or elevate the cars upward in a repetitive "hopping" or "dancing" motion that can be demonstrated during hopping contests sponsored by clubs and organizations. Similarly, the use of hydraulic systems permits the creation of mobile light shows in which the cruiser drops "his ride" atop a magnesium scrape plate affixed to the underside of the automobile carriage. By so doing, the scrape plate makes contact with the asphalt, thereby producing a hail of magnesium sparks and light. Not all lowrider automobiles maintain all of the features noted here; however, the deployment of hydraulic systems is now widespread within Low Rider circles.

While lowrider automobiles are customarily developed around a variety of automobile makes and models, vintage 1930s through 1960s models remain the most popular, with 1970s and later models following on their heels. Where vintage automobiles are concerned, lowrider enthusiasts often modify their vehicles so as to alter the stock suspension system; this is done by installing hydraulics in place of springs and shocks, then proceeding to the transformation of the chassis and the application of exterior paint and interior details. Essential custom options include elaborate airbrushed murals and hand-painted designs; the integration of modified grill and fender work; upgraded upholstery and carpeting; and the addition of chain or molded steering wheels, custom rims and tires, glass etchings, chrome and other metal plating, custom lighting, stereo and CD/DVD (compact disc/digital video disc) entertainment systems, and related accoutrements.

Such elaborate custom detailing is often available to lowrider enthusiasts through their membership in a lowrider automobile club and those "happenings" sponsored by such clubs, other corporate and commercial sponsors, lowrider media organizations, and auto parts manufacturers and distributors. A lowrider automobile happening is essentially a car show or exhibition that features both local-club and sponsored-corporate customized lowriders. At such events, which vary considerably in terms of participation and attendance by car club members and the general public, lowrider automobiles of every make and model, and lowrider minitrucks, older vintage and custom-panel vans, lowrider bikes and motorcycles, and lowrider trucks may be featured. A program for such a show typically includes car-hopping, best paint and custom, and theme competitions in which lowrider enthusiasts compete for trophies and related awards.

Because the lowrider phenomenon is the by-product of a social and cultural dynamic that hinges on the maintenance and modification of the low-rider automobile, and one that acquires much of its meaning and existence from those dynamics surrounding the formation of car clubs and caravans devoted to lowrider customization and social interaction, many variations of what it means to be a Low Rider have evolved. In an effort to capture the diversity that exists, Low Riders can be divided into five primary groups. These include "Solo Cruisers"; "Car Clubbers," or "Members"; "Veterans," or "*veteranos*"; lowrider club participant, or fellow "homeboys"; and other members of the lowrider fraternity, including "minitruckers" "bikers"; "two-wheelers"; or lowrider bicyclists; and other low-profile vehicle enthusiasts.

Ultimately, the car clubs themselves are fashioned after the mutual aid societies, or Mexican American *mutualistas*. of earlier times. Mutual aid societies are generally formed by immigrant groups for the purposes of assisting and supporting other recent immi-grants, and similarly, lowrider automobile clubs frequently promote social interaction and the pool-ing of technical talents and expertise among its members. A typical club will admit those who have varying proficiencies with respect to custom car modification, paint, upholstery, promotion, and lead-ership. It is precisely this point of departure that so benefits and promotes the proliferation of lowrider automobile clubs across the U.S. Southwest and, more generally, North America.

Today lowriding boasts an international follow-ing spanning North America, Mexico, and such far-flung regions of lowrider enthusiasm as Japan and Europe. Lowrider automobile happenings organized by *Lowrider Magazine,* and a host of other corporate sponsors, make possible both annual and regional car shows in which awards are given for custom paint, detail, and related categories. Vehicles include a di-verse array of low-profile two- and four-wheel cruis-ing machines. The hopping contest has become a prominent official and unofficial pastime or sport among Chicano and other Latino as well as African

Chevrolet in a car-dance competition, Los Angeles.

American lowrider enthusiasts—including females—across the country. Notably, a number of renowned national art and natural history museums have added lowriders and lowrider art to their permanent collections. Moreover, it is no longer unusual to spy the occasional low-slung custom cruiser hopping its way through a scene of a major motion picture or in television commercials for national and international products such as Pepsi, Coca-Cola, among myriad other commodities and services.

RELATED ARTICLES

Mexican Americans; Mutual Aid Societies; Popular Culture.

FURTHER READING

Barker, George C. "Pachuco: An American Spanish Argot and Its Social Functions." In *Social Science Bulletin,* no. 18: 5–38.

Mazón, Mauricio. *The Zoot-Suit Riots: The Psychology of Symbolic Annihilation.* Austin: Univ. of Tex. Press, 1984.

Mendoza, Rubén G. "Journey to Aztlán: An Anthropologist among the Lowriders." *Q-vo Magazine* 3, no. 2 (1981): 18–19.

Mendoza, Rubén G. "The Low Rider Ritual: Social Mobility on Wheels." *Minority Notes* 2, no. 1-2 (1981): 10–11, 30.

Mendoza, Rubén G. "The Lowrider Happening: Hydraulics and the Hopping Competition." *Caminos Magazine* 4, no. 7 (1983): 34, 44.

Mendoza, Rubén G. "Cruising Art and Culture in Aztlán: Lowriding in the Mexican American Southwest." In *U.S. Latino Literatures and Cultures: Transnational Perspectives.* Ed. by Francisco A. Lomelí and Karin Ikas. Heidelberg, Germany: Carl Winter–Verlag, 2000.

Mendoza, Rubén G., and Cruz Torres. "Hispanic Traditional Technology and Material Culture in the United States." In *Handbook of Hispanic Cultures in the United States: Anthropology.* Ed. by Thomas Weaver. Houston: Univ. of Houston/Arte Público Press, 1994.

Parsons, Jack. *Low 'n Slow: Lowriding in New Mexico.* Santa Fe: Mus. of N.Mex. Press, 1999.

Plascencia, Luis F. B. "Lowriding in the Southwest: Cultural Symbols in the Mexican Community." In *History, Culture, and Society: Chicano Studies in the 1980's.* Ed. by Mario T. Garcia et al. Ypsilanti, Mich.: Bilingual Press/Editorial Bilingue, 1983.

RUBÉN G. MENDOZA

LULAC. *See* LEAGUE OF UNITED LATIN AMERICAN CITIZENS.

M

MACHISMO

Machismo is the word used to express an exaggerated sense of manhood, or hypermasculinity. The expression derives from the word *macho,* which indicates the male sex of any animal. The term, according to some critics, expresses the Latino version of the myth of male supremacy and female subordination, which is upheld by most cultures throughout the world. But there are conflicting definitions of the word, and in fact *machismo* is used and understood in many ways. In its negative sense, critics have defined it as the traditional Latino cult of virility and aggressive masculinity, which is characterized by arrogant sexist attitudes, heavy drinking, domestic violence, male-to-male competition, and of having a large family (frequently in more than one household) as a signifier of virility, homophobia, and violence that includes notions of bravery, honor, and respect. The concepts of bravery, honor, and respect are important in this definition since, until not long ago, these ideas were the bedrock for enacting laws that bestowed on husbands the entire control over the couple's children (*patria potestad*) and, under certain circumstances, also the right to kill adulterous wives, "bad women," with impunity. By law these murders were very often classified as desperate crimes of passion, as deeds committed out of a profound loss of self-esteem. In the contemporary context and modern construction of femininity and masculinity, this definition still suggests the double standard that the man is allowed to enjoy sex both with his wife and in extramarital relationships while the woman is expected not to enjoy sex, to be submissive, long-suffering, respectful, and faithful to her husband—that is, to be a "good woman." In the positive definition of *machismo,* the term becomes an idealized form of masculinity, that is, a way of life; a set of ethical tenets where inner strength, self-respect, responsibility, assertiveness, generosity, courage, pride, honesty, respect, humility, and striving for excellence are desirable personal traits and cultural values that should be aimed at. Scholars have found that this definition of *machismo* is not restricted to men only, but that it extends to women, encouraging them to be strong and assertive *hembras* (the female sex for any animal), since these traits may be found in females, too, and should be a sought-after way of life for either gender.

Origins of Machismo

Much has been written about the possible origins of machismo. When tracing its origins some Chicana feminists have tended to question the Catholic Church, the folkloristic Book of Genesis, and the Old and New Testaments, which have served a patriarchal civilization that considers it proper for women to be docile servants subordinated to men in order to reach recognition as worthy. Chicana queer theorists have problematized Christian ideology for its propagation, naturalization, and sanctification of heterosexuality as well as its tendency, through the cult of the Virgin Mother as a role model, to enhance the image of women as essentially asexual beings and mothers. Further, some feminists have argued that many women have found this iconic model unfeasible to follow, since the Virgin reminds them of the impossibility of being a virgin mother. These scholars have also questioned the dualistic and polarizing principles of the faith that divide humanity between good and evil, male and female, with no gradations in between. At the same time some theorists have considered that the origin of machismo is to be found in the patriarchal order that already predominated in pre-Columbian America, while other academics have expressed the possibility that this social behavior might also have its roots in the preconquest history of the Americas. The Chicana theorist Ana Castillo has suggested that many Muslim attitudes and customs reached the New World via the Spanish conquest, and proposes that since the Moorish conquest of Spain lasted eight centuries, it is relevant to be aware of the influence the Arab world might have had on Spanish culture in relation to the way women are viewed and the hierarchical social relations between the genders. Castillo has put forward that many customs related to the systematic subordination and exclusion of women from economic and social life, which traditionally have been assigned to Islam and Catholicism as religions that worship female virginity and purity, had their origin in Berber Arab ancient cultural traditions of peoples from the Maghreb region that predate both monotheistic religions by many centuries. In this case Morocco is viewed as the bridge that facilitated the exchange of Spanish and Berber Arab traditions and attitudes. Among the similarities this scholar has found throughout some of the Mediterranean cultures influenced by the North African Maghreb societies and traditions, she highlights, among others, the tendency to crown with privileges, responsibilities, and power the first born male in relation to his other siblings; the predilection of sons at the detriment of the girls; crimes of passion committed against women; family vendettas.

Other scholars have attempted to trace back machismo to the Spanish *caballerismo,* or "chivalry," which had its roots in the long period of the Reconquista, the Spanish Christian crusade to expel the Moors from its territory. In this conflict, which started in 711 and ended in 1492—longest of all European wars—historians tend to agree that the strength and devotion of the Spanish Orders of Chivalry played a crucial role in the recuperation of lost territories and the resulting liberation of the nation from the invader. Some of these scholars also argue that the roots of machismo lie in the code of honor that ruled most aspects of the life of the *caballeros.* Ideally, the harshly disciplined and individualistic *caballero* was expected to treat women with deference; to stoically fight his battles of liberation against the aggressor with pride and integrity; to protect the defenseless. These scholars suggest that by the time of the discovery of the New World, those aristocratic ideals of the past had already collapsed in Spain, and that the negative masculine ideals the Spanish conquistadores propagated in the Americas were a degenerated version of the medieval noble ideals.

A significant number of theorists, making use of Freudian psychoanalytical theory, have endeavored to link the historical emergence of machismo in the New World with the devastating psychological impact the Spanish conquest had on the psyches of the defeated peoples of Spanish America. These scholars suggest that the ideal of masculinity, the macho, and its poignant characteristics were implanted by the Spanish conquistador Hernán Cortés at the time of the traumatic conquest of Mexico, when the Spaniard and his companions played the role of aggressive masculine invaders who violently penetrated the victimized Native American cultures despite their bravery and resistance. Thus, some scholars view machismo as the desperate attempt of the insecure Latino mestizos to cope with the primal trauma and to exorcise the inferior effeminate Indian role imposed on them during the Conquest by stressing their Hispanic masculinity. Others see it as the daily struggle of the contemporary mestizo in his desire to prove himself as a man and to avoid the trauma of another conquest. In this context, mestizos build an aggressive and narcissistic masculinity that, in order to resolve gender insecurities and fears of bisexuality or homosexuality, emphasizes sexual intercourse as indispensable and leads men to become conquistador and *chingadores* (in this specific context the word means to make use of violent behavior and cruelty in dealing with women) of members of the "weaker" sex. According to these scholars the mestizo, born of the Spanish and Indian encounter, unconsciously both disdains and admires his mythical violent and oppressive "father," maintaining a distant and ambivalent relationship with him. At the same time, the mestizo loathes his mythical subservient Indian mother and all that is submissive, passive, and feminine in her.

At this point the controversial role played by the Indian princess Malitzin Tenépal, or Doña Marina (La Malinche), the concubine-interpreter for Cortés, who is still viewed by many Mexicans as a symbol of betrayal and surrender to the hated Spaniards, also contributes to the devaluation of the Indian mother and the feelings of suspicion toward her. Scholars of the psychoanalytical approach suggest that the same applies to the Indian father, the emasculated Montezuma, who left Mexicans without a national masculine role model to be proud of. The absence of this primal father—his inability to protect and defend his son from the aggressor—has been used to explain the ambivalent relationships some male Mexicans have with their fathers. Some scholars have also made use of these ideas to elucidate the periodic appearance of caudillos, rebels, and dictators in certain Latin American countries, arguing that these figures are the unconscious return of the aggressive conquistador who strives to control the feminine masses.

Theorists who have a preference for empirical support argue that machismo is not as ancient a Mexican and Latino phenomenon as some tend to believe. Don Américo Paredes has suggested that close study of folksongs from the colonial, independence, and the Mexican reform periods show no traces of macho bravado in their lyrics. He has explained that when boastful male characters appear in the lyrics of *décimas* of prerevolutionary times, they might confer on themselves noble traits, such as true courage, strength, and endurance, but do not refer to themselves as being true *machos,* (a word that otherwise was viewed as improper and offensive). Only with the beginning of the revolutionary period does the foolish swagger of those fearless men take a stern dimension as the threat of death becomes a daily reality to the heroic man. Paredes's study of *corridos* of the time not only has brought to light that this transition started to take place with the increasing imperialistic Anglo-American intrusion into Mexican affairs, but also that only during the postrevolutionary period, at the time of World War II, does the figure of the bully macho appear in a popular middle-class *corrido* for the first time, making the word acceptable. In fact, scholars tend to agree that from this time the *corridos* that made Mexico popular also disseminated a violent macho image of Mexican men abroad and contributed to consolidation of the perception of

Mexico as the land of the *puros machos*. Another scholar suggests that in the 1940s, in the desire to fashion a stable and coherent national identity, golden-age Mexican cinema—with its superstars Jorge Negrete and Pedro Infante and its incorporation of the folkloristic larger-than-life macho image—unwittingly contributed to the creation of the Mexican male self-perception as macho and to the propagation of the macho frame of mind in the country.

Scholars tend to agree that the reflective work by the celebrated Mexican poet and philosopher Octavio Paz *El laberinto de la soledad* (The Labyrinth of Solitude: Life and Thought in Mexico) fostered and facilitated the propagation of some of the categories perceived as quintessential traits of the male Mexican identity: machismo, aggressivity, and loneliness. Additionally, feminist scholars have been critical of Paz's negative portrayal of the mythic Indian mother La Malinche, one of the most complex cultural icons of postconquest America, in the chapter of *The Labyrinth of Solitude* titled "The Sons of La Malinche." These scholars suggest that Paz's repudiating view of La Malinche strongly contributed to the prevalence of a negative view of Cortés's translator in the 20th century. These theorists have objected to Paz's inability to provide Mexicans and other Latinos, as mestizos, with a positive interpretation of *mestizaje* and the Indian mother in order to stimulate a positive conception of themselves and their history. Chicana theorists have remarked that despite his awareness of the power of this historical cultural icon to engender self-hatred and misogyny in the Mexican and Latino psyche and identity, Paz, in his dealing with the Indian princess, remains oblivious to the pre-Columbian Indian world order and thus to the complex historical, sociopolitical conditions at the time of the conquest. In Paz's examination of the mestizos' Indian mother, the historical Malitzin loses all her human complexity and remains a prostitute, the first *chingada*—the ultimate symbol of woman's betrayal, passivity, surrender, and nothingness. Some theorists have ironically interpreted Paz's limited view of Malitzin as his own passivity and inability to revise history, to rewrite debilitating myths, and in this way enforcing their violent perpetuation.

The View of Machismo in *Caballero*

During the last decade the research of Chicano scholars María Cotera and José Limón has contributed a more complex view of the Mexican nationalist period, its male-centered nationalist discourse, and its propagation of the macho masculine image; they have found unpublished literary works by women that question the representation of the intrepid macho hero reacting against American imperialism in the popular *corridos.* Scholars agree that the discovery of the work by the Texan Chicana scholar and writer Jovita Gonzáles de Mireles and her friend Margaret Eimer, *Caballero: A Historical Novel,* contributes to the deconstruction of ideological assumptions about women and women of Mexican descent as passive, politically naive, and submissive beings. Cotera suggests that these two authors (who throughout their work question the masculine *caballero* image and criticize his patriarchal worldview, which limits women's and men's options) can be viewed as predecessors of major Chicana writers and theorists.

Among the outstanding Chicana feminist and queer studies scholars are Ana Castillo, Cherríe Moraga, Gloria Anzaldúa, Adelaida del Castillo, and Norma Alarcón, who have often been dismissed as *malinchistas,* or sellouts, for radically questioning the legitimacy of the assumptions of their own cultures and the universal male Chicano subject. The challenging work of the two friends—which remained unpublished because it was considered unmarketable in 1938—depicts a nationalist *corrido* hero, a traditional male-centered image of opposition, who essentially fights for his own masculine right and the rights of other heterosexual men to secure the unquestionable order of things based on patriarchal verities in the face of the Anglo-American threat. In other words, this would constitute a world order that consciously or unconsciously inhibits, excludes, and qualifies as *malinchistas* all persons who reject, contextualize, and defy absolutist traditional principles and values as well as fixed gender categories in their quest for some kind of autonomous identities.

Alternative Explanations of Machismo

Other social theorists who do not support the idea of machismo as the ancient and deep-rooted Mexican and Latino male identity, have, in a sense, drawn attention to the newness of the phenomenon. In fact, they claim that the masculine traits so openly denigrated as indispensable expressions of Mexican and Latino machismo can be found in many cultures, including the Anglo-American, and are almost universal. These theorists suggest that the negative magnification of Latino machismo is pervaded with

Anglo-American racist overtones that reveal oppressive colonizing practices aimed at supporting political and theoretical agendas in order to maintain Mexicans, Chicanos, and Latin Americans in a subordinate position. In this monolithic discourse about Latino masculinity—which, until not long ago, lacked scholarly research and attention and still remains a vast field in need of exploration—the conception of the Mexican *corrido* violent masculine figure has been stretched to the whole of Latin America. The tendency to conceive of Latino cultures as a homogeneous group having an incontestable common cultural heritage neurotically concerned with a distinctive Latino masculinity based on machismo and hierarchical gender relations has been a reason for this generalization.

Some of these theorists emphasize that the term *machismo* has been adapted by Anglo-American popular culture; in this popular discourse, when the term *macho* is applied to heroes or male superstars, it tends to have positive connotations such as attractiveness and assertive manhood. Otherwise, they suggest, in Anglo-American discourse the expression has generally been associated with negative male character traits that do not apply to all men in general, but have been, specifically, forced on unsophisticated Mexicans, Chicanos, and Latin American men by mainstream society and social policies that have had an impact on the environment in which many boys and girls grow up. Consequently, these scholars suggest that it is not quite accurate to understand machismo traits as essentially unique traits of Mexican or Latin American macho men victimizing submissive Latino women, since not all Latino males and females exhibit or subscribe to the negative traits paraded through the machismo paradigm; some reject them outright. Some scholars have proposed that the magnification of denigrating aspects in Mexican and Latino gender relations, such as wife beating, unfaithfulness, or male jealousy, might be understood as part of a belittling, hegemonic, discursive practice that also aims at obscuring, negating, and safeguarding unequal and abusive gender relations in Anglo-American spheres.

Theorists tend to agree that Latino stereotypical behaviors might be reactions to oppressive and hostile social conditions to which Latino men and women are subjected, or products of a profound sense of being threatened or excluded. They suggest that the dissemination of these stereotypes through the media have significantly contributed to the way Latino groups are viewed and perceived by mainstream culture and the rest of the world. Some theorists worry that such manipulation might lead public opinion toward the perception that Latino cultures are problematic, deficient, and violent. At the same time they suggest negative representations cannot only engender destructive self-images among Latinos but might also accentuate and naturalize negative images that some colonized Chicanos and Latinos already have of themselves.

Under these circumstances machismo can be viewed as having a racist history. Debasing generalizations have been supported by fabrications about intrinsic ethnic characteristics, which include swaggering and abusive Latino masculinity as well as irrational and immature gender relations in backward Latino cultures. Scholars have thus pointed out that this homogenizing popular and "colonial" discourse—based on assumptions and perceived truths—tends to refer to a stereotypical Mexican and Latino masculine identity. However, it does not allow for varieties of manhood or masculinity among Latinos or for variables of class, generation, age, life cycles, education, country, region, and ethnicity. Some theorists stress that many of these assumed, fixed, and ahistorical gender categories have contributed to the perpetuation of Latino ideal types and stereotypes and have occasionally biased some mainstream anthropologists, social scientists, and thinkers toward grand conclusions about gender relations in Mexico, among Latinos in the United States, and in Latin America as a whole. In fact, the groundbreaking work of the scholar Matthew C. Gutmann, in the vicinity of Santo Domingo in Mexico City, has brought to light the precariousness of attempts to provide all-encompassing statements about a distinctive Mexican macho masculinity or, for that matter, of a representative male identity or gender relation within the very neighborhood he studied.

Machismo and the Latino Family

The machismo conversation has also had an impact on the way Chicano and Latino families have been represented in the Anglo-American context. That is, in the scientific discussion of traditional Latino family structure with the overriding male head, the term *machismo* has been used to hold Chicano and Latino cultures in the United States responsible for all the failures and problems of socialization they ex-

perienced inside and outside of school. Chicano scholar Alfredo Mirandé posits that mainstream discourse, which stresses education as the key to social progress and success, views existence in an authoritarian, macho-oriented family life—where the needs of individuals are subordinated to those of the patriarch—as a constraint to the development of the individual, leading to damaging fatalism and intellectual indifference. In other words, it has been proposed that cultures with undemocratic family lives have consistently brought forward individuals who have been encouraged to become meek, lazy, submissive, dependent, fatalistic, masochistic, emotional, irrational, religious, authoritarian, unreliable, criminally prone, and with limited intellectual capacities. Thus, according to scientific discussion, the repression within the macho family encourages violent and criminal outbursts outside the family, since the male adolescent has to confirm his masculinity outside the authoritarian home and compensate for his feelings of inferiority.

Nonetheless, Chicano scholarship has stressed that such observations (in an endeavor to shift attention away from external oppression by the imperialistic culture and to blur its own inadequacy) have ignored the fact that more often than not Chicano and Latino children have attended schools that tend to denigrate Catholic religion; to pathologize their family values, the marriages of their parents, and family relationships; to view their cultures and their language as naturally inferior and not worthy of study or interest. In addition, in the case of Chicano children, these schools have tended to minimize and distort their long history on the soil of the United States and to deny or degrade the Catholic and Mexican influence and contribution to the development of the Southwest. In fact, because children have often been ridiculed for speaking Spanish, many of them have come to view Spanish as a source of embarrassment.

Several scholars have observed among Chicano and Latino families the proclivity for intensive contact with the extended-family, encouraging frequent visits and affectionate relationships with such family members as *abuelos,* "grandfathers"; *abuelas,* "grandmothers"; *tios,* "uncles"; *tias,* "aunts"; *sobrinas,* "nieces"; and *sobrinos,* "nephews." Sociology scholar Maxine Baca Zinn has suggested that, maybe more than a traditional Latino family value, such close kinship can be understood as an important force of minority preservation and opposition to cultural domination and as a result of structural discrimination and the absence of support from the competitive surrounding American society. Chicano and Latino scholars suggest that it is not productive either to idolize or to vilify Latino family life and structure. They emphasize that there is no static or uniform Chicano or Latino type of family; rather, it is an organic unit. In this sense, there are many types of family, which vary according to external conditions such as country of origin, region, education, social class, age, and length of residency in the United States.

Contemporary studies of machismo attempt to redefine it and tend to depict it as a cultural myth forced on Latino men and cultures. These studies make readers aware of the difficulties that Chicanos, Mexicans, and other Latino minorities have had in controlling, rejecting, and redefining the biased stereotypical cultural definitions placed on them by the media and social scientists. Studies have found that Latinos, in their desire to obtain the approval of Anglo-American opinion, have unwittingly contributed to their own denigration and destruction by negating their cultures and those parts of themselves that are viewed as deficient and unworthy by the colonizer's discourse. In this way, some Latinos have contributed to the legitimatization of the colonizing process that victimizes them. Other theorists have dealt with cases of internal colonization that have led many Chicanos and Latinos to fulfill the inculcated stereotypes. These researchers have stressed the importance of joining efforts and engaging in a decolonizing process in which Latinos and Chicanos are encouraged to make sense of their diverse existences and experiences in order to re-create themselves, their lives, and their cultures in empowering ways.

Feminist sociologists recognize the importance of research done on machismo and its contribution to the redefinition of the damaging stereotype. At the same time, these scholars point out that in the impatient desire to deconstruct and question the racist, arbitrary, and simplistic stereotype of Latino violent machismo, it is imperative to recognize the presence of violent male dominance. That it exists in Chicano, Latino, and non-Latino communities at institutional, social, and interpersonal levels, remains an issue that cannot be left unattended. Several scholars have suggested that the contemporary rise of male violence against women, not only in some Latino communities, might be a result of the women's increasing independence, which challenges traditional roles. Feminist sociologists agree with other social theorists and ethnographers about the need to emphasize and take into consideration the instability and changeability of gender identities and relations in their research in order to attain and produce more nuanced, contextualized, and balanced knowledge. They understand the necessity to attempt to analyze, shake, and redefine traditional dichotomous gender roles. Scholars continue to question the paradigm of patriarchal male dominance, which is an almost universal phenomenon in human societies. Nonetheless, they insist that gender inequalities and machismo do exist in Latino cultures and that it would be a mistake to assume otherwise.

RELATED ARTICLES

Family; Homosexuality, Male; Marianismo; Stereotypes and Stereotyping.

FURTHER READING

Baca Zinn, Maxine. "Political Familialism: Toward Sex Role Equality in Chicano Families." *Aztlán: Chicano Journal of the Social Sciences and the Arts* 6 (Spring): 13–26.

Castillo, Ana. *Massacre of the Dreamers. Essays on Xicanisma.* Albuquerque: Univ. of N.Mex. Press, 1994.

Cotera, María. "Deconstructing the Corrido Hero: *Caballero* and Its Gendered Critique of Nationalist Discourse." In *Perspectives in Mexican American Studies. Mexican American Women Changing Images.* Ed. by Juan R. Garcia. Tucson: Univ. of Ariz., 1995.

Goldwert, Marvin. *Machismo and Conquest.* New York: Univ. Press of Am., 1983.

González, Ray, ed. *Muy Macho: Latino Men Confront Their Manhood.* New York: Doubleday, 1996.

Gutmann, Matthew C. *The Meanings of Macho: Being a Man in Mexico City.* Berkeley: Univ. of Calif. Press, 1996.

Mirandé, Alfredo. *The Chicano Experience. An Alternative Perspective.* Notre Dame, Ind.: Univ. of Notre Dame Press, 1985.

Mirandé, Alfredo. *Hombres y Machos: Masculinity and Latino Culture.* Boulder, Colo.: Westview Press, 1996.

Paredes, Américo. "The United States, Mexico, and Machismo." In *Perspectives on Las Américas. A Reader in Culture, History, and Representation.* Ed. by Matthew C. Gutmann et al. Malden, Mass.: Blackwell, 2003.

Paz, Octavio. *The Labyrinth of Solitude: Life and Thought in Mexico.* Tr. by Lysander Kemp. New York: Grove, 1961.

LUZ ANGÉLICA KIRSCHNER

MALDEF. See MEXICAN AMERICAN LEGAL DEFENSE AND EDUCATION FUND.

MALINCHE, LA

The controversial historical character of La Malinche is at the heart of Mexican ethnology and psychology. Also known as Doña Marina, she was the American Indian woman who played a key role in the conquest of the Aztec empire by Hernán Cortés. In the course of her relationship with Cortés, she became his interpreter, guide, mistress, mother of their son, and confidante. Over the years her image has undergone numerous alterations, from the gently virtuous Marina of some early chroniclers to the perfidious and treacherous betrayer of her people. More recently, late-20th- and early-21st-century feminist critics have been reevaluating her in more sympathetic ways, seeing in her situation a paradigm for the tensions, contradictions, and oppression surrounding the female condition. Her myth is omnipresent in Mexican culture but has also influenced writers around the world, though in both cases the myth often obscures the reality.

Facts about the woman known as La Malinche are few. None of what we know comes from the primary source; she left no written record. There is general agreement that she was probably highborn because of her level of linguistic and diplomatic skill. She enters history as one of a group of 20 women who were presented to Cortés by the Tabascan people as part of other tributes early in his march toward the Aztec capital of Tenochtitlán. She was probably about 15 at the time. Initially she was given

Aztec drawing of Doña Marina "La Malinche" (right), interpreting during the meeting of Montezuma II (seated on left) and Hernán Cortés at Tenochtitlán, Mexico, November 1519.

to Alonso Hernández Puerto Carrero, but her knowledge of languages brought her to the attention of Cortés. She spoke both Nahuatl—the language of the Aztecs—and Mayan; in particular, she understood the aristocratic language of the Nahuatl-speaking elite, and she learned to speak Spanish. Her son with Cortés, Martin, became his father's main heir and returned with him to Spain, where he was legitimized and knighted. Martin is often depicted in art and literature as the first mestizo prototype for the Mexican nation, although it is likely he was among a number of children produced by relationships between Spaniards and indigenous women.

Cortés subsequently married Marina to Juan Jaramillo, with whom she had a daughter. As a dowry, he gave the newly married couple the *encomiendas* (estates) of Olutla and Jilotepec, near Coatzacoalcos. Little is known of Marina after that time; even the date of her death is disputed, some contending it was 1527, others claiming that records show she was present in Mexico City in 1537 and probably died by 1541, when Jaramillo remarried.

Controversy about her name stems from the different ways chroniclers have construed their accounts. Malinal or Malinalli is thought to have been her Indian name, thus leading Cortés, after baptism, to call her Marina, his Spanish version. He mentions her by that name in his letters to King Charles. The other two contemporary chroniclers, López de Gómara and Bernal Díaz del Castillo, also use the name Marina when alluding to her, although Díaz more courteously refers to her as Doña Marina. Unlike Gómara, Díaz was present during the march to conquest, and he gives her a heroic and key role. She is also prominent in the indigenous drawings of the time, in particular the pictorial record known as the *Lienzo de Tlaxcala,* which documents the alliance against Montezuma. It is significant that the Indians called Cortés "El Malinche," which is thought to mean "the captain of Marina" in their language. Malintzin is another common name for her, the explanation for this version being that the *tzin* ending added to her name denotes a person of high estate, comparable to Doña in Spanish.

Important in literature, but also in ethnohistory, Malinche's actions situate her in positions analogous to Pocahontas and Sacajawea, as cultural mediators, alternately saviors and guides for European conquerors. As such her reputation, like theirs, is subject to the political vagaries of the times. During the colonial period, as long as the Spanish were in power, Marina was portrayed respectfully, but with Mexican independence from Spain, her characterization began to change. It was then that the concept of *malinchismo* developed. Broadly defined, *malinchismo* is the rejection and betrayal of one's own as a byproduct of admiration for the foreign and novel. A *malinchista* is one who sells out to foreign interest. Concurrently, 19th-century Mexican literature began to focus increasingly on her sexuality. This led to several mythic and folkloric associations. One emphasized her portrayal as La Chingada (the Violated One), thus reflecting a quasi-schizophrenic cultural conundrum as the sons of La Chingada struggled to synthesize the dual nature of their European and American Indian heritages. At root, the concept of *malinchismo* is misogynistic, scapegoating a young female who was little more than disposable property, handed from man to man, and revictimizing her by associating her name with traitorous behavior. In that nationalistic vein, she is also seen as an Eve figure, one who welcomed the snake into paradise, a temptress and yet still the first mother of Mexico. In the hostility toward the conqueror, she is blamed for the downfall of her country and her sexuality is emphasized. Rather than seeing the lack of power she had in terms of her own body, Malinche is turned into a seductress, wanton and lascivious. The mother-whore contradiction is highlighted in her association with La Lloron (the Weeping Woman), a figure to both frighten and pity, a ghostly mother crying for her lost children. Marina's son, Martin, and her daughter, Maria, were taken from her and raised by others.

Recent female writers have, in their transformation of her, challenged the misogynistic depiction of her. Like feminist scholars who have recaptured other victims of patriarchally oppressive characterizations, such as Lilith, witches, and Medea, the writers have emphasized the intelligence, strength, and will to survive that it must have taken for her to occupy the position she did. In particular, Chicana writers have "read" the negative "Malinche" epithet as an attempt to keep girls and women subordinated and have thus begun the work of resuscitating her. Writer Sandra Cisneros in *The House on Mango Street* amplifies the difficult duality imposed on the characterization of women in Mexican literature by the binary archetypes of La Virgen (Virgin) de Guadalupe and La Malinche, trying to negotiate for herself and other

Chicana writers role models that transcend the threat to Mexican masculinity represented by Malinche. In her fiction Cisneros revises and recasts the two myths from the perspective of their female protagonists, delivering a vision of Chicana womanhood that is autonomous and independent, neither the worshipped nor the conquered. A recent biography produces little new factual information but does call for a reevaluation of this much vilified character, pointing out how precarious her situation was—a powerless girl-child, presented as tribute—and how the "Mexico" she is blamed for helping destroy did not exist. In the cause of Mexican nationalism, Malinche has been scapegoated for a combination of factors, such as tribal hatred for the Aztecs, combined with the devastating effect of European diseases that brought about the end of Montezuma's empire. Poets such as Helen Silva, Naomi Quiñónez, Adaljiza Sosa Riddell, and Carmen Tafolla give Malinche her voice, explore her betrayal, and resymbolize her, repudiating gendered nationalist interpretations. Thus, in the last quarter of the 20th century, La Malinche became a sympathetic figure in the poetry, drama, and fiction as well as the revisionist histories of our times.

RELATED ARTICLES

Colonialism; Feminism; Indigenous Heritage; Llorona, La; Nahuas.

FURTHER READING

Cypress, Sandra Messinger. *La Malinche in Mexican Literature: From History to Myth.* Austin: Univ. of Tex. Press, 1991.

Díaz del Castillo, Bernal. *The Conquest of New Spain.* Tr. by J. M. Cohen. Baltimore: Penguin, 1963.

Lanyon, Anna. *Malinche's Conquest.* Allen & Unwin, 2000.

Moraga, Cherríe. "A Long Line of Vendidas." In *Loving in the War Years.* Boston: South End Press, 1983.

Paz, Octavio. *The Labyrinth of Solitude: Life and Thought in Mexico.* Tr. by Lysander Kemp. New York: Grove, 1961.

Pratt, Mary Louise. "'Yo Soy La Malinche': Chicana Writers and the Poetics of Ethnonationalism." *Callaloo* 16, no. 4 (Fall 1993): 859–873.

Prescott, W. H. *The Conquest of Mexico.* Vols. 1 and 2. New York: Dutton, 1965.

Stavans, Ilan. "Translation and Identity." In *The Essential Ilan Stavans.* New York: Routledge, 2000.

MIMI R. GLADSTEIN

MAMBO

In Latin music the word *mambo* refers to three things: first, a constantly repeating musical phrase or passage; second, a hybrid instrumental musical form, created in Cuba during the early 1940s; third, and perhaps most famously, a dance craze, which began in the United States during the 1940s and was eventually overlapped in the middle of the 1950s by yet another (although lesser) dance craze called *cha cha cha* (cha-cha).

In musical band arrangements, when one instrument (such as trumpet) is improvising a solo, other instruments (such as the horn section of the orchestra) may begin playing a repeating, predetermined phrase underneath the solo in order to punctuate it in some musical way. This phrase is called a *mambo*.

Taking this idea a step further, in the early 1940s Orestes López and his brother Israel ("Cachao") Lopez, respectively pianist and bassist for Orquesta Arcaño y sus Maravillas, wrote a fourth or "D" section to *danzon*. At first they called it *el ritmo nuevo* (the new rhythm), and then later *el mambo*. Orestes actually wrote an instrumental song, using this new form, which he called *El Mambo.* In the meantime, Arsenio Rodríguez, a well-known *tresista* and orchestra leader of the period, also experimented with this new form, calling it *el ritmo Diablo,* and added a new instrument, the *tumbadora*—or conga drum—to the sound of his band. (Soon thereafter, the conga drum was also added to Orquesta Arcaño y sus Maravillas.) In 1950 Damasio Pérez Prado, who played piano for Orquesta Casino de la Playa during the 1940s, formed an orchestra in Mexico and began playing his own mambo compositions. These brass-oriented, highly energetic tunes—such as *Que Rico El Mambo, Mambo No. 5,* and *Mambo No. 8*—were designed for mass-audience consumption, and quickly made Prado famous all over the world (erroneously, of course) as the inventor of the mambo.

Toward the end of the decade, when this new hybrid form started being played in such U.S. dance halls as the New York Palladium by groups such as Machito and His Afro Cubans, the mambo craze exploded onto the scene. As a dance form, mambo was similar to the Cuban way of dancing of that period, but its timing was quite different. In its fundamental, defining pattern of movement, steps were taken in a forward and back slot formation on the second, third, and fourth beats of each 4/4 musical

Professional Cuban dance team Pete and Millie show variations of the mambo, at New York City's Palladium ballroom, 1954.

measure, with a rest or weight shift on the "one." Eventually, this manner of dancing was called, "breaking on two," and was considered (at least by the cognoscenti) the only truly appropriate rhythmic approach to this new and exciting music—since it coincided with the infectious, underlying rhythm of the conga drum. Furthermore, breaks and turns from American swing were incorporated into mambo, and later in the 1970s from American hustle. Because the basic timing of mambo is comparatively difficult to master, it has fallen out of favor in the present day, replaced by a more rudimentary manner of dancing, which is often called salsa.

RELATED ARTICLES

Dance; Music, Popular; Salsa.

FURTHER READING

Boggs, Vernon W. *Salsiology: Afro-Cuban Music and the Evolution of Salsa in New York City.* New York: Excelsior Music Pub., 1992.

Roberts, John Storm. *The Latin Tinge: The Impact of Latin American Music on the United States.* New York: Oxford Univ. Press, 1999.

Salazar, Max. *Mambo Kingdom: Latin Music in New York.* New York: Schirmer Bks., 2002.

FRAN CHESLEIGH

MANIFEST DESTINY

A phrase coined in 1839 by John L. O'Sullivan, the editor of the magazine *Democratic Review,* "Manifest Destiny" was used frequently in the mid- to late 1800s as both ideology and public policy and was expressed, for example, in the writings of Ralph Waldo Emerson and the art of George Crofutt. It had its roots in Puritan ideals built into the very structure of United States government and guiding documents. The concept includes ideas such as the Puritan work ethic, Euro-American supremacy, and Providence and the hand of God ordaining Americans as a chosen people, predestined, naturally, to spread democracy to everyone in the hemisphere.

The ideology of Manifest Destiny became public policy in relationship to Mexico and its northern territories in the early 1800s. Walt Whitman, the American poet, wrote in 1846 in the *Democratic Eagle,* "It is for the interest of mankind that its power and territory be extended—the farther the better." O'Sullivan wrote: "This is our high destiny, and in nature's eternal, inevitable decree of cause and effect we must accomplish it." The notion that Christianity was superior to the polytheism of American Indians, and to the supposed "idolatry" practiced by Mexican Catholics, drove expansion as did Anglo-Americans' beliefs that they had superior governmental organizations and economics in the forms of democracy and capitalism. Imbedded in Manifest Destiny was the belief that nonwhite people were not capable of self-government through democracy, and it became meshed with notions of "free labor" and slavery, implying that nonwhite, nonfree peoples were not destined to be successful in capitalism, which was driven by thoughts of acquiring private property and individualism.

Manifest Destiny affected public policy and foreign relations, particularly in relationship to Latin America. After U.S. victories in the American Revolution and the British War of 1812, the nation believed it natural and fated for it to expand their borders. Coinciding with U.S. expansion was Mexico's economic and political struggling after gaining its independence from Spain in 1821. These struggles supported the U.S. belief that Mexico was economically and politically inferior and therefore destined to be ruled by its northern neighbor "extending the area of freedom." It romanticized the frontier expansion as a noble enterprise. This ideology led to the creation of the Texas Rangers in 1823, the famed Battle of the Alamo, and Mexico's eventual loss of Texas to the United States in 1836, with Texas joining the Union in 1845. It also shaped the Bear Flag Revolt in California in 1846, and eventually the Mexican War with the United States from 1846 to 1848. According to historian K. Jack Bauer, "to the American exponents of Manifest Destiny, California had an attraction like that of a crowd for a politician." Obtaining California's coast was essential to securing ports on both shores and preventing other nations such as Great Britain from thwarting U.S. economic and political progression.

The doctrine of Manifest Destiny rationalized and justified imperial expansion and allowed Anglo-Americans to absolve themselves of fault and guilt of taking Mexico's land in 1848, under the Treaty of Guadalupe Hidalgo, and in 1853, under the Gadsden Purchase Treaty—because it was God's will. Manifest Destiny also justified post-1848 treatment of nonwhite Mexicans and Indians because Anglo-Americans believed they knew the best use of land, which was through capitalism and individual property rights. Examples such as whites' transgression of Mexican American land rights (violating the terms of the treaty), lynchings of Chicanos by "forty-niners" during the California gold rush, or the imposition of foreign miners taxes, fueled a long-held Chicano distrust of the United States and Anglo-Americans.

The significance of Manifest Destiny for Mexican Americans and other Hispanics in the United States cannot be overstated. As Gilbert G. González and Raúl Fernández write:

> Clearly in the post-1848 years in the newly acquired southwestern frontier, Anglo settlers frequently treated the Hispanic population much like it dealt with the native Indian population: as people without rights who were merely obstacles to the acquisition and exploitation of natural resources and land. And, to be sure, the violence of the conquerors was often met with the resistance of the conquered. But these cultural struggles and racial conflicts have become for many Chicano historians the principal bases for understanding Chicano history.

RELATED ARTICLES

Gadsden Purchase; Guadalupe Hidalgo, Treaty of; Homestead Act; Louisiana Purchase; Mexican-American War.

FURTHER READING

Acuña, Rodolfo. *Occupied America: A History of Chicanos.* New York: Pearson Longman, 2004.

Almaguer, Tomás. *Racial Fault Lines: The Historical Origins of White Supremacy in California.* Berkeley: Univ. of Calif. Press, 1994.

Bauer, K. Jack. *The Mexican War 1846–1848.* Lincoln: Univ. of Nebr. Press, 1974.

Christensen, Carol, and Thomas Christensen. *The U.S.-Mexican War.* San Francisco: Bay Bks., 1998.

González, Gilbert G., and Raúl Fernández. *A Century of Chicano History: Empire, Nations, and Migration.* New York: Routledge, 2003.

Saxton, Alexander. *The Rise and Fall of the White Republic: Class Politics and Mass Culture in Nineteenth-Century America.* New York: Verso, 1990.

SUSAN GREEN

Workers sewing at a maquiladora, or factory, in Central America.

MAQUILADORAS

Maquiladoras are foreign-owned (mostly U.S.) export-processing factories that employ a labor-intensive assembly-line workforce. These factories began in northern Mexico in 1965 (well before NAFTA, the North American Free Trade Agreement of 1994) to take advantage both of Mexico's Border Industrialization Program and of U.S. tariffs charged only on the value added of "off shore" processing in a fragmented production process. The shore is merely the line drawn in the sand after the mid-19th century wars and purchases that redrew the United States–Mexico border. Now, in the 21st century, the maquiladora industry is critical to the consolidation of Mexico and the United States as primary trading partners, importing and exporting goods associated with the low-cost hands of assembly-line production workers.

Maquiladora production workers are in the majority female, a pattern that has held since the 1960s. These Latina workers, who identify themselves as Mexicanas with respect to their national rather than cultural identity, once made up 80 percent of production workers, a figure now decreased to about 60 percent. Recruitment strategies "gender" the division of labor, with Latinos and Mexicanos more likely to work in auto-assembly plants, and Mexicanas in electronic and garment plants, where their supposed nimble figures are viewed as assets. Each plant has distinctive ways of "constructing gender," but plants share common globalized production, distribution, and control strategies in Mexico and elsewhere in the world.

A pioneering study set the tone and methodology for early critical analysis on maquiladoras and their labor forces. Using a combination of interviews and work inside plants to allow in-depth observation, Maria Patricia Fernandez-Kelley (1983) painted a negative picture of plants with overpaid male (mostly foreign) managers and underpaid female workers. Early accounts like these generalized from the few to all maquiladoras. Later accounts did little to differentiate among maquiladoras, except for the foreign- versus Mexican-owned, but stressed the positive aspects of job creation in a Mexican economy with insufficient job opportunities.

No dispute exists about the low-cost labor that makes up the bulk of maquiladora employees. The legal Mexican minimum wage in its northern border states is equivalent to approximately $4 (U.S.) per day (post 2000) plus employer contributions to fringe benefits, whether for meal and transport programs or for social security and access to the national health and housing programs, or all of these. But critical studies and workers' voices usually focus on net pay, while the industry frets about the total pay package. Many workers belong to unions, but few unions are independent advocates of workers' interests; rather, most unions are affiliated with the once-dominant Partido Revolucionario Institucional (PRI) and seek stability and good management relations. Nevertheless, workers are not the docile labor force once assumed; sabotage occurs on occasion, and labor turnover rates are high. Workers organize on their own, and some affiliate with independent unions and cross-border organizing efforts. The Coalition for Justice in the Maquiladoras is a well-known example of the latter.

Ciudad Juarez is the maquila capital of Mexico, with the number of plants hovering around 300, employing in 2000 a quarter of a million workers. In a comparison of formal and informal labor in the pre-peso devaluation of 1994, workers report earnings at two times the minimum wage in maquilas, lower than wages of informal workers who took advantage of border opportunities. These northern border cities serve as magnets for internal migration of workers from the south, creating difficulties in local governance in a federal system that grants little revenue-generating authority to *municipios*. In Ciudad Juarez, total numbers of employees diminished by the year 2003, owing to economic recession in the United States and the low-skill plants moving their operations to places with far cheaper labor costs, such as China. Nevertheless, maquiladoras are likely to persist for many decades, given their border locations and transportation benefits, both for goods and residential opportunities afforded U.S. managers who live on *el otro lado* (the other side, that is, the United States).

RELATED ARTICLES

Border, United States-Mexico; Labor; Sweatshops.

FURTHER READING

Fernandez-Kelly, Maria Patricia. *For We Are Sold, I and My People: Women and Industry in Mexico's Frontier.* Albany: State Univ. of N.Y. Press, 1983.

Kamel, Rachel, and Anya Hoffman, eds. *The Maquiladora Reader: Cross-Border Organizing since NAFTA.* Philadelphia: Am. Friends Service Committee, 1999.

Pena, Devon. *The Terror of the Machine: Technology, Work, Gender, and Ecology on the U.S.-Mexico Border.* Austin: Univ. of Tex. Press, 1997.

Ruiz, Vicki, and Susan Tiano, eds. *Women on the U.S.-Mexico Border: Responses to Change.* Boston: Allen & Unwin, 1987.

Salzinger, Leslie. *Genders in Production: Making Workers in Mexico's Global Factories.* Berkeley: Univ. of Calif. Press, 2003.

Sklair, Leslie. *Assembling for Development: The Maquila Industry in Mexico and the United States.* Boston: Unwin Hyman, 1989.

Staudt, Kathleen. *Free Trade? Informal Economies at the U.S.-Mexico Border.* Philadelphia: Temple Univ. Press, 1998.

Staudt, Kathleen, and Irasema Coronado. *Fronteras No Mas: Toward Social Justice at the U.S.-Mexico Border.* New York: Palgrave, 2002.

Stoddard, Elwyn. *Maquila: Assembly Plants in Northern Mexico.* El Paso: Tex. Western Press, 1987.

Tiano, Susan. *Patriarchy on the Line: Labor, Gender and Ideology in the Mexican Maquila Industry.* Philadelphia: Temple Univ. Press, 1994.

KATHLEEN STAUDT

MARIACHI

As a noun, *mariachi* refers to a single musician or to an ensemble playing music. (A group of musicians is referred to in the singular, such as, for example, El Mariachi México de Pepe Villa.) As an adjective, *mariachi* refers to a style of music originating in Mexico. Despite the common folk etymology that derives *mariachi* from the French *mariage,* the word is actually of Náhuatl origin, indicating a platform for musical and dance performance. From there, the term came to designate a dance gathering, and finally the orchestra playing for the dance. Mariachi began—presumably sometime in Mexico's pre-Columbian past—as a regional style heard mainly in Jalisco, Nayarit, and Michoacán states. No discernible traces remain in modern mariachi of the music played by rattles, drums, reed and clay flutes, and conch-shell horns in the time of Aztec rule. These gave way after the conquest to stringed instruments adapted from the Spanish, and by the time of its first documentation, mariachi was dominated by strings, with the folk harp transmitting the melody. The basic 19th-century ensemble of harp, violins, and guitars was probably modeled on the typical Spanish theater orchestra. Two distinctive mariachi string instruments, the *vihuela* and the *gitarron,* represent uniquely Mexican modifications to Spanish instruments. A letter of May 7, 1852, from Catholic priest Cosme Santa Anna to the archibishop of Guadalajara, contains the first—negative—reference to mariachi as an unrestrained music-making spoiling the solemnity of Holy Saturday. This remark may refer not so much to the music as to the accompanying dance, the vigorous *zapateado* that can reduce a dance platform to splinters. This negative attitude toward a rustic and popular musical form would continue for many decades. Mariachi records were made starting in 1908, and the music became diffused throughout Mexico beginning in the 1930s through the media of radio (especially station XEW) and cinema, and under the nationalist mood of the regime of Lázaro Cárdenas, who began the practice of contracting mariachi groups for appearances at state functions. The expansion of mariachi into these media brought about the introduction of an instrument considered essential to mariachi today, the trumpet (usually at least two). Although the trumpet had been too loud and blaring for most live audiences, it became essential for carrying the melody over radio and film soundtracks. Today, mariachi can be seen as an indigenous Mexican "classical" music, sharing with its European counterpart the characteristics of cultural prestige, formality of dress and performance, level of musicianship and complexity of ensemble interaction, and presence at similar venues, such as formal restaurants, concerts, weddings, anniversaries, receptions, and *quinceañeras* (girls' 15th birthday celebrations), both in Mexico and in the United States.

Since the 1930s there have really existed two mariachis. One is regionally based in western Mexico, folkloric, and played by local amateur or semiprofessional string players, either without costume or in peasant garb. The diatonic folk harp is the central instrument for this kind of mariachi. The other, urban mariachi, is played by professional musicians (who generally number between 7 and 11) dressed in *charro* outfits. The trumpet and violin are important instruments, while the harp is optional. The rhythmic and harmonic backbone of both types is provided by the *gitarrón* (a large bass instrument played like a guitar) and the *vihuela* (a smallish, round-backed guitar). The remainder of this article deals solely with the latter form of mariachi, which has achieved national and international prominence.

Like American jazz, mariachi music embraces a wide variety of styles and instrumentation and has the capacity to adapt itself to new types of music. To the basic texture noted above can be added voice for those songs with lyrics (and the familiar *grito* or yell for those without); folk harp; marimba; drums; or a host of other instruments in various combinations. Accordion is almost never present, undoubtedly to keep mariachi distinguishable from *norteña* music. Also essential is the *charro* outfit, derived from the formal dress of well-to-do ranchers, including a set of buttons up both pant legs (or for women, up both sides of the skirt) called a *botonadura.* Musically, the most basic and traditional mariachi genre is called a *son.* In addition, mariachi performances nearly always include several of the following types of music: ranchera, corrido, polka, vals, paso doble, bolero, huapango, cumbia, and joropa. Some groups also attempt transcriptions of classical or pop songs. Traditional mariachi groups rarely venture into Caribbean styles such as mambo, merengue, or salsa, because the syncopation and off-beats of those dances conflict with their fundamentally "square" rhythmic orientation.

Professional, trumpet-based mariachi is now considered to be the national musical style of Mexico. As such, it is a source of pride and ethnic identity for many Mexican Americans, and instruction in it is offered in several school systems in heavily Latino areas of the United States. Hundreds of professional and semiprofessional bands ply their existence in every large U.S. city hosting significant numbers of Chicanos, including Los Angeles, San José, San Francisco, and San Diego, California; Tuscon and Phoenix, Arizona; Las Vegas, Nevada; El Paso, San Antonio, and Houston, Texas; Chicago, Illinois; Orlando, Florida; Washington, D.C.; and New York City. Mariachi followed Mexican workers into the United States during and after World War II, when it was performed in the cantinas where those workers would eat and relax, paying for their music *al talón* (that is, per song). In this environment the music acquired a somewhat dubious reputation, although its centrality to Mexican culture was recognized.

United States–based mariachi has contributed greatly to several developments in the genre. In the mid-1960s, Nati Cano of Los Angeles, for example, is credited with having held the first dinner-concert

Female mariachi members practice before a show at the Hollywood Bowl in California.

performances by his Mariachi Los Camperos, which raised mariachi from the all-male *cantina* to a more middle-class, mixed-gender ambience. In the 1970s, under the influence of the Chicano movement and calls for multicultural education, several school districts in Latino urban areas began offering mariachi as an alternative to classical orchestra or choir. The first university-based mariachi group was Mariachi Ucatlán, hosted by the Institute of Ethnomusicology at the University of California, Los Angeles. In 1979 the first mariachi conference was organized in San Antonio, Texas, by Belle San Miguel Ortiz. From 1982 on, a Tuscon mariachi, Mariachi Cobre, formed out of an extracurricular activity for children at risk founded by an Irish Catholic priest, was contracted to play at the Mexico Pavilion in the EPCOT Center at Disney World, thus exposing visitors from around the world to mariachi music. The Mariachi U.S.A. festival was begun in Los Angeles in 1990 by Rodri Rodríguez. Mariachi groups in the United States tend to be heterogeneous, consisting of Mexicans, Chicanos, other Latinos, and Anglos, thus further spreading and internationalizing the form. Finally, recording artists such as Herb Alpert and Linda Ronstadt have helped widen the appeal of mariachi.

The United States has been an important site for women to enter the mariachi profession. A number of all-female groups have become popular in both the United States and Mexico, and integrated groups also exist, although anecdotes of male musicians' refusal to play alongside women persist. Latino women who enter mariachi must overcome lingering associations of the music with society's seamier side (a perception reinforced by the 1993 film *El mariachi*). However, women frequently welcome mariachi as a pathway for resisting feminine stereotypes. Leonor Xóchitl Pérez, a mariachi violinist for many years, has told how at 15 she could not wait to replace her white *quinceañera* dress with her black *charro* outfit.

RELATED ARTICLES

Music, Classical; Music, Popular; Musical Instruments.

FURTHER READING

Ballard, Keith R. "Mariachi: Ethnic Music as a Teaching Tool." *Teaching Music* 9 (Feb. 2002): 22–27.

Jáquez, Cándida F. "*El Mariachi*: Musical Repertoire as Socio-cultural Investment." In *Musical Migrations*. Ed. by Frances R. Aparicio and Cándida F. Jáquez. New York: Palgrave, 2003.

Nevin, Jeff. *Virtuoso Mariachi*. Lanham, Md.: Univ. Press of Am., 2002.

Sheehy, Daniel. "Mexican Mariachi Music: Made in the U.S.A." In *Musics of Multicultural America: A Study of Twelve Musical Communities*. Ed. by Kip Lornell and Anne K. Rasmussen. Toronto: Schirmer, 1997.

Xóchitl Pérez, Leonor. "Transgressing the Taboo: A Chicana's Voice in the Mariachi World." In *Chicana Traditions: Continuity and Change*. Ed. by Norma E. Cantú and Olga Nájera-Ramírez. Urbana: Univ. of Ill. Press, 2002.

THOMAS O. BEEBEE

MARIANISMO

One of the most controversial and least understood traditional cultural values associated with female gender-role socialization is *marianismo*, characterized as the self-sacrificing, nurturing, humble, and virtuous woman. This construct is often viewed as the opposite of *machismo*, which is described and popularized as the sexually aggressive, domineering, and self-confident Latino man. *Marianismo* has its roots in the Roman Catholic religion and is associated with the Virgin Mary. Thus, Latina mothers are responsible for providing the religious and spiritual strength in a family, while young women must remain virgins until they are married. Some argue that these traditional gender-role expectations are associated with women in general, not just Latinas. Nonetheless, *marianismo* is still considered a Latino cultural value based on its prevalence in Latin American countries.

In order to fully capture the complexity of this gender role and how it is manifested in today's society, a review of its historical origins is warranted. In particular, Evelyn Stevens in "Marianismo: The Other Face of Machismo" (1994) noted that the roots go back to primitive times when women were idealized because they could create life within their bodies. In many parts of the world, including the Mediterranean region, the female figure was portrayed as a goddess and worshiped. Early Christianity also played an important role by giving Mary, mother of Jesus, celestial qualities. Thus, the worship of the Virgin Mary became known as "Marianism" or the Marian cult; however, it is not a religious practice.

Stevens speculated that the Marian cult may have arrived in the New World during the Spanish conquest. In particular, the Virgin Mary is said to have appeared in Mexico and was given the name la Virgen de Guadalupe. Symbolizing hope, love, and self-sacrifice, she became the patron saint of Mexico in the 18th century, and later of all Latin America. According to Stevens it is difficult to discern how these characteristics became associated with women in Latin American society, but she surmises that the widespread influence of religion significantly contributes to the present-day stereotypic image of the "ideal" Latins as submissive, spiritually and morally superior, and without sexual desires. This historic characterization of Latinas is deeply embedded in the culture, and a number of scholars claim that its roots can be traced to the colonial period, when a rigid social structure dictated women's roles.

The extent to which Latinas in contemporary U.S. society adhere to *marianista* attitudes and behaviors is a topic of much debate and is being challenged in light of changing cultural patterns in the United States. Rosa Maria Gil and Carmen Inoa Vazquez in *The Maria Paradox* (1996) formulated ten behaviors, called "commandments," that epitomize this traditional gender role. These include the following: Do not forget a woman's place; Do not forsake tradition; Do not be single, self-supporting, or independent; Do not put your own needs first; Do not forget that sex is for making babies; and Do not discuss personal problems outside the home. Gil and Vazquez offer a compelling case that Latinas may be conflicted about these gender-role expectations for themselves, especially among those who value independence and want a different lifestyle, such as a career and egalitarian relationships with men. Given the increased opportunities for women to actively participate in economic, political, and social arenas, Latinas are assertively making decisions about postponing marriage and whether or not to have children. Latinas in greater numbers are pursuing higher education and focusing on careers. However, the pressure from older generations of women (such as mothers and grandmothers) who hold fast to traditions may result in feelings of guilt and shame. In essence, the push to preserve aspects of traditional gender role expectations could be related to a strong sense of family obligation.

While the focus has been to examine *marianismo* in the context of American society, efforts to study its presence and transformation in contemporary Latin America have also emerged. In fact, an alternative perspective is offered that centers on an economic basis for its very existence. Tracy Bachrach Ehlers, in "Debunking Marianismo: Economic Vulnerability and Survival Strategies among Guatemalan Wives" (1991), proposed that women's *marianista* behaviors are a direct result of their economic, social, and sexual dependence in a society where men are in a position of power. Ehlers set out to examine the division of labor among Guatemalan men and women of Maya descent in two contrasting communities that were undergoing market integration: one that had a subsistence economy but was experiencing rapid growth in commercial weaving; and the other, a rapidly developing economy with a variety of employment opportunities for both sexes. The findings of her study confirm that the women in both communities were at a distinct disadvantage in several ways. First, men controlled the commercial weaving business once dominated by women and were profiting from this enterprise, more so than the women. Second, the types of occupations held by the Maya women became limited, whereas the job possibilities for men had expanded as a result of educational opportunities afforded to them. Finally, women continued to be solely responsible for household duties even though they, too, were contributing to the household income. Furthermore, many of them no longer participated in the labor market because the men were earning more money. According to Ehlers, the consequences of this change in labor participation places women in a vulnerable position in that there is increased dependency on the male for the financial stability of the family. She concluded that aspects of *marianismo* play out in this scenario because women, who once associated work with increased self-esteem and a higher social status, had become dependent on and subordinate to men.

In sum, some scholars claim that Latinas are faced with many challenges in a male-dominated society. While they may want to uphold aspects of traditional values, they also struggle to incorporate egalitarian ideals. This is evident in the rise of the Chicana feminist movement that began in the 1960s and remained strong into the 21st century.

RELATED ARTICLES

Catholicism; Family; Feminism; Machismo; Religion; Spirituality.

FURTHER READING

Ehlers, Tracy Bachrach. "Debunking Marianismo: Economic Vulnerability and Survival Strategies among Guatemalan Wives." *Ethnology* 30 (January 1991): 1–15.

Gil, Rosa Maria, and Carmen Inoa Vazquez. *The Maria Paradox*. New York: Putnam, 1996.

Stevens, Evelyn P. "Marianismo: The Other Face of Machismo." *Confronting Change, Challenging Tradition: Women in Latin American History*. Ed. by Gertrude M. Yeager. Wilmington, Del.: Scholarly Resources, 1994.

AZARA SANTIAGO-RIVERA

MARIEL BOAT LIFT

From April 21 to September 26, 1980, as part of the so-called Mariel boat lift, 125,266 Cubans migrated to the United States, making that event the largest uncontrolled, direct migration in American history. More than 2,000 private vessels participated in the boat lift, which at its peak averaged 2,800 daily arrivals, including a record of 6,000 arrivals on June 3. The oceanic exodus resulted in the death of 26 people and set off a humanitarian and political crisis in the United States as the state of Florida coped with the rapid migrant influx and the Carter administration lost control over U.S. immigration policy.

Leading up to the Mariel boat lift was a dispute, beginning in January 1980, between the Peruvian and Cuban governments over asylum rights. On April 1, 1980, the tension reached its boiling point when a group of six asylum seekers broke into the Peruvian embassy in Cuba by crashing a hijacked public bus through the embassy compound gate. The bus crashers requested and received political asylum from the Peruvian government. As a retaliatory measure, on April 4, 1980, the Cuban government publicly announced that anyone wishing to emigrate from Cuba could do so by going to the Peruvian embassy in Havana to receive exit visas. The announcement also explained that the Cuban soldiers who usually guarded the embassy had been removed, providing easy and unfettered access to the embassy to all.

Asylum seekers and embassy break-ins were not new to Cuba. Several hundred Cubans had sought and received political asylum in foreign embassies since 1959, and most cases were resolved peacefully. However, because this particular incident resulted in the death of a Cuban guard on duty at the embassy, the Cuban government demanded the surrender of the bus crashers. Peru's refusal to grant Cuba's request led to the latter government's decision to remove the guards and to announce the opportunities available at the Peruvian embassy for quick and simple emigration.

The Cuban government and most Cubans in Cuba and in exile were stunned by the fast and overwhelming response to the government's proclamation. Within 48 hours after the announcement, more than 10,000 people had crowded the small embassy compound, markedly exceeding its capacity. As a response to the unexpected turnout, the Cuban government unilaterally authorized and encouraged a boat lift of its disaffected citizens to the United States and explained that transportation would be provided by Cuban exiles willing to sail to Cuba to pick up relatives. The exile community interpreted the announcement as an act of desperation that could possibly be the beginning of the end of Fidel Castro's government.

The reaction to the emigration open door was swift, and within hours, dozens of boats arrived at the port of Mariel, Cuba, and as promised, they were allowed to transport their human cargo back to Key West, Florida, where most were welcomed as heroes by relatives, U.S. immigration officials, Cuban American political leaders, and community organizers. The boat lift, however, was just the beginning of what still stands as one of the most dramatic and traumatic experiences in the history of U.S. immigration. For Cuba the event was also extremely significant; the then 20-year-old revolution was struggling with the effects of a serious economic crisis, diminishing popular support for the revolutionary process, and the pressures of a foreign policy that was often at odds with the Soviet Union, the country's main ally and supporter in international affairs.

As the boat lift intensified during summer 1980, the media in the United States began reporting that Castro was using the boat lift to get rid of Cuba's hardened criminals and other social deviants. As a result, all Mariel entrants were labeled Marielitos, a pejorative label that characterized and stigmatized all

© JACQUES LANGEVIN/AP/WIDE WORLD PHOTOS

Cuban refugees wait aboard a boat in Mariel, Cuba, bound for Key West, Florida, as part of the Mariel boat lift, 1980.

entrants as criminals. In reality, only about 2 percent of the Mariel entrants had criminal records in Cuba. The other 98 percent were hard-working, decent people hoping to start a new life in the United States. Nonetheless, the label stuck, and, more tragically still, more than 5,000 entrants were detained by the Immigration and Naturalization Service (INS) and determined to be "excludable" aliens, not fit for United States society. Most of those "excludables" served long prison terms in U.S. federal prisons for crimes committed in Cuba, others were deported back to Cuba, and as of 2004 there were still 1,000 held in American prisons, suspended in a legal limbo since 1980.

In an attempt to settle the excludables issue and to normalize the migration flow between Cuba and the United States, in 1984 the two countries signed a historic immigration agreement that called for the deportation of all excludable Mariel entrants and set a quota of 20,000 Cuban legal immigrants per year. Unfortunately, the Cuban Government suspended the agreement to protest the Reagan administration's establishment of Radio Martí, a U.S.-based radio transmission program dedicated to broadcasting anti–Cuban government propaganda to Cuba.

Contrary to popular belief, the boat lift was not a unique incident. A similar but smaller boat lift from the port of Camarioca, Cuba, took place in 1965 and led to a massive airlift that resulted in the migration of 265,000 Cubans to the United States. Likewise, the history of Cuban migration to the United States since the Cuban revolution suggests that rather than unexpected, the Mariel boat lift was a direct and almost predictable consequence of U.S. immigration policy toward Cuba dating back to 1959. Since the triumph of the Cuban revolution, Cubans wishing to emigrate have been welcomed in the United States, where they are claimed as a political victory of capitalism over communism.

RELATED ARTICLES

Balseros; Castro, Fidel; Cuba; Immigration, Latino; Politics, Cuban American.

FURTHER READING

Doss, Joe Morris. *Let the Bastards Go: From Cuba to Freedom on God's Mercy.* Baton Rouge: La. State Univ. Press, 2003.

Engstrom, David W. *Decision Making Adrift: The Carter Administration and the Mariel Boatlift.* Lanham, Md.: Rowman & Littlefield, 1997.

Fernández, Gastón A. *The Mariel Exodus: Twenty Years Later, A Study on the Politics of Stigma and a Research Bibliography.* Miami: Ediciones Universal, 2002.

Hamm, Mark S. *The Abandoned Ones: The Imprisonment and Uprising of the Mariel Boat People.* Boston: Northeastern Univ. Press, 1995.

Larzelere, Alex. *The 1980 Cuban Boatlift: Castro's Ploy, America's Dilemma.* Washington, D.C.: Natl. Defense Univ. Press, 1988.

FELÍX MASUD-PILOTO

MARÍN, CHEECH

Born: July 13, 1946; South Central Los Angeles, California

Cheech Marín is famous for his irreverent, subversive, and humorous portraits of stereotypical Chicanos in the movies he made with his Asian American partner, Tommy Chong. He is also recognized as a major collector of Mexican American art, his wealth of paintings having been exhibited nationwide, increasing the attention to this artistic tradition.

The son of a police officer, Ricardo Marín was born shortly after World War II and was raised in the suburb of Granada Hills, in the San Fernando Valley. Marín attended California State University at Northridge, but he left eight credits short of a degree in English. He moved to Vancouver, British Columbia, to avoid the Vietnam draft, and it was there that he met the Canadian-born Thomas Chong, who is the product of a mixed lineage—Chinese, French, Scottish, and Irish. A musician and high school dropout, Chong at the time was the owner of a club, where Marín worked for nine months.

The two eventually became partners in a stand-up comedy routine and moved to Los Angeles, where they performed until, at a club called the Troubador, the music impresario Lou Adler discovered them. Over a decade and a half, the duo, known as Cheech and Chong, teamed together to costar in eight movies. Considered by reviewers as low-brow, B-quality films at the time of their release, some have become cult classics.

Cheech and Chong's first movie was *Up in Smoke*, which generated record-breaking revenues in excess of $100 million in 1978. It was followed by a series of low-budget but popular films in the early half of the 1980s, Marín's most prolific period: *Cheech and Chong's Next Movie* (1980), *Cheech and Chong's Nice Dream* (1981), *Things Are Tough All Over* (1982), *Cheech and Chong: Still Smoking* (1983), and *Cheech and Chong: The Corsican Brothers* (1984). The pair also appeared in Martin Scorsese's *After Hours* (1985) and *Rude Awakening* (1989), among other films with different directors.

The duo split and Marín continued with a solo career that was ignited in 1987 with his successful directorial debut, *Born in East L.A.,* arguably his most important movie, and one in which he also had the leading role. The protagonist is a Chicano who by mistake crosses the United States–Mexico border only to find out he is not allowed to return home because of his physical appearance. A humorous exploration, and exploitation, of ethnic stereotypes, the film is regularly featured on campuses across the country. Its final scene—in which, after many attempts to reenter the United States, the protagonist persuades numerous Mexicans to cross the border with him by foot at the exact same time—has become an emblem of incessant south-of-the-border immigration to the United States.

Other credits include films by Mexican American director Robert Rodríguez (*From Dusk till Dawn, Desperado, Spy Kids, Once upon a Time in Mexico,* among others), as well as roles in movies such as *Luminarias* (2001) and *The Original Latin Kings of Comedy* (2003). Martín has also done voiceovers in animated features—for example, the voice of the character Banzai in Walt Disney's *Lion King.* He released an album of children's songs with Latin American rhythms called *My Name Is Cheech, the School Bus Driver,* which became quite popular and was followed by *My Name Is Cheech, the School Bus Driver "Coast to Coast."* In the latter the protagonist drives from Los Angeles to Miami.

According to lore, Marín's nickname "Cheech" comes from his fondness for Mexican American food, in particular *chicarrones* (pronounced chee-cha-roh-nehs), a popular fried pork-skin snack. In the early 1990s the name Cheech Marín was synonymous with cheap ethnic culture. But a new generation of Latinos has fruitfully committed itself to revitalizing and redefining his image. As a result, Marín is perceived today as a forerunner of a defiant attitude toward popular art that is connected with the esthetic concept of *rascuachismo,* the view that cheap, second-rate art is an empowering tool in the struggle to find a suitable collective identity for Latinos.

The other side of Marín's career is less known, yet equally important. Over the years he has become a private art collector with an impressive selection of paintings by artists such as Frank Romero, Gronk Patssi Valdez, George Yepes, Rupert García, Leo Limón, Eloy Torres, and Carlos Almaráz. Individual items in the collection have been seen in museums nationwide. Collectively, the 96 paintings by 20 artists was turned into a traveling exhibit called *Chicano Visions: American Painters on the Verge,* and a catalog was published in 2002. Marín has brought attention to the Chicano artistic tradition in significant ways. It has alerted people to a diverse, politically engaged tradition that is no longer on the fringes of the artistic world; encouraged museums and galleries to expand their collections not only of Mexican American but of other Latino groups' art, as well; and heightened interest in more detailed, more narrowly defined exhibits. In this sense the marriage between art and celebrity status has proved rewarding.

Marín, as an entrepreneur, has developed his own line of gourmet hot sauces. Married to Rikki Morley in 1975, he adopted a daughter with her, but they divorced in 1984. He then married Patti Heid, with whom he has two children.

RELATED ARTICLES

Art, Mexican American and Chicano; Art, Popular; Film; Popular Culture.

FURTHER READING

Marín, Cheech. *Chicano Visions: American Painters on the Verge.* New York: Bulfinch Press, 2002.

Menard, Valerie. *The Latino Holiday Book: From Cinco de Mayo to Día de los Muertos; The Celebrations and Traditions of Hispanic-Americans.* Foreword by Cheech Marín. Collingdale, Pa.: Diane Publ., 2000.

ILAN STAVANS

MARRIAGE

Marriage among the various Latino groups has a rich history influenced by Spanish traditions that were introduced during the colonial period. Many of the rituals and rites of marriage that are practiced today come from a combination of Spanish and indigenous cultural and religious traditions that are unique to each country of origin. In addition, Catholicism has heavily influenced courtship and marriage ceremonies among the Latino groups where church weddings, performed by a priest, are common. In contemporary U.S. society, Latino weddings may look very much like the traditional American ceremony, where bridesmaids and their escorts, a maid of honor, a best man, a flower girl, and a ring bearer are all part of the event. However, there are a variety of unique Latino cultural traditions, many of which are still practiced today.

Traditions

Norma Williams, the author of *The Mexican American Family* (1990), points out that in traditional Mexican weddings, *arras* (13 coins symbolizing the desire for both the bride and groom to be financially secure) are blessed by the priest and given to the couple. Also, the *lazo* (a large rosary) is placed around the couple representing their union. Immediate and extended family members as well as close friends attend the marriage ceremony. According to Williams, traditional Mexican weddings often have *primeros padrinos* (first godparents to witness the wedding), who are selected to provide support and advice to the wedding couple.

One of the unique traditions that carried over into the early part of the 20th century, but no longer is a popular practice, was the formal presentation of the marriage proposal by a *portador*, a highly respected older male from the community, such as a godfather, clergy member, or relative, who would deliver the marriage proposal to the young woman's parents. Often this individual would serve as the intermediary between the young couple's parents during the decision-making process about the marriage proposal. Typically, the discussion about the marriage would be conducted by the young woman's parents (primarily the father or *portador*) and the young man's parents.

In traditional Puerto Rican weddings the newlyweds greet each guest and pin them with *capias*, souvenirs that may consist of ornately decorated ribbon printed with the bride and groom's name and the wedding date. While this small gift symbolizes the couple's union, it also expresses their appreciation to guests for attending the wedding ceremony and festivities. Another tradition is to place a bridal doll, wearing a dress that is identical to the bride's, on the head table.

Cuban traditions are somewhat similar to those of Puerto Rican and Mexican weddings; they are festive occasions with lively music and dancing. In addition, the famous money dance, in which each man who dances with the bride must pin money to her dress, is often seen at Cuban weddings. The purpose of this tradition is to help the bride and groom with their honeymoon expenses.

Demographic Marriage Patterns

In general Latinos tend to marry at a younger age than do non-Latino whites and African Americans in the United States. This is partly because Latinos as a group are relatively younger than the overall U.S. population.

Because the Catholic religion has historically played a central role in Latino culture, the incidence of divorce among Latinos is relatively low. In recent years, however, there has been a rise in the rates of separation and divorce. Based on current U.S. census information, it appears that the Latino group most affected by this trend is the Puerto Rican population. It has been reported that compared with all other Latino groups, Puerto Rican women are less likely to marry by age 25; and compared with Mexicans, Cubans, and Central and South Americans, Puerto Ricans have the lowest rate of marriage and the highest rate of women heading households with no spouse present. In contrast, Cubans appear to have the highest rate of marriage compared to all other Latino groups.

The differing marital patterns among these various Latino groups can be attributed to a variety of factors such as age, place of birth (born in the "home" country versus born in the United States), and socioeconomic indicators such as income. However, the experts who study this phenomenon note that Latino marriage patterns are complex, influenced not only by the factors mentioned above but also by religious affiliation, education, gender, place of residency, and migration history. This is particularly important because Latinos are a diverse group of people who come from different Spanish-speaking countries, each with a unique history, cultural traditions, foods, and indigenous roots.

While the Spanish language is considered a common characteristic among Latinos, there are differences in size and in historical and present-day migration patterns, including geographic areas of settlement in the United States. Specifically, about 60 percent of the Latino population are of Mexican heritage and live primarily in the western and southwestern United States, most notably, California and Texas. The second largest group, Puerto Ricans account for about 11 percent of the Latino population and live primarily in the Northeast, in particular, New York. Cubans, make up the third largest group; they account for about 3 percent of Latinos and reside for the most part in Florida. Central and South

Americans come from a variety of Spanish-speaking countries such as El Salvador, Honduras, Nicaragua, Argentina, Colombia, Chile, and Peru. Central and South Americans, as a group, make up about 9 percent of the total Latino population. Their migration patterns are more difficult to discern, partly because the numbers from each of these countries are relatively small compared with the Mexican, Puerto Rican, and Cuban populations. Dominicans, considered one of the newer immigrant groups, have settled in the Northeast, primarily in New York and New Jersey. The differences in migration patterns, geographic settlement areas, socioeconomic backgrounds, and cultural traditions undeniably influence marriage behaviors.

Changing Values and Beliefs

It is well recognized that family formation in the United States underwent considerable transformation during the last several decades of the 20th century. The fact that couples live together without being married (cohabitation), marry at an older age, engage in premarital sex, and have children out of wedlock are examples of how this transformation manifests itself. In essence, the normative pattern of getting married, staying married, and having children appears to be declining in the United States, while cohabitation is on the rise.

Given this trend, there has been an interest in determining if this phenomenon is also occurring among the various Latino groups in the United States. One of the driving forces behind studying Latino marriage patterns is the notion that as a group Latinos have a strong familistic orientation. The importance of the family, known as *familismo,* is said to be one of the traditional values that has remained relatively strong, even among U.S.-born Latinos. This familistic orientation appears to be reinforced because a large segment of the population consists of recent immigrants, who are more likely to adhere to traditional beliefs and customs and settle in geographic regions where Latino communities already exist. Whether or not this trend will continue to hold true has been a subject of interest among social scientists.

In "Normative Beliefs about Marriage and Cohabitation: A Comparison of Non-Latino Whites, Mexican Americans, and Puerto Ricans" (1996), R. S. Oropesa states that there are considerable differences in marriage norms across ethnic and racial groups stemming from cultural traditions (such as the socialization of women to believe that marriage, children, and family are priorities), and economic conditions (employment opportunities). In particular, Oropesa claims that Mexican Americans more strongly favor marriage, especially among the foreign born, than non-Latino whites. Conversely, Puerto Ricans are more accepting of cohabitation than non-Latino whites and Mexican Americans. A plausible explanation offered is that Puerto Ricans in the United States are considered the most disadvantaged compared with all other Latino groups, with the lowest level of educational attainment and labor-market participation as well as the highest rate of unemployment. Therefore, informal unions, sometimes referred to as consensual unions, might be the best alternative because of low socioeconomic status. Furthermore, consensual unions are said to have originated in the 16th century during the Spanish conquest when the *conquistadors* (Spanish colonizers) endorsed sexual unions with the indigenous women of the island of Puerto Rico. This type of union remained common throughout the 19th century but steadily declined

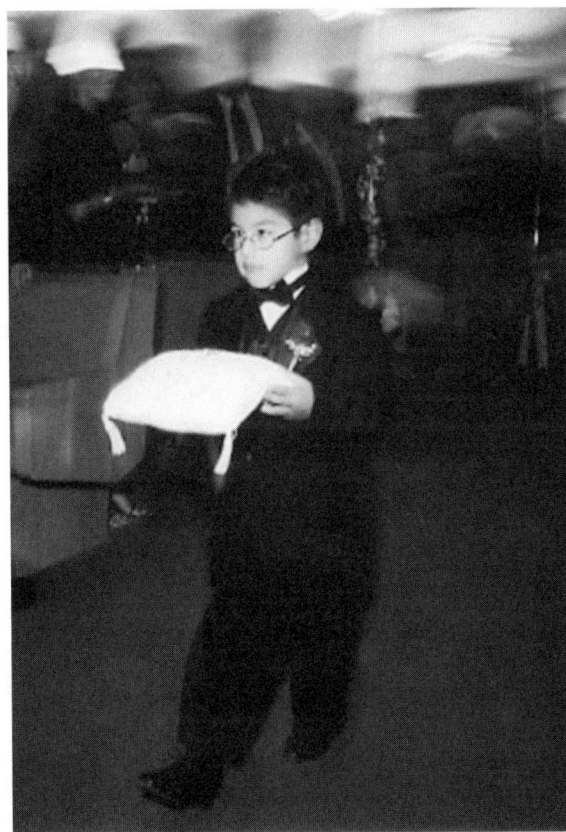

© JESSE HERRERA

Ring bearer during a wedding ceremony.

during the 20th century. It is believed that some Puerto Ricans who migrated to and settled in the United States during the 20th century continued the practice.

The trend toward cohabiting rather than marrying has different consequences for Latinos, according to sociologists such as Nancy Landale and Renata Forste, authors of "Patterns of Entry into Cohabitation and Marriage among Mainland Puerto Rican Women" (1991). They point out that the shift toward informal unions rather than marriage among Puerto Ricans parallels that of the U.S. population as a whole; however, cohabitation is not seen as a stage that will eventually lead to marriage but rather as an end point. Puerto Rican women are opting to have and raise children without marriage, even though the informal unions are often unstable. Although increased sexual activity and pregnancy in adolescents often leads to early marriage (in fact, it has been noted that there has been an increase in adolescent marriages), the rate of adolescent girls' giving birth has declined. Landale and Forste also conclude that remaining in school decreases the likelihood of early union formation.

Intermarriage

Demographic trends indicate that U.S society is becoming increasingly diverse with different cultural, racial, and ethnic groups coming into contact more frequently than ever before. In theory, people who work or live in close proximity develop commonalities. Douglas Gurak and Joseph Fitzpatrick call it "social proximity" and suggest that it promotes an expanded worldview, reduces prejudice, and increases awareness and tolerance of ethnic and cultural differences. Evidence of this phenomenon is reflected in the shift toward intermarriage among ethnic and racial groups that occurred during the last several decades of the 20th century, particularly among Latinos. As Gurak and Fitzpatrick emphasize, intermarriage is a strong indicator of a group's "interethnic social distance"; yet one cannot conclude that all intermarriages lead to assimilation. For instance, a Dominican who marries a Puerto Rican may have similar cultural traditions and experiences, and thus the interethnic social distance between the two is relatively small. That does not mean, however, that they have become part of the mainstream U.S. culture and society. On the contrary, it has been argued that multiple barriers such as discrimination in housing, employment, and education prevent minorities from fully participating in all aspects of mainstream society.

Formal unions between Latinos and non-Latino ethnic and racial groups, known as "out-group marriage," have also been explored; again, caution must be taken in concluding that one culture is lost at the expense of the other. Specifically, Gurak and Fitzpatrick elaborate on the out-marriage rates of five Latino groups living in New York City in 1975 and assert that Puerto Ricans were the least likely to marry outside their ethnic group regardless of generational status (that is, first, second, and third generation living in the United States) compared with Cubans, Dominicans, and Central and South Americans. In addition, the rate of intermarriage between Puerto Ricans and other Latinos was higher than the other groups. For example, formal unions between Puerto Ricans and Dominicans appeared to be more common than marriages between other Latino groups. In contrast, Cubans had the highest rate of marriage with third-generation, non-Latino Americans.

Based on these tendencies, a number of interesting observations emerge. First, Gurak and Fitzpatrick suggest that the degree to which marriage occurs outside one's ethnic group may be a function of socioeconomic background and residency. In this case, Puerto Ricans may be less likely to intermarry because of their relatively low socioeconomic status and high concentration in New York City. Second, generational status also plays an important role in the tendency to intermarry. That is, the higher rates of intermarriage that occur among the second and third generation indicates that Latinos are assimilating. Finally, the differences noted are evidence of the complexity involved in identifying the conditions and characteristics that result in these varying patterns.

Later reports on Latino intermarriages indicate that gender, generation, country of origin, and place of residence greatly influence these trends. For instance, Kevin Heubusch and Shannon Dortch note in "Meet the New Hispanic Family" (1996) that men are more likely to intermarry than are women. Second-generation South American men are forming cross-ethnic unions, and Cubans continue to have the highest rate of marriage outside their own ethnic group.

Roberto Suro's "Mixed Doubles" (1999) coined the phrase "the beginning of the blend," emphasizing that interracial and interethnic marriages have dramatically increased since the 1980s. Such unions are heavily concentrated among those who are under the age of 35 and have at least some college education and incomes in the top 50 percent. According to Suros new patterns are emerging. For instance, Latino and non-Latino white marriages appear to be more common than any other mix (Latino and Asian, Latino and black) and are heavily concentrated in states such as California, Texas, Florida, and New York where the Latino population is fairly large.

The diversity of the Latino population in the United States also increases the potential for cross-cultural unions, for example, Puerto Ricans marrying Dominicans, Cubans marrying Puerto Ricans, and Mexicans marrying Costa Ricans. As noted elsewhere, cultural similarities such as language, cuisine, religion, and some traditions encourage such unions. These marriage patterns clearly show that Latino families are experiencing considerable change, not only structurally but also in the blending of cultural beliefs, traditions, and practices.

Migration and Marital Stability

In recent years social scientists have been interested in identifying the causes of the dramatic increases in separation and divorce rates and out-of-wedlock births in contemporary U.S. society. They claim that these trends have resulted in a rising number of women, especially poor minority women, heading families with no spouse present. The major concern is that divorce or separation often leads to a decline in the economic stability of the family, thus placing these women and their children at greater risk for disenfranchisement and isolation. In the case of Latinos, one important dimension to consider is how migration might be affecting the institution of marriage.

Understanding the effects of migration on marriage has become a focal point among investigators because a main source of the Latino population's growth is, in fact, due to immigration. Although there may be intragroup (across Latino groups) differences with respect to the reasons for migrating to the United States, the process of adaptation to a new way of life often leads to increased stress and social isolation. Therefore, these negative consequences may be affecting the individual's and family's well-being.

Some scholars propose that the stress and strain associated with migration, particularly among Latinos, is related to marital disruption or dissolution as well as to family instability. Nancy Landale and Nimfa Ogena in "Migration and Union Dissolution among Puerto Rican Women" (1995) set out to investigate this premise. Specifically, they looked at the relationship between migration and first union disruption among Puerto Rican women by comparing five different migration status groups:

(1) "nonmigrant" women (born and living in Puerto Rico);

(2) "return migrants" (born and living on the island with prior residency in the United States);

(3) "first-generation U.S. migrants" (born on the island and living in the United States;

(4) "second-generation migrants" (born and residing in the United States); and

(5) "U.S. born return migrants" (born in the United States and living on the island of Puerto Rico).

A number of interesting patterns emerge from the data obtained on these various migrant groups. First, the authors found that the rate of union dissolution increased with the length of residency in the United States. Second, there were numerous clear distinctions between the Puerto Rican nonmigrant women (Puerto Rico–born and living on the island with no U.S. exposure) compared with the migrant women (first- and second-generation living in the United States). In particular, there was a tendency for the migrant women to be pregnant before the actual marriage or to have children without a formal union. In addition, the migrant women had a markedly higher rate of union dissolution compared with the nonmigrant women. Third, the rate of union dissolution was strongly related to a number of characteristics that appear to be consistent with previous research. Specifically, Puerto Rican women who were employed before marriage showed lower rates of marital disruption compared with women who were unemployed. Also, women with children before marriage or who were pregnant at the time of marriage were more likely to experience marital disruption than were other women, However, that rate declined as women remained in a marriage longer and for those women whose children were under the age of six and born in the union. Finally, the authors emphasize that one of the most important factors related to marriage stability is the migration experience, concluding that recent immigrants who do not have the necessary social support system in place are more likely to experience marital disruption.

Given the rapid and steady growth of the Latino population in the United States and the increasing diversity within it, it is imperative that examination continues of these and other characteristics that influence marriage and informal unions, as well as marital disruption such as divorce and separation. Furthermore, as intermarriage rates increase, the blending of traditions between two or more cultures will undoubtedly continue to transform U.S society.

RELATED ARTICLES

Family; Intermarriage; Love, Latino Conceptions of; Parenting; Religion.

FURTHER READING

Fitzpatrick, Joseph P. "The Puerto Rican Family." In *Ethnic Families in America: Patterns and Variation*. Ed. by Charles H. Mindel and Robert W. Habenstein. New York: Elsvier, 1981.

Gurak, Douglas T., and Joseph P. Fitzpatrick. "Intermarriage among Hispanic Ethnic Groups in New York City." *American Journal of Sociology* 87 (January 1982): 921–934.

Heubusch, Kevin, and Shannon Dortch. "Meet the New Hispanic Family." *American Demographics* 18 (October 1996): 29.

Landale, Nancy S., and Renata Forste. "Patterns of Entry into Cohabitation and Marriage among Mainland Puerto Rican Women." *Demography* 28 (November 1991): 587–607.

Landale, Nancy S., and Nimfa B. Ogena. "Migration and Union Dissolution among Puerto Rican Women." *International Migration Review* 29 (Autumn 1995): 671–692.

Oropesa, R. S. "Normative Beliefs about Marriage and Cohabitation: A Comparison of Non-Latino Whites, Mexican Americans, and Puerto Ricans." *Journal of Marriage and the Family* 58 (November 1991): 49–62.

Suros, Roberto. "Mixed Doubles." *American Demographics* 21 (November 1999): 56–63.

Thorton, Arland. "Changing Attitudes toward Family Issues in the United States." *Journal of Marriage and the Family* 51 (November 1989): 873–893.

Williams, Norma. *The Mexican American Family: Traditions and Change*. New York: General Hall, 1990.

AZARA SANTIAGO-RIVERA

MARTÍ, JOSÉ

Born: January 28, 1853; Havana, Cuba
Died: May 19, 1895; Cuba

"I am at last in a country where each one seems to be his own master," José Martí wrote shortly after he set foot in North America. "One can breathe freely. For here, freedom is the foundation, the shield, the essence of life." These words are indicative of the exuberance he felt on his arrival in New York City.

Martí had a high forehead, a receding hairline, bushy eyebrows and mustache, deep-set eyes, a gaunt face, and ears that stuck out. During the last 14 years of his life, the man Cubans see as their singular historical hero lived in exile in New York City. In those years he organized, agitated on behalf of and raised funds for Cuban independence from Spain. He led the Partido Revolucionario Cubano (Cuban Revolutionary Party), and published its newspaper, *Patria,* to spread its philosophy. He gave dynamic public speeches, attended clandestine meetings, and was involved in the secret purchase of arms. His tireless efforts stitching together the financial and popular support for war against Spain ran concurrent with his literary life, which included translations, plays, essays, journalism, short stories, poetry, children's works, polemics and tracts, boundless correspondence, and one novel. He supported his passion for Cuba Libre (a Free Cuba) not only working for publishers and newspapers but also teaching Spanish at night and working for export-import concerns. On the diplomatic front, Martí represented, at various times, the governments of Uruguay, Argentina, and Paraguay in the United States. His concept of *nuestra América* (our America) augured strongly for links between all countries of the hemisphere. To understand Martí's life in the United States is to grasp the initial currents of Latin American immigration to this country, as well as the seeds of binational relations.

Martí's father, a native of Valencia, Spain, was a sergeant in the Spanish army. His mother came from the Canary Islands. When José, informally known throughout his life as Pepe, was two years old, the Martí family moved to Spain for two years, then returned to Cuba. Young Pepe grew up in Havana, but spent enough time in the countryside to appreciate the tempo and flavor of life there as well. Martí was inspired by Carlos Manuel de Céspedes's 1868 Grito de Yara (Cry of Yara) for Cuban independence that, among other things, demanded that slavery be phased out. A year later Martí was arrested for disloyalty—primarily for his writing advocating liberty for the island—and sentenced to work in a stone quarry. After six months of injurious hard labor he was exiled from Cuba to Spain, where he

DOS PATRIAS

Dos patrias tengo yo: Cuba y la noche.
¿O son una las dos? No bien retira
so majestad el sol, con largos velos
y un clavel en la mano, silenciosa
Cuba cual viuda triste me aparece.
¡Yo sé cuál es ese clavel sangriento
que en la mano le tiembla! Está vacío
mi pecho, destrozado está y vacío
en donde estaba el corazón. Ya es hora
de empezar a morir. La noche es buena
para decir adiós. La luz estorba
y la palabra humana. El universo
habla mejor que el hombre.

Cual bandera
que invita a batallar, la llama roja
de la vela flama. Las ventanas
abro, ya estrecho en mí. Muda, rompiendo
las hojas del clavel, como una nube
que enturbia el cielo, Cuba, viuda, pasa . . .

"Dos Patrias" by José Martí.

TWO HOMELANDS

I have two motherlands: Cuba and the night.
Or are they one and the same?
No sooner does the sun withdraw
its majesty, that Cuba, with long veils,
and a carnation in hand, appears
silently before me.

I know what the bleeding carnation is
that trembles in her hand! Empty,
my breast is destroyed and empty
where the heart once was. It's time
to begin dying. The night is fitting
for a good-bye. The light is vexing
and the word, human. The universe
speaks better than man.

Like a flag
calling to battle, the candle's red flame
flickers. I open
the windows, overwhelmed already. Mute,
tearing
the carnation's leaves,
in the overcast sky, Cuba widowed, passes by
. . .

"Two Homelands," translated by Ilan Stavans.

enrolled in a Madrid university and wrote pamphlets, tracts, treatises, and public letters about the misery, especially in prisons, that Cubans suffered under Spanish rule. Toward the end of 1874, having earned degrees from the University of Zaragoza, he traveled to Mexico City to visit his since-relocated family, stopping in France, England, and, briefly, New York, before sailing for Veracruz, Mexico. From there he took a train to Mexico City.

Martí lived for two years in Mexico as a journalist and high school teacher. Early in 1877 he entered Cuba surreptitiously as Julián Pérez—his middle name and his mother's surname—and stayed two months. That spring Martí moved to Guatemala where he took a teaching job and, on a year-end trip to Mexico City, married Carmen Zayas-Bazán, a Cuban woman he had met in that city's Cuban exile community. His writing, constant throughout, continued to focus on the need for Cuban independence from Spain.

In the fall of the following year, Martí returned to Havana under his own name with his wife, having soured on the politics of Guatemala, and in late November they had a baby boy, José Francisco Martí y Zayas-Bazán. Ten months later Martí was again arrested—this time for conspiring against the mother country—and was once more exiled to Spain. By the end of that year, he had traveled through France to Le Havre, where he took second-class passage on the S.S. *France*. When the ship docked in New York on a snowy January 3, 1880, Martí gave his occupation to the immigration officer in one English word: "advocate."

Three weeks after his arrival in Manhattan, Martí gave a speech at Steck Hall to the Cuban exile community about relations between Cuba and Spain. It began a flurry of activities that included assuming the presidency of the Comité Revolucionario Cubano for a while, public speaking, printing his Steck Hall talk into a pamphlet, and traveling to Cape May, New Jersey, and Philadelphia. For his tireless devotion to Cuba Libre, the Spanish government had detectives, including the Pinkertons, spy on him

In March 1880 his wife and son arrived from Havana, but he and Carmen had very different attitudes about Cuban independence, and Carmen and young José left seven months later. The following month his landlady, Carmen Miyares de Mantilla, whose husband was an invalid, gave birth to a daughter that

Martí treated as his own the rest of his life. The baby's birth certificate in Brooklyn lists Martí as godfather. Although there is scant positive evidence, it was assumed by all who knew Martí that the child, María, was his daughter.

In the first half of 1881, Martí lived in Venezuela, where his major accomplishment was publishing a literary magazine, *Revista Venezolana.* He was critical of the country's dictator, and in July he was asked to leave. He took the next ship back to New York, his primary residence until the end of his life.

Martí took comfort in New York's literary scene and its Latin American cultural clubs. He traveled on occasion to other states, principally Florida, and a few times to Latin American countries, but New York City became his true home. For many years he lived on West 29th Street, eventually moving uptown to lodgings in the West 50s and 60s. He roomed in Brooklyn, briefly. His writing during his New York years reflected his humanism and opti-

mism. His grief-stricken verse often dealt with nature and love, frequently infused with a subtle sensuality. "If you could see me struggling to conquer this beautiful but rebellious English," Martí wrote a friend shortly after arriving in New York; "three or four months more and I shall open a way for myself."

Over the next few years Martí published an enormous output of literature, starting with *Ismaelillo,* poetry devoted to his distant son Pepito written while in Caracas. ("I know arms that are strong, soft and fragrant; I know when they encircle my fragile neck, my body, like a kissed rose, opens . . . ") During this period he translated a number of books from English into Spanish; the best known among them is *Romana* by Helen Hunt Jackson. He also began what was, in retrospect, a singular and groundbreaking vocation of writing essays about life in the United States. These descriptive and lively literary commentaries were published Uruguay, Venezuela, Argentina, Honduras, and Mexico, and farther, in Spain.

A child looks at a display of photographs of José Martí at the Casa Museo, the house where Martí was born in Havana, Cuba.

In the closing decades of the 19th century, the United States flexed its muscles at sea and in industry, its culture expanded enormously, and advances in publishing brought inexpensive books to the masses. It was an exuberant era to be a part of, and Martí was active, front and center.

Readers in Latin America were exposed to Martí on Walt Whitman (his poetry, offered Martí, contains "grandiose priestly apothegms, like outbursts of light"), Ralph Waldo Emerson ("he felt divine bliss and indulged in delightful, celestial communion"), Mark Twain ("his wit derives from the originality and gross vitality of his own life"), Louisa May Alcott ("virtue gradually enters the soul as one reads [her books], the way balsam enters a wound"), and Oscar Wilde ("a noble sincerity radiates from the young poet's face"). His romantic journalism covered domestic U.S. politics, which he saw as increasingly corrupt, and U.S. foreign policy, whose frightful expansionism alarmed him. He wrote of women's suffrage, the streets of New York, the Brooklyn Bridge, Chanukah, Ellis Island, and the memorial service for Karl Marx. He sympathized with the anarchists hanged for the Haymarket Square labor riot in 1886. "This Republic," he wrote, "has fallen into the injustice and violence of monarchies." He had begun what was, in effect, the first syndicated newspaper column throughout Latin America. He was, literally, a foreign correspondent.

Even as he contributed to the literature of the Americas, Martí's passion to rid Cuba of Spain formed the molten core and the outer moons of his world. It attracted attention for its unceasing fury, for its velocity and trajectory, and for its universal righteousness. The 1880s, however, was not a decade for a war of independence but rather for developing a grand political and military strategy that would end the face-off in which the Cuban insurrectionists and their Spanish rulers found themselves. For example, in late 1882, shortly before his son and wife visited again, Martí took an active role in establishing the New York Patriotic Organizing Committee for Cuban Emigration. On occasion he visited with Tomás Estrada Palma, a Cuban American living in Central Valley, New York, who ran a private school and was, like Martí, exiled from his homeland and desirous of a free Cuba. (In 1902 Estrada Palma was tapped by the U.S. government to be a candidate for Cuba's first presidency after the four-year U.S. occupation following the Spanish-American War. He won.) Martí stayed in touch with military leaders from the island such as Calixto García, Máximo Gómez, and Antonio Maceo. With the latter two he disagreed vehemently over the role of the military in a postwar Cuba, but they reconciled for the greater good of the island.

Over the years Martí made valuable New York friendships, including with Charles Dana, distinguished publisher of the *Sun,* a newspaper, and Horatio Rubens, a well-connected young lawyer with an office on Broadway. Martí met Dana soon after arriving in the city, and the two maintained a close personal and professional relationship until Martí's death. Martí met Rubens in 1893, initially enlisting him to represent striking tobacco workers in Key West, Florida, and then in other matters of the Partido Revolucionario Cubano. So taken was Rubens by the concept of Cuba Libre that he devoted enormous time and energy to the cause, writing a book about it in his later years (*Liberty, The Story of Cuba*; 1932). He called Martí "a man equipped by Divine Providence."

Political meetings, family discord, rallying the workers—these took time and drained energy. Martí seemed to relax only when partaking in literary *tertulias*—informal literary gatherings. He was a colleague of the Puerto Rican poet, journalist, and typesetter Francisco Gonzalo "Pachín" Marín, likewise in the struggle for his *patria*'s independence and likewise having adopted New York as his home. Martí was also a contemporary of Puerto Rican writer and ethicist Eugenio María de Hostos, who preceded Martí in New York. Hostos was part of the struggle to free the Caribbean of Spanish rule, and he envisioned the region's strength in its unity rather than its separate countries. Martí's activities also created the political space for the Dos Antilles Political Club, founded in 1892 by Arthur Schomburg, among others, to promote Cuban and Puerto Rican separation from Spain. Martí took part in activities of the Sociedad Literaria Hispano-Americana and often relaxed with writers and other comrades at Delmonico's at the corner of Beaver and South William streets. (In his expense report, one Pinkerton undercover agent listed 75¢ for a bottle of wine at Delmonico's restaurant.) He routinely put in 18-hour work days.

Martí's political activities, both overt and covert, accelerated in the early 1890s with organizing and fund-raising trips to Tampa and Key West, as well as to Caribbean nations. In early 1895, having secretly bought arms in the United States, insurrectionists were ready to ship them out from Fernandina Beach, Florida, but U.S. government officers, tipped off to the clandestine cargo, confiscated the ship and the goods. Martí, mortified that the careful planning had gone awry, made plans to go to Cuba himself. Through the late winter and early spring of 1895, Martí, who had left his papers, books, and other possessions with friends in New York, traveled to the Dominican Republic, then Haiti, with plans to join military operations in Cuba. On April 11 he landed in La Playita, Cuba, in the country's far east, and together with General Máximo Gómez, with whom he had been traveling, set out to defeat the Spanish in what he hoped would be the final phase of the struggle. Confronted by Spanish troops on May 19, the poet countermanded an order from Gómez not to charge. Forty-two-year-old José Julián Martí y Pérez rode out front of his comrades-in-arms and was instantly killed. A sculptor's impression of that moment can be seen at the Avenue of the Americas entrance to Central Park in New York City. (When the city of New York was prepared to erect that statue in the early 1960s, a brouhaha broke out between anti- and pro-Castro Cuban Americans over which faction could claim his heritage.)

In death Martí has taken on religious, literary, and even sexual identity far beyond what his 42 years demonstrated. Starting in the 1920s he was referred to by Cubans as "The Apostle," a disturbing connotation that elevates him beyond the mortal. His wide-ranging literary career produced such quantity as well as quality that today Cubans and others of all political stripes can find something by him that articulates a given point of view. More than a century after they were written, Martí's aphorisms and metaphors now seem quaint, yet he was among the first generation of Latin American modernists. Martí's poetry is studied in schools throughout the Americas with good reason, for its language was lush and its similes fulsome. Within the United States his name softens the faces of anti-Castro hardliners and inspires non-Cuban Latinos who rightly see him as one of their historical heroes. "I love simplicity," he wrote of his style, "and believe in the need to express emotion in plain and honest forms." His poetry has made him a one-size-fits-all champion of the downtrodden and romantic.

Among his works that remain most popular are *La edad de oro* (The Golden Age), a touching children's magazine that lasted four issues; and *Versos sencillos* (Simple Verses), poetry that reflected nature, sadness, and an ample vision. (Lines from a few of the stanzas were appropriated in the 1960s and put to an already-composed tune called *Guantanamera*.) Among Cubans the conventional wisdom holds that the sad-eyed Martí was quite a ladies' man, a notion obliquely referred to in his own writing.

Statues of Martí stand in plazas throughout Europe and Latin America, and the Cuban communities of South Florida and northern New Jersey have constant reminders of the intellectual rabble-rouser as well. In Cuba it is impossible to walk more than a block in any town without seeing a chalk-white bust of Martí, or to drive many kilometers on a highway without spotting a billboard with his likeness and a pithy quote. He has posthumously been anointed the "intellectual author" of the revolution that brought the Castro government to power in 1959. The U.S. government, in an effort to disseminate anti-Castro attitudes into Cuba, named its radio and television stations aimed at the island after Martí. Although Martí was enamored of his new country in his initial years, by the end he despaired its international impulses. "It is my duty," he wrote near the end of his life, "to prevent by the independence of Cuba, the United States from spreading over the West Indies and falling, with that added weight, upon other lands of Our America. All I have done up to now, and shall do hereafter I do to that end . . . I have lived inside the monster and know its entrails, and my weapon is only the slingshot of David." Symbolically, Martí has come to represent a 19th-century vision of dedication, brilliance, and glory.

RELATED ARTICLES

Cuba; Literature, Cuban American; Politics, Cuban American.

FURTHER READING

Gray, Richard B. *José Martí: Cuban Patriot.* Gainesville: Univ. of Fla. Press, 1962.

Kirk, John M. *José Martí: Mentor of the Cuban Nation.* Gainesville: Univ. of Fla. Press, 1983.

Mañach, Jorge. *Martí: Apostle of Freedom.* Tr. by Coley Taylor. New York: Devin-Adair Co., 1950.

Martí, José. *Obras completas.* (28 vols.) Havana: Editorial de Ciencias Sociales, 1963–1973.

Martí, José. *Selected Writings.* Tr. by Esther Allen. New York: Penguin, 2002.

Poyo, Gerald E. *"With All, and for the Good of All": The Emergence of Popular Nationalism in the Cuban Communities of the United States, 1848–1898.* Durham, N.C.: Duke Univ. Press, 1989.

TOM MILLER

MARXISM

Marxism is frequently defined as the system of thought developed by two German philosophers, Karl Marx (1818–1883) and Friedrich Engels (1820–1895). Commonly associated with socialism and communism, Marxism focuses primarily on understanding issues pertinent to the unequal distribution of social and economic resources in capitalist societies. Much of the Marxist interpretation of economic relations is based on what Marxists call the social relations of production. This presumes that economic relationships act as the primary influence in the development of societal relationships and therefore exert a high level of influence over class relations. According to Marxism, class relations influence how individuals perceive themselves and others and are therefore the key determinants of social structures and social change. Marxism tries to understand this complex relationship of class and the capitalist economy by exploring relationships of subordination and domination, particularly in areas such as the individual's relationship to the products of his or her labor.

Due to the rigor with which Marxism takes on conflicts of economic alienation and social inequality, this system of thought offers an attractive political proxy to groups in the economic underclass. As Latinos have lobbied for social, cultural, political, and economic stability in the United States, some of the more politically progressive Latino groups have pursued Marxist principles. During the highly politicized period of the 1960s and early 1970s, several Hispanic organizations (League of United Latin American Citizens [LULAC], United Farm Workers [UFW], La Raza Unida, Brown Berets, Centro de Acción Social Autónoma [CASA], El Movimiento Estudiantil Chicano de Aztlán [MECHA]) espoused Marxist-like viewpoints. It should be noted, however, that subsequent scholars have struggled to reconcile Marxism's European origins with these groups' strong commitment to nationalism and indigenous cultural roots.

Marxist influence has also extended to scholarly analyses of the historical political climate for Latinos in the United States. The Marxist framework has provided a lens for analyzing the economic and political relationships between the United States and various Latin American and Caribbean countries. These critical examinations have explored the results of various direct and indirect U.S. military interventions in Latin America, including the 1848 Treaty of Guadalupe Hidalgo and the 1898 annexation of Puerto Rico. In addition, Marxism has provided a format for scholarly discussions about the social, political, and economic conditions facing Latinos in the United States. These discussions have focused primarily on critiques of U.S. economic policies, foreign and domestic, that are perceived to create unfavorable conditions for Latinos *en locale* and abroad (one topic, for example, is the North American Free Trade Agreement, or NAFTA).

More conservative Latino political groups have been critical of Marxist philosophy contending that it undermines the values of democracy and capitalism. Groups such as the early 1970s Nixon administration's Cabinet Committee on Opportunities for Spanish Speaking People and the more recent Republican National Hispanic Assembly have lobbied for more conservative economic policies, which contrast starkly with Marxist ideology.

RELATED ARTICLES

Politics, Latino.

FURTHER READING

Darder, Antonia, and Rodolfo D. Torres. *The Latino Studies Reader: Culture, Economy, and Society.* Malden, Mass., and Oxford, England: Blackwell, 1998.

Deutschmann, David, ed. *Che Guevara Reader.* 2d expanded ed. Melbourne, N.Y.: Ocean Press, 2003.

Mindiola, Tatcho. "Marxism and the Chicano Movement: Preliminary Remarks." In *Perspectivas en chicano studies* "Perspectives in Chicano Studies." Ed. by R. F. Macías. Los Angeles, Calif.: Aztlán Pubns./NACCS (Natl. Assn. for Chicana and Chicano Studies), 1977.

Torres, Carlos A. *Democracy, Education, and Multiculturalism: Dilemmas of Citizenship in a Global World.* New York: Rowman & Littlefield, 1998.

Tucker, Robert C., ed. *The Marx-Engels Reader.* 2d ed. New York: Norton, 1978.

JEFFREY M. R. DUNCAN-ANDRADE

MAS CANOSA, JORGE

Born: September 21, 1939; Santiago de Cuba
Died: November 23, 1997; Miami, Florida

Jorge Mas Canosa came to the United States as a penniless immigrant in 1960 and became a multimillionaire, arguably the most influential Cuban American in the United States. Although he fled the Cuban revolution in 1960, he was determined to overthrow Fidel Castro. He joined other anti-Communist exiles in Miami and participated in the disastrous Bay of Pigs invasion.

Turning from politics to business after settling in Miami, Mas Canosa did odd jobs to earn a living and feed his family, working as a milkman and a stevedore. In 1971 he borrowed $50,000 to start a telecommunications company and turned it into the center of his family business empire. His rags-to-riches business success story embodied the values and work ethic generally associated with the Cuban exile community. As chairman of the board of Mas Tec, he was one of the few Latinos in the United States to chair the board of a public company.

But Mas Canosa is best known for his tireless and uncompromising campaign to topple Castro's revolutionary government. He founded the Cuban American National Foundation (CANF) in 1981 to promote a democratic transition in his homeland. As the chair of CANF until his death in 1997, Mas Canosa used his considerable charisma and passion to develop the most powerful Cuban American lobby in the United States. His first great success came during the administration of President Ronald Reagan, when the United States began broadcasting Radio Marti with Mas Canosa serving as the chairman of the President's Advisory Board for Cuba Broadcasting. In 1990 Mas Canosa persuaded President George H. W. Bush to launch TV Marti, even though the Cuban government jammed all broadcasts. Mas Canosa scored his greatest political successes when Congress passed the Cuban Democracy Act of 1992 and the Cuban Liberty and Democratic Solidarity Act of 1996 (Helms-Burton), both designed to tighten the economic embargo on Cuba. The Helms-Burton law contained a controversial provision that allowed Cuban Americans to sue foreign companies in U.S. courts for properties lost in Cuba. Despite international protests, President Clinton signed the bill into law, a reflection of the power of the Cuban American lobby headed by Mas Canosa.

A fiery and passionate orator, Mas Canosa tolerated little dissent, displaying an authoritarian flair in his political behavior that critics compared to Castro's. The determined Cuban American maintained a firm grip on the CANF, and through it he gained a virtual veto power over U.S. policy toward Cuba. Those who did not agree with him were often derided as Communist sympathizers, even if they simply pointed out that TV Marti could not be seen on the island. For better or worse, Mas Canosa represented the Cuban American exile community to presidents Ronald Reagan, George H. W. Bush, and Bill Clinton. After his death the presidency of the CANF passed to his son, Jorge Mas Santos, and the organization is still the most powerful Cuban organization in the country.

© MARTA LAVANDIER/AP/WIDE WORLD PHOTOS

Cuban American National Foundation chairman Jorge Mas Canosa, speaking to the media in Miami after meeting with President Bill Clinton, 1996.

RELATED ARTICLES

Cuban American National Foundation; Cuban Americans; Politics, Cuban American.

FURTHER READING

Fernández, Damián. "From Little Havana to Washington, D.C.: The Impact of Cuban-Americans on U.S. Foreign Policy." In *Ethnic Groups and U.S. Foreign Policy*. Ed. by Mohammed E. Ahrari. Westport, Conn.: Greenwood Press, 1987.

Fonzi, Gaeton. "Who Is Jorge Mas Canosa?" *Esquire Magazine*. (January 1993).

Garcia, Maria Cristina. *Havana, USA: Cuban Exiles and Cuban Americans in South Florida, 1959–1994*. Berkeley: Univ. of Calif. Press, 1997.

Newhouse, John. "A Reporter at Large: Socialism or Death." *The New Yorker* 68 (April 27, 1992): 52–83.

Smith, Wayne S. *The U.S.-Cuba Imbroglio: Anatomy of a Crisis*. Washington, D.C.: Ctr. for Intl. Policy, 1996.

PAUL DOSAL

MASSACHUSETTS

Before the arrival of the Europeans, the original inhabitants of the Massachusetts area were the Massachusetts Indians, who are believed to have been of Algonquian origin. However, the first Europeans reached the shore of this region early in the 17th century, and Massachusetts became the site of the second permanent English settlement in North America when the Pilgrims landed at Plymouth Rock in 1620. On February 6, 1788, 168 years later, following the successful completion of the American Revolution, the state of Massachusetts became one of the first American states.

During the 19th century, a small but steady stream of Cuban and Puerto Rican *tabaqueros* (tobacco laborers) made their way to Boston to find work as shop owners, factory workers, or farmworkers. Famous throughout the world for their skill in making quality cigars, Cubans and Puerto Ricans were valued for their expertise in this field.

In 1917 the Jones Act granted all Puerto Ricans American citizenship, which gave them unrestricted movement between the mainland and the island of Puerto Rico. As a result, a small stream of Puerto Ricans moved to Boston, taking up residence in the South End and Jamaica Plain. By 1920 the federal census counted 48 Puerto Ricans as residing in the city of Boston.

In 1940 the first Latino social organization—the Club Hispano-Progresivo (Hispanic-Progressive Club)—was founded for Latinos living in the Boston area. During World War II, Puerto Ricans had begun arriving in significant numbers in the New England states as farm- and orchard workers. After the war, however, the migration of Puerto Ricans to Massachusetts—officially encouraged by the United States government—accelerated significantly. A considerable number of these new residents took menial jobs in the manufacturing districts of Boston and Springfield.

By 1956 the Migration Office of the Commonwealth of Puerto Rico was opened in Boston in order to facilitate the contracting of Puerto Rican labor by farmers and factory owners in various areas of Massachusetts. Frequently the office collaborated with the Massachusetts Department of Employment Services to recruit Puerto Rican labor.

In the 1960 census, 5,217 Puerto Ricans were tallied as residents of Massachusetts, representing 0.6 percent of the total Puerto Rican population in the United States. Later in that decade, in 1968, Alex Rodriguez became the first Puerto Rican in the Boston area to run for state representative in Boston's South End. However, his bid for state office was defeated even though he had received the endorsement of the Citizens for Participation in Political Action (CPPAX).

During the late 1960s and early 1970s, the Latino community of Boston became more active in the city's social and political direction. Residing primarily in the South End, Roxbury, and Dorchester, Puerto Ricans and other Hispanics organized several organizations to deal with the issues that most strongly affected the Puerto Rican community in the Boston area.

In 1969 Puerto Rican Entering and Settling Services was set up to welcome Puerto Ricans and other Latin Americans as they arrived at Logan Airport from abroad. This organization helped Latino families get established with a place to stay and gainful employment. A year later, in the 1970 census, a total of 23,332 Puerto Ricans were tallied as residents of Massachusetts, representing a significant increase from the 1960 census.

In 1967 the first Festival Puertorriqueño de Massachusetts (Puerto Rican Festival of Massachusetts) was organized in Blackstone Park in the South End of Boston. This celebration of Puerto Rican culture and history has become a yearly event that draws thousands of visitors each July. In recent years, the festival has been moved to Franklin Park. The 34th Annual Puerto Rican Festival, held in July 2001, attracted 200,000 celebrants. This and other celebrations of the Puerto Rican community are frequently timed to coincide with Constitution Day, July 25, the date on which, in 1952, Puerto Rico's constitution became effective.

At the start of the new decade, advocates for the Puerto Rican community were expressing concerns about the education of Puerto Rican children in the Boston area. A task force report in 1970 had revealed that a large number of Puerto Rican high school students—frustrated by language barriers—were dropping out of school at an alarming rate. Later in the year community leaders were able to secure the approval of the Transitional Bilingual Education Law, making Massachusetts one of the first states to require bilingual education for its Latino students.

In the same year, La Alianza Hispana (The Hispanic Alliance) was founded in the Roxbury–North Dorchester area as a multiservice, community-based, nonprofit organization dedicated to promoting Latino self-determination and advocating equal access for Puerto Ricans to basic services in the greater Boston area. By providing linguistically and culturally appropriate services to Latinos, the alliance accomplished a great deal in combating the effects of poverty and discrimination.

The alliance has been instrumental in training Latino leaders in the Boston area, including Nelson Merced, who became the first Latino to serve as a Massachusetts state representative (from the 5th Suffolk District) from 1988 to 1992. Even in the 21st century, La Alianza has continued to provide mentoring services, ESL (English as a second language) classes, and educational counseling to help Spanish-speaking students make their way through Massachusetts's educational system.

The West Broadway development in South Boston became embroiled in racial conflict during the 1973–1974 crisis over forced busing. In March 1973, two Puerto Rican residents in the neighborhood killed a white youth. This event sparked a four-day rampage by white friends of the victim in July 1973. The Blackstone Park riots led to the firebombing and stoning of Puerto Rican stores and apartments and caused many Puerto Rican families to flee the projects, undoing a decade of integration efforts.

However, it was also during 1973 that the Betances Festival was first organized at Villa Victoria to help Puerto Ricans in the South End celebrate their culture and heritage. The festival commemorates the life and achievements of Ramón Emeterio Betances (1827–1898), a Puerto Rican patriot, poet, medical doctor, and abolitionist. This event has become a tradition among Latinos in New England and has evolved into an annual summer festival, sponsored by Inquilinos Boricuas en Acción (IBA; Puerto Rican Tenants in Action). IBA is a community development corporation that was originally established in 1976 to serve the Villa Victoria community. Its cultural component, Arte y Cultura (Art and Culture), has organized various cultural awareness programs and workshops in an effort to help Latino youth appreciate their cultural roots.

The 1980 U.S. Census tallied 76,450 Puerto Ricans living in Massachusetts, with 18,899 of this group residing in the city of Boston. With the increasing leverage provided by their growing numbers, Puerto Ricans were fast becoming a respected cultural group within Boston's diverse ethnic mix.

In 1990 the federal census tallied 287,549 Hispanics living in Massachusetts, representing 4.8 percent of Massachusetts's total population of 6,016,425. Puerto Ricans were the largest Latino group, accounting for 53 percent of the Hispanic population of the state, followed by Dominicans, who were estimated to make up 11 percent. Mexican Americans made up only 4 percent of the Latino population in that year. In 1990, 25,767 Puerto Ricans were living within the city limits of Boston, where they made up 42 percent of all Latinos living in the city.

In 1989 the Mauricio Gastón Institute for Latino Community Development and Public Policy was established at the University of Massachusetts in Boston, in large part through the efforts of Puerto Rican academics and community activists. Gastón, a native of Cuba in whose memory the institute is named, was a Latino community activist and urban planner who served on the faculty of the University of Massachusetts–Boston's College of Public and Community Service until his death in 1986. The institution's primary purpose was to provide an improved understanding of the Latino experience in Massachusetts. It has become the most important Latino research center in New England.

From 1990 to 1995, estimates suggested that the Latino population of Massachusetts grew by almost 20 percent, from 287,549 to 344,068, increasing their percentage to 5.6 percent of the state population. But the growth of the Latino community in Massachusetts from 1990 to 2000 was even more impressive. With an increase of 141,180 people (49.1 percent), the Hispanic population of Massachusetts reached 428,729 persons, representing 6.8 percent of the entire state population. In the 2000 census, Puerto Rican residents of Massachusetts numbered 199,207, or 46.5 percent of the Latino population, giving that state the fifth largest population of Puerto Ricans (after New York, Florida, New Jersey, and Pennsylvania).

In 2000, 49,913 Dominicans were tallied in the 2000 census, accounting for 11.6 percent of the total Latino population of Massachusetts and giving Massachusetts the fourth largest population of Dominicans (after New York, New Jersey, and Florida). Migrants from Miraflores and other towns in the Dominican Republic first started arriving in Boston in the late 1960s.

A 20-block section of Jamaica Plain—once part of an Irish American neighborhood—became the main destination of Dominican migrants. By the beginning of the 21st century, Dominicans had also established a strong presence in Lawrence and Lynn,

the old shoe-manufacturing town. The Dominican influence in the Jamaican Plain area has inspired the frequent Caribbean music and dance festivals in neighboring Franklin Park.

The 2000 U.S. Census reported that 49,101 residents of Massachusetts had immigrated from El Salvador, Colombia, Guatemala, and Honduras. Of these four groups, however, the Salvadorians experienced a 137 percent increase between 1990 and 2000. By the end of the 1990s, several thousand Salvadorians had made their homes in Chelsea, Cambridge, and Somerville.

Until the 1990s, Mexican immigrants traditionally headed for Texas, California, or midwestern states to seek employment. In the 1990s, however, larger numbers of Mexicans made their way to East Boston where they found employment and low-rent apartments. In the 2000 census the Mexican American population made up 5.2 percent of the Latino population of the state. There appears to be a greater

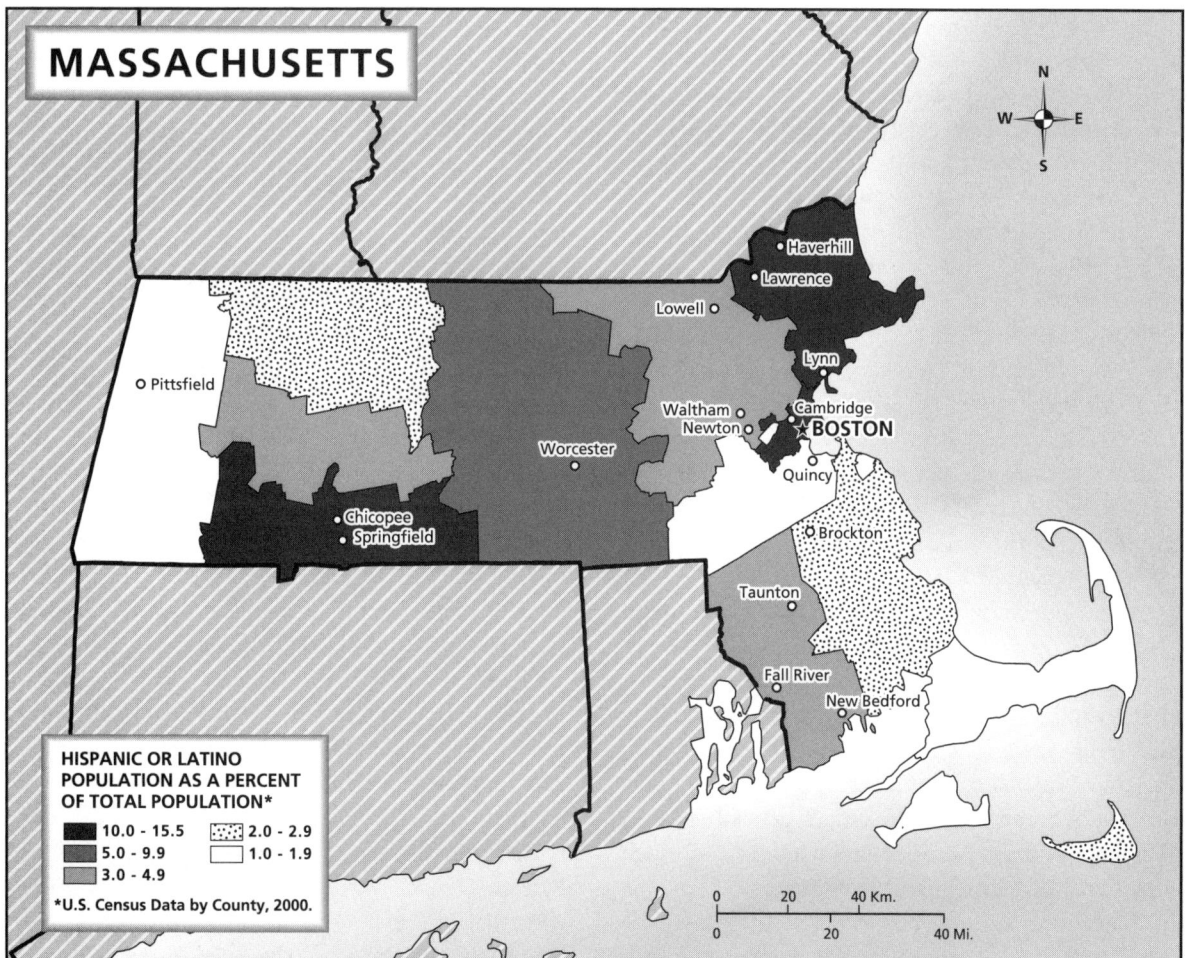

MASSACHUSETTS

HISPANIC OR LATINO
POPULATION AS A PERCENT
OF TOTAL POPULATION*

- 10.0 - 15.5
- 5.0 - 9.9
- 3.0 - 4.9
- 2.0 - 2.9
- 1.0 - 1.9

*U.S. Census Data by County, 2000.

dispersal of Mexican Americans to a wide range of Massachusetts communities, possibly explained by their higher average educational attainment and income than Dominicans and Puerto Ricans. Other Latino groups represented in Massachusetts's diverse Hispanic population in 2000 included Guatemalans (11,437) and Cuban Americans (8,867).

Suffolk County, with a population of 107,031 Latinos in the 2000 census, had the largest percentage of Latinos: 15.5 percent. Hampden County, with a population of 69,197 Latinos, had the second largest percentage of Latinos with 15.2 percent, followed by Essex County, with 79,871 Latino residents representing 11.0 percent of the county population.

The November 1998 elections marked a turning point in the political representation of Latinos in Massachusetts. These elections brought three Latinos to the state legislature simultaneously. Cheryl A. Rivera, a lawyer of Puerto Rican heritage, was elected to represent the 10th Hampden District, including the city of Springfield where Latinos represented about 20 percent of the population. Representative Rivera was instrumental as one of the founders of the first Latino-American Caucus for the Massachusetts Legislature and was named 1999 Woman of the Year by the Massachusetts Association of Hispanic Attorneys and the City of Springfield's Woman's Commission.

The second Latino to be elected to state office in the 1998 election was Jarret T. Barrios, the grandson of Cuban immigrants. Born in Florida, the son of a carpenter and social worker, Mr. Barrios graduated from Harvard University with honors and went to work on the Boston City Council. After receiving his law degree from Georgetown Law School, Barrios was elected state representative for the 28th Middlesex District, which had a 5 percent Latino population at the time.

Representative Barrios is well respected by his peers for his commitment to the issues of housing, child care, education, and access to quality healthcare. In 2002, after serving two terms as state representative, Barrios claimed the seat previously held by Senate president Thomas Birmingham, after defeating four primary opponents in September and running unopposed in the November general election. Senator Barrios's constituency includes Cambridge, Chelsea, Charlestown, and Everett.

The third Latino to be elected to the Massachusetts House of Representatives in 1998 was José L.

Santiago, a native of Yabucoa, Puerto Rico. Mr. Santiago was elected as representative of the 16th Essex District, which includes Lawrence, a city with a significant Latino population. Lawrence is located 25 miles (40 km) north of Boston and, as an important industrial town along the Merrimack River, drew large numbers of Latino migrants in the second half of the 20th century.

A resident of Lawrence from the age of eight, José Santiago had served as the city's first Latino councilor in 1993. Already by 1990, Latinos had represented 42 percent of the city's total population, and it was this community that provided the bulk of his support. In the 2000 census, the Latino population reached the status of a full majority group, boasting a population of 43,019, making up 59.7 percent of the city's total population of 72,043. With a voting age population of 54.1 percent in 2000, Latinos made up 40 percent of the city's registered voters, a formidable force.

However, in the 2002 general elections Representative Santiago was opposed by William Lantigua, a native of the Dominican Republic and a seasoned political activist. Although the two men had been political allies for a time, they had a falling out and Lantigua decided to challenge Santiago for representation of the 16th District. In order to run against Santiago, Lantigua left the Democratic Party. When the final tally was counted, Lantigua had won the election by only 183 votes, becoming the first Dominican American representative to run for statewide office in Massachusetts.

In 2001 Lantigua had spearheaded Isabel Meléndez's campaign for the mayor of Lawrence. A well-known community activist, Meléndez had become the first Latina to run for that office. However, she lost the election to Michael J. Sullivan by a mere 957 votes. In the first years of the new century, many Latinos have made their appearance on the political scene. A native of the Dominican Republic, Marcos Devers was elected as an at-large city councilor in 1998. Then, in 2001, Councilman Devers was elected interim mayor of Lawrence for five weeks by a vote of five to four. Soon after, Mayor Devers was elected council president of Lawrence.

In the November 2003 City Council elections, four Hispanics councilors—Carlos Matos, Israel Reyes, Marcos Devers, and Nilka I. Alvarez-Rodriguez—were elected, giving the Latinos four of the seats on the nine-member board. This event earned Lawrence the title of "New England's most Hispanic city." With increasing political representation in Massachusetts becoming a reality, young Latino activists are coming of age in Boston and Lawrence, poised to make critical decisions in an electoral process that formerly excluded them.

Organizations that advocate for Latino youth and students have been established in almost every corner of Massachusetts, in an attempt to offset the negative effects of poverty, language barriers, and low educational attainment. The Puerto Rican Cultural Center of Springfield, established in 1976, sponsors GED (General Educational Development) and ESL classes in both English and Spanish to help young Latinos in their educational pursuits. La Familia Hispana, Inc., is a nonprofit organization that has fostered an appreciation of Hispanic culture, music, and literature in the Pioneer Valley for almost two decades.

The Latino Parents Association (LPA) of Jamaica Plain was organized in 1988 to help involve Latino parents in their children's education. Concerned about the high dropout rates among Latino students in the Boston Public School System, the LPA gave Hispanic parents an opportunity to work collectively to obtain equal educational opportunities and the highest quality instruction for their children.

Latinos in Massachusetts have also made great strides in acquiring media outlets to educate and inform the community. For two decades, LA PLAZA, a weekly television program on Boston's WGBH station, has presented the culture and concerns of Boston's Latino community to its audience. In Worcester, New England's second largest city, two noncommercial radio stations have provided programming on subject matter relating to Puerto Ricans, Colombians, and Central Americans.

Spanish and bilingual newspapers have been well established in Massachusetts for three decades. Boston's principal Spanish-language newspaper, *El Mundo,* first started operating in 1974. The weekly newspaper has become the primary source of news for Latino residents of Boston, Lowell, Jamaica Plain, Dorchester, Cambridge, and Chelsea. *La Semana* has also served the Spanish-speaking community of Boston since 1978.

In other parts of Massachusetts, many Spanish-language newspapers have started to provide news for their communities. Since 1996 *Rumbo* has been the primary bilingual newspaper published in Lawrence. Published by the husband and wife team of Alberto M. Suris and Dalia Díaz, *Rumbo* has offered a wide range of newspaper services for both Lawrence and an extended area of the Merrimack Valley.

Candela Boston, a popular online magazine, provides information about "la Vida Latina" in the greater Boston area. The Web site won the Internet Tips Excellent Site Award. The Massachusetts House of Representatives even presented a citation for Candela's outstanding contribution to the Boston Hispanic community.

The Latino Resources Network (LRN) was originally organized in 1998 as a support group for Latino professionals in the human services fields. However, the LRN has grown to include Latinos from a wide range of fields and businesses in an effort to promote Latino culture while developing leadership potential for Latinos in the Merrimack Valley. In 2003–2004, the LRN and the Department of Training and Development of Lawrence created the New Paths Program to recruit out-of-school youth seeking educational services.

Baseball is the most popular sport in Puerto Rico. In moving from Puerto Rico to Massachusetts, most Puerto Ricans bring their passion for baseball with them. During the 1990s, several talented Latino ballplayers on the Boston Red Sox attracted the attention of both the Latino community and the nation. Young shortstop Nomar Garciaparra and pitcher Pedro Martínez became star players on the Red Sox. A native of the Dominican Republic, Martínez was the best pitcher in baseball from 1998 to 2000, until shoulder injuries took their toll on his performance in 2001. When Manny Ramírez signed on to his second season with the Red Sox, he received an eight-year, $160 million contract in December 2000 and became the first player of color to sign a free-agent contract with the Red Sox while in the prime of his career.

Hispanic Magazine publishes a yearly list of "superior centers of higher learning where Hispanic students are thriving." The March 2004 edition of the magazine published "The Top 25 Colleges for Latinos," which included three Massachusetts institutions of higher learning in the top ten colleges. Listed in second place was Massachusetts Institute of Technology in Cambridge, where the Latino student population stands at 12 percent. Another Cambridge institution, Harvard University, made third place. At Harvard, the Hispanic population stands at 8 percent. Tufts University in Medford was listed as the tenth best college for Hispanics.

Although their population at Harvard has remained relatively small, Latino students there have made great efforts to preserve their culture and pride on campus. Concilio Latino was founded to serve as an umbrella organization for all the Latin American organizations on the Harvard campus. Founded in the early 1990s, Concilio has encouraged Latino students from diverse backgrounds to take part in and endorse their cultures. La Organización de Puertorriqueños was organized at Harvard by Puerto Rican students who portray positive images of Puerto Rican culture on campus.

Founded in 1971, the Harvard Ballet Folklórico de Aztlán (BFA) is the oldest Latino cultural organization at Harvard. As a student-run organization, BFA has been committed to the celebration of Mexican folk culture through the traditional dances of many regions of Mexico. The BFA actively participates in campus and community celebrations of the important Mexican festivals on Día de los Muertos (Day of the Dead) and Cinco de Mayo.

The Latinos who came to Massachusetts in the 1940s and 1950s came from very humble origins. They came to labor in orchards and factories and to put food on their families' tables. Their assimilation into the mainstream Anglo society was a slow and sometimes painful process, in which community activists advocated for their fair treatment.

Since the 1990s, however, Dominicans, Puerto Ricans, Salvadorans, and Mexican Americans have established themselves in many communities across the state. With this increased presence, Latinos have earned a position of both respect and power. Politicians, advertising agencies, baseball franchises, and corporations have all begun to recognize and seek the attention of the Latino community in Massachusetts.

RELATED ARTICLES

Education, Higher; Immigration, Latino; Politics, Latino.

FURTHER READING

Donata, Alison. "The Hispanic Population of Massachusetts." *Massachusetts State Data Center Newsletter* 3, Issue 1 (2002).
Garcia, Kimberly. "The Top 25 Colleges for Latinos." *Hispanic Magazine* (March 2004).
Hardy-Fanta, Carol. *Latina Politics, Latino Politics: Gender, Culture, and Political Participation in Boston.* Philadelphia: Temple Univ. Press, 1993.
Hardy-Fanta, Carol, and Jeffrey N. Gerson, eds. *Latino Politics in Massachusetts: Struggles, Strategies and Prospects (Race and Politics).* New York: Garland, 2001.
Torres, Andrés, and Lisa Chaves. *Latinos in Massachusetts: An Update.* Boston: Mauricio Gastón Inst., Univ. of Mass. Press, 1998.
U.S. Commission on Civil Rights. *Issues of Concern to Puerto Ricans in Boston and Springfield.* Boston: Mass. Advisory Committee, 1972.

SELECTED WEB SITES

Boston Family History: Puerto Rican. http://www.bostonfamilyhistory.net/ancestors/ puertorican/pr_1950.html
Candela Boston. http://www.candelaboston.com/form.htm

JOHN P. SCHMAL

MASS STERILIZATION CAMPAIGN

Mass sterilization programs (sterilization is the irreversible method of surgical birth control, for either males or females) directed at various groups of people have been undertaken a number of times in the United States. These programs have been both formal and informal, voluntary and involuntary. Mass sterilization of Latinos and Latinas has been advocated and practiced even though it violates many laws and this group's constitutional rights. Francis Galton first proposed in 1883 that the biologically "fit" should reproduce, while the "unfit" should not, and since that time sterilization has been applied to those who are deemed socially, physically, or economically unfit.

The use of sterilization as birth control is best seen in the case of Puerto Ricans both on the island and on the mainland. In the 1930s, through the Puerto Rican Emergency Relief Fund, the U.S. government opened birth control clinics, later to be joined by private family-planning organizations and municipal public programs, to address Puerto Rico's high birthrate. Theories about the links between economic hardship in developing regions and population growth suggested to the U.S. government and private associations that sterilization was the best solution to the island's economic deprivation. By 1940, 7 percent of the island's women had been sterilized; by 1954, 16 percent; and by 1965, 34 percent of all married women ages 20 to 49 had been sterilized. Studies conducted in the 1950s indicated that sterilization was the best-known and most popular method of birth control, indicating the emphasis placed on the surgical option. In popular discourse the procedure is simply referred to as *la operación* (the operation).

Women of Mexican ancestry in the United States faced a similar situation throughout the 20th century. Ideologies of cultural difference, inferiority, and the notion that Mexicans with large families were an economic burden on the government and society as a whole were used to justify mass-sterilization programs directed at Mexican and Mexican American women. One of the best documented examples of a mass sterilization program in the Mexican community was that of the University of Southern California—Los Angeles Medical Center in the 1970s. A class-action lawsuit filed in 1975 on behalf of 11 Spanish-speaking women, *Madrigal* v. *Quilligan,* detailed that what was characterized as "voluntary sterilization" was anything but this. Evidence in the suit demonstrated that women had been pressured into agreeing to sterilization during labor and had been sterilized without informed consent—often after the use of substantial pain medication; anti-Mexican and antiworking-class sentiments were commonly cited as justification for these practices. The plaintiffs in *Madrigal* claimed damages and sought an end to coercive sterilization. The Comisión Feminíl Mexicana Nacional (Mexican National Women's Commission) joined the suit, and although judgment was found for the defendants, the suit helped achieve the use of bilingual consent forms, increased enforcement of a 72-hour waiting period prior to the operation, and a moratorium on coercion in sterilization.

Mass sterilization programs remain controversial, owing to their targeting the poor and communities of color. Sterilization as part of judicial sentencing for drug offenses or nonpayment of spousal support, as well as voluntary programs run by private foundations that offer cash incentives for sterilization of men and women with several children, continue to the present.

RELATED ARTICLES

Birth Control; Health; Politics, Puerto Rican.

FURTHER READING

Dietz, James L. *Economic History of Puerto Rico: Institutional Change and Capitalist Development.* Princeton, N.J.: Princeton Univ. Press, 1986.

Mora, Magdalena, and Adelaida Del Castillo, eds. *Mexican Women in the United States: Struggles Past and Present.* Los Angeles: Univ. of Calif. Chicano Studies Res. Ctr., 1980.

SUSAN GREEN

MAYAS

Various cities across the sunbelt of the United States are home to indigenous Maya immigrants from different countries, language groups, and communities. Ten thousand live in Los Angeles, the largest settlement of Maya north of the Rio Grande, and significant Maya colonies also exist in cities such as Houston; Indiantown, Florida; and Morganton, North Carolina. Guatemala is the nation of origin for the majority of these Maya, who first came to the United States in large numbers as war refugees seeking asylum from the Guatemalan internal fighting of the 1970s and 1980s, when America backed military dictatorships that implemented state violence and guerrilla witch hunts resulting in decimation of the indigenous population. Maya now come to the United States as economic refugees escaping the poverty and unemployment of their devastated home regions. Many follow the seasonal and episodic work cycles established by undocumented Mexican migrant farmworkers, while others have taken advantage of work permits granted to them when applying for asylum, procuring jobs in the visible economy in construction, landscaping, and various industrial milieus.

Modern Maya in Latin America and the United States are genetic and cultural heirs to the ancient indigenous peoples who originally inhabited southern Mesoamerica, an area that today includes southeastern Mexico, Belize, Guatemala, Honduras, and El Salvador. Pre-Columbian Maya civilization was one of the most accomplished societies in the Western Hemisphere; by as early as 900 B.C., the Maya had developed an elaborate system of religious beliefs and symbols, invented the zero and the only ancient writing system in the Americas containing phonetic symbols, and amassed an outstanding astronomical corpus, including different and precise calendars.

Like other indigenous societies, Maya civilization was dismantled after the arrival of Europeans in Latin America. Over the hundreds of years since the conquest of the Maya empire, efforts to modernize and homogenize Central America have involved consistent and aggressive attacks on indigenous Maya culture, their economic viability, and their very existence. In present-day Latin America, the majority of indigenous Maya reside in the rural countryside, working as *campesinos,* or subsistence farmers. Many vestiges of their ancestral culture still thrive, such as language,

Detail from the *Panel of the Slaves,* a bas-relief in the Palenque Maya ruins, Mexico; figure is probably a priest making an offering.

the integrity and importance of the village as a community unit, and the use of the *traje*, a traditional garb.

Maya living in the United States retain similar cultural inheritances; however, the extremely disparate natures of U.S. and Maya cultures have forced them to adapt to the demands of their new, very different settings. Facing a variety of adverse conditions and dangers north of the Rio Grande—poverty, unstable employment, homelessness, prejudice, threat of deportation, often an ability to communicate only in a Maya language, unfamiliarity with the host culture, and so on—they have transformed their own culture and sense of identity to accommodate their pressing need for solidarity. Whereas in Latin America the existence of isolated town units and regional languages and dialects presents a source of separation for indigenous Maya, in the United States these rifts partially erode and are replaced by a sense of ethnic cohesion that distinguishes them from other Latinos and emphasizes the unique racial and cultural discrimination to which they are subjected.

Many Maya settlements in the United States foster solidarity by constructing a community-based social structure that reflects the traditional social structure of Maya towns and villages in Latin America. In Florida, for example, Maya immigrants have established a foundation of cultural institutions and support networks such as stores and businesses, churches, social groups, soccer leagues, burial societies, and Maya-language radio programs. The Maya also utilize modern forms of communication and transportation to contact their hometowns and villages in Latin America. This practice has built transnational communities that allow for a constant exchange of traditional Maya culture and modern American influences, as well as providing a crucial influx of economic support to the Maya of Latin America.

At the same time that indigenous Maya live and work in the United States, the legacy of pre-Columbian Maya society exists as a source of pride for many mestizo Latinos. Countless U.S. Hispanic artists, authors, and intellectuals have mythicized the Maya as ancient cultural heroes in their works, depicting the civilization as a venerable and mystical element of Latino identity. The reverence paid to the ancient Maya, however, is frequently not outstretched to their contemporary indigenous descendants, including those within the United States. Rather, a dichotomy exists between the idealized "noble" ancient Maya and the present-day Maya immigrant, who is too often painted as ignorant, backward, and hopelessly destitute. Yet, if Maya in the United States are successful in continuing to establish communities that promote ethnic solidarity and economic stability, they may help to bridge the gap between ancient Maya legends and the modern Maya population.

RELATED ARTICLES

Guatemalan Americans; Indigenous Heritage; Mesoamerica; Mexico; Nahuas; Popol Vuh.

FURTHER READING

Adams, Richard E. W., and Murdo J. MacLeod, eds. "The Cambridge History of the Native Peoples of the Americas." In *Mesoamerica.* Vol. 2. Cambridge, Mass.: Cambridge Univ. Press, 2000.

Burns, Allan F. *Maya in Exile: Guatemalans in Florida.* Philadelphia: Temple Univ. Press, 1993.

Fink, Leon. *The Maya of Morganton: Work and Community in the Nuevo New South.* Chapel Hill: Univ. of N.C. Press, 2003.

Freidel, David, et al. *Maya Cosmos. Three Thousand Years on the Shaman's Path.* New York: William Morrow, 1993.

Loucky, James, and Marilyn M. Moors. *The Maya Diaspora: Guatemalan Roots, New American Lives.* Philadelphia: Temple Univ. Press, 2000.

Ross, John. *Rebellion from the Roots: Indian Uprising in Chiapas.* Monroe, Canada: Common Courage Press, 1995.

Popol Vuh: The Mayan Book of the Dawn of Life. Tr. by Dennis Tedlock. New York: Touchstone Bks., 1996.

SELECTED WEB SITE

Foundation for the Advancement of Mesoamerican Studies, Inc. www.famsi.org

ALEJANDRA GARCÍA QUINTANILLA
ADAM JUDE GONZALES

MECHA. *See* MOVIMIENTO ESTUDANTIL CHICANO DE AZTLAN.

MEDICINE

With the rapid growth of the Latino population in the United States, there has been a great demand for medical care in disease areas that particularly affect this group—obesity, diabetes, mental illness, asthma, tuberculosis, HIV (human immunodeficiency virus) infection, and high blood pressure. Providing adequate medical care, however, will require overcoming language, cultural, and belief barriers that the U.S. medical system may not be ready to address. There are very few incentives for non-Latino physicians to practice in indigent, physician-shortage areas, and learning Spanish or becoming familiar with the Latino culture so as to be able to provide culturally competent services is not a priority. A lack of Hispanics in the medical profession has further negatively affected the provision of services to Latino patients. Only 3.4 percent of practicing physicians and 6.4 percent of medical students enrolled in U.S. medical schools are Hispanic. As a result of these factors, Latinos are separated from any medical services by an ever-widening chasm. Even when access to medical services is available, differences in beliefs and language and the presence of condescending attitudes of medical professionals toward Hispanics may undermine the integrity of these services.

Latino attitudes toward health care in the United States today are shaped by these contemporary issues as well as many other, historical factors. It is inevitable that pre-Columbian indigenous and African roots, beliefs, and cultural practices that are part of the heritage of the diverse Latino population of the United States will influence this group's views on medical issues and will come into play in making health-care decisions. Traditional practices such as *curanderismo, sobadores, remedios caseros,* and *ofrendas* are still adhered to by many Latinos today. *Curanderismo* is a very common practice among Latinos, and it is believed to have evolved from the merging of Spanish conquistador Judeo-Christian religious beliefs and the indigenous herbal medicine already practiced in the New World. The art of *Curanderismo* entails *limpias,* a cleansing of the electromagnetic field surrounding the body, prescription of herbal drinks, prayers, tinctures, and ointments. *Sobadores* are a form of massage therapists use to heal sprains, strains, and muscle aches. *Remedios caseros,* or "home remedies," consisting of herbal drinks and ointments, are commonly used to treat aches and pains. *Ofrendas*—"offerings" to God, the Virgin Mary (as well as the Virgin of Guadalupe), or Christian saints, who may also represent deities of the African pantheon— are frequently made to request healing for a loved one or as thanksgiving for a successful recovery from illness or injury.

Many traditional Latinos regard conventional medicine as just one of several approaches to use for treatment of illness or injury, or as means of preventing illness. As Latinos are faced with choosing health care, they often opt for the choices that are not only most familiar but are also those to which they have

the best access. It is estimated that nearly 40 percent of Latinos under the age of 65 do not have health insurance. More than 29 percent of the uninsured under 18 years of age are Latino children. One-fourth of the nation's 44 million uninsured individuals are Latino. The states of California, Florida, New York, and Texas account for 73 percent of all uninsured Latinos.

U.S. Hispanics disproportionately lack health insurance for a number of reasons. Those in the workforce tend to hold jobs that do not offer benefits and that are lower paying, less stable, and more hazardous than the norm. Indigent Latinos who, but for their lack of legal residency, might otherwise be qualified for Medicaid benefits are disqualified because of their immigration status. Even some lawful permanent residents are denied access to government-funded health-care benefits. Immigrants are often hesitant to access medical services to which they are entitled, even for their U.S. citizen children, for fear of deportation. Furthermore, Latinos, especially immigrants with language barriers, find it overwhelming to navigate the insurance and health-care system in the United States to acquire the medical care they need. Lack of knowledge of their rights, as well, keeps them from acquiring the services they need. Although traditional health practices may be effective in healing and be efficient in disease prevention, access to modern science is needed so that Latinos, like other members of society, can make the wise and prompt choices that can be crucial in the diagnosis and treatment of disease.

Access to health care through health insurance, although vitally important, does not, in and of itself, guarantee quality care. In 1979 the United States Department of Health and Human Services (DHHS) embarked on a national planning process to establish national health objectives for all Americans. The process resulted in a report and action plan entitled "Healthy People: The Surgeon General's Report on Health Promotion and Disease Prevention." This initiative was renewed and continued in 1990 as Healthy People 2000, a program identifying the nation's health-care needs and incorporating strategies to meet them. In 2000, Healthy People 2010 was launched with specific plans of action to end disparities in health care, to provide health insurance coverage to all Americans, and to increase access to health-care providers through satisfactory communication skills, including the ability to communicate in a culturally and linguistically appropriate manner.

To render guidance and facilitate provision of culturally and linguistically competent care, the Office of the Secretary of the DHHS's Office of Minority Health launched an initiative to develop federally recognized standards for the provision of these services. This initiative gave rise to the Culturally and Linguistically Appropriate Services (CLAS) standards, published in the Federal Register on December 22, 2000. The 14 standards are organized into three themes: "Culturally Competent Care," "Language Access Services," and "Organizational Supports for Cultural Competence." The standards serve as guiding principles in supplying culturally competent health care to diverse populations, and while the standards are directed primarily toward health-care organizations, at the same time individual providers, policymakers, and accreditation and credentialing agencies also are encouraged to use them. It is important that all health providers are familiar with the standards and implement them at all levels of health services, since the ultimate aim of the standards is to contribute to the elimination of racial and ethnic health disparities and to improve the health of all Americans.

Culturally and linguistically appropriate care in a physician's office is crucial for Latino patients, whereas culture competence in the medical profession requires more. Conducting Latino-focused research is key in determining the health needs of the U.S. Hispanic community and serving them in a more culturally competent way. The limited availability of Latino health data has hindered the development of Latino-customized public health policies, in turn, taking a toll on the kind of treatment given to the Latino community and the effectiveness of that treatment. Data that *are* available are aggregated into national data sets that hide the particular needs of the different Latino subgroups. A good example of the misleading nature of aggregate data is evident in the area of infant mortality. The aggregate data for Latinos in the United States show a decline in infant mortality and in low birth weight. However, the data for mainland Puerto Ricans show an increased risk in both of these indicators. The Latino population of the United States is composed of many distinct sub-

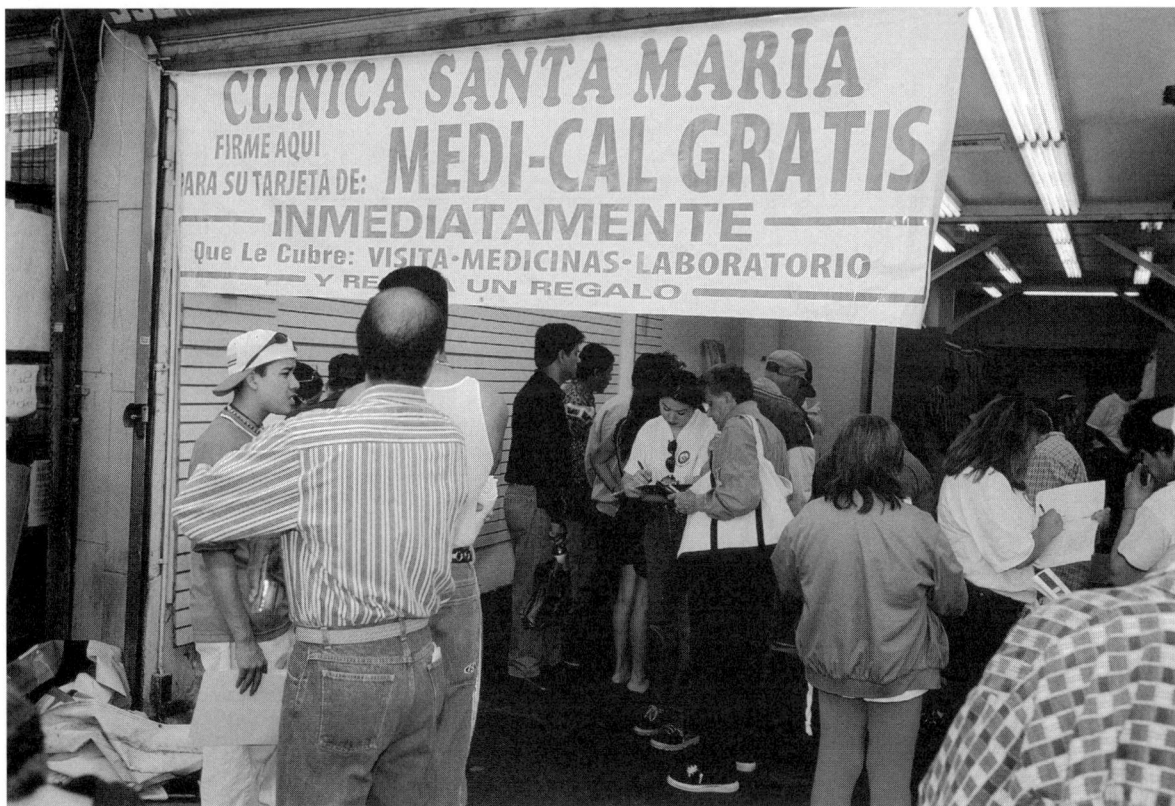

Waiting in a hallway at a clinic in Santa Maria, California.

groups that should be taken into consideration when conducting research. Approximately 65 percent of Latinos are Mexican American, 14 percent Central or South American, 11 percent Puerto Rican, 8 percent other Latino, and 5 percent Cuban.

Latino research can benefit much more than just the Latino population. There is an existing strong link between culture and health. Research leading to an understanding of this relationship, and its application across cultures, benefits all Americans. Cultural factors conducive to positive health outcomes in the Latino community could have a positive effect among other groups when implemented. An example of a cross-cultural benefit of Latino-specific research can be seen in the concept recognized by researchers as the "epidemiological paradox." Despite negative economic and other factors that would be expected to negatively effect Latinos' health, the health profile of the group appears to be unaffected in some areas; some research findings, for instance, show that Latinos have reduced risk, as compared with non-Hispanic whites, for the top three causes of death in the United States—heart disease, cancers, and stroke. Reasons for these findings need to be investigated, and further findings and conclusive evidence could lead to development of treatment and prevention strategies beneficial to other cultural groups.

Before cultural competence in any form is achieved, either through provision of linguistically and culturally competent care or through research, adequate Latino representation in the health fields must be achieved. The Hispanic population of the United States continues to grow steadily, as a result of immigration and a high birthrate. Unfortunately, the percentage of Latinos in the health-care professions and in the educational "pipeline"—that is, medical and health professions schools—are not increasing. Additionally, Latino students are not attending and graduating from colleges and universities in numbers proportionate to their percentage of the population. This situation is further exacerbated by the battle over "affirmative action," which is causing a drop-off in Latinos' applications to state colleges, universities, and graduate schools.

However, even in the face of a severe shortage of Latino physicians, certain measures could alleviate the situation. The lack of Hispanic physicians could be somewhat compensated for by giving training to non-Latino physicians to assist them in providing culturally and linguistically competent services. According to David Hayes Bautista, the issue is not about the need for Latino medical practitioners, but about the need for practitioners willing to make an effort to speak Spanish and to serve in physician shortage areas. This solution, however, presupposes the interest of non-Latino physicians in making these efforts. Bautista notes that 51 percent of Latino physicians have indicated they would be willing to do so, as compared with 0.5 percent of non-Latinos. A statewide survey of all physicians in Colorado showed that Latino physicians spent more hours per week in direct patient care, were more likely to have a primary care specialty, and were less often specialty board certified than were white, non-Hispanic doctors. The survey also indicated that Latino physicians tended to be more involved with the needs of Medicaid patients and to practice in either poor or Hispanic neighborhoods. These findings confirm the need for providing educational opportunities and support for Latino students in the health sciences. They also highlight the need to identify ways to make non-Latino physicians more open to take the training and to develop other steps necessary to effect culturally competent care for Latino patients.

Just as patient services are negatively impacted by the shortage of Latino practitioners, Hispanic-oriented research is hampered by the severe shortage of Latino health researchers. Exceedingly limited effort has been made by government, academic institutions, and the private sector to provide health data on U.S. Hispanics. Very small numbers of studies have been conducted among the Latino population as a whole, but they have been excluded from surveys conducted for research. Exciting research on Latino subjects and issues has by and large been conducted by non-Latinos without the meaningful participation of representatives from the Latino community. Just as in the documented case in the area of patient care, it is more likely that Latino researchers would take more interest in conducting research that would benefit the Latino community than do their non-Latino counterparts.

In addition to language barriers, lack of access to culturally competent care, and a marked dearth of Latino health professionals, there is yet an even greater barrier to the health-care system for Latinos: the issue of trust. The Hispanic population often seeks alternative help or no help at all because of a lack of trust in the medical system, owing to various factors. A physician may spend as little as five minutes with a patient. During this time the doctor is frequently unwilling or unable to demonstrate an effort to communicate important health issues in a way the patient can understand, or to provide a comfortable atmosphere for the patient. The initial encounter between a patient and physician is crucial for establishing a positive relationship between the two parties. A relationship of trust is based on time spent between two people, and that relationship is often vital for the patient's disclosure of symptoms that may not be detected by any other means. If a doctor does not make an effort to honor a patient as a person of a different culture and attempt to speak his or her language in order to reach this trusting relationship, it can a make a person very reluctant to come back for another visit and share anything at all. Physicians need to be prepared to recognize that the Latino culture operates differently and be open to flexible ways of practicing—for example, welcoming family members in a clinical encounter and soliciting their opinions in a health decision. Traditional healers (mentioned earlier) recognize these factors, which explains Latinos' greater inclination to consult these individuals.

Ending the disparity in access to health-care services for members of the U.S. Hispanic community is highly dependent on cultural competence in the medical profession. While the more substantial presence of Latinos in health professions is believed to be the best solution to achieve this result, other elements of medicine are important, as well. There should be a more timely intervention in the provision of treatment for diseases affecting the Latino community today, in addition to preventive health care and other public health services. More Hispanics in health professions, in and of itself, is not a panacea for the elimination of health disparities between Hispanic and non-Hispanic white Americans. Latinos must have economic access to health care through insurance. Culturally competent services in our medical practices today must be available through Latino and other health-care professionals practicing in their communities. Research is needed in the areas of specific Latino health issues, and data must be made available to the various Latino subgroups. The development of all of these factors will create a strong foundation for the improvement of the Latino health status.

RELATED ARTICLES

Health; HIV/AIDS; Infectious Diseases; Mental Health.

FURTHER READING

Aguirre-Molina, Marylin, et al. *Health Issues in the Latino Community.* San Francisco: Jossey-Bass, 2001.

Chong, Nilda. *The Latino Patient.* Yarmouth, Mass.: Intercultural Press, 2002.

Fryer, George E., Jr., et al. "Hispanic vs. White Non-Hispanic Physician Medical Practices in Colorado." *Journal of Health Care for the Poor and Underserved* 12, no. 3 (2001).

Garza, Mary Jane. "Healing Spirits." *Hispanic* (June 1998): 30–38.

Giachello, Aida L. "Challenges and Opportunities in Establishing a Latino Health Research Center in a Majority Academic Institution." *Journal of Medical Systems* 20, no. 5 (1996).

Hayes-Bautista, David. "Research on Culturally Competent Healthcare Systems: Less Sensitivity, More Statistics." *American Journal of Preventive Medicine* (April 2003).

Hayes-Bautista, David, et al. "Health and Medicine in the Southwest: A Window to Medicine in the US in 2050." *Med Am* 1 (2000): 4–12.

Markides, Kyriakos S., and Jeanniene Coreil. "The Health of Hispanics in the Southwestern United States: An Epidemiological Paradox." *Public Health Reports* 101, no. 3 (1986): 253–262.

U.S. Department of Health and Human Services. *Healthy People 2010.* Washington, D.C.: USGPO, 1997.

U.S. Department of Health and Human Services. *National Standards for Culturally and Linguistically Appropriate Services in Health Care.* USGPO, 2001 [prepared by IQ Solutions for Office of Minority Health].

Zambrana, Ruth E., "Health Data Issues for Hispanics: Implications for Public Health Research." *Journal of Health Care for the Poor and Underserved.* Forthcoming.

GUADALUPE PACHECO

MELA. *See* MOTHERS OF EAST LOS ANGELES.

MENCHÚ, RIGOBERTA

Born: January 9, 1959; Chimel, Guatemala

Rigoberta Menchú is a famous if also controversial Maya Indian from the highlands of Guatemala who became an advocate for aboriginal and women's rights in her native country and all over the Hispanic world. She was born and raised in a poor Quiché peasant family of coffee pickers. (The Quichés are part of the Maya culture.) At an early age she became involved, through the Catholic Church, in activism. She taught herself Spanish and other Maya languages. Menchú's family apparently took part in guerrilla activities, which led to her father being imprisoned and tortured. He joined the Committee of the Peasant Union (CUC) and in 1979–the same year Rigoberta's brother was arrested, tortured, and killed by the Guatemalan Army—she also joined the CUC. Her father was killed a year later by security forces in the nation's capital. Then her mother was arrested, raped, and killed.

Soon Menchú was involved in strikes to improve labor conditions and she became part of the 31st of January Front, in charge of educating the aboriginal population and resisting the military. In 1981 she went into hiding and eventually left for Mexico, where she began to organize an international opposition to the abuse of Indians in Guatemala. While in Paris in 1983, she was interviewed for hours by Elisabeth Burgos-Debray, a Venezuelan anthropologist and then-wife of French intellectual Regis Debray. Burgos-Debray transcribed and edited the interviews, turning them into a book, *Yo soy Rigoberta Menchú y así me nació la conciencia,* which appeared in Spanish in 1984 (Eng. tr., 1984; *I Rigoberta Menchú, an Indian Woman in Guatemala*). Around that time she also was part of an important documentary film, *When the Mountains Tremble* (1983), directed by Pamela Yates and Thomas Sigel. It describes the struggle of the Indian peasantry in Guatemala against state and foreign oppression.

Menchú was awarded the Nobel Peace Prize in 1992, the year of the quincentennial celebration of Christopher Columbus's first trip and landing in the Bahamas. In 1997 she published her second book, *Crossing Borders: An Autobiography,* which was released in Spanish and English the following year.

In 1999 Menchú became the center of a polemical debate of global proportions when the Stanford-trained anthropologist David Stoll, in his book *Menchú and the Story of All Poor Guatemalans,* offered an exposé that tested the accuracy of her life story. Stoll used interviews with local Mayans and Menchú's acquaintances to research her past. He concluded that some of the events she presents, even some she claimed to have been an eyewitness to, are incorrect. The controversy reached the Norwegian Nobel Committee. One of its members, Geir Lundestad, announced that Menchú's Nobel Prize "was not based exclusively or primarily on the autobiography." He proceeded to dismiss the idea that the award should be revoked. Meanwhile, the controversy surrounding her is a staple of the American academy.

In the United States Menchú is not only popular but also a role model on campuses and in left-wing circles. She is connected, as well, with groups advocating for the rights of feminists and Native Americans. Among Latinos—particularly among Chicanos and Puerto Ricans—she serves as a bridge to a pre-Columbian past that is not stressed often enough.

RELATED ARTICLES

Activism; Guatemalan Americans.

FURTHER READING

Arias, Arturo, ed. *The Rigoberta Menchú Controversy.* With a Response by David Stoll. Minneapolis: Univ. of Minn. Press, 2001.

Calvert, Peter. *Guatemala: A Nation in Turmoil.* Boulder, Colo.: Westview Press, 1985.

Menchú, Rigoberta. *I Rigoberta Menchú, an Indian Woman in Guatemala.* Ed. by Elisabeth Burgos-Debray. New York: Verso, 1984.

Menchú, Rigoberta. *Crossing Borders: An Autobiography.* New York: Verso, 1998.

Perera, Victor. *Unfinished Conquest: The Guatemalan Tragedy.* Berkeley: Univ. of Calif. Press, 1993.

Stavans, Ilan. "Rigoberta Menchú: Truth or Dare." In *The Essential Ilan Stavans.* New York: Routledge, 2000.

Stoll, David. *Menchú and the Story of All Poor Guatemalans.* Boulder, Colo.: Westview Press, 1999.

ILAN STAVANS

MENDEZ V. WESTMINSTER SCHOOL DISTRICT

For the first half of the 20th century, those of Mexican origin or descent living and working in the United States were victims of innumerable expressions of implicit and explicit social and institutional discrimination. One of the most visible instances of discrimination was in the context of residential segregation. Residential segregation was predicated on the notion that those of Mexican lineage were essentially unsuited to live within proximity of white citizens. Thus, it was necessary for whites to formally eschew interaction with unfit people of color. Apparatuses for separating Mexicans from—then, primarily—white communities took many forms, including residential covenants, gerrymandering of political districts, and of course unapologetic racist expulsion from communities. In 1896 the Supreme Court ruling from *Plessy* v. *Fergusson* (which upheld the principle of racial segregation) provided the federal government with a new doctrine, "separate but equal," and with it came the opportunity to extend to states the legal prerogative to segregate blacks from whites. This piece of jurisprudence was eventually used to justify the legal separation of all people of color, in all possible respects, from whites. Now, with a legal mandate in hand, states and local municipalities were unabated in their segregationist interpretation of the separate-but-equal finding, and they would inevitably extended prevailing opinions regarding the need to separate whites from people of color to include the delivery of educational services. The separate-but-equal clause was used throughout the U.S. Southwest to justify segregated schooling opportunities for the children of Mexican immigrants in the United States.

In 1944 a chain of events unfolded that would lead to the official end of de jure segregation in California and furnish a portion of the legal basis for the abolition of educational segregation across the country. Beginning in 1930 Mexican parents in Lemon Grove, California, refused to accept the placement of their children in a "Mexican" school that was widely regarded as academically inferior to that of the school for white children. In September 1944, in the course of attempting to register their children for school in Orange County, California, Gonzalo and Felicitas Mendez, who had recently moved to the area to manage a small farm that belonged to interned Japanese owners, were informed that their children would not be admitted to the 17th Street School. The family had to decide whether to accept the white school's refusal to admit their children, based on physical appearance and their Spanish surname, or to demand their enrollment in the all-white school. Choosing the latter, a lawsuit was filed by Gonzalo Mendez challenging the legal grounds of *Plessy*'s separate-but-equal doctrine. The prevailing legal footing culled from the *Plessy* edict for educational segregation was found by then U.S. district judge Paul McCormick as possessing no "constitutional or congressional basis for which states could legally segregate Mexican Americans." In his 1946 ruling, Judge McCormick found that segregation of children of color, in general, violated the protections accorded them by the 14th Amendment to the Constitution. In pursuing their rights, the successful appeal for educational equity finalized in *Mendez* v. *Westminster* in 1947 led to the end of de jure segregation in general, and in particular educational segregation in California. In 1954–1955, *Mendez* v. *Westminster* was cited as legal precedent by Thurgood Marshall

in the case of *Brown* v. *Board of Education* on behalf of black families in Topeka, Kansas.

RELATED ARTICLES

Discrimination; Education; Supreme Court, United States.

FURTHER READING

Acuna, R. *Anything but Mexican: Chicanos in Contemporary Los Angeles.* New York: Verso, 1996.

Donato, R., M. Menchaca, and R. Valencia. "Segregation, Desegregation, and Integration." In *Chicano School Failure and Success: Past, Present and Future.* 2d. ed. New York: Routledge, 2002.

Menchaca, M., and R. Valencia. "Anglo-Saxon Ideologies and Their Impact on the Segregation of Mexican Students in California, the 1920–1930s." *Anthropology and Education Quarterly* 21 (1990): 222–249.

JUAN SANCHEZ MUÑOZ

MENÉNDEZ DE AVILÉS, PEDRO

Born: 1519; Avilés, Spain
Died: 1574; Santander, Spain

One of the most controversial Iberian explorers and colonizers in the Americas, best known for his settlement in St. Augustine, Florida, and for fighting the French, English, and aboriginal populations on this side of the Atlantic Ocean, Pedro Menéndez de Avilés was born in a coastal town in the Asturias region of northern Spain. His parents were landowners but did not belong to the nobility. In 1533, at the age of 14, he left his home and ran away to sea without parental consent. In 1549, after going through the various ranks, he was commissioned by the Holy Roman Emperor Charles V (Charles I of Spain) to drive pirates away from the coasts of Spain. In 1554 he was appointed captain of the Indies Fleet. Menéndez de Avilés was very impulsive and with time he made many enemies. He was imprisoned in 1563 and freed in 1565 after regaining the favor of the new king, Phillip II.

King Phillip II had become upset after learning of a Huguenot settlement on the coast of Florida. The Huguenots were a reformist Protestant church that followed the teachings of Jean Calvin and had left France—owing to the persecution they experienced there, which evolved into the Wars of Religion starting around 1562—and settled in northern Florida. The fact that they were Protestant, thus heretics in the eyes of King Phillip II, combined with the territorial intrusion in Florida angered the Spanish monarch. He sent Menéndez de Avilés there, in 1565, to expel the Huguenots and to establish a colony. Instead Menéndez Avilés massacred all the Frenchmen in the settlement; he hung them from trees with an inscription that read, "not as Frenchmen but as heretics."

Menéndez de Avilés and a contingent of 1,500 Spanish settlers established themselves in St. Augustine in 1565. They occupied and rebuilt the French Fort Caroline, and began the construction of the town. At the beginning they were on good terms with the native Timucua Indians. Their chief, Seloy, welcomed the trading opportunity that came with the Spanish presence, but after a while the Indians realized that the intention of the Spaniards was to settle there permanently, so Seloy turned against the Spaniards and burned the fort. Menéndez de Avilés did not give up. He built another fort on the other side of the St. Augustine Bay. He also built a series of nine forts along the Florida coast, reaching as far north as South Carolina.

In 1567 he was recalled by King Phillip II. After a period of inactivity, Menéndez de Avilés was called again by the monarch; this time his task was to create a squadron of ships that would engage the English, who at that time were encouraging acts of piracy and sabotage against the Spaniards by means of privateer commissions. His task was to create a squadron that would hunt down and eliminate the privateers sent out by England, including Sir Francis Drake and John Hawkins. After some months of preparation, Menéndez de Avilés died in a port city in northern Spain in the midst of creating a fighting force to keep the English at bay.

RELATED ARTICLES

Colonialism; Colonial Period; Explorers and Chroniclers; Florida; Saint Augustine.

FURTHER READING

Cumming, W. P. "The Parreus Map (1562) of French Florida." *Imago Mundi* 17 (1963): 27–40.

Richardson, Sarah. "The Spanish Plymouth Rock." *Discover* 15, no. 1 (January 1994): 80.

Weisenmiller, Mark. "St. Augustine: America's First City." *Hispanic* 13 (November 2002): 70.

CÉSAR ALEGRE

THE GRANGER COLLECTION

Spanish postage stamp featuring explorer Pedro Menéndez de Avilés.

MENTAL HEALTH

The steady growth of the Latino population in the United States has drawn attention to culturally related health issues, including mental illness. Mental illness refers to difficulties related to cognition, emotion, and behavior. It affects Latinos of all ages, genders, ethnicities, religions, and nationalities. However, little research has been done to understand biological, psychological, social, and cultural factors specific to Latino groups or to study the impact of mental illness on the Latino community.

The antecedent, or cause, of a disorder can be linked to a variety of sources. Rather than limiting each disorder to one cause, most illnesses are considered to be the product of multiple causes. These often include a combination of biological, psychological, and sociocultural factors. Cultural differences that Latinos experience are important in understanding the etiology of mental illness within the Latino population. As immigrants arrive in the United States, the introduction to new cultures and a new language is often difficult and stressful. The stress of acculturation—the process of adopting the attributes of another culture—is often cited as a cause of various psychological disorders that Latinos experience. As acculturation takes place, however, Latinos in the United States adapt to new ideas regarding mental health, including new treatments and preventative measures. Some studies, however, suggest that good mental health among Latinos might actually decrease with acculturation and assimilation. For example, longitudinal studies of U.S.-born Mexicans and Puerto Ricans indicate higher rates of depression in second-generation Latinos than in first-generation Latinos. Adolescents in the Latino community tend to have higher rates of attempted suicide (over 10 percent) than do other groups (7 percent of African Americans and 6 percent of non-Hispanic whites).

Lack of information about causes and effects of mental illness is prevalent in the Latino community, where superstitions sometimes prevail. Religion and spiritualism may play a role in the perspectives that some Latinos hold toward mental illness. In cultural terms, mental illness is sometimes understood as *un castigo y un pecado,* at once a punishment and a sin. Some Latinos believe that a mentally ill individual might have behaved in an immoral way, nurtured deep envy, or been the target of some sort of curse, resulting in mental illness. Supernatural forces or bad luck (*la mala suerte*) may also be considered a cause of mental illness. The belief that *brujos* (witches) cause mental illness is still present in the belief system of some Latinos. Rather than seeking help from a physician or psychiatrist, Latinos might resort to prayer and religious devotion as forms of therapy. Also, a distrust in Western medicine may lead some Latinos to traditional folk healers such as *espiritistas, curanderos,* and *santeros,* healers whose rituals combine Catholic and African traditional beliefs.

Access to a properly trained mental health provider is not readily available to many in the Latino community. Adequate resources, language barriers, and health insurance (or lack of it) have an impact on the availability and the effectiveness of mental health services. Of all the ethnic groups in the United States, Latinos are the least likely to have health insurance. According to the U.S. Census Bureau, in 2001 almost one out of every three Latinos—approximately 33 percent of the Hispanic population in the United States—did not have health insurance. The Latino population is also less likely than non-Latino

whites to seek treatment for mental health problems. Often when Latinos do have health insurance and seek help from doctors, they consult a primary-care physician rather than a mental health professional.

Language barriers can also have an impact on the level of effective communication, confidence, and understanding between Latino patients and physicians. A recent immigrant who speaks only Spanish may need an interpreter who might not convey or express a patient's precise feelings or symptoms. Bilingual patients and health-care providers might also find it challenging to communicate in a chosen code. Additionally, the varieties of Spanish used by different national groups (Mexican Americans, Cuban Americans, Puerto Ricans, and so on) and literacy levels are also likely to have an impact on clear and effective communication and trust.

The use of family therapy is generally an effective method of treatment for Latinos owing to the importance of close family ties. Some Latin American cultures believe that mental health disturbances are a result of structural problems within the family. Therapy that includes the entire family aims at promoting healthy interactions among family members and resolving as a close-knit unit the issues that contribute to mental illness.

Ethnopsychopharmacology is a relatively new field of study that examines the relationship between a patient's ethnic and cultural background and his or her response to certain medications. This connection applies specifically to new immigrants since their diets and overall health behaviors may differ from those of acculturated individuals.

Health behaviors such as diet, exercise, athletic activity, and sleep patterns—as well as genetic and societal influences—may impact the effect of medications on patients. Future research and better understanding of cultural and socioeconomic factors affecting the Latino community will result in more effective assessment and treatment plans.

RELATED ARTICLES

Botanicas; Curanderismo; Family; Health; Medicine.

FURTHER READING

Altarriba, Jeanette, and Lisa M. Bauer. "Counseling Cuban Americans." In *Counseling American Minorities: A Cross-Cultural Perspective.* 5th ed. Ed. by Donald R. Atkinson, et al. New York: McGraw-Hill, 1998.

Altarriba, Jeanette, and Lisa M. Bauer."Counseling the Hispanic Client: Cuban Americans, Mexican Americans, and Puerto Ricans." *Journal of Counseling and Development* 76, no. 4 (Fall 1998): 389–396.

López, Alberto G., and Ernestina Carrillo, eds. *The Latino Psychiatric Patient: Assessment and Treatment.* Washington, D.C.: American Psychiatric Pub., 2001.

Pedersen, Paul B., et al., eds. *Counseling across Cultures.* 5th ed. Thousand Oaks, Calif.: Sage Pubns., 2002.

Santiago-Rivera, Azara L., et al. *Counseling Latinos and la Familia: A Practical Guide.* Thousand Oaks, Calif.: Sage Pubns., 2002

Vega, W. A., and M. Alegría. "Latino Mental Health and Treatment in the United States." In *Health Issues in the Latino Community.* Ed. by Marilyn Aguirre-Molina, et al. San Francisco: Jossey Bass, 2001.

JEANETTE ALTARRIBA
BRIANNA L. WATTIE

MERCADOS. *See* BODEGAS, COLMADOS, MERCADOS.

MERENGUE

The Dominican Republic has given birth to a variety of Afro-Hispanic musical idioms, but the only Dominican form that has made a significant impact abroad—at least until the *bachata* boom of the 1990s—is the snappy 2/4 rhythm called merengue. There are other dances called merengue elsewhere that do not share the same sensually brisk rhythm.

Although it is believed to be older, merengue's first public references date back to the 1840s, when it was played by the string-and-percussion ensembles known as *bandurrias criollas*. Merengue's initial percussive component—the autochthonous double-headed tambora bass drum and the scraper called *güiro* or *güira*—survived the passage of time, but the Spanish-derived strings were replaced by the diatonic German accordions imported from Germany. Nowadays, an accordion, metallic *güiro* (or *güira*) and tambora are still regarded as the classical merengue ensemble known as *perico ripiao*. After the saxophone was added to the merengue format, an evolved form emerged in the northern province of El Cibao by 1915. The sax became a vital element of the brassy merengue big bands that would prevail in subsequent decades. Influenced by various U.S. and Cuban genres, the merengue generated various 20th-century by-products, such as *pambiche, bolerengue,* and *magulina.*

Although Damirón and Chapuseau had already played an Americanized form of merengue in New York during the 1940s, the authentic El Cibao–style merengue was not introduced to New York City until the early 1950s by none other than Angel Villoria. As a matter of fact, some of Villoria's sidemen—including but not limited to vocalist Dioris Valladares and tambora player Luis Quintero—would become a vital part of New York's Latin music scene in the years to come. Rudolph Mangual, Jr., *Latin Beat* magazine's publisher, points out that the Dominican merengue "did not catch on abroad until Ralph Pérez, founder of Ansonia Records, recorded the Conjunto Típico Cibaeño on 78-rpm records in the early 1950s. Their recordings spread like wildfire elsewhere around the globe and gave international exposure to the Dominican rhythm of merengue."

In 1993 the New York–based Dominican saxophonist Mario Rivera elaborated an unprecedented fusion of jazz and merengue in his bandleading debut (*El Comandante,* Groovin' High/RTC). Never mind that he had already introduced the tambora within a jazz context four years earlier, during his tenure with the late Dizzy Gillespie's United Nation Orchestra. It was right around that time that a Berklee School of Music graduate, the guitar-playing singer-songwriter Juan Luis Guerra, revived his native country's musical heritage by tastefully blending merengue and *bachata* ingredients with pop and jazz elements, among other things.

On the other hand, taking advantage of the rhythmic deficiency found in the prevailing *salsa romántica* scene, merengue invaded and conquered both Puerto Rico and New York City, where large numbers of Dominican immigrants had arrived since the late 1980s, thus explaining why the exuberantly sensual Puerto Rican songstress Olga Tañón has become the undisputed merengue queen of our time.

Since the mid-1990s countless "merenhouse" or "technomerengue" groups have emerged in the mostly Dominican New York City enclave of Washington Heights and other Hispanic neighborhoods of the city, where they have fused merengue grooves with techniques and gadgets extracted from hip-hop and house-music styles.

RELATED ARTICLES

Dominican Americans; Musical Instruments; Music, Popular; Washington Heights.

© J. EMILIO FLORES/GETTY IMAGES

Merengue rock group Los Ilegales performs at the EMI Latin Music post–Grammy Awards party in West Hollywood, California, 2002.

FURTHER READING

Austerlitz, Paul. *Dominican Music and Merengue: Dominican Identity*. Philadelphia: Temple Univ. Press, 1997.

Brito Ureña, Luis Manuel. *El merengue y la realidad existencial del hombre dominicano* (Merengue and the Dominican Man's Existential Reality). Santo Domingo: Editora Universitaria, 1987.

Del Castillo, José, and Manuel A. García Arevalo. *Antología del merengue* (Anthology of Merengue). Santo Domingo: Editora Corripio, 1992.

LUIS TAMARGO

MESOAMERICA

The term conventionally used for the pre-Spanish area that stretched from south of the Mexican desert through Guatemala and other Central American nations, Mesoamerica is better defined by its cultural characteristics than by the blurred borders of its geography. Mesoamerica produced one of the world's early original civilizations, one of three original phonetic writing systems, and early developments in mathematics, astronomy, architecture, agriculture, and literature. The best-known Mesoamerican societies were those of the Aztecs and Maya, but there were many others; more than 100 distinct languages and a well-established system of trade among the tribes and city-states existed. At the time of the invasion by Europeans, the population of Mesoamerica may have been as high as 25 million. There are no undisputed estimates, because the ravages of disease, war, and famine brought about by the introduction of European germs, animals, plants, and farming methods greatly reduced the population before a census could be taken. Nonetheless, we can speak of a Mesoamerican legacy, both cultural and linguistic, in communities where original languages predominate, in a very large bilingual and multilingual population, and as an influence in the monolingual Spanish population of the area. In recent years the area inhabited by Mesoamerican descendants has extended north into the United States through the migration of indigenous people, including monolingual speakers of Mesoamerican languages. Of these immigrants, some are Nahuatl speakers returning to the very land from which their ancestors are thought to have emigrated more than 700 years ago.

Physical Features and Vegetation

The two great volcanoes, Popocatepetl (Smoking Mountain) and Iztaccihuatl (Sleeping Woman), that lie at the outskirts of the Mexican Federal District are the best-known physical features of the region formerly known as Mesoamerica. The southern lowlands have a subtropical climate—black jungle in the southwest and low jungle in the southeast—with steep mountain ranges in the northern states of Chiapas and Oaxaca, Mexico, and south of the Usumacinta River in Guatemala. Many of the original features of the land have been changed by European farming methods, lumber cutting, and animal husbandry. The forests that existed before the European invasion have been turned into savanna in the *bajío,* Mexico's breadbasket. The clear-cutting of hardwoods in the south has changed much of the forestland into low jungle.

Rainfall in what was Mesoamerica is erratic. In the Yucatán Peninsula there are no rivers; water for drinking must be drawn from cenotes, places where the surface rock collapsed allowing access to subsurface water. City-states were often built around these cenotes, which could not be used by the ancient Maya for crop irrigation but often had religious significance as well as providing drinking water. There is a large cenote at Chichén Itzá, a restored Toltec-influenced city in the present state of Yucatán. Some Maya cities, like Palenque in Chiapas, were built near rivers, as were the cities in Guatemala.

Climatic events played a large role in Mesoamerican history. The Maya codices (folded books) record droughts and invasions of locusts, and Chaac, the Rain God of the Maya, is known also by the names Storm and Hurricane. In the valley of Mexico, the supply of potable water has been a problem since pre-Hispanic times. During a drought in the late 15th century, the bellicose Aztec ruler Ahuitzotl ordered a dam built to divert water from Coyoacán to supply Tenochtitlán and the surrounding lake. So much water came into the city that everything was flooded. Dikes could not save it. Ahuitzotl's dam had to be destroyed, and the Mexicans had to depend once again on Tlaloc, the rain god.

Much of Mesoamerica was mountainous, which made farming difficult. In the current Mexican state of Oaxaca, the Zapotec and Mixtec civilizations flourished in what appear now to be inhospitable conditions, but may not have been so before the introduction of European farming and animal husbandry, which led to depletion of nutrients in the soil through large plantings of single crops, destruction of groundcover by large herds of animals, and a general misunderstanding of climatic conditions for agriculture. Chalco, near Mexico City, like many other Mesoamerican city-states grew up around a lake. Fish provided the main source of protein for them as for many of the Mazatecs and the Purépecha of the present state of Michoacán (*michi* means "fish").

History

Mesoamerican cultures evolved with the development of corn from grasses (teosinte; Nahuatl, *teōsintli*) in about 3000 B.C. in Tehuacán, Puebla, or perhaps even earlier. This enabled the hunter-gatherer cultures to settle in one place. Since corn is the only grain that cannot reproduce without human assistance, it had to be tended throughout the growing cycle; a sedentary existence was required. Soon the corn farmers built permanent dwellings and began the division of labor characteristic of more socially stratified civilizations. A class of priests and scholars arose beside the warriors and the farmers, the latter of whom continually bred the corn to develop strains more resistant to drought, heat, and flood. The work was slow and hard, employing the slash and burn method, which both cleared the land and provided ash to fertilize the corn. Although corn quickly depletes the soil, the newly sedentary people soon devised the *tres santos* (corn, beans, and squash) of the milpa (small farm) system. They plowed the legumes under, the corn grew on the same cleared land year after year, a new class of laborers who constructed temples and palaces could be afforded, and large city-states emerged out of the jungles and in the mountain valleys. They were primarily religious centers in the beginning, but the Mesoamericans soon had enough leisure to produce full-time astronomers, mathematicians, philosophers, and artists as well as artisans. It was during this Classic Period (300 through 900 A.D.) that the Maya originated a form of phonetic writing.

The evolution of Mesoamerican civilizations appears to have begun with the Olmecs, along the southeastern coast of Mexico in the present state of

Tabasco. Olmec is a Nahuatl word meaning Rubber People; however, no one knows what language the Olmecs themselves spoke. They seem to have worshiped a jaguar god, but they also dragged (the wheel was not used in Mesoamerica before the Spaniards arrived) great pieces of basalt about 50 miles (80 km) to their city-state—if it had developed to that extent—and sculpted immense heads, with infantile faces and skulls covered by what look very much like leather football helmets. They invented a calendar, had a complex society, spread their ideas and inventions south to the Maya and west to Teotihuacán and beyond, and disappeared. No one knows how or why.

By 250 C.E. the Teotihuacán civilization had begun to flourish in the Mexican basin. At its peak

Conquest of Mexico and Peru, by Diego Homem, on a page from a portolan atlas (circa 1588).

Teotihuacán may have had as many as 125,000 residents, including people from various parts of Mesoamerica who lived in large compounds like modern apartment houses. Some were foreigners from as far away as Oaxaca. It is not known why they lived in Teotihuacán, nor what language was spoken there, how the Teotihuacanos managed their trade networks, why they built great pyramids along what is known now as the Street of the Dead. Their chief deity was female, and, as in much of Mesoamerica, they also worshiped a Storm God. They made black pottery and elaborately painted vessels, sculpted various kinds of stone, and were adept at fresco painting. A feathered serpent appears in various places in Teotihuacán, which may be the god known as Quetzalcóatl (Kukulkan to the Maya), the culture-bearer, or may simply signify high status. The monumental architecture was built early on. By 750 C.E. Teotihuacán was abandoned. It may have declined slowly over a period of 150–200 years. Only its art, both delicate and monumental, remains. No word, no memory, nothing other than art remains in the massive stillness.

The Zapotec civilization, about which much more is known, flourished at the same time as Teotihuacán and engaged in trade with the Teotihuacanos, probably to get obsidian to use for cutting tools and weapons—in return for what we do not know. Teotihuacán and Monte Alban, the two great city-states of the time, do not appear to have worshiped the same gods or have had a similar social structure. The Zapotec culture began earlier and lasted far longer than that of Teotihuacán, until the Spanish invasion, and is even manifest today in the forms of literature in Zapoteco and some of the greatest post-muralist Mexican art by such painters as Rufino Tamayo and Francisco Toledo. As the Zapotecans grew more prosperous, they were able to build a separate city, Mitla, to serve as a religious center and a home for their high priest, who lived in papal splendor. Unlike the Teotihuacanos, the Zapotecans developed a useful system of glyphic writing. From these glyphs and the two calendars—one ceremonial (of 260 days) and the other a highly accurate 365-day system—it is possible to understand names of persons, places, dates, and some events. From examination of stone carvings and information written in Latin script by Zapotecans after the Spanish conquest, anthropologists have described Zapotecan religious rites as involving the seeking of another form of con-

sciousness, but there is no record of what the Zapotecan priests saw, heard, or thought while in the ecstatic conditions. The search into other modes of consciousness was not limited to the Zapotecs; it was also practiced by the Maya and Aztecs, using hallucinogenic drugs and the painful piercing of the tongue and the penis to achieve a state of religious ecstasy.

The Maya developed earlier than the Zapotecs, entered their Classic Period at about the same time, but did not "disappear" like other Mesoamerican societies—beginning with their precursors, the Olmecs. Calendars (both annual and ritual) bear striking similarities to those of the rest of the Mesoamerican world. How much contact and of what kind the Maya and Olmecs had before the disappearance of the Olmecs is not known; nonetheless, the relation is clear. The great flowering of Maya society began somewhere between 100 and 300 C.E., with cities rising from Palenque in the north all through the Yucatán Peninsula and Guatemala.

There remain many Maya-speaking villages and towns. They have survived an invasion by the Toltecs (see below) from the north and the Spaniards and other Europeans from the east. A system of shamans, organized along military lines, still practices in the present-day state of Quintana Roo, Maya literature appears regularly in magazines, and a novel has been written in Maya. Mesoamerican descendants here, as elsewhere, have adapted to the new realities of the contemporary world. It is this living legacy of Mesoamerica even more than the documents on deerskin or the bark of the fig tree or painted on pottery and walls that provides access to the ancient world. Readings of Maya writings, for example, assume that the language spoken by the ancient writers was similar to Chol, a contemporary Maya language.

After the fall of Tenochtitlán another city-state arose in central Mexico, Tula, which became known as the city of craftsmen (but also warriors). The Toltecs, as Tula's inhabitants were called, developed an elaborate (stratified) social organization and culture, both of which (including aspects of their language, Nahuatl) spread throughout much of Mesoamerica—sometimes through coercion. Chichén Itzá, for example, in present-day Yucatán was invaded by Toltec culture. The city of Mayapán was deeply influenced by the Toltecs (Mayapán has a Náhuatl suffix meaning "place of").

In Tula, religion and political history were so entwined they cannot be separated. The most extraordinary person or god, or both, lived there. His name comes down to us as Ce Acatl Topiltzin Quetzalcóatl, which means One Reed Our Beloved Prince Feathered Serpent. One Reed is his birthdate name; Feathered Serpent is the name of a deity known all across Mesoamerica as Quetzalcóatl or Kukulkan or Gucumatz. The historical Quetzalcóatl, a monk or spiritual leader, apparently differed with other factions in Tula over the question of human sacrifice, Quetzalcóatl preferring the sacrifice of butterflies. He was ousted from his leadership post, fled to the eastern shore, and, according to legend, set sail in a boat made of paper (or perhaps of snakes). Quetzalcóatl set fire to the boat and rose into the heavens to become the Morning Star, the older Precious Twin, the Sun being the other (the Morning Star precedes the sun in the dawn sky).

Another version of the story holds that three wizards (Tezcatlipocas, or Smoking Mirrors) got Quetzalcóatal drunk, after which the monk slept with his sister, then fled in shame. Yet another Quetzalcóatl saved human beings from extinction at the end of the fourth sun by bleeding his penis on their ground-up bones in the underworld and thus bringing them back to life. In this same version he is the bringer of corn, which was the foundation of Mesoamerican civilization, making him the Mesoamerican culture-bearer.

The Toltecs were great artisans; the word *toltecay-otl* came to mean "artistry" or "artisanship" in Mesoamerica. But the Toltecs, too, seem to have disappeared, leaving behind culture, language, and the glory of Quetzalcóatl, who was born in the year Ce Acatl, died in the year Ce Acatl, and was predicted to return in that year, which would be 1519 in the European calendar, the year of the Spanish invasion. But that was far in the future. By then another group had supplanted the Toltecs in central Mexico.

In the 14th century a people with a reputation for ferocity from the north, thought to be from Aztlán (which most likely meant what is now the U.S. Southwest, although it may have referred to an island off the west coast of Mexico), journeyed south through the desert in search of a prophesied place where an eagle stood on a cactus with a snake in its mouth. The Nahuatl word for the cactus, said to have grown out of the buried heart of the evil wizard Copil, is *tenochtli*—hence Tenochtitlán, Place of the Cactus. The people from the north had found

their prophesied place. Unfortunately, they found it occupied by a people whose king was anxious to make an alliance with the strangers by marrying off his daughter to one of their eligible young men. According to legend, he sent the young woman to them to meet her bridegroom, and when she came back for the wedding ceremony, the king saw something unimaginably bizarre. It was not his daughter, but one of the strangers dressed in his daughter's skin.

Horrified, the king drove the strangers out, forcing them into an area near a lake where there was nothing to eat but rattlesnakes. The strangers, who had been toughened by years of wandering as they searched for their foretold land, took easily to the new diet, and to raise food for themselves developed a method for making floating islands in the lake (*chinampas*), enjoying the food they grew there. The strangers became known as the Mexica, probably for Mex-tli, the name of their war god. From 1325 to 1519 the Mexica ruled central Mexico, sending out traders to much of Mesoamerica, developing philosophy, literature, art, architecture, governance, trade, educational systems, everything but phonetic writing. They were expert in war and possessed of a penchant for human sacrifice that eventually cost the lives of thousands.

The crisis from which Mesoamerica still struggles to fully regain its autonomy, the maintenance of its languages, customs, and religion, began with the arrival of Christopher Columbus in the Americas, followed by the depredations led by Hernán (the name he preferred) Cortés in the north in 1519–1521 and by the Montejos—Francisco and his son known as El Mozo—beginning in 1526. All but five of the Maya codices were destroyed in a great auto-da-fé conducted by Bishop Diego de Landa in 1562.

In the Valley of Mexico, the Tlaxcalans, following a terrible slaughter and destruction of the temples by Cortés, chose to ally themselves with the Spaniards. Through a combined effort lasting for months through the summer of 1521, the Spaniards and their indigenous allies defeated the Mexica. Motecuhzoma Xocoyotzin (the younger) was murdered. There was a frightful slaughter of Mexica inside a temple during the Feast of Toxcatl. Cuauhtémoc, the last *huey tlahtoani* (great speaker) of the Mexica, was captured, and after being tortured was forced to accompany the Spanish expedition to the south led by Pedro de

Page from the Codex Becker depicting two war chiefs. The figure on the left indicates submission, while the one on the right issues orders; pre-Columbian, probably Mixtec.

Alvarado. Cuauhtémoc was nailed to a ceiba tree (the cruciform "world tree" of the Maya), where he died.

Alvarado, known as Tonatiuh (Sun God) because of his red hair, was the most vicious of the Spanish captains. He looted and murdered until he commanded the Spanish troops at Miztón in 1541, putting down the last Aztec uprising, but this battle against native people, who were led by Tenamaztle, was also Alvarado's last. He was thrown from his horse and killed.

Maya resistance continued into the 20th century, when the Caste War finally came to an end on the Yucatán Peninsula. Resistance in Chiapas was more sporadic, but as late as the end of the 20th century, the traditional Tzotziles Maya in San Juan Chamula expelled both Catholic followers of the papal hierarchy and Protestants from their indigenous village.

The effect of Spanish attempts to Christianize native people varied from place to place. One of the two surviving accounts of the first phase of conversion is the Coloquios of 1524, in which Spanish priests explained both their religion and the hierarchy of church and state to surviving Aztec nobles and religious. Later, Fray Bernardino de Sahagún, a Franciscan, employed some of the surviving Mexica to help him gather a vast amount of information about the way they had lived and thought prior to the invasion. Although it was Fray Sahagún's stated purpose to use the material to understand the Mesoamerican cultures in order to replace them with Christianity, his work was the first systematic ethnography and has been one of the great sources for the maintenance of the classical Nahuatl language and native culture.

Art and Religion

The early Mesoamericans observed the heavens and the seasons and developed a sense of time similar to that of Isaac Newton. Time, in their view, existed at two levels: first, what might be called a grand level, encompassing all existence prior to the beginning and after the end—the Maya said that at the beginning of the world there were already footprints. Within this grand time exist both the "no longer" and the "not yet." Time is an equation, according to Newton as well as the Maya, both of whom said that time might go in either direction, as an equation can go in either direction. One of the best-known Maya works is translated as "The Ancient Future of the Itzá."

Mesoamerican calendars (that is, those of the Maya and the Aztec) were astonishingly accurate in astronomical terms, but calendars interested the original peoples even more from a religious standpoint. They interpreted time in cycles and extrapolated from these the cycles of creation, widely known by the Aztec as the five suns. Life depended on these great cycles, which were marked by intersections of the solar and lunar calendars. The Maya believed the world would end in our year 2012, the Aztecs believed that year was to be the fifth and final sun or creation, prophesying that the world would end in earthquake and fire. Since Mesoamerica, like ancient Greece, had no concept of heaven or hell, the end of the world was simply that, the end. The hope of heaven did not exist. Therefore, in order to maintain their earthly well-being, Mesoamericans sought to propitiate the gods, and they did that by sacrificing the most precious thing, human life.

This concept of human sacrifice, although alien to contemporary society, has been compared to the willingness of Abraham to sacrifice Isaac in the Old Testament and to the sacrifice of Jesus in the New Testament. However, the number of persons sacrificed by the Mesoamericans was awing. The Cakchiquel Maya play *Rabinal Achí* and a similar Aztec story offer testament to the acceptance of sacrifice by Mesoamerican warriors and royalty, for in both instances the warriors preferred to be sacrificed rather than marry into the family of the ruler of another city-state.

People were most often sacrificed to the sun, the offering of the precious liquor of life expected to put off the end of the fifth and final sun. But there were also sacrifices to Huitzilopochtli, the god of war who represented the sun, as well, and whose name was also Mex-tli, and to Tlaloc, the god of rain. Mesoamerican views of deities were generally dualistic. The Aztecs called the great god by the name Ometeotl (Two-God) or the God of Duality (similar to the Maya Junab Kuj, or Unified God), comprising Totatzin (Our Honored Father) and Tonantzin (Our Honored Mother). It is interesting to note that in Mexico the apparition of the Virgin of Guadalupe is said to have occurred in 1531, at Tepeyac, formerly a shrine to Tonantzin. Thus the patron saint of Mexicans and Mexican Americans is the blending of the two cultures, of two religions: indigenous and Christian.

Of the gods who were not dual, Tlaloc and Quetzalcóatl (Gucumatz or Kukulkan) were the most important, for one brought the rain that supported life and the other was the culture-bearer, the one who brought corn to Mesoamerica and was also the keeper of the arts of metalwork, painting, and so on. The mother god of the Aztecs was Coatlicue, who gave birth to the moon and to her brother, the god Huitzilopochtli. As in many cultures, these came of a virgin birth: Coatlicue swallowed a feather and became pregnant.

Philosophy and religion in Mesoamerica embraced, among other beliefs and practices, sympathetic magic as well as the most sophisticated notions about the meaning of life. The Maya imitated frogs to bring rain, and the Aztecs caused children to cry, expecting that their tears would bring tears from the skies. Tlaloc (or Chaac of the Yucatecan Maya) determined the physical quality of life in a land where droughts were common and severe and irrigation systems were generally insufficient to sustain crops during a dry period. Although the Mesoamerican pantheon was complex, it did not determine all thought or behavior, however. In writings such as the Maya *Popol Vuh* or *Pop Wuj* (Book of Counsel; sometimes known as the Maya Bible) or information collected from the Cantares Mexicanos, Florentine Codex, or Huehuehtlahtolli (Words of the Elders) of the Aztecs, an unsystematic yet highly developed set of morals and a view of life not unlike European existentialism can be found. Social behavior is codified in the Huehuehtlahtolli, and the materialist origins of the cosmology are clear in the descent of the hero twins of the *Popol Vuh* to the underworld, where they battle the dark creatures and emerge again, like the corn planted in the ground and emerging after the spring rains. The sine qua non of life itself is cyclical, like the sun, the seasons, the planets, even creations. Humans, however, are not reborn.

Intellectual pursuits, often connected to or justified by religion, as in other civilizations, occupied much of the time and energy of the classes of priests, scholars, and nobles. The Zapotecs constructed the city of Mitla for such purpose; the Maya priestly intellectuals developed a system of writing, mixing phonograms (drawings denoting sounds) with logograms (signs denoting whole words); and the Aztecs devoted a formal school, the *calmecac,* to educating its nobles in literature, theology, art, and philosophy. There was a powerful sense of history in much of Mesoamerica, and it can still be seen in the surviving Maya codices, many stelae, and other inscriptions. Aztec history, on the other hand, is quite another matter, because Tlacaelel (an early revisionist) had the history of the Aztecs rewritten to comport with their greatness. He did this from his position as Cihuacóatl (literally, Serpent Woman), the adviser, and second in command, to several Great Speakers, as the rulers were called. Tlacaelel also invented the Flowery War, in which there were no massed attacks, only the taking of prisoners by a battalion of 8,000 or 16,000 men (divisions were in multiples of 4) to supply the people of Tenochtitlán, Tlaxcala, Chalco, and other cities and towns with sacrificial victims.

The classes and occupations at all levels in Mesoamerica—farmer, merchant, trader, builder, priest, soldier, scholar, noble—were separate, and the intellectual disciplines, including arcane religious knowledge, were limited to the upper classes, although no small knot of houses existed without its local deity. The worldview was expressed in art, literature, and the rules of daily life, but the societies were complex; at the time of the Spanish invasion, Motecuhzoma Xocoyotzin (the Great Speaker or ruler of the Aztecs) lived in splendor, prostitutes worked the dark streets, the priests wore the blood of sacrifices in their hair, and those living in poverty lived a meager and difficult life. It was no different among the Maya, where one can still see the complex entrance to the central part of Mayapán, a little maze where those coming from outside the central city could be sorted.

The humanities held an extremely important place in Mesoamerica. The *Popol Vuh* contains a brief section in which the author or authors speak of the sacrifice one must make for art. Art, not mere artisanry, began early in Mesoamerica and has survived, although not always flourishing, through plague, conquest, and the destruction of many of the most important works. Three thousand years ago the Olmecs, excellent sculptors, buried a group of small statues in a formation preserved by the archaeologists who unearthed them. All the figures were made of greenstone, save one, and that one faced the others, perhaps addressing them, but more likely different from the others in some social, political, or ethnic respect. From the Olmecs forward, Mesoamerican art and literature were devoted to what the British critic Clive Bell called "significant form." Bell spoke of Mesoamerican art as among the greatest examples of expression through form ever produced. This is not to say that Mesoamerican artists were unconcerned with content but that the highest aesthetic experience was for them in the apperception of the beauty of form. The Olmec work was carried on by the Maya sculptors, painters, and architects to the south and by those of Teotihuacán and the Zapotecs in the center and the west. In the 14th and 15th centuries, the Aztecs carried on the devotion to form they had learned from the Toltecs as well as what they may have seen in the ruins of Teotihuacán and gathered from the Maya and Zapotecs through trade.

Literature in Mesoamerica was produced by priests and nobles for the consumption of priests and nobles. The other classes, with the possible exception of merchants, did not have access to literature, although some works would surely have interested them. Language held a place of defining importance throughout Mesoamerica, as evidenced by the name of those people now commonly grouped under the name Aztecs (the word Aztec was first used in the 18th century by Fray Francisco Clavijero); they were Nahuas, which means "clear speakers." Unlike many societies throughout human history, they did not call themselves "the people"; they viewed language as the defining human characteristic.

While the Maya utilized writing in the form of glyphs, the Nahuas and others used the standard preliterate mnemonic device of rhythm and form. They taught philosophy and history through various kinds of songs, each of which was a distinct form. All through Mesoamerica, literature, history, philosophy, science, and religion were inseparable. Inscriptions on Maya stelae generally began with the retelling of a myth and then moved into history. The architectural ordering of Teotihuacán, while still puzzling, may hold the key to the history and language of the Place of the Gods. When combined with the sculpture and pottery, it tells us a great deal about the religion, the military and trade alliances, and the multicultural aspect of the civilization.

The *Popol Vuh,* which contains many delightful and frightening stories, a history, and the basic philosophy of the Maya, is magnificently told—rich in humor and horror—intricate enough that one can study it for years, comparing it with the books of the Chilam Balams (Jaguar Priests) written centuries later and to the extant codices. The calendrical notations connected to the *Popol Vuh* had been lost by the time the book was first redacted in the 17th century; had this not happened, it would have been a much more complex work and readers might be able to more easily comprehend the great metaphor of Xibalba (the Underworld), where the sun went at the end of the day, and the daily cycle's relation to time, the cosmos, corn, and life itself.

Mesoamerican literature, which contains a wealth of history and storytelling, is largely devoted to a philosophy that has about it the sense of resignation common to millenarianism, but which lacks the hope for heaven that enables Christian millenarians to overcome the sadness of an inevitable end-time. Prayer and sacrifice therefore had to do with the near time, and it was often guided by time itself. Among the Maya the seating of the cycle designated a city as "holy" and gave certain city-states a hegemonic aspect in all areas—intellectual, religious, military, and economic. At the end of the cycle the city was destroyed, either physically or symbolically, and the next cycle was seated in another city. Wars were fought over the seating of the cycle of years, and great cities were destroyed. The literature of the Maya Postclassic Period documents such wars—for example, the destruction of Mayapán—but does not clarify earlier periods on the Yucatán Peninsula or in Guatemala, although a great deal of information is being gathered at present from such magnificent sites as Copán. In the west the Mixtec-Zapotec wars are well known, but history and myth come together there, as in all Mesoamerican accounts of the pre-Hispanic period, because, in general, Mesoamerica assigned a unique value to historical events, seeing them as revelations of the confluence of human will and worldly power with supernatural forces and the ineluctable path of time.

In Aztec literature the mood of that area of Mesoamerica as well as its thoughts and activities has been preserved. There are "tickling" poems (*icnocuicatl*), but for the most part the poems exhibit what would now be described as existential angst. The poets ask again and again, "Is it true we only live but once?" And they answer the question by speaking of the ends of earthly things—jade shatters, feathers are torn. "Friends," the prince Ayocuan says in the "Dialogue of Flowers and Song"(a *difrasismo,* meaning art or poetry), "listen to the dream of a word," and he goes on to speak of the coming of spring, of the quieting of one's heart.

A question about the provenance of art begins the dialogue. The princes muse on it and come to the inevitable conclusion that life is short and art is long. There is no more useful key to Mesoamerican thought than that. The Aztecs did not expect to return to earth after death. Heroes lived in memory; they did not return. "Only a little while here on earth," the poets said. They believed in courage and history, and what they could not explain through science or philosophy they consigned to myth.

Science

Mathematics, astronomy, architecture, and medicine came to Mesoamerica through meticulous observation and a sense of order based on the natural order of the universe. The Maya date 13.0.0.0.0 was by their calculations the moment when nothing existed within time. To mark it required a symbol and a concept, zero. The thought came to the Maya long before it was imported from the east to Europe. Their science and mathematics helped enable them to engineer *sacbeob* (white roads) of extraordinary dimensions. The *sacbe* from Cobá to Yaxuná runs for 62 miles (100 km) in an almost perfectly straight line. The terrain is completely flat. How the Maya were able to plot the course of the road without an Archimedian point of vantage or modern navigational instruments remains one of the mysteries of their science.

Mesoamerican architects had not developed the true arch by the time of the European invasion, but vaulted constructions were not uncommon. They often used the pyramid's sturdy shape, they were able to build ball courts that returned a given number of echoes, and they had a bead on magnetic north without having iron for use in a compass. With their horticultural knowledge, Mesoamericans bred several types of corn, using as many as five types in a single hole to be sure of acceptable growth no matter what the level of rainfall. In the use of medicinal plants and herbs, they had found palliatives or cures for a great many afflictions. Through a vast trade network the medicinal plants and herbs, along with foodstuffs, precious cacao, and some semiprecious stones and metal, were widely available.

As urban planners and managers, they had leapt far ahead of other cultures. The Spaniards, arriving at Tenochtitlán, pronounced it the cleanest and most beautiful city in the world, with the most orderly and carefully policed market. Since there were no beasts of burden in Mesoamerica, the use of the wheel except for toys was unknown. Scientific development moved along a path very different from that of Europe, but the intellectual requirements were no less rigorous, and perhaps more rigorous. Intellectual growth was rapid, until the course of scientific progress came to an abrupt end early in the 16th century.

21st Century

A Mesoamerican legacy exists now in several forms. There are more than a million monolingual speakers of indigenous languages, and the native populations are increasing despite the killings in Guatemala and the economic poverty of indigenous peoples in Mexico. Millions more are bilingual while still retaining much of their original language and culture. Dictionaries based on historical principles are now able to show the changes in meanings of words over time, one proof of the living character of a language such as Nahuatl. Similarly, dictionaries of Yucatecan Maya show changes over time, including now a new spelling for most words, one closer to actual sounds and more indicative of the accented and inflected character of the language. Most of the rest of the former Mesoamerican region is now of mixed ancestry: indigenous, European, and African, as well as Asian. In recent years a large number of people from the area have joined those from northern Mexico as immigrants to the United States; thus "Mesoamerica" now extends from Alaska to El Salvador. Works in Mesoamerican languages are written and published

in California as well as in Mexico and Guatemala. The civilizations begun with the domestication of teosinte have not merely survived, they are once again thriving.

RELATED ARTICLES

Archeology; Aztlan; Colonialism; Gamio, Manuel; Leon-Portilla, Miguel; Mayas; Nahuas; Popol Vuh; Quetzalcóatl.

FURTHER READING

Edmonson, Munro. *The Ancient Future of the Itzá.* Austin: Univ. of Tex. Press, 1982.

León-Portilla, Miguel. *Aztec Thought and Culture.* Norman: Univ. of Okla. Press, 1968.

León-Portilla, Miguel. *La filosofía Náhuatl estuiada en sus Fuentes* ("The Nahuatl Philosophy") Rev. ed. Mexico City: Nat. Autonomous Univ. of Mex., 1997.

León-Portilla, Miguel, and Earl Shorris, eds. *In the Language of Kings: An Anthology of Mesoamerican Literature—Pre-Columbian to the Present.* New York, W. W. Norton, 2001.

Lockhart, James. *The Nahuas after the Conquest.* Palo Alto, Calif.: Stanford Univ. Press, 1992.

Schele, Linda, et al. *Maya Cosmos.* New York: Morrow, 1993.

Tedlock, Dennis, tr. *Popol Vuh: The Definitive Edition of the Mayan Book of the Dawn of Life and the Glories of Gods and Kings.* New York: Simon & Schuster, 1985.

EARL SHORRIS

MESTIZAJE

Mestizaje is a Spanish word that refers to the racial and cultural mixing of European, American Indian, and African blood in Latin American and Latino peoples. The word originates at the point of contact between the Europeans, the Indigenous people of the Americas, and the arrival of African slaves. Conceptually *mestizaje* is associated with mixture, hybridity, transculturation, and racial miscegenation. The term is widely used in Latin American and Latino communities to reflect cultural, political, and racial identity. Culturally *mestizaje* refers to a broad synthesis of social, political, artistic, and linguistic ideas and identities. It has been viewed as a foundational concept for Latino, specifically Chicano, identity in the United States. A person who is a product of *mestizaje* is called a mestizo.

Latin America

Mestizaje begins to exist with the conquest of the Americas by the Spaniards. The figure of Doña Marina, or La Malinche, as she is often called, has come to embody the concept of *mestizaje* in relation to the conquest and the ability to move between different linguistic and cultural spaces. Speaking Nahuatl, Maya, and eventually Spanish, Doña Marina facilitated Spanish victory over the Aztecs by acting as Cortés's translator. She also had a son with Cortés—Martín Cortés—who would be one of the earliest mestizos in Latin America.

One of the initial meditations on *mestizaje* can be found in the Inca Garcilaso de la Vega's *Comentarios Reales*; he was the first colonial writer to employ the term *mestizaje* as a cultural concept or category. During the colonial period the concept of *mestizaje* became central to the construction of Creole (European American) identity and, ultimately, to the struggle for independence. The colonial *criollos* used the discursive category of *mestizaje* to rhetorically base their struggle for independence from Spain and Portugal on American Indian resistance. In the newly independent Latin America countries, especially Mexico, the new national identity was built, in great part, on an affirmation of a heterogeneous mestizo identity.

It was in the early 20th century that the concept of *mestizaje* began to play a central role in philosophical and political discussions about culture, race, and identity, especially in Mexico. Throughout the 19th century the national project of Porfirio Díaz privileged whiteness, wealth, and those of European descent. The Mexican Revolution of 1910–1917, however, ushered in a need to evaluate changed historic conditions in the context of race, culture, and national identity. Three works provide the foundation for *mestizaje* as a nationalist discourse: Andrés Molina Enríquez's *Los grandes problemas nacionales* (1909), José Vasconcelos's *La raza cósmica* (1925), and Manuel Gamio's *Forjando patria* (1916). These intellectuals promoted the idea that *mestizaje* was fundamental to the Mexican nation's well-being and future, and that a nationalist ideology promoting *mestizaje* would provide unity, economic progress, and a defense against foreign intrusions.

In *Los grandes problemas nacionales,* Enríquez argued that mestizos are the most powerful and most patriotic of all races in Mexico. On the other hand, Gamio, whose ideas were particularly influential in the 1940s, explored different ways to integrate the Indian into mainstream society in *Forjando patria,* thus creating a national *mestizaje.* He argued specifically that mestizos were the true leaders in Mexico and that their intellectual superiority led to the fight

against injustice and oppression. While Enríquez and Gamio were to play central roles in the evolution of a nationalist program based on *mestizaje* in the 1940s and 1950s in Mexico, it was the work of Vasconcelos that would have the greatest impact on the Latino community—specifically the Chicano community—in the United States.

Vasconcelos, in *La raza cósmica,* champions *mestizaje* as the key to progress and advancement of the Mexican nation. He argues that a focus on *mestizaje* will lead to the creation of a new fifth, or cosmic, race that would be superior to the four others (the black, the Indian, the Mongol, and the white, according to Vasconcelos). It was through racial mixing, and the subsequent creation of a new mestizo race, that a more powerful Mexican identity would emerge. This cosmic race, according to Vasconcelos, would embody racial purity and cultural superiority.

The ideologies proposed by Molina Enríquez, Gamio, Vasconcelos, and later Alfonso Caso would form the basis for a national ideology in Mexico in the 1940s and 1950s. The official indigenization of the Mexican state during this period would focus on *mestizaje* as the basis for integrating the Indian into the framework of the nation project. This nationalist ideology of *mestizaje* would also be reflected in the art, literature, and film of Mexico in the 1940s and 1950s.

The idea of *mestizaje* is also articulated in the writings of Peruvian José Carlos Mariátegui. In his *Seven Interpretive Essays on Peruvian Reality* (1928), Mariátegui juxtaposes Marxist ideology and Latin American *mestizaje* to promote a new nationalist project for Peru. He argues for the creation of a new Latin American Marxism that will emerge through the mixing of European and American Indian cultures and traditions. At the core of Mariátegui's proposal is a complete rejection of colonial *criollo* society and a reevaluation of the American Indian cultures. He proposes an alternative political, social, and cultural project for Peru based on *mestizaje* and Indo-American socialism.

As a result of the slave trade—ironically, supported by, among others, Fray Bartolomé de Las Casas, the so-called "defender of the Indians," to ensure that the aboriginal population would not be decimated by the careless Spaniards—Cuba, Puerto Rico, the Dominican Republic, and other Caribbean islands where the Spanish colonial influence was felt have a different racial and ethnic—and thus, cultural—texture. As a result, the idea of *mestizaje* does not apply to the region. Instead, the concepts in vogue are Creolization and Negritude, which are defined by different parameters and by a dependency on Africa as an original source.

The Chicano Movement

The idea of *mestizaje* played a central role in shaping the ideology of the Chicano civil rights movement of the 1960s and 1970s. Specifically, the ideas put forth by Vasconcelos in *La raza cósmica* formed the basis for the political discourse heralded by Chicano foundational texts such as the "Plan Espiritual de Aztlán" and Corky González's *Yo soy Joaquín* (I am Joaquín). While the ideology of Chicanismo looked to indigenous pre-Columbian culture as the point of departure for Chicano identity, most Chicanos were mestizos and their political and cultural discourse reflected that ancestry. Therefore, it is not surprising that in the context of the Chicano movement, *mestizaje* referred not only to a mixing of races but also to a historical reinterpretation that linked Chicano identity directly to the pre-Columbian cultures of the Aztecs and the Maya.

The quest to come to terms with Chicano mestizo identity led directly to Vasconcelos's ideas on the cosmic fifth race. The idea of a mixed-blood race that would overshadow and overpower all other races on an intellectual, cultural, and spiritual level intrigued Chicano activists. To this extent, the Chicano movement, which heralded an independent political, cultural, and historical identity for Mexican Americans, was anchored largely by the belief that Chicanos were the cosmic, "bronze race" to which Vasconcelos had referred in his 1925 publication. This allowed for the creation and construction of "brown" as a racial category that was politically, culturally, and economically relevant in the United States. The concept of brown power and the bronze race, which were discursive unifying forces in the Chicano movement, embodied the power of *mestizaje* by affirming the power of hybrid identity. Through the creation of *la raza*, Chicanos heralded racial difference and pushed for a reinterpretation of the past linked to *indigenismo* and pre-Columbian cultures.

At the same time, a common understanding of *mestizaje* as an identifying factor for Chicanos promoted a sense of community within the Chicano movement. Chicanos began to refer to themselves as "La Familia Cósmica," or "La Familia de La Raza." Similarly, *la raza,* a politically charged term identified with the Chicano nation and the ideology of Chicanismo in the 1960s and 1970s, literally meant "the race." However, the term was a clear reference to Vasoncelos's fifth race as articulated in *La raza cósmica.*

The affirmation by Chicanos of *la raza* as the bronze race is clearly articulated in the "Plan Espiritual de Aztlán," which firmly positions the ideology of *mestizaje* within the nationalist project of the Chicano movement. This manifesto, adopted in March 1969 at the first National Chicano Youth Liberation Conference in Denver, Colorado, boldly promotes Chicano nationalism and self-determination through unity, economy, education, institutions, self-defense, culture, and political liberation. The document constituted the ideological framework of the Chicano movement and promoted *mestizaje* as the driving force behind Chicanismo.

On many levels the idea of Aztlán became the spatial embodiment of *mestizaje* for Chicanos in the 1960s and 1970s. It represented the symbolic space where Chicanos could build a future based on "brown power" and a revitalized pride in indigenous culture. While Aztlán is historically understood to be the mythical homeland of the ancient Aztecs, for Chicano nationalists it came to represent a utopian geographical homeland for the Chicano people. Although Aztlán existed mostly as a poetic idea, it also became a metaphor for cultural and racial *mestizaje* within the Chicano movement.

One of the clearest affirmations of *mestizaje* as a marker of identity within the Chicano movement is González's epic poem *Yo soy Joaquín* (1967). The poem, which narrates Chicano history from pre-Columbian times to the present, was written in 1965 and published in 1967 by González, who founded the Crusade for Justice in 1966. By March of the same year, Luis Valdez's Teatro Campesino had already adapted the poem for public performance. As the most influential poem of the Chicano movement, *Yo soy Joaquín* calls on Chicanos to embrace mestizo culture and identity in order to define themselves and their movement.

González's *mestizaje* is simultaneously a historical, cultural, and racial category. *Yo soy Joaquín* is subdivided into historical epochs that extend back to pre-Columbian times and forward to the 20th century.

Each section highlights indigenous, Mexican, and Chicano events, as well as historical figures who played key roles in Chicano history. Special attention is paid to indigenous resistance and opposition to the Anglo-American state. The poem argues against assimilation to Anglo-American culture, and the end of *Yo soy Joaquín* boldly claims *mestizaje* as the source of Chicano identity. González ultimately declares a new revolutionary identity for Chicanos that is grounded in *mestizaje*. In the last lines he cries out that *la raza* represents a mixture of Mexican, Indian, and Spanish blood, histories, and cultural identity, and that the revolutionary future of the Chicano depends on embracing this *mestizaje*.

The visual art of the Chicano movement also affirmed the centrality of *mestizaje* to Chicano identity. The visual representations of the *raza de bronze* complement the themes of Alurista's poetry and the theatrical works of the Teatro Campesino, which fused Aztec, Maya, and Catholic symbols into their theatrical skits. Visual articulations of *mestizaje* can be seen in art that was exhibited in both public and private spaces. For example, Emanuel Martínez's *Farm Workers' Altar* (1967) brings together Catholic and pre-Columbian imagery with references to the brown power movement and the struggle of the United Farm Workers. José Gamaliel González's mural *Raza de oro* (1975), painted with the youth of Westtown on Hubbard Street in Chicago, uses the Maya motif of the "vision serpent" to communicate the direct historical line between pre-Columbian cultures and the Chicano movement. In Zarco Guerrero's 1976 mural titled *Culture, Brotherhood, and Pride,* painted on the side of a building, images of an Aztec deity and an Aztec warrior frame a doorway. Above the door is the black eagle logo of the United Farm Workers, along with the words *La Raza Cósmica,* an obvious reference to Vasconcelos. In the center of the mural, Guerrero also painted two Maya profiles, which reaffirm the theme of neoindigenism as linked to the discourse of *mestizaje*.

A more recent visual articulation of *mestizaje* can be found in Judith Baca's *La mestizaje* from 1991, which shows a Chicana woman in the center of the canvas framed by varied indigenous profiles that refer to different races and cultures. This work, which is done in pastel on canvas, also reinterprets the traditionally masculine discourse of Chicano *mestizaje* within a gendered, feminist framework. By directing the observer's eye to a Chicana, as the dominant figure in the composition, Baca integrates gender and sexuality into the Chicano discourse of *mestizaje,* thereby creating concrete dialogue with the work of writer Gloria Anzaldúa.

The New Latino

The idea of *mestizaje* does not apply to Latinos with Caribbean roots (for example, Dominican Americans, Puerto Ricans on the mainland, and Cuban Americans). But it is a quintessential concept among Mexican Americans and even among people from Central American nations including Guatemala, Nicaragua, and El Salvador. Anzaldúa's seminal work, *Borderlands/La Frontera* (1987), takes the concept of *mestizaje* beyond a racial and cultural mixture of Spanish and Indian blood. Her work develops the discursive category of the border as a metaphor for *mestizaje* and hybridity in general. As Anzaldúa attempts to find her own place within this liminal space of the border, she theorizes about living in the margins and about the possibilities that such a location might possess for communicating across cultures. The borderlands, therefore, become an evocation of postcolonial *mestizaje* that shatters homogenous comfort zones of heterosexual, monolingual, and monocultural subjects.

With Anzaldúa, the discourse of *mestizaje* becomes an ethnic, sexual, and political quest to revise traditional boundaries and celebrate the plural consciousness of the Chicana and Chicano. Her essay "La conciencia de la mestiza/Towards a new mestiza consciousness" traces the oppression of indigenous identity in Anglo culture, and even within the Chicano community. As a response to this repression, Anzaldúa calls for a plural subject that challenges the oppressor and affirms the validity and power of Mexican indigenous cultures. This resistance is embodied in the subject of the "new mestiza," who embraces contradictions, ambiguity, hybridity, and plurality. According to Anzaldúa, the new mestiza moves between different racial, ethnic, and gendered boundaries—learning to be Indian in Mexican culture or to be Mexican from an Anglo perspective. She has a tolerance for contradictions and a passion for plurality, relying on biological, racial, ideological, linguistic, and cultural advantages presented by overlapping spaces and discourses.

It is important to note that while Anzaldúa does affirm the importance of Vasconcelos's philosophy of *mestizaje* for contemporary Chicano theory, she does not embrace the idea of a homogenous cosmic race that will be all things—and belong—to all cultures. For Anzaldúa, *mestizaje* is heterogeneous and multicultural. As such, the new mestiza transforms the process of miscegenation and cultural interaction into a space of power through the celebration of difference, and hybridity. The borderland becomes the space of the new mestiza.

Mestizaje is recodified in the writing of Richard Rodríguez as the "browning of America." In contrast to Anzaldúa, Rodríguez's reading of *mestizaje* directly appropriates Vasconcelos's utopian ideal of the cosmic race as a homogenous goal and projects it onto the U.S. cultural and racial landscape of the late 20th and early 21st century. Writing from a largely autobiographical perspective, Rodríguez, in *Days of Obligation: An Argument with My Mexican Father* (1992) and *Brown: The Last Discovery of America* (2002), posits that Vasconcelos's concept of the cosmic race provides the necessary framework for understanding the complex racial and ethnic politics of the U.S. cultural landscape. He argues specifically that Mexico's racial and cultural *mestizaje* prefigures the proliferation of languages, races, and cultures in the United States. This miscegenation leads to the

"browning of America," in which Latinos are empowered through *mestizaje*.

Rodríguez's first book, *Hunger of Memory: The Education of Richard Rodríguez* (1982), simultaneously presents a critical approximation to bilingual education and affirmative action, and affirms race and ethnicity as markers of difference that prevent Rodríguez from assimilating into the U.S. middle class. Following Vasconcelos, he argues for the elimination of ethnic and racial difference, for it is the shedding of racial markers that will allow Chicanos to assimilate into U.S. middle-class culture and discard the need to function differently in public and private spheres.

Rodríguez's second book, *Days of Obligation: An Argument with My Mexican Father* (1992), focuses even more concretely on race and articulates an acute awareness of brownness as an index of identity. In this text his discussions of miscegenation as a force that is shaping the cultural and ethnic landscape of the United States leads Rodríguez to embrace *mestizaje* as the discourse of choice. Moving beyond the binary opposition of white and nonwhite, he discusses the way in which mestizo (brown) reality is permeating all spaces in the United States. Much like

City of Dreams, River of History, a mural in the Amtrak-Metrolink Union Station in Los Angeles, by Richard Wyatt, shows the diversity of California's population.

Vasconcelos's utopian argument that *mestizaje* will lead to a cosmic race, Rodríguez posits that the opposition between Mexicans and U.S. Americans will be slowly erased as ethnic and racial differences are blurred. If Chicanos embrace *mestizaje* or miscegenation, the categories of white and black begin to lose their validity. Brown, instead, becomes the defining ethnic marker and the new cosmic race.

It is important to note that Rodríguez does not blindly embrace Vasconcelos's philosophy. While his reading of *mestizaje* is largely based on an appropriation of the concept of the cosmic race, he subverts Vasconcelos's discourse at various points. In contrast to Vasconcelos, who believes that Latin America is the privileged location of the cosmic race, Rodríguez views the United States as the space where *mestizaje* will evolve in its fullest form. He also erases from the equation of miscegenation Vasconcelos's view of the European as the most powerful force. *Mestizaje,* instead, becomes an opportunity for the Indian to erase the European, as opposed to Vasconcelos's dream of having the European slowly blot out the Indian race. While Vasconcelos embraces whiteness, Rodríguez embraces brownness. Furthermore, Rodríguez does not identify the Indian with only the ancient Aztecs or the Maya, as the Chicano movement often did. Instead, he embraces the contemporary indigenous peoples of Mexico and Central America as the key to *mestizaje* and the future browning of America. Unlike Anzaldúa, whose "new mestiza consciousness" is based on plurality and heterogeneity, Rodríguez links hybridity to a homogenous mestizo culture. Cultural interaction and racial miscegenation will lead to a new "brown" reality in the United States that will provide new opportunities for Latinos in all spheres.

RELATED ARTICLES

Anzaldúa, Gloria; Aztlan; Brownness; Chicano Movement; Intermarriage; Race; Vasconcelos, José.

FURTHER READING

Aldama, Arturo. *Disrupting Savagism: Intersecting Chicana/o, Mexican Immigrant, and Native American Struggles for Self-Representation.* Durham, N.C.: Duke Univ. Press, 2001.

Anzaldúa, Gloria. *Borderlands/La Frontera.* San Francisco: Aunt Lute Bks., 1987.

Caso, Alfonso. *Métodos y resultados de la politica indigenista en Mexico* (Methods and Results of Indigenous Policies in Mexico). Mexico City: Instituto Nacional Indigenista, 1954.

Dávalos, Karen. *Exhibiting Mestizaje: Mexican (American) Museums in the Diaspora.* Albuquerque: Univ. of N.Mex. Press, 2001.

De Castro, Juan. *Nations: Culture, Race, and Conformity in Latin American Literature.* Tucson: Univ. of Ariz. Press, 2002.

Doremus, Anne. "Indigenism, Mestizaje, and Nacional Identity in Mexico in the 1940's and 1950's." *Mexican Studies/Estudios Mexicanos.* 17, no. 2 (Summer 2001): 375–402.

Enríquez, Andrés Molina. *Los grandes problemas nacionales* (The Big National Problems). Mexico City: Ediciones ERA, 1978.

Gamio, Manuel. *Forjando Patria* (Creating the Homeland). Mexico City: Ediciones Porrúa, 1971.

García, Ignacio. *Chicanismo: The Forging of a Militant Ethos among Mexican Americans.* Tucson: Univ. of Ariz. Press, 1997.

González, Corky. *I am Joaquín: An Epic Poem.* New York: Bantam Bks., 1972.

Mariátegui, José Carlos. *Seven Interpretive Essays on Peruvian Reality.* Tr. by Marjory Urquidi. Austin: Univ. of Tex. Press, 1971.

"Plan Espiritual de Aztlán." In *Documents of the Chicano Struggle.* New York: Pathfinder Press, 1971.

Rodríguez, Richard. *Hunger of Memory: The Education of Richard Rodriguez.* Boston: D. R. Godine, 1982.

Rodríguez, Richard. *Days of Obligation: An Argument with my Mexican Father.* New York: Viking Press, 1992.

Rodríguez, Richard. *Brown: The Last Discovery of America.* New York: Viking Press, 2002.

Stavans, Ilan. "How Hispanics Became Brown." In *The Riddle of Cantinflas: Essays on Hispanic Popular Culture.* Albuquerque: Univ. of N.Mex. Press, 1998.

Vasconcelos, José. *The Cosmic Race: A Bilingual Edition.* Tr. by Didier T. Jaén. Baltimore: Johns Hopkins Univ. Press, 1997.

ROXANNE DÁVILA

MEXICAN AMERICAN LEGAL DEFENSE AND EDUCATION FUND

Founded in 1968, the Mexican American Legal Defense and Education Fund (MALDEF) is a nonprofit charitable organization dedicated to promoting and protecting the civil rights of the nearly 40 million Latinos who live and work in the United States. Although MALDEF pursues a variety of initiatives, its principal activity has long been the prosecution of civil litigation, usually in the areas of education, employment, immigration, and voting rights.

Peter Tijerina, a Chicano lawyer from Texas, was most responsible for creating MALDEF. In 1946, while still in college, Tijerina joined the League of United Latin American Citizens (LULAC) to fight discrimination against Chicanos then common in the Lone Star State. Later, he became one of the few Latinos to serve as judge there. By the mid-1960s

Tijerina was state civil rights chairman for LULAC's San Antonio branch. LULAC ran "truth squads," or teams of volunteers who investigated problems affecting the Mexican American community. These truth squads looked into a variety of matters, such as the mysterious deaths of rural Chicano workers and the persistent segregation of Chicano schoolchildren. Although this work was important, Tijerina believed that Chicanos needed to mount a sustained legal attack on discrimination in public institutions if they were to escape second-class citizenship. But no Mexican American organization had been able to muster the resources to do so.

In 1966, a case Tijerina was handling convinced him that the time to establish such an organization had come. He was representing a woman named Muñoz, who had lost her right leg in an accident. Fearing that no all-white Texas jury would award her fair compensation, Tijerina tried, but failed, to select a more representative jury that would have included Mexican Americans. Although existing law was on his side, the resources to enforce it were not; Tijerina estimated that it would cost $10,000 to bring a separate challenge alleging that Chicanos were illegally excluded from the jury pool. So he decided to raise the stakes.

In spring 1967, Tijerina, along with Bexar County commissioner Albert Peña and former San Antonio city councilman Roy Padilla, traveled to New York City to meet with officials of the Ford Foundation. The meeting had been arranged by civil rights lawyer Jack Greenberg of the NAACP Legal Defense and Education Fund (LDF). The success of the LDF in *Brown* v. *Board of Education* and other landmark cases had shown what a litigation-oriented group could accomplish, even with modest resources. At the meeting the foundation expressed interest in granting funds to create a Chicano civil rights organization modeled after the LDF and invited the trio to submit a grant application.

Over the next year Tijerina, Gregory Luna, and other Texas lawyers, drawing on their LULAC contacts, organized support for MALDEF in Arizona, California, Colorado, and New Mexico. Meanwhile, Vilma S. Martinez, a young staff attorney with the LDF, helped prepare the grant application. On May 1, 1968, the group's board of directors convened in San Antonio, where it established headquarters. (A field office was opened in Los Angeles.) Tijerina became the first executive director and Carlos Cadena

the first president. The Ford Foundation announced a five-year grant to fund legal work on behalf of Mexican Americans in the sum of $2.2 million—more than twice the amount requested. Of this sum, $250,000 was earmarked for scholarships for Chicano law students. MALDEF had been born.

In 1970, to project a more national image, MALDEF moved its headquarters to San Francisco. The year before, Tijerina had stepped down as director in favor of Mario Obledo, a longtime LULAC leader who was then serving as deputy attorney general in Texas. As president and general counsel, Obledo implemented the strategy of filing test cases on constitutional grounds. When possible, MALDEF would take those cases to higher courts to set new legal precedents. He also opened offices in Albuquerque, Denver, and Washington, D.C.

In 1973 Obledo's strategy began to pay off with two U.S. Supreme Court cases. In *White* v. *Regester,* MALDEF successfully challenged Texas's system of "at large" elections. The Court agreed that such elections unfairly diluted the voting power of Mexican Americans. In *San Antonio Independent School District* v. *Rodriguez,* MALDEF argued that Texas's system of financing public schools through local property taxes violated the federal equal protection rights of Mexican American schoolchildren. The trial court had agreed, but the Supreme Court reversed. The defeat, however, set the stage for a later victory. In 1989, in *Edgewood Independent School District* v. *Kirby,* MALDEF presented evidence that, under the same system of financing, per pupil spending in the Lone Star State ranged from as little as $2,112 in predominantly Chicano schools to as much as $19,333 in predominantly Anglo schools. The Texas Supreme Court found that the practice violated the state constitution and ordered that it be dismantled.

From 1973 to 1982, Martinez served as president and general counsel, overseeing MALDEF's rise to prominence. Inside the organization, she created the Chicana Rights Project, an initiative to challenge sex discrimination against Mexican American women, and an internship program to train young Chicano lawyers. Outside it, she vigorously pursued the MALDEF agenda of opening doors to educational opportunity and political access. In 1982, in *Plyler* v. *Doe,* Martinez helped persuade the U.S. Supreme Court to strike down a Texas statute denying public education to the children of undocumented aliens.

By 1986, when Antonia Hernandez assumed leadership, the organization that Tijerina had founded to assist Chicanos in the Southwest was dedicated to helping Latinos throughout the country. The Los Angeles office became its headquarters. MALDEF played a key role in successful challenges to Proposition 187, an initiative denying undocumented aliens access to public education and other services in California, and to gerrymandering, which had kept Latinos off the Los Angeles County Board of Supervisors for over a century. In 1991 the election of Supervisor Gloria Molina, largely the result of a districting plan negotiated by MALDEF, changed that.

RELATED ARTICLES

Galarza, Ernesto; Politics, Mexican American; Puerto Rican Legal Defense and Education Fund.

FURTHER READING

Acuña, Rodolfo F. *Occupied America: A History of Chicanos.* 3d ed. New York: Harper & Row, 1988.

Hernandez, Antonia. "Pete Tijerina." In *Memorandum to MALDEF Board of Directors.* www.maldef.org.htm

Meier, Matt S., and Margo Gutiérrez. "Mexican American Legal Defense and Educational Fund (MALDEF)." In *Encyclopedia of the Mexican American Civil Rights Movement.* Westport, Conn.: Greenwood Press, 2000.

O'Connor, Karen, and Lee Epstein. "A Legal Voice for the Chicano Community: The Activities of the Mexican American Legal Defense and Education Fund." In *The Mexican American Experience,* Ed. by Rodolfo O. de la Garza et al. Austin: Univ. of Tex. Press, 1985.

Rosales, F. Arturo. *Chicano! The History of the Mexican American Civil Rights Movement.* Rev. 2d ed. Houston, Tex.: Arte Publico Press, 1997.

CHRISTOPHER DAVID RUIZ CAMERON

MEXICAN AMERICAN POLITICAL ASSOCIATION

Founded in 1959, the Mexican American Political Association (MAPA) is dedicated to "the constitutional and democratic principle of political freedom" for Mexican American and Hispanic people. Inspired by the black civil rights movement of the 1960s, MAPA was one of the first Chicano organizations to declare its primary purpose as political rather than social or economic. It has long sought to elect politicians, seat judges, and enact legislation to increase the influence of Chicanos in the United States. Although officially nonpartisan, MAPA has tended to favor Democratic candidates and causes.

Among the 150 people who attended MAPA's founding meeting in Fresno, California, were most of the early leaders of the Chicano civil rights movement. Humberto "Bert" Corona, the prominent community activist, was later appointed to the U.S. Civil Rights Commission. Herman E. Gallegos, the veteran community organizer, academic, and foundation and business consultant, would serve as the first executive director of the Southwest (now National) Council of La Raza. Eduardo Quevedo, cofounder of the Congreso de Los Pueblos de Habla Española, became MAPA's first president. Edward R. Roybal, the first Chicano elected to the Los Angeles City Council in the 20th century, went on to serve 30 years in the U.S. House of Representatives.

In 1962 MAPA played an instrumental role in electing Roybal to Congress from his heavily Chicano East Los Angeles district. Thereafter, it helped secure the appointment of several Mexican Americans to judgeships in California. For a time during the 1960s, these successes established MAPA as a model for political organizing among Chicanos in the Southwest. Despite efforts during the 1970s to expand nationally, MAPA has remained a California-based organization.

Like other new groups of its era, MAPA departed from traditional Mexican Americanism in two ways. First, it disputed the notion that a lack of education doomed Chicanos to political vulnerability. Second, it used the rhetoric of racism to identify problems affecting the community. Both positions foreshadowed the tactics of the Chicano student movement of the early 1970s. MAPA drew attention to language barriers, police brutality, and school segregation, among other issues.

For much of its existence, MAPA's loose organizational structure permitted militant and moderate members to cooperate. In recent times MAPA has been beset by internal strife. At least two causes are at work: an inability to adapt to the challenges of representing a more diverse Latino population, and the widening gap between members favoring aggressive tactics and those favoring self-empowerment through community education. In August 2002 the group's general endorsement convention was canceled owing to threats of violence. Today there are two MAPAs: the first, headed by Ben Benavidez, continues to call itself MAPA; the second, headed by Steven Figueroa, calls itself MAPA Voter Registration Project and Education Corporation.

RELATED ARTICLES

Chicano Movement; Civil Rights; Corona, Humberto; Discrimination; Mexican Americans; Politics, Mexican American; Voting.

FURTHER READING

Carreon, Hector. "The Sad Degeneration of the Mexican-American Political Association (MAPA)." *La Voz de Aztlán* (August 27, 2002) www.aztlan.net/sadmapa.htm

Meier, Matt S., and Margo Gutiérrez. "Mexican American Political Association (MAPA)." In *Encyclopedia of the Mexican American Civil Rights Movement*. Westport, Conn.: Greenwood Press, 2000.

Rosales, F. Arturo. *Chicano! The History of the Mexican American Civil Rights Movement*. 2d rev. ed. Houston, Tex.: Arte Publico Press, 1997.

SELECTED WEB SITE

Mexican American Political Association.
www.mapa.historical_highlights.org

CHRISTOPHER DAVID RUIZ CAMERON

MEXICAN AMERICANS

The historical experience of Mexican Americans (commonly known as Chicanos and Chicanas) in the United States is a complex and heterogeneous one and is characterized by a blend of Western and non-Western cultures. Mexican American culture and identity can be traced to indigenous cultures that predate European arrival to the Americas. The notion of *mestizaje,* or interbreeding in the New World, presents an argument that Mexican American origins are part Indian and part European. In fact two different books have as part of their respective titles "From Indians to Chicanos" and "From Conquistadors to Chicanos." Thus such approaches demonstrate a progeny in which Mexican Americans are represented as both vanquished and conqueror. Still, other scholars argue that small numbers of African, Burmese, Siamese, Indonesian, and Filipino slaves entered as part of the Spanish conquest and colonization of Mexico. More research needs to be conducted in order to explore the impact and contributions of such populations, however slight, on the larger Mexican population.

Some scholars argue that indigenous groups, including Nahuatl (Aztec and Mexica) cultures from Mesoamerica, in present-day Mexico, as well as indigenous cultures from the present-day southwestern United States contributed to the emergence of Chicana and Chicano culture and identity. In the Southwest the process of acculturation resulted in a cultural and ideological *mestizaje,* through which many Indian converts remained physically Indian yet became culturally and at times ideologically Spanish or Mexican. In these ideological cases of *mestizaje,* the Mexicanization of Indians resulted in a repressive inclusion of this subaltern population. That is, inclusion of Indians into colonial Spanish and Mexican institutions and societies usually came with a downward social mobility, the result largely of legislation and social expectations that normalized Eurocentric ideals at the expense of indigenous ones.

The Spanish Mexican Period

Spanish imperial expansion to the northern frontier (including today's U.S. Southwest) was facilitated by assertive and defensive purposes. Various population or settlement campaigns including *entradas* (military expeditions), convict colonies, private colonies, and others were initiated to explore the potential wealth and geopolitical advantages of routes and natural harbors in order to incorporate the region into the developing global economy. On the other hand, such campaigns emerged in direct response to competing colonial interests such as that of the Russians, French, and British.

During the Spanish colonial and Mexican national period (1492–1848), Indians were granted legal rights, yet de facto practices sought to maintain Indians in a subordinate social position. A major rationale for such practices included the infantilization of adult Indians who were commonly referred to as *niños* (children) by Euro-Mexicans, owing to their perceived infantile state of mind. By contrast, elites commonly referred to themselves as *gente de razón* (people of reason). These social designations were part of the attempt to establish a racialized order in which indigenous physical and intellectual characteristics were socially constructed to be perceived as inferior to European ones. Such perceptions guided legislation and other forms of policies that sought to acculturate Indians into the mainstream.

Indians at this time were incorporated into the developing global economy as subjects of the Catholic missions, where they performed different tasks. Despite the popularized mythology of "rugged individualist" cowboys pacifying or civilizing "savage" Indians, the first cowboys in what is now the U.S. West were in fact early Indian *vaqueros,* who tended to cattle and were members of a Spanish cavalry known as the Barcelona Light Cavalry in the 1810s and 1820s, predating the United States Cavalry.

A commission established in 1824 to address the matter of Indians in the present-day Southwest, who were to be affected by the secularization of missions, reported that "the first and most important step that must be taken to lead the Indian to civilization was to teach him the value of his right to own land." The commission later determined that land should be given only to "those Indians who have the necessary disposition and faculties for agricultural work." Indians thus had to adapt to Spanish Mexican notions of economic productivity in order to be elevated from workers to landowners. The fact that this edict became legal doctrine further demonstrates the willingness on the part of Spanish Mexican elites to tolerate perceived racialized differences in exchange for the assimilation of cultural, ideological, and economic values. Moreover, it confirms the institutionalization of one group's values over those of another, subordinate one. The Spanish Mexican period has had a lasting effect on internal ethnic relations among Mexican Americans.

The European American Conquest, 1850–1900

Early scholars argued that Mexican American culture and identity originated as a consequence of the 1846–1848 Mexican War with America. Preludes to the war included the Monroe Doctrine of 1823, which marked Latin America as "off limits" for further European colonization and involved repeated attempts by the United States to purchase parts of Mexico. In fact, in 1835, President Andrew Jackson dispatched a diplomat to Mexico in order to offer $500,000 for the purchase of San Francisco Bay and the northern part of Alta California. Mexico—never having accepted the U.S. annexation of Texas in 1845 and angered by its admission into the Union—chose to fight for its territorial integrity; while the United States rationalized the war through Manifest Destiny, the postulation that the nation was preor-

© GORDON KING/YAKIMA HERALD-REPUBLIC/AP/WIDE WORLD PHOTOS

A customer in Yakima, Washington, waits for a receipt after wiring money home to Mexico. For many Latinos living in the United States, sending money to relatives back home is part of their monthly routine.

dained by God to expand its borders to the Pacific Ocean.

The legacy of Mexican Americans as conquered subjects has been quite diverse. Following the Mexican War many *ricos* (elite, wealthy Mexicans) were part of the various constitutional conventions that established the southwestern states. During the postwar transitional period, elites were actively involved in state legislatures as elected officials. Some, especially those who were enfranchised, accommodated themselves to the new ways. In New Mexico and Texas the alliances between elites and American political and economic interests resulted in political machines that controlled resources and politics.

Another example of accommodation was that of the New Mexican Chicano Rafael Chacón, a career military man whose several campaigns included service in the Mexican Army during the Mexican War and for the Union forces during the Civil War. Among Chacón's rationales for serving in the U.S. Army despite having fought against it during the Mexican War were his sense of professionalism and his belief in honor and chivalry.

Not all *ricos* found accommodation to the new order a viable alternative, however. Some well-off Mexicans, including those who were enfranchised politically and economically, were barred from legal and political participation. For example, in April 1857 Los Angeles supervisor and wealthy landowner Manuel Dominguez was denied the right to testify in court because he was suspected of having Indian blood. In addition to being a wealthy politician, Dominguez had been one of several Californios who participated in drafting the first California constitution.

Dominguez's compatriot Pablo de la Guerra, son of one of the original white settlers of California, was a rich landowner who served as a diplomat during the Mexican and American periods in California as a customs official, senator, and judge. De la Guerra was prosecuted in 1870 by the state of California in *People* v. *de la Guerra* for "attempting to exercise the rights of a white citizen." Thus, although de la Guerra came from a background that, during the Spanish Mexican period, enjoyed the racial designation of whiteness, his status was demoted to that of a person of color during the American period in an attempt to disenfranchise him and others.

In response to repeated attempts at disenfranchisement, de la Guerra's wife, Josefa, filed a lawsuit against the city of Santa Barbara, claiming the latter had unlawfully usurped her land and constructed the city's civic center, including city hall, atop said land without compensating her. She ultimately lost her case and appeal, but the case nonetheless demonstrated her attempt at redress and the complications of conflicting legal traditions (Spanish Mexican and English American) as they pertained to landownership. In a twist of irony, Fiestas, the annual celebration in Santa Barbara that purports to celebrate that city's Spanish heritage, and, in particular, the de la Guerra family, is held on this exact site.

The California Land Act of 1851 eventually dispossessed hundreds of thousands of acreage from landed elite Mexicans. Though Mexicans and Mexican Americans were able to verify land claims, many lost their land because of exorbitant attorney fees and a series of floods that damaged crops and cattle, the major staple of Mexican economy in most regions.

Those Mexican residents who were not wealthy were subjected to laws that were intended to disenfranchise them and simultaneously create exclusive access to economic and political opportunities for westward-migrating white Americans. Demographic displacement also included voluntary repatriation in New Mexico of approximately 1,200 Mexicans to northern Mexico between 1848–1849. In California laws such as the Foreign Miner's Tax of April 13, 1850, during the Gold Rush, placed a $20 monthly tariff on "foreigners." Though ambiguous in its designation of "foreigners," this law affirmed the rights of white Americans to exclude Mexicans, Chinese, and others from public mines and thus denied them access to capital necessary for upward mobility. Perhaps a more significant impact of this law was the rise of vigilante groups in the absence of policing agencies to enforce the law. Nondeputized individuals took the law into their own hands and initiated a period of racial violence that is still the subject of popular folklore and has been glorified if not oversimplified in Hollywood movies.

An Immigrant People, 1900–1930

At the turn of the 20th century, masses of Mexicans immigrated into the United States to work in agricultural and industrial sectors. These newly arrived immigrants joined those of the "conquered" generation, many members of which had experienced social and economic decline. Together the Mexican immigrants and Chicanos formed barrios throughout the Southwest and Midwest during the early 20th century.

The mass migration resulted from "push" and "pull" factors. Push factors included the political and economic instability in Mexico caused by the Mexican Revolution. After Mexican dictator Porfirio Díaz was ousted in 1910, various revolutionary factions—aided in part by competing foreign interest from the United States, England, France, and Germany—continued to battle for control of the country. Such instability and bloodshed caused massive migrations within Mexico as people moved away from rural areas and toward *pueblos* (Spanish colonial towns) and urban *ciudades*. Many Mexicans began to migrate north to the United States in an attempt to get away from the continued violence and lack of stability.

At the same time, numerous Mexicans were drawn to the United States by the promise of jobs and social stability, which constituted "pull" factors. Labor recruiters encouraged Mexicans to immigrate into the United States, and thousands of Mexican immigrants entered through Texas and California in order to work in the fields picking cotton, fruits, vegetables, and nuts. A considerable number of immigrants who entered Texas moved on to the fields in the Midwest, where agricultural work provided an entry point for Mexican laborers into that region. For example, in 1927 the Mexican population in the Midwest was estimated at 63,700, which, during the summer months, increased to 80,000 owing to an increase in farmworkers. This also reflects the seasonality of a good deal of labor, families following crops from the Southwest to the Midwest where Mexican migrant farmworkers picked sugar beets, among other crops.

As Mexican immigrants entered the Midwest, they began to settle there and looked to other, less seasonal forms of employment. Thus Mexican workers entered the railroad industry, steel mills, meatpacking plants, and automobile factories in urban areas, such as Gary, Indiana, and Detroit. The immigrants settled in barrios throughout the Southwest and Midwest. In some states, such as Kansas and parts of California, Mexican railroad workers lived in "boxcar" communities on railroad yards.

Transformed by the areas in which they settled, Mexican immigrants in turn transformed their new environment. They brought with them their music, folklore, and political ideologies, which had lasting consequences; indeed in some areas, cultural continuity persisted. And the mainstream culture was enriched through its borrowing from Chicano music, cuisine, art, and so on.

On the other hand, this period was also characterized by a rent in Mexican patriarchy. Having always resisted patriarchy, young Mexican American women began joining the waged labor force at increased rates. As new wage earners, many of them affirmed their liberty by breaking from traditional household expectations and moving away from home prior to marriage. Expressions of "freedom" were demonstrated in consumer practices that further affirmed their acculturation into American society. Tastes in American-made consumer goods, culture, and the like contributed to an increased Americanization of some members of the Mexican American community. Still, while these young women liberated themselves from patriarchal households, they submerged themselves into another form of oppression, namely as waged workers in a capitalist economy.

The story of Pedro J. González provides a classic if unusual example of a Mexican immigrant. Immortalized by the film *Break of Dawn,* González participated in the Mexican Revolution as part of the forces of Francisco "Pancho" Villa. After his revolutionary activity, González fled to Los Angeles in 1923 in order to spare his life. Once there, he auditioned as a singer for a live program at radio station KMPC, where he was turned away because he sang in Spanish. The persistent singer turned to selling commercials for the Spanish-speaking radio audience. Soon, González was able to convince station management to allow him to have his own show in Spanish, which began at 4:00 A.M.. Along with his group, Los Madrugadores (the Early Risers), he became a local folk hero for his rapid success.

Filled with a social conscience from his days as a revolutionary, González began to address the many injustices against Mexicans through his radio program. For instance, during the 1930s in response to the Great Depression, the INS (Immigration and Naturalization Service) initiated roundups of Mexicans for the purpose of deportation. Such deportations included American-born Mexicans and angered an entire community. During one broadcast González proclaimed that those behind the deportations were "the real criminals. . . . They say that this deportation campaign is to secure jobs for North American citizens. It's a trick. It isn't true. It's really nothing more than a racist attack against all Mexicans. We are neither illegals nor undesirables."

Such pronouncements caught the ire of Los Angeles district attorney Buron Fitts, who later indicted González on trumped-up rape charges; he was falsely convicted of raping a 16-year-old girl, who later recanted her story, claiming that authorities had gotten her to lie about the accusations. González was sent to San Quentin prison for six years. While in prison, steady protests by Mexican residents and protests led by his wife Maria in Los Angeles and abroad brought much publicity to his case.

After his parole the Gonzálezes were deported. On their way to Tijuana, Mexico, González stopped at Los Angeles's Grand Union Station, were he was met by thousands of fans. Prior to the train's leaving, it is reported that he entertained his fans with ballads and other songs for several hours. The Gonzálezes settled in the vicinity of Tijuana and in 1971 were allowed to return to the United States to be reunited with their children. González continued his advocacy until his death in San Diego in 1995 at the age of 99.

A Segregated People

Segregation of Mexican Americans has occurred at the legal and personal levels; thus it has not simply been a matter of separation among groups. Rather, segregation embodied exclusion from participation in public, political, or economic opportunities, which had direct consequences on the distribution of capital, wealth, political access, and educational opportunities.

The development of Mexican immigrant and Chicano communities resulted in a variety of responses by American society, among which was the attempt to establish segregated "Mexican schools" in the early half of the 20th century. The existence of such schools proved to have several consequences. First, they segregated Mexican American schoolchildren on a racial basis. Second, they offered inferior instruction through a curriculum that systemically held lower expectations of Mexican students and tracked them into manual forms of labor. Third, as a direct consequence of a "working-class" curriculum and lowered teacher expectations, the schools were furnished with inferior resources. Fourth, these schools were intended to Americanize Mexican schoolchildren, under the presumption that "American" culture was superior to Mexican culture. And, fifth, several

successful lawsuits were filed by parents and civic organizations, which served as precedents to the historic *Brown* v. *Topeka Board of Education* in 1954.

Indeed, in response to the Mexican schools, Chicanos filed lawsuits to challenge the legality of school segregation. Such cases were filed in Del Rio, Texas (1930); Lemon Grove, California (1931): and Westminster, California (1946). These cases found that Mexican schoolchildren had been unlawfully denied access to equal educational opportunities—equal to those enjoyed by white children. They also helped to set precedents for the above-mentioned landmark federal case *Brown* v. *Topeka Board of Education,* which outlawed school segregation at the federal level.

Housing discrimination also persisted. The application of restrictive covenants prohibited non-Caucasians from buying homes in desirable areas. A major consequence of this practice was the inability by Mexican Americans, among others, to develop capital on equal terms vis-à-vis whites. Despite rhetoric by federal officials regarding the need for equality, many federal laws were left to local enforcement, thereby undermining the intent of equal opportunity laws. As generations passed, wealth was inherited by those whose parents had access to such capital, while disproportionate economic opportunities and poverty were inherited by those whose parents were denied equal access to such capital.

In addition to these segregation practices, Chicanos were prohibited in some areas from swimming in public pools, were relegated to segregated seats in theaters, and were not allowed to frequent restaurants and hotels. Indeed, "No Mexicans Allowed" signs were not uncommon during the era of segregation.

An Integrated People

Mexican Americans worked to integrate themselves into the U.S. mainstream at various levels. Beginning with World War II and through subsequent foreign wars, the level of military participation among Mexican Americans increased as many sought to demonstrate their patriotism, while others simply wanted to demonstrate that despite discriminatory treatment, they, too, were American.

In addition, Chicanos participated in various reformist social movements throughout their history in the United States. Working- and middle-class organizations flourished with particular attention paid to improving the social, economic, political, and cultural conditions of Chicanos. Moreover, Mexican Americans have been central to the development of working-class movements and middle-class civil rights movements.

In response to a tradition of racial exclusion by labor unions, such unions as La Confederación de Uniones de Campesinos y Obreros Mexicanos (CUCOM) and United Cannery, Agricultural, Packing, and Allied Workers of America (UCAPAWA) began to recruit among Mexican American workers in the 1930s. These efforts included, as well, the organizing of Filipino and Japanese workers along with those of other nationalities for better wages and working conditions.

The Asociación Nacional México-Americana (ANMA) was formed during this period. ANMA was organized by militant Mexican and Mexican American unionists who saw a need to address issues beyond labor. Thus their platform included issues such as education, undocumented immigrant rights, housing, political representation, youth-related issues, police brutality, and promotion of Chicano culture. The focus of ANMA shifted attention from localized issues to a more national arena. By 1950 ANMA reached 4,000 members who enlisted in as many as 35 locals through six states.

Professional organizations such as the League of United Latin American Citizens (LULAC), the Mexican American Legal Defense and Education Fund (MALDEF), the National Council of La Raza, the Southwest Voter Registration Project, and others have been central to the development of a national awareness of the plight of Mexican Americans. In many instances such organizations have been at the forefront of public debate and policy formation. Indeed, many of the advances Chicanos have enjoyed are the direct result of organizations such as LULAC and MALDEF.

In contrast to the left-oriented politics of ANMA, these organizations have immersed themselves in mainstream politics. Despite their efforts, however, they have been criticized by some people on the grounds that their corporate sponsorships limit their full potential. For example, certain organizations have been criticized for taking money from alcohol and tobacco corporations, the critics insisting that accepting such money limits the advocacy against tobacco and alcohol abuse in Mexican American and other Latino communities.

On the other hand, those who rationalize such relationships with corporate funding argue that the visibility of issues that are pertinent to Chicanos and other Latinos increases as a result of such funding. In either case, the emergence of Mexican Americans on the national political scene has resulted from years of organizing.

The Chicano movement of the 1960s and 1970s, while seen as a militant revolutionary cause in some contemporary circles, emerged as a reformist movement in retrospect. The cultural renaissance that helped to fuel the movement included advances in the arts, educational achievement, and gains in political representation.

Many of these gains came as a result of affirmative-action programs. Though under attack in recent years, these programs dramatically increased the level of participation of Mexican Americans and other marginalized populations in education, employment, and other areas that brought these groups into the mainstream. It is still too early to determine the actual impact of such programs. For now, it can be said that the Chicano movement and accompanying programs and policies have had diverse consequences. On one hand, more participation in and access to mainstream America has resulted from the movement. On the other hand, critics of the movement's aftermath have decried what they perceive to be the "co-optation" of movement ideals, especially in the area of political representation by elite interests. Whatever the case, such a discussion sheds light on the meaning of democratic reform and the representations of various competing constituencies.

The Urban Experience

Beginning in the 1950s, urban renewal programs attempted to rid cities of perceived "urban blight." In areas such as Los Angeles this became a euphemism for land-use rezoning and the consequent uprooting and dislocation of the Mexican American population. Among the first major projects during this time was the building of the infamous East Los Angeles interchange, which today is one of the most congested freeway intersections in the world. The use of eminent domain helped to clear land in order to build access roads to downtown for mostly white commuters who left the inner city as part of what some call white flight. The community of Boyle Heights, a predominantly Mexican American community in Los Angeles, was dissected by the 5, 10,

Mexican American culture and identity can be traced to indigenous cultures that predate European arrival to the Americas.

60, and 101 freeways. Still another example of urban dislocation for Chicanos was the clearing of the Chavez Ravine neighborhood in order to construct Dodger Stadium and the expansive parking lots that surround it.

Such practices continued until the 1980s, when a group of mothers known as Mothers of East Los Angeles—and, later, Madres del Este de Los Angeles–Santa Isabel (MELASI)—spearheaded a fight against a proposed state prison in their neighborhood. This grassroots movement formalized an informal network of PTA (Parent-Teacher Association) moms, and neighborhood watch organizers whose network extended into the 1960s and 1970s, when their children were young.

The activism and moral outrage of not being taken into account when such land-use decisions were made resonated in the core of mothers, many of whom were uprooted themselves in the 1950s to make way for the freeways. While taking on the state of California against the proposed prison, MELASI began to address other quality-of-life issues, including the attempts to install a pipeline through the middle of East Los Angeles and to build toxic-waste incinerators in nearby industrial areas.

Under the leadership of women such as Juana Beatríz Gutiérrez, Erlinda Robles, Juanita Centeno, and Rosa Villaseñor, the Mothers successfully defeated all of these unwanted projects and became part of national networks for environmental justice. In the process they have helped to transform the political landscape of their cities. The Mothers took a further proactive approach to improving quality of life, including the establishment of a scholarship fund, the creation of a community garden, a graffiti abatement program, lead-paint awareness education, an inoculation program for children without health care, and countless other contributions. It is their legacy that solidifies the plight of Mexican Americans and announces a brighter future.

RELATED ARTICLES

Art, Mexican American and Chicano; Aztlán; Bilingual Education; Bilingualism; Border, United States–Mexico;

Brownness; Catolicos Por La Raza; Chicanismo; Chicano Movement; Chicano Studies; Cinco de Mayo; Corrido; Coyotes; Cuisine, Mexican American; Cuisine, Tex-Mex; Día de la Raza; Día de los Muertos; Durst Ranch Affair; East Los Angeles School Walkout; English as a Second Language; Espiritismo; Farmworkers Movement; Folklore, Mexican American; Gangs; Good Neighbor Policy; Greaser Act; Huelga; Literature, Mexican American; Los Angeles; Low Riders; Mexican American Legal Defense and Education Fund; Mexican American Political Association; Mexican American Unity Council; Milagro Beanfield War; Movimiento Estudantil Chicano de Aztlán; Narcocorrido; National Chicano Moratorium of Vietnam; Operation Wetback; Pachuco; Passing; Politics, Mexican American; Raza Unida Party, La; Spiritual Plan of Aztlán; Zoot Suit Riots.

FURTHER READING

Acuña, Rodolfo. *Occupied America: A History of Chicanos.* 5th ed. New York: Pearson/Longman, 2004.

De la Torre, Adela, and Beatríz Pesquera. *Building with Our Hands: New Directions in Chicana Studies.* Berkeley: Univ. of Calif. Press, 1993.

García, Mario. *Mexican Americans: Leadership, Ideology, and Identity, 1930–1960.* New Haven, Conn.: Yale Univ. Press, 1989.

Menchaca, Martha. *Recovering History, Constructing Race: The Indian, Black, and White Roots of Mexican Americans.* Austin: Univ. of Tex. Press, 2001.

Pérez, Emma. *The Decolonial Imaginary: Writing Chicanas into History.* Bloomington: Ind. Univ. Press, 1999.

Prado, Mary. *Mexican American Women Activists: Identity and Resistance in Two Los Angeles Communities.* Philadelphia: Temple Univ. Press, 1998.

Vargas, Zaragosa. *Major Problems in Mexican American History.* Boston: Houghton Mifflin, 1999.

Vigil, James Diego. *From Indians to Chicanos: The Dynamics of Mexican American Culture.* Prospect Heights, Ill.: Waveland Press, 1984.

GABRIEL GUTIÉRREZ

MEXICAN AMERICAN UNITY COUNCIL

The Mexican American Unity Council (MAUC) is a nonprofit community organization based in San Antonio, Texas. Founded in 1967, MAUC reflects the Chicano movement's commitment to the political and economic well-being of the Latino community. The organization was founded by Charles Cotrell, Juan Patlán, Albert Peña, and William C. Velásquez, active figures in the Chicano movement who forged strong ties between MAUC and other leading Latino advocacy organizations, such as the Mexican American Legal Defense and Education Fund, the National Council of La Raza, and the Southwestern Voter Registration Project.

MAUC was created for the initial purpose of improving economic opportunities in the predominantly Mexican American and low-income communities of west and southwest San Antonio. Many of the organization's early efforts were focused on promoting economic development by raising funds to invest directly in the community. As part of its early strategy, it established a for-profit arm through which to invest venture capital. The money it made was reinvested in community businesses, thus providing the community with a constant flow of capital. Other projects followed a similar strategy of community empowerment. Among its first and most notable projects was the revitalization of Prospect Hill, a historically Latino community suffering from urban decay. MAUC was able to purchase an abandoned elementary school in the neighborhood to use as the new site of its headquarters. It was then able to pump money into the community's economy and provide an incentive to neighborhood residents to follow suit with similar renovation projects.

MAUC also recognized the disastrous side effects of economic inequality. It provided information and advocacy services on a diverse range of matters and set up programs to address mental health and substance abuse issues. In 1975 it established the Child and Family Mental Health Program, offering comprehensive psychiatric treatment to individuals with emotional, behavioral, and substance abuse problems. As part of its effort, MAUC founded Casa del Sol, a bilingual treatment facility for alcohol abuse. Casa del Sol sought to treat substance abuse and its underlying causes by offering patients medical services as well as counseling, economic support, and vocational rehabilitation. MAUC's programs also targeted Latino youth and, in 1979, operated the Youth Community Conservation and Improvement Program. Working with the Department of Housing and Urban Development, MAUC and other organizations offered employment training and jobs to local at-risk youth.

Continuing to address issues affecting the Latino population, in July 2003 MAUC joined the National Council of La Raza and other community-based organizations in launching a state program aimed at offering alternatives to incarceration for nonviolent, low-level offenders. The program was part of an effort to reduce the disparity in the criminal justice system and lower the disproportionate number of Latino and African American inmates in prison.

Through the decades, the various efforts of the Mexican American Unity Council have helped raise awareness of the issues affecting the Latino community.

RELATED ARTICLES

Chicano Movement; Mexican American Legal Defense and Education Fund; National Council of La Raza; Politics, Mexican American.

FURTHER READING

Martinez, Douglas R. "Hispanic Youth Employment: Programs and Problems." *Agenda: A Journal of Hispanic Issues* 9, no. 1 (1979): 14–16.

Saavedra-Vela, Pilar. "Unity Brings Hope to the San Antonio Barrio." *Agenda: A Journal of Hispanic Issues* 8, no. 4 (1978): 23–26.

SELECTED WEB SITE

Hispanic Research Center. "Personal Papers of Judge Albert Peña." Making Connections.
http://hrc.utsa.edu/hrc/archives_pena.htm

LUPE GARCÍA

MEXICAN-AMERICAN WAR

Although it is often overlooked in discussions of major military conflicts in which the United States of America was involved, the Mexican-American War had a significant impact on the geography and demography of the United States. While casualties were low, the result was the transfer of hundreds of thousands of acres of territory to the United States, including warm-water ports in the Pacific and millions of dollars in gold bullion extracted from California's mines, and, particularly, a transfer of population and a transformation of southwestern sensibility from the centuries-old Spanish, Creole, and mestizo (mixed-blood) population to the sovereignty of the Anglo-dominated United States of America.

The war was fought between 1846 and 1848; however, its origins lie in the 1820s and 1830s, particularly with the articulation by James Monroe in his second inaugural of the doctrine of European nonintervention in the Americas. This bold challenge to European colonialism by a relatively young nation evolved into the concept of Manifest Destiny by which the United States of America was "destined" to rule from sea to sea. The concept was outlined by many politicians in the 1820s and early 1830s but given its final name in 1845 by John L. O'Sullivan, editor of the *Democratic Review*; it resonates to the contemporary era in such conflicts as the wars in Vietnam and Iraq.

A second condition that played a major role in bringing about the war was the ongoing conflict in the federal legislatures over which states and territories would allow slavery. In 1835 Texas, after an influx of many Anglo-Americans, had declared independence from Mexico, which brought about a war of rebellion between Texans and Mexicans and finally ended with Texas's independence after the famous battle of the Alamo mission, a massacre of Texan troops at Goliad, and a decisive victory by Sam Houston over Antonio López de Santa Anna at San Jacinto. When in the early 1840s both the United States and Texas governments made overtures about Texas's becoming a state, the Republic became a political crucible for pro- and antislavery forces in Washington.

Historians suspect that when James Polk became president in March 1845, he had already decided that the United States should stretch from the Atlantic to the Pacific, and he coveted Mexican territory north of the Rio Grande. This led him to the annexation of Texas, to provoke a border conflict with an unstable Mexican government and then to destabilize the democratically elected government in Mexico. In an 11th-hour maneuver, on the eve of the end of his presidency, Polk's lame duck predecessor, John Tyler, offered to annex Texas, but Polk could have withdrawn the offer had he seen fit. On July 4 Texas accepted, enraging the Mexican government, which feared U.S. expansionism. The U.S. government further provoked the Mexican government by insisting that the Texas-Mexico border lay along the Rio Grande, while the Mexicans insisted it stood at the Rio Nueces, about 20 miles (32 km) to the north.

In June 1845, as anger at the U.S. offer of annexation and fear of its hegemony grew, the Mexican government refused to allow Polk's envoy, John Slidell, to enter the country. At the same time Polk ordered General Zachary Taylor, the future president of the United States, to move his troops to southern Texas and to secure ports in the Gulf of Mexico. The new Mexican government under Manuel Paredes responded, and by the beginning of 1846, both sides had stationed forces on either side of the contested border. An uneasy truce resulted until, after several changes of Mexican command, on April 25, 1846, General Mariano Arista sent a small force across the river, where it was surrounded by the American army, and all its troops were taken prisoner.

News of the opening of hostilities took two weeks to reach Washington, D.C., where outrage erupted; Congress declared war in early May 1846. According to most observers at the time, the United States had a military force inadequate to the task of fighting the Mexicans, and many European commentators noted from the first that the Mexican army would easily overrun the Americans, though at the begin-

Painting shows General Porfirio Díaz leading the Juarez army to victory at Puebla, May 5, 1862.

ning of the war, the U.S. government quickly expanded its military strength. As hostilities progressed, the American military decided on a combined policy of invasions and blockades. The army would push south from Texas and other border states, and the navy would block entrances and exits in ports in the Gulf of Mexico and the Pacific.

In the meantime Mexico's presidents were changing. Many Mexicans attributed the inability to meet the American threat or to find a diplomatic solution short of war to presidential inexperience, incompetence, or corrupt self-interest. Faced with American aggression, the legislature recalled former president General Antonio López de Santa Anna from disgraced exile in Havana, the same Santa Anna who had defeated Anglo-Texan and Texas Mexican troops during the Texas Rebellion. During that conflict he had won the Battle of the Alamo, where he had earned the enmity of many Anglo-Americans and Texas Mexicans because of his cruelty, had ordered the slaughter of Texan prisoners of war after the battle of Goliad, and had been defeated at San Jacinto. In the end, however, Mexico lost the war for Texas, which then became an independent republic.

After the declaration of war, from north of the Rio Grande, Taylor advanced south and west through Matamoros. On September 23, after a long march, several bombardments of the city, and subsequent infantry attacks, he then took the city of Monterrey. With the American advance only lightly checked by Mexican troops, Santa Anna decided to confront Taylor at the town of Buena Vista, where he marshaled tens of thousands of Mexican troops. After a pitched battle Taylor's forces defeated those of Santa Anna, and Buena Vista became one of the decisive battles of the Mexican-American War, allowing Taylor to consolidate territorial control north of Mexico City. At the same time, Commodore P. S. P. Conner attacked the Gulf Coast city of Tampico from the sea, which gave the Americans control of important Mexican ports, and forces under the command of Brigadier General Stephen W. Kearny in New Mexico and Commodore Robert Stockton in California occupied those territories. Among the four, all of northern Mexico had been secured.

The next step for the Americans was to invade Mexico City itself. Under the command of General Winfield Scott, they sailed south from near Tampico to a site on the Gulf Coast near Vera Cruz, consolidated their positions, and then headed inland toward the capital—along a similar route taken by Hernán Cortés more than three centuries earlier—and a confrontation with Santa Anna, who had assured his countrymen he would turn back the threat. Despite his preparations, Santa Anna was defeated, and on September 14, 1847, the American flag was raised over the city. The Americans occupied Mexico City and held the government and its people hostage, though for a brief period of time resistance continued from pockets of the Mexican Army and local citizenry. Santa Anna resigned the presidency, though he would return several times for short stints until his ultimate political defeat later that year.

Despite these military victories, the war was unpopular in the United States—heavy taxes were levied to support the military—where it was often called "Mr. Polk's War," particularly by representatives of the Whig Party whose candidate, Henry Clay, Polk had defeated at the polls in 1844. The Congress and Senate, especially antislavery and antitaxation forces who believed Polk was more interested in expanding slavery and U.S. territory than in the merits of the conflict itself, were vehemently opposed. Newspaper editorials on both sides fanned the flames of the conflict. Finally, with little more to gain by remaining in the Mexican capital as an occupying force, Polk sent envoys to broker a treaty. In fact, throughout much of the war, its unpopularity at home led Polk to negotiate a peace with a series of Mexican presidents, to no avail. Early in the war, however, before he had sufficient leverage, these attempts may have been half-hearted; now that his troops had occupied the capital, he was able to dictate terms to a Mexican government in disarray.

In the fall of 1847, as the United States began to gain the upper hand, in order to negotiate favorable peace terms with Mexico, Polk selected the chief clerk of the State Department, Nicholas Trist. Trist immediately ran into problems over whom to deal with, now that Santa Anna was again disgraced. During the subsequent few months, Trist made little progress on a treaty, and Polk recalled him, reasoning that Mexico was now a defeated nation and should be forced to approach Washington to sue for terms. However, it took six weeks for the message to reach Trist, during which time he was able to negotiate a treaty with the Mexican government. On February 2, 1848, Trist signed the Treaty of Guadalupe Hidalgo, which effectively ended the war on highly favorable terms to the American government.

This put Polk in an odd position: he had received a treaty from an aide whom he had recalled prior to the signing of that treaty. However, rather than reject it, he decided to send it to Congress with the tacit understanding that Mexico was now a defeated country and that terms could be dictated, as far as the political climate would allow.

According to the treaty, the Mexican government was forced to cede about half its territory, which now makes up the states of New Mexico, Arizona, California, Utah, Colorado, Nevada, and parts of Wyoming. In return, Mexico would receive $15 million and protection for its citizens in the newly purchased territories. In fact, the United States Senate rejected Article X of the treaty, thereby removing most of the property protections and, in the end, many Mexican landowners lost their lands. Former Mexican citizens were invited to remain in the newly acquired American territories, supposedly with all the personal protections of American citizens, though in practice this was not generally the case. Gold was discovered in California just after the treaty's signing, and the hundreds of millions of dollars in gold dust extracted from its hills and valleys dwarfed the American payments to the Mexican government as part of the settlement. After the treaty was ratified, American troops withdrew to their own soil, which now extended from the Atlantic to the Pacific, and included hundreds of thousands of former Mexican residents. The Mexican government, unhappy over the deletion of Article X, asked the American government to reconsider protections for former Mexican citizens, and in May 1848, in order to remedy this situation, representatives of both governments signed the Protocol of Queretaro. The American government later rejected this agreement as well.

The Latino population of the United States of America until that time was limited to scattered pockets in the Northeast, South, and Midwest. However, with the defeat of the Mexican army and the cession to the United States of what had been previously Mexican land, the American polity would later change to reflect new Mexican American cultural attributes, including place names, an artificial national border and cross-border family connections, and the introduction of a language bloc. Mexican American alienation from the dominant Anglo-American culture was later reflected in the re-creation of a metaphor of a homeland, the mythical Aztlán; in the late 20th century some Mexican Americans designated the American Southwest as "occupied America." Many historians have also suggested that the United States's war with Mexico, and its subsequent treatment of Mexico as an "inferior nation," is a partial cause of the ongoing instability of the government of Mexico itself and an indirect cause of later large-scale political and economic migrations from the south to the United States, particularly during and after the Mexican Revolution in 1910 and in the post–World War II period.

On the other hand, the war did little to solve the slavery question, which would erupt only 13 years later in the War between the States. Military techniques and careers that developed during the war were widely employed on those battlefields, and historians have noted that the Mexican-American War was like a dress rehearsal for that conflict.

RELATED ARTICLES

Arizona; Border, United States–Mexico; California; Californios; Guadalupe Hidalgo, Treaty of; Manifest Destiny; Mexico; New Mexico; Protocol of Queretaro; Texas; United States–Mexico Relations.

FURTHER READING

Bauer, K. Jack. *The Mexican War, 1846–1848.* New York: Macmillan, 1947.

Bergeron, Paul H. *The Presidency of James K. Polk.* Lawrence: Univ. Press of Kans., 1987.

Brack, Gene M. *Mexico Views Manifest Destiny, 1821–1846: An Essay on the Origins of the Mexican War.* Albuquerque: Univ. of N.Mex. Press, 1975.

Eisenhower, John S. D. *So Far from God: The U.S. War with Mexico 1846–1848.* New York: Random House, 1989.

Singletary, Otis A. *The Mexican War.* Chicago: Univ. of Chicago Press, 1960.

Smith, Justin H. *The War with Mexico.* New York: Macmillan, 1919.

Weems, John Edward. *To Conquer a Peace: The War between the United States and Mexico.* New York: Doubleday, 1974.

Winders, Richard Bruce. *Mr. Polk's Army: The American Military Experience in the Mexican War.* College Station: Texas A&M Univ. Press, 1997.

HAROLD AUGENBRAUM

MEXICAN REVOLUTION

The Mexican Revolution (1910–1920) was a series of social and political upheavals and popular rebellions that produced fundamental changes in Mexico and established many important themes and trends that still resonate in Latino society today. One of the most important themes of the revolution was that *los de abajo* (the downtrodden and dispossessed) could have a voice and power if they organized themselves and fought centralized government for what they wanted. Yet these mass political and military movements, personified by Francisco "Pancho" Villa and Emiliano Zapata, took on a logic of their own, beyond the control of well-intentioned and idealistic elites. These movements also found it difficult to compromise their localized goals and were not interested in or capable of seizing national power. *Los de arriba* (the elite in power, or those wanting to displace an older generation in power) soon allied themselves with reactionary forces (Francisco Madero with Victoriano Huerta) to control the plebian "storm" engulfing the country. But the eventual victors, Venustiano Carranza and Alvaro Obregón, were pragmatic and often ruthless revolutionaries who were able to take advantage of divisions between mass movements and form effective political alliances for national power.

At the end of the 19th century, Porfirio Díaz—who fought against the French as a liberal during the 1860s and who eventually defeated his fellow liberals, including Benito Juárez, during the 1870s—inaugurated a powerful dictatorship that deftly created and maintained political and economic alliances with other elites throughout Mexico. During the Porfiriato (1876–1910), a national political stability was achieved from the center, through client relationships between Díaz and regional *jefe políticos,* such as Luis García Pimentel, a sugar planter from Morelos, and Luis Terrazas, a cattle rancher from Chihuahua. These plutocrats benefited not only from the nationalization and centralization of the Mexican government but also from the integration of the Mexican economy into the world economy. Instead of being a hodgepodge of regions with little economic relation to each other or to potential export markets, Mexico became increasingly connected internationally through a national railway system that was a priority during the Porfiriato.

But these very same successes, for the benefit of a few, created the groundwork for the tumultuous decade after 1910. Many of the state governors and other political elites were old men at the eve of the revolution; Díaz himself was 78 in 1908. So there was little political turnover and there were no concrete plans for political succession to allow a new generation to take control of Mexico. Also, newly appointed governors, including Enrique Creel in Chihuahua in 1904 and Pablo Escandón in Morelos in 1909, were political neophytes who aggravated social tensions by ignoring and then destroying traditional relationships with villages. Most important, social and political tensions were reaching a high point because of the integration of the Mexican economy into the world economy and the rapid centralization of political power. In the south, the ancient communal lands of villages were often arbitrarily and brutally usurped by vast haciendas, which had become economic enterprises focused on the export market. In Chihuahua, Creel passed laws that replaced municipally elected officials with his own appointments and that allowed the sale and expropriation of land belonging to free villages to outsiders.

Into this tense and already violent milieu, Porfirio Díaz granted a widely publicized interview, in February 1908, to James Creelman, in which the old dictator mused about retiring in 1910 and not running for reelection, and invited an opposition party to participate in "free" elections. Although Díaz had not been serious about his promises, he unwittingly released a small tremor in the political landscape that soon became an earthquake. The gutsy Francisco I. Madero—the son of a wealthy, northern Mexican family who owned cotton plantations, mines, and textile factories—took up the liberal cause for free elections and against the "boss rule" of the Porfiriato. As his Anti-Reelectionist Party campaigned throughout the country in 1909, Madero gained adherents among some of the liberal elite, in the urban middle and working classes, and even in the countryside. The democratic movement endured increasing persecution, fraudulent elections in 1910 (when Díaz scored another landslide victory for the presidency), and finally the arrest and exile of Madero. But the fragile façade of the Porfiriato had already irreparably cracked. What was politically possible had been collectively seized in the air. Long-standing grievances against arbitrary land seizures, corrupt politicians, and even excessive taxation had surfaced and coalesced at regional and national levels. Madero called for an armed revolt from his base in Texas. As federal troops fought regional *caudillos* (military leaders) and their village armies, political riots broke out in Mexico City and other communities. Revolutionary forces seized the border city of Juárez, and Madero declared it the provisional capital of Mexico. Díaz resigned from the presidency in May 1911 and boarded a ship at Veracruz to escape the chaos.

Two critical focal points of this early part of the revolution (1911–1912) were Morelos in the south and Chihuahua in the north. Zapata was fighting on behalf of the villages of Morelos, to gain back the lands taken unjustly by the haciendas and to establish a political system that would not revert to the destruction of traditional village life. His revolution was a class warfare between peasant farmers and the landed elite. In November 1911, Zapata's principles were spelled out clearly in his Plan de Ayala: fundamental agrarian reform must be implemented locally, by local authorities, and not by outsiders bent on betraying the revolution. For Zapata, Madero's Plan de San Luis Potosi—which had earlier denounced Porfirio Díaz, called for free elections, and declared Madero to be provisional president—seemed at first only a start, and then a liberal betrayal of promises for fundamental change. The revolution was not over simply because Madero had replaced Díaz and his cronies with other elites now demanding disarmament and the reestablishment of order. In Chihuahua, Pascual Orozco conducted the largest northern army at the time of Díaz's resignation, and gave impetus to the Maderista revolution just when it might have failed to topple the dictator. With armies of miners, railwaymen, muleteers, ranchers, lumberjacks, and other tough men of the northern sierra, Orozco and Villa fought against the oppressive Terraza regime and its *jefe políticos*.

But while Villa, out of personal loyalty to Madero (whom he admired for his education and courage), supported the newly elected liberal president, Orozco refused to disarm and fought against Villa at Parral; he was finally defeated by federal armies in May 1912. Madero relied increasingly on Victoriano Huerta to gain control of the country and secure his liberal victory, but Huerta was a ruthless military man from the Porfiriato who was sympathetic to the conservative elite appalled at the "dirt" that had risen to the top during the revolution. Moreover, Madero began to implement policies that undermined the most fundamental changes in agrarian reform and local political control. Thus, conservative elements made a comeback, with Madero acquiescing to Huerta's ferocious campaigns against Zapata and Orozco. Fellow revolutionaries also abandoned Madero for his tepid reforms, and such leaders as Venustiano Carranza, the governor of Coahuila, did not trust Madero's weak resolve to deal with the conservative opposition once and for all. The culmination of these events

THE GRANGER COLLECTION

María Gutierrez, one of Pancho Villa's lieutenants during the Mexican Revolution.

was the Decena Trágica of February 1913, when Huerta led a military coup that toppled the liberal government, and Madero was assassinated in Mexico City.

Huerta's counterrevolution, with its military persecution and draconian policies, reunited and reinvigorated the old Madero alliance against him. While Zapata gathered his forces in the hills of Morelos for strikes against Huerta's federal army in the villages and towns, Villa scored his most spectacular victories of the revolution against Huerta in the north. In October 1913, Villa's troops captured the strategic city of Torreón, and Villa further organized not only his División del Norte but also the administration of the territory under his control. Then, in November, Villa employed an unorthodox but brilliant military strategy to take the important border city of Juárez: after intercepting a federal supply train, Villa loaded this "Trojan horse" with his own troops and stunned Huerta's federal garrison into surrender, capturing scores of prisoners and tons of ammunition. Later that month, at Tierra Blanca, where a federal force of 7,000 had regrouped to take back Juárez, Rodolfo Fierro, a Villa lieutenant, sent a locomotive loaded with dynamite—*a máquina loca*—crashing into the federal army train. Simultaneously Villa and his cavalry attacked the enemy flanks. The federals panicked and retreated. Later, after shooting the captured federal officers, Villa celebrated at a tumultuous fiesta in Juárez. By April 1914, Villa and his jubilant but exhausted troops had demolished the federal army in the north. Meanwhile, Alvaro Obregón, the revolutionary general from Sonora who had become Carranza's ally, slowly and methodically professionalized his fighting force and chose only limited battles against Huerta's troops, a strategy that would leave Obregón in good shape for the coming battle of winners. Victoriano Huerta finally resigned from the presidency in July 1914 and fled the country.

At crucial moments during the revolution, both Villa and Zapata refused to solidify their military positions with bids to take over Mexico City and establish national political power. For different reasons, these revolutionary *caudillos* distrusted city mores and sophistication, and maybe distrusted themselves in an environment of political negotiation and compromise. Zapata fought for the villages of Morelos and the principles of the Plan de Ayala, while Villa fought for the people of Chihuahua and their freedom. But this loyalty to place and culture not only made them more representative of *los de abajo,* but it also prevented a real, coordinated alliance between Zapata and Villa, and encouraged their self-limitation, amid victory, to the places that mattered the most to them. Thus, in the summer of 1914 it was Obregón who marched triumphantly into Mexico City and began to neutralize the isolated Zapata with remnants of the federal army and his forces.

Despite the convening of a constitutional convention in Mexico City to codify and legitimize the political gains of the Mexican Revolution in late 1914, it was military power and position that would ultimately determine who would win and what the terms of victory would be. While the astute Carranza proclaimed social and political reforms to gain crucial allies and co-opt enemies, Obregón undertook a systematic military strategy of focusing his forces on limited fronts to enhance his national military supremacy. These "Constitutionalist" leaders, from Coahuila and Sonora, would also not make the mistakes Madero made: whoever did not support their revolutionary effort was to be encircled and then eliminated.

Free to more or less ignore Zapata by early 1915, Obregón prepared for the final series of battles against Villa. Obregón won the military support of urban workers from La Casa del Obrero Mundial, concentrated his military forces, and chose the time and place of battle in central Mexico, at Celaya in April 1915. After stretching Villa's supply and communication lines, but not his own, Obregón arrayed his forces behind canals and ditches and withstood Villa's famed assaults. At crucial moments Obregón repeatedly unleashed his reserve forces onto Villa's flanks, and the Villistas, without a reserve, exhausted and confused and not as disciplined as Obregón's army, were disseminated. In May at León, Obregón's forces again took up a defensive position while the Villistas regrouped for an attack, to avenge Celaya. But while Obregón lost his right arm at León, he again won a pivotal battle of the Mexican Revolution by enduring Villa's successive assaults, draining his power and ammunition, and then systematically counterattacking with well-supplied reserves. At the battles of Celaya, León, and finally, Aguascalientes in July 1915, about 20,000 men died in combat, two-thirds of them Villistas, and the División del Norte ceased being a threat to national power.

The Constitution of 1917, and the use of its radical articles (Articles 27 and 123) to gain political support for the Constitutionalists, exemplified how Carranza and Obregón were more able to broker political and military deals at a national level, appeal to exhausted combatants in the countryside as well as the emerging working class in the cities, and form and manipulate effective bureaucracies for their benefit. Eventually, a systematic and professional military force defeated charismatic but chaotic *caudillos,* and a somewhat reformist regime began to channel the unleashed demands of *los de abajo* into official government policy. But much of what the Mexican Revolution fundamentally changed was unofficial: a new elite became at least aware of the suffering and grievances of *los de abajo* and wary of their potential power; a new history of violent confrontation, especially in rural Mexico, reformed centuries-old traditions and relationships; and the new political imperative became an attempt to channel popular grievances first, instead of simply ignoring or brutally suppressing them immediately. Carranza assumed the presidency in 1917, and three years later Obregón overthrew Carranza, who was subsequently killed. And so ended the first major revolution of the 20th century.

Throughout the Mexican Revolution the strategic role of the border region, particularly the cities of Juárez and El Paso, meant that the influences of the revolution also crossed international boundaries to reach Mexican Americans. Revolutionaries including Madero, Orozco, Villa, and Carranza used the El Paso–Juárez area to gain money, arms, and even combatants for their armies. Attacks against Mexicans and Mexican Americans in El Paso by American military forces bent on selectively enforcing neutrality laws, and by Americans fearful of the radical politics of the revolution, further politicized parts of the Mexican American community. Finally, the social and economic chaos of the revolution provoked many more Mexicans to immigrate to the United States. By 1920, Mexicans in El Paso became the majority of the city's population. Exodus from Mexico, which affected the entire American Southwest, continued long after 1920, when Mexico was mired in an economic depression and continued political upheaval, while the United States enjoyed an economic resurgence.

Beyond the reform in elite attitudes toward *los de abajo,* the change in social relationships in rural Mexico, and the transformation of the state to an organization that was somewhat responsive to, and often manipulative of, popular demands, the ten traumatic years of the Mexican Revolution created other important themes that still resonate in the Mexican American community today. A sympathy for the dispossessed and the downtrodden also included the realization that *los de abajo* had lost the revolution. Thus on the one hand, a romanticism arose for the causes of Villa and Zapata, but on the other hand, a lingering sense of their tragic fate also took hold. *Los de abajo* rose to temporary glory because of who they were, and what they sincerely believed, but they also lost, in large part, because of their own limitations and how they were rooted to the people and places they loved. Sometimes a sense of defeatism also surfaced, one in which others—especially the United States, with its military aggression or often xenophobic culture—became the "bogeymen" preventing ultimate success. The subsequent "revolutionary"

government in Mexico, with its manipulation of popular demands and its "institutional revolution," also engendered a distrust of elections and the political process and a reliance on political machinations and connections to effect real change. But at the beginning of the 21st century, Mexico has changed once again: recent democratic elections, for the first time since the Mexican Revolution, removed the official political party from the presidency and many governorships. And so a new era of self-determination and real democratic pluralism and debate may be at hand in Mexico.

RELATED ARTICLES

Mexico; Villa, Francisco; Zapata, Emiliano.

FURTHER READING

Azuela, Mariano. *The Underdogs: A Novel of the Mexican Revolution.* Intro. by Ilan Stavans. New York: Modern Library, 2002 [a new rendition, with notes, by Beth E. Jörgensen, based on the E. Munguía, Jr., translation].
García, Mario T. *Desert Immigrants: The Mexicans of El Paso, 1880–1920.* New Haven: Yale Univ. Press, 1981.
Katz, Friedrich. *The Life and Times of Pancho Villa.* Stanford, Calif.: Stanford Univ. Press, 1998.
Knight, Alan. *The Mexican Revolution: Porfirians, Liberals and Peasants.* Vol. 1. Cambridge: Cambridge Univ. Press, 1986.
Knight, Alan. *The Mexican Revolution: Counter-revolution and Reconstruction.* Vol. 2. Cambridge, England: Cambridge Univ. Press, 1986.
Smith, Peter H. *Labyrinths of Power: Political Recruitment in Twentieth Century Mexico.* Princeton, N.J.: Princeton Univ. Press, 1979.
Womack, John, Jr. *Zapata and the Mexican Revolution.* New York: Vintage Bks., 1968.

SERGIO TRONCOSO

MEXICO

It is often said that the United States and Mexico are not two distant neighbors, but close friends who have much in common and who need each other. Americans' interest in the history of Mexico is largely a result of the presence in the United States of millions of Mexican immigrants, some of them the descendants of the Mexicans who arrived in Texas around 1836 and in 1848 in the Southwest. With few exceptions, and especially since the 1960s, Mexican Americans have searched for their roots and identity in the cultures of Mexico. It is for these reasons, as well as the important trade and cultural relations existing between the two countries, that Mexico's history is so important to all Americans.

Origins

By coming north, Mexican immigrants have reversed the pilgrimage of their ancestors, the Aztecs, who, led by their god Huitzilopochtli, abandoned their place of origin, Aztlán, in search of the promised land somewhere in the south. They found it in the Valley of Anáhuac, and there they built, on an island in the center of Lake Texcoco in the year 1325, their cultural center, Tenochtitlán, today Mexico City. At first persecuted, the Aztecs soon were able to conquer most of the other peoples who had earlier settled in the valley, establishing an empire that included most of what is today central Mexico as well as parts of Central America. The only people who competed with them were the Maya of Yucatán, who had writing, mathematics (use of the concept zero), and an advanced astronomical system, as demonstrated by the various codices and stella, and after the Spanish conquest by the histories of several Spanish friars, among them Fray Bernardino de Sahagún, Fray Diego Durán, Motolinía, and Torquemada.

Colonial Mexico

The cultural development achieved by the Aztecs under Moctezuma and the Maya in their city-states came to an end on August 13, 1521, with the imprisonment of Cuauhtémoc, the last *tlatoani* (king; literally "he who speaks") of the Aztecs. The Spanish conqueror Hernán Cortés was able to defeat the Aztecs with the aid of firearms and horses; the help of the Tlaxcalans, enemies of the Aztecs; and the presence of the translators La Malinche (baptized as Doña Marina) and Jerónimo de Aguilar. Although Tenochtitlán was destroyed, Cortés chose to rebuild it and made it the capital of the conquered territories, which he named New Spain. A contemporary Chicano dramatist, Luis Valdez, in one of his *Actos*, the puppet show "La conquista de México" (1968, 1971), attributes the defeat of the Aztecs to their not being united, a fact he uses to urge the California *campesinos* (field workers) to join César Chávez's United Farm Workers union.

The desire to expand the conquered land resulted in the undertaking of new expeditions, south of what is now Central and South America and north of what is now the U.S. South and Southwest. A Spanish exploration sent to Florida from Cuba, under the command of Pánfilo de Narváez, was less successful than that of Cortés: Narváez's fleet was destroyed by a storm. Four of the survivors, Alvar Núñez Cabeza de Vaca, Diego Dorantes, Alonso del Castillo, and the black man Estevánico, crossed the continent on foot in a long and perilous journey from Texas to Sonora. Although this early history is speculative, it is believed that once in Mexico, Cabeza de Vaca, the author of the chronicle *Naufragios y relación* (1541), gave an exaggerated oral report of the richness of the region. He spoke about people living in structures of four and five stories high who traded in emeralds and turquoise. Antonio de Mendoza, first viceroy (1535–1550), believing Cabeza de Vaca's glowing oral report, organized an expedition under the command of Fray Marcos de Niza to explore what is now the state of New Mexico. Niza's vivid imagination led him to believe, as he told Mendoza in his report, *Descubrimiento de las siete ciudades* (Discovery of the Seven Cities, 1539), that what he had found were the mythical seven cities, with Cíbola as its capital, a city he compared in grandeur to Tenochtitlán. Other *entradas* (expeditions) followed, all looking in vain for rich mythical cities. The most important were those of Francisco Vázquez de Coronado (1540–1542), documented by Pedro Castañeda de Nájera in his own *Relación de la jornada a Cíbola*; and Juan de Oñate to New Mexico in 1598, accompanied by the poet Gaspar Pérez de Villagrá, author of the *Historia de la Nueva México* (1610), considered to be, although written in verse, the first history of a state of the Union. With Gaspar de Portalá's expedition to California came Fray Junípero Serra, the founder of the missions. Descendants of these early settlers have lived uninterruptedly in these lands.

Colonial Mexico became the *crisol* (crucible) in which the character of the Mexican nation and its people was formed. The creation of the *raza mestiza* (mixed race) began with the two sons of Cortés and La Malinche. The presence of another racial group, the Africans (brought as slaves), gave rise to what José Vasconcelos was later to call "the cosmic race." There were also the *criollos* (American-born Spanish), who dominated culturally during the colonial period and even today constitute Mexico's elite. Along with the *conquistadores* (conquerors) came the friars, who established colleges (the first in Tlatelolco in 1536), introduced the printing press and published the first book in the Americas in 1539, and founded the university in 1553. The *criollos* produced three outstanding writers: the dramatist Juan Ruiz de Alarcón (1580–1639), who competed with the great Golden Age dramatists in Spain; Sor Juana Inés de la

Cruz (1648–1695), the first feminist of the Americas and author of one of Mexico's great poems, *Primero sueño* (First dream, circa 1685); and the scholar Carlos de Sigüenza y Góngora (1645–1700), the author of *Infortunios de Alonso Ramírez* (1690), considered to be a forerunner of the novel, and a journalistic narrative, *Mercuio Volante* (Flying Mercury, 1693), about the reconquest of New Mexico by Don Diego de Vargas in 1692. (The story was re-created by Fray Angélico Chávez in his novel *La Conquistadora* [1954].) An aspect of religious *mestizaje* is the Virgin of Guadalupe, who appeared in Tepeyac in 1531 to an Indian, Juan Diego, and was recently made a saint by the pope. The mestizos, and not the *criollos* or Indians, were later to predominate, and Mexico today is considered to be a mestizo nation. Indian cultures, however, have not disappeared. The English historian Arnold J. Toynbee gives Mexico as an example of how one culture can substitute another; however, when he visited Mexico he realized

that he had been mistaken, since he could see that the Indian past had not disappeared. The theme of the presence of Indian cultures in contemporary Mexico has been treated by Carlos Fuentes in his fiction.

From Independence to 1847

Inspired by the independence of the United States in 1776, the French revolution of 1789, and the invasion of Spain by Napoleon in 1805, a group of *criollos* led by Father Miguel Hidalgo began to plan for Mexico's independence. The armed struggle, however, did not start until the night of September 15, 1810. Although Hidalgo was imprisoned and executed in 1811, the fight continued, led by José María Morelos (1765–1815), Vicente Guerrero (1782–1831), and others. It was not, however, until 1821 that independence from Spain was finally achieved. In 1822 Agustín de Iturbide, instrumental in obtaining Mexico's independence, declared himself em-

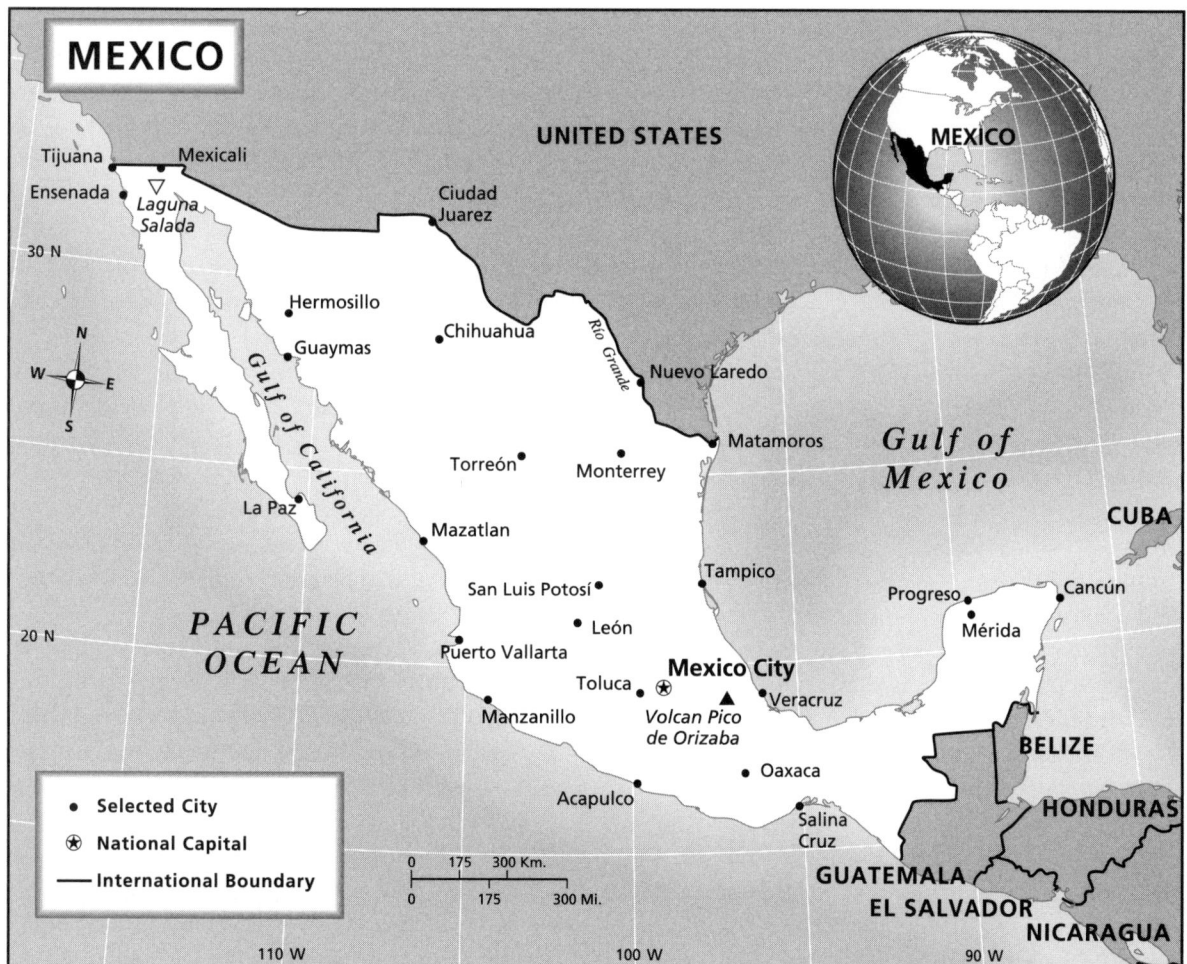

MEXICO

UNITED STATES

Tijuana • Mexicali
Ensenada • ▽ *Laguna Salada*
Ciudad Juarez
30 N
Hermosillo •
• Guaymas
Chihuahua •
Rio Grande
Nuevo Laredo •
• Matamoros
Torreón • Monterrey •
La Paz •
Mazatlan •
San Luis Potosí •
• León
PACIFIC OCEAN
20 N
Puerto Vallarta •
Manzanillo •
Toluca •
Mexico City ⊛
Volcan Pico de Orizaba ▲
Veracruz
Tampico •
Progreso • Cancún •
Mérida •
• Oaxaca
Acapulco •
Salina Cruz
BELIZE
HONDURAS
GUATEMALA
EL SALVADOR
NICARAGUA

Gulf of California

Gulf of Mexico

CUBA

MEXICO

• Selected City
⊛ National Capital
— International Boundary

0 175 300 Km.
0 175 300 Mi.

110 W   100 W   90 W

peror, thus postponing the creation of a federal government until his abdication the following year. The United States, under President Monroe, recognized Mexico and named Joel R. Poinsett as its first minister. He is remembered for having brought to the United States the red Mexican Christmas plant that bears his name and for having founded in Mexico the York Rite Masons.

In 1823, the year that Guadalupe Victoria (1786–1843) was elected president, a federal form of government was established, and a constitution, similar to that of the United States, was approved. The conservatives, who preferred a centralized system, rejected the federal republic. In June 1829 Spain tried to reconquer Mexico and sent an army under the command of Isidro Barradas, who was defeated by Antonio López de Santa Anna. From that year on, this *caudillo* (military leader) was to dominate the chaotic political life of the period.

Busy fighting each other for power, political leaders did not pay attention to what was happening in the northern provinces. By 1836 enough Americans had settled in Texas to form a majority and declare themselves independent. Santa Anna fought them at the Alamo, in San Antonio, but soon after that he was defeated at San Jacinto and had to accept the independence of that large province. A dispute about borders and the annexation of Texas led to the Mexican-American War of 1846, which ended with the taking of Mexico City in 1847 and the signing of the Treaty of Guadalupe Hidalgo on December 2, 1848. Mexico ceded half its territory to the United States—an area that included California, Nevada, Utah, Arizona, New Mexico, and parts of Colorado—in effect creating the Mexican American people, later to be called Chicanos.

From 1848 to 1910

In spite of all his faults, lack of administrative skills, and other defects, Santa Anna was able to return to power in 1853, declaring himself dictator. Lacking funds, he sold to the United States the land known as La Mesilla, bordering the states of Arizona and New Mexico, in the so-called Gadsden Purchase. Not able to stand his misgoverning, finally in March 1854 a group of liberals proclaimed the Plan de Ayutla. This movement marked the end of the dictator and the appearance of Benito Juárez on the political scene. A Zapotec Indian, Juárez became the leader of the liberals, first as president of the Supreme

Court, then as vice president, and finally as president from 1858 to 1872, the year of his death. It was under Juárez's leadership that a new liberal constitution was approved in 1857. The conservatives immediately opposed it, thus beginning a three-year war (1858–1860). In 1861 the country was in ruins and the treasury empty, so Juárez declared a moratorium of Mexico's foreign debt. England, France, and Spain sent troops to Mexico to collect; however, England and Spain withdrew and only France stayed, occupying the country after a temporary setback at Puebla on May 5, 1862, when a ragged Mexican army under the command of General Ignacio Zaragoza defeated Europe's best army. That date, celebrated annually as Cinco de Mayo, became the most important civic festivity among Chicanos.

Because the American Civil War had begun, Napoleon III decided to set up a colony in Mexico and he sent Maximilian and Carlota to rule as sovereigns. Juárez, however, continued fighting, and when in 1867 Napoleon withdrew his troops to defend France against Bismarck's Germany, the empire collapsed. General Mariano Escobedo captured Maximilian in Querétaro, and a military tribunal condemned him and his two generals, Miguel Miramón and Tomás Mejía, to death. They were executed on June 19, 1867, at the Cerro de las Campanas near the city of Querétaro. The republic was reestablished.

When Juárez died in 1872, he was succeeded by the chief justice, Sebastián Lerdo de Tejada, who ruled as interim president until he was elected by popular vote the same year. He was reelected in 1876, but General Porfirio Díaz revolted and forced him to leave the country. In New York de Tejada was visited by other exiled Díaz opponents, among them Adolfo Carrillo, who published in Brownsville, Texas, in 1889, the year of Lerdo's death, the *Memorias íntimas del Licenciado Don Sebastián Lerdo de Tejada*, a satirical book used by the enemies of Díaz's 30 years of dictatorship.

The Revolution (1910–1940)

Francisco I. Madero (1873–1913) announced that if Díaz did not resign, the people would take up arms on November 20, 1910. Since Don Porfirio paid no attention to the threats, the revolution began as announced. The *revolución anunciada* changed the course of Mexican history. With the fall of Ciudad Juárez to Francisco (Pancho) Villa and others, the revolutionaries triumphed on May 21, 1911. Díaz left the country and went to France, where he died in 1915. Madero was elected president, but his term was cut short in February 1913, when followers of Victoriano Huerta, the leader of a counterrevolution, assassinated him. Huerta's government was immediately opposed militarily by the northern leaders Francisco Villa (1880–1923), Venustiano Carranza, Alvaro Obregón, Lucio Blanco, and others, and in the south by Emiliano Zapata (1877–1919), whose struggle to recover the common lands had started in 1908. After the fall of Zacatecas to Villa's army, the demise of Huerta was assured. Carranza became president in 1917 and ruled until 1920, the year he was assassinated by the armies of Obregón, who became president that year. His election marked the end of the armed revolution. On April 10, 1919, Zapata also was betrayed and assassinated. These two popular revolutionaries, Villa and Zapata, became the heroes of the people during the Chicano social *movimiento* of the 1960s.

In the struggle for power among the winners of this first Mexican Revolution of the 20th century, the leaders, after their triumph, turned their armies against each other in an internal struggle for power, as is often the case. Carranza turned against Villa, and Obregón turned against both Carranza and Villa. However, a new constitution was accepted on February 5, 1917, at a constitutional convention in the city of Querétaro attended by all the revolutionary leaders. Articles of this constitution that reflect the ideals of the early leaders are the call for a socialist education, the ownership of mines and oil by the nation, the rights of workers to unionize, and most important, the *no re-elección* of the president in order to avoid a 30-year dictatorship like that of Porfirio Díaz.

Obregón, elected president in 1920, was followed in 1924 by Plutarco Elías Calles. Although diplomatic relations with the United States were rather tense during the tenure of Ambassador Dwight W. Morrow, who had been appointed in 1927 by President Coolidge, his classmate at Amherst College, the principal conflicts were peacefully resolved. Calles was followed by Emilio Portes Gil (1928–1929), Pascual Ortiz Rubio (1930–1932), Abelardo Rodríguez (1932–1934), and Lázaro Cárdenas (1934–1940).

The major events that took place from 1920 to 1940 were the Cristero Rebellion (1926–1929); the creation of the PRI (Partido Revolucionario Institucional) in 1929, in power until the year 2000; the distribution of land, which began under Calles (although General Lucio Blanco was the first to distribute the lands of a hacienda to the *campesinos* in Tamaulipas in 1913); and the expropriation of the British and American oil fields, which took place in 1938 under Cárdenas. Other social reforms were the abolition of the death penalty (1930) and the establishment of Social Security (1934) and the right of women to vote (1938).

An important consequence of the ten-year revolution was the large number of people who emigrated. Emigration from Mexico to the United States between 1848 and 1910 was negligible, but after 1910 a large influx of Mexicans crossed the border in search of security and work in the green fields of Texas, New Mexico, and California, as well as in the factories of more remote states. Most of these immigrants never returned to their native land except during the depression years of the 1930s. The Great Depression affected all aspects of their lives; thousands of *mexicanos* were deported, as their labor was no longer needed.

Another aspect of the revolution was the artistic and literary renaissance it sparked. Under José Vasconcelos, secretary of education for Obregón, important government buildings were placed in the hands of the famous muralists Diego Rivera, José Clemente Orozco, and David Alfaro Siqueiros, whose murals served to teach Mexico's history to the masses and turned out to be a great attraction for tourists. In literature the revolution provided material for a new novel, *Andrés Pérez, Maderista* (1911), by Mariano Azuela, a prophetic work in which the author foresaw the failure of the revolution. Azuela was to become famous with his classic *Los de abajo*, published in El Paso, Texas, in 1915, and translated as *The Underdogs* in 1929. During the presidency of Cárdenas, narratives about the Indians reached their highest point with novels such as *El Indio* (1935) by Gregorio López y Fuentes. In music, Carlos Chávez's *Sinfonía India* (1938) for pre-Hispanic instruments became well-known in the United States.

Post-Revolutionary Mexico (1940–1968)

The year 1940 marked the end of an era in the history of Mexico. Beginning with Manuel Ávila Camacho's presidency (1940–1946), social reforms were abandoned and emphasis was given to material progress. Relations with the United States were strengthened, as Mexico entered World War II in

139

May 1942 and later sent an air squadron to the Pacific front. As the result of this military alliance, the United States agreed on a settlement of the oil well expropriation, renewed buying silver, and canceled the interest on Mexico's debt. The Reciprocal Trade Agreement, signed in 1942 and in force until 1950, can be considered as a precursor to the North American Free Trade Agreement (NAFTA). Since the United States needed a labor force, the Bracero (farmhand) Program was established. The program, which began in 1942, continued under the governments of Miguel Alemán (1946–1952), Adolfo Ruiz Cortínez (1952–1958), and Adolfo López Mateos (1958–1964) and ended in 1964, the first year of Gustavo Díaz Ordaz's (1964–1970) term as president. During those 22 years, 5 million *braceros* came to the United States, many of whom did not return to Mexico.

In 1947 President Harry Truman visited Mexico and paid homage to the "Niños Héroes," the cadets who had died in Chapultepec in 1847 fighting the American soldiers. President Alemán visited Washington, D.C., and invited U.S. interests to invest in Mexico, and the American government agreed to support projects to be proposed by Mexico. For the first time, the United States opened a line of credit of $150 million for Mexico to be used to develop the oil industry and $56 million to reorganize the railroads. President Truman also signed an agreement on immigration. This diplomatic interchange has been called "Mexico's first honeymoon with the United States."

In 1968 the Olympic Games were to take place in Mexico and President Díaz Ordaz did not want to be confronted with the student uprising that had begun in a high school and had spread to the university. On October 2 the students, accompanied by friends and relatives, held a meeting at the Plaza de las Tres Culturas in Tlatelolco, where the army fired on them, killing about 300 participants. The nation was in shock and the president lost all his effectiveness as a ruler.

Contemporary Mexico

By focusing on industrialization and urban development, the poor and the *campesinos* (peasants), most of whom lived in poverty, were forgotten. Díaz Ordaz's successor, Luis Echeverría (1970–1978), tried to help them but his policies were not followed by his successors. This poverty in rural Mexico is one

Heading toward the main plaza in Mexico City.

of the reasons why so many *campesinos* leave their lands and migrate to the United States, most of them entering the country without documents.

In 1972 great oil discoveries were made in Chiapas, Tabasco, and Campeche, but this was not made public until the first year of José López Portillo's presidency (1976–1982). Owing to gross mismanagement, Mexico suffered one of the worst economic crises in its history. During López Portillo's last year in office, he nationalized the banks and set the exchange rate of the peso, thus causing its devaluation to the lowest level in the history of the nation.

When the next president, Miguel de la Madrid Hurtado (1982–1988), came to power the economic crisis had not yet been resolved. De la Madrid was a friend of López Portillo and had been his finance secretary, so he was well-acquainted with the problem. The large foreign debt reached a high point, and when President Ronald Reagan refused to intervene, Mexico had to default. As a result, the number of people migrating reached previously unseen numbers. The sending of illegal drugs from Colombia through Mexico and from Mexico itself also presented a problem. Relations with the United States deteriorated in 1985 as a result of the murder in Mexico of Enrique Camarena, a U.S. drug enforcement agent. De la Madrid's successor, Carlos Salinas de Gortari (1988–1994), surrounded by young U.S.-trained technocrats (he himself had studied political economy at the John F. Kennedy School of Government at Harvard University), turned his attention to the economy. He privatized a large number of unproductive industries and balanced the budget, and by 1991 he had a surplus. Gotari's greatest triumph was having the U.S. Congress approve NAFTA in November 17, 1993, which went into effect January 1, 1994. Unexpectedly, that year the Zapatista uprising exploded in Chiapas, led by the masked subcomandante Marcos, a rebellion that received international attention and obscured Salinas's constitutional reforms and the successful Solaridad program, directed to help the *campesinos* and the poor. Salinas continued Echeverrías's policy of establishing relations with the Chicano people and was the first to confer the Order of the Aztec Eagle to several leaders, among them Américo Paredes, César Chávez, Antonia Hernández, Gloria Molina, Luis Valdez, and others. This practice was not continued by Salinas's successor, Ernesto Zedillo (1994–2000), the last president elected by the PRI. The PRI candidate was defeated in 2000 by Vicente Fox, the PAN (Partido Acción Nacional) candidate, from whom the people expected great changes. Since the events of September 11, 2001, however, relations between Mexico and the United States have deteriorated, and no agreement has been reached about the urgent problem of immigration.

United States–Mexico Cultural Relations

The cultural relations between Mexico and the United States began during the last decades of the 19th century. In 1872 the poet William Cullen Bryant visited Mexico, where he was warmly received. He was recognized as being the first to translate the work of a Mexican author, the fables of José Rosas Moreno, into English. From Mexico, Bryant sent long letters to the New York *Evening Post* about his impressions. President Porfirio Díaz, although it is claimed that he said, "Poor Mexico, so far from God and so close to the United States," made a treaty with American contractors to build Mexico's railroads, The act greatly increased the commercial relations between the two countries, but it also facilitated a means for immigrants to enter the United States to work. Their number was greatly increased after 1910, owing to the effects of the Mexican Revolution and the boom in business and agriculture in the United States, where laborers were needed. At present the money sent to Mexico by these workers constitutes one of its most important sources of income.

American cultural influence in Mexico was first the result of the large number of tourists visiting the country, especially centers such as Mexico City, Yucatán, and Acapulco, and more recently Cancún. After the tourists came the influence of Hollywood, television, and the internet. This influence increased after 1985, when the National Aeronautics and Space Administration (NASA) carried into space the first Mexican satellite, *Morelos I*, followed soon after by *Morelos II*. The results are noticeable in all spheres of Mexican life, but principally in the adoption of many English words, the interest in American sports, and the competition of U.S. television programs with the popular Mexican *telenovelas* (soap operas). Very obvious is also the presence of American business firms such Sears, McDonald's, and even Taco Bell and Starbucks. This influence in the food market has been reciprocal, as Mexico's food and drinks—its tacos, enchiladas, burritos, tamales, salsas, nachos, margaritas, and tequila—have become very popular in the

United States. At the same time, in Mexico all types of American products can be found even in the small cities. This exchange of cultural values has enriched the two countries to the point that new subcultures are beginning to appear. These interchanges are most visible at the border, where thousands of people cross in both directions.

RELATED ARTICLES

Alamo, Battle of the; Alliance for Progress; Aztlán; Bear Flag Revolt; Border, United States–Mexico; Bracero Program; Cinco de Mayo; Cuisine, Mexican; Cuisine, Tex-Mex; Día de los Muertos; Gadsden Purchase; Guadalupe Hidalgo, Treaty of; Maquiladoras; Mexican Americans; Mexican-American War; Mexican Revolution; Quetzalcóatl; United States–Mexico Relations; Vasconcelos, José; Virgen de Guadalupe; Zapata, Emiliano.

FURTHER READING

Camp, Roderic Ai. *Mexican Political Biographies 1935–1993.* Austin: Univ. of Tex. Press, 1995.
Carrasco, David, and Eduardo Matos Moctezuma. *Moctezuma's Mexico: Visions of the Aztec World.* Rev. ed. Boulder: Univ. Press of Colo., 2003.
Krauze, Enrique. *Mexico, Biography of Power: A History of Modern Mexico, 1810–1996.* Tr. by Hank Heifetz. Austin: Univ. of Tex. Press, 1997.
Leonard, Irving. *Baroque Times in Old Mexico: Seventeenth-Century Persons, Places, and Practices.* Ann Arbor: Univ. of Mich. Press, 1959.
Paz, Octavio. *Sor Juana, or The Traps of Faith.* Tr. by Margaret Sayers Peden. Cambridge, Mass.: Harvard Univ. Press, 1988.
Werner, Michael S., ed. *Encyclopedia of Mexico: History, Society and Culture.* Chicago: Fitzroy Dearborn Pubs., 1997.

LUIS LEAL

MIAMI

Located in the extreme southeastern portion of the Florida mainland, Miami-Dade County (2000 population: 2,253,362), better known simply as Miami, is the eighth largest county in the United States by population and is second only to Los Angeles County in the number of Latinos (1,291,737 in 2000). Miami-Dade County comprises the Miami-Hialeah Metropolitan Statistical Area (MSA) and is a sociologically more relevant unit of analysis than is the city of Miami, a political division that represents only about 15 percent of the population of the metropolitan area. The largest MSA in the nation by population with a Latino majority (57.3 percent in 2000), Miami is nearly 80 percent "minority." The city of Miami is the only metropolis in the United States

where immigrants are a majority; in 2000, 50.9 percent of the city's population was foreign born.

One of the major gateways for immigration to the United States since the 1960s, Miami at the beginning of the 21st century is a unique example of immigrant economic and political empowerment. Cubans began migrating in massive numbers shortly after the 1959 revolution led by Fidel Castro. Their influence and that of later waves of immigrants from other countries of Latin America and the Caribbean transformed dramatically the area's cultural, linguistic, political, and economic conditions in a single generation. Latinos in Miami own proportionately more businesses than do Latinos in any other metropolitan area, and they have attained positions of power and influence in the area's major public, private, and civic institutions.

As of 2004 the mayors of Miami-Dade County (Alex Penelas), the city of Miami (Manny Diaz), and the city of Hialeah (Raul Martinez); the presidents of the state university (Modesto Maidique, Florida International University) and the community college system (Eduardo Padrón, Miami-Dade College); the state's attorney (Kathy Fernandez-Rundle) and the U.S. attorney (Marcos Jimenez); the head of one of the largest private law firms in North America (Cesar L. Alvarez, Greenberg Traurig); and three members of the U.S. House of Representatives (Republicans Ileana Ros-Lehtinen, Lincoln Diaz-Balart, and Mario Diaz-Balart) were all Cuban American. Non-Cuban Latinos, who constitute the fastest-growing sector of the Latino population in Miami, have established a large number of businesses and include a significant number of professionals, but they have yet to attain strong representation in the highest spheres of local political and economic power. In 2002, however, Juan Carlos Zapata, a Republican, was the first Colombian American elected to the Florida legislature.

Miami is a major Latin American–Latino media and entertainment center and is the headquarters for Univisión, the largest Latino-oriented television network in the United States. The Spanish language is widely spoken, and there are two Spanish-language dailies, *El Nuevo Herald* and *Diario de las Américas,* as well as numerous tabloids, many aimed at specific national groups. In 1962 Miami's Coral Way Elementary Bilingual School implemented the first public school bilingual education program of the modern era. In 1973 the Board of County Commissioners, which at the time had no Latino members, declared the county officially bilingual and bicultural. But in 1980, in what was to become the first battle of the "English only" controversy, Dade County (renamed Miami-Dade County in 1997) voters overwhelmingly approved an antibilingual ordinance prohibiting the expenditure of government funds to promote any language other than English or any culture other than that of the United States. The County Commission rescinded the ordinance in the 1990s but did not restore the official bilingual-bicultural designation.

Miami's warm and sunny climate (average annual low temperature of 69.1° F, or 20.6° C; average annual high temperature of 76.7° F, or 24.8° C; percentage of days sunshine, 58 percent) and its abundant beaches are among the main reasons for its success as an international tourist destination. The weather is one of the attractions of Miami frequently cited by Latinos, particularly those from the Caribbean and those migrating from New York City and other cities from the Northeast as well as those in the Midwest.

The county has a total area of 1,944 square miles (5,035 sq km), which include large environmentally sensitive wetlands. The topography is flat. It is bounded on the north by Broward County (principal city, Ft. Lauderdale); on the south by Monroe County, including the Florida Keys (principal city, Key West); on the west by Collier County (principal city, Naples); and on the east by Biscayne Bay and the Atlantic Ocean.

Until the 20th century, large areas of Miami-Dade County were underwater for at least part of the year, and early settlement concentrated along the coastal ridge. In the 20th century, massive drainage projects greatly increased the area subject to development but damaged the ecosystem, including the wetlands and the offshore reefs. To prevent further deterioration, Everglades National Park was founded in 1947, and Biscayne National Park, an underwater park, in 1980. City planning councils have established urban development boundaries, but population and political pressures have led to frequent expansion of the areas subject to development. Although Miami was made possible by the railroad, it developed to accommodate the automobile era, and it remains a horizontal, relatively low-density urban and suburban area connected to a greater extent by expressways than by mass transit.

The Tequesta Indians, a small tribe of hunters and gatherers numbering probably in the hundreds at the time of European contact, inhabited southeastern Florida for thousands of years. They made pottery and had settlements along Biscayne Bay. Contact with the Spanish beginning in the 1500s brought diseases that, along with warfare, apparently decimated them to the point of extinction by the year 1800. In 1998, developers excavating for high-rise construction near the mouth of the Miami River in downtown Miami uncovered a 38-foot (12-meter) limestone circle built by the Tequesta at what may have been their capital. The circle, unlike many other Indian and non-Indian historical sites destroyed in Miami's rush to development and redevelopment, will be preserved.

The first white settlers in the late 19th century encountered, traded with, and battled another Native American nation, the Seminole tribe. The Seminoles and a related group, the Miccosukees, came into north Florida from the Creek Nation territory of north Georgia in the 1700s at the invitation of the Spanish. After Spain's sale of Florida to the United States in 1812, the Seminoles were displaced and relocated on a reservation in central Florida. The Indian Removal Act of 1830 provided for the ethnic cleansing of Indians from the southeastern United States and their forced relocation to the West. Resisting forcible removal for decades, the Seminoles and Miccosukees battled federal troops, retreating into the vast, swampy recesses of what later came to be known as the Everglades. Today's Miccosukees are descendants of the few Indians who survived the wars. The tribe has a reservation in the western section of the county and operates a gaming facility, a resort, and other tourist attractions.

Named after a Tequesta word meaning either "sweet water" or "big water" (the sources differ on this score), Miami is by some accounts the youngest major American city. Certainly it is a neoteric urban center compared with the large cities of the Northeast, the Midwest, and the South. Even other Florida cities predate Miami, including Tampa and Jacksonville to the north and Key West to the south.

The story of the coming of the railroad is Miami's foundational narrative. There were few residents before the railroad and no city. When the railroad came, the city of Miami was incorporated and the new town grew quickly. The pattern of settlement on the east coast of Florida flowed from north to south, following the extension of the railroad. Before the railroad there were a few hundred inhabitants living in small settlements near the mouth of the Miami River, the Coconut Grove area a few miles south, the Cutler area at the extreme south of the county, and the Lemon City area about 5 miles (8 km) north of today's downtown. A Florida state census of 1885 enumerated only 335 inhabitants in the entire county.

Real estate speculation surrounding the coming of the railroad was a major catalyst to Miami's growth. In 1891 a young widow named Julia Tuttle purchased 640 acres (260 ha) on the north bank of the Miami River near present-day downtown. Four years later, on the wake of the freeze of 1895–1896 that devastated the citrus crop in areas of the state north of Miami, Tuttle convinced railroad magnate Henry Flagler to extend his Florida East Coast (FEC) railroad tracks south from West Palm Beach to the warmer climate of Miami. On April 15, 1896, the first train roared into Miami. On July 28 of that year, the city was incorporated on the strength of the votes of 344 men, many of whom worked on building Flagler's railroad, and a third of whom were black. By 1900 the population of Dade County was 4,955, of which 1,681 lived in the city of Miami.

African Americans provided much of the labor for construction of the railroad, which made the city possible and supplied part of the political backing to create the city as a legal entity. Yet, for more than half a century, blacks were not heard from as significant political actors. Although in many ways Miami, founded three decades after the Civil War and settled by people from myriad places, is not a typical southern city, Jim Crow was there from day one. In 1896 Tuttle and Flagler—the latter having agreed to lay out the town at his expense—drafted a city plan that segregated black residents of Miami into an area called "Colored Town." This was located west of the railroad tracks, as in other Florida cities. Until the civil rights movement of the 1950s and 1960s swept de jure segregation away, "separate but not equal" held sway in Miami, from the schools to the drinking fountains to the beaches. Blacks in Miami since then have made significant advances in politics, the professions, and many other areas, but the legacy of segregation and discrimination lives on in myriad ways.

Tourism, a mainstay of the economy today and throughout its history, was there at the beginning as well. Flagler wasted no time capitalizing on Miami's tourist-friendly atmosphere; having decided to bring the railroad, he immediately set out to build a hotel, the Royal Palm, inaugurated in 1897. With it came not only tourism but also progress; the Royal Palm Hotel had the first electric lights in the city.

The first 25 years of the 20th century saw the construction of luxury residences for the rich elite as well as the first middle-class suburbs. The population increased by a factor of eight in the two decades, reaching 42,753 in 1920. But the real boom came during the next decade, which featured a frenzy of real estate development, swindles, and the creation of Coral Gables and expansion of Miami Beach. In the 1920s the population increased to 142,555. George Merrick, the developer of Coral Gables, built the upscale city on a Mediterranean theme. Many of the streets were named after Spanish cities and historical places, such as Alhambra; 50 years later, well-off Latinos, people who actually knew the original pronunciation of the street names, began moving there in significant numbers. By 2000, Latinos were 46.6 percent of the population of Coral Gables.

The late 1920s were tough for Miami: a devastating hurricane in 1926, the bursting of the real estate bubble, and the 1929 stock market crash. But in the 1930s many new hotels, most of them built in the art deco or moderne style, sprang up in the southern end of Miami Beach. Fifty years later, this architecture would be the basis for the renaissance in South Beach.

World War II put Miami's development on hold and brought many servicemen and -women to Miami for training. Some of them went back to settle in Miami in the late 1940s and 1950s, contributing to a postwar boom that brought the population of greater Miami to almost a million by 1960.

The Transformation of Miami

The ethnic makeup of Miami was radically transformed in the second half of the 20th century with the immigration of hundreds of thousands of Cubans and other Latin Americans. In 1950, of the total county population (495,000), Hispanics accounted for only 4 percent (20,000), whites (not of Hispanic origin) for 83 percent (410,000), and blacks for 13 percent (65,000). By 2000 not only had the area's population increased fourfold, but Latinos now made up 57.3 percent of the population (with a projected 69 percent by 2000); whites not of Latino origin,

20.7 percent; African Americans, or blacks (not including black Latinos), 19.0 percent; Asians, 1.4 percent; and all other races, 1.6 percent. No other major American city has experienced such a rapid and profound ethnic transition toward an overwhelming demographic majority in such a short period of time.

Approximately half of the Latino population is of Cuban national origin, and the other half comprises all other Hispanic national origins combined. Cubans easily are the largest Latino national origin group in Miami-Dade, but despite the continuing growth of the Cuban population, its share of the Hispanic population has declined steadily, from approximately 90 percent in 1970 to 50 percent in 2000 as a result of faster growth among other Latino groups, owing to massive immigration and higher birthrates. This process of diversification is ongoing despite the entry of tens of thousands of rafters in the 1990s and the U.S.-Cuban immigration agreement of 1994, which grants Cubans 20,000 visas annually. In 1990–2000 the Cuban-origin population grew by 15.4 percent, while the non-Cuban Latino population grew by 64.6 percent, or roughly four times as fast. The result is that the Latino population is increasingly diverse in national origin. Still, with 28.9 percent of the area's population, Cubans constitute the largest

single ethnic group in Miami, exceeding all other black, white, and Latino populations (Puerto Rican, 3.6 percent of total Miami population; Nicaraguan, 3.1 percent; Colombian, 3.1 percent; Mexican, 1.7 percent; Dominican, 1.6 percent; and all other Latinos, 23.2 percent). The vast majority of Miami Cubans, more than 90 percent, in their answer to the U.S. Census question on race, identify themselves as Hispanic white.

Looking specifically at the Latino population, in rank order in 2000 it was 50.3 percent Cuban (650,601), 6.2 percent Puerto Rican (80,327), 5.4 percent Colombian (70,066), 5.3 percent Nicaraguan (69,257), 2.9 percent Mexican (38,095), 2.8 percent Dominican (36,454), 2.1 percent Honduran (26,829), 1.8 percent Peruvian (23,327), 1.7 percent Venezuelan (21,593), and 1.0 percent Argentinean (13,341). The formation of the diverse Latino population that currently exists in Miami reflects historical events in different regions of Latin America and the successive immigrant waves they generated.

The Cuban revolution itself was responsible for several distinct waves of international migration. The early 1970s were dominated by the arrival of Cubans disaffected by the radicalization of the Cuban revolution, including expropriation of property, the establishment of a one-party Communist rule and

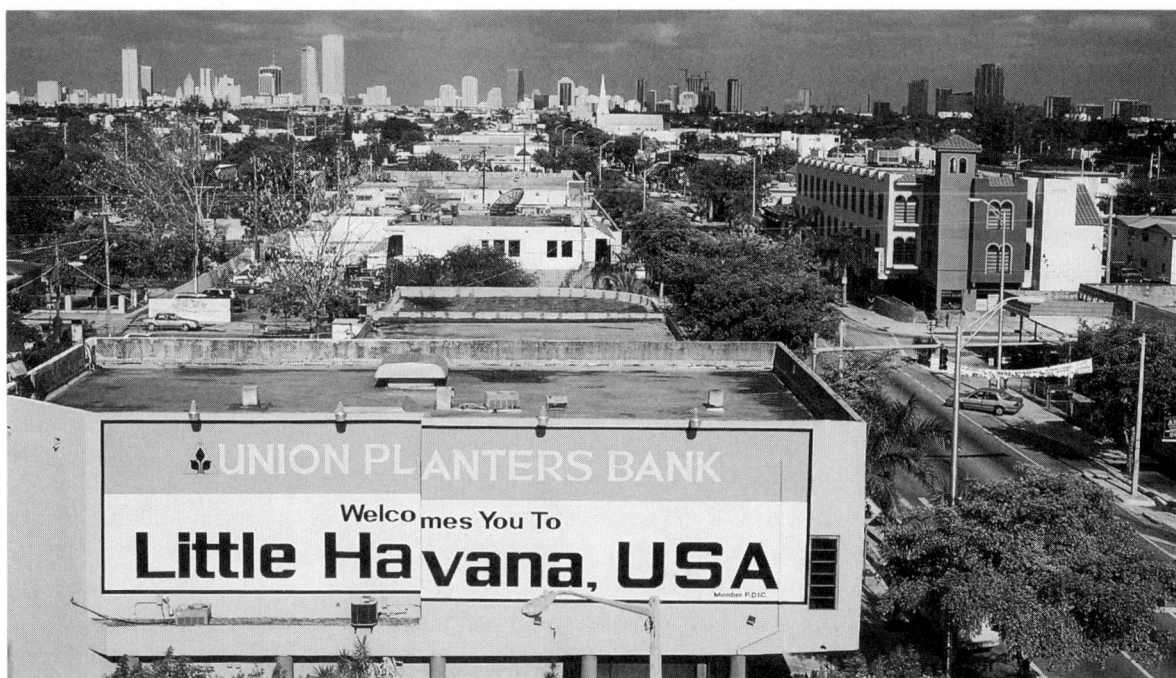

"Little Havana, USA" billboard hangs on the Union Planter's Bank, with the skyline of Miami beyond.

an officially atheist state, alignment with the Soviet bloc, and shortages of consumer goods.

In the context of the Cold War and the U.S. campaign to overthrow Fidel Castro, the U.S. government assisted and encouraged Cuban immigration through a number of policies, including a visa waiver program, a program for the migration of unaccompanied minors ("Pedro Pan") facilitated by the Catholic Church in Miami and anti-Castro Cubans on the island, the granting of refugee status to political prisoners and other persecuted individuals, and assistance including income support, medical care, and student loans. The motives for the open arms policy appear to have included humanitarian considerations; the desire to develop political opposition and an exile army to topple Castro (deployed in the disastrous Bay of Pigs invasion); promotion of a brain drain of professionals and managers to cripple the Cuban economy; and raising anti-Communist propaganda useful in the contest over Latin America and developing nations.

The failure of the Bay of Pigs invasion accelerated Cuban immigration to Miami and led the U.S. government to establish a Cuban refugee relocation program, which eventually settled thousands of Cubans in communities throughout the United States. But the majority of Cubans stayed in Miami, and many of those who had moved elsewhere have filtered back in the ensuing decades, including a good number who have gone back upon retirement.

The first wave of Cuban immigration, beginning with the overthrow of the regime of Fulgencio Batista on January 1, 1959, ended abruptly with the October 1962 Cuban missile crisis. A second wave, which began in 1965 with a boat lift from the Cuban port of Camarioca that segued into a U.S.-sponsored airlift, ended in 1973. Commencing in 1980, a third wave, known as the Mariel boat lift for the port city through which the migration took place, brought 125,000 Cubans in a five-month period. A fourth wave, starting in the early 1990s with a gradual increase of rafters in the wake of the collapse of the Cuban economy, exploded in 1994, when the Cuban government allowed free emigration by sea. This led to an agreement between the U.S. and Cuban governments to discourage irregular migration, including an agreement by the United States to provide Cubans 20,000 immigration visas per year. This wave is ongoing.

While Cuban immigration was modest from 1973 to 1994 (except for the Mariel boat lift), Central American immigration increased rapidly in the late 1970s and 1980s as a result of war, repression, and revolution. Nicaraguans opposed to the Sandinista revolution of 1979 were the largest group of Central American arrivals. As had occurred in the 1960s, Miami became the capital of an exile group opposed to this leftist Latin American revolution, a group organized and backed by the United States to overthrow the revolutionary government through violent means.

Although Nicaraguans did not receive the same privileged treatment as refugees that Cubans had received since the 1960s, the U.S. government directed and funded the "contra" war and approved Nicaraguan asylum claims at a much higher rate than they did those of Salvadorans and Guatemalans fleeing repression by death squads or governments backed by the United States. The Cuban-Nicaraguan relation was characterized by political solidarity coupled with ethnic tensions. Whereas Cuban and Nicaraguan exiles found ideological common ground in their anti-Communism, they frequently expressed ethnic prejudices and encountered cultural frictions at the grassroots level.

The coming of the Nicaraguans and other Central Americans in the 1980s led to the establishment of a "Little Managua" in and around the city of Sweetwater in the western section of the county. Sections of Little Havana, the area of heaviest Cuban settlement in the 1960s, have become more Central American than Cuban. On today's Calle Ocho, the heart of Little Havana, one can find Nicaraguan, Peruvian, Mexican, and Dominican restaurants alongside long-established Cuban favorites.

The electoral defeat of the Sandinistas in 1989 and the subsequent settlement of the conflicts in El Salvador and Guatemala led to a reduction in the Central American immigrant flow in the 1990s. Indeed, the Nicaraguan population of Miami actually dropped by 4,987, or nearly 7 percent, during the decade.

The story in the 1990s was South American immigration, driven by economic, political, and security concerns. Increasing by 42 percent in this decade, South Americans, who had numbered 108,768 to 119,534 Central Americans in 1990, overtook Central Americans, 154,348 versus 128,903, by 2000. If the 1980s was the decade that saw the establishment of myriad Central American restaurants and other business establishments, the 1990s and early 2000s has been the decade that has witnessed the emergence of many Argentine, Peruvian, and Venezuelan enterprises. The move to south Florida of the headquarters of the Cisneros Group, a giant Venezuelan communications conglomerate, is emblematic of this phenomenon.

Economy, Culture, and Social Relations

Challenges to racial discrimination brought violence to Miami as early as the 1950s, and not only violence against blacks but also against Jews—as with the bombing of a synagogue by racists opposed to Jewish support for integration. Nonetheless, it was only with the riot of 1968 that racial turmoil in Miami drew national attention. The bloody Liberty City riot of 1980, one of four that took place in the city in that decade, tarnished the public relations image of Miami as the Magic City. Drug wars, uncontrolled immigrant flows, battles over language, and crime further changed the city's reputation. Miami became an "ethnic cauldron," a "paradise lost," and a "city on the edge."

White (Anglo) flight accelerated in the 1980s, and in 1992 Hurricane Andrew gave the process another big boost. In the 1980s, annual domestic net in-migration averaged −13,423; in the 1990s it grew to 17,501 a year. Meanwhile, international net migration (net immigration) averaged +36,717 a year in the 1980s and +32,213 in the 1990s.

While civic efforts to fight racial and ethnic polarization, poverty, drugs, and crime and to increase jobs and minority economic development undoubtedly did some good, larger structural forces such as the economic boom, the aging of the population, and increased black representation in elected office probably account for much of the improvements in the 1990s—declining crime rates, the end of the drug wars, and relative racial peace. Nonetheless, by the end of the decade, the poverty rate in the metropolitan area was among the ten highest in the country, and the city of Miami topped all cities of 250,000 or more in this dire social indicator. Black-Cuban relations remained tense, and the preferential immigration treatment of Cubans over Haitians was a perennial issue.

In the 1970s, ideological conflicts regarding U.S.-Cuban relations became a heated point of contention for Miami Cubans as exile militants targeted those who favored dialogue with the Cuban government, those who did business with Cuba, and even a radio

personality who spoke out against terrorism. By the 1980s and 1990s, intolerance in the Cuban community had taken on less violent forms but had nevertheless become a national issue and threatened to torpedo Miami's aspirations to host major events, such as the Junior Olympics and Pan American Games, because they included athletes from Cuba.

The saga of Elián González, the Cuban rafter boy rescued from the waters that claimed his mother's life, divided the city from 1999 to 2000, with the overwhelming majority of Cubans insisting the boy stay in the United States and the rest of the community siding with the father's wish to be reunited with his son in Cuba and decide his future. The federal raid to remove the boy from the home of the Miami relatives enraged large sectors of the Cuban community, while others in the city and the nation saw the attitudes and actions of Miami Cubans in a negative light. In the wake of the Elián affair, Cuban American leaders sought to improve the community's image by adopting a more moderate tone, but in 2001 the Latin Grammy Awards event scheduled to take place in Miami was moved to avoid possible confrontations. The awards ceremony returned to the city in 2003, but performers from Cuba were not present, and Latin Grammy organizers were quoted as saying the awards ceremony would not be returning because of the political climate.

Miami is mainly a service-centered economy, with tourism (10.5 million visitors in 2003), commerce, real estate, construction, banking, health care, education, and entertainment among the major industries in this sector. There is also a substantial light-manufacturing sector and some agriculture in the extreme southern section of the county. In 1990 the top five categories of employment by industry were professional and related services (22 percent), retail trade (18 percent), manufacturing (11 percent), utilities (10 percent), and finance, insurance, and real estate (8 percent).

Miami is characterized by a plethora of small- and medium-size businesses, but only two Fortune 500 companies have their headquarters in the area. International trade, especially with Latin America and the Caribbean, is a centerpiece of the economy. The city is "the business center of the Americas," according to the area's economic development promoters. Indeed, a large number of U.S. and global companies, as well as banks, base all or a substantial part of their Latin American operations there. Miami leaders want the city to play a pivotal role in the process of economic hemispheric integration that is expected to advance in the early decades of the 21st century.

The busiest cruise port in the world (3.6 million cruise passengers a year), Miami also boasts a major container port (8.6 million tons of cargo per year) and one of the major airports in the nation (30 million passengers a year come through Miami International Airport). The city is the major airport hub connecting the United States with Latin America and the Caribbean. In many cases, the most convenient air route between Latin American capitals goes through Miami, bolstering its claim as "the capital of Latin America."

Latino culture is not merely preserved in Miami; it has become the fundamental element of a unique Miami style that reflects the mélange of distinct ethnic, racial, and cultural influences within the county. Beginning in the 1970s Cuban salsa singers such as Willy Chirino pioneered the eclectic Miami Sound, a musical style that fuses traditional Cuban rhythms with American jazz and rock and roll. Miami's countless discos and nightclubs are considered some of the world's most glamorous, and the cultural mix of Latino and Caribbean influences resonates in the Cuban salsa, Jamaican reggae, Dominican merengue, and American hip-hop that provide the soundtrack to Miami's exotic nightlife.

The city offers a diversity of restaurants, cafés, and *bodegas* (Latino grocery stores) that serve traditional Latin American dishes, especially those from Brazil, Nicaragua, Colombia, Puerto Rico, and, of course, Cuba. Beginning in the 1990s Miami restaurateurs also began to develop their own regional style, pioneering a "Nuevo Latino" cuisine that draws flavors from West Indian and Asian ingredients.

Miami presents Latino and exiled Latin American artists, writers, and musicians with a unique artistic environment; Latin American cultural ties merge with multicultural modernity, giving artists free reign to make Latino art that is both contemporary and traditional. There are many galleries, festivals, and exhibitions in the area that showcase local Latino artists and their work; and a staple of the arts community, the Bridge Theater, presents Hispanic American stage works and radio plays as well as works in English by world-renowned Latino playwrights. The county also resembles a "Latino Hollywood," home to many of the county's highest-paid and most famous Latino stars.

Several questions loom over the future of Miami in the first decade of the 21st century. Can the city's leaders overcome poverty and racial tensions, or will these once again tear the city apart? How will Miami respond to hemispheric integration, and what will be the city's role if a free trade area of the Americas is constructed? Will Miami be able to realize the dream of being the "Capital of the Americas" and the Latino entertainment capital, or will ideological intolerance stand in the way? What will happen when Fidel Castro dies, when there is a change in U.S.-Cuban relations, or when there is transition in the political and economic systems in Cuba? What is not in question is that Miami is both a forerunner in the demographic and cultural Latinization of the United States as well as a singular case in the Latino experience in this nation.

RELATED ARTICLES

Calle Ocho; Cuba; Cuban Americans; Florida; Immigration, Latino; Little Havana; Mariel Boat Lift.

FURTHER READING

Bardach, Anne Louise. *Cuba Confidential: Love and Vengeance in Miami and Havana.* New York: Random House, 2002.

Castro, Max J. "The Politics of Language in Miami." In *Miami Now: Immigration, Ethnicity and Social Change.* Ed. by Guillermo Grenier and Alex Stepick. Gainesville: Univ. Press of Fla., 1992.

Didion, Joan. *Miami.* New York: Pocket Bks., 1997.

Grenier, Guillermo J., and Max J. Castro. "Triadic Politics: Ethnicity, Race and Politics in Miami." *Pacific Historical Review* 68, no. 2 (May 1999): 273–292.

Grenier, Guillermo J., and Lisandro Perez. *The Legacy of Exile: Cubans in the United States.* Boston: Allyn and Bacon, 2003.

Levine, Robert M. *Secret Missions to Cuba: Fidel Castro, Bernardo Benes and Cuban Miami.* New York: Palgrave, 2001.

Metropolitan Dade County, Office of Community and Economic Development, Historic Preservation Division. *From Wilderness to Metropolis: The History and Architecture of Dade County, Florida (1825–1940).* 2d ed. 1982. Reprint; Miami: Metropolitan Dade County, 1992.

Miami-Dade County, Department of Planning and Zoning, Research Section. *Miami-Dade County Facts— 2003: A Compendium of Selected Statistics.* Miami: May 2003.

Portes, Alejandro, and Alex Stepick. *City on the Edge: The Transformation of Miami.* Berkeley: Univ. of Calif. Press, 1993.

Stepick, Alex, et al. *This Land Is Our Land: Immigrants and Power in Miami.* Berkeley: Univ. of Calif. Press, 2003.

U.S. Census Bureau. *2000 Census of Population and Housing.* Miami-Dade County QuickFacts. http://quickfacts.census.gov/qfd/states/12/12086.html

SELECTED WEB SITE

City of Miami (official site). www.ci.maimi.fl.us

MAX J. CASTRO

MIAMI HERALD, THE

South Florida's oldest newspaper, the *Miami Herald* is one of the largest newspaper publications in the United States. While its journalism has won numerous awards over the years, much of its significance lies in its development along with the "latinization" of the city around it. Begun on September 15, 1903, as the *Miami Evening Record,* in 2003 the *Miami Herald* celebrated 100 years of publishing history, which is intricately intertwined with the history of Miami itself. During the course of the 20th century, Miami evolved from a small trading town to a thriving, multicultural metropolis. Along the way, the *Miami Herald* has had to acknowledge, respond to, and, in some cases, direct that transformation.

The *Miami Evening Record* was first owned and published in 1903 by businessman Frank Stoneman, one year after the U.S. occupation of Cuba ended with the insertion of the Platt Amendment into the Cuban constitution. The amendment allowed the United States to intervene in Cuban affairs if deemed necessary to maintain order in the Caribbean. While the stage was set for conflict in Cuba over American foreign policy, the city of Miami would not feel the first reverberations of it for several decades to come.

The paper changed hands in 1910 when Frank Shutts bought it with the financial assistance of Henry Flagler and Stoneman. The newly named *Miami Herald* was printed daily and thrived over the next two decades, reporting on such major stories as the sinking of the *Titanic,* the events of World War I, and the boom in Florida real estate speculation during the 1920s. After the Stock Market Crash of 1929 and the ensuing Great Depression, the paper underwent a major change.

On October 15, 1937, John S. Knight bought the *Miami Herald* from Shutts for approximately $2.25 million. In the 1930s Miami became known for its tourist attractions and somewhat notorious for its gambling and other vices. Knight took firm editorial control of the paper. He lived in Miami for five months of the year and took it upon himself to expand and reorganize the paper into business and editorial sections.

In the early 1930s the city of Miami had its first major encounter with political refugees from the south. Hundreds of Cubans arrived there after successfully fleeing the ascendancy of the tumultuous regime of Gerardo Machado. Led by former Cuban president Mario Menocal, the Cuban émigrés were given a warm send-off three years later when the Machado regime collapsed and the Cubans returned home. Promising that the city would always be open to newcomers, the *Miami Herald* pledged itself to a political position that would be tested in decades to come.

During the years leading to and immediately following World War II, U.S. foreign policy sought security in hemispheric solidarity from the Axis pow-

THE MIAMI HERALD/AP/WIDE WORLD PHOTOS

Front page of the redesigned *Miami Herald,* September 15, 2003, celebrating its first century in circulation.

ers. The sharing of information between the United States and Latin American countries played a large part in forging this solidarity, and the print media became one of the chief means of promoting mutual understanding and cooperation among the nations of the Western Hemisphere. In January 1946 the *Miami Herald* launched the Clipper edition, an abridged version of the larger paper that could be shipped to various Latin American countries by air. The increased hemispheric awareness of the paper was rewarded when later that year the *Herald*'s managing editor, Lee Hills, won the Maria Moore Cabot award for writing about and increasing the popular awareness of certain Latin American issues. In 1951 the paper won its first of what to date is a total of 17 Pulitzer Prizes for investigative journalism.

Throughout the 1960s Miami experienced a major influx of Cuban political refugees from the Castro regime. Unlike the group who had come in the 1930s, the Cubans who later fled Castro came to the United States to stay. Miami, like many major urban centers in the mid- to late 20th century, underwent a process of "latinization," and the city's Cuban population contributed to its emergence as a multicultural metropolis. The *Miami Herald* did little to respond to this process over the first major decade of Cuban immigration. By the 1970s, however, the political situation in Cuba had deteriorated to such an extent that the émigré community in Miami stepped up their efforts to force the paper to take notice. While the paper later explained its silence as having been motivated by a lack of reliable information from Cuba, others like Ramon Mestre, a future *Herald* staff member, believed that the paper had been simply unresponsive. Although the *Miami Herald* launched a supplement in 1976 called "El Herald," an insert that would deliver the *Herald* to Miami's Spanish speakers and readers, it nevertheless failed to address the concerns of its changing community. Importantly, however, it marked the first time a major U.S. daily paper published a Spanish-language insert, and within three years it was received in more than 76,000 households.

In November 1987, *El Nuevo Herald* began publication as more than a supplement. With its own publisher, Roberto Suarez (who had started at the *Herald* in 1962 as a mailer and later, in 1990, became president of the company), *El Nuevo Herald* was committed to better understanding and representing Miami's Latino population. In 1998 *El Nuevo*

Herald became its own entity, owned by the Miami Herald Publishing Company, with independent sales and subscriptions. *El Nuevo Herald* has become a leader in its field, serving a diverse Florida audience of 470,000 with an equally diverse staff. It has won numerous prestigious awards, including that given by the National Association of Hispanic Publications, an organization founded in 1982, and the coveted Ortega y Gasset Prize in 2002.

RELATED ARTICLES

Journalism; Miami; Newspapers and Magazines; *Nuevo Herald, El.*

FURTHER READING

Balmaseda, Liz. "Chaos, Change, Common Future: The Newspaper Meets Exile." *Miami Herald.* Oct. 6, 2002.

Grenier, Guillermo J. *The Legacy of Exile: Cubans in the United States.* Boston: Allyn & Bacon, 2003.

Kanellos, Nicolás. *Hispanic Firsts: 500 Years of Extraordinary Achievement.* Detroit: Visible Ink Press, 1997.

Smiley, Nixon. *Knights of the Fourth Estate: The Story of the Miami Herald.* Miami: E.A. Seemann Pub., 1974.

DESIRÉE GARCIA

MICHIGAN

Latin Americans have been streaming into Michigan for the past 100 years. Some 600 Hispanics of diverse national backgrounds lived in Detroit as early as 1880. Their settlement in Michigan follows a pattern common to that of Latinos in many other Midwestern states. Mexican *traqueros,* or "track workers," pioneered the trek to the Great Lakes region. *Enganchistas,* or "labor recruiters," also led several thousand Tejanos and Mexicanos yearly to Michigan's sugar beet farms in the 1920s. The labor of the *betabeleros,* as the beet workers came to be known, helped to keep the sugar beet industry afloat after World War I temporarily disrupted European immigration to the Midwest.

The Puerto Ricans came next, starting in 1950, as a result of a combination of "push" and "pull" factors. Operation Bootstrap, an industrialization scheme launched on the island in the late 1940s, could not keep up with the rising demand for jobs. Inexpensive airfares, ample employment opportunities in the United States, and their status as American citizens facilitated the migration of Puerto Ricans to the U.S. mainland. Midwest companies, under fire for employing foreign workers, actively recruited Puerto Ricans for the region's farms, railroads, found-ries, automobile plants, and mines. In 1950 Michigan beet growers contracted over 5,000 Puerto Rican farmworkers under an arrangement dubbed Operation Farmlift.

The latest Latino newcomers in Michigan include Cubans arriving under the federally funded Cuban Refugee Assistance Program of 1961–1984; Central Americans fleeing war-torn Nicaragua, Guatemala, and El Salvador, many of them sponsored by the Texas- and Chicago-based Sanctuary Movement; and South Americans, led by Argentines and Colombians, driven to exile in the United States by domestic political instability and economic dislocation in the post-1950s.

The first Latino communities in Michigan emerged out of the laboring experiences of Mexicanos and Puerto Ricans. Those unable to earn enough money to get back to Mexico, Texas, or Puerto Rico or those who abandoned the fields for better jobs in factories, steel plants, and automobile assembly lines

put down roots in the state. As a result, Latino *colonias,* or "communities," sprang up across the state, especially in Saginaw, Port Huron, Flint, Adrian, Pontiac, Dearborn, and Detroit. By the 1920s a Mexican consulate, El Círculo Mutualista Mexicano, and a church dedicated to Nuestra Señora de Guadalupe were in place in Detroit.

The state's Mexican-descent population plunged during the Great Depression, when rampant unemployment and xenophobic sentiments sparked the repatriation and deportation of Mexican nationals and their U.S.-born children across the nation. The Mexican artist Diego Rivera, who painted the mural *Man and Machine* at the Detroit Institute of Arts in 1932–1933, assisted destitute Mexicans' return to their homeland. Statewide, the Mexican population fell from 9,739 in 1930, to 3,694 in 1940, a nearly 40 percent drop. Despite this setback, immigration and a high fertility rate in the post-1940s regenerated the Latino population.

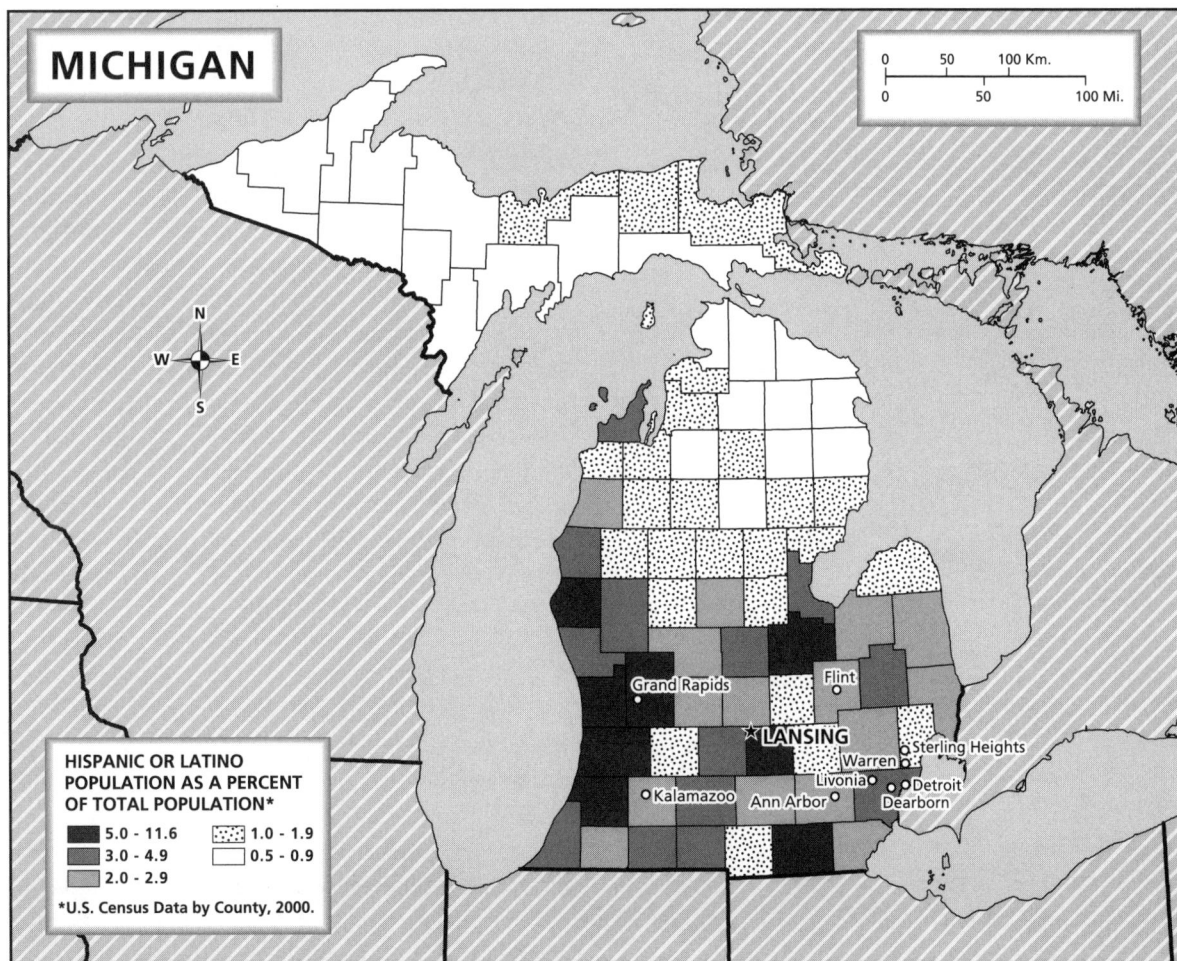

MICHIGAN

HISPANIC OR LATINO
POPULATION AS A PERCENT
OF TOTAL POPULATION*

- 5.0 - 11.6
- 1.0 - 1.9
- 3.0 - 4.9
- 0.5 - 0.9
- 2.0 - 2.9

*U.S. Census Data by County, 2000.

By the 1960s, Latinos established a multiservice center, Latin Americans for Social and Economic Development (LA SED), in Detroit. LA SED, in turn, was instrumental in organizing Latino en Marcha, the predecessor of Wayne State University's Center for Chicano-Boricua Studies, one of the oldest and most successful undergraduate ethnic studies programs for Latinos in the Midwest. Wayne State's Walter P. Reuther Library is a major repository for the records of the United Farm Workers of America. The Julián Samora Research Institute at Michigan State University, in operation since 1989, is the premier Latino research center in the Midwest. Today, over 300,000 Mexicans, Puerto Ricans, Cubans, and Central and South Americans live in Michigan, which has the second-largest Latino population in the Midwest.

RELATED ARTICLES

Immigration, Latino.

FURTHER READING

Baba, Marietta L., and Malvina H. Abonyi. *Mexicans of Detroit.* Detroit: Wayne State University, Center for Urban Studies, 1979.

Chinea, Jorge L. "Ethnic Prejudice and Anti-Immigrant Policies in Times of Economic Stress: Mexican Repatriation from the United States, 1929–1939." *East Wind/West Wind* (Winter 1996): 9–13.

Maldonado, Edwin. "Contract Workers and the Origins of Puerto Rican Communities in the United States." *International Migration Review* 13:1 (1979): 103–121.

Skendzel, Eduard A. *Detroit's Pioneer Mexicans: A Historical Study of the Mexican Colony in Detroit.* Grand Rapids, Mich.: Littleshield Press, 1980.

Salas, Gumecindo, and Isabel Salas. "The Mexican Community of Detroit." In *Immigrants and Migrants: The Detroit Ethnic Experience.* Ed. by David W. Hartman Detroit: Wayne State Univ.: University Studies and Weekend College, 1974.

Salas, Gumecindo, Jesse Gonzales, and Severiano Resendez. "Hispanics." In *Ethnic Groups in Michigan.* Ed. by James M. Anderson and Iva A. Smith. Detroit: Michigan Council for the Arts, 1983.

Valdés, Dennis N. *Al Norte: Agricultural Workers in the Great Lakes Region, 1917–1970.* Austin: Univ. of Tex. Press, 1991.

Vargas, Zaragosa. *Proletarians of the North: A History of Mexican Industrial Workers in Detroit and the Midwest, 1917–1933.* Berkeley: Univ. of Calif. Press, 1993.

JORGE LUIS CHINEA

MILAGRO BEANFIELD WAR

The Milagro Beanfield War (1974), the first novel in author John Nichols's New Mexico trilogy, tells of a haphazard battle between the impoverished townspeople of Milagro, in the north end of the state, and land speculators and politicos who want to usurp centuries' old water rights. Nichols, who moved to Taos, New Mexico, in 1969, had been active in and written about similar local struggles since his arrival, and he drew on some of the personalities, places, and incidents he had encountered. The New Mexico town of Costilla, on the Colorado border, inspired much of *Milagro* and its dilemma, and the Tres Rios Association, a group of acequia-users whose livelihood in the early 1970s was threatened by a proposed dam and water conservancy, motivated Nichols's writing. Nichols's predominantly Hispanic neighbors saw him as an honorable and dedicated propagandist and adviser for their cause. Like the residents of Milagro, they eventually won their battle. Elements in their struggle included preterritorial Spanish customs, interpreted as allotting water use to the farmers, and U.S. law, complicated further by the Treaty of Guadalupe Hidalgo. Since that era most of the water rights in New Mexico's Middle and Upper Rio Grande Basin have been adjudicated.

The novel's skirmish begins when Joe Mondragón, a jackass-of-all-trades, impulsively irrigates his fallow 0.7-acre (0.3-ha) bean field with water from an irrigation channel that would have otherwise benefited a developer. The state's powerful wrongfully interpret this petty act of ornery disobedience as unruly civil defiance, and they overreact with their own disorderly conduct. The novel includes cockeyed legends and half-baked visions, petty miracles and mischievous angels. Race and class are perceptible subtexts. A goofy VISTA (Volunteers in Service to America) volunteer and mangy farm animals round out the essential power and zaniness of the novel. In a region where tradition and suspicion go hand in hand, *Milagro* takes a stand for righteousness and unity. Referring to the movie *Salt of the Earth* about a New Mexico miners' strike, Nichols wrote that he hoped his book "could emulate successfully the message and the humanity of that film." *Milagro* was published within a few years of the English translations by works from Latin America's boom generation authors Gabriel García Márquez, Manuel Puig, and Mario Vargas Llosa, and the reading public was ready for an in-country book that accepted superstitions and wonders as part of daily life in rural Latino America. The critic Peter Wild called *Milagro* "ribald good fun with a bittersweet social message."

The other two books in Nichols's New Mexico trilogy are *The Nirvana Blues* and *The Magic Journey,* the latter of which the author himself believes "a far better and more comprehensive book than *Milagro.*" Together, the three reveal northern New Mexico in the last quarter of the 20th century.

The Milagro Beanfield War provoked a number of potential movie producers to consider a film, but not until 12 years after *Milagro*'s publication, after many false starts, did the right script, financing, cast, and crew coalesce into a bankable effort. The movie's producer was Moctezona Esparza, who had earned a reputation with documentaries and PBS (Public Broadcasting Service) films focusing on Latino America. Robert Redford was the director, and its cast included Rubén Blades, Sonia Braga, Freddy Fender, and Christopher Walken, among others. Many local residents were used as extras, and local mariachis provided the music.

Filming took place in Truchas, New Mexico, after the town of Chimayo, the filmmakers' first choice, decided that a Hollywood invasion was not for them. Curiously, a few weeks into filming, New Mexico land-grant activist Reies Tijerina sued the moviemakers, insisting that the movie was based on him and his activities. (The suit was dropped a month later.) The movie was released in spring 1988 to generally favorable reviews and gained release worldwide. The book, often used in college courses focusing on the Southwest, has been translated into at least eight languages for publication throughout Europe and Latin America. Cheech Marin reads an audio cassette version of *The Milagro Beanfield War.*

RELATED ARTICLES

Agriculture; Film; New Mexico.

FURTHER READING
Miller, Tom. *Jack Ruby's Kitchen Sink: Offbeat Travels through America's Southwest.* Washington, D.C.: Natl. Geographic Soc., 2000.
Nichols, John. *The Milagro Beanfield War.* New York; Henry Holt, 1974.
Nichols, John. *A Fragile Beauty: John Nichols' Milagro Country—Text and Photographs from His Life and Work.* Salt Lake City: Peregrine Smith Bks., 1987.
Nichols, John. *Dancing on the Stones—Selected Essays.* Albuquerque: Univ. of N.Mex. Press, 2000.
Wild, Peter. *John Nichols.* Western Writers Series. Boise, Idaho: Boise State Univ., 1986.

TOM MILLER

MILITARY, UNITED STATES

The United States military has played prominent roles in the national identity and daily lives of Latinos and Latinas in the United States, marked by two recurring features: the "wars" fought against intolerance and discrimination at home and in the services and those fought against the nation's declared enemies. The initial relationship between Mexican-origin populations and Puerto Ricans emerged in the aftermath of the expansion of the United States through military conquest. The relationship among the U.S. military, the U.S. society, and these populations were qualitatively very different from those of all other populations except Native Americans, who themselves were conquered by both the U.S. military and the Spanish and Mexican ancestors of U.S. Latinos. Nevertheless, Latinas and Latinos have not only fulfilled their military duty but they have also used the experience as the basis from which to further their civil rights and to fight for employment, education, and social justice. Equally important were the many roles that women filled and the changes they initiated, from espionage to suffering in combat—which helped create the social templates used for fighting sexual discrimination and harassment, access to crucial jobs in wartime, and for developing the spiritual and emotional foundations for men overseas.

While commentators have suggested that the initial U.S. military participation of Latinas and Latinos can be traced to the American Revolutionary War and the use of Mexican, Puerto Rican, and Cuban troops by Governor Bernardo de Galvez of Florida and the Spanish Imperial Army against the English crown, this argument of inclusion stretches the fundamental relations between Latinos and the U.S. military and the national state. This essay departs from such an assumption and concentrates solely on the relationship initiated between Latino populations and the U.S. military and the national society.

Early Military Relations with Latino Populations

The Mexican-American War of 1846–1848 produced the often contradictory relations between populations of what then was Mexico and the United States. That war itself was part of U.S. territorial expansionism following the dictums of manifest destiny and those in the United States partial to the further increase of slave-holding states. Slave-holding populations earlier had successfully overthrown the neophyte Mexican nation's political control in Texas in 1836, and some Mexican Texans had in fact fought against Mexico and later against the United States in the Mexican-American War.

The Civil War

The importance of the Mexican-American War cannot be understated; it set the stage for the American Civil War in which Mexican-origin populations would fight for both the Union and the Confederacy. Over 13,000 Mexicans and Cubans served for the Confederacy, especially those from Texas, Louisiana, and Florida. On the other hand, numerous companies of Mexican-origin peoples organized Union companies; among the many was Jose Alba Clemente's Company, 1st Co. New Mexico USA Military. Latinas were well represented in the war. Loretta Janeta Velázquez, a Cuban woman, was said to have fought disguised as a Confederate soldier. (*The Woman in Battle* is her account of her adventures as Lieutenant Harry Buford.) She enlisted in the Confederate Army disguised as a man and fought at First Manassas, Ball's Bluff, and Fort Pillow. Discharged when her gender was discovered, she rejoined and fought at Shiloh. Discovered again, she became a successful Confederate spy.

Spanish-American War

Latinos continued to serve in the U.S. military throughout the 19th century and even fought against Spaniards in the Spanish-American War with the assistance of Cuban irregulars who had defeated the Spaniards earlier. Mexican-origin populations from New Mexico, Texas, and California fought with Theodore Roosevelt's Rough Riders, as well as with other units at San Juan Hill and other engagements. Thus F Troop (a platoon-sized unit of about 100 Spanish speaking citizens from the state of New Mexico) was led by Captain Maximiliano Luna of Santa Fe, New Mexico.

This war also formed the basis of the relationship between Puerto Rico and the United States. On the cusp of becoming independent from Spain, Puerto Rico became and remained a territorial annex of the United States; its people, as territorial citizens of the United States, would extensively serve in the U.S. military from annexation to the present.

World War I

World War I engaged 200,000 Latinos, especially Mexican Americans. Puerto Ricans served in all–Puerto Rican units, which, in the aftermath of the Spanish-American War, were formed in six segregated infantry regiments, guarding key installations in Puerto Rico and the Panama Canal Zone. For those of Mexican origin, the United States-Mexico border did present an opportunity to express their dissatisfaction with discrimination in the United States. Although little studied, there were numerous young men who, although born in the United States, chose to move to Mexico rather than serve in the bloody trenches of France. Yet many others did serve with distinction, such as Private First Class Jose C. Salazar, U.S. Army 128th Infantry Regiment, 32d Infantry Division, who died on November 10, 1918, the last day of the war. Others wrote of their experiences, for example J. Luz Saenz of South Texas, who published a diary that illustrates the desire to serve faithfully in the U.S. military while simultaneously having to cope with the discriminatory reality of Texas racism and ethnocentrism in that period. In spite of mistreatment and the fact that others were fleeing across the border to escape military service, David Barkley a Mexican American from Laredo, Texas, chose to serve in the 89th Infantry Division's 356th Infantry Regiment and won the Medal of Honor posthumously for his actions near Pouilly, France, on November 9, 1918.

Fighting Discrimination

Military service did move returning veterans to fight for their rights and against discrimination. While not a veterans' organization, the League of United Latin American Congress (LULAC) was founded in 1929 and influenced by returning veterans such as Saenz who served on its board of directors early on. However, the role of Mexican-origin women in developing LULAC cannot be underestimated since its auxiliary organization was crucial in the total organization's development. It is more than likely that Latinas served among the 33,000 women who were enlisted in the armed services during World War I, while other Latinas served in crucial labor roles in factories, businesses, and in agriculture.

World War II

The pattern of returning veterans' influencing and organizing associations in the struggle against racial and ethnic discrimination had its apogee after the intense service in all branches of the military by Mexican Americans, Puerto Ricans, and some Cubans. Yet, there were also internal struggles in the services themselves with Latinos at times being less eligible for promotion and unrecognized for their actions on the battlefield. On the other hand many Latinos were honored, receiving accolades for valor and leadership. For example during World War II, the 158th Infantry Regiment, known as the "Bushmasters"—a quarter of whom were Mexican Americans—was lauded by General Douglas MacArthur as "one of the greatest fighting combat teams ever deployed for battle."

Large segments of the Mexican American population, U.S. citizens and noncitizens alike, joined either elite units of the army, such as the paratroopers or the Marines, or were drafted in large numbers into combat units. Some, for example Antonio Alcaraz and his sisters, whose parents had migrated to Tucson, Arizona, from Sinaloa, Mexico, shortly after the Mexican Revolution, were all sent back to Mexico during the infamous "repatriation" period in the 1930s while Antonio was enrolled at Tucson High School. Shortly afterwards he "illegally" returned to the United States to enlist and he served with the 551st Parachute Regiment. Later, only a few weeks after becoming a U.S. citizen, he was wounded in the battle for Salerno. Others became aces, such as Francis Perdomos and Richard Candelaria, both born in El Paso, Texas, but raised in Los Angeles, California. The former became the last United States Air Force pilot to become an "Ace in a Day" when he shot down five Japanese planes in a single day while serving with the 464th Fighter Squadron in the Far East. The latter, on April 7, 1945, single-handedly engaged 17 German combat aircraft and shot down four German fighters to add to the two he had downed previously. Marine Edward Romero of Tucson survived two wounds in the battles of Saipan, Tinian, and was in the first wave of the invasion of Iwo Jima in which 90 percent casualties were suffered and fierce hand-to-hand combat ensued.

Many combat units were made up almost exclusively of Mexican-origin soldiers, such as E Company of the 141st Infantry Regiment of the 36th Division; the 7th, 30th, and 142d Infantry Regiments of the 3d Division; the 22d Infantry Regiment of the 4th Division; the 23d Infantry Regiment of the 2d Division; and the 79th Infantry Regiment of the 7th Division. In all, 11 Mexican-origin soldiers were awarded the Medal of Honor; among them was Marcario Garcia of Villa de Castaño, Mexico, of the 4th Infantry Division.

Like many of their World War I compatriots, this generation struggled for civil rights and declared *no mas* (no more) against discrimination, founding the American GI Forum. The Forum was made up entirely of returning veterans who, on returning home, were denied their earned educational, housing, and medical benefits. In addition, some funeral homes refused to bury the bodies of battle-slain Mexican American veterans in other than segregated cemeteries. The American GI Forum was responsible for many of the gains made in the areas of education and school desegregation, housing and restricted covenants, voting rights, and employment opportunities; its members were among the many who took advantage of the GI Bill to earn university degrees.

About 65,000 Puerto Ricans also served in the armed forces during World War II, but many served in segregated units, such as the Regular Army's 65th Infantry Regiment and the Puerto Rican National Guard's 295th and 296th Infantry Regiments in

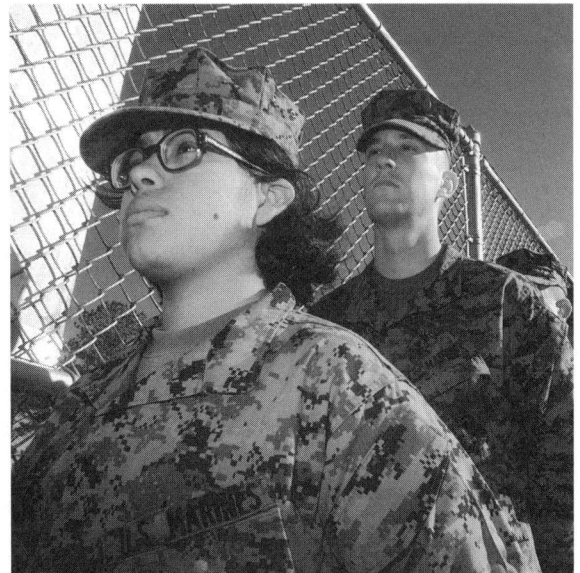

© RANDY DAVEY/POLARIS

A Marine private at the armory at Camp Geiger, Jacksonville, North Carolina, waiting to be issued weapons, 2003.

Puerto Rico, Panama, the Caribbean, Hawaii, North Africa, Italy, the Maritime Alps of France, and Germany. Annapolis graduate Pedro del Valle, United States Marine Corps of Puerto Rico, was the architect of all artillery on Guadacanal. Without his tactical and strategic use of arms, that very tenuous battle would certainly have been lost. He commanded the 11th Marines (artillery regiment of the 1st Marine Division), the Artillery of the 3d Amphibious Corps on Guadalcanal and Guam, and the 1st Marine Division during the Okinawa Campaign. Among his numerous awards, decorations, and medals is the Distinguished Service Medal and the Legion of Merit with Gold Star.

Puerto Ricans faced appalling social and economic conditions when they returned to the island, and thousands migrated from there to New York City where they faced issues similar to those of Mexicans in the Southwest: poor employment opportunities, limited educational opportunities, racial and linguistic discrimination, housing covenants, and economic disparities in salaries and wages, as well as exclusion from union representation. They, too, developed veteran-led independent organizations under the GI Forum banner, and, as part of the basis for their legitimate claims, they pointed to four Puerto Ricans who received Congressional Medal of Honor medals and hundreds of Boriquas who died in the Pacific and Europe.

Watershed for Women

World War II was also a watershed for most American women and for Latinas especially. There are four main areas in which Latinas especially contributed to U.S. efforts in World War II: first, because of the much higher birth rates of Latino families, Latina mothers especially suffered with multiple children deployed overseas. Second, many Latinas served in the navy, Marine Corps, army, and Army Air Force as officers, enlisted women, nurses, and so on. Third, Latinas took jobs they had previously been denied and created new ones when millions of men joined the services, thus Latinas fought ethnic and gender discrimination on the job and in the military.

Mexican-origin women replaced male railroad workers in firing up locomotive engines for the Southern Pacific Railroad, taking the first important steps toward breaking down the color barriers encountered by Mexican men. In addition they successfully had men fired for sexual harassment, possibly among the first women in the United States to do so in the workplace. Mexican-origin women, represented by the Amalgamated Clothing Workers of America, worked in the copper mines of Arizona. These women organized a series of wildcat strikes protesting poor working conditions and sexual harassment. Many would form auxiliary women's organizations with their returning husbands and brothers, who once again faced employment discrimination for the very jobs their spouses and sisters had filled.

The Soldiers of Agriculture and the Railroads

A little-known, important fact is that while thousands of Mexico-born U.S. armed forces volunteers served the United States in World War II, about 300,000 Mexicans, under the Mexico–United States Borrowed Workmanship Program—also known as the Bracero Program—replaced their brethren and non-Latino workers who had gone off to war, in jobs in California, Montana, Washington, Colorado, Michigan, Arizona, Wisconsin, and Minnesota between 1942 and 1946. Some considered themselves "soldiers of agriculture, construction, and of the railroads."

Korea

Unlike World War II, the Korean War was often a contentious event; there was little understanding as to the whys and whens of the "police action" that cost many lives. This war was also, however, a mixed proposition for many Latinos and Latinas since those who went into combat in Korea had been in the midst of fighting civil rights battles at home. President Truman's 1948 integration order had many implications, especially for Puerto Rican soldiers, many of whom served in nonsegregated units. However, in Korea, Puerto Ricans were placed in segregated units, including the well-regarded 65th Army Regiment that had served both world wars. In Korea the regiment was subject to much criticism after 100 of its men refused to fight in one badly organized and futile battle. They had already faced heavy casualties owing to incompetent leadership and non-Spanish-speaking noncommissioned officers. Eventually, the men of the 65th were exonerated and all courts-martial were rescinded. The 65th also served with distinction in helping guard the flanks of the First Marine Division, many of whom were of Mexican descent, as it extricated itself from the infamous Chosen Reservoir.

About 80 percent of Marine Reserve Easy Company were Mexicans and Mexican Americans from Tucson, Arizona. Some, only 17 years old and still in high school, were called up in June 1950. With very limited training they fought valiantly through the Inchon invasion, the battle for the city of Seoul, and to the Yalu River bordering China. Some returned to graduate from Tucson High School, many wounded and all suffering from different levels of battle shock.

Here, too, the Medal of Honor would be awarded, mostly posthumously, to eight Latinos: six of Mexican descent, one Puerto Rican, and one Cuban. This important generation would also return to the United States to fight for civil rights; they would attain college degrees and create many opportunities for following generations, as did Sergeant Eugene Suarez, the only Mexican American Marine combat photographer to have served in either World War II or Korea.

The Korean War, like World War II, also served as an important step toward greater civil and educational equity for Latinas and Latinos, with many returning men and women joining the GI Forum; developing civil associations such as the Mexican American Political Association, the Mexican American League, and others; and taking advantage of the GI Bill, which offered similar support to that of the World War II version.

Vietnam

Participation in combat was not to cease for Latinos. Between 1961 and 2004 many casualties were suffered, terrible psychic wounds incurred, and families were torn apart. Among the costliest wars in terms of disproportionate number of Latino casualties was Vietnam. An analysis of the distribution of Latino-origin soldiers, marines, and sailors in combat units, their total casualty rates, and the after effects on families has not yet been accomplished. However, it is known that between January 1961 and February 1967, slightly less than 20 percent of those killed in Vietnam from the U.S. Southwest were of Mexican origin; and between December 1967 and March 1969, 19 percent were of Mexican origin—U.S.- and Mexican-born. For the duration of the war, 1961–1973, of those who served one in two Latinos served

in combat units, one in three was wounded, and one in five was killed.

Especially between 1968 and 1973, these casualty rates were felt by many communities whose sons had perished in what had become a very unpopular war. These statistics also became known and were questioned among many sectors of the Latino community. Widespread protests, not unlike those expressed by millions of other Americans, were organized and carried out by Latino university and high school students, professionals, farmworkers, blue-collar workers, and numerous community organizations and individuals. The Chicano Moratorium of Los Angeles against the War, attended by thousands on August 29, 1970, was among the largest organized protests but it ended ignominiously in a skirmish with Los Angeles riot police and Los Angeles County sheriffs' deputies.

Returning Latino Vietnam veterans, unlike their fathers and grandfathers, did not generally join veterans' associations. Instead, like many others, they hid from the open hostility heaped on them and escaped into neighborhoods to attend school or find jobs. In many cases they suffered alone for many years from the shock of battle. According to the National Vietnam Veterans Readjustment Study, 29 percent of Latinos who went to Vietnam at some point in their adult lives met the full diagnostic criteria for Post Traumatic Stress Disorder, compared with a lifetime prevalence rate of 20 percent and 14 percent for African Americans and Anglo-Americans, respectively. The Latino percentage is only surpassed by Native American veterans, at 30 percent.

Like their fathers and grandfathers before them, this generation earned ten Medals of Honor, and, while whole units were no longer segregated or composed mostly of Latinos, the sheer percentage of Latinos serving in combat units supported the conclusion that Vietnam was fought by too many youths whose main recommendation for combat was the lack of a college deferment. Yet, as in World War II and Korea, noncitizens gave their lives for others and were awarded the Medal of Honor. Puerto Ricans won as many Medals of Honor Awards (four) in Vietnam as they had in World War II.

1990–2004

Twenty thousand Latinos served in operations Desert Storm and Desert Shield (1990–1991), and by 1997 a third of the combat troops in Bosnia were Latinos.

But the U.S. intervention in Iraq in 2004 once again raised the issue of Latinos engaged mostly in combat units and often in harm's way, regardless of citizenship. The first two Marines killed in that war were not citizens of the United States but of Guatemala and Mexico; the third was an immigrant son from Mexico.

Indeed, in Iraq the Marine Corps had the highest percentage of Latinos and Latinas (14 percent) compared with the other branches of the military, in part because of the allure of an elite combat force and, in many cases, the quest for opportunity through the military.

Conclusion

The association of the U.S. military and Latino communities has been a long one, beginning with the expansion of U.S. military power into Mexico and the Caribbean in the middle and late 19th century. This relationship is characterized by both accommodation and participation and rejection and resistance, depending on the political and social circumstances of the time. The United States was seen as a benefactor by some during the Texas Revolt and by some as an enemy during the Mexican-American War. During the Civil War, Mexicans, who had themselves been conquered only 18 years earlier, fought for both the Confederacy and the Union; and 33 years later they also served with distinction in the Spanish-American War against other Spanish-speaking populations. During this entire process, however, both Mexicans and Puerto Ricans had been compressed into rural and urban enclaves; in the latter case especially, racial segregation had played a major role in differentiating this population from the rest of the U.S. citizenry. For Mexicans, the border created citizenship in the United States but also a permeable membrane that now forced some relatives to be "Americans" and others "Mexicans." In addition, most Mexicans in the United States—now U.S. citizens—were denied many of the civil liberties, job opportunities, educational access, housing accommodations, and political voting rights that were available to the majority population.

Each war has provided a means by which returning veterans were able to resist such conditions, and

The widow and son of a U.S. Marine, pictured in the photograph, who was killed in Iraq in 2003.

the war dead were constant reminders that Latinos did not have to accept the status quo. Thus, in the Civil War, the Spanish-American War, World War I, World War II, Korea, Vietnam, Desert Storm, Desert Shield, and later in Iraq, Latinos have served the United States valiantly and with distinction.

RELATED ARTICLES

65th Infantry; American GI Forum; Chicano Movement; Civil War; Gulf Wars; Korean War; Mexican-American War; National Chicano Moratorium of Vietnam; Spanish-American War; Vietnam War; World War I; World War II.

FURTHER READING

del Valle, Pedro. *Semper Fidelis: An Autobiography: Lt. Gen. Pedro A. del Valle.* Hawthorne, Calif.: Christian Book Club of Am., 1976.

Grant, Ulysses S. *The Personal Memoirs of Ulysses S. Grant.* 1885. Reprint. Old Saybrook, Conn.: Konecky & Konecky Press, 1992.

Meketa, Jacqueline Dorgan. *Legacy of Honor: The Life of Rafael Chacon.* Las Cruces, N.Mex.: Yucca Tree Press, 2000.

Ramirez, Juan. *A Patriot After All: The Story of a Chicano Vietnam Vet.* Albuquerque: Univ. of N.Mex. Press, 1999.

Ramos, Henry A. J. *The American G.I. Forum: In Pursuit of the Dream, 1948–1983.* Houston, Tex.: Arte Publico Press, 1998.

Rivas, Maggie, ed. *Narratives: Stories of U.S. Latinos and Latinas in World War II.* Austin: School of Journalism, Univ. of Tex., 2000–2004.

Roosevelt, Theodore. *The Rough Riders.* New York: Scribner's, 1899.

Trujillo, Charly. *Soldados: Chicanos in Viet Nam.* San Jose, Calif.: Chusma Press, 1990.

Velazquez, Loreta Janeta. *The Woman in Battle: A Narrative of the Exploits, Adventures, and Travels of Madame Loreta Janeta Velazquez, Otherwise Known as Lieutenant Harry T. Buford, Confederate States Army.* Richmond, Va.: Dustin, Gilman & Co., 1876 [electronic copy: http://docsouth.unc.edu/velazquez/velazquez.html].

Velez, Carlos G. *Border Visions: The Cultures of Mexicans of the Southwest United States.* Tucson: Univ. of Ariz. Press, 1996.

CARLOS G. VELEZ-IBANEZ

MIRANDA, CARMEN

Born: February 9, 1909; Marco de Canvezes, Portugal
Died: August 5, 1955; Los Angeles, California

Born Maria do Carmo Miranda da Cunha, actor and entertainer Carmen Miranda moved with her family to Rio de Janeiro, Brazil, when she was very young, so she always considered herself a carioca, as natives of Rio are called. Her father owned a prosperous wholesale fruit business, and the family lived a comfortable middle-class life. Maria, or Carmen, was sent to a fine convent school. She showed early talent as a singer, and soon began performing on local radio stations. Eventually she became a popular recording star, which, in turn, led to appearances in Brazilian films.

The Shubert brothers, successful Broadway producers, were impressed enough to bring Miranda to New York to appear in their popular musical comedy, *The Streets of Paris.* She received excellent reviews and was later offered an engagement at the Starlight Roof of the Waldorf-Astoria. This was a venue much-watched by Hollywood talent scouts because in those days the studios were making many musical comedies. A talent scout from Twentieth Century-Fox liked what he saw and heard and set up a screen test at the studio.

Miranda was cast in musicals with stars such as Betty Grable, Alice Faye, and Don Ameche as well as in big budget films, including *Down Argentine Way* in 1940, *That Night in Rio* and *Weekend in Havana* in 1941, and *The Gang's All Here* in 1943, which featured a very suggestive number involving bananas (barely getting through the censors).

Miranda was given substantial roles, and she managed to steal every scene she was in. Her fractured English, colorful costumes, and turbans piled high with tropical fruits were huge hits with audiences. The Portuguese language itself added to the hilarity, with its strange "a-ow" sounds at the ends of words and its sibilant "shhhs," throughout.

During the 1940s her impact was so great that a new nightclub in New York called itself the Copacabana, after the famed beach in Rio. It featured a chorus line of gorgeous women, all wearing turbans loaded with fruit. The turbans became the club's logo.

While Miranda was enjoying her success in Hollywood, her compatriots were not. They considered her a sellout, an entertainer who was reinforcing the stereotype of the hot-blooded Latina. They felt that the world was laughing at her, not with her. Miranda herself was a willing coconspirator. In her eagerness to please, and in appreciation for what she had been given, she never uttered a word of complaint about the parts she was asked to play. Nor did she make any suggestions that might have cooled down her overheated image.

Carmen Miranda in the Busby Berkeley movie *The Gang's All Here*, 1943.

The actor's roles were basically the same: the clueless, oversexed nightclub entertainer who spoke funny English. Her costumes were skimpy (she was probably the first entertainer, outside of a burlesque show, to bare her midriff), her platform shoes ridiculously high, and her jealous fits dependably comic. There was no way the studio would change that formula; it had worked too well.

Until she went back to Brazil for her first visit home, Miranda was seemingly unaware of what was happening to her in Hollywood. Instead of a triumphant return, she got angry protests in front of her hotel. She returned to Hollywood shocked and disappointed.

Miranda returned to making the films that were such money makers for the studio, but inevitably depression set in, exacerbated by the use of her face for the Chiquita Banana logo. A brief, unhappy marriage only made things worse. Miranda, a real professional, continued to work, appearing to be as happy-go-lucky as ever.

On August 5, 1955, while appearing on the Jimmy Durante television show, she suffered a fatal heart attack. Her body was shipped back to her homeland for burial. Brazil declared a national day of mourning.

As the 1980s drew to a close, Miranda became a symbol of the sexual and economic exploitation of Latin women. In 1995 a documentary about Miranda's life, called *Bananas Is My Business,* was shown on public television. It revealed, at last, the tragedy of her life.

RELATED ARTICLES

Film; Stereotypes and Stereotyping.

FURTHER READING

Guera, Lucia. *Las noches de Carmen Miranda.* Buenos Aires: Editorial Sud Americana, 2002.

Montero, Marta Gil. *Brazilian Bombshell.* New York: Donald I. Fine, 1989.

SYLVIA SHORRIS

MISSIONS

Missions served multiple roles in the Latino community as well as in the non-Latino communities in which they were situated. They first emerged as Spanish colonial institutions and served religious, economic, and imperial purposes in the late 16th century. As religious institutions, missions were responsible for providing spiritual guidance to the colonizing class as well as for the attempted conversion of indigenous communities. As economic institutions with agricultural developments and ranches, missions were instrumental in sustaining local settlements.

Historical and Geographic Overview

Missions were vital to the European settlement of frontier regions because of the infrastructure they provided. For example, mission assets included water reservoirs, aqueducts, carpenters' shops, tanneries, jail houses, ranches, cattle, crops such as wheat, and other resources that exemplified a complex existence. Most of the heavy labor, such as construction of buildings and aqueducts, was conducted by Indians.

Throughout their existence, missions have held historical, religious, architectural, economic, and cultural significance. Missions were often complexes in themselves, initially serving as Spanish colonial institutions and complementing other colonial institutions such as presidios (military forts) and pueblos (towns) on the northern Spanish frontier. While missions were not located in all the modern states, they served the expansive northern Spanish frontier that included the modern-day states of Florida, South Carolina, Georgia, Virginia, Alabama, Mississippi, Louisiana, Texas, New Mexico, Arizona, California, Oklahoma, Kansas, Colorado, Utah, and Nevada.

The earliest missions were established by Jesuits while the later ones were built by Franciscans. Between 1566 and 1572, Jesuits built ten missions in Ajacán, the name Spaniards had given to the present-day state of Virginia (in the vicinity of Jamestown), to south Florida (in the vicinity of Miami). The mission in Virginia is significant because it was built in 1570, 37 years before the English established a permanent colony at Jamestown. After the turn of the century and by 1675, Franciscans had expanded the domain of Spanish missions to more than 250 miles (400 km) west of the Atlantic coast. Four mission provinces in Florida included Guale in the modern state of Georgia, Timucua along the northern Atlantic coastline of Florida, Apalachee on the Gulf coast along the Florida panhandle, and Apalachicola in the westernmost part of Florida.

As colonial efforts moved northwest, missions were established in northern New Mexico beginning in 1581 among the Pueblo Indians. The Pueblo were considered ideal for missionization by Franciscan friars owing to their sedentary social organization. Indian labor was utilized for the building of mission compounds; Pueblo women built the walls of missions, while Pueblo men did much of the carpentry. This region was also significant because it helped to facilitate further colonization from the interior of New Spain toward the northwestern frontier. The Pueblo did not respond positively, however. In 1680 they revolted and expelled, if only for a short time, their Spanish colonizers.

In the modern-day state of Arizona, Franciscan friars tried to convert Hopis at the village of Awatovi. They established San Bernardo Mission there in 1629. By 1641 missions had been established at Shongopovi and Oraibi, but the Pueblo Revolt of 1680 had consequences in Arizona as well; four Franciscans were killed by the Hopis, and further missionization attempts failed over the next three decades.

After the failures of the Franciscan missionaries, Arizona missions were run by Jesuits from 1730 until their expulsion from New Spain in 1767. The Jesuit entries into modern southern Arizona were preceded by the establishment of missions along the California Gulf in what are today the central and northern Mexican states of Sinaloa and Sonora. The Jesuit Eusebio Francisco Kino is credited with directing the first missions in southern Arizona, including Guevavi and San Xavier del Bac along the Santa Cruz River in 1701.

French ventures into the Gulf coast during the late 17th century prompted Spain to establish missions in the interior and along the Gulf coast of Texas. Missions were established along the present-day Texas and Louisiana border in the early 18th century. Five missions were built along the San Antonio River between 1718 and 1731. While successful, the number of Indian converts in the five San Antonio missions remained small compared with missions in Florida and New Mexico, perhaps owing to the larger number of nomadic indigenous peoples who lived in the San Antonio area.

Missions were started in California for the purpose of establishing a colonial presence as well as for converting the native populations. Owing to imperial rivalries among the Spanish, Russians, and English, missions helped to settle the strategically valuable coastal region that included natural bays and harbors in San Francisco, Monterrey, Los Angeles, and San Diego. The Channel Islands off the coast of Santa Barbara also provided a waterway for the emerging shipping industry. Among the many missions established in the modern-day state of California were those at San Diego (1769), San Antonio de Padua (1771), San Gabriel (1771), San Luis Obispo (1772), San Francisco (1776), San Juan Capistrano (1776), San Jose (1777), and Santa Barbara (1782).

California's missions are perhaps the most romanticized because of their restoration and incorporation into the tourist industry as sights of interest. As with other missions, California's were assigned to a corresponding presidio, which normally had several missions within its jurisdiction. A significant task of the California missions was to provide food for the soldiers and their families.

A primary function of missions during the colonial era was to bring the various localities into a developing global economy and under the domain of Spain. Thus, evangelization took on religious, economic, cultural, and political meaning. The goals were to acculturate Indians of the different missions, to assist in the settlement of outlying areas for political and economic purposes, and to fend off imperial rivals. In order to accomplish this, Spanish missionaries at times attempted to develop an ideological form of *mestizaje* (mixture).

In an effort to offset Indian resistance to colonization—and more importantly to incorporate Indians into the mainstream—cultural, racial, and ideological forms of *mestizaje* proved to be strategies of Spanish Mexican conquest. For some Indians different forms of *mestizaje* later became strategies of survival. Yet, *mestizaje* was based on the notion of negotiated, and at times forced, acculturation through the conglomeration of presumably superior Eurocentric values and the appropriation, subjugation, and suppression of presumably inferior indigenous worldviews. This was effected through an inclusive, repressive process that sought to incorporate Indians into

mainstream society, yet at subservient levels; although Indians were allowed and even encouraged to participate in social functions, their level of participation was limited until they were able to demonstrate a full understanding of Spanish ways. An attempt was made to destroy the native understanding of the natural world and replace it with a Eurocentric one. This included efforts by the Spanish missionaries to change the dress and the mode of economic productivity of the Indians, for example, teaching them that nudity was shameful and that surplus productivity was superior to subsistence productivity.

Institutionally, Indians could vote, but their vote was restricted to the election of local majordomos of Indian *rancherías,* communal villages that were situated in close proximity to the missions, and they could not vote to elect Spanish Mexican officials. In 1824 a special commission was convened and concluded that because the mission system was "anti-republican . . . the first and most important step that must be taken to lead the Indian to civilization was to teach him the value of his right to own land." Upon completing this task the commission determined that land should only be given to those Indians "who have the necessary disposition and faculties for agricultural work." California's Indians thus had to demonstrate their adaptability to Spanish notions of economic productivity in order to be elevated from workers to land owners.

Conversion for Indians also meant a shift to the Spanish language and a change to Spanish names. Mission Indians were renamed and an attempt was made to place an alternative identity on them. In February 1822 a Chumash Indian from the area of Mission San Buenaventura in California testified in a criminal case that in spite of earlier attempts by Franciscan missionaries to rename him Francisco, his name was Alizanahuit. That assertion, along with numerous acts of resistance on the part of mission Indians, demonstrates that the process of constructing an ideological *mestizaje* consisted of negotiation with, rejection of, and resistance to dominant ideals. Indians were not simply absorbed into Spanish culture and ideals. They often "spoke back" to the colonial process.

The attempt to convert Indians to Catholicism was complemented by the development of an economic infrastructure. Thus, while religious conversion was a primary goal, missionaries incorporated Indians as workers who performed different tasks such as building missions and surrounding buildings, aqueducts, and canals.

Indians provided labor in the service sector as well, and many became servants for colonial families, tended to cattle, and were central to the development of an early agricultural economy that helped to sustain other colonial institutions such as the presidios, the soldiers and their families, and the local pueblos and their correspondent inhabitants.

Mission Indians, known as neophytes, lived on local *rancherías*. Young girls and women were often placed in *monjerios* (nunneries) and kept under lock and key by a *llavera* who was usually an older Christianized Indian woman. The separation of unwedded young men and women seemed to be a preoccupation of missionaries who often complained of what they perceived to be "sexual transgressions" among the Indians. Indians who refused or otherwise were excluded from mission life were known as gentiles.

Often infantalized, Indians, including adults, were generally known by the designation *niños* (children).

Economic Resources and Functions of the Mission Complex

Contrary to popular notions that the American West was "civilized" as a result of constant battles that pitted "cowboys" against "Indians," California's mission Indians were in fact the first cowboys in the Western Hemisphere. Californian Indians functioned as vaqueros in a complex and oftentimes vibrant setting.

Some missions built *lavanderias,* or wash basins, where clothes and other items were washed. The building of such mission facilities demonstrated a combination of Spanish and Indian ideals. At Mission Santa Barbara in California, for example, the *lavanderia* was adorned by sculptures of bear and mountain lion heads that were created by Chumash

THE GRANGER COLLECTION

Earliest known view of California, this 1786 illustration shows Native Americans at the mission at Carmel, welcoming the Comte de La Perouse and his expedition.

Indians who resided in the local area. Such Indian artistry demonstrates that a conglomeration of Spanish and Indian worldviews characterized the mission experience, and it is important to note that although the Spanish worldview dominated such proceedings, the mission process was not simply an imposition of Spanish norms upon indigenous populations.

Remnants of a pottery room exist in some missions. Pottery rooms were essential because they helped to facilitate the fabrication of containers and vessels that were significant for storing foodstuffs and water supply. As with other facilities in the mission complexes, Indians provided a bulk of this work.

In other instances, missions were in charge of reservoirs that supplied the mission and surroundings with water. Much of the water supply was diverted from local mountain creeks through aqueducts that were constructed by Indians. Irrigation systems were developed in order to grow crops in mission farmlands.

Cattle and wheat were essential staples for the missions' survival. Along the California coast, cattle were used to feed the local populace, and hide was in demand from industrial areas. The hide was prepared for market in tanning vats that existed on mission grounds. Indian workers slaughtered cattle, dressed and processed the hides, and were responsible for maintenance of the grounds.

Wheat was used as a local food source as well, but perhaps carried more value as an item for maritime trade with the ships that sailed the Pacific coast. Such trade was forbidden by the Spanish crown, yet Franciscan missionaries and government officials sometimes engaged in the black market economy to satisfy local needs and desires. For example, in October 1821, when the impact of revolution had not yet hit the *frontera* regions, Franciscans engaged in illicit trade with a Russian ship anchored off the coast of California. Much of the wheat that was traded was exchanged for goods that were needed in the local missions. Government officials were so surprised at the amount of surplus wheat relative to the low taxes collected for that year that they launched an investigation. Among the findings were Indian complaints of hunger, attributed to the confiscation of the Indian wheat allotment by missionaries.

Economic developments had ecological consequences for the local environment. The introduction of cattle and other livestock by the missions resulted in grazing and trampling of local native vegetation.

As cattle and other livestock took over the feeding grounds of local native game, such as deer, the latter moved out to the fringes at an increased rate. This disturbed the traditional reliance by local Indians on such food sources. As a result, they were more inclined to come into communication with missions.

Military Support of Missions

The Royal Orders for New Discoveries of 1573 prohibited the use of military force as a means of conquest of the *fronteras*. However, the historical record demonstrates repeated incidents of use of force against mission Indians. Indeed, military presence in the vicinity of missions had a variety of consequences.

On the one hand, it helped to stabilize the mission efforts by providing an armed force that protected missionaries as well as civilians from what were considered to be uncivilized Indians. On the other hand, the behavior of some soldiers caused great concern among missionaries and civilian officials alike because of the consequences it had on Indians. Acts of sexual violence on the part of soldiers against indigenous women became cause for concern in California in the late 18th century. Missionaries submitted numerous complaints to civilian officials about the rape and murder of young Indian women. The missionaries played a role in trying to avert such incidents because they felt among other things that it would negatively affect their evangelization efforts. Thus, Franciscan missionaries attempted to affect policies that would deter soldiers from engaging in sexually violent acts.

Soldiers also posed a threat to mission intents in a case that involved trade among Amajava Indians from the Colorado River region bordering California and Arizona with missionaries in Mission San Buenaventura in 1819. In the spring of that year Amajava Indians traveled to the coastal mission to trade with Franciscan missionaries. When they arrived, they were held and incarcerated with plans to be released and expelled from the region the following Monday. During Sunday Mass, several of the imprisoned Amajavas forced their way out, leading Franciscan missionaries to arm local Chumash Indians and to call on soldiers to recapture them. A battle ensued in which two Spanish soldiers and one neophyte soldier were killed. Ten Amajavas were killed as well. All ten were decapitated and their heads impaled on stakes for public display in the plaza. The episode resulted in a short yet tumultuous period of conflict between the Amajava Indians and Spanish soldiers.

Indian Revolts

Perceived sexual transgressions, theft, idolatry, and other acts among mission Indians were punishable by flogging, incarceration, and placement in stocks. Whether they were affected by harsh treatment at the hands of the missionaries or by military repression, Indians living in the vicinity of missions openly revolted when they did not engage in passive resistance. These acts included numerous assassinations of Franciscan friars and others affiliated with the missions. Two of the most well-known cases of Indian revolt against missions included the Pueblo Revolt of 1680 and the Chumash Revolt of 1824.

The Pueblo Revolt of 1680 was led by Popé from the Tewa pueblo of San Juan. Popé had previously been accused of witchcraft and idolatry and arrested by Spanish authorities. Of 40 Tewa who were arrested, 3 were hanged and the others whipped and condemned to servitude. Popé fled north to Taos where he remained in hiding as he developed his plans for revenge.

At Taos, Popé planned, along with several others, a full-scale assault on Spaniards in the region with the intent to destroy them or drive them out. The assault began in early August 1680 and resulted in the killing of 21 Franciscans and 380 colonists. Those Spaniards who survived fled south. The independence gained by the Pueblo Indians lasted until 1692 when Spanish authorities reconquered the region.

The Chumash revolt of 1824 involved attacks by Indians against missions in the Santa Barbara area. They set fire to the mission building in Santa Ynez and engaged Spanish troops at Mission Santa Barbara. At the latter mission, Chumash Indians took Padre Antonio Jaime captive and put him against a wall used to screen troops from frontal enemy fire as the Indians fired from behind the wall. Several Spaniards in the vicinity were killed. There is some debate concerning the origin of the Chumash Revolt, but it is likely that the combined effects of harsh treatment by Franciscans of Indians, scarcity of supplies, lack of freedom, sexual repression, punishment for practice of indigenous religious ways, and several other causes all contributed to the Indians' frustration.

Secularization of Missions

As Spain and later Mexico eyed imperial rivals to the north and east, various attempts to settle the northern frontier were made. The Colonization Act of 1824 attempted to stimulate settlement of the northern frontier by liberalizing land policy. Mexico invited Anglos to migrate to Texas and establish settlements. A convict colony was sent to California in 1829; women were encouraged to migrate north from Mexico for the purpose of stabilizing the frontier; and the privately and publicly financed Hijar-Padrés colony was settled in California in 1834. These and other attempts to populate the frontier with civilians led to an increased demand on their part for more control over resources and politics.

Indeed, the increased lay population of Spanish Mexican homesteaders and retired military officials and their families in the vicinity of the missions during the 1820s and 1830s led to anticlericism that was embedded in economic more than spiritual concerns, attesting more to the economic viability of the Franciscan missionaries as managers and the missions as institutions than to anti-Catholicism. Because the Catholic Church was among the biggest holders of property, the homesteaders began to move toward secularization of mission lands, driven by competition for material and social control over the wealth and laborers in the regions under question.

Some of the anti-Spanish and anticleric sentiment that fed the War of Independence did carry over to the move to privatize land and other mission resources. Many civilians criticized the control missionaries had over land and Indians. Government officials soon began to heed the calls of these civilians. On August 17, 1833, the Mexican Congress passed a bill of secularization, which decreed that vast mission land holdings were to be redistributed to civilians. Indians under the care of missionaries were to be emancipated and given their freedom. In addition, Article 5 of the secularization bill gave land to mission Indians.

Still, many questions remained regarding the plight of mission Indians. For example, Father Durán wrote to Alt California governor José María de Echeandía,

> " . . . the ideas of the Indians, of the non-Indians, and of the government are so very different. The latter wants the Indians [to] be private owners of lands and other property, which is very just. The Indians want the freedom of vagabonds, and the rest want the absolute emancipation of the neo-

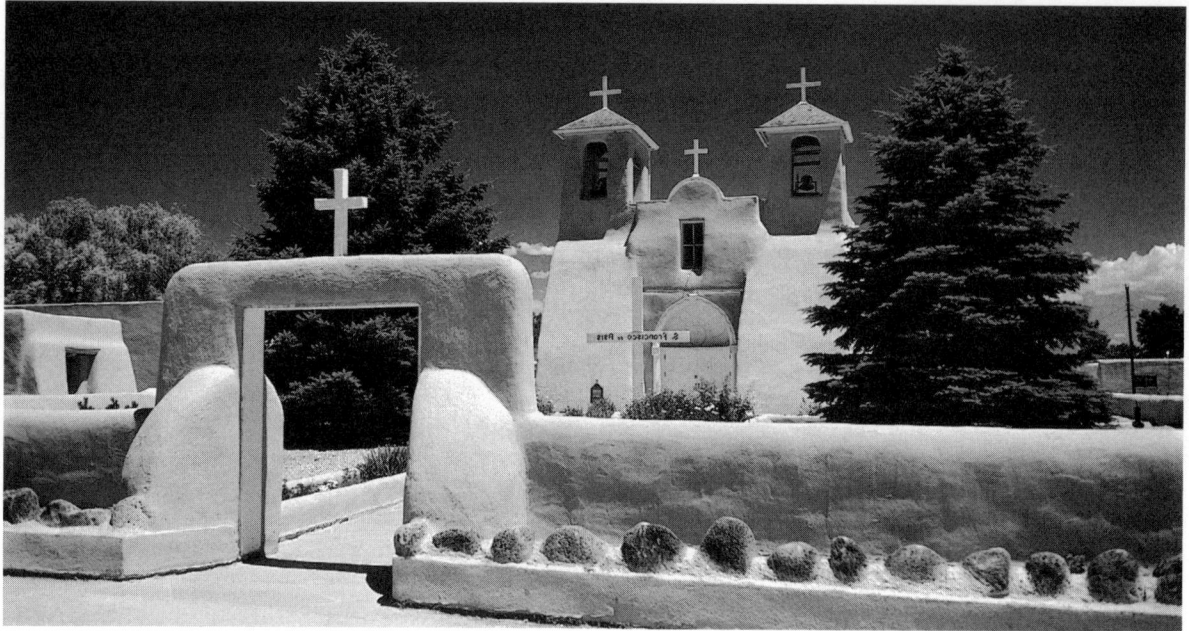

San Francisco de Asis Mission church, dating to circa 1772, Ranchos de Taos, New Mexico.

phytes and without the order of townships formed according to the manner of civilized settlements . . . . I do not understand how such opposite interests can be reconciled."

Whatever the concerns, the secularization bill's aim was to provide an institutional framework for privatization efforts. Thus, beginning in 1834, nearly 8 million acres (3 million ha) were granted or sold to former Spanish Mexican officials, soldiers, and civilians, including women. This gave rise to a new *ranchero* and *ranchera* class.

Spanish Fantasy Heritage

The decline of missions began shortly after the secularization decree, when private land holders were granted land and other property formerly held by the missions. However, while Indians were among the grantees, their ownership of land was short-lived in most cases. Thus, many former mission Indians entered the new order as workers on the large private estates or *ranchos*.

This began a period of deterioration of mission buildings and their surroundings that was accelerated by the U.S. conquest of Mexico. New demands caused by westward migration and the Gold Rush after the Mexican-American War resulted in the further appropriation and neglect of the former mission compounds. Indeed, mass overland migrations in the mid-19th century resulted in a new and increased demand that was satisfied by squatting and other means. Corporate interests began to take their toll in the latter part of the 19th century.

At the turn of the 20th century, however, a movement was launched to preserve the mission buildings and their environs. This resulted in part from a conscious effort to create a tourist industry in various areas where missions were located. During the revivalist era, mission buildings and their environs were reconstructed and preserved as part of what Carey McWilliams called the Spanish "Fantasy Heritage." That is, in spite of a subjective exclusion of Spanish Mexican contributions in the historical accounts of frontier development, and despite the fact that the founding of many settlements in the formerly held Spanish Mexican territories was exercised by people of mixed racial background, including Indians, Africans, and Chinese, the culture that was credited with the settlement of such places was Spanish.

According to McWilliams, "Once the Spanish past was resurrected, this early neglect was greatly compensated. Discovered as a tourist-promotion in the 1880s, the Spanish mission background in Southern California was inflated to mythical proportions." Such a statement is mitigated by the existence of evidence that contradicted the popular notion of a benevolent and peaceful coexistence between Spanish colonizers and their colonial subjects, especially where the missions were concerned.

Writing in 1948, McWilliams noted that "Today community after community is busily resurrecting its 'Spanish' ruins and, in a number of cases, masterplans have been adopted—as in Saint Augustine in 1936; Monterey in 1939; and San Antonio in 1938—to rebuild whole communities along lines consonant with the original Spanish conception." In part because of the revitalization efforts, missions are today a vital part of the tourist industry, and some missions continue to serve as local parishes. The revitalization efforts continue to this day.

Missions as Pedagogical Tools

In addition to their significance as tourist attractions, missions also serve as important research and pedagogical units, acting as centers where elementary school children are taught about the Spanish, Mexican, and Indian contributions to the early frontier regions. Most missions house museums that engage visitors in a public historical discourse through visual displays and accompanying narratives about local people and events, and some missions have archival units that house historical documents for research purposes. The documents they hold are pertinent to the missions as well as to those individuals who made the mission communities viable. Thus they contain the stories not only of missionaries but of civilians, Indians, soldiers, government officials, and many others.

Lamentably, public knowledge about missions is sometimes limited because generalizations about their histories persist. In spite of this, our understanding of missions continues to grow and our interpretations of their past continue to change owing to evolving questions and insights. Indeed, missions provide an appropriate and oftentimes exciting window through which to view the complex history of their surroundings, as well as being reflective of the present state of affairs.

RELATED ARTICLES

Boscana, Geronimo; California; Californios; Catholicism; Colonialism; Colonial Period; Florida; Jesuits; New Mexico; Religion; Serra, Junipero; Texas.

FURTHER READING

Boyd, Mark F., et al. *Here They Once Stood: The Tragic End of the Apalachee Missions.* Gainesville: Univ. of Fla. Press, 1999.

Espinosa, J. Manuel. *The Pueblo Indian Revolt of 1696 and the Franciscan Mission in New Mexico: Letters of the Missionaries and Related Documents.* Norman: Univ. of Okla. Press, 1988.

Jackson, Robert H. *Indian Population Decline: The Missions of Northwestern New Spain, 1687–1840.* Albuquerque: Univ. of N.Mex. Press, 1994.

McWilliams, Carey. *North from Mexico: The Spanish Speaking People of the United States.* New York: Praeger, 1990.

Monroy, Douglas. *Thrown among Strangers: The Making of Mexican Culture in Frontier California.* Berkeley: Univ. of Calif. Press, 1990.

Officer, James E. *Hispanic Arizona, 1536–1856.* Tucson: Univ. of Ariz. Press, 1987.

Weber, David J. *The Spanish Frontier in North America.* New Haven, Conn.: Yale Univ. Press, 1992.

GABRIEL GUTIÉRREZ

MISSISSIPPI

The state of Mississippi is located in the southern portion of the United States along the northern coast of the Gulf of Mexico. The word *mississippi* is believed to have been derived from the Ojibwa (Chippewa) term *mici zibi,* which means "great river." Most of the area that makes up present-day Mississippi was originally inhabited by the Choctaw, Chickasaw, and Natchez tribes. However, by 1840 the majority of these Native American groups had been exterminated, assimilated, or forced to relocate to other parts of the United States.

The Gulf region of the southern United States was explored and claimed by Spain long before the English established their first North American settlement at Jamestown (1607). In fact, Spain's original claim to Florida in the early 16th century included parts of southern Mississippi. One of the first Europeans to enter the area of present-day Mississippi was Hernando de Soto, who led a force of about 600 Spanish soldiers and explored large parts of at least six southern states from 1539 to 1543.

During the American Revolution (1775–1783), Spain declared war on Great Britain and assisted the rebels by attacking British posts in the Mississippi region. The Spanish governor of Louisiana, Bernardo de Gálvez, putting together an army of Indians, free Africans, Creoles, and Spanish regulars, marched on and seized the British-held fort at Natchez in 1779. In the years following the Revolution, however,

Spanish influence in the Mississippi area declined considerably. A large influx of Anglo settlers and African slaves in the next few decades eliminated most vestiges of the former French and Spanish cultures.

For the better part of two centuries, Latinos have traditionally had a limited presence in Mississippi. In addition to migrating to and inhabiting many parts of the American Southwest, the Mexican immigrants of the 20th century traveled to disparate parts of the United States to seek employment in the railroad, meatpacking, and agricultural industries. However, Mississippi—generally regarded as poor when compared to sister states—was not a center of attraction for Latino immigrants until the last years of the 20th century. In 1980 the Hispanic population of Mississippi numbered 24,731 persons, representing less than 1 percent of the total state population. By 1990 this figure had dropped to 15,931, representing only 0.62 percent of the population.

In 1947 the Mississippi Southern College (now the University of Southern Mississippi) in Hattiesburg, Mississippi, established the Latin American Institute to teach Spanish-speaking students English prior to their admittance to regular university classes. This organization continues to serve immigrant students from Latin America and other parts of the world. Many Latinos who came to Mississippi to study in the 1970s and 1980s decided to remain in the state because of the educational and economic opportunities that were available to them in some parts of the state.

In the 1990s the first significant numbers of Hispanics began moving to Mississippi in search of employment in the gaming, poultry-processing, light manufacturing, construction, and agricultural components of the state economy. This wave of immigrant laborers caused the number of Hispanic residents in the state to more than double from 15,931 in 1990

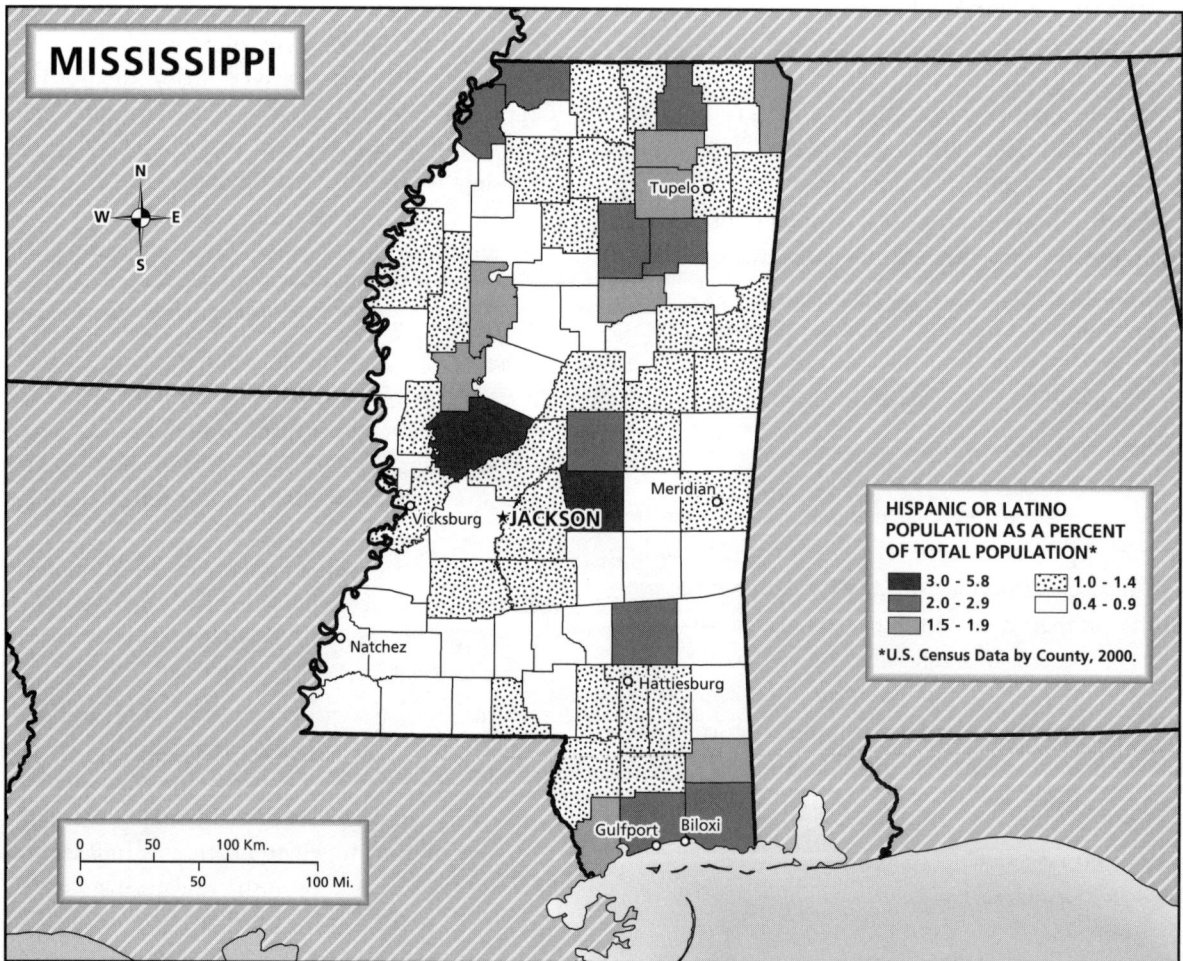

MISSISSIPPI

HISPANIC OR LATINO POPULATION AS A PERCENT OF TOTAL POPULATION*

3.0 - 5.8   1.0 - 1.4
2.0 - 2.9   0.4 - 0.9
1.5 - 1.9

*U.S. Census Data by County, 2000.

to 39,569 in the 2000 census, representing 1.4 percent of the state's population. Of this number, 21,616 were of Mexican descent, representing 54.6 percent of all the Hispanics in the state. Natives of Mexico actually accounted for almost one-quarter (23.8 percent) of all the state's foreign-born population in 2000. Central Americans and South Americans numbered 2,882, representing 7.3 percent of the state's Hispanic population, and Puerto Ricans numbered 2,881, representing the same percentage. The Cuban population was tallied at 1,508, or 3.8 percent. In 2000, 48 of Mississippi's 82 counties had 200 or more Hispanic residents, compared with 19 counties in 1990.

Unfortunately the influx of immigrants to a predominantly English-speaking environment has led to some problems for the newcomers. As in other parts of the United States, Latino workers who do not speak English take low paying jobs as poultry workers, day laborers, and service workers and become easy targets for discrimination and human rights abuses. Many Hispanics involved in the construction industry have been illegally denied overtime wages because their employers know that undocumented workers, fearing deportation, cannot report them.

Concerns have also been expressed on the issue of workplace injuries. In a four-year period (2000–2004), 15 Latino workers were killed on the job in Mississippi. Although Latinos make up less than 2 percent of the state population, they accounted for roughly 14 percent of all workplace deaths, primarily because they were not provided with Spanish-language materials relating to job safety.

The Mississippi Immigrant Rights Alliance (MIRA) is an organization of labor, religious, community, civil rights, business, and social service organizations from various parts of Mississippi. In 2002 MIRA, the Equal Justice Center, and the Southern Migrant Legal Services pooled their resources in an effort to educate immigrant laborers.

This campaign, dubbed the Poultry Workers Justice Project, conducted employment-rights workshops for immigrant Latinos working in poultry-processing factories of central and northern Mississippi. Hundreds of workers took part in these workshops, which were conducted in Spanish and covered basic rights relating to wages, job safety, discrimination, and labor contracts.

Other organizations supporting Latinos have been established in Mississippi. Founded in 1996, the Mississippi Hispanic Association (Asociación Hispana de Mississippi), located in Jackson, provides information and referrals to government and human services organizations. The organization also promotes awareness of Hispanic culture through the production of the Festival Latino, an annual festival held in Jackson. The association also publishes a quarterly newsletter, *Gaceta Hispana*.

The Latino community of Mississippi has not yet achieved any form of political representation in the state mainly because it lacks the numbers to elect its own representatives. In the November 2002 elections, approximately 23,000 Latinos living in Mississippi were classified as American citizens. However, only about 6,000 Hispanics were registered to vote, and only 4,000 actually voted.

As of 2004 Mississippi had only four representatives serving in the U.S. House of Representatives. With a qualified voting population of less than 1 percent, the prospects for the election of a Hispanic to the House seem remote. However, in 2003, Julio del Castillo, a naturalized immigrant from South America, challenged the two-term Democratic incumbent, Eric Clark, for the statewide elected position of secretary of state. Del Castillo lost the election but garnered an impressive 201,765 votes, representing 23.47 percent of the total vote.

At the beginning of the 21st century, Mississippi appears to be moving toward greater ethnic diversity. The Hispanic population growth rates were three to four times those of Caucasians and African Americans, and the U.S. Census Bureau has projected that between 1995 and 2025 the number of Hispanics in Mississippi will grow 101 percent, a faster rate than in 43 other states. It is expected that the increase in the Latino population in the next decades will affect both the cultural and political landscape of Mississippi.

RELATED ARTICLES

Immigration, Latino; Politics, Latino.

FURTHER READING

Brown, Timothy R. "Hispanics Seek Better Life in Mississippi." *Clarion-Ledger Mississippi News*. (June 25, 2003).

Murphy, Arthur D., et al. *Latino Workers in the Contemporary South. Southern Anthropological Society Proceedings 34.* Athens: Univ. of Ga. Press, 2001.

169 ☀

Musgrave, Beth. "Hispanics Make Up Increasing Percentage of Gulfport, Miss.-Area Worker Deaths." *Biloxi Sun Herald.* (May 11, 2004).

Torres, Cruz C. *Emerging Latino Communities: A New Challenge for the Rural South.* No. 12. Mississippi State: Southern Rural Development Center, August 2000. http://srdc.msstate.edu/publications/torres.pdf

SELECTED WEB SITE

CensusScope: Mississippi: Population by Race: Race and Ethnicity Selections, 1980–2000. http://www.census.gov/prod/2003pubs/02statab/election.pdf

JOHN P. SCHMAL

MISSOURI

The state of Missouri was originally inhabited by several indigenous tribes, the most prominent of which was the Missouri tribe. The Missouri, whose name means "people who have wooden canoes," belonged to a division of the Siouxan linguistic family.

French explorers were the first Europeans to venture into the present-day region of Missouri. Eventually, Missouri became one small part of the large French colony of Louisiana (named for King Louis XIV). However, after the French and Indian War (1754–1763), France ceded the entire Louisiana colony—including Missouri—to Spain.

In 1775 the American Revolution commenced on the eastern seaboard as the 13 original American colonies sought independence from Great Britain. Spain and France—both rivals of England's power—signed a military alliance in April 1779, promising to help the American revolutionaries in their struggle for autonomy. Then, on June 21, 1779, Spain formally declared war on Great Britain and surreptitiously began to funnel financial support to the rebels.

In May 1780—as the American Revolution raged on the eastern coast—Spain made preparations to oppose English campaigns in the Louisiana territories. On May 16, St. Louis—a small Spanish fortress at the time—came under attack by British and Indian forces, numbering up to 1,200. The Spanish lieutenant governor Fernando De Leyba successfully defended the town and ended the siege. Later, Spanish campaigns in the Missouri area were able to end the British threat in Louisiana. And, by 1783 the American Revolution had accomplished its goal of independence.

On October 1, 1800, by the secret Treaty of St. Ildefonso, Emperor Napoleon Bonaparte forced the Spanish government to return the Louisiana Territory—including Missouri—to French control. However, the Spanish continued to administer the territory from New Orleans. Then, in March 1803 Emperor Napoleon shocked the world by offering all of the Louisiana Territory to the United States. The 909,000 square miles (350,950 sq km) of the Louisiana Territory—some 43,000 square miles (16,600 sq km) larger than the United States at that time—was sold for $23,213,567.73, which worked out to about 4¢ an acre.

In October 1804, the Spanish governor and his troops departed from St. Louis, turning over effective control of the area to the United States. Seventeen years later in 1821, Missouri was the 24th state to join the Union. With large numbers of German and Irish immigrants moving there, it became an important agricultural state of America's Midwest. During this time, the Spanish influence in Missouri virtually disappeared, in large part owing to the fact that their rule over the area had lasted less than four decades.

Early in the 20th century, large numbers of Mexican immigrants were recruited to work in railroad yards throughout the United States. The railroad yards of Kansas City, Missouri, and Kansas City, Kansas, were crisscrossed by 12 railroads entering from all directions, providing an important manufacturing sector in both cities. The Santa Fe and Southern Pacific railroads primarily employed Mexican track laborers, bringing many Mexican immigrants into the area.

In 1900, only 77 Mexicans had been counted as residents in the St. Louis area. However, in 1904 the St. Louis, Brownsville and Mexican Railroad was completed, providing St. Louis with a direct rail link to the Mexican border. It was in this year that small numbers of Mexican laborers began to make their way to St. Louis to seek employment on track maintenance crews. By 1930 their numbers had increased to 1,731 in the greater St. Louis area.

However, Mexican people in St. Louis and other Missouri cities were frequently the victims of vicious discrimination and were often barred from hospitals, theaters, and restaurants. In addition, the Great Depression of the 1930s and the Mexican Repatriation Program of 1931–1934 caused a sharp decline in Mexican immigration to Missouri. For most of the 20th century and well into the 1980s, Mexican immigration never reached the same levels that it did

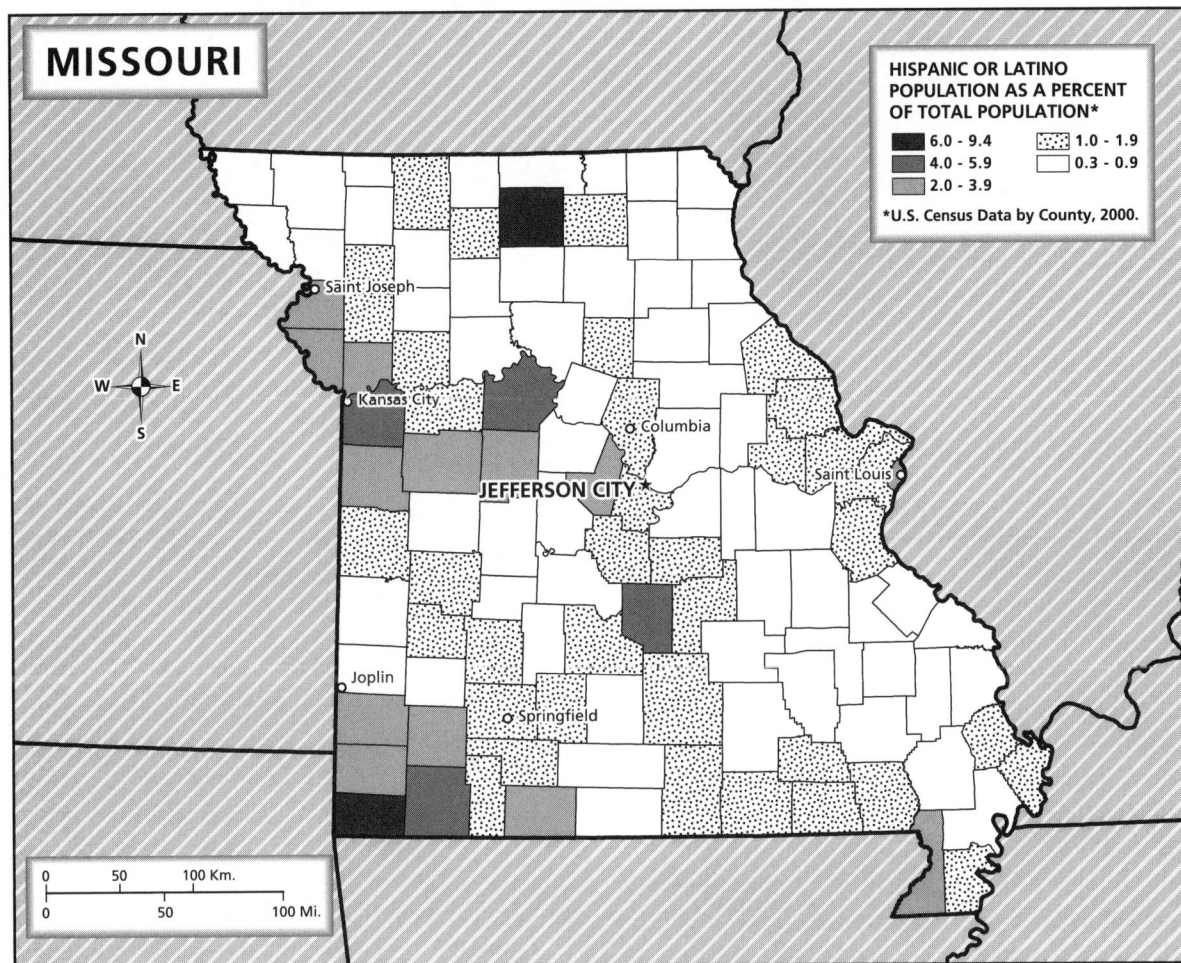

MISSOURI

HISPANIC OR LATINO
POPULATION AS A PERCENT
OF TOTAL POPULATION*

- 6.0 - 9.4
- 4.0 - 5.9
- 2.0 - 3.9
- 1.0 - 1.9
- 0.3 - 0.9

*U.S. Census Data by County, 2000.

in its western neighbor, Kansas. The 51,653 Latinos tallied in Missouri's 1980 census represented only 1 percent of the entire state population.

The number of Latinos counted in Missouri at the time of the 1990 census was 61,702, a growth rate of 19.4 percent from 1980. In contrast, Missouri's total population increase amounted to only 4.1 percent for the same period. According to the 1990 census, Missouri's Hispanic population was spread across several counties, with Pulaski County boasting the largest Latino percentage (4.7 percent). Some Mexican immigrants also had made their way to Sullivan and McDonald counties, in large part to seek employment in the beef and poultry processing industries of those areas. At the same time the service sector of Kansas City represented another magnet for Mexican immigration.

The population of Missouri's Latino community increased from 61,702 in 1990 to 118,592 in 2000—an increase of 92.2 percent, and an unprecedented

130 percent increase from the 1980 population figure. Mexican Americans were the largest Hispanic group, with 77,887 individuals representing almost 66 percent of all Latinos. Puerto Ricans numbered 6,677 in 2000, representing 5.6 percent of the state's Latino population.

Although their overall share of the Missouri population remained modest at 2.2 percent, Latinos had increased their numbers in many Missouri counties. Jackson County, in which Kansas City is located, boasted the largest concentration of Latinos, which saw an increase of 16,270 persons between 1990 and 2000. The Hispanic population in Kansas City, Missouri, was tallied at 30,604 in 2000 and represented 6.9 percent of the city's total population. The city of St. Louis had the second largest concentration of Latinos, with 7,022 persons, or 2 percent of the population, followed by Independence, which boasted a Latino population of 4,175 (3.7 percent of the total).

Even the rural counties of Pettis, Lawrence, Saline, and Jasper—with their meatpacking industries—saw significant increases in their Hispanic populations during the 1990s. The city of Carthage in Jasper County witnessed a spectacular 2,688 percent growth in its Hispanic population between 1980 and 2000. With its diverse economic base, Carthage was home to 1,589 Latinos in 2000, a figure representing 12.5 percent of the total population.

In recent years several institutions have been established to help the Spanish-speaking population adjust to their new lives in an English-language-dominant society. Based in Kansas City, Missouri, the Coalition of Hispanic Organizations (COHO) is a group of 24 organizations that have pooled their resources to help improve the quality of life for Latinos throughout Missouri.

El Centro Latino, founded in 2000 under the guidance of Eduardo Crespi, is a nonprofit, primarily volunteer-run organization established to help the Latino population of central Missouri acculturate to their new environment with its new laws, customs, and language. In recent years, the center has provided health information on HIV and AIDS, STDs (sexually transmitted diseases), and diabetes to Spanish-speaking persons in the Boone County area.

Part of making Latinos comfortable in a new environment is providing them with Spanish-language news. In Columbia, *Adelante!* became the primary bilingual newspaper available to Hispanics in central Missouri. In Kansas City, bilingual *Dos Mundos* (Two Worlds) has been the primary newspaper for the Hispanic population of the Kansas City area since 1981.

In 1977 a group of Latino business leaders in Kansas City, Missouri, founded the Hispanic Chamber of Commerce of Greater Kansas City, which was designed to help develop a business network that would provide the Hispanic business community with cohesion and strength. Over time, the Chamber has also specialized in promoting business relationships between Hispanic businesses and the non-Hispanic business environment of the Kansas City metropolitan area.

Although Hispanics only accounted for 2 percent of Missouri's population in 2000, the percent of Hispanic children enrolled in school increased significantly during the 1990s and will undoubtedly continue to increase during the early decades of the 21st century. In 1990 there were 6,131 Hispanic students enrolled in Missouri public schools. By 2000 the enrollment of Hispanics in Missouri schools had reached 16,269—an increase of more than 165 percent.

Latino students in the Missouri university system continue to represent a small minority of the overall student population. For this reason a number of organizations have been established to help young Latinos in their transition to college life. The Hispanic and Latin American Faculty and Staff Association (HLAFSA) was established in 1999 to communicate interests, concerns, and awareness of Hispanics and Latin Americans at the University of Missouri. In addition to fostering multicultural awareness among faculty and staff members, HLAFSA also plays a role in the recruitment and retention of Latino faculty and students at the University.

With the enthusiastic support of the University of Missouri System, HLAFSA initiated a three-day conference entitled Cambio de Colores (Change of Colors): Latinos in Missouri: A Call to Action! in March 2002. This event, held at the University of Missouri-Columbia, was attended by 250 people and highlighted various issues affecting Latino immigrants in the state. The conference was so successful that Cambio de Colores has evolved into an annual conference dedicated to promoting understanding of Missouri's Latino immigrant population.

Although the Latino population of Missouri has not yet achieved political representation in the electoral process, the efforts of Latino-focused organizations will undoubtedly play a role in such future campaigns as their population grows and their economic and cultural influence becomes recognized.

RELATED ARTICLES

Immigration, Latino; Louisiana Purchase; Mexican Americans.

FURTHER READING

Lazos Vargas, Sylvia R., and Stephen C. Jeanetta. *Cambio de Colores. Immigration of Latinos to Missouri*. Columbia: Univ. of Mo., 2002.

Rynearson, Ann Manry. *Hiding within the Melting Pot: Mexican Americans in St. Louis*. St. Louis, Missouri: Ph.D. Dissertation, Washington Univ., 1980.

Shirmer, Sherry Lamb. *Historical Overview of the Ethnic Communities in Kansas City*. Kansas City, Missouri: Pan-Educational Institute, 1976.

SELECTED WEB SITES

HLAFSA: Hispanic and Latin American Faculty and Staff Association. http://www.missouri.edu/hlafsa/

Missouri Economic Research and Information Center: *"Hispanic Growth in Missouri."*
http://www.ded.state.mo.us/business/ researchandplanning/indicators/population/hispanic/ hispanic_en.shtml
Mo-River.Net—*Hispanic / Latino.*
http://www.mo-river.net/Hispanic_Latino/

JOHN P. SCHMAL

MOHR, NICHOLASA

Born: November 1, 1938; New York, New York

A leading mainland Puerto Rican literary voice and an influential feminist figure in the Latino canon, Nicholasa Mohr was raised in the Bronx, New York City, by her Puerto Rican parents. She was the youngest of seven children and the only girl. Her mother was part of an early wave of immigrants who settled in New York during the Depression.

Art was Mohr's first calling; she studied at the Art Students League in Manhattan, New York, and went to Mexico in the late 1950s, where she attended the Taller de Artes Gráficas. After returning to New York, she continued her studies at the New School for Social Research, the Brooklyn Museum Art School, and the Pratt Graphics Center. She married Irwin Mohr, a child psychologist, and had two children.

While working as a printmaker and an art teacher in New York and New Jersey, she wrote some vignettes about the coming-of-age experiences of a young girl. They became the basis for her first novel *Nilda* (1973), which was about life among Puerto Rican families in New York during World War II from a feminine viewpoint. The book was immediately recognized as a contribution to the growing genre of literature documenting the Puerto Rican experience in the city. It was selected as Best Book of the Year by the *School Library Journal* and Outstanding Book of the Year by the *New York Times.* Several other books followed: *El Bronx Remembered* (1975); *In Nueva York* (1977); *Felita* (1979), a novel; and *Rituals of Survival: A Woman's Portfolio* (1985), a collection of stories about Latina women who survive under difficult circumstances.

After that came *Going Home* (1986), a children's novel; *All for the Better: A Story of El Barrio* (1995), a biography of Evelyn López Antonetty, a Hispanic community leader; and *In My Own Words: Growing Up inside the Sanctuary of My Imagination* (1994), a memoir of her early years. Since the middle of the 1990s, Mohr has written several children's books, among them *The Song of El Coqui* (1995), which she illustrated in collaboration with Puerto Rican graphic artist Antonio Martorell, and *Old Letivia and the Mountain of Sorrows* (1996).

Mohr's work was groundbreaking because it introduced a feminine perspective into the literature of the Puerto Rican diaspora. Earlier works, such as Jesús Colón's *A Puerto Rican in New York and Other Sketches* and Piri Thomas's *Down These Mean Streets,* recorded the experience of male Puerto Rican youths growing up in the inner city ghettos. Mohr focused on the very different experiences of young girls, Nilda and Felita, who were not as exposed to violence in the streets as were their male counterparts, but who were more enmeshed in sometimes tense and difficult family relationships, suffering another kind of prejudice—against women—within that context.

In her essay "Puerto Rican Writers in the United States, Puerto Rican Writers in Puerto Rico: A Separation beyond Language," in *Barrios and Borderlines: Cultures of Latinos and Latinas in the United States,* Mohr was the first to point out that differences between island Puerto Ricans and those raised in the United States were not only in language but also in culture and outlook. This proved controversial with island intellectuals and writers. Nevertheless, she is one of the writers who has most closely worked with an island artist (Antonio Martorell) in her books for children.

Mohr has been awarded an honorary doctorate of letters by the State University of New York at Albany. She was a visiting professor at Queens College and a writer in residence at the Smithsonian Institution and at the American University in London. She received the Hispanic Heritage Award for Literature in 1997.

RELATED ARTICLES

Literature, Puerto Rican on the Mainland.

FURTHER READING

Aparicio, Frances. "From Ethnicity to Multiculturalism: An Historical Overview of Puerto Rican Literature in the United States." In *Handbook of Hispanic Cultures in the United States: Literature and Art.* Ed. by Nicolás Kanellos and Claudio Esteva-Fabregat. Houston, Tex.: Arte Público Press, 1993.
Barradas, Efraín. "Nicholasa Mohr, narradora 'neorrican.'" In *Partes de un todo.* Río Piedras: Editorial de la Universidad de Puerto Rico, 1998.

Flores, Juan. "Puerto Rican Literature in the United States: Stages and Perspectives." In *Divided Borders: Essays on Puerto Rican Identity.* Houston, Tex.: Arte Público Press, 1993.

Hernández, Carmen Dolores. "Nicholasa Mohr." In *Puerto Rican Voices in English: Interviews with Writers.* Westport, Conn.: Praeger, 1997.

CARMEN DOLORES HERNÁNDEZ

MOLINA, MARIO

Born: March 19, 1943; Mexico City, Mexico

Mario J. Molina is the first Mexican-born winner of the Nobel Prize for chemistry. He was born in Mexico City on March 19, 1943, to Roberto Molina Pasquel and Leonor Henriquez de Molina. His father was a lawyer who later served as Mexican ambassador to Ethiopia, Australia, and the Philippines. The young Molina's budding interest in chemistry was supported by his aunt Esther Molina, a chemist in the sugar industry, and by his parents, who con-

© STEVEN SENNE/AP/WIDE WORLD PHOTOS

Massachusetts Institute of Technology professor Mario Molina, who shared the 1995 Nobel Prize for Chemistry for his work in atmospheric chemistry.

verted a bathroom into a laboratory for his use. At age 11 Molina attended boarding school in Switzerland. In 1960 he enrolled in the chemical engineering program at the Universidad Nacional Autonoma de Mexico (UNAM) (National University of Mexico). After graduation, Molina's need for additional training in mathematics, physics, and other areas took him to Germany and Paris. He returned to Mexico as an assistant professor at the UNAM, where he established the first graduate program in chemical engineering. In 1968 he left for the University of California at Berkeley to pursue a Ph.D. in physical chemistry, a degree not available in Mexico at the time. Molina joined the research group of Professor George C. Pimentel, which studied molecular dynamics using chemical lasers. There he met Luisa Tan who would become his wife and a research collaborator.

The social dynamics at Berkeley brought Molina to reflect on the significance of science and technology to society. After completing his Ph.D., Molina moved to the University of California at Irvine for a postdoctoral fellowship with Sherwood Rowland. Both he and Rowland shared an interest in atmospheric chemistry and environmental studies, and Molina chose to study chlorofluorocarbons (CFCs). Their 1974 paper published in *Nature* suggested a connection between CFCs and destruction of the ozone layer that shields the earth from harmful ultraviolet radiation. When the media eventually picked up the CFC story, and the effect of CFCs on the ozone layer became a publicly debated issue, Molina had to balance the role of scientist as impartial observer with the need to communicate with media and policymakers. He and Rowland testified at legislative hearings on potential controls on CFC emissions, which contributed to the development of the Montreal Protocol on Substances That Deplete the Ozone Layer. Molina became a faculty member at Irvine in 1975 and established his own atmospheric science laboratory. In 1987, while working at the National Aeronautic and Space Administration's Jet Propulsion Laboratory, he and his wife drew connections between the Antarctic ozone hole and CFCs, which were later confirmed. In 1989 he became a professor at the Massachusetts Institute of Technology (MIT). He was appointed a scientific adviser to the Clinton administration in 1994, and in 1995 Molina and Rowland won the Nobel Prize for chemistry, along with Paul J. Crutzen of the Max Planck Institute for Chemistry.

Molina returns regularly to Mexico City to work on environmental concerns through MIT's Integrated Program on Urban, Regional, and Global Air Pollution. In 2002 he and his wife coedited *Air Quality in the Mexico Megacity: An Integrated Assessment,* a compilation of the research done through this program. He established the Molina Fellowship in Environmental Science to bring young scientists from emerging nations to MIT to study environmental sciences in the hope that the fellows will return to their countries better able to address complex environmental concerns.

RELATED ARTICLES

Education, Higher; Science.

FURTHER READING

Molina, Luisa T., and Mario J. Molina, eds. *Air Quality in the Mexico Megacity: An Integrated Assessment.* Boston: Kluwer Acad. Pubs., 2002.

Molina, Mario J., and F. Sherwood Rowland. "Stratospheric Sink for Chlorofluoromethanes-chlorine Atom Catalyzed Destruction of Ozone." *Nature* 249 (1974): 810–812.

Nemecek, Sasha. "Mario Molina: Rescuing the Ozone Layer." *Scientific American* 277 (November 1997): 40–42.

Stevenson, Richard. "Mario Molina: Telling the World." *Chemistry in Britain* 35 (June 1999): 20–22.

SELECTED WEB SITES

Official Website of the Nobel Foundation. *"Mario J. Molina—Autobiography."*
http://www.nobel.se/chemistry/laureates/1995/molina-autobio.html

Mario J. Molina, Professor, Massachusetts Institute of Technology. http://www-eaps.mit.edu/molina/

KRISTINE M. ALPI

MONROE DOCTRINE

In 1832 President James Monroe set forth a U.S. foreign policy, the Monroe Doctrine, which was authored by Secretary of State John Quincy Adams, opposing European intervention in the Western Hemisphere. The United States feared that Spain, having restored its monarchy after Napoleon's downfall, might try to regain her colonies in the Americas. The Holy Alliance—Russia, Austria, and Prussia—also posed the threat of extending to the Americas its fight against representative governments. This doctrine was to have a profound effect on U.S. relations with the countries in the Americas but also with countries worldwide.

President Monroe stated in his second inaugural speech, eventually to be known as the Monroe Doctrine: "The American continents, by the free and independent condition which they have assumed and maintained, are henceforth not to be considered as subjects for future colonization by any European power. We should consider any attempt on their part to extend their system to any part of this hemisphere as dangerous to our peace and safety."

In return, the United States agreed not to interfere in existing European colonies or the internal affairs of Europe. But future U.S. administrations' reinterpretations of the doctrine prohibited the transfer of territory in the Americas from one European country to another and granted the United States exclusive control over any canal connecting the Atlantic and Pacific oceans through Central America. Furthermore, the Monroe Doctrine became the legal framework for the U.S. expansionist drive toward becoming a world power, known as Manifest Destiny. In 1898 the United States entered a war with Spain over the independence of Cuba. From the Spanish-American War the United States won Guam, Puerto Rico, and the Philippine Islands. Most important, the United States emerged as a military and colonial power.

The Roosevelt Corollary added in 1904 granted the United States the right to intervene in any Latin American nation undergoing internal turmoil or engaged in external misconduct. The Roosevelt Corollary justified U.S. intervention in Caribbean states during the administrations of presidents William Taft and Woodrow Wilson. During the first quarter of the 20th century, the scope of the Monroe Doctrine narrowed as the Great Depression humbled American character and Pan-Americanism gained popularity.

The Monroe Doctrine again became central during World War II and throughout the Cold War. It was evoked when the Soviet Union installed nuclear missiles in Cuba, to prevent Soviet subversion in Chile in 1970–1973, and again in Central America between 1980–1989. A time the United States failed to invoke the Monroe Doctrine was during the Falklands War of 1982 between Argentina and England, when it chose to support England, its NATO (North Atlantic Treaty Organization) ally.

THE BIG STICK IN THE CARIBBEAN SEA

"The Big Stick in the Caribbean Sea," by W. A. Rogers, *New York Herald,* 1904, depicts Theodore Roosevelt enforcing his concept of the Monroe Doctrine by having the U.S. Navy steam from one Caribbean port to another.

The Monroe Doctrine has been the single most significant factor in determining U.S. foreign policy in the Western Hemisphere. It also has had a profound impact in the domestic arena with regard to Hispanics. By fueling American expansionism in the 19th century, the doctrine transformed the nation's demographics. After the Mexican-American War of 1846–1848, the United States acquired the northern half of Mexico, along with its inhabitants, which became the states of California, Nevada, Arizona, New Mexico, and Utah. The area's inhabitants were the predecessors of today's Hispanics (the term Hispanic as an ethnic category was created by the United States Census Bureau in 1970). Puerto Rico has remained an unincorporated U.S. territory since 1898. Its people were granted American citizenship under the Jones Act in 1917. The status of Puerto Rico remains an unresolved legacy of the Monroe Doctrine, even when the validity of the doctrine itself has come into debate.

RELATED ARTICLES

United States–Central America Relations; United States–Mexico Relations; United States Presidents, and Latinos; United States–South America Relations.

FURTHER READING

Dent, David W. *The Legacy of the Monroe Doctrine: A Reference Guide to U.S. Involvement in Latin America and the Caribbean.* Westport, Conn.: Greenwood Press, 1999.

Smith, Gaddis. *The Last Years of the Monroe Doctrine, 1945–1993.* New York: Hill & Wang, 1995.

Van Alstyne, Richard W. *Encyclopedia of American Foreign Policy,* 2d ed., vol. 2. New York: Scribner, 2001.

RAÚL GUERRERO

MONTALVO, SERGIO. *See* KID CHOCOLATE.

MORENO, MARIO. *See* CANTINFLAS.

MORENO, RITA

Born: December 11, 1932; Humacao, Puerto Rico

A performer of extraordinary vitality, Rita Moreno was the first Latina to win an Academy Award and the only actress to win an Oscar, a Tony, a Grammy, and two Emmys. This multitalented performer was born Rosita Dolores Alverio to a family of small independent farmers, or *jibaros*. At the age of five she left Puerto Rico to join her mother, who was working in the garment industry in New York City.

It was not long before her talent manifested itself, and by the age of 7 she was performing at a Green- wich Village nightclub. At age 11 Moreno was dubbing Spanish-language versions of American films. When she was 13, she landed her first Broadway role, which brought her to the attention of Holly- wood talent scouts. Soon after, she appeared in the film *A Medal for Benny* (1945).

Moreno continued to take acting classes while performing professionally as a singer and dancer. In 1950 she returned to the big screen in several films, *So Young, So Bad; The Toast of New Orleans;* and *Pagan Love Song*. It was MGM (Metro-Goldwyn-Mayer) studio chief Louis B. Mayer who suggested that she shorten her name from Rosita to Rita. She also took the surname of her mother's third hus- band. She would henceforth be known as Rita Moreno.

A major breakthrough for Moreno was landing the role of Anita in the phenomenally successful film *West Side Story* (1961). Her performance of the mu- sical number "America," with its feminist undertones,

PHOTOS12.COM / POLARIS IMAGES

Rita Moreno (center) in a film still from Robert Wise and Jerome Robbins's *West Side Story,* 1961.

is legendary. Moreno conveys the energy of all Puerto Rican women seeking to better their lives in a society that allows them to express themselves in full. This was the role that earned her an Oscar for best supporting actress. Hoping that such recognition would open new doors, Moreno instead found that most of the scripts sent to her after *West Side Story* merely called for her to replay stereotypical Latin spitfires. She turned to the theater for a broader range of roles that would allow her to display her many talents. Moreno returned to film in 1969, playing Alan Arkin's girlfriend in the comedy *Popi*. In 1971 she played a small role in Mike Nichols's *Carnal Knowledge*.

In the 1970s Moreno made appearances on the television series *Sesame Street* and joined the cast of *The Electric Company,* also a children's television series. Her participation in *The Electric Company* soundtrack album earned her a Grammy in 1972. During this time she did not, however, abandon the theater or television. In 1975 she received a Tony for her performance in the Broadway show *The Ritz*. She was also given an Emmy award in 1977 for her performance in *Sesame Street* and again in 1978 for her role in *The Rockford Files*.

Throughout her career Moreno has advocated for greater diversity in the roles offered Latinos in films and other venues. Her triumph over tremendous odds, and her success in film, television, music, and theater, has inspired many young actors of different ethnic groups to pursue their dreams.

RELATED ARTICLES

Film; Popular Culture; Theater.

FURTHER READING

Acker, Ally. *Reel women: Pioneers of the Cinema, 1896–Present.* New York: Continuum, 1991.
Hadley-Garcia, George. *Hispanic Hollywood: The Latins in Motion Pictures.* New York: Carol Pub., 1990.
Kanellos, Nicolás. "Moreno, Rita." *St. James Encyclopedia of Popular Culture.* Ed. by Tom Pendergast and Sara Pendergast. Detroit: St. James Press, 2000.
Suntree, Susan. "Rita Moreno." In *Hispanics of Achievement.* New York: Chelsea House, 1993.

RAÚL DAMACIO TOVARES

MORMONISM

Mormonism refers to the set of ideas and practices that trace their origins to the teachings of Joseph Smith (1805–1844). The largest and best-known Mormon group, numbering perhaps 10 million members worldwide, is the Church of Jesus Christ of Latter-day Saints (LDS) based in Salt Lake City, Utah. The preferred self-designation is the Church of Jesus Christ, but the LDS Church is still popular in scholarly and historical literature.

Distinctive doctrines include:

(1) Recognition of Joseph Smith as a true prophet of God.
(2) The authority of the Book of Mormon and other Mormon scriptures as equal to that of the Bible.
(3) "Celestial marriage," which claims the continuation of marriage into the afterlife.
(4) Vicarious baptism for those who have died without the opportunity to accept the Gospel.
(5) Restoration of full divinity for preexisting souls.

Almost from the beginning Mormonism showed a special interest in the indigenous peoples of the Americas. In Mormon theology the native peoples are regarded as Lamanites, a group believed to have descended from the biblical Joseph. The acceptance of the Gospel by these peoples can expedite the restoration of Christ's kingdom. Mormons believe that Jesus himself came to preach among the pre-Columbian peoples of the Americas.

The Mormon message was taken to Latin America as early as 1851 by Parley Pratt. In 1874 Brigham Young (1801–1877), the successor to Joseph Smith, insisted that the Mormon message be communicated to Mexicans, who were viewed as descendants of Lehi, another Hebrew figure in the Book of Mormon. Parts of the Mormon scriptures were published in Spanish by 1875.

Mormonism has managed to attract significant proportions of U.S. Latinos. The reasons are numerous and complex, but they bear similarities to those that attract converts to Protestantism. Services specifically designed for Hispanics can be traced at least to the creation, in the 1920s, of the Rama Mexicana (Mexican Branch), a Spanish-speaking unit in Salt Lake City that was later reorganized as a larger administrative unit owing to phenomenal growth rates.

Nonetheless, racial and ethnic discrimination has been a main concern of many LDS Hispanics. It was not until 1978 that the priesthood, which was normally granted to all European American Mormon males in good standing, was extended to all Mormon males regardless of ethnicity or color. Yet the proportions of Hispanics in the upper echelons of the LDS Church still do not match the proportion of Hispanic membership. Debates continue on whether Latino units should assimilate or insist on cultural independence.

Although the study of Hispanic Mormons is still in its infancy, most experts predict that larger proportions of Mormons will be U.S. Latinos. One estimate for 1998 noted that 21 of the 46 congregations of Mormons in New York City were Spanish speaking, and that half of all LDS members in New York City were Hispanic. Some estimate that by 2050 more than 25 percent of all Mormons in Utah will be Hispanic.

RELATED ARTICLES
Religion.

FURTHER READING

Brooke, John L. *The Refiner's Fire: The Making of Mormon Cosmology, 1644–1844.* Cambridge: Cambridge Univ. Press, 1994.

Embry, Jessie L. *In His Own Language: Mormon Spanish-Speaking Congregations in the United States.* Salt Lake City: Signature Bks., 1997.

Iber, Jorge. *Hispanics in the Mormon Zion, 1912–1999.* College Station: Tex. A&M Univ. Press, 2000.

Lucas, James. W. "Mormons in New York City." In *New York Glory: Religions in the City.* Ed. by Tony Carnes and Anna Karpathakis. New York: N.Y. Univ. Press, 2001.

Shipps, Jan. *Mormonism: The Story of a New Religious Tradition.* Urbana: Univ. of Ill., 1987.

Tullis, F. Lamond. *Mormons in Mexico: The Dynamics of Faith and Culture.* Logan: Utah State Univ. Press, 1987.

HECTOR AVALOS

MOTHERS OF EAST LOS ANGELES

Founded in 1985 in the East Los Angeles community of Boyle Heights, California, the Mothers of East Los Angeles (MELA) was formed in response to neighborhood opposition to the construction of a state prison in East Los Angeles. During the course of its seven-year struggle against the prison, MELA became an active participant in community politics and went on to address environmental and political issues affecting the Latino community.

MELA sprang into existence after leaders and residents of Boyle Heights learned that the California Department of Corrections (DOC) had chosen the predominantly working-class and Latino community to house the next correctional facility in the city of Los Angeles. Opposition to the DOC's decision centered on the proximity of the proposed site to the community of Boyle Heights and 34 neighborhood schools. "Environmental racism" also was an issue, especially after it was learned that the DOC had failed to test the site for hazardous waste, develop an environmental impact report detailing the environmental costs of the prison on the community, or provide residents with adequate notice. Soon, neighborhood residents and local leaders began organizing a coalition to stop construction of the prison. Responding to the need to have women involved in community efforts, Father John Moretta of the Church of Resurrection approached a few of the women in his congregation and informed them of the prison project. He named the group the Mothers of East Los Angeles and put them into contact with others organizing in the Boyle Heights area. Women recruited from local church parishes, the founding members of MELA were active in church politics or had children attending local Catholic schools. The organization that began with a few local women soon grew to include over 400 people. MELA held press conferences and community meetings and participated in convoys to Sacramento, the state capital, to meet with and lobby politicians on the prison issue. During the summers of 1986 and 1987, it organized weekly protest marches to highlight local opposition to the prison and help counter the notion that East Los Angeles residents were apathetic to the project. The effort to stop construction of the prison successfully ended in 1992, when California governor Pete Wilson signed a bill putting an end to the project.

MELA worked hard to keep the needs of its members at the center of its political agenda, and it was able to retain its identity as a grassroots organization. Many of its members were local women who were married and had young children, and meetings and marches were often organized around their needs. Instead of competing or interfering with the home lives of its members, MELA was able to use the traditional role of women as caretakers of the family to strengthen women's involvement in community politics.

Among the issues MELA addressed were the construction of a toxic waste incinerator planned for the neighboring city of Vernon and the construction of an oil pipeline that would have detoured through East Los Angeles. The organization viewed both projects as potential health hazards and, with the aid of other organizations, was successful in putting an end to their construction. MELA eventually split into two independent branches, largely along parish lines, over competing visions of the future of the organization. Despite the split, Mothers of East Los Angeles continues to play an active role in community politics.

RELATED ARTICLES

Activism; Gangs; Los Angeles.

FURTHER READING

Gutiérrez, Gabriel. "Mothers of East Los Angeles Strike Back." In *Unequal Protection: Environmental Justice and Communities of Color.* Ed. by Robert D. Bullard. San Francisco: Sierra Club Bks., 1994.

Platt, Kamala. "Chicana Strategies for Success and Survival: Cultural Poetics of Environmental Justice from the Mothers of East Los Angeles." *Frontiers* 8, no. 2 (1997): 48–72.

Pardo, Mary S. *Mexican American Women Activists: Identity and Resistance in Two Los Angeles Communities.* Philadelphia: Temple Univ. Press, 1998.

Pardo, Mary S. "Mexican American Women Grassroots Community Activists: 'Mothers of East Los Angeles.'" *Frontiers* 11, no. 1 (1990): 1–7.

LUPE GARCÍA

MOVIMIENTO ESTUDIANTIL CHICANO DE AZTLÁN

El Movimiento Estudiantil Chicano de Aztlán (MEChA; the Chicano Student Movement of Aztlán) was founded by students of Mexican origin during the Chicano civil rights movement in the 1960s and 1970s. It became one of the most prominent student organizations, catapulting educational issues to the forefront of the civil rights reform era.

During the First National Chicano Youth Liberation Conference held in Denver, Colorado, in March 1969, the term *Chicano* was adopted to unite students under a common political and cultural identity. The adoption of *Chicano* symbolized the emergence of a new generation of Mexican Americans coming of age in the United States, the Chicano generation. This generation embodied the recognition of a positive Mexican identity and an affirmation of *mestizaje,* a hybrid identity and history bridging Mexico and the United States.

After the Denver conference Chicanos met at the University of California, Santa Barbara, to discuss the "plan of action" for Chicano self-determination. Conference participants agreed to rename Chicano

student organizations to MEChA. Students also delineated a series of goals for MEChA to implement in local communities. This plan is known as El Plan de Santa Barbara. The goals were broadly stated as education and community development.

Chicanos considered education the most critical issue. Given the low educational attainment of Chicanos, MEChA provided leadership to increase the numbers of educated Chicanos, thus the use of the term *Estudiantil* (student). MEChA developed a master plan for the creation of educational curriculum sensitive to Chicano history and culture. Additionally, MEChA redirected university resources to meet the needs of Chicano students through the creation and implementation of support programs and services, such as tutoring and mentoring. Finally, MEChA played a substantive role in the creation of Chicano studies programs and hiring of Chicano faculty.

MEChA provided leadership in Mexican communities, or barrios. One goal was to create and maintain a network of community organizations to promote advancement and self-determination. Also, MEChA increased Chicanos' participation in politics through the training of community members. Another goal was the formation of a Chicano political party to address issues affecting Chicano communities neglected by mainstream political parties. This became a reality through the formation of La Raza Unida Party.

By the mid-1980s, internal and external forces contributed to weakening the visibility and effectiveness of MEChA. The organization suffered from splits over competing ideologies and strategies. Some Chicanos adopted a nationalist and militant stance while others promoted assimilation to mainstream society. Students utilized strikes, walk-outs, and sit-ins to voice their frustrations. The notorious 1968 strike at an East Los Angeles high school culminated in the arrest of 13 Chicanos involved in educational reform. Their indictment by a Los Angeles County grand jury for conspiracy symbolized the risk of being associated with the Chicano movement. Despite the dangers, thousands of students joined MEChA and contributed to building the Chicano civil rights movement. However, the proposals, tactics, and effectiveness differed across the state of California and the nation.

Involvement in MEChA provided training for learning organizational skills and developing leadership. Many *mechistas* graduated from college and were among the first Chicanos to enter academia and other professional fields. Others entered into electoral politics and community service organizations. Although MEChA has had a problematic evolution, the work of student activists continues to influence many areas of civil rights.

RELATED ARTICLES

Chicanismo; Chicano Movement; Politics, Mexican American; Raza Unida Party, La.

FURTHER READING

Acuña, Rodolfo. *Occupied America: A History of Chicanos.* 4th ed. New York: Longman, 2000.

Gomez-Quiñonez, Juan. *Chicano Politics: Reality and Promise, 1940–1990.* Albuquerque: Univ. of N.Mex. Press, 1990.

Muñoz, Carlos, Jr. *Youth, Identity, Power: The Chicano Movement.* London, New York: Verso, 1989.

Navarro, Armando. *Mexican American Youth Organization: Avant-Garde of the Chicano Movement in Texas.* Austin: Univ. of Tex. Press, 1995.

ARCELA NUÑEZ-ALVAREZ

MOYA PONS, FRANK

Born: March 13, 1944; La Vega, Santo Domingo

Moya Pons is one of the best-known and most prolific of contemporary Dominican historians. He came of age during the years that followed the death of dictator Rafael Leonidas Trujillo and the 1965 U.S. intervention in the Dominican Republic. He participated actively in the political student movements of the Autonomous University of Santo Domingo (UASD), where he had moved after completing his primary education in his native town La Vega. He received a degree in philosophy from the university in 1966, studied Latin American history at Georgetown University, and obtained a master's and doctorate from Columbia University in 1987. He has taught Latin American and Caribbean history at the University of Florida, Gainesville, and Columbia University, besides serving as a visiting fellow at the Woodrow Wilson Center for the International Scholars, Smithsonian Institution. He began his teaching career at the Universidad Católica Madre y Maestra (UCMM) in Santiago, his home institution for many years and where he edited the journal *Eme-Eme: Estudios Sociales* (Eme-Eme: Dominican Studies) and secured the Ford Foundation project (Fondo para el Avance de las Ciencias Sociales), a unit within the

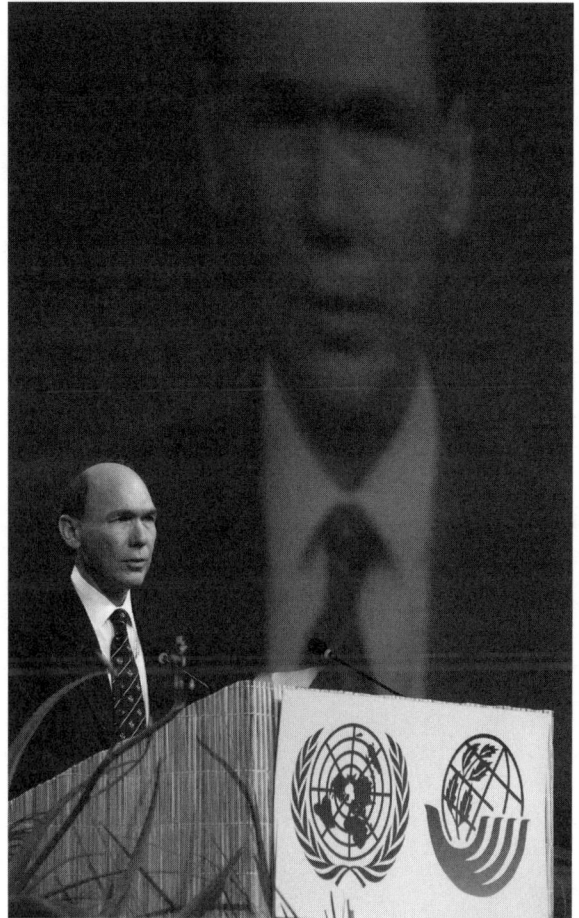

UNITED NATIONS

Frank Moya Pons speaking at the World Summit on Sustainable Development, 2002.

university to conduct research. He directed the Museo de las Casas Reales in Santo Domingo for four years and served as research director of FondoMicro (the fund for the financing of small businesses).

Moya Pons is considered to be a pioneer in the field of Dominican history and has been an inspiration to Dominican American scholars. His first book, *La Española en el siglo XVI: 1493–1520* (Hispaniola in the Sixteenth Century: 1493–1520), published in 1971, won the Dominican Republic National History Prize, although the award was not officially recognized by the government since the book highlighted issues that had been obscured by the traditional Dominican historiography. The book represents a major undertaking of vigorous analysis of an important period of Caribbean history. Since then he has authored more than 20 books and some 60 scholarly articles. His book *Manual de historia dominicana*, now in its tenth edition, is considered a seminal text in Dominican historiography. While serving as visiting research director of the City University of New York (CUNY) Dominican Studies Institute at City College (a research unit within CUNY dedicated to Dominican studies) he published *Dominican Republic: A National History* (1995), which is the first Dominican history book of importance written in English since 1928. For a period of six years, he kept a weekly column in *Rumbo* magazine under the title "La historia tiene otra historia" (The other story in history). These one-page articles are particularly noteworthy as compact, pithy accounts of key events that have shaped Dominican history yet have been neglected in the textbooks and manuals of the Dominican experience from colonial times to the present.

In 2000 Moya Pons was appointed to head the newly created Ministry of the Environment and Natural Resources of the Dominican Republic. His ecological initiatives are serving as models in the implementation of environmental policies in Latin America. He also serves as the vice president of OGM Central de Datos—a data research service of Dominican newspapers and journals that he founded in the 1990s. Although he has occasionally been described as a political conservative, his practice and his writings reveal the opposite. Despite his government post, Moya Pons has continued to use his voice critically to express his concerns about the present and uncharted future of the Dominican Republic. He has also been among the first to consider the Dominican diaspora in the United States as an integral part of Dominican history.

RELATED ARTICLES

Dominican Studies; Education, Higher.

FURTHER READING

Alonso, María E. "Frank Moya Pons: 'No quiero que mi país siga siendo un basurero'" (Frank Moya Pons: I Do Not Want My Country To Be a Litter Can). *Rumbo* (November 4, 2002): 44–46.

Moquete, Clodomiro. "Frank Moya Pons: 'Confesiones imprevistas de un homo sapiens militante' " (Frank Moya Pons: Unexpected Confessions of a Militant Homo Sapiens). *Vetas* 3, no. 14 (December 1995): 16–21.

Torres-Saillant, Silvio. "¿Historiador conservador o intelectual subversivo?: Hacia una relectura de Frank Moya Pons " (Conservative Historian or Subversive Intellectual?: Toward a Rereading of Frank Moya Pons). *Rumbo* (May 29, 1995) : 1–15.

SARAH APONTE

MUÑOZ MARÍN, LUIS

Born: February 18, 1898; San Juan, Puerto Rico
Died: April 30, 1980; Puerto Rico

Writer, statesman, and architect of modern Puerto Rico, Luis Muñoz Marín was born in San Juan four months before the U.S. military invasion. The son of Amalia Marín and Luis Muñoz Rivera, the island's most influential late-19th-century politician, the younger Muñoz was at the epicenter of island politics since birth. His father had successfully advocated for autonomy under Spain and served in the short-lived 1897 autonomous administration. He was later elected as the island's nonvoting resident commissioner in the U.S. Congress in 1910.

Owing to his father's political career, Muñoz Marín grew up in Puerto Rico, New York City, and Washington, D.C.; some have called him the "first Nuyorican." He was bilingual, bicultural, and fully conversant in the ways of Washington politics, a skill that would prove invaluable two decades later when he founded his own party. Initially, however, Muñoz Marín showed little interest in party politics and was instead known as "El Vate" (the Bard), a "bohemian" poet, editor, and a writer of essays on a broad range of political and cultural topics.

In 1919 Muñoz Marín met and married Muna Lee, a leading Pan Americanist, author, translator, feminist, poet, and U.S. government official. The couple had two children; they divorced in 1946.

Ideologically, the young Muñoz Marín was influenced by the "mystic" socialist philosophy of Edwin Markham, whose 1899 poem "The Man with the Hoe," prophesying the awakening of exploited workers, he translated. An active part of intellectual circles in New York and San Juan, Muñoz Marín also read and discussed "free-thinking" philosophy, Karl Marx's *Communist Manifesto,* and Fabianism. A decade before returning to Puerto Rico in 1931, he campaigned for the Socialist Party but did not formally run for public office until 1932, when he was elected as a senator-at-large on the Liberal Party ticket.

A defender of independence from his youth, Muñoz Marín was taken by Franklin Delano Roosevelt's New Deal legislation. Whereas previously he viewed the United States as an obstacle to Puerto Rico's economic and political self-determination, he came to perceive the federal government as a means to reform the crudest forms of economic and colonial domination. Appealing directly to President Roosevelt, Muñoz Marín succeeded in attracting New Deal and other programs to Puerto Rico, but a series of political setbacks resulted in his expulsion from the Liberal Party, and the languishing of reformist projects. His response to the lowest point of his political life, however, had a lasting impact on Puerto Ricans and Americans.

As it has become legendary, Muñoz Marín got into a beat-up Ford with a loudspeaker to promote the creation of a new party: the Popular Democratic Party (PDP). Founded on July 22, 1938, the party adopted as its symbol the peasant's (*jíbaro's*) straw hat, underscored by the slogan "Bread, Land, and Liberty." In contrast to all other existing party heads, Muñoz Marín declared that Puerto Rico's political relationship with the United States was not at issue during the election, and he promoted a program aimed at curbing the exploitative power of the sugar monopolies. In an unprecedented campaign strategy, he requested the support of the impoverished agricultural workers, visiting every town on the island and urging laborers not to allow themselves to "sell their vote" for a few dollars or in exchange for goods, as was the custom.

Muñoz Marín stunned the establishment when in 1940 the PDP won the elections by a large enough margin to elect him to the Senate. Over the next eight years, Muñoz and his party passed legislation to end the sugar land monopoly, supply basic services such as electricity to the poor, and reform education. With the support of the last American appointed governor to the island, Rexford Guy Tugwell, Muñoz Marín also advocated for Puerto Ricans to elect their own governor. Not surprisingly, the majority of voters elected El Vate by a landslide in 1948.

The PDP's electoral success did not end the status debate. Rejecting independence and statehood as economically punitive, Muñoz Marín championed the creation of the Commonwealth of Puerto Rico on July 25, 1952. The Commonwealth (or Estado Libre Asociado) provided for further autonomy over

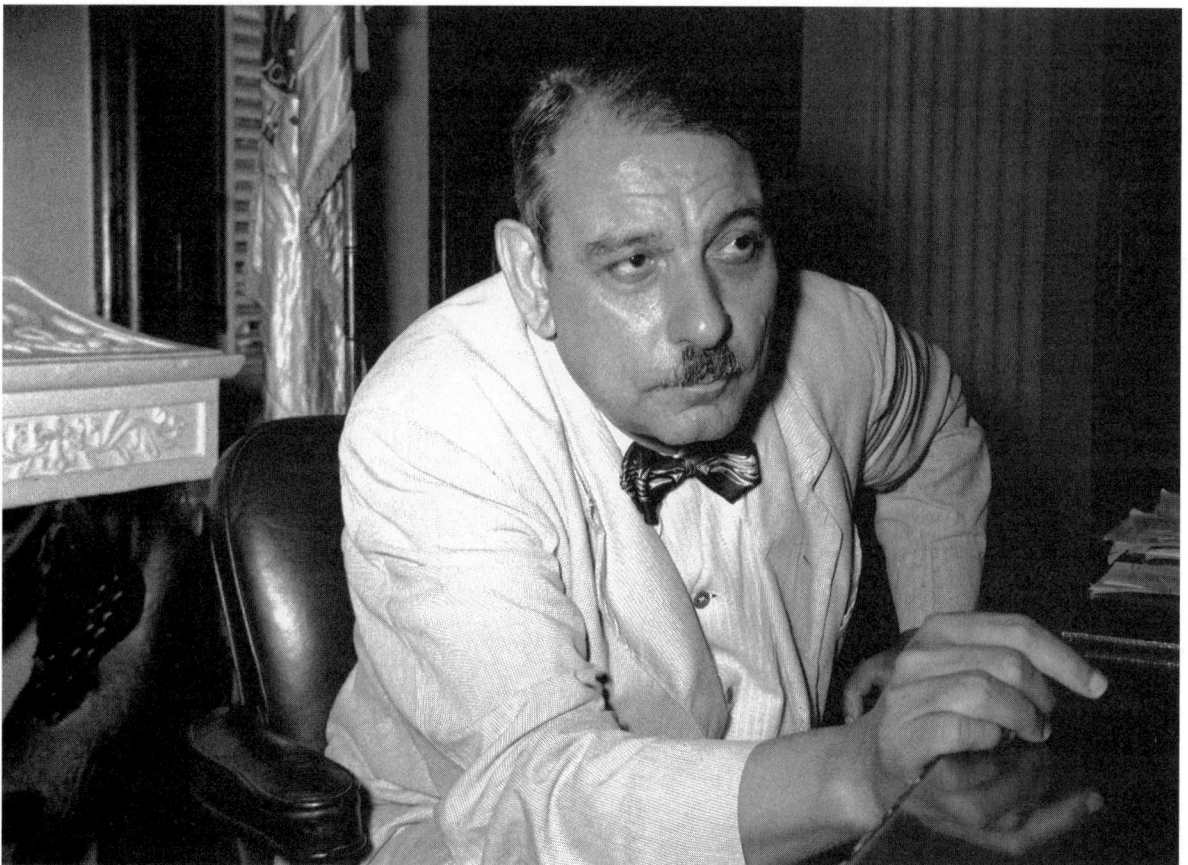

Puerto Rico's Governor Luis Muñoz Marín at La Fortaleza, an old Spanish palace in San Juan, 1952.

ON RECENT DISTURBANCES IN PUERTO RICO

The people of Puerto Rico are profoundly indignant at the attempt made at Blair House, in which two Puerto Rican nationalists were involved. We would feel ashamed of calling ourselves Puerto Ricans, if it were not for the fact that the nationalist gangsters are less than 500 in number, among the more than two million decent, democracy-loving American citizens that make up our community. We have a genuine admiration and affection for President Truman, not only because of his leadership in these troubled times of the world, but in a more intimate sense, because of his constant, fair-minded, generous attitude in helping Puerto Rico to help itself. We are deeply relieved that this criminal attempt was as futile as the violence that we have experienced from the same source and under the same guidance in Puerto Rico during the last two days. This crime confirms my conviction of the connection of these mad, grotesque, and futile nationalist violence-makers in Puerto Rico with communistic propaganda strategy all over the world.

Excerpt from "On Recent Disturbances in Puerto Rico," a speech delivered by Luis Muñoz Marín in Barranquitas, Puerto Rico (July 1951).

local affairs, economic integration without federal taxation, and the retaining of U.S. citizenship. Following the founding of the Commonwealth, Muñoz Marín's administration implemented "Operation Bootstrap," an export-led industrialization program that transformed the island's economy through mostly U.S. private investment and mass migration of the "excess" labor force to the United States, most notably New York City. Operation Bootstrap was complemented by Operation Serenity, a policy that sought to provide a "spiritual" balance to modernization through the redefinition of culture—not national sovereignty—as the essence of national identity.

After serving as governor from 1940 to 1964, Muñoz Marín declined the nomination for a fifth term and returned to the Senate, where he served until 1970. He was constantly reminded of the implications that came with his project of economic modernization under enduring colonial conditions. After his death he was mourned by thousands of friends, foes, and the people whose lives he dramatically changed. He left a complex legacy: substantially higher standards of living, over two-thirds of Puerto Ricans residing in the United States, Puerto Rico's relative local autonomy, and a largely consensual colonial society.

RELATED ARTICLES

Lee, Muna; Operation Bootstrap; Politics, Puerto Rican; Puerto Rico.

FURTHER READING

Aitken, Thomas, Jr. *Poet in the Fortress*. New York: New Am. Lib., 1964.

De Heredia, Manuel. *Luis Muñoz Marín: Biografía Abierta* (Luis Muñoz Marín: Biography). Rio Piedras: Ediciones Puerto, 1973.

López Rojas, Luis A. *Luis Muñoz Marín y las estrategias del poder, 1936–1946* (Luis Muñoz Marín and the Strategies of Power). San Juan: Isla Negra Editores, 1998.

Matthews, Thomas. *Luis Muñoz Marín: A Concise Biography*. New York: Am. R. D. M. Corp., 1967.

Muñoz Marín, Luis. *Memorias, Volumes 1–3* (Memoirs . . .). Rio Piedras: Universidad Interamericana de Puerto Rico, 1982.

Natal, Carmelo Rosario. *La juventud de Luis Muñoz Marín* (The Youth of Luis Muñoz Marín). San Juan, 1976.

Tugwell, Rexford Guy. *The Stricken Land: The Story of Puerto Rico*. New York: Doubleday, 1947.

FRANCES NEGRÓN-MUNTANER

MURALISM

Muralism, or *muralismo* in Spanish, generally refers to the practice of transferring images or designs to architectural surfaces, using any of a variety of techniques—including fresco, brush painting, mosaic tile, aerosol or airbrush, or more recently, digital "wallpapering." The root term in Spanish is *muro,* meaning "wall," indicating perhaps the most common surface of choice for muralists. Given the architectural placement and often monumental size of the mural image, muralism can be distinguished from other forms of image production by its greater attentiveness to the technical problem of integrating the visual image to the details of its inhabited spatial context, such as adjacent architectural forms, multiple sight lines, and routes of traffic. Notably, the Spanish cognate, as a consequence of Mexico's 20th-century revolutionary mural movement and the important role of murals in articulating the goals of the Chicano movement in the United States from the 1960s onward, is often freighted with political connotations not comprehended by technical definition.

This semantic distinction between *muralism* and *muralismo* underscores problems with speaking of muralism in exclusively technical terms. A strictly technical definition obscures several significant dimensions of mural practice. First, muralism in this sense comprehends a broad spectrum of work on the many surfaces of the built environment. Mural artistry most famously involves the elaboration of an image or series of images that aspire to recognition as art or object of specialized attention and experience. But mural work may also be as simple as the visual adornment of walls, ceilings, or floors, of interiors or exteriors, with decorative motifs. In addition, some mural practices (such as graffiti) may eschew the status of artwork entirely, emphasizing communication over artistry in their use of urban surfaces to publicize an opinion or point of view, mark social territory, or express support for a political candidate or concern. Second, the numerous modalities of modern mural practice have contributed to continued controversy—most dramatically with respect to aerosol techniques and graffiti "writing"—over what merits the designation of mural art, and whether *muralism* is a term best reserved exclusively for artistic work. Third, because the "canvas" that must be secured for the mural work represents a portion of the built environment, muralists frequently must negotiate through an array of social actors, institutions, interests, and relationships in addition to resolving the technical problems of image transfer.

As a consequence of its unique social dimensions, muralism is embedded in different historical times and places in a variety of social, political, and cultural contexts that give mural practices a range of different functions and meanings not exhausted by traditional notions of art. Hence, both the work of Michelangelo in the Sistine Chapel in early 16th-century Italy and that of an aerosol street artist in the early 21st century on New York's Lower East Side can be classified as muralism, but the purpose and significance of the artist's mural practice and art is distinct to each respective architectural environment, cultural milieu, social setting, and institutional circumstance. The Sistine Chapel situates mural artistry within Catholic religious discourse and an art world constituted by elite patrons and a guild system. In contrast, the aerosol artist operates at the margins of the established art world, negotiating with local, non-expert patrons when not poaching wall space outright, and often articulates an overt challenge to dominant social norms.

Latino mural practice has included the full range of muralism, from graffiti slogan to decorative detail to monumental public artwork. In fact, historically, muralism has been a significant cultural component of Latino experience in the United States, representing both an important Latino contribution to U.S. national culture and public life and an expressive medium useful for negotiating the public visibility of Latino identities and concerns in relation to dominant Anglo-Saxon U.S. culture and society. Latino muralists and mural art have contributed to the aesthetic shaping of public and communal spaces, most visibly in U.S. cities that are home to large Latino populations, such as Los Angeles and San Diego, California; Denver, Colorado; El Paso, Texas; Chicago; New York City; and Miami, among others. Latino muralism is vital also as a communicative practice, not only via the mural image itself but also through the involvement of communities in aesthetic and symbolic decision-making related to mural production. As a communicative medium, mural art has facilitated and strengthened the formation of Latino collective identity and community sensibility within the United States, and it has aided in identifying emerging issues of common concern.

Of Latino mural art, Chicano variants have enjoyed the greatest defined public profile and most extensive presence across the United States. In fact, Chicano muralism emerged in the 1960s and 1970s as one of the richest tendencies within the community murals phenomenon in the United States generally. The special strength of the Chicano mural arts derives from several related factors: the U.S. Latino population is predominantly of Mexican heritage (Latinos of Mexican background representing two-thirds of the whole), as are many of the largest urban Latino settlements in the country; the Chicano civil rights and culture movement formed the leading edge of Latino social and cultural activism in the United States in the second half of the 20th century; and Mexican mural art was at the forefront of the development of modern mural aesthetics and practice in the 20th century.

Present-day U.S. Latino mural artists are influenced by a wide range of stylistic currents, as well as a broad spectrum of non-Latino cultural heritages that inform both individual mural works and the artistic corpus of the individual artist. However, there are a number of historical sources for the vitality of Latino muralism generally and Chicano muralism in particular. The most frequently referenced historical antecedents for modern Latino mural artistry correspond geographically to present-day Mexico and the U.S. Southwest, and they follow the uneven trajectory of Latin American cultural formation from its origins in early non-European civilizations to the conquest and colonial period and through to the modern nation-state. The most prominent historical predecessors and influences for U.S. Latino muralists are pre-Columbian, indigenous mural traditions; Catholic religious arts originating in the colonial period; murals as an element of popular culture and everyday life; and the socially committed and politically engaged muralism of the revolutionary Mexican school of the first half of the 20th century. Latter-day mural artists continue to draw on these mural traditions in both form and content, and—especially in the case of Chicano muralism—often as frame of reference for elevating the mural form itself to the status of symbol of cultural identity.

Pre-Columbian Murals

Prior to the European conquest of the Americas in the 16th century, muralism had been a significant feature of the more technologically advanced indigenous civilizations (for example, Aztec and Maya), whose prominent architectural works, chiefly pyramids and temples, were often adorned with mural frescos. Archaeological sites in Bonampak, Teotihuacán, Chichén Itzá, and Tlaxcala in present-day Mexico contain some of the most well-known pre-Columbian murals. Wall paintings also have been uncovered in the Andean region of South America and in the kivas of the U.S. Southwest (Arizona, Colorado, and New Mexico), but it is Mexico's indigenous cultural ancestry that most commonly makes an appearance in modern Latino mural art.

Modern Latino muralists, like their Mexican counterparts, sometimes evoke the muralism of the pre-conquest in order to illustrate the connections between their own artistic practice and regional cultural histo-

DARTMOUTH COLLEGE

Departure of Quetzalcóatl by José Clemente Orozco, from the Orozco Frescoes (completed in 1934) in the Baker Library, Dartmouth College, Hanover, New Hampshire.

ries, as well as to identify contemporary cultural materials with millennial indigenous legacies. Despite this frequent emphasis on the non-Western facets of mestizo heritage in contemporary mural form, the practical continuity such linkage implies for regional mural traditions—from the precolonial through to the contemporary period—is questionable. Most of the visual culture of the early indigenous peoples of Latin America was in fact destroyed by the religious zealotry of the European conquerors, and the study and preservation of remaining indigenous monuments is itself an artifact of the current era.

Nevertheless, modern Latino mural art connects to the indigenous civilizations of the past through the prevalence of visual motifs, symbols, deities, and historic personages preserved in frescos, statuary, and other cultural artifacts of the precolonial period. It is not uncommon for Latino muralists to include in their works elements from historical indigenous visual cultures, such as the planar representational style of an Aztec or Mixtec codex, or even specific figures from Mexico's rich pre-Hispanic narrative pictography. Other common sources for modern mural imagery are widely recognizable precolonial architectural, sculptural, and ceremonial forms. Especially prevalent in Chicano murals are such details as depictions of pyramids and the corbeled Maya arch; sun and moon calendars cut from stone; Olmec heads; ceremonial artifacts such as the chac mool, a reclining stone figure of obscure function with a bowl in its belly; and deities including Quetzalcóatl, the plumed serpent of both Maya and Aztec derivation, and Coatlicue, the Aztec earth goddess. Pre-Columbian figures often serve in Chicano murals as visual counterpoint to critical representations of a technocratic Western modernity.

Religious Art

Latino culture in the United States, as in Latin America more broadly, includes a strong tradition of religious art, largely Catholic in character. Because Catholicism provided the chief ideological justification for the conquest and propagated the cultural dominance of Europeans in the colonization of the Americas by the Iberian powers, Catholic cultural production—including the construction of churches and missions and the painting of murals in their interiors—aggressively sought to replace preexisting non-Christian cosmogonies and their media of diffusion. Vestiges of Spanish colonial culture are present across the U.S. Southwest and from Florida as far west as Louisiana.

Among the influences on latter-day Latino visual culture generally, and mural art in particular, can be found much of the same New Testament pictorial idiom that predominated in the religious artwork of the colonial era. Images of the Virgin Mary and Jesus Christ are not uncommon, even when the murals that bear them are characterized by a secular location or message. The Virgin of Guadalupe, whose image is said to have miraculously appeared on the tunic of an indigenous man in 1531 at Tepeyac, is the most prolifically reproduced figure of all. Her close association with Mexican national identity and popular culture has made her image and cult meaningful far beyond her strictly Catholic status. Chicano visual artists have adapted her image north of the border as an amulet of Chicano identity and as a medium for negotiating tensions, especially as regards the role of women, between traditional values and social progress. Muralists and mural historians have also noted the presence of other traditions of religious art in the murals of the modern era, such as retablos, votive paintings that document personal spiritual experiences. Chicana artist Yreina Cervántes's mural La ofrenda (1989; Los Angeles), for example, integrates a hagiographic likeness of United Farm Workers leader Dolores Huerta to a visual field filled with ritual objects and folk spiritual offerings.

Church murals in a variety of styles are an important feature of many Latino communities today. The modern Catholic Church, influenced in part by social movements and the famed "preferential option for the poor" adopted after the Vatican II Council in 1968, has supported more recent popular styles as well. For example, so-called primitivist styles made popular by liberation theology in Central America during the 1980s (especially in Fernando Llort's influential fusion of folk sensibilities with religious artifacts in El Salvador) have had some influence in the adornment of church walls with brightly colored scenes of rural life combined with doves and other symbols of Christian inspiration. Many Chicano artists have created murals for churches, often blending social issues, a color-rich palette, and dynamic human figures with Christian symbols. Modern Latino church murals in the United States have gone largely undocumented.

Popular Culture

Contemporary Mexican and Mexican American traditions of mural art are steeped in popular culture and working-class histories. In Mexico the secular lineage of present-day mural art includes the *pulquería* murals of the 19th and the early 20th century. Painted on interior or exterior walls of cantinas and *pulquerías*—popular drinking establishments specializing in *pulque* (an alcoholic beverage derived from the maguey plant)—these murals commonly offered postcardlike visions of beautiful women or tropical escape for the enjoyment of the bar's working-class male clientele. Famed Mexican artist Frida Kahlo, herself an important icon for Chicana muralists, embraced this mural genre during the heyday of revolutionary Mexican muralism in the 1920s and 1930s. Murals remain a distinctive feature of many Latino-owned businesses—restaurants, bars, barbershops, groceries, and the like—in U.S. cities today.

The visual dimensions of popular culture and working-class sensibilities have provided a wealth of materials and styles of aesthetic representation for Latino muralists. Calendar and poster art from Mexico has circulated widely within the United States as Latino communities have expanded, and, as a consequence, images such as guardian angels, the Aztec prince Cuauhtémoc, and the legendary romantic figures of Popocateptl and Ixtaccihuatl have become commonplace in Latino community murals. Similarly, Mexican American cultural pride has found visual support in the red, white, and green Mexican tricolor, which is sometimes added as a detail to other mural figures coincidental to barrio life in the United States, like lowrider cars or the Virgin of Guadalupe. Similar use of the Puerto Rican, Cuban, and Dominican flags in street murals in New York testify to the strong nationalism of Latino popular culture. Other kinds of popular image production and consumption sometimes inform the aesthetic choices of mural artists, as with the fanciful forms of tattoo, or *paño,* art. *Calaveras*—animated skeletal renderings of the dead—also are a major contribution of Latino popular culture, deriving from annual Day of the Dead celebrations. Muralists have often mimicked the famous *grabados* (engravings) of Mexican graphic artist José Guadalupe Posada when integrating *calaveras* into their murals.

More recently, aerosol art, stylized graffiti lettering, hip-hop youth culture (including the emergence of Latin rap and spoken word poetry) have become significant sources of inspiration and points of reference for Latino visual artists. In the late 1980s, Latino aerosol artists in New York City began painting memorial murals, honoring young people who had died as a result of police brutality, gang violence, or drug use. The practice has since spread nationally and is now an important genre of community muralism.

Mexican Muralism

The single greatest modern influence on muralism in the United States undoubtedly has been the work of the so-called Mexican school. Originating in a public arts program promulgated by José Vasconcelos, Mexico's secretary of public education from 1921 to 1924, the Mexican mural movement emerged from the conjunction of a revolutionary political atmosphere, strong state funding for the arts, and a dynamic group of artists that included Diego Rivera, José Clemente Orozco, and David Alfaro Siqueiros. These three, often referred to as *los tres grandes* (the three great ones), are most closely identified with the resultant school of painting characterized by social realist aesthetics, the active joining of art and politics, and the use of the mural as a medium for narrating social progress and the advancement of social movements. All of these elements are visible in Chicano muralism and have left a vital impression on U.S. community murals in general.

Although the Mexican school's influence can be partly ascribed to the weight of Mexican national cultural heritage within U.S. Latino communities, it is also important to note that the *tres grandes* all produced significant mural works within the United States. Controversy surrounding many of these works served to elevate the public profile of this brand of muralism. Orozco painted mural cycles at Pomona College in California (1930), at the New School for Social Research in New York City (1931), and at Dartmouth College in New Hampshire (*American Civilization;* 1932). Siqueiros's *América Tropical* (1932; Los Angeles), which includes the depiction of a crucified mestizo, was nearly obliterated soon after its completion because its sponsors were displeased with the mural's critique of U.S. racism. Rivera painted murals in San Francisco, Detroit, and New York City, and achieved international notoriety after his mural for the latter city's Rockefeller Center (*Man at the Crossroads;* 1933) was destroyed because he refused to remove a favorable portrait of Soviet leader V. I. Lenin. The federal arts program of the Roosevelt administration during the Great Depression was modeled in part on the Mexican experience.

Although the work of Rivera and others is a touchstone for mural artists throughout the hemisphere, the influence of the Mexican school is especially pronounced in Chicano muralism. Chicano murals have been similarly marked by the responsiveness of the artwork to issues of social import and have drawn energy and inspiration from Chicanismo, the civil rights movement, and other progressive social formations. Many Chicano artists have traveled to Mexico for artistic study, including Texas artist Raul Valdez, who was able to train with Siqueiros before the Mexican artist's death in 1973. Aesthetic influences can be seen in the heroic proportions of immigrant fieldworkers and other subjects of Chicano social struggle, in monumental portraiture of Chicano leaders and activists, and in the use of murals to visually narrate community histories. Occasionally, the Mexican school legacy is directly referenced, as with Daniel Galvez's mural *Viva la Raza* (1977; San Francisco), which includes a rendering of Siqueiros's *New Democracy* mural (1944; Mexico City) on the side of a tractor trailer. Alessandra Moctezuma and Eva Cockcroft reproduced Siqueiros's *América Tropical* in their *Homage to Siqueiros* (2001; Los Angeles).

Importantly, because of the proximity of Mexico to the United States and the strength of Mexican cultural heritage within the United States, Mexican artists continue the cross-border work initiated by the Mexican school, carrying out mural commissions in the U.S. Southwest with some frequency. As Mexican American communities have grown and extended farther north, cross-border mural collaborations have followed. Mexico City muralist Daniel Manrique painted a mural for the United Electrical Workers in Chicago in 1997, for example, and the Taller de Investigación Plástica, a public arts collective from Michoacán, produced a noteworthy mosaic tile mural, *Mosaic of the Americas,* in Minneapolis, Minnesota, in 2001.

Chicano Muralism

Chicano muralism is closely linked to the historic emergence of the Chicano movement in the 1960s. As Mexican Americans and Mexican migrant workers fought for equal rights and equitable treatment in U.S. society, a cultural renaissance of sorts took place. The political work of the United Farm Work-

ers (UFW), the Raza Unida Party, and other insurgent Chicano organizations was fortified by the diffusion of Chicano publications and graphic arts work. Alongside flyers and posters, murals became a vital part of the visual culture through which Chicano cultural pride and social demands were defined and propagated. Chicano mural-making played a vital role as a cultural mediator of histories, revitalizing the connections between Mexico's revolutionary history and Chicano civil rights activism, while also cross-referencing Chicano experience with that of other U.S. minorities, or with regional efforts at social transformation. Significantly, in Chicano murals the figure of UFW leader César Chávez often shares the wall with African American civil rights leader Martin Luther King or Cuban revolutionist Ché Guevara, or indigenous rights activist Rigoberta Menchú. Murals were also important as a community-building mechanism, drawing people together around the common public experience of reclaiming and celebrating a cultural heritage. And, because of the urban character of the mural form, muralism proved an effective means for securing community public space against the pressures of commercialization, urban violence, and real estate development.

Chicano cultural activism spawned a number of arts collectives and cultural organizations, a great many of these in California. Arts collectives frequently operated to facilitate large-scale mural production. Examples of such groups are the Sacramento-based Royal Chicano Air Force, founded in 1970; East Los Streetscapers, active during 1979–1985; and two separate groups calling themselves Mujeres Muralistas organized for the purpose of mural painting, first in San Francisco between 1974 and 1976 and later in San Diego in 1977. Chroniclers of Chicano art history cite institutions such as the Goez Gallery, founded by mural artists Joe and John González and David Botello in Los Angeles in 1969; the Social and Public Art Resource Center (SPARC), founded by muralist Judy Baca in 1976 to promote the creation and conservation of murals; or El Grito de Aztlán Gallery in Denver, founded by Carlos Santistevan in 1968 as examples of the many galleries and cultural centers established by Chicano activists throughout the Southwest in their aim for community-controlled resources and alternate venues for cultural expression and recognition. The nascent institutional structures allowed mural art to proliferate throughout the region of highest concentration of

A mural in downtown Belvidere, Illinois, celebrates the town's Hispanic heritage (2001).

Latino communities and made possible greater visibility for emerging artists and their work. In 1975, for example, the Goez Gallery published a mural map of East Los Angeles, documenting more than 270 murals in the area. For their part, arts groups nurtured a collaborative ethic, organically linked the arts to social struggle, and provided a working social context for individual artistic development.

According to art historian Shifra Goldman, the first Chicano murals in California were painted in 1968 by Antonio Bernal on the UFW Teatro Campesino Center in Del Rey, California. Historian Ricardo Romo has noted that UFW headquarters were also important sites for murals in Texas during the early period of Chicano activism. It should be noted, of course, that adequate mural documentation practice and scholarly interest in the mural phenomenon developed more slowly than the mural movement itself. Murals are almost by definition a local medium, and consequently the public reception and appreciation of Chicano murals were fragmented and uneven in the initial period. With few exceptions mural histories treating U.S. community muralism, whether Latino or other variants, have centered on individual states or cities; a generation after its inception, a comprehensive study of the Chicano mural movement has yet to be written.

Chicano murals—whether through their public locations, thematic contents, or the controversies they have generated—are monuments to collective negotiation of urban space, cultural defense and appropriation, and critical perspectives on mainstream U.S. society and values. Judy Baca's *Great Wall of Los Angeles* (1976–1983), painted along a half mile (8.8 km) of cement flood channel, involved the participation of a multiethnic cohort of a dozen artists and more than 300 area youth. The mural treats the history of Los Angeles, but with a critical eye to the immigrant experience, establishing historical continuity in the contributions of U.S. minorities to the progress and defense of the nation while unflinchingly depicting the occasional racist hostility of U.S. dominant culture. The expulsion of Mexican immigrants and the World War II internment of Japanese Americans are depicted as part of the same problematic national history. One of the most celebrated episodes in Chicano muralism is the defense of Chicano Park in San Diego, where a land takeover initiated in 1970 by local residents opposed to a city urbanization plan resulted in the painting of a long series of support columns under the Coronado Bay bridge. The unique mural series, painted by many different artists and community members over more than a decade, carved out a communal public space with images such as that of a proud UFW family painted by José Montoya and the Royal Chicano Air Force in 1975. The concrete banks of the Rio Grande, particularly around the El Paso–Ciudad Juárez area have been the site of multiple murals since the late 1980s commenting on U.S.-Mexico border tensions. In Chicago the Pilsen neighborhood, at one time a major eastern European immigrant settlement, has been transformed into a Mexican immigrant barrio where murals abound amid concerns with surrounding urban renewal. In 1997 Marcos Raya, a leading figure in Chicago's Chicano mural movement, painted *Cataclysm*, a large portable mural composed of angular thrusting antagonism between Pilsen's minority community and the machinations of capitalist modernity.

The Chicano movement launched the careers of a number of important public artists. There were, of course, predecessors to the generation of mural artists allied to Chicanismo in the 1960s and 1970s. Especially worthy of note and further study are those Latinos who contributed to the Works Progress Administration public arts program of the 1930s, such as Xavier González and José Aceves, both of whom painted murals in Texas post offices. Some artists, like El Paso–based Manuel Acosta, bridged the gap between an older generation of Latino artists and the Chicano mural movement. A distinctively Chicano muralism responded to new cultural strengths and challenges and hence has been multifaceted in character. For some artists, such as José Antonio Burciaga, mural practice was one component of a lively intellectual contribution. For others, such as Judy Baca, muralism would be the centerpiece of a far-reaching urban community activism. Still more painted murals but were better known for other modalities of cultural activism, as was the case with René Yañez, whose curatorial work was critical in creating exposure for Chicano art, or George Yepes, whose murals and studio work are equally acclaimed.

Too numerous to mention here, a host of mural works and a corresponding range of aesthetic styles have provided the impulse for continued development of Chicano muralism, from Willie Herron's

provocative *The Wall That Cracked Open* (1972; Los Angeles), which absorbed existing graffiti into a street mural commentary on conflictive social conditions, to Jaime Longoria's *La llorona* (1996; Minneapolis), whose expressionist use of color and fanciful animal forms bring the legend of the wailing woman to bear on the problem of adolescent pregnancies. Lastly, one of the more interesting features of the Chicano mural phenomenon is the prominence of female artists relative to the male-dominated Mexican tradition of muralism. Mujeres Muralistas (initially Patricia Rodríguez, Graciela Carillo, Consuelo Méndez, and Irene Pérez, and later a group of San Diego students led by Yolanda López) is a feminist grouping unheard of in the Mexican mural tradition. More recently, Alma López has been at the leading edge of mural work using digital technology, as with her 1997 series of digital murals on vinyl for the Estrada Courts Community Center in Los Angeles, in which the technique allows for photomontage juxtaposing community women with historical counterparts such as 17th-century protofeminist Sor Juana Inés de la Cruz.

RELATED ARTICLES
Art, Mexican American and Chicano; Baca, Judith; Chicano Movement; Painting; Popular Culture; Rivera, Diego.

FURTHER READING
Cockcroft, Eva, and Holly Barnet-Sánchez. *Signs from the Heart: California Chicano Murals.* Albuquerque: Univ. of N.Mex. Press, 1999.
Cockcroft, Eva, et al. *Toward a People's Art.* Albuquerque: Univ. of N.Mex. Press, 1999.
Cooper, Martha, and Joseph Sciarra. *R.I.P.: Memorial Wall Art.* London: Thames & Hudson, 1994.
Fernández, Justino. *A Guide to Mexican Art.* Chicago: Univ. of Chicago Press, 1969.
Folgarait, Leonard. *Mural Painting and Social Revolution in Mexico, 1920–1940: Art of the New Order.* Cambridge, Mass.: Cambridge Univ. Press, 1998.
Gray, Mary Lackritz. *A Guide to Chicago's Murals.* Chicago: Univ. of Chicago Press, 2001.
Juárez, Miguel. *Colors on Desert Walls: The Murals of El Paso.* El Paso: Tex. Western Press, 1997.

BRUCE CAMPBELL

MURRIETA, JOAQUÍN

Born: Probably 1820s; Sonora, Mexico
Died: July 24, 1854; Arroyo Cantúa, California

Joaquín Murrieta's legend is more significant in U.S. Latino history than his life and deeds. Most likely the leader of a gang of horse thieves, he has been written into history as a figure wronged by a racist Anglo population of California during the days of the gold rush, and taken up by the Mexican American community as a symbol of resistance.

Murrieta (also spelled Murieta and, sometimes, Murietta) was probably born in the 1820s in the Mexican state of Sonora, which was then in the center of the country and, after 1848, a northern province. He most likely emigrated to Upper California during the gold rush heading a band of thieves who stole horses north of the border, driving them into Mexico and selling them there—one of several gang leaders who terrorized the countryside at the time and included Joaquín Juan Murrieta (a cousin) and Joaquín Valenzuela.

After the cession of Upper California to the United States in 1848, as a result of the Mexican War with America, and following the granting of statehood in 1850, the population of California grew from about 20,000 to 100,000. The need for the new state legislature to demonstrate social order resulted in a crackdown on bandits. A bounty of $5,000 was put on the head of "Joaquín," most likely a con-

flation of several contemporary *bandidos* (bandits), and one Captain Harry Love was authorized to use all means to capture him, dead or alive.

Love scoured the state until July 24, 1854, just before the bounty's time limit was to expire, when he purportedly caught up to the Murrieta gang in Arroyo Cantúa, near Tulare Lake, in the center of the state. Two of the four or five men reported killed were, according to Love, Murrieta and his henchman Tres Dedos (Three-Fingered Jack). The head of what was alleged to be Murrieta was cut off, placed in a jar with preserving liquid, and used as proof of the capture. For several years, this head was exhibited in various cities and towns throughout California, until it was lost, though several men who supposedly knew Murrieta denied it was his.

The legend of Murrieta as a beneficent, wronged subaltern was created soon thereafter by the half-Cherokee, half-Anglo journalist John Rollin Ridge, who wrote under the name of Yellow Bird. His *Life and Adventures of Joaquín Murieta, the Celebrated California Bandit* reformulated Murrieta as a well-educated, peaceable Mexican whose brother was lynched and wife raped and killed by drunken Anglos, and who turned to crime out of revenge. At one time or another, Chilean and French writers have also claimed Murrieta as one of their own; he appears in Pablo Neruda's play *Fulgor y muerte de Joaquín Murrieta* (Splendor and Death of Joaquín Murrieta), for example. As time passed, the Mexican American community adopted the legendary Murrieta as a symbol of resistance.

During the second half of the 20th century, several authors, such as Remi Nadeau and Frank Latta, attempted to uncover the "real" Joaquín Murrieta, but the legend persists through such works as Walter Noble Burns's *Robin Hood of El Dorado* and Isabel Allende's *Daughter of Fortune*.

RELATED ARTICLES

California; Criminals and Bandidos; Folklore, Mexican American.

FURTHER READING

Allende, Isabel. *Daughter of Fortune*. New York: HarperCollins, 1999.

Burns, Walter Noble. *The Robin Hood of El Dorado: The Saga of Joaquín Murrieta, Famous Outlaw of California's Age of Gold*. New York: Coward-McCann, 1932.

Joaquín Murieta, The Brigand Chief of California. San Francisco: Calif. Police Gazette, 1859. Reprint. San Francisco: Grabhorn Press, 1932.

WILL BE EXHIBITED
FOR ONE DAY ONLY!

AT THE STOCKTON HOUSE!
THIS DAY, AUG. 12, FROM 9 A. M., UNTIL 6 P. M.

THE HEAD
Of the renowned Bandit!

JOAQUIN!
AND THE
HAND OF THREE FINGERED JACK!
THE NOTORIOUS ROBBER AND MURDERER.

"JOAQUIN" and "THREE-FINGERED JACK" were captured by the State Rangers, under the command of Capt. Harry Love, at the Arroyo Cantua, July 24th. No reasonable doubt can be entertained in regard to the identification of the head now on exhibition, as being that of the notorious robber, Joaquin Murrietta, as it has been recognized by hundreds of persons who have formerly seen him.

BUREAU OF LAND MANAGEMENT, HOLLISTER FIELD OFFICE

Poster announcing a one-day exhibit in California of "The Head of the Renowned Bandit Joaquin [Murrieta] and the Hand of Three Fingered Jack."

Latta, Frank F. *Joaquín Murrieta and His Horse Gangs.* Santa Cruz, Calif.: Bear State Bks., 1980.

Nadeau, Remi. *The Real Joaquín Murieta, California's Gold Rush Bandit: Truth v. Myth.* Santa Barbara, Calif.: Crest Pubs., 1974.

Varley, James F. *The Legend of Joaquín Murrieta, California's Gold Rush Bandit.* Twin Falls, Idaho: Big Lost River Press, 1995.

Yellow Bird (John Rollin Ridge). *The Life and Adventures of Joaquín Murieta, the Celebrated California Bandit.* 1954. Reprint. Norman: Univ. of Okla. Press, 1955.

HAROLD AUGENBRAUM

MUSEUMS

Museums have played an important role in the development of Latino culture and its dissemination to a wider audience in the United States. They serve as resources for U.S. Hispanics seeking to learn more about their ethnic and cultural origins, and as points of contact between Latino and non–Latino segments of society. Two types of institutions have, since the mid-20th century, collected and presented Latino and Latin American art: general art museums located in areas of Hispanic culture and museums founded by Latinos themselves.

United States institutions with Latino interests have been strengthened by the active museum world throughout Latin America. Robust museum infrastructures exist in Brazil, Venezuela, and, especially, Mexico, which can be said to be among the foremost nations in the world (and well in advance of the United States) in the support it gives to museums and similar cultural organizations. Emerging or reviving museum networks can also be found in Argentina, Chile, and Peru. Puerto Rico's museums and galleries, along with those in Miami, Florida, and Texas, are significant agents in bridging North American and Latin American cultural interests. We can assume that the Dominican Republic and Cuba will make increasing contributions to this interchange in the near future.

Pre-Columbian art and artifacts are widely dispersed across the United States. Almost every major museum has a collection of quality objects representing a variety of pre-Hispanic New World cultures. In the case of colonial (or as Latin Americans prefer to say, viceregal) art, collections are fewer and more randomly located. Significant resources are found at the Brooklyn Museum and the Hispanic Society of America in New York City, the Philadelphia Museum of Art, the Davenport (Iowa) Museum of Art,

the New Orleans Museum of Art, the San Antonio (Texas) Museum of Art, the University of Texas at Austin, the Denver Art Museum, the Colorado Springs Fine Arts Center, the Tucson (Arizona) Museum of Art, and the University of Arizona Museum of Art, as well as the various branches of the Museum of New Mexico, particularly the Palace of the Governors and the Museum of International Folk Art, along with private museums such as the Museum of Spanish Colonial Art in Santa Fe, New Mexico.

Latin American art from the 19th century is very poorly represented in U.S. museums. Collections can be found at the Brooklyn Museum, el Museo del Barrio, and the Hispanic Society of America in New York City; museums and collections in Puerto Rico; the various branches of the Smithsonian Institution in Washington, D.C.; the San Antonio Museum of Art (Nelson A. Rockefeller Center for Latin American Art); the New Mexico State University Art Gallery (NMSU), Las Cruces, and the Museum of International Folk Art and other institutions in Santa Fe; the Colorado Springs Fine Arts Center; and in collections emphasizing the American West, such as the Gilcrease Museum in Tulsa, (Oklahoma) and the Gene Autry Museum in Los Angeles. In most collections the majority of objects are Mexican or U.S. Southwest images of popular religious devotion. South American academic painting is almost absent. The scant representation and scattered nature of these collections is a significant handicap for U.S. Hispanic artists, since so much Latino visual culture derives from 19th-century sources. Moreover, major exhibitions have not focused on this area.

In contrast, early-20th-century Latin American art is well represented in North American museums. Above all, the Mexican muralists (such as Diego Rivera, José Clemente Orozco, David Alfaro Siqueiros, and Juan O'Gorman), associated artists (such as Frida Kahlo and Rufino Tamayo), and internationally recognized Latin American expatriate artists (such as Wilfredo Lam, Roberto Matta, and Claudio Bravo) are found in U.S. collections. All of the Mexicans, along with other masters such as Carlos Mérida and Gunther Gerzso, worked from time to time in the United States. Indeed, Rivera's mural cycle at the Detroit Institute of Arts is arguably the foremost monumental art commission in North America. Despite this widespread coverage, however, few large collections of 20th-century Latin American art have been assembled in the United States, outside of those found at the University of Texas (now managed by the Jack S. Blanton Museum of Art); the San Antonio Museum of Art; the Rhode Island School of Design; the Los Angeles County Museum of Art (LACMA—the largest general fine arts collection of Latino works); the Museum of Modern Art, New York City (MoMA—whose holdings have been reunited in an exhibition for el Museo del Barrio); and the Houston Museum of Fine Arts (particularly strong in photographs and prints). In contrast to the general acceptance of Latin American art, Latino and Latina artists of the period 1900–1960 have been treated as an aspect of American regionalism. Their works are typically found in local museums serving Hispanic areas in Texas, New Mexico, and, to a lesser extent, California, or in collections focused on specific Latino groups, as in the case of the Puerto Rican and Nuyorican artists collected by el Museo del Barrio.

New Mexico represents an anomaly in the history of museums addressing Latino values, because the region has enjoyed four centuries of Hispanic culture, with no cultural breaks between the colonial period and the 19th century and relatively few between the periods of Mexican and U.S. sovereignty. Instead, an additive process and a sense of cross-fertilization among the Native American, Hispanic, and Anglo segments of New Mexico society have produced a great deal of respect and institutional support for the values of each tradition—although of course artists and ethnic groups continue to vie for public support. New Mexico museums of Hispanic interest such as the Museum of Fine Arts (modern and contemporary), the Palace of the Governors (colonial), the Museum of Spanish Colonial Art, the Museum of International Folk Art, and New Mexico State University at Las Cruces have already been mentioned.

In the late 1960s and 1970s, the increasing social and economic power of Hispanic communities, the organizing of Hispanic labor groups such as the United Farm Workers, and a significant increase in the number of active Latino and Latina studio artists led to demands for the inclusion of more Hispanics in exhibitions and collections at civic museums. Frustrated in this effort to seek wider recognition, Hispanics in several areas created independent Latino art museums and exhibition centers. These included el Museo del Barrio in New York City (1969) and

© MARTHA COOPER/CITY LORE

Three Kings procession, sponsored by el Museo del Barrio in New York City.

the Mexican Museum in San Francisco (1975), joined somewhat later by the Mexican Cultural Center Museum in Chicago (1987). Today Latino museums or exhibiting arts centers can be found in New Mexico, Texas (Corpus Christi, Austin, and Dallas), Florida (Miami and Coral Gables), California (Long Beach), and other locations.

El Museo del Barrio, the Mexican Museum, and the Mexican Cultural Center Museum share many characteristics. In New York a group of Puerto Rican educators and artists under the leadership of the artist Rafael Montañez Ortiz and Marta Moreno Vega, an educator, joined with community leaders in East Harlem, or El Barrio to its Puerto Rican and Nuyorican inhabitants, to form the parent organization. In San Francisco members of the Mexican immigrant and Chicano communities responded to the vision of artist Peter Rodríguez in founding the Mexican Museum. Similarly, in Chicago, a group of artists and educators provided the initial motivation for the Mexican Cultural Center Museum.

In other ways, the three organizations differ. The Mexican Cultural Center has continued to focus on the Mexican American community in Chicago, while el Museo del Barrio in New York and the Mexican Museum in California have explicitly widened their field of interest to include all of Latin America and every type of U.S. Hispanic group, although this has occasioned controversy among those seeking to preserve the original narrow ethnic focus of each institution. At the time of their founding, the New York and San Francisco organizations were closely associated with politically progressive groups. In both cases, transition to a stable institutional structure in a capitalist society has meant finding a modus vivendi between, on the one hand, a popular audience and exhibiting artists who may maintain radical political ideas and, on the other, a patron class whose interests may be socially, but not necessarily artistically, more conservative.

One should also note the recent phenomenon, both in the United States and in Latin America, of foundations being set up to perpetuate the work of collectors of Latin American art. In one case, that of the Robert Gumbiner Foundation of Long Beach, California, the collecting interests have led to the establishment, in 1996, of the Museum of Latin American Art at Long Beach. More institutions of this sort should emerge in the first decades of the 21st century.

The success of the Latino museums' exhibitions and educational programs, along with popular social pressures and the desires of a new Hispanic patron class, have finally led many public museums to cultivate contemporary Hispanic art from both the United States and Latin America. Hence museums in Miami, Austin, Corpus Christi (Texas), Long Beach, and other locations throughout the Southwest and California regularly address Latino audiences and exhibit Latino and Latina artists. Recently curatorships in Latin American art have been established in major museums, such as LACMA and the Houston Museum of Fine Arts. These curators also provide support for colleagues in contemporary art departments who seek to collect U.S. Hispanic art. Ironically, New York's museums, despite a large Hispanic population and the significant Latino presence in commercial art galleries, lag behind those of other centers in according attention to modern and contemporary Hispanic art. As of this writing, only the limited programs of Museo del Barrio address this need.

RELATED ARTICLES

Art, Colonial; Art Criticism; Art, Cuban American; Art, Dominican American; Art, Folk; Art, Galleries and Collections; Art, Mexican American and Chicano; Art, Popular; Art, Puerto Rican on the Mainland; Kahlo, Frida; Painting; Rivera, Diego; Sculpture.

FURTHER READING

Burke, Marcus B. *Treasures of Mexican Colonial Painting: The Davenport Museum of Art Collection.* Davenport, Iowa/Santa Fe, N.Mex.: Davenport Mus. of Art/Mus. of N.Mex. Press, 1998.

Dávalos, Karen Mary. *Exhibiting Mestizaje: Mexican (American) Museums in the Diaspora.* Albuquerque: Univ. of N.Mex. Press, 2001 [with extensive prior bibliography].

Fane, Diana, et al., eds. *Converging Cultures: Art and Identity in Spanish America.* Brooklyn, N.Y.: Brooklyn Mus. of Art, 1996.

Oettinger, Marion, Jr. *Folk Treasures of Mexico: The Nelson A. Rockefeller Collection.* New York: Abrams, 1990.

Pierce, Donna, et al. *Conexiones: Connections in Spanish Colonial Art.* Santa Fe, N.Mex.: Mus. of Spanish Colonial Art/Spanish Colonial Arts Society, 2002.

Quirarte, Jacinto. *Mexican American Artists.* Austin and London: Univ. of Tex. Press, 1973.

SELECTED WEB SITES

Los Angeles County Museum of Art. http://www.collectionsonline.lacma.org/lacma.asp?mypage=latinamer

El Museo del Barrio. http://www.elmuseo.org

Mexican Museum. http://www.mexicanmuseum.org/information/index.asp

Mexican Fine Arts Center Museum.
    http://www.mfacmchicago.org
San Antonio Museum.
    http://www.samuseum.org/laac/laac_cd/INDEH.HTM
Museum of New Mexico.
    http://www.museumofnewmexico.org/home.html
Museum of International Folk Art.
    http://www.moifa.org/home.php

MARCUS BURKE

MUSIC, CLASSICAL

The complex repertoire defined as Latin American classical music—also called concert, erudite, or art music—has different historic origins and contexts. Like all classical music it has been inherited from the past, transcending original social contexts through specific aesthetic merits; or it has been composed to achieve high aesthetic standards while communicating the composers' personal views. Its definitive descriptor may be that art music, as performed in the concert hall, is not consumed for dancing or mere entertainment; it purportedly conveys higher aesthetic or even spiritual values through technical sophistication. Its professional practice among Latin Americans in the United States has occurred mostly, if not exclusively, among members of the educated middle classes, and it is enjoyed by them and the upper classes from all ethnic origins who support it through charitable donations and concert attendance.

Latin American classical musicians have struggled to gain acceptance within the art music mainstream, where Germanic and Russian Jewish communities with a longer record of support for art music in the United States dominate. The working-class Latino communities, although never a homogeneous block, tend to endorse popular dance music instead. Conversely, as orchestras and other art-music institutions reach wider audiences in the United States, more crossover between Latin American art and popular music have taken place in concert halls since the end of the 20th century.

The earliest Hispanic repertoire in the United States was found in the missions of California and New Mexico, now undergoing a reconsideration by scholars and early music ensembles on the concert circuit. The extant manuscripts, including Gregorian chants and compositions written between the 17th and 19th centuries, were copied by the Franciscan missionaries and recopied by their Native American apprentices. The repertoire included works imported from Spain or Mexico, such as Masses by Francisco López Capillas or Ignacio Jerusalem, as well as a few original works, presumably composed in California, such as the unattributed *Missa Viscaina*, and the *Pastorela* by Florencio Ibáñez.

The missionaries used music as a tool for the Christian evangelization of the Indians, an approach that was imitated by French missionaries in Louisiana and other French colonies. The educational objective determined the relative simplicity of the music's texture, as compared with contemporary works from European cathedrals, written in Renaissance polyphony or early Baroque concert styles. Set to sacred Latin texts from the Catholic Mass or Office, or to devotional texts in Spanish, mission music shows a prevalence of simple polyphony, voice against voice homophony, short sectional dimensions, and narrow vocal ranges. Interestingly, centuries later, a certain pervasiveness of parallel thirds in the upper voices has been retained in Mexican popular music.

Examples of hybridization produced the more original music, including *alabados* on devotional texts, perhaps accompanied by native percussion. The recently discovered *Once misas Mexicanas*, found in Tomé, New Mexico, represented the practice of using folk and popular elements within the religious context. During the 18th century and later, the missions sponsored instrumental ensembles in which mestizo musicians performed. Beautiful examples of music from the Hispanic Southwest involve the synthesis of Baroque instrumental practices, such as *continuo accompaniment,* with devotional chanting of Gregorian or folk melodies. Most of this anonymous repertoire is being gradually reconstructed by scholars and appreciated for its pure and touching expression.

Latin American art music in the United States in the 19th century has only recently become an area of musicological investigation. In the Southwest, Mexican and American cultures remained in constant exchange. The private musical activity by the landowning Spanish families arguably reproduced European salon styles. The Spanish Mexican composers Manuel Ferrer (1828–1904) and Miguel Arévalo performed and published in 19th-century California, producing many guitar compositions and arrangements of the dances of the time, including those not of Spanish origin circulating in California society. It has also been argued that melodies from zarzuelas, the traditional Spanish musical theater, may have been transmitted from Cuba and Mexico to eastern and southwestern regions of the United States, through piano and dance-band arrangements and recital songs. Paradoxically, it is the popular genre of the *corrido,* with its sung narratives of the misadventures of southwestern heroes and common men and women, that has gained the attention of scholars and critics for its intrinsic poetic power, with some of its examples beginning to achieve art-music status.

The upper classes supporting the development of orchestras, choruses, and opera houses in the northeastern United States identified with European art music, neglecting compositions by American composers in general. However, the pioneering Louisiana composer and virtuoso pianist Louis Moreau Gottschalk (1829–1869) began to introduce Latin American elements into his music. While touring in Spain, Cuba, Brazil, and other Latin American countries, Gottschalk synthesized the folk melodies and syncopated rhythms of the region within European genres, in pieces such as *Souvenir de Porto Rico (Marche des Gibaros), Souvenir de la Havane,* and *Grande fantaisie triomphale sur l'hymne national brésilien.* The power of Latin rhythms blended with European salon genres permeated all coastal regions in the Caribbean and the Atlantic, eventually reaching France and Argentina. By the mid-19th century the use of Latin rhythms to represent sensuality and exoticism began to become established in French art music (as in Bizet's opera *Carmen*) just as the same formula served the incipient Latin American musical nationalism trying to separate from European colonialism. The treatment by composers in the French milieu bounced back to Spain, Latin America, and the United States, providing the roots of modern Latin styles for orchestra.

As classical music venues and touring circuits continued to develop in the United States, Latin American classical musicians exerted influence through performance of the European repertoire, in a manner usually judged to be highly individualistic. Among them, pianist Teresa Carreño, born in Venezuela in 1853, came to the United States at a young age to be trained by Gottschalk, after which she lived and toured alternatively in the United States, Europe, and Venezuela, becoming one of the greatest pianists of her generation and the first woman to conduct an opera. She in turn taught and promoted the American pianist and composer Edward MacDowell. She died in New York in 1917. The Spanish cellist Pablo Casals (1876–1973) enjoyed a long career as a soloist and chamber-music player, transplanted from Europe to Puerto Rico in 1956, where he founded the Casals Festival. He was an equal among the greatest artists of his time; although he avoided the United States because of its recognition of Franco's dictatorial regime in Spain, his friendship with many American performers and the importance of his festival translated into real prestige in the American musical milieu. He accepted an invitation to perform at the White House for President Kennedy in 1961.

The Brazilian pianist Guiomar Novaes (1895–1979) gave regular presentations in New York between 1915 and 1972, earning rave reviews for her poetic eloquence. The Chilean pianist Claudio Arrau (1903–1991) chose the United States as his home in 1941, touring worldwide until his death. He was universally praised for his deep interpretations of Beethoven's sonatas. Some of his students have continued to exert an influence on American piano teaching—otherwise dominated by Russian pianism—including the pedagogues Rafael De Silva, German Díez, and Rosalina Sackstein, and the virtuoso pianist and composer Alfonso Montecino. The Cuban-born pianist Jorge Bolet (1914–1990) trained at the Curtis Institute of Philadelphia from a very young age, but lacking a professional network, his career had a slow start in spite of outstanding gifts. A period in the army led him to conduct the Japanese premiere of Gilbert and Sullivan's *The Mikado* in 1944. A recital at Carnegie Hall in New York in 1974 suddenly consecrated him as one of the greatest pianists of the age, hailed as the last representative of the grand European Romantic tradition of piano playing. Bolet signed a recording contract with Decca Records, which left many documents of his extraordinary artistry. Along with Claudio Arrau—who recorded for Phillips Records—Bolet was the most recorded Latin American classical musician living in the United States.

Following these giants, the U.S. classical music world has witnessed the brilliant careers of several major resident Latin American performers born after 1950, including the virtuoso pianists Horacio Gutiérrez, Santiago Rodríguez, and José Feghali (the latter the winner of the famed Van Cliburn Piano Competition in Texas); the violinists Andrés Cárdenes and Elmar Oliveira; violist Roberto Díaz; cellist Andrés

Díaz (winner of the New York Naumburg Prize); and the clarinetist Ricardo Morales (who at 21 was appointed principal clarinetist of the Metropolitan Opera Orchestra). Although all of them have established their prestige through the European repertoire, they have gradually inserted important Latin American classical compositions in their recitals and commissioned new Latin American works. The Cuarteto Latinoamericano, a string quartet straddling residencies in the United States and Mexico, has devoted its career to the promotion of Latin American composers, winning several awards along the way.

The operatic milieu has also witnessed the rise of brilliant Hispanic singers. Although there exists a long-standing mythology that Latin cultures produce high male voices, it has been apparent that prominent opera houses in the United States wait for Latin singers to achieve fame in Europe before sanctioning their appearances on U.S. stages. This contributes to the migration of rising Latin American stars first to Europe, as happened with the emerging Argentinean tenors José Cura (b. 1962) and Marcelo Alvarez (b. 1962). In spite of this, Puerto Rican basso cantante Justino Díaz (b. 1940) was a regular presence at New York's Metropolitan Opera House in the 1960s and 1970s, and Chilean soprano Verónica Villarroel has been a frequent star in the same house since the 1990s. Díaz sang the premiere of Argentinean composer Alberto Ginastera's opera *Beatrix Cenci* at the inauguration of the Kennedy Center's Opera House in Washington, D.C., in 1971.

The most notable Latino opera artist in modern times has been the tenor Plácido Domingo, born in Spain in 1941 and raised in Mexico, who has been a luminary of New York's Metropolitan Opera since the 1970s, general director of the National Opera in Washington since 1996, and artistic director of the Los Angeles Opera since 2000. Interestingly, Domingo rose to prominence in the United States through his performance of the title role in Ginastera's opera *Don Rodrigo* in 1966 with the New York City Opera. With his international reputation established as one of the greatest tenors of all time, Domingo has not hesitated to promote the zarzuela, where he gained his initial training as a singer. He has also recorded tangos and other popular Latin songs, confirming their artistic merits to new audiences, and expanding the range of what can be considered Latin American art music. He was also responsible for the revival of the late Romantic opera *Il Guarany* by Brazilian composer Carlos Gomes (1836–1896).

The Spanish zarzuela has regained prominence since the 1970s, as Latino communities achieve higher economic and social levels and do not identify exclusively with European opera as a status symbol. Besides Domingo, pianist and arranger Pablo Zinger has promoted the genre, as has producer Silvia Brito of the Thalia Spanish Theater, both in New York. The zarzuela's future on the American musical stage will depend on a more efficient publication and distribution of performing materials, an economic factor revealing the underlying fabric on which of all art music depends.

Recordings represent an important subsection of the classical music field. Recordings of Latin American music by American labels usually have been prompted by political or social fashions, rather than by economic demand. Latin American conductors have been proactive in recording Latin American classical repertoire, along with North American conductors who would direct contemporary music from all provenances. The Mexican conductor Eduardo Mata (1942–1995) achieved the highest professional levels as the music director of the Dallas Symphony between 1977 and 1993. His dashing advocacy of Spanish and Latin American music alongside the mainstream repertoire gained him worldwide recognition before his untimely death. His prestige encouraged the production of a series of Latin American recordings by the Dorian record label with the Simón Bolívar orchestra of Venezuela in the 1990s. Daniel Barenboim, born in Argentina of Jewish descent, was one of the most celebrated conductors and pianists in the world in the late 20th and into the 21st century. Since the late 1990s he has also turned his attention to performances of Latin American piano music, notably of Argentinean tangos by compatriot Astor Piazzolla. Nonetheless, a tendency of the classical music establishment to prefer Latin American music with distinct popular elements has been objected to by Latin American contemporary composers, who believe the public in Europe and the United States seeks to experience a blanket exoticism and "otherness" through their work, instead of accepting their individual messages, some of which can be quite different from Latin traditional or urban popular music. Still, Latin American music has been increasingly recorded since 1992 (with the celebrations of the "Encounter of the Two Worlds"). Filling

Latin American gaps in the record labels' catalogs has helped to offset the decline in overall sales of all other classical repertoire.

Modern Latin American art music composers have availed themselves of all techniques and styles circulating in European and American art music. They argue that they are heirs to European as much as to Native American and African traditions, all components of Latin American culture. Musical identity versus reception in the European and North American market has been an endemic topic of controversy among Latin American composers in the United States. At the same time, Latin American traditional and urban popular music components have maintained a rhetorical power over American composers as a whole, who continue to relate it to telluric and sensuous expression, and by extension to feminist and political references, as witnessed in many works by Aaron Copland, Leonard Bernstein, and, later, John Adams.

The modern exchange of art music between the United States and Latin American countries has occurred over four main phases. During the first three decades of the 20th century, the tourist and economic trade between the United States and prerevolutionary Cuba facilitated the professional activities of Cuban performers and composers in the United States. The composer, pianist, and bandleader Ernesto Lecuona (1896–1963) worked in Hollywood and on Broadway while still composing virtuoso concert music infused with Cuban melodies and rhythms, in the tradition of the Americans Gottschalk and Scott Joplin, the Spaniards Enrique Granados and Isaac Albéniz, and the Cubans Manuel Saumell and Ignacio Cervantes. Some Mexican salon music also crossed to the United States through sheet music and at the beginning of radio, such as the waltzes of the Mexican Juventino Rosas and the famous song *Estrellita* by his compatriot Manuel Ponce. This repertory has maintained favor with concert pianists and singers seeking to promote Latin American music within the mainstream, and it has many parallels in art music from all other countries in Latin America.

From the 1920s to the 1940s, at the onset of musical modernism, composers from the United States and Latin America sought to create a continental musical identity separate from Europe, based on the use of indigenous materials or experimental processes. This philosophy flourished with the Pan-American Association of Composers, founded by the French-born American composer Edgard Varèse and his Mexican colleague Carlos Chávez in 1928. Their promotion of contemporary music concerts and commissions favored exchanges with Latin American composers.

Latin American compositions heard in the United States at this time ran the gamut of contemporary styles, with the exception of strict 12-tone serialism. A regionalist modernism used Latin American folk materials to deviate from European common practice, by the addition of stratified and irregular rhythms, modular melodies, or unusual Latin instruments. The *Afrocubanismo* of Cuban Amadeo Roldán followed this style, producing the influential composition *Rítmica V* for percussion ensemble (1929–1931), the first work of its kind in Western music, and contemporary with *Ionisations* by Varèse, also for percussion alone. Carlos Chávez speculated on the characteristics of Aztec music and applied his theories to his composition *Xochipili* (1940), which he premiered at New York's Museum of Modern Art. He also explored modernist rituals in his commission by Martha Graham's dance company, the ballet *La hija de Cólquide*. In the meantime, postimpressionist nationalism, using extended tonal harmonies and rhapsodic development, was practiced by Brazilians Heitor Villa-Lobos and Camargo Guarnieri in orchestral symphonic poems depicting, overtly or subliminally, the vast Brazilian jungle or its frenetic urban life. All these composers frequently visited American orchestras as guest conductors or composers.

Besides these modernist trends, a neoclassicist tendency has endured in most Latin American art music in the United States to this day, at least during substantial periods in most composers' output. In 1939 the composer Joaquin Nin-Culmell settled in California after studies with the Spanish composer Manuel de Falla, and unrelated to the modernist experimentation of his colleagues in New York, maintained a neoclassical style throughout his career. His compositions continued to explore the relationship between Cuban and Spanish folk music using the refined elegance of postimpressionist harmonic language. Variations of this approach persist in the music of many composers, especially in choral and chamber music genres.

Between the 1940s and 1960s the Guggenheim and Rockefeller foundations, along with other programs, sponsored many Latin American composers to study in the United States with Aaron Copland

and others. Several of the artists stayed to pursue successful careers as creators and pedagogues, among them Julián Orbón, Aurelio de la Vega, Héctor Campos Parsi, Roque Cordero, and Juan Orrego Salas. The latter founded the Latin American Music Center at Indiana University, a very important effort to document the breadth and depth of Latin American art music within the United States. All these composers have received commissions by major orchestras and ensembles at some point in their careers, but none broke through to mainstream recognition—beyond unquestionable professional prestige—a feat quite difficult for any art-music composer. Nonetheless, a Pulitzer Prize rewarded the unique contributions of Argentinean-born Mario Davidovsky (b. 1934) who, through his series of Synchronisms, developed an influential genre combining acoustic instruments and electronic sounds. Davidovsky, along with Spanish-born Leonardo Balada (b. 1933), broke through to the experimental avantgarde. As adopted by younger generations, these expansions of the meaning and language of music have retained the lyricism and playfulness that pervades much Latin American music.

Formal inter-American musical exchanges have endured in the United States; organizations and composers have utilized festivals as locations for the exchange of creative ideas and for publicizing new achievements, in place of a broad-based marketing structure and commercial distribution of Latin American classical music. The Inter-American Music Festivals in Washington, D.C., have been the most significant. Sponsored by the Organization of American States and directed by the indefatigable conductor Guillermo Espinosa from 1953 to 1975, they intersected with American state policies toward Latin America and therefore had extraordinary public recognition and artistic importance. These festivals produced the American premieres of major compositions, especially those by Alberto Ginastera, who never settled in the United States but gained international fame in the 1960s and 1970s through this forum. These festivals were then promoted worldwide by Voice of America broadcasts. Concert series by the New York–based group North/South Consonance, led by Mexican-born composer and conductor Max Lifschitz (b. 1948), and the New Music Miami Festival, led by composer Orlando Jacinto Garcia (b. 1954), followed in this spirit, as did the well publicized concert series *Sonidos de las Américas,* produced by the American Composers Orchestra of New York with American conductor Dennis Russell Davies during the mid-1990s.

Since 1992 most orchestras and art-music organizations in the United States have made deliberate efforts to program Latin American music, with the purpose of reaching out to Latino communities and expanding their audiences. Most efforts are circumscribed to special concerts celebrating Hispanic History Month or other Hispanic events. This trend has revealed much about the nature of the reception of classical music and how it intersects with class and culture. These ventures have included repertoire by some popular composers, who, being classically trained, cross over to the art-music world with surprising success, like tango composer Astor Piazzolla, timbales virtuoso Tito Puente, and jazz pianist Chick Corea; film composers whose orchestral music fits the concert hall, such as Lalo Schifrin, composer of the *Mission: Impossible* and *Dirty Harry* themes; and, not surprisingly, well known pseudo-Spanish music by eminent French composers such as Ravel and Debussy. However, the *Armonia* program of the Chicago Symphony, led by Venezuelan composer Ricardo Lorenz (b. 1961) between 1998 and 2002, broke new ground by commissioning music in which both the orchestra members and popular musicians in the city would perform together.

Since the 1980s Latin American music within the United States art-music milieu has reached a level of maturity and received a more enlightened reception. Although stereotypes still persist, especially among groups who use music as educational and audience-building tools, several Latin American composers have reached and maintained a presence in the higher echelons of classical music in the United States. Robert Xavier Rodriguez (b. San Antonio, 1946) is perhaps the first U.S.-born Latino composer to establish a successful career in art music. His many orchestral works and the opera *Frida,* based on the life of the famous painter Frida Kahlo, have been performed at important venues in the country. Puerto Rican composer Roberto Sierra's brilliant career has included residencies with the Milwaukee and Philadelphia orchestras; and Cuban-born Tania León attends festivals and conducts her own music around the world. The extraordinary success in 2000 of *La pasión según San Marcos* by Osvaldo Golijov (b. Argentina, 1960) has broken through to the classical music mainstream. A collage of academic and popular components, it earned the composer a MacArthur "genius" Award, at a time when well-established performers such as the Kronos Quartet and Yo-Yo Ma regularly record Latin American music. It has been suggested, however, that Latin American music, classical or popular, is a musical stream of such complexity that it is best examined as unique and self-referential, distinct from other streams. Its impact in the United States is undeniable.

RELATED ARTICLES

Corrido; Domingo, Plácido; Musical Instruments; Music, Popular; Popular Culture; Puente, Tito.

FURTHER READING

Béhague, Gerard. *Music in Latin America: An Introduction.* New Jersey: Prentice Hall, 1991.

Koegel, John. "After Columbus: The Musical Journey." *Ars Musica Denver* 7, no. 1 (Fall 1994): 31–55 [a collection of essays on musical interchange in 18th-century imperial Spain].

Koegel, John. "Mexican and Mexican-American Musical Life in Southern California." *Inter-American Music Review* 13, no. 2 (Spring-Summer 1993): 111–114.

Manuel, Peter, ed. *Essays on Cuban Music: North American and Cuban Perspectives.* Lanham, Md.: Univ. Press of Am., 1991.

Roberts, John Storm. *The Latin Tinge: The Impact of Latin American Music on the United States.* New York: Oxford Univ. Press, 1979.

Sadie, Stanley, ed. *The New Grove Dictionary of Music and Musicians.* 2d ed. London: Macmillan, 2002.

Summers, William. "Spanish Music in California, 1769–1840: A Reassessment." In *IMS Report.* Kassel, Germany: Barenreiter, 1981.

SELECTED WEB SITE

Latin American Music Center at Indiana University. http://www.music.indiana.edu/som/lamc

CARMEN TELLEZ

MUSIC, POPULAR

The term *Latin music* identifies a wide range of genres and styles generated in Latin America and the Iberian Peninsula, as well as a few forms developed by the Latino communities. Rooted in three cultural sources (European, African, and American Indian), Latin music is as diverse as one would expect from such an extensive transatlantic area. The music of Cuba and the other Spanish-speaking Antilles for example, has no distinctive American Indian traits, whereas most Mexican styles have scarce African elements.

Most of the popular Latin forms that affected the music in the United States in an enduring fashion came from Cuba, a small Caribbean island that has given birth to numerous musical idioms, including but not limited to *punto guajiro, contradanza,* habanera, *danzón, danzonete,* bolero, *trova,* rumba, *guaguancó, columbia,* conga, *son, guaracha,* mambo, *chachachá* (cha cha), *pachanga, guapachá, pilón, pa'cá, mozambique, songo,* and *timba.* In addition, what is known today as salsa is mostly derived from *son* and *guaracha,* and Latin jazz was created simultaneously in Havana and New York, back in the days when it was accurately identified as Afro-Cuban jazz. The sounds of Cuba dominated the Latin music world throughout the 20th century and seem set to continue to do so into the new millennium.

It must be noted that Puerto Rico's native idioms (*bomba, plena, seis*) have been a good deal less influential in the popular music of the United States than were Cuba's, although Puerto Rican and Nuyorican musicians have played a vital role in Latino music history, particularly in the fields of salsa and Latin jazz. Keep in mind that the development of Puerto Rican music became inseparable from the migration process beginning in the 1920s. The two greatest Puerto Rican popular music composers, Rafael Hernández and Pedro Flores, lived in Puerto Rico and in New York and scored hits in both places.

Second only to Cuba in order of importance is the impact of the largest Latin American nation, Brazil, for as many reasons as there are types of Brazilian music—*maxixe, choro, marcha,* samba, *baião, frevo,* bossa nova, *MPB, fricote, afoxé, maracatu, coco, embolada, carimbó, lambada, trio eléctrico,* and so on. Bossa nova, like samba, is now a solid part of the international repertoire, particularly in the jazz realm.

Another significant Latin source is Mexico, whose music was "naturalized" as a result of the Mexican-American War and the subsequent Treaty of Guadalupe Hidalgo. *Corridos* based on specifically Chicano subjects have been penned in the Southwest since the 19th century.

Cuban rhythms began to spread to other regions of the Western Hemisphere by the middle of the 19th century. It is likely that a great part of what has been classified as "Creole" in New Orleans is Cuban-derived music. Louis Moreau Gottchalk (1829–1869), allegedly the first piano virtuoso in the United States, managed to combine the habanera (a byproduct of the Cuban contradanza) with the Afro-American cakewalk by the 1850s. As a matter of fact, the habanera had made its mark on ragtime and early jazz by the 1880s, approximately two decades before another New Orleans pianist, Ferdinand "Jelly Roll" Morton, used said Cuban rhythm in his *New Orleans Blues* (1902). Jelly Roll was precisely the one who described jazz as possessing a "Spanish tinge."

Ironically, the first mass fad in America for a Latin style came from a remote South American country, Argentina. The tango took the United States by storm in 1913 and flourished throughout the following decade, giving a mighty boost to the Latin influence on popular music north of the Rio Grande.

The music of Brazil first acquired international attention with the success of the *maxixe* in the United States and Europe around World War I. The North American public was briefly captivated by this vivacious dance, derived from a fusion of the Afro-Brazilian *lundu* with the tango, the habanera, and the polka.

The opening shot of the 20th-century Cuban music invasion was fired by Don Azpiazu and his New York–based Havana Casino Orchestra, whose 1921 recording of the *son-pregón El Manicero* (*The Peanut Vendor*) sold 5 million copies and led to the American craze for rumba (frequently spelled *rhumba*). Most of these rhumbas were actually *sones,* but the fashion for Cuban music started by *The Peanut Vendor* grew and matured throughout the next three decades.

In the mid-1920s Rafael Hernández showed up in New York, where he set the standards for the city's numerous guitar trios with his first group (Trío Boringuen), while becoming the most sought-after Puerto Rican composer of his era. Hernández authored more than 2,000 songs, including the unofficial Puerto Rican anthem *Lamento borincano.*

By the end of the 1920s, New York had bands entirely composed of Latin musicians. One of the first Latin-style orchestras was led by the Cuban trumpeter Vicente Sigler. A young Cuban flutist, Alberto Socarrás, played briefly with Sigler before organizing his own band. Socarrás, by the way, was the first flutist to record a jazz solo, back in 1929.

During the 1930s many Puerto Ricans moved to New York, driven from their native island by the Depression. The Puerto Rican trombonist Juan Tizol incorporated Antillean colors into Duke Ellington's 1930s repertoire, while Manuel "Canario" Jiménez

introduced the *plena* to Spanish Harlem. By then, Latin music was divided in separate scenes in New York: The "uptown" scene catered to Latino immigrants while the "downtown" scene's trendy hotels and clubs catered to North Americans. The Cuban conga rhythm began to reach the United States by the end of the decade, when its simplified U.S. version became firmly associated with Desiderio "Desi" Arnaz.

Although it was introduced to Texas and Northern Mexico in the 1890s by Bohemian and Czech railroad engineers, the accordion first appeared in Chicano recordings in the 1930s, when a large number of *corridos* were issued by the American labels, and Chicano music had an impact on the style called "Western swing." Texas served as the ideal breeding ground for an indigenous Chicano style known as *norteño* (northern), in which the accordion would become the dominant instrument during the following decade.

Hollywood films, and to a lesser degree the Broadway stage, were important to the spread of Latin music throughout the United States in the 1940s. Hollywood's most successful Latin performer at the time was the Catalonian-Cuban bandleader Francisco de Asís Javier Cougat (better known as Xavier Cougat), who appeared in numerous kitsch musicals featuring exotic song-and-dance intervals. Coincidentally, the 1940s saw the first export of Brazilian samba to the United States, when songs such as Ary Barroso's *Aquarela de Brasil* were featured in Walt Disney's animated films and covered in other Hollywood productions by the extravagant Portuguese-Brazilian vocalist Carmen Miranda, who was known to wear a veritable orchard atop her head.

The 1940s were marked by the consolidation of two major Cuban-rooted movements—mambo and Afro-Cuban jazz (also known as Cubop). Founded in 1940 by the Havanese singer-*maraquero* Frank "Machito" Grillo, the Afro-Cubans became the most important Latin New York big band of the 1940s and 1950s, when they did much to promote the mambo and put Afro-Cuban jazz (subsequently known as Latin jazz) on the map. Machito's Afro-Cubans redefined the music of Latin New York, moving between uptown and downtown audiences. Their musical director, Mario Bauzá, successfully merged Cuba's dance rhythms with American horns to create a new entity. Bauzá must also be credited with introducing the newly arrived Cuban percussionist Luciano Pozo González (better known as Chano Pozo) to Dizzy Gillespie, thus facilitating one of the most significant collaborations in the history of jazz. Perhaps the only legend that is shared by both *rumberos* and jazzmen, Pozo was able to adjust his *tumbadoras* (conga drums) to the rhythmic patterns of bebop during his brief tenure with Gillespie, with whom he authored such Cuban jazz classics as *Manteca* and *Tin Tin Deo,* while popularizing Cuban percussion in the American jazz scene. One must not ignore, of course, the fruitful role played since the late 1940s by another Cuban expatriate, Arturo "Chico" O'Farrill, whose innovative compositions and arrangements allowed the North American jazz musicians to expand their rhythmic horizons. O'Farrill's compositions for Machito's big band included the refined *Afro-Cuban Jazz Suite,* featuring Charlie Parker on saxophone.

During the 1940s and 1950s, the growth of the Puerto Rican community increased steadily on the mainland's East Coast, and a new style of orchestrated Antillean folk music ruffled to the surface of Latin New York when trumpeter César Concepción brought the Puerto Rican *plena* to the metropolis, adapting it to the big band format. By the end of the 1940s, a number of small record companies sprang up in New York, providing an outlet for a couple of young bandleaders of Puerto Rican origin who shared the same nickname—the instrumentalist Ernest "Tito" Puente and the vocalist Pablo "Tito" Rodríguez.

Right around that time numerous local Mexican labels were emerging in the Southwest, mostly in Texas and California. The postwar prosperity in southern California gave birth to a new generation of Chicano bandleaders, whose combo recordings fused jump blues and mambo with Spanglish lyrics, reflecting the rebellious nature of Los Angeles's pachuco (zoot-suiter) subculture.

The first important Latin jazz name on the West Coast was Stan Kenton, who foreshadowed the jazz-bossa era of the early 1960s by hiring Brazilian guitarist Laurindo Almeida in the fall of 1947. When Kenton's orchestra was disbanded by the end of the decade, some of his top alumni (Pete Condoli, Bob Cooper, Art Pepper) were hired by a Cuban bandleader named René Touzet, the author of *La noche de anoche* and other memorable bolero classics.

Introduced in New York in 1949 by the Cuban revue Las Mulatas del Fuego, the mambo overtook the rumba and the conga a few years later. Although the standard for the growing New York–style big-band mambo was mainly developed by the three most influential bandleaders in town (Machito, Puente, and Rodríguez), the musician most responsible for the mambo's global rise was a Cuban pianist named Dámaso Pérez Prado, nicknamed "Cara de foca" (Sealface) and inevitably associated with a couple of instrumental hits, *Cherry Pink and Apple Blossom White* (1955) and *Patricia* (1958). In the era before rock-and-roll, Pérez Prado became a counterculture hero with his lacquered pompadour and his Dizzy-style goatee. Not to mention his flashy jewelry and trademark grunts. In 1954 he moved to his main American turf, the City of Angels (Los Angeles), where his main bandleading rivals also were piano players—the native Angelino Eddie Cano and the Antillean expatriate René Touzet.

Destined to exercise a major influence over a musical movement to be labeled much later as salsa, the blind Cuban tresero and composer Arsenio Rodríguez arrived in New York when the Cuban presence was already felt throughout the nation by way of the television situation comedy *I Love Lucy,* produced and protagonized from 1951 to 1959 by Desi Arnaz and his gifted spouse, the comedienne Lucille Ball. Desi was not a great singer, but he managed to deliver Cuban music straight into Anglo-America's living rooms.

By the middle of the decade, the popularity of Latin music peaked in the United States with cha cha mania, when this imported danceable rhythm swept the entire country. Never mind that the U.S. imitations of the Cuban cha cha—erroneously applied to simplified or exaggerated big band arrangements—failed to duplicate the original explosive charm of the island's *charanga* (flute-and-fiddle) format.

In addition to the aforementioned Cuban idioms, other Latin forms had an impact during the 1950s. The Puerto Rican percussionist Rafael Cortijo brought the *plena* back into fashion and introduced the bomba to the dance format in 1957, four years after a quartet led by Laurindo Almeida and Bud Shank recorded a ten-inch jazz-*baião* album in Hollywood. This was probably the first American-made Brazilian jazz session, as well as an amazing prefiguration of the bossa nova invasion.

The 1950s were a time of flux for Chicano music. Within the sphere of *música tejana,* the *rancheras* began to rival the older *corridos* in importance. In 1958 the Los Angeles Chicano Ritchie Valens scored a rock-and-roll hit with his simplified version of *La Bamba,* an old *son jarocho* from the Mexican seaport of Veracruz. More than 150 additional versions of *La Bamba* have been recorded since then.

The 1960s brought about changes around the world in virtually everything, and Latin music was no exception. The severance of diplomatic ties between the United States and Cuba, as a result of Fidel Castro's ascent to power in Havana, struck a serious blow to the Latin music scene north of the Rio Grande, since it was cut off from its primordial source of inspiration. On the other hand, scores of renowned Cuban musicians went into exile. Many of them (Celia Cruz, Israel "Cachao" López, José Fajardo, Julio Gutierrez, La Lupe) made their way to New York, where they would contribute in the years to come to the initial impetus of the salsa movement, mostly in conjunction with a new generation of Nuyorican musicians. In addition, a few former participants in Havana's legendary Panart jam sessions brought the *descarga* bug to the Big Apple (New York City), where the Alegre All Stars, under the musical direction of the Nuyorican pianist Charlie Palmieri, recorded a series of influential *descarga* albums from 1962 to 1967.

Developed in Havana by Eduardo Davidson and transplanted to New York by another Cuban exile, flutist José Fajardo, the *pachanga* ousted the cha cha from the city during the summer of 1961. Played by Palmieri's Orquesta Duboney and other blossoming *charangas,* this energetic dance was the rage among Latino adolescents when the million-selling hit *El Watusi*—recorded in 1963 by the Nuyorican *tumbador* Ray Barretto's *charanga*—ushered in another dance fad known as *bugalú* (or Latin boogaloo), which would displace the *pachanga* sooner than later.

A brash and extroverted product of the Nuyoricans' hybrid culture, the *bugalú* mixed a simplified mambo with bilingual lyrics and rhythm-and-blues inflections, and even threw up a few hits, including Joe Cuba's million-selling *Bang Bang.* The *bugalú* died out by the end of the decade, when it gave way to the New York movement that would eventually be identified as salsa.

Following the path established in the previous decade by British pianist George Shearing's San Francisco–based quintet, St. Louis–born vibraphonist Cal Tjader maintained his reputation as one of the most consistent exponents of the small-group, West Coast style of Latin jazz during the 1960s. His former sideman, the Havanese *tumbador* Ramón "Mongo" Santamaría, hit the top of the American charts in 1963 with his catchy version of Herbie Hancock's *Watermelon Man.* On the other hand, John Coltrane's cover of *Afro Blue* turned that Mongo original into the one Cuban tune that practically every jazz musician knows.

Brazilian music got a boost when one of samba's modern by-products, bossa nova, entered the world spotlight through the 1959 film *Black Orpheus.* Developed in the 1950s by Antonio Carlos Jobim, João Gilberto, and other Carioca bohemians who mixed urban samba with cool jazz influences, the bossa nova sounds were transplanted to North America by guitarist Charlie Byrd and saxophonist Stan Getz, whose 1962 smash hit album *Jazz Samba* (Verve) shot to the number one position on the Billboard pop chart, although it was really jazz-bossa—a new dimension of Latin jazz—rather than bona fide Brazilian bossa nova. Four years later, just as the bossa craze seemed to be dying out, Brazilian pianist Sergio Mendes's light blend of bossa and American pop had an enormous success when his LP *Sergio Mendes and Brasil '66* hit number seven on the pop charts. Despite its commercial dilution, the bossa nova movement incorporated numbers such as *Desafinado* and *Girl from Ipanema* into the North American songbook and brought about a revival of the guitar in American jazz.

An adulterated Mexican version of the Colombian *cumbia* rhythm invaded the Southwest by the mid-1960s, resulting in the emergence of the substyle called *cumbia norteña* on both sides of the Rio Grande. Simultaneously, a couple of Texan singers came to the fore: Freddie Fender proved to be equally fluent in his native state's country and Chicano styles, and Trini López became the original Tejano "folknick" by elaborating a popular mixture of Mexican and Anglo-American elements.

The 1970s saw the consolidation of a couple of American musical movements—New York's salsa and California's Latin rock. Founded in 1964 by the Italian American divorce attorney Jerry Masucci (in conjunction with the Dominican bandleader Johnny Pacheco), Fania Records became the most influential Latin label in the United States by the following decade, when it successfully repackaged and sold New York's Cuban-derived sounds under the label of "salsa," thus profiting from the musical vacuum created years earlier by the rupture of U.S. relations with Cuba. Despite its unquestionable Cuban *son* backbone, salsa's first performers and audiences were mainly Puerto Rican, and as it gained ground in the Caribbean and South America, it broadened its range by incorporating elements of Puerto Rican *bomba* and *plena,* Dominican merengue, Colombian *cumbia,* Panamanian *tamborito,* and even Brazilian samba. Attracting new audiences, the seasoned Cuban vocalist Celia Cruz became the undisputed "Queen of Salsa," often collaborating with other top-selling Fania artists. From 1972 to 1977, the Nuyorican trombonist Willie Colón and the Panamanian singer-songwriter Rubén Blades engaged in one of Fania's most powerful partnerships. Blades's compositions shifted salsa lyrics from the limitations of romance to socially realistic chronicles.

Latin rock began as a California phenomenon by the end of the 1960s, when the young San Francisco–based Mexican guitarist Carlos Santana developed a style that fused acid rock with blues and Cuban ingredients. Santana popularized the new sound in the 1970s through such hits as *Oye como va* and *Para los rumberos,* taking these Tito Puente originals to rock audiences around the world. His group was the tip of a California Latin rock iceberg, which included such bands as Malo, Azteca, and El Chicano. Eventually, Santana overshadowed all of its rivals, most of whom disbanded by the end of the decade.

The influence of Brazilian elements in jazz and popular music was renewed in the 1970s, when percussionist Airto Moreira and vocalist Flora Purim appeared (separately or together) on landmark albums that helped establish the new subgenre called "jazz-fusion." The jazz world also felt the impact of the Argentine tenorist Leandro "Gato" Barbieri, who recorded a series of experiments with a wide range of Latin American forms. He even revived such venerable tangos as *Mi Buenos Aires querido* and *El día que tu me quieras.*

Cumbia norteña recordings continued to sell like hot tortillas throughout the Southwest in the 1970s, displacing most surviving West Coast practitioners of Cuban-derived dance music, while a prominent Tejano group—Little Joe and La Familia—incorporated salsa-influenced brass arrangements, although his sound remained firmly rooted on the *rancheras* that had swept into popularity two decades earlier in the Lone Star State. Generally speaking, Mexican touches became increasingly common in country music by the end of the decade.

The Fania monopoly came to an end around 1980, when Jerry Masucci moved to Argentina and left Pacheco in charge of a rapidly fading salsa empire. By the mid-1980s Puerto Rico replaced New York as the main center of the salsa industry and began to promote the bland style known as "salsa romantica." The 1980s also saw waves of immigrants who brought diverse musical styles to various major American cities, from Dominican merengue to Colombian *vallenato* to Central American *punta.*

The 1980 Mariel Boat Lift brought fresh Cuban talents to the United States, including such notable percussionists as *tumbador* Daniel Ponce and trap drummer Ignacio Berroa. The Latin jazz movement in America was revitalized a year later with the arrival of the Cuban reedman Paquito D'Rivera, who consolidated his position as one of the aristocrats of the jazz world in the years to come. The 1980s also witnessed the emergence of other distinguished Latin jazz entities, such as Jerry González and the Fort Apache Band and Jorge Dalto's Inter-American Band. Back on the West Coast the Los Angeles–based Chicano tumbador Idelfonso "Poncho" Sánchez would become the top selling bandleader for Concord Picante, a Latin jazz sublabel established in 1979 by the California record impresario Carl Jefferson.

Following a dramatic plunge in the Dominican economy, a large number of merengue bands arrived in New York. Initially confined to the Washington Heights (in northern Manhattan) Dominican neighborhoods, the merengue eventually spread to the rest of the city, and then to Puerto Rico, where it almost overshadowed salsa.

Meanwhile, Gloria Estefan and the Miami Sound Machine successfully combined south Florida's funk-pop sound with a spicing of Cuban rhythms, as exemplified in their huge 1985 hit *Conga.* They broke the American pop barrier in 1987, when their record *Primitive Love* sold over 1.5 million copies.

The Brazilian influence in American jazz was strengthened during the 1980s with the rise of not one but two female pianists from the largest South American nation—Tania Maria and Eliane Elias. By the end of the decade, another Brazilian dance had gained international currency, as the lambada briefly conquered the United States and Europe with its sensual moves.

Comprising mostly Chicano musicians, Los Lobos started to attract widespread attention by the early 1980s, as they fused rock, country, rhythm and blues, blues, and *norteño* music into an eloquent Los Angeles brew. A major commercial breakthrough came when the Los Lobos–powered soundtrack for the hit movie *La Bamba* shot to the top of the pop album charts in the summer of 1987.

By the 1990s the merengue boom had slowed somewhat, while another Dominican form, the *bachata,* came to the fore. At the same time, the New York impresario Ralph Mercado produced, on his now-defunct RMM label, extremely polished but bland salsa albums, cornering a large share of the market previously controlled by Fania.

When New York salsa lost most of the young Latino audience to rap and other forms, many of the top salsa musicians moved into (or back into) the wider jazz field. This resulted in an apparent growth of the Latin jazz market, which was reinforced with the arrival of various Cuban jazz newcomers, such as Arturo Sandoval, Gonzalo Rubalcaba, and Juan Pablo Torres, all of whom contributed to the rapid growth in the new wave of Cuban influence on Latin jazz during the 1990s.

Although most Latin jazz practitioners remained within the Cuban or Brazilian confines of their hybrid idiom, others branched out in many different directions. Backed by his Salsa Refugees, the Dominican instrumentalist Mario Rivera brought about the marriage of jazz and merengue, while the Panamanian pianist Danilo Pérez passionately explored the rhythms of his native country, and the Los Angeles–based reedman Justo Almario sought inspiration from *cumbia, bambuco, vallenato, pasillo,* and other Colombian forms. As a result of this exciting process of cross-fertilization, Latin jazz is gaining increasing exposure and becoming an ideal creative vehicle for many adventurous musicians.

The Cuban connection was firmly reestablished in the 1990s, after the Los Angeles bluesman Ry Cooder traveled to the island to record with native

© WANDERLAN P. SILVA/AP/WIDE WORLD PHOTOS

Joquinha Gonzaga plays accordion during a 1999 tribute to his uncle, Brazilian folk musician Luiz Gonzaga, known as the "king of Baiao," at New York's Lincoln Center.

musicians. The combined result—the album *Buena Vista Social Club* and Wim Wenders's musical documentary of the same name—turned into a global blockbuster and led to the revival of *son* and other traditional Cuban genres, offsetting the formulaic timba trends in contemporary Cuban music.

Last but not least, a simplistic fusion of the *norteño* style with the tuba—anchored sounds of village brass bands from the Mexican state of Sinaloa—came to virtually dominate the Southwest in the last decade of the 20th century. *Banda* music took over the aforesaid region of the United States with popular *narcocorridos,* whose amusing lyrics relate the trials and tribulations of Mexican drug traffickers on both sides of the border.

RELATED ARTICLES

Bachata; Bolero; Bomba; Cha-Cha; Colón, Willie; Cruz, Celia; Danzon; D'Rivera, Paquito; Estefan, Gloria; Guaracha; Jazz; Miranda, Carmen; Norteño; Palmieri, Charlie; Plena; Popular Culture; Rap; Rhumba; Rumba; Salsa; Sandoval, Arturo; Santana, Carlos; Son; Tejano; Valens, Ritchie.

FURTHER READING

Austerlitz, Paul. *Dominican Music and Merengue: Dominican Identity.* Philadelphia: Temple Univ. Press, 1997.

Carpentier, Alejo. *Music in Cuba.* Tr. by Alan West Durán. Minneapolis: Univ. of Minn. Press, 2001.

Chediak, Nat. *Diccionario de jazz Latino* (Latin Jazz Dictionary). Madrid, Spain: Fundación Autor, 1998.

Clark, Walter Aaron, ed. *From Tejano to Tango: Latin American Popular Music.* New York: Routledge, 2002.

Díaz Ayala, Cristóbal. *Música cubana: Del areyto a la nueva trova* (Cuban Music: From Areyto to Nueva Trova). Hato Rey, Puerto Rico: Editorial Cubanacán, 1981.

Díaz Ayala, Cristóbal. *La marcha de los Jíbaros, 1898–1997: Cien años de música Puertorriqueña por el mundo* (The March of the Jíbaros, 1898–1997: A Hundred Years of Puerto Rican Music around the World). San Juan, Puerto Rico: Fundación Musicalia/Editorial Plaza Mayor, 1998.

Figueroa, Frank. *Encyclopedia of Latin American Music in New York.* St. Petersburg, Fla.: Pillar Pubs., 1995.

Giro, Radamés. *El mambo* (The Mambo). Havana, Cuba: Editorial Letras Cubanas, 1993.

Krich, John. *Why Is This Country Dancing? A One-Man Samba to the Beat of Brazil.* New York: Simon & Schuster, 1993.

Morales, Ed. *The Latin Beat: The Rhythms and Roots of Latin Music from Bossa Nova to Salsa and Beyond.* Cambridge, Mass.: Da Capo Press, 2003.

Orovio, Hélio. *Diccionario de la música Cubana* (Dictionary of Cuban Music). Havana, Cuba: Editorial Letras Cubanas, 1992.

Padura Fuentes, Leonardo. *Los rostros de la salsa* (The Faces of Salsa). Havana, Cuba: Ediciones Unión, 1997.

Roberts, John Storm. *The Latin Tinge: The Impact of Latin American Music on the United States.* Tivoli, N.Y.: Original Music, 1985.

LUIS TAMARGO

MUSICAL INSTRUMENTS

The making of music has evolved throughout the world into a highly diverse and complex art form in which we use not only our hands and feet to keep rhythm while we shout and sing but also employ highly sophisticated musical instruments to enhance our creative endeavors. Generally, most Latin American musical ensembles today use many of the same instruments as those of European and North American ensembles. Thus in the popular Latin American musical traditions of countries such as Cuba, Puerto Rico, the Dominican Republic, Mexico, and Brazil, many instruments are used that are fairly common to the rest of the western world, including the piano, bass, "standard" drum kit, tympani, ancillary percussion, guitar, accordion, vibraphone, trumpet, trombone, saxophone, clarinet, violin, and flute.

On the other hand, there are many instruments used in the music of Latin America that do not derive from the European/North American traditions. These instruments are native to their countries of origin, or in many cases they are part of the legacy of African people who were forcibly brought to these countries as slaves between the 15th and the 17th century. The instruments described below are used today not only in their own native folkloric and popular music traditions, but within the past century they have also become part of the growing tradition of Latin American music in the United States. The instruments defined in this article represent only a few of the myriad native instruments found in countries throughout Latin America.

Cuba

The following musical instruments are generally thought of as part of the Cuban musical instrument tradition (although several are simultaneously part of the traditions of other Caribbean countries as well). Some of these instruments originally came from Africa, while others were developed in Cuba itself during the past three centuries.

Bata. *Bata* consist of three double-membrane, hourglass-shaped hand drums, called *iya, itotele,* and *okonkolo.* These instruments originated in Nigeria among the Yoruba people and are used in Cuba as well as in other parts of the world for worship within an African-based religion, known as Lucumi or Santería. The sounds produced by these sacred drums, played in concert by three drummers, emulate phrases and prayers to individual *orishas* (deities) of the Lucumi religion. In modern times, *bata* have been utilized more and more in the secular context in order to add rhythmic diversity and exotic interest to popular music orchestrations.

Botija. A *botija* is a large, open-mouthed, earthenware jug, originally used to carry olive oil from Spain and used in the 19th and the early 20th century as a musical instrument to add a bass sound to popular

Cuban music such as *son.* The sound of the *botija* is made by blowing across its open mouth, thereby producing a low-pitched, basslike hum. Eventually, the *botija* was replaced as a musical instrument, first by the *marimbula* (see below) and later by the bass fiddle. Today, the *botija* is used principally by ensembles that play popular Cuban music such as *changui* and *son* in its original manner.

Bongos. Bongos consist of two small, wooden or fiberglass hand drums, joined together by a support centerpiece and traditionally played between the percussionist's knees (although today they are often found mounted on stands). The smaller of the two drums, called the *macho,* is tuned higher in pitch than the larger, called the *hembra.* During the 1920s and

Mexican Orchestra, woven wool tapestry by the Raymond Picaud Studio, Aubusson, France, 1951, designed by Raoul Dufy.

later, bongos were played in a highly improvisational manner within the context of the Cuban *son*. They were tuned by the use of heat or flame to tighten the skins. Today, bongos have become virtually standard in salsa bands from every country and they are tuned manually, by hand-tightening metal tuning rods with a wrench. In general the contemporary role of bongos is to provide a 4/4 rhythm, called *martillo*, and its variations, with the occasional improvised "solo," in order to add rhythmic richness and excitement to popular music orchestrations. Bongos are also employed quite often in musical aggregations that play non-Latin music.

Cajon. A *cajon* is simply a wooden box played with the hands in order to simulate the sound of a drum. During the time of colonial oppression in Cuba, slaves were not permitted to possess drums or other artifacts of their native culture. In order to play a form of secular music called rumba, they resorted to finding substitutes that could serve as drums. Favorite choices were the boxes that had held imported codfish, candles, and spirits such as cognac. These boxes were reputed to make the best sounds and were therefore utilized in the developing local tradition. Today, *cajones* are used particularly in the playing of *yambu*, one of the Cuban folkloric rumba secular forms. They are also occasionally chosen in popular music as a substitute for bongos (see above).

Chekere. A *chekere* (also spelled *shekere*) is a medium-sized gourd (or calabash) that has been gutted, dried and cured, and strung with colorful beads. Often known by its Yoruba name, *agbe*, the *chekere* is most commonly used in the music of Lucumi (Santería). Sounds are made with the *chekere* by shaking it, thereby causing the beads to rattle against its sides, or by striking its flat bottom, producing a low-pitched, drumlike sound accompanied by the rattling of the beads. A group of three *chekeres*, each of a different size and musical pitch, played by three percussionists in concert, is utilized in a type of religious ceremony sometimes referred to simply as *guiro*. Today, a single *chekere* may be used in a salsa band to add visual interest as well as unique musical coloration.

Claves. *Claves* consist of a pair of sticks, often made of teak or rosewood, that are used to play the rhythm called *clave*, which is central to most Caribbean music. For a right-handed percussionist, one stick is cradled in the left hand, while the other, held in the right hand, strikes the first crossways to produce a sharp, piercing sound. In recent times, another type of *claves*, called African *claves*, also have been introduced into Latin American music. With African *claves*, the stick that is struck is larger than the other. It is also hollow in the center and has a groove, which is cupped in the hand to enhance the produced sound. *Claves* are used extensively in Cuban folkloric music today. At one time it was standard to see *claves* in virtually every Cuban musical ensemble; however, in the contemporary scene *claves* are utilized only occasionally in salsa bands as ancillary percussion instruments.

Congas. Congas (known in Cuba and other parts of Latin America as *tumbadoras*) are large, barrel-shaped, single-membrane wooden or sometimes fiberglass hand drums that are used today both in folkloric and popular music throughout the world. Descendents of Congolese *makuta* drums, conga drums were originally used in Cuba in festival street music such as *conga de comparsa*, from which they no doubt derived their name, *tambores de conga* (drums of the conga), and eventually simply congas. They were (and are) also used in secular folkloric music such as *guaguanco* and *rumba columbia*, and in the music of various religious sects and secret societies, including Lucumi and *palo mayombe*. According to most sources, conga drums were introduced into Cuban popular music by the renowned *tresista* Arsenio Rodríguez under great protest and rejection by high society, who considered this instrument to be "of the streets." Through Arsenio's influence, however, the conga drum soon found its way into the Orquesta Arcaño y sus Maravillas, one of the most popular "society" ensembles of the period. Finding themselves unable to reject a musical "innovation" by the well-regarded Antonio Arcaño, high society reluctantly went along, and the conga drum quickly revolutionized the sound of the rhythm section of virtually every type of popular Latin American musical aggregation. Like its cousin the bongo, the conga drum was originally tuned by heating the membrane over a flame until the skin had become tight enough to achieve the desirable pitch. By the early 1950s, the skin was tuned far more efficiently—by tightening a series of metal tuning rods with a wrench. In the present day, conga drums and their signature 4/4-

time rhythm, *tumbao,* have become a standard component of virtually every salsa band in the world. They are also used extensively in Latin jazz, in various kinds of Dominican, Mexican, and Brazilian music, and often to punctuate the rhythm sections of various types of non-Latin ensembles.

Cowbell. The cowbell (known in Cuba as *cencerro* or *campana*) is an ancillary or support rhythm instrument that is found in both secular and religious music. A descendant of the *ekon,* an instrument utilized in Cuba by the Abakua religious sect, the cowbell has had its clapper removed for use as an instrument and is found in many different sizes and shapes. It is made to sound by striking it with a wooden stick, often called a "beater." In popular salsa music today, the cowbell will often be part of the equipment played by the *timbalero,* who may have one or more bells of various sizes, mounted on the timbales. The *bongosero* will generally also have a large cowbell (usually called the bongo bell) and beater nearby, which will be played alternatively with the bongos during various parts of the musical arrangement. A sound similar to that of the cowbell is played by either a *guataca* (literally, a hoe blade) or an *agogo.*

Guataca. A *guataca* is literally the blade of a hoe. The sound it makes is similar to that of a cowbell (*cencerro* or *campana*), of which it is a predecessor in Cuban music. The *guataca* was originally used during the colonial period in Cuba by people who had no ordinary access to musical instruments. It is traditionally played by using a large railroad spike or nail as a beater. The *guataca* is used today by Cuban folkloric music ensembles in playing such forms as *rumba columbia* in its original manner.

Guiro. The *guiro* is a gourd or calabash that is used in Cuban religious, folkloric, and popular music as well as in the music of many other Latin American countries today. In order to function as a musical instrument, the *guiro* must first be hollowed of its contents, then dried and cured. Unlike its cousin, the *chekere* (see above), the *guiro* is not strung with beads, nor is it struck by the hand to produce its unique sound. Rather, it is opened at its top end and serrated along one side, often having finger holes for gripping, and it is scraped or struck with a thin wooden or plastic stick. The *guiro* is utilized exten-

sively in popular Latin American music today as an ancillary or support instrument that is used to keep time in musical ensembles.

Maracas. Maracas consist of a pair of round or pear-shaped, rattlelike instruments that are used as ancillary percussion in Cuban religious, folkloric, and popular music. Originally, maracas were gutted, dried, and cured gourds, into which small, hard objects such as pebbles or fruit pips were added to create the sound when the maracas were shaken. The holes were filled by tightly inserting wooden handles in the bottoms of the gourds. Eventually, maracas were also fashioned out of wood, coconut shells, or leather. Today, maracas are most often made of molded plastic. Cuban *son* ensembles of the 1920s and 1930s almost always had a *maracero* (maracas player) in the rhythm section. This tradition extended into the larger *conjuntos* and *orquestas* during the 1940s and 1950s. In the United States, one of the most famous *maraceros* was Frank Grillo ("Machito"), who was reputed to have elevated the playing of maracas to an art form unto itself. Currently, maracas are used occasionally in salsa bands—often by the lead singer—to punctuate the rhythm of the music and to add a colorful visual aspect to the overall presentation.

Marimbula. The *marimbula* is an instrument of Congolese origin, which at one time was utilized in Cuba as a more melodic and sophisticated replacement for the *botija* (earthenware jug, see above) in providing a bass sound for *changui* (and later *son*) ensembles. Physically, the *marimbula* is constructed as a wooden box in the shape of a cube, a rectangle, or a solid trapezoid. It is hollow with a sound hole on one side and includes a series of metal, tonguelike slats that are plucked by the fingers to produce individual sounds of different musical pitches. Today the *marimbula* is most often found in ensembles that play Cuban *changui* in its original form. It is also occasionally seen in small groups playing non-Latin music.

Palitos. *Palitos* are simply a pair of wooden sticks that are used as rhythmic support instruments in the context of Cuban folkloric rumba (*guaguanco, rumba columbia,* and *yambu*). The word *palitos* also refers to the specific support rhythm being played. The sticks are played against the sides of a drum or on a thick, stand-mounted bamboo wooden block, called a *gua gua.* (Curiously, the word *gua gua* also means a bus or van—the double entendre refers no doubt to the role of the *palitos* and *gua gua* being used to rhythmically impel or drive the music being played.) In rumba ensembles the wooden sticks are often replaced by *cucharas* (spoons), particularly in *yambu,* in which *cajones* replace *tumbadoras* (conga drums) in order to maintain the tradition of utilizing "found" substitutes instead of standard instruments.

Quijada. The *quijada* is the skeletal jawbone of a donkey, horse, or mule. When struck by the fist or palm, it makes a clattering sound as the loosened teeth of the jawbone rattle against the bone. The *quijada* is often used as a novelty percussion instrument in the context of popular music ensembles throughout Latin America. In recent years the distinctive sound of the *quijada* has been recreated effectively through a man-made instrument called a vibraslap.

Timbales. Timbales consist of a pair of cylindrical metal drum shells, known as *cascaras,* each of which has a tunable head on one side and is open on the bottom. The drums are tuned to different pitches (high and low) and are mounted side by side on a metal stand. They are made to sound by percussive hammer strokes with the fingers or through the use of sticks, which may strike the heads, the rims, or the sides of the metal shells. Timbales descend from classical tympani or kettle drums (known as *timbales* in French), which were utilized in *orquestas tipicas* in Cuba toward the end of the 19th century. Tympani were quite large and cumbersome, and, in order to create drums that were more portable, *timbales criollos* were developed. These were as described above and were used in *charangas francesas* (literally, French orchestras), which were smaller ensembles that utilized flute and violin rather than brass instruments to interpret *danzon,* the popular music of the day. Eventually, tympani were phased out of Cuban *orquestas,* perhaps because of their size, but also because the sound of the more modern timbales became extremely popular. Currently, timbales are used in salsa bands all over the world, as well as in non-Latin groups as part of larger standard drum kits. Today, timbales come equipped with many extras, including cowbells of various sizes, *gua guas* (wood blocks), cymbals, and any number of other percussion options. Timbales are also available in a smaller version, called *timbalitos* or *pailas,* which are generally used

for high-energy solos, and in a larger version, called *timbalones,* which make a deeper, more powerful sound, and are therefore often found in large *orquestas.*

Tres. Descended from the Spanish guitar, the *tres* is a string instrument, played with a plectrum or pick that was originally used in Cuban ensembles that interpreted the *son.* The shape of the *tres* is similar to that of a guitar; however it is smaller, it has a shorter neck, and its string set is divided into three double courses (originally three triple courses for a total of nine strings), spaced more widely apart than standard guitar strings. The strings were originally tuned to a D minor triad (D, F, A), but, because of the influence of prominent *tresistas* such as Arsenio Rodríguez, it is currently tuned to the second inversion of a C-major triad (G, C, E). The two G strings are tuned in octaves, the C strings are tuned in unison, and the E strings are tuned in octaves. It is this special tuning combination that gives the *tres* its unique sound. The *tres* is used in the musical ensemble as a support or rhythm instrument, playing repetitive rhythm patterns that are known as *guajeos.* It is also often utilized as a frontline solo instrument. Today, the *tres* is found in groups that play Cuban *son* in its original manner and occasionally in salsa bands—particularly those that attempt to emulate the older, more traditional sound of the *son.*

Puerto Rico

The following musical instruments are generally thought of as part of the Puerto Rican musical instrument tradition. Some of these instruments originally came from Africa, while others were developed in Puerto Rico itself during the past three centuries.

Bomba. The *bomba* is a large, single-membrane, barrel-shaped wooden drum that is utilized in Puerto Rico to play rhythm accompaniment within the musical form that also is called *bomba.* The instrument is constructed in the same manner as the Cuban *tumbadora* (or conga drum), except that it is considerably wider and squatter in shape. Originally, *bombas* were tuned using heat or flame, but in modern times this is accomplished through the use of metal tuning rods adjusted with a wrench. The rhythm structure of *bomba* is set by a group of three musicians playing drums tuned to different pitches (high, medium, and low) in concert. Today, *bomba* drums are seen in the United States almost exclusively within musical ensembles that play this indigenous Puerto Rican music.

Cuatro. Like its Cuban cousin the *tres,* the Puerto Rican *cuatro* is a string instrument, played with a plectrum or pick, and descended from the Spanish guitar. The silhouette of many *cuatros* resembles the shape of a violin—with its decorative, incurved cutouts near the sound hole. Originally, the *cuatro* was, in fact, a 4-string guitar; hence, its name. However, sometime in the 19th century *cuatros* began to appear with 10 and even 15 strings, strung in five courses. The modern *cuatro* has five double courses, tuned as follows: B in octaves, E in octaves, A in unison (or sometimes by older players in octaves), D in unison, and G in unison. The *cuatro* was originally utilized as an instrument for accompanying folkloric and popular songs. Today it is occasionally found in salsa bands, following a tradition begun by the famous *cuatrista* Yomo Toro.

Guicharo. The *guicharo* is a small gourd that is utilized in the music of Puerto Rican *bomba* and *plena.* The gourd has been gutted, dried, and cured, but its curving top has been left on as a handle (unlike the larger Cuban *guiro* [see above], which has had its top removed). One side has been serrated for scraping, and a small sound hole has been cut into its bottom. The *guicharo* is played by scraping or striking its side with a thin stick. This instrument is seen in the United States almost exclusively in groups that play Puerto Rican *bomba* and *plena.*

Pandereta. A *pandereta* is a small, flat, single-membrane, tunable hand drum that is functionally the same as a tambourine, but without the flat, metal discs, which are sometimes called "jingles." In the popular Puerto Rican *plena,* a group of three *panderetas,* each tuned to a different pitch, keep the rhythm—two of the *panderetistas* playing support parts while one improvises over their constant rhythm. The *panderetas* are joined by a *guicharo* (see above) and an accordion, which plays the melody and accompanies the singers in this lively, energetic, urban song form.

Dominican Republic

The following musical instruments are generally thought of as part of the musical instrument tradition of the Dominican Republic. Some of these instruments originally came from Africa, while others were developed in the Dominican Republic itself during the past three centuries.

Guira. The *guira* is an ancillary or support rhythm instrument that is standard in orchestras from the Dominican Republic. Generally, it is a lightweight metal cylinder, closed at both ends by conical end pieces. It possesses a handle, which enables it to be easily held in one hand, and is serrated all around its rounded sides. The *guira* is played by scraping or striking it, using a special metal comblike device (similar in shape to an "Afro" hair comb). *Guiras* are used extensively today in bands that play such popular Dominican song forms as merengue and *bachata.*

Tambora. The *tambora* is a medium-sized, double-membrane, barrel- or cylinder-shaped, tunable wooden drum that is used in Dominican orchestras. The instrument may be played while the musician is standing, in which case it is generally hung from the neck by a strap, or while sitting, in which case it may optionally be strapped around the waist for better stability. The *tambora* is played by striking one side alternatively with the hand or a wooden beater (which may also be used to strike the wooden sides of the drum), and the other side with the hand only. Although in modern times the majority of *tamboras* are tunable through the use of tuning rods and a wrench, ensembles that play a more folkloric style of merengue—using only *tambora, guira,* accordion, and voices—may purposely choose a more primitive version of this unique drum in order to preserve authenticity. In this case the instrument is tuned by tightening a network of interlocking cords or leather thongs. Like the *guira,* the *tambora* is standard in Dominican orchestras that play popular music such as merengue and *bachata.*

Mexico

The following musical instruments are generally thought of as part of the musical instrument tradition of Mexico. Some of these instruments originally came from Spain, while others were developed in Mexico during the past three centuries.

Bajo sexto. The *bajo sexto* is a Mexican version of a 12-string guitar, often utilized in mariachi and other popular Mexican music. It consists of six double courses of strings, tuned in octaves as E, A, D, G, B, and E (in the same manner as a guitar from lowest to highest string). The *bajo sexto* is tuned a full octave lower than an ordinary guitar, since it functions as a bass instrument within the ensemble.

Guitarron. The *guitarron* (sometimes referred to as a *guitarron de Toloche*) is an oversized, six-string guitar, most likely developed in the Mexican state of Jalisco, as a replacement for the cumbersome harp, which was originally a part of the mariachi orchestra. The *guitarron* has a very wide body and a short neck, is strapped over the shoulder, and is usually played with the fingers. It is generally tuned through wooden pegs in its headstock. The tuning is like that of a guitar (E, A, D, G, B, E—from lowest to highest strings), although at times it will be tuned as follows (from lowest to highest): A, D, G, C, E, A. The *guitarron* has become a standard instrument in mariachi, both in Mexico and in the United States.

Marimba. The marimba, reputedly named after a Zulu goddess of the same name, is a mallet percussion instrument of African origin, which was brought to the new world during the era of slave trade, probably sometime during the 16th century. It is a member of the xylophone family and is played by striking its bars (often made of rosewood) with rubber or yarn-wound mallets. The contemporary marimba's 36- to 54-bar keyboard is laid out like that of a piano. It is said that a Guatemalan named Sebastian Hurtado developed the first modern marimba by substituting resonator pipes for its primitive, hanging gourds, which had been used up to that time to create the sound of the instrument. Marimbas have become a standard part of the Mexican musical instrument tradition over many years. Entire ensembles consisting only of marimbas are found both in Mexico and in the United States. Marimbas are also utilized today both as support and solo instruments in musical contexts of all kinds throughout the world.

Brazil

The following musical instruments are generally thought of as part of the musical instrument tradition of Brazil. Some of these instruments originally came from Africa, while others were developed in Brazil itself during the past three centuries.

Ago-go. The *ago-go* consists of two small cowbell-like instruments, used for playing Brazilian folkloric song forms such as samba and *baion*. The bells are generally shaped like cones, open at one end, and joined together by a bent metal rod that has been welded to the closed end of each bell. The *ago-go* is held in one hand while being struck by a beater with the other.

Berimbao. Originally from Africa, the *berimbao* is a unique instrument, used primarily in Brazil as part of the Afro-Brazilian ritual called *capoeira*. It is, in fact, a bow, attached to which is an open-ended gourd; both are strung in a special way with a metal wire. The player holds the shaft of the bow in the left hand at the point where the gourd is attached. In this same hand is also held a small coin. In the other hand, the player holds a thin wooden stick and a small shaker known as a *caxixi*. The complex sound of the *berimbao* is made by tapping the stick against the wire, while pressing the coin with the other hand against the wire to raise and lower the pitch. At the same time, the gourd may be moved back and forth against the player's stomach, thereby producing a "wah-wah" sound. The *berimbao* is used today to add special effects and visual excitement to musical ensembles of all types.

Cabasa. The *cabasa* (sometimes called *afoxe* or *afuche*) is a small gourd that is used as a support rhythm instrument in Brazilian folkloric and popular song forms such as samba, *baion* and *bossa nova*. To prepare the gourd for use, it must be dried and cured, after which grooves must be cut into its outer shell. It is then strung with beads. The *cabasa* is played by placing one hand on the beads and rotating the shell sharply left or right to produce the instrument's unique sound. A modern version of the *cabasa* consists of a metal cylinder with a handle, around which is a network of small beads. It is played in the same manner as its more authentic cousin, but it produces a sharper sound.

Chocalho. The *chocalho* (sometimes called a *ganza*) is a metal shaker, used for playing Brazilian folkloric and popular song forms such as samba, *baion,* and *bossa nova*. The instrument consists of one or two closed, cylindrical containers, which generally contain sand. The *chocalho* is played with both hands by moving it sharply toward and away from the body, usually at about shoulder level or slightly higher.

Cuica. The *cuica* is a small, cylindrical, tunable, single-membrane drum (constructed much like a standard drum-kit snare or tom tom), which is used in a Brazilian samba variation known as *batacuda*. The shell of the *cuica* is made of metal, wood, or fiberglass, and the instrument is strapped around the neck of the player for use. A unique aspect of the *cuica* is that a thin bamboo stick is fastened to the center of the membrane so that it protrudes inside the shell of the drum. The *cuica* is played by rubbing a damp piece of cloth (held between the fingers) up and down the length of the bamboo stick at various speeds while raising or lowering the pitch of the membrane by depressing it with the free hand. This produces a variety of unusual sounds, ranging from what seems like moaning to the barking of a dog.

Pandeiro. The *pandeiro,* sometimes called the national musical instrument of Brazil, is a single-membrane, tunable tambourine, played by hand in all manner of folkloric and popular song forms in Brazil. The instrument's distinctive sound is said to come from its "jinglers," groups of two discs in placed in six locations around the shell of the *pandeiro.* These must be made of tin to create the characteristic dry sound. This instrument is so well loved in Brazil that during carnival each year a special prize is awarded to the best *pandeiro* player.

Reco-reco. The *reco-reco* is a hollow bamboo instrument that is used as a support rhythm instrument in samba. About 12 to 15 inches (30 to 38 cm) in length with a serrated side, the *reco-reco* is held in one hand while it is scraped with a thin metal stick. A larger, more elaborate version of the *reco-reco,* often found in carnival bands, consists of a hollow metal container with a hornlike opening at one end and several springs attached to one side. These springs are scraped to produce the instrument's unique sound.

Surdo. The *surdo* is a large, cylindrical, tunable, double-membrane drum (constructed much like a standard snare drum) that is used for keeping the bass rhythm in Brazilian folkloric song forms such as samba and *baion*. It is strapped over the shoulder and played with a large beater in one hand, while the other hand serves to muffle certain sounds within the drum's rhythm patterns.

Tamborim. Similar to the *pandeiro,* the *tamborim* is a single-membrane, tunable, tambourine-like instrument used in Brazilian samba. It is small, its shell is generally made of metal, and it is held in one hand while being struck with a stick by the other.

RELATED ARTICLES

Afro-Latino Influences; Bachata; Bomba; Danzón; Jazz; Mariachi; Music, Classical; Music, Popular; Plena; Rumba; Salsa; Son.

FURTHER READING

Adato, Joseph, and Judy George, eds. *The Percussionist's Dictionary: Translations, Descriptions and Photographs of Percussion Instruments from around the World.* Melville, N.Y.: Belwin Mills, 1984.

Amira, John, and Steven Cornelius. *The Music of Santería: Traditional Rhythms of the Batá Drums.* Crown Point, Ind.: White Cliffs Media Co., 1992.

Gerard, Charley, and Marty Sheller. *Salsa!: The Rhythm of Latin Music.* New ed. Tempe, Ariz.: White Cliffs Media Co., 1998.

Mauleon, Rebeca. *The Salsa Guide Book.* Petaluma: Sher Music, 1993.

Orovio, Helio. *Diccionario de la música Cubana: Biográfico y teenico* (Dictionary of Cuban Music). Havana, Cuba: Letras Cubanas, 1981.

Ortiz, Fernando. *La africanía de la música folklórica Cubana* (The Africanization of Cuban Folkloric Music). 1950. Reprint. Havana, Cuba: Letras Cubanas, 1993.

Ortiz, Fernando. *Los instrumentos de la música afrocubana* (The Instruments of Afro-Cuban Music). 1951. Reprint. Havana, Cuba: Letras Cubanas, 1995.

Roberts, John Storm. *The Latin Tinge: The Impact of Latin American Music on the United States.* New York: Oxford Univ. Press, 1999.

Sulsbrück, Birger. *Latin-American Percussion: Rhythms and Rhythm Instruments from Cuba and Brazil.* Copenhagen: Edition Wilhelm Hansen, 1986.

Uribe, Ed. *The Essence of Afro-Cuban Percussion & Drum Set.* Miami, Fla.: Warner Brothers, 1996.

FRAN CHESLEIGH

MUSLIMS. *See* ISLAM.

MUTUAL AID SOCIETIES

Mutual aid societies have long been used by immigrant groups to help meet basic human needs and to help in the adjustment of newcomers to life in the United States. In the early 1900s, at the time of greatest immigration to the United States, Irish, German, and Jewish communities all established a form of mutual aid societies to assist their own. *Sociedades mutualistas* had been established in Mexico and other parts of Latin America, and they became a popular organizing strategy, providing resources and leadership on an informal, nongovernmental basis, for Latinos in the late 19th and the early 20th century throughout Spanish-speaking communities in the Southwest and into the Midwest as far as Indiana and Michigan. *Mutualismo* (fraternity) was created along geographic, trade, ethnic, or religious lines. Often these groups maintained close ties to other organizations in the community and served as conduits of information, or networks. Mutualism demonstrated strength and ingenuity in the face of hostility and countered the prevailing stereotype of the lazy, apathetic Mexican or Latino. *Mutualistas* were particularly popular and valuable among recent immigrants.

Mutual aid societies varied greatly in size and scope. While many were informal and organized strictly for charitable purposes, others evolved into complex hierarchies involving dues-paying membership organizations. They provided a number of economic, social, and educational services and benefits to members, such as credit unions, burial insurance, disability insurance, health care, legal aid, newsletters, support for civic or religious celebrations, and programs for women and youth. As such, their membership consisted of working- and lower-middle-class people. Societies could be exclusively male (as were fraternal organizations), all female, or mixed. Some were able to provide emergency loans and mediation of disputes among community members. Many evolved into elaborate economic organizations, providing medical insurance and job training. At a time when ethnic minorities were excluded from educational opportunities or when public educational facilities were inferior, some societies opened their own local schools for children and adults and established communal libraries. For Mexicans in the Southwest who were denied entry into existing labor unions, some *mutualistas* also became trade unions. In advocating for their own communities, *sociedades mutualistas* sometimes formed the organizational foundation for later civil rights efforts, political activism, and self-help coalitions throughout the Southwest, whose focus was combating all forms of discrimination in Latino communities.

As important as the concrete benefits of *mutualistas* were, the emotional, linguistic, and psychological support they provided was equally important. Frequently these organizations had names of important Hispanic heroes, held meetings in Spanish, and reinforced historical, cultural, linguistic, and religious traditions in the face of assimilationist pressures in the United States.

One of the earliest examples of mutualism in the United States among Latinos was the Club Recíproco (Reciprocal Club) of Corpus Christi, Texas, founded in 1873. The Alianza Hispano Americana (Hispanic American Alliance) of Tucson, Arizona, established in 1894, was among the largest and most successful of the *sociedades mutualistas*. It expanded to over 200 chapters nationwide; by 1897 it had its first national convention, and by 1939 it had grown to over 17,000 members in the southwestern United States and Mexico.

As was the case for many charitable-philanthropic organizations, the Great Depression strained the collective capacity of mutual aid societies to meet community needs. With no working members to contribute to programs, many societies shut their doors. Another explanation for their disappearance relates to the rise in the expectation that government would contribute to the provision of welfare programs. By the 1930s New Deal era, government was playing an increasing role in providing workers' compensation insurance, mothers' pensions, and care to the indigent elderly, with the advent of the Social Security Act. Many of the Latino mutual aid societies persist today as social or charitable rather than economic organizations, often linked to Catholic church efforts.

Both small and complex mutual aid societies have played a key role in the survival, adaptation, and advancement of many immigrant groups in the United States. The practices of cooperative ventures, mutual protection, community development, and service have been effective survival mechanisms. *Sociedades mutualistas* have played a significant part in helping many Latinos negotiate the difficulties of starting a new life.

RELATED ARTICLES

Alianza Hispano-Americana; Banking.

FURTHER READING

Acuña, Rodolfo. *Occupied America: A History of Chicanos* (2d ed.). 1981. Reprint. New York: Pearson Longman, 2004.
García, Mario T. *Mexican Americans: Leadership, Ideology, and Identity, 1930–1960.* New Haven: Yale Univ. Press, 1989.

Gómez-Quiñones, Juan. *Mexican American Labor 1790–1990.* Albuquerque: Univ. of N.Mex. Press, 1994.

McVetty, Suzanne. "Help Is at Hand: Immigrant Aid Societies, Part 1." *Ancestry Magazine* 14 no. 4 (July–August, 1996): 1–4.

Reisler, Mark. *By the Sweat of Their Brow: Mexican Immigrant Labor in the United States, 1900–1940.* Westport, Conn.: Greenwood Press, 1976

Valdés, Dennis Nodín. *Barrios Norteños: St. Paul and Midwestern Mexican Communities in the Twentieth Century.* Austin: Univ. of Tex. Press, 2000.

REBECCA LÓPEZ
SUSAN GREEN

N

NAHUAS

The Nahua, or Nahuas (pronounced NAH-wah), are all those people of indigenous origin in the territories of the former Mesoamerica who speak any dialect of the Nahuatl (pronounced NAH-wahtl) language (Mexicano, Azteca, Pipil) or who have inherited the cultural and social mores of that tradition, or both. The word *Nahuatlaca* means people who explain themselves and speak distinctly, according to the 16th-century Codex Ramirez, which acknowledged the arts of rhetoric and statesmanship for which Nahua tradition became known. *In naoa: iehoantin in naoatlatolli ic tlatoa, in achi Mexica tlatoa, in maca nel iuh tlanqui,* or "The Nahua: they are the ones who speak the Nahuatl language. They speak a little like the Mexica, although not perfectly," is how one of Fray Bernardino de Sahagún's informants identified them.

Currently some 1.5 million–1.6 million speakers of Nahuatl still live in Mexico (1,448,936 over the age of five according to the National Institute of Statistics, 2000; according to the Summer Institute of Linguistics, 1,697,000), more than any other native group in Mexico. They are concentrated largely in villages and municipalities in the states of Puebla, Guerrero, Vera Cruz, Tlaxcala, Morelos, Oaxaca, Durango, Mexico, and San Luis Potosí. The Pipil speakers are descendants of pre-Hispanic migrations into what is now Nicaragua and El Salvador. Many Pipil speakers were part of the migrations of Mexican workers into the United States.

The original founders of Teotihuacán (c. 200 B.C. to 700 A.D.) may have spoken Nahuatl—no one knows for sure—but by the time of the Aztec Triple Alliance in the 15th century, the Nahua cities of Mexico-Tenochtitlán, Tlacopán, and Texcoco were the inheritors of everything ancient and civilized in the great cities of the Mexican Altiplano. Not all Nahuas were Aztec, however; the province of Tlaxcala, though contiguous to Texcoco, was still unsubdued by the Alliance in 1519 and became the principal ally in Hernán Cortés's campaign against the power of Montezuma II. Whatever their original ethnicity or language, all "Toltec" settled cities surrounding the basin of Lake Texcoco inherited and taught the rich oral traditions of the Nahuatl language.

In the colonial period the Nahua cities and villages continued for some time with the traditional social and political structures of the *altepetl,* or ethnic state, under dynastic rulers. Gradually, however, under the pressures of *encomienda* (tribute labor), forced relocation to centralized towns, evangelization, an increasingly refined caste system, and epidemics, the Nahua cities and villages—along with every other Indian culture—became increasingly Hispanized and autonomous. Although the revolutionary Emiliano Zapata was a Nahua and used his language extensively in official communication and public proclamations, villages of Nahua people were largely unaware of themselves as a dispersed but significant native people throughout much of the 20th century. However, owing to publication efforts such as Miguel Barrios's Nahuatl-language newspaper,

A Nahua woman plays a small guitar at the entrance to Mexico City's Basilica, in anticipation of a visit by Pope John Paul II, who offered mass in the Nahua language (2002).

Mexihkatl Itonalama (Mexican's Daily), and, in the 1950s, the bilingual education and publication movement promoted by the National Autonomous University under prominent intellectuals such as Miguel León Portilla, by 1987 Nahua poet Joel Martínez Hernández could write, "We Nahua people are not found in one place, we are dispersed, we are scattered in sixteen states, in eight-hundred-and-eight towns. And so we must recognize we exist not only in our hamlet, not only in our own town; we Nahua people live throughout all the lands of Mexico."

RELATED ARTICLES

Colonialism; Gamio, Manuel; Indigenous Heritage; Leon-Portilla, Miguel; Mayas; Mesoamerica; Taino.

FURTHER READING

Lockhart, James. *The Nahuas after the Conquest.* Stanford, Calif.: Stanford Univ. Press, 1992.
Martínez Hernández, Joel. "How Many Native Nahuas Are We?" In *New Voices in Native American Literary Criticism.* Ed. by Arnold Krupat. Washington, D.C.: Smithsonian Inst. Press, 1993.
Radin, Paul, ed. and tr. "The Codex Ramirez." *The Sources and Authenticity of the History of the Ancient Mexicans: Publications in American Archeology and Ethnology* 17, no. 1 (1920). New York: Kraus Reprint, 1965.
Sahagún, Fray Bernardino de, ed. *Florentine Codex: General History of the Things of New Spain.* Tr. and ed. by Arthur J. O. Anderson and Charles E. Dibble. 13 parts. Salt Lake City: Univ. of Utah Press, 1950–1982.

SELECTED WEB SITES

Instituto Nacional de Estadistica—geografica e informatica (INE). www.inegi.gob.mx/est/default.asp?c=2397
Summer Institute of Linguistics (SIL). www.sil.org/mexico/nahuatl/familia-nahuatl.htm

WILLARD GINGERICH

NARCOCORRIDO

A subgenre of the 200-year-old *corrido,* the *narcocorrido* (drug ballad) has its roots in the 1920s, when dozens of songs were written about the bootleggers who smuggled alcohol into the United States from

Mexico. With the end of Prohibition, some of the smuggling gangs turned to other illegal drugs, and by 1934 a Texan duo had recorded *El contrabandista*, the song of a bootlegger who was now smuggling marijuana, morphine, and cocaine.

Drug-smuggling ballads remained a staple of the border repertoire for the next few decades, but the *narcocorrido* wave is usually dated from 1972, when Los Tigres del Norte recorded *Contrabando y traición* (Smuggling and Betrayal), the ballad of Camelia the Texan, who crosses the border with her boyfriend carrying marijuana to sell in Los Angeles. This became a huge international hit, launching Los Tigres on their career as the most popular band in *norteño* music, and hundreds of other groups rushed to imitate their model.

The most influential composer of *narcocorridos* was Paulino Vargas, whose *Corrido de Lamberto Quintero* and "La banda del carro rojo" (The Red Car Gang) were classically styled epics of the modern Mexican crime world. He was followed by Teodoro Bello, who added a new twist by writing in clever code language, as in "Pacas de a kilo" (One Kilo Packets), wherein he suggests a marijuana grower's pride in his crop with the phrase *qué chulas se ven mis vacas con colitas de borrego* (how cute my cows look with their little rams' tails).

In the 1990s Chalino Sánchez pioneered a new wave of drug-world balladeers. Born in the Mexican state of Sinaloa but based in Los Angeles, Sánchez had a harder-edged, streetwise style, and after he was murdered in 1992, he was elevated to legend. His harsh singing voice and gunfighter image have been copied by a generation of young singers, who have made Los Angeles into the new center of the *corrido* form. During the same period, groups such as Los Tucanes de Tijuana went beyond epical lyrics about brave smugglers and started singing about the pleasures of drug parties.

Like gangsta rap, with which it shares a largely overlapping audience, the *narcocorridos* have been attacked as a public menace, and they are banned from radio programs by many stations on both sides of the border. To their fans, though, they are less symbols of drugs and crime than of a fierce pride in Mexican roots and traditions. They continue to be accompanied by accordion *conjuntos* and polka-flavored brass bands and have resisted musical modernization, despite the rap connection and the fact that many *corridistas* now dress in urban gangsta styles.

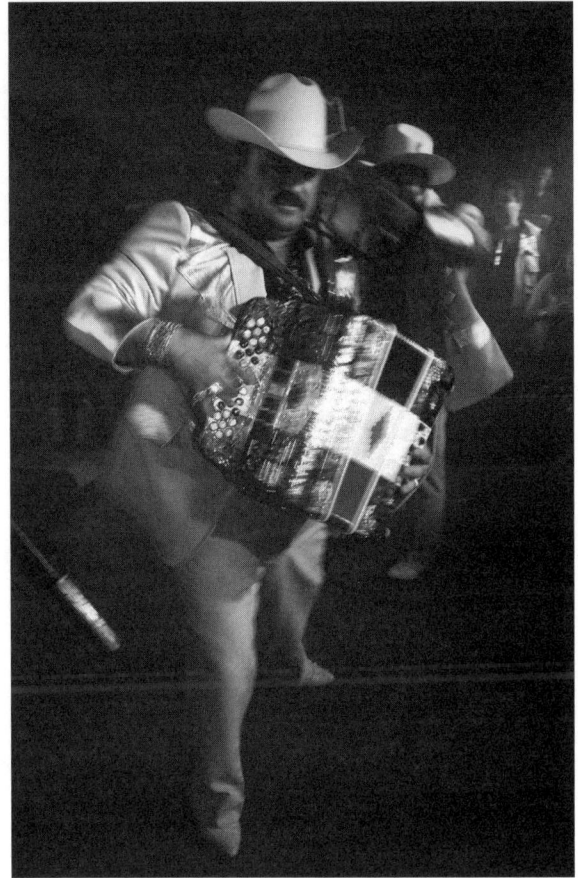

LA OPINION PHOTOS / NEWSCOM

An accordion player in the Mexican *narcocorrido* musical group Los Razos, in Los Angeles, California.

Their fans typically show up dressed in cowboy gear and silk shirts bearing symbols that include both marijuana leaves and the Virgin of Guadalupe. Thus the *narcocorrido* has become a unique blend of traditionalism and cutting-edge street style as well as a symbol of the re-Mexicanization of the southwestern United States.

RELATED ARTICLES

Border, United States-Mexico; Corrido; Drugs; Music, Popular; Rap.

FURTHER READING

Edberg, Mark C. *El Narcotraficante*. Austin: Univ. of Tex. Press, 2004.

Quinones, Sam. *True Tales from Another Mexico*. Albuquerque: Univ. of N.Mex. Press, 2001.

Simonett, Helena. *Banda: Mexican Musical Life across Borders*. Middletown, Conn.: Wesleyan Univ. Press, 2001.

Stavans, Ilan. "Hispanic U.S.A.: Literature, Music, Language." In *The Cambridge Companion to Modern Latin American Culture*. Ed. by John King. Cambridge: Cambridge Univ. Press, 2004.

Wald, Elijah. *Narcocorrido*. New York: Rayo, 2002.

SELECTED WEB SITE
Elijah Wald—Narcocorrido.
www.elijahwald.com/corrido.html

ELIJAH WALD

NATIONAL ASSOCIATION TO PROMOTE LIBRARY AND INFORMATION SERVICES TO THE SPANISH SPEAKING. See REFORMA.

NATIONAL CHICANO MORATORIUM OF VIETNAM

As the Vietnam War entered the 1970s, it became evident that an ungainly number of minority youth had been drafted and sent off to Southeast Asia and that a disproportionate number of soldiers killed in the war were Latino and black, a percentage far out of line with their numbers in the population at large. Among Mexican Americans, outrage at the war and its effect on their community took the form of demonstrations, culminating in a major war protest in Los Angeles on August 29, 1970, called the National Chicano Moratorium. Despite intramural squabbles between different organizations that made up the Moratorium coalition, the atmosphere that Sunday morning was festive and positive. A multiethnic crowd of more than 20,000 marchers, many carrying placards and banners, took up six lanes of Whittier Boulevard as they headed toward the rally at Laguna Park. Speakers were militant in their opposition to the Vietnam War and used the occasion to promote issues of racial identity, fraternity, and justice.

As the hot afternoon wore on, however, a number of people drifted over to a nearby liquor store for beer and soda, so many that the store's owner locked the door to prevent more customers from entering and to make sure those that did, paid for their refreshments. "After a half-hour with the doors still locked," author Ernesto Chávez relates in *Mi Raza Primero!* (My People First!), "[the owner] panicked and called the sheriffs." Three sheriffs with clubs and a riot gun appeared, and after an empty can was tossed at the sheriffs' car, two dozen deputies arrived. This drama unfolded behind most of the unwitting crowd at the rally but within view of the stage, where the speaker implored police to hold their line. Law enforcement's response was the opposite, and rapidly reinforcements from the sheriff's office and Los Angeles police arrived and waded into the crowd to arrest unsuspecting demonstrators. Some in the crowd threw rocks and bottles at the police, but most tried to leave the park, taking refuge in neighborhood houses and on buses. Police countered by shooting tear gas at private homes and following passengers onto buses and beating them. Author Luis J. Rodriguez was among the many beaten and jailed. "A line of deputies at the park's edge—armed with high-powered rifles, billy-clubs and tear gas launchers—swaggered toward the crowd," he wrote in *Always Running*. "They mowed down anybody in their path. . . . Before I knew it, officers drove my face into the dirt." The brutal police action caused a violent reaction by some, who broke windows of some stores along Whittier Boulevard. By day's end, Laguna Park was filled not with antiwar demonstrators but with 1,500 police.

The statistics were as follows: damaged buildings, 158; destroyed buildings, 4; arrested, approximately 400; killed, 3. Most notable in this last category was Rubén Salazar, news director of KMEX television and a columnist and former reporter for the *Los Angeles Times*. Salazar, who attended the antiwar rally, witnessed much of the trouble and, with some colleagues, went to the Silver Dollar Café to sit out the most intense police violence. Instead, a tear-gas projectile fired into the café by a sheriff's deputy hit Salazar and killed him. "There was absolutely no misconduct on the part of the deputies involved," said Los Angeles County sheriff Peter Pitchess. The 16-day televised inquest into Salazar's death concluded, by a 4-3 vote, that the deputy had killed Salazar. Still, the Los Angeles district attorney refused to prosecute, and the U.S. Justice Department declined to act on community requests to investigate civil rights violations. Later it was revealed that a Los Angeles police provocateur had infiltrated the Moratorium leadership.

Subsequent Chicano demonstrations in Los Angeles and elsewhere in California were marred by violence, mainly instigated by police, but also by a nasty and omnipresent cadre of troublemakers among the peaceful protesters. One result of the excessive law enforcement activity was that the issue of police brutality rose to the top of local community concerns.

Laguna Park is now named for Rubén Salazar, whose death symbolized the tragic events of the day. And the August 29, 1970, National Chicano Moratorium has become a significant part of the history of the anti–Vietnam War movement.

RELATED ARTICLES

Activism; Civil Rights; Salazar, Rubén; Vietnam War.

FURTHER READING

Chávez, Ernesto. *"Mi Raza Primero!": Nationalism, Identity, and Insurgency in the Chicano Movement in Los Angeles, 1966–1978.* Berkeley: Univ. of Calif. Press, 2002.

Escobar, Edward J. "The Dialectics of Repression: The Los Angeles Police Department and the Chicano Movement, 1968–1971." *Journal of American History* 79 (March 1993): 1483–1514.

García, Mario T. *Memories of Chicano History: the Life and Narrative of Bert Corona.* Berkeley: Univ. of Calif. Press, 1994.

García, Mario T. *Rubén Salazar: Border Correspondent.* Berkeley: Univ. of Calif. Press, 1995.

Rodriguez, Luis J. *Always Running—La Vida Loca: Gang Days in L.A.* Willimantic, Conn.: Curbstone Press, 1993.

TOM MILLER

NATIONAL COUNCIL OF LA RAZA

The National Council of La Raza (NCLR), originally known as the Southwest Council of La Raza (SWCLR), was founded in February 1968. Since the 1980s the NCLR has focused on two main goals. The first objective is to provide support for capacity-building endeavors of Hispanic community-based organizations. The Council provides organizational assistance in management, governance, program operations, and resource development in urban and rural communities. The second objective is to support applied research, policy analysis, and advocacy on issues related to education, immigration, housing, health, employment, and civil rights enforcement. Additionally, the NCLR provides education on policies and programs affecting Hispanics.

The concept of "La Raza" grew out of the historic La Raza Unida Conference in El Paso, Texas, in October 1967, which was held to discuss the role of the federal government in Mexican American affairs. An organizing committee, elected at the La Raza Unida Conference, proceeded to structure the organization. Formed in Phoenix, Arizona, and with a satellite office in San Francisco, the Council began providing training and financial resources for local organizations to serve the Mexican American com-

munity. The Council's main focus was the coordination of political activities and involvement in civic organizations to reduce poverty and discrimination.

The initial funding for the NCLR came from the Ford Foundation. From fall 1967 to spring 1968, Herman Gallegos, Ernesto Galarza, and Julian Samora worked on developing the organizational structure and in February 1968 incorporated the entity as the Southwest Council of La Raza. By June 1968 the SWCLR received its first grant from the Ford Foundation in the amount of $630,000 to support local activities, and it began working at the local level to effect political change. The SWCLR contributed to funding the Mexican American Legal Defense and Educational Fund (MALDEF) and the Southwest Voter Registration Education Project (SVREP). These organizations were actively involved in various legal battles to protect the civil rights of Mexican Americans and to increase political participation in the electoral process.

New legislation enacted by Congress caused the SWCLR to further reorganize. The Tax Reform Act of 1969 included significant provisions affecting the types of activities philanthropic organizations could fund. As a result of this law, the SWCLR was unable to utilize funds for political action groups and voter registration drives. Thus the focus was changed from political organizing to community economic development. Further, the SWCLR became a private, nonprofit, and politically unaffiliated national Hispanic organization. Although its main efforts were concentrated in Arizona, California, Colorado, New Mexico, and Texas, it opened its National Services Office in Washington, D.C., in 1970 and gradually adopted a national focus. Herman Gallegos was the first executive director and Moclavio Barraza was appointed chairman of the board of directors. In July 1969 Gallegos and Humberto "Bert" Corona, board of directors member, had resigned in protest of the organization's restructuring. Henry Santiestevan became the second president and executive director. The Ford Foundation contributed $1,353,700 for a two-year period.

From 1971 until 1974 the SWCLR underwent several reforms. Following a recommendation of the Ford Foundation, the SWCLR reorganized as the National Council of La Raza in January 1973. On June 8, 1974, Raúl Yzaguirre was appointed the new national director. He replaced previous staff with handpicked individuals from his research consultancy firm, and was the president and CEO (chief executive officer) of the NCLR for over 25 years.

The original vision of the NCLR was to facilitate and advocate for the integration of Mexican Americans into mainstream society, to coordinate activities, and disseminate information. Under the direction of Yzaguirre, the organization focused on fund-raising and economic development. In 1974 it, along with the Mexican American Unity Council (MAUC) from San Antonio, helped to form the Association of Western Spanish Speaking Community Development Organizations. The NCLR was well established in Washington, D.C., by 1976. During the presidential administration of Jimmy Carter, it received funding from the federal government, and in 1977 federal funds constituted the bulk of the Council's revenue.

In 1978 the NCLR held its first national conference in Washington, D.C. That same year, the NCLR underwent a second major reorganization. It changed from being a community-based entity to a corporate structure.

A prominent Hispanic organization, the NCLR has over 270 affiliates in 40 states, Puerto Rico, and the District of Columbia. In addition, it has a na-tional membership of 30,000 groups and individuals. Currently, the Council has field offices in Los Angeles, Phoenix, Chicago, San Antonio, and San Juan, Puerto Rico. These offices provide services to affiliates and local organizations working on health, education, leadership, and community development.

The NCLR's policy and programs promote economic mobility and equality of opportunity for Hispanics in the United States. In addition, the organization conducts research on such topics as population demographics, civil rights, economic mobility, education, farmworkers, foreign policy, health, housing and economic development, immigration, leadership development, social security reform, and welfare reform. The NCLR has published over 80 significant congressional testimonies, research and policy reports, handbooks, training and other manuals, statistical analyses, fact sheets, issue updates, and selected speeches on a wide range of issues in the last 25 years. Publications include *Latino Community Cardiovascular Disease Prevention and Outreach Initiative: Background Report* (1996); *Untapped Potential: A Look at Hispanic Women in the U.S.* (1996); *Locked Out: Hispanic Underrepresentation in Federally-Assisted Housing*

Four businessmen hold an oversized $3.6 million check, donated to the National Council of La Raza, Austin, Texas.

Programs (1997); *State of Hispanic America 1998: Latino Education, Status and Prospects* (1998); *Beyond Ellis Island: Latino Immigration to the United States* (1999); *The Latino Vote in the '90s* (1999); *The Mainstream of Hate: A Report on Latinos and Harassment, Hate Violence, and Law Enforcement Abuse in the '90s* (1999); *Moving up the Economic Ladder: Latino Workers and the Nation's Future Prosperity* (2000); *U.S. Latino Children: A Status Report* (2000); *Testimony on Election Reform* (2001); *Welfare Reform Implementation in Puerto Rico: A Status Report* (2001); *Testimony on Drug Sentencing and its Effects on the Latino Community* (2002); and *Testimony on Terrorism, Immigration, and Civil Rights* (2002). The NCLR also publishes a quarterly newsletter and holds an annual conference to disseminate public information.

The overarching goal of the Council is to influence "macro-level" national policy to help Hispanics move out of poverty and into the nation's economic mainstream. Since a historic meeting in 1980 with President Ronald Reagan, Vice President George Bush, White House Chief of Staff James Baker, and other top administration officials, the NCLR has maintained national credibility as an organization of Hispanics from various Latin American nationalities pursuing economic integration. The organization's wide affiliation with the private sector, foundations, and government facilitates its ability to carry out its projects and objectives.

RELATED ARTICLES

Galarza, Ernesto; Politics, Mexican American; Yzaguirre, Raúl.

FURTHER READING

Fisher, Maria, and Sonia M. Pérez. *Latino Education: Status and Prospects.* Washington, D.C.: Nat. Council of La Raza, 1998.

Gomez-Quinonez, Juan. *Chicano Politics: Reality and Promise, 1940–1990.* Albuquerque: Univ. of N.Mex. Press, 1990.

National Council of La Raza. *The Road to Equality: 25 Years of Commitment.* Washington, D.C., 1993.

National Council of La Raza. *National Council of La Raza: Home-to-Own Program.* Washington, D.C., 1996.

Njus, Jonathan. *Burden or Relief?: The Impact of Tax Policy on Hispanic Working Families.* Washington, D.C.: Nat. Council of La Raza, 1997.

Pérez, Sonia M. *Moving from the Margins: Puerto Rican Young Men and Family Poverty.* Washington, D.C.: Nat. Council of La Raza, 1993.

Sullivan, Kathleen M., and Cecilia Muñoz. *Racing toward "Big Brother": Computer Verification, National ID Cards, and Immigration Control.* Washington, D.C.: Nat. Council of La Raza, 1995.

SELECTED WEB SITE

National Council of La Raza Official Website. http://www.nclr.org/

ARCELA NUÑEZ-ALVAREZ

NATIONAL HISPANIC MEDIA COALITION

Since its 1986 founding, the National Hispanic Media Coalition (NHMC) has influentially advocated for the U.S media industry's increased engagement with the country's Latino population. Focusing on television, radio, and film, the NHMC has called attention to allegedly marginalizing effects of industry practices on Latino industry employees (including actors and screenwriters) and on Latino consumers of media. To this end, the NHMC has used a variety of tactics, including dialogue with industry executives, the publication of reports evaluating industry efforts at hiring and programming diversification, petitions to the FCC (Federal Communications Commission) requesting the revocation of certain stations' television and radio broadcasting licenses, boycotts of selected programming, and street protests.

A not-for-profit umbrella organization of over 50 Latino advocacy groups with offices in many of the country's largest Latino communities, including Los Angeles (its headquarters), New York City, Chicago and San Antonio, Texas, the NHMC has worked with different Latino groups, while steadfastly arguing that all Latino groups in the United States experience similar forms of misrepresentation and exclusion by the media industry. The Coalition, aware of the importance of concerted action to effecting changes within the industry, has sought alliances with Latino and non-Latino advocacy groups alike, including the National Council of La Raza (NCLR), the National Association for the Advancement of Colored People (NAACP), and the National Asian Pacific American Legal Consortium (NAPALC).

The NHMC has viewed the low numbers of Latino employees at all levels of media production as the root cause of what many see as the industry's apparent tendencies to perpetuate stereotypes about Latinos and to omit Latinos and issues important to Latinos from their productions. One factor spurring the NHMC's 1986 founding was the sale of the Spanish International Network (SIN)—which since 1961 had dominated the U.S. Spanish-language television market—by Mexican owner Emilio Azcarraga to Hallmark, Inc. Hallmark renamed the network Univisión. Critics of the sale, the NHMC founders were pleased with Azcarraga's departure but concerned that, without U.S. Latino ownership, Univisión's productions would not reflect adequately the needs of the U.S. Latino community. The NHMC has demonstrated ambivalence toward Latin America–based Spanish-language media groups, criticizing their historical control over programming aimed at U.S. Latinos. In 1992 the Coalition unsuccessfully filed suit against the FCC to protest their approval of the sale of Univisión to a group of investors that included Azcarraga, on the grounds that Hispanics in the United States are better suited to advance the image and employment of Hispanics in the media than are foreigners. However, the NHMC has not turned a blind eye to U.S. Latino media groups. For example, it has taken legal action against Spanish-language radio stations for airing programs with excessive vulgar content.

NHMC efforts to compel English-language media groups to present Latinos in a more balanced light have met considerable resistance. In general, these groups have not perceived sufficient economic incentives to warrant changes. Not until the year 2000 were Memoranda of Understanding signed between the NHMC and ABC (American Broadcasting Co.), CBS (Columbia Broadcasting System), NBC (National Broadcasting Corp.), and FOX, stipulating hiring and programming diversification plans. In 2003, however, the NHMC reported that all major networks had begun to make significant advances in these areas.

RELATED ARTICLES

Film; Journalism; Radio; Television.

FURTHER READING

BOOKS

Rodríguez, América. *Making Latino News: Race, Language, Class.* Thousand Oaks, Calif.: Sage Pubns., 1999.

Rodríguez, Clara E., ed. *Latin Looks: Images of Latinas and Latinos in the U.S. Media.* Boulder, Colo.: Westview Press, 1997.

SELECTED WEB SITES

National Hispanic Media Coalition. www.nhmc.org

ADRIAN ALTHOFF

NATIONAL PUERTO RICAN COALITION

In 1977 a select group of Puerto Rican community leaders met in Washington, D.C., at the invitation of the U.S. Commission on Civil Rights, to discuss the future of Puerto Ricans in the United States and Puerto Rico. Emerging from this meeting was the agreement to institute an organization that would represent the interest of the Puerto Rican community before politicians and policymakers. The result was the creation, in that year, of the National Puerto Rican Coalition, Inc. (NPRC). Located in Washington, D.C., the NPRC is a nonprofit organization dedicated to the development of public policy issues central to the Puerto Rican community.

Since its inception, the NPRC has had an impressive record of achievement as the foremost national Puerto Rican advocacy and policy organization. Its accomplishments include the development of a national public policy agenda, the preparation of reports concerning the impact of legislative changes on the welfare of the Puerto Rican community, and the creation of an educational policy program for the development of student leadership. Known as the Puerto Rican/Latino Youth Leadership Development Initiative, the educational policy program was designed to encourage the participation of Puerto Rican and Latino and Latina students by offering fellowships and workshops in areas of public policy and political affairs. More recently the Coalition has announced a joint venture with Mortgage Bankers Association (MBA) in an effort to increase Latino and Latina home ownership.

The NPRC also produces various publications, among them the NPRC Reports and *Adelante,* a student newsletter. Through its publications, the Coalition has been able to provide relevant pubic policy and community information to a network of hundreds of Puerto Rican community-based organizations. Included among their reports was an important article entitled "Fighting Back: Puerto Ricans Respond to the AIDS Epidemic," which was devoted to the rise of HIV (human immunodeficiency virus) within the Puerto Rican community.

Furthering their commitment to Puerto Rican awareness, representatives from the NPRC organized the first National Puerto Rican Affirmation Day. Held on March 29, 1996, the event drew an estimated 7,000 people to Washington, D.C., to commemorate Puerto Rican war veterans and to bring awareness to Puerto Rican public policy issues. The NPRC also participated in the National Day of Solidarity with the People of Vieques, contesting the United States role in the bombing of Vieques, Puerto Rico.

Today the NPRC is recognized as a world leader within the Puerto Rican community. Through its commitment to community work and interaction with numerous associations and institutions, the NPRC now represents the interest of 7 million Puerto Ricans, by way of a network of over 1,000 community-based organizations. In the words of the Coalition, "Our work is dedicated to building the capacity of local leadership to develop strategic action plans; utilize their collective strengths and to address issues . . . we are certain will make a positive contribution to our community and society."

Elected in 1995, Manuel Mirabel currently serves as the president of the National Puerto Rican Coalition as well as chair of the board of directors of the Hispanic Association for Corporate Responsibility (HACR), which is the leading national Hispanic leadership coalition addressing issues of corporate responsibility.

RELATED ARTICLES

Politics, Puerto Rican; Puerto Ricans on the Mainland.

FURTHER READING

Hernández, José. *Conquered Peoples in America*. Dubuque, Iowa: Kendall Hunt, 1994.

SELECTED WEB SITE

National Puerto Rican Coalition.
   http://www.bateylink.org/about.htm

BRIAN MONTES

NATIVE AMERICANS. *See* INDIGENOUS HERITAGE.

NATIVISM

A form of racism directed at ethnic immigrant groups, nativism is a social phenomenon that has been practiced in the United States since the earliest days of the republic. The targeted groups are usually very recent immigrants, whose entry into the United States coincides with some kind of cultural change or economic decline (such as a recession) in the United States. To explain the economic or social imbalances taking place, nativists will use the immigrant group as a convenient scapegoat to explain to the American people that the solution to the problem is very simple: reduce or stop the immigration of the group in question and there will be a gradual return to the status quo.

American nativism has been practiced more often—although not exclusively—by people of European descent. It is regarded by some historians as a cyclical phenomenon, variously directed toward Asians, eastern Europeans, Catholics, Jews, Mexicans, Germans, Puerto Ricans, Central Americans, and Cubans. In the United States the first major nativist movement was manifested in the late 19th century against German and French immigrants from Europe. The Alien and Sedition Acts of 1798 gave the president of the United States authority to banish or imprison any foreigners deemed to be a threat to the U.S. government.

The Irish Potato Famine of 1846 led to an unprecedented level of immigration from Ireland to the United States. At the same time, agricultural famine and political upheaval in Germany resulted in increased emigration of Germans seeking to create a new life for themselves in America. The huge influx of immigrants arriving at eastern seaports caused consternation among many Americans, which found expression in the American Party.

More popularly known as the Know-Nothing Party, this strongly anti-immigrant organization came into prominence in the late 1840s and 1850s. The Know-Nothings, in addition to opposing the massive migration of German and Irish immigrants from Europe, were virulently anti-Catholic, the native religion of many of the arriving immigrants. Even Millard Fillmore (U.S. president from 1850 to 1853) joined their ranks. However, common sense prevailed, and when the Know-Nothings nominated Fillmore for president in 1956, he carried only one state, Maryland, losing by a landslide to the Democratic candidate, James Buchanan.

The annexation of Texas (1844) and the Mexican War with America (1846–1848) led to significant demographic changes for the United States. In accordance with the Treaty of Guadalupe Hidalgo, signed on February 2, 1848, and ending all hostilities between Mexico and the United States, Mexico handed over to the United States 525,000 square miles (1.36 million sq km) of land, including the present-day states of Arizona, California, Colorado, Montana, Nevada, New Mexico, Texas, and Utah. By provisions of the treaty, the 82,500 Mexican citizens living in the annexed territories were offered American citizenship and full protection of the law. Article XI, section 21 of California's 1849 constitution reflected the treaty's guarantee that the former Mexican citizens were to be permitted to maintain their Spanish language and participate fully as citizens through bilingual publication of statutes and regulations.

However, the new legislators of California came to regard the Spanish-speaking population and their culture as something foreign and proceeded to ignore the state constitution's protective provisions. In 1879 this guarantee was officially rescinded from the constitution, and documents relating to elections were no longer published in Spanish. Then, in 1894, the Mexican American population was further restricted when an English literacy requirement was adopted as a state constitutional amendment. This provision excluded from the electoral process any Mexican Californian male who could not read in English or write his name. This anti-immigrant intent was even written into the California election laws. Section 5567 of the California Elections Code, as adopted in 1941, required that elections be conducted in the English language and prohibited election officials from speaking any language other than English while on duty at the polling stations.

Bearing a strong resemblance to nativism, such political actions against Mexican Americans in California and Texas were commonplace for the better part of the next century, and fair political representation of Hispanics did not become a reality until the 1960s. The literacy law remained on the books in California until it was challenged in the California courts. In the landmark court case *Castro* v. *State of California,* a California court found that "fear and hatred played a significant role" in the legislature's passage of the English literacy voting requirement.

American politicians have often turned waves of nativist feeling to political advantage, voting for anti-immigrant legislation to appease a fearful and anxious native population. The Chinese Exclusion Act of 1882, which led directly to a reduction in the immigration of Chinese laborers, was a prime example of this during the 19th century. Large numbers of Chinese had come to the United States in response to the need for inexpensive labor, especially in the construction of the transcontinental railroad. However,

competition between Chinese laborers and American workers led to a growing nativist movement, resulting in the Chinese Exclusion Act of May 6, 1882, in which Congress suspended immigration of Chinese laborers for ten years. With the conclusion of the 1907 Gentlemen's Agreement between Japan and the United States, the flow of Japanese laborers into the United States was also severely restricted.

The restriction of Asian labor, however, came at a very inconvenient time. The American economy was starting to evolve into a powerful dynamo with a strong need for foreign labor. To fill this ever-growing need, American industries looked southward to Mexico. Yet, although the need for Mexican labor was very obvious to American industry, some of the most virulent anti-immigrant sentiment during the 20th century would be directed toward Mexican migrants.

In 1894 the Immigration Restriction League (IRL) was founded by a group of Boston lawyers and professors, who had become alarmed by the large influx of immigrants from foreign countries. The IRL and other organizations played a role in getting Congress to pass a literacy bill in 1897, but President Grover Cleveland vetoed the bill.

It was during the first decade of the 20th century that the U.S. Department of Commerce started to monitor the entry of immigrants along the Mexican and Canadian borders. Concerns had developed that criminal elements within the immigrant groups might cause problems in the United States. One of the most potent influences on this sentiment was the assassination of President William McKinley on September 6, 1901, by a Polish anarchist. By 1908, Customs officers stationed at the border were filling out a Report of Inspection for each immigrant crossing the southern border. Among the many questions each immigrant was asked was whether he or she was a polygamist, an anarchist, or a former prison inmate.

Notwithstanding the tightened immigration policy, Mexican migration north continued to occur. With the turn of the century, American companies began a vigorous campaign to recruit Mexican laborers to work in the railroad, construction, and agricultural industries. The ten-year Mexican Revolution, starting in 1910, swept from one corner of Mexico to the other, taking the lives of a million and a half Mexicans. Another million Mexican nationals fled northward into the United States to seek both work and refuge.

In April 1917 the United States entered World War I with its declaration of war on Germany. With American soldiers marching off to fight, the labor needs of the business sector became even more acute, and more Mexican laborers were invited to help relieve the shortage. However, in the first year of the war, American xenophobia played into the hands of nativists.

Worried about a huge influx of refugees from central and eastern Europe following the end of the war, nativists convinced American politicians to pass the Immigration Act of 1917. Before this act was passed, almost no restrictions were in effect against Mexicans, who could cross the border at will. After the act was signed, however, prospective immigrants—including Mexicans—had to pay a head tax of eight dollars. The act also imposed a literacy test on immigrants over the age of 16. During the first months after the law's enactment, 5,745 Mexicans were turned away at the border for being unwilling or unable to pay the head tax.

Although the nativist intent was clearly aimed at all immigrant groups, including Mexicans, the U.S. Labor Department, responding to the pressure of the railroad and agricultural industries, asked Congress in May 1917 to waive the literacy and head taxes for Mexican agricultural workers. In 1918, the year World War I ended, the waiver was extended to allow the importation of Mexicans to work on railroads, in coal mines, and in government construction work. The waiver of the Immigration Act lasted from May 1917 until May 1921 and permitted the entry of some 73,000 temporary workers into the United States through 1923.

The Great Depression of the 1930s further inflamed nativist sentiments. With 13 million Americans out of work by 1933, many people came to believe that immigrants were stealing the jobs of Americans. In order to appease an uneasy and fearful population, government officials began a systematic eviction of Mexicans and Mexican Americans from U.S. soil. Massive and indiscriminate raids conducted by immigration officials led to the forced removal of at least half a million Mexicans from the United States between 1930 and 1939.

Two decades later, in 1954, when the migration of undocumented Mexicans across the border reached unprecedented levels, a national reaction against illegal immigration led to "Operation Wetback." Within a three-year period, it is believed that the Immigra-tion and Naturalization Service (INS) forcibly removed and returned to Mexico more than a million immigrants.

In 1980 the mass exodus of Cuban refugees fired up nativist sentiments in the Miami area. The "Mariel boat lift," as it was called, brought at least 125,000 Spanish-speaking individuals to southern Florida. This, in turn, led to the 1980 antibilingual referendum in Miami, which was passed by 59 percent of the vote. Although this measure hoped to make southern Florida a less hospitable place for Latinos, in the long run it failed, since large numbers of Cubans continued to make their way to Miami to live and prosper.

One of the most recent manifestations of nativism took place in California in 1994. Hispanics had increased from 12 percent of the population in 1970 to 26 percent in 1990. The large influx of Spanish-speaking people moving into all parts of the state aroused the fears of several nativist groups, in particular the Federation for American Immigration Reform (FAIR). That coupled with the prolonged recession of the early 1990s probably contributed to the anti-immigrant sentiment leading to the ballot initiative Proposition 187. Known as the "Save Our State Initiative," it would deny public social services, publicly funded health care, and public education to people who were suspected of being illegal immigrants. The proponents of Proposition 187 convinced many California voters that the state had become a welfare magnet for illegal aliens who cost California taxpayers more than $5 billion a year. Opponents of the initiative claimed that nativists were greatly exaggerating the true figures. However, when the final tally was counted, the controversial proposal was approved by 59 percent of California voters in November 1994. A federal district court judge later ruled that the primary provisions of the law were unconstitutional and invalidated some of its provisions.

Similar initiatives have been brought before the voting public in other states, with mixed results. But to immigrant activists the Illegal Immigration Reform and Immigrant Responsibility Act of 1996, signed into law on September 30, 1996, contained many draconian measures aimed at controlling illegal immigration and fulfilling some of the objectives of nativist groups who advocated similar legislation.

The terrorist attacks of September 11, 2001, have contributed to renewed anti-immigrant reaction, chiefly targeting Muslims from a wide variety of

Middle Eastern and Asian nations. As America ponders new restrictions on immigration, it is clear to most analysts that Latin Americans will suffer as much as any other immigrant group with the passing of such legislation.

RELATED ARTICLES

Discrimination; Politics, Latino.

FURTHER READING

Alarcón, Rafael. *Proposition 187: An Effective Measure to Deter Undocumented Migration to California? A Report.* San Francisco: Multicultural Education, Training and Advocacy, 1994.

Balderrama, Francisco E., and Raymond Rodríguez. *Decade of Betrayal: Mexican Repatriation in the 1930s.* Albuquerque: Univ. of N.Mex. Press, 1995.

Chinea, Jorge L. "Ethnic Prejudice and Anti-Immigrant Policies in Times of Economic Stress: Mexican Repatriation from the United States, 1929–1939." *East Wind/West Wind* (Winter 1996): 9–13, 16.

Cornelius, Wayne A. *America in the Era of Limits: Migrants, Nativists, and the Future of U.S.-Mexican Relations.* La Jolla, Calif.: Ctr. for U.S.-Mexican Studies, Univ. of Calif. at San Diego, 1982.

García, Juan Ramon. *Operation Wetback: The Mass Deportation of Mexican Undocumented Workers in 1954.* Westport, Conn.: Greenwood Press, 1980.

Hoffman, Abraham. *Unwanted Mexican Americans in the Great Depression: Repatriation Pressures, 1929–1939.* Tucson: Univ. of Ariz. Press, 1974.

Perea, Juan F., ed. *Immigrants Out! The New Nativism and the Anti-Immigrant Impulse in the United States.* New York: N.Y. Univ. Press, 1997.

Samora, Julian. *Los Mojados: The Wetback Story.* Notre Dame, Ind.: Univ. of Notre Dame Press, 1971.

JOHN P. SCHMAL

NAVA, GREGORY

Born: April 10, 1949; San Diego, California

Gregory Nava is one of the most successful Latino filmmakers of his time. Born in 1949 to parents of Mexican and Basque ancestry, Nava grew up in the multicultural milieu of San Diego, California, and was exposed to cultural diversity at a young age. He proved his cultural affinity for Latino subjects when as a film student at the University of California at Los Angeles (UCLA), he wrote, produced, and directed his first award-winning film, *The Journal of Diego Rodriguez Silva.*

Encouraged by the film's being named "Best Dramatic Film" at the National Student Film Festival, Nava went on to produce many other lauded works that would secure him a place in Latino film history. His 1973 film, *The Confessions of Aman,* earned broad attention and the "Best Feature" accolade at the Chicago International Film Festival. Yet it was not until the release of *El Norte* (1984), a low-budget film about the struggle of Guatemalan peasants trying to make it in the United States, that Nava received his most significant acclaim. A mix of endearing characters, a clear story line, and a compelling visual style, the film won over audiences in U.S. theaters while debates raged in the streets over the U.S. role in Central America. The film was a huge success and brought attention both to Nava and the plight of Central American refugees in the United States. As an independent film, cowritten by Nava's wife, Anna Thomas, *El Norte* faced significant obstacles during its production. Not the least of these was the kidnapping of the crew's film and its production manager while the project was on location in Mexico. After ransoming back both, the production crew relocated to Los Angeles. Such hardships were rewarded when the movie received a standing ovation at the Telluride Film Festival and an Oscar nomination for best screenplay.

Following the success of *El Norte,* Nava went on to produce other feature films, but the transition from independent filmmaker to Hollywood director proved difficult and he stumbled along the way. Nava's first Hollywood-produced feature film, *A Time of Destiny* (1988) starring William Hurt and Timothy Hutton, was referred to as "overblown" by one critic, and it fell far short of the success enjoyed by *El Norte.* In 1995 he wrote and directed *My Family, Mi Familia,* the saga of a Mexican American family in Los Angeles. Nava achieved commercial success with *Selena* (1997), the true-life story of the Tejano pop star Selena, starring Jennifer Lopez. The film did not receive the critical praise awarded *El Norte,* but *Selena* was nonetheless important because of its success in the Hollywood marketplace. The overtly commercial film was a rare "crossover" success. Nava then went on to direct Halle Berry, Lela Rochon, and Vivica A. Fox in *Why Do Fools Fall in Love?* (1998). He remains one of the few Latino directors to work both in both Latino and mainstream pictures—no small feat. Nava's most recent feature film accomplishment came when the screenplay for *Frida,* the epic story of the Mexican artist Frida Kahlo starring Selma Hayek, was awarded an Oscar at the 2002 Academy Awards.

Continually interested in the diverse, multicultural society that is the United States, Nava went on to create the public television series *American Family,* which debuted on PBS stations in 2002. Starring Edward James Olmos as a Mexican American patriarch in East Los Angeles, the television series traces the many joys and hardships faced by his children and grandchildren as people of color living in the United States. The series received a cool reception from public television programmers who questioned *American Family*'s ability to pull in viewers and by others in the system who objected to the program's high cost—by public television standards, and it was cancelled in 2004.

RELATED ARTICLES

Film; Television.

FURTHER READING

Reyes, Luis, and Peter Rubie. *Hispanics in Hollywood: A Celebration of 100 Years in Film and Television.* Hollywood: Lone Eagle Publ., 2000.

Rosen, David. "Crossover: Hispanic Specialty Films in the U.S. Movie Marketplace." In *Chicanos and Film: Representation and Resistance.* Ed. by Chon Noriega. Minneapolis: Univ. of Minn. Press, 1992.

JOSEPH TOVARES

NAVIDAD

Navidad is Spanish for Christmas, the celebration of the nativity of Jesus Christ. Most of the customs and traditions of Christmas have pagan roots and have little to do with the Western Christian belief that the day is the date on which Mary gave birth to Jesus Christ. For the ancient agrarian peoples of the Northern Hemisphere, this time of the year had always been an occasion of festivity, rejoicing, excess, and thanksgiving as they celebrated the lengthening of daylight following the winter solstice around December 22. For those societies that lived close to the soil, the return of the sun not only represented the rebirth of the powerful sun god but also the promises of survival and restoration of light and life, since nature would soon regain power and planting could begin. The date of December 25 probably originated with the pagan celebration of the birthday of the pre-Zarathustrian Persian sun god Mithra. The celebration of this pagan divinity also became widespread during the 2d and the 4th centuries in the Roman Empire, where it was called the Birthday of the Unconquered Sun, Natalis Solis Invicti. This midwinter festival also encompassed the presiding Saturnalia, in honor of the god of agriculture and

fertility, Saturn, from December 17 to 23, and was followed by Kalends, from January 1 to 5, their New Year celebration. The Roman carnival was characterized by home decoration with greenery, feasting, gift giving and receiving, drinking of liquor, singing, processions, fortune telling, sexual license, gambling, good wishes for the next year, and promises of personal transformation as the world was being renovated by the return of the power of the sun.

Until the 2d century, Christians did not consider it relevant to know the exact date of the birth of Jesus Christ. The period of the year and the exact year when Christ was born, as well as his place of birth, are still subjects of speculation and controversy among scholars. Church documents suggest that the celebration of Christian Christmas itself began around 336 C.E., in a time when the early Christian church struggled to expand and to become established as a legitimate faith. Between 354 and 360, under the authority of Pope Liberius, Christian authorities agreed on the night of December 24–25 as the date for the Feast of Jesus Christ's Nativity. Scholars propose that Christian fathers, understanding the powerful hold the midwinter Mithraic festival of the Unconquered Sun had on pagan worshipers, and in their efforts to turn sun worshipers into worshipers of the creator of the sun, saw fit to place the major festivity of the church at a time of the year when the most celebrated pagan festivals took place. Originally the Christian celebration was called the Birthday of the Lord, Dies Natalis Domini.

Documents from the Middle Ages reveal that the celebration was often viewed as offensive although it had already become an important Christian religious holiday. Even after Christianity had become a firmly rooted religion, some devout people condemned the pagan customs and moral attitudes associated with the Roman Saturnalia and Kalends that had been transferred into the Christian festivity and that persisted despite the rejection of these celebrations and customs by the Roman Catholic authorities. Some scholars propose that regardless of the complaints, in 567, church leaders, remembering that it was easier to appropriate than to fight the popular inclination to celebrate, expanded Christmas from December 25 to January 5, turning it into a period that became the Twelve Days of Christmas, or Christmastide. During this time, on New Year's Day, the nobility exchanged gifts and gave gifts to their kings as a way to show prestige; peasants offered gifts to their lords, and as a response the lords invited them to a Christmas feast. Historians agree that there are no records suggesting a gift exchange occurred on Christmas day. At the same time, religious observers who wished to follow the Bible verbatim opposed a celebration, during which gluttony and drinking were significant and cross-dressing was permitted, suggesting that it had nothing to do with Christian tradition. They argued that if the Gospels did not provide an exact date for the celebration of the event, it was a sign that God did not request the festivity be observed.

In the 16th century the Protestant Reformation started to be felt across Europe. As a result, Christian indulgence and excessive Christmas customs were more strongly condemned and there were efforts to abolish Christmas for being irreconcilable with the scripture. In England the sect of the Puritans lobbied for church reformation, to promote prayer and commitment to God, but the sect was opposed by high-ranking officials of the Church of England. By the mid-17th century the aim of the Puritan majority in the Parliament was no longer the reformation of the church but the abolition of the Christian festivity. Supporters of the event were declared enemies of the Christian faith by the Puritans. Eventually, under Oliver Cromwell, in 1647, the observance of the festivity was forbidden. Only in 1660 with the restoration of the monarchy by the Parliament, and the ascension of King Charles II to the throne were Christmas and previous holidays reestablished.

In the New World, in the colony of New England, from 1659 to 1681, Puritans legally banned the celebration; for many religious people in the colonies, the festivity became a meaningless, vulgar, and socially disturbing occasion. Other immigrants with different religious affiliations—Anglican, Lutheran, Mennonite, Roman Catholic—tended to approve of the festivity, but their observance was relatively simple. The first Christmas celebration by English settlers in the colonies had taken place in Jamestown, Virginia, in 1607, but some scholars propose that the first Christmas celebration in the territory, which would later be known as the United States, was actually presided over by Father Francisco López de Mendoza in St. Augustine, Florida, in 1565. Other scholars speculate that it might have already taken place in 1539, when troops of Spanish colonists camped over the winter season near the place that today is known as Tallahassee.

It was only during the 19th century, during the onset of the Industrial Revolution and the creation of the potbellied gift bringer Santa Claus that the Christmas celebration turned into the American sentimental and old-fashioned-looking tradition that is well known to the contemporary Christian and non-Christian observers of the festival. Scholars agree that the embellished construction of Christmas coincided with the emergence of middle-class sensibilities and values in an age of industrialized overproduction, that is, the growing cult of domesticity and motherhood and the discovery of childhood. Christmas was transformed into a capitalist family value; it was a modern-family-centered gift giving by parents to children that aimed at bringing consumerism and the idealized American nuclear family together. Few Latino Christmas traditions have been incorporated into the American customs associated with the celebration of Jesus Christ's birth. Scholars agree that though consistently and predominantly Catholic in its orientation, Latino Christmas celebration developed in accordance with the mixing and blending that has been a primordial element of Latin American cultures and identities since the discovery of the continent and the subsequent colonization by Spain, along with the contemporary Anglo-American political and cultural dominance in the continent. Thus the Latino Christmas has been an ongoing merging of Native American, African, and European elements, religions, and traditions.

But this complex process of amalgamation has often been an excruciating one for the colonized peoples. For Latinos in the United States and the rest of the Latin American continent, it has involved constant negotiation in the face of the Anglo-American geographical and cultural expansion. Scholars agree as well that, initially, for Catholic Latinos in the United States, the steady stream of Protestant Anglo-Americans colonists into their territory caused a high degree of anxiety. This was not only due to the threat the imposition of a new language and new political, legal, and educational systems represented to their political and cultural existence but also to Latinos' feelings of betraying their history, religion, cultural traditions, and identity that the clash, negotiation, and compromise with the invading culture often engendered. By now some Latinos have embraced Protestantism; the figure of Santa Claus and the Christmas tree have become an integral part of Latino Christmas tradition among the Latino communities in the United States and even in the rest of the Latin American countries.

In the United States, Latino celebrations, though different from family to family, include a Christmas Eve feast; midnight Christmas Mass; Misa de Gallo; and nativity scenes with Jesus, Mary, Joseph, the shepherds, and the Three Magi, *pesebres*. These remain important rituals for Cuban, Ecuadorian, Colombian, and Puerto Rican families. On December 12, Mexican Americans celebrate the day of the patron saint "The Mother of the Americas"—that is, the dark-skinned Holy Virgin Our Lady of Guadalupe, Nuestra Señora de Guadalupe, that embodies the blending of American Indian and European beliefs. Afterward, from December 16 through 24, Mexican American communities inaugurate the Christmas season either with the processions called *las posadas*—which commemorate the difficult journey of Mary and Joseph from Nazareth to Bethlehem looking for lodging—or by staging the miracle play *La Pastorela,* or *Los Pastores* (The Shepherds), the journey of the three shepherds following the star to Bethlehem to adore the child. These two folk dramas, which also combine indigenous and Christian rituals, have their roots in medieval Spain and were introduced in the New World by Spanish missioners in their effort to teach American Indians elements of the Christian religion. In some Mexican American and Puerto Rican families gift giving has remained a tradition reserved for January 6, Three Kings' Day, which it will be noted concludes the original Twelve Days of Christmas not preserved in the dominant Anglo-American practice. Puerto Ricans celebrate their *asaltos navideños* or *parrandas* (caroling block parties), which, on Christmas Eve and the Epiphany, can go through the night and into the next day when the *parranda* ends with a breakfast. Ideally, this breakfast consists of a *sopón,* a chicken and rice soup. *Parranda* musicians play Puerto Rican music, which is a blend of Afro-Caribbean music, sometimes making use of traditional instruments, such as guitars, the triangle, maracas, and *güiro*—made from a gourd.

When it comes to food, many Latino families have adopted the Anglo-American Christmas menu, but they combine it with traditional holy day food. Mexican Americans prepare rice, beans, and the Native American corn-based dish tamales, which are cooked in a communal effort called *la tamalada*. Mexican Americans attempt to pass on the commu-

© JIMMY DORANTES/LATIN FOCUS

Young girl ponders her gifts on Christmas morning.

nal tradition and the recipe from generation to generation even if the recipe has undergone slight modifications to satisfy changing tastes. Many Puerto Rican families get together to cook the time-consuming *pasteles,* a potato and meat pie wrapped in banana leaves; and Cubans feature both *lechón asado,* roasted pork—which is another family project—and *turrones,* special almond candies from Spain. Latino Christmas celebrations are hybrid practices that nonetheless preserve the uniqueness and richness of their specific cultures and heritages.

Latinos are the fastest-growing minority groups in the United States, and among many of these groups is the awareness that Christmas has become the religious expression of capitalistic consumerism. Some of them have become dissatisfied with the celebration; others have become sensitive to the expectations of consumer society that very often clash with the poverty, marginalization, and discrimination—the struggle to survive faced by many newly arrived Latino immigrants or second-, third-, and longer-generation Latinos who have settled in the United States. Nevertheless, for Latinos Christmas remains an important religious and spiritual celebration, a means of agency to contest oppressive discourses and to affirm the diversity of Latino identity in the United States in particular and in the Americas, in general. Latino Christmas is a complex celebration that confirms and affirms the perseverance, and the malleability, of Latinos' identities in their desire to corroborate their presence in the hemisphere, and to preserve the specificity of their particular identities and heritages in a process that has been taking place for many centuries and in which they have often been portrayed as irrevocably "other" with the resulting homogenization and negation of their specific identities, histories, and cultures.

RELATED ARTICLES

Holidays; Religion; Tres Reyes Magos.

FURTHER READING

Cubría, Jorge. *La navidad: Historias, leyendas, tradiciones y cuentos* (Christmas: Stories, Legends, Traditions, and Tales). Mexico: Edames, 1999.

Gulevich, Tanya. *Encyclopedia of Christmas and New Year's Celebrations.* 2d ed., rev. Detroit, Mich.: Omnographics, 2003.

Horsley, Richard, and James Tracy, eds. *Christmas Unwrapped: Consumerism, Christ, and Culture.* Harrisburg, Pa.: Trinity Press Int., 2001.

Kanellos, Nicolás. *Noche Buena: Hispanic American Christmas Stories.* Oxford: Oxford Univ. Press, 2000.

Menard, Valerie. *The Latino Holiday Book: From Cinco de Mayo to Día de los Muertos—the Celebrations and Traditions of Hispanic-Americans.* New York: Marlowe & Co., 2000.

Nissenbaum, Stephen. *The Battle for Christmas.* New York: Knopf, 1996.

Rodríguez, Pepe. *Mitos y ritos de la Navidad: Origen y significado de las celebraciones navideñas* (Christmas Myths and Rites: Origin and Meanings of Christmas Celebrations). Madrid: Ediciones Grupo Zeta, 1997.

LUZ ANGÉLICA KIRSCHNER

NERUDA, PABLO

Born: July 12, 1904; Parral, Chile
Died: September 23, 1973; Santiago, Chile

Neftalí Ricardo Basoalto was born in the small village of Parral, Chile, to a mother who taught school and a father who worked for the railroad. He adopted his pen name, Pablo Neruda (the surname after a Czech writer), for fear of his family's disapproval of having embarked on a poetic life. His early poetry was romantic in nature, but then it became more politically engaged as Neruda's interest and experience in world affairs developed. Neruda served as a diplomat in various parts of the world, including Burma, Java, Madrid, Mexico, and Paris. He witnessed the Spanish Civil War, visited and wrote about the Soviet Union, opposed the American invasion of Vietnam, and ran for president of Chile. Winning the Nobel Prize for literature in 1971 for, according to the Swedish committee, "a poetry that

HULTON/ARCHIVE BY GETTY IMAGES

The Chilean poet and activist Pablo Neruda, New York City, 1966.

with the action of an elemental force brings alive a continent's destiny and dreams," he was by then one of the most popular poets in the world (his oeuvre is translated into three dozen languages). His deepest connection was to the people of the Americas, including Latinos in the United States. Neruda died of cancer a few months after the coup d'état of General Augusto Pinochet in Santiago.

Neruda's first success was *Viente poemas de amor y una canción desperada* (*Twenty Love Poems and a Song of Despair*), which was published in 1924, when he was 19 years old. Starting with *Residencia en la tierra* (1933, 1935; *Residence on Earth*), his ideological stand becomes evident. The collection includes poems such as "Explico algunas cosas" ("I Explain a Few Things"), where Neruda chronicles the fall of Madrid to the Republican forces, and another one, "Oda a Frederico García Lorca" ("Ode to Federico García Lorca"), where he denounces the assassination of his friend the Andalusian poet and playwright.

Canto General (1950; *The General's Song*) is Neruda's masterpiece. In it he attempted an all-encompassing portrait of Latin America, from its mineral life, flora, and fauna, to a detailed chronicle of its human history, from before the time of the conquest in the 16th century to the hard labor of miners and laborers in the 20th. The volume includes the famous segment "Alturas de Macchu Picchu" (1945; "The

Heights of Macchu Picchu"), about the then recently discovered Inca ruins in Peru.

Some of the most moving, intimate poems Neruda wrote are part of *Los versos del capitán* (1952; *The Captain's Verses*), *Extravadaria* (1958), and *Isla Negra* (1964). In these collections he returned to a more domestic and existential, less public approach to literature. But he is perhaps best known for the countless odes he wrote to common objects that populate our life and to which we pay little attention: a sock, a watermelon, a dictionary, an artichoke, maize, and a movie theater.

Neruda's connection to Latinos has not been left unnoticed. In his work he often wrote about the United States, making a distinction between its people, to whom he felt connected (he adored Walt Whitman and portrayed himself as "the Whitman of the Hispanic world"), and its government, which he accused of conducting a misguided foreign policy (he described Richard Nixon as a murderer). One of his plays, *Fulgor y muerte de Joaquín Murieta, bandido chileno injusticiado en California el 23 de julio de 1853* (*Splendor and Death of Joaquín Murieta*, 1966), centered on the legendary 19th-century U.S. border outlaw, whom Neruda identified as one of the hundreds of Chileans engaged in the California gold rush. He also wrote about the Cuban revolution and the American colonization of Puerto Rico, topics that made him a cause célèbre among Chicanos during the civil rights era.

A number of American poets have translated Neruda (Robert Bly, W. S. Merwin, Mark Strand, James Wright, among others). Latinos such as Miguel Algarín of the Nuyorican Poets' Café, Martín Espada, and Gary Soto have also offered inspiring renditions of his poems and have even turned him into a protagonist in some of their own work. The following is a translation by Ilan Stavans of Neruda's poem "In Vietnam," from *The Poetry of Pablo Neruda* (2003):

And who made war?

It's been pounding since the day before yesterday.

I'm afraid.

It pounds like a stone
against the wall,
like thunder with blood,
like a dying mountain.
This is a world
I didn't make.

You didn't make it.
They made it.
Who threatens it with terrible fingers?
Who wants it decapitated?
Wasn't it about to come into being?
And who kills it now it is born?

The cyclist is afraid,
so is the architect.
The mother with a child and her breasts
hides in the mud.
This mother sleeps in the cave and suddenly,
war,
war arrives big,
arrives full of fire
and already dead,
dead
are the mother with her milk and her son.

They died in the mud.

Oh pain! From then
till now,
should one stay covered with mud
up to the temples,
singing and shooting? Holy God!
If only you had been told
before you lived, almost before you lived . . .
If at least
they had whispered it
to your relatives and nonrelatives,
children of love's laughter,
children of human sperm,
of that fragrance
in a new Monday and with a fresh shirt . . .
But they had to die so suddenly,
without ever knowing what it was all about!

They are the same ones
who come to kill us,
yes, the same ones
who come to burn us,
yes, the same ones,
the winners and the braggers,
the smiling ones who enjoyed so much
and took so much,
now
by air
they come, will come, they came,
to kill the world within us.

They have left a pool
made of father, mother, and child.
Let us look
in it,
look for our own blood and bones,
look for them in the mud of Vietnam,
look for them among so many other bones;
they're charred, they no longer belong to anyone
but to everyone,

our bones are burnt,
look for your death in that death,
because they are after you too,
and the fate they bring you is that selfsame mud.

RELATED ARTICLES

Literature, Latin American.

FURTHER READING

Bloom, Harold, ed. *Pablo Neruda.* New York: Chelsea House, 1989.

Feinstein, Adam. *Pablo Neruda: A Biography.* New York and Boston: Bloomsbury, 2004.

Guibert, Rita. *Seven Voices.* New York: Knopf, 1973.

Stavans, Ilan, ed. *The Poetry of Pablo Neruda.* New York: Farrar, Straus, 2003.

ILAN STAVANS

NEVADA

Known as the Sagebrush State, Nevada is the 7th largest state in total land area, but is only 35th in terms of population. The state was originally inhabited by several indigenous tribes, including the Shoshone, Paiute, and Pueblo Indians. As early as 1776, Spanish missionaries are believed to have explored the area while crossing the southern portion of the state on their way from Mexico to California. Early Spanish explorers named this region *Nevada,* a Spanish word meaning "snow-clad," a probable reference to the snowcapped Sierra Nevada Mountains.

The Las Vegas Valley was discovered in December 1829 by Rafael Rivera, a young Mexican scout, with Antonio Armijo. The Armijo party was attempting to discover a new trade route from New Mexico to Los Angeles, California. After the party had set up camp, Rivera went out into the desert to find water for the group. According to legend, he came to an oasis with an abundance of artesian springs. Rivera's discovery resulted in the "missing link" of what came to be known as the Old Spanish Trail. Because of the abundance of wild grasses in the area, the Spaniards soon began to refer to the valley as Las Vegas, the Spanish words for "the meadows." From that point on, Spanish traders, traveling to California, commonly used Las Vegas as a campground.

At the time of Rivera's discovery, the territory of Nevada was still part of Mexico. However, on February 2, 1848, as a result of the Treaty of Guadalupe Hidalgo, Mexico ceded a large portion of the southwestern United States, including all of present-day Nevada, to its northern neighbor. Once its mineral wealth was realized, Nevada was quickly admitted to the United States on October 31, 1864.

Under American jurisdiction Nevada's mineral wealth became a magnet for migrants from far and wide. The most prominent of the Latino groups to take part in the mining industry of Nevada were miners from the northwestern Mexican state of Sonora. It is believed that Ignacio Paredes, a miner from Sonora, was the first person to discover what later became the Comstock Mine near Virginia City. However, after Paredes prematurely abandoned the mine, other miners came along in 1859 and reopened it; it was named for one of its claimants, the Canadian-born Henry Comstock.

During the 1860s a group of Mexican prospectors established the Columbus Mining District, but eventually they lost control of the district to Anglo-Americans. It is believed that Sonora miners introduced the *batea* (pan) that was used in placer mining. The Nevada State Census of 1875 counted 311 Hispanic individuals, with 34 percent of the residents living in Storey County, the jurisdiction containing Virginia City. A large portion of the Latinos tallied in the 1875 census had come from the American states of California, New Mexico, and Texas, while others came from Mexico, Chile, Spain, and Portugal. Most of the adult Hispanic males were employed as mule packers, miners, and laborers.

The completion of the San Pedro, Los Angeles, and Salt Lake Railroad, linking Salt Lake City, Utah, with Los Angeles in 1905, gave birth to Las Vegas as a railroad town. The construction of the railroads in the area created a need for Mexican laborers, and, as a result, Latinos were among the earliest residents of the nascent city of Las Vegas. For a quarter of a century, the railroad became the primary industry of the Las Vegas area, employing thousands of Mexican immigrants on track-maintenance crews.

The Federal Census of 1970 enumerated 27,142 "persons of Spanish language" in Nevada, a group that represented 5.6 percent of the state's population. It was during the early 1970s that Hispanic organizations began advocating for the rights and benefits of Latinos living in Nevada. Concerned about racism directed against Latinos, the Nevada Association of Latin Americans (NALA) filed a complaint against the Clark County Economic Opportunity Board, charging that Hispanics were not receiving equal benefits from government programs.

PLATE 1 • A family is reunited in San Pedro, California, following a U.S. Coast Guardsman's six-month deployment to the Persian Gulf, April 9, 2002.

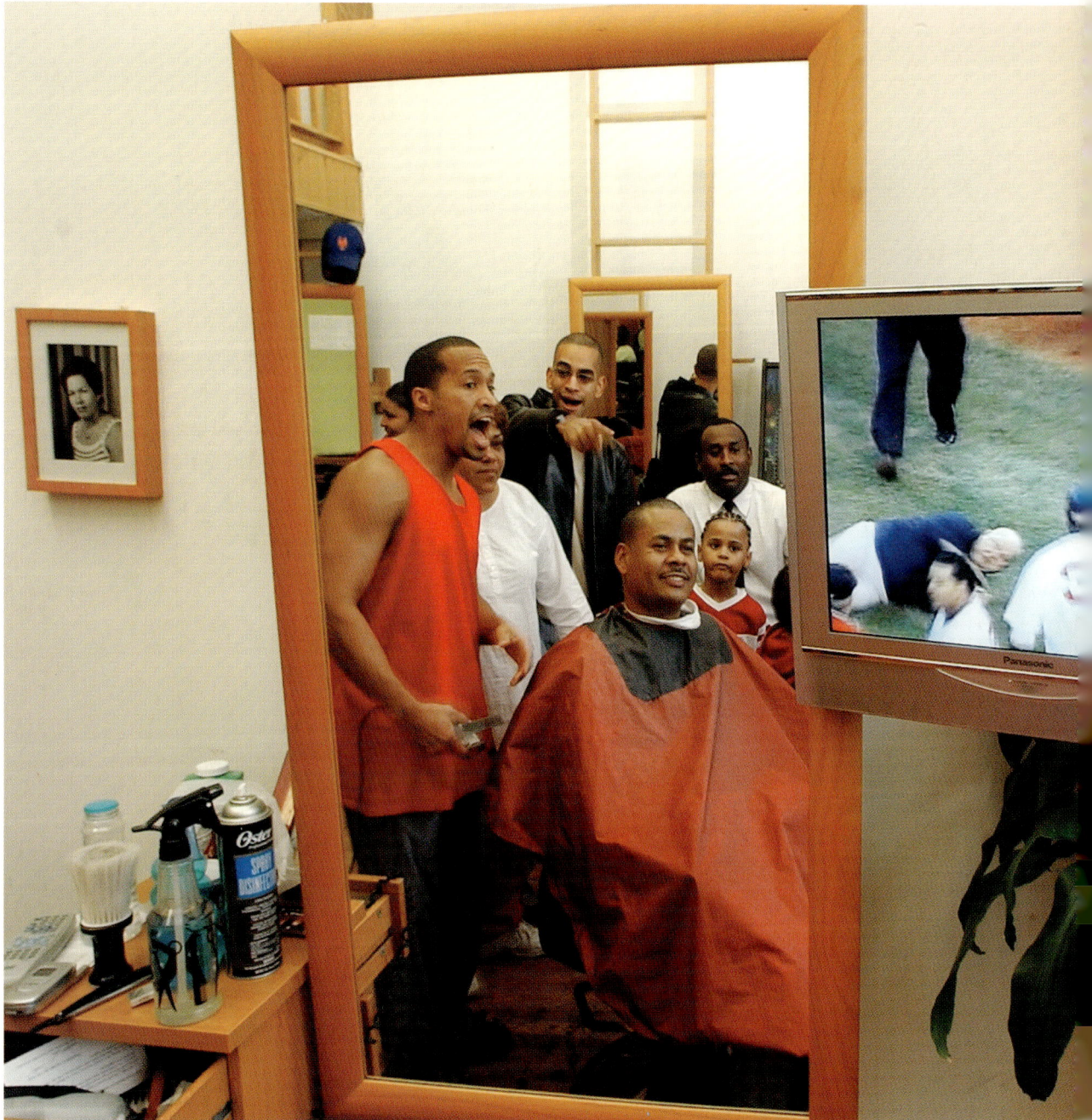

PLATE 2 • In a Dominican barbershop in New York City's Washington Heights neighborhood, watching Boston Red Sox pitcher Pedro Martinez, also Dominican, in an altercation with New York Yankees' bench coach Don Zimmer, 2003.

© KEN GIGER / DALLAS MORNING NEWS / KRT

PLATE 3 • U.S. Olympic swimmer Pablo Morales after winning the gold medal in the mens' 100-meter butterfly at the XXV Summer Olympics, Barcelona, Spain (1993).

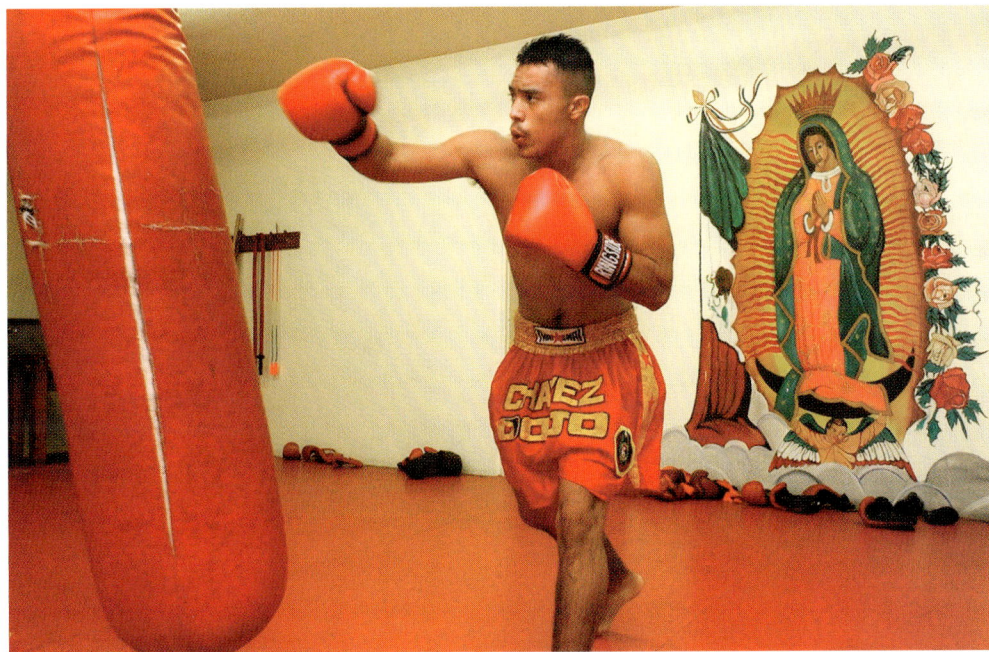

© KITTY CLARK FRITZ / AP/WIDE WORLD PHOTOS

PLATE 4 • A young boxer at the Chávez Dojo Gym in Albuquerque, New Mexico, is one of a group of local high school boys who is a member of a home-grown La Raza Unida club.

PLATE 5 • Chita Rivera (right) and Liane Plane dancing in a scene from the Broadway production of *West Side Story*, 1957.

PLATE 6 •
A piece in an exhibit titled Diego Rivera: Art and Revolution, at the Los Angeles County Museum of Art, 1999.

PLATE 7 • A group of children take part in the International Day Festival outside Public School 89 in the Elmhurst section of Queens, New York, 1999.

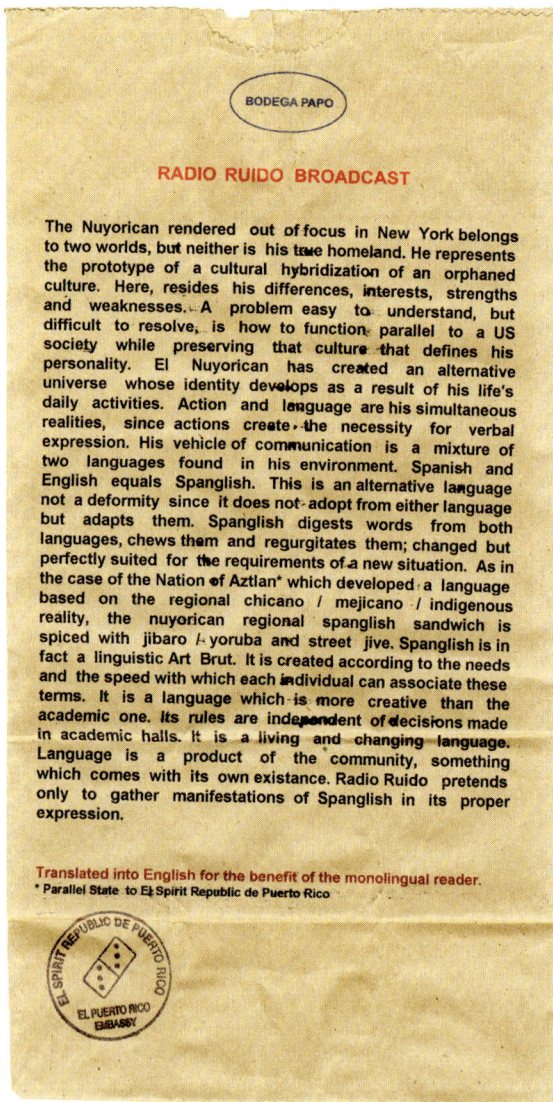

PLATE 8 • Spanish Language Analysis, artwork on a paper bag. In the permanent collection of El Museo del Barrio, New York.

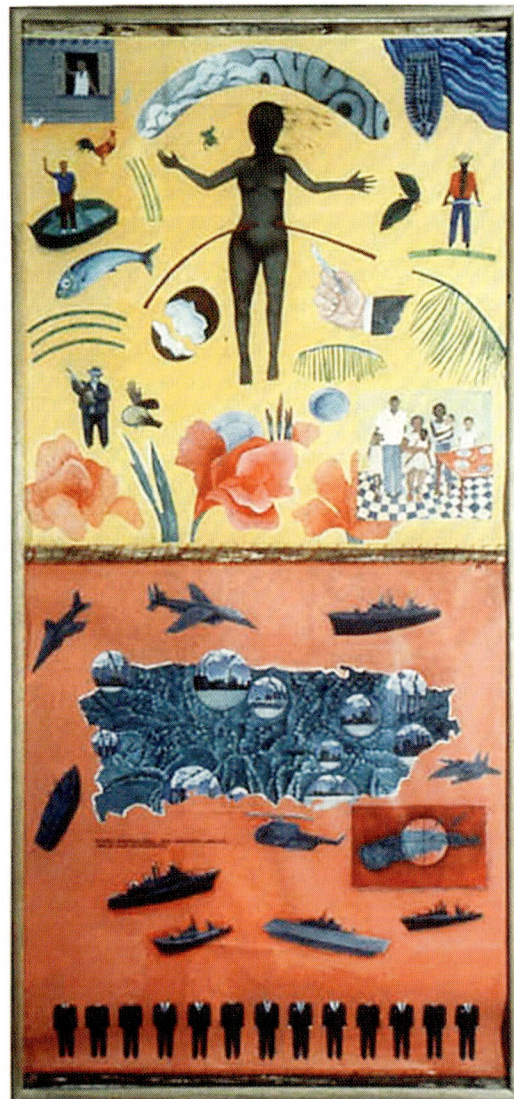

PLATE 9 • Isla del Encanto (Island of Enchantment; 1986) by Marina Gutiérrez; acrylic on paper, in the permanent collection at El Museo del Barrio, in New York City.

PLATE 10 • Pyro by Jean Michel Basquiat (1984); acrylic and mixed media on canvas.

PLATE 11 • *Las Castas* (Human Races), oil on canvas; anonymous, 18th century.

NEVADA

HISPANIC OR LATINO
POPULATION AS A PERCENT
OF TOTAL POPULATION*

- 19.0 - 22.0
- 15.0 - 18.9
- 12.0 - 14.9
- 8.0 - 11.9
- 5.1 - 7.9

*U.S. Census Data by County, 2000.

Reno

★ CARSON CITY

Las Vegas
Henderson

0   50   100 Km.
0   50   100 Mi.

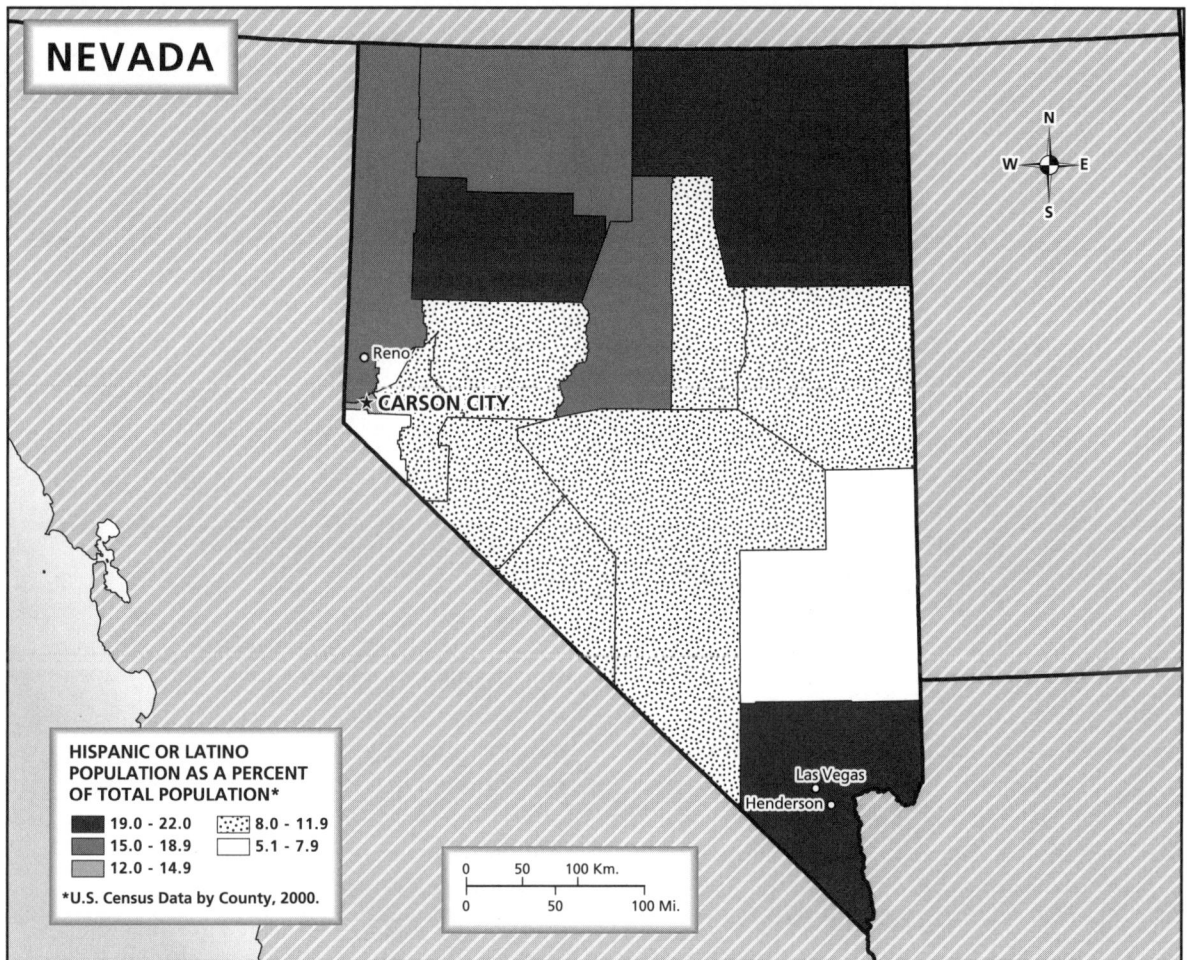

In 1972 eight Latino organizations in Clark County united to form the Nevada Spanish-Speaking Coalition in an effort to jointly solve the problems faced by Latinos living in their jurisdiction. Pooling the resources of several organizations helped the coalition to address a wide range of concerns, including the education, employment, and housing problems of Latinos in Clark county. In 1976 the Latin Chamber of Commerce of Nevada was founded by a small group of Cubans in Las Vegas. This organization advocated for the economic advancement of the Latino community in Las Vegas and, in 1978, opened offices in Clark County and Reno with the hope of encouraging the economic development of Latinos in northern Nevada.

By 1980 Nevada's Latino population had increased to 53,879, representing 6.7 percent of the state population. Ten years later, in 1990, the Latino community more than doubled, increasing to 124,419, or 10.4 percent of the total population. It was the eco-

nomic boom in Nevada's casino economy in the 1990s that created an abundance of service and construction jobs and drew large numbers of Latinos from other states and from Mexico.

Because many of the new jobs did not require skilled workers, the barrios of Los Angeles and other poor Hispanic communities became the primary sources of Latino labor for Nevada. The casinos created opportunities, even for people with limited English-language skills or those lacking high school degrees. The lower rents and inexpensive housing available in the Las Vegas area became added incentive for Latinos to relocate.

From 1990 to 1999 Nevada experienced a 145 percent growth rate in its Hispanic population, second only to the state of Georgia. According to Otto Merida, executive director of the Las Vegas Latin Chamber of Commerce, Latino-owned enterprises in Nevada more than doubled between 1987 and

1992 to 3,900, with the majority of the businesses in Las Vegas.

With the influx of Hispanics to Nevada, businesses dedicated primarily to immigrants began to proliferate. In some neighborhoods money transfer outlets and immigration consulting companies began to appear in shopping malls surrounding immigrant neighborhoods. In order to provide an ethnic flavor for Latino cuisine in Las Vegas, Tacos Mexico, a Los Angeles chain, opened up several restaurants in Las Vegas in less than a decade.

In 1980 *El Mundo* became the first Spanish newspaper in the Las Vegas area. Six years later *Univisión* became the first Spanish-language television station in the Reno area, with Leslie Ann Mix as first station manager. In 1989 the Hispanic Chamber of Commerce of Northern Nevada was established as the Hispanic Business Council, with Mix as its founding president. Mix, an Anglo-American who was raised in Puerto Rico, later became the editor of the *Telemundo Times,* a 26-page bilingual promotional newspaper that was mailed to Hispanics in the Las Vegas area.

By the beginning of the 21st century, Las Vegas had become the home of three Spanish-language weekly newspapers, one of which was purchased by the *Las Vegas Review Journal,* the city's main daily newspaper. Other forms of Spanish-language media followed the newspapers, and eventually three radio stations and two television networks became focused on the Spanish-speaking population of Las Vegas.

The 2000 census merely confirmed what the analysts had predicted for more than a decade. In this census, the Hispanic population of Nevada was tallied at 393,970, representing 19.7 percent of the state population. Of this total, 285,764 persons claimed to be of Mexican American heritage, representing 14.3 percent of the state population and almost 73 percent of the total Latino population. In contrast, Cuban Americans and Puerto Ricans numbered less than 22,000 individuals, representing less than 6 percent of the Latino community. Nevada's Latino population grew another 15 percent from 402,000 in July 2000 to more than 462,000 in July 2002, the third fastest growth rate among all American states.

Las Vegas, the capital of Clark County, witnessed the largest influx of both immigrants and Latinos, most of them to fill jobs in home construction and in hotels and casinos. The overall population of Clark County increased 66 percent between 1990 and 2000, while the number of Latino residents tripled to about 375,000, representing 22 percent of the entire county's population. In recognition of Las Vegas's potential value to Latinos, in 1996, 1999, and 2003 *Hispanic Magazine* included Las Vegas in its list of top ten cities for Hispanics to live in.

In spite of their increasing numbers, the political representation of Latinos in Nevada has been slow in coming. Gus Núñez, an engineer and a native of Cuba, served for eight years on the Reno City Council until 1993. Bob Coffin, whose mother was of Mexican heritage, was elected to the Nevada Assembly in 1983 and moved on to the Senate, where he represented Clark County's Tenth District from 1987 to 2003.

Although the Latino population of Clark County is almost 400,000, only about 65,000 of these persons are citizens who are registered to vote. Nevada's foreign-born population increased 202 percent between 1990 and 2000 with the addition of 212,000 immigrants. Foreign-born residents now number 317,000, representing 16 percent of the total state population, much higher than the national average of 11 percent. Many of these people are noncitizen Latinos who are not yet eligible to vote.

Assembly District 28 was drawn in 1991 as a majority Latino district. However, even with a Latino population of more than 70 percent, the district has never had a Hispanic serve as its representative. The two Hispanic candidates who ran in District 28 in 1992 split the Hispanic vote, and the seat went to a third candidate, Vonne Chowning, who as of this writing was still in office.

In 1994 Emma Sepulveda, a literature professor, became the first Latina to run for the state legislature. After she lost the Senate race, Professor Sepulveda, frustrated with the lack of Hispanic voter turnout, founded a nonprofit organization in northern Nevada called Latinos for Political Education. Fidel Salcedo, a native-born Nevadan, was elected to serve as the Reno justice of the peace by the Washoe County Board of Commissioners in 1981. Judge Salcedo has continued to hold this position for more than two decades, having been reelected to the position several times.

Another Latino politician was Dario Herrera, a native of Miami and the son of refuges from Castro's Cuba. In 1996, at the age of 23, Herrera was elected to the Nevada State Assembly as one of the youngest state officials in Nevada's history. Two years later, Assemblyman Herrera was appointed to the post of Clark County Commissioner, making him the youngest person and only the second Hispanic to hold the prestigious seat.

In the 2002 primary elections, 27 Hispanic candidates ran for Nevada state offices; however, only 5 of these candidates survived the primary races, while 12 automatically advanced to the November general election. After the final tallies were counted in November, only five of the Latino candidates were declared victorious. The most noteworthy victory of a Latino candidate in 2002 was Brian Sandoval's successful bid for the office of Nevada attorney general. When Sandoval took office on January 6, 2003, he became the first Latino in Nevada history to be elected to statewide office.

Most Latino representatives in Nevada now openly admit that they cannot rely on the Hispanic population alone to gain elected office. Instead, they rely on the vote of all Nevadans to accomplish their objectives and to best serve their constituency.

No one person in Nevada has been able to bring about awareness of the presence and contributions of Latinos to Nevada history more than Malvin Lane (Tony) Miranda, chairman of the department of anthropology and ethnic studies at the University of Nevada, Las Vegas. At the behest of the Latino community, Miranda coauthored *Hispanic Profiles in Nevada History, 1829–1991,* as a means of educating Nevada's junior high and high school students about Hispanic involvement in Nevada's history.

Miranda also wrote a scholarly work critically acclaimed as "a landmark study in Nevada's ethnic history," entitled *A History of Hispanics in Southern Nevada,* published in 1997 by the University of Nevada Press. The efforts of individuals such as Miranda and Mix have created a cultural environment that has given Nevada's Latino community a new sense of pride and direction.

RELATED ARTICLES

Immigration, Latino.

FURTHER READING

Miranda, M. L. *A History of Hispanics in Southern Nevada.* Reno: Univ. of Nev. Press, 1997.

Miranda, M. L. "Some Observations on Hispanics in Nevada in the 1980s." *Nevada Public Affairs Review* 2 (1988): 36–42.

Miranda, M. L., and Thomas Rodriguez. *Hispanic Profiles in Nevada History: 1829–1991.* Las Vegas: Latin Chamber of Commerce, 1991.

SELECTED WEB SITES

El Mundo Demographics: The Hispanic Market.
  http://www.elmundo.net/pages/eng/demo.html
Hispanic Chamber of Commerce Northern Nevada.
  http://www.hccnn.org/home.htm

JOHN P. SCHMAL

NEW DEAL

The New Deal was a series of economic programs and social reforms enacted between 1933 and 1935 by the U.S. president Franklin Delano Roosevelt in response to the Great Depression and its widespread economic and social destruction. Of the programs affecting Latinos the most important were the Agricultural Adjustment Act (AAA), the Federal Emergency Relief Administration (FERA, and its Puerto Rican counterpart, PRERA), the National Labor Relations Act (NLRA), the Civilian Conservation Corps (CCC), the Homeowner's Loan Corporation (HLC), the Puerto Rican Reconstruction Administration (PRRA), and the Works Progress Administration (WPA). Taken collectively this amalgam of acronyms was referred to as Roosevelt's "Alphabet Soup." Although some of the reforms and programs proposed by Roosevelt were later ruled to be unconstitutional, others, such as Social Security, or unemployment compensation, survive today.

The Depression seriously affected the Latino population in the United States mainland and on the island of Puerto Rico. The notion that work and relief should be reserved for "real Americans," which was frequently applied to mean non-Latinos, had devastating impacts. Hispanics in general were reluctant to partake in New Deal programs, seeing them as a distasteful last resort when long stretches of unemployment drained families' meager savings. However, Mexicans identified strongly with Roosevelt, the Democratic Party, and the goals of the New Deal. Prior to the New Deal and federal safety net programs, *sociedades mutualistas* ("mutual-aid societies") helped provide crucial economic and social support for Latinos in times of need. In addition, Puerto Ricans identified with Roosevelt, since their governor at the time was a relative of the U.S. president.

New Deal programs offered work or stable income to those who could access them. However for local administrators frequently denied benefits to Mexicans and other Latinos, and federal laws governing minimum wages, social security, collective bargaining, and unemployment benefits under the National Labor Relations Act specifically excluded agricultural workers. Additionally, the Works Progress Administration (WPA) as amended by the 1937 Relief Appropriation Act, excluded foreign nationals who had not taken out their citizenship papers, thus excluding thousands of Mexicans, even those of long-standing residence in the United States, from relief (exceptions were made for the spouses of U.S. citizens and veterans who had served in the U.S. military). Programs such as the CCC also increasingly excluded Mexicans. Consequently, women and children often labored in the fields or in the informal economy to help their families survive. New Deal administrators occasionally helped lessen the repatriation (deportation) efforts targeting Mexicans in the United States, because the deportation of the family's main income earner could cause remaining family members to rely on public relief.

Certain of the New Deal programs, such as those supporting agriculture (AAA) or housing and urban redevelopment had the sometimes unintended but real impacts of hurting Latinos, as, for example, public works projects that comprised or destroyed parts of vibrant barrios through the use eminent domain, or the segregation of FHA (Federal Housing Administration) loan recipients through the use of restrictive covenants. And some programs, such as the NLRA, which allowed urban workers to unionize, were difficult to enforce, with Latinos facing termination, threats, and violence in trying to exercise their rights under the New Deal. Moreover, many unions refused Latino members or would not organize where Latinos were a majority of the workers. Important exceptions exist, however, such as the International Ladies Garment Workers Union (ILGWU), which, with a Hispanic contingency, led a successful strike in Los Angeles in the 1930s.

New Deal programs in Puerto Rico also followed the Great Depression, as well as a series of hurricanes, much like the environmental destruction caused by the Dust Bowl on the mainland. As a commonwealth of the United States, Puerto Rico and its residents received different treatment under the New Deal than did Hispanics on the mainland. While the government did intervene on the island, the stability created by the New Deal on the mainland eluded the island, with programs more focused on temporary relief than on long-lasting, meaningful reform to compensate for centuries of colonialism and transfer to the United States. The governor of Puerto Rico at the time of the Great Depression was Theodore Roosevelt, Jr., the son of the former president. Thus, while PRERA distributed hundreds of thousands of dollars to needy Puerto Ricans in 1933 and helped build roads, train young professionals, and modestly advance some industries, it was wholly inadequate for the tens of thousands of families in need.

In 1934 the U.S. government helped created the Puerto Rican Policy Commission (PRPC) to study the island's specific situation and mold New Deal policies to their specific needs. The result was the Chardón Plan to reorient the economy, and its implementation was given to the new Puerto Rican Reconstruction Administration created by President Roosevelt in 1935. The PRRA was successful in reducing unemployment and lessening the suffering of Puerto Ricans, but when funding for the administration ran out in the late 1930s, the programs it supported did, as well. As with some New Deal programs on the mainland that were designed to help segments of the population but wound up hurting Latinos, the tax placed on products under the AAA, which helped U.S. farmers, hurt island consumers; Puerto Ricans had a difficult time affording food imports. One benefit enjoyed on the island and not

THE GRANGER COLLECTION

"The Galloping Snail," by Burt Thomas for the *Detroit News,* depicts President Franklin Roosevelt urging a slow Congress to pass his New Deal programs in his first 100 days, March 1933.

the mainland was embodied in the Insular Labor Relations Act (ILRA) of 1945, modeled after the NLRA, which extended the right to collectively organize and bargain to agricultural workers. Provisions of the National Industrial Relations Act (NIRA) later incorporated into the NLRA—such as the raising of wages, lowering of workweek hours, and improvement of working conditions under a "code of conduct"—did benefit workers, particularly women.

RELATED ARTICLES

Mutual Aid Societies; United States Presidents, and Latinos.

FURTHER READING

Acuña, Rodolfo. *Occupied America: A History of Chicanos.* New York: Longman, 1994.

Balderrama, Francisco E., and Raymond Rodríguez. *Decade of Betrayal: Mexican Repatriation in the 1930s.* Albuquerque: Univ. of N.Mex. Press, 1995.

Dietz, James L. *Economic History of Puerto Rico: Institutional Change and Capitalist Development.* Princeton N.J.: Princeton Univ. Press, 1986.

Gómez-Quiñones, Juan. *Mexican American Labor 1790–1990.* Albuquerque: Univ. of N.Mex. Press, 1994.

Guerín-Gonzáles, Camille. *Mexican Workers and American Dreams: Immigration, Repatriation, and California Farm Labor 1900–1939.* New Brunswick, N.J.: Rutgers Univ. Press, 1994.

Valdés, Dionicio Nodin. *Barrios Norteños: St. Paul and Midwestern Mexican Communities in the Twentieth Century.* Austin: Univ. of Tex. Press, 2000.

SUSAN GREEN

NEW JERSEY

Statistics from the 1990s revealed that New Jersey boasted the country's second largest concentrations of Cuban, Puerto Rican, and Dominican Americans. By 2000 the U.S. Census Bureau estimated that Latinos made up 13.3 percent of New Jersey's population. In 2002 New Jersey had the seventh largest Latino population in the country. The 2000 census estimates reveal that Latinos are a numerical presence in Essex and Union counties, which have Latino populations between 15 and 20 percent, and in Hudson and Passaic counties, which have Latino populations of 30 and approximately 40 percent, respectively.

Latinos have settled in New Jersey for a variety of reasons. Puerto Ricans came to New Jersey in the early part of the 20th century to work as seasonal agricultural laborers. Some workers went back to Puerto Rico, but others stayed, settling in the communities where they worked. Currently, there is a large Puerto Rican population in Newark, concentrated in the North Ward but also present in other parts of the city.

Puerto Ricans have played a significant role in racial and ethnic politics in Newark since the late 1960s. Racial animosity between whites and nonwhites remained palpable in the city after the 1967 riots there. The situation was exacerbated by the election of two white extremists to the Newark municipal council in a 1968 special election. One of the candidates, Anthony Giuliano, the former president of the Police Benevolent Association, refused to support residents' attempts to establish a police review board to look into claims of police brutality. The other candidate, Anthony Imperiale, was later linked to segregationist presidential candidate and former Alabama governor George Wallace and would lead a vigilante squad of white men who patrolled the North Ward by terrorizing blacks and Latinos who entered their territory.

Black Newarkers had begun to organize politically to claim political power in the 1970 municipal election. Poet Amiri Baraka organized the first all-black convention in 1968, but by 1969 he was forging ties with Puerto Ricans, who were also targets of Imperiale's violence. As a result the black Committee for a United New-Ark (CFUN), represented by Baraka, joined in a mutual defense agreement with the Young Lords, who were represented in Newark by Baraka's friend and fellow poet Felipe Luciano. Their efforts led to the organization of the joint black and Puerto Rican convention in 1969, at which black and Puerto Rican community leaders, elected officials, and prominent residents of moderate to radical ideologies joined forces to create an electoral strategy for the 1970 municipal elections. The convention raised and endorsed a slate of candidates under the banner of the "Community Choice" slate. This slate included Ramon Aneses, who was a candidate for an at-large seat on the municipal council.

Aneses lost the 1970 election, but other Latinos have since attained elected office in Newark. In 1974 Henry Martinez was elected East Ward councilman. He was unseated in 1998 by Augusto Amador, who became the city's first Portuguese representative for the largely Portuguese and Brazilian ward. In 1994 Luis Quintana became Newark's first Latino councilmember-at-large. In 2002 Deputy Mayor Hector

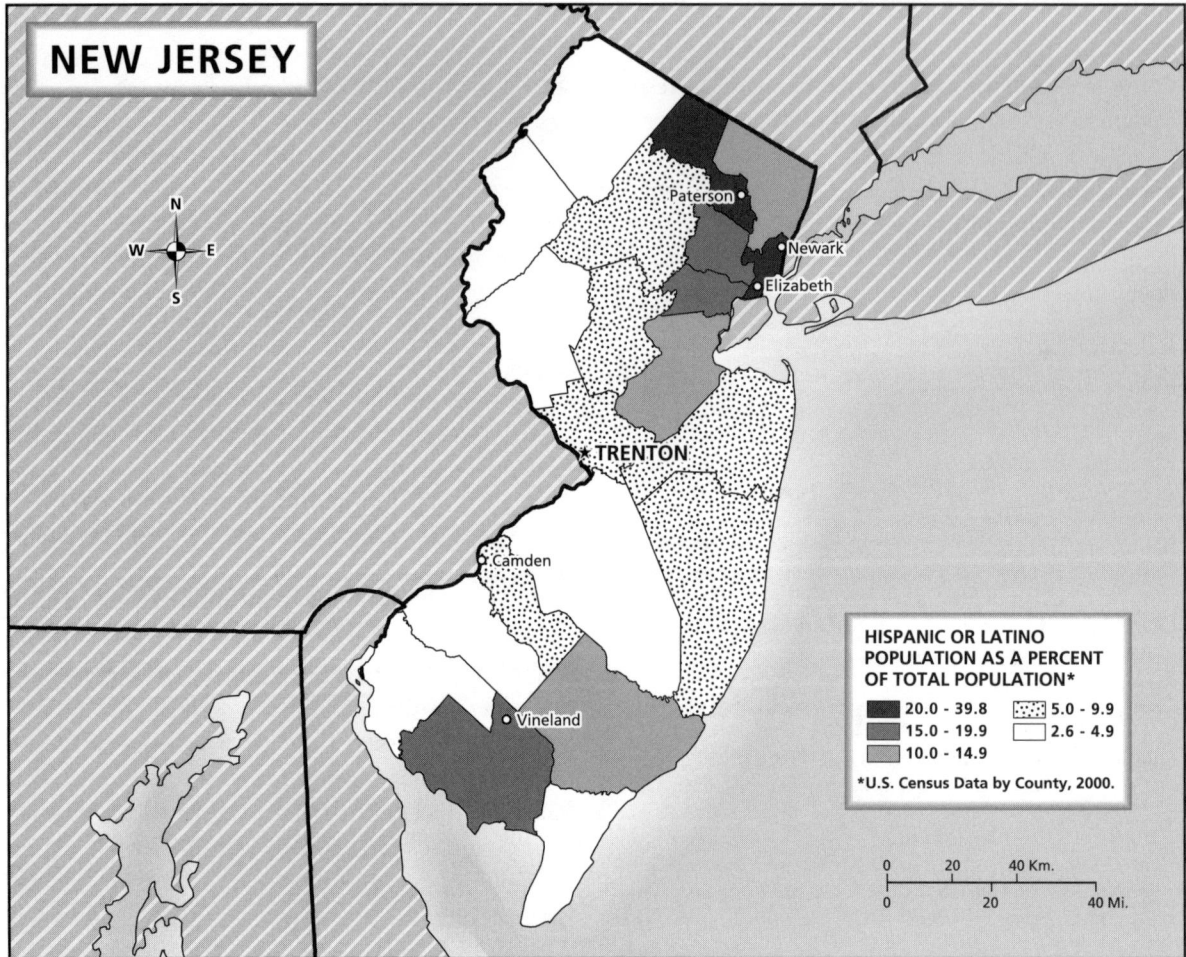

NEW JERSEY

Paterson
Newark
Elizabeth
*TRENTON
Camden
Vineland

HISPANIC OR LATINO POPULATION AS A PERCENT OF TOTAL POPULATION*

20.0 - 39.8 | 5.0 - 9.9
15.0 - 19.9 | 2.6 - 4.9
10.0 - 14.9

*U.S. Census Data by County, 2000.

Corchado became the majority Latino North Ward's first Latino councilmember.

Newark was not the only New Jersey city to witness racial and ethnic unrest. In 1971 Latinos took to the streets in Camden after reports surfaced that police had beaten a young Latino. As a result of that incident, a young Latino lawyer, Joe Rodríguez, emerged as a mediator, helping to bring Latino interests to the attention of Camden's elected officials. Rodríguez would go on to achieve many firsts, including becoming the first Latino head of the state board of education in 1971 and the first Latino president of the New Jersey Bar Association and he eventually became a federal district judge. John Dios was appointed New Jersey's first Latino judge in 1974.

Cuban migration to New Jersey began in earnest after Fidel Castro's 1959 Cuban revolution. While most exiles settled in the Miami area, the federal government, through the Cuban Refugee Program, actively encouraged others to settle outside that city. Many of those exiles settled in northern Hudson County, New Jersey, which includes Union City and West New York. Many of the immigrants were from Havana or Las Villas, Cuba, and most of them spent little if any time in Miami before coming to New Jersey.

A 1980 study by the Hispanic Research Center at Fordham University investigated the sociological characteristics of northern New Jersey's Cuban community. Its findings underscore the importance of kinship and friendship networks among the residents. Many people followed friends and family to the area when they chose to settle in Hudson county and credit those ties with easing their adjustment. While the residents indicated a high degree of civic-mindedness (they reported high levels of voter registration and turnout), they indicated that they were not active members of civic or ethnic organizations, although they were actively involved in labor unions.

Thus it is not surprising that more modern analyses of Cuban American politics considered the northern New Jersey community to be far less politicized than its Miami counterpart.

Although New Jersey's Cuban citizens are perceived to wield less political power than Miami's, they do exert a considerable amount of political influence. For instance, Robert Menendez, the former mayor of Union City, served in the U.S. House of Representatives as, at the time, the country's only Cuban American Democrat. As chair of the Hudson County Democratic Party, Menendez wielded considerable influence at the local and state levels. For instance, he was instrumental in persuading Governor James McGreevey to appoint Assemblyman Albio Sires, who was also mayor of West New York, as New Jersey's first Latino speaker of the State Assembly in 2002. Menendez was also a force to be reckoned with at the national level. In 2002 he was elected as chair of the House Democratic Caucus, becoming the highest ranking Latino and the highest ranking New Jerseyan in Congress. He was even considered a leading contender to replace Robert Torricelli as the New Jersey Democratic Party's nominee for the U.S. Senate in 2002, after Torricelli withdrew from the race because of an ethics scandal.

Dominican immigration to the United States increased in the 1960s after the death of dictator Rafael Trujillo, who had restricted Dominican emigration. Immigration steadily climbed in the 1980s and 1990s as people came to the United States looking for work. While many of the Dominican job seekers coming were unskilled laborers, middle-class and professional Dominicans also immigrated in search of economic opportunity. The majority of Dominicans settled in New York, but a sizeable portion chose northern New Jersey as home. In fact, New Jersey's Dominican population is larger than its Cuban population. Five of the country's ten fastest-growing Dominican American enclaves are in New Jersey. Many Dominicans have settled in Passaic County, particularly in the cities of Paterson and Passaic, and Paterson's Dominican Day parade has become an annual highlight.

Dominicans settling in New York and New Jersey have established an economic niche for themselves in their new homes. Many small urban markets, or bodegas, in Dominican enclaves such as Paterson and Passaic are Dominican-owned. There are also Dominican hair salons and travel agencies.

Cities such as Elizabeth and Newark have also witnessed the growth in Honduran and Nicaraguan populations. Immigration from these countries began in earnest after Hurricane Mitch devastated Honduras and Nicaragua in 1998.

The diversity of New Jersey's Latino population is still increasing. Whereas the bulk of the state's Latinos came from Cuba and Puerto Rico two generations ago, by 2000, Latinos were arriving from 21 different countries. Notably, there are large numbers of Ecuadorians, Nicaraguans, Peruvians, and Colombians settling in the state. While there are noticeable ethnic enclaves, particularly in northern New Jersey, the Latino population is growing in all parts of the state, even the small towns. These groups have established or are establishing ethnic communities and businesses and are positioning themselves to participate in state and local politics. In short, they are integrating themselves into their communities.

The process of political integration has not been without its challenges. While Latinos have made many strides politically, there are still obstacles to overcome. For instance, while Latinos made up over 13 percent of the New Jersey population, they made up a little more than 6 percent of state government employees. In 2004 only 6 of the 80 state assemblypersons were Latino. There were no Latino state senators in 2004, and Latinos made up less than 4 percent of the state judicial branch in 2002. Furthermore, Latinos often live in cities that are dominated by non-Latino political machines. In 2001, however, Samuel Rivera became the first Latino mayor of Passaic. This first was followed in 2002 by the election of José Torres in nearby Paterson. The election of Rivera and Torres brought the number of Latino mayors in the state to four, including Albio Sires of West New York and Joseph Vas of Perth Amboy.

New Jersey politicians are still learning how to reach out to Latino voters. For instance, when former governor Christine Whitman was elected to her first term in 1993, she won 60 percent of the Latino vote by building political alliances with Latino groups. She made a huge misstep, however, when she launched her diversity campaign, called "Many Faces, One Family," and neglected to include Latinos as part of the "family." She also appointed only one Latino to her cabinet during her first term. Nevertheless her Democratic opponent received only 48 percent of the Latino vote when she won her reelection bid in 1997.

Governor James McGreevey may have been a little more successful with outreach to Latino constituents in 2001. McGreevey's wife, Dina Matos-McGreevey, who is Portuguese, figured prominently in the campaign, making Spanish-language commercials on behalf of her husband. The McGreevey campaign also conducted polling in Latino communities to inform their targeted political communication. McGreevey learned that Latinos were concerned about crime, and his organization used this information to attack Republican Bret Schundler's support for carrying concealed weapons. Schundler had been popular with his Latino constituents when he was mayor of Jersey City. In the end, McGreevey won over 70 percent of the Latino vote. Once in office, McGreevey faced criticism from Latinos in the state. He made two prominent Latino appointments, but he encountered criticism from Latino leaders in the summer of 2003 for failing to nominate Zulima Farber, a Cuban American lawyer, to the New Jersey Supreme Court. In August 2004, McGreevey announced that he would resign from office as a result of a sex scandal involving a former appointee.

While one cannot predict the circumstances under which Latinos will obtain a more equitable share of power in New Jersey, some observers wonder if the Farber incident may prove to be a catalyst to greater Latino political organization. In the wake of Farber's not receiving a nomination, Latino leaders have identified that coalescing across nationality groups and across the state regional divides (urban-rural-suburban, and northern and southern New Jersey) is critical to gaining more political clout in the state.

Latinos have contributed more to New Jersey than political leadership. Major League Soccer's New Jersey MetroStars features numerous Latino players. One of them, midfielder Amada Guevara, represented his native Honduras in the 2004 World Cup.

Additionally, Latino writers have drawn on their experiences in New Jersey to win critical acclaim in the literary world. Judith Ortiz Cofer uses her experiences growing up in Puerto Rico and New Jersey to create prose and poetry that addresses the duality of being Puerto Rican and living on the mainland. Ortiz Cofer is notable in particular for distinguishing herself from the Nuyorican school of poetry made famous by her neighbors in New York City,

such as Pedro Pietri. In 1989 she was nominated for a Pulitzer Prize for her book *In the Line of the Sun*.

Junot Díaz represents a later generation of literary talent. Born in the Dominican Republic and raised in New Jersey, Díaz won critical acclaim for his first book of short stories, *Drown* (1996), in which he captured the struggles of growing up in both the Dominican Republic and in inner-city United States. Díaz went on to win a prestigious Guggenheim fellowship in 1999 and a PEN/Malamud award in 2002.

RELATED ARTICLES
Cuban Americans; Díaz, Junot; Dominican Americans; Immigration, Latino; Politics, Cuban American; Politics, Latino; Politics, Puerto Rican; Puerto Ricans on the Mainland.

FURTHER READING
Pérez y González, María E. *Puerto Ricans in the United States.* Westport, CT: Greenwood Press, 2000.
Rogg, Eleanor Meyer, and Rosemary Santana Cooney. *Adaptation and Adjustment of Cubans: West New York, New Jersey.* Bronx, N.Y.: Hispanic Research Center, 1980.
Torres-Saillant, Silvio, and Ramona Hernández. *The Dominican Americans.* Westport, CT: Greenwood Press, 1998.
Woodard, Komozi. *A Nation within a Nation: Amiri Baraka (LeRoi Jones) and Black Power Politics.* Chapel Hill: Univ. of N.C. Press, 1999.

ANDRA GILLESPIE

NEW MEXICO

New Mexico shares a Latino heritage with the other U.S. southwestern states of Arizona and Texas, and with the Pacific coastal state of California. New Mexico's Spanish heritage of language, culture, and way of life began in the late 1500s, giving it, perhaps, the most Latino-oriented culture in the United States, rich in Hispanic history and culture. Its European-founded state capital, Santa Fe, has been continually in use for 400 years. Although New Mexico has the oldest capital city in the nation, paradoxically it was one of the last (the 47th) states to join the Union, on January 6, 1912.

Spanish explorers had initially searched for another Mexico, rich in gold and silver, and for the site of the fabled seven cities of Cibola (gold) through the explorations of Fray Marcos de Niza in 1539 and Francisco Coronado in 1540. Years later, in 1598, Juan de Oñate led his expedition from Mexico and founded San Gabriel del Yunque, the first capital of the provincial government. These expeditions of de Niza, de Oñate, and Coronado, whose expedition went as far as the middle of what today is Kansas, laid the ground work for future trade routes such as El Camino Real (Royal Road). In 1610, ten years before the English pilgrims landed at Plymouth Rock, Pedro de Peralta, the third governor of the state, founded Santa Fe as the new capital of the province between the Pecos River and the Rio Grande. Except for a major uprising in 1680, which drove out the Spanish colonizers, the natives and the newcomers lived in peace after the Spanish settlers returned under the leadership of Diego de Vargas in 1692. Other explorations followed, as well. The Dominguez–Escalante expedition of 1776 would make known areas in Colorado, Utah, Arizona, and New Mexico never before seen by white men. Also, in a short time, the provincial state capital became a center of missions with churches and schools. Missionary priests arrived to teach the Catholic faith to native peoples. New Mexico became, in time, the oldest and most important and populous internal province governed by the viceroyalty of New Spain.

In 1778 Teodoro de Croix, commandant of the Internal Provinces, named Juan Bautista de Anza, who in 1776 had led an expedition to found San Francisco, California, to the governorship of New Mexico. He pacified the warring Comanche and ably governed the state. In addition to the pacification and evangelization of native peoples, the Spaniards sought domestic economic support for their administrative work and a profit for their investments in their colonizing efforts. The Spanish crown through the viceroy in Mexico City provided numerous land grants over the years. Spain granted common pueblo lands to small villages as they grew up in the mountain canyons and valleys. These were pueblo common land grants. The Spanish government also granted grazing rights to sheep raisers near the mountain pastures.

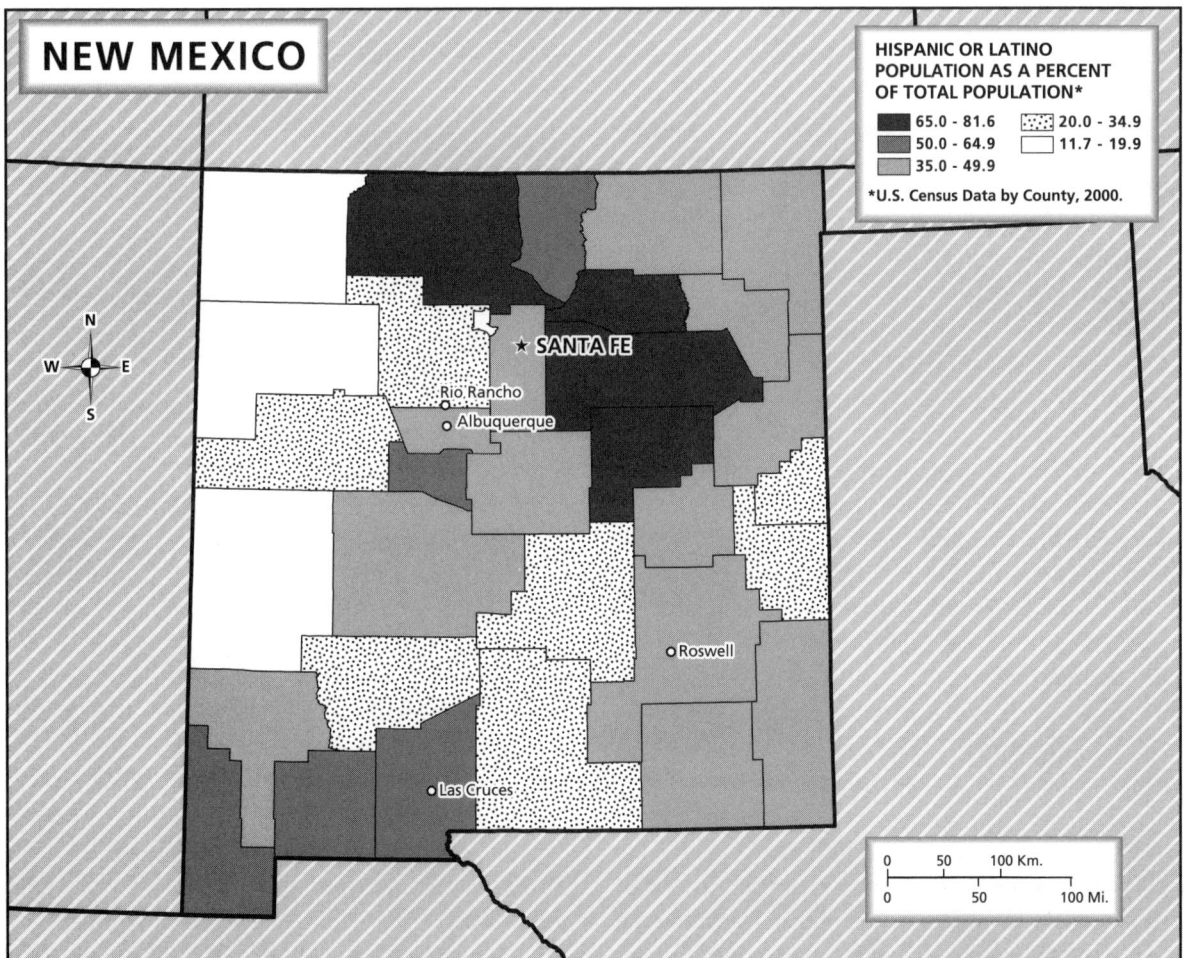

NEW MEXICO

HISPANIC OR LATINO POPULATION AS A PERCENT OF TOTAL POPULATION*

65.0 - 81.6 | 20.0 - 34.9
50.0 - 64.9 | 11.7 - 19.9
35.0 - 49.9

*U.S. Census Data by County, 2000.

Following El Camino Real from Mexico trekked New Mexico's future Latino citizens, and with them came the state's future economic industries. Mexican *vaqueros* (cowhands) on horseback herded cattle, shepherds guided flocks of sheep, miners brought their skills and tools, mules and oxen pulled wagons carrying seeds for fruit orchards and crops for farm lands. The products from these industries would in some future time be transported to Missouri, Chihuahua, Sonora, and to California. First, however, there would be the need to establish trade routes. Also, all of these past economic developments by Spanish and Mexican settlers later help would modern New Mexico to excel in trade with other states, countries, and especially with Mexico through the North American Free Trade Agreement (NAFTA).

The Spaniards and Mexican settlers from Mexico never found the cities of gold, but discovered other types of riches. The new settlers discovered in New Mexico not only a geographic beauty of land, rivers, and climate but mountains with minerals and lands suitable for farming and grazing. In time farms and ranches developed, at first around the areas near Santa Fe but progressively extended out to other areas of the state. Prospecting led to the discovery of gold and silver. Mines were dug and formed in mountain areas. Modern New Mexico developed coal production, natural gas, copper, uranium, and potash. New Mexico provides about 50 percent of the United States's uranium. Just as *vaqueros* worked the cattle and farmers developed large farms, the Mexican miners worked the mines. In addition there developed sheep raising, and shepherds drove flocks to summer pastures in mountains. There were also architects, builders, teachers, and arts and crafts with metals, silver, wood, and leather. Various service occupations developed in complexity and number. Trade initially was local but eventually extended to Mexico and the United States. Their early work and trade became foundations conducive to New Mexico's later economic interests and developments.

New Mexico's Spanish and Mexican settlers initial traded with Native American people they encountered living on top of high mesas in clustered adobe villages, which the Spaniards called *pueblos,* or towns. The two groups of people interacted profitably with each other for centuries, and learned life skills and arts and crafts from each other. The Hispanic settlers introduced new crops, and farm animals such as cattle, sheep, donkeys, horses, and mules.

They shared their ranching skills, silversmith crafts, tin and wood arts, architecture, language, and music. The settlers learned new survival skills, and about native foods and arts and crafts from the native peoples who had lived in the land for thousands of years. The missions and churches grew in number owing to the hard work of priests who shared their faith in Christianity and converted the Native Americans to Catholicism. Santa Fe grew in population, and in time it developed a large public plaza with beautiful and functional government and religious buildings built around the square. The government building stands to this day and is still in use.

Anglo-Americans immigrated to New Mexico in substantial numbers after the state became part of the United States in 1848, and at the end of that century when the railroads provided easier transportation. Americans from other states continued to settle in New Mexico or visit as tourists throughout the subsequent centuries. Many tourists participate in the visual arts exhibitions held in Santa Fe each year, visit museums, or purchase native arts and crafts.

Because of the longevity of its Latino way of life, in addition to its buildings New Mexico is world famous for its rich creativity and culture. Its Latino heritage has served the state very well. The predominant philosophical thread in the vital fabric of life in Latino New Mexico was the collision and mixing of cultures in their struggles for survival. When the Anglo immigrants arrived in the late 1800s many joined the cultural mix; the resultant culture was pluralistic, incorporating the best of each: Native American, Anglo, and Latino. The present-day Latinos of New Mexico inherited a cultural mosaic, a new *mestizaje* (mixture) blending ethnic types and cultures from which emerged a new type of ethnic American Latino, incorporating the characteristics of the others. The process of *mestizaje* has deep historical roots; it began in Spain and continued over centuries, creating a new Spanish people who combined ancient Iberians, Romans, Visigoths, Greeks, Celts, and many other ethnic types into a new Spanish ethnic group, culture, and language. These Spaniards went to Mexico where the *mestizaje* continued with Mexican native tribal peoples. This process of *mestizaje* continued into the Southwest and New Mexico with Spanish and Mexican settlers. In New Mexico some people call themselves *Hispanos* after their ancestors who came directly from Spain or who have a long-standing cultural affinity with Hispanic culture. Nevertheless, the Spanish and Mexicans who ventured north from Mexico made lasting contributions to the state in language, music, dance, religion, and economic and cultural aspects.

Like Colorado, New Mexico is divided into numerous counties. Whereas Arizona only has 15 counties, New Mexico comprises 66 counties and 102 municipalities. Of the population 38 percent is Latino and 9 percent is Native American. The governor of New Mexico from 2003 to 2006 was Bill Richardson, a Latino. Latinos serve in many state official positions such as the secretary of state, state treasurer, and state auditor. Latinos serve as justices of the state Supreme Court and judges of the Court of Appeals. They are also well represented in the ranks of state representatives and senators, and district judges, as well as at the municipal government level. In 2004, out of 70 representatives 29 were Latino, and out of 42 state senators 15 were Latino. Latinos have deep historical roots in public service. Well remembered are former U.S. senators Dennis (Dionisio) Chávez and Joseph Montoya. Representative Manuel Lujan served New Mexico in Washington for many years before serving as secretary of the interior. Following are some other examples of Hispano leaders.

Manuel Armijo (1792–1853) as territorial governor of Nuevo Mexico (1827–1829, 1845–1846), authorized 15 million acres (6 million ha) in land grants, many of which were motivated by the need to politically protect Nuevo Mexico. In 1841 Texas had speared a malintentioned expedition against New Mexico. Although territorial governor Armijo repelled the Texas–Santa Fe expedition of 1841, he failed to engage the enemy forces of Colonel Stephen W. Kearny during the American invasion of Nuevo Mexico. After the Mexico-American War of 1846, through the Treaty of Guadalupe Hidalgo (1848), New Mexico would become part of the United States.

Another Latino, Diego Archuleta (1814–1884) served the Mexican and U.S. governments in political matters. First, he served as a Nuevo Mexicano representative to the national congress in Mexico (1843–1845), when Nuevo Mexico was still part of Mexico. Then during the 1850s he was elected to the New Mexico legislative assembly. During and after the Civil War, he was elected to the upper house Legislative Council for seven terms.

In time New Mexicans became more accepting of American control and turned their attention to

CENSUS Year	Total Population	Percent	Hispanic Origin (of any race)	Percent
2000	1,819,046	100	765,386	42.1
1990	1,515,069	100	579,225	38.2
1980	1,302,894	100	477,222	36.6

NEW MEXICO—POPULATION BY HISPANIC ORIGIN, 1980 TO 2000

Source: U.S. Census Bureau, 2000.

making the best of it all. At this time the controversy over slavery raged throughout the United States. In the compromise of 1850 New Mexico became a territory. Hispano leaders like Miguel Otero, Father Antonio Jose Martinez, and Diego Archuleta served in the territorial assembly. Hispanos, despite efforts by Confederates to gain their support, remained loyal to the United States. During the Civil War thousands of Hispanos served with the Union forces. A Confederate force of 3,000 from Texas, commanded by General Sibley, invaded New Mexico, occupying Albuquerque and Santa Fe. At Glorieta Pass, not far from Santa Fe, Colonel Manuel Chávez commanded Union forces and destroyed the Confederate supply base, forcing the Confederate troops' return to Texas.

The period following the Civil War was one of violence and lawlessness involving Indian agitations and range wars between Anglo cattle ranchers and Hispano sheep raisers. The so-called Lincoln County War in 1876–1878 added to the conflicts in the southeastern part of the state. From these trying times of criminal activity in southern New Mexico emerged the legendary people's hero—Elfego Baca—later sheriff and politico to keep peace, law, and order.

The arrival of the railroads changed the political, economic, and social relationships among Hispanos when they were overwhelmed by Anglo immigration from the United States. Soon they were greatly outnumbered and suffered similar setbacks similar to those experienced in Texas, California, and Arizona. Landholders lost lands to Anglos employing dubious legal and political means. New Mexico land-grant holders, like those Spanish and Mexican land holders in other states of the Southwest, had lost their land titles over the passage of 300 years, the turmoil of wars, and conflicts arising from the change of national sovereignty from Mexico to the United States.

HISPANIC OR LATINO AND RACE—NEW MEXICO, 2000

Total Population	1,819,046	100 %
Hispanic or Latino (of any race)	765,386	42.1%
Mexican	330,049	18.1%
Puerto Rican	4,488	0.2%
Cuban	2,588	0.1%
Other Hispanic or Latino	428,261	23.5%
Not Hispanic or Latino	1,053,660	57.9%

Source: U.S. Census Bureau, 2000 summary.

Thus they presented easy targets for the U.S. Court of Private Land Claims that worked in narrow legalistic ways. The attorneys representing land claimants and the infamous Santa Fe Ring dishonestly acquired millions of acres of land. Dispossessed of lands and having to communicate in a new language, in a new law, and out-populated by Anglo immigrants whose country now controlled the state, New Mexico Latinos had to begin at the bottom on the climb toward recuperation. They would in time make inroads toward recapturing their economic, political, cultural, and social lives in some fashion of equality as citizens of the United States. This can be seen today.

However, a land issue continues to irritate many Latinos. Land rights in the Southwest for Mexican Americans incorporated into the United States after the 1848 war with Mexico were based on the Treaty of Guadalupe Hidalgo. However, Article IX, which specified protection of property, was not approved by the United States, which instead relied on the U.S. Constitution's protection of citizen rights for protection of property rights. Patricia Bell Blawis in her book *Tijerina and the Land Grants: Mexican Americans in Struggle for their Heritage* (1971) states that those rights were not honored. In 1897 the *United States* v. *Sandoval* decided that Spanish and Mexican community grants were United States public domain, to be administered by the U.S. Forest Service. The New Mexican villages dependent on grazing lands and common farming areas around their pueblos were plunged onto a trajectory toward poverty. Their economic way of life for the previous 300 years had ended.

During the Great Depression until World War II, these New Mexican villagers were dependent on the U.S. Government. (That is why great interest in obtaining their land rights persists.) During the Chicano movement of the 1960s, Rodolfo ("Corky")

Gonzáles organized the Crusade for Justice, which advocated for urban social justice and equal rights; José Angel Gutiérrez organized La Raza Unida political party in Texas to seek Mexican American political power; César Chávez organized the United Farm Workers to seek recognition for field laborers and to negotiate work contracts. But in New Mexico the main interest was land-grant recovery. Reies López Tijerina, a militant Mexican American leader, had investigated the land-grant issue in New Mexico in 1960. He created in 1963 the Alianza Federal de Mercedes (Federal Alliance of Land Grants) with the objective of returning pueblo common lands to their rightful owners. Spanish and Mexican custom and law form the basis for land use in the Southwest. In his book *Spanish and Mexican Land Grants and the Law* (1989), Malcolm Ebright affirmed that the Spanish king gave pueblo or municipal governments control over crown lands. Both Spain and Mexico gave land grants to settlers to help colonize Mexico's northern frontiers.

Tijerina's menu of activities included a 60-mile (96-km) march from Albuquerque to Santa Fe to present their demands to then governor Jack Campbell. More emboldened, the Alianza in October 1966 occupied a parcel of land in the Kit Carson National Forest. A year later the event for which his group gained world recognition occurred: Tijerina led a raid on New Mexico's County Courthouse in Rio Arriba Tierra Amarilla to arrest authorities held responsible by the Alianza for withholding the disputed land.

In May 1967, the organization changed its name. It became the Alianza Federal de Pueblos Libres (Federal Alliance of Free Towns). The Alianza, in a more sophisticated manner, attempted through legal appeals to convince the United States government to return common lands to the villages. There were no substantial results, despite its nonconfrontational efforts, such as when the organization had forcefully taken over the Rio Arriba courthouse.

In addition to land, water has always been a bone of contention in the southwest. Spanish law had governed the use of water in the Southwest for centuries. Expert-witness testimony about Hispanic water law has served as the basis for judicial decisions of water rights cases in the Southwest. The Treaty of Guadalupe Hidalgo protected Mexican properties, such as village common lands. After 1848 the United States government discovered the diverse land and water usage as prescribed by law in the Southwest. For example, New Mexico villages, communities dating to the 1600s, maintained successful cooperative associations that administered water rights. Those dry farming areas that relied on irrigation had systems for the division of water; a method for maintaining the *acequia madre,* or main channel; and the lateral ditches, *sangrias,* that led the water into the fields proper. Each family water user has a responsibility to make arrangements for a family member to help clean the *acequia madre.* In New Mexico, during the 300-year tradition, the *alcalde* or "mayor" administers the distribution of water and the allocation of times for watering depending on the amount of land to be irrigated. As in Arizona, irrigation is carried out during the night by the *zanjero,* or irrigator of fields.

In the Southwest the practice of publishing Spanish-language newspapers that provide political news, community interest articles, information, and *corridos* (ballads) on social issues antedated the United States war with Mexico in 1848. In this long southwestern tradition, *El Grito del Norte* (The Northern Cry) was published in Albuquerque as an independent newspaper to cover the Chicano movement, events, activists, and experiences during the 1960s and 1970s. Elizabeth "Betita" Martinez, an out-of-state activist and writer, was the publisher and editor. The paper offered political information on the Chicano movement as well as providing a historical perspective. The 1960s to the 1970s was a period of political activity for Latinos in New Mexico, California, Texas, and Arizona.

Jerry Apodaca began his political career when he was first elected to the New Mexico state senate in 1966. After eight years in the state legislature, on January 1, 1975, he became the 22d governor of the state and the first Hispanic governor in 50 years. His interests in energy issues led him to serve the Four Corners Regional Commission.

After Toney Anaya earned his law degree in 1967 at the Washington College of Law, American University, and had gained experience by working in the office of Senator Dennis Chavez from New Mexico, he returned to New Mexico as administrative assistant to Governor Bruce King. In 1974 Anaya was elected New Mexico's attorney general. In November 1982 he was elected governor, taking controversial stands against conventional politics by increasing state income taxes, promoting a strong affirmative action program, and proclaiming New

Mexico a sanctuary state for Central American refugees. For some time after 1984 Anaya was spoken of as a potential vice-presidential candidate.

New Mexico is also the setting for important fiction dealing with Latinos. Anglo authors include Willa Cather, whose novel *Death Comes to the Archbishop* is about Spanish missionaries in colonial times. Fray Angélico Chávez, famous for his *New Mexico Triptych* (it includes three stories: "The Angel's New Wings," "The Penitente Thief," and "Hunchback Madonna"), infused Catholic motifs in this oeuvre. The Chicano Rudolfo Anaya, author of *Bless Me Ultima,* among scores of books, explores the Mexican heritage of the place in thrillers, stories, and novels. Along with José Diego Maestas, he edited *Cuentos: Tales from the Hispanic Southwest* in 1980.

RELATED ARTICLES

Comanches; Gadsden Purchase; Gorras Blancas, Las; Guadalupe Hidalgo, Treaty of; Indian Wars; Mexican-American War; Southwestern United States, Anglo Immigration to; Taos Rebellion.

FURTHER READING

Bargas, Kita. *Valiente! Heritage of Texas, New Mexico, and Arizona to Statehood.* Nogales, Ariz.: Saxon Publications, 1985.

Blawis, Patricia Bell. *Tijerina and the Land Grants: Mexican Americans in Struggle for Their Heritage.* New York: International Pubs., 1971.

Briggs, Charles L., and John R. Van Ness, eds. *Land, Water, and Culture: New Perspectives on Hispanic Land Grants.* Albuquerque: Univ. of N.Mex. Press, 1987.

Ebright, Malcolm, ed. *Spanish and Mexican Land Grants and the Law.* Manhattan, Kans.: Sunflower Univ. Press, 1989.

Maestas, José Griego y., and Rudolfo A. Anaya. *Cuentos: Tales from the Hispanic Southwest.* Santa Fe: Museum of N.Mex. Press, 1980.

Meier, Matt S., and Feliciano Ribera. *Mexican Americans/ American Mexicans From Conquistadors to Chicanos.* New York: Hill and Wang, 1993.

Ortega, Pedro Ribera. *Christmas In Old Santa Fe.* Santa Fe: Sunstone Press, 1973.

Simmons, Marc. *New Mexico An Interpretive History.* Albuquerque: Univ. of N.Mex. Press, 1988.

Warner, Ted J., ed. *The Dominguez-Escalante Journal Their Expedition through Colorado, Utah, Arizona, and New Mexico in 1776.* Tr. by Fray Angélico Chávez. Salt Lake City: Univ. of Utah Press, 1995.

SANTOS C. VEGA

NEWSPAPERS AND MAGAZINES

For years Latino leaders have protested the negative portrayal or nonrepresentation of the Latino community in the mass media. This complaint can be seen in texts dating back to the beginning of the 19th century. It continued unabated well into the 1990s and into the early years of the 21st century. Not only is the lack of knowledge press leaders have regarding the problems surrounding the U.S. Hispanic community partly responsible for the negative representation, but the paucity of Latino editors and reporters within the mainstream English-language press is also a significant factor.

Since the passing of the Civil Rights Act in 1964, a greater minority representation in the newsroom has been sought. A couple of pioneering national associations strive to achieve this goal of incorporating ethnic minorities into newsrooms. One of them is the American Society of Newspaper Editors (ASNE) founded in 1922, which since 1978, has advocated for multiculturalism to increase diversity in U.S. newspaper newsrooms. It had established as a goal for the year 2000 "to have the nation's nonwhite newsroom population equal in percentage to that in the U.S. population." Likewise, in April 1984, the National Association of Hispanic Journalists (NAHJ) was established. With 1,700 members, this association is dedicated to the recognition and professional advancement of Latinos in the news industry.

Yet, despite the existence of the above-mentioned associations, the number of Latinos in the nation's most important newsrooms is far from representative of the population. According to a survey conducted by the *Boston Globe,* "only nine of the top 100 newspapers had a percentage of minority journalists on par with the percentage of minorities in their circulation areas." Latinos made up 4.04 percent of all newsroom employees in 2003. According to Nicolás Kanellos and Helvetia Martell's book *Hispanic Periodicals in the United States* (2000), *The Daily Worker,* the Communist Party newspaper published in New York, was the only paper to grant Jesús Colón (considered to be the first Latino reporter to make the transition to English-language press) an employment opportunity in 1955.

In recent history more Latino journalists have gained prestige and recognition within the national press, such as Gilbert Bailon of the *Dallas Morning News;* Mirta Ojito of the *New York Times;* Rick Rodríguez of the *Sacramento Bee;* Carolina García of the *San Antonio Express-News;* Alberto Ibarguen of the *Miami Herald;* Marie Arana of the *Washington Post;* Frank del Olmo of the *Los Angeles Times;* and Juan González of the *New York Daily News.*

Their participation in mainstream news brings a new vision and better understanding of the Latino community; however, the community's representation is still limited. In the process to achieve an objective representation of the Latino community within the mainstream press, the Latino press, written in Spanish as well as in English, has been active in its publications in the United States for almost two centuries.

The Latino press, which is vibrant and productive, with an extensive market, reflects the rapid growth of the community. The final decade of the 20th century witnessed a boom within Latino journalism. The figures confirm it; in 1999 the National Hispanic Media Directory identified more than 1,250 publications directed to the U.S. Hispanic market. The production of newspapers and magazines in particular enjoyed an increase of 50 percent. Just as imported as quantity, however, is quality, and the prestige of the Spanish-language press is evident in the directory, with its inclusion of at least two Spanish-language dailies, *La Opinión* and *¡Hoy!,* both of which are considered to be among the 50 best newspapers of the country, confirm the Latino press's excellence.

The first representative texts of Hispanic journalism in the United States date back to the beginning of the 19th century, a period in which the press became a form of mass-media communication in modern societies. The Hispanic press in the United States emerged at a time when the Latino community was registered as an ethnic minority, the first Hispanic communities having been formed during the 19th-century territorial expansion of the United States.

Some of the newly incorporated communities had their own journalistic traditions prior to U.S. annexation. With some effort they were able to keep these traditions alive. The first Spanish-language newspapers in the United States were published in New Orleans in 1808 (*El Misisipí*) and 1809 (*El Mensajero* and *Luisianés*), only five years after its annexation. Texas, Florida, and New Mexico already had established papers before the United States acquired these lands, as confirmed by the Texan newspapers *La Gaceta de Texas* and *El Mexicano,* published in 1813; *El Telégrafo de las Floridas* in 1817; and *El Crepúsculo de la Libertad,* published in New Mexico in 1834. In New York the Hispanic press tradition began early with the 1824 publication *El Habanero.* The majority of these newspapers preceded the *New York Sun,* recognized as the first mass-circulation press in the United States, and published in 1833.

This early surge of the U.S. Hispanic press can be explained by the fact that the ethnic minority was not a community of immigrants, but instead an invaded community. In *Occupied America* (2000) Rodolfo Acuña states that during the 19th century, 136 Spanish-language newspapers were published in the Southwest alone. The spread of Spanish-language newspapers in the Southwest, Florida, and elsewhere in the nation during the second half of the 19th century provides a view into life in Latino communities in the United States. For instance, the trials and tribulations of the tobacco industry in Ybor City (Florida) and New York City, was reflected in local dailies, which documented the domestic and labor conditions of Cubans and Puerto Ricans at the time.

The Spanish language has played an important role in the history of the Latino press. The majority of publications, past and present, are published in Spanish or in a bilingual version. The purpose of publishing in the native language of immigrant communities is a response to linguistic discrimination. At the same time, maintaining the use of Spanish for established Latino communities goes further; it validates one of the most basic cultural elements: language. The Latino press preserves the use of the native language as a representation of cultural pride and family traditions, and it keeps the language itself alive.

After World War II, English-language publications emerged within the Latino press. They reflected, on one hand, an agenda to integrate into the larger society and, on the other, the existence of an English monolingual Latino community. The theme of linguistic identification has been a controversial matter within the Latino community. Nonetheless, Spanish use demonstrates granting a prestigious status to the native language and, at the same time, the Latino culture.

Favorable circumstances existed in the United States for the establishment of the Latino press. Latino communities took advantage of the free press in the United States and generated a wide range of publications. Today one can identify, reviewing the history of the Latino press, publications that have served a diverse community. There are those looking to strengthen new communities; those defending the rights of their readers and offering civic education; those promoting the independence of their countries of origin, or the removal of a foreign dictatorship; others that worry about the establishment of commercial alliances or the exportation of technological advances; and so on.

Latinos constitute a heterogeneous minority, from different nations of origin, social backgrounds, and migration experiences. Nonetheless, on the current political agenda is a pan-Hispanic concept. And with ancestral pluralism characterizing the 38.8 million Latinos who live in the United States (according to the U.S. Census figures of July 2002), it is clear that uniting this community represents a tremendous challenge, even more so if pan-Hispanicism comes to include those beyond U.S. borders.

A similar challenge is facing Latino press specialists when they attempt to reach such a varied readership. The press is at once a public service and a business. With this in mind, the first great division that should be established is ownership, those whose owners are not part of the Hispanic community and the press written by and for Latinos.

Publications that do not belong to the community—which usually have as their sole interest economic gains—typically take advantage of private corporation or government financing available for the fair representation of minorities. These publications limit themselves to offering only a translation of the mainstream press news; they are not concerned with objectively representing the community, nor do they try to satisfy the specific interests of their audience.

The newspapers and magazines written and published by Latinos consider it their journalistic responsibility to find and elaborate the information the community needs and has the right to have to educate, make aware, and offer a fair representation of the community it serves. Throughout the history of the Latino press in the United States, it has been confirmed that only when the community possesses the media can it efficiently serve the community, thus becoming an alternate source of information.

Traditionally, the expense of mass-media production has made its existence virtually impossible without federal aid or private financing. Maintaining a stable economic base is one of the major challenges facing minority publications. The short lifespan of most Latino-owned publications proves this to be true. In fact, many newspapers and magazines struggle to survive for more than a few months or years, and frequently they are not able to maintain regular publishing schedules.

During the 19th century, for example, few publications maintained their production for more than 20 years. Of those few, the following can be cited. From New Mexico are *El Tiempo* (1882–1911), published in Las Cruces; *El Boletín Popular* (1885–1908); and *La Voz del Pueblo* (1889–1924), published in Santa Fe, and *El Combate* (1892–1919) of Albuquerque. From California is *La Sociedad* (1869–1895), published in San Francisco. From Texas is *El Correo Mexicano* (1890–1914), published in San Antonio. From New York is *Noticioso de Ambos Mundos* (1836–1859), and finally, from Trinidad, Colorado, *El Progreso* (1891–1914).

Journals and magazines from the 19th and the 20th centuries were published irregularly owing to inadequate financial support. However, they covered a range of different subject areas, from religious (*La Revista Católica*, 1875–1962, published in Las Vegas, New Mexico; and *Revista Evangelica*, 1937–1956, published in El Paso, Texas) to literary (*El Ateneo: Repertorio Ilustrado de Arte, Ciencia y Literatura*, 1874–1877, published in New York; *Revista Ilustrada*, 1907–1931, published in New Mexico; and *Con Safos* and *El Grito*, both from California and funded in 1968). In addition were political and civic groups' monthly newsletters (*LULAC News*, founded by the League of United Latin American Citizens, 1931–1979; the *Forumeer*, published by the American GI Forum; and *El Malcriado*, published in California by the United Farm Workers Organizing Committees, 1964–1975), which kept people informed about their rights and benefits as citizens of the United States.

Later there was a proliferation of diverse publications targeted to U.S. Latinos. These are illustrated magazines, mainly published in English or bilingual versions that started after the 1970s. The most prominent of this group are *VISTA* (1985), *Hispanic* (1988), *Hispanic Business* (1979), and *Latina Magazine* (1997). Since the last decades of the 20th century, there has been tremendous growth in Latino magazines. The majority of these, however, are highly commercial publications that cover mass-market, tabloid-style topics and are mainly advertising vehicles trying to capture the U.S. Hispanic market. Some magazines of this type have had overseas circulations as well as U.S. distribution. For example, *Geomundo*, *Cristina*, *People en Español*, or *ERES* (with a biweekly circulation of about 500,000).

On the other hand, there are stories of successful publications established during the first decades of the 20th century that remain strong in the current century, such as the newspaper *La Opinión*, in Los Angeles and, in New York City, *el diario/LA PRENSA* and its primary competitor *¡Hoy!* in New York City. Other publications that were founded in the second half of the 20th century and are still publishing with daily circulations above 50,000 editions, can also be cited. Among them are the newspapers *Noticias del Mundo*, in New York; in Miami, *El Nuevo Herald* and *Diario de las Américas*; in El Paso, Texas, *Diario de Juárez*; and in Chicago, *El Mañana*. These newspapers are characterized by their adaptability, which has kept them active through the years. All of these enterprises have had to consider drastic demographic changes throughout the 20th century—for example, the shifting percentage of the immigrant population versus native-born Hispanic communities—in order to serve their specific needs.

Besides having to redefine the ideal reader or target audience, these publications have also had to implement other economic strategies to survive in the market. One of the most common and successful strategies has been the merger of two or more journalistic enterprises. This was the case for two of the largest publications of the 20th century. *La Prensa*, founded by Ignacio E. Lozano in San Antonio, Texas, in 1913, expanded its influence with the creation of its sister publication, *La Opinión*, in Los Angeles in 1926. *La Opinión* remains under the patronage of the Lozano family. *La Prensa*, however, facing financial difficulties, merged in 1963 with *Diario de Nueva York* (1948–1963) to form *el diario/LA PRENSA*.

Another strategy has been to make the transition from a Spanish-language supplement of a mainstream paper to an independent publication. Thus was the case of *El Miami Herald*, which from 1976, until 1987, was a supplement of the *Miami Herald*, when it became *El Nuevo Herald*.

Nicolás Kanellos suggests a three-tiered classification system for the Latino press: the press in exile, the immigrant press, and the native Hispanic press, based on diverse models of readers who select the publications being analyzed. This classification system facilitates understanding the political and social realities that the Hispanic community has endured, since this reality determines the type of publications published during different periods of time and the readers these publications sought to address.

The first division, or the press in exile, includes publications written by political leaders or intellectuals who promoted the independence or revolutionary movements of their countries of origin. These publications, although printed in the United States, were distributed primarily abroad. Included in this classification are those publications related to the political schisms and armed struggles in the Hispanic world, such as the independence movements in Puerto Rico and Cuba during the 19th century and the independence and revolutionary movements in Mexico during the beginning of the 19th and 20th century. This category of press can also include publications that supported the Republican cause during the Spanish Civil War of the 1930s, or, during the second half of the 20th century, the publications that denounced the wars and genocides in Central and South America.

The second group, or the immigrant press, is perhaps best represented by Spanish-language publications. In the 19th and 20th centuries, the political and social instability that characterized the Hispanic world, and the strong political and economic intervention by the United States in the region, motivated a constant immigration to and exile in the United States. Along with the southwestern states, the locations that mainly welcomed these immigrant communities were Florida, New York City, Chicago, and Washington, D.C. Nonetheless, during the second half of the 20th century, the Latino presence became dispersed throughout the United States—a demographic change that called for the creation of new media. The objectives of this type of press are diverse and include topics such as the defense of immigrant rights and the struggle against discrimination. However, the kind of information it offers is focused for the most part on Latin American countries.

The third group, the native Hispanic press, covers the needs of the established communities in the country. This press concerns itself primarily with national issues affecting the community, the promotion of civil rights, and political representation in the com-

© TIM BOYLE/GETTY IMAGES

The Spanish-language newspaper ¡Hoy! in Chicago's mainly Latino Little Village neighborhood.

munity. It differs from the previous two categories because of its use of the English language. The editions frequently are bilingual.

These three types of press have had a direct influence in the Latino community. The exile press, for example, has an effect on local communities since such publications create a deep political and social consciousness.

Cases in which freedom of the press was restricted have not been uncommon for the Latino press, occurring mainly when the country is at war, or when a war affects the United States directly. Many dedicated Latino journalists have experienced repercussions because of their dedication to the community, sometimes offending the local status quo. Throughout the history of the Latino press, cases of repression against journalists can be cited. For example, Félix Martínez, editor of *La Voz del Pueblo* (1889–1924) published in New Mexico, had to leave the United States because of repercussions and censorship. A later notorious event involved Rubén Salazar, a legendary Chicano reporter for *The Los Angeles Times,* who was killed by police during a riot in 1970.

Kanellos's classification scheme is not always the most precise way to analyze the immense Latino press in the United States in the 21st century. Some of these publications, which may begin by representing an exile or immigrant community, are transformed into a native Hispanic press, or vice versa. To understand these assimilations, demographic changes within the Latino community, as well as the socioeconomic conditions of the country, must be taken into consideration. For example, it is common to observe, looking at the history of the Latino press, publications adjusting the profiles of their readership during strong periods of immigration.

Newspapers for the Hispanic community reflect the social reality in which they are produced. Consequently, the Latino community press is considered to be the principal investigative instrument with which the community has recovered its history.

By studying the history of this press, several different topics can be identified, including the areas of greatest demographic representation, waves of immigration, major historical events, the political orientation of the Latino community, moral values, cultural richness, topics of interest, and problems that affect the daily lives of members of the community.

The 21st century offers important possibilities for the Latino press but also poses considerable challenges, particularly that of ownership. Currently, European American companies, not Hispanic businesses, control the main Latino dailies. Two hundred years of history illustrate that when the Latino press is in the hands of members of its community, the possibilities of achieving its objectives become more viable.

The demographic studies that show Latino's constituting the largest minority group in the United States also place Latinos among those with the lowest income, and the least amount of education. Maintaining an alternative press could mean not only fair representation but also political, economic, and educational advancement and empowerment in the Latino community.

RELATED ARTICLES

El Diario/LA PRENSA; Journalism; *Miami Herald, The*; *Nuevo Herald, El*; *Opinión, La*; Popular Culture; Radio; Salazar, Rubén; Television.

FURTHER READING

Acuña, Rodolfo. *Occupied America: A History of Chicanos.* 4th ed. New York: Longman, 2000.

Carreira, María M. "The Media, Marketing and Critical Mass: Portents of Linguistic Maintenance." *Southwest Journal of Linguistics* 21 no. 2 (2002): 37–54.

Kanellos, Nicolás, and Helvetia Martell. *Hispanic Periodicals in the United States: Origins to 1960; A Brief History and Comprehensive Bibliography.* Houston, Tex.: Arte Público Press, 2000.

Riggins, Stephen Harold. *Ethnic Minority Media: An International Perspective.* Thousand Oaks, Calif.: Sage Pubns., 1992.

Rodríguez, América. *Making Latino News: Race, Language, Class.* Thousand Oaks, Calif.: Sage Pubns., 1999.

Villarreal, Roberto E., and Norma G. Hernández. *Latinos and Political Coalitions: Political Empowerment for the 1990s.* Westport, Conn.: Greenwood Press, 1991.

Wilson, Clint C., II, and Félix Gutiérrez. *Race, Multiculturalism, and the Media.* 2d ed. Thousand Oaks, Calif.: Sage Pubns., 1995.

SELECTED WEB SITES

American Society of Newspaper Editors.
   http://www.asne.org/
El Diario/La Prensa Online. www.eldiariony.com
National Association of Hispanic Journalists.
   http://www.nahj.org/

REBECA ACEVEDO

NEW YORK CITY

The history of Latinos in New York City is vast, complex, and politically charged. Historians have dated it back to the early 19th century. Since then, the Latino subcultures there have burgeoned, in number and breadth, and have in recent years become the center of attention for Hollywood, the media, and major corporations looking to target a market with major buying power. Latinos can be found in all major neighborhoods within the five boroughs of New York City: Manhattan, Staten Island, Queens, the Bronx, and Brooklyn. Their heritage as well as their skin color and traditions reflect the diverse array of their countries of origin—Mexico, Spain, the Caribbean (largely Puerto Rico, Cuba, and the Dominican Republic), Central America, and South America.

According to the U.S. Census of 1870 and 1890, the Latino and Hispanic population was estimated at about 6,000 people toward the end of the 19th century. At the time those living in New York City included Mexicans, Spaniards, Puerto Ricans, and Cubans. In the year 2000 the estimated number of Latinos grew to 2,160,554, constituting 27 percent of the city's population and showing an increase in what might be termed a *pan-Latinization*. Present-day Latinos are a mixture of skilled and unskilled workers who are steadfastly becoming the largest minority group in New York City, playing a prominent role in the community's development and labor force; yet many of them are still considered second-class citizens. Even the most recent Hispanic arrivals face discrimination, housing shortages, overcrowding, and unjust immigration laws.

Early 19th-century migrants were a mixture of skilled and semiskilled merchants and laborers, optimistic in a new land with a promising future. World War I and the United States's intervention in the politics of Cuba and Puerto Rico created a wave of political exiles aspiring to escape international exploitation and oppression in their homelands. For Cubans and Puerto Ricans, the accessibility of New York City facilitated easy passage and departure, for gaining independence or for a quick return to the native soil. Cubans, Puerto Ricans, and Spanish exiles—who brought with them their culture, food, and music—soon became the Latino working class of New York.

Bernardo Vega, a political activist from Puerto Rico who arrived in New York in 1916, wrote accurate and thorough memoirs during the period from 1910 to the 1940s. Vega discussed his job in munitions and tobacco factories and the issue in the community of intellectuals versus working class. The cigar factories hired men and women for the position of "El Lector" (the reader) whose job it was to read to the workers during business hours, creating many political discussions about socialism and anarchism. According to Vega, the readers were considered the intellectuals of the Latino working class. Cigar workers were also known to occupy standing-room sections in the Metropolitan Opera House and in local theaters. Puerto Ricans, known to be active supporters of any politician concerned with their plight, were the largest, most influential group among these Latinos, having gained citizenship and the right to vote in 1917. Despite their cultured backgrounds and citizenship status, however, these Puerto Ricans were treated as cheap labor and second-class citizens, and dissatisfaction with this treatment resonated in Latino music and politics. Numerous social activists were born out of this experience. For example, an influential female reader was Luisa Capetillo, a union organizer, who demanded equality among female and male cigar laborers. Jesús Colón, a labor organizer and an active participant in Puerto Rican affairs, was another effective leader.

The numerous organizations, newspapers, and rallies served as examples of the political sentiment in New York City during this era. The Tammany Hall political machine, which governed New York City politics, allowed immigrants to obtain jobs and housing and became the politician's target for electoral ballots. Many Hispanics saw New York as an escape from unemployment and poverty and were reported to have migrated to sections of Harlem and the Lower East Side of Manhattan as well as to Brooklyn. According to Vega, Latinos, except those who were of darker skin, faced little housing discrimination and enjoyed vibrant and social lives. They lived in neighborhoods previously built for Jewish, Italian, and Irish immigrants, which because of constant use, overcrowding, and little or no upkeep, were considered slums.

One popular area, located in northeastern Manhattan, was called *El Barrio,* or "the Neighborhood," and was externally known as Spanish Harlem. This section of Manhattan soon became the home to many Puerto Rican pioneers. It was the cradle for popular Latin beats such as salsa, merengue, mambo, rumba, and Latin soul, and made superstars of numerous artists such as Tito Puente, Celia Cruz, Marc Anthony, and Carlos Santana. Music and rhythm, which originated in El Barrio, is now the essence of

New York's Latino beat and has had a monumental impact on the sound of American music today.

The early 1930s marked the beginning of the Great Depression, World War II, and a shift from cigar and sugar manufacturing. As cigarette smoking and mechanized factories became the norm, U.S. Hispanics found themselves out of work and in desperate situations. The years after the Depression and World War II and until 1970 saw an influx of unemployed and impoverished immigrants from Puerto Rico, Cuba, and the Dominican Republic. Between 1945 and the late 1960s, U.S. government leaders actively patronized the United States in Puerto Rico, promoting migration and promising work and housing.

During approximately the same period, anti-Castro Cuban political refugees entered the country, and the death of dictator Leonidas Trujillo marked a change in immigration policies for natives of the Dominican Republic who were no longer bound to Trujillo's regime. Meanwhile Puerto Ricans were becoming the largest Latino group in New York City and "the Puerto Rican" would soon be synonymous with the stereotypical "Latino." As Juan González said in *Harvest of Empire,* "It didn't take long for the white, English-speaking majority to start casting uneasy glances at the growing number of brown-skinned, Spanish-speaking teenagers who didn't seem to fit into any established racial group." These new migrants arrived with the expectation of finding a place in the city's postwar market but soon found themselves within an unfavorable society and labor force. Racial tensions between Italians and Puerto Ricans flared in the 1950s, after Vito Marcantonio, a local Italian congressman, lost the election. Street gangs in both groups were popular.

The social unrest among Puerto Ricans and other ethnic groups was depicted on Broadway and in Hollywood in such shows as *West Side Story,* which gained international acclaim. The film made a star out of Rita Moreno, one of Puerto Rico's great entertainers. Moreno became the only female artist to date to win an Oscar, a Tony, a Grammy, and an Emmy. The 1950s also gave rise to Latin dance clubs such as the famous Latin Quarter and the Copacabana, making the mambo, cha-cha, and the *pachanga* internationally popular. Music rapidly became part of New York City's cross-cultural change; it was not rare to see Puerto Ricans, Afro-Americans, Upper East Side WASPs (white Anglo-Saxon Protestants),

and Jews dancing to the rhythms of Tito Rodríguez and Desi Arnaz.

Puerto Ricans' desire for social justice prevailed in the 1960s, a time of political activism and boycotts. Caught in the middle of a violent and dangerous ethnic war, dark skinned Puerto Ricans and other Latinos became prey to de facto segregation and gang beatings. To protect themselves, Puerto Ricans formed organizations and held rallies and meetings. An extremely influential mobilization was the Young Lords, comprising mostly young Puerto Ricans whose goal was to fight for equality, housing, and the poor. The first Latino leadership groups were formed in the Puerto Rican community; their aims were to strive for education and quality of living. Even today the number of people attending the annual Puerto Rican day parade, established in the 1960s, is a manifestation of the high regard that many Latinos have for their cultural heritage in New York City.

Some of the most politically effective artists of the era were Julia de Burgos, a Puerto Rican poet who wrote on the controversies between the homeland and New York City life, and Pedro Pietri, whose book of poetry *Puerto Rican Obituary*—in which he covers such topics as exploitation by employers, drug addiction, and segregation—received noteworthy praise. Another esteemed playwright was Miguel Piñero, the author of *Short Eyes* and one of the founders of the Nuyorican Poets Café, a landmark club where poets, playwrights, singers, and others from all walks of life gather to perform, display, and discuss artistic work. Popular neologisms became the norm: *Nuyorican* was and is used to describe a Puerto Rican New York resident; the term *Spanglish* refers to the language containing a mixture of English and Spanish spoken interchangeably. With their automatic U.S. citizenship and a long active political presence in New York, Puerto Ricans have played an important role in New York's history.

The year 1965 marked an end to the national origins quota law and stamped passage into the United States. Thousands of immigrants from Colombia, the Dominican Republic, Ecuador, Peru, and other countries in Central and South America migrated to the United States. Newcomers created social unrest for a city that feared a decline in American values and in the economy. Puerto Ricans soon lost jobs to migrants who were accustomed to a lower quality of life and did not complain about low wages

Mural on a wall along a New York City sidewalk depicts Puerto Rican cultural heritage.

and exploitation. A once overwhelmingly Puerto Rican society was being dominated by other Latino groups. Dominicans were the fastest-growing group in the city, and the northwestern Manhattan neighborhood of Washington Heights became known as their home away from home.

Supermarkets, bodegas (grocery stores), restaurants, and other places that were commonly owned by or employed Puerto Ricans were now being run by other Latino groups. Locations of these large communities were Spanish Harlem, the Lower East and West sides of Manhattan; Sunset Park, Bushwick, Brownsville, Red Hook, and Williamsburg sections of Brooklyn. These neighborhoods became known for their bodegas, sales, corner markets, and multicultural, diverse, lower-economic-class citizens. Spanish descendants were found in areas such as Manhattan's Chelsea, south Brooklyn, Williamsburg, and the Brooklyn Navy Yard. Latin food invariably made its way into the city's ethnic cuisine, and it soon was a hot trend, helping to create a household name out of Goya Foods, Inc., and a popular fast-food chain restaurant out of Taco Bell. Over the last half century stickball (a version of baseball), handball, soccer, and other street games became popular among Latino youths in the city. Latino influence has notably increased in competitive and professional sports, and numbers of Latinos can be found on the rosters of New York City's two Major League baseball teams, the Yankees and the Mets.

The 1980s and 1990s brought a generation of Latino immigrants struggling for identity in neighborhoods that threatened to drown them in drugs and violence. The majority of them had less than a high school diploma and were unskilled and uneducated. Between 1980 and 1993, the need for public assistance rose dramatically. The years to come would bring about a drastic change among first-, second-, and third-generation Latinos, who would now see themselves as Americans and would surpass their parents' education, living standards, and housing situations.

By the year 2000 New York City was home to a full spectrum of diversity and was being shaped by a prodigious Latino community. According to the 2000 U.S. Census, Mexicans constituted 186,872 of

New York City's population, but most Mexicans were undocumented and thus were not included in this deceptive number. Puerto Ricans had reached a staggering 789,172 and were the poorest of all Latino groups. Cubans numbered 41,123 and were considered the Latino "elite," while Dominicans accounted for 406,806, making them the second largest Latino group. Central Americans, South Americans, and other Latinos accounted for approximately 736,581 of the city's residents. Although today Latinos, in general, have a higher standard of living compared with their predecessors, many still face housing shortages and overcrowding. According to the Centro de Estudios Puertoriqueños at Hunter College, City University of New York, "the increase in migration from Latin America and high fertility rates among Latinos, while benefiting the city and the state of New York as a whole, has come at a disproportionate cost to the Latino population of the city." The result has been overcrowding and substandard liv-

ing, an issue that Latinos must focus on if they hope to move forward and find political, sociocultural, and intellectual prosperity.

Early Latino migrants fought for nationalism, independence, and one day returning to their homelands. These migrants struggled to maintain a social status and quietly accepted their second-level class. The political struggle of the 1950s and 1960s reconstructed life for second-generation Latinos who fought for political rights, better housing, job security, and the American dream. They also introduced to New York City their food, language, and other aspects of Hispanic culture, enhancing the city's cross-cultural richness. Latinos can be found in all levels of society and in most every major neighborhood of New York. The issues of housing, overcrowding and higher education are still prevalent among Latinos, but these issues have more of an impact on today's first-generation immigrants. The sons and daughters of New York's early immigrants have surmounted

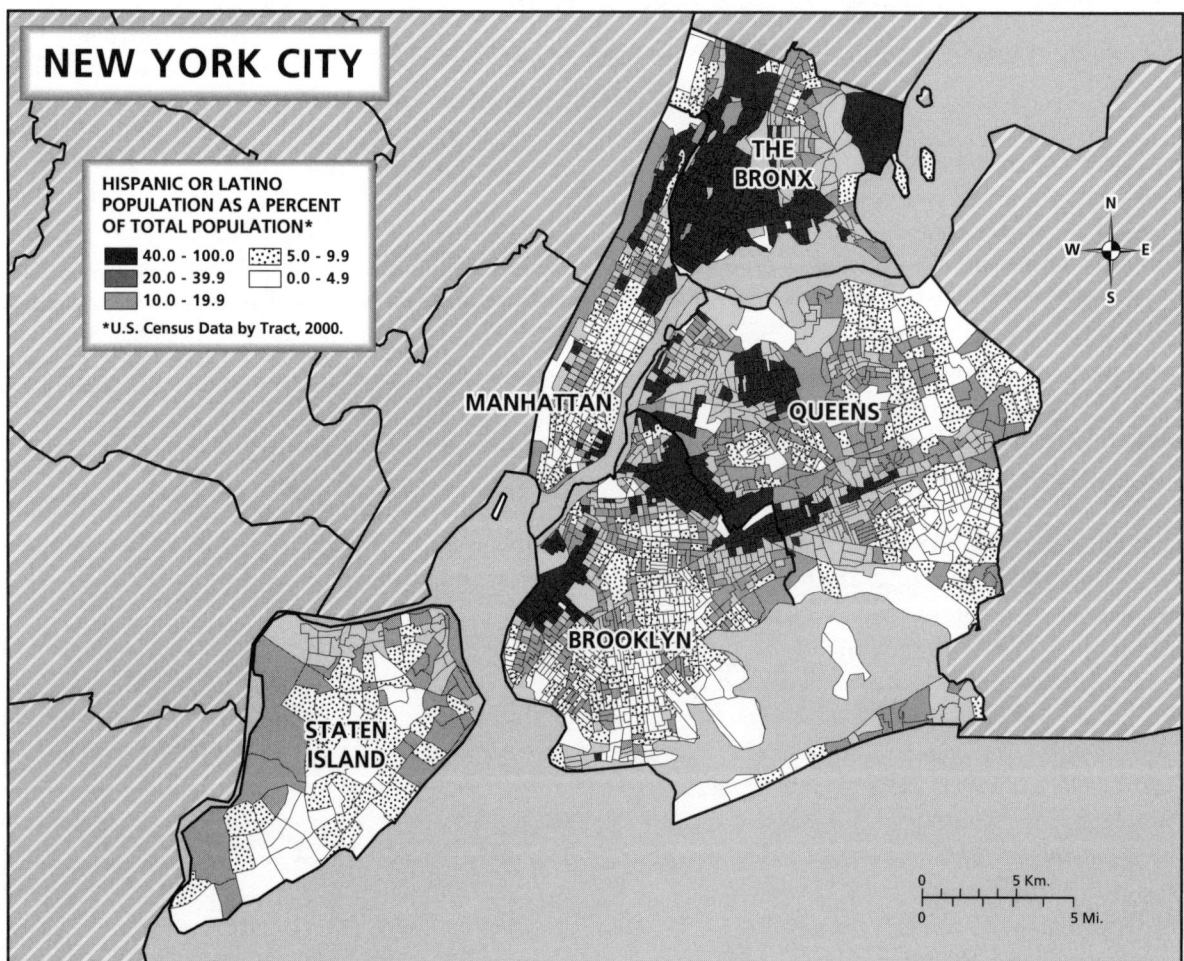

NEW YORK CITY

HISPANIC OR LATINO POPULATION AS A PERCENT OF TOTAL POPULATION*

40.0 - 100.0   5.0 - 9.9
20.0 - 39.9   0.0 - 4.9
10.0 - 19.9

*U.S. Census Data by Tract, 2000.

THE BRONX

MANHATTAN

QUEENS

BROOKLYN

STATEN ISLAND

0   5 Km.
0   5 Mi.

obstacles and can be found in the theater, academia, the arts, politics, and business.

RELATED ARTICLES

Barrio, El; Barrio Life; Brazilian Americans; Chilean Americans; Colombian Americans; Costa Rican Americans; Cuban Americans; Dominican Americans; Guatemalan Americans; Immigration, Latino; Loisaida; Mexican Americans; New York State; Nicaraguan Americans; Nuyorican Poets Café; Panamanian Americans; Political Parties; Politics, Latino; Politics, Puerto Rican; Puerto Rican Day Parade; Puerto Ricans on the Mainland; Restaurants; Spanish Americans; Spanish Harlem; Stonewall Movement; Venezuelan Americans; Washington Heights; *West Side Story.*

FURTHER READING

Centro de Estudios Puertoriqueños. *Housing Emergency and Overcrowding: Latinos in New York City.* New York: Hunter College, City Univ. of N.Y., 2003.

Flores, Juan. *From Bomba to Hip-Hop: Puerto Rican Culture and Latino Identity.* New York: Columbia Univ. Press, 2000.

Gonzáles, Juan. *Harvest of Empire: A History of Latinos in America.* New York: Viking Penguin, 2000.

Haslip-Viera, Gabriel, and Sherrie L. Baver. *Latinos in New York: Communities in Transition.* Notre Dame, Ind.: Univ. of Notre Dame Press, 1996.

SANDRA DUQUE

NEW YORK STATE

In 2000 Hispanics made up more than 15 percent of the state population of New York and 27 percent of the population in New York City's five boroughs, according to the U.S. Census. More than 75 percent of the state's Hispanic population resided in New York City, considered the largest Hispanic community in the nation. In the Census 2000, the New York state counties with the largest Hispanic populations included the Bronx, with 644,705 Hispanics; Queens, with 556,605; Kings, with 487,878; New York, with 417,816; Suffolk, with 149,411; Westchester, with 144,124; and Nassau, with 133,282.

In 2000 the state's Hispanic population of 2,867,583 was diverse. It has grown 29.5 percent from 1990, mirroring a national trend in the burgeoning Hispanic population. Puerto Ricans continued to make up the largest Hispanic subgroup in New York state, with 1,050,293 habitants, or 37 percent. The next largest group was Dominicans, with 455,061 habitants, or 16 percent; followed by Mexicans, with 260,889 habitants, or 9 percent. Cubans made up 62,590 of the Hispanic population, at 2

percent; South Americans were 318,387, or 11 percent; and Central Americans were 181,875, or 6 percent of the Hispanic population. Other Latinos composed 19 percent of the Hispanic population.

Latino migration from the city to Long Island has grown. More than 282,000 Hispanics lived in Nassau and Suffolk counties of Long Island, more than 10 percent of Long Island's population. The Hispanic population was centered in communities such as Brentwood, Hempstead, Freeport, and Central Islip. There also was a small but growing presence on the eastern end in towns such as Southampton. Puerto Ricans made up about 27 percent of Long Island's Hispanic population. Mexicans accounted for 5 percent, Cubans 3 percent, and Hispanics from other countries accounted for almost 66 percent; many of them came from Central America, particularly El Salvador.

The Long Island community of Farmingville has been a flashpoint of ethnic tensions in recent years. In July 2003 the home of a family of Mexican immigrants was firebombed; nobody was injured. In 2000 a couple of white supremacists masquerading as contractors picked up and attacked two Mexican immigrant workers; the attackers were convicted of attempted manslaughter. Mexican and Central American immigrants, many of them undocumented, have been steadily moving to towns and villages on Long Island in search of contracting work. An anti-immigrant group that formed in the late 1990s, Sachem Quality of Life Organization, has virulently opposed day laborers and undocumented immigrants. They were not, however, directly linked to any of the crimes in Farmingville. Immigration advocates have launched an effort to set up day-labor sites in other communities such as Freeport, and Hispanic political groups have sought representation in Long Island in recent years. A Hispanic Democratic Club was founded in Brentwood in the late 1990s and in Nassau a Republican Hispanic Assembly also was founded; however, there was almost no Hispanic representation among elected officials.

In Yonkers in Westchester County the 2000 census counted 51,852 Hispanics, a growth of nearly 62 percent over 1990 population figures, or 26 percent of the city residents. Only a few Hispanics were recorded in Yonkers in the 1900 census, with the first Hispanic group to move there in large numbers being Cubans. They eventually established La Lojia, a Cuban community center. Puerto Ricans had moved to Yonkers in large numbers by the 1950s, and in the 1960s Dominicans were moving in as well. In 1978 Colombians established the Colombian Community Center, and around this time the annual Puerto Rican Parade celebrations began. Since the 1980s the area has seen a gradual increase in its Mexican population, which formed the Mexican Chamber of Commerce in 2001. Still, Puerto Ricans were the largest Hispanic group in Yonkers in the 2000 census.

Hispanics in Yonkers have fought for political representation. Fernando Fuentes became the first Latino to hold elected office in Yonkers after he was appointed in 1994. An organization of Hispanic Democrats of Westchester also formed there. One of the early community groups to assist the Hispanic community's social service needs was the Spanish Community Progress Foundation, founded in a storefront in the late 1960s. Recent community groups that

have formed include YALIS (Yonkers Alliance for Latino and Immigrant Services).

Outside of the metropolitan area, cities with growing Hispanic populations include Albany, Buffalo, Rochester, and Syracuse. The 1880 census showed only small numbers of Latino families in these communities, mostly from Cuba, Spain, Mexico, and South America. Latinos started arriving in larger

NEW YORK—POPULATION BY HISPANIC ORIGIN, 1980 TO 2000

Census Year	Total Population	Percentage	Hispanic Origin	Percentage
2000	18,976,457	100	2,867583	15.1
1990	17,990,455	100	2,214,026	12.3
1980	17,558,072	100	1,659,300	9.5

Source: U.S. Census Bureau, 2000.

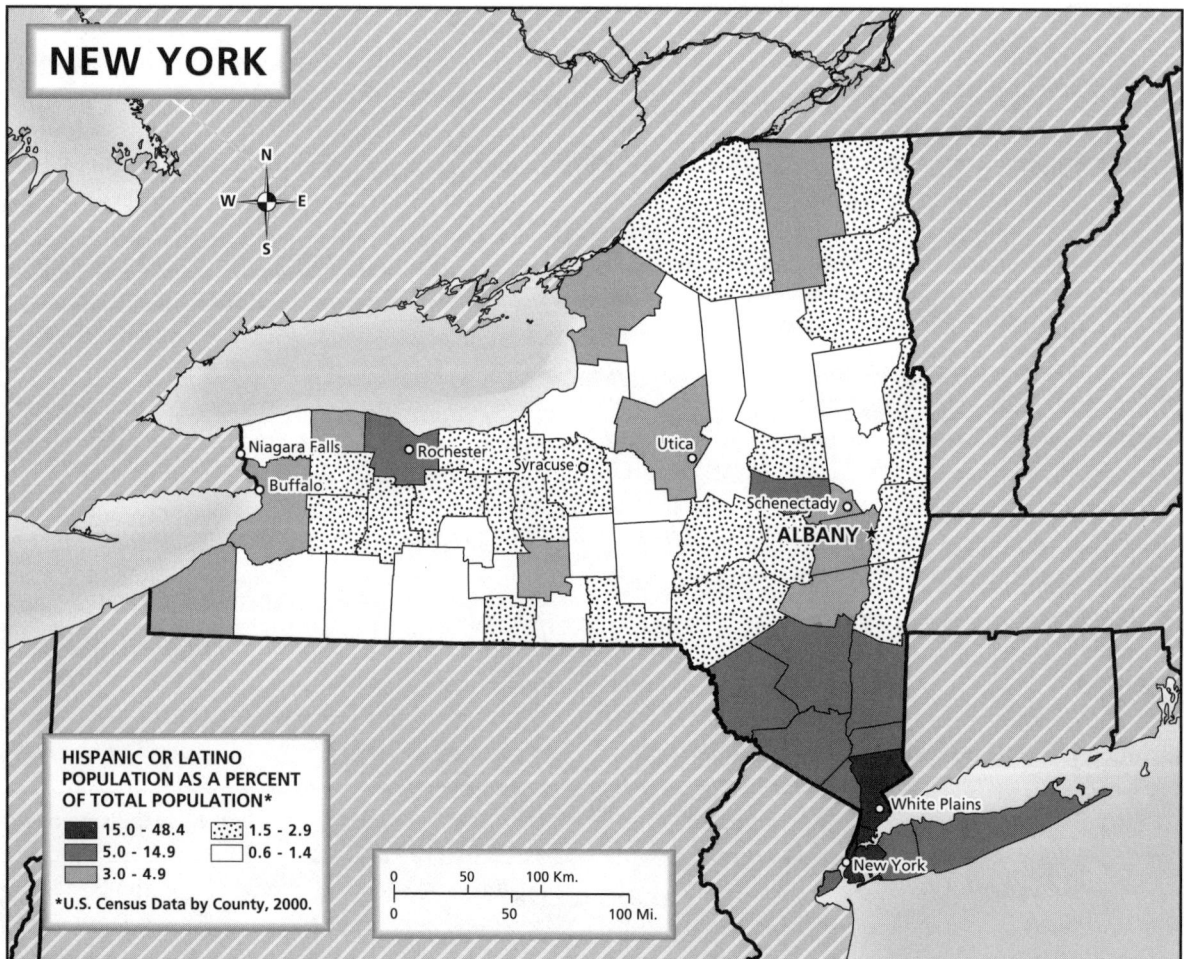

NEW YORK

HISPANIC OR LATINO POPULATION AS A PERCENT OF TOTAL POPULATION*

- 15.0 - 48.4
- 5.0 - 14.9
- 3.0 - 4.9
- 1.5 - 2.9
- 0.6 - 1.4

*U.S. Census Data by County, 2000.

numbers from the 1940s to the 1960s. In Albany County the Hispanic population grew from 5,311 to more than 9,000 from 1990 to 2000, when Hispanics made up around 6 percent of the Albany city population. The Hispanic population grew from 2,703 to 3,433 in Montgomery County, where Amsterdam is located. In the late 1940s Mohawk Mills in Amsterdam began recruiting Puerto Rican laborers by advertising in newspapers on the island. Dominicans also began to settle in the area in the 1960s, and the Latino community began forming social clubs, one of the earliest being the Spanish American Club. In 1975 the Centro Civico Hispano American was founded in Albany and the Centro Civico of Amsterdam was formed in 1986. In April 2004 Joe Cavazos was appointed the commissioner of administrative services in Albany, making him the city's first Hispanic commissioner.

In western New York cities, such as Buffalo, there were 22,076 Hispanics, who made up 7.5 percent of the population in 2000, but their history in the area goes back to 1924 when a Spanish American club was founded to serve the 140 people of Spanish descent living there. Mexicans also had an early presence and formed the Centro Social Club Mexicano in 1947. The Puerto Rican community is still the largest in Buffalo, dating back to the 1940s. By 1950 there were approximately 1,500 Puerto Ricans in the area; they formed the Borinquen Club. Augustine "Pucho" Olivencia founded the Puerto Rican-American Community Organization on Swan Street in 1969. Cubans and Dominicans moved to Buffalo in greater numbers in the 1960s. In 1970 Hispanics United of Buffalo was formed as a community organization. By 2000 the Lower West Side of Buffalo was the center of the Hispanic community.

The Hispanic population was the fastest growing group in Rochester. Hispanics migrated to this part of western New York more than a half century ago. According to Census 2000, there were 28,032 Hispanics in Rochester, totaling 13 percent of the population. In Monroe County alone, the Hispanic population increased from 26,450 to 39,065 from 1990 to 2000. In the six-county Rochester region, the Hispanic population nearly doubled to 48,000. Puerto Ricans were the largest group, representing 78 percent of the Hispanic population in the city. Cubans made up about 4 percent of the Hispanic population, and Mexicans 3 percent. The Hispanic population also increased in the suburbs of Rochester. In 1990, 87 percent of Monroe County's Hispanic population lived in the city. By 2000, only 72 percent lived in the city, although Hispanics still account for only a small percentage of the total suburban population. Hispanics in Rochester have made some political gains; there has been at least one Hispanic representative on every board, including the Monroe County legislature, the Rochester board of education, and the city council.

In Syracuse in Onondaga County, the Latino community grew in the 1950s when migrant farmworkers, mostly from Puerto Rico, came to pick crops in the region. By the 1960s these families had left farm work for factory and restaurant work, settling mostly on the south and west sides of the city. With support from Saint Lucy's Church, residents formed the Spanish Action League in 1969. This nonsectarian social service agency had a million-dollar budget in 2001. By 1974 community leaders had formed the Borinquen Latin American Club, which sponsored dances and recreational activities for families. In 1989 the ANCLA (Association of Neighbors Concerned with Latino Affairs), was created to involve Latinos in the political process. In 2001 the Onondaga Latino Caucus, focusing on voter registration and education forums, was founded. That same year Bethaida Gonzalez was elected president of the Syracuse common council, having served on the Syracuse city school board from 1991 to 1994. The 2000 census found 5,349 Latinos in Syracuse with the population having grown by 55 percent to 11,175 in Onondaga County.

New York State counties with smaller Hispanic populations also saw a dramatic increase in growth from 1990 to 2000. The greatest percentage increase of Hispanic population in the state was in Putnam County, which saw an increase of more than 166 percent, to almost 6,000. In Fulton County the Hispanic population grew by 115 percent, to 882, and in Genesee County the Hispanic population grew by 100 percent, to 904. Dutchess County's Hispanic population grew by 85 percent, to more than 18,000, and in Broome County it grew by 61 percent, to almost 4,000 residents. The Hispanic population grew by 60 percent in Ulster County, to 10,941, and in Erie County it grew by 40 percent, to more than 31,054.

As their numbers have grown, more Latinos have been elected to statewide office. In 1937 Oscar Riv-

HISPANIC OR LATINO AND RACE NEW YORK 2000

Total Population	18,976,457	100.0%
Hispanic or Latino (of any race)	2,867,583	15.1%
Mexican	260,889	1.4%
Puerto Rican	1,050,293	5.5%
Cuban	62,590	0.3%
Other Hispanic or Latino	1,493,811	7.9%
Not Hispanic or Latino	16,108,874	84.9%

Source: U.S. Census Bureau, 2000.

era, of Puerto Rican heritage, was elected to the state Assembly. In 1970 Herman Badillo was elected to the U.S. House of Representatives from New York's 21st District in the South Bronx. He became the first congressman born in Puerto Rico to represent a district in the continental United States. In 1964 Robert Garcia was elected to the New York Assembly and two years later became the first Puerto Rican elected to the New York State Senate. In 1978 he was elected to the U.S. House of Representatives. As of 2002 there were 4 Latinos in the state Senate and 11 Latinos in the state Assembly. New York State was represented by two Latinos in the U.S. Congress, representatives Jose E. Serrano and Nydia M. Velasquez, both Democrats, although Latinos made up only around 8 percent of the voting electorate in the state.

The growth of the Hispanic population in the state is also reflected in the growth of the Latino and Spanish-language media. The Spanish-language newspaper *¡Hoy!* debuted in New York in 1998. Another major Spanish-language newspaper is *El Diario/LA PRENSA*. *El Nacional,* another daily, targets the New York Dominican audience. There are more than a dozen weekly or monthly newspapers and magazines in New York City that focus on specific countries such as Colombia, Mexico, and Puerto Rico. Among the other Hispanic publications in the state are *El Aguila del Hudson Valley,* published in White Plains, *Noticias del Mundo,* published on Long Island, and *Panorama Hispano* and *La Ultima Hora,* both published in Buffalo. There are numerous radio stations in New York with Spanish-language programs or Latin music formats.

The cultural influence of Latinos also is widespread in the state. The Association of Hispanic Arts, Inc. (AHA) is a nonprofit organization dedicated to the advancement of Latino arts, artists, and arts organiza-

tions, which supports grants throughout the New York tristate area. In Buffalo the nonprofit Latin American Cultural Association operates El Buen Amigo, an art gallery and shop with imported goods from Latin America. Buffalo is also home to El Museo Francisco Oller y Diego Rivera, a nonprofit arts organization dedicated to the exhibition of fine art by Latin American and African American artists and other artists of color. The city of Albany, in collaboration with the Albany Latin Festival Association, holds an annual Latinfest, a family festival event with Latin music and jazz bands.

The fraternal service organization La Unidad Latina, Lambda Upsilon Lambda, was founded at Cornell University in Ithaca in 1982. It was the first Latino fraternity chartered at an Ivy League university. Today, it has chapters across New York state and the country.

Latinos have also played key roles in New York's sports world. Soccer is one of the most popular sports among Latinos in the United States, as it is in their home countries. New York's Major League baseball teams boast numerous Latino players. Latinos also figure prominently in the state's boxing community (José "Chegui" Torres, from New York, won a silver medal in the 1956 Olympics and in 1965 became the world light-heavyweight boxing champion. He also served as the commissioner and chairman of the New York State Athletic Commission, the first Hispanic to hold either position.

Overall, Hispanics in New York state lag behind the general population in median household income. The median household income for Hispanics of any race in New York state in 1999 was $30,499, according to census figures. Of the Hispanic subgroups, South Americans were among the highest earners, with a median household income of $40,046; followed by Cubans, with $36,201; and Central Americans, with $36,055. The average household income for Mexicans was $34,589; for Dominicans, it was $26,873; and for Puerto Ricans, $25,878. A census sampling of households found 28 percent of Hispanics in New York State had an income level below the poverty line in 1999.

RELATED ARTICLES

Brazilian Americans; Chilean Americans; Colombian Americans; Costa Rican Americans; Cuban Americans; Dominican Americans; Guatemalan Americans; Immigration, Latino; Mexican Americans; New York City; Nicaraguan Americans; Panamanian Americans; Puerto

Ricans on the Mainland; Spanish Americans; Venezuelan Americans.

FURTHER READING

Ayala, César J. "The Decline of the Plantation Economy and the Puerto Rican Migration of the 1950s." *Latino Studies Journal* 7, no. 1 (Winter 1996): 61–90.

Chenault, Lawrence. *The Puerto Rican Migrant in New York City.* 1938. Reprint. New York: Russell & Russell, 1970.

Hernández, Ramona, and Francisco L. Rivera-Batiz. "Dominicans in the United States: A Socioeconomic Profile, 2000." *Dominican Research Monographs, The CUNY Dominican Studies Institute* (October 6, 2003).

TERESA PUENTE

NICARAGUAN AMERICANS

Nicaraguans have immigrated to the United States in small groups since the early 1900s, but their presence was especially felt over the last three decades of the 20th century. The Nicaraguan community has concentrated in three major urban areas: Miami, Los Angeles, and New York City. According to the U.S. census 1997 yearbook, more than 50 percent of Nicaraguans lived in Florida; 35 percent reported living in California, mostly around Los Angeles; and only 7 percent were registered in the New York–New Jersey area. In general, the Nicaraguan American community is financially better off than most Central American national groups except the Costa Rican. Nevertheless, there are major differences within the Nicaraguan American community: the most affluent community is located in the New York–New Jersey area, and the poorest is found in the Miami area. Nicaraguan Americans are Spanish speaking and predominantly Catholic. They celebrate the patron saints of the church with festivals and processions, which also provide a context for artistic and cultural expressions of the local identity. The most important patronal festivals celebrated in the Nicaraguan communities in Florida are Santa Ana, San Sebastián, La Purísima, San Jerónimo, and La Griteria.

The U.S. Census 1997 yearbook reported that approximately 239,000 Nicaraguans lived in the United States. The figures published by the Immigration and Naturalization Service (INS) statistical yearbooks are preferred by some analysts and policymakers mostly because the large majority of Nicaraguans have appealed for refugee status in the United States and, therefore, have filed a request for political asylum with INS offices. According to INS figures 23,261 were admitted as permanent residents between 1976 and 1985; 75,264 were admitted between 1986 and 1993; and 94,582 between 1994 and 2002, with a total of 193,107 Nicaraguan immigrants being granted legal status since 1976.

The territory that is now Nicaragua was occupied by the Spanish in 1522 under Gil Gonzáles de Avila and became part of the captaincy general of Guatemala. After declaring independence from Spain in 1821, Nicaragua was briefly part of the Central American Federation. Politics in Nicaragua can be described as a long conflict between liberals and conservatives, with several foreign interests trying to determine the direction of the country. British forces established a siege in San Juan del Norte in 1848, commencing a period of conflict over the control of the Mosquito Coast.

The United States was interested in a passage (the Nicaragua Canal) between the Atlantic and Pacific oceans, and that interest was certainly heightened by the discovery of gold in California. In 1912 U.S. marines landed to support the provisional president, Adolfo Día, in a civil war. In an attempt to justify American occupation, the Bryan-Chamorro Treaty, which gave the United States exclusive rights for a Nicaraguan canal as well as other privileges, was signed in 1916. It was not terminated until 1970. Nicaraguan Liberals opposed the U.S. intervention, and a guerrilla war led by Augusto César Sandino was carried out against the U.S.-supported regime for years. The U.S. marines withdrew in 1933, and three years later Anastasio Somoza emerged as the strongman in Nicaragua. His dictatorship lasted almost 20 years, from 1937 until 1956, when he was assassinated. His sons, Luis and Anastasio Somoza, continued to engineer the presidential elections and government of Nicaragua, which was corrupt and full of abuses, for many years. For example, after the 1972 earthquake that devastated Managua, Anastasio Somoza became director of the emergency relief operations and diverted most of the international aid to himself and his associates. By 1974 two major opposition factions, the Sandinista National Liberation Front (FSLN) and the Democratic Liberation Union (UDEL), had developed. Violent fighting between the Somoza government and the opposition occurred throughout the 1970s and by 1979 the FSLN and UDEL had defeated the Somoza government. The more radical, left-wing FSLN, or Sandinistas, took control of the government, instituting widespread social, political, and economic changes. Many economic institutions and resources were nationalized, land was redistributed, and social services such as health care and education were improved.

In 1981 the United States, politically unsupportive of the Sandinista government and suspicious of its relations with the Soviet Union and Cuba, cut off economic aid to Nicaragua and began supporting the counterrevolutionary military forces, or "contras." In 1984 Daniel Ortega was chosen as president of the Sandinista party. Although his government was popular, especially with the urban poor and peasants, the contras began an active military campaign against the Sandinista regime, which in reality affected all aspects of Nicaraguan life. It was at this time that the exodus to the United States, especially to the cities of Miami and Los Angeles, became massive. Although they believed at first that their return home would be imminent, the Nicaraguans soon realized that their exile would be more permanent, as matters in Nicaragua continued to worsen.

Stable Nicaraguan communities in the United States took shape as the immigrants established small businesses or found other employment, reproducing the internal patterns they had left in the home country. Especially in Miami, where the climate was favorable for educated, middle-class refugees from a leftist revolutionary government, which also supported the socialist Cuban government, Nicaraguans have developed a well-established community. In the 1980s they could (like Cubans) apply for political asylum from a socialist government at home.

In 1990, supported by the contra movement and ex-Somocista National Guard officers, Violeta Chamorro won the elections against the Sandinistas. The United States soon lifted its trade embargo and the contras ceased fighting. Chamorro tried, with mixed success, to revive the economy and generate a conciliatory political environment. In 1996 José Alemán, who was the leader of the Liberal Alliance, won the elections. This conservative coalition also retained the presidency in 2001 with the election of Enrique Bolaños.

Although the news of Chamorro's election was received with joy by a large number of those in the U.S. Nicaraguan community, this change in the government at home did not create a sizable return of expatriates. By this time many Nicaraguans had lived in the States for five to ten years, establishing themselves and their families in the community, and they were reluctant to go back to the uncertainties of a post–civil war period. The high rates of unemployment or underemployment (nearly 60 percent) in Nicaragua was another major deterrent to their returning.

In November 1998 Hurricane Mitch killed 4,000 people in Nicaragua, which has a population of barely over 4 million. Nicaraguans were granted the right to immigrate to the United States under the Nicaraguan Adjustment and Central American Relief Act (NACARA); 63,329 Nicaraguans were admitted between 1999 and 2002.

Nicaraguan Americans have added their rich culture heritage to their American communities. In the film *Carla's Song* (1996), Oyanka Cabezas, a well-known Nicaraguan actress, portrays a Nicaraguan dancer in a love story between a rebellious Scottish bus driver and a Nicaraguan refugee during the Sandinista-contra war.

Daisy Zamora, a Nicaraguan-born, San Francisco–based writer, was a combatant in the National Sandinista Liberation Front and director of Radio Sandino's clandestine programs during the revolution. In the Sandinista government she served as vice minister of culture and as the executive director of the Institute of Economic and Social Research of Nicaragua. She has published three books of poetry: *En limpio se escribe la vida* (1988); *La violenta espuma;* and *A cada quien la vida,* as well as an anthology, *The Nicaraguan Woman in Poetry.* Three books of her poems are available in English: *Clean Slate* (1993), *Riverbed of Memory* (1992), and *The Violent Foam* (2002). She is presented in the Bill Moyers's *Language of Life* series that first aired on the Public Broadcasting Service in 1995, and she is also well-known as a painter and a psychologist.

Gioconda Belli is another well-published Nicaraguan writer who lives in Managua, Nicaragua, and Santa Monica, California. Belli's poetry and fiction have been translated into several languages. For her second collection of poems, *Línea de Fuego* (1978; Line of Fire), Belli won the prestigious Casa de las Americas Prize. Her poetry has been described as one of the most beautiful and natural voices of the Nicaraguan revolution and of Nicaraguan women. Her first novel, *The Inhabited Woman/Amor Insurrecto* (1984), was an international best-seller. Some of her books are to be found in English translation, including *De la costilla de Eva* (1987), which was translated and published as *From Eve's Rib* in 1989. Her autobiography, *The Country under My Skin: A*

Memoir of Love and War (2002) *(El país bajo mis pies)*, tells of her extraordinary life as a mother, poet, and revolutionary, but above all as a Nicaraguan woman. "This book is about American history, North and South; about power and the seeds of revolution; about one woman's life and choices entangled among many lives—and deaths—expended in the unkillable hope for human freedom and love" (Adrienne Rich). As the Nicaraguan community in the United States grows, a new generation of Nicaraguan Americans will become established in the cultural, political, and economic environments of the United States.

RELATED ARTICLES

Immigration, Latino; Literature, Latin American; United States-Central America Relations.

FURTHER READING

Cortázar, Julio. *Nicaraguan Sketches*. Tr. by Kathleen Weaver. New York: Norton 1989.

Lipski, John. "The Linguistic Situation of Central Americans." In *New Immigrants in the United States; Readings for Second Language Educators*. Ed. by Sandra Lee McKay and Sau-ling Cynthia Wong. Cambridge, England: Cambridge Univ. Press 2000.

U.S. Immigration and Naturalization Service. *Statistical Yearbook of the Immigration and Naturalization Service, 2002.* Washington, DC: USGPO.

M. CECILIA COLOMBI

NORTEÑO

At its bare essence *norteño,* Spanish for "northern," is a folk-based music similar to American country. Like conjunto and Tejano, it originated along the U.S.-Mexico border, especially the then sparsely populated areas of the northern Mexican states of Chihuahua, Coahuila, Nuevo León, and Tamaulipas. Like country music, *norteño* was stigmatized as hillbilly and blue-collar music. Owing to its rural background, *norteño* music appealed to farmworkers, ranchers, and their displaced brethren who ventured to Monterrey, Nuevo León, Mexico, in search of factory work. It was often sung in a raspy, relaxed style but with lively European-rooted polka and waltz rhythms; the music made people dance. The quintessentially Mexican story-songs known as *corridos* became part of the repertoire, and accordion players adopted a staccato, high-pitched tone that is uniquely Mexican.

One of the seminal *norteño* groups was Los Alegres de Terán, formed in 1948 in General Terán, Nuevo

León, Mexico, by accordionist Eugenio Abrego and bajo sexto player Tomás Ortiz. The duo, known for its spry rhythms and descriptive *corridos,* scored hits with the romantic *Alma Enamorada* and corridos *Carta Jugada* and *El Güero Estrada*. It was one of the first *norteño* groups to sign with a major recording label. The music's instrumentation grew fuller over time, with many groups adding drums and saxophone by the 1950s. Los Relámpagos del Norte, the most influential *norteño* group of the 1960s, was formed in the border city of Reynosa. Including Ramón Ayala and Cornelio Reyna, the group ruled the charts throughout the decade thanks to Reyna's romantic touch on *Hay Ojitos* and *Me Caí de la Nube*. He also incorporated the Cuban ballad rhythm of bolero with his classic *Mi Tesoro*. Bolero would become an important rhythm with many *norteño* bands from northeastern Mexico. Ayala and Reyna went on to outstanding solo careers, occasionally reuniting. Reyna

REFORMA-EN RED / NEWSCOM

Mexico-born accordion player Celso Pina, left, accompanies Texan Flaco Jiménez during a *norteño* concert, Mexico City, 2001.

died in 1997, and in 2000 Ayala produced an album by Cornelio Reyna, Jr.

Slowly, *norteño* began catching on in the northwestern Mexico states of Sinaloa, Sonora, and Baja California, and in 1968 another major group emerged in the form of Los Tigres del Norte. Originally from Sinaloa, Los Tigres formed in San Jose, California, playing a harsher sound that included bouncy electric bass and fierce accordion and sax introductions. Their signature sound included the *narcocorrido,* or story-song about drug trafficking. Their first hit, in 1972, was *Contrabando y Traición.* By the 1980s, Los Tigres began recording *corridos* about the immigrant experience such as *La Tumba del Mojado* and *La Jaula del Oro* that empathized with their nostalgia for home. Slowly, *norteño* music began gaining noteworthy sales. By 2003 Los Tigres had seven gold albums, awarded by the Recording Industry Association of America for sales exceeding 500,000.

Although the top *norteño* groups routinely sold as well in the United States as Spanish releases by crossover stars Marc Anthony, Shakira, and Paulina Rubio, they did not receive anywhere near the attention. However, the *norteño* stars, with their accordion-based music, cowboy hats, and polyester suits, worried little about appealing to English-speaking audiences. Then, in the mid-1990s, a new subgenre called *norteño*-lite became popular thanks to artists such as Michael Salgado, Intocable, and Pesado, which added rock-inspired guitar feedback, tropical congas, and Britpop-derived harmonies. These groups did not sing outlaw *corridos* or press for open borders. The groups' successes inspired a wave of Rio Grande Valley–based boy bands like Costumbre, Duelo, Iman, and Siggno, with a sound that infused romance and intimacy in a tradition-bound genre. Another subtle rock influence comes from these groups' names—all are one-word monikers like many classic rock groups. These touches helped *norteño* gain popularity among Mexico's middle class, especially in Monterrey.

In 1995 Grupo Limite from Monterrey, Mexico, shot up the charts by fusing *norteño* with the danceable Colombian rhythm known as *cumbia.* The group also featured a female lead singer, Alicia Villarreal, whose girlishly charismatic vocals helped her become a star in a genre dominated by males and macho lyrics. Other groups, such as Priscila y sus Balas de Plata, Dinora y la Juventud, and the all-female La Conquista picked up on the formula, helping to give

norteño a photogenic face. By the early 2000s Límite and La Conquista were adding hip-hop scratches and bubblegum raps to their music, expanding their appeal even further. Some of these groups even replaced the *bajo sexto* with the electric bass and eschewed Western-style outfits in favor of popular fashion.

Northern Mexico's increasing influence in Mexican society also contributed to the rise in *norteño* popularity. In 1895, on the eve of *norteño*'s birth, Mexico's six northern border states accounted for only 9.7 percent of the country's population. But irrigation, electrification, and finally NAFTA (the North American Free Trade Agreement) made the north more habitable. By 2000 its share had soared to 17.1 percent.

By combining *norteño* with gangsta rap and making *corridos* more explicit, *norteño* began to catch on among second-generation Mexican Americans, especially on the West Coast. Driving this fascination was the cult interest in a singer named Chalino Sanchez. Born in Guayabo, Sinaloa, in 1960, Sanchez snuck into the United States in 1977 and found employment in the Los Angeles area. He formed his own band, but because of his controversial *narcocorridos*, he was unable to get radio play. However, his tapes sold briskly at swap meets and flea markets. On May 16, 1992, the day after a performance in Culiacan, Sinaloa, Sanchez was found shot to death beside a highway. His death earned him even more notoriety, turning him into a folk legend.

Today, especially in the Los Angeles area, Sanchez's legacy has helped popularize California-based hardcore *narcocorrido* artists such as Los Razos and Jessie Morales. Morales's *Homenaje a Chalino Sanchez* debuted at number one on the Billboard Latin 50 for the week ending July 7, 2001. Los Tucanes de Tijuana was another popular group whose *narcocorridos* expressed barely concealed admiration for traffickers. In Mexico, many civic organizations and state legislatures tried to ban these groups' *narcocorridos* from the airwaves.

Norteño's ability to assimilate modern trends while retaining its accordion roots and Mexican feel demonstrates a flexibility few could have predicted when the genre emerged from the dusty ranchos in the early 20th century. *Norteño* music has enjoyed a massive resurgence in the United States in the new millennium, thanks to its timeless roots appeal and continually increasing audience of Mexican immigrants.

RELATED ARTICLES
Corrido; Music, Popular; Narcocorrido; Rap; Tejano.

FURTHER READING
Burr, Ramiro. *The Billboard Guide to Tejano and Regional Mexican Music.* New York: Billboard Bks., 1999.
Quiñones, Sam. *True Tales From Another Mexico: The Lynch Mob, The Popsicle Kings, Chalino and The Bronx.* Albuquerque: Univ. of N.Mex. Press, 2001.
Wald, Elijah. *Narcocorrido: A Journey Into the Music of Drugs, Guns and Guerrillas.* New York: HarperCollins, 2001.

RAMIRO BURR
DOUG SHANNON

NORTH CAROLINA

Latinos are changing the face of the American South, particularly North Carolina, where a dramatic demographic shift has taken place. Indeed, North Carolina has the fastest-growing Latino population in the entire country.

Although hard data is seldom readily available and is often inaccurate, the U.S. Census Bureau calculates that from 1990 to 2000, the Latino population grew by almost 400 percent. This growth included five of the country's 30 fastest-growing counties in terms of Latino population (Wake, Mecklenburg, Forsyth, Guilford, and Durham—all in North Carolina). The cities of Raleigh, Greensboro, and Charlotte have three of the four fastest-growing Latino populations in the nation.

The significant growth in the new Latino diaspora is attributed by and large to recent immigration. Initially males were most likely to immigrate to North Carolina to work, but over the past several years entire families have settled there, and some women have come alone. Most are of Mexican origin, followed by Puerto Ricans, Cubans, and Central and South Americans, and a large percentage are migrating from California, Texas, Florida, and New York. The next largest group are migrating from other states, such as New Jersey, Virginia, and Georgia. A portion of the growth is attributed, as well, to the rising number of Latino births. Latino births in North Carolina have a higher rate than do other population groups, and by the year 2000 the rate had increased more than sevenfold since 1990. Additionally, there are many migrant farmworkers who live seasonally in North Carolina (the fifth most populous farmworker state), who are often not included in population figures.

The potential for continued demographic growth is very great, since more than half of the state's Latino immigrants are between the ages of 18 and 35. This indicates, too, that Latina females are in their peak childbearing years. Also, almost twice as many Latinos in North Carolina are under five years old, as compared to the general state population.

Social life is changing for both Latinos and non-Latinos, and numerous public visible markers of Latino culture appear throughout the state, in cities and rural towns alike. There are now countless restaurants and bodegas (grocery stores) where Latino food and other products can be purchased. Sunday Mass is readily available in Spanish in numerous churches, new educational programs have developed in public schools, and a large, well-organized Latino soccer league exists. There are many Spanish-language radio stations, two Spanish-language newspapers, and an internet resource guide. The state has recently seen its first Latino elected to municipal office and a Latino appointed to a Mexican consulate. There is a Latino Community Credit Union, with more than 8,000 members and $12 million in assets. The presence of self-help and advocacy groups, such as "El Centro Hispano," offer social and educational services from court translations to after-school programs, and El Pueblo, a statewide group that works to shape policy, among other things, is expanding.

The arrival of Hispanics should be appropriately heralded as an opportunity to increase diversity in North Carolina, strengthen the tax, labor, consumption, and investment pools, and increase ties with Mexico and the rest of Latin America. However, few North Carolinians have yet grasped its full meaning. Of 700 adults surveyed in 1997, 42 percent disliked the influx of Latinos into the state (about 33 percent approved; 20 percent were unsure). When asked how their neighbors would feel if Latinos moved into their neighborhood, 54 percent thought people who lived near them would disapprove. Whites were more likely to say that their neighbors would disapprove. Further, many North Carolinians, as a whole, have no clear idea of who Latinos are, and there has been a tremendous tendency to "racialize" this group. Most often, Hispanic immigrants have been labeled *Hispanic,* the umbrella term used by the Census Bureau, and commonly referred to as an "ethnic group." But in reality most immigrants

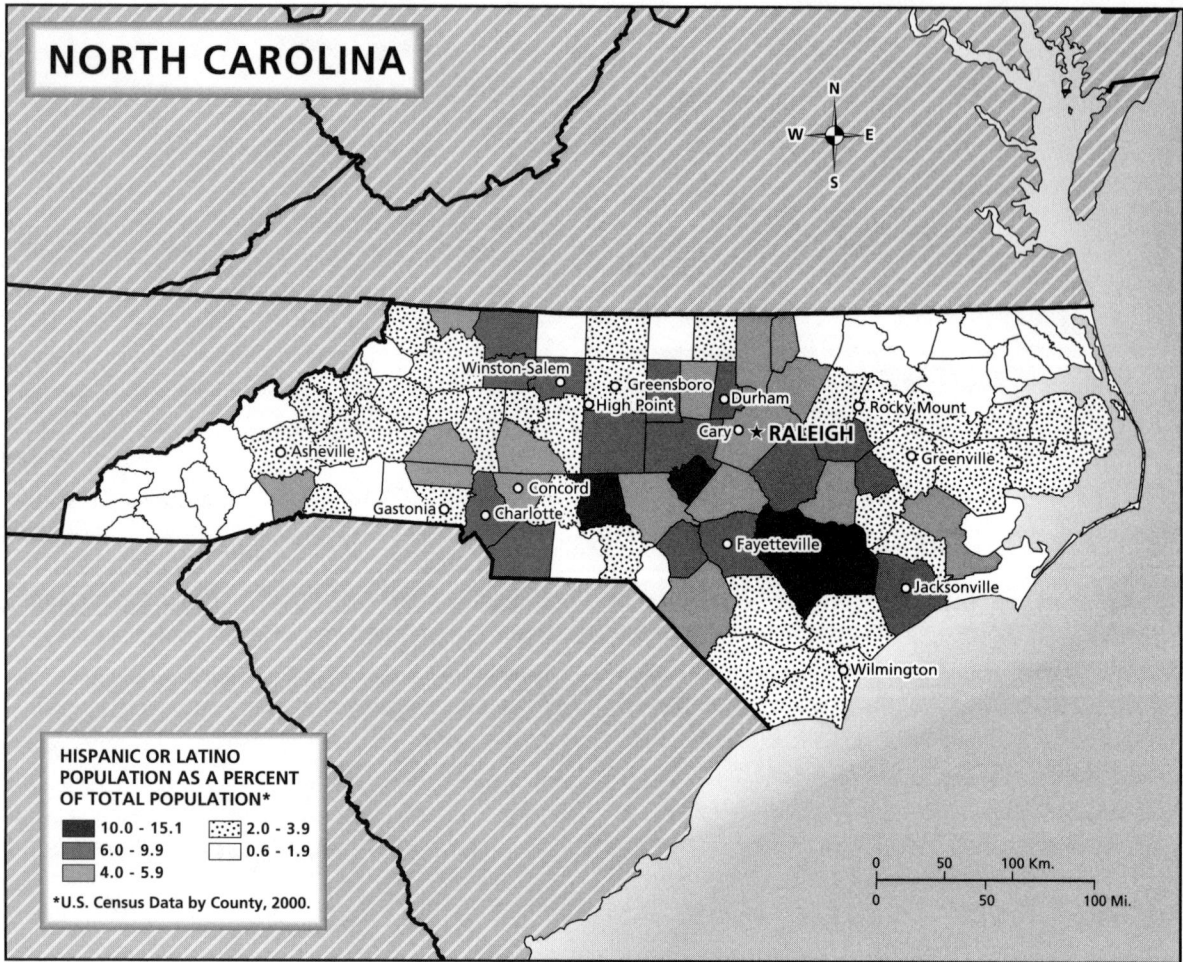

NORTH CAROLINA

HISPANIC OR LATINO
POPULATION AS A PERCENT
OF TOTAL POPULATION*

- 10.0 - 15.1
- 6.0 - 9.9
- 4.0 - 5.9
- 2.0 - 3.9
- 0.6 - 1.9

*U.S. Census Data by County, 2000.

have not been any one ethnic group at all, but a mix of many different groups, the major heritage being Mexicans.

The Latino population has become an integral part of the North Carolina economy, providing a valuable human resource and labor for agriculture, construction, and manufacturing industries across the state. Moreover, the Latino workforce represents not only an important and needed supply of labor, but also its earning and spending power exerts a huge impact. North Carolina was the top-ranked state for rate of growth of Latino buying power over 1990–2002, with an increase of 912 percent. It is the author's opinion that one barrier facing Hispanic immigrants has much less to do with any lack of jobs available than with the harsh reality of most undocumented immigrants being unable to fully participate in the state's formal economy, where opportunities come with full economic rights and responsibilities. Many hard-working immigrants who share common

values of education, family, and work ethic are often being forced to operate in a shadow economy full of false identities, cash transactions, and much economic uncertainty.

Some Latino advocates have argued that the early 1990s could be considered the honeymoon period, since many North Carolinians were excited by the new population group. However, as the Latino population grew rapidly, many communities, particularly rural, felt threatened, and the negative media coverage of topics such as Hispanic gangs and violence tainted views about the Hispanic community. For example, in the western section of Chatham County, concentrated in the small town of Siler City, significant change in the ethnic composition has taken place since 1990. Immigrants from Mexico, El Salvador, and Guatemala, tired of the high transience and difficulties of farmwork, began settling there to work the year-round jobs offered by the chicken plants. The number of Latino poultry workers increased steadily as relatives of workers (and others through word of mouth) began moving to the area when they learned there was work available.

In Siler City the settlement or intermediate relocation of entire families has placed particular unforeseen stresses on the social services, housing, legal system, and health and education facilities of the town. In other words, the local poultry plants actively recruited and lured workers, but the local infrastructure could not keep up with the growth. There has been a lack of affordable housing and thus the persistence of crowded and unhealthy living conditions. High incidents of tuberculosis and occupational injuries and illnesses as well as a paucity of appropriate instruction in local schools for the school-age children of the new laborers also characterizes the situation. But, very important, the current strength of the local economy has been, in part, a result of the contributions of the Latino immigrant community, both in terms of the cheap exploitable labor they have provided and their patronage of local businesses. However, the frustrations over the corporate offices' externalization of indirect costs become directed at the Latino newcomers rather than at the industry.

The example of Siler City gives a general indication of the experiences of the new Latino diaspora throughout North Carolina and the American South. Additionally, the social organization of the Hispanic population in these areas has been hampered by the fragmentation that Latinos face in terms of where they live and work. Often there are no defined Latino barrios, and gathering spaces are few and far between. In response, in just under a decade, the increase of the Latino population in North Carolina has brought a substantial increase in the number of nonprofit organizations, state agencies, and programs that are attempting to assist the Latino population.

RELATED ARTICLES

Agriculture; Cuban Americans; Immigration, Latino; Labor; Mexican Americans; Puerto Ricans on the Mainland.

FURTHER READING

Institute for Research in the Social Sciences. Carolina Poll. Univ. of N.C. at Chapel Hill, Spring 1997.

Larson, Alice C. *Migrant and Seasonal Farmworker Enumeration Profiles Study: North Carolina.* Vashon Island, Wash.: Larson Assistance Servs., September 2000 [prepared for Migrant Health Program, Bureau of Primary Health Care, Health Resources and Services Administration].

Murillo, Enrique G., Jr. "Pedagogy of a Latin American Festival." *The Urban Review* 29, no. 4: 263–281.

Murillo, Enrique G., Jr. *Growing Pains: Cartographies of Change, Contestation and Social Division in North Carolina.* Unpublished diss. Chapel Hill: Univ. of N.C., 1999.

Murillo, Enrique G., Jr. "How Does It Feel to Be a Problem?: Disciplining the Transnational Subject in the American South." In *Education in the New Latino Diaspora: Policy and the Politics of Identity.* Ed. by Stanton Wortham et al. Westport, Conn.: Ablex Publ., 2001.

Noblit, G., Sofia Villenas, et al. *Latino Cultures and Services Study: Perspectives on Children and Families.* Chapel Hill: Univ. of N.C., 1995 [final report of a Frank Porter Graham Child Development Ctr. small grant].

Wortham, Stanton, et al., eds. *Education in the New Latino Diaspora: Policy and the Politics of Identity.* Westport, Conn.: Ablex Publ., 2001.

SELECTED WEB SITES

Partnership of NC Governor's office for Latino/Hispanic Affairs, NC Cooperative Extension Service and El Pueblo, Inc. www.ayudate.org

El Pueblo, Inc. www.elpueblo.org [Raleigh-based statewide advocacy and policy organization dedicated to strengthening the Latino community].

Las Culturas. com www.lasculturas.com/lib/libNorthCarolina.php [Latino groups, portals, and resources about Hispanic life and culture in North Carolina].

North Carolina Department of Agriculture and Consumer Services, Agricultural Statistics Division. www.ncagr.com/stats/cashrcpt/cshcomyr.htm

North Carolina Latinos. N.C. Latino Health, 2003. www.nciom.org/projects/latino/latinopub/C2.pdf

North Carolina Society of Hispanic Professionals. www.thencshp.org/ [a networking and encouragement program for professionals and aspiring students].

ENRIQUE G. MURILLO, JR.

NUEVO HERALD, EL

El Nuevo Herald is one of the largest and fastest-growing newspapers in the United States. Published by the Miami Herald Publishing Company, which is owned by Knight Ridder, *El Nuevo Herald* serves a weekly readership of 470,000 in the south and central Florida area. Its staff hails from Cuba, Puerto Rico, Mexico, Colombia, the Dominican Republic, Venezuela, Spain, Peru, Nicaragua, Bolivia, the Philippines, Chile, Costa Rica, and the United States. The paper's readership is also heterogeneous, reflect-

© JIMMY DORANTES/LATIN FOCUS

Cover of *El Nuevo Herald,* a Spanish-language newspaper in Miami.

ing a multiethnic population that makes up Dade, Broward, and Monroe counties.

El Nuevo Herald began as a feature section of the *Miami Herald* in 1977. Owing in large part to the growing influence of the Hispanic community in Florida, *El Nuevo Herald* was spun off in 1998, given editorial freedom, and quickly growing to prominence. It soon became one of the most popular Spanish-language papers in the United States and the most widely read on Sundays.

The newspaper produces about 52 pages of color and black-and-white material on a daily basis and about 82 pages on Sundays. Among the special features of the paper are "Domingo Social," a weekly society tabloid; "Viernes," which offers weekly entertainment information; "Negocios," the weekly business section; and "Arte & Letras," the Sunday "Arts and Letters" section. In addition *El Nuevo Herald* supplies its readers with local, national, and hemispheric news, opinion editorials, classifieds, sports, the arts, horoscopes, and immigration issues.

El Nuevo Herald is remarkable in that it is among a small handful of Spanish-language dailies that are backed by large publishing companies. Its connections with the *Miami Herald* and its national advertisers facilitated the success of the paper.

The newspaper's laurels are numerous. For five consecutive years the National Association of Hispanic Publications (NAHP) honored the publication as the best Spanish-language daily newspaper in the United States. In 2002 the paper was awarded the Ortega y Gasset Prize, one of the most prestigious

and coveted in Spanish-language journalism. It has also been the recipient of the Goldsmith Prize from Harvard University, which awards excellence in public debate about government and the press.

Involved with its local community, the paper participates in the Copa Latina soccer tournament and in *tertulias,* round-table discussions. It contributes, as well, to community recognition awards and projects.

RELATED ARTICLES

Journalism; Miami Herald, The; Newspapers and Magazines.

FURTHER READING

Matera, Fran R. *The Miami Herald's Coverage of Cuban Issues: Tropes as Indicators of Bias.* Coral Gables, Fla.: Res. Inst. for Cuban Studies, Grad. School of Int'l. Studies, Univ. of Fla., 1990.

SELECTED WEB SITES

Knight Ridder Company Profile.
http://www.knightridder.com/working/profiles/nuevo_miami.html
The Miami Herald. http://www.miamiheraldadvertising.com

DESIRÉE GARCIA

NÚÑEZ CABEZA DE VACA, ALVAR

**Born: Circa 1485–1490; Jerez de la Frontera, Spain
Died: Circa 1556–1564; Seville, Spain**

Alvar Núñez Cabeza de Vaca was born in Jerez de la Frontera (Andalucia), Spain, between 1485 and 1490, the fourth son of a prominent family; his grandfather, Pedro de Vera, was the well-known conqueror of the Canary Islands. The name Cabeza de Vaca, which means "cow's head" was for many years thought to come from Núñez Cabeza de Vaca's ancestor, the shepherd Martín Alhaja, who in the 13th century marked a mountain pass with the skull of a cow to help the Christian king Sancho defeat the Moors, though recent research has called this story into question.

Núñez Cabeza de Vaca entered military service at a young age and distinguished himself in the service of the dukes of Medina Sidonia in the wars the Spanish crown waged in Italy to hold on to its Italian possessions. Although few details of his life in the first two decades of the 16th century remain, his appearance as a prominent member of the expedition to the North American continent under the governorship of Pánfilo de Narváez attests to his status at the Spanish court.

In June 1527 Narváez and approximately 600 men left the port of San Lucar de Barrameda, near the mouth of the Guadalquivir River in southern Spain, with the objective of traveling to the southern coast of North America and claiming it for the Spanish crown. Although administrative documents of the time provide some details of the effort, most information comes from Cabeza de Vaca's own account of the disaster.

After stops in Hispaniola and Cuba, at Easter time, 1528, the expedition landed on the western coast of Florida. According to Núñez Cabeza de Vaca's *La Relación* (1542; *The Chronicle*), Narváez proceeded to make one bad decision after another, until only four members of the original party were left, living near the eastern coast of Texas. During the following eight years, Núñez Cabeza de Vaca and his companions traveled slowly in the direction of Mexico

THE GRANGER COLLECTION

Postage stamp from Spain featuring explorer Alvar Núñez Cabeza de Vaca.

THE ACCOUNT

From the place where we landed to this village and land of Apalachee, the country is mostly flat, the soil sandy and firm. Throughout it there are many large trees and open woodlands in which there are walnut trees and laurels and others called sweet-gums, cedars, junipers, live oaks, pines, oaks and low-growing palmettos like those in Castile. Throughout it there are many large and small lakes, some of them very difficult to cross, partly because they are so deep and partly because there are so many fallen trees in them. They have sandy bottoms, and the ones we found in Apalachee are much larger than any we had encountered on the way. There are many cornfields in this province, and the houses are as spread out through the countryside as those of the Gelves.

The animals that we saw in those lands were three kinds of deer, rabbits and hares, bears and lions and other wild animals, among which we saw one which carries its young in a pouch on its belly. While they are small they carry them in that manner until they can get their own food. If they happen to be out of the pouch searching for food when people approach, the mother does not flee until she has gathered them all in her pouch. The country there is very cold and has good pastures for livestock. There are many kinds of birds: very many geese, ducks, large ducks, royal ducks, ibises, egrets and herons and quail. We saw many falcons, marsh hawks, sparrow hawks, goshawks and many other birds.

Excerpt from "The Account" ("La Relación"; 1542) by Alvar Núñez Cabeza de Vaca, in *Herencia: The Anthology of Hispanic Literature of the United States* (2002).

City, through various means transforming themselves from slaves into faith healers and holy men, until finally they encountered Spanish soldiers seeking slaves. *The Chronicle,* also known as *The Account,* is a combination of observation, history, and self-aggrandizing fiction, prized by ethnographers for its information on the indigenous peoples of the area, and by literary critics for its complex structure and personal story of transformation and redemption, containing many elements echoed in Latino literature of the late 20th century.

Núñez Cabeza de Vaca's description of his role as an intermediary between the Spanish and American indigenous populations resulted in his being given, in 1541, the governorship of the Río de la Plata region of South America. There, according to his later account, his attempts to bring just rule were resented by resident Spaniards, who mutinied, clapped him in irons, and sent him ignominiously back to Spain. Not allowed by Spanish law to call witnesses in his own defense, he was disgraced. The appearance of his written defense, *Commentaries,* along with a second edition of his *Chronicle of the Narváez Expedition* (1555), rehabilitated him, and he was awarded a state pension. It is believed that he died in Seville between 1556 and 1564.

Critics and historians have often called Núñez Cabeza de Vaca "the first Latino" because his chronicle was the first written work to express the personal changes experienced by a Hispanic living in North America, in addition to providing ethnographic and biospheric information. The work has been translated numerous times and in 1991 was made into a feature film by Nicolás Echeverría.

RELATED ARTICLES

Colonialism; Colonial Period; Explorers and Chroniclers.

FURTHER READING

Adorno, Rolena, and Patrick Charles Pautz, eds. *Alvar Núñez Cabeza de Vaca: His Account, His Life, and the Expedition of Pánfilo de Narváez.* Lincoln: Univ. of Nebr. Press, 1999.

Bishop, Morris. *The Odyssey of Cabeza de Vaca.* New York: Century, 1933.

Pastor Bodmer, Beatriz. *The Armature of Conquest: Spanish Accounts of the Discovery of America, 1492–1589.* Tr. by Lydia Longstreth Hunt. Stanford, Calif.: Stanford Univ. Press, 1992.

Núñez Cabeza de Vaca, Alavar. *Chronicle of the Narváez Expedition.* Tr. by Fanny Bandelier, rev. by Harold Augenbraum. New York: Penguin 2002.

HAROLD AUGENBRAUM

NUYORICAN POETS CAFÉ

"There were a few of us who used the name Nuyorican," says poet Americo Casiano, offering the origins of the phrase born in the mid-1960s for second- and third-generation Puerto Ricans living in New York City. "It was originally intended by the community as a negative social label, but we used it as a positive one," he is quick to add, referring to himself and fellow poets Sandra Maria Esteves, Jesus Papoleto Melendez, Tato Laviera, and Luis Reyes Rivera. It was these core poets, following both the protests and policies of the 1960s and the later literary accomplishments of Piri Thomas and Victor Hernandez Cruz (who gave readings throughout the city, carrying their cultural label with pride), who inspired Brooklyn College professor Miguel Algarin to find a space for their burgeoning art. Thus the Nuyorican Poets Café (NPC) was built, reactively, on New York's Lower East Side in 1973, when there was a need for physically and culturally displaced Puerto Rican writers and their audiences to congregate. The NPC became their home. When, after closing for several years owing to financial difficulties, it reopened in the late 1980s, spurred on by the death of Lower East Side artist Miguel "Miky" Pinero, it brought into its repertoire a new form of poetry presentation, with which (in New York) it has become synonymous: slam.

Slam is a literary movement, created to make poetry more accessible to the people, and poets more responsive to their audiences. This sharing, however, may be harming the art, with some saying that the competitive nature of the slam and the concept of judging poems is deleterious to the art form.

Originating in Chicago around 1984, slam was the idea of construction worker and poet Marc Smith, who believed that a poet had a responsibility to his or her audience to keep it engaged in the performance. Smith's idea of a poetry reading was to create a space where the arts of poetry and performance connected. That space, originally at the Get Me High Lounge's Sunday Night Reading Series, became slam.

A slam is a poetry competition, where poems are judged Olympic-style—with scores ranging from 0 to 10. Judging is based on the whims of randomly picked judges whose one defining qualification is they themselves are not slamming. Since there are no common standards to be met, yet there are prizes to be won, this causes problems. Tempers flare, egos abound, and the performances arguably count as much as the words of a poem as poets try to gain fame and cash.

Bob Holman, a coproducer of the reopened NPC, had traveled to Chicago and witnessed slam firsthand. Believing it to be something the café and its denizens needed, he brought slam to New York. Since 1990 the slam competitions at the NPC have had phenomenal success—bringing the café and its slammers recognition, but sometimes leading them to doubt its original intentions.

Paul Beatty, the Nuyorican Poets Café's first slam champion (1990), attacked the poetry scene in an interview, saying that the performances at the Nuyorican started outweighing everything, even the writing. Beatty felt there was a sense of self-righteousness among poets on the slam scene, which has led to the rumored division between academia and slam. Guy LeCharles González, of the 1998 Nuyorican team—the café's only national-winning team, wrote an article for the April 1999 issue of *Poet's & Writer's Magazine,* in which he claimed that slam was becoming a poetry revolution.

In this essay Gonzalez posited that there is a schism between academic poets and slammers; however, there is little or no evidence to back up the claim. Jim Fitzgerald, an editor at St. Martin's Press (in Paul Devlin's 1998 documentary *SlamNation*), states that slam is a "fad," that much of slam writing does not work on the page. His interview is interspersed with comments by Jessica Care Moore, a former Nuyorican slam team member and now a published writer herself, who is obviously angered at Fitzgerald's having rejected her work.

But Fitzgerald is not the only person who feels that much slam poetry is weak. Poet and professor Tony Medina, in an interview with poet and NPC slam champion Willie Perdomo, accused many slam poets of the crime of illiteracy. "They write but they don't read," he says, often citing the performances of poets such as Perdomo and himself as the catalyst for their poetic license.

From literature as well as experience one can see a schism between slam as an ideal and its often much baser reality. In the introduction to *Aloud: Voices from the Nuyorican Poets Café,* one learns that slam has created a living, supportive community of "people who are listening to others speak." Other slam books also promote this humanitarian ideal. *Burning Down the House,* by the 1998 Nuyorican Slam team, ends not with a poem but with LeCharles Gonzalez's slam essay from *Poets & Writers.* Sonia Sohn, in the film *Slam* (1998)—which contains the screenplay and journals of the movie's producers and actors—describes both *Slam* the movie and slam politic as "beautiful, life saving, the ultimate."

In contrast, in Devlin's *SlamNation* many famous slam poets are shown ranting and whining about scores, seedings, and how they want to beat other

NUYORICAN POET'S CAFÉ

A logo commemorating an event held at Town Hall in New York City, November 2003, honoring 30 years of the Nuyorican Poets Café.

teams and individuals. Nuyorican team poet Mums da Schemer was given a four, leading teammate Saul Williams to insult the judge, saying, "If you, in your life, need to give a four to 'The Truth,' then you can't survive." Counterpoised with this is the attitude represented by Gary Glazner. Producer of the first National Poetry Slam, Glazner quotes García Lorca in the introduction of his book *Poetry Slam* (subtitled *The Competitive Art of Performance Poetry*): "There is poetry that rises from the book and becomes human enough to talk and shout, weep and despair." Referring to the quotation, Glazner writes, "That is the spirit of Slam poetry."

RELATED ARTICLES

Laviera, Jesus; Literature, Puerto Rican on the Mainland; New York City; Puerto Ricans on the Mainland.

FURTHER READING

Algarin, Miguel, and Bob Holman. *Aloud: Voices from the Nuyorican Café.* New York: Henry Holt, 1994.

Bonair-Agard, Roger, et al. *Burning Down the House.* New York: Soft Skull Press, 2000.

Glazner, Gary Mex. *Poetry Slam: The Competitive Art of Performance Poetry.* San Francisco: Manic D Press, 2000.

Stratton, Richard, and Kim Wozencraft, eds. *Slam.* New York: Grove, 1998.

JOHN RODRÍGUEZ

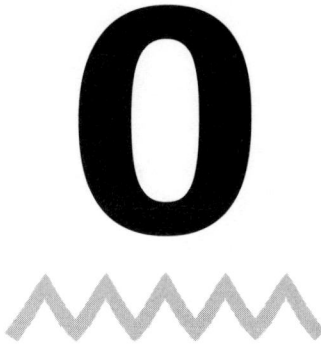

O

OCHOA, ELLEN

Born: May 10, 1958; Los Angeles, California

Scientist, engineer, and astronaut Ellen Ochoa, the daughter of Louis Zak and Rosanne Ochoa, was brought up by her mother in La Mesa, California (her parents divorced when she was in junior high school). She chose to use her mother's family name, to recognize her mother's support while she was a student. Ochoa married Coe Fulmer Miles, with whom she had two sons.

As a teenager Ochoa took to music with the idea of becoming a classical flutist, but owing to her mother's advice to finish her studies, Ochoa attended Grossmont High School in La Mesa, and in 1975, she decided to pursue a bachelor's degree in physics at San Diego State University, where she graduated as valedictorian of her class. In 1980 she entered graduate school at Stanford University, earning a master of science and a doctorate in electrical engineering in 1981 and 1985, respectively. Between 1985 and 1988 Ochoa worked at Sandia National Laboratories in Albuquerque, New Mexico, and NASA's (National Aeronautics and Space Administration) Ames Research Center in Mountain View, California, where she investigated optical systems that could process information and developed computer programs to be used on aeronautical expeditions. As a result of her research, she patented an optical inspection system, an optical object recognition method, and a system to remove "noise," or interference, from images.

Inspired in 1983 by Sally Ride, the first female U.S. astronaut, Ochoa applied to NASA, a formerly male-dominated program. She was selected in January 1990 on the basis of the potential of her inventions to increase the collection of data and to evaluate the status of the equipment. In July 1991, she trained at the Johnson Space Center in Houston, becoming the first Hispanic female astronaut in history. Her duties consisted of developing and testing flight software, computer hardware, and robotics.

After four expeditions Ochoa had accumulated more than 970 hours of spaceflight. She was appointed as mission specialist on the STS-56 ATLAS-2 *Discovery* (April 4–17, 1993) to study the effect of solar activity on the earth's climate and environment; as payload commander on STS-66 ATLAS-3 (November 3–14, 1994) to analyze the energy of the sun at that point in its 11-year cycle and its possible changes; and as mission specialist again and flight engineer on STS-96 *Discovery* (May 27–June 6, 1999), in charge of preparing the arrival of the first crew to live in the International Space Station, and on STS-110 *Atlantis* (April 8–19, 2002), their mission being to deliver and install the SO (S-Zero) Truss, using the station's robotic arm to maneuver spacewalkers for the first time.

Ochoa has received many awards, including the Congressional Hispanic Caucus Medallion of Excellence in 1993; Space Flight Medals in 1993, 1994, 1999, and 2002; the Women in Aerospace Outstanding Achievement Award; the Hispanic Engineer Albert Baez Award for Outstanding Technical Con-

NASA

Astronaut Ellen Ochoa, STS-110 mission specialist, looks through the earth observation window in the *Destiny* laboratory aboard the International Space Station, 2002.

tribution to Humanity; and the Hispanic Heritage Leadership Award. In 1999 President Bill Clinton chose Ochoa—considered one of the most successful Hispanic women in the 20th century—to serve on the Presidential Commission on the Celebration of Women in American History. Her outstanding scientific research has opened up new possibilities in optics and its application to aeronautics.

She has collaborated with the California Center for Teaching Careers (CalTeach), a recruitment program administered by California State University whose purpose is to attract people to teaching. She has visited high schools in California to instill in students the belief that hard work is always well rewarded. Ochoa is a role model for Latinos who want to excel in education and break social prejudice barriers, and for women who struggle to compete in traditionally male-oriented careers.

RELATED ARTICLES

Science; Technology.

FURTHER READING

González-Jensen, Margarita, and Peter Rillero.** *Blast off with Ellen Ochoa.* Crystal Lake, Ill.: Rigby, 1999.
Triana, Estrella M. *Stepping into the Future: Hispanics in Science and Engineering.* Washington, D.C.: Directorate for Education and Human Resources Programs, AAAS (Am. Assn. for the Advancement of Science), 1992.
Woodmansee, Laura S. *Women Astronauts.* Burlington, Ontario: Apogee Bks., 2002.

JORGE ABRIL-SÁNCHEZ

O'FARRILL, ARTURO

Born: October 28, 1921; Havana, Cuba
Died: June 27, 2001; New York, New York

One could argue whether Arturo "Chico" O'Farrill is the muse of Latin Jazz, but beyond question he was one of its three great figures, along with Mario Bauzá and Machito (Francisco Grillo). Sent to a military school in Georgia (1936–1940), O'Farrill was expected to go to law school after graduation. However, his love for big-band music compelled him to take up trumpet. He studied with Cuban classical composer Félix Guerrero and played with the Orquesta Bellemar. By 1948 he was in New York City, ghost-composing for Gil Fuller; then he wrote a hit for Benny Goodman (*Undercurrent Blues*) and subsequently composed for Dizzy Gillespie, Noro Morales, Stan Kenton (*Cuban Episode*), and Machito. O'Farrill abandoned the trumpet and dedicated his career to composing, directing, and arranging. His *Afro-Cuban Jazz Suite* (1950), recorded with Charlie Parker, Flip Phillips, and Buddy Rich, is a recognized masterpiece of the genre and was followed by a *Second Afro-Cuban Jazz Suite* (1952) and the *Manteca Suite* (1954), adding three movements to the Gillespie-Pozo original to form the latter suite. From 1951 to 1954 he released six landmark recordings of Latin big-band jazz, which included the Afro-Cuban suites, as well as *Cuban Blues,* the latter rereleased as an eponymous two-CD set (1996). Although composing prolifically and still popular in the United States in the 1950s, he moved to Mexico in 1957, where he composed *The Aztec Suite* (1959). His son Arturo, an accomplished pianist, was born in Mexico (1960).

O'Farrill returned to the United States in 1965, and from 1967 to 1994 he did not record as a bandleader but, instead, arranged prolifically for La Lupe, Cal Tjader, Count Basie, Ringo Starr, Clark Terry, Charles Mingus, David Bowie, and Gato Barbieri, among others. He also wrote extensively for television commercials. O'Farrill made a comeback in the mid-1990s with three extraordinary recordings, the first being *Pure Emotion* (1995), which won a Grammy nomination and features *Variations on a Well-Known Theme,* a 12-minute version of *La Cucaracha* that mixes in Ellington with show tunes to 12-tone passages; it is a masterful conversion of this melody into a suite that is a telescoped panorama of 20th-century music. *Heart of a Legend* (1999) features vintage O'Farrill, from the gorgeous *guajira* (a type of musical genre from the Cuban countryside) *La Campiña* to his *Trumpet Fantasy* (1995) for Wynton Marsalis, a moody, then driving and bouncy piece that showcases the instrument. *Carambola* (2000) was a fitting end to a prolific career. With his classical training, O'Farrill showed a remarkable handling of form that always seemed effortless and elegant, buoyed by infectious rhythms. He was comfortable composing *sones* (a Euro-African mix that is Cuba's most popular music genre), cha-chas, rumbas, and *guajiras,* as well as blues and jazz, often going from genre to genre within a song almost unnoticeably. Included in Fernando Trueba's film on Latin Jazz, *Calle 54,* O'Farrill also wrote classical pieces: Symphony No. 1 (1944), Winds Quintet (1945), Saxophone Quartet (1948–1949), Clarinet Fantasy, and *Three Cuban Dances,* which was performed by the Caracas Philharmonic in 1981.

RELATED ARTICLES

Jazz; Music, Popular.

FURTHER READING

Acosta, Leonardo. *Raíces del jazz Latino, Un siglo de jazz en Cuba.* Baranquilla, Colombia: Editorial la Iguana Ciega, 2001.

Chediak, Nat. *Diccionario de jazz Latino.* Madrid: Fundación Autor, 1998.

Roberts, John Storm, *Latin Jazz, the First of the Fusions: 1880s to Today.* New York: Schirmer, 1999.

Yarnow, Scott. *Afro-Cuban Jazz.* San Francisco: Freeman, 2000.

ALAN WEST-DURÁN

OHIO

Scholarship committed to the emigration of Mexicans from the Southwest and Mexico into the Midwest has been scant. Information concerning their migration to Ohio is even scarcer. However, the presence of Latinos in the Midwest is significant, considering their impact on American industry and agriculture.

Beginning roughly in 1914 and because of a wartime economy, young unattached male nationals from Mexico began to move to the Midwest owing to a temporary economic opportunity. Scholars note that the movement of Mexicans into the Southwest and northward into the Midwest was affected by the severe depression that hit the Central Plateau of Mexico in 1907, which had an impact on mining and ranching and caused general starvation and the debasement of Mexican currency. The subsequent Mexican Revolution in 1910 raised fears of economic and political instability. Meanwhile, north of the border the realities of an American labor shortage, largely a result of reduced Asian immigration and European immigrant preferences for higher wages and more secure employment, created opportunities for Mexican laborers to move northward. The vast majority of these first immigrant workers labored in the sugar beet fields, in the railway construction industry, and on maintenance crews.

Railroad companies heavily recruited Mexican laborers from the Southwest with promises of high wages, free transportation, and discounts on their return trips. Advertising in Spanish-language newspapers, pool halls, and employment agencies, railroad companies also made use of recruiters, who earned money from providing Midwest companies with workers. Recruiters therefore created mass advertisements and fliers, and even assisted workers in crossing the border into the United States, regardless of the violation of Contract Labor Law. Often enough, workers used the contract offers to obtain passage to the United States or to the Midwest, particularly to cities such as Cincinnati, but on arrival many workers would desert their contracts and seek out other work. The shortages caused by these situations thus increased recruitment. Mexican laborers, who had been frequently mistaken as passive because of lan-

guage barriers and inexperience, learned the value of their unified labor when it came time to negotiate better wages and living conditions. They discovered that both the government and their employers desired their services regardless of the variety of immigration laws that might have been initially discouraging.

From the early 1900s into the 1930s, there was a serious disparity between the number of Mexican male laborers and Mexican women. In the majority of Midwest states, particularly Kansas and Missouri, where meatpacking plants and sugar beet factories represented most labor opportunities for women, the ratio was nearly 100 to 1. Mexican women were usually employed as daily workers, at half the wages offered to men. As a result, women often took in laundry and worked as domestics, which spurred the growing independence and Americanization of young Mexican women. Out of necessity Mexican families would allow their older daughters to work outside

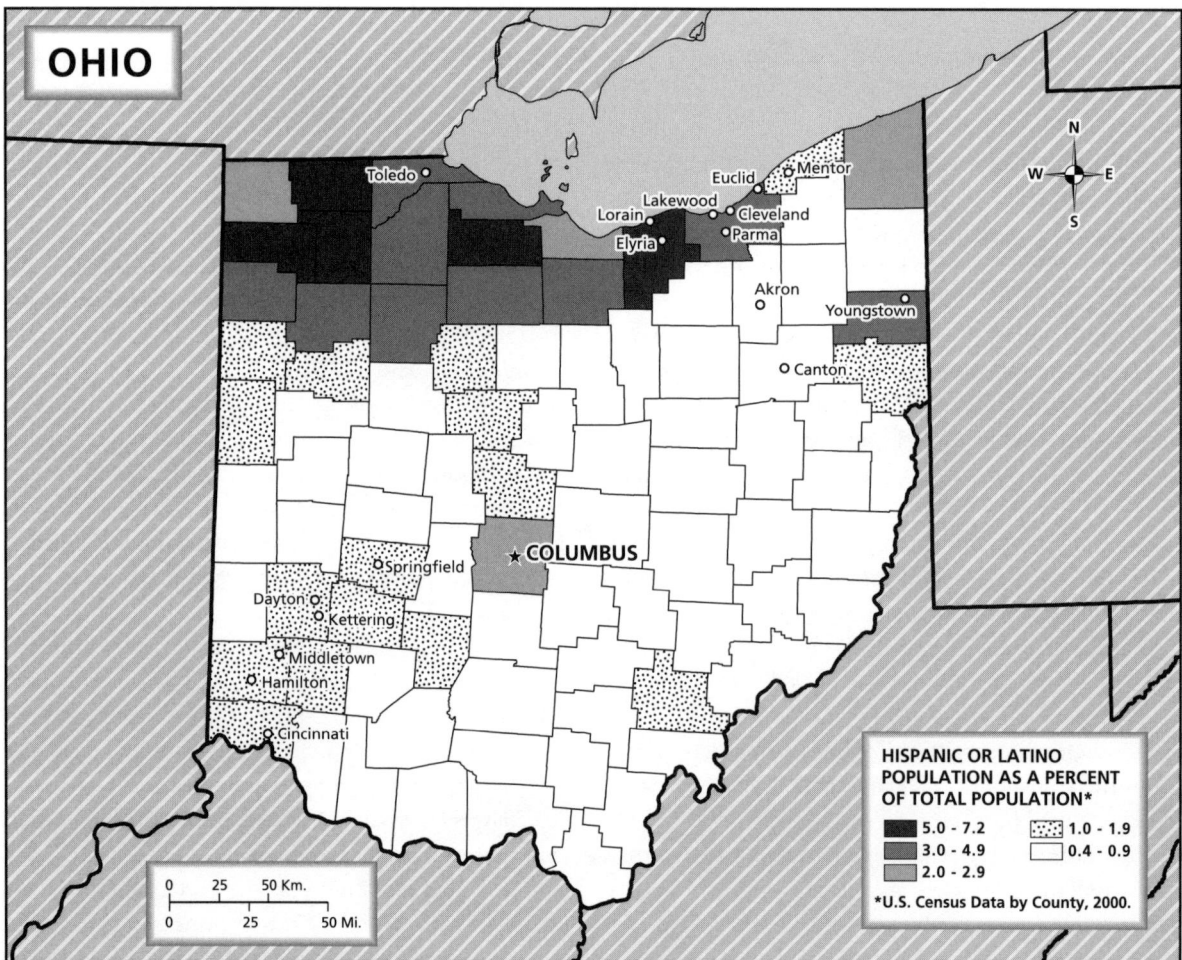

OHIO

HISPANIC OR LATINO
POPULATION AS A PERCENT
OF TOTAL POPULATION*

- 5.0 - 7.2
- 3.0 - 4.9
- 2.0 - 2.9
- 1.0 - 1.9
- 0.4 - 0.9

*U.S. Census Data by County, 2000.

the home. However, it was feared that the unbalanced ratio of men to women, and the opportunity for unmarried Mexican women to learn English while working would lead to desertion of Mexican men, which contributed to already fervent Mexican male attitudes against Mexican women working outside the home. As a result, many of the contributions made by Mexican women to the labor force, and the development of social and activist impulses with respect to these women, have been largely ignored and overshadowed by those of their male counterparts.

Modern Ohio boasts a growing Latino population, which continues to provide opportunities and development of Latino organizations and publications. Its major cities contain the largest Latino populations in the state: Cleveland, Columbus, and Cincinnati.

Cleveland's Latino population has historically been dominated by Puerto Ricans, who exceeded 46,000 in the 2000 U.S. Census. Cleveland is the site of an annual Puerto Rican parade and Latino Festival, as well as the widely celebrated Latino Heritage Day. It is home to the only Spanish-language soccer publication in Ohio; and it claims the Latino Media Group, the state's first and only Latino advertising agency, which generates three community newspapers and is affiliated with a Latino radio station. Cleveland State University also provides a variety of radio shows in Spanish.

Among other organizations working diligently to service the needs of growing Latino populations in Cleveland is the Spanish American Committee (SAC), the oldest and largest nonprofit Latino service agency in the city. Established in 1966, SAC provides social services, employment, housing, ESL (English as a second language), bilingual daycare, immigration services, translation and interpretive services, bilingual scouting, notarizations, and educational and employment discrimination counseling. Notably, in the heart of the Latino community is El Barrio, a free, neighborhood-based program of empowerment and cultural integration founded in 1990 as a 501(c)(3)—charitable organization—but operating as an independent agency since 1993. El Barrio focuses on community integration, education and job skills development, and job placement and retention as their major programming thrusts.

As Ohio's capital, Columbus boasts a wide variety of programming and organizations to service the

state's second largest Latino population. Certainly with the largest newspaper dedicated to Latinos in Ohio, *La Voz Hispana,* Columbus claims a prominent position for gathering and communicating local, Mexican, and Latin American information.

In Columbus the Commission on Hispanic/Latino Affairs deals directly with issues concerning Ohioans. Created by legislative act and signed into law by Governor James Rhodes on July 8, 1977, the commission is led by 11 members on the Board of Commissioners, all of whom must speak Spanish; be of Hispanic origin; be American citizens or "lawful, permanent resident aliens"; and be appointed by the governor under consultation with and approval of the Senate. The commission also purports to have a membership representative of the Latino population's distribution, both geographically and numerically, in Ohio. Its monthly meetings are held in Columbus, except on occasions when the members determine to make the commission more accessible to its constituents in other areas of the state.

Columbus is the site of Festival Latino, whose mission is "to provide the community with an opportunity to experience traditional and contemporary Latin American culture through the presentation of the performing and visual arts, educational workshops and authentic cuisine." It is arguably the largest Latino festival—and Latino event in general—in Ohio, attracting multicultural audiences from inside and outside the state. The festival has been the venue for countless Latino performers. Going beyond entertainment, however, the festival is also the occasion for and the site of visual art exhibitions; children's workshops; employment and educational opportunities; a community marketplace; health and human services information, including free health screenings; and more than 40 restaurants and food booths that feature traditional and contemporary Latino foods.

In addition, the Latino Outreach Program in central Ohio is a relatively new organization committed to addressing financial and educational needs for the state's growing Latino population. Out of this program, the Ohio Health, Telhio, Big Bear/Members First, and Western credit unions, along with the Ohio State University Extension and the Ohio Credit Union Foundation, formed the Latino Financial Education Partnership to address these needs. Classes are held in churches, schools, and credit union lobbies and businesses, as well as over the telephone. The Ohio Latino Arts Association provides for the exhibition of artists of Latino descent, endeavoring to represent the ethnic and cultural variety of Hispanic populations in Ohio. They juxtapose the work of internationally renowned artists with up-and-coming artists to create a mosaic of sculpture, ceramics, photography, and painting. The Ohio Latino-Hispanic Health Coalition, founded by Lydia Alejandro of Toledo, conducted the first statewide survey of health issues that focused on medical problems, insurance, and accessibility issues, pointing up health disparities among Latino populations.

While Cincinnati has the smallest population of Latinos of the three cities, the first wave of Cincinnati's Latino population comprised professionals who typically bonded more with corporate and academic cultures than with ethnic groups, primarily attributable to the small numbers and variety of Latinos who arrived. The majority of this first wave arrived from Brazil, Ecuador, Bolivia, and Cuba to work as professionals in large corporations in the area, such as Procter & Gamble and General Electric; as professors at the University of Cincinnati; and as executives at Chiquita. Ethnic interactions were usually in the form of intimate gatherings, in living rooms and kitchens, among people from the same country.

Cincinnati's Hispanic population since the first wave has expanded to include more immigrants, not only from other states but also from Guatemala, Puerto Rico, Colombia, Peru, and Mexico. Groups such as Awareness for Latinos Arriving in the States, or ALAS (meaning "wings"), which provides assistance to Spanish-speaking immigrants, are influencing the opportunities for Spanish-speaking populations in the area. Certainly the influx has created an audience of almost 20,000 for such media publications and productions as *La Jornada Latina,* a biweekly, bilingual Latino newspaper with a circulation of 15,000 across greater Cincinnati, Dayton, and northern Kentucky; *Noticiero Latino-USA,* the first commercial radio news program in Spanish in the tristate area; *Buenos Dias America,* a Spanish-language radio show in the area; and *Deporte Gráfico,* a weekly publication in Spanish of sports and entertainment; *Nuestro Ohio,* which offers "news, ideas and information" for Hispanics living in Ohio; the area's first Latin cable show, Time Warner's *Ritmo Latino*; and alternative sources such as *¡Oye! Que Pasa? La Cadena Latina,* a bimonthly communication link for Hispanics. With a growing Latino population in a city struggling with its racial politics, grassroots organiza-

tions such as Lafricano, though in its embryonic stage, set the pace for joint efforts to create a common force among Latinos and African Americans in the area. On the religious front, Su Casa Hispanic Ministries, a Catholic social service organization, is at the center of grassroots organizing of undocumented immigrants in the local communities and labor force. While Ohio does not often come to mind as a hub of Latino activity, certainly the changing diversity in demographics, as in other states, continues to require another look at local politics of accessibility, the notion of race and ethnicity, economics, and representation.

RELATED ARTICLES

Immigration, Latino; Mexican Americans; Puerto Ricans on the Mainland.

FURTHER READING

García, Juan. *Mexicans in the Midwest: 1900–1932.* Tucson: Univ. of Ariz. Press, 1996.

Vargas, Zaragosa. *Proletarians of the North: A History of Mexican Industrial Workers in Detroit and the Midwest, 1917–1933.* Berkeley: Univ. of Calif. Press, 1993.

SELECTED WEB SITES

Nuestro Ohio. http://www.nuestroohio.com

Ohio Commission on Hispanic/Latino Affairs. http://www.state.oh.us/spa

HELANE D. ADAMS

OLMOS, EDWARD JAMES

Born: February 24, 1947; East Los Angeles, California

Edward James Olmos has had an acting and producing career that has been distinguished by a sincere commitment to social activism. He won a Tony Award for his striking portrayal of El Pachuco in Luis Valdez's play *Zoot Suit* (1978), an Emmy Award for his role in the hit television series *Miami Vice,* and an Academy Award nomination for his character Jaime Escalante in the critically acclaimed film *Stand and Deliver* (1987). Olmos has chosen roles based on their ability to convey certain ethnic and social themes. When roles that deal with explicit Latino themes are short in coming, the actor shapes his character to deal with such subjects implicitly, such as in his portrayal of Lieutenant Martin Costillo in *Miami Vice* (1984–1989) and a racially complex police detective in *Blade Runner* (1982).

Olmos has attributed his social activism to his childhood days in East Los Angeles, where he was born to a Mexican-born father and Mexican American mother in the barrio of Boyle Heights. While the neighborhood harbored a significant Latino population, it was nevertheless home to a diverse array of ethnic groups including Russians, Koreans, and Chinese. It is this peaceful cohabitation of different peoples that Olmos has striven for in his work as an actor and as an activist.

As a student at Motebello High School, Olmos became interested in music and formed a band called Pacific Ocean with fellow students. He later went on to attend East Los Angeles College and California State University, all the while playing at nightclubs on the Sunset Strip. It was there that he met his first wife, Kaija, the daughter of actor Howard Keel, with whom he had two sons. It was not until he auditioned and got the part of El Pachuco in *Zoot Suit* that he met with success as a performer. The true story about young Mexican Americans in Los Angeles during World War II was particularly familiar to Olmos. Drawing from his childhood experiences, he played the role to critical acclaim.

The success of *Zoot Suit* ensured bigger and better roles for the young actor. After *Miami Vice* and *Blade Runner,* he directed his first film, *American Me* (1992), and starred in *Mi Familia/My Family* (1995) and the television series *American Family* (2001). Throughout his successful projects, however, Olmos has used his star status to promote a variety of causes. He has been actively involved with community-service projects and affiliated with numerous nonprofit organizations. Among the groups are Michael Jackson's Heal the World Foundation and FASE, the Foundation for Advancement in Science and Education.

In 2001 Olmos participated in a movement to end trial bombing runs by the U.S. Navy on the inhabited island of Vieques in Puerto Rico. There, Olmos, Robert Kennedy, Jr., Dennis Rivera, and numerous others were arrested for trespassing. Their subsequent prison sentences brought a great deal of attention to the issue and helped force the departure of the navy from the island in 2003. Merging his professional and personal goals, Olmos continued to

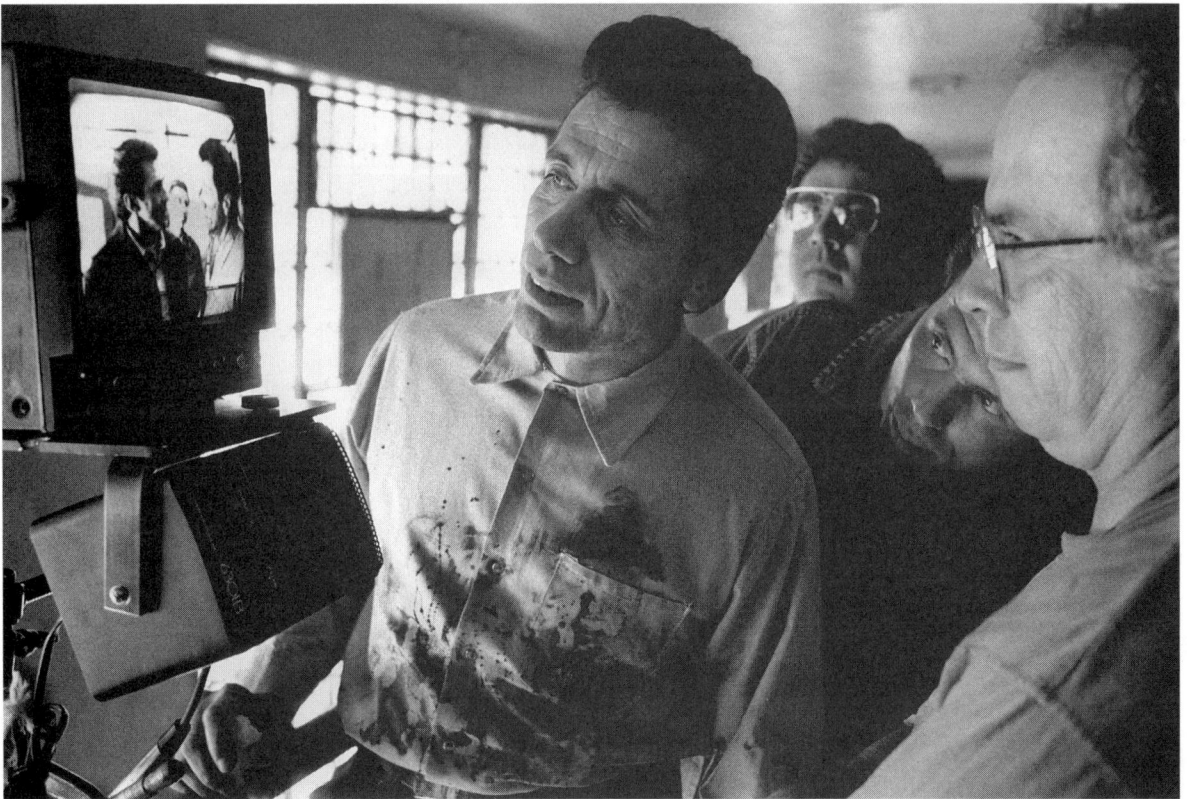

Actor and director Edward James Olmos watches a scene during the shooting of the film *American Me.*

succeed at promoting racial harmony and social justice through his work in media and activism.

RELATED ARTICLES
Activism; Film; Television.

FURTHER READING
Olmos, Edward James, with Lea Ybarra and Manuel Monterrey. *Americanos: Latino Life in the United States/La vida Latina en los Estados Unidos.* Boston: Little, Brown, 1999.
Reyes, Luis, and Peter Rubie. *Hispanics in Hollywood, A Celebration of 100 Years in Film and Television.* Hollywood, Calif.: ifilm Publ., 2000.
Stavans, Ilan. "Edward James Olmos." *Word of Mouth.* Tucson: Univ. of Ariz. Press, 2005.

JOSEPH TOVARES

OLYMPIC GAMES

When historians Antonio Rios-Bustamante and William Estrada published their booklet on Latino participation in the Olympics, in time for the 1984 Games in heavily Latino-populated Los Angeles, only 50 U.S. Latinos could be counted among Olympic competitors since 1896. Over the course of the 20th century, Latino participation steadily increased, and Latinos won nearly 40 cumulative medals in various arenas, more than any Latin American countries except Cuba, Spain, Brazil, Mexico, and Argentina.

Despite relatively small numbers, Latinos have a long history of medal-winning, and they have had particular success in the boxing division. Indeed, the first medal to be won by a U.S. Latino was the silver received by boxer Joe Salas in the flyweight boxing division, in Paris, France, in 1924. Since that time a total of seven medals have been won in boxing. In 1956 Jose Torres won the silver in boxing at the Olympic Games in Melbourne, Australia. Torres was followed by two bronze-medal winners, Ricardo Carreras and Jesse Valdez, at the 1972 competition in Munich, Germany. These added to an impressive nine medals won by Latin Americans from Cuba, Mexico, Colombia, and Spain.

The first U.S. Latino to win a gold medal in the boxing competition was Paul Gonzales, who distinguished himself in the light flyweight division at the 23d Olympiad in Los Angeles in 1984. After Gonzales, Michael Carbajal secured the silver medal in 1988 for the light flyweight division as well. In 1992 Oscar de la Hoya won the gold medal in Barcelona, Spain. Fighting at 132 pounds, de la Hoya defeated Marco

Rudolph with a knockdown punch in the third round. Exhibiting his Mexican American roots in East Los Angeles, de la Hoya capped his victory by waving both an American and a Mexican flag in the boxing ring. The U.S. Latino heritage in the Olympic boxing championships continued into the 21st century with Olympic hopefuls Ricardo "Rocky" Juárez in the featherweight division and Jose Navarro in the flyweight division.

Beyond boxing, U.S. Latinos have distinguished themselves in other areas of the Olympic Games. In fencing, the legendary Miguel de Capriles won bronze medals in both the 1932 competition in Los Angeles and in the 1948 Games in London. And in baseball, Flavio Alfaro won the silver medal in 1984 and Augie Ojeda won the bronze in 1996. Second to boxing for the number of medals earned, swimming has been a successful area of competition as well. At the 1984 Games in Los Angeles, Pablo Morales won an astonishing three medals, two silver and one gold, in the 100-meter butterfly, and the 200- and 400-meter individual medley swimming competitions. His success was followed by Tracie Ruiz-Conforto's silver medal in the synchronized swimming event in 1988 and Dara Torres's bronze medal for swimming that same year. In 1992, Morales returned to win two more gold medals. Torres also won an additional gold medal in that competition. They were joined by Heather Simmons-Carrasco who won the silver medal for synchronized swimming.

Tennis has been another Olympic sport in which U.S. Latinas have garnered distinction. In 1992, at the Olympiad in Barcelona, Mary Joe Fernandez won the bronze medal in singles and paired with Gigi Fernandez to win the gold medal in the women's tennis doubles. At the next Olympiad in 1996, both women one the gold once more in the doubles category.

In the 1984 Games in Los Angeles, Joseph Vargas won the silver medal for water polo, Mario Martinez won the silver for weight lifting, and James Martinez won the bronze for wrestling. The Games in 1988 saw Raoul Rodriguez win the silver medal for rowing. At the 1992 Barcelona Games, Trent Dimas won the gold medal in gymnastics and Juan Moreno secured the silver medal for tae kwon do. The Atlanta Games in 1996 saw U.S. Latina Lisa Fernandez secure the gold medal for softball.

Derek Parra won the gold medal in 2002 for speed skating. This sport is a recent addition to the Olym-

© ITSUO INOUYE/AP/WIDE WORLD PHOTOS

Gold-medal winner Derek Parra of the United States on his way to renewing the world record in the men's 1,500-meter speed-skating competition at the 2002 Winter Olympics, Salt Lake City, Utah.

pic Games and reflects both its popularity and its inner-city origins. For his positive impact on Latino youth, Parra was also given a Hispanic Heritage Award in 2002.

Although the competitive landscape is slowly changing, there are obstacles in evidence. Latinos often lack the financial backing required to pay for top-notch training and coaching, and historically they have not been pursued by collegiate athletic programs, the springboard for many Olympic teams. In 1996 only 1 Latino athlete among 44 was recruited for the U.S. Olympic baseball trials, a sport that attracts significant numbers of Latinos, notably at the professional level. The absence of role models is also cited as a challenge for young Latino athletes.

In terms of institutional support, the United States Olympic Committee (USOC) has begun to strengthen its outreach to minority communities and development of women and minority leaders. In 1996 the special subcommittee Minorities in Sports Task Force was formed to try to draw from underserved populations. Project GOLD (Guaranteed Olympic Leadership Development) was created to

host workshops to develop ethnic minorities and women interested in becoming leaders in the U.S. Olympic movement. The USOC's Finding Leaders Among Minorities Everywhere (FLAME) program is an effort to reach youth leaders from Boys and Girls Clubs of America, rewarding them for excelling in athletics, academics, and community involvement with a four-day visit to the Olympic Training Center in Colorado Springs.

RELATED ARTICLES

Baseball; Boxing; de la Hoya, Oscar; Sports in Latino Life; Tennis.

FURTHER READING

Bustamente, Antonio Ríos, and William Estrada. "The Latino Olympians: A History of Latino American Participation in the Olympic Games, 1896–1984." *Caminos Magazine* (1984).

Harris, Jaime C. "Black, Latino Athletes: The New Faces of the Winter Olympics?" *New York Amsterdam News* (February 28–March 6, 2002).

Menard, Valerie. "Out of the Loop." *Hispanic* 9, no. 7 (July 1996).

Toohey, Kristine, and A. J. Veal, eds. *The Olympic Games: A Social Science Perspective.* New York : CABI Pub., 2000.

SELECTED WEB SITE

Latino Legends in Sports.
http://www.latinosportslegends.com/

DESIRÉE GARCIA

ONOMASTICS

The *Real Academia Española* defines the term *onomastics* as the system underlying the origins of words, especially proper names; also the science that classifies and studies proper names; and finally as the day a person celebrates the patron saint associated with his or her name. The initial definition by the *Real Academia Española* sets the tone for our understanding of onomastics within the framework of Latino culture. In addition, *onomastics* also refers to last names or family names. This article will explain the Spanish onomastic tradition, follow the tradition to the American continent, and look at its impact on Latino name traditions today.

Formation of Last Names

The function of a last name is to establish a difference between people who share a first name. Initially, and still common in some rural areas in Spain and Latin America, a technique that was employed was to associate nicknames with people. With the increasing need for legal documents and notarized transactions it became necessary to include more information than just a first name on the documents in order to give them some validity—thus the need for a hereditary last name.

The use of a last name became commonplace in the 11th and 12th centuries because in the Middle Ages, similar to today, there were naming fashions, and people would name their children according to the given fashion, thus creating a cumulus of people who shared a first name.

In the kingdoms of Navarre, León, and Castille (Spain) it became the standard to add to the son's name, the name of the father, plus the suffix "-ez," which meant "son of." A name such as Juan Martinez was equivalent to saying "Juan son of Martin." This tradition was first started by the upper class and then it became popular and was extended among all classes.

In the 13th and 14th centuries, the practice of making the second name hereditary became extended mostly because of the need to pass along an inheritance to the newer generations. During the Middle Ages professions were passed on from parents to children; thus in official and commercial documents they would be reflected. Juan Herrero (Juan, horseshoe maker) would transfer his profession to his descendants, and also his last name; such was the case with commoners. In the noble classes the same was done with titles of nobility. Juan Caballero (knight) would also transfer his last name to his offspring as a way of passing on his noble title. During the Middle Ages the adoption of a last name was a voluntary process, and there was complete freedom regarding the types of last names that could be adopted. It was not atypical to find a priest with an Islamic last name. Offspring could often choose among all their ancestors for the last name that they liked best and adopt it. Thus in those times there was much variation owing to personal preference, the orthographic criteria of the scribe, or even the accent of a particular geographical area.

In the 15th century hereditary last names were consolidated, thanks to the ecclesiastic proposal by Cardinal Cisneros that all births and deaths must be accounted for in the parish records. In spite of this, in the poorest sectors of society the hereditary paternal last name was not fixed until 1870, when the civil registry of Spain came into existence. In the case of the Americas one can see that the ecclesiastic proposal of Cardinal Cisneros, coupled with the need to have proper documentation on ship manifests that went to the New World, created a standard practice to include the hereditary last name associated with each person who undertook the crossing of the Atlantic.

The practice since 1870, with the new regulations of the civil registry, is to use two last names. The first last name is traditionally passed on from fathers to sons and the second last name is passed from the mother.

All of the above practices are part of today's Latino naming tradition. Latinos also incorporate traditional U.S. naming practices. The freedom that exists in the United States with regard to changing one's name upon becoming a citizen, coupled with large numbers of undocumented persons, have fostered the adoption of a naming technique considered more American, such as using proper names from the Anglo tradition to create a link with the new cultural setting. It is very common to find Latinos with an Anglo first name and a Spanish last name.

Classification of Last Names

Today's last names can be classified in seven basic categories. They are presented here in order of importance and frequency of use:

Patronymic Last Names. This process is characteristic of human communities. The common practice is to specify the name of the father in order to be able to establish differences between people with the same first names. This process was then expanded into a hereditary process (in some instances the name of the mother is used instead). This is the case of last names that are traditionally first names, such as "Miguel," which then becomes "de Miguel" when used as a last name.

A last name that comes from the father's first name is the most common occurrence in Spanish. Such names, as mentioned earlier, are formed by adding the suffix "ez" to the father's proper name. These are extremely common last names.

Toponym Last Names. The custom of using the name of the place of a person's origin as a last name can be traced to ancient Greece. Names that refer to a place of origin or residence are varied, ranging from the name of a country or a region to the name of a small river or a small property or building. Therefore, one can speak of names that come from "minor toponyms" such as small properties, mounts, and small rivers, and names that come from "major toponyms," such as towns or cities, regions, countries, and large rivers. Minor toponym last names were at first used by members of the same town to differentiate among residents with the same first name. It is also common to use a last name associated with a *partida,* or property. For example, one could say that if a person named Juan resided near the village fountain he would likely be referred to as "Juan de la Fuente" (Juan of the Fountain).

In order to establish a classification of the toponym last names, the next six categories must be considered: (1) names that come from countries, regions, towns, or villages, such as España, Aragón, and Almagro; (2) names that come from the common appellative of a population nuclei, such as Aldea, Barrio, or Villa; (3) names that come from the common appellative of buildings, such as Torres, Castillo, Corral, Puente, or Iglesia; (4) names that come from hydrographic words such as Ebro, Río, Torrente, Ribera, or Fuentes; (5) names that come from the common referents to the terrain, such as Roca, Monte, Sierra, Valle, Cueva, or Peña; and (6) names that come from the common appellatives of vegetation, such as Encina, Perales, Manzano, or Robles.

© MICHAEL NEWMAN/PHOTOEDIT

Street sign for Cesar E. Chavez Avenue, with Chinese translation, in Los Angeles.

Office or Title Last Names. This category includes all of those last names that come from ecclesiastical offices, from administrative offices, and from titles of nobility. It is important to note that if a last name comes from one of the above categories, it can be because of two reasons, affinity to the office or to hereditary.

For instance, a person who exhibited very pious behavior might have been called Abad (abbot), but it might also be that the last name is used because that person is indeed a descendant of an abbot. This may seem controversial if the celibate nature of the ecclesiastic offices is taken into account, but such is not the case. Celibacy was enforced by the Roman Catholic Church only after the Council of Trento (1563), which came after the period when the use of last names became a standard practice.

Also, a last name such as Rey (king) might mean a person who worked for the king, looked like the king, or had a kinglike attitude. Such last names can be classified into three distinct categories: (1) names based on ecclesiastical offices, such as Abad, Cardenal, or Sacristán; (2) names based on administrative offices, such as Alcalde, Escribano, or Capitán; and (3) names based on titles of nobility, such as Duque, Conde, Rey, or Caballero.

Profession Last Names. Last names based on a family's profession were used to differentiate a first name by means of establishing some additional classificatory parameter, such as the profession. Owing to the strength of trade unions during the Middle Ages, such appellatives became more like heredity, as were the professions themselves. These last names can be classified into three distinct categories: (1) names that come from professions related to commerce and manufacturing, such as Molinero, Herrero, or Sastre; (2) names that come from professions related to agriculture and rural endeavors, such as Pastor, Vaquero, or Cazador; and (3) names that come from other professions such as Caminero or Criado.

Last Names from Nicknames. This can be considered the oldest of the systems employed to tell people apart. Even today the use of nicknames is extensive in the Spanish language and cultures. Nicknames are found in rural as well as urban areas. In urban areas ranging from Santiago, Chile, to Chicago, Illinois, there has been an increase in the use of nicknames, especially those related to gang activities and the subcultures associated with them, such as music and, to a lesser extent, literary manifestations. The association of a person with a nickname can be made for many reasons. Physical or moral simile is the most common. Sometimes the reason for the equivalence can just be an anecdote.

Last names that come from nicknames can be classified into the following groups: physical characteristics such as Bajo, Gordo, or Calvo; moral characteristics such as Feliz, Bueno, or Salado; animal characteristics such as Borrego, Buey, or Vaca; plant characteristics such as Limón, Cebolla, Trigo, or Oliva; family related characteristics such as Nieto or Sobrino; and age or status characteristics such as Casado, Joven, Mayor, or Viejo. This last category would include all other nicknames that normally refer to circumstances or anecdotes relating to the person's life. In this category can be included last names that refer to objects, in which case, the name of an object was used instead of the profession. Some examples include Cuerda, Cadenas, Botella, or Porras.

Last Names from Blessings, Benedictions, and Wishes for the Newborn.

Such last names are the additional names that the parents would give to an infant at his or her christening. These names sometimes have become, with the passing of time, last names. The names are related to the circumstances surrounding the birth of an infant. Some of the last names referred to issues of legitimacy and paternity. Names such as Bastardo, Expósito, Temprano, or Tirado, for example. Names in this category might stigmatize the person to whom it was given.

Additional names were given in order to satisfy the popular belief that a favorable name would result in positive life experiences or perhaps would determine in some fashion the future endeavors of that child. Names such as Lozano (healthy or beautiful), Tierno, Bello, Bueno, and so on, provided praise to the newborn. Names such as Feliz or Buendía, for example, were given in hopes of providing good luck for the infant. Names related to blessings or the ecclesiastical rite were also believed to be beneficial, such as Diosdado, de Jesús, and de Dios.

Lastly are those last names that come from the name of the month of the birth, such as Abril, Febrero, or Mayo, for example. These names were erroneously believed to belong to children of uncertain parenthood.

Last Names of Uncertain or Unknown Origin.

In some instances there are last names that cannot be explained etymologically with any degree of certainty. These last names are normally of pre-Roman origin, such as García or Muñoz. Sometimes the words come from Latin, Germanic, or Arab traditions but the changes that they have undergone through the years have rendered them unrecognizable. Also, as we have seen before, some of the last names are formed with reference to geographical names that are normally very old and difficult to trace.

History of Last Names

This section explores the origin of the last names in Spanish. They are grouped into chronological sections to facilitate the understanding of the mechanisms that have acted on the onomastic processes in Spanish.

Pre-Roman Names. There is little information regarding the formation of tribal names of the Celts, Iberians, and the other cultures of the peninsula before the time of the Romans. During the Roman colonization they adopted the Roman standard of using their last names, which explains why some names, such as García, Pacheco, Velasco, and so on, are still in use today.

Roman Names. The Romans of the higher classes had a very elaborate onomastic system for naming. The first name, or *praenomen,* was equivalent to today's Anglo first name. That name was followed by the name associated with the tribe, *gentilicium*. The next name that was used was equivalent to the last name, it was called *cognomen*. The last name that they added to this equation was the *agnomen,* which was a nickname that had some relevance to the person in question. The process of Romanization on the Iberian peninsula brought this system to the natives. This elaborate system was typical only of the higher classes; the plebeians continued to use only a name or a nickname.

Judeo-Christian Names. With the advent of Christianity on the Iberian peninsula, after the 4th and 5th centuries, there were substantial changes that affected the onomastic system. The names that were used were those of the saints and martyrs. These names displaced the Roman names that were in use before and also made obsolete the four-name system, which was replaced by a more simplified one-name system. The name used was the baptism name. After the fall of the Roman Empire, Germanic tribes took over the Iberian peninsula, bringing with them a new onomastic scenario; Germanic names quickly became trendy and replaced the Roman names during the Middle Ages. Part of the reason for the popularity of Germanic names was the fact that they were the ruling class and they had prestige. These names are related to the waging of war.

Jewish Names. In spite of the long history of the Jews in Spain, there are very few Spanish last names that are of Jewish origin. This is because of the political situation in Spain that was hostile, to say the least, to its Jewish population. The Jews as a community were discriminated against during the Middle Ages, becoming the scapegoat for all the ailments that plagued the kingdoms. This friction culminated with the expulsion from Spain of the Jews (and the Muslims) in 1492. The Jewish names that are found today in Spain are mostly the result of 20th-century migrations.

Muslim Names. Unlike the fate of Jewish names, Muslim names did not completely vanish from Spanish onomastics. Muslim names sometimes were associated with crafts and also with toponyms, and have withstood the passage of time. They can still be found in the southern and southeastern regions of Spain.

Muslims stayed in Spain from 711 until 1609, the date of their final expulsion from the Spanish kingdom. Their presence in the region for almost 900 years left an undeniable mark on all aspects of life and, by association, the onomastic processes.

Gypsy Names. There are not many Gypsy last names in Spain, but owing to their marital practices there are some family names that are more common among the Gypsy families. Gypsies have been on the Iberian peninsula since the Middle Ages; through the years they have adopted the standard Spanish naming system.

The contribution that makes this collective different from other groups is that they have continued to use first names from the Caló, such as Adonay,

Sandojé, Sujamí, and so on. This use of Caló is in contrast to the Spanish trend of following the different naming fashions (Germanic, biblical, or other).

Castilian Names. These names are generally classified by adding the suffix "ez" to the name, which means "son of." An alternate way to produce last names that was typical of Castile was the use of "de." This practice was also common in France; however, in France it was a sign of nobility. Because of this, in Spain it was also perceived as an indication of nobility.

American Names. The people who made the first Atlantic crossings were, for the most part, citizens of the kingdom of Castile. They brought with them the onomastic system that was dominant in Castile in the 15th century, with all the characteristics that

© RUDI VON BRIEL/PHOTOEDIT

Signs outside campaign headquarters for Dominican councilman candidate Ydánis Rodríguez, in the Washington Heights neighborhood of New York City.

were described earlier. The people who first populated the colonies came from the southern sections of the kingdom of Castile, which meant that there were also last names that followed the Muslim tradition.

For the most part the naming system on the North American continent was based on first names and, in the cases of the upper classes, there were toponyms associated with the first names. The Spaniards adapted indigenous names to the Spanish phonetic system, thus changing some of the original pronunciations. Another common practice that was associated with Christianization was to change the non-Christian names of the indigenous people to Christian names. This practice left intact many indigenous last names that were associated with toponyms. Another of the common practices by the Spaniards was to provide last names to the indigenous people who served the Spanish ruling class. In such instances, servants would adopt the name of the master. This was also common among the slave populations of the Caribbean, although sometimes names were randomly assigned to slaves.

The administrative requirements already in place in the Spanish empire created a need for the establishment of an onomastic system in the New World in order to properly document the new population in a rational fashion. Thus the Spanish onomastic system was imposed on the new population.

Since the indigenous heritage movements of the late 20th century, there has been a resurgence of indigenous names, mostly in areas of Central America and Mexico. Persons in the former colonies have sought to gain some autochthonous identity by rescuing some indigenous names and using them as first or last names.

Another trend today is the use of names common to the United States, resulting from U.S. influence on its Latino population and Latin America. For example, in the United States it is common to employ one last name, a first name, and a middle name, which is often referred to by its initial. In the U.S. Latino community the adoption of this system has led to the omission of the mother's last name from the last name pair that is dictated by Spanish tradition. In a way the adoption of the U.S. system has brought Latino onomastics to where they were prior to the 1870s. This backward trend has created a mass of commonly used last names, such as López, González, Rodríguez, and García, for example. This clustering has led to the use, in some instances, of the second last name as a compound of the first.

Compound Names. Compound names are sometimes used in Spanish. During the Middle Ages and the Renaissance, noble families used this technique in order to emphasize the nobility of both branches of the family. Today the U.S. Latino population has adopted this practice in order to preserve the mother's last name, which would otherwise disappear under the U.S. onomastic system. Such usage also allows Latinos to further identify themselves by the use of last names.

Orphans. There are many popular beliefs that identify certain names with those given to orphaned children, one of which is Expósito, meaning "orphaned" in Spanish. In general there were several naming conventions associated with orphaned children, and none was dominant or exclusive. It is popularly thought that last names associated with saints belong to orphaned children, although such names can also indicate a toponym.

RELATED ARTICLES
Family; Spanish in the United States; Toponymy.

FURTHER READING
Algeo, John. *On Defining the Proper Name.* Gainesville: Univ. Press of Fla., 1973.

Bright, William, ed. *International Encyclopedia of Linguistics.* New York: Oxford Univ. Press, 1992.

Feld, Steven, and Keith H. Basso, eds. *Senses of Place.* Santa Fe, N.Mex.: School of Am. Res. Press, 1996.

Lamarque, P. V. "Names and descriptions." *Encyclopedia of Language and Linguistics.* Ed. by R. E. Asher. Oxford: Pergamon, 1994.

Lehrer, Adrienne. "Names and Naming: Why We Need Fields and Frames." In *Frames, Fields, and Contrasts: New Essays in Semantic and Lexical Organization.* Ed. by A. Lehrer and E. F. Kittay. Hillsdale, N.J.: Erlbaum, 1992.

Lehrer, Adrienne. "Proper Names: Linguistic Aspects." *Encyclopedia of Language and Linguistics.* Vol. 6. Ed. by R. E. Asher. Oxford: Pergamon, 1994.

Menn, Lise, and Brian MacWhinney. "The Repeated Morph Constraint: Towards an Explanation." *Language* 60 (1984): 419–541.

Tooker, Elisabeth, ed. *Naming Systems: Proceedings of the American Ethnological Society 1980.* Washington, D.C.: Am. Ethnological Society, 1984.

CÉSAR ALEGRE

OPERATION BOOTSTRAP

Operation Bootstrap is the popular name for a strategy of economic development initiated by the Commonwealth of Puerto Rico during the 1940s. It was formally initiated by the passage of the Industrial Incentives Act of 1947. This legislation substituted a program of state-controlled industrialization for a system of state-sponsored incentives and tax exemptions to attract private investment. Operation Bootstrap was the name for the advertising campaign that followed passage of the legislation, but it quickly became shorthand for industrialization, agrarian reform, and population control.

The industrialization component of Operation Bootstrap revolved around a set of incentives including the construction of factory buildings and other infrastructure, training programs for Puerto Rican workers, and a publicity campaign emphasizing the existence of an abundant and cheap supply of labor on the island, all at the government's expense. Companies were also offered generous tax exemptions on their profits.

Agrarian reform was predicated on the need to wrest control of the economy from sugar interests because of their inability to sustain economic development. The agricultural economy was characterized by small enterprises, which, by definition, did not produce capital goods, had low rates of fixed capital investment, and employed few workers. The sugar industry was a case in point. Not only did it import its capital goods, it also neither provided steady employment nor made any contribution to urbanization—a key ingredient of modernization.

Before industrialization created an imbalance between the supply and demand of labor, the island's political leadership was convinced that Puerto Rico's economic ills were the result of overpopulation. This belief was buttressed in the 1940s by the perception of a deepening population crisis. The crisis was not so much the result of high fertility rates but an aftereffect of the Great Depression and of the inability of industries to fully absorb the increased supply of labor generated by the collapse of the agricultural sector and the migration of displaced workers from the rural countryside into the island's cities. Nevertheless, the government embarked on a program of family planning that included sterilization and a campaign to persuade workers to migrate to the United States.

Operation Bootstrap was significant in a number of ways. It was the first strategy of its kind in the so-called capitalist periphery. It made the Puerto Rican pattern of development fundamentally different from Latin America's and a model for the so-called *maquiladora* pattern of production (referring to a Mexican program that allows foreign ownership of companies organized to import merchandise that is assembled, manufactured, or repaired with low-wage labor and then exported to the country of origin or a third country under special customs arrangements). Between 1950 and 1990 average family income on the island increased by 93 percent, life expectancy increased by 14 years, and access to higher education was up by 92 percent. On the other hand, dramatic economic growth occurred at the expense of autonomous economic development. Operation Bootstrap failed to maintain Puerto Rico's comparative advantage over other developing nations. It did not minimize the costs associated with a reliance on tax incentives to attract capital investment and was unable to control growing unemployment. It has been said that Operation Bootstrap produced a century of economic development in one decade. At the turn of the 20th century, however, it was considered a failing strategy. Whatever its costs and benefits, there is no doubt that Operation Bootstrap ushered in Puerto Rico's colonial modernity.

RELATED ARTICLES

Politics, Puerto Rican; Puerto Ricans on the Mainland.

FURTHER READING

Alicea, Marisa. "The Latino Immigration Experience: The Case of Mexicanos, Puertorriqueños, and Cubanos." In *Handbook of Hispanic Cultures in the United States: Sociology.* Ed. by Félix Padilla et al. Houston, Tex.: Arte Público Press, 1994.

Maldonado, A. W. *Teodoro Moscoso and Puerto Rico's Operation Bootstrap.* Gainesville: Univ. Press of Fla., 1997.

Pantojas-García, Emilio. *Development Strategies as Ideology, Puerto Rico's Export-Led Industrialization Experience.* Boulder, Colo.: Lynne Rienner, 1990.

Rivera-Batiz, Francisco L., and Carlos E. Santiago. *Island Paradox, Puerto Rico in the 1990s.* New York: Russell Sage Fnd., 1996.

JOSÉ E. CRUZ

OPERATION HAMMER

Unprecedented increases in street gang membership, gang-related killings, and rock, or "crack," cocaine consumption in Los Angeles during the 1980s provoked vigorous law enforcement responses. Operation Hammer, also referred to as "The Hammer," was one of the most publicized aspects of the Los Angeles Police Department's (LAPD's) simultaneous "wars" on gang violence and drug dealers and consumers under Chief Daryl Gates. Operation Hammer entailed the coordination of weekend night sweeps of areas of reputed gang and drug activity by contingents of as many as 1,000 police officers and elite tactical squads working on an overtime basis. With the alleged goal of restoring "law and order" to affected neighborhoods, mostly in the predominantly African American and Latino south-central area, officers made between 300 and over 1,000 arrests per night, and an estimated 20,000 total arrests during the duration of the operation, from February to August 1988.

Although Hammer disrupted some gang and drug-dealing activities, gang killings and assaults increased steadily during the late 1980s. The high cost of the sweeps influenced the Los Angeles city council's decision to cut off the operation's funding after only six months. Some also questioned the sweeps' effectiveness. The existing state prison infrastructure was inadequate to absorb many new arrivals. Moreover, of the thousands arrested during the sweeps, a majority were guilty of minor offenses, such as jaywalking, loitering, and parking violations. The police created intelligence files of scores of gang members, but the fact that between 25 and 30 percent of those detained by police were undocumented immigrants (mostly from Mexico and Central America) severely hindered police efforts to track gang members. Some of those taken into custody were innocent of any wrongdoing, and on many nights criminal charges were filed against less than 10 percent of those arrested.

Although short lived, Operation Hammer was viewed favorably by most Los Angeles residents at the time. The January 1988 murder of Karen Toshima, a woman caught in the crossfire between two rival African American gangs in upscale Westwood, agitated already generalized fears of drug dealing and gang violence and increased popular demand for more forceful police action. Although the citywide uproar following Toshima's murder helped to make the implementation of the Hammer politically viable, most south-central Los Angeles residents had favored a more aggressive police role in their neighborhoods throughout the crime upswing of the 1980s.

The fact that south-central residents were widely considered a "pro-police" constituency did not, however, imply the absence of community-police tensions. Nearly all of the people arrested under Operation Hammer were either African American or Latino, a fact that troubled civil-rights advocacy groups. Since the tenure of Chief William Parker (1950–1966), the LAPD had been virtually free from political and civilian supervision. Most scholars believe this phenomenon gave bigoted officers more latitude in their treatment of suspects and isolated the LAPD from the communities they served. A "proactive" campaign entailing the use of aggressive policing tactics, sometimes on innocent people, the Hammer further distanced the LAPD from many low-income minorities. Fines paid by the LAPD to resolve excessive-force suits increased steadily in the years immediately following the operation, and reached over $20 million in 1992. Since the Rodney King trial and the Los Angeles riots in 1992, popular approval in Los Angeles and in other parts of the United States for law enforcement tactics modeled after those associated with Operation Hammer has dramatically declined.

RELATED ARTICLES

Crime and Latinos; Drugs; Gangs; Law Enforcement; Los Angeles.

FURTHER READING

Cannon, Lou. *Official Negligence: How Rodney King and the Riots Changed Los Angeles and the LAPD.* New York: Random House, 1997.

Domanick, Joe. *To Protect and to Serve: The LAPD's Century of War in the City of Dreams.* New York: Pocket Bks., 1994.

Gates, Daryl F., and Diane K. Shah. *Chief: My Life in the LAPD.* New York: Bantam, 1992.

Independent Commission on the Los Angeles Police Department. *Report of the Independent Commission.* Los Angeles, 1991.

ADRIAN ALTHOFF

OPERATION PETER PAN

In 1959, when Fidel Castro's revolution triumphed in Cuba, many Cuban parents who feared for their children's future under the new regime sent them to the United States to be temporarily taken care of. This exodus to the United States of over 14,000 unaccompanied Cuban children between ages 6 and

A tearful 20-month-old who was temporarily separated from her parents during Operation Peter Pan in Miami in 1962.

18 has become known as Operation Peter Pan, or Operación Pedro Pan.

Beginning on December 26, 1960, as a secret effort, Operation Peter Pan was framed within a number of ideological concerns. Rumors had circulated throughout Cuba that parents would lose *patria potestad*, the right to make decisions while raising their children. Since education was a part of Castro's national project and schools were temporarily being closed down for a national literacy campaign, many parents wanted to save their children from communist indoctrination. Backed by U.S. propaganda, a fear of communism quickly spread among Cuban parents, particularly those involved in the underground rebellion against Castro's new regime who feared that their children would be left abandoned if they were jailed or executed.

Operation Peter Pan is best understood as a symbol of the continuing tense relations between the United States, the Cuban exile community, and Cuba. It was not simply a humanitarian mission devoid of politics. In the 1960s, U.S. refugee policy was sensitive to the needs of the Cold War and visa requirements were waived for Cuban applicants. Although the United States proclaimed to aid refugees on humanitarian grounds, there were also military and political interests in doing so. Government officials counted on the propaganda value of Cuban escapees serving as examples of U.S. democracy as well their potential for providing intelligence. Thus there were operational reasons to expedite the visas for family members because having children of the underground served multiple purposes. Not only did children require different security checks than adults, but Cuban parents also could continue fighting the regime without pressure of having to tend to their children. Meanwhile CIA (Central Intelligence Agency) control over their children ensured compliance from Cuban parents. Many were willing to fight in the resistance as long as their children were safe.

Despite these military and political objectives, Operation Peter Pan was carried out under a religious cloak of humanitarian assistance.

For the operation to begin, a local school in Cuba was needed to provide the request for student visas, as well as a social service agency that could plan for the total care of children on their arrival to the United States. With federal funding and donations from various organizations and companies, James Baker, the headmaster of Ruston Academy, an American school in Havana, teamed up with Father Bryan Walsh, the director of the Catholic Welfare Bureau. They were granted blanket authority to issue waivers to any children ages 6–16 years of age, while Father Walsh assumed responsibility for caring for the children in foster or group homes until they were reunited with their parents. Friends or relatives looked after approximately 6,000 of the children, while two-thirds of the remaining 8,000 were under the care of the federal government. Yet because this was a child-welfare program and not an educational project, Congress questioned the constitutionality of a federal program that paid money to the Catholic Church to take care of refugee children.

Conducted in secret for the majority of two years, Operation Peter Pan was made public in February 1962. Authorities feared that any publicity of the program might endanger families or inhibit the possibility of other children migrating. Yet the operation would only last until immigration was closed between the United States and Cuba on October 22, 1962, with the onset of the Cuban Missile Crisis. It was not until the opening of the Camarioca port and the freedom flights in 1965 that many children were reunited with their parents. However, not all families were reunited, and when immigration was halted again in 1973, many families were left divided.

There are conflicting views about the origins and purposes of Operation Peter Pan. The Cuban government saw the plan as an example of unscrupulous psychological warfare, a CIA plan to undermine the Cuban family, and an act of U.S. aggression whereby the U.S. government kidnapped Cuba's youth. The Peter Pan children were central to the propaganda campaigns of both governments. The political struggles between the United States and Cuba were played out through these refugee children such that their safety and emotional needs were overshadowed by politics and military objectives.

RELATED ARTICLES

Castro, Fidel; Cuba; Cuban Americans; Exile; Immigration, Latino; Politics, Cuban American.

FURTHER READING

Conde, Yvonne. *Operation Peter Pan: The Untold Exodus of 14,048 Cuban Children.* New York: Routledge, 1999.

Torreira Crespo, Ramón, and José Buajasán Marrawi. *Operación Peter Pan: Un Caso de Guerra Psicológica Contra Cuba* (Operation Peter Pan: A Case of Psychological Warfare Against Cuba). La Habana: Editora Política, 2000.

Torres, Maria de los Angeles. *The Lost Apple: Operation Pedro Pan, Cuban Children in the U.S., and the Promise of a Better Future.* Boston: Beacon Press, 2003.

SELECTED WEB SITE

Operation Pedro Pan Group, Inc. http://www.pedropan.org/

ALYSSA GARCIA

OPERATION WETBACK

The immigration enforcement drive code-named Operation Wetback was the second largest Mexican repatriation project of the United States Immigration and Naturalization Service (the first occurred during the Great Depression). Launched under the administration of President Dwight Eisenhower, Attorney General Herbert Brownell, and immigration commissioner general Joseph Swing, Operation Wetback was carried out from the careful planning phase in August 1953 to its full-fledged implementation on June 9, 1954. State governors, police departments, and Native American tribal governments in California, Arizona, Texas, and the Midwest helped the Immigration and Naturalization Services (INS) to implement the campaign.

During World War II the United States and Mexico negotiated a bilateral agreement to import Mexican workers to fill the labor demand resulting from the deployment of U.S. workers. The agreement, called the Emergency Labor Program, or the Bracero Program, was approved on April 4, 1942, in Mexico, and the U.S. Congress enacted Public Law 45 on April 29, 1943. In 22 years, the foreign worker program imported approximately 5 million *braceros* to work in 24 states.

The contradictory relationship between the INS, growers, and labor organizations made Mexican immigration a thorny issue. Pull factors (those incentives that drew Mexican immigrants to the United States) in the United States economy shaped immigration policy to allow Mexican laborers to cross the border with few restrictions during harvests and prosperous economic times. Push factors (those conditions that forced Mexicans out of the country) consisting of economic downturns and nativism or xenophobia led to immigration restrictions and massive deportation campaigns. The increase in Mexican immigration coupled with the U.S. economic recession of the early 1950s caused nativists to turn against Mexicans. Anti-Mexican rhetoric portrayed Mexican immigrants as dangerous and subversive.

Between 1944 and 1954, during the "wetback decade," a national sentiment against Mexican immigrants peaked with the enactment of restrictive immigration legislation. Undocumented workers were labeled "wetbacks" or *mojados* (literally, "wet people") because many crossed the Rio Grande to reach the United States. The Border Patrol carried out a quasi-military operation of mass roundups and deportations of Mexicans to the interior of Mexico. On July 15, 1954, the first day of the operation, 4,800 Mexicans were apprehended and deported. They were sent across the border on trucks, buses, trains, and by sea. When Operation Wetback moved to the midwestern United States, the INS created the Border Patrol Air Transport Arm to airlift "illegals" to the border. At the border they were loaded onto ships and sent as far south as the port of Veracruz. During the first year, 11,459 Mexicans were airlifted from the midwestern states. The targets of this project were "illegal aliens"; however, implementation focused on Mexicans in general. In some cases undocumented immigrants were deported along with their U.S.-born children. The Border Patrol sought "suspected" undocumented Mexicans on the streets, in private residences, and at work sites and asked for identification. Many Mexicans were shipped across the border without due process. Native American tribal governments in Yuma, Arizona, were contracted to supervise the "hunt down" of undocumented Mexicans. They were paid a bounty of $2.50 to $3.00 per person caught crossing through their reservation.

The exact number of deportees is unknown. According to the INS, as many as 1.3 million Mexicans were apprehended and deported. During 1953, 875,000 were deported and 20,174 were airlifted from Spokane (Washington), Chicago, Kansas City, and St. Louis. In 1954 over 1 million Mexicans were deported. In 1955 the number decreased to 256,290. And in 1956 the deportations totaled 90,122.

The dominant national current at the time was for restriction of Mexican immigration. Labor leaders, United States politicians, and many Mexican American organizations supported measures to halt Mexican immigration. Mexican American organizations including the American GI Forum and the League of United Latin American Citizens (LULAC) opposed Mexican immigration, arguing that it had an adverse effect on the socioeconomic conditions of U.S.-born citizens of Latin American descent. In a report entitled *What Price Wetbacks?* (1955), the American GI Forum of Texas urged the federal government for immediate immigration control. Politicians such as Hubert Humphrey, Paul Douglas, and Herbert Lehman argued for the need to enact restrictive legislation. They espoused the belief that Mexican immigrants were taking away jobs from other Americans and were lowering wage standards. Attorney General Herbert Brownell called for higher budgets to implement stricter legislation. President Eisenhower supported the plan.

Commissioner Swing, President Eisenhower's classmate at West Point, developed the strategic plan to patrol the border, to reorganize the Border Patrol command structure, to introduce new equipment and uniforms, and to increase the budget of the Border Patrol. Also, Swing developed the media campaign to publicize the operation and portray the "Mexican menace" as the enemy. Most important, he created the Mobile Task Force in charge of deporting Mexicans to the interior of the country. In addition, he requested a $10 million budget increase to build a 150-mile- (240-km-) long fence to separate Mexico from the United States.

The ramifications of McCarthyism during the Cold War limited opposition to Operation Wetback. One of the selling points of the operation was the promise of limiting the flow of "subversives" across the United States–Mexico border. The assistant secretary of labor, Rocco Siciliano; the chief of the Border Patrol, Willard Kelly; and Senator Pat McCarran urged for immigration control to counteract subversive activities, particularly in the labor movement. With the exception of the Asociación Nacional Mexico-Americana (ANMA), formed in 1948 to advocate for the rights of Mexicans, few other organizations overtly opposed Operation Wetback. The ANMA condemned the violations of due process and the discriminate persecution of Mexicans in general. As a result of their advocacy, the organization's leadership came under the scrutiny of the House Un-American Activities Committee (HUAC). Other organizations opposing Operation Wetback were the Independent Progressive Party, the Los Angeles Committee for the Protection of the Foreign Born, and some locals of the International Longshoremen's and Warehousemen's Union (ILWU). On April 17, 1959, a group of concerned individuals presented a petition to the United Nations charging that the United States government, by carrying out racist and arbitrary procedures during the deportations, had violated the rights of Mexicans.

Operation Wetback did not end Mexican immigration; however, it established a negative standard for the treatment of Mexicans. It also increased police surveillance and began the militarization of the United States–Mexico border. By the end of Operation Wetback, in mid-September 1956, the Border Patrol's budget had doubled. Undocumented immigration to the United States was curtailed but has continued into the present.

RELATED ARTICLES

Border, United States-Mexico; Bracero Program; Deportation; Immigration, Latino; Labor; United States Congress; United States–Mexico Relations.

FURTHER READING

Acuña, Rodolfo. *Occupied America: A History of Chicanos.* 4th ed. New York: Longman, 2000.

Calavita, Kitty. *Inside the State: The Bracero Program, Immigration, and the I.N.S.* New York : Routledge, 1992.

Cavazos, Sylvia. *The Disposable Mexican: Operation Wetback, 1954 ; the Deportation of Undocumented Workers in California and Texas.* Ann Arbor, Mich.: UMI, 1998.

Down in the Valley; A Supplementary Report on Developments in the Wetback and Bracero Situation of the Lower Rio Grande Valley of Texas since Publication of "What Price Wetbacks?." Austin, Tex.: American GI Forum of Texas/Texas State Federation of Labor. 1955.

Driscoll, Barbara A. *The Tracks North: The Railroad Bracero Program of World War II.* 1st ed. Austin, Tex.: CMAS Bks., Ctr. for Mexican Am. Studies, Univ. of Tex. at Austin, 1999.

García, Juan Ramon. *Operation Wetback: The Mass Deportation of Mexican Undocumented Workers in 1954.* Westport, Conn.: Greenwood Press, 1980.

ARCELA NUÑEZ-ALVAREZ

OPINIÓN, LA

Los Angeles–based *La Opinión* is the most widely read and long-running Spanish-language newspaper in the United States. Founded on September 16, 1926, to coincide with Mexican Independence Day, in its growth and development it mirrors the Hispanic population in southern California. In its early years the newspaper's coverage focused primarily on Mexico, reflecting both the composition of Los Angeles's Spanish-speaking population at the time and founder Ignacio E. Lozano's journalistic vision of *La Opinión* as a Mexican newspaper in exile.

Escaping political turmoil in Mexico, Lozano arrived in the United States in 1908 committed to establishing an independent newspaper. Settling in San Antonio, Texas, he founded *La Prensa,* a daily Spanish-language newspaper that primarily reported on political and social developments in Mexico and was highly critical of the administration of President Plutarco E. Calles. As the pattern of Mexican immigration shifted from Texas to California, Lozano seized the opportunity to launch *La Opinión.* With the founder's death in 1953, son Ignacio E. Lozano, Jr., assumed leadership of *La Opinión,* while *La Prensa* came under the management of Lozano's widow Alicia Elizondo de Lozano. *La Prensa* was sold in 1959 and published its last issue in 1963. *La Opinión* suffered losses during its first years, but by 1930 it was turning a profit and had a sizable a readership base that extended beyond California to Texas, New Mexico, Arizona, Oregon, Utah, and Illinois.

From its inception *La Opinión* distinguished itself for its coverage of issues that were either ignored by the English-language media or were treated from a perspective that did not reflect the point of view of Mexicans in the United States. Predicated on the notion that these immigrants would return to their homeland, the paper initially saw its role as one of bringing about reform in Mexican society and guiding refugees both through their stay in the United States and their eventual return home. To these ends *La Opinión* offered a critical look at issues believed to be the root causes of mass emigration from Mexico—namely, political corruption, poverty, and social injustice. The daily was highly critical of the United States, as well, exposing the plight of Mexicans at the hands of an Anglo majority that was prejudiced and exploitive of this population. Frequent editorials advised Mexican parents to maintain their cultural and linguistic roots at home so as to pave the way for the repatriation of their children. To this end the paper also sponsored Mexican cultural events in southern California and educational initiatives aimed at improving the Spanish-language skills of Mexican children.

La Opinión's treatment of issues such as the deportation and repatriation of Mexicans in the 1930s and the Zoot Suit Riots of 1943 established its reputation as a champion of the rights of Mexican immigrants. (The Zoot Suit Riots were a violent upheaval that pitted Mexicans in Los Angeles against the city's white majority and exposed the incendiary portrayals of Mexicans in the mainstream media.) In the 1950s the paper broadened its treatment of U.S. domestic issues, in an effort to better serve the growing number of readers for whom repatriation to Mexico was no longer a goal. These readers increasingly relied on *La Opinión* to shepherd them through the process of making a home in the United States. Accordingly, in 1970 Lozano, Jr., described the daily's mission as "no longer to be a Mexican newspaper published in Los Angeles, but an American newspaper that happens to be published in Spanish." More recently, the influx of Central and South Americans to the Los Angeles area has also precipitated a shift in coverage from primarily Mexican and Mexican American topics to more pan-Hispanic ones. In 1986 *La Opinión* played a pivotal role in the passage of the Immigration Reform and Control Act, which extended amnesty to millions of immigrants in California. The paper's aggressive campaign on behalf of voter registration and its series of editorials emphasizing the importance of political participation galvanized Latinos and raised their political and economic visibility in southern California.

In 1976, when Lozano, Jr., was appointed as U.S. ambassador to El Salvador, his children José and Leticia took over as copublishers of the paper. The Times Mirror Company, the communication conglomerate that publishes the *Los Angeles Times,* acquired 50 percent ownership of *La Opinión* in 1990. Ten years later the Tribune Company assumed this share of ownership, when it purchased the Times Mirror Company. However, editorial and operational control of *La Opinión* remains in the Lozano family. In 1999 and 2000 *La Opinión* was recognized as the Outstanding Hispanic Daily by the National Association of Hispanic Publications.

La Opinión Today

With a daily readership of nearly 700,000, *La Opinión* is the second most read paper in southern California, after the *Los Angeles Times*. The paper's readership includes foreign-born Latinos who are unfamiliar with the American system and are not proficient in English, as well as acculturated Spanish-English bilinguals. For the former, the paper fills the need for vital information in Spanish, while for the latter, it offers cultural identity and fosters community connections.

La Opinión's daily sections include "News," "Metro," "Sports," "Entertainment," "Commentary," and "Business." Weekly sections cover technology, personal finances, real estate, education, and personal advice. The Sunday paper is similar to that of other major metropolitan papers with coupons, home improvement tips, help wanted ads, a television guide, and a magazine covering cultural topics. In addition, the Sunday paper features Tío Caimán, a children's section specially designed to promote reading in Spanish. *La Opinión Digital* (www.laopinión.com) is an online extension of the daily with free access to archived articles. Proprietary news is available to other media through syndication service.

Under the leadership of José Lozano and sister Monica, the paper continues its longtime commitment to public-service journalism. It publishes a

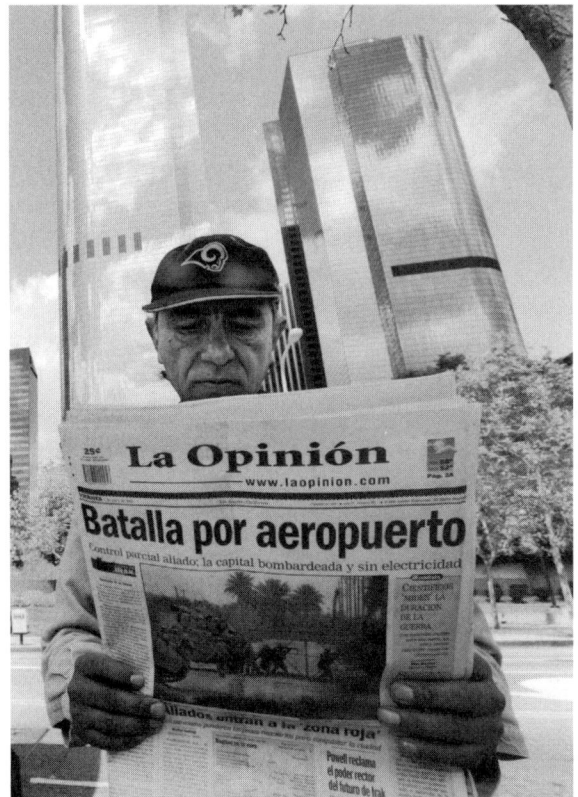

In Los Angeles a man reads the Spanish-language newspaper *La Opinión*.

293 ✺

number of supplements spotlighting topics such as education, health care, civic responsibility, finances, early childhood, and so on. It also sponsors election debates, scholastic and artistic contests, and scholarships for children.

Future goals for the daily include a greater electronic presence as well as expansion into other markets. With a population of over 4 million Hispanics, Los Angeles County is the largest Hispanic county in the United States and the highest ranked market in buying power for the Hispanic population.

RELATED ARTICLES

Journalism; Newspapers and Magazines.

FURTHER READING

Laezman, Rick. "Seventy-Five Years and Counting." *Hispanic Business* (March 2001): 20.

Medeiros, Francine. "La Opinión, a Mexican Exile Newspaper: A Content Analysis of Its First Years, 1926–1929." *Aztlán* 11, no. 1: 65–87.

Veciana-Suarez, Ana. *Hispanic Media, USA.* Washington, D.C.: Media Inst., 1988.

SELECTED WEB SITE

Conozca La Opinión.
www.laopinion.com/corporate/about/
index.phtml?lang=sp

MARÍA M. CARREIRA

ORDEN HIJOS DE AMÉRICA

The Orden Hijos de América, also known as the Order of Sons of America (OSA), was founded in 1921 in San Antonio, Texas, to combat civil rights abuses against Hispanics. Among its concerns were irregularities in wages, education, and housing. One of the first statewide Mexican American civil rights organizations founded in Texas, the organization's first meeting was held in October 1921 at a local barbershop owned by Ramon H. Carvajal; by November of that year more than 150 people attended a meeting in a town hall.

The OSA's state charter, obtained in January 1922, stated that the organization's purpose was to use its "influence in all fields of social, economic, and political action in order to realize the greatest enjoyment possible of all the rights and privileges and prerogatives extended by the American constitution." The group's constitution, written in English in 1922 and in Spanish in 1927, stated that the OSA would serve as a mutual aid society, pro-labor organization, civic group, and political association.

The order's membership was limited to U.S. citizens, native born or naturalized, of Mexican or Spanish descent, over age 16. The founders included John C. Solis, Francisco and Melchor Leyton, and Santiago G. Tafolla, who was the group's president. In 1925 the organization opened a headquarters on Main Street in downtown San Antonio, and formed additional chapters in Corpus Christi, Somerset, Pearsall, Kingsville, Alice, and Beeville, Texas. In 1923 the San Antonio chapter had 250 members and by 1928 the Corpus Christi chapter had more than 175 members.

The OSA was formed at a time when Jim Crow laws had increased the segregation of the races in the South. These laws were also enforced against Mexicans and Tejanos, who were relegated to separate residential areas and designated spaces in public facilities. They attended separate schools and worshipped in mostly segregated churches. Among the problems facing Mexicans and Mexican Americans in Texas in the early 1900s were lynchings, expulsion from their land, and educational inequality.

Against this backdrop, the OSA took on many causes. The San Antonio chapter paid for an attorney for two men, Juan Morales and Victor Fuentes, who were accused of murder in Corpus Christi. As a result of the OSA's fight for a new Mexican school in Corpus Christi, the Cheston L. Heath school was dedicated in September 1925. In 1927 the OSA advocated for the first Mexican American to serve on a jury in Nueces County, and its members fought for the removal of a "No Mexicans Allowed" sign in North Beach. They also provided aid to a Mexican tenant family suing a white landlord and helped two Mexican girls attend a white school in Banquete.

Over time there were changes in the all-male leadership of the organization and some splintering off from the main body. In 1922 a former member formed another group called the Sons of Texas; in 1927 some younger members left the OSA and formed the Knights of America; by 1929 the Corpus Christi chapter broke with the OSA and joined the Latin American Citizens League of the Valley. As the Orden lost members to other organizations, the group eventually ceased to exist by the late 1920s. Three early Texas organizations, including the Orden de Hijos de America, the Knights of America, and the League of Latin American Citizens, formed the

League of United Latin American Citizens (LULAC) in Corpus Christi in 1929. Today, LULAC has become one of the largest, most influential, and most long-lasting Mexican American organizations.

RELATED ARTICLES
Civil Rights; League of United Latin American Citizens.

FURTHER READING

Leininger Pycior, Julie. *La Raza Organizes: Mexican American Life in San Antonio 1915–1930, as Reflected in Mutualista Activities.* Ph.D. dissertation, South Bend, Ind: Univ. of Notre Dame, 1979.

Orozco, Cynthia. *The Handbook of Texas Online.* Austin: The Texas State Historical Assn. and the General Libraries at the Univ. of Tex. at Austin, 2002. www.tsha.utexas.edu/handbook/online/

Weeks, O. Douglas. "The League of United Latin-American Citizens: A Texas-Mexican Civic Organization." *Southwestern Political and Social Science Quarterly* (December 1929).

TERESA PUENTE

OREGON

The state of Oregon, located along the Pacific coastline of the United States, was originally inhabited by several indigenous groups, including the Klamath, Modoc, Multnomah, and Chinook peoples. In 1602 the Spanish explorer Sebastian Vizcaino, searching for the fabled Northwest Passage, was one the first Europeans to explore and map the Oregon coastline. Much later, in 1774 the Spanish explorer Juan Pérez, traveling north from San Francisco, also sailed along the Oregon coastline, claiming the entire region for the king of Spain.

However, Spain's reach along the Oregon coastline was very tentative, and it was contested by two powerful European rivals, England and Russia. Preoccupied by internal problems and widespread rebellions in her American colonies, Spain signed the Adams-Onis Treaty in 1819, relinquishing its claims to all areas north of the 42d parallel, including all of present-day Oregon. Two years later Mexico declared independence and Spain's presence in the region was eliminated forever.

Oregon became the 33d American state on February 14, 1859. But it was not until the 20th century that Mexican laborers entered the state in significant numbers. The Mexican Revolution (1910–1920) was a major catalyst for Mexican immigrants, sending laborers from the central states of Zacatecas, Jalisco, Michoacán, Guanajuato, and other parts of Mexico northward in search of railroad and agricultural employment. The shortage of workers after the United States entered World War I in 1917 prompted several railroad companies to recruit Mexican laborers to help maintain their tracks.

With America's entry into World War II in December 1941, another prolonged labor shortage prompted the United States government to sign the Migrant Labor Agreement with Mexico on August 4, 1942. It was through this program that more than 15,000 Mexican *braceros* (laborers) were contracted to work on farms in Oregon's agricultural fields.

Mexican American laborers from California and Texas also went north to work in the fertile Willamette Valley, which has been regarded as the agricultural heartland of Oregon for more than a century. Although many of the Latinos arrived as seasonal laborers to take part in the harvesting of beans, potatoes, apples, sugar beets, cherries, and strawberries, some of these itinerant workers gradually settled down with their families to establish permanent roots in the areas where they worked.

The growth of Oregon's Hispanic community in later decades has been impressive. In the 1980 census, the total Hispanic population of Oregon was tallied at 65,847, or 2.5 percent of the total state population. By 1990 this ethnic group had increased to 112,707, which still represented only 4 percent of Oregon's total population. But in the 2000 census, Oregon's Hispanic population increased dramatically to 275,314, a 318 percent increase from 1980.

Mexican Americans were the largest Hispanic group tallied in the 2000 census, accounting for 214,662 individuals, representing 77.9 percent of the Latino population and 6.3 percent of the overall state population. The number of Puerto Ricans was tallied at 5,092, and the Cuban American population was represented by 3,091 individuals, both constituting less than 2 percent of the total Hispanic population in that census year.

The bulk of the Latino population is concentrated in the tricounty area of Washington, Multnomah, and Clackamas counties, which saw a population increase of 116,068—or 191 percent—between 1990 and 2000. Multnomah County alone saw a 170 percent increase from 18,390 residents in 1990 to 49,607 residents in 2000.

Given the growth of their numbers, Latinos now represent a tremendous economic force in the Portland-Willamette area. In recognition of its growing

Latino population, Portland was listed in 1996 by *Hispanic Magazine* as one of the top ten cities for Hispanics to live, in terms of quality of life and other issues.

Several organizations have been established in recent decades to address the needs of Oregon's rapidly growing Hispanic community. Centro Latino Americano was established in 1972 in Eugene as an advocate for the social, economic, and political rights of Latino residents in Lane County. The Hacienda Community Development Corporation (HCDC) of Portland was established in 1992 for the purpose of helping Hispanic residents in northeast Portland to get affordable housing and other economic assistance. The Oregon Council for Hispanic Advancement (OCHA) was founded in Portland in 1985 with the mission of finding and creating educational and economic opportunities for Latinos in Oregon and southwest Washington.

The farmworker and migrant populations of Oregon—largely made up of Mexican Americans—have struggled to assert their economic and political rights. In May 1977 the Willamette Valley Immigration Project (WVIP) was founded after several INS (Immigration and Naturalization Services) raids targeted the Latino community. The organization provided legal advice and representation to undocumented laborers. Another organization, Pineros y Campesinos Unidos del Noroeste (PCUN; Northwest Treeplanters and Farmworkers United) was founded in 1985 by 80 farmworkers and has become the primary advocate for Oregon's farmworker community. Based in Woodburn, the PCUN has played a crucial role in educating and empowering newly arriving Latino farmworkers to help them avoid the systematic exploitation that plagues migrant communities.

Political representation has come very slowly to Oregon's Latino community. In 1997 Susan Castillo,

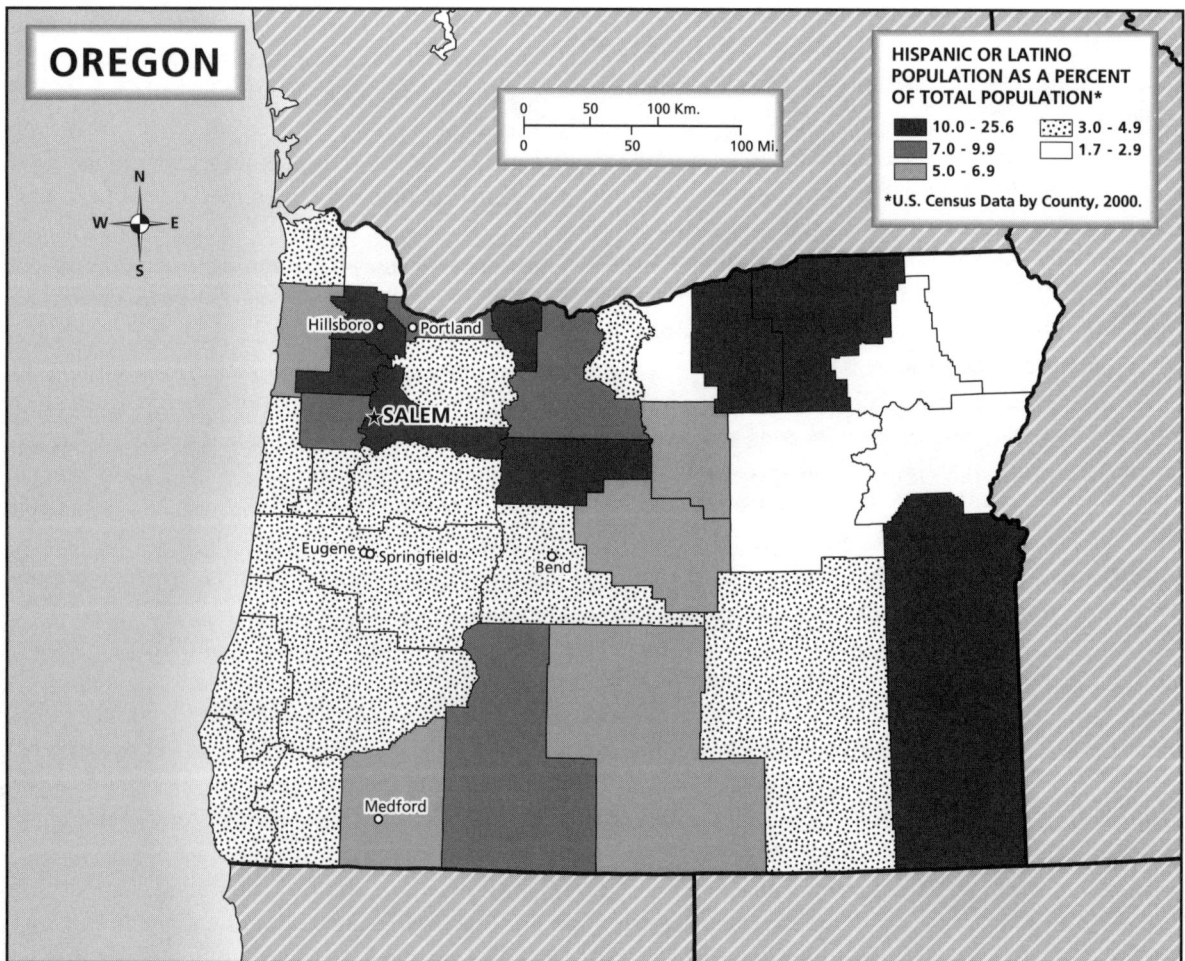

OREGON

HISPANIC OR LATINO POPULATION AS A PERCENT OF TOTAL POPULATION*

10.0 - 25.6   3.0 - 4.9
7.0 - 9.9   1.7 - 2.9
5.0 - 6.9

*U.S. Census Data by County, 2000.

Hillsboro · Portland

★ SALEM

Eugene ∞ Springfield   Bend

Medford

who enjoyed a long career as an award-winning television journalist, became the first Latina to serve in the Oregon Legislative Assembly. Five years later, in 2002, Senator Castillo broke new ground when she was appointed the superintendent of public instruction in Oregon. With this appointment, Oregon became only the second state in the country to elect a Latina to statewide office.

RELATED ARTICLES

Adams-Onis, Treaty of; Immigration, Latino.

FURTHER READING

Gamboa, Erasmo. "Mexican Migration Into Washington State: A History, 1940–1960." *Pacific Northwest Quarterly,* 72, no. 1 (January 1981).

Gamboa, Erasmo. *Mexican Labor and World War II: Braceros in the Pacific Northwest, 1942–1947.* Austin: Univ. of Tex. Press, 1990.

Gamboa, Erasmo, and Carolyn M. Buan, eds. *Nosotros: The Hispanic People of Oregon: Essays and Recollections.* Portland: Oregon Council for the Humanities, 1995.

SELECTED WEB SITES

Oregon Council for Hispanic Achievement.
  http://www.ocha-nw.org/history.html

PCUN—Northwest Treeplanters and Farmworkers United.
  http://www.pcun.org/

JOHN P. SCHMAL

COURTESY OF MUSEUM OF NEW MEXICO, NEG. NO. 152218

Portrait of Miguel A. Otero, Sr., 1881.

OTERO FAMILY

Prominent in New Mexico, the Otero family comprises congressional representatives, governors, a suffragist, and writers whose roles in the shaping of the state's identity have been decisive. The family traced its roots to a mid-18th-century Spanish settler, Pedro Otero. However, genealogical research suggests that Pedro was born Pedro Durán y Chávez in New Mexico, not Spain. He was orphaned as a child and possibly raised by Fray Cayetano Otero, the only Otero living in New Mexico at the time.

Pedro and his wife, Maria, had several children, including Vicente Antonio, who was born in 1781. Vicente became the patriarch of a clan that would shape New Mexico's history well into the 20th century. He served as judge and mayor during both the Spanish and Mexican periods. His wife, Gertrudis Aragón, bore at least nine children.

Their most famous son, Miguel Antonio I, was born on June 21, 1829, in Valencia, New Mexico, when it was part of Mexico. After basic instruction in Spanish, he was sent to school in St. Louis, Missouri, and then earned a law degree in New York. When Miguel Antonio returned home in the early 1850s, New Mexico was a territory of the United States. One of his first jobs was as personal secretary to the territorial governor. He next served in the territorial legislature and then as attorney general. In 1855 he ran for Congress, narrowly losing the popular vote, but he successfully contested the election in the House of Representatives; he accused his opponent, José Manuel Gallegos—a former Mexican priest who spoke limited English—of stealing the election with votes from Mexican citizens and questioned his loyalty to the United States.

In Congress, Otero lobbied for a railroad link to New Mexico and allied himself with the South to pursue a southern route for the transcontinental railroad. In return for support of southern politicians, he advocated for New Mexico's admission to the Union as a slave state. When the Civil War broke out, he did not support the Confederacy, but his proslavery positions ended his political career, although he remained influential on railroad causes. While serving in Congress, Otero married Mary Josephine Blackwood, a staunch southerner.

In 1861 Otero headed to Kansas and operated several successful warehousing and merchandising businesses tied to the railroad. The Oteros had four children, including Miguel Antonio II, born October 17, 1861. As a boy, Miguel Antonio II met "Wild Bill" Hickok, "Buffalo" Bill Cody, and "Calamity" Jane. As teenagers, Miguel Antonio and his brother Page were sent east to attend school, but never lasted very long in any one place. Miguel Antonio, at age 17, joined his father's firm in the newly formed town of Otero, the first New Mexico stop on the Atchison, Topeka and Santa Fe Railroad, named after the elder Miguel Antonio, who worked tirelessly to secure the right-of-way. Two years later the Oteros founded the San Miguel National Bank, with father and both sons serving as officers. The family further diversified economically, obtaining telephone franchise rights in New Mexico and northern Mexico. In 1882 Miguel Antonio I died suddenly of pneumonia. According to contemporary press accounts, he was a millionaire but Miguel Antonio II said that while his father's investments had considerable potential, they had little monetary value.

Miguel Antonio II continued his father's business interests and became active in politics, holding several local elected offices. In 1888 he married Caroline Virginia Emmett, the daughter of a former chief justice of the Minnesota supreme court. Their first son, Miguel Antonio Otero III, lived only a few days. A second child, named Miguel Antonio Otero IV, was born a year later, on August 30, 1892. In 1897 President McKinley rather unexpectedly made Miguel Antonio II governor of New Mexico after political leaders in the territory were unable to agree on a nominee. He served nine years, the longest term of office of any Hispanic governor in U.S. history.

After leaving office, Otero devoted himself to business and then wrote a three-volume memoir describing his adventures on the frontier, in business, and in politics. He died in 1944. His son became a judge, ran unsuccessfully for Congress, and married Katherine Stinson, a pioneering aviator and stunt pilot.

A number of other Oteros rose to prominence in New Mexico. Mariano S. Otero, Miguel Antonio I's cousin, served as a territorial delegate to Congress, defeating his uncle Manuel Antonio Otero in the election. Following his term in Washington, Mariano was a successful banker and rancher and was described in the *New York Times* in 1890 as the richest man in New Mexico.

Despite the wealth and influence of the Oteros, the family fell victim to the land grant injustices that dispossessed many Hispanos of their property. Miguel Antonio I and his brother Manuel Antonio owned more than 1 million acres (400,000 ha) of ranch land. When the two brothers died, Miguel Antonio II and Manuel B. Otero, son of Manuel Antonio, inherited it. James Whitney of Boston challenged their ownership; a gunfight ensued leaving Whitney and Manuel B. Otero dead. Eventually the Supreme Court declared the land grant void, and Anglo settlers quickly took possession.

Manuel B. Otero's daughter, Adelina "Nina" Otero, was a prominent suffragist. After the 19th Amendment passed, she ran unsuccessfully for New Mexico's seat in the House of Representatives. She remained active in politics, serving in many appointed posts. In 1936 she published *Old Spain in Our Southwest,* a collection of vignettes and observations on Hispanic life and culture in New Mexico.

The Oteros, despite their prominence and accomplishments, have attracted relatively little scholarly attention, possibly owing to stances on political and social issues that are unfashionable now. Miguel Antonio I stole an election and promoted slavery. His son gave little attention to his Hispanic heritage in his voluminous memoirs, leading Genaro Padilla to dismiss him as "self-denying." Nina Otero, despite her efforts on behalf of women, is accused of displaying a New Mexican plantation (or hacienda) mentality in her writing. All of the Oteros are charged with claiming "Spanish" origins, when the family patriarch was an orphan who took an assumed name. Whatever their moral failings, however, the Oteros were among the most prominent Hispanics of their time and their legacy, however ambivalent, merits further study.

RELATED ARTICLES

New Mexico.

FURTHER READING

Chavez, Angélico. "Otero." In *Origins of New Mexico Families: A Genealogy of the Spanish Colonial Period.* Rev. ed. Santa Fe : Mus. of N.Mex. Press, 1992.

Lomelí, Francisco, and Genaro M. Padilla, eds. *Nuevomexicano Cultural Legacy: Forms, Agencies, and Discourse.* Albuquerque: Univ. of N.Mex. Press, 2002.

Otero, Miguel Antonio. *Otero: An Autobiographical Trilogy.* New York: Arno Press, 1974.

Otero, Nina. *Old Spain in Our Southwest.* New York: Harcourt, 1936.

Padilla, Genaro M. *My History, Not Yours: The Formation of Mexican American Autobiography.* Madison: Univ. of Wis. Press, 1993.

Whaley, Charlotte. *Nina Otero-Warren of Santa Fe.* Albuquerque: Univ. of N.Mex. Press, 1994.

P. SCOTT BROWN

P

PACHUCO

The pachuco youth subculture of second-generation Mexican Americans emerged throughout the Southwest during World War II. Pachucos blatantly rebelled against both traditional Mexican and mainstream U.S. culture by frequenting public city streets in zoot suit attire—a controversial style consisting of an expensive, tailor-made fingertip jacket, draped trousers tapered at the ankles, and hair in a duck-tail cut. Some pachucas—their female counterparts—also wore draped pants; others adorned themselves with short skirts, socks pulled up to mid-calf, huaraches, and either a tight sweater or the broad-shouldered fingertip coat of the male attire. Pachucas' ostentatious look also included stark make-up and an elaborate pompadour. The actual label *pachuco* is a contested term that carries different meanings depending on the frame of reference. Anglo and Mexican populations generally associated pachucos and pachucas with gang activities; yet, in reality, involvement in the pachuco subculture varied in degree from one individual to another. Some of the young men and women did participate in a street-based culture of gang life, but most simply flirted with the image of disrepute. An anxious wartime populace, however, largely failed to distinguish between those flaunting the look and those engaging in a criminal lifestyle. Many mistakenly confused delinquent pachucas and pachucos with any young Mexican American woman or man who defied social norms by dressing in the zoot suit style.

The pachuco phenomenon of the war years represented a unique generational response to the Mexican community's exclusion from U.S. society. During the late 1930s and 1940s, the Mexican population was transformed from a primarily foreign-born immigrant population to one composed mainly of American-born daughters and sons. As Americans, this new generation grew increasingly dissatisfied with their second-class treatment. Officially, wartime propaganda hailed ethnic and racial pluralism as an American ideal to be celebrated; but for the Mexican community, the historical realities of poverty, discrimination in public facilities, poor housing and educational opportunities, and confinement to menial labor told a different story. For the second generation, the stinging hardships of racism and the unrelenting lack of opportunities available in their daily lives proved a great contradiction to the wartime rhetoric of "Americans All."

One of the most noticeable markers of the second generation's alienation and discontent was the zoot suit. Wages earned from war production created new opportunities for working-class youths to experiment with consumer culture, and increasing numbers of young Mexican American men and women began to assertively frequent public venues in this conspicuous fashion. Amid patriotic appeals for conformity and austerity, wearing this spectacular attire signified both an effort to be stylish and to demonstrate disaffection with American society.

For the larger Anglo populace, pachucos and pachucas threatened wartime stability. In the midst of

Pachucos near their "bomber" car at a low-rider show in Los Angeles.

a cloth scarcity resulting from federal rationing regulations, many viewed the excess material used to make the zoot outfit as an unpatriotic waste. More problematic was the tendency of zoot suiters to leave barrios and frequent the busy streets and dance halls of urban centers. The flamboyant presence of ethnic women and men in areas outside segregated neighborhoods increasingly spelled trouble to authorities.

Fear of pachucos peaked in summer 1942 when a young Mexican man named José Díaz was found dead near a reservoir in Los Angeles. Police rounded up hundreds of second-generation youths of Mexican descent in connection with the so-called Sleepy Lagoon case. In a notoriously bigoted trial, 17 young men—all but one of Mexican or Mexican American ancestry—were tried and convicted for involvement in the murder. Additionally, a group of Spanish-surnamed young women were eventually sent to the Ventura School for Girls—a California correctional facility—for their alleged connection to the crime.

Although two years later the male Sleepy Lagoon defendants won acquittal on appeal, negative stereotypes of pachucas and pachucos continued unabated throughout the war years. Few groups of Mexican

Americans donning zoot suit attire could congregate in public areas without encountering discrimination and police harassment, and local newspapers highlighted dramatic acts of crime allegedly committed by zoot suited teens of Mexican descent. Numerous contemporary observers estimated that only 5 percent or less of Mexican American youths could be classified as delinquents, but law enforcement and the press warned of a dangerous Mexican gang crime wave. Events came to a head in June 1943 when a week of violent clashes—popularly known as the Zoot Suit Riots—erupted between Mexican Americans and Anglo servicemen on Los Angeles streets. Taking matters into their own hands, military personnel sought to remind the rebellious minority youths of their place in segregated Los Angeles.

Despite their negative reputation, in reality most pachucas and pachucos simply used fashion and public behavior as a means to create a distinctive ethnic and gender identity. Clothing and make-up enabled the youths to play with identities separate from the old-fashioned ethos of their parents' generation; for pachucas in particular, their brash appearance and bold public conduct violated strict moral codes and societal expectations of proper feminine behavior. By subverting mainstream consumer culture and visibly expressing discontent with the dominant society, pachucos and pachucas fashioned a racialized, collective identity that helped many Mexican Americans escape feeling like outsiders in the United States. Their shared adoption of zoot suit clothing styles signified a sense of belonging to a distinctly Mexican American subculture.

Over time the pachuco secured a place in popular lore and legacy. During the Chicano movement of the late 1960s and 1970s, a generation of activists looked to the zoot suiter as an early model of protest against the second-class citizenship of Mexican Americans in U.S. society. Poetry such as José Montoya's "El Louie" (1970), Virginia Granado's "Para Mi Jefe" (1974), and Tino Villanueva's "Pachuco Remembered" (1974), in addition to Luis Valdez's play and later film *Zoot Suit* (1982), all pay tribute to the rebellious man in drapes. Similarly, Chicana artist Judith Baca's multimedia triptych *Las Tres Marías* (1976) and Carmen Lomas Garza's painting *Las Pachucas, Razor Blade 'do* (1989) portray the controversial pachuca figure as a symbol of female strength and resistance. The pachuco subculture helped to redefine an ethnic identity of difference for a new generation of Mexican Americans.

RELATED ARTICLES

Calo; Chicano Movement; Gangs; Paz, Octavio; Politics, Mexican American; Sleepy Lagoon Case; Stereotypes and Stereotyping; Zoot Suit Riots.

FURTHER READING

Escobar, Edward J. *Race, Police, and the Making of a Political Identity: Mexican Americans and the Los Angeles Police Department, 1940–1945*. Berkeley: Univ. of Calif. Press, 1999.

Escobedo, Elizabeth. *Mexican American Home Front: The Politics of Gender, Culture, and Community in World War II Los Angeles*. Ph.D. dissertation. Seattle: Univ. of Wash., 2004.

Pagán, Eduardo Obregón. *Murder at the Sleepy Lagoon: Zoot Suits, Race, and Riot in Wartime L.A.* Chapel Hill: Univ. of N.C. Press, 2003.

Ramírez, Catherine Sue. *The Pachuca in Chicana/o Art, Literature and History: Reexamining Nation, Cultural Nationalism and Resistance*. Ph.D. dissertation. Berkeley: Univ. of Calif., 2000.

ELIZABETH R. ESCOBEDO

PAINTING

Painting by Latino artists in what is now the United States and its dependencies has a 300-year history. During the Spanish colonial era New Mexico, California, Texas, Puerto Rico, and Spanish Louisiana supported centers of artistic production and patronage, and the Spanish American tradition has remained unbroken in areas such as New Mexico and Puerto Rico, where both popular and "high" art forms continue to flourish in a clear awareness of the Latino past. Moreover, Latino painting was energetically revived in the later 20th and into the 21st century across a wide portion of the country, including the major metropolitan areas of California, the Southwest, Texas, New York, and Florida. Today, no survey of contemporary painting in the United States could fail to include Latino and Latina artists working in a wide variety of artistic idioms.

While it is impossible to generalize about so diverse a group of artists, certain themes will recur in the discussion. These include religious imagery, generally Roman Catholic in nature but often including local religious traditions, such as the Day of the Dead in Mexico or African spiritualist elements from Brazil and Cuba; surrealism, in both its abstract and realist (magic realist) manifestations; folk art, and themes derived from popular art; new figuration; bright colors; expressionist brushwork (neo-Expressionism); and social engagement, either through allied political movements or in the sense of social criticism (for example, of violence, machismo, or economic privilege).

Puerto Rico

Although technically a dependent commonwealth, Puerto Rico will be treated here as though it were fully integrated with the other United States. Puerto Rican painting first flourished in the 18th century, beginning with the arrival, in 1775, of the exiled Spanish rococo master Luis Paret y Alcázar (in Puerto Rico until 1778). Paret's Puerto Rican follower, José Campeche (José de Rivafrecha y Jordán, 1751–1809), was one of the most important late Spanish-colonial artists at any location. His works have been esteemed from his lifetime to the present day, and he left a direct legacy in the atelier of his family. During the 19th century numerous artists visited Puerto Rico, including the Spanish Romantic landscape artist Jenaro Pérez Villaamil, on the island in the early 1830s. The best-known 19th-century Puerto Rican painter is, however, the impressionist Francisco Oller y Cestero (1833–1917). Trained in France from 1858, Oller formed close, if also stormy relationships with Paul Cézanne and (more smoothly) Camille Pissarro. Active in San Juan and in Europe, Oller's long life spanned the transition from Spanish to U.S. rule, and his work established *plein air* realism and impressionist techniques as the standards for early 20th-century Puerto Rican painting. Oller's choice of idiom is also seen in the work of his younger contemporaries such as Ramón Frade (1875–1954), who trained in the Dominican Republic and in Europe and whose 1905 image of a *jíbaro,* or Puerto Rican peasant, with a stalk of plantains, entitled *El pan nuestro,* has become an icon of Hispanic Caribbean culture. After 1909 Frade returned to his native Carey, where he worked in relative isolation for the remainder of his long life.

In the 1920s and 1930s North American influence began to be felt in Puerto Rico, for example in the appointment of the U.S. painter and watercolorist Walt Dehner, who had been associated with the Ashcan school artists, as professor of painting at the university in 1929. In addition to stimulating and training island artists, Dehner organized highly important exhibitions of international modernist art. At the same time Puerto Ricans such as Rafael D. Palacios (b. 1905; in New York by 1913), Luis Quero Chiesa (b. 1911), and Lorenzo Homar (b. 1913), became part of the first immigrations to New York and therefore studied and exhibited in the United States. Homar, for example, trained at New York City's Art Students' League and Pratt Institute; he would return to Puerto Rico in 1950. Just the opposite was the case with Rafael Tufiño, who was actually born in Brooklyn, New York, in 1922 but returned to Puerto Rico in 1936. The efforts of both local and New York-based artists found support in the officially sponsored art exhibitions mounted in 1929, 1931, and 1936, as well as the independent artists' exhibition in 1937. Also in 1936–1939, there began an exodus from Spain of artists fleeing the Spanish Civil War and its fascist aftermath. Among those arriving in Puerto Rico were Esteban Vicente, Alejandro Sánchez Felipe, Ángel Botello Barros, and Cristóbal Ruiz Pulido. Vicente would move on to New York, but Botello (1913–1986) and Ruiz (1881–1962) would make important contributions to the Puerto Rican school. Ruiz's highly abstracted, light-shot figural compositions anticipate the Califor-

nia artists of the 1960s and the work of David Hockney, while Botello, who principally worked in the Dominican Republic and Haiti before settling in Puerto Rico in the 1950s, is better known for his subsequent sculptures. Botello also opened a pair of art galleries in San Juan that became important focal points for local artistic culture. Sánchez (1875–1971) would become one of the most important art teachers on the island, training Tufiño among many others.

After World War II Puerto Rico began to come into its own as an independent society bridging the United States and Latin America. In 1947 Operation Bootstrap (Operación Manos a la Obra), an industrial and economic development initiative, was begun, and in the next year, the first Puerto Rican governor, Luis Muñoz Martín, was elected. Not only by virtue of increased government support, but also because of the emergence of a local patron class, Puerto Rican artists could find employment in greater numbers on the island itself. In these same years, increased contacts between Puerto Rican and Mexican artists (Tufiño, for example, was in Mexico from about 1946 to 1950) injected new energy into many aspects of Puerto Rican art and provided a second source of inspiration to counteract the influence of New York. By the 1950s the combination of social and artistic forces had led to a notable flowering of artistic talent, usually referred to as the "Generation of 1950."

Of particular importance was the development of graphic arts, which, while just outside the scope of this essay, are essential to any understanding of painting in Puerto Rico during the 1950s. In 1950 Félix Rodríguez Baez (b. 1929), Julio Rosado del Valle (b. 1922), and others formed the Centro de Arte Puertorriqueño (CAP), the graphic production of which linked Puerto Rican art and popular culture but whose radical politics (as in the Mexican tradition) fell afoul of more conservative political forces in 1954. Also in 1954 an associated printmaker, Carlos Raquel Rivera (b. 1923), who had trained, like Homar, at the Art Students' League, visited Mexico and returned to Puerto Rico strongly influenced by the politicized social imagery of Mexico's Taller de la Gráfica Popular. In 1957 Homar organized a Taller de Artes Gráficas at the Instituto de Cultura Puertorriqueña and became in the process the mentor for an entire generation of younger artists. Since the printmakers were painters and occasionally sculptors as well, the developments in the graphic arts were reflected immediately throughout all aspects of Puerto Rican art.

Other artists had different associations. Francisco Rodón (b. 1934) developed a specialty in still lifes and highly psychological portraiture, the latter expressed in a large series of painterly images of notable Latin Americans called *Personajes*. Domingo García (b. 1932), who trained in New York and Chicago, returned to Puerto Rico in 1958 with a figurative style energized by abstract expressionist elements. Manuel Hernández Acevedo (1921–1988) worked in a naive style in both painting and silkscreen prints. Myrna Báez (b. 1931), a printmaker as well as a painter, places ambiguous figures in mysterious, surrealist interiors, often lit from a landscape beyond. Geometric abstraction also emerged in Puerto Rico in the 1960s, following the lead of both New York and Venezuela (again showing the bridge function of Puerto Rican visual culture). Distinguished among these artists are Luis Hernández Cruz (b. 1936), Marcos Irizarry (1936–1995), and Noemí Ruiz (b. 1931). Later Puerto Rican art has followed postmodern and neo-Expressionist currents in Europe and New York. Leading the way in this regard was Rafael Ferrer (b. 1933), who already in the 1960s was rebelling against the socially oriented works of the generation of 1950. The best-known of the younger artists is Arnaldo Roche-Rabell (b. 1955), active in Puerto Rico and Chicago; his violently colored, pigment-laden canvases with inclusions of leaves and other objects have summed up emotionally expressive postmodern art for many viewers.

Nuyoricans

In the late 1960s and the 1970s, New York City's large Puerto Rican community began to develop a sense of its own cultural power and uniqueness. At the same time the significant changes in Puerto Rican island society had begun to separate social and cultural developments there from those in New York. In 1969, for example, Puerto Rican educators and artists under the leadership of the sculptor and destructive theater artist Rafael Montañez Ortiz (b. 1934) organized a museum in East Harlem ("El Barrio") to its Puerto Rican and Nuyorican inhabitants now known as El Museo del Barrio. Furthermore, for over three decades, the literary movement centered on the Nuyorican Poets Café has been a hotbed of poetry, drama, prose, and popular music truly in the city's avant-garde. Nevertheless, apart from grassroots or popular artistic circles, it is extremely difficult to separate Nuyorican and Puerto Rican contributions in the visual arts. In the first place, island-born and New York-born Puerto Rican painters tend to move back and forth. No Nuyorican painters' group has coalesced to impress itself on the art world in a way analogous to the various Chicano groups (the Nuyorican Poets Café, for example, lists no associated visual artists' groups at all). Part of the problem is social. All Puerto Ricans have been U.S. citizens since 1917. In this sense "immigration" is only partially correct in describing the Puerto Rican experience in New York; movement back and forth is possible, often affordable, and frequent. The disintegration of the Puerto Rican barrios in East Harlem and Brooklyn, an inevitable result of the movement of families into the middle class (and therefore to the suburbs in many cases), and the tendency of Nuyorican intellectual culture to be comparatively radical in political terms, have also worked against socially engaged Nuyorican artists seeking patronage in a capitalist society. By the end of the 20th century, a much diminished number of artists were seeking or willing to be identified as "Nuyorican." Two contemporary artists in this category are Soraida Martínez, born in Spanish Harlem (1956), who combines hard-edged figurative abstraction with radical social commentary, and Yasmin Hernández of Brooklyn, who takes a softer political stance but is no less committed to social causes, including those related to questions of African racial origins. The brief but spectacular career of graffiti artist Jean Michel Basquiat (1960–1988), who was of both Haitian and Puerto Rican descent, may perhaps be offered as the greatest success story to date among New York Afro-Latino artists.

New Mexico

Of all the Hispanic regions of the United States, New Mexico offers the greatest continuity of artistic traditions from the 18th century to the present day. Eighteenth-century painting in the region embraces provincial works in the European style, such as the devotional paintings of Bernardo Miera y Pacheco (fl. 1780), and what has been called Indo-Christian art in other contexts—that is, the works of the *santeros,* or painters of holy images, who created panels for altarpieces in mission churches attached to Native American communities. Among the names from the late 1700s are the Laguna Santero, A. J. Santero, Pedro Antonio Fresquis, and, into the 19th century, José Aragón and the artist known as Molleno. An artistic explosion in this idiom followed in the first half of the 19th century, with the name of [José] Rafael Aragón being most prominent. The *santero* style has the attributes of naive folk art, with linear depictions, almost ink drawings, and subtle colorism. Many works express a stunning sense of direct artistic communication. In the context of ongoing cultural cross-fertilization between the Latino community (subsequently the Latino and Anglo-American communities) and the Native American groups, the style was kept remarkably stable into the late 19th and early 20th century in the hands of artists such as José Benito Ortega and José de Gracia Gonzales, and has been revived in contemporary art by painters such as Roxanne Shaw, Arturo Olivas, Sarah Valdez, and Cecilia N. Leitner—although one should also add the *santeros* who work in polychromed wood (painted as well as sculpted), of whom the best known are Horacio Valdez, Gustavo Victor Goler, the Ortega family, and Luis Eligio Tapia (b. 1950), who has appeared in numerous contemporary art exhibitions nationally. Because of the large numbers of wealthy cultural tourists attracted particularly to Santa Fe, New Mexico has become an important marketplace for all kinds of Latino art, including contemporary painting in avant-garde idioms.

In the 1930s a number of New Mexican artists came of age working in what is usually called the American scene movement. Among them were Margaret Herrera Chávez (b. 1912), a watercolorist and graphic artist as well as oil painter, and a large group working for the Works Progress Administration (WPA) Federal Art Project. The WPA artists included Eliseo José Rodríguez (b. 1915), who began his career painting murals for the Texas centennial celebration in 1936 and became the dean of New Mexico painters; Esquípula Romero de Romero (1889–1975), who traveled widely in Latin America and studied at the Academy of San Carlos in Mexico, moving from a realist style connected with the Taos artists to more surreal and expressive figure and landscape compositions; and Edward Arcenio Chávez (1917–1995) and Pedro López Cervántez (1915–1987), the two best-known of the New Deal–era artists. Cervántez, who described himself as "painter: oils in primitive realism" later in his career, painted in a style analogous to that of Grant Wood and Charles Sheeler. Chávez's work for the WPA in Colorado, as well as his subsequent movable pictures, combined influences from the Mexican muralists with those of American artists such as John Steuart Curry. In the 1960s Chávez, who resided in New York after the war, moved into abstract surrealism, with occasional experiments in harder-edged compositions as well as sculpture and assemblage. In contrast, Joel Tito Ramírez (b. 1923) continued the WPA style in landscapes after World War II. Connections with Mexico were augmented by the Good Neighbor Policy during the war, and attracted Mexican artists such as Jesús Guerrero Galván (1910–1973), who came in 1942 to teach at the University of New Mexico at Albuquerque, where he also painted a mural.

Like Chávez, New Mexican artists at the turn of the 21st century have confronted a dilemma: a gallery and patronage structure selecting strongly for traditional forms and folk art, or for Latino avant-garde pictures brought in from other centers, but not for local avant-garde products. Some artists, such as Belarmino Esquibel, have solved the problem by creating modern images of traditional subjects. Others, such Glynn Gómez (b. 1945), who spent several years in Vietnam as a Marine in the late 1960s, incorporating imagery from that experience into drawings, paintings, and assemblages with drawing elements from 1968 onwards, have simply forged ahead in the modernist idiom. Gómez's oil wash techniques in the 1970s produced ghostlike surreal figures set in sharply abstract contexts, offering strong resonance with contemporary Latin American art. Some contemporary Rio Grande valley artists have surprising affinities with the older generations. For example, Rudy Fernández, born in Colorado in 1948 and active in Arizona, has made mixed-media assemblage paintings, the still-life elements of which seem like postmodern echoes of López Cervántez's still lifes. (A similar resonance can be felt in the works of Rudy Treviño of Texas.)

Texas

Like New Mexico, Texas has enjoyed three centuries of Latino presence, but local artistic traditions were severely dislocated in the 19th century by the influx of Anglo-American settlers, except for popular art forms in South Texas and the Rio Grande valley. Nevertheless, both Texas-born Latinos and Mexican immigrants found increasing opportunities for artistic expression throughout the 20th century, and in the opening years of the 21st they can be said to dominate in many ways the contemporary art scene.

In the colonial period the many mission churches in Texas were decorated, principally by local artists, but the development of *santero* ateliers that one finds continuing into the 19th century in New Mexico is not so well documented in Texas. In the early years of the 20th century, new immigration brought a number of Mexicans who would develop into artists, such as Antonio García, for many years the senior Mexican American artist in Texas. Born in Monterrey, Mexico, in 1901, García came to Texas at age 12; he trained at the Art Institute of Chicago, 1927–1930. An important teacher at Corpus Christi in South Texas, he served as a role model for several generations of Texas artists. His style has relationships both with Mexican art and with American art of the 1930s, particularly Edward Hopper and Reginald Marsh. Of special merit are his murals and frescoes in churches in Corpus Christi, Goliad, and elsewhere, and the socially themed murals he produced for the WPA in 1933 under the direct inspiration of Mexican muralism. (García's work for the San Diego, Texas, high school, *March on Washington,* offered a criticism of Herbert Hoover's policies and celebrated those of Franklin D. Roosevelt.) A WPA colleague Xavier González, better known as a sculptor, painted murals in San Antonio in the same year.

Almost the complete opposite of García is the self-taught artist Consuelo (Chelo) González Amézcua, who was born in Mexico in 1903 but spent her life in the small town of Del Rio, Texas. Her compositions, largely ink on paper, often concern mythical and historical Aztec figures and historical women, presented with thousands of intricate linear patterns making almost a mosaic effect. The ancient Mexican and proto-feminist aspects of her imagery are important precedents for Chicano art. The Texas art scene was also energized in the 1940s and 1950s by distinguished Mexican painters coming to work in Texas. For example, the biomorphic abstract painter Carlos Mérida (1891–1984) taught at North Texas State University near Dallas in 1942 and subsequently designed murals for San Antonio in the 1950s. The even more famous Rufino Tamayo (1899–1991) painted murals in Dallas in 1953 and in Houston in 1955–1956.

In the late 1950s and 1960s, a large group of Mexican American painters from Texas came of age simultaneously. The best-known of these is Melesio (Mel) Casas, born in El Paso in 1929. Active in San Antonio, Casas brought Hispanic imagery to large-scale pop art creations in the 1960s; his ironic depictions of ethnic relations between Latinos and Anglos set the tone for much subsequent Chicano imagery. Associated with Casas in San Antonio was the Chicano artists group C/F (Con Safo), including the Mexican-born photo-realist and tile muralist Jesse Treviño. The city also supported Emilio Aguirre (b. 1929) and Rudy Treviño (b. 1945), both Texas-born, and both of whom bridged the transition from pop art into postmodern imagery. César Augusto Martínez (b. 1944), another Texas-born painter and photographer active in San Antonio, was originally part of Con Safo and extremely active as a promoter of Chicano art and culture. His paintings present existentialist figures isolated against vivid textured backgrounds surprisingly reminiscent of those of Vincent Van Gogh. Although principally a sculptor, Jiménez (born, like Casas, in El Paso in 1940) paints his figures and creates life-sized colored figural drawings, cut out and mounted on plywood in installation ensembles. Finally, Carmen Lomas Garza (b. 1948), a native of the lower Rio Grande valley in Texas, has maintained the closest connection with the popular art traditions of the region. She seeks to depict Mexican American life (especially of an earlier time) in a neonaive popular idiom.

Texas has also contributed a long list of painters of all ethnic backgrounds to the New York art world. Among these is Ray Smith, born in Texas (1959) but raised and trained in Mexico before going to New York in 1985. His postmodern figurative works juxtapose animals with images from art history in striking, dynamic compositions. The inverse situation is found in the career of Ibsen Espada (b. 1952), who was born in New York and raised in Puerto Rico but trained and worked in Houston, painting in a nonobjective, biomorphic-abstract style.

Tejano versus Chicano

An extremely close relationship exists between Mexican American artists in Texas and the wider movement since the late 1960s and 1970 of Chicano art. Indeed, "Tex-Mex" artists who seek to be ethnically identified have been increasingly subsumed under the category of *Chicano,* a term many Mexican Americans in Texas still reject. In an interview from 1970, San Antonio artist Mel Casas, perhaps the best-known Mexican American painter from Texas (Luis Jiménez is the best-known Mexican American sculptor), was hesitant to use the Chicano label, perhaps because of its close association with radical political causes and agricultural union organizing, which were not artistic issues. (Casas preferred at the time to think of himself as an "outsider"—neither Anglo nor Mexican.) By 1972 Casas and an associated group of Texas Latinos had embraced *Chicano,* largely because it implied this sense of not quite belonging yet offered the possibility of a synthesis of Mexican and Anglo-American cultures.

California before 1970

By the early 20th century, almost every aspect of living Latino culture (except perhaps the architecture of the original missions) had been pushed to the margins of society. As California artists of Latino descent thereafter sought to reclaim their heritage, they found tremendous inspiration in the astounding developments of the Mexican school, particularly in the mural work of Diego Rivera, José Clemente Orozco, and David Alfaro Siqueiros, all of whom were in California in 1930–1931. Orozco (1883–1949) painted murals in Claremont, and Rivera (1886–1957) in San Francisco on several occasions. Frida Kahlo (1907–1954) also had close connections with California patrons, and Siqueiros (1896–1974) actually taught briefly in 1932 in Los Angeles, where he painted two highly controversial murals, both of which were suppressed, although one, *American Tropical,* is the subject of restoration efforts. A more permanent influence emerged from the residence of the Mexican painter and teacher Alfredo Rámos Martínez (1872–1946), in California from the 1930s. In addition to producing movable works, Rámos Martínez painted murals, including an enormous, 100-foot-wide (30-meter), example at Scripps College. Another famous Mexican artist active in California was Miguel Covarrubias (1904–1957) who painted two murals in San Francisco in 1940, alongside Rivera.

A pioneer group of California Latinos, coming of age in the 1940s, were able to look to the Mexicans' achievements as models. Among them was the northern California painter Peter Rodríguez (b. 1926), who worked in a painterly, nonfigurative abstract mode. Another northern Californian, Louis Gutiér-rez (b. 1933), trained in Mexico as well as San José, developing an abstract expressive figural style with links to European abstraction, looking forward to postmodern or neo-Expressionist forms in the 1970s. A slightly younger group, already thinking of themselves as Chicano, came of age in the 1960s. Eduardo Carrillo (b. 1937) trained in California and in Spain and has been active in Sacramento; his works have blended symbolist and surrealist elements, often with architectural elements and landscapes; he was active as a Chicano muralist, but also produced realist views of the urban environment. Even the older generation of California Latino artists has typically been born in California, in contrast with the higher percentage of immigrant origins among the older Texas group. Finally, one should note the extraordinary artistic production of Martín Ramírez (1885–1960), a Mexican immigrant folk artist institutionalized for severe schizophrenia but who created exquisite tempera drawings beginning in the 1940s.

Mexican American and Chicano Art

Interacting with the regional developments in New Mexico, Texas, and California has been the rise of Chicano culture. As complicated as Chicano may be as an ethnic and cultural descriptor, in the fine arts it can be taken to refer to the work of Mexican-American and Mexican immigrant artists coming of age since the late 1960s in the context of the sort of grass-roots political, social, cultural, and labor organizing typified by the Raza Unida party, the United Farm Workers Union, and the Mexican American Youth Organization. While the linguistic and cultural values and geographic distances dividing the Mexican American community across the Southwest are very great, a number of factors offer common ground. Among these are: radical political theory; solidarity with industrial and agricultural workers and poor urban immigrants; a strong sense of common ethnic identity and pride in the face of a hypothesized Euro-centric hostility going back to the Spanish conquest of Mexico, including the Mexican Revolution's positing of a special aspect of *mestizaje,* usually referred to as *la raza* (the race); certain other common myths, such as that of Atzlán; common iconography, for example the Virgin of Guadalupe Tepeyac; a collective awareness of 20th-century Mexican art, both at the elevated level of artists such as Diego Rivera, José Clemente Orozco, David Alfaro Siquieros, Juan O'Gorman, Frida Kahlo, María Izquierda, Rufino Tamayo, and Francisco Toledo, as well as the vast resources of Mexican popular arts; and engagement, where possible, with local Latino artistic traditions.

An extremely important aspect of Chicano art has been the mural movement. Chicano muralism has its origin in the much earlier phenomenon of Mexican muralism, a highly important modernist art form originating in the 1920s in the political aftermath of the Mexican Revolution, and involving artists such as Rivera, Orozco, and Siqueiros, all of whom worked in the United States from the 1930s. The U.S.-born Hispanic WPA and postwar muralists also served as models. From the late 1960s, Hispanic mural artists in California, Arizona, New Mexico, and Texas used specific Chicano imagery to express the hopes, fears, and social aspirations of the mostly Mexican American communities in which they lived. (Initially there was also significant interaction with political theater groups attached to movements such as the farmworkers.) One of the earliest Chicano murals understood as such was Manuel Acosta's *Iwo Jima,* painted in El Paso in 1966. However, the signature work of the mural movement in the Chicano barrio of East Los Angeles was Willie Herron's (b. 1951) *The Wall that Cracked Open,* 1972, a response to youth gang violence against his brother. Herron's partners in the Chicano activist group ASCO (Nausea) in the 1970s—Glugio "Gronk" Nicandro (b. 1954), Harry Gamboa, Jr. (b. 1951), and Patssi Valdez—have also created murals, as have Carlos Almaraz (1941–1989), Paul and David Botello, and Wayne Alaniz Healy (the East Los Streetscapers), Ernesto de la Loza, Frederico Vigil, Raymond Patlán (b. 1946), George Yepes, Eloy Torrez, and Frank Romero (b. 1941). (Almaraz, Romero, Gilbert "Magu" Luján, and Roberto "Beto" de la Rocha also formed a slightly older group known as Los Four in the 1970s.) To the Texas muralists already mentioned can be added Leo Tanguma in Houston and Raúl Valdez in Austin.

The impact of Chicano murals on the reformation of the urban landscape in the southwestern United States and even as far afield as Chicago, should not be underestimated. According to Teresa Palomo Acosta, in El Paso, Texas, alone over 100 murals were painted between the mid-1960s and about 2000. In 1993 Tucson, Arizona, counted 135 Chicano-related murals, many of which had replaced earlier images. The numbers are many times greater for the Los Angeles area. Because of the public locales and often radical nature of the imagery, Chicano murals have often encountered official hostility and political censorship, resulting in the destruction or covering over of many murals, a problem going back to the North American works of Rivera and Siqueiros in the 1930s. Indeed, the production of new murals peaked in the early 1990s, with many later efforts devoted to restoring or re-creating earlier murals, now that the social climate favors their preservation.

Awareness of Chicano painting on the part of the Los Angeles artistic establishment dates from 1972, when Gamboa, Herron, Gronk, and Valdez spray-painted the Los Angeles Country Museum of Art (LACMA) in protest after Gamboa became enraged at its lack of contemporary Latino art. (Four years earlier Luis Jiménez had opted for a similar guerrilla tactic in New York City, surreptitiously installing three sculptures in the Castelli Gallery.) Within 18 months LACMA presented a show of the competing artists in Los Four. In portable works, Gronk's large-scale, cartoon-like imagery is rendered in an explosive, neo-Expressionist manner, with glimpses of influence from the German expressionists and Ensor, while Patssi Valdez offers dreamlike visions in vivid colors clearly influenced by Mexico's María Izquierdo. Among the Los Four artists, Carlos Almaraz produces large-scale oils using pastel-like brushwork in animated, luminously colored compositions with occasional touches of violence and threat; Frank Romero, on the other hand, offers brightly colored, playful compositions filled with humor and irony. Humor is also a watchword of Gilbert Luján's (b. 1940) large-scale postmodern pastels depicting half-length pairs of young men with dogs dressed as humans. ASCO also functioned as a conceptual and performance group, with Gamboa in particular becoming an important author and theorist.

John Valadez (b. 1951), who worked with the Los Four artists, is a particularly astute observer of the Chicano scene; his large-scale photo-realist compositions are often technical tours-de-force executed in pastel as well as oil that reveal his involvement with the theater. Equally related to theater and cinema are the dark and often violent images of Adan Hernández, which have been called a mixture of neo-Expressionist and Chicano-noir. Realistic figures dominate the more surreal art of portraitist Eloy Torrez and symbolist George Yepes.

A highly important aspect of the Chicano movement is the role of Chicana artists, such as Patssi Valdez and Carmen Lomas Garza, both discussed earlier. Indeed, among Hispanic muralists, arguably the best known is the Chicana painter Judith Baca (b. 1946), whose *Great Wall of Los Angeles* (1976–1984) covers 2,435 running feet (742 meters) of mural with Latino history, myth, and symbolism, and involved scores of professional and volunteer painters.

Other women active in the California mural movement include Yreina Cervantes and Juana Alicia (b. 1953), while a large group of women have created murals in Texas, including Mago Orona Gándara, Irene Martínez, and Monika Acevedo in El Paso. Among painters of moveable pictures, Diane Gamboa's cartoon-like, harshly colored figural compositions and expressionist close-ups exude a disquieting, decadent mood, in contrast with the lush, sensual but also harshly colored compositions of Margaret García. Equally lush, but calmer and more spiritual are the garden and forest scenes of Patricia González. Two San Francisco area artists, Yolanda López (b. 1942) and Amalia Mesa-Baines (b. 1943), have provided archtypical Chicano and Chicana imagery—López with personalized reinterpretations of traditional religious subjects and Mesa-Baines with altarlike installations blending paintings and objects.

South Florida and the Cuban Diaspora

The complexities of Latino art are particularly evident in the Latino culture of south Florida. As the home of one of the largest Latino communities in the United States, as well as the gateway connecting North America to the Latin Caribbean and South America, Miami has become one of the most important art marketplaces in the world and a breeding ground for large-scale art collectors with a passionate interest in Latino and Latin American contemporary art. Since the Cuban Revolution of 1959, two generations of Cuban expatriot artists—coming in two principal waves of immigration, the first in the early 1960s and the second in the Mariel exodus of 1980—have joined immigrant artists from all corners of Latin America, Puerto Rican artists, and now a younger generation of Florida-born Latinos, usually of Cuban American descent, to offer a variety of contemporary artistic styles. Dominating the cultural scene is the Cuban American community, whose leadership is decidedly conservative, locked in opposition to cultural and economic exchange with Com-

munist Cuba, although well aware of the reality of persistent artistic interchange. The immigrant flow is literally one-way, with not even the hope, while the current regime survives, of return after success abroad. Much Cuban exile art is consequently marked by a nostalgia and longing of a very specific type quite different from the evocations of homeland in Chicano and Nuyorican art.

The history of 20th-century Cuban art before 1959 lies outside the scope of this essay, but one should note the flourishing artistic establishment in Havana from the early years of the century and the development at midcentury of Cuban abstract art, particularly the oeuvres of Amelia Peláez (1896–1968), a follower of Fernand Léger, and Wilfredo Lam (1902–1982), who blended cubist, surrealist, and Afro-Cuban cultural elements and remained a major influence on all subsequent Cuban artists. (The Afro-Cuban element was also developed by Cundo Bermúdez, b. 1914, whose works are more patterned and geometrical in the manner of Torres-García; after the revolution, Bermúdez immigrated first to Puerto Rico and then to Miami.) Antonio Gattorno (1904–1980) developed a magic-realist variety of surrealism, strongly influenced by Salvador Dalí, after coming to the United States in the 1940s. In the 1950s Agustín Fernández (b. 1928) developed an abstract-surreal style with strong ties to Matta (Eduardo Matta Echaurren, the Chilean abstract expressionist, 1911–2002), which he brought to New York in 1972. In general, a surrealist influence, whether abstract or figurative, pervades the work of nearly every Cuban painter. In addition, overtly Roman Catholic imagery is much less prevalent in Cuban art than it is, for example, in Mexican American works, and when religion is present, it is often syncretic Afro-Cuban spiritualism rather than traditional Catholic motifs.

Surrealist influence can readily be seen in the works of the architect-painter Humberto Calzada (b. 1944), who immigrated in 1960 and trained in the United States. Calzada paints sharply delineated, surreal images of buildings and architectural elements, including his signature doorways with their luminous stained-glass transoms evoking (as they did in Peláez's works) the urban context of old Havana. Similarly, Julio Larraz's (b. 1944) still lifes and other realistic motifs are set into decidedly surreal contexts, often against backgrounds suggesting outer space or other unusual locations. Surrealism is equally evident in the eerie, luminous jungle landscapes of Tomás

Sánchez (b. 1948), with their clearly spiritual intent. Sánchez trained and began his career in Cuba, leaving with the Mariel exodus in 1980. Another artist in the Mariel group, Carlos Alfonso (1950–1991) worked in an abstract surrealist manner with affinities to Paul Klee. Similarly, Hugo Consuegra, while exhibiting the strong influence of abstract expressionism and subsequent U.S. artistic developments, presents abstracted natural motifs, such as might be found in the tropical jungle, in a dreamlike atmosphere.

Among other artists Humberto Benitez (b. 1960), who comes from a commercial art background, develops isolated figures or still life motifs in luminous pastel colors with ties to artists such as Klee and Francisco Toledo. Baruj Salinas's (b. 1938) work involves painterly, oversize floral imagery. Salinas, who works in Europe as well as the United States, has been linked to the so-called neo-Baroque movement in Latin American contemporary art, along with Cuban American artists such as Arturo Rodríguez, Emilio Falero, María Brito, Rafaél Soriano, and Alberto Rey.

Frank García produces evocations of Italian Renaissance painting in the context of the Cuban diaspora, while painter-attorney Xavier Cortada's ironic folk images in bright tropical colors conjure up Caribbean and Afro-Cuban roots, celebrating the new transplanted Hispanic world of Miami, even to the extent of decorating the outside of a plane used by a Cuban family to escape to North America. Cortada's work is a reminder us that Miami, in clear imitation of the Mexican and Chicano movements, has its own mural renaissance. In contrast, José Bedia (b. 1959) fuses neo-Expressionist gestures with symbolist elements in a decidedly postmodern idiom.

South Florida was not the only destination of Cuban immigrants. Pedro Pérez (b. 1951) went with his family to New Jersey in 1966, trained in Tampa, then went to New York. His postmodern, abstract-surreal oil pastels and humorous mixed media ensembles, in part inspired by his parents' jewelry business in Cuba, exhibit vivid but carefully tempered colors. Also in New York, Luis Cruz Azaceta (b. 1942), who was not involved in art before leaving Cuba, eventually allied himself with the predominant neo-Expressionist styles of the 1980s while maintaining clearly Latino imagery. Paul Sierra (b. 1944) went to Chicago with his family in 1961. His works offer postmodern compositions with neo-Ex-

pressionist brushwork and decidedly macabre imagery, again often set against lush, surreal backgrounds.

Younger Cuban Americans, born at many locations within the United States and coming of age at the turn of the 21st century, find their inspiration in wider sources; two representative examples include Miami-born Roland Becerra and Gustavo Souto, who was born in Puerto Rico of Cuban exile parents. Becerra received a master of fine arts degree in 1971 from Yale University. His works, when they offer Latino elements, may as well refer to Siqueiros as to specifically Cuban motifs, but like many other painters of Cuban origin, he presents a decidedly surrealist affect in disturbing, almost cinematic images of violence and overweight subjects. Souto paints postmodern reformulations of motifs from artists such as René Magritte (a Cuban touch in the sense of being linked to surrealism) but also neo-Expressionist personal images.

Latin American Immigrant Artists

It is worthwhile noting a representative sample of the many South and Central American painters who have actually immigrated to the United States on a permanent basis and are therefore properly considered "Latino." The styles and attachments of these artists are wildly diverse, often reflecting artistic currents in their countries of origin and international aesthetic movements, particularly the various forms of surrealism. Several of the artists have European Jewish origins, adding an important international element to their work.

Among the best-known painters is the Nicaraguan Armando Morales (b. 1927), whose mysterious compositions with nude figures in textured, shadowy landscapes carefully balance abstraction and figuration. A truly international artist is the Venezuelan-born Alirio Palacios (b. 1940), who studied in China and Warsaw as well as Geneva before moving to New York in 1978; his human and animal figures often reveal Asian sources. The Brazilian Vik Muniz (b. 1961), also active in New York City, uses large-scale photography to create painterly compositions. From Uruguay have come several painters associated with Joaquín Torres-García's school. Julio Alpuy (b. 1919), for example, was the director of the Taller Torres-García, 1946–1951, and has had a wide international following. Another Uruguayan, José Gurvich (1927–1974), was born in Lithuania but went to Uruguay as a child; he worked in Israel and Uruguay before moving to New York in 1970. The Argentine assemblage artist, Elena Presser, active in South Florida, creates exquisitely detailed compositions using parts of musical instruments, astronomical imagery, and color. She works in series, inspired by the musical compositions of Bach, and acknowledges the direct influence of Joseph Cornell, the American surrealist, and international modernists such as Klee. Ismael Frigerio (b. 1955), who went to New York from his native Chile in 1979, blends expressionist and surrealist elements in his sketchily painted large canvases, which suggest influences from Europe, the postwar United States, and Asia. Finally, there is Luis Stand, born in Colombia in 1950 but trained in New York, including under the Cuban American, Rafael Ferrer. His new-figurative imagery explores themes of violence and machismo, with animals and humans confronting (or merging) against lushly patterned backgrounds.

RELATED ARTICLES

Art, Colonial; Art, Cuban American; Art, Dominican American; Art, Folk; Art, Galleries and Collections; Art, Mexican American and Chicano; Art, Popular; Art, Puerto Rican on the Mainland; Art Criticism; Arts, Graphic; Baca, Judith; Campeche, José; Charlot, Jean; Con Safo; Goldman, Shifra; Graffiti; Graphic Arts; Kahlo, Frida; López, Yolanda; Muralism; Paz, Octavio; Ramírez, Martín; Rivera, Diego.

FURTHER READING

Ades, Dawn, and Stanton L. Catlin, et al. *Art in Latin America: The Modern Era, 1820–1980.* New Haven, Conn.: Yale Univ. Press, 1989.

Beardsley, John, and Jane Livingston, *Hispanic Art in the United States: Thirty Contemporary Painters & Sculptors.* Houston, Tex.: Houston Mus. of Fine Arts; New York: Cross Abbeville Press, 1987 [includes an essay by Octavio Paz].

Bosch, Lynette M. F. *Cuban-American Art in Miami: Exile, Identity and the Neo-Baroque.* London: Lund Humphreys, 2004.

Cancel, Luis R., ed. *The Latin American Spirit: Art and Artists in the United States, 1920–1970.* New York: Bronx Museum of the Arts; Abrams, 1988.

Cockcroft, Eva Sperling, and Holly Barnet-Sánchez. *Signs From the Heart: California Chicano Murals.* Albuquerque: Univ. of N.Mex. Press, 1993.

Davalos, Karen Mary. *Exhibiting Mestizaje: Mexican (American) Museums in the Diaspora.* Albuquerque: Univ. of N.Mex. Press, 2001.

Gaspar de Alba, Alicia. *Chicano Art Inside / Outside the Master's House: Cultural Politics and the CARA Exhibition.* Austin: Univ. of Tex. Press, 1998.

Gaya Nuño, Juan Antonio. *La pintura puertorriqueña.* Río Piedras, Puerto Rico: Editorial de la Univ. de Puerto Rico, 1994.

Goldman, Shifra, and Tomás Ybarra-Fausto. *Arte Chicano: A Comprehensive Annotated Bibliography of Chicano Art, 1965–1981.* Berkeley: Chicano Studies Library Pubs. Unit, Univ. of Calif., 1985.

Griswold del Castillo, Richard, Teresa McKenna, and Yvonne Yarbro-Bejarano, eds. *Chicano Art: Resistance and Affirmation.* Exhibition catalog. Los Angeles: Wight Art Gallery, Univ. of Calif., 1991.

Marin, Cheech, et al. *Chicano Visions: American Painters on the Verge.* Boston: Little, Brown, 2002.

Noriega, Chon A., et al. *East of the River: Chicano Art Collectors Anonymous. From the Collections of Martha Abeytia Canales and Charles Canales.* Santa Monica, Calif.: Santa Monica Mus. of Art, 2000.

Nunn, Tey Marianna. *Sin Nombre: Hispana & Hispano Artists of the New Deal Era.* Albuquerque: Univ. of N.Mex. Press, 2001.

Oettinger, Marion, Jr. *Folk Treasures of Mexico: The Nelson A. Rockefeller Collection.* New York: Abrams, 1990.

Padilla, Carmella, ed. *Conexiones: Connections in Spanish Colonial Art.* Santa Fe, N.Mex.: Mus. of Spanish Colonial Art, 2002.

Palomo Acosta, Teresa. "Chicano Mural Movement." In *Handbook of Texas Online.* Austin: General Libraries of the Univ. of Tex. and the Tex. State Historical Assoc., 2004. http://www.tsha.utexas.edu/handbook/online/articles/view/CC/kjc3.html

Quirarte, Jacinto. *Mexican American Artists.* Austin: Univ. of Tex. Press, 1973.

Quirarte, Jacinto. *The Art and Architecture of the Texas Missions.* Austin: Univ. of Tex. Press, 2002.

Riggs, Thomas, ed. *St. James Guide to Hispanic Artists: Profiles of Latino and Latin American Artists.* Detroit, Mich.: St. James Press, 2002.

Sullivan, Edward, ed. *Latin American Art in the Twentieth Century.* London: Phaidon, 1996.

Yorba, Jonathan. *Arte Latino: Treasures from the Smithsonian American Art Museum.* New York: Watson-Guptill Pubns., 2001.

MARCUS BURKE

PALMIERI, CHARLIE

Born: November 21, 1927; New York, New York
Died: September 12, 1988; Bronx, New York

The Nuyorican pianist Carlos "Charlie" Palmieri, Jr., was born a year after his parents had migrated from Ponce, Puerto Rico, to New York City's Spanish Harlem neighborhood as part of the first wave of Puerto Ricans who sought a better way of life on the U.S. mainland. Palmieri's younger brother Eddie, another highly regarded Latin musician, was born nine years later.

Palmieri began his piano training at the age of seven, and seven years later he was already playing with professional Latin dance orchestras and hotel bands. Since his first solo recording in 1948, as leader of Conjunto Pin-Pin, he never failed to exhibit his

© CARLOS ORTIZ

Jazz pianist Charlie Palmieri.

passionate approach and awesome technique as a pianist. He was probably the first keyboardist to introduce the electric organ to the New York Latin music scene, but he never abandoned or neglected his first love—the acoustic piano.

After leading various *conjuntos* (trumpet-led ensembles) in the 1950s, Palmieri organized, at the dawn of New York's *pachanga* dance craze, the second *charanga* (flute-and-fiddle orchestra) ever formed in the music industry of New York City: Orquesta Duboney. This four-violin *charanga* (featuring a future salsa star and impresario named Johnny Pacheco on flute) became enormously popular in the early 1960s, sometimes playing four dances a night. Like many other New York bandleaders, Palmieri returned eventually to the brassy *conjunto* sound.

In 1961 Palmieri became the musical director of the Alegre All Stars, whose half-dozen recordings were inspired by the legendary Panart *descargas* (Cuban-style jam sessions) recorded in Havana. Elaborated intermittently during the following six years,

the Alegre All Stars' *descargas* provided some of the finest Cuban-derived moments in 1960s U.S. music history and highlighted the improvisational talents of some of the top Latin musicians and singers outside of Havana—for example, Chombo Silva, Barry Rodgers, Bobby Rodríguez, Kako, Louie Ramírez, Cheo Feliciano, and Rudy Calzado.

From the late 1940s to his death at the age of 61, Palmieri's solo discography oscillated between Latin jazz and popular dance music. As a bandleader, and through his guidance and talent, Palmieri inspired scores of young musicians in the 1960s and 1970s, including Willie Colón, Papo Lucca, and Jimmy Sabater.

After recuperating from a heart attack in the mid-1980s, Palmieri was told that he would not regain the full use of his hands, but he returned eventually to a regular performing and recording schedule with his own group, El Combo Gigante, as well as with the bands led by Joe Quijano and Orlando Marín, among others. He even managed to record one of the greatest albums of his career (*A Giant Step,* 1984; Tropical Budda).

On September 12, 1988, Palmieri died of a heart attack in the Bronx. He had just returned to his native city from San Juan, where—along with a lifetime friend, singer composer Bobby Capó—he had performed for the Puerto Rican governor at his official residence, La Fortaleza.

Palmieri, despite his characteristic modesty, was one of the most talented U.S.-based Latin pianists of the 20th century, as demonstrated in his extensive solo discography as well as his collaborations with Tito Puente, Tito Rodríguez, Herbie Mann, Eddie Palmieri, Cal Tjader, Machito, Mongo Santamaría and Cachao, among others.

RELATED ARTICLES

Colón, Willie; Jazz; Music, Popular; Salsa.

FURTHER READING

Boggs, Vernon W. "Salsiology: Afro-Cuban Music and the Evolution of Salsa in New York." In *City.* New York: Excelsior Music Publ., 1992.

Chediak, Nat. *Diccionario de jazz latino* (Dictionary of Latin Jazz). Madrid: Fundación Autor, 1998.

Salazar, Max. "Remembering Charlie Palmieri (Part 1)." *Latin Beat Magazine* (August 1999): 24–28.

Salazar, Max. "Remembering Charlie Palmieri (Part 2)." *Latin Beat Magazine* (September 1999): 24–28.

LUIS TAMARGO

PANAMANIAN AMERICANS

Located within the most narrow and southern segment of Central America, Panama borders Costa Rica, Colombia, the Caribbean Sea, and the Pacific Ocean. The ethnic population is divided among mestizos (65 percent), blacks and mulattos (14 percent), whites (10 percent), and American Indians (8 percent). Although the official language is Spanish, bilingual programs, businesses and even personal households teach English as a second language. Most of the population consider themselves Roman Catholic, however there is representation from other faiths, including Buddhism, Baha'i, Islam, Judaism, and Protestantism.

The history of Panamanian Americans in the United States begins with the relationship between Panama and the United States, which perhaps begins with the building of the Panama Railroad in the mid-19th century. A response to the California Gold Rush, the railroad provided opportunities for Panamanian railway workers and others to enter the United States. The opening of the Panama Canal in 1914 provided for even more significant Panamanian immigration patterns. The Panama Canal Act of 1979 guaranteed entry as residents into the United States for longtime workers associated with the operation of the canal. Another significant immigration pattern occurred as a result of the United Fruit Company's operation of banana plantations, railroads, wharves, and ships, which facilitated the immigration of former canal workers who were English-speaking residents and citizens of Panama. With subsequent events, including the Great Depression of the 1930s and World War II, Panamanian immigration fluctuated according to the demand for labor and economic hardship in Panama resulting from U.S. streamlining of canal operations and facilities, and reduction of residential communities and military bases. Some Panamanians also immigrated to enlist in the U.S. armed forces during the Korean War. After 1970 the trend of immigration by working- and middle-class people of color from Panama changed again; for a time thereafter, there was a pronounced immigrant body of business class and white elites who immigrated as political exiles, some of whom remained in the United States. As a result of political conflicts between the United States and the Noriega regime in the early 1980s, and plummeting confidence in Panamanian economic security and growth, another increase in immigration occurred. Subsequent better relations between the United States and Panama have not necessarily produced any prominent changes in such movement.

While the number of legal immigrants from Panama to the United States is smaller than those from other Central American countries other than Belize and Costa Rica, Panamanians have a higher rate of naturalization. And although Panamanians do not have as clear and large a concentration of population in any one section of the United States, there are marked populations in metropolitan areas of New York, Miami, Chicago, Los Angeles, Boston, Atlanta, and Washington, D.C.

Similar to other Central American immigrant communities, the Panamanian American community in the United States has been shaped by the politics between Panama and the United States. Panamanians have a significant exposure to and comfort with American culture and norms, which are considered crucial to upward mobility and success. The relationship of Panamanian Americans to Panama is also distinct from other Central American immigrants relationships to their countries of origin, particularly with regard to family remittances to home countries and the prosperity enjoyed by Panama, largely attributed to American presence there. Scholars also cite the wide distribution of Panamanian Americans throughout the United States and the resentments, past and present, toward immigrants as a reason for the difference between Panamanian Americans' relationships with Panama compared with other immigrant communities' relationships with their countries of origin.

Cultural and social activities in Panamanian communities are often national events that involve Panamanian holiday celebrations, observed with patriotic speeches, artistic productions, and ecumenical services combined with announcements, awards, and nostalgia through traditional foods, music, dance, dress, and decorations. One example of such an event is the annual celebration of the Panamanian Family Reunion, which includes thousands of families and social groups from across the United States, not all of whom are Panamanians. There are social and community activities to celebrate successes and achievements by Panamanian Americans; for example individual prominence and achievement in particular fields such as politics, sports, and the arts.

Some well-known Panamanian Americans include United States Army specialist Shoshana Johnson, who, during the Iraq War, was kidnapped by Iraqi soldiers and later found by American soldiers; Raul Romero, a Panama native who served as an adviser on Latino issues under George W. Bush; Rubén Blades, Grammy Award winning musician and actor, who ran for president of Panama in 1994; boxing great Roberto Duran; and actress Tatyana Ali, best known for her role on the television series *Fresh Prince of Bel Air*. Other sports figures include Rolando Blackman of the Dallas Mavericks, Mariano Rivera of the New York Yankees, and Laffit Pincay, the jockey who broke Bill Shoemaker's record when he became the first to reach 9,000 wins.

Panamanian Americans remain politically active through debates and keen interest in political activities that involve Panama and its terminal cities. While there is a relative absence of distinctively Panamanian organizations and publications, there are broader based ethnic and political interest groups to which many belong. To remain abreast of political perspectives, many Panamanian Americans rely on contacts with relatives and friends in Panama as well as national and international television networks. Younger generations seem to have grown more comfortable with expanded definitions of Latino heritage, joining multiethnic organizations. Older generations are described as more isolated and selective about their participation in such groups. Most Panamanians in the United States strive to retain links to Panama for the benefit of their children and their relatives residing in Panama, and to secure ethnic, cultural, and social connections to future migration possibilities to and from the United States.

RELATED ARTICLES

Blades, Rubén; United States–Central America Relations.

FURTHER READING

Orozco, Manuel. *International Norms and Mobilization for Democracy: Nicaragua in the World.* Burlington, Vt.: Ashgate, 2002.

Bayne-Smith, M., and R. S. Bryce-Laporte. "Panamanians in New York." In *Encyclopedia of New York City.* Ed. by Kenneth Jackson. New Haven, Conn.: Yale Univ. Press, 1995.

Conniff, M. *Black Labor on a White Canal:* Panama, 1904–1981. Pittsburgh: Univ. of Pittsburgh Press, 1985.

Levinson, David, and Melvin Ember, eds. *American Immigrant Cultures: Builders of a Nation.* Vol. 2. New York: Macmillan Reference, 1997.

Priestly, G. "Ethnicity, Class, and National Questions in Panama: The Emerging Literature." In *Emerging Perspectives on the Black Diaspora.* Ed. by A. W. Bonnett and G. L. Watson. Lanham, Md.: Univ. Press of America, 1989.

Westerman, George. *Los Inmigrantes Antillanos en Panama.* Panama: Instituto Nacional de Cultura, 1980.

HELANE D. ADAMS

PANTOJA, ANTONIA

Born: September 13, 1922; San Juan, Puerto Rico
Died: May 25, 2002; New York, New York

Antonia Pantoja was a brilliant and effective community activist, social worker, educator, and one of the true pioneers in advocating for better education for Puerto Ricans and all Latinos in New York. She was the founder of two important organizations that sought to transform higher education for minorities; Aspira and Universidad Boricua.

Despite her humble origins, the absence of her father, and a childhood filled with great poverty in the working community of Barrio Obrero, Pantoja was able to successfully gain an education, owing to her intelligence, tenacity and self-determination, and the support and encouragement of her grandmother and others. She received a teaching degree from the Normal School of the University of Puerto Rico in 1942. For two years she taught in rural schools on the island before, like thousands of other Puerto Ricans, migrating to New York City in search of better opportunities. She worked first in factories; unlike her peers, however, she was determined to improve her English, to change the working conditions of herself and her peers, and to explore the rich cultural life of the city. In 1952, with the help of a scholarship, she graduated from Hunter College with a degree in sociology; she obtained a master's degree in social work from Columbia University in 1954.

In the 1950s and 1960s most Puerto Ricans in New York lived below the poverty line, worked in the lowest-paying jobs, had little or no education or knowledge of English, lived in crowded spaces or inadequate housing, and lacked technical training. In addition their children faced one of the highest dropout rates in the U.S. school system. The community also lacked organization and political power. It is within the context of those realities that the contributions of Pantoja must be highlighted. She saw inequalities and disadvantages for Puerto Ricans and committed herself to seeking change. Her founding of the Puerto Rican Forum (later known as the National Puerto Rican Forum) in 1957 was the first step to professionally beginning to deal with the "Puerto Rican problem," particularly within education. In 1961 she founded Aspira, Incorporated, whose motto, "Excellence through the Pursuit of Education," synthesized its mission to provide well-organized programs to assist students in gaining college admission and receiving financial aid while attending college. Through Aspira's efforts, Puerto Ricans began to push for reforms in terms of curriculum relevancy, adult education, and school-community relations.

In 1972 Aspira sued the City of New York in federal court. The court, in 1974, ruled in favor of Aspira, and the city was ordered to begin bilingual education and English-as-a-second-language programs for Latino students. In the 1970s Pantaja also founded in Washington, D.C., the Universidad Boricua (1970), becoming its chancellor. Earning a doctoral degree in 1973 from Union Graduate School in Ohio, she also established the Puerto Rican Research and Resource Center in Washington, D.C.

Health problems contributed to her decision to move west, and in 1978 Pantoja became a faculty member of San Diego State University's School of Social Work, where she created the Graduate School for Community Development. Back in Puerto Rico (1984–1998), she continued her leadership by establishing Producir, an organization to help small businesses in neglected areas, and Providencia, to develop affordable housing. She returned to New York City to resume her work in the community, defend the Spanish language against the "English Only" movement, and to fully accept her identity as a Nuyorican. She received numerous awards; notably she was the first Puerto Rican to receive the Presidential Medal for Freedom, which was awarded to her by President Bill Clinton in 1996. Her autobiography, *Memoir of a Visionary: Antonia Pantoja* (2002), is a moving account of her life, aspirations, and achievements.

RELATED ARTICLES

Activism; Bilingual Education; Education; Education, Higher; Puerto Ricans on the Mainland.

FURTHER READING

Pantoja, Antonia. *Memoir of a Visionary: Antonia Pantoja.* Houston: Arte Público, 2002.

Perry, Wilhelmina. "Memories of a Life of Work: An Interview with Antonia Pantoja." *Harvard Educational Review: Symposium: Colonialism and Working-Class Resistance: Puerto Rican Education in the United States* 66 (1998): 244–258.

ASELA RODRÍGUEZ DE LAGUNA

PAREDES, AMÉRICO

Born: September 3, 1915; Brownsville, Texas
Died: May 5, 1999; Austin, Texas

Américo Paredes was an acclaimed Mexican American folklorist and ethnographer and one of the most respected contemporary Chicano intellectuals. Not only did he lay the foundation for a new and compelling Mexican American intellectual tradition, but he also trained an entire generation of borderland folklorists. Paredes became the editor of the U.S. military newspaper *Stars and Stripes* during his years in the U.S. Army. In 1950, a time when few Hispanics had opportunities in higher education in Brownsville, Texas, Paredes, at age 35, enrolled at the University of Texas. He went on to have a 33-year

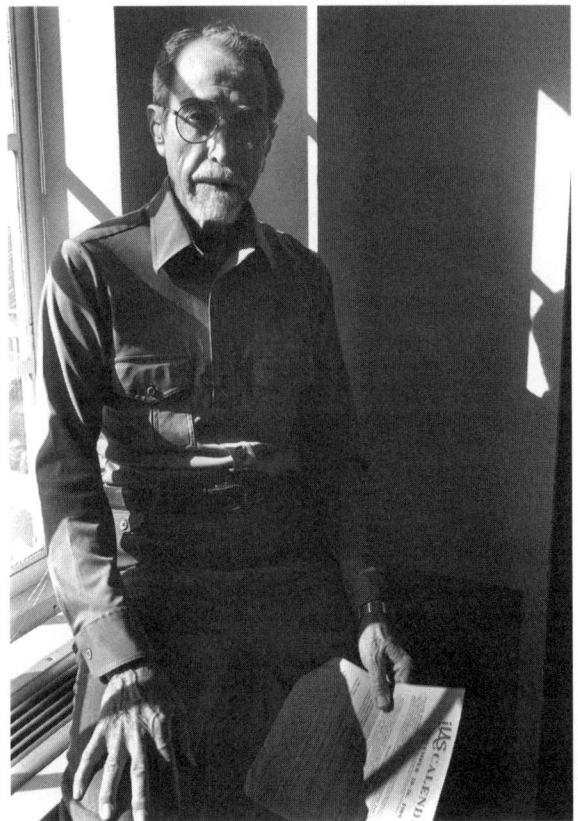

© JESSE HERRERA

Américo Paredes.

teaching career at his alma mater, during which time he organized the folklore archives in 1970, founded the university's Mexican American studies program in 1972, edited the *Journal of American Folklore* from 1969 to 1973, and founded and directed the Center for Intercultural Studies in Folklore and Ethnomusicology.

While at the University of Texas, Paredes dedicated a substantial portion of his career to the study of Mexican folklore in south Texas. His revolutionary approach to writing about "tradition" in early Texas helped shape a positive cultural identity among Mexican Americans. Paredes traveled to the Rio Grande border region collecting folktales and *corridos,* or Mexican American ballads. In doing so he considered the way that traditional music forms speak and record historical events for communities to artistically render their perspectives. Paredes's 1958 influential work *With His Pistol in His Hand: A Border Ballad and Its Hero,* about the legend of Gregorio Cortez, challenged stereotypical views of life in the Texas-Mexico borderlands.

Throughout his scholarship Paredes developed a theory that Chicano folklore emerged from a process of cultural conflict generated by the invasion of Anglo culture into south Texas during the 1800s. Resistance to an encroaching foreign culture, the loss of political and economic power, feelings of social marginality, and the resulting conflict of cultures all contributed to the legends, jokes, and songs that have become part of Chicano folklore.

By refuting racist characterizations of Mexicans, Paredes offers an unrepressed critique of past and present racial discrimination from the early 20th century to contemporary Texas. He paints a portrait of the Texas Rangers killing Mexicans indiscriminately, critiquing the work of William Madsen and Texas historian Walter Prescott Webb, who created the myth of the Texas Rangers as bringing order and civilization to the state. Paredes also critiques the very notion of anthropological "objectivity" in scholarship. He enumerates how various errors and misunderstandings about language and culture are accepted as literal truths. In so doing, he engendered a new wave a scholarship and academic achievement.

Paredes's humanistic approach to conducting research has brought a new consciousness to the study of folklore, teaching that the examination of cultural or folkloric phenomenon cannot be divorced from the social context in which it is performed or ex-

pressed. His research emphasized the importance of the informant's culture, history, and social setting of community. In documenting the imaginative styles concerned with Mexican American struggles for social justice, Paredes created a new historiographical space, critiquing the process of history making itself. During his life Paredes received prestigious awards, recognitions, and creative-writing prizes from the National Endowment for the Humanities, the Mexican government, and the 76th Texas Legislature. Américo Paredes persistently pursued his goal of validating Mexican American studies, remaining active in civil rights, bicultural education, and ethnic minority affairs for Texas and the University of Texas.

RELATED ARTICLES
Border, United States-Mexico; Corrido; Folklore, Mexican American; Mexican Americans.

FURTHER READING
Limón, José E. *Dancing With the Devil: Society and Cultural Poetics in Mexican-American South Texas.* Madison: Univ. of Wis. Press, 1994.
Paredes, Américo. *With His Pistol in His Hand: A Border Ballad and Its Hero.* Austin: Univ. of Tex. Press, 1958.
Paredes, Américo. *A Texas-Mexican Cancionero: Folksongs of the Lower Border.* Urbana: Univ. of Ill. Press, 1976.
Paredes, Américo. *Between Two Worlds.* Houston: Arte Público Press, 1991.
Paredes, Américo. *Folklore and Culture of the Texas-American Border.* Austin, Tex.: Ctr. for Mex. Am. Studies Bks., 1993.
Rosaldo, Renato. *Culture and Truth: The Remaking of Social Analysis.* Boston: Beacon Press, 1989.
Saldívar, José. "Chicano Border Narratives as Cultural Critique." In *Criticism in the Borderlands: Studies in Chicano Literature, Culture, and Ideology.* Ed. by Hector Calderón and Jose David Saldívar. Durham, N.C.: Duke Univ. Press, 1991.
Saldívar, Ramón. *Chicano Narrative: The Dialects of Difference.* Madison: Univ. of Wis. Press, 1990.

ALYSSA GARCÍA

PARENTING

A fundamental task of families is to carry out the socialization of their children. Children who are born into any society need to learn the behaviors that are acceptable to their families as well as the language, beliefs, thoughts and emotions, and motivations characteristic of the culture, or cultures into which they are born. Every child must learn these attributes in order to achieve the social and economic status of adulthood. Parents develop or choose strategies for socializing their children that are guided by cultural values and a desire to instill these values in their children and, in turn, promote in their children healthy development and competencies consistent with the family's cultural beliefs.

In traditional Latino cultures the socialization role is grounded in cultural notions of what it means to be well educated. *Un niño o una niña bien educados* (a well-educated boy or girl) is a child who emulates the traditional values of respect, familism, cooperation, interdependence, and humility. Children are viewed as mirrors of the family; their behaviors are a reflection of how well the parents have raised them. Therefore, the parenting of Hispanic children in traditional U.S. families has been described as a blend of authoritativeness and indulgence; in order to mold obedient, well-behaved children who respect their fathers and adore their mothers, the fathers or male figures discipline and the mothers love and indulge the children. Moreover, for Latino parents the task entails preparing the children to live in two different and, at times, conflictual cultural spaces.

What factors inform the way Latino parents raise their children in increasingly complex and multicultural contexts? And what are some salient issues faced by single, teen, and gay and lesbian parents?

The Challenge of Diversity

A key characteristic of Latino families is their diversity in terms of nationality, generational level, class status, and education. While most Hispanics in the United States have been socialized themselves with strong values of family and the importance of parenting, the extent to which their parenting practices reflect traditional values will depend largely on the adults' level of acculturation and their own childhood experiences. Likewise, the impact of poverty, undereducation, difficult living conditions, and stresses inherent in urban living also influence child-rearing practices, irrespective of cultural ideals and values.

Despite the large numbers of Latinos and the high reproductive rates of several Latino subgroups, little research attention has been paid to how Latinos of diverse backgrounds parent their children. In fact, some scholars criticize most research on Latino parenting because of its reliance on a deficit model, which holds Anglo parenting as the norm and views any practices differing from those of middle-class European American parents as problematic or dysfunctional. In addition, most studies of Latino parenting have utilized primarily poor families and low-income

single parents as participants, thus confounding economic status with cultural beliefs or practices that may influence parenting behaviors. Instead, studies should focus on within-group variation and compare only Latinos and other groups from the same socioeconomic classes, since parents cross-culturally may hold similar parenting goals, but the values and contextual factors that influence how children are raised will differ across and within cultural groups.

Child-Rearing Beliefs

In general, Latinos of varying social classes are described as holding interdependent parenting values that emphasize the interconnectedness of human beings to one another. European Americans are described as valuing self-control and mastery; thus their parenting practices aim to foster a more independent self than is valued by Latinos. In contrast, Latinos tend to emphasize interdependence, connection, and loyalty to family over individuality and self-control.

Child-centered cultural beliefs influence parenting from conception. A number of folk beliefs in traditional Latino subcultures posit that pregnant women should be treated well, catered to, and provided with familial and social support for the optimal development of the fetus. *La cuarentena,* the 40-day postpartum period, is a time for parents and baby to bond; women are encouraged to refrain from any housework and to avoid any unpleasant situation that could lead to *corajes,* or getting angry, since strong emotions could affect the milk of nursing mothers. This system relies on strong familial and friendship bonds, which will ensure that new parents will have assistance. Cultural views also influence feeding and sleeping preferences. For example, while European Americans may prefer children to develop regular feeding and sleeping schedules in infancy, Latino parents are more likely to follow the child's "schedule" and value close physical contact with the infant. European American parents and more acculturated Latinos may prefer for the baby to sleep in his or her own room, while traditional parents are likely to have the infant in their room and even in the same bed with them.

The goal of parenting in early childhood across cultures is to facilitate the optimal development of the child and to prepare him or her for school. In their 2002 study of Puerto Rican middle class mothers, Harwood and associates describe the concept of "proper demeanor" as key to parenting in early childhood. Specifically, parents expect that the child should develop an awareness of the "proper level of courtesy and decorum required in a given situation in relation to other people of a particular age, sex and social status." The cultural rule governing proper demeanor is respect. Parenting strategies in early childhood should thus foster knowledge of who merits respect and under what circumstances, as well as the development of a behavioral repertoire that demonstrates respect. These authors have found evidence of this cultural belief among socioeconomically diverse Puerto Rican groups on both the island and the mainland.

Many Mexican and Central American immigrants also espouse the notion of proper demeanor (*buena conducta*). Among rural immigrants from this region, proper demeanor is also grounded in the cultural construct of respect; consequently, children are taught not to speak out of turn, not to question adult au-

thority, not to look at elders in the eye, and, for girls, to exhibit physical modesty at all times. Clearly, these behaviors will be rewarded in the family but may be problematic in non-Latino contexts, including schools where these behaviors may be misunderstood as disinterest or inattention.

The task of raising children is made more difficult by the cultural changes families face postmigration. Similarly, new environmental factors, such as increased pollution and racial segregation in urban centers, will influence the extent to which parents rely on "tried and true" child-rearing strategies that worked in their country of origin. Some studies suggest that immigrant parents who reside in multiracial urban contexts may experience these communities as frightening or threatening. As a result, they may adopt parenting strategies to protect their children from harm without being fully aware or concerned as to how these practices may affect their children's ability to succeed socially or in school at a later point. Thus many parents will not allow their children to socialize with neighbors, which can result in delays in their acquisition of English language or create difficulties for social development. In the same way, new environmental demands may determine the extent to which parents attempt to instill in their children their own cultural values or modify or develop new ones.

Parenting Processes

Traditional gender roles continue to influence how Latinos of varying national origins and socioeconomic classes raise their children, although with significant variation. In general Latino parents encourage their sons to be more independent than their daughters. Girls are expected to obey the family's moral code and avoid bringing shame to the family.

These traditional roles reflect the values of machismo and *marianismo*. Machismo is the code of male behavior that evolved from patriarchal notions of male chivalry, the valuing of physical prowess and stoicism, with an emphasis on the man's role as the head of the household. Influenced by Catholic ideology, *marianismo* is the counterpart of machismo. This value emphasizes a woman's role as a mother and celebrates her self-sacrifice and suffering for her children. Families who adhere strictly to these values are more likely to foster more rigid gender-role socialization wherein males are encouraged to have great independence from the family while females are ex-

© BILL ARON / PHOTOEDIT

Parents of school-age children emphasize the importance of education.

pected to emulate their mother and the Virgin Mother. As a result, males are accorded more freedom of time, thought, and expression and females are trained to serve others—they typically are expected to help raise younger siblings, cook, clean, and serve the men, including brothers. In such families, postsecondary education for females may not be encouraged. Traditional families who emphasize adherence to traditional Latino values may not fully prepare their children for living in a multicultural context. Furthermore, these families may face greater parent-child conflicts during adolescence.

Central to raising children is the importance of preparing offspring for a good life. Latino parents are described as highly valuing education, which is inextricably connected to more basic beliefs about children's moral development. In studies examining Latino parental involvement in education, a metaphor that emerged is the concept of *el buen camino,* or following the good path of life, to explain parents' developmental goals for their children. Latino parents see the home and the school as sites where children will be prepared for life. While the school is supposed to furnish the necessary knowledge for academic advancement and success in life, parents are expected to provide a solid moral foundation through the teaching of values in the home. The ethical and moral foundation laid down by parents is believed to be necessary for their children's internalization of what the family, community, and society expect of them.

Adolescence is seen as a critical transitional stage, where the parents' influence diminishes and that of the child's peers increases. Latino parents face many challenges during this stage, and immigrant Hispanic parents in particular express concerns about the decreased control over their children in the United States. Also, the task of preparing children for a good life is made more complex by migration to the new culture, since many Latino parents have inadequate knowledge of the dominant culture or lack the economic resources to provide their children with access to better schools.

In 2000, psychologists Margarita Azmitia and Jane Brown interviewed Latino parents of adolescents regarding their views on the path of life; the majority of them described the good path as being respectful and maintaining high moral values. They noted the importance of the family to guide and instruct children before adolescence, since the youth would then

be exposed to a more complex world outside the family. Parents described the good path as relating to desirable character traits that were instilled in the home and the bad path as behaviors and activities, particularly using drugs and alcohol or joining gangs, that their children faced outside the home.

These researchers also investigated how the parents attempted to lead their children toward the good path. Three principal strategies emerged. First, parents relied on *consejos,* giving advice through the use of cultural narratives or stories that emphasized morality and good behavior. Second, the parents attempted to provide children with strong moral support and to be their child's friend and advocate. Third, if parents perceived the children as deviating from the good path or succumbing to bad influences, the parents exercised greater control by restricting and monitoring their children's activities.

Parents of elementary- and middle-school-aged children highlighted the importance of school and schoolwork and supported their children's educational efforts. The Latino immigrant parents in the sample feared the transition to middle school and concomitant entry to adolescence. They expressed concern that the children's focus on school and learning could be adversely affected by adolescent pressures and worried about the possible negative influence of their children's peers. Parents also acknowledged that peers could exercise a positive influence on their children if they were "good children from good families." Most parents in this study knew and approved of their children's friends, and few of their children evidenced behavioral problems; thus it is not clear whether parents of youth who experienced academic or behavioral problems utilized the same parenting strategies. The parent participants in the study however, expressed greater concern about their older children and worried more about their daughters' friends as potential negative influences. They also worried about the dangers their sons faced "on the street." Several of the boys in the study experienced academic difficulties; their parents expressed concern that their dreams of a better life for their children were beginning to slip away.

Both immigrant and U.S.-born Hispanic parents value education. Studies also point to the high priority given to good moral character and familial interdependence. Azmitia and Brown underscored in their 2000 findings the importance of American schools engaging the participation of Latino parents with respect to their cultural values. Yet, contrary to stereotypes, Latino parents value education and are involved in their children's schooling, although their participation may be less "visible" to teachers, since it may occur mostly in the home. Moreover, there is ample evidence that when needed, these parents will mobilize on behalf of their children's education.

Co-parenting

Defined by researcher Yvonne Caldera and associates as the extent to which "husbands and wives function as partners or adversaries in the parenting role," co-parenting is characterized by multidimensional processes reflecting how parents support, assist, or sabotage each other's parenting efforts. The general assumption has been that women in most cultures continue to have primary responsibility for the socialization of their children. However, since the 1970s, with women's increased presence in the paid labor force, a softening of traditional gender roles has occurred. In middle-class and professional families, men have become more involved in the parenting of children. Baca Zinn, among other social scientists, found in a 1994 study greater role flexibility among Chicano working-class couples; however, most of the changes were in terms of a household division of labor; the greater role flexibility does not necessarily reflect significant changes in ideology. In fact, many Latinas continue to show some reluctance to let go of the notion that men should be the head of household, both in terms of being the breadwinner and representing the family to the outside world. This ideology is likely to influence how they raise their sons and daughters. Yet few studies have examined parenting strategies in two-parent Latino families. A notable exception is the 2002 study by Caldera and associates of co-parenting among heterosexual Mexican American couples.

Caldera and her colleagues studied 14 lower- to middle-class Mexican American couples. Their findings contradict the traditional view of Latino men as uninvolved in parenting and support a growing research trend that both Latino and European American fathers are highly involved with their children. The study found that Mexican American couples in their sample preferred a cooperative model of co-parenting and a broad range of cooperative dynamics through which they aimed for an equal distribution of parenting tasks. In addition, these parents identified a process of compensation, reflecting a parenting alliance, whereby the parent with stronger skills in certain areas would engage in those parenting domains, or would fill in when the other parent was unavailable. In general the traditional view was evident, with fathers providing relief for the mothers, while mothers were not viewed in the same manner. The main source of co-parenting conflict apparent in this study was the parents' report that sometimes they contradicted each other in front of the children, despite their awareness that this could undermine the other's authority. Nevertheless, the study points to the fact that Latino parents are aware of the value of providing a united front to the children, supporting each other's parenting efforts and utilizing culturally endorsed strategies to guide and promote the healthy development of their children. Couples who engaged in cooperative co-parenting also reported experiencing marital satisfaction, and their children were described as well behaved and developing normally in preschool.

Families at Risk

The few studies of Latino parenting suggest that most Latinos still hold traditional views and believe in developing a solid moral base in their offspring. Likewise, Latino parents promote strong family ties yet are willing to modify their practices to assist their children's educational development. To what extent their parenting processes are affected by acculturation has not been systematically studied. However, Celia Falicov argues that the multiple losses immigrants experience as a result of their migration can undermine their parenting abilities, particularly of children in adolescence, when strategies successful in their country of origin do not adequately prepare the children for a bicultural life. Most authors note the importance of understanding Latino families contextually, in order to identify risk factors as well as those protective factors that families bring along with them, which can aid in the parenting role.

Cross-cultural studies of family functioning point to poverty as a major risk factor for successful parenting. Moreover, several studies have focused on the challenges faced by "nontraditional families"—notably teen mothers and poor, single-parent families.

A number of studies find that teen parenting, when compared with adult parenting, is less optimal; teen mothers are more likely to respond to their infants and children with more negative affect and to be less responsive to their children's needs than are adult mothers. Ultimately, it is assumed that both teen mothers and their children will suffer more negative outcomes, principally owing to the higher likelihood that teen mothers will be poor and have less education and less opportunity for upward mobility. It is more likely that teen mothers will reside in neighborhoods with fewer resources and thus will raise their children in poverty. This is a serious concern given the high rates of Latina teen mothers. Despite these high numbers, few studies examine their unique experience and particular parenting processes. Clinical psychologist Josefina Contreras proposed (2002) a conceptual model to determine parenting among Latina teens. The model urges an examination of the teen's contextual factors (sources of stress and support, developmental history, her own characteristics, including psychological well-being, and school or career opportunities) as well as the characteristics of her child and other socialization agents (extended family, mentors, and so on). Indeed, an examination of parenting among Latina teens is critical in order to avoid generalizing from the findings of studies with European American and African American teen mothers.

Single and Blended Families

While no studies of single, middle-class Latino parents exist, single parenting is identified as a risk factor by most family research. Other studies generally point to the absence of a parent, typically the father, as a key factor in educational underachievement and conduct problems of children and youth. Similarly, no studies have examined the particular challenges of parenting children in blended families (divorced and remarried individuals who bring their own children into a new marriage) or ethnically or racially mixed homes. The fact that single parents often utilize members of extended families as co-parents is well documented among Latino families, but research has not been undertaken to investigate how this co-parenting occurs and to what extent it is satisfying for all involved.

To date, no studies of parenting practices have focused on Latino gay or lesbian couples. Psychologists Charlotte Patterson and Richard Chan reviewed (1999) research on children of gay and lesbian parents and found no significant differences between these children and those of heterosexual couples in terms of gender identity, gender-role behavior, sexual orientation, or psychological well-being. Further-

© TOMAS OVALLE/AP/WIDE WORLD PHOTOS

Men have become more involved in parenting in middle-class and professional families.

more, they saw no evidence of social problems or stigmatization of these children by their peers. The authors caution that most studies included only white, middle- to upper-middle-class families in their samples; thus their findings cannot be generalized for more ethnically or socioeconomically diverse groups. Also, because the studies reviewed did not center on parenting of children per se, it is not clear if differences exist in how lesbian or gay parents negotiate the multiple tasks of parenting. A 1997 study of lesbian couples found that those couples negotiated household and child care based on interests, time, ability to afford help, and agreements on how and when tasks would be completed. It would appear, then, that collaborative parenting was the preference. Nevertheless, there is an absence of information about the particular challenges Latino gay and lesbian couples face or the unique experiences they encounter.

There is much to study about Latino parenting beliefs, processes, and outcomes. As the Latino minority assumes an increasingly higher profile in U.S. society, it is crucial to pay careful attention to its socioeconomic, educational, national, and sexual diversity. The extent to which Latinos acculturate depends on the success of parents as teachers, caregivers, and role models.

RELATED ARTICLES

Adoption; Assimilation; Childhood and Adolescence; Education; Family; Feminism; Homosexuality, Female; Homosexuality, Male; Mental Health.

FURTHER READING

Baca Zinn, Maxine. "Adaptation and Continuity in Mexican-Origin Families. " In *Minority Families in the United States: A Multicultural Perspective.* Ed. by Ronald L. Taylor, 1994. Upper Saddle River, N.J.: Prentice Hall, 1994.

Bialeschki, M. Deborah, and Kimberly D. Pearce. "I Don't Want a Lifestyle—I Want a Life: The Effects of Role Negotiations on the Leisure of Lesbian Mothers." *Journal of Leisure Research* 1 (1997): 113–131.

Contreras, Josefina M., ed. *Latino Children and Families in the United States: Current Research and Future Directions.* Westport, Conn.: Praeger, 2002.

Delgado, Jane. *Salud: A Latina's Guide to Total Health.* New York: HarperCollins, 2002.

Delgado-Gaitan, Concha. "School Matters in the Mexican American Home: Socializing Children to Education." *American Educational Research Journal* 29 (1992): 495–513.

Delgado-Gaitan, Concha. "Consejos: The Power of Cultural Narratives." *Anthropology and Education Quarterly* 25 (1994): 298–316.

Falicov, Celia. "The Challenge of School and Work." In *Latino Families in Therapy: A Guide to Multicultural Practice.* New York: Guilford Press, 115–130, 1998.

Patterson, Charlotte J., and Richard W. Chan. "Families Headed by Lesbian and Gay Parents." In *Parenting and Child Development in "Nontraditional Families."* Ed. by M. E. Lamb. Mahwah, N.J.: Erlbaum Pubs., 1999.

YVETTE G. FLORES

PAROCHIAL SCHOOLS

Parochial schools are private religious schools that operate parallel to the public school system. In the United States, some of the religious groups that support parochial schools include Lutherans, Seventh-Day Adventists, Orthodox Jews, Muslims, and evangelical Protestants. The most numerous parochial schools, however, are those attached to Roman Catholic parishes.

Catholic parochial schools usually provide primary education for children from kindergarten through eighth grade and sometimes a secondary program for high school students. According to the National Parochial School Directory (January 2004) there are over 7,250 Catholic parochial schools throughout the United States. For example, in California there are 577 Catholic schools; of those, 468 offer elementary education and middle education (grades prekindergarten–8); 107 offer high school education (grades 9–12), and 2 that offer only middle school education (grades 7–8). Catholic parochial schools are widespread, mostly in urban areas, where they are considered a valuable alternative to many public schools. (For example, in the area of San Diego there are more than 40 parochial schools; or 7 percent of all the parochial schools in California.) Catholic school children generally wear uniforms and are taught by nuns and lay teachers in a religious atmosphere. Some parochial schools also offer or allow Saturday Spanish schools to function on their premises. Saturday Spanish schools are mostly free, taught by volunteers to emphasize Latino culture and values. There are also private Catholic colleges and universities operated by the many different Catholic devotional or public-service orders all over the country where millions of students are educated. In addition, Catholic charities and hospitals are widespread.

Although the vast majority of Latinos in the United States are Roman Catholic, only a small proportion attend Catholic schools. It has been estimated that in the 1990s, 80 percent or more of Latinos were Roman Catholic, but only 20 percent attended Catholic schools. One reason for this low figure could be economic. Catholic schools are relatively expensive, and Latinos are among the groups with the lowest socioeconomic status in the country. In spite of this, and as more Latinos enter the middle classes, many Latino parents send their children to Catholic parochial schools, and they have become an increasingly large and influential group within these organizations. Latino parents see parochial schools as a vehicle for the transmission of their religious and cultural heritage to their children.

Although Catholic schools have existed in the United States since colonial times, the Catholic parochial school system as it is known today developed in the 19th century as an answer to what was then seen as a Protestant domination of the public school system. By 1890 the now common 12-grade system, whereby the child enters kindergarten at age five, goes to grammar or elementary school for grades 1 through 8, high or secondary school for grades 9 through 12, and then enters college, had evolved.

Attendance at schools was compulsory and legislated in all states, although the age of attendance and length of the school year could vary considerably.

Until the 1963 federal ban on prayer in schools, religion played a major role in the public school system. In a country that was overwhelmingly Protestant, most of the prayers and the religious lessons taught at school were Protestant based. In 1884 a group of American bishops met at the Third Plenary Council of Baltimore with the idea of organizing a parochial school system that could offer an alternative to the dominant Protestantism taught at schools. Soon after, local Catholic churches set up elementary schools, and in time the number of secondary and high schools increased. Every diocese supported a number of parish schools. The curriculum of the elementary and secondary schools was similar to that of the public schools with the addition of a strong emphasis on the Catholic doctrine.

In the middle of the 20th century, the traditional structure of parochial education changed. The Second Vatican Council (1962–1965) created an ecumenical spirit that convinced many Roman Catholics of the disadvantages of a separatist religious education. Furthermore, many critics of parochial education claimed that public schools provided a better secular education at a lower cost. Because of such criticism, parochial schools were obliged to hire lay teachers who were responsible for an increasingly larger proportion of the curriculum. In the middle of the 1960s, with Catholic schools facing severe financial problems, many parish schools were closed and the number of students in Catholic schools diminished sharply. The percentage of Catholic students attending Catholic grade schools in January 2004 was only half what it was in the 1950s (down from 45 percent to 20 percent). Meanwhile, the percentage of Catholic children who were not in parochial schools but were in parish-based religious education programs increased from 37 percent to 61 percent. Although 80 percent of Catholic students attended public institutions, the enrollment at Catholic colleges and universities tripled since 1950 from 230,000 to over 700,000.

There were other changes in the profile of parochial schools in the 20th century that reflected the

© BILL ARON/PHOTOEDIT

Parochial school children during math class, in Hialeah, Florida.

general characteristics of the Catholic population in the United States. According to the 2004 Official Catholic Directory (which relies on parishes and dioceses for its data) there were about 63 million Catholics in this country, although the total number of Americans who identified as Catholic was considerably higher, as two-thirds were registered parishioners and one-third were not. Only 20 percent of today's Catholics belong to the pre–Vatican II generation (born in or before 1940), one-third belong to the Vatican II generation (born between 1941 and 1960), and nearly half are members of the post–Vatican II generation (born since 1961). Catholics in the United States have gone from being a relatively small, working-class, and highly segregated population of largely white Europeans to being a larger, more middle-class, and increasingly non-European population that is more integrated into American society and culture. Over the last 100 years, white Catholics of European ancestry have experienced a marked upward mobility, becoming more prosperous and educated. At the same time, during that period the church has been absorbing a large wave of non-European immigrants. The estimates of how many U.S. Catholics are Latinos range between 15 and 40 percent. About 4 percent of Catholics are African American, 2 percent are Asian, and 1 percent are Native American. The population of Latino students is becoming more significant in these days as many Latino parents believe in the importance of preserving the religious and family heritage through education.

Parochial schools still account for the majority of the attendance at private schools, but their financial difficulties and loss of students have forced them to look for aid from other sources, primarily from their students' families. The government can provide some aid to parochial schools, but only to support the secular curriculum, following the 1963 federal ban on prayer in schools and the separation of state and church. The Elementary and Secondary Education Act (1965, amended 1966, 1967) was the first national general-aid education program in the United States to provide support for students in private as well as public schools. It makes available funds for school library and textbook services and helps with the education of poor and disabled children; but federal aid can not be used for religious materials, which form a significant part of the schools' costs.

The American idea of separation of state and church, that is, complete noninterference on both sides, dates back to Thomas Jefferson's Virginia statute for religious freedom, and it is expressed in the First Amendment to the U.S. Constitution. Today there is little friction between the roles of church and state except in the area of education. There have been many debates over such questions as religious education in tax-supported schools and public aid to parochial schools. By the end of 1999 school vouchers had become a controversial topic and federal courts were coming to terms with its political repercussions. When the voucher system resulted in most recipients attending religious schools instead of public schools, it was argued that the system violated the Constitution.

Until the 1970s most instruction in parochial schools in the United States was conducted in English, which was also true of public schools, following an assimilationist educational philosophy that was prevalent in the country. An example of a Catholic education delivered in English for Latino students is described by Richard Rodriguez in his book *Hunger of Memory: The Education of Richard Rodriguez*. A Mexican American, Rodriguez attended elementary school at a Catholic school in Sacramento in the 1950s. The following is an excerpt describing his first day of classes:

> I remember to start with that day in Sacramento—a California now nearly thirty years past—when I first entered a classroom, able to understand some fifty stray English words. The third of four children, I had been preceded to a neighborhood Roman Catholic school by an older brother and sister. . . .

> The nun said, in a friendly but oddly impersonal voice, "Boys and girls, this is Richard Rodriguez." (I heard her sound out: Rich-heard Road-ree-guess.) It was the first time I had heard anyone name me in English. "Richard" the nun repeated more slowly, writing my name down in her black leather book. Quickly I turned to see my mother's face dissolve in a watery blur behind the pebbled glass door.

Bilingual education was introduced in public and parochial schools in the middle of the 1970s. In 1974 two major events occurred on that front, the Equal Educational Opportunity Act was approved, granting citizens greater rights to bilingual education, and the Office of Bilingual Education and Minority Language Affairs was created. In the Latino community, bilingual education is often preferred as a way of maintaining the native language as well as the ethnic and cultural identity.

Latino parents with the financial means to do so are more likely to send their children to Catholic schools. Catholic schools offer a number of positive attributes for many Latino parents apart from religion. Latino neighborhood schools are still rarely integrated, despite government attempts at integration. Because Catholic schools are independently run and accept students of many ethnic and national backgrounds, they represent an opportunity for Latino parents to send their children to integrated schools. In addition Catholic schools historically have had more strict disciplinary standards than public schools. Some Latino parents who live in urban areas that are riddled with violence, drug addiction, and other criminal activities, find it desirable to educate their children in an environment with stronger discipline.

Bilingual education in Catholic schools is fairly recent. Its success will not be measurable until this first generation of bilingual students reaches adulthood. In recent years, especially in California and other southwestern states, there have been attacks on bilingual education, such as California's Proposition 227 in 1998 that banned bilingual education in public schools. Catholic parochial schools that offer bilingual education provide a choice for Latino parents who believe in maintaining their language and culture as a family heritage.

RELATED ARTICLES

Bilingual Education; Catholicism; Childhood and Adolescence; Education; Education, Higher; Religion.

FURTHER READING

Hunt, Thomas C., et al., eds. *Catholic School Leadership: An Invitation to Lead*. New York: Falmer Press, 2000.

McLaughlin, Terence H., et al., eds. *Contemporary Catholic School: Context, Identity and Diversity*. London and Washington, D.C.: Falmer Press, 1996.

Rodriguez, Richard. *Hunger of Memory: The Education of Richard Rodriguez: An Autobiography*. Boston: Bantam, 2004.

U.S. Immigration and Naturalization Service. *Statistical Yearbook of the Immigration and Naturalization Service, 2002*. Washington, DC: USGPO, 2002.

SELECTED WEB SITES

Bosi Center for Religion and American Public Life at Boston College.
http://www.bc.edu/bc_org/research/rapl/ church-in-america/intro.html

M. CECILIA COLOMBI

PASSING

The verb *to pass* has many meanings, but one in particular holds strong racial implications. In terms of race, if one "passes," one succeeds in presenting oneself as a member of a race to which one does not actually belong. The most common use of this verb refers to the phenomenon of nonwhites pretending to be white. In English-speaking countries such as the United States and Great Britain, membership in the white race has historically entailed certain economic and political advantages, so the most common form of passing has involved racial minorities (such as African Americans or Native Americans) hiding their nonwhite ancestry and, if possible, manipulating their appearance and mannerisms to appear physically and culturally indistinguishable from whites.

In the context of Latinos, it is impossible to discuss passing without referring to the long and controversial history of light-skinned African Americans who chose to hide their black roots and pass as white people, from the time of slavery and long after. Before Latinos were a racially defined group and classified in popular parlance as distinct from whites (a trend that is far from universal or consistent), it was mostly blacks in the United States who confronted the issue of passing.

To confront the issue of passing is to confront the biological falsehood of discrete and separate races. In some senses, given the extent of interracial relationships and biracial children in the New World, it is absurd to talk about one group passing as another, since the groups themselves are so inextricably mixed together in the first place. Yet in the context of the United States, the country's legal and social institutions gave rise to a particularly strong illusion that whites, blacks, and Indians were discreet races with biologically real distinctions. (It is interesting to note that genetics have shown racial categories to be biologically false, since there are not enough meaningful differences among the so-called races. Thus "race" is a cultural concept, based on seemingly apparent similarities and dissimilarities.) One traditional explanation for this difference between racial sensibilities in Anglo America and Latin America has to do with the differences between English and Spanish techniques of conquest in the New World.

When the Spanish began conquering the New World in the 16th century, their soldiers tended to pursue relationships with Indian women, producing a sizable population of mestizos, or "mixed," children of both white and Indian parents. The English did not begin wholesale occupation of the New World until the following century. While some miscegenation occurred between English settlers and Indians, it was not as common, and in the United States there was never a distinct class of mestizos comparable to the large numbers in Latin America.

With the introduction of African slaves to the New World, the precedent set by patterns of white-Indian miscegenation influenced the way Spanish and English colonialists dealt with the question of white-black miscegenation. In Latin American territories with many slaves, such as the Caribbean and Brazil, there were high rates of miscegenation and large classes of mulattoes (*mulatos*), or "mixed" children of white and black parents. The mulattoes were viewed in Latin America as somewhat different from pure-blooded Africans, although the laws varied from place to place. By contrast, in English-speaking slave territories, such as the American South, whites knew that mulattoes existed, but they tended to view them, both legally and socially, as members of the black race rather than as members of both races or as a different category altogether. The English-speaking Americas followed a "one-drop" rule, by which any small amount of African blood made a person entirely black.

There were important differences in the racial sensibilities of Spain and England. Spain is geographically close to Africa. In the 15th and 16th centuries, Spaniards still had fresh memories of Islamic colonization; they were already fairly familiar with a wide range of skin colors and facial features. England, by contrast, is geographically remote and was more exclusively familiar with ethnic groups who shared the features of fair skin (such as the Scots, the Welsh, the Irish, and so on).

The result of these various racial differences was that in English-speaking America, light-skinned blacks had a clear incentive to try to "pass" as white—that is, to pretend that their African ancestry did not exist after enough generations of miscegenation had produced descendants who looked physically European. The obsession with passing dominates 19th-century and early 20th-century African American literature (as in, for example, *Running a Thousand Miles to Freedom* by William and Ellen Craft, *Iola Leroy* by Frances Harper, and *Passing* by Nella Larsen), particularly since laws in the American South made it such that

people who passed could obtain legal rights otherwise denied to them.

Latinos in the United States inherit all the same controversies surrounding passing, now that they are the largest minority group in the country. Whereas in the early 21st century passing is no longer as important an issue for African Americans as it once was, U.S. Hispanics are constantly dealing with the circumstances of their racial identity's ambiguous visual status. "Latino" or "Hispanic" is now used as a category comparable to "African American," which grew out of what were perceived as racial rather than cultural factors (someone was considered "black" originally if he or she had "black blood" and ancestors who looked black). Yet U.S. Hispanics have no racial commonality, and to conceptualize them as a race requires one to pretend that there is a mythical physical basis to their identity, which in fact does not exist. While it would be difficult to quantify what percentage of Latinos look Latino in some crudely stereotypical sense, it is fair to say that many Latinos grow up in the United States with the vague sense that they do not look the way they are supposed to. Many Latinos are told that they look white, while others hear that they look black—making the group as a whole likely candidates for passing.

On the street and at school, in the household and in politics, not looking the part has strong implications. The individual is made to feel illegitimate and unworthy. Spanish-language television often deals, humorously and otherwise, with Hispanic characters passing for Anglos and vice versa. Performance artist John Leguizamo, in one-man-shows such as *Mambo Mouth* and *Spic-o-Rama,* impersonates Latinos passing for Asian executives, Irish police officers, and so forth. Film actors such as Anthony Quinn, Raul Julia, and Antonio Banderas have been accused of not emphasizing enough their Latino selves. At times the characters they play on the silver screen deal with this hidden identity as well.

Compared with the earlier African American preoccupation with passing, U.S. Hispanic literature has not dealt very much with the scenario of a Latino or Latina who hides his or her ancestry and pretends to be purely Anglo-American in order to avoid some kind of prejudice or hardship. Latino authors who have written on the subject of passing include José Antonio Villarreal, Julia Alvarez, and Piri Thomas. Just as it did for African Americans before them, as memorialized in, among other novels, Charles Chestnutt's 1900 work *The House behind the Cedars,* the decision to pass can cause a great deal of discomfort for Latinos. They have to restrict how much they deal with Latino family members and worry about saying or doing the wrong thing that might expose their ancestry. As depicted in the short story "Edison, New Jersey," by Junot Díaz (included in his 1996 collection *Drown*), Latinos who are "hiding" from public scrutiny of their heritage will find it stressful to meet other Latinos. In the case of Díaz's short story, a Dominican housemaid and a Dominican deliveryman come across each other in a predominantly white New Jersey suburb. While neither has been trying to "pass" in the 19th-century sense, the woman is concealing her identity by staying inside a white man's house, and she does everything she can to forestall interactions with the deliveryman, who has the cultural sensibility to identify her and expose her lifestyle. For those who pass, another Latino will most likely sense traces of a bilingual upbringing in the person's speech patterns or mannerisms, as was the case in this short story. Depending on the community in which a person lives, the decision to pass is often made based on a deep awareness of racism and discrimination. Sometimes the sense of shame about being different can be traced back to the pain that parents or grandparents went through in earlier decades when there was even less tolerance for Latinos than there is now.

Another phenomenon to consider is the Hispanic who resents being told that he or she does not look Hispanic. In the same short story by Díaz, for instance, in their first conversation, the housemaid tells the deliveryman that he does not look Dominican, which only motivates the deliveryman to prove his ethnic identity more vehemently. One might call this "antipassing," or the painful act of having to publicly reaffirm one's Latino status to counteract having the physical appearance of another race.

Both passing and antipassing, besides having a political side, are extremely personal acts that can have a far deeper emotional impact on Latinos than outsiders might guess. Comments such as, "You don't look Latino," may tap into lifelong internal struggles and cause a great deal of pain for the person to whom the remark is directed. In an ideal society everyone would understand the connection between what we call "race" and what we actually understand as "culture," and an absence of prejudice would make passing and antipassing entirely unnecessary.

RELATED ARTICLES
Discrimination; Mestizaje; Race.

FURTHER READING
Chestnutt, Charles. *House behind the Cedars.* 1900. Reprint. London: Penguin, 1993.
Craft, William, and Ellen Craft. *Running a Thousand Miles to Freedom.* New York: Arno Press, 1969.
Díaz, Junot. "Edison, New Jersey." In *Drown.* New York: Riverhead Bks., 1996.
Fanon, Frantz. *Black Skin, White Masks.* New York: Grove, 1967.
Foster, Frances Smith. *Witnessing Slavery: the Development of the Ante-Bellum Slave Narratives.* Westport, Conn.: Greenwood Press, 1979.
Harper, Frances E. W. "Iola Leroy." In *Three Classic African-American Novels.* Ed. by Henry Louis Gates, Jr. New York: Vintage, 1990.
Larsen, Nella. *Passing.* New York: Modern Lib., 2000.
Radcliffe, Sarah, and Sallie Westwood. *Remaking the Nation: Place, Identity and Politics in Latin America.* London: Routledge, 1996.
Rodriguez, America. *Making Latino News: Race, Language, Class.* Thousand Oaks, Calif.: Sage Pubns., 1999.
Sollers, Werner. *Neither Black nor White yet Both: Thematic Explorations of Interracial Literature.* New York: Oxford Univ. Press, 1997.

ROBERT OSCAR LOPEZ

PAU-LLOSA, RICARDO

Born: May 17, 1954; Havana, Cuba

A major poet writing primarily in English and an art critic and curator focusing on 20th-century Latin American art, Ricardo Manuel Pau-Llosa was born to working-class parents, Ricardo Pau and Maria Llosa, who fled Cuba soon after the communists rose to power in 1959. Pau-Llosa, who has lived in the United States since 1960, received a bachelor's degree from Florida International University in 1974 and a master's degree in English from Florida Atlantic University in 1976. His five books of poetry are *Sorting Metaphors* (1983; winner of the first national competition for the Anhinga Prize), *Bread of the Imagined* (1992), *Cuba* (1993; the 100th title in the Carnegie-Mellon University Press Poetry Series), *Vereda Tropical* (1999), and *The Mastery Impulse* (2003).

Influenced by philosopher Edmund Husserl and phenomenology, Pau-Llosa's early poetry expanded metaphor and other forms of figurative language (or tropes) with the aim of giving everyday perceptions the ambiguity and panoramic quality of the dream state. Expounding on Pablo Neruda's *Odas Elemen-*

tales, Pau-Llosa composed poems—many without syntax—whose overpowering chain of metaphors linked common images (such as a thumb print in "Swirling Lines," in *Bread*) to numerous other events and objects. His goal was to ground contemplation of the infinite and the poetic act in the physical world. As Richard Wilbur wrote about Pau-Llosa's first collection, "This is a poetry of great imaginative strength, in which oddity sharpens one's sense of the real." Other early influences included Rainer Maria Rilke, Wallace Stevens, Jorge Luis Borges, and Derek Walcott.

With *Cuba,* the first major book by a Cuban American poet that dealt entirely with the island and exile, Pau-Llosa turned the conventions of autobiographical verse into an exploration of the mechanics of memory. He projected, in a conversational tone, the loss of Cuba as a historical, rather than a personal, catastrophe. In a widely anthologized poem from this collection, "Frutas," the speaker recalls his first childhood encounter in exile with Cuba's tropical fruits in a manner that evokes Plato's Allegory of the Cave and Proust, yet is free of nostalgia. His fourth collection, *Vereda Tropical,* heightens the poet's interest in what he calls the "theatrical nature" of all experience, with poems set in Miami cabarets. In "Wikly at the Conga Drums," the immediacy of the performance is what awakens the music's link to personal identity and the forces of history. *The Mastery Impulse* closes this trilogy with a paean to the imagination as the saving force that binds experience to memory and the pursuit of meaning in life. In "Parable" it is trope-making rather than worship that guides transcendence. As Eric Ormsby has said, Pau-Llosa may be the "only American poet now writing who combines an intense lyric gift with a tragic historical sense." Pamela Stewart has observed that Pau-Llosa's is "a poetry of complicated optimism."

Pau-Llosa's ground-breaking art criticism spans a quarter century, devising a theoretical basis on which to see Latin American art as distinct yet part of the Western tradition. He has concentrated on how the region's visual artists use tropes to enrich representation, rather than reduce or eliminate it as has been largely the case in North American and European modernism. For Pau-Llosa, this distinction is pivotal for understanding even nonreferential artists such as Rogelio Polesello and Jesús Soto. He cocurated the traveling survey of exile art, Outside Cuba/Fuera de Cuba, at Rutgers in 1987 and authored the critical text in its book-length catalog. He has published studies on Rafael Soriano, Rolando López Dirube, Fernando de Szyszlo, Olga de Amaral, Clarence Holbrook Carter, Arnaldo Roche-Rabell, and Humberto Calzada. From 1982 to 1993 Pau-Llosa was a senior editor of *Art International.* He has served as curator and juror in numerous group exhibitions, including the 1997 and 1999 Lima Biennials (Peru) and the 1992 Eco-Art exhibition in Rio de Janeiro, Brazil.

Poetry and art criticism have had an impact on each other in Pau-Llosa's aesthetics. Not only are a significant portion of his poems inspired by specific paintings, sculptures, and photographs, but art has also shaped the visual intensity and originality of his literary work. Conversely, his sensitivity to ideas and the workings of metaphor and other tropes, as well as his ability to shed light on the creative process, make him one of the most respected art critics of his generation.

RELATED ARTICLES

Art Criticism; Literature, Latin American.

FURTHER READING

Dick, Bruce Allen. *Poet's Truth: Conversations with Latino/a Poets.* Tucson: Univ. of Ariz. Press, 2003.

Luís, William. *Dance between Two Cultures: Latino Caribbean Literature Written in the United States.* Nashville, Tenn.: Vanderbilt Univ. Press, 1997.

Martínez, Dionisio D. "A Voice for an Inarticulate Hunger." Prologue to *Bread of the Imagined,* by Ricardo Pau-Llosa. Tempe, Ariz.: Bilingual Press, 1991.

Milián, Alberto. "Defying Time and History: Interview with Ricardo Pau-Llosa." *Mercury Rising* 15, no. 1 (Summer 2003).

Moreno, Gean. "A New, Unique Reality–The Poem Itself: An Interview with Ricardo Pau-Llosa." *Bloomsbury Review* 15, no. 1 (January-February 1995).

Pau-Llosa, Ricardo. "The Wages of Exile." In *Re-membering Cuba: Legacy of a Diaspora.* Ed. by Andrea O'Reilly Herrera. Austin: Univ. of Tex. Press, 2001.

Pulido, José. "Rompiendo el silencio de la cotidianidad: entrevista con Ricardo Pau-Llosa." *BCV Cultural* Caracas, Venezuela; October 2002.

ALBERTO MILIÁN

PAZ, OCTAVIO

Born: March 31, 1914; Mexico City, Mexico
Died: April 20, 1998; Mexico City, Mexico

For many years Octavio Paz's 1950 essay *The Labyrinth of Solitude* (translated in 1961) has been the paradigm for polemical views of the role and psychic composition of Mexicans (and by extension Latinos) in the United States. This is particularly evident in the chapter "Pachucos and other Extremes," whose impact on Latino literatures can be perceived in their representation of youth as a symbol of love, horror, and loathing; an embodiment of liberty and the forbidden; and, above all, as an enigma. Paz's vision was roughly translated into "craziness" by Latino writers, and his imprint can be traced from Alurista's (Alberto H. Urista) poetry in *El ombligo de Aztlán* to Luis J. Rodríguez's *Always Running: La vida loca; Gang Days in L.A.* (1993), and Yxta Maya Murray's *Locas* (1997).

As Paz's worldwide fame increased, he and his work became exemplary for the universality Latino writers can achieve. A volume published after he received the Nobel Prize in 1990, *The Double Flame: Love and Eroticism* (1993, translated in 1995), reiterated his worth as one of the most original essayists in any language, a polymath who held his own, and then some, with Eliot, Pound, Valery, and many others. That essay, emblematic of his lifelong thematic interests (love, human alienation, religion, history) also proves that "Latin roots" were always a motherlode for the hundreds of poems, essays, social philosophy, and literary and art criticism he wrote, as well as for the worldview that emerges from the flouting and mixing of those fields.

There is also no denying his interest in Mexico's indigenous past, as well as his own ethnic hybridity (his ancestry was Spanish and Indian). The mere fact that he is still a sought-after authority for understanding New World culture, especially as he describes its mixed roots in another classic essay, *Sor Juana; or, The Traps of Faith* (1982, translated in 1988), speaks wonders for the need to have his work as a constant reference for the acculturation problems still facing Latinos in the 21st century. He is like a pebble inside a shoe, and that is his great contribution toward understanding differences based on objective views of the Latino condition.

When Paz died in 1998, at the age of 84, writer Mario Vargas Llosa said that what defined Paz was "the language of passion." Indeed, from his earliest poems he was daring and original, partaking of just about every cultural interest or influence that came to the Americas. That is his intellectual bequest, and from *Luna silvestre* (Rustic Moon, 1933) to *Tree Within* (1987, translated in 1988) his poetry is a constant search for the ultimate relationship between

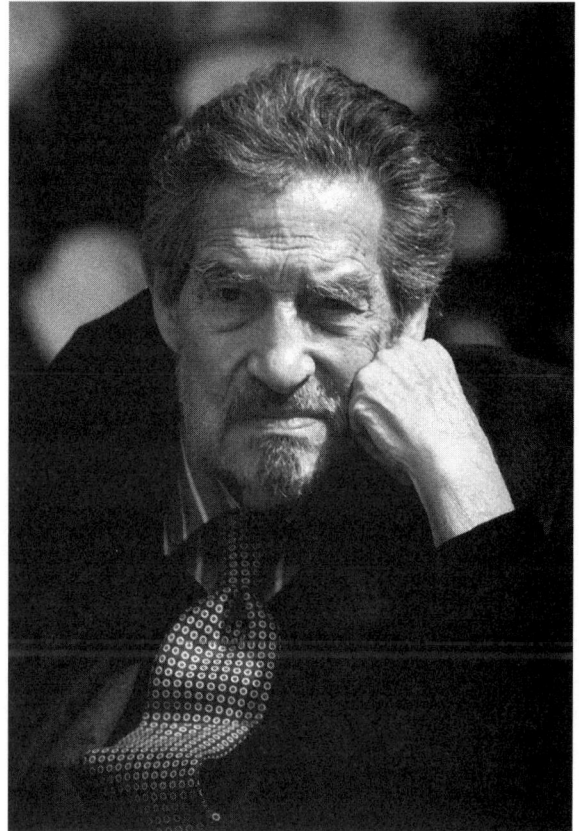

REUTERS / LANDOV

Mexico's Nobel Laureate poet and writer Octavio Paz, December 1997.

representations of human knowledge and the self-referentiality of poetic forms. He succeeded by drawing from sources as disparate as John Cage's theories on music, Eastern philosophy, and his travel experience.

Octavio Paz was born into a middle-class family in Mexico City. He was in Spain at the time of the Spanish Civil War and eventually became a diplomat in France and India. He founded a series of influential magazines in Mexico City and was astonishingly prolific, publishing more than 120 books. His interest in Latinos in the United States was small and unsustained. He wrote a couple of essays on Latino identity and discussed the work of painters such as Martín Ramírez. But mostly he was concerned with foreign policy, especially with the relationship between the United States and Mexico, a topic that appears in several of his books.

He really found a niche in his essays that, while not as personal as his poetry (which does not seem to have had a lasting effect on Latino writers), possess a clarity and elegance rarely found among his very few peers. Although he wrote on Duchamp and Lévi-Strauss, his critical essays on poetry (*The Bow and the Lyre* [1973], *Conjunctions and Disjunctions* [1974], *The Other Mexico* [1972]), and political ones like *The Philanthropic Ogre* (1985) show him to be one of the greatest witnesses to the 20th century, which is when Latino culture came into its own. Still, his greatest legacy is defining Mexico's soul (and to a good degree, Latin America's), and we also owe him for the introduction of pluralism to trite political debate.

RELATED ARTICLES

Art Criticism; Literature, Latin American.

FURTHER READING

Anuario de la Fundación Octavio Paz 1 (1999). Mexico City: Fundación Octavio Paz, 1999.

Fein, John. *Octavio Paz. A Reading of his Major Poems, 1957–1976.* Lexington: Univ. Press of Ky., 1986.

Grenier, Yvon. "Octavio Paz and the Changing Role of Intellectuals in Mexico." *Discourse* 23, no. 2 (Spring 2001): 124–43.

Ivask, Ivar, ed. *The Perpetual Present: The Poetry and Prose of Octavio Paz.* Norman: Univ. of Okla. Press, 1973.

Leal, Luis. "Octavio Paz and the Chicano." *Latin American Literary Review* 10 (1977): 115–123.

Lewis, Bart L. "Fostering the Critical Debate: Octavio Paz on Latin American Literature." *Antípodas* 4 (December 1992): 215–27.

Quiroga, José. *Understanding Octavio Paz.* Columbia: Univ. of S.C. Press, 1999.

Santí, Enrico Mario. *El acto de las palabras: estudios y diálogos con Octavio Paz.* Mexico City: Fondo de Cultura Económica, 1997.

Stavans, Ilan. *Octavio Paz: A Meditation.* Tucson: Univ. of Ariz. Press, 2001.

Wilson, Jason. *Octavio Paz.* Boston: Twayne, 1986.

WILL H. CORRAL

PENITENTES

Los Hermanos Penitentes, also known as La Hermandad de Nuestro Padre Jesús Nazareno, is a lay religious society that has been active in northern New Mexico and southern Colorado since at least the 1830s. Composed of mostly independent local chapters known as *moradas,* the brotherhood has been instrumental both in maintaining religious traditions and in attending to the welfare and spiritual needs of village communities.

As suggested by their name, the Penitentes are devoted to the practice of penance and to the Passion of Jesus. Lenten and Holy Week observances figure centrally in their religious calendar; however, the brotherhood remains active throughout the year in charitable and devotional activities. Its members render aid to families in times of illness, death, and hardship; they assist one another with heavy work; and they organize wakes, funerals, burials, and other religious ceremonies.

By convention Lenten and Holy Week observances were seldom attended by outsiders, but they have been the subject of popular intrigue and commentary for more than a century. Resembling medieval penitential traditions, the observances have included (among other things) prayer, incantation, procession, nighttime worship, cross bearing, self-flagellation and, sometimes, mortification or crucifixion. The sacred lives of the Penitentes encompass a wide range of traditions and sacred commitments that extend beyond the Lenten season. Holy Week rituals remain mostly closed to the public, although some are now openly carried out.

During the 19th century, penitential practices met with stern disapproval from the Catholic Church and the English-reading public, which learned of them through the highly sensationalized accounts of American travel writers, such as Josiah Gregg, whose *Commerce of the Prairies* appeared in 1843, and Charles Lummis, who photographed and described a Lenten procession in his 1888 contribution to *Cosmopolitan.* When Santa Fe Archbishops Jean Baptiste Lamy (1850–1885) and Jean Baptiste Salpointe (1885–1894) attempted to abolish the society and its practices or to bring the society under church authority, their efforts failed. Rather than submit to church authority, the Penitente leadership safeguarded the society's autonomy by legal incorporation of the *moradas.* During the 20th century the church grew more accommodating to the brotherhood and, in 1947, granted the Penitentes official church recognition.

The origins of New Mexico's Penitentes have been a matter of considerable speculation. Many scholars believe the society grew out of the Third Order of Saint Francis, introduced to the region in the 18th century. Some suggest that the brotherhood arose, more precisely, between 1790 and 1810, in the absence of sufficient clergy to attend to the spiritual needs of New Spain's northern frontier settlements. Whatever their origins, it is clear that the brotherhood flourished during the 19th century as Americans flowed into the region, displacing many villagers from their lands. Thus many scholars and lay observers view the Penitentes as a symbol of Nuevo Mexicano ethnic identity and spiritual vitality.

RELATED ARTICLES

Catholicism; Holidays; New Mexico; Religion.

FURTHER READING

Carroll, Michael P. *The Penitente Brotherhood: Patriarchy and Hispano-Catholicism in New Mexico.* Baltimore: Johns Hopkins Univ. Press, 2002.

López Pulido, Alberto. *The Sacred World of the Penitentes.* Washington, D.C.: Smithsonian Inst. Press, 2000.

Wiegle, Marta. *Brothers of Light, Brothers of Blood: The Penitentes of the Southwest.* Albuquerque: Univ. of N.M. Press, 1976.

JOHN NIETO-PHILLIPS

PENNSYLVANIA

The Delaware, Shawnee, and Seneca Indians were the primary indigenous groups to inhabit the present-day state of Pennsylvania. In the 17th century Dutch and English traders made their way into Pennsylvania, followed by Germans and Swedes. But the most famous settlers of Pennsylvania were the Quakers, who sought refuge in William Penn's colony in order to practice religious freedom and live by their own laws. The state of Pennsylvania was admitted as one of the first American states on December 12, 1787.

The presence of Hispanics in Pennsylvania dates to the early 19th century, when Spain ran profitable tobacco and sugar industries in its Caribbean possessions (Cuba and Puerto Rico). As trading relations between the two nations grew stronger, Puerto Rican and Cuban businesspeople, sailors, and merchants frequently made their homes in Philadelphia. By the 1820s Spain had opened a consulate in Philadelphia to facilitate the growing commercial exchange between the United States and Spain's Caribbean colonies.

Philadelphia, however, also provided an early home and base for Cubans and Puerto Ricans who openly advocated independence for their homelands. In 1823 the first Spanish-language newspaper, *El Habanero,* a political, scientific, and literary newspaper, was published in Philadelphia by the Cuban political exile Felix Varela. Later in the century the Cuban revolutionary leader and poet José Martí came to Philadelphia at least twice to discuss political issues with the Latino community. Highly respected for his struggle to achieve independence for his native

land, Martí lost his life in Cuba on May 19, 1895, while fighting to achieve his goals.

For most of the 19th century, a steady stream of Cubans and Puerto Ricans made their way to Philadelphia, usually to work as *tabaqueros* (tobacco laborers) in Philadelphia's expanding tobacco industry. Famous throughout the world for their skill in producing quality cigars, Cuban and Puerto Rican businesspeople established the Spanish-Cuban Auxiliary of the Cigar Makers International Union in Philadelphia in 1877.

In 1917 the Jones Act granted all Puerto Ricans American citizenship, which gave them unrestricted movement between the mainland and the island of Puerto Rico, leading to an influx of Puerto Rican migrants in the 1920s. This migration picked up in the next three decades as Puerto Ricans sought employment in the agricultural industry and the steel mills of eastern and southeastern Pennsylvania.

Only 7,350 persons of Hispanic origin were tallied in the entire state of Pennsylvania in the 1940 census. But, in the aftermath of World War II, larger numbers of Puerto Ricans made their way to Pennsylvania to work as migrant farm laborers in the farm areas surrounding Philadelphia, Allentown, and Reading. Other Latinos were recruited by the poultry trade of Lancaster County. However, sometimes disputes broke out between the Puerto Ricans and their neighbors. After the 1953 Spring Garden Riots, an office for Hispanic Affairs was established in Philadelphia.

In the 1960s and 1970s many Puerto Ricans living in the New York and Massachusetts areas moved a short distance to Pennsylvania to find better job opportunities. By the time of the 1960 census, 21,206 Puerto Ricans were living in the state of Pennsylvania, representing the fifth largest population of Puerto Ricans, after New York, New Jersey, Illinois, and California. However, many Latino families in Pennsylvania faced a language barrier within the dominant Anglo society. As a result, they sometimes had difficulty getting access to basic social and health services.

The Latino population of Pennsylvania was tallied in 1970 at 44,263. By 1980 the population of Latinos had more than tripled to 153,961. Of this total, 91,802 were Puerto Ricans, representing 60 percent of the Latino population. The Hispanic population of Pennsylvania in 1990 was tallied at 232,262 persons, or 2 percent of the state's 11.9 million inhabitants.

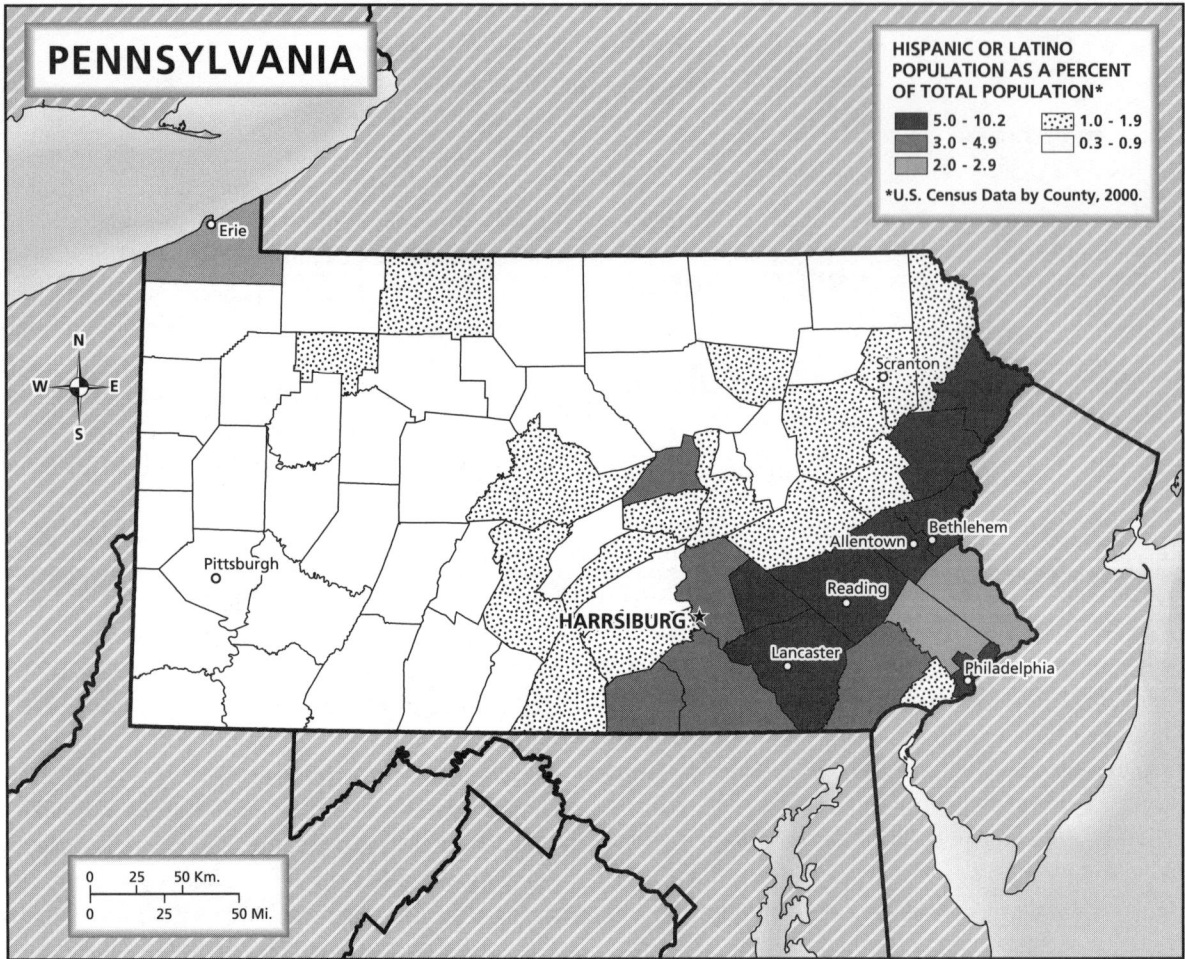

Although Pennsylvania is only the 32d largest state in terms of land area, it was, by 2000, the 6th most populous American state, with a population of 12,281,054. Persons of Hispanic or Latino origin numbered 394,088, or 3.2 percent of the state population, much smaller than the national percentage of 12.5 percent. Of the 394,088 Hispanics, 228,557 Puerto Ricans lived in Pennsylvania, giving it the fourth largest Puerto Rican population (after New York, Florida, and New Jersey). Puerto Ricans also represented almost 58 percent of the total Hispanic population and 1.9 percent of the state population. Mexican Americans, on the other hand, had a population of 55,178, representing only 14 percent of the total Hispanic population. In addition, 12,186 Dominicans were also tallied in the census, giving Pennsylvania the sixth largest population of that ethnic group. Pennsylvania, with 10,363 Cuban Americans residing within its borders, had the ninth largest population of Cubans in the United States.

In 2000 Philadelphia County saw a significant increase in its own Hispanic population to 128,928, a 45 percent increase from 89,193 in 1990. This is true despite the fact that the population of the whole city fell by 4 percent between 1990 and 2000. With 8.5 percent of the city's population, Latinos were concentrated in several communities, including North Philadelphia, Kensington, Olney, and Spring Garden. To the north the Latino population of Monroe County in northeast Pennsylvania increased by more than 300 percent, reaching 6.6 percent. The lion's share of this growth was a result of the county's proximity to the Puerto Rican communities of New York and New Jersey.

The influx of Mexican laborers in the 1960s produced enclaves of migrant laborers in Pennsylvania, primarily in Chester county, where many of the Mexican laborers found employment in the local mushroom industry. In the following decades the intensification of crop production created a greater need for farmworkers, a large number of whom were from the Mexican state of Guanajuato.

At the request of several Latino leaders from the Philadelphia area, Governor Milton Shapp, on December 7, 1971, issued an executive order establishing the Governor's Council on Opportunity for the Spanish Speaking. The council was established to help remove obstacles in the hiring of bilingual employees in state government. Then, on December 4, 1979, Governor Dick Thornburgh created the Governor's Council on the Hispanic Community. The Council was given the responsibility of ensuring that Latinos receive equal opportunities and treatment under the laws of the Commonwealth. In addition, the Council had the authority to evaluate the effectiveness of state programs, which affected the Latino community.

On January 26, 1989, following a historic meeting with Pennsylvania Latino leaders, Governor Robert P. Casey signed Executive Order 1989-1 and rescinded Executive Order 1979-16, establishing the Governor's Advisory Commission on Latino Affairs (GACLA). To support statewide economic development, GACLA helped to establish the Pennsylvania Latino Chamber of Commerce. GACLA also facilitated the creation of the Pennsylvania Association of Latino Organizations (PALO), a statewide nonprofit organization dedicated to strengthening local community-based organizations. Both organizations have actively worked with the Pennsylvania Department of Education to establish community learning centers throughout the state.

On April 2, 2003, Governor Edward G. Rendell appointed Pedro Cortés the acting secretary of the Commonwealth. The appointment was confirmed by the Pennsylvania Senate on May 13, 2003, making Secretary Cortés the first Latino state cabinet member in the Commonwealth. Prior to taking the reins at the Department of State, Cortés was the executive director of the Pennsylvania Governor's Advisory Commission on Latino Affairs. A native of Puerto Rico, Cortés has lived in Harrisburg since 1990 and was educated in both Massachusetts and Pennsylvania.

In recognition of Pennsylvania's growing Latino community, former vice president Albert Gore and secretary of energy Bill Richardson addressed Latino elected and appointed officials from all over the United States at the National Association of Latino Elected and Appointed Officials (NALEO) 16th Annual Conference, which was held in Philadelphia in June 1999.

Benjamin Ramos, a native of Aguas Buenas, Puerto Rico, was elected as the representative for Pennsylvania's 180th Legislative District, where he served from 1994 through 2000. Ramos had also served as the deputy mayor for the city of Philadelphia from 1992 to 1994. As a state representative, Ramos had worked to improve adult basic education and curb school violence.

In 2000 Angel Cruz defeated Representative Cortés and was elected as the new representative of the 180th District in Pennsylvania's State House of Representatives. Before his election, Representative Cruz had worked as a union organizer and as a former aide to Philadelphia city councilman Rick Mariano. In 2002, Representative Cruz was reelected for his second term and at the time was Pennsylvania's only Hispanic member of the House of Representatives.

By the beginning of the 21st century, Philadelphia had at least 50 community-based Latino service organizations that were able to provide social and educational resources for the Spanish-speaking community. The Pennsylvania Statewide Latino Coalition (PSLC) is a nonprofit, nonpartisan alliance of Latino leaders, organizations, community activists, students, and individuals that serves as a statewide institutional catalyst for positive social change and political advancement. This wide array of organizations are working to help Latinos adjust to changing demographics and issues in various parts of the state.

Congreso de Latinos Unidos was founded in 1977 by Puerto Rican activists as a community-based organization that works in the impoverished neighborhoods of eastern North Philadelphia, where most of the city's Latino community resides. Through a variety of social services and community development projects, Congreso works to empower people and creates opportunities for learning and self-development. The Asociación De Puertorriqueños En Marcha (APM) was founded in the northeastern section of Philadelphia to provide for the needs of Puerto Ricans living in the urban areas.

ASPIRA of Pennsylvania was established in 1971 as an advocate agency for Latino residents. Its mission is to assist the Latino community to grow and prosper in Pennsylvania. GACLA makes recommendations to the governor on policies, procedures, and legislation, to make the state more responsive to the needs of Latino residents.

In 1992 Hernán Guaracao and his wife, Elizabeth, began publication of a Spanish-language newspaper, *Al Día*. This weekly newspaper provides news and information to the Latino Community in the Greater "Filadelfia" area and the Delaware Valley. That year the Hispanic Chamber of Commerce in Western Pennsylvania was established in Pittsburgh to create opportunities for the Hispanic community in commerce and business development. Their Web site offers many links to important resources for Spanish-speaking individuals.

RELATED ARTICLES

Immigration, Latino.

FURTHER READING

Escobar-Haskins, Lillian. *Latinos in Erie, Pennsylvania. Myths and Realities: Growing Beyond the Stereotypes.* Erie, Penn.: Hispanic Am. Council of Erie, 1995.

Garcia, Victor Q. *Mexican Enclaves in the U.S. Northeast: Immigrant and Migrant Mushroom Workers in Southern Chester County, Pennsylvania.* East Lansing, Mich.: Julian Samora Res. Inst., Mich. State Univ., 1997 [JSRI Research Report 27].

Koss, Joan Dee. *Puerto Ricans in Philadelphia: Migration and Accommodation.* Doctoral thesis, 1965. Philadelphia: Univ. of Penn.

Whalen, Carmen Teresa. *From Puerto Rico to Philadelphia: Puerto Rican Workers and Postwar Economies.* Philadelphia: Temple Univ. Press, 2001.

JOHN P. SCHMAL

PEREZ, SELENA QUINTANILLA. *See* SELENA.

PÉREZ DE VILLAGRÁ, GASPAR

Born: 1555; Puebla de los Ángeles, Mexico
Died: 1620; Unknown

Known not only as one of the early chroniclers of the conquest of the Americas but as one of the forerunners of Latino literature in the United States for his epic poem *Historia de la Nueva México,* Gaspar Pérez de Villagrá was born in Puebla de los Angeles (near Mexico City) in 1555. His father, Hernán Pérez de Villagrá, was a Spaniard from Campos de Villagrán. Although Gaspar Pérez de Villagrá was a creole by birth, his generation of Spaniards born in the New World did not feel any less Spanish than those born in Spain. Little is known about his youth or his early adulthood. He was, however, part of the small group of privileged creoles who studied in

Spain, obtaining his degree from the University of Salamanca.

It is not known when Pérez de Villagrá returned to New Spain, but it must have been prior to his association with Don Juan de Oñate, in 1596. He was made captain and legal officer of Juan de Oñate's expedition into New Mexico. During that expedition Pérez de Villagrá composed the reputed epic poem *Historia de la Nueva México,* in which he is also one of the protagonists who help in the pacification and the political and social organization of the new territory.

After the expedition ended, his whereabouts are not fully known. He served as a major from 1601–1603, in Guanacevi and Nuestra Señora de Alancón in Nueva Vizcaya, before returning to Spain in 1605. While in Spain it is believed that he followed the court from Madrid to Valladolid in 1605 and that later he established himself in Alcalá de Henares, where his work *Historia de la Nueva México* was published in 1610.

It was Pérez de Villagrá's intention that his epic poem constitute a plea to King Phillip III for a position in the New World. The king, however, did not hear his petitions, because in 1614 Pérez de Villagrá was convicted in absentia of the death of two deserters from the Juan de Oñate expedition. Pérez de Villagrá finally succeeded in his pleas, and in 1620 he was appointed mayor of Zapotitlán in Guatemala. He died on his way to the post in 1620.

Pérez de Villagrá's importance lies more in his literary work than in his role as a captain or mayor. His *Historia de la Nueva México* is a historical account of the conquest of New Mexico written in the characteristic epic poetry common in the Renaissance: hendecasyllabic (11-syllable) verse separated into cantos. An excerpt from the 34-canto poem, with English translation (Encinias, Rodríguez, and Sánchez, 1992), follows:

> Las armas y el varón heroico canto,
> El ser, valor, prudencia y alto esfuerzo
> De aquel cuya paciencia no rendida,
> Por un mar de disgustos arrojada,
> A pesar de a envidia ponzoñosa
> Los hechos y prohezas va encumbrando
> De aquellos españoles valerosos (Canto I)

> I sing of arms and the heroic man
> The being, courage, care, and high emprise
> Of him whose unconquered patience
> Though cast upon a sea of cares,

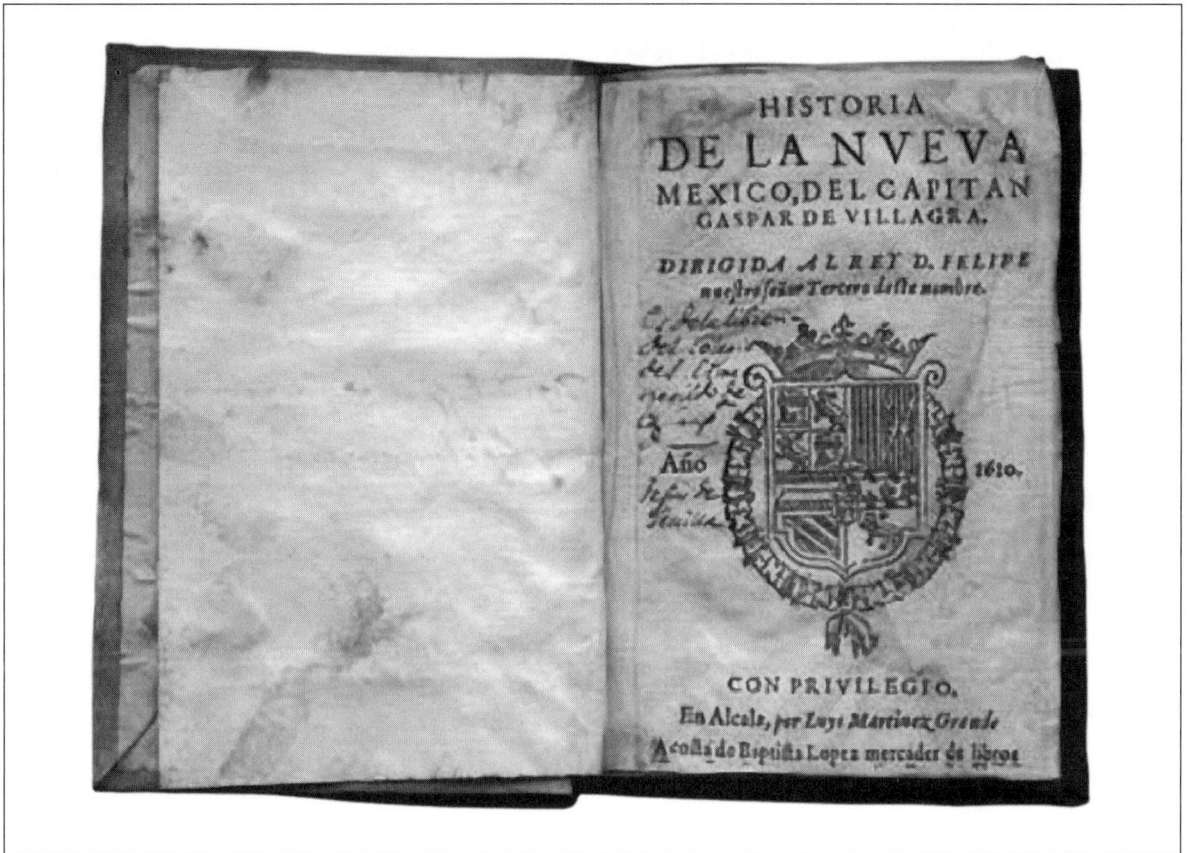

Title page of the *Historia de la Nueva México,* by Gaspar Pérez de Villagrá, 1610.

In spite of envy slanderous,
In raising to new heights the feats, the deeds
Of those brave spaniards

Some critics have considered the *Historia* to be an advance to what would later become the historical novels of 19th-century Europe, but within the poetic tradition of the Renaissance. Although Pérez de Villagrá was in Spain at the same time that Cervantes published *Don Quixote,* it is not known if the authors had knowledge of each other's works.

In recent years—and especially since the publication by the University of New Mexico Press of the critical edition of *Historia de la Nueva México* in 1992—there has been an attempt to place Pérez de Villagrá as one of the foundational figures in the Latino literary tradition. He is untrustworthy when it comes to historical and chronological events, his depiction of the aboriginal population has been criticized as paternalistic, and as a poet Pérez de Villagrá can be uninspiring and repetitive. Still, his work announces some of the leitmotifs that would define the tradition for future generations, in particular from the late 19th century onward.

RELATED ARTICLES

Colonial Period; de Oñate, Juan; Explorers and Chroniclers; History; New Mexico.

FURTHER READING

Leal, Luis. "Poetic Discourse in Pérez de Villagrá's *Historia de la Nueva México.*" In *Reconstructing a Chicano/a Literary Heritage: Hispanic Colonial Literature of the Southwest.* Ed. by María Herrera-Sobek. Tucson: Univ. of Ariz. Press, 1993.

Pérez de Villagrá, Gaspar. *Historia de Nuevo México.* Ed. by Mercedes Junquera. Madrid: Historia 16, 1989.

Pérez de Villagrá, Gaspar. *Historia de la Nueva México, 1610: A Critical and Annotated Spanish/English Edition.* Tr. and ed. by Miguel Encinias, Alfred Rodríguez, and Joseph Sánchez. Albuquerque: Univ. of N.Mex. Press, 1992.

CÉSAR ALEGRE

PERSIAN GULF WARS

On August 2, 1990, President Saddam Hussein of Iraq invaded the small neighboring state of Kuwait, accusing the Arab emirate of overproduction of oil and theft of Iraqi oil. The small emirate was overwhelmed and occupied very quickly by an army that was numerically superior to Kuwait's small military force. On November 29, 1990, in response to Iraq's unilateral action, the United Nations Security Council authorized the use of force against Iraq if Saddam failed to withdraw his forces from Kuwait by January 15, 1991.

In the next two months a massive military buildup of United States forces took place. By the time that Operation Desert Storm—the liberation of Kuwait—had commenced on January 16, 1991, the United States had mobilized a military force of 532,000 men and women in strategic positions throughout the Persian Gulf area. Out of this considerable force, some 25,000 Hispanic men and women served in uniform, representing less than 5 percent of all armed forces personnel. By the time the war ended on April 6, 1991, 367 servicemen and women had died while on active duty, including 147 who were killed in combat action. When the final count was tallied, 17 Latinos—or 5 percent of the total casualties—had died in combat.

In the period of demobilization following the Gulf War, the representation of Latinos in the armed forces dropped considerably. However, in 1999 the Department of Defense, recognizing that Hispanic Americans had a greater propensity than most other ethnic groups to enlist in the armed forces, initiated recruitment efforts designed to bring more Hispanic soldiers into the armed services. The aggressive recruitment campaign was very successful, and by the end of September 2001, the Pew Hispanic Center reported that there were 109,487 Hispanics in the enlisted ranks, representing about 9.5 percent of the active-duty enlisted force. The service with the largest percentage of Latinos was the Marine Corps, where almost 14 percent of the personnel were Hispanic. In contrast, the representation of Hispanics in the U.S. Air Force was only 5.57 percent, the least of all the services.

With the terrorist attacks on American soil of September 11, 2001, and the subsequent invasion of Afghanistan, the American people experienced a surge in their collective patriotism that had not been seen since World War II. This patriotic fervor touched the Latino community as much as it did any other ethnic group, and by 2002 the Pentagon reported that the total number of Latinos serving in the military as a whole was 129,254 persons, or 6 percent of the total American military force. Of this number, 55,380 were of Mexican origin, 22,881 came from Puerto Rican background, and another 1,740 were of Cuban descent.

Twelve years after the Desert Storm campaign, President George W. Bush, son of the first President Bush, sent American forces back to the Persian Gulf area with the express intention of overthrowing Saddam Hussein. This campaign, dubbed Operation Iraqi Freedom, was set into motion on March 21, 2003, and within five weeks the Iraqi dictator was forced to flee his capital.

By the time American forces had stepped inside Iraq, some 15,000 soldiers of Hispanic background were actually deployed in the Persian Gulf, representing 6 percent of the total U.S. forces involved in the operation. In the first month of the war, as the casualties began to mount, several Latinos serving in uniform were listed among those who were killed in action. According to the Department of Defense, total military deaths in Operation Iraqi Freedom through April 30, 2003—the end of regular combat operations—amounted to 138 soldiers. Of this total, 24 soldiers—or 18 percent—were classified as Hispanic or Latino.

On May 1 President Bush declared that major combat in the Iraqi theater was over. However, the subsequent occupation of Iraq by American forces turned out to be a more difficult task than the administration had anticipated. As a result, from May 1, 2003, to February 26, 2004, the total number of military deaths reached 411 men and women, including 40 Latinos, who represented 10 percent of the military deaths. Among the Latinos who died in combat, at least 12 were from California and another 13 from Texas.

In the first Gulf War, America's military commitment had been associated with the liberation of Kuwait. However, in the second Gulf War, America's preemptive strike against the Iraqi dictatorship became a divisive issue for some Latino communities. Although Hispanic Americans have traditionally jumped at the opportunity to serve their nation in a

A U.S. Marine Force protection specialist from the Combined Joint Task Force Consequence Management, in Operation Iraqi Freedom, Camp Doha, Kuwait, 2003.

time of need, some community leaders, like other Americans, questioned American motives for the war.

One of the most important issues among Latinos involved the well-known fact that some young Chicano men and women in California and Texas had enlisted in the armed forces in order to learn a profession and to escape the poverty of their barrio communities. Latino activists and military statisticians also made note of Latinos' preference for enlisting in the Marine Corps, possibly the result of the Marines' aggressive recruiting techniques. It was this preference that put Latinos on the front lines in great numbers and, as a result, led to a high rate of combat deaths during the first month of the war.

On July 3, 2002, President Bush had signed Executive Order 13269, providing "expedited naturalization for aliens and noncitizen nationals" serving in the period following the September 11, terrorist attacks. With this decree, foreign residents who enrolled in the armed forces would qualify for citizenship in less than the five years required for other noncitizens. Newspaper columnists lamented the fact that this executive order provided young Latinos born in other countries with a strong incentive to join the armed services to speed up the citizenship process.

Of great concern to the Latino community was the fact that the majority of Hispanic soldiers were privates, the lowest rank of enlisted military personnel. The presence of so many Latinos in the lower rungs of the military hierarchy may have been due, in large part, to the lower educational level of many Hispanics. And, unfortunately, the lower-level functions of Hispanic enlisted personnel put many of these soldiers on the front lines, in the line of fire.

According to 2001 Department of Defense statistics, Latinos made up 17.7 percent of the "infantry, gun crews, and seamanship" occupations in all the service branches. Of the Latinos and Latinas in the army, 24.7 percent occupied these jobs; for the Marine Corps, the figure was 19.7 percent. Although women are not permitted to serve in the infantry, they are given responsibilities with gun crews and supply crews. The presence of women in these potentially dangerous situations became sadly apparent when 15 soldiers of the 507th Maintenance Company were killed or captured by Iraqi forces.

With the end of major combat operations and the occupation of Iraq by American forces, insurgent forces began to wage a hit-and-run terrorist campaign against coalition forces. As the year progressed, the terrorist attacks against American targets grew more determined and more deadly. As a result, many of the Latinas assigned to marine and army units had become as vulnerable to attack as their male compatriots.

Although Latinos and Latinas in the military were overrepresented in hazardous combat positions, their presence in the higher ranks was less conspicuous. The Pew Hispanic Center pointed out that Hispanics made up only 3.8 percent of the entire active-duty officer corps. However, on June 14, 2003, Lieutenant General Ricardo S. Sánchez was appointed as the commander of all coalition ground forces in Iraq. A native of Rio Grande City in southern Texas, Sánchez had been commissioned into the United States Army after his graduation from Texas A&M University as a distinguished military graduate. During the next three decades, he achieved a steady string of promotions, leading up to his promotion as a three-star general.

As commanding officer of 120,000 U.S. troops and some 30,000 military staff from coalition countries, Sánchez became the highest-ranking Hispanic in the U.S. Army. Recognizing Sánchez as an important role model for Latino youth, *Hispanic Magazine* selected him as "Hispanic of the Year" in its December 2003 edition.

Although the controversy over America's preemptive strike against Saddam Hussein continued to be a topic of discussion, Latinos have remained staunch in their support for their sons and daughters who have served in the Persian Gulf. Many Americans, in fact, have pointed out the strong sense of patriotism and duty exhibited by young men and women of Latino communities across the country. On October 2, 2003, President Bush, in a White House ceremony celebrating the beginning of Hispanic Heritage Month, paid tribute to the achievement of Hispanic Americans and their contributions to America and referred to Latinos as "an incredibly important part of our country."

RELATED ARTICLES
Military, United States.

FURTHER READING
Cevallos, Diego. "Iraq-Mexico: Mexicans on the Front-Line." *Inter Press Service News Agency* (April 3, 2003).
Executive Order 13269. *Expedited Naturalization of Aliens and Noncitizen Nationals Serving in an Active-Duty Status during the War on Terrorism. Federal Register.* 67 FR 45287 (July 8, 2002).
Giordono, Joseph. "Brand New Day: More Hispanics Taking Charge in the Military." *Stripes Sunday Magazine* (October 5, 2003.)
Hoffman, Lisa, and Thomas Hargrove. "Death Has No Bias among U.S. Soldiers in Iraq." *Scripps Howard News Service* (January 14, 2004).
Holston, Mark. "Soldier of Fortune: Far from Home, Lt. Gen. Ricardo Sánchez Leads the Effort to Stabilize Postwar Iraq." *Hispanic Magazine* (December 2003).
Pew Hispanic Center. *Fact Sheet: Hispanics in the Military* (March 27, 2003).

SELECTED WEB SITE
Directorate for Information Operations and Reports. Military Casualty Reports.
http://www.dior.whs.mil/mmid/casualty/castop.htm

JOHN P. SCHMAL

PERUVIAN AMERICANS

Some 2 million Peruvians currently reside outside of Peru, mostly in the United States, South America, and Western Europe. Between 1971 and 2001 the Immigration and Naturalization Service (INS) admitted 209,618 documented Peruvian immigrants, and the U.S. Census counted 60,440 Peruvian immigrants in 1980, 151,837 in 1990, and 276,981 in 2000 (381,850 by adjusted 2000 Hispanic/Latino figures). In 1990 Peruvians were the second largest South American immigrant group in the United States (behind Colombians), but by 2000 they were the third largest (behind Colombians and Ecuadorians). In 1999 Peru received $800 million in remittances from migrants abroad.

There are five broad phases of U.S.-bound Peruvian migration. In the first phase (late 19th century), Peruvian and other South American laborers migrated to California during the Gold Rush. In the second phase (early 20th century), new pioneer Peruvian migrants were recruited to work in textile mills near Paterson, New Jersey. After World War II, migration increased in response to rising U.S. demand for industrial labor, as well as to oil boom and modernization policies in Peru, which uprooted more Peruvians from their traditional rural lifestyles and provided them with new incentives to migrate abroad (usually to the larger cities in Peru but later to other countries, too). Owing to these earlier migrations, there is now a sizable number of second- and third-generation Peruvians living in the United States.

In the third phase (late 1960s through 1980s), U.S.-bound Peruvian migration increased and diversified. Highly skilled professionals and technicians began migrating in response to 1965 changes in U.S. immigration law and new employment-based economic policies instituted under the Carter and Reagan administrations. By the early 1980s Peruvian immigrants exhibited great socioeconomic diversity, and most had migrated because economic and social mobility were becoming increasingly harder to attain in Peru.

The fourth phase of Peruvian migration (1980s to 1992) was both economic and political. Economically, Peruvian industrial, export agriculture, and *estancamiento* policies uprooted more manual workers, who had fewer skills and were more likely to come from the Sierra (mountainous regions in the Andes) than were their professional predecessors. During the "lost decade" of the 1980s, urban poverty was exacerbated by an acute economic crisis, rising unemployment and underemployment, and the overcrowding of Peruvian cities owing to continued internal migration from the Sierra and rural areas. Politically, Peru witnessed a massive increase in violence and human rights abuses, starting with the appearance of Shining Path and the Túpac Amaru revolutionary movements and then matched by the rise of a state-sponsored governmental opposition force. This guerrilla and counterguerrilla warfare terrorized the Andean highlands and urban Lima, resulting in thousands of deaths, massive rural displacements, and declines in ordinary Peruvians' confidence in their government. All of these factors combined motivated large numbers of Peruvians to leave their country in the 1980s. Estimated numbers stand somewhere between 200,000 and 600,000, mostly self-identified *andinos* (indigenous persons of rural, lower-class origins). And out of 112,687 Peruvians who left Peru between 1985 and early 1988, 45,095 (40 percent) went to the United States.

The Peruvian military's capture of Shining Path's leader in 1992 ushered in a new period of hope and stability for Peruvians abroad, and many returned home. However, the fifth phase of Peruvian emigration began in the late 1990s, owing to new economic declines and political insecurity in Peru. The "lost decade" of the 1980s, known even in the indigenous language quechua as *década de chaqwa* (decade of chaos), was never fully recovered. Peruvian and Ecuadorian emigration rates hit new highs in 1998, 1999, and 2000. In 2000 alone, 183,000 Peruvians left their home country, a figure more than double that of previous years. Teófilo Altamirano shows that today more women than men are leaving Peru, the "brain drain" emigration of Peruvian professionals continues to be of great concern, roughly one in three Peruvians and Ecuadorians in the United States is undocumented, and Peruvians' migration destinations in the United States have expanded to include all 50 states. In 2000, Peruvian immigrants resided primarily in California (18.3 percent), Florida (18.2 percent), New Jersey (15.9 percent), New York (14.7 percent), and Virginia (6.2 percent), and Paterson, New Jersey, remains the unofficial center of "Little Peru" on the East Coast.

By education and occupation, Peruvians rank on the low end of South American immigrant groups, but higher than Mexicans and most other Central American immigrant groups. Internally, Peruvian immigrants are diverse. Upper-class Peruvian immigrants are likely to have migrated in the 1970s and 1980s, to be of European descent, and to be well adapted in terms of English-language ability, residence, and relationship to American mainstream cultural models. Middle-class Peruvians are likely to have migrated for a more diverse range of reasons and to identify more with the mestizo character of Peruvian national identity. Many hit "glass ceilings" at their jobs or suffer downward mobility because they cannot successfully transfer their professional statuses from Peru to the United States. Finally, lower-class Peruvian immigrants, while the smallest in number, tend to come from rural areas in the Peruvian Sierra. Many speak indigenous languages, such as Quechua or Aymara, instead of or in addition to Spanish, and many are located on the bottom rungs of the U.S. labor market in precarious positions such as factory, construction, and agricultural workers. (For example, several researchers have called attention to the plight of indigenous Peruvian shepherds working on ranches in the American Northwest.)

Peruvian immigrants also differ by region of origin, ethnicity, race, language, and cultural identity.

For example, as Ulises Juan Zevallos Aguilar illustrates, Andean immigrants in the United States broaden traditional ethnolinguistic ideas of the "Andean archipelago" in South America, linking them with Andean migrant settlements in Lima, Guayaquil, and La Paz. He describes how over the past few decades new developments in Peru have resulted in greater emphasis being put on Andean identity there, and argues that this "andeanization" is extending to immigrants in the United States as well. He has identified four broad groups of Peruvians with Andean ancestry in the United States: "bicultural" Quechua-Spanish speaking immigrants; "tricultural" Quechua-Spanish-English-speaking immigrants; "locally indigenous identified" immigrants; and immigrants who have never considered themselves Andean. Within these groups he finds both Incan and local indigenous forms of Andean identification.

Finally, Peruvians are well organized compared with other Latin American immigrant groups. They now have over 450 voluntary associations in the United States, which help new immigrants maintain important cultural values, manage adaptation pressures, organize politically, and collect money to remit home. Among them are large Peruvian American chambers of commerce as well as small Peruvian businesses (especially in the restaurant and tourism industries), immigrant advocacy groups, and an even larger variety of Peruvian churches, restaurants, soccer leagues, and music, dance, and cultural groups (such as the Peru-Inka Cultural Association in Coral Gables, Florida, and the Así es Mi Perú in Lake Worth, Florida). But, as is the case with many immigrant groups, these associations tend to be organized along—and thus also to exclude others by—lines such as class status, region of origin, race, or ethnicity. Therefore, the diversity of recent Peruvian immigration presents new challenges to the community as a whole as it works to define its identity and achieve success in the United States.

RELATED ARTICLES

Cuisine, South American; Immigration, Latino; United States-South America Relations.

FURTHER READING

Altamirano, Teófilo. *Los que se fueron: Peruanos en los Estados Unidos (Those Who Left: Peruvians in the United States).* Lima, Peru: Pontificia Universidad Católica del Peru, Fondo Editorial, 1990.

Altamirano, Teófilo. *Éxodo: Peruanos en el exterior (Exodus: Peruvians Abroad).* Lima, Peru: Pontificia Universidad Católica del Peru, Fondo Editorial, 1992.

Jones–Correa, Michael. *Between Two Nations: The Political Predicament of Latinos in New York City.* Ithaca, N.Y.: Cornell Univ. Press, 1998.

Zevallos Aguilar, Ulises Juan. "Hácia una topografía del archipiélago cultural andino (Toward a Topography of the Andean Cultural Archipelago)." *Socialismo y participacíon* 87 (May 2000): 101–110.

Zevallos Aguilar, Ulises Juan. "Baile, comida y música en la construcción de una identidad cultural subalterna andina en el exilio norteamericano (Dance, Food, and Music in the Construction of a Subaltern Andean Cultural Identity in North American Exile)." In *Convergencia de tiempos: estudios subalternos/contextos latinoamericanos estado, cultura, subalternidad.* Ed. by Ileana Rodríguez. Atlanta, Ga.: Ed. Rodopi, 2001.

HELEN B. MARROW

PEYOTE

Peyote is a cactus plant native to southern Texas and Northern Mexico, known for its hallucinogenic effects when eaten. Peyote "buttons" are harvested and dried crowns of *Lophophora williamsii* and *L. diffusa,* two species of a globular, spineless, and furrowed cactus plant, a little under softball size, found along the Rio Grande and the Chihuahuan plateau. Archeological evidence indicates that peyote, along with other mind-altering plants, was used thousands of years before the arrival of Europeans. In 1560 con-

© RICARDO SANDOVAL/DALLAS MORNING NEWS / KRT

A ripe peyote bulb in the desert near Real de Catorce, Mexico.

quering Spaniards reported its use in northern Mexico by indigenous societies for religious and healing purposes. Its use was proscribed by the Spanish Inquisition, which declared it to be the "work of the devil." Despite centuries of effort to suppress its use, however, it remains as a central community focus in some Mexican Indian groups, as, for example, among the Tarahumaras in their healing practices, and it is deeply embedded in the community and spiritual life of the Huichols, who stubbornly cling to traditions such as the ceremonial peyote hunt.

Religious use of peyote spread north through Indian reservations in the United States in the late 1800s. Combined with Christian concepts, it became part of the ceremonies of the Native American Church (NAC) and was considered to have both spiritual and healing properties. Its emergence was met by missionary and governmental efforts to outlaw its use, but it was also defended by some religious and civil liberties groups as an authentic religious practice. Peyote was eventually legalized for use as an NAC sacrament under principles of religious freedom by acts of the U.S. Congress, last amended in 1994. Other possession of peyote, classified as a Schedule I drug, is forbidden under federal drug laws.

Extolled by writers such as Aldous Huxley and Carlos Castaneda, use of peyote as a psychedelic drug in the United States peaked sharply during the countercultural movement in the decades of the 1960s and 1970s, later to decline. It is classified by the Substance Abuse and Mental Health Services Administration (SAMHSA) as a hallucinogen, but its use is not tracked separately from the substances LSD (lysergic acid diethylamide), PCP (phencyclidine), and "Ecstasy," among others. Although rates vary among different Latino subgroups, illicit use of hallucinogens among Hispanics parallels that of the general population, but peyote tends not to be a drug of choice for casual psychedelic experiences because of its initial unpleasant effects, which are described below.

The primary hallucinatory ingredient of peyote is mescaline, which affects neurotransmission in the brain. Typically it is ingested by eating the ground-up peyote buttons or drinking a tea made from the peyote material. It initially produces nausea and vomiting. Rapid heart rate and feelings of panic are possible. A second, hallucinatory stage follows with alterations of color and form perception and experiences involving "visions," a sense of depersonalization

or "dual existence," and introspective and contemplative moods. In NAC ceremonies it is used in a group setting under the guidance of a "roadman." Repeated use may result in tolerance, but it does not generally produce dependence.

While some Chicanos and other Latinos may reject their Indian connections, others seek to exalt their heritage and proudly identify themselves as either Indian or mestizo. They see a parallel between their own discrimination experiences and the plight of the Huichols, whose spiritual equilibrium as well as the integrity of their traditional territory are threatened by Western inroads. Further, they feel a spiritual connection with this beleaguered but persevering people. For these Chicanos and other mestizo populations, peyote represents both pre-Columbian mystical practices and resistance to European cultural domination and discrimination. Their interest in peyote symbolizes solidarity with indigenous groups and a uniquely Native American spiritual identity.

In the popular imagination, peyote is associated with the character of Don Juan Matus, the shaman in Carlos Castaneda's *Teachings of Don Juan,* a controversial book that stands as a cornerstone of the New Age philosophy. Matus is presented as a Yaqui aboriginal who uses peyote to bring about alternative ways of experiencing reality.

RELATED ARTICLES

Castaneda, Carlos; Drugs; Indigenous Heritage; Religion; Spirituality.

FURTHER READING

Anderson, Edward F. *Peyote: The Divine Cactus.* 2d ed. Tucson: Univ. of Ariz. Press, 1996

Castaneda, Carlos. *The Teachings of Don Juan: A Yaqui Way of Knowledge.* Berkeley: Univ. of Calif. Press, 1968.

National Institute of Drug Abuse. *Drug Use among Racial Minorities.* NIH publication no. 03-3888, rev. September 2003.

Gonzáles, Patrisia, and Roberto Rodríguez. "Indians and Mestizos in the Americas." *Chronicle Features.* http://inform.umd.edu/EdRes/Topic/Diversity/Specific/Race/Specific/Hispanic.

Schaefer, Stacy B. and Peter T. Furst, eds. *People of the Peyote: Huichol Indian History, Religion and Survival.* Albuquerque: Univ. of N.Mex. Press, 1996.

Stewart, Omer C. *Peyote Religion: A History.* Norman: Univ. of Okla. Press, 1987.

United States Congress. *American Indian Religious Freedom Act Amendments of 1994.* Washington, D.C.: USGPO, 1994

CHARLES W. ACKER

PHILIPPINES

Perhaps the least known of all the Latino communities in the United States are the Filipinos. In Southeast Asia, however, distinct from their Muslim, Confucian, and Buddhist neighbors, they are often referred to as "Latinos of the East," reflecting popular images of them as musicians, dancers, and singers. Indeed, their history, Spanish names, mestizo features, religion, and culture—particularly in language and the arts—reflect more than 300 years of Spanish colonization. From 1564 to 1898 the Iberians ruled *Las Islas Filipinas* (now known as the Philippines) and implanted their culture in the archipelago in ways that remain indelibly part of the modern Filipino psyche.

The Philippines was Spain's only colony in Asia, the result of the Portuguese navigator Ferdinand Magellan's globe-girdling expedition on behalf of the Spanish Crown, to find a new route to the Spice Islands. The expedition, down to three ships out of the original five, came across the islands on March 16, 1521, after a harrowing voyage across the Pacific. There, Magellan was slain by Lapu Lapu, a native chief; only one ship managed the return to Spain. It was in 1565, however, that the Philippines, after four exploratory expeditions (1525–1542), was finally settled as a Spanish colony. Its center was Manila, which the conquistador Lopez de Legazpi had wrested from its Muslim rulers, razed to the ground, and, in its place, erected a Spanish-type city with a plaza, church, and town hall making up its focal point—the prototype of other cities and towns in the archipelago. Spanish rule, however, never extended fully over Mindanao, which had been Islamized in the 14th century.

The country's name—derived from Philip II, the Spanish monarch at the time the islands were appropriated—indicates the country's historical beginnings as a legal geographical and political entity of more than 7,000 islands that had, except for the Sultanate in Jolo and cities such as Manila and Cebu (whose rulers held sway over surrounding settlements), existed as a loose collection of towns, or *baranggays,* independent of each other, headed by *datus,* or chieftains.

Originally the term *Filipino* was reserved for the Spaniards, both expatriates and those born on Philippine soil. The indigenous populace was simply referred to as *Indios,* the same term used by the Spanish for the various indigenous groups throughout Latin America. Only after the successful 1896 revolution against Spain (the first in Asia against a Western colonizer) did the term come to include the local population.

The Philippines was ruled administratively through New Spain, or Mexico, both in terms of civil and ecclesiastical authority. Many of the Spanish clergy and civil servants assigned to the Philippines spent years of service in Mexico before crossing the Pacific. However, with Mexico's independence in 1821, the colony was then governed directly from Madrid. The two-and-a-half centuries of contact with Mexico left an indelible imprint on the Asian colony, with Mexicans coming over as soldiers and officers, colonists, or exiles, and settling in Manila and nearby provinces. Two of the most popular religious icons in the country—the Virgin of Antipolo and the Black Nazarene—originated in Mexico and are venerated for their reputed miraculous powers. Mexico's impact on the Asian colony can also be seen in agricultural products brought from the New World, such as the tomato, peanut, chico, avocado, lima bean, achuete, maize, and cacao.

The major link between Mexico and the Philippines lay in the galleon trade, first begun in 1573 and lasting until 1815, when increasing foreign competition rendered the route less profitable. Until then the annual round-trip voyage between Manila and Acapulco, while fraught with danger, was quite lucrative. Ships out of Manila, which served as a major entrepot in Southeast Asia, carried gold, spices from the Moluccas, silks and porcelain from China, and pearls from the Sulu Archipelago. On the return trip the cargo consisted mostly of Mexican silver, which helped pay for the costs of running the colony. The voyages also resulted in arguably the oldest Asian communities in North America, when Manila Men (as Filipino crewmen were called) jumped ship—in Malo, New Orleans, and Acapulco and San Blas in Mexico—to escape abusive masters.

By the late 19th century a nationalist movement emerged, fueled in part by a growing clamor for more autonomy and much needed reforms in civil and ecclesiastical rule, and the influential writings, in Spanish, of intellectuals known as *los ilustrados* (the enlightened ones)—young Filipino men who had lived and studied in Spain and Europe, and thus were exposed to liberal ideas. The most influential ilustrado was José Rizal, a brilliant polymath and doctor, whose two great novels *Noli Me Tangere* (Touch Me Not) and *El Filibusterismo* (The Subversive) were scathing critiques of Spanish abuse and repression, especially on the part of the friars. The colonial authorities banned the books and accused Rizal of aiding the revolution that had erupted in August of 1896. Imprisoned and subjected to a mock trial, the 35-year-old Rizal was shot by the Spanish at dawn on December 30, 1896. His martyr's death further fanned the flames of revolution.

With the outbreak of the three-month-long Spanish-American War of 1898, the Spanish position became untenable. By then Filipino forces had control of all of Luzon, the main island, except for Manila. A republic, headed by General Emilio Aguinaldo, had been established with a democratic constitution—the first, like the revolution, in Asia. However, the 1898 Treaty of Paris between the Spanish government and the United States resulted in the latter taking over the fledgling nation. The

American takeover was fiercely resisted, though, by the Filipinos in the brutal 1899 Philippine-American War. Hostilities officially lasted until 1902, when the United States declared victory, although in reality they continued for close to a decade. American occupation of the islands ended on July 4, 1946, when Philippine independence was finally restored. Spain may have been ousted, yet her legacies in the Philippines remain deeply rooted in widely disparate areas such as the law—the civil code has its origins in the Spanish *Codigo Civil*—and in cuisine, but principally in religion, language, and the arts.

Today, the Philippines is the only predominantly Catholic nation in the whole of Asia, with Roman Catholics making up more than 80 percent of the population—a testament to the proselytizing zeal and far-reaching influence of the Spanish friars. The colonial administrators and the friars required the local population to live "under the bells," that is, within hearing distance of the church bells. This made it

PHILIPPINES

easier to govern and Christianize the locals. Infants were christened with the names of saints while families registering at the *municipio* (town hall) were required to change their native names to Hispanic ones. Thus Spanish surnames such as "Reyes," "de los Santos," "Cruz," "Garcia," and "de Leon" are common throughout the country. Indeed, the Filipino equivalent of John Doe is Juan de la Cruz.

Like those in other Latin American nations, Filipino Catholics fuse indigenous beliefs and mores with church ritual and doctrine, and venerate especially the Virgin Mary and the Santo Nino (Holy Infant), whose most well-known icon in the Philippines resides in Cebu City's basilica, a gift of Magellan to the queen of Cebu at the time of his arrival. Like Mexicans, Filipino Catholics engage in feverish, often bloody observances of Holy Week, manifested in flagellations and the occasional crucifixion.

The faith that came through Spain is reflected most evidently in the baroque Spanish colonial-era churches, with their ornate facades and altars, to be found throughout the island nation. It is also through the Church that the fiesta evolved into the permanent cultural fixture it is now—the highlight of a town's or neighborhood's social calendar. Centered on a religious procession devoted to the town's patron saint, the fiesta is an occasion for lavish merrymaking, dining, drinking, and dancing.

The longest fiesta may be Christmas, or Pasko (from the Spanish Pascua), which can begin in early November and culminates with the Feast of the Three Kings, on January 6. The holiday period means carolers on the streets or in homes, with a repertoire of songs that invariably includes the Spanish "Nacio, Nacio Pastores." It means attending the *Missa de Gallo* (the Rooster's Mass) for several nights, culminating with the Christmas Eve midnight Mass. There follows the *Noche Buena* (the Good Night), a grand repast for the family. The dishes reflect the abundant, Hispanicized table with *jamon* (ham), *morcon* (sausage), and *arroz a la valenciana* (Valencia-style paella) among the main dishes, and *leche flan* (caramel custard) and *brazo de Mercedes* (meringue roll) among the desserts.

During the colonial period Spanish was the archipelago's sole official language. Thereafter, and until 1987, it was one of three, the other two being English and Pilipino. Until the 1970s students were required to study the Spanish language. While no longer an official tongue, its lasting influence is evident in Pilipino. Linguists estimate that at least 5,000 words of contemporary Pilipino are Spanish or Spanish-derived words, from *sapatos* (shoes) and *mesa* (table) to *pantalon* (pants) and *cine* (film), from *makinilya* (typewriter) to *pan de sal* (sourdough bread). Indeed, the everyday greeting of *Kumusta* is a variation of *Como esta?* Spanish survives as well in *Chavacano*—a creolized mix of Spanish and Pilipino—both in the province of Cavite just south of Manila, and in Zamboanga Province in Mindanao.

In literature, a body of work exists in Spanish dating from the 16th century to the early part of the 20th, the best known works being Rizal's aforementioned novels, the *Noli* and *Fili*. And while contemporary Filipino writers no longer employ Spanish, through temperament and history their writings exhibit a decidedly Latino flavor, influenced as much by Latin American novelists and poets as by Anglo authors. In the works of the National Artist for Literature, Nick Joaquin, for instance, one sees a strongly Hispanicized world beset by modernity and loss.

Hispanicization is also evident in movies and television where talents with mestizo features are preferred, and where the plots resemble those of the Latin *telenovela*. In theater, the Spanish *zarsuela* (musical comedy) has influenced the development of Philippine theater. In dance, a number of standards in the repertory of Filipino dance groups reveal their Hispanic roots, such as the *Pandannggo sa Ilaw* and the *Jota Moncadeña,* adaptations of Spanish regional dances, the fandango and the *jota*.

In the United States these Hispanic roots manifest themselves in various ways in the different Filipino communities, through annual fiestas such as the Santacruzan, which commemorates the discovery of Christ's cross by Saint Helena. The elaborate procession features religious rites and local beauties acting as Reina Elenas, each with a consort. Local dance troupes are formed, whose repertory includes indigenous and colonial-era dances. In Hollywood such affinities have meant that Filipino-American actors are usually cast as Latinos, two of the best-known examples being Lou Diamond Phillips and Tia Carrere.

The felt kinship between Filipinos and other Latinos is best exemplified in the history of the United Farm Workers (UFW). The UFW was formed in 1965 with the merger of the predominantly Filipino Agricultural Workers Organizing Committee (AWOC), led by Dolores Huerta, a Mexican American, and Larry Itliong, a Filipino, and the predominantly Chicano National Farm Workers Association (NFWA), led by César Chávez. AWOC members had initiated a strike in the grape fields of California on September 8, 1964; they were soon joined by the NFWA. The merger was the natural outcome of both Filipino and Mexican migrant laborers working the farms and fields of agribusiness on the West Coast. Indeed, serving as vice president to Chávez was Philip Vera Cruz, a Filipino. The Filipino migrant workers' struggles and their hardscrabble lives, alongside other migrant workers such as the Mexicans, are described vividly in *America Is in the Heart,* the powerful semiautobiographical novel of Carlos Bulosan (1911–1956), himself a farmworker and labor organizer.

RELATED ARTICLES

Farmworkers Movement; Spanish-American War.

FURTHER READING

Bulosan, Carlos. *America Is in the Heart.* Seattle: Univ. of Wash. Press, 2000.

Constantino, Renato. *A History of the Philippines: From the Spanish Colonization to the Second World War.* New York: Monthly Review Press, 1975.

Cordova, Fred. *Forgotten Asian Americans: A Pictorial Essay, 1763–1963.* 1983. Reprint. Dubuque, Iowa: Kendall/Hunt, 1999.

Corpuz, O. D. *Roots of the Filipino Nation.* Vols. 1 and 2. Quezon City, Philippines: Aklahi Fnd., 1989.

Ileto, Reynaldo. *Pasyon and Revolution: Popular Movements in the Philippines, 1840–1910.* Manila: Ateneo de Manila Univ. Press, 1979; 1989.

Rafael, Vicente. *Contracting Colonialism: Translation and Christian Conversion in Tagalog Society Under Early Spanish Rule.* Durham, N.C.: Duke Univ. Press, 1993.

Scharlin, Craig, and Lilia Villanueva. *Philip Vera Cruz: A Personal History of Filipino Immigrants and the Farmworkers Movement.* Los Angeles: UCLA Labor Center, Institute of Industrial Relations and UCLA Asian American Studies Center, 1997.

Scott, W. H. *Baranggay: Sixteenth Century Philippine Culture and Society.* Manila: Ateneo de Manila Univ. Press, 1994.

Takaki, Ronald. *Strangers from a Different Shore: A History of Asian America.* Rev. ed. Boston: Little, Brown, 1998.

SELECTED WEB SITES

Los Indios Bravos: The Filipino Solidarity Project.
www.los-indios-bravos.com

Filipino American National Historical Society.
www.fanhs-national.org

LUIS H. FRANCIA

PHILOSOPHY

Latino philosophy is a relatively new area of study that became current in the United States at the end of the 20th century. At times it refers to the philosophy practiced in the United States by people of Latin American origin, and at other times to the philosophy of any Hispanic philosopher working in the United States.

Latin American philosophy begins within the Iberian clergy sent by the Spanish and Portuguese crowns to convert the indigenous people of Latin America. The main philosophical centers during the early colonial period were Mexico and Peru, the two places where empires and rich natural resources coexisted. For Latin American thinkers, like their European counterparts, logical and metaphysical questions dominated philosophical discussion. Antonio Rubio's (1548–1615) *Logica mexicana* was one of the most important scholarly texts written in the New World.

Although adherence to scholarly thinkers was central and many thinkers continued to write within this tradition, others were guided by humanism, and still others were more concerned with the political and legal questions raised by the colonization of the Americas. Arguably, the most important of these thinkers was Bartolomé de Las Casas (1484–1566), a Dominican friar from Spain who became the leading champion of the rights of American Indians. His long life was devoted to arguing before the crown that "Indians," although different, were just as human as the Spaniards and so entitled to the same basic human rights. As early as 1515 Las Casas petitioned the Spanish crown to eliminate the slavery of American Indians. In 1550 he participated in a famous debate with another Spaniard, the Aristotelian Juan Ginés de Sepúlveda (1490–1573), arguing that it was unjust to wage war against the indigenous peoples of the Americas and to enslave them.

A significant break with scholasticism began during the independentist period with a growing interest in early modern philosophies, especially Descartes's epistemology and Rousseau's political philosophy, which was used to formulate an intellectual platform that would help support independence from Spain and Portugal. There was a strong influence of Utilitarianism reflected in the emphasis on progress and the move to make ideas tools for social change. According to utilitarians, the morality of an action is determined by its consequences. Another source of this period consisted of the liberal ideas of the French *philosophes,* who made reason a measure of legitimacy in social and governmental matters.

Not all of the leading figures from this time were philosophers in the strict sense. Rather, they were men of action who used ideas for practical ends. Simón Bolívar (Venezuela, 1783–1830), José Joaquin Fernández de Lizardi (Mexico, 1776–1827), Mariano Moreno (Argentina, 1778–1811), and José Cecilio del Valle (Honduras, 1780–1834) can be most accurately characterized as political leaders rather than philosophers. Instead of devoting their lives to developing systems of thought, they were more interested in concrete political and military action that would lead to political independence.

Bolívar, known as "El Libertador," successfully led northern South America to independence from Spain and was the founding father of five republics (Colombia, Venezuela, Ecuador, Peru, and Bolivia). Although monumental deeds such as these, rather than his writings, are Bolívar's legacy, some leaders attempted to also develop ideas that would help to secure stability after independence had been won. Francisco de Miranda (Venezuela, 1750–1816), for example, was not only an active participant in the battles for independence, he also developed some of the ideas that Bolívar used to change the political structures in the Americas.

The independentist period was followed by positivism. This was in part a response to the social, financial, and political needs of the newly liberated countries of Latin America. Juan Bautista Alberdi (Argentina, 1812–1884), Domingo Faustino Sarmiento (Argentina, 1811–1888), and Andrés Bello (Venezuela, 1781–1865) were important figures of this movement. Each favored experience over theoretical speculation and was interested in issues of social justice, educational reform, and progress. In general, positivists emphasized the explicative value of empirical science and rejected metaphysics.

Positivism exerted an unusually strong influence in Latin American society. Testifying to this is the preservation of the positivist inscription "Order and Progress" on the Brazilian national flag. In Mexico the dictatorship of Porfirio Díaz adopted positivism as its official philosophy. Among the most original positivists were the Cuban Enrique José Varona (1849–1933) and the Argentine Enrique José Ingenieros (1877–1925). Indeed, these two men introduced such fundamental modifications to traditional posi-

tivism that their thought paved the way toward a move away from it.

The contemporary period can be broken down into three phases. It includes the foundational stage, the period of normalcy, and the period of maturity.

This stage begins with the decline of positivism. The generation of thinkers who adamantly rejected the central principles of positivism became known as the "founders," a designation coined by Francisco Romero, and included among others: Alejandro Octavio Deústua (Peru, 1849–1945), Alejandro Korn (Argentina, 1860–1936), Enrique Molina (Chile, 1871–1964), Carlos Vaz Ferreira (Uruguay, 1872–1958), Raimundo de Farias Brito (Brazil, 1862–1917), José Vasconcelos (Mexico, 1882–1959), and Antonio Caso (Mexico, 1883–1946). These thinkers began to develop ideas that culminated in the formulation of what can be called philosophical anthropology.

Vasconcelos was not only an accomplished philosopher but, like so many other Latin American philosophers, he was also a devoted educator and political activist. Much of his work focuses on the meaning of Mexican culture in particular and the on destiny of Latin America in general. In two of his most popular works, *La raza cósmica* (1925; The Cosmic Race, 1997) and *Indología* (1926; Indology), he claims that in the future of humanity will be a cosmic race, a synthesis of the four basic races of the world that will emerge in the region of the Amazon and fulfill "the divine mission of America." He contrasts this to the ethnic egoism and nationalism that dominates Anglo-Saxon culture and claims that the new race of which he speaks will be characterized by a universalistic spirit based on love.

In addition to the work of the founders, other crucial influences in overcoming positivism and its legacy were vitalism and intuitionism, especially the versions imported from French philosophers such as Emile Boutroux (1845–1921) and Henri Bergson (1859–1941). Vitalism conceived reality in living terms, as spontaneous, organic, and dynamic, whereas intuitionism emphasized the intuitive source of human values. Yet arguably the most important force in the transition away from positivism was the influence of the Spanish philosopher José Ortega y Gasset (1883–1955). Ortega introduced the thought of German philosophers such as Max Scheler (1874–1928) and Nicolai Hartmann (1882–1950) to a generation of

Latin American thinkers, thereby expanding the philosophical dialogue of the entire region.

The generation shaped by the founders and by the ideas imported from Spain, France, and Germany have been characterized by Francisco Miró Quesada (Peru, b. 1918), as "the generation of forgers." A major figure of this generation who played a central role in the development of philosophical anthropology was Samuel Ramos (Mexico, 1897–1959). He focused on Mexican culture, thereby inspiring interest in what is culturally unique to Latin American nations. Ramos's book *El perfil del hombre y la cultura en México* (1934; *Profile of Man and Culture in Mexico*, 1962) was the first attempt at interpreting Mexican culture.

Francisco Romero (Argentina, 1891–1962) also was an important thinker devoted to the development of philosophical anthropology, and his *Teoría del hombre* (1952; *Theory of Man*, 1964) was highly influential. Romero sought to develop a view of human beings in terms of intentionality (that is, the direction of human activity and consciousness) and spirituality and defined this in universal terms rather than the culturally specific parameters outlined by Ramos.

Throughout the history of Latin American thought there has been a tension between those philosophers who focus on the universal human condition and those whose concern is the particular situation determined by specific cultural circumstances. In Mexico, for example, many philosophers have discussed the impact of colonization on the development of culture in Mexico. This emphasis on the particular grew as a result of a historical event that brought two traditions into even closer contact with one another and heralded yet another stage in the development of Latin American philosophy.

During the late 1930s and 1940s, owing to the upheavals created by the Spanish Civil War, a significant group of thinkers from Spain arrived in Latin America. These philosophers became known as the *transterrados*. Among these are Joaquín Xirau (1895–1946), Eduardo Nicol (1907–1986), José Ferrater Mora (1912–1991), José Gaos (1900–1969), Luis Recaséns Siches (1903–1977), and Juan David García Bacca (1901–1992). Their presence helped to break some of the national barriers that had existed in Latin America before their arrival. The conception of *hispanidad* (Hispanicity) that they inherited from the Spanish philosopher Miguel de Unamuno and the

need to establish themselves in their adopted land helped the process; they went from country to country, spreading ideas and contributing to an ever broadening philosophical dialogue. Their influence showed itself most strongly when the generation born around 1910 reached maturity.

One of the most influential of the *transterrados* was Gaos, a student of Ortega and eventually the teacher of one of Mexico's most important philosophers, Leopoldo Zea (1912–2004). Gaos encouraged Zea to study the history of Mexican thought, and this resulted in one of Zea's best known books, *El positivismo en México* (1968; *Positivism in Mexico*, 1974). Through Gaos, Ortega had a strong impact on Zea's views. Zea was also influenced by the psychoanalytic approach to the problem of cultural identity developed by Samuel Ramos, which he used to develop a critique of philosophy and to articulate a mestizo (mixed) consciousness. The term *mestizo* reveals an interest in issues associated with race and culture, as it relates to the implications of Latin Americans having both Spanish and American Indian heritages. Zea's work on *mestizaje* was taken up by the Argentine philosopher Arturo Andrés Roig (b. 1922) and the Peruvian Miró-Quesada.

Although during the previous period philosophers from different countries in Latin America began to interact critically with one another, it was at this time that the trend actually blossomed. During the last 50 years, the level of philosophical activity in several Latin American countries has improved significantly, owing, in part, to the institutionalization of philosophy. The number of national philosophical societies and centers, institutes, faculties, and departments that have as their exclusive end the teaching and investigation of philosophy has increased substantially, as have the number of philosophy journals. This activity has begun to awaken interest outside of Latin America.

Most European and American philosophical schools and trends have practitioners in Latin America today, and some have important representatives who are not content with copying foreign ideas, but attempt to develop original positions. Among the most widespread are phenomenology, analytic philosophy, and, more recently, postmodernism.

One movement that deserves mention because it originated in Latin America is the philosophy of liberation. It grew out of liberation theology, which itself began in Peru and Brazil. The origins of liberation philosophy can be traced to the 1970s in Argentina, to a group of thinkers that includes Arturo Andrés Roig, Horacio Cerutti Guldberg (b. 1950), and Enrique Dussel (b. 1934). Because of the political turmoil during this period, many of these philosophers were forced into exile, thus disrupting the continuity of the movement and leading to the creation of two distinct strands: the historicist and the essentialist. In spite of differences both strands share a common concern with what it means to study philosophy from the periphery, that is, from the condition of dependence that these thinkers claim characterizes Latin American culture. The philosophy of liberation has been shaped in part by Marxist and Catholic ideas.

Finally, Latino and Latina philosophers are an ever-growing presence in the United States. Héctor Neri Castañeda (1924–1991) and Mario Bunge (b. 1919) stand out as older major figures; but the list of younger members of the group keeps growing. Most of them work in well-established philosophical traditions, ranging from analytic philosophy to postmodernism. Many of them, as in the case of their Latin American counterparts, have a distinct interest in Latin American philosophy and sociopolitical issues, but they are also concerned with the universal philosophical concerns that are part and parcel of the human condition.

Among the most active Latino and Latina philosophers are Ernest Sosa (b. 1940), who works in epistemology and metaphysics from an analytic perspective; Jorge J. E. Gracia (b. 1942), a historian of medieval and Hispanic philosophy who has written extensively in metaphysics, philosophical historiography, and interpretation; and Ofelia Schutte (b. 1945), who concentrates on issues of feminism and Latin American thought. Younger but very active are Linda Alcoff, who works in epistemology and feminism; Susana Nuccetelli, who publishes on the philosophy of mind and Latin American philosophy; and Eduardo Mendieta, whose research concerns primarily contemporary Latin American philosophy.

RELATED ARTICLES

Latino Studies; Liberation Theology; Politics, Latino; Vasconcelos, José.

FURTHER READING

Beuchot, Mauricio. *The History of Philosophy in Colonial Mexico.* Tr. by Elizabeth Millán, with a foreword by Jorge J. E. Gracia. Washington, D.C.: Catholic Univ. of Am. Press, 1998.

Crawford, **William Rex.** *A Century of Latin American Thought.* 3d ed. Cambridge, Mass.: Harvard Univ. Press, 1961.

Davis, Harold Eugene. *Latin American Thought: A Historical Introduction.* Baton Rouge: La. State Univ. Press, 1972.

Ferrater Mora, José. *Unamuno: A Philosophy of Tragedy.* Tr. by Philip Sliver. 1962. Reprint. Westport, Conn.: Greenwood Press, 1981.

Gracía, Jorge J. E., et al., eds. *Philosophical Analysis in Latin America.* Dordrecht, Holland, and Boston: Reidel Pub. Co., 1984.

Gracía, Jorge J. E., ed. "Latin American Philosophy Today." Double issue of *The Philosophical Forum* (1988–1989).

Gracía, Jorge J. E., and Elizabeth Millán-Zaibert, eds. *Latin American Philosophy for the 21st Century: The Human Condition, Values, and the Search for Identity.* Amherst, N.Y.: Prometheus, 2003.

Mendieta, Eduardo, ed. *Latin American Philosophy: Currents, Issues, Debates.* Bloomington: Ind. Univ. Press, 2003.

Nuccetelli, Susana. *Latin American Thought: Philosophical Problems and Arguments.* Boulder, Colo: Westview Press, 2002.

Nuccetelli, Susana, and Gary Seai, eds. *Latin American Philosophy: An Introduction with Readings.* Upper Saddle River, N.J.: Prentice Hall, 2003.

Sáenz, Mario. *The Identity of Liberation in Latin American Thought: Latin American Historicism and the Phenomenology of Leopoldo Zea.* Lanham, Md: Rowman and Littlefield, 1999.

Schutte, Ofelia. *Cultural Identity and Social Liberation in Latin American Thought.* Albany: State Univ. of N.Y. Press, 1993.

JORGE J. E. GRACÍA
LEO ZAIBERT

PHOTOGRAPHY

One of the least studied aspects of Latino visual arts, Latino photography primarily encompasses the efforts of Cuban American, Mexican American and Chicano, and Puerto Rican photographers. The majority of this work dates from the mid-1960s to the present, although there are important precursors from prior decades, particularly in the Mexican American and Puerto Rican communities. Photography by Latino artists defies overarching definitions and mirrors the broad approaches evident in contemporary photographic practice in the United States. In fact, there is no single, unifying history of Latino photography; rather, the field comprises a plurality of histories that at times intersect, and at other times remain distinct. Work by Latinos ranges from documentary essays and "straight" fine-art photography to staged or constructed images and those resulting from forms of darkroom manipulation to photographic work combined with other media—painting, assemblages, or installations. In recent years digitally produced imagery has played an increasingly important role for Latino photographers and artists alike.

A handful of characteristics link Chicano, Cuban American, Puerto Rican, and other Latino photographers, particularly shared roots in colonized, Spanish-speaking cultures, as well as the frequent use of the photographic medium to explore identity and aspects of the Latino experience in the United States. These photographers also speak to the discrete historical and cultural factors that shape their own communities. For example, among Cuban American photographers who were born in Cuba and left their homeland as children or as young adults, the themes of political exile and cultural displacement have been expansively investigated. For Chicano photographers, their relation to Mexico, border issues, and the experience of socioeconomic marginalization and its cultural ramifications have been expressed in both documentary and nontraditional work. Puerto Rican photographers, on the other hand, have frequently interpreted the specificities of the Puerto Rican experience, particularly issues related to political autonomy, the struggle to maintain cultural identity, and Boricua or Nuyorican culture in New York, where a significant number of Puerto Rican artists live either permanently or for periods of their careers. However, not all Latino photographers create work that is identifiably "Latino." Many convey universal themes ranging from spirituality to the nature of visual representation, while others have dealt with political and social issues. Especially among the generation that emerged in the 1990s, cultural and racial identity is often implied in more oblique terms, and visual languages are deployed that rely on irony and metaphor.

Scant research has been undertaken on pioneering Latino photographers in the United States. The earliest were principally studio portraitists, such as Bertha Gil Rodríguez (b. 1920), a female photographer in Texas who worked professionally for nearly four decades, first as a studio apprentice beginning in 1935 in the border town of Eagle Pass, and later as the owner of a San Antonio portrait studio from 1958 to 1970. Much earlier, in New York from the 1870s through the turn of the century, the Cuban José María Mora was a well-known portraitist specializing in theater personalities. Among the celebrities who sat for his camera were Buffalo Bill Cody, the English Vokes sisters, and Charlotte "Lotta" Crabtree. In Puerto Rico daguerreotypists offered their services as early as 1844, and in the 19th and early 20th centuries, portraitists and itinerant photographers were active on the island. Regrettably, much early photography by Puerto Ricans has been destroyed or exists in a fragile state because of the island's humid climate.

The most significant modern-era photographer in Puerto Rico was Jack Delano (1914–1997), who adopted the island as his home. He was born in Kiev (Ukraine), raised in the United States from the age of nine, and went to Puerto Rico in 1941 as a photographer for the Farm Security Administration (FSA). Delano spent three months there and in the U.S. Virgin Islands, traveling extensively and producing over 2,000 negatives depicting landscapes, towns, workers, customs, and everyday life. After World War II, Delano returned to Puerto Rico where he taught, wrote, made films, continued to photograph, and engaged in other activities that fostered the development of a cultural community. Lesser known FSA photographers in Puerto Rico are Edwin and Louise Rosskam. Edwin Rosskam (1903–1985) originally went to the island in 1937 as a freelance photojournalist covering the nationalist movement for *Life* magazine. The FSA subsequently hired Edwin and Louise (1910–2003), and for several months in 1937–1938 they created a rich visual record of the living conditions, landscapes, and towns on the island. Delano's work, however, became well known in Puerto Rico and served as a model for younger photographers interested in documenting the changing character of life on their island as well as political and social concerns.

Another pioneer in the field of Latino photography is John Candelario (1916–1993), a seventh-generation New Mexican who documented Hispanic culture in the state with a strong modernist sensibility. He pursued photography in the 1930s and 1940s and in these years was a member of the cultural circle in northern New Mexico that centered around Georgia O'Keeffe. She introduced Candelario to Edward Stieglitz, who exhibited some of his photographs at his New York gallery, An American Place. This led to Candelario's inclusion in a 1944 photography exhibition at the Museum of Modern Art in New York. Candelario also knew Edward Weston and Ansel Adams and introduced them to the Indian pueblos where they photographed.

The contemporary era in Latino photography began in the 1970s, a period when Latinos as well as African American and female artists were develop-

Dos Mujeres, Familia López, by Luis Carlos Bernal, 1978.

ing visual languages that signaled a growing sense of self-affirmation and concomitant resistance from main-stream culture. Within the field of photography this was also the era that witnessed the first Coloquios Latinoamericano de Fotografía. Held in Mexico City in 1979 and 1981, these were watershed events in the history of Latin American photography that brought together for the first time photographers from throughout the Americas, including Latinos. Many of the most influential voices at the Coloquios asserted the preeminent role of socially committed

documentary photography as a means of influencing social and political change. This ethos not only guided the evolution of Latin American photography in the 1980s, but also influenced Latino photographers coming of age in this period.

A leading figure in this era was the Puerto Rican Héctor Méndez Caratini (b. 1949). Throughout his career he has strived to construct an image of Puerto Rican, and more broadly, Caribbean identity, by documenting such subjects as *carnaval* (carnival) and other fiestas, colonial coffee and sugarcane plantations, the tradition of the *vaquero* (cowboy), and, in the Dominican Republic, the secretive Afro-Caribbean spiritual practices of Gagá and Vudú. He has also worked with experimental modes. In the 2001 series Vieques: Crónicas del Calvario (Vieques: Chronicles from Calvary), he created boldly expressionistic collages that combine photographs with texts and painting to protest the U.S. Navy's occupation of the Puerto Rican island of Vieques.

Among the first generation of Cuban Americans to work in the documentary mode is Mario Algaze (b. 1947), whose photographs are poetic evocations of quotidian life in Latin America encountered during his extensive travels from the 1970s through the mid-1990s. Following in the tradition of Manuel Alvarez Bravo's lyrical form of documentation, Algaze focused on picturing in black and white realms that appear to be untouched by modern influence. In a 1999 2000 series made during his first visit to Cuba since leaving in 1960, Algaze similarly captured environments suffuse with a timeless sense of place. These works reveal the photographer's nostalgia for his homeland while ironically underscoring economic realities in contemporary Cuba where physically little has changed since the Revolution.

Chicanos working in the documentary mode have also been inspired by the strong tradition of Mexican documentary photography, as well as by the example of photographers who witnessed the birth of the Chicano civil rights movement and chronicled César Chávez's labor-organizing activities in California in the 1960s. Cris Sánchez and Manuel Echavarria were two of the leading photographers documenting Chávez and the activities of the United Farm Workers, as well as the lives of seasonal farm workers in California's central valley. More recently, Genaro Molina, a California photojournalist, continued in the tradition of these activist photographers. In an early 1990s photo essay titled Fields of Pain, he recorded the influx of Mexicans into central California and the appalling working and living conditions they faced as migrant farmworkers. While such photographers were driven by social and political concerns, rather than artistic motivations, their work provided inspiration to later generations of Latino photographers who have explored the possibilities of merging a social message with a more conscious aesthetic sensibility.

Louis Carlos Bernal (1941–1993) is notable for being among the first photographers associated with the Chicano art movement as well as the first to produce a sustained study of Mexican American life in the Southwest. Working in black and white and in color, Bernal sympathetically captured scenes that no other photographer had ever comprehensively studied—Mexican American people in their modest homes, portraits of cholos and cholas, *quincañeras* (a girl's 15th-birthday celebration), and domestic religious shrines. Among his most elegiac works are those of The Benitez Suite of 1977, a series of black-and-white photographs that record the house and belongings of an elderly woman who had gone to live in a nursing home. In this series Bernal constructed a hauntingly eloquent image of the remnants of a human life. Bernal intimately knew the worlds he photographed and endowed his photographs with emotional intensity and honesty. As he stated in 1978, "The Chicano artist cannot isolate himself from the community, but finds himself in the midst of his people, creating art of and for the people."

Ricardo Valverde (1946–1998) began his career as a street photographer in the early 1970s, chronicling members of the local art community as well as people and scenes he encountered walking around with a camera in Los Angeles. He also recorded some of the activities of Asco, a pioneering conceptual artists group that staged satiric outdoor performance pieces in East Los Angeles in the 1970s. When the print workshop and cultural center Self-Help Graphics introduced Day of the Dead parades in East Los Angeles in the early 1970s, Valverde provided some of its rare documentation.

By the late 1980s Latinos began to increasingly pursue various forms of manipulated imagery, ranging from painting on photographic prints to staging and constructing scenes to combining photography with collage and text and later to experimenting with digital processes. Valverde, for example, moved away from documentary photography when he decided that he wanted to mesh reality with fantasy as well as to challenge notions of photographic reality. In the early 1990s he began to paint with pastels on his prints, and he later added the techniques of cutting and abrading silver gelatin prints. The resulting images appear to be more painterly than photographic, and also reveal the influence of graffiti, a ubiquitous, popular art form on the streets of East Los Angeles. With Valverde's fluid approach to his artistic media, his late work became a phantasmagoria of images that vividly melded evocations of the subconscious with life's stark realities.

Charles Biasiny Rivera has pursued a similar approach, transforming street scenes he took of New York Puerto Ricans by painting on and along the borders of his compositions and adding poetic, sometimes plaintive handwritten texts. These methods endow his works with a spiritual or otherworldly quality, and elevate his everyday subjects into emblems of hope and grace. Biasiny Rivera has also been a preeminent promoter of Latino photography as a cofounder in 1974 of EnFoco, a New York-based organization dedicated to providing Latino and other photographers outside the mainstream with opportunities to expose their work to a broad audience. EnFoco continues to provide support to the Latino photographic community by organizing exhibitions, presenting educational programs, and publishing the magazine *Nueva Luz*.

Another form of manipulated photography has involved the construction of staged or directed images. Harry Gamboa (b. 1951), a Chicano artist whose work involves multimedia performance, installation, video, fotonovela, writing, and other creative forms, has also worked with photography since the early 1970s. Gamboa was a member of the aforementioned artist group Asco, which presented absurdist public performances including a series of "No Movies," acted scenes that resulted in photographic "stills" from nonexistent films. The photograph *Decoy Gang War Victim,* 1974, for example, pictures an invented scene of an East Los Angeles gang shooting that was distributed and then broadcast by the local media as a presumed real news event. Gamboa also produced more conventional photographs in the 1970s, documenting street life in his native East Los Angeles. In 1991 he began an ongoing series, Chicano Male Unbonded, full-length portraits of Chicano men in confrontational poses photographed on dimly lit streets. The captions accompanying the portraits identify these subjects as artists, lawyers, and academics, thereby undermining the stereotypical notions that some may hold toward Chicano men.

Robert Buitrón (b. 1953) has staged narrative sequences infused with humor and irony to comment on the marginalized position of Chicanos in American society. In the 1989–1991 series The Legend of Ixtacchihuatl and Popocatepetl, he referenced the tradition of garishly illustrated Mexican popular calendars that often feature scenes of these mythic pre-Columbian lovers. In Buitrón's version, Ixta and Popo are contemporary Aztecs wearing feather headdresses and other traditional accoutrements while engaging in activities that suggest a futile quest to assimilate into mainstream society—having a rooftop barbecue, attending a meeting in a corporate boardroom, or visiting Tijuana. With such images Buitrón satirized many aspects of the Chicano experience, from the dual pressures to preserve tradition or assimilate into the mainstream to gender issues to the ambivalent feelings Chicanos often hold toward Mexico.

A visual strategy employed by many Latino photographers is to assemble imagery and symbols in constructed spaces for the camera, a metaphorical means of referring to the hybrid quality that is a defining characteristic of the Latino experience. The Puerto Rican artist and New York native Juan Sanchez aims to articulate the complexity of Puerto Rican identity, whose character emerges from the fact that the island is a colonized entity that does not fully share in the civil rights and economic opportunities enjoyed by U.S. citizens; as an island whose population is a mix of Taino (indigenous Caribbean), Spanish, African races; and as a people who are divided between their homeland and the mainland, especially New York. His works are dense, painted collages that include symbols drawn from Taino and Afro-Caribbean cultures, Catholicism, Puerto Rican popular culture and folk traditions, and contemporary life. Photography plays a central role in these compositions. Images of children, the Puerto Rican flag, and religious figures take on symbolic roles in his oeuvre, lending a poignant air to politically charged works that interpret the reality of a people who struggle to maintain a distinct identity and political voice.

The Texas-based Chicana photographer Kathy Vargas (b. 1950) reflects her consciousness of the layers of history that have shaped her identity by assembling and layering symbolic forms in her studio, which she photographs with a 4 x 5 view camera. She has typically pictured X-rays and skeletons; flowers, thorns, and other plant forms; birds and feathers; and milagros, objects that conjure such an array of influences as pre-Columbian philosophies, the Mexican Day of the Dead (Dia de los Muertos) tradition, and popular religious practices, especially the small shrines that Vargas encounters in her San Antonio neighborhood. She then tones or hand-colors the resulting works, which function as intimate spaces for the contemplation of life, death, and time's passage.

Maria Martinez Cañas (b. 1960) developed distinctive means to produce photographic imagery in the early 1990s when she produced collage-like works created from large, intricately devised negatives that are printed as contact prints. Her themes are characteristic of those that have concerned the first generation of Cuban American photographers who came to the United States in the early years of Castro's regime—the experience of exile, nostalgia for homeland, and family. Martinez Cañas's initial images were composed of abstract, biomorphic, and totemic forms, and paid homage to the formal language of the pioneering Cuban modernist artist Wifredo Lam. Later works combined photographs and actual two-dimensional objects such as maps and postage stamps. In the series Quince Sellos Cubanos/ Fifteen Cuban Stamps, she juxtaposed postage stamps with larger-scale representations of the subjects they memorialized to suggest the themes of travel, national identity, and communication. By focusing on subject matter that symbolizes geography, distance, history, and communication, she underscored a desire to maintain a strong connection to her native Cuba.

Abelardo Morrell (b. 1948), who came to the United States when he was 14, has similarly shown a preoccupation with place that he expresses with camera obscura images that merge views of inside and outside worlds. His first photographs applying this technique were made in the late 1980s in his child's bedroom, and the resulting works convey both a magical sense of a transformed place and an uneasy sense of dislocation. He has also made camera obscura images in which the Brooklyn Bridge or the Umbrian countryside, for example, inexplicably appear in intimate bedroom settings. In the late 1990s, during his first return visit to Cuba, he made a series of images in interior settings that are haunting for their emptiness and sense of history. Although the human form is absent from all of these compositions, these are psychologically charged works that infuse architectural spaces with deep emotional resonances.

Eduardo Muñoz, who left Cuba in 1992, represents a younger generation of Cuban Americans. His compositions involve a complex layering of images— projections of film stills and old family portraits often shown in disjunctive scales when seen against the walls of his home, domestic furniture, and incongruously placed objects, photographed and printed as large-scale color photographs. With these compositions, Muñoz conjures personal memory, family history, and a palpable sense of nostalgia. A key work in his oeuvre is from the series Marea Baja (Low Tide; 2001–2003), and was inspired by a visit to Cuba after a long absence. The central image in the composition depicts Muñoz as an adolescent, before a wave-swept coast, his arms stretched outward in an expression of youthful freedom. The artist projected the image at home, photographing it through the window of his car, and adding a recent self-portrait taken at the same locale and positioned in the frame of the car's rearview mirror. This merging of images from past and present, metaphorical collapsing of geographical boundaries, and creative recollection of personal history, is characteristic of his photographic practice and speaks of the exile's desire to preserve memories and maintain a connection to family and place.

Another theme that has been central to the work of Latino photographers is that of the body, a politically and psychologically charged site for the exploration of ethnic and cultural identity, gender and sexuality, and spirituality. An important precursor in this regard is Ana Mendieta (1984–1985), the pioneering Cuban American artist who undertook ritual performances in nature that richly connoted a reverence for the earth, a heightened state of physical and spiritual consciousness, and the cycle of life and death. Her example has inspired many Latino and Latin American photographers to use self-portraiture or the depiction of others in a ritualistic, highly symbolic manner. In addition, the interest in the body held by Latino photographers can be linked to the focus on this theme by several influential Latin American photographers, such as the Mexican Gerardo Suter or the Guatemalan Luis González Palma.

Among the leading contemporary Latino photographers working with the human body is the Puerto Rican Víctor Vázquez (b. 1950), who depicts elaborate stagings of male and female nudes. In his large-scale, hand-toned photographs from the mid-1990s, he shows his figures accompanied by such organic elements as plants, feathers, and chicken parts, signifying a ritual communion with nature. Santería, animism, and other Afro-Caribbean spiritual practices inspire the photographer's symbolic vocabulary, but Vázquez has emphasized that his aim is not to interpret these traditions, but rather to express the human condition at its most primal and at intense moments of physical and spiritual consciousness. His mode of picturing the body projects a plurality of meanings; about spirituality, individual and collective history, culture and tradition, and physical desire. In the late 1990s Vázquez broadened his practice to include objects, installation, and video. In a 2000 exhibition held in San Juan, *Natura Cultura,* he presented his photographs of nudes in a large installation with totemic objects and symbolic assemblages, thus casting the photograph as an object, and the body as the key element in a broad symbolic repertoire.

The female body is central to the work of Laura Aguilar (b. 1959), a Los Angeles–based Chicana photographer who has examined issues of gender, race, and class. Her late 1980s Latina Lesbian series consists of portraits accompanied by autobiographical texts that express the struggles and sense of self-affirmation of individuals who are doubly socially marginalized as a result of their identity as Latinas and lesbians. In 1990 Aguilar produced one of the most provocative images in the corpus of Chicano photography, *Three Eagles Flying,* a triptych depicting the nude artist wrapped and bound by flags of the United States and Mexico and flanked by photographs of the two flags. This image of the body in bondage holds strong sexual as well as political connotations; with the body, Aguilar has constructed an allegory of the Chicano and Chicana body as encompassing ambivalent dualities, whether expressed as clashing geographic entities, social values, or desires.

Andres Serrano (b. 1950) gained international notoriety in 1987 for *Piss Christ,* a color photograph of a small crucifix submerged in the artist's urine. Seen as blasphemous by conservative Christians and politicians, this image became steeped in the cultural

© ROBERT C. BUITRON

Ixtaccihuatl y Popocatepetl . . . The Legend Continues, 1990; gelatin silver print by Robert C. Buitron.

politics of the 1980s, a period when the AIDS crisis dominated social discourse in the United States. This image was one of a larger body of works meant not to provoke controversy but to directly confront such issues as spirituality, moral values, sexuality, and mortality. Among the themes Serrano has depicted in starkly focused, large, color photographs are body fluids pictured as abstract forms and as the backgrounds of still-life compositions, portraits of Ku Klux Klan members and homeless people, scenes of extreme sexuality, and human corpses. By aestheticizing such unsettling subject matter, Serrano produces images that are often simultaneously beautiful and frightening. But the artist's goal, as he has stated, is to "take a formal tradition and subvert it by inverting the images, abstracting that which we take for granted, in an attempt to question not only photography, but my own experience and social reality."

Since the 1990s several Latino artists—like their colleagues in many parts of the world—have made photography a central part of their work, which might also include installations, objects, video, or painting. Particularly for Cuban Americans, this approach is rooted in the strategies devised by the generation of artists that emerged in Cuba in the late 1970s and 1980s. These artists articulated a variety of conceptual languages to critique the state of affairs in their country, thus laying the groundwork for a new sense of expressive freedom in Cuban visual arts. Significantly, many either referenced the photographic medium or used photography itself in their work. Among the first Cuban American artists to deploy the photographic medium in a conceptual manner was Felix Gonzalez Torres (1957–1996), whose work encompassed installations and public art projects. Gonzalez Torres used photographs in such works as *Aparición* (1991), presented as a stack of posters illustrated with an image of clouds that recalls the geometric perfection of minimalist sculpture while functioning as a gift (the spectator may take a copy, and the stack is continually replenished while on public display). In its endless repetition, the work also makes reference to one of the defining qualities of the photographic image. *Untitled* (1992) was a public art piece, an outdoor billboard featuring a photograph of an unmade bed. Dedicated to the artist's male companion, Gonzalez Torres used monumentally scaled photographic images to transform a scene of private intimacy into a politically loaded statement on public policy. Other conceptually based artists who have incorporated photography into their work include the Cuban Americans Gory (Rogelio López Marín), Arturo Cuenca, and Ernesto Pujol, and the Puerto Rican Adal Maldonado.

In recent years Latino photographers have also turned to digital technologies to construct imagery. Chicana photographer Martina Lopez has worked with digital imagery since the late 1980s, initially appropriating portraits of family members to construct autobiographical images symbolizing memory, loss, and time's passing. In proceeding bodies of work she incorporated portraits from turn-of-the-century photo albums into fabricated landscapes, thus creating allegorical scenes that refer, more universally, to a collective history, the passing of generations, and cultural memory. The effects that Lopez achieves through computer manipulation—disjointed topographies and deep vistas, shifts in scale, and the mixing of color, black-and-white, and toned images—produce dreamlike spaces for the contemplation of one's own history.

Mexican-born Alma Lopez gained national media attention in 2001 when her 1999 digital print, "Our Lady" was exhibited in Santa Fe, New Mexico. This contemporary version of a Virgin of Guadalupe, nude and festooned with garlands of flowers, deeply offended some public officials and members of the clergy who saw it as sacrilegious. The artist's intent, however, was to create a positive symbol of Latina identity as well as to express her emotional connection to the Virgin. While Lopez's career has become identified with this single image, she has also used digital processes to compose images that explore cultural and social issues related to the Chicano community. She has portrayed seamstresses, children, figures at the border, and Juan Soldado, popularly known as the patron saint of illegal immigrants, often setting her figures before the Los Angeles skyline and juxtaposed against pre-Columbian symbols, maps of Mexico, and news photos relating to Mexican Americans. With digital manipulation she seamlessly merges disparate forms into a single picture field, thus vividly denoting the multiplicity of influences that have shaped or are transforming Latino culture.

RELATED ARTICLES

Art, Cuban American; Art, Dominican American; Art, Galleries and Collections; Art, Mexican American and Chicano; Art, Popular; Art, Puerto Rican on the Mainland; Art Criticism.

FURTHER READING

From the West: Chicano Narrative Photography. San Francisco: The Mexican Museum, 1995.

Island Journey. Bronx, New York: En Foco, and the Hostos Center for Art and Culture, 1995.

Sichel, Berta. *Aztlán Hoy: La Posnación Chicana*. Madrid: Dirección General de Archivos, Museos y Bibliotecas de la Consejería de Cultura de la Comunidad de Madrid, 1999.

Viera, Ricardo. *Latin American Artist-Photographers from the Lehigh University Art Galleries Collection*. Bethlehem, Penn.: Lehigh Univ. Art Galleries– Museum Operation, 2001.

ELIZABETH FERRER

PIÑERO, MIGUEL

Born: 1946; Gurabo, Puerto Rico
Died: June 4, 1988; New York, New York

Miguel (Mikey) Piñero is one of the most important Nuyorrican playwrights and poets and a figure whose legacy has turned him into an icon. Piñero, the oldest of the four children of his mother's first marriage, moved in 1950 with his family to the Lower East Side of New York City. When the father abandoned the family, they lived on the streets for a time.

Piñero's education was highly irregular; he liked to read and he wrote poetry from an early age, encouraged by his mother who also wrote poetry. His increasingly delinquent lifestyle, however, landed him in juvenile detention centers such as the New York City correctional institution on Rikers Island. Paroled at 19, he joined the Puerto Rican Young Lords, but he had become a heroin addict and was again committed to several institutions, including the New York State Penitentiary at Ossining (Sing Sing).

There he attended a workshop given by Marvin Felix Camillo and began to write plays. *Short Eyes*, which made him famous, is a human drama set in prison dealing with the codes of a closed system that reflect those who govern the outside world. The play portrays the need for a scapegoat to satisfy deep frustrations and prejudices and deals with racial, ethnic, and national alliances. Its powerful scope is reminis-

© JERRY T. MOSEY/AP/WIDE WORLD PHOTOS

Director Marvin Félix Camillo, left, and playwright Miguel Gómez Piñero, in New York City, 1974.

cent of classical tragedy as it moves inexorably to a violent ending.

Short Eyes was performed in 1974 in the Theater of Riverside Church by The Family, a company formed by former inmates. It was acclaimed by critics and theater-lovers, and Piñero was hailed as an American Jean Genet. Joseph Papp took the play to the Public Theater and then to the Vivian Beaumont Theatre in Lincoln Center, where it opened on May 9, 1974. It was a resounding success, winning the New York Drama Critics Circle Award, an Obie, and a Tony nomination. A film, with a script by Piñero, was made in 1977.

Piñero continued writing for the theater. Among his plays are *Eulogy for a Small Time Thief* (produced in 1977), *The Sun Always Shines for the Cool* (produced in 1978), and *Midnight Moon at the Greasy Spoon* (produced in 1981). He moved briefly to Los Angeles, where he wrote scripts for television series and appeared in some episodes, while also acting in such films as *Fort Apache, the Bronx* (1981) and *Breathless* (1983). In 1984 he scripted several episodes of *Miami Vice,* a hit television series, and acted in others.

Piñero was also a poet, belonging to the Nuyorican poetry movement of together with Miguel Algarín—with whom he founded the Nuyorican Poets Café—and poets Jesús (Papoleto) Meléndez, Lucky Cienfuegos, and Sandra María Esteves, among others. The word *Nuyorican* was used by Algarín and Piñero as a way of defining a Puerto Rican culture developed in New York in close contact with Anglos and with people of diverse backgrounds. As a description of the group's poetry, it symbolized an aesthetic that included oral delivery of poetry, frequent code switching, and themes that dealt with life as it was lived on the streets of Manhattan's Lower East Side. Drink, drugs, delinquency, violence, and homosexuality—besides the racial and ethnic differences between Puerto Ricans and white Americans and the prejudices they engendered—were among the most frequent themes of this poetry, which documented and dramatized the circumstances of their lives. Piñero co-edited, with Algarín, the anthology *Nuyorican Poetry: An Anthology of Puerto Rican Words and Feelings* (1975) and later published a book of poetry: *La Bodega Sold Dreams* (1980). He became a legend in his own time. *Piñero,* a movie, was made about his life in 2001.

RELATED ARTICLES

Literature, Puerto Rican on the Mainland; Nuyorican Poets Cafe; Theater.

FURTHER READING

Aparicio, Frances. "From Ethnicity to Multiculturalism: An Historical Overview of Puerto Rican Literature in the United States." In *Handbook of Hispanic Cultures in the United States: Literature and Art.* Ed. by Nicolás Kanellos and Claudio Esteva-Fabregat. Houston, Tex.: Arte Público Press, 1993.

Flores, Juan. "Puerto Rican Literature in the United States: Stages and Perspectives." In *Divided Borders. Essays on Puerto Rican Identity.* Houston, Tex.: Arte Público Press, 1993.

Hernández, Carmen Dolores. "Miguel Algarín." In *Puerto Rican Voices in English. Interviews with Writers.* Westport, Conn.: Praeger, 1997.

Mohr, Eugene. *The Nuyorican Experience: Literature of the Puerto Rican Minority.* Westport, Conn.: Greenwood Press, 1982.

CARMEN DOLORES HERNÁNDEZ

PLAN DE DELANO. *See* DELANO, PLAN DE.

PLAN DE SAN DIEGO. *See* SAN DIEGO, PLAN DE.

PLAN DE SANTA BARBARA. *See* SANTA BARBARA, PLAN DE.

PLENA

Although its most basic features were derived directly or indirectly from the native *bomba* genre, it appears that the influences brought to the southern seaport of Ponce, Puerto Rico, by former slaves from various English-speaking Caribbean islands served as a catalyst for the emergence of *plena* at the beginning of the 20th century. Known for its syncopated rhythms, improvised instrumentation, and call-and-response vocal cadences, the *plena*'s four- or six-line verses generally deal with current events or social commentary in a satirical and humorous manner, bringing the news of the day to the general public, similar to Trinidadian calypso.

The main rhythmic instruments of *plena* are the *panderetas* or *panderos* (large, rattleless tambourines with different pitches), and the *güiro* (a gourd scraper also found in Cuban and Dominican music), but melodic and harmonic instruments have been integrated

Los Pleneros de la 21, the biggest *bomba y plena* group in New York City.

into this Afro-European form since its beginning, from the so-called *sinfonía de mano* (a Puerto Rican derivation of the German accordion) to the autochthonous ten-string *cuatro*.

The first *plena* recording was made by a group led by Manuel "El Canario" Jiménez in New York City, circa 1927. Within a few years the *plena* had already supplanted the traditions of both *bomba* and *música jíbara* among large segments of the working-class Puerto Rican population at home and abroad.

During the next two decades the *plena* extended its popularity when it was introduced by César Concepción and other San Juan figures into a danceable big-band repertoire geared toward the island's middle and upper classes. Never mind that such bandleaders failed to adapt the *plena*'s genuine essence to their U.S.-influenced orchestral format.

Nevertheless, the *plena* returned to the streets where it had begun, as its proper manifestations were eventually transmitted by percussionist Rafael Cortijo's combo (featuring Ismael Rivera's energetic vocals) to the younger generations. Without even utilizing the traditional *panderetas,* Cortijo revitalized

the *plena* in the 1960s with the compatible sounds of the Cuban *guaracha*.

The *plena*'s popularity was also increased in 1961 by the trombonist Efraín "Mon" Rivera, whose New York City–based band fused a powerful trombone section with the aforesaid Puerto Rican idiom. Mon's influence would be felt in the U.S. salsa scene through the remaining years of the 20th century.

With the passing of Cortijo and other vital *plena* exponents, the genre faded from the commercial mainstream, although a *plena* resurgence (spearheaded by the 12-piece band Plena Libre) has taken place in Puerto Rico since the 1990s, while traditional groups, such as Los Pleneros de la 110 and Los Pleneros de la 21, have kept the tradition alive in New York City.

Plena may be dwarfed in commercial terms by salsa and merengue, but the genre is still of considerable significance to younger generations of Puerto Rican musicians, as exemplified by the recent recordings of New York's Viento de Agua, a youthful ensemble that must be credited for taking both *plena* and *bomba,* at the dawn of the 21st century, to a creative level never experienced by prior practitioners of these ancestral expressions.

RELATED ARTICLES

Afro-Latino Influences; Music, Popular.

FURTHER READING

Echevarría Alvarado, Félix. *La plena: Origen, sentido y desarrollo en el fo1klore puertorriqueño* (Plena: Origin, Meaning and Development in Puerto Rican Folklore). Santurce: Epress, 1984.

Glasser, Ruth. *My Music Is My Flag: Puerto Rican Musicians and Their New York Communities, 1917–1940.* Berkeley: Univ. of Calif. Press, 1995.

LUIS TAMARGO

POLITICAL ASSOCIATION OF SPANISH SPEAKING ORGANIZATIONS

Founded in 1960, the Political Association of Spanish Speaking Associations (PASSO) was originally intended to be a national organization, but it is better known as an influential Texas organization. PASSO, along with the Mexican American Political Association (MAPA) in California, was one of the first overtly political Latino organizations, and its founding symbolized the shift in tactical strategy leading up to the Chicano movement of the late 1960s.

Prior to 1959 prominent Latino organizations focused on integrating new immigrants into their communities or on pushing for Mexican American integration into mainstream society. As such, their orientation was more social and civic than political and more moderate than radical. The first ethnic organizations were the *mutualistas,* or mutual aid societies, which provided insurance and other forms of economic assistance to Mexican American immigrants. They were followed by the League of Latin American Citizens (LULAC) whose goal was the economic and sociopolitical integration of Chicanos into mainstream society. Some critics charged the organization with focusing on the integration of middle-class Mexican Americans at the expense of those who were poor. Other organizations, including the American GI Forum, followed. The GI Forum was founded to ensure that Mexican American veterans of World War II received their fair share of benefits owed to them. While organizations such as LULAC and the GI Forum did address issues of discrimination, they took care to maintain at least the facade of nonpartisanship (the GI Forum did, however, cam-

paign for Democratic candidates in the 1950s). In many ways these groups were characterized as operating above the fray of electoral politics.

PASSO, in contrast, was explicitly political and electoral. Its goal was to educate Mexican American voters and to increase Mexican American voter registration and turnout. PASSO organizers wanted to use that electoral power to assert Chicano political power and influence. The association reached the peak of its power in 1963 in Crystal City, Texas, where the population was 80 percent Mexican American—many being migrant farmworkers—yet Anglos controlled the city and its agriculturally based economy. At the end of a wildly successful voter registration drive, which for the first time made Mexican American voters the majority of the city's electorate, PASSO fielded an all-Latino slate of city council candidates, called *los cinco,* "the five," after their number. In a stunning upset, the PASSO slate unseated the entire Anglo council, becoming the Southwest's first all Mexican American city council. That election demonstrated the power and self-determination of the Chicano electorate.

After the Crystal City victory, other cities hoped to organize similar campaigns. More moderate members of PASSO urged caution, wanting to ensure that political candidates were prepared to govern. There was open concern that *los cinco* had not been the most ideal political candidates. This discussion revealed an ideological rift between the moderate and more radial elements within the organization. This rift never healed. Nevertheless, the PASSO victory in Crystal City demonstrated the latent power of the Mexican American electorate and inspired other groups to push for Chicano political power.

RELATED ARTICLES

Inter-Latino Relations; Mutual Aid Societies; Politics, Latino.

FURTHER READING

García, Ignacio. *Viva Kennedy: Mexican Americans in Search of a Camelot.* College Station: Tex. A&M Univ. Press, 2000.

Hero, Rodney E. *Latinos and the U.S. Political System: Two-Tiered Pluralism.* Philadelphia: Temple Univ. Press, 1992.

McClain, Paula D., and Joseph Stewart, Jr. *"Can We All Get Along?" Racial and Ethnic Minorities in American Politics.* 2d ed. Boulder, Colo: Westview Press, 1999.

ANDRA GILLESPIE

POLITICAL PARTIES

The role of Latinos in presidential elections since the one that brought Ronald Reagan to office for the first time has become increasingly important. Unlike African Americans, Latinos are not solidly Democratic. Although only 20 percent of Latinos nationwide are registered Republican, President George W. Bush received approximately 35 percent of the Latino vote in the 2000 election. Since 45 percent of Latinos are registered Democrats, the Democratic Party has launched a renewed campaign to re-ignite their traditional support within the Latino community. New Mexico governor Bill Richardson was chosen to chair the 2004 Democratic National Convention in Boston, becoming the first Hispanic American ever in this role. Since approximately 35 percent of Latinos are registered independents, both political parties have actively pursued them in hopes of bringing them into their coalition.

The Republican Party has involved Latinos in its apparatus nationally and locally. President Reagan was elected president with strong Latino support, while in 1996 Robert Dole received a very small percentage of the Latino vote. In recent years, however, the Republican Party has alienated many Latino voters with such policies as English-only, welfare-reform, and anti-immigration legislation. In order to win Latino support, the Republicans have tried to moderate their extremist image and adopt a more reasonable, compassionate-conservative agenda that involves family values, lower taxes, and community control.

Hispanics in the United States cover the political spectrum. Fifty-two percent of Cuban Americans, for example, say they are Republican, while 47 percent of Mexican Americans are registered Democrats. This trend, however, is not always so clear. Comparing and contrasting different Latino groups' assimilation into American culture helps explain the diversity of opinions within the Latino community. An analysis of the dominant political ideologies among U.S. Hispanics is necessary in order to understand why Latino voters attach themselves to one political party or another.

History

Latinos are a politically and ethnically diverse group; not all Latinos can be classified in the same manner. Mexican Americans, for example, have resided in the Southwest for hundreds of years. Their unique cultural history is part of the political culture in states such as Texas, California, and New Mexico. Puerto Rican and Cuban immigrants, however, have more recently immigrated to the mainland United States for economic and political reasons, respectively. It was not until the 1960s that the number of Latino immigrants swelled, making the United States the fifth largest Spanish-speaking country in the world. A closer look at the history of Mexican Americans, Puerto Rican Americans, and Cuban Americans can help explain their varying political allegiances.

Mexican Americans

Mexican Americans are the largest and oldest Latino group in the United States. Much of the Southwest was part of Mexico until the Treaty of Guadalupe Hidalgo in 1848, whereby Mexico ceded to the United States territory that would become eight states. Many Mexicans lived on this land and remained there despite American control. Once Americans began to arrive in the new region, prejudice emerged against the Chicanos, who were seen by Americans as "cowardly, ignorant, lazy, and addicted to gambling and alcohol."

Most Mexican Americans in the United States have a mestizo origin; that is, they are a mixture of Caucasian and Native American. Mexican Americans currently represent one-quarter of the electorate in such crucial states as Texas and California. Traditionally, Chicanos have been loyal members of the Democratic Party, although in places such as New Mexico, Republicans have had a long tradition of incorporating Latinos into their fold. In New Mexico approximately 16 percent of Latinos are registered Republicans. The number of tepid Democrats is nearly 30 percent for Mexican Americans, higher than the number of Democrats in any other Latino group. Older Mexican Americans tend to be stronger partisans, while Spanish speakers are more likely to be weak partisans. Thus Chicanos are more likely to be Democrats, but are not as intense in their support for the Democratic Party as Cuban Americans are for the Republican Party.

Puerto Ricans

Unlike other Latinos, Puerto Ricans are already American citizens before entering the contiguous United States. Consequently, they are not branded as "illegals." Puerto Ricans have traditionally settled in New York City, to which they first migrated following the Spanish-American War. It was not until after World War II that Puerto Ricans migrated en masse to New York. In his book *Latinos and the U.S. Political System,* Rodney Hero attributes their immigration to the United States to "the economic policies of the United States and the island's government, which have encouraged industrialization and capitalist investment." Like today's Mexican immigrants, Puerto Ricans have come to the U.S. mainland for economic improvement and prosperity. Puerto Ricans have traditionally been heavily involved in the Democratic Party, and approximately 50 percent are registered Democrats. They are in accord with increased government support for the poor and see the Democratic Party as more willing to implement programs designed to help the economically disadvantaged. Unlike Republican Mexican Americans, Republican Puerto Ricans, especially men, are more likely to have had higher levels of education.

In recent elections Puerto Ricans have used their influence in the Democratic Party apparatus to deliver votes for fellow Democrats. In 1996 former president Clinton captured 93 percent of the Puerto Rican vote. On the other hand, the Republican former New York City mayor Rudolph Giuliani captured 37 percent of the Puerto Rican vote in his successful mayoral reelection campaign, and New York City Republican mayor Michael R. Bloomberg won his 2001 race with strong support from the Latino community, which is mostly Puerto Rican and Dominican. Dominicans have consistently supported a Republican mayor in greater numbers than have Puerto Ricans, however. One could argue that these numbers merely indicate the failure of the Republicans at the national level and the success of Giuliani and Bloomberg at the local level. Puerto Ricans clearly do not vote on any single issue, but the survey data and election choices seem to be somewhat counterintuitive. With numbers exceeding the rate at which African Americans vote for Democratic candidates, many Puerto Rican elites are concerned with responsiveness of the party to Puerto Rican constituents and the fear that votes may be assumed won without any persuasion. At the same time, the Democratic Party in New York counts many Puerto Ricans as leaders within the city and state party structure, thus enabling the party to be more responsive.

© STEVE YEATER/AP/WIDE WORLD PHOTOS

On election night 2003 California lieutenant governor Cruz Bustamante comments on Proposition 54, an initiative that would ban state and local governments from tracking race.

Cuban Americans

Unlike other Latinos, Cuban Americans primarily came to the United States (most settling in Miami) because of adverse political conditions, following Fidel Castro's revolution of 1959. In 2000 the Elián González controversy ignited the passions of many Cuban Americans who believed that the Clinton administration's Department of Justice, headed by Janet Reno, improperly sent the young boy back to an oppressive tyrannical regime. Many Cuban Americans who themselves left behind mothers, fathers, and siblings in Cuba in the early 1960s saw this incident as an affront to the principle that the ability to live in freedom outweighs the rights of a father. Presidential candidate Al Gore broke with former president Clinton, believing that the boy should have been allowed to stay in the United States. Despite this position, Gore received fewer Cuban American votes in Florida than did Bill Clinton in 1996, thus costing him Florida's crucial electoral votes. Most Cuban Americans are in this country for political rather than economic reasons. Lewis Gann and Peter Duignan note that "when many Mexican or Puerto Rican intellectuals turned to anti-establishment politics in the United States, most Cubans looked upon the United States as a refuge against tyranny." This distinction is crucial when determining the reason for Cuban Americans largely voting Republican in contrast to other Latinos. Traditionally, the Republican Party has been more supportive than the Democratic Party of tightening the trade embargo on Cuba. In addition, the GOP was perceived as more anti-communist during the Cold War. Better than 66.7 percent of Cuban Americans oppose U.S. relations with Cuba, and, surprisingly, Mexican Americans and Puerto Ricans also oppose U.S. relations with Cuba, at 56.3 percent and 59.7 percent, respectively. Forty-eight percent of Cubans surveyed classified themselves as strong Republicans. This figure exceeds the number of Puerto Ricans and Mexican Americans who claim to be strong Democrats by approximately 10 percentage points and 16 percentage points, respectively. In addition, Cuban Americans born in Cuba are less likely to be Republicans, while Cuban Americans who speak at least some Spanish are more likely to be Republicans. It appears that immigrants who left Cuba after 1959 but before the Mariel boat lift in 1980 are more likely to identify as partisan Republicans.

California

California's Hispanic demography is primarily Mexican American. In the 1990s the Republican Party failed to present a clear and winning strategy in this state. The 1998 elections resulted in a new Democratic governor, Gray Davis, and the reelection of Democratic senator Barbara Boxer.

Many attributed this anti-Republican mood among Latinos in the state to former governor Pete Wilson, who was elected to that office in 1990. During his tenure he alienated many Latinos because of his anti-immigration stance in support of Proposition 187, which aimed to limit state services to undocumented immigrants and their children. An article in *The Economist* noted: "Pete Wilson has done the impossible. He has succeeded in uniting most of the state's very varied Latinos behind a single cause . . . hatred of Mr. Wilson's party, the Republicans." The state of California saw a Democratic surge beginning in 1996, with Wilson's alienation of Latinos certainly contributing to this phenomenon. There were three factors for the surge: the out-migration of Republican voters, the growth of the Latino vote, and the economic shift of the state's huge defense-oriented and aerospace industrial base to information-age technology.

There were three major issues that contributed to the Democratic surge in California—immigration policy, English-only, and affirmative action. With regard to immigration, the Republicans fostered a climate of hostility toward Latinos entering the country. Republican congressman Bob Dornan, for example, advocated a tough immigration policy that, according to many Latinos, was tantamount to racism. Latino voters overwhelmingly opposed Proposition 187, and they expressed this through the ballot box. The proposition, however, passed in the statewide election because of strong white support. Many Latinos felt that this was a racist attack on Latinos, who are the majority of immigrants in California. Furthermore, they saw the Republican agenda as a disguise for anti-Latino policies, certainly a result of restrictive legislation like Proposition 187.

Secondly, a substantial number of Republicans pushed for an English-only law that would curb bilingual education in public schools. A high percentage of Hispanics saw this policy as unfair because it discriminated against them, since they are the main beneficiaries of bilingual education. In California, Republican politicians have generally supported English-only policies.

Thirdly, the Republican policy of ending affirmative action in California alienated many Latinos. The enactment of Proposition 209 effectively banned affirmative action in the state's higher education admission policies. Not only has this policy angered African Americans, it has also angered Latinos who feel that affirmative action is necessary for upward mobility. However, following a recall election in November 2003, Republican movie actor Arnold Schwarzenegger was elected governor, replacing Gray Davis.

Texas

The 1990 U.S. Census showed that Mexican Americans constituted 26 percent of the population in Texas, which in 2000 rose to 33 percent. In addition, according to Charles Elliott and his associates, Texas has elected more Latinos to public office than any other state. With a growing number of Latino officeholders and coalitions, it is evident that Latinos have been a major force in both political parties in Texas. A study of Latinos in Texas in the 1990s found that "28 percent of Hispanics identified themselves as liberals, 34 percent as moderates, and 37 percent as conservatives," which indicates that Republicans have made gains among Latinos.

Republican George W. Bush had focused on education, tort, and welfare-system reform, as well as juvenile justice laws for his 1994 gubernatorial victory. In 1998 Bush was reelected with 68.6 percent of the vote, significantly garnering 49 percent of the Hispanic vote, 27 percent of the black vote, 65 percent of the female vote, and 27 percent of the Democratic vote. In addition, he was the first gubernatorial candidate to have won in the strongly Hispanic and Democratic border counties of El Paso, Cameron, and Hidalgo. Thus some Republicans have argued that Bush's election campaign should serve as an example to Republicans.

Republicans in Texas have capitalized on the notion that the majority of Latinos are moderate to conservative, especially on social issues. Bush, in his first presidential campaign, was related to Latinos by offering them a conservative philosophy. Furthermore, education was a major platform item.

Given his success with Latinos, Bush may have taken cues from Henry Bonilla. Bonilla has served as a Republican congressman from the San Antonio area for almost ten years in a Democratic district. His district was 65 percent Latino, and he was the first Latino Republican congressman elected in Texas history. Winning office with over 65 percent of the vote each time, Bonilla combined a personal appeal—being sensitive to his constituents' concerns—with the Republican message of lower taxes and less government spending to achieve his electoral coalition.

Bonilla proposes that Republicans actively court the Latino vote and campaign in their neighborhoods. That Hispanics are an active part of Republican Party politics in Texas is another advantage to the party, since they can help mobilize other voters during elections. This is not the case in California, where the Republicans have in recent years been inhospitable to the inclusion of Latinos in their party apparatus precisely because of the perceived anti-immigrant policies of the state party.

In Texas, Republican politicians proved that their message can win Latino support. Latinos will be more receptive to GOP candidates if there is a community outreach campaign that addresses the needs of the Latino community along with those of other Americans.

Observations

The demographics in the United States are changing, and the American political parties are beginning to respond to the burgeoning Latino voting bloc. Latinos are becoming major candidates in races all

© GEORGE BRIDGES/KRT

George W. Bush greets Representative Ileana Ros-Lehtinen (Republican, Florida) after speaking about U.S. policy toward Cuba.

over the country. New Latino U.S. House members are entering the chamber every two years; in 2002 Representatives Mario Diaz-Balart (Republican, Florida), Linda Sanchez (Democrat, California), and Raul Grijalva (Democrat, Arizona) were all elected to the House. It is only a matter of time before the U.S. Senate counts Hispanics in that body, and before more states in addition to New Mexico elect Latino governors. Already, in many states, Latinos have risen to powerful party positions—among them, Democrat Albio Sires, the Cuban-born speaker of the New Jersey Assembly; and Al Cardenas, the chairman of the Florida Republican Party. Both political parties have appointed high-profile Latinos to important cabinet positions. Latinos will continue to be involved in the political administrations of both parties and will undoubtedly be influential decision-makers for years to come. Everyone wins in a competitive political culture. Rivalry between the two major parties within the Latino community will inevitably lead to a more responsive and representative government. The relationship between Latinos and the political parties is complex and fluid. Competitive two-party politics will result in a stronger Latino community in the 21st century.

RELATED ARTICLES

Democratic Party; League of United Latin American Citizens; Politics, Cuban American; Politics, Latino; Politics, Mexican American; Politics, Puerto Rican; Republican Party; United States Presidents and Latinos.

FURTHER READING

Conde, Carlos. "Republicans on the Mend." *Hispanic.* 11 (May 1998): 36–42.

DeSipio, Louis. *Counting on the Latino Vote.* Charlottesville: Univ. of Va. Press, 1996.

Dickens, E. Larry. *Texas Politics.* Boston: Houghton Mifflin, 1997.

Elliott, Charles P. *The World of Texas Politics.* New York: St. Martin's, 1998.

Gann, Lewis H., and Peter J. Duignan. *The Hispanics in the United States: A History.* Boulder, Colo.: Westview Press, 1986.

Hero, Rodney E. *Latinos and the U.S. Political System: Two Tiered Pluralism.* Philadelphia: Temple Univ. Press, 1992.

JASON P. CASELLAS

POLITICS, CUBAN AMERICAN

Beginning in 1890, first under the leadership of José Martí and later Tomás Estrada Palma, a New York–based Cuban junta founded patriotic clubs of Cuban workers throughout the United States resulting in monthly financial contributions for the purchase of weapons and ammunition. By 1896 they were sufficiently organized to hold a week-long Cuban American Fair at Madison Square Garden in New York City and to establish a league of non-Cuban supporters including future president Theodore Roosevelt and celebrated millionaire John Jacob Astor.

The rebels also exploited tabloid newspaper competition between Joseph Pulitzer's *New York World* and William Randolph Hearst's *New York Journal* to demonize the Spaniards and publicize a sympathetic, though not necessarily factual, presentation of the rebel cause that hastened U.S. entry into the war. They endorsed the Teller Amendment, which disclaimed any intention on the part of the United States to control Cuba except for purposes of pacification, asserting that the U.S. forces would leave once independence was achieved. At the end of the Spanish-American War, the amendment came back to haunt Cuban-U.S. relations when it was reinterpreted in the Platt Amendment as a U.S. right of intervention when necessary. In the independence era, as with successive ones, it was difficult for those in Cuba and their exile counterparts to maintain lines of communication, authority, and trust.

Similarly, in the late 1950s Fidel Castro's 26th of July Movement and other revolutionary groups organized in the United States to raise funds, buy weapons, and lobby in favor of ending U.S. support to Fulgencio Batista. In November 1957 representa-

tives of the seven leading groups negotiated and signed an agreement in Miami creating a Cuban Liberation Council. Castro denounced the pact, demonstrating the inherent tensions between U.S.- and Cuban-based revolutionaries, saying that "the leaders of the other organizations that signed this pact are living in exile, making an imaginary revolution, while the leaders of the July 26 Movement are in Cuba, making a real revolution." Under Castro's leadership a second pact, signed in Caracas, Venezuela, in 1958, affirmed the unity of the major groups without specifying a program. Political control of the insurrection shifted to Castro where it remained until the revolutionary triumph of 1959.

Following the departure of Cuban dictator Batista on December 31, 1958, and the radicalization of politics on the island, many Cubans went into exile, with approximately 135,000 settling mainly in South Florida during the first three years. Initially, exiles assumed that U.S.-led or U.S.-supported intervention would quickly lead to the installation of a democratic regime and to what they called *regreso* (return) on favorable terms. History gave them every reason to believe in "return," since prior generations of Cubans had experienced only brief exiles during tense political contests in the homeland, and U.S. troops had intervened in the Cuban War of Independence and again in 1906, 1912, and 1917.

The pervasiveness of the "return" mentality can be seen in Miami newspapers from the 1960s, where appliance and furniture advertisements reveal then-popular expectations. The ads pitched portable models of furniture and appliances, urging customers to buy now what they will take home later. Many young families put off having children with the expectation that, within a few years, they could begin their families in Cuba. Like domestic life, political involvement in the United States was simply a means to hasten "return." Thousands of exiles joined Brigade 2506, a United States-Central Intelligence Agency organized, financed, and trained assault force that invaded Cuba in 1961. A parallel group of civilian exile leaders formed the Consejo Revolucionario Cubano (Cuban Revolutionary Council), which was intended as a transitional governing junta once the invasion succeeded.

When this first postrevolutionary political alliance ended in unexpected defeat at the Bay of Pigs, both exiles and academic experts blamed a number of factors, including political naiveté on the part of the

Supporters of the Brothers to the Rescue watch a tape of leader José Basulto, in Miami, 2003.

exiles, exclusion of exile leaders from planning, their detention by the U.S. government during the invasion, poor site selection for the initial invasion, and the failure of President Kennedy to authorize effective air cover for the invasion or to commit U.S. ground forces. Whatever the reasons for defeat, for many Cubans it marked their future partisan political choices. The North American leaders who had thwarted their return were from the Democratic Party; this would not be forgotten when Cuban exiles eventually resigned themselves to staying in the United States, becoming citizens, and engaging in domestic politics.

A year later the 1962 Cuban missile crisis ended with a U.S.-Soviet agreement that the United States would not invade Cuba in exchange for Soviet withdrawal of the missiles. Cold war negotiation had prevented nuclear war and favored U.S. national security but thwarted any lingering hope of a quick and easy "return" for the nearly 200,000 Cubans who had arrived by that time. The disillusioned exiles were relocated throughout the United States by the federally sponsored Cuban Refugee Program. At the

time it seemed that Cuban American politics would be the politics of assimilation that had characterized other immigrant groups.

However, in 1965 another surge of Cubans entered the United States, first through the Camarioca boatlift and then by way of the "air bridge" that continued until 1973. Another 340,000 Cubans arrived in these years, and despite their resettlement many voluntarily returned to the Miami area. By the late 1970s, 65 percent of Cuban Americans lived in south Florida. Had they remained scattered, the small numbers of Cuban Americans relative to the population of the United States would have made it unlikely that they could gain collective and continuing political power. By settling mainly in south Florida or by returning to the area after initial relocation, exiles established Miami as the unofficial capital of the largest Cuban community outside the island.

More important, the Cubans established themselves on favorable terms. Geographic concentration combined with mutual aid, government benefits, preexisting Cuban capital, women entering the workforce, and educational attainment helped form a

Cuban American enclave rather than a ghettoized, dependent minority. That is, through a variety of favorable circumstances, Cubans were able to establish an economically viable community that remained socially and culturally their own. Fortunately for the Cubans, the location itself became powerful as Florida evolved into a key electoral state. Those who could affect voting in Florida could influence presidents and their foreign policies.

For over a decade Cuban exiles did not act on their domestic political potential in the United States for several reasons. First, they were not yet citizens and they lacked the vote even though they had growing numbers. A second factor was the relative strength of continuing ties to Cuba. Eduardo Padrón, now the president of Miami-Dade College, remembers that in 1970 when he and other political activists began to urge Cuban Americans to run for elected office they were denounced on local radio stations as Communists. Candidacy and citizenship implied

that the Cubans were "giving up" on going home, thereby bolstering Castro's position. As late as 1978 no Cuban American held an elected state or county office in Florida, although elites such as Alfredo Durán in the Democratic Party and Alfredo Cardenas in the Republican Party had not only joined but had come to lead state and county political organizations for their parties.

By the early 1980s, however, a combination of economic integration and social discrimination made mass political participation desirable. Nativist sentiment, aroused by the large numbers of Cubans and increased use of Spanish in public places, led some non-Hispanic groups to propose an English-only referendum in Dade County. The measure passed with combined support of Anglo and black voters. The English-only ordinance prohibited the bilingualism that was evolving and meant that civil proceedings such as marriages could not be performed in Spanish. It reversed the positive multicultural philosophy

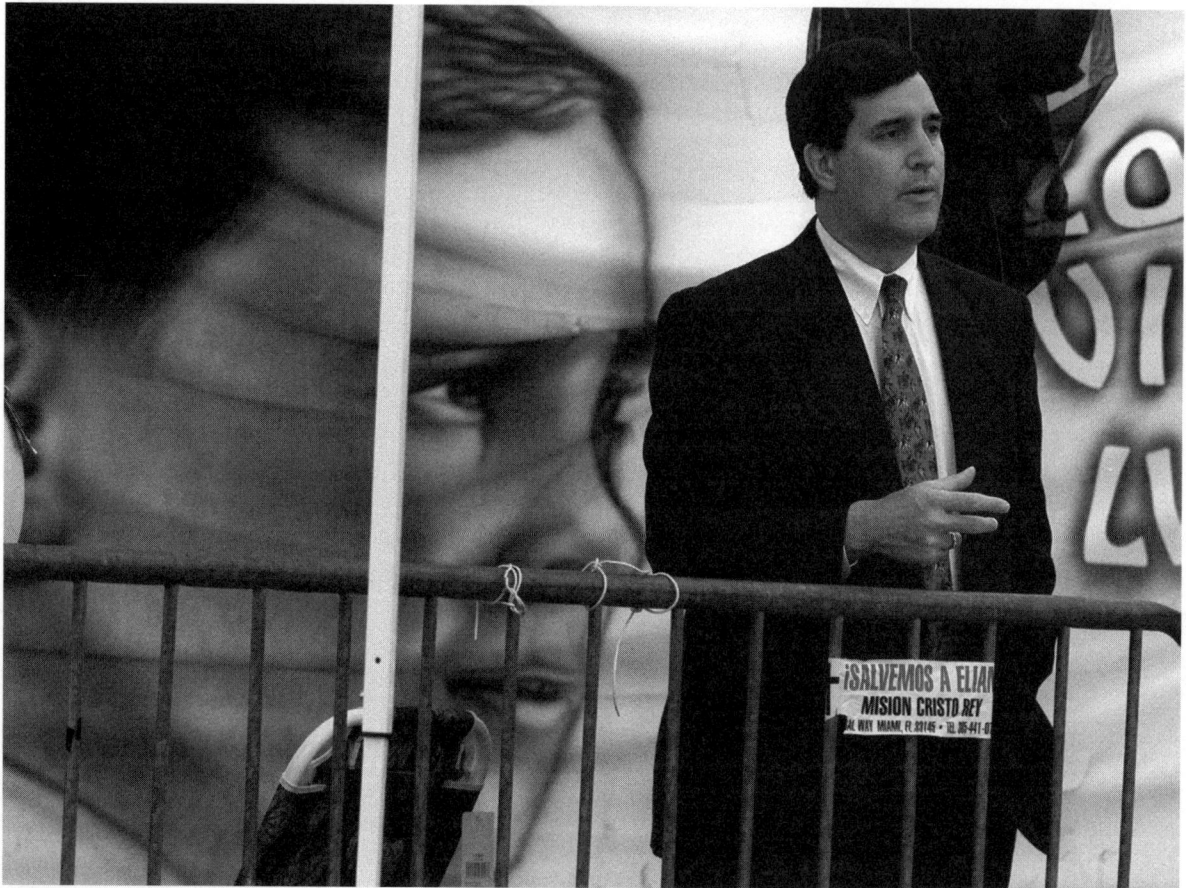

© CHUCK FADELY / MIAMI HERALD / GETTY IMAGES

Miami mayor Joe Carollo speaks across the barricades to protesters staging a vigil at the Little Havana home of Elián González's relatives during U.S. government efforts to return the boy to his father in Cuba.

that had resulted in a 1970 ordinance endorsing bilingualism and revealed deep resentment in the non-Latino community.

Offended by the measure, Cubans took immediate and direct political action, registering to vote for the first time in large numbers. In 1976 Cuban Americans accounted for only 8 percent of registered voters in Dade County but by 1983 they claimed 20 percent of all registrations. By 1983 in south Florida they could be found in elected positions extending from the local Dade County school board to the mayoral offices of suburban Hialeah and Sweetwater and in three seats in the Florida legislature. When President Ronald Reagan boasted of having appointed 125 Latinos to high positions during his first term, it turned out that 100 of them were Cuban Americans. Cuban Americans were outstripping other Latino groups in prominence and power.

When the English-only ordinance was finally rescinded in 1993 it was accomplished by a county commission composed of a majority of Cuban American commissioners in a metropolitan area that was home to over 585,000 persons of Cuban descent. In 30 years time, Cuban Americans became the majority.

Although Cuban Americans, unlike other Latinos, joined both major political parties, their voting patterns and political culture were profoundly conservative. In 1989 when conservative Republican Ileana Ros Lehtinen, the daughter of a Bay of Pigs brigade member, became the first Cuban American elected to the U.S. Congress, she replaced a retiring 20-year veteran, liberal Democrat Claude Pepper. Ros received 94 percent of all Cuban American votes despite the fact that Republicans accounted for less than 40 percent of registered voters, and the election further divided the area by race and ethnicity. At least five factors can explain the persistent conservative tendency in Cuban American politics.

First, the founders of the Cuban American community were wealthy and they were white. Unlike other Latino groups, Cubans came to the United States in a reverse order, led by wealthy conservatives, followed by professionals, and finally by the working classes. Likely Democratic supporters such as unskilled laborers and those who would have been rejected based on race never came in significant numbers, and those few who did settled outside of Miami. The financial ability to rebuild businesses, combined

with whiteness, which afforded access to civic boards and committees—quickly extended to financial power. This foundation served as a springboard for the middle and working classes that followed. Although Cuban American communities had their share of poor and needy groups, the image of the "miracle" of Cuban American success and the need to support an anti-Castro foreign policy agenda always came first for Cuban American leaders. Social welfare activism, a customary linking point to partisan politics in other Latino communities, was handled through more traditional channels of *amiguismo* (networks of favors based on friendship) in the Cuban community.

Secondly, the experience of losing a way of life and real property to a Soviet-supported revolution made the Cuban Americans profoundly anti-Communist. The relatively radical temper of the times in the United States during the late 1960s and early 1970s ran counter to Cuban Americans' experience and further isolated them, reinforcing the need to stick together and to take a conservative position. In addition, Cubans believed that the Democratic Party had betrayed them at the Bay of Pigs and that the Republicans had just taken a turn to the right under Richard Nixon.

A third factor that created a conservative political culture was the fact that moderate to left-of-center forces in the Cuban polity were missing in the exile in any significant numbers until the late 1970s and 1980s. There simply was no substantial counterweight to conservative ideas. From 1961 on, most of those still in Cuba who broke with Fidel Castro and advocated center to left-of-center political views had been executed or were in prison. Through the joint efforts of exiles in the United States and Venezuela, together with officials of the Carter administration, many of these political prisoners were released in the late 1970s and took their families with them into exile. There, they faced the dual problems of reestablishing their lives and their politics in a well organized and politically vengeful community that blamed them for loss of the homeland. The most reactionary forces had declared a "war through all the paths of the world" during the 1970s as a way to continue resisting the revolutionary consolidation on the island. This involved terrorist activity aimed at Cuban diplomats, their missions, and their supporters. During the late 1970s and early 1980s, centrist and leftist perspectives were silenced in the Cuban American community through violence and ostracism.

A fourth powerful element assuring that Cuban American politics would be conservative was the preeminence of a single lobbying group. In 1981 the Cuban American National Foundation (CANF) and its associated political action committee were formed. Control of the organization was soon consolidated under the leadership of Jorge Mas Canosa, a Cuban American, self-made multimillionaire. Essentially, CANF used a strategy of controlling U.S. foreign policy toward Cuba through political contributions and lobbying at a time that was propitious for their cause. Florida was a key electoral state critical to presidential candidates. By supporting a conservative policy toward Cuba, candidates could gain a crucial swing vote without having to trade away other domestic or foreign policy issues to obtain it. The Cuban Americans were seen as single-issue voters where contact with a single group, CANF, could achieve results. Although CANF had its headquarters in Miami, it had active chapters in every significant diaspora community both in the United States and abroad. With the exception of Jimmy Carter's brief dialogue in 1978, CANF funds and lobbying would successfully reward or pressure, or both, presidential and congressional candidates into maintaining a conservative and punitive foreign policy and a liberal immigration policy toward Cuba for two decades.

The foundation and Mas Canosa not only came to epitomize Cuban American politics for most political pundits and the media but also to link Miami in the public imagination with a particularly monolithic conservatism. Invoking "the Cubans in Miami" became indistinguishable from saying "conservative politics." When discussing Latino political views taken together, it was not uncommon to hear general support for liberal to leftist policy preferences qualified by "except for those in Miami." In many places this stereotype persists despite changes in the demography and diversity of political views in Miami.

A final ingredient that promoted conservatism was lack of communication with the island population during the 1970s and the separation of Cuban families that accompanied it. With the acceptance of a Soviet-style administration in 1968, the island became relatively closed to Westerners. Families in Cuba could lose opportunities for and access to work and education if they were found to be in contact with their *gusano* (worm) relatives in the United States. Communication that might have tempered conservative views and healed personal relationships in Miami was cut off from both sides of the Straits of Florida.

In the late 1970s, when a dialogue did occur between the Cuban government and more moderate exiles, those Cuban Americans who participated paid a high price in lost jobs, ruined businesses, and truncated socioeconomic opportunities. It also contributed to Carter's failure to gain a second term. Although the 1978 "dialogue" opened the way for return visits by Cuban Americans, people did not advertise their visits within what was now a presumptively punitive and conservative context. Nonetheless, seeds of alternative political thinking were sown in the late 1970s.

In 1980 and again in 1994, the small but growing numbers of people who favored contact with the island were supplemented with two substantial surges of new arrivals born and raised entirely under the revolution. In 1980 approximately 125,000 Cubans arrived in the United States through the Mariel Boat Lift, and by 1994 over 45,000 came as rafters. These groups denied political struggle and eventual "return" as their prime motivations and have did not become active in exile political life. Rather, they endured life-threatening ordeals in order to escape politics permanently and to make private lives in the United States. They have strong ties to family and friends in Cuba and see deficiencies in both the exile and the island social systems. They are more likely to criticize the U.S. embargo and to want a resolution of U.S.-Cuba differences so that conditions will improve for their relatives in Cuba. As the Cuban American population ages, the demography of the exile is shifting toward the perspective of the moderate groups who arrived in the 1970s and the more apolitical groups from the post-1980s. Since most of the post-1980 arrivals do not vote, they have made an impact on public opinion but not on politics.

There are, however, other powerful domestic groups, such as traditionally Republican agribusiness wanting to sell products to Cuba, that are affecting Cuban American politics by taking an aggressive antiembargo, protrade position. As a consequence, the CANF formula is no longer working. Senators and representatives now have local constituents who offer a different counsel when it comes to U.S. foreign policy and trade with Cuba.

Additionally, the foundational leader, Mas Canosa, died in 1997 leaving his son, Jorge Mas Santos to run CANF. Since then, conservative elements have become factionalized. The hard-line associates of Canosa left CANF to form the Cuban Liberty Council, calling the new CANF president disrespectful. Mas Santos's leadership of CANF has been less purposeful, zealous, and astute than his father's. Rather than successfully twisting some political arms, in August 2003, in response to the return of Cuban asylum seekers, the various conservative factions fell into a bout of public name calling that occupied the Cuban American media for several days. Mas Santos accused the two Republican congressional representatives, Lincoln Díaz-Balart and Ileana Ros, of "allowing" President George W. Bush to abandon the Cuban American cause by failing to restrain repatriation and for lack of action on the massive human rights violations that occurred in Cuba in March 2003. Ros and Díaz-Balart took a straight party line, defending the president and making ad hominem attacks against Mas Santos, while the Cuban Liberty Council stormed Florida governor Jeb Bush's offices demanding that he call his brother to account. The once solid and formidable conservative wing of Cuban American politics showed signs of internal strife and a lack of strategic direction.

At the same time, the U.S. Congress came close to passing legislation easing the travel ban on Cuba and expanding trade. Although President Bush promised to veto any such legislation, the growing success of the measure illustrated the rising political influence of Cuban American moderates. These groups have worked in coalition with North American nongovernmental organizations opposed to the embargo and with corporate agricultural interests to draft and lobby the legislation.

Not only are views changing within the Cuban American community but other, traditionally more liberal Latino groups have established themselves in what had been exclusively Cuban American political territory in Florida. Puerto Ricans, who are citizens by birth and can vote on arrival, doubled their numbers in Florida during the 1990s with 482,000 living mostly around Orlando by 2000. Both Democratic and Republican political parties have formed "Caribbean Caucuses" in their Florida chapters to facilitate the inclusion of approximately 500,000

West Indians living there. Add to these groups more than 400,000 Mexicans who made up South Florida's fastest rising Latino population in the 2000 census, and continued exclusive control by Cuban Americans seems unlikely.

In preparation for the 2004 presidential election, the Southwest Voter Registration Project, a predominantly Mexican American group, sent organizers to Florida to accelerate voter registration among Latinos of all origins. Clearly, the critical electoral status of Florida that has empowered Cuban American politicians is increasingly contested territory. Interestingly, a poll conducted by the Southwest Voter Registration Project revealed that 62 percent of Cuban Americans feel that improving their quality of life is a higher priority than changing the government in Cuba. Among those under age 45 the percentage jumps to 72 percent. Within the traditional electorate priorities have changed.

Despite demographic shifts and constituent preferences, the majority of elected leaders in Cuban American communities are conservative and Republican. Over time they have developed mechanisms for serving constituents and have amassed seniority and influence in state and federal legislatures that help them retain office. Alfredo Duran, the former chair of the Florida Democratic Party, offered this summary of the situation: "Cuban-Americans will continue to have unmatched economic control for the foreseeable future and, for winning in politics, that's what counts."

RELATED ARTICLES

Brothers to the Rescue; Castro, Fidel; Cuban American National Council; Cuban American National Foundation; Cuban Missile Crisis; Cuban Revolution; Democratic Party; Dialogo, El; Exile; Guevara, Ernesto; Mas Canosa, Jorge; Republican Party.

FURTHER READING

Arboleya, Jesus. *The Cuban Counterrevolution.* Athens, Ohio: Ohio Univ. Center for International Studies, 2000.

Bardach, Ann Louise. *Cuba Confidential: Love and Vengeance in Miami and Havana.* New York: Random House, 2002.

Boswell, Thomas D., and Guarione Díaz. *A Demographic Profile of Cuban Americans.* Miami: Cuban Am. National Council, 2002.

Portes, Alejandro, and Alex Stepick. *City on the Edge: The Transformation of Miami.* Berkeley: Univ. of Calif. Press, 1993.

HOLLY ACKERMAN

POLITICS, LATINO

To speak about Latino politics, one must first understand who is included or counted as a Latino. Some commentators explain that the term *Latino* is a sociolegal construction of a loosely identifiable ethnic community, which encompasses, in turn, members of different ethnic groups. The term *Hispanic* has become a proxy in the United States for categorizing all people whose ancestry is primarily from a Spanish-speaking country. A growing majority of Latinos in the United States reject being categorized as *Hispanic*, because of the term's association with Spanish conquest and colonial power. In addition, the term does not take into account the diverse racial, class, linguistic, cultural, historical, and national-origin distinctiveness of people grouped under this category. Most prefer the term *Latino,* short for Latinoamericano, because it is a more inclusive and perhaps more descriptive term.

Latino political participation is historically rich, reflecting oppositional politics, political compromise, or accommodation politics and protest politics. Although some commentators indicate that Latino politics proper only began to emerge in the 1970s, and was shaped by the civil rights agenda, others point out that Latino politics—specifically, Chicano politics—can be traced to the Mexican-American War. Whenever its origin, virtually all Latino political involvement began with organizational politics, as represented by social action organizations, unions, and service clubs. Two of the most important organizations to emerge during the early 1920s were La Orden de los Hijos de America, and the League of Latin American Citizens. The United Farm Workers, founded in 1962 by César Chávez in California, was a catalyst in the subsequent development of labor politics. Latinos in the United States have a lengthy history of organizing communally dynamic groups to shield themselves against American political domination as well as ethnic discrimination and all of its manifestations.

The origins of Latino political power were concentrated in the local politics of the Southwest, without much impact on the national arena. For example, during the period of accommodation politics (1920s–1930s), few if any of the grass-roots organizations had the power to challenge and change American political hegemony. Impediments to reaching a national audience or having an effect of national scope were rooted in a lack of resources, institutional discrimination, gerrymandering, threats of deportation, and lack of expertise. As new political organizations and leaders emerged, the move toward registering Latino voters began to gather momentum.

But the drive toward involvement and inclusion has encountered severe obstacles. Naturalization and voter registration are two of the most significant barriers to full Latino political participation. According to the 2000 census, Latinos account for 13 percent of the population, or 35 million people. Yet, only 5.9 million Latinos voted in the 2000 election. Although Latino voter turnout has historically been low, the 2000 elections show an increasing gap between the size of the population and those eligible or willing to vote. Low participation is the result of a variety of demographic factors, including a young population—over 12 million Latinos are under 18 years of age—and a large percentage of first-generation immigrants, who make up more than half the voting-age population. For example, as of the year 2000, four in ten Latinos residing in the United States lacked U.S. citizenship. As of 2004, 60 percent of Latinos were not eligible to vote. The challenges presented by the rapidly growing Latino population—soon to become the largest minority group in the United States—are significant because with such a large presence comes the promise of increased political participation and empowerment in the face of difficult cultural, linguistic, and demographic barriers to such empowerment.

One's categorization as a Latino has legal consequences. Since 1997 federal law, through the White House's Office of Management and Budget (OMB) Directive Number 15, has imposed the categorization of Hispanic or Latino to "a person of Cuban, Mexican, Puerto Rican, South or Central American, or other Spanish culture or origin regardless of race." Latinos are not a monolith, yet the federal government relies on official data collected under OMB Directive 15 to enforce civil-rights laws, legislative redistricting and voting rights, affirmative action programs, school desegregation, minority business development, and fair housing provisions, and to conduct the census.

Understanding that the Latino population measured by the 2000 U.S. Census suffers from both under inclusiveness and over inclusiveness, when the Latino population reaches majority by 2015, Latino politics will propel an important shift in national politics in the United States. Immigration is and has been the single most important force influencing and shaping Latino politics. In this context, studies about immigration patterns and policies show that immigration shapes political attitudes and behavior, and influences interest-group mobilization. Addressing immigration issues as well as focusing on the imperative of naturalization as central organizing political principles will present some of the most difficult challenges to the Latino political effort in the coming years.

Political involvement depends considerably on political enlistment and mobilization, and political organizations play an essential role in securing and enabling participation. Political organizations and coalitions are formed with the intent to create some unity among Latinos. While some organizations have an exclusive political focus, others are more diversified, targeting the politics as well as the ideals of the Latino community. One of the first organizations to form was the League of United Latin Americans (LULAC), in 1921 in Corpus Christi, Texas. The initial goals of LULAC were to promote civil and social equality, full integration of Spanish-speaking Americans, improved education, active participation in U.S. politics, and an end to discrimination in schools and employment.

The largest and oldest Latino organization in the United States, LULAC became an effective lobbying group quite rapidly as a result of its well thought-out efforts to achieve its organizing goals. It undertook writing educational voter guides and information. Its policy and education arm undertook numerous studies of legislation affecting Latinos. Today LULAC is actively involved in a variety of educational, social, and political projects aimed at changing the national political agenda. For example, citizenship awareness programs; corporate alliances; the Empower Hispanic America with Technology Project; LULAC National Educational Service Centers; housing, immigration, employment, leadership, literacy, and scholarship programs; a voter registration project; and SER Jobs for Progress.

The 1960s ushered in the creation of additional social and political organizations, each with varying degrees of success. Those with the ability to raise funds from private and public sources have been the most successful. An important group created in the 1960s is the National Council of La Raza (NCLR), of Washington, D.C. Its original mission was to reduce poverty and discrimination and improve life opportunities for Hispanic Americans. Toward this goal NCLR enabled the creation of community-based organizations, and engaged in applied research, policy analysis, and advocacy on behalf of Latino communities' interests and needs regarding such important issues as education, immigration, housing, health, employment, discrimination, and other issues affecting Latino communities.

Two additional organizations tied to Latino politics are the Congressional Hispanic Caucus (CHC) and the National Association of Latino Elected and Appointed Officials (NALEO). The CHC was founded in 1976 by Herman Badillo and four other Latino Democrats then in Congress. CHC was originally organized as a legislative service organization under the rules of Congress and today is a congressional member organization, which had 25 members in the 108th Congress. The goals of the CHC are to voice and advance through the legislative process issues affecting Latinos in the United States and insular areas. The function of the CHC is to serve as a forum through which Latino members of Congress can coalesce around a collective legislative agenda and, among other tasks, to monitor executive and judicial policies affecting Latinos. The CHC also has an educational foundation arm, which has as a primary focus the education and empowerment of future Latino political leaders.

NALEO was formed in 1976 as a nonprofit, nonpartisan, member organization of the nation's elected and appointed officials and supporters. NALEO membership increased from 3,128 members in 1984 to 4,464 in 2002. NALEO is focused on increasing Latino participation in areas that are of national and salient concern to a majority of Latino communities. In 1981 NALEO expanded to create an Educational Fund, which develops and implements programs that promote the integration of Latino immigrants. Much like the efforts of the CHC, NALEO conducts programs that focus on educating and developing future political and community leaders, trains Latino elected and appointed officials, and conducts research on a variety of issues affecting Latinos.

The research, studies, and policy projects many of these organizations undertake provide extremely useful information to educate leaders and grass-roots organizations about the problems confronting Latino participation, which in turn help to strategize em-

The 1998 victory of former mayor of Miami, Florida, Xavier Suárez, was nullified owing to allegations that some of the people who voted for him were dead.

powerment efforts. Since the 1970s Latinos have been motivated by recognizing the potential they hold for economic and political empowerment. For example, one study conducted by NALEO shows that between 1984 and 1994, the total number of Latino elected officials increased nationally from 3,128 to 4,625—an increase of approximately 50 percent. The increase is most commonly attributed to the adoption of bilingual ballot laws, a surge in Latino political activism, and an increase in the number of Latino candidates competing in local, state, and federal elections.

Latino political participation, while still lagging behind its population presence, has increased significantly since 1990. As described by authors Louis DeSipio and Rodolfo O. de la Garza, there is a rise of a "new cadre of Latino elites and new institutions to shape candidate outreach to Latinos." These new elites are described as being primarily "young, highly educated Latinos who have begun to populate campaigns." As the new Latino elites participate more actively and in greater numbers in political campaigns, they bring with them the power to draw attention to the concerns of the Latino community, to educate non-Latino candidates about Latino communities, and to set an example and become role models for others to follow. Some of the more promising organizations include Latino political action committees and Latino associations within state and national political parties. Although most Latino organizations struggle with fundraising and gaining influence at the national level, there is hope that this situation will change as more Latinos gain citizenship, education, wealth, and status. For example, although Latino participation in presidential campaign staffs had been minimal prior to 1992, about 20 percent of the Clinton political campaign workers of 1992 and 1996 were Latino, and Latinos were subsequently involved in many aspects of and held posts within the Clinton administration.

Informal and formal networks of influential Latinos have also fueled local grass-roots efforts to encourage involvement in politics. The Republican Party offers the best example of an organization with a formal Latino network that includes leadership training for local Latino Republican leaders. In addition to education programs and mentorship opportunities, the party frequently distributes updates on policy issues taking center stage in Washington, and explains how these could affect Latinos. There is also a network of supporters for both state and national Republican candidates on which to rely when the party needs to mobilize the Latino vote. An example of such efforts could be seen during the 2000 presidential election when Latinos gathered support for George Bush in Texas and New Mexico.

The Latino members of the Democratic Party in California offer an example of a successful informal network. Beginning in the mid-1990s non-Latino Democrats designated certain state legislative seats as belonging to Latino candidates. These seats were off limits to non-Latinos who expected support from the state party.

A debate exists on the policy positions most Latinos prefer. Some commentators suggest that Democrats are more in tune with Latino concerns and interests than are Republicans. Others suggest that Republicans obtain a significant proportion of the Latino vote. However, studies indicate that the majority of Latinos vote for Democrats, both at the local and national levels. For example, in the 2000 presidential election, 54 percent of Latinos voted for Gore, 28 percent for Bush, and 15 percent were undecided. When these percentages are disaggregated, 70 percent of Cubans supported Bush, while Mexican and Puerto Rican respondents were more likely to support Gore. These percentages were consistent at the state and the national levels.

The richly diverse composition of the Latino community yields no collective self-identity or shared politics. Latinos in the United States come from many different countries. Some speak Spanish and some do not. Some are naturalized U.S. citizens, while others are undocumented. People who classify themselves as Latino might be able to trace their ancestry in the United States back to the American Revolution, while others—from university professors to farm laborers—might have arrived in the last calendar year. It is therefore not surprising that there are major differences in political views within the Latino community. There is not a "Latino" position on civil rights, affirmative action, immigration, welfare, or abortion, for example. Voting patterns and policy preferences, while not widely divergent, vary with income, education, age, gender, and national origin. Even when controlling for demographic factors, the key issues overall are, in order of importance, education, race relations, unemployment, the economy, and immigration.

According to the Latino National Political Survey (LNPS), Latinos generally are concerned with social, economic, and ethnic issues. The importance of this identification sheds light on local politics because the LNPS shows that these issues tend to drive Latino community politics. Latinos appear to be disproportionately concerned with domestic issues, in comparison with the general electorate's interest in foreign policy issues, especially those that may involve their nations of origin or ancestry. Surprisingly, the LNPS reveals a low level of concern for affirmative action programs and other civil-rights era measures.

The Voting Rights Act and other civil-rights laws of the 1960s paved the way for Latinos' political, educational, and economic gains. Data show that second-generation Latinos achieve economically, educationally, and socially with greater success than did their predecessors.

The Voting Rights Act (VRA), although enacted primarily to protect and enfranchise Black voters, has had a dramatic effect on Latinos and their political empowerment. The act prompted changes in the elimination of anti-Latino voter dilution efforts, made available bilingual election materials, and paved the way for the creation of Latino districts. While Congress did not take into account Latino voters in enacting the original VRA of 1965, subsequent amendments addressed some of the oversights in the original statute. Numerous Latino organizations, including the Mexican American Legal Defense and Education Fund (MALDEF), offered testimony to

SOMETIMES THE KING IS A WOMAN - ARTWORK BY DE LA VEGA; PHOTOGRAPHY BY DENNIS FLORES

A promotional postcard for New York City Council candidate Melissa Mark Viverito features an art work by De La Vega titled *Sometimes the King Is a Woman*.

Congress when the VRA was under consideration for amendment and extension in 1975.

Latino congressional leaders identified problems with intimidation, exclusion, educational segregation, antiminority gerrymandering, registration difficulties, and, among others, stringent third-party ballot access requirements for Latino voters. Congress amended the VRA and extended the statute for 25 years in 1982, and again in 1992, until 2007. The amendments addressed the concerns of the Latino community, especially those dealing with access to the ballot and availability of bilingual election materials. These changes allowed for greater participation in the political process and the election of a larger proportion of Latino leaders.

Latino candidates, both men and women, were elected to office at unprecedented levels during the 1970s, 1980s, and 1990s as a result of these policy and statutory changes. In California, which has the largest Latino population in the country, the number of Latino state representatives increased to 24 in the 1998 election. Latino representation at various levels of political office—state and national—has resulted in increased Latino employment in government, an increased number of Latino teachers, and more responsive public policies with respect to government contracts and representation on boards and commissions. These are direct consequences of increased political participation.

RELATED ARTICLES

Activism; Civil Rights; Congressional Hispanic Caucus; Democratic Party; League of United Latin American Citizens; Politics, Cuban American; Politics, Mexican American; Politics, Puerto Rican; Republican Party; United States Congress; Voting.

FURTHER READING

Affigne, Tony. "Latino Politics in the United States: An Introduction, in Latino Politics in the United States Symposium." *Political Science* (September 2000).

Barreto, Matt, et al. *A Glimpse Into Latino Policy and Voting Preferences*. Policy Brief. Los Angeles, Calif.: Tomás Rivera Policy Institute, 2002.

De la Garza, et al. *Latino Voices: Mexican, Puerto Rican, and Cuban Perspectives on American Politics*. Boulder, Colo.: Westview Press, 1992.

De Sipio, Louis and Rodolfo De La Garza. *Immigrants, Immigrant Policy, and the Foundation of the Next Century's Latino Politics: The Declining Saliente of the Civil Rights Agenda in an Era of High Immigration.* 2000. http://www.civilrightsproject.harvard.edu/research/latino97/DeSipio.pdf

Duignan, Peter J., and L. H. Gann. *The Hispanics in the United States.* Boulder, Colo.: Westview Press, 1986.

González Baker, Susan. "Su Voto es Su Voz: Latino Political Empowerment and the Immigration Challenge" *PS: Political Science and Politics* 29, no. 3 (September 1996): 465–468.

Laney, Garrine P. "Hispanic Tradition and Achievement in the United States." In *Hispanic Americans, Issues and Bibliography.* Ed. by Karl A. Lawrence. New York: Nova, 2002.

Sierra, Christine Marie. "In Search of National Power: Chicanos Working the System of Immigration Reform, 1976–1986." In *Chicano Politics and Society in the Late Twentieth Century.* Ed. by David Montejano. Austin: Univ. of Tex. Press, 1999.

Toro, Luis Angel. "Race, Identity, and Box Checking: The Hispanic Classification in OMB Directive No. 15." In *The Latino/a Condition.* Ed. by Richard Delgado, et al. New York: N.Y. Univ. Press, 1998.

SELECTED WEB SITES

The Congressional Hispanic Caucus Institute. http://www.chci.org

Library of Congress, Hispanic Reading Room. www.loc.gov/rr/Hispanic/congress

National Association of Latino Elected and Appointed Officials Education Fund. http://www.naleo.org

ANA MARIA MERICO-STEPHENS

POLITICS, MEXICAN AMERICAN

The struggle for self-determination among Mexican Americans has been a slow and arduous one. The minority is known to have heterogeneous political agendas and is difficult to unify at the national, state, and local levels. A lack of leadership and the deterioration of civil representation have been consistent problems.

After decades of silence the Chicano movement, which coincided with the civil rights era, finally allowed for the economic and ideological dilemmas affecting people of Mexican descent to be recognized in the national arena. But the aftermath of the civil rights era again watered down political activism in the community. By the late 1990s, the attempt to bring recognition to the plight of Mexican Americans was increasingly being seen as part of Latino politics in general.

After the Treaty of Guadalupe Hidalgo

Although its roots reach farther back in time, Mexican American political consciousness was born in 1848 when the Treaty of Guadalupe Hidalgo was signed, thereby transferring to the United States the southwestern provinces that had belonged to Mexico (Arizona, California, New Mexico, and Texas, and parts of Utah, Nevada, Colorado, Wyoming, and Oklahoma). The signing of this pact officially ended the Mexican-American War. The invasion of Mexican territory by U.S. troops had devastating consequences. Bigotry and xenophobia were immediately tangible for the Spanish-speaking population of the Southwest, traditionally seen as disconnected from Mexican political affairs. Plus, in Washington, D.C., Mexico, as a free and independent nation, was perceived as unworthy of balanced partnership. Its mestizo culture was seen by some in the United States as barbarous.

After the treaty was signed, a period of rapid economic expansion took place (1848–1857), followed by the consolidation of the new American empire (1865–1898). Thus, the Anglo presence in the newly acquired western territories symbolized the age of colonization from the start. A hierarchical structure was immediately established. Mexicans were considered second-class citizens. In the short run this resulted in instances of animosity and rebellion. In the long run it encouraged a sense of nonconformity, the impact of which would be tangible more than a century later during the civil rights era.

Once the treaty was in place, former Mexican political leaders north of the Rio Grande quickly recognized the fact that their power either had been diminished or had altogether disappeared. For instance, Juan Nepucemeno Seguín, a hero of the Texas revolution who also had a role in the slave trade, was embittered when he was not included in Texan power sharing, which was controlled by Anglos. Likewise, Californio lands were left unprotected by the treaty, and within 20 years had been lost, an occurrence that was chronicled by Juan Antonio Ocasio in *The History of Alta California* and Mariano Guadalupe Hidalgo in his unpublished memoirs.

Indeed, from about 1850 to 1950 Mexican Americans lived under oppressive conditions. Infamous judicial cases and xenophobic explosions such as the Sleepy Lagoon case and the Zoot Suit Riots evidenced the limited role Latino community leaders had in defending their constituents. Anti-Mexicanism was rampant in states such as Arizona, Colorado, and New Mexico, as well as Texas and California. Historians, including Rudolfo Acuña in his popular

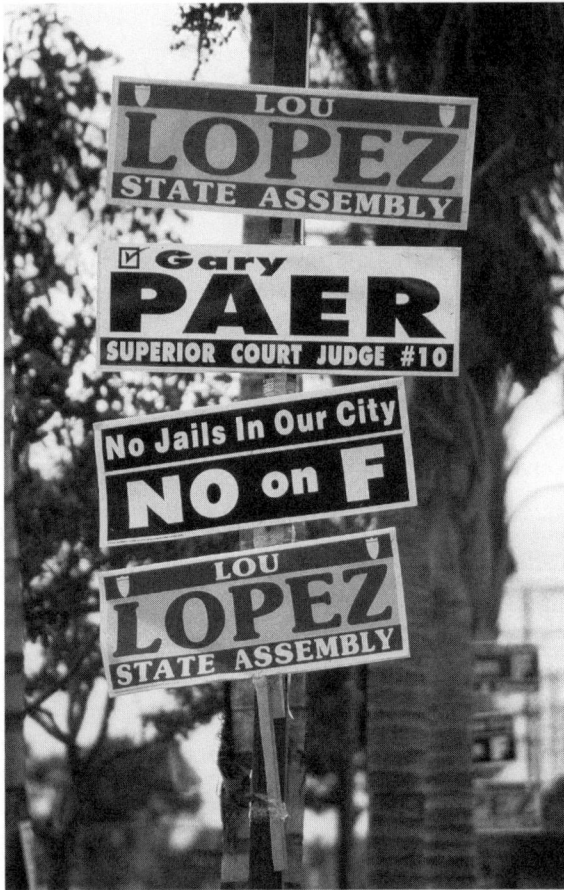

© SPENCER GRANT/PHOTOEDIT

Signs for candidates and a local proposition in Santa Ana, California.

Occupied America, have described the ordeal of oppression under which Spanish-speaking people lived. But little by way of change was forthcoming locally or at the national level.

California. The demise of the political power of Mexican Americans in the state of California was essentially complete by the 1880s, caused, in part at least, by the substantial influx of European Americans to southern California, especially to San Diego, Los Angeles, Santa Barbara, Ventura, and San Bernardino counties. In the 125-year-period following the treaty, only nine Mexican Americans, a meager number, served in the state Senate and 24 in the Assembly. These included state senators Romualdo Pacheco, who later became a congressman; R. F. Del Valle; and Miguel Estudillo. Plus, the Roybal family from Los Angeles, whose members included Edward and Lucille Roybal-Allard, was a welcome respite. Its political service lasted a couple of genera-

tions, an astonishing achievement by all accounts, in particular when one considers the dismal representation of Mexican Americans in the state.

In response to the worsening situation of Mexican Americans, several so-called pressure groups, entities whose business it was to improve social conditions through political means, took shape in the late 1940s and throughout the 1950s. The first one was a committee formed to help Edward Roybal's unsuccessful bid for election in 1947 to the Los Angeles City Council. The committee later transformed itself into the influential Community Service Organization (CSO), whose impact on Mexican American life was significant. Indeed, historians agree that the CSO was instrumental in Roybal's successful City Council campaign two years later. Its advocacy included guarding and furthering Mexican American democratic rights, increasing awareness of Mexican American citizenship responsibilities, coordinating Mexican American efforts that would benefit the entire minority, and registering all U.S. citizens of Mexican ancestry to vote.

Groups that offered counseling services and information to the Mexican American community of East Los Angeles included the Council of Mexican American Affairs (CMAA), founded in 1953, and the Mexican American Political Association (MAPA), an organization with political interests that were somewhat similar to CSO, established in 1959. MAPA came into its own when, in 1962, it endorsed the successful campaigns of Edward Roybal for Congress and Philip Soto and John Moreno for the California Legislature. It became even more important in the 1960s, at the height of the Chicano movement, after the June 1968 arrest of the "East Los Angeles 13" and the August 1970 killing by police of *Los Angeles Times* journalist Rubén Salazar. MAPA voiced the frustration and resentment of Mexican Americans. It supported the initiatives of the Chicano movement and helped crystallize smoldering distrust among Mexican Americans of the Los Angeles political establishment and of law-enforcement agencies, widely acknowledged to be biased and patently violent against nonwhites, especially blacks and Mexicans.

But none of the pressure groups was able to change the status quo. It is estimated that in 1972, while Mexican Americans accounted for almost 59 percent of the ethnic population of California, only about 20 percent of legislators could be identified as emerging from this minority. Indeed, it was in 1972 that the United States Commission on Civil Rights asserted that "racism has been a major factor in denying Mexican Americans' access to our political and government institutions in [the state] today."

Colorado. The demographically Native counties—Conejos, Costilla, Huérfano, and Las Animas—have given Colorado over 86 percent of its Mexican American elected officials and have had an impact on its political history. Among the highlights of the state's Mexican American political participation are the service of eight Mexican Americans on the Territorial Council between 1861 and 1876 and the election of five state senators during the 1877–1973 period, three in the State House in 1904, 1926, and 1970. In addition, there are the political legacies of politicians such as Casimiro Barela and Felipe Baca, whose impact on the Mexican American minority in Colorado has been significant.

New Mexico. Powerful and consistent participation by Mexican Americans in politics is the norm in New Mexico. Some scholars have defined this norm as "deviant," and explain it by pointing to the geographic and cultural isolation of this minority in the state population. Mexican Americans have historically served in most New Mexico state and local offices, and as chiefs in the state and Santa Fe city police departments. Other examples of this vigorous political life include the 24 Mexican Americans who have been members of the state's Council and House of Representatives, and three Mexican Americans who have served as either territorial or state governors. In fact, a total of 57 percent of the state's registered voters at the time of statehood (1912) were Mexican Americans. Since then, a pragmatic approach to collaborations with the Democratic and Republican parties has been established. Strong organizational links between the Hispano and Republican parties took place in the early 20th century. Also, Dennis Chávez's New Deal politics were supported by a majority of the population during the mid-1930s. Later, Governor Bill Richardson, a Democrat whose mother is Mexican, pushed for greater recognition of Mexican American culture in New Mexico. Ironically, in New Mexico, Mexican Americans are the most economically impoverished group.

Texas. The perceived abuse of force by an Anglo sheriff in Brownsville during the arrest of one of Juan Cortina's former *vaqueros* turned into a major debacle, which culminated in attempts at emancipation from U.S. rule. The result was a proclamation in the Plan of San Diego for an independent state for Mexicans, blacks, and Indians in south Texas. The attempt at emancipation followed decades of overt and tacit racism.

Emancipation was not to be, of course. Actually, the situation deteriorated as time went by. In the early 20th century, violence in Texas against Mexican nationals and Mexican Americans in general increased. For instance, on November 2, 1910, Antonio Rodríguez was arrested by a sheriff's deputy near Rocksprings. He was accused of murdering a European American woman at a nearby ranch. Before he could be brought to justice, Rodríguez was burned alive by a mob. Similarly, León Cárdenas Martínez was put on trial in 1911 for the alleged murder of two Anglo-American women. Neither case was ever able to prove the murders.

The Chicano Movement

It was not until the late 1960s, at the time of the civil rights movement, that Mexican American political awareness was brought to national attention. It was then that Mexican Americans adopted the rubric *Chicano* as a symbol of pride and self-affirmation. This new awareness benefited from additional grassroots organizing, which often took a cultural tack.

The political climate at the time was conducive to a combination of individual struggle and organizational development against American internal colonialism. It also coincided with the fight for independence and self-determination of small countries in the so-called Third World. Plus, the U.S. war in Vietnam galvanized many people to rebel against what was seen as an imperialist drive. This drive was not only a matter of foreign policy but also a strategy within the nation to keep minorities from having access to the power structure. But the Chicano movement (*El Movimiento*) was an anomaly because Mexican Americans had traditionally engaged in heterogeneous political activity and, as a minority, were known to be difficult to coordinate when it came to clear-cut objectives and strategies. Thus, the seven objectives established by *El Plan Espiritual de Aztlán* of 1969, composed in Crystal City, Texas, were a break from the past. These objectives were unity, economy, education, institutions, self-defense, culture, and political liberation. They were connected to six action steps: awareness and distribution, call for walk-outs, self-defense, community organization, economic programs, and creation of an independent political party.

El movimiento came to life in the 1960s with broadly shared goals carried out among generally unrelated politically active organizations located in several cities and states throughout the West. Its origins can be traced to a combination of grass-roots movements that emerged in response to discriminatory practices in both the private and public sectors in the American West and Southwest. The new Chicano activism attempted to transform the very nature of earlier, more passive organizations, including mutual aid societies, and used the examples of the African American civil rights movement of the 1950s and early 1960s, increased Mexican American participation in higher education in the early 1960s, and even the model of Latin American political activism to develop theoretical manifestos as blueprints for the development of a public Chicano political identity

through organized activism. The foremost of these many organizations were the United Farm Workers, founded by César Chávez in California; the Crusade for Justice, founded by Rodolfo "Corky" González in Colorado; the Alianza Federal, founded by Reies López Tijerina in New Mexico; and La Raza Unida, a political party founded by José Angel Gutiérrez in Texas. Campus activism, also a model taken from other sources, resulted in the Movimiento Estudiantil Chicano de Aztlán (MEChA), based on dozens of college campuses across the country. The movement also included artistic developments such as *muralismo* (muralism) and theater (especially the Teatro Campesino), which was generally known as the Chicano Renaissance.

The idea of a "movement," however, was the creation of commentators who felt a need to group these local or regional organizations into a national grass-roots upheaval, rather than the development of many separate organizations with parallel or related objectives. The effectiveness of these organizations was based primarily in the local nature of their struggles, and often the ad hoc nature of their struc-

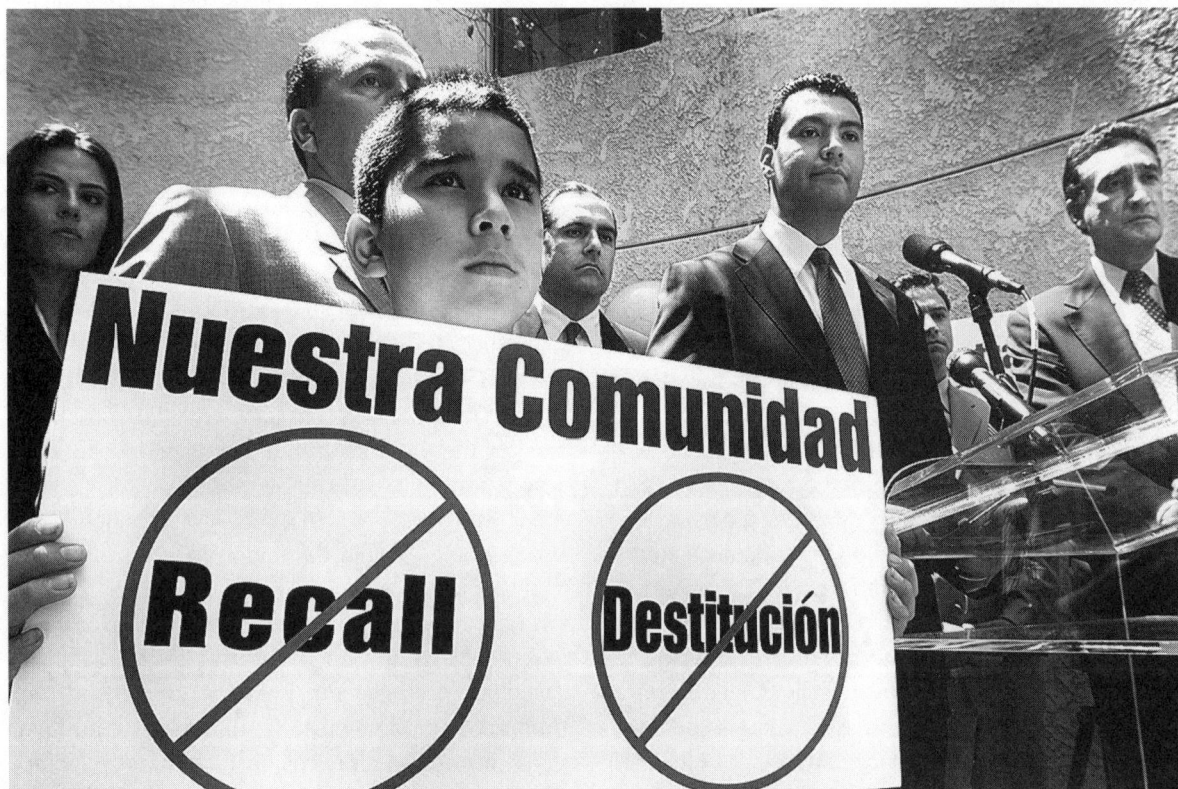

© AURELIA VENTURA/LA OPINION/NEWSCOM

In Los Angeles former secretary of Housing and Urban Development Henry Cisneros holds a press conference to denounce the recall of Governor Gray Davis, 2003.

ture. This became more obvious when several of these groups came together to protest the Vietnam War and the overrepresentation of Chicanos in the draft because of low income levels and the lack of access to student and other deferments. The lack of connections among these groups did not diminish their effectiveness in local and regional spheres, however, and apart from their work, they provided the next generation of Chicanos with a "founding structure" for political and social involvement and an activist identity.

Future of Consciousness

Scholarship on the Mexican American experience has flourished since the 1970s. A number of significant works have been published. They include Ignacio M. García's *Chicanismo: The Forging of a Militant Ethos among Mexican Americans;* Carlos Muñoz's *Youth, Identity, Power;* as well as *A Century of Chicano History: Empire, Nations, and Migration,* by Gilbert G. González and Raul A. Fernández; *Chicano Politics and Society in the Late Twentieth Century,* edited by David Montejano; and the encyclopedic *Mexican American Experience,* edited by Matt S. Meier and Margo Gutiérrez. There have also teen television documentaries such as the four-episode miniseries *Chicano!,* and motion pictures addressing Chicano politics. These materials pose important questions about the crossroads at which ethnicity and ideology meet in the United States and about political participation among Mexican Americans. Clearly, since *El movimiento* a new generation has come of age reflecting on the ethnic, political, and cultural place that people of Mexican descent have had in the United States.

What, then, are likely to be the burning issues affecting Mexican Americans in the 21st century? Does the picketing, the wearing of khakis, the ethnic pride of the civil rights era, and the socialist hopes that arose from the Chicano movement have any relevance? In the age of Latino politics, will Mexican Americans tone down their particular demands in favor of a Pan-Hispanic agenda likening them to Cuban Americans, Dominican Americans, and Puerto Ricans on the mainland? Or will full acculturation carry the day?

If the past is an indicator, Mexican Americans are likely to retain a sense of ethnic pride and unity. Although assimilation to mainstream culture is unquestionably being achieved through education and social and political means, the transformation is slow. Immigration is high, a large number of people in the community live below the poverty line, do not have health insurance, and often fall through the cracks in the school system. In large urban centers such as Los Angeles, Houston, and Chicago, drugs as well as domestic and street violence are rampant. Offensive stereotypes prevail and language barriers impede politicians to improve the situation. As long as these abysmal conditions continue, the deep feeling of frustration will endure, and with it the belief that the "American Dream" does not make room for Mexican Americans. Thus, in spite of its century-and-a-half history, the political struggle for affirmation and a better life is still an uphill one.

RELATED ARTICLES

Activism; Arizona; California; Chicano Movement; Civil Rights; Corona, Humberto; Discrimination; East Los Angeles School Walkout; Gonzáles, Rodolfo; Gorras Blancas, Las; Mexican American Political Association; Mexican Americans; Movimiento Estudantil Chicano de Aztlán; New Mexico; Raza Unida Party, La; Texas; Tijerina, Reies López; Varela, Félix.

FURTHER READING

Acuña, Rodolfo. *America: A History of Mexican-Americans.* New York: Harper and Row, 1988.

Anaya, Rodolfo A., and Francisco A. Lomeli, eds. *Aztlán: Essays on the chicano Homeland.* Albuquerque: Univ. of N.Mex. Press, 1989.

García, Ignacio M. *Chicanismo: The Forging of a Militant Ethos among Mexican Americans.* Tucson: Univ. of Ariz. Press, 1997.

Gómez-Peña, Guillermo. *The New World Border: Prophecies, Poems and Loqueras for the End of the Century.* San Francisco: City Lights Books, 1996.

Gómez-Quiñones, Juan. *On Culture.* Los Angeles: Univ. of Calif., Los Angeles Mexican-American Studies Ctr., 1977.

González, Gilbert G., and Raul A. Fernández. *A Century of Chicano History: Empire, Nations, and Migration.* New York: Routledge, 2003.

Gutiérrez, David G., ed. *Between Two Worlds: Mexican Immigrants in the United States.* Wilmington, Del.: Scholarly Resources, 1996.

Hurtado, Aída, and Patricia Gurin. *Chicana/o Identity in a Changing U.S. Society: quién soy? quiénes somos?* Tucson: Univ. of Ariz. Press, 2004.

Meier, Matt S., and Margo Gutiérrez. *The Mexican American Experience.* Westport, Conn.: Greenwood Press, 2003.

Montejano, David, ed. *Chicano Politics and Society in the Late Twentieth Century.* Austin: Univ. of Tex. Press, 1999.

Muñoz, Carlos. *Youth, Identity, Power: The Chicano Movement.* New York: Verso, 1989.

Nathan, Debbie. *Women and Other Aliens: Essays From the U.S.-México Border.* El Paso, Tex.: Cinco Puntos Press, 1991.

Noriega, Chon, et al., eds. *The Mexican-American Studies Reader: An Anthology of Aztlán, 1970–2000.* Los Angeles: Univ. of Calif., Los Angeles Mexican-Am. Studies Ctr., 2001.

Stavans, Ilan. *The Hispanic Condition.* New York: Harper-Collins, 1995.

Steiner, Stan. *The Mexican Americans.* London: Minority Rights Group, 1979.

Vento, Arnaldo C. *Mestizo: The History, Culture, and Politics of the Mexican and Chicano: The Emerging Mestizo-Americans.* Lanham, Md.: Univ. Press of Am., 1998.

MARTÍN CARRERA

POLITICS, PUERTO RICAN

The history of Puerto Rican politics on the mainland can be divided into four periods, based on distinctive characteristics. From 1920 to 1950 the most prominent activities were community organizing and institution building. Mobilization centered on sociocultural projects. Politics was nationalist in focus and content. From 1950 until the mid-1960s sociocultural organization also predominated. Politics was still nationalist but increasingly less so. From the mid-1960s until 1975 politics took a new turn, simultaneously becoming more attentive to electoral processes while shifting to a bureaucratic style. Radicalism also grew during this period. Since 1975, the main arena of participation has been the electoral and policy process. The goals of representation, agenda-setting, and policymaking have been its target.

Homeland issues prevailed in the Puerto Rican community during settlement. The cast of parades and demonstrations was nationalist with a focus on campaigns in support of independence for Puerto Rico. In Brooklyn in the early 20th century, although some attention was paid to local agendas and incorporation issues, this did not represent the bulk of most energies in the community. There was activity in support of politicians such as Vito Marcantonio and Fiorello La Guardia, but political parties paid little attention to Puerto Ricans except during key elections.

Political representation was achieved as early as 1937 with the election of Oscar García Rivera of Manhattan to the New York State legislature. Yet, Puerto Ricans were mostly marginal to the leading political parties. This was reinforced by their occasional support of reform politicians. In 1948 the community shifted its reliance from the Marcantonio political organization to the Office of the Commonwealth of Puerto Rico. This agency sponsored voter registration drives, lobbying, and community organizing but its primary emphasis was social and cultural. By 1950, elections failed to attract the interest of most.

From 1950 until the mid-1960s Puerto Rican groups maintained their sociocultural focus. Vocational interest groups, professional associations, hometown clubs, and sports organizations predominated. The Puerto Rican Parade began in this postwar period. While many of these groups showed interest in the political process, the tie between island and mainland remained paramount in their concerns. This link was most intensely upheld by nationalist groups. In 1950 two members of the Puerto Rican Nationalist Party, Oscar Collazo and Griselio Torresola, extended the reach of a political uprising on the island by trying to assassinate President Harry S. Truman. Four years later, Lolita Lebrón, Rafael Cancel Miranda, Irving Flores, and Andrés Figueroa Cordero called attention to Puerto Rico's colonial status by shooting at members of the U.S. House of Representatives.

After these actions the movement went into a spiral of decline. It was not until the 1960s that nationalist agitation began to show new signs of life with the establishment of the Movimiento Pro Independencia in New York.

By 1959, observers noted increased political awareness among Puerto Ricans in the United States. This change was mostly a reflection of increases in electoral turnout. Thirteen years after Oscar García Rivera's incumbency ended in 1940, Felipe N. Torres made it to the state assembly, to serve until 1962. For the most part the few Puerto Ricans who were politically prominent during this period were upper-class, island-born individuals.

Until the mid-1960s Puerto Ricans lacked the influence to shape public policy and thus were not able to benefit fully from public services. Initiatives to improve socioeconomic conditions were profitable in the short-term but did not achieve lasting results. During the 1960s' War on Poverty, Puerto Rican elites were more successful in the local antipoverty establishment than in other arenas of representation. Accomplishments at this level contributed to a patron-client model of politics that hindered increases in political representation. The capacity of the community to develop independent political power was also limited.

The period from the mid-1960s to the early 1970s ushered in a new style of political action. Characterized by sporadic instances of collective behavior, as well as by radical ferment, Puerto Rican politics began to focus on bureaucratic political incorporation. This was the era of the Harlem Riot in New York City, of the Division Street riot in Chicago, and of the Comanchero and Labor Day riots in Hartford, Connecticut.

During this stage Puerto Ricans organized the Young Lords Party, the Puerto Rican Socialist Party, El Comité-MINP (Movimiento de Izquierda Nacional Puertorriqueño), and the Puerto Rican Student Union. Simultaneously, Puerto Rican leaders were active in the Community Action Program agencies and antipoverty programs of the time. Although the Movimiento de Liberación Nacional and the Fuerzas Armadas de Liberación Nacional emerged after 1975, they were the extreme wing of a radical movement that was nearly spent by the end of this period.

While politics acquired a bureaucratic emphasis, increases in electoral participation were evident as well. In 1970 the most prominent Puerto Rican appointed official was Herman Badillo, a native of Caguas, Puerto Rico, who served as New York City's Commissioner of Relocation from 1962 to 1965, and became the first Puerto Rican elected to Congress. In 1965 Badillo was elected Bronx borough president—an important accomplishment—but for the community his election to Congress was the high point of political incorporation. He represented New York's 21st District in the South Bronx. In 1972 a significant voter registration drive took place, under the direction of the Cruzada Cívica del Voto. In the same year, Puerto Ricans achieved some visibility within the Democratic party with the assignment of 11 delegates to the national convention, where they joined Chicanos in forming the Latino Caucus. After Badillo's victory the number of electoral candidates grew significantly.

© SHANA RAAB / GETTY IMAGES

Representative José Serrano poses in his Washington, D.C., office with portraits of his heroes Martin Luther King, Jr., and Robert F. Kennedy, 1999.

From the mid-1970s to the present, Puerto Rican politics focused on mainland-based partisan and extrapartisan political incorporation. More Puerto Ricans were elected to various offices, and voter registration drives as well as redistricting efforts were an important part of political strategy.

Service provision and organizational maintenance were the primary focus of many organizations. Grassroots mobilization and agenda-setting efforts were critical. Concern about the status of Puerto Rican women was also prominent and led to the formation, in 1972 in Washington, D.C., of the National Conference of Puerto Rican Women. This group was emblematic of the important role played by Puerto Rican women in the mainland political process.

Several groups dedicated to the political and policy process emerged during the 1970s and early 1980s. The Puerto Rican Legal Defense and Education Fund was founded in 1972 to protect the civil rights of Puerto Ricans and other Latinos. The National Puerto Rican Coalition, a policy advocacy organization based in Washington, D.C., was established in 1977. Two other important organizations were the National Congress of Puerto Rican Rights and the Institute for Puerto Rican Policy, both founded in 1981. The former advocated for the civil and human rights of Puerto Ricans and to oppose U.S. intervention in Latin America and the Caribbean. The latter acted as an independent watchdog and advocacy group.

In Puerto Rico roughly 71 percent of eligible voters went to the polls in 1948; only 45 percent of Puerto Ricans did so on the mainland. By 1950 less than half of the Puerto Ricans in New York had voted at any time. Political behavior in Puerto Rico was not replicated in the United States. The migrants' lack of familiarity with the mainland political process was overwhelming. The prevailing political style did not entice them to participate. Further, political parties did very little to bring Puerto Rican voters into their fold.

Yet a strong desire for access to the political system always characterized the mainland community. From 1954 to 1956 the number of Puerto Rican voters in New York City rose from roughly 35,000 to 85,000, in large part owing to extensive registration campaigns conducted by interested organizations. By 1957 the city's Puerto Rican population had reached more than half a million but demo-graphy had little impact on representation. In that year Puerto Ricans held the distinction of having never gained a seat on the New York City Council nor to any elective city office.

By 1959 political participation reflected increased determination and sense of purpose, with a political elite seeking electoral success. Community events showcased Puerto Ricans as an electorate deserving attention. Their awareness of the need to take control of their own political destiny was evidenced in discussions to establish a "Spanish party." Some, on the other hand, worried about the destructive power of "nationalist agitators." The balance of these forces was zero: neither nationalist agitation nor independent political organization took root.

For the most part Puerto Rican elites have been clear about the relationship between political participation and progress. During the 1960s, public expressions reflecting growing political awareness and aspirations were frequent. Yet, according to some analysts Puerto Rican organization and mobilization during this period was weak. In their view, a close connection between island and mainland hindered community organization and leadership development. No evidence was offered to support this. Later research showed that the emphasis on island interests and concerns did not arrest organizational or leadership development.

By 1961 the future of Puerto Rican political incorporation seemed bright, given the number of elected and appointed Puerto Rican officials in New York. Among these officials were three state legislators, two city magistrates, a number of commissioners, members on 17 of the 25 city school boards, and five district party leaders. Badillo's victory in 1970 was followed by the election of Maurice Ferré as mayor of Miami in 1973. Ferré's success was due to the mobilization of a largely Cuban constituency and it was celebrated more in Puerto Rico than in El Barrio. Nevertheless, his accomplishment had great symbolic power.

During the 1960s and 1970s, antipoverty agencies were important sites for the development of Puerto Rican politics. Some of these organizations were the only available inroads into political mobilization or electoral politics. For the most part they discouraged independent community activism. Their existence closed off avenues for mobilization for anything other than routine politics. These agencies were a de facto pressure-group system for Puerto Ricans in a context of great resistance to their political mobilization on the part of established groups and institutions.

Antipoverty programs provided opportunities to further the organization of the community. By controlling large umbrella groups, Puerto Ricans were able to finance a wide variety of programs. In Connecticut, Illinois, Massachusetts, New Jersey, New York, and Pennsylvania, community leaders used antipoverty agencies for political purposes. These programs were also emblematic of a contradiction between individual and community advancement. To wit, the upward mobility experienced by service providers contrasted with the lack of progress that afflicted a substantial portion of the community.

During the 1970s, population growth led to further institutional development. Community organizations became professionalized. In this process, external funding was a critical factor. Professionalization meant an expanded source of white-collar employment and a larger pool of candidates for leadership positions. It also meant that services substituted for advocacy. Many potential leaders became mere administrators. In some cases, agency directors conflated organizational and community interests. As a result, organizational maintenance was rationalized as community well-being. In many cases politics became a means to secure funding rather than community advancement.

Organization at this level did not always translate into electoral participation. Throughout the 1970s, 1980s, and 1990s, electoral participation among Puerto Ricans was consistently low. In Puerto Rico voter turnout in general elections had averaged 85 percent from 1972 to the 1990s. In contrast, during the 1996 presidential election, in New York City districts with concentrations of 70 percent or more of the group identified, 69 percent of Puerto Ricans registered to vote and 42 percent of those registered turned out. Compared to Latinos, Puerto Ricans had higher registration but lower turnout rates. Both whites and blacks registered below the Puerto Rican mark at 63 and 65 percent, respectively. However, turnout among white and black registered voters was higher at 60 percent for whites and 52 percent for African Americans.

Interestingly, low turnout was not a symptom of alienation. According to de la Garza's Latino National Political Survey (1992), a majority of *Boricuas* on the mainland favored a permanent relationship between Puerto Rico and the United States: 69.4 percent preferred the Commonwealth and 27 percent supported statehood; only 3.5 percent supported independence. Moreover, in response to the question, "How strong is your love for the United States?" 31.5 percent of respondents said "extremely strong" and 37.1 percent said "very strong"; only 8.1 percent responded "not very strong." To the question, "How proud are you to be an American?" 38.5 percent responded "extremely proud" and 44.6 percent said "very proud." A small minority of 2.3 percent of respondents said they were "not very proud" of their citizenship.

In New York State, Puerto Rican legislators joined African Americans in 1966 to form the State Assembly's Black and Puerto Rican Caucus. This alliance sought to force concessions from the Assembly leadership to benefit minority interests. During the 1970s the Caucus was often described as rudderless, fraught with conflict, and focused on the wrong battles even by its own members. But there were also instances of successful cooperation. The 1975 New York City fiscal crisis provided one crucial opportunity for collaboration between Puerto Rican and black legislators.

After Badillo left Congress in 1978, he was succeeded by Robert García, who served in the New York State Assembly and Senate from 1964 to 1978. When García resigned in 1990, he was replaced by New York State assemblyman José E. Serrano. Until 1993 Serrano was the sole Puerto Rican in Congress. In that year he was joined by Nydia Velázquez, who was elected from New York's 12th Congressional District, and Luis Gutiérrez, from District 4 in Chicago. These elections were precedent setting: Velázquez was the first Puerto Rican woman to serve in Congress; Gutiérrez was the first Hispanic from Illinois to win a congressional seat. These victories were examples of growing political power. Locally, this was best illustrated in Hartford, Connecticut. By 1991, two state representatives from that city were Puerto Rican, as well as a department head, several members of commissions, the corporation counsel, the deputy city manager, and three of the nine-member city council. In 2001, after a period of stagnation for Puerto Rican politics, the city elected Eddie Pérez as mayor and later approved a reform of the charter that gave Pérez expanded powers.

Despite low voter turnout during the 1980s and 1990s, the process of representation did not stagnate.

Between 1989 and 1992, Puerto Rican electoral representation increased by 16 percent. In Connecticut, Massachusetts, New Jersey, New York, Ohio, and Pennsylvania, Hispanic elected officials were overwhelmingly Puerto Rican. Even in California and Indiana, Puerto Ricans had representation. However, compared to their proportion of the population, the level of Puerto Rican representation was low: they made up more than 1 percent of the U.S. population but less than one-tenth of 1 percent of U.S. elected officials.

In Congress, Badillo included job training for unemployed non-English-speaking citizens in the Comprehensive Manpower Act of 1973. He supported legislation promoting community development programs, tax credits for educational expenses, and career opportunities in the health professions for disadvantaged youth. This was in contrast to his actions in the 1990s as chairman of the City University of New York. There he opposed open admissions and remedial education, a stand that was harshly criticized by many. When he suggested that uneducated immigrants from Mexico and the Dominican Republic were the city's biggest problem, some demanded his resignation.

The effectiveness of Robert García in Congress was diluted by his attention to issues that did not directly affect Puerto Ricans. Elected officials often focus on certain issues to secure broad standing, which they can use to better promote the interests of their constituents. In García's case, with the exception of his 1980 partnership with Republican Jack Kemp to introduce Enterprise Zones legislation, this strategy failed to produce the desired result. This was compounded by his implication in the Wedtech scandal, an incident involving large-scale corruption among corporate executives and government officials. Battered by multiple criminal charges, García resigned from the House of Representatives in 1990.

José Serrano focused his energy on issues critical to his Puerto Rican constituency. During his first term he sponsored a bill to reduce dropout rates in schools. In the 102nd Congress (1991–1992) he was the principal sponsor of a bill that expanded the protections of the Voting Rights Act of 1965 to linguistic minorities. As chairman of the Congressional Hispanic Caucus during the 103rd Congress (1993–1994), he led the battle against the establishment of English as the official language of the United States. His work on child nutrition programs, food stamps,

Head Start, AIDS prevention, and tuberculosis control was steady and substantial. But his attention to other issues of minor relevance to Puerto Ricans detracted him from a more single-minded focus on a Puerto Rican agenda and did not make him more prominent among his peers.

The commitment of Nydia Velázquez and Luis Gutiérrez to a legislative and service agenda focused on Puerto Ricans has been evident. After surviving serious challenges to her incumbency—her district was considered unconstitutional—she was named Ranking Democrat in the House Small Business Committee in 1998. From this position she promoted business growth and employment opportunities in her district. Gutiérrez was a strong supporter of the earned income credit tax and a staunch advocate of an increase in the minimum wage. He worked to save from budget cuts programs such as Medicare, Medicaid, home-heating assistance, and school lunches. He also supported legislation providing priority health care to members of the armed services who became ill after their tours of duty in the Persian Gulf.

Some argue that the U.S. political system has failed Puerto Ricans. The promise of politics—representation, benefits, upward mobility—remains largely unfulfilled. More specifically, the argument suggests that despite laudable performance, the impact of Puerto Rican elected officials at all levels on the well-being of the community has been limited. Contextual and structural factors are, for the most part, responsible for this shortcoming. The focus of representatives on amelioration and the short-term has also played a role.

Some have suggested that Puerto Ricans gained more from the civil rights and antiwar movements than they gained from Puerto Rican participation. Others have claimed that even though Puerto Ricans emulated African Americans, they did so in a context of competition for goods and services. What is true about the political process and the political society—that Puerto Ricans were excluded from full incorporation by a combination of circumstances—could be true of social movements as well, a claim that has been made with regard to the gay and lesbian movement. Yet, the case of the environmentalist movement suggests that Puerto Rican attitudes also played a role in how they participated.

Extant accounts of Puerto Rican participation in the civil rights, antiwar, environmental, and feminist

Women wearing U.S. flags as scarves in support of U.S. statehood for Puerto Rico, prior to Governor Sila Calderón's state of the commonwealth speech in San Juan, 2003.

movements suggest a consistent thread of activism as well as faint connections. One link is well-established: Gilberto Gerena Valentín, a community activist who migrated to the United States in the mid-1930s, has been widely recognized for his participation in the civil rights movement. Others are not well-known. Puerto Rican participation in the antiwar and feminist movements lacks figures as prominent as Gerena Valentín. There is evidence that the gay and lesbian movement largely rejected Puerto Ricans. On the other hand, research shows that environmentalists in Puerto Rico were disdainful of their mainland counterparts. This attitude was reproduced in Puerto Rican radical circles on the mainland.

Puerto Rican social movements in the United States emerged as expressions of two tendencies. One purported to develop the community's human capital, to build institutional resources, and join labor unions or political parties to achieve full political incorporation. Some efforts within this category challenged the status quo, but the basic emphasis of campaigns was on reform. During the late 1960s the community control movement in education in New York City was one of the most prominent expressions of this variant.

The second tendency proposed the development of political capacity necessary to achieve Puerto Rican independence and to transform American society. In this approach, the emphasis was on creative destruction and separatism. The means used to effect change were, for the most part, legal and acceptable. Illegal actions were few and largely ineffective. The most significant representatives of this approach were the Puerto Rican Socialist Party (PSP) and the Young Lords Party.

Puerto Rican social movements sought to integrate the struggle against colonialism on the island with the struggle for democratic rights on the mainland. In practice, these concerns were more often than not juxtaposed. For example, the PSP consistently held the view that the struggles for national liberation and for Puerto Rican democratic rights should be linked. In reality, the party's foremost priority was the achievement of Puerto Rico's independence. In fact, the dissonance between intent and action was an important cause of the party's demise.

Many tried hard to overcome this dichotomy but intersections were rare and riddled with unintended effects. In places such as Hartford and Philadelphia convergence did take place. There Puerto Rican radicals combined bargaining and compromise tactics with demand-protest actions, challenging established political organizations to achieve representation. Convergence, however, did not produce the type of linkage between self-determination for Puerto Rico and the achievement of democratic rights for Puerto Ricans in the United States originally contemplated by radicals. In the new articulation, electoral representation substituted for anticolonialism. The achievement of democratic rights was conceived as a stepping stone for radical change but the result was different. Interest group politics substituted for systemic transformation.

Another unintended consequence of convergence was the weakening of radical social movements. As insiders, radicals did not forget the link between island and mainland politics but the connection was limited to episodic debates on the status question, usually centered on federally sponsored plebiscites. Ironically, by toning down their rhetoric to meet the requirements of electoral politics, radicals limited the content of their substantive message without necessarily becoming more credible. Yet, many continued pushing for change in their communities as organizers, politicians, artists, and educators.

A consensus exists that Puerto Rican politics in the United States needs further examination. Areas such as electoral behavior, the relationship between descriptive and substantive representation, gender politics, the effectiveness of social movements, the impact of political socialization on the island on political behavior on the mainland, and the role of political leaders in promoting community progress are but some of the key issues that researchers have identified as needing closer scrutiny.

On the policy side, some have all but abandoned hope of achieving progress in the absence of systemic change. Others have suggested that a two-pronged policy agenda, seeking economic growth and equality, is necessary. According to some of the leading analysts of Puerto Rican politics in the United States, the basic attitude of policymakers toward Puerto Ricans is one of oblivious disregard. This is a most significant obstacle in the community's pursuit of greater social influence and more effective political power.

RELATED ARTICLES

Muñoz Marín, Luis; National Puerto Rican Coalition; Pantoja, Antonia; Politics, Latino; Puerto Ricans on the Mainland; Vieques.

FURTHER READING

Cruz, José E., ed. "Puerto Rican Politics in the United States." *Centro* (Spring 2003).

Cruz, José E. *Identity and Power, Puerto Rican Politics and the Challenge of Ethnicity.* Philadelphia: Temple Univ. Press, 1998.

de la Garza, Rodolfo O., et al. *Latino Voices.* Boulder, Colo.: Westview Press 1992.

Estades, Rosa. *Patterns of Political Participation of Puerto Ricans in New York City.* Rio Piedras, P.R.: Editorial Universitaria, 1978.

Falcón, Angelo. "Puerto Rican Political Participation: New York City and Puerto Rico." In *Time for Decision: The United States and Puerto Rico.* Ed. by Jorge Heine. Lanham, Md.: North-South Pubs., 1983.

Glazer, Nathan, and Daniel P. Moynihan. *Beyond the Melting Pot; The Negroes, Puerto Ricans, Jews, Italians, and Irish of New York City.* Cambridge, Mass.: MIT Press, 1970.

Jennings, James, and Monte Rivera, eds. *Puerto Rican Politics in Urban America.* Westport, Conn.: Greenwood Press, 1984.

Nelson, Dale. "The Political Behavior of New York Puerto Ricans: Assimilation or Survival?" In *The Puerto Rican Struggle.* Ed. by Clara Rodríguez, et al. Maplewood, N.J.: Waterfront Press, 1984.

Padilla, Félix M. *Puerto Rican Chicago.* Notre Dame, Ind.: Univ. of Notre Dame Press, 1987.

Sánchez, José Ramón. "Puerto Ricans and the Door of Participation in U.S. Politics." In *Handbook of Hispanic Cultures in the United States: Sociology.* Ed. by Félix Padilla, et al. Houston, Tex.: Arte Público Press, 1994.

Torres, Andrés, and José E. Velázquez, eds. *The Puerto Rican Movement: Voices from the Diaspora.* Philadelphia: Temple Univ. Press, 1998.

JOSÉ E. CRUZ

POPOL VUH

Popol Vuh is the title of the sacred book of the Quiché Maya. The literal translation is either "Council Book" or "Book of the Community." Its stories and chronicles originated in the pre-Columbian era, and part of the book recounts the exodus of the Quiché from the Yucatán Peninsula south into Guatemala about 1000 A.D. The *Popol Vuh* represents the most complete and sophisticated record of pre-Columbian religion in the Americas. Besides religious feeling and cultural identity, it also demonstrates imagination, humor, literary sophistication, poetic sensibility, and close observation of the natural world.

The *Popol Vuh* is divided into four parts. The first part records the creation of the world by Heart of Sky, as well as several failed attempts at creating humans as animals from wood and mud. The second part recounts a duel between sets of hero twins from the upper world and demonic princes of the netherworld, Xibalba. The third part tells of the creation of the sun and of true humans from maize. The fourth part, which is clearly concerned with documenting the origins of the Quiché and their difference from other peoples of the region, gives details of cult origins and tribal wars.

The stories were apparently preserved and transmitted in hieroglyphic books of the Maya painted on leaves. The Quiché were conquered by Pedro de Alvarado in 1524, subsequent to which Spanish friars were sent to convert them to Christianity and to acculturate them. An unknown Maya or Mayas wrote down the *Popol Vuh* in Quiché, using the Roman characters they had learned from the Spanish to approximate the sounds of the language. Dominican friar Francisco de Ximénez found the manuscript and translated it into Spanish; it was re-translated several times during the 19th and 20th centuries into a number of European languages; Dennis Tedlock has produced an authoritative verse translation into English.

The author(s) of the *Popol Vuh* made very clear that the purpose for writing it down was to preserve their own culture in the face of enforced assimilation: "We shall write about [creation] now amid the preaching of God, in Christendom now. We shall bring it out because there is no longer a place to see it, a Council Book." In this quote, the words for God and Christendom are Spanish-derived, indicating the foreignness of Catholic thought to the Quiché worldview; however, the creation story that begins the text bears the imprint of Genesis while retaining its fundamentally Maya character. Hence, the book in its present form can be considered the product of cultural confrontation and synthesis.

The continuing influence of the *Popol Vuh* can be described as a set of concentric circles radiating outward from the geographic and ethnographic center of its composition. Each circle finds a different set of themes and preoccupations in the book. The *Popol Vuh* retains its vitality among the Quiché. Tedlock's translation is prefaced by photographs of Maya "daykeepers," that is, of those who use the *Popol Vuh* for divination, astronomy, and other activities. The Guatemalan Miguel Ángel Asturias drew heavily on the *Popol Vuh* for his Nobel Prize–winning novel, *Hombres de maíz* (1949), a landmark of the magic realism that signaled a distinctively American form of writing. Guatemalan-Quiché Rigoberta Menchú uses epigraphs from the *Popol Vuh* for approximately half the chapters of her testimonial, *I, Rigoberta Menchú*.

Moving to the next circle, the book has become a symbol of the tenacity and literary genius of native peoples of the Americas. Leslie Marmon Silko has her characters quote from the *Popol Vuh* in her novel, *Almanac of the Dead* (1991), which takes its readers on a nightmare journey through the drug-infested world of the American Southwest and Mexico. The presence of the *Popol Vuh* serves to prophesy the passing away of white culture from the land and its return to its original possessors.

Chicana playwright Cherríe Moraga finds similar hope in the Maya text, but one tied more specifically to language. Her play *Heart of the Earth: A Popol Vuh Story* uses a variety of languages, including Maya, English, Spanish, and Spanglish. Moraga writes in her foreword that "the world of language I hope to evoke is one of a diverse and people-of-color América that more closely reflects its changing and beautifully darkening face as we enter the twenty-first century."

There is, finally, the circle of anthropologists, archaeologists, choreographers, filmmakers, philosophers, theologians, writers, and artists from around the world who have seen in the *Popol Vuh* that which most fascinated them and who have used it as a fount of creativity. Rolando Klein's 1975 film, *Chac*, provides a good example of the complexities of *Popol Vuh* adaptation and reception. Filmed in the Chiapas region of Mexico using Maya nonactors, the film, which is loosely based on accounts of the rain god given in the *Popol Vuh*, was promoted by the Mexican government as a message of "national culture." It was well received in France and Germany, but in the United States it remained a cult film, appealing mainly to New Agers and to Native Americans. Klein, meanwhile, now resides in Pasadena, California, having tried unsuccessfully to break into the Hollywood movie industry.

In general, the *Popol Vuh* has not had the pan-Latino appeal of the Virgin of Guadalupe, nor has it entered the Latino school curriculum to the extent that mariachi music has. Its influence remains strongest among Latinos with a strong native heritage and among Native Americans.

RELATED ARTICLES

Mayas; Religion.

FURTHER READING

Brotherston, Gordon, and Lúcia de Sà. "First Peoples of the Americas and Their Literature." *CLCWeb: Comparative Literature and Culture* 4 no. 2 (June 2002). clcwebjournal.lib.purdue.edu/clcweb02-2/ brotherston&sa02.html

Coe, Michael D. "The Hero Twins: Myth and Image." In *The Maya Vase Book: A Corpus of Rollout Photographs of Maya Vases.* Vol. 1., ed. by Justin Kerr. New York: Kerr Assoc., 1989.

González, Servando. *Popol Vuh: An Interactive Text/Graphics Adventure.* San Francisco, 1991 [self-published].

Menchú, Rigoberta. *I, Rigoberta Menchú: An Indian Woman in Guatemala.* Ed. by Elisabeth Burgos-Debray, tr. by Ann Wright. New York: Verso, 1984.

Moraga, Cherrié. "Heart of the Earth: A *Popol Vuh* Story." In *Puro Teatro: A Latina Anthology.* Ed. by Alberto Sandoval-Sánchez and Nancy Saporta Sternbach. Tucson: Univ. of Ariz. Press, 2000.

Popol Vuh: The Definitive Edition of the Mayan Book of the Dawn of Life and the Glories of Gods and Kings. 2d ed. Tr. by Dennis Tedlock. New York: Touchstone-Simon & Schuster, 1996.

Popol Vuh: The Sacred Book of the Ancient Quiché Maya. Tr. by Delia Goetz and Sylvanus G. Morley. From a Spanish translation by Adrián Recinos. Norman: Univ. of Okla. Press, 1950.

Preuss, Mary H. *Gods of the Popol Vuh: Xmukne', K'ucumatz, Tojil, and Jurakán.* Culver City, Calif.: Labyrinthos, 1988.

Silko, Leslie Marmon. *Almanac of the Dead: A Novel.* New York: Simon & Schuster, 1991.

THOMAS O. BEEBEE

POPULAR ART. *See* ART, POPULAR.

POPULAR CULTURE

Popular culture can be defined as a set of generally available artifacts, including food, art, fashion, music, games, films, and television programs, which has roots in common knowledge, frequent expression in nonwritten form, and is accepted or consumed by significant numbers of people. However, popular culture changes across societies over time, and the definition is subject to change according to these shifts. For some, popular culture serves the purpose of obscuring dominant ideology; others see the pro-

liferation of popular artifacts as simply a vehicle to perpetuate capitalism by reflecting the interests and desires of the dominant group. Feminist critiques of popular culture express concerns that it is a form of patriarchal ideology, which favors the interests of men over those of women. Postmodernists have found that popular culture represents a unique space in which the boundaries between image and reality are blurred. Some critics, in particular those affiliated with postcolonialism, also believe that through popular culture a sense of political empowerment can take place in a particular society.

In the case of Latino cultural production in the United States, any and all of the above definitions apply at some point in its history. The proliferation of things Latino in daily consumption and practice can be traced alongside trends of Latin American immigration to and migration within the United States. The "Latinization" of the United States, which takes the form of the appropriation and reformulation of cultural icons, mirrors the slightly more pervasive "Americanization" of many Latin American countries, varying in intensity with regional populations. In places such as the U.S.-Mexico border, popular cultural production has taken a hybrid form, where material items serve as testimony to the centuries of multicultural influences converged upon one social and political space.

Some cultural critics express concerns about the form that the expropriation or adaptation of Latin American popular culture often takes in the United States. Avant-garde performance artist Guillermo Gómez-Peña sees the dangers of essentializing *latinidad* in his 1989 essay "The Multicultural Paradigm: An Open Letter to the National Arts Community," in which he cautions against the adoption of spiritual and aesthetic models of Latin culture without a profound understanding of the political outrage and cultural contradiction that often drives such artistic production. He faults the contemporary art world for applying such monikers as "colorful," "passionate," and "mysterious" to Latin popular culture as euphemisms for irrationalism and primitivism. This approach has come to be known as "Tropicalization," that is to say, the infusion of exotic, dreamlike qualities to Hispanic culture in the United States. Another particularly important concept relevant to the Mexican American community, *rascuachismo,* defined by critics such as Tomás Ybarra-Frausto and Ilan Stavans, suggests that low-class popular items, similar in manufacturing quality to what is known in German as *kitsch* and in Spanish as *cursi,* have an ideological power in mass culture that gives Chicanos a sense of dignity and collective consciousness. This term does not have an equivalent for Cuban Americans and Puerto Ricans on the mainland. While popular culture encompasses a broad array of forms, an examination of food, music, and television helps to illuminate the trajectory of Latino cultural production and consumption in the United States.

Food

Reports of consumer trends in the mid-1990s claimed that salsa had surpassed ketchup in sales in the United States, a fact that for some might point to a greater cultural shift in the country. The salsa phenomenon serves as a marker in the decades-long process of mainstreaming Latin American foods in the U.S. consumer market. The increased presence of Mexican workers in the American Southwest owing to the Bracero Program (a guest worker program initiated during World War II to alleviate labor shortages in the United States by inviting Mexican workers on a temporary basis) naturally led to the increased presence of Mexican restaurants and ingredients in markets, as well as tamales sold on street corners, but these remained largely confined to predominantly Mexican American neighborhoods. Altered versions of Mexican recipes were most famously introduced to the American palate during the fast-food boom that characterized the postwar era. California entrepreneur Glen Bell capitalized on the demographic shift that he was observing in his home state, and in 1952 opened Bell's Drive-In, which in a few short years would blossom into the nationwide Taco Bell chain. Bell learned to adapt spicy Mexican ingredients to American tastes, and over the years he successfully introduced tacos, burritos, fajitas, and gorditos into the shopping centers, airports, and strip malls where Taco Bell franchises cropped up.

The history of a popular dessert provides an example of the unconventional ways in which a food product might acquire a "Latin" origin. In the 1920s Carnation Concentrated Milk Company concocted a recipe for a cream cake and printed it on the label of its condensed milk cans in hopes of boosting sales. The company experienced an increase of sales to Latin American countries in the following decades, and before long the dessert now known as *tres leches* became associated with confectionaries in Puerto Rico, and Mexico; Nicaragua adopted *tres leches* as its national sweet. In the United States, the three-milk cake appears on menus of Mexican and Caribbean restaurants as a traditional regional dessert, despite its inauspicious origins in U.S. test kitchens.

Music

Latin rhythms have seamlessly worked their way into mainstream American music, leaving an indelible imprint on jazz, pop, ballad, and dance music traditions. Tourism Cuba in the 1920s and 1930s exposed visitors from the United States to such rhythms as cha-cha-chá and rumba. Consequently, the evolution of big-band music became infused with Latin rhythms, leading to the invention of the mambo, and escalating into the "mambo craze" of the 1950s closely associated with the brilliant musical career of Tito Puente. The close proximity of New Orleans, Louisiana, and Havana, Cuba, allowed for artistic collaboration between jazz musicians, and jazz absorbed many Cuban influences, especially evident in the expressions of Dizzy Gillespie and Charlie Parker. The 1960s also saw the introduction of Brazilian-based bossa nova into American jazz, marked especially by collaborations between Stan Getz and Charlie Byrd with Brazilian musicians Antonio Carlos Jobim, Astrud Gilberto, and João Gilberto. An electronic version of the bossa nova rhythm found its way onto the synthesizer invented by Robert Moog and first commercially available in 1965.

The trajectory of salsa most vividly illustrates the popular appeal of Latin-based musical forms in the United States, as well as their adaptation and incorporation into mainstream American music. Salsa, which translates into "sauce" in Spanish, is a literal fusion of musical flavors in its combination of *son* vocals, jazz improvisation, *clave* beat, Cuban rhythms, and often electric instrumentation. Salsa was born in the late 1960s and early 1970s in New York City, and quickly evolved into what author Peter Manuel called "the soundtrack for the Latino pride movement." At their conception, salsa lyrics were heavily charged with political messages, disparaging the inequitable socioeconomic conditions suffered by Latinos in the United States. Politician and actor Rubén Blades, originally from Panama, enjoyed recognition as a salsa musician and incorporated sometimes scathing political critiques into his lyrics. Salsa's sensibility struck notes initially with Puerto Ricans and Nuyoricans, and quickly spread to embody a Pan-Latino ethnic identity.

By the 1980s salsa had evolved from a vehicle of political commentary to a popular dance rhythm, and it began to experience increased exposure on mainstream radio stations. However, alongside heightened popular appeal, the politicized lyrics that characterized the form in its early days began to favor more innocuous themes of love and relationships. Bands such as Gloria Estefan's Miami Sound Machine helped to catapult the music form fully into the American music scene in the 1980s by increasing electric instrumentation, almost at the expense of the original *son* and rumba rhythms, and by incorporating rock-star glamour into the bands' looks. Salsa in its popular form enjoyed wide acceptance in Latin America, where it was frequently appropriated as a national art form. The late 1990s saw a return to Latin music's authentic roots, most notably with the popularity of Cuba's Buena Vista Social Club, a group of elderly musicians "discovered" on the streets of Havana by American musician Ry Cooder (who captured the group's performance in a feature film and sound track both titled the *Buena Vista Social Club*. Ibrahim Ferrer and Ruben González, two of the most prominent members of the group, sang boleros and cha-chas and became famous for their renditions of salsa songs. Los Van Van, a world-renowned Cuban salsa band, provides another example of salsa music coming to rest in the land of its roots after having been concocted in New York City. As an example of salsa's international appeal, in 1989 the Japanese salsa band Orquesta de la Luz made its debut in New York, perfectly executing salsa rhythms despite the fact that none of the band members spoke Spanish.

In the pop music realm, Latino groups eased their way into mainstream genres by embracing the stereotype of the Latin lover, infusing radio waves with English-language ballads peppered with Spanish words and phrases easily identifiable to the Anglo ear. Puerto Rican boy-band Menudo enjoyed success in the United States for much of the 1980s, fronted by adolescent crooner Ricky Martin. From the late 1990s to the early 2000s, many female musicians chose to self-identify as Latina, most notably the singer-danceractress Jennifer Lopez and Colombian teen sensation Shakira.

Entertainment

A few iconic figures stand out as purveyors of Latin American culture to American media and daily life. Carmen Miranda remains one of the most recognizable and colorful Latina characters, teetering her fruit-laden way through television and cinematic productions on platform shoes. Although born in Portugal, Miranda fostered her image in Bahia, a coastal region of Brazil, where Afro-Brazilian peasant women are mythologized for their distinctive dress (which, incidentally, did not include headdresses made of bananas). Miranda arrived in New York in 1939, an unofficial cultural ambassador in Roosevelt's Good Neighbor era. Her kooky, sweet, exotic persona endeared her to the American public as the "Brazilian Bombshell." However, she was more frequently cast in roles as a Spanish-speaking spitfire, and often the distinctions between Portuguese and Spanish became blurred to the point of being interchangeable in her roles. While she continued to delight audiences as a comic actress, she had difficulty convincing producers to see her as a serious actor; in one instance a producer threatened her to not lose her Brazilian accent or she would no longer be marketable as an exotic "other." Meanwhile, Brazilians were dismayed by Miranda's exaggerated and inaccurate representation, and cultural officials treated her coldly on her 1954 return visit to Brazil. Miranda died of heart failure in 1955, but her bejeweled tropical image has been perpetuated throughout popular culture, influencing women's fashion trends in toned-down versions of her tropical styles, taking form in a Bugs Bunny parody, insinuated on the Chiquita banana label, and finding resonance in the exaggerated feminine manifestations of drag-queen culture.

Desi Arnaz's character Ricky Ricardo on the 1951–1957 television comedy show *I Love Lucy* served as another foundational Latin icon. His on-screen persona provided one of the first visual models of the hot-blooded Latin lover, appearing opposite his red-haired American wife, Lucille Ball. The program gave Arnaz ample air time as a Cuban musician, with many scenes featuring mambo and cha-cha-chá interludes taking place in his character's Latin nightclub. Producers allowed Ricky Ricardo's Spanish tirades to run untranslated, exposing audiences to a rapid-fire barrage of exclamations in another language. His flashy, hot-tempered, dashing screen presence helped to promote the image of the Latin lover in popular culture, a convention that found repeated

Billboard promoting *Enough*, a 2004 film starring Latina pop star Jennifer Lopez.

expression in further television programs, soap operas, movies, and commercials.

Speedy Gonzáles, Warner Brothers' fast-talking and faster-racing mouse from Sonora, Mexico, first appeared in cartoon history in 1953. Speedy, dubbed "The Fastest Mouse in All Mexico," appeared dressed as a Mexican peasant, complete with giant sombrero, bare feet, and red neckerchief. Expressions of *Arriba, ándale!* peppered his language and his cartoons (*Tortilla Flaps, Tabasco Road, Mexicali Schmoes, The Wild Chase,* among Speedy's popular titles) often took place in idealized Mexican pueblos. The chatty rodent was removed from airwaves in 1999 amid concerns that the cartoon character was stereotypical and would offend Mexican Americans. Ironically, the removal of Speedy from television spurred a "Free the Mouse" movement among Latino viewers who considered Speedy to be a positive role model for children, and appreciated an English-speaking yet distinctly Mexican character being represented in cartoons. The movement has gained the endorsement of the League of United Latin American Citizens (LULAC) and other Hispanic American organizations.

Other icons of Latin American origin found their way into the pantheon of Latino popular-culture heroes over the course of the 20th century. Mexican painter Frida Kahlo, wife of muralist Diego Rivera, gained widespread popularity in the United States decades after her death in 1954. Her work, rife with themes of fragmented identity, indigenous heritage, and uncertain sexuality, has been adopted by Chicano, feminist, and fringe culture groups alike as representative of their respective quests for identity. Likewise, the ubiquitous photograph of the Argentine revolutionary Ché Guevara, who was credited with helping Fidel Castro instigate the 1959 Cuban Revolution, has been appropriated in endless ways in the United States as a generic symbol of rebellion. Although Guevara despised the United States and spurned capitalist ideology, his image crops up on album covers (Rage Against the Machine), on tee-shirts, bathing suits, action figures, and posters. Guevara's image has become affiliated with a broad trend of Latin American revolution, and his image can now be just as easily found on the beach in Sonora as in Cuba or Los Angeles.

Telenovelas, Latin American television serials resembling soap operas, have their roots in 19th-century serial novels and stories popularized in Europe. The form became adapted to mass media in Cuba, where the radio soap opera flourished thanks to sponsorship by U.S. household marketers such as Colgate-Palmolive, Proctor and Gamble, and Gessy-Lever. In 1948 the serial drama *El derecho de nacer* became a radio hit in Cuba, and has seen revivals in television versions produced in many countries. In the 1950s the introduction of television helped the epic romance dramas to evolve into the telenovela and enjoyed prolific production in Cuba throughout the decade until Fidel Castro's 1959 revolution brought a halt to the industry. By that time, telenovelas were already widespread throughout Latin America, and Mexico's Televisa, Venezuela's Venevision, and Brazil's Globo assumed production and international exportation of the popular entertainment form. Telenovelas differ from soap operas in that they are usually broadcast during prime-time hours, frequently feature politically or socially controversial issues, and the finite plot line finite revolves around a romantic couple whose suspense-filled escapades last a brief 180 to 200 episodes before culminating in a narrative conclusion. Telenovelas attract audiences across gender and generational lines, and emerged as a central element in Latin American domestic life in the second half of the 20th century. Televisa serves as the leading supplier of telenovelas in the U.S. market, burgeoning in the 1980s with Los Angeles as the demographic target. In 1994 Televisa teamed with the Fox Network to produce *Empire,* the first English-language telenovela. The popularity of telenovelas in the United States transcends the strictly Latino audience, capturing fans of diverse cultural and national backgrounds, a phenomenon that defies the North-to-South trend of cultural imperialism.

RELATED ARTICLES

Advertising; Bracero Program; Cuisine; Fast Food; Film; Guevara, Ernesto; Music, Popular; Restaurants; Stereotypes and Stereotyping; Telenovelas; Television.

FURTHER READING

Andrews, Bart. *The "I Love Lucy" Book.* New York: Doubleday, 1985.

Aparicio, Frances R., and Susana Chávez-Silverman, eds. *Tropicalizations: Transcultural Representations of Latinidad.* Hanover, N.H.: Univ. Press of New England, 1997.

Helena Solberg. "Bananas is my Business." In *Latin American Popular Culture.* Ed. by William H. Beezley and Linda A. Curcio-Nagy. Wilmington, Del.: SR Bks., 2000.

Delgado, Celeste Fraser, and José Esteban Muñoz, eds. *Everynight Life: Culture and Dance in Latin/o America.* Durham, N.C.: Duke Univ. Press, 1997.

Gómez-Peña, Guillermo. *Warrior for Gringostroika.* Saint Paul, Minn.: Graywolf Press, 1993.

Habell-Pallan, Michelle, and Mary Romero, eds. *Latino/a Popular Culture.* New York: N.Y. Univ. Press, 2002.

Katz, Elihu, and George Wedell, et al. *Broadcasting in the Third World: Promise and Performance.* Cambridge, Mass.: Harvard Univ. Press, 1977.

Matelski, Marilyn. *Soap Operas Worldwide: Cultural and Serial Realities.* Jefferson, N.C.: McFarland & Co., 1999.

Pike, Frederick B. *The United States and Latin America: Myths and Stereotypes of Civilization and Nature.* Austin: Univ. of Tex. Press, 1992.

Stavans, Ilan. *The Riddle of Cantinflas: Essays on Hispanic Popular Culture.* Albuquerque: Univ. of N.Mex. Press, 1998.

Strinati, Dominic. *An Introduction to Theories of Popular Culture.* London: Routledge, 1995.

ELENA JACKSON ALBARRÁN

POPULAR MUSIC. *See* MUSIC, POPULAR.

PORTILLO, LOURDES

Born: November 11, 1944; Chihuahua, Mexico

Acclaimed filmmaker Lourdes Portillo is often described as "Mexican born and Chicana identified." The inherent transition referred to in that description has served as a catalyst for Portillo's film work, which, according to her official Web site, has "focused on the search for Latino identity." Since the 1980s Portillo has produced an important body of work and is regarded as one of the leading documentary producers in the country.

Portillo began working on documentary films at the age of 21 when a friend asked her to assist on a movie in Los Angeles. According to Portillo, "I knew from that moment what I was going to do for the rest of my life." An apprenticeship at the San Francisco National Association of Broadcast Employees and Technicians (NABET) led to a job in 1975 as a camera assistant to Stephen Lighthill on *Over, Under, Sideways, Down.* The film was produced by Cine Manifest, a collective that Lighthill had helped organize four years earlier for the expressed purpose of making interesting, low-budget features. Portillo's experience at Cine Manifest dovetailed with her dual interests in filmmaking and politics. In an interview with scholar Rosa Linda Fregoso, Portillo described Cine Manifest as a group of Marxist filmmakers. She claimed to have received two different kinds of education: a political education and a free associative filmic education, which is how she began working in film. From that time on Portillo remained in San Francisco working almost exclusively as an independent producer.

Portillo's first film was *Después del Terremoto* (After the Earthquake), made in 1979. The film is about a Nicaraguan woman who moves to San Francisco following the devastating earthquake of 1976. That the protagonist is a woman is no accident. Portillo's films almost always deal with issues of gender. Portillo has said that one of the things that she finds interesting and important about this film is that gender is at the center of cultural conflict. The film was made during a time of exceptional strife in Central America, when many refugees were coming to the United States—and a good number to San Francisco. Unlike most other political films of the era, *Después del Terremoto*, produced with Nina Serrano, is a narrative film and not a documentary. The film is set in the Bay area but addresses the political situation in Nicaragua through the lives of the protagonists.

Portillo continued to explore the themes of identity, race, gender, and class in her later films. In 1986 she produced *Las Madres de la Plaza de Mayo*, which chronicles the story of the mothers of those who "disappeared" during Argentina's "dirty war." The film was nominated for an Oscar in 1986. Portillo followed with *Ofrenda* in 1990, about Chicano and Mexican views of death. Portillo's contention that her films are produced "in service to the Chicano community first," is supported by her choice of film topics.

To coincide with the quincentennial of the arrival of European explorers to the Americas, in 1992 Portillo released *Columbus on Trial,* a satire that explored the ugly side of the Genoan admiral, who opened the door for the systematic destruction of the aboriginal population on this side of the Atlantic Ocean. The trial in the film is presided over by a female judge of Latino descent.

The Devil Never Sleeps, which Portillo made in 1994, tells the deeply personal story of the death of her uncle, Oscar Ruíz, in her home state of Chihuahua, Mexico. Portillo returns home and investigates the controversy surrounding Ruiz's death from a gunshot wound to the head. In 1999 Portillo produced *Corpus: A Home Movie for Selena,* about the slain Tejano music singer and what she meant to Chicanas. The film proved problematic and even Portillo recognized it as minor.

Arguably the most visible and perhaps the most important of Portillo's films is *Señorita Extraviada,* released in 2001. Produced in collaboration with the Center for Independent Documentary and Independent Television Service, it is a soul-searching exploration of the still-unsolved mass murder of young women in Ciudad Juárez, on the U.S.-Mexico bor-

der. Portillo interviewed dozens of relatives, victims, police officers, investigators, and politicians, and produced an exposé of Mexican corruption. Applauded at the Sundance Film Festival and other forums for nontraditional films, it is a controversial piece that helped draw attention to a crime that politicians wanted to avoid.

Después del Terremoto, Corpus: A Home Movie for Selena, and *Señorita Extraviada,* among other films, all reflect Portillo's identity as a strident Chicana independent filmmaker. Despite the inconsistency of her work, her oeuvre remains impressive.

RELATED ARTICLES
Film; Mexican Americans.

FURTHER READING
Salas, Fred. "Interview with Lourdes Portillo." *Motion Magazine* (December 6, 1998).
"Screening Resistance: A Conversation between Lourdes Portillo and Rosa Linda" *www.lordespotillo.com*
Fregoso, Rosa Linda, ed. *The Devil Never Sleeps, and Other Films.* Austin: Univ. of Tex., Press, 2001.

SELECTED WEB SITES
The Films and Videos of Lourdes Portillo. www.lourdesportillo.com

JOSÉ ANDRADE

POSADA, JOSÉ GUADALUPE

Born: 1852; Aguascalientes, Mexico
Died: 1913; Mexico City, Mexico

As Mexico's greatest printmaker, José Guadalupe Posada deeply influenced the course of Mexican and Chicano art. During his lifetime Posada was regarded as a commercial artisan rather than as a serious artist. Commencing in the 1920s the Mexican mural renaissance brought about a reevaluation of art and culture in the aftermath of the Mexican Revolution. Jean Charlot deemed Posada the preeminent artist of the Mexican people. Surrealist leader André Breton subsequently introduced Posada to an international audience.

In the introduction to *Posada, Messenger of Mortality* (1989), Peter Wollen argues that Posada's name and legend provided both a role model for and "an alternative tradition" to the academic conventions that had been favored by the creole elites: "It gave credibility to claims to be part of an authentically Mexican artistic tradition, crossing both the class gap and the historic divide of the Revolution itself and,

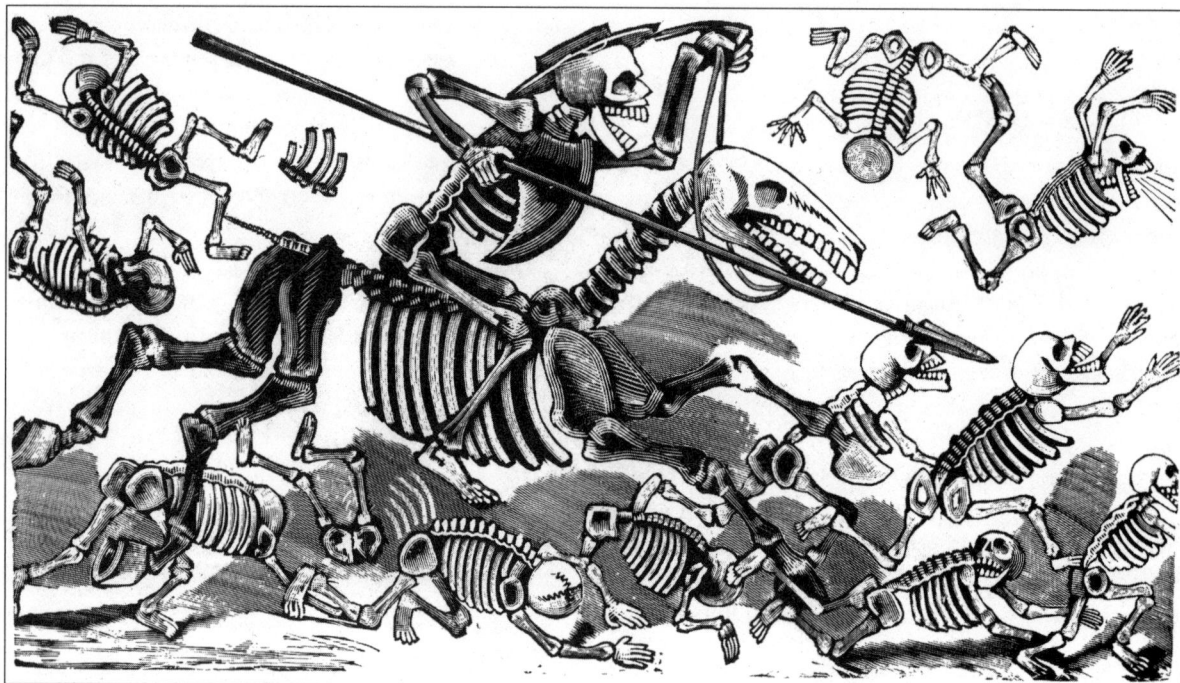

"*Calavera*" of *Don Quixote*, engraving by José Posada.

at the same time, guaranteed the modernity of the tradition by aligning it with the revival of interest in popular imagery among the European avant-garde."

Posada's brother Cirilio taught him to draw; he later studied briefly at an Aguascalientes drawing academy. An apprentice in the lithography shop run by Trinidad Pedroza in 1870, Posada quickly developed facility in the medium. His satirical illustrations for Pedrozo's *El Jicote* (a Sunday newspaper) won immediate attention. Having offended local elites, Pedroza and Posada moved to León in 1873, where they produced a broad range of commercial work. From 1884 to 1888 Posada also taught lithography at a high school in León.

Posada illustrated more than 50 magazines and newspapers, some with rather conventional images. His most admired works are the broadsheets (irregularly issued single sheets) made for Antonio Venegas Arroyo after moving to Mexico City in 1888. In "Posada and the 'Popular'" (1994), Thomas Gretton argues that Posada disguised his facility and made deliberately crude prints designed to appeal to Venegas Arroyo's moderately literate, lower-class, urbanized mestizo audience. In "Posada's Prints as Photomechanical Artefacts" (1992) Gretton holds

that these rustic-looking images were made with the most modern photographic technologies.

Two types of broadsheets stand out: *calaveras* (issued on the Day of the Dead [Día de los Muertos]) and crime. In *Posada's Broadsheets* (1998), Patrick Frank notes Posada's focus on the most sensationalistic crimes of passion—those directed against members of one's own family (which often include a demonic presence). Frank emphasizes the vitality of Posada's murderous protagonists.

Even the skulls and skeletons in Posada's *calaveras* possess an uncommon vigor and expressivity. Posada's most famous print, the *Calavera Catrina* (illustrated), was elaborated into a full figure by Diego Rivera in a mural called *Dream of a Sunday Afternoon in the Alameda Park* (1947–1948). Numerous Latin American and Latino artists have produced variations of the *Calavera Catrina*. About 2,000 prints by Posada are extant and are in museum collections in cities throughout the United States.

RELATED ARTICLES

Art, Popular; Arts, Graphic; Charlot, Jean; Newspapers and Magazines.

FURTHER READING

Frank, Patrick. *Posada's Broadsheets: Mexican Popular Imagery 1890–1910.* Albuquerque: Univ. of N.Mex. Press, 1998.

Gretton, Thomas. "Posada's Prints as Photomechanical Artefacts." *Print Quarterly* 9 (December 1992): 335–356.

Gretton, Thomas. "Posada and the 'Popular': Commodities and Social Constructs in Mexico before the Revolution." *Oxford Art Journal* 17, no. 2 (1994): 335–356.

Instituto Nacional de Bellas Artes. *Posada y la prensa ilustrada: Signos de modernización y resistencias.* Mexico: Museo Nacional de Arte, 1996.

Posada's Mexico. Ed. by Ron Tyler. Washington, D.C.: Lib. of Congress, 1979.

Wollen, Peter. Intro., *J. G. Posada. Messenger of Mortality.* Ed. by Julian Rothenstein. Mt. Kisco, N.Y.: Moyer Bell Ltd., 1989.

RUBEN C. CORDOVA

POSADAS

The nine-day Christmas celebrations (December 16–24) known as *posadas* are community events that reenact María and José's (Mary and Joseph's) search for shelter the days before their son Jesus was born in Bethlehem. *Las posadas,* meaning inns or places of rest for weary travelers, have resonated among many Latino communities in the United States, particularly because they reflect the search for a place to call home for many immigrants, and because these nightly strolls through neighborhoods during the days before Christmas bring families and neighbors together in an often indifferent and even hostile world.

Las posadas have been vibrant celebrations in Mexico for centuries, thus many Mexican American communities, from El Paso, Texas, to Los Angeles to Durham, North Carolina, have imported this holiday tradition and even reinterpreted it in the United States. But Puerto Rico and Colombia, for example, also have similar Christmas traditions (sometimes called Las Novenas or Misas de Aguinaldo), and so *posadas* also serve to join all Latinos in a festive atmosphere of goodwill and religious observance.

Originally, *las posadas* emerged from the Misas de Aguinaldo that began in 1587 after the Augustinian friar Diego de Soria petitioned the pope for permission to have a series of nine outdoor masses in Mexico, with allegorical scenes (*pastorelas*) to portray and explain the Christmas story to huge and enthusiastic crowds of Indians. The pope granted permission for the Misas de Aguinaldo, but by the late 1700s these outdoor masses had become too raucous and disrespectful for the archbishop of Mexico

City, who preferred a more solemn observance of the traditional Mass. So the church slowly went indoors during Christmastime, so to speak, and left these celebrations of food and noise to neighborhoods and families in Mexico. After a while the focus of these folk festivals became María and José's search for a place to have their baby, and they became known as *las posadas.*

A typical *posada* in the United States begins in the early evening hours at a predetermined house in the neighborhood. Often two children, playing the roles of María and José, dress up in white tunics with colorful headbands, maybe with a makeshift staff for José and a donkey for María to ride. She might also have a pillow tucked in her tunic to display the urgency of finding a place to stay for the night. Adults and children follow behind María and José to the first stop. In the United States, the church has begun to include itself again in these community events, and so a priest sometimes walks beside the holy couple, and leads the throng in prayer. Everyone carries a candle, and a few adults briefly stop the neighborhood traffic as the crowd marches along, singing under the stars.

At the first house, the owners, and several preselected individuals from the crowd, go inside and wait for José to rap on the door with his staff. Then a beautiful hymn of query and response, in an archaic and hypnotic Spanish, begins between the "innkeepers" inside the house, and María and José and the "pilgrims" outside. The pilgrims beseech the innkeepers to let them have a place to stay. The innkeepers respond with suspicion and question whether they may be vagrants or even dangerous criminals. The pilgrims reply that they are just poor and about to have a baby, who is to be the Son of God. The innkeepers respond by telling them to go away. José implores the owners of the house to let them stay just one night. After more polite, yet heartbreaking, exchanges María, José, and the pilgrims finally decide to try the next house. Often, three or four houses are visited during a *posada.* At the last house, the pilgrims are finally welcomed inside.

In their haven for the night, the pilgrims (*peregrinos*) sing a few final songs of reverence, and then they are served punch, hot chocolate, perhaps a few sandwiches, *buñuelos,* tamales, *champurado,* and *menudo.* Children take wild swings at a piñata stuffed with candy. On Christmas Eve, the night ends with the Misa de Gallo, or midnight Mass, at a local

© RIC VASQUEZ/AP/WIDE WORLD PHOTOS

Grandparents, escorted by their grandchildren, start the *posada* on Christmas Eve in Rio Hondo, Texas, 2003.

church. *Las posadas* are indeed a community celebration of public togetherness for many Latinos; they provide an opportunity for Latinos to feel they belong and to profess their faith and link neighbor to neighbor, under the stars, and finally find a place to call home.

RELATED ARTICLES
Holidays; Navidad.

FURTHER READING
Cavazos-González, Gilbero. "Whom Will You Welcome This Christmas?" *U.S. Catholic Magazine* (December 2002).
Davidow, Joie, and Esmeralda Santiago. *Las Christmas: Latino Authors Share Their Holiday Memories.* New York: Knopf, 1998.
De Paola, Tomie. *The Night of Las Posadas.* New York: Putnam, 1999.
Ramírez, Josephine. "A Tale of Los Angeles: Posadas: Nourishing Community." *Harvard Review of Latin America* (Winter 2003).
Ross, Corinne. *Christmas in Mexico.* New York: McGraw Hill, 1991.
Troncoso, Sergio. "The Last Tortilla." In *The Last Tortilla and Other Stories.* Tucson: Univ. of Ariz. Press, 1999.

SERGIO TRONCOSO

PRESIDENTS AND LATINOS. *See*
UNITED STATES PRESIDENTS, AND LATINOS.

PRLDEF. *See* PUERTO RICAN LEGAL DEFENSE AND EDUCATION FUND.

PROPOSITION 187

Proposition 187, also known as the "Save Our State" initiative and "California's Anti-Immigration Law" because it purports to deny public social, educational, and health services to undocumented immigrants in California, was written by Alan Nelson, former federal immigration commissioner under President Ronald Reagan and Harold Ezell, western region commissioner of the Immigration Naturalization Service (INS). The initiative was backed and funded by Republicans with the primary proponent Assemblyman Dick Mountjoy (R Monrovia). Proposition 187 was submitted to California voters in the November 8, 1994, general election, passed with 59 percent approval, and became law the next day.

The text of Proposition 187 identifies undocumented immigrants as the source of economic hardship, personal injury, and damages of criminal conduct suffered by Californians. The proposition also asserts the rights of Californians to demand protection from unlawful entrance into the country and cooperation among local, state, and federal agencies to ensure that undocumented immigrants will not receive public services and benefits. Ten sections of the proposition outline this desire for protection from the presence of undocumented immigrants in California; the crime and punishment as a felony for the manufacture, distribution or sale of false citizenship or resident alien documents; the crime and punishment for use of these documents; the expectation of information collection and verification and cooperation from all law enforcement agencies with the INS; the specifics of exclusion of undocumented immigrants for public social services; the exclusion of undocumented immigrants from publicly funded health care; the exclusion of undocumented immigrants from public elementary and secondary schools; the exclusion of undocumented immigrants from public postsecondary educational institutions; the expectations for the attorney general's cooperation with the INS; and the disallowance of amendment or severability of the various provisions of the proposition.

The distinct and heavily debated features of Proposition 187 are in its demands that California's law enforcement, social services, health care, and public personnel require citizenship status verification from those suspected to be illegal before rendering services other than emergency care as required by law. The proposition outlines penalties and criminal punishment for falsification and usage of citizenship documents and makes provision for law enforcement agencies to question persons "suspected of being present in the United States in violation of federal immigration laws" regarding date of birth and entry into the United States, and to demand documentation of citizenship status. In excluding undocumented immigrants from public social services until verification is made of the citizenship status of the suspected persons, Proposition 187 demands that persons found to be illegal must be reported to the state director of social services, the attorney general of California, and the U.S. INS. In addition, the Education Code requires a similar suspicion, reporting, and denial of services, but also specifies that each term public postsecondary schools must verify the citizenship of its masses to ensure the identification and removal of undocumented immigrants.

The debates concerning Proposition 187 hinge on questions of constitutionality, but many have assessed the damage from a fiscal perspective. The legislative analyst has reported three major concerns. Based on INS estimates, state and local governments would save roughly $200 million dollars annually from the denial of benefits and services to people who cannot provide evidence of citizenship. While that may seem like a much desired option, the analyst finds that the verification of the citizenship status of persons in need of health care, students and their parents, and every "suspect" person arrested, however, would cost in the tens of millions of dollars for the state, local governments, and schools. Since getting started is considerably more expensive than budgeted maintenance, projected costs of the first year exceeded $100 million. The third fiscal consideration outlined by the legislative analyst finds that the state could expect roughly $15 billion of federal funding out of reach owing to conflicts in federal requirements for education, health and welfare programs.

The arguments for Proposition 187 usually focus on supply and demand logic. If access to social services is what draws undocumented immigrants, then it stands to reason that cutting off these services off would seriously disable the state's attractiveness. Proponents argue that unsuccessful border control that puts California in such a condition of fiscal, criminal, and social mayhem requires the state to use the proposition to chastise politicians concerning their duty to protect California's borders. They also argue that the opposition to the proposition stems from those who stand to gain the most from illegal residents: public unions and medical clinics.

The arguments against Proposition 187 typically consider the proposition as a dangerously misplaced bandage on a wide and gaping wound. Although many opponents to the proposition agree that there is a growing problem with the entrance and residence of illegal immigrants, they suggest that border enforcement and corporate crackdowns should be at the heart of any resolution to deal with the problem, rather than a denial of public services. They argue that incurring new costs to the state while attempting to identify undocumented immigrants does not address the employers who consistently hire illegal immigrants without significant repercussion while simultaneously creating a potentially volatile social and health risk. They argue that the fiscal risk amounts to almost $150 used for every dollar saved, and they point out the obvious hazard of controlling communicable diseases given the continued opportunities for employment despite the denial of public services.

Other opponents of the proposition argue the clear threat to civil liberties inherent in the proposition's provision for reporting "suspicious" persons. They attack the language of the proposition as legal jargon concealing hatred and fear reminiscent of the treatment of free blacks during slavery, suspected Communists, and Asian populations in U.S. history. The California Association of Hospitals and Health Systems, the League of Women Voters, and the Congress of California Seniors opposed the proposition. The proposition was backed and funded by various Republican interest groups and politicians.

The proposition was approved, yet owing to its main provisions being ruled unconstitutional, it never went into effect. Of the ten sections, the only felony penalty that is currently enforced is for using or creating false documents that would allow illegal immigrants access to public benefits or employment. Full enforcement of the proposition could mean a significant jail sentence for undocumented parents receiving health care or attempting to send their children to school. The passing of such a proposition, in a state

© FRANK WIESE/AP/WIDE WORLD PHOTOS

Activists for and against Proposition 187 during a rally outside the Federal Building in Los Angeles, California, 1996.

as ethnically diverse as California, publicized and formalized hostilities and divisions among and between ethnic groups and continues to act as a sign of the complexity of race and class relations in California.

RELATED ARTICLES

California; Discrimination; Education; Health; Immigration, Latino.

FURTHER READING

Aldama, Arturo J., and Naomi H. Quiñonez, eds. *Decolonial Voices: Chicana and Chicano Cultural Studies in the 21st Century.* Bloomington: Ind. Univ. Press, 2002.

Gracía, Jorge J. E., and Pablo De Greiff. *Hispanics/Latinos in the United States: Ethnicity, Race, and Rights.* New York: Routledge, 2000.

Mailman, Stanley. "California's Proposition 187 and Its Lessons." *New York Law Journal* (January 3, 1995): 3. http://ssbb.com/article1/html.

Stavans, Ilan. *The Hispanic Condition: The Power of a People,* 2d ed. New York: HarperCollins, 2001.

Trueba, Enrique T. *Latinos Unidos: From Cultural Diversity to the Politics of Solidarity.* New York: Rowman & Littlefield, 1999.

SELECTED WEB SITES

California Voter Foundation.
http://www.calvoter.org/archive/94general/props/187.html

Online News Hour.
http://www.pbs.org/newshour/bb/congress/immigrant_benefits1_3-26.html

HELANE D. ADAMS

PROTESTANTISM

Protestantism is a major branch of Christianity derived from groups that separated from the Roman Catholic Church beginning in the 16th century, particularly in central and northern Europe and in England. Protestant churches comprise large denominations (Southern Baptists, Presbyterians) and individual congregations not affiliated with larger bodies. Although Protestantism is a varied phenomenon, one generally can identify the following commonalities:

(1) The pope and his hierarchy are not considered religious authorities;

(2) the Bible is used as the primary religious authority;

(3) personal conscience is considered the primary religious interpreter of the Bible (priesthood of all believers);

(4) the sacraments (especially Baptism and Holy Communion) are de-emphasized as means of salvation;

(5) the idea of salvation as a free gift ("grace") of God, and not something that can be achieved by "works," is emphasized; and

(6) veneration of the Virgin Mary and the saints is eliminated or de-emphasized.

The rise of Protestantism among Latinos and Latinas in the United States constitutes perhaps one of the most significant revolutions in Christianity since the 16th century. Figures from an interim report of the Hispanic Churches in American Public Life Project (HCAPL), published in 2003, the largest survey of U.S. Latino religious behavior to date, reports that 23 percent of U.S. Latinos identify themselves as Protestant. More importantly, the HCAPL confirms earlier estimates that about 600,000 U.S. Latinos per year convert to Protestantism. If so, this rate is probably higher than the conversion rate of 16th-century Europe.

Beginnings of Protestantism in Europe

The Protestant Reformation was part of a long series of earlier attempts to reform or dethrone Roman Catholicism in Europe. The primary initial Protestant figure was Martin Luther (1483–1546), an Augustinian monk and professor of theology at Wittenberg University in Germany. Luther complained that the building of St. Peter's Basilica in Rome was being financed by the sale of "indulgences," which, in effect, promised the forgiveness of sins in exchange for payment. On October 31, 1517, Luther reportedly posted, on the door of the main church in Wittenberg, an invitation to debate 95 theses that outlined his complaints. Although Luther had intended only to reform Catholicism, not abandon it, his acts spawned a series of events that led to his excommunication and eventually to the founding of what came to be known as Protestantism.

The success of Luther spawned other groups, some of which sought more radical departures from Roman Catholic theology and practice, including the Baptists, Presbyterians, and Methodists. European kingdoms began to identify themselves as Catholic or Protestant, showing the link between nationalism and the rise of Protestantism. Thus England, much of Germany, and Scandinavia became predominantly Protestant; Spain, Portugal, and Italy remained predominantly Catholic.

Protestantism in Latin America

For most of the last 500 years, Protestantism had a relatively insignificant presence among Latin Americans, owing to the long colonization and dominance of the Spanish Catholic Church. Even at the beginning of the 20th century there were only a few Protestant churches (particularly Episcopalian, Presbyterian, and Methodist) in Latin America. Protestantism gained a foothold in the Americas only in the wake of American expansion into Latin America.

Protestantism had made its first significant inroads into Mexico with the rise of Porfirio Díaz, a dictator who held power for most of 1881–1911. Although the northern Mexican states held high concentrations of Protestants relative to other regions of Mexico, the number of Protestants was still very small at the turn of the 20th century. According to Deborah Baldwin, there were 1,913 Protestants in 1905 in Sonora, a state with a population of approximately 221,000. The best-represented groups were Methodists, Baptists, and Episcopalians.

Protestantism made its first significant inroads into Puerto Rico and Cuba when the United States gained control of those islands in the aftermath of the Spanish-American War of 1898. By 1910, Protestants had some 15 missionary societies, 120 churches, and 326 missions in Puerto Rico alone. These developments have influenced the rise of Protestantism among Puerto Ricans who have moved to the U.S. mainland, particularly since 1950. Although many Cubans who converted to Protestantism in the United States in the early 20th century sometimes returned to Cuba in order to gain new converts there, both Protestantism and Catholicism were adversely affected in Cuba with the assumption to power of Fidel Castro in 1959.

In Central and South America the growth of Protestantism today derives from missionary work rather than just through American military expansion. Of particular importance is the rise of television in these areas. American televangelists are able to broadcast their programs all over Latin America, often followed by enormous "crusades" in which they preach in public. The popularity of such televangelists plays a strong marketing role, especially in Chile and Guatemala, which have some of the largest proportions of Protestants in all of Latin America.

Protestantism among U.S. Latinos

Protestantism among U.S. Latinos has two main sources. One is the immigrants from Latin America who come into the United States as Protestants. The other source is conversion in the United States. Both sources yield subsequent generations of Protestants. In many cases, Protestantism arises in a truly transnational environment, as was the case in the U.S.-Mexican borderlands, where some missionaries established churches on both sides of the border.

Mexicans living in what is now the American Southwest were among the first Latinos to interact on a significant level with Protestants, particularly with Anglo-Protestant settlers in Texas. The end of the Mexican War in 1848 provided a new impetus for the work of Protestant missionaries, who sometimes saw Mexican Americans as an initial step to the conversion of Mexico to Protestantism. One of these early missionaries was Melinda Rankin (1811–1888), a young Presbyterian New Englander who used Brownsville, Texas, as a base for missionary work in the U.S.-Mexico borderlands. About 1853 Ambrosio González of New Mexico became the first recorded Latino convert to Protestantism, according to some traditions. Some 15.5 percent of Mexican Americans are now Protestants (de la Garza).

Some scholars estimate that over 10 percent of Puerto Ricans in New York were Protestant by the 1970s, with Pentecostal varieties being dominant. By the 1990s, some 20.7 percent of Puerto Ricans born in the U.S. mainland were Protestant (de la Garza). Some 5 percent of the Cuban population was estimated to be Protestant at the beginning of the Fidel Castro era in 1959, and, while the Castro revolution had a negative impact on Protestants, it did not eliminate them completely. Many Cuban exiles established Protestant churches in the United States, especially in Miami, and now about 10.2 percent of Cuban Americans (born in the United States) are Protestant, according to de la Garza.

The socioeconomic profile of Latino Protestants has yet to be studied in great detail. In 1988 Andrew Greeley estimated that second-generation Latino and Latina Protestants had an average of 11.3 years of education, with an annual income of about $27,000, compared with an annual income of about $19,000 for Latino Catholics. Fifty-two percent of these second-generation Protestants were employed in white-collar jobs, 28 percent being described as managers. Greeley also reported that, compared with

Catholic Latinos, Hispanic Protestants were "happier in their marriages, family life, and personal life."

Evangelical Protestants

Within Protestantism, evangelicals, as opposed to "mainline" Protestants, are gaining a lion's share of conversions from Catholicism. Mainline Protestant denominations are those that were established in the 16th and 17th centuries or that have been part of the ruling establishment, or both. Primary examples are Lutherans, Presbyterians, Methodists, and Southern Baptists (although there is a large assortment of other Baptist groups). HCAPL reports that mainline churches constitute about 14.8 percent, or 1.6 million, of all Latino Protestants.

By contrast, some 88 percent (6.2 million) of all Latino Protestants describe themselves as "Evangelicals" or "born again." Evangelical is a term with a complex history and meaning. Today, most Evangelicals speak of being "born again." Evangelicals believe in the virgin birth, deity, and imminent return of Jesus Christ and that society ought to be ruled by biblical principles, and they advocate a very active and vigorous form of proselytization. In addition, conservative Protestant Evangelicals may be strongly anti-Catholic. Some mainline denominations (such as Southern Baptists) identify themselves as Evangelicals.

One of the most often used criteria for identifying Anglo-Evangelicals has been the "born again" self-identification. The term derives from John 3:3, where Jesus tells a certain Nicodemus that in order to enter the kingdom of God, he must be "born again," although the original Greek phrase more precisely means "born from above," as indicated by the New Revised Standard Version. Gallup and Castelli, who use the born-again experience to identify Evangelicals, estimate that 6 percent of American Evangelicals are Hispanics and that the vast majority of Hispanic Protestants are Evangelicals. De la Garza, however, reports that 20.2 percent of Cuban Americans consider themselves born-again, along with 29.2 percent of Puerto Ricans (U.S. born) and 30.1 percent of Mexican Americans, even though the percentages of self-professed Protestants in each of those Latino subgroups is lower in the same survey. This disparity indicates that the born-again criterion must be used with great caution in identifying Hispanic Evangelicals. Indeed, new figures from the HCAPL survey, which also uses the born-again criterion for

some of its measures, indicates that some 26 percent of Catholic Latinos now describe themselves as born again, representing the influence of Protestant terminology on Catholics.

Latino Evangelicals also continue the Anglo-American evangelical tradition of distinguishing themselves from groups such as the Jehovah's Witnesses and Mormons, who are perceived to be unorthodox in some central teachings. For example, Jehovah's Witnesses deny that Jesus is God, although there are similar positions among Evangelicals (for example, "Oneness Pentecostalism"). Nonetheless, perhaps one in ten non-Catholic Latinos are Jehovah's Witnesses or Mormons, according to some estimates.

Pentecostal Protestants

One of the major movements within Hispanic Evangelicalism is called Pentecostalism, an American-born movement that stresses that miracles and other supernatural phenomena (speaking in tongues, faith healing, and Holy Spirit baptism) depicted in early Christianity are still achievable and should be actively cultivated. According to the HCAPL, some 64 percent (or 4.5 million) of all Latino Protestants are members of "Pentecostal or Charismatic denominations or claim to be Pentecostal, Charismatic, or spirit-filled." In New York City, Pentecostal Puerto Ricans reportedly outnumber all other Protestant Puerto Ricans combined.

The biblical origins of Pentecostalism are found in Acts 2, which speaks of the baptism of the Holy Spirit. This event apparently refers to the endowment of the believer with divine power in order to carry out the Christian mission. For example, the power of healing and exorcism are meant to provide signs useful for proselytization (Mark 16:17–18). In addition, it was believed that the increased manifestation of these supernatural gifts signaled the nearness of the Second Coming of Jesus.

Equally significant for Pentecostalism is that the first Christians who received the baptism of the Holy Spirit believed they were able to speak in foreign languages, a skill that would be useful for evangelizing other nations. The phenomenon of "speaking in tongues," known technically as glossolalia, became the hallmark of Pentecostalism. According to most Pentecostals, one knows that one has received the baptism of the Holy Spirit only when one speaks in tongues. While mainline denominations usually believe that Holy Spirit baptism is automatically provided at conversion, Pentecostals believe Holy Spirit baptism is an event that one must strive for after conversion. For this and other reasons, some mainline denominations sometimes see Pentecostalism as an emotional or even demonic phenomenon.

An organizational hallmark of Pentecostalism is congregational and denominational fragmentation. Since the Holy Spirit's power is theoretically available to anyone, people will follow leaders who are believed to possess the most power. Thus it is common for small groups to break away from larger denominations if individual congregations or pastors feel that the Holy Spirit is leading them to do so. Consequently, new congregations are constantly being formed from previous congregations. A related phenomenon is the "cult of personality," which has been quite pronounced, especially among Pentecostal Hispanics. Rather than denominations, often particular figures become rallying points for organization.

Reasons for Protestantization

Explaining Protestantization has become a main preoccupation of the academic study of U.S. Latino/a and Latin American Protestantism. Some of the initial impetus to explain Protestantization comes from Catholic academics' wishing to forge strategies to stop the erosion in Catholic membership. For example, Andrew Greeley, who became one of the foremost sociologists of Protestantization, is also a Catholic priest who warns about what he terms "defection" among Hispanic Catholics. Many Protestant writers, on the other hand, view the growth of Protestants as the triumph of God's plan.

From a secular perspective, there is no single reason to explain the shift to Protestantism, but perhaps the simplest theory appeals to the fragmentation of audiences that occurs when new choices are introduced. Catholicism was the only official choice for much of the last 500 years in Latin America; when Protestant groups came along with American expansion, people had new choices, and the Catholic audience fragmented.

Another theory emphasizes that Catholicism was never evenly distributed in Latin America. Thus, Protestantism simply filled the "empty niches." For example, about 1934, when the Church of God established one of its early missions in the border town of Agua Prieta, in the state of Sonora, Mexico, there was no Catholic priest or Catholic church at all in that town. When the nuns of the Company of Mary

attempted, in the 1930s, to recruit young Latina women to attend their newly founded school in Douglas, Arizona, just on the other side of the border from Agua Prieta, they were hindered by the lack of a strong Catholic tradition in those parts of the U.S.-Mexican borderlands.

Another explanation notes that Hispanic Catholics in the United States often feel alienated from an American brand of Catholicism that is not willing to adjust to their cultural distinctness. Even after Vatican II, which sought flexibility in catering to the cultural worship practices of Catholics around the world, many Latinos still felt that American Catholic officials sought to Americanize rather than accept them. Thus, in New York City, Puerto Rican Catholics have complained about being relegated to the basement of Anglo-American churches. Predominantly Mexican American parishes in Texas have complained that they receive fewer resources than their predominantly Anglo-American counterparts. Converting to Protestantism was, therefore, partly a reaction to alienation from the Catholic Church.

In contrast to Catholicism, Protestantism has been more willing to provide Hispanic divisions that help retain Latino cultural practices and worship styles. The Church of God, for example, had a Spanish-speaking division from at least the 1950s. Southern Baptist Spanish-speaking denominations are now some of the largest Southern Baptist churches in the nation. At the same time some sociologists note that many Latinos and Latin Americans "indigenize" as well as adopt American brands of Protestantism.

The democratization of power and social mobility also are important reasons for Protestantization. While becoming a priest can be a lengthy process, Protestant ministry and leadership can be achieved relatively quickly. Pentecostalism, with its emphasis on the power of the Holy Spirit, is perhaps the most liberal in terms of accepting leadership abilities in converts. Congregations often fracture and spawn new groups, reinforcing the idea that individuals and groups are free to decide what is best for themselves.

A related attraction of Protestantism is the possibility for the enhanced role of women. Pentecostals, in particular, have been quite accepting of female leadership. Famous examples include Aimee Semple McPherson (1890–1944), founder of the Four Square Gospel, and Maria Atkinson (1879–1963), founder of the Church of God in the U.S.-Mexican borderlands. As was the case with Atkinson, however, women who achieve a leadership position are sometimes later disempowered by the very men they help to train. While women still are not well represented in the top leadership of most Protestant denominations, they are relatively better represented than in the Catholic church.

Many converts to Pentecostal Protestantism report first visiting Pentecostal churches because of their emphasis on healing. Pentecostalism can function as an alternative health-care system in areas where conventional health care is not accessible or has not yielded satisfactory results. Even if religious practice does not yield the desired health outcome, converts may stay in those churches for other benefits that the group may provide (such as social networking or new leadership opportunities). Pentecostalism must also compete in Latin America and in many parts of the United States with other alternative health-care systems, such as the variegated traditions known collectively as *curanderismo,* which can combine indigenous practices with Christian beliefs. Likewise, healing practices associated with Afro-Caribbean traditions (such as Santería), prominent in Florida and New York, can compete with those of the Pentecostal Church. The latter will often see these practices as demonic, although the church may accept certain traditional elements such as herbal remedies.

Protestantism may also be part of an Americanization process. Atkinson, for example, often promoted the idea that American-style Protestantism was an antidote for what she saw as superstitious Catholicism among Mexicans, and she believed that Americanization would improve their lives. Protestantism, which has often been perceived as basic to the American character, thus functioned as a strategy for upward social mobility among many Hispanics. Likewise, many Latin Americans adopt Protestantism after viewing American televangelists who link material prosperity with following Protestant theology.

These explanations have largely superseded earlier explanations based on "social pathology," especially in regard to Pentecostalism. In the early 1960s Pentecostalism was seen as a psychiatric phenomenon or as a sort of delusional response to socioeconomic stress and alienation; however, studies by Vivian Garrison, among others, showed that Pentecostal converts are not necessarily any more socially deprived than converts to non-Pentecostal groups.

Protestantism and Latino Culture

Protestantism is already having significant effects on Latino culture in the United States. First, there is the continued erosion of the Catholic "essentialism" that has permeated Latino and Latina identity for much of their history in America. Although the ranks of American Catholics are increasingly composed of Latinos, assuming that all Latinos are Catholic is fast becoming an obsolete idea.

Latino religious art is also changing with the rise of Protestantism. Historically, Protestantism has eschewed religious art. Thus one does not often find images of the Virgin of Guadalupe in Protestant homes. The wearing of personal religious art such as crucifixes is usually frowned upon, especially among Pentecostals, and participation in large or flamboyant quasireligious Latino celebrations (fiestas), which have been historically important and usually filled with Catholic icons, diminishes among Protestants. Instead, many Protestants shift to seeing sermons and other oral and aural religious activities ("witnessing" and "scripture memorization") as works of art.

Protestantism, as a theme, is not a significant part of U.S. Latino literature, despite the fact that a few well-known authors have been or are Protestants, including Oscar "Zeta" Acosta, Ed Vega, and Thomas. Protestantism is seen as comical, foreign, and disingenuous in Rolando Hinojosa's *Klail City* (1987). In *Savior, Savior, Hold My Hand* (1972), Piri Thomas portrays Protestantism as only a temporary solution for his life. It is particularly difficult to find conservative Protestant views (as in Nicky Cruz's *Run, Baby, Run,* 1968) represented in the U.S. Latino canons. In part, the long history of Catholicism has meant that Catholic themes would predominate. On the other hand, Protestantism has come to the fore in U.S. Latino culture at a time when Latino authors, who often represent elite educated segments of the Anglo-American population, are pursuing a more pluralistic and eclectic religious experience.

Musical forms have been quite varied among U.S. Latino Protestants. The mainline Protestant churches tend to be the most conservative, using organs and more standardized musical forms that date back to medieval Europe. Many U.S. Latino Pentecostals, on the other hand, were evangelized by missionaries who used musical forms that are distinctly American. For example, the Church of God, a Pentecostal denomination based in Cleveland, Tennessee, brought musical traditions that originated in Appalachia and

Pastor Leo Bernal from the First Hispanic Baptist Church of Duncanville, Texas, in preparation for the metroplex mission with Billy Graham, 2002.

the American South to newly formed Latino Pentecostal churches in the U.S.-Mexican borderlands. Recently, there has been more flexibility in the use of Latino and Latin American forms as sacred music among Latino Protestants.

Politically, it is difficult to gauge the effects of Protestantism. It has often been the case that political interests have outweighed purely religious ones. For example, historically Cuban Americans have voted Republican because of the anticommunism ideology usually associated with that party. In 1998 George W. Bush won a large portion of the Latino vote in his reelection as governor of Texas; however, in 1996, Cuban Americans voted in large numbers in favor of Bill Clinton. The 2000 presidential elections demonstrated the volatility and independence of Protestant Latinos. HCAPL reported that, weeks prior to the election, Pentecostals planned to split their vote evenly for Al Gore (35 percent) and George W. Bush (35 percent). However, those labeled as "evangelicals" favored Bush (42 percent) over Gore (29 percent).

The Future

Although Protestantism among Latinos in the United States is not monolithic, many scholars see the movement toward further independence from Anglo de-

nominational hierarchies as a major trend. The Assemblies of God and other denominations now have large Spanish divisions managed almost entirely by Hispanic ministers, and there are some churches that have always been exclusively in the hands of Latinos (for example, The Puerto Rican Assembly of Christian Churches). Central and South American immigrants, particularly from Honduras and Guatemala, may add significantly to the proportion of Hispanic Protestants in the United States.

Women usually have been able to ascend to higher positions in many Latino Protestant churches. One must be careful, however, to distinguish between mainline and Pentecostal churches in this regard. Conservative mainline denominations, such as the Southern Baptists, are still quite resistant to women serving as pastors, a policy that has been enforced by Latino Southern Baptists. Nonetheless, the increasing participation of women is expected in most Latino Protestant denominations in the future.

Latino Protestants are also impacting Catholic policy, with three, sometimes paradoxical, results. One is a counteroffensive to stop the shift to Protestantism, as is reflected in the National Pastoral Plan for Hispanic Ministry approved by the U.S. bishops in 1987. Another response is a type of ecumenism that acknowledges the future vitality of Hispanic Protestantism and stresses common interests between Catholics and Protestants (for example, the anti-abortion movement). The third response is the adoption of some of the ideas of Protestants, especially those of Pentecostals, to create new forms of Charismatic and Pentecostal Catholics. According to the HCAPL, some 22 percent of Catholics now describe themselves as "Charismatic," reflecting the Pentecostalization of Catholicism.

The future also will probably bring a further revision in the traditional historiography of American Pentecostalism and Protestantism. For example, early Pentecostalism had at least two foci in America, according to standard histories. One focus was in the Appalachian mountains, where the first Pentecostals broke away from mainline churches that were perceived as being too modern. Another focus was in urban Los Angeles, where an African American preacher, William Seymour (1870–1922), is credited with popularizing the movement.

Although the role of Latino Pentecostal pioneers often has been ignored by Anglo-American historians, Latino scholars of religion are now focusing on the Pentecostal pioneer Francisco "El Azteca" Olazábal (1886–1937), an immigrant from Mexico who was probably one of the foremost evangelists of his time. By the time of his death, Olazabal had founded the Latin American Council of Churches, which united some 150 churches in Puerto Rico and the United States. This organization, which reflected the alienation from Anglo Protestantism, became one of the early assertions of a common Latino Protestant identity in the United States. Likewise, Maria Atkinson, who founded the Church of God in the U.S.-Mexican borderlands, has only recently been the subject of academic study.

RELATED ARTICLES

Bible in Spanish; Catholicism; Evangelism; Religion.

FURTHER READING

Avalos, Héctor. "Maria Atkinson and the Rise of Pentecostalism in the U.S.-Mexico Borderlands." *Journal of Religion and Society,* 3 (2001). http: moses//creighton.edu/JRS/2001/2001-5.html

Baldwin, Deborah. *Protestants and the Mexican Revolution: Missionaries, Ministers, and Social Change.* Urbana: Univ. of Ill., 1990.

de la Garza, Rodolfo O., et al. *Latino Voices: Mexican, Puerto Rican, and Cuban Perspectives on American Politics.* Boulder, Colo.: Westview Press, 1992.

Espinosa, Gastón. "*El Azteca*: Francisco Olazábal and Latino Pentecostal Charisma, Power, and Faith Healing in the Borderlands." *Journal of the American Academy of Religion* 67:3 (1999): 597–616.

Gallup, George, Jr., and Jim Castelli. *The People's Religion: American Faith in the 90's.* New York: Macmillan, 1989.

Garrison, Vivian. "Sectarianism and Psychosocial Adjustment: A Controlled Comparison of Puerto Rican Pentecostals and Catholics." In *Religious Movements in Contemporary America.* Ed. by Irving I. Zaretzky and Mark P. Leone. Princeton, N.J.: Princeton Univ. Press, 1974.

Greeley, Andrew M. "Defection among Hispanics." *America* (July 30, 1988): 61–62.

Greeley, Andrew M. "Defection among Hispanics." *America* (September 27, 1997): 12–13.

Iber, Jorge. *Hispanics in the Mormon Zion, 1912–1999.* College Station: Texas A&M Univ. Press, 2000.

Jenkins, Philip. *The Next Christendom: The Coming of Global Christianity.* New York: Oxford Univ. Press, 2002.

Stoll, David. *Is Latin America Turning Protestant? The Politics of Evangelical Growth.* Berkeley: Univ. of Calif. Press, 1990.

HECTOR AVALOS

PROTOCOL OF QUERÉTARO

The war between the United States and Mexico was officially over with the signing of the Treaty of Guadalupe Hidalgo on February 2, 1848. The treaty ended many years of fighting, principally over the southwestern expansion of the United States into what Mexico believed to be its territory. The Treaty of Guadalupe Hidalgo sought to find a compromise for the two countries by preserving many property, political, and civil rights for the Mexican citizens who would now be living in U.S. territory. Many of these early Mexican settlers to the Southwest had been granted land ownership by the early Spanish government in Mexico and had lived in the disputed territories for many generations.

The U.S. Senate, in its ratification of the final version of the Treaty of Guadalupe Hidalgo, made several changes to the treaty that threatened to annul the guarantees of the original treaty. The Senate version amended the original ninth article and deleted the tenth article of the Treaty. This version, in effect, softened or even eliminated some stronger language in the original treaty protecting the religious rights of Mexican inhabitants, protecting Mexican landowners in Texas, and protecting other property and claims of longtime Mexican residents.

Mexico protested these revisions, and both countries came together to work out a compromise document known as the Protocol of Querétaro. The protocol was actually signed by representatives from both countries on May 26, 1848, in the city of Querétaro, Mexico. This agreement sought to clarify that the United States did not intend to annul the civil, political, and religious protections named in the original treaty. The protocol contained three articles that reiterated the intent of the treaty to preserve the legal and property rights of Mexicans in the ceded territories. Mexican property owners were assured of fair treatment, and that the U.S. government intended to honor the original provisions of the treaty. However, shortly after the protocol was signed by representatives at the scene, the U.S. government disavowed the protocol, stating that the signers did not have any official authority to sign such a statement.

Without the stronger, protective wording in the treaty, Mexican and Mexican-Indian property owners became more vulnerable to efforts to deprive them of ancestral lands, mining rights, citizenship rights, and civil rights. Many claims for property violations of the treaty were now left to individual state legislatures and courts for their own interpretation, and most of these interpretations favored the Anglo claimants who wanted to expand their lands. Al-

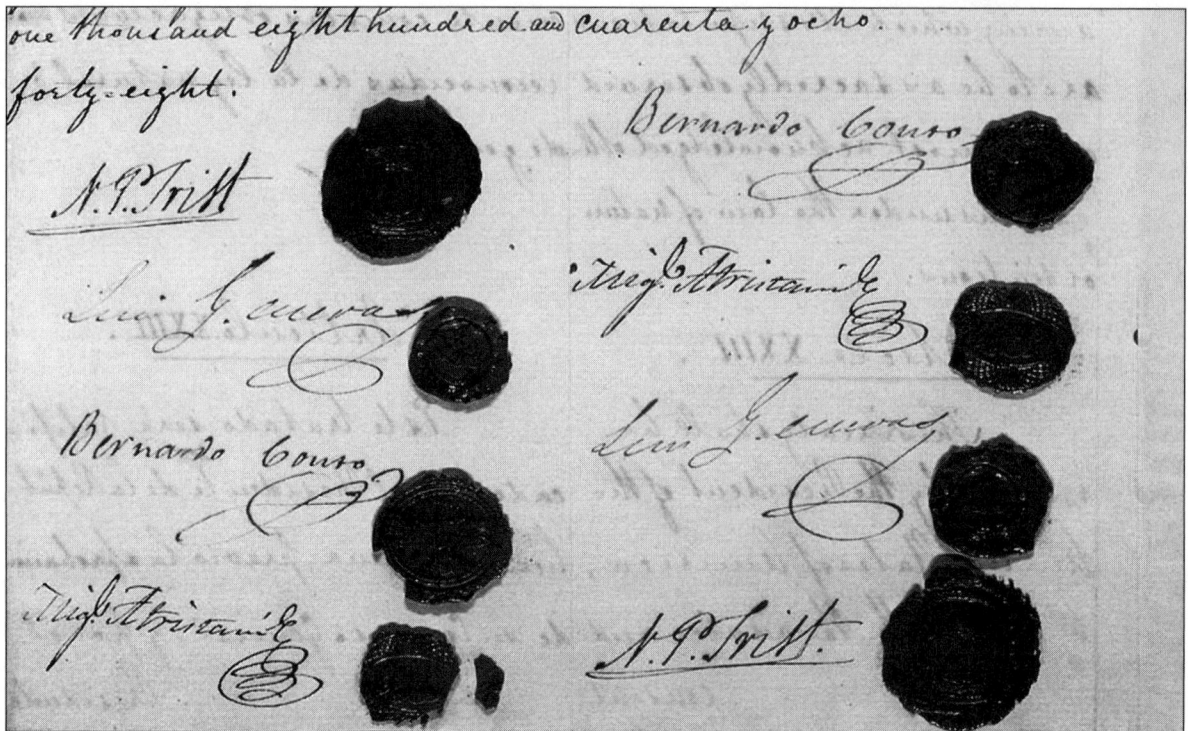

Last page of the Treaty of Guadalupe Hidalgo, with signatures and seals, 1848.

though the treaty had originally granted U.S. citizenship to all Mexican citizens in the ceded territories, states now refused to honor those benefits. The result of this loss of rights for numerous once-prosperous Mexican inhabitants resulted in their economic collapse and their movement into second-class status. Many individuals of Mexican descent in the southwestern United States can point to land grants that were taken away from their families because of the changes to the Treaty of Guadalupe Hidalgo and because of the annulment of the Protocol of Querétaro.

RELATED ARTICLES

Guadalupe Hidalgo, Treaty of; Mexican-American War; Mexico; United States-Mexico Relations.

FURTHER READING

Blawis, Patricia Bell. *Tijerina and the Land Grants: Mexican Americans in Struggle for Their Heritage.* New York: International Pubs., 1971.

Griswold del Castillo, Richard. *The Treaty of Guadalupe Hidalgo: A Legacy of Conflict.* Norman: Univ. of Okla. Press, 1990.

Menchaca, Martha. *Recovering History, Constructing Race: The Indian, Black and White Roots of Mexican Americans.* Austin: Univ. of Tex. Press, 2001.

Miller, David Hunter. *Treaties and Other International Acts of the United States of America.* Vol. 5. Washington, D.C.: USGPO, 1937.

Sedillo López, Antoinette, ed. *Land Grants, Housing and Political Power.* New York: Garland, 1995.

REBECCA A. LÓPEZ

PUBLISHING

It is often mistakenly assumed that Latino literature in the United States is a recent phenomenon. In fact, its rich and diverse history is more than four centuries old. The production, manufacture, and distribution of books also has a long and solid tradition in the United States. This entry seeks to explore the history of Latino literature in the U.S. book publishing industry, dividing the topic between English-Language publishing and the history and reach of Spanish-language publishing.

PUBLISHING, ENGLISH-LANGUAGE

The publication of Latino literature in the English language generally has taken the form of pieces written originally in Spanish and translated into English, or work written in English. The former was published more readily in the English-language publishing houses in the 19th and early 20th century, but Latino literature written originally in English has a publishing history of only about 125 years, and mostly since the last quarter of the 20th century.

The first Latino-related publishing in English arrived in the mid-19th century when English-language publishing houses began to bring out documents pertaining to Spanish explorers in the Americas. That was also the era in which William Hickling Prescott's historical accounts of the discovery of Mexico and Peru were released, as well as some early translations of works by Fray Bartolomé de Las Casas. By the turn of the century, many of these had been brought into print, including the earliest known accounts such as Alvar Núñez Cabeza de Vaca's *Chronicle of the Narváez Expedition,* his account of his journey across what would become the southern United States, released mainly by literary presses specializing in scholarly and historical literature. Subsequent books on the explorers were published in the 1920s and 1930s by private presses such as the Quivira Society.

However, few works written originally in English were published at that time. One of the earliest Latino authors to have her English-language work appear was María Amparo Ruíz de Burton, whose *Who Would Have Thought It?* was published anonymously by J. B. Lippincott and Company in 1872. Her second book, *The Squatter and the Don*, appeared in 1881 with the name "C. Loyal" on the title page (a common epithet in Mexican literature at the time, standing for *ciudadano loyal* or "loyal citizen"). At that point an enterprising journalist tracked down the copyright of her work in the Library of Congress, and her authorship was made public.

Although William Carlos Williams published in the early part of the century, his work was generally not considered "Latino." Few other original works were published in English, except for isolated scholarly work on Latino topics, such as the sociology of Latino communities, or stories in limited-run journals and magazines, such as the stories written by Mario Suárez in the late 1940s. However, even Suárez was not able to find a publisher for his full-length work.

Small Presses

Latino-run small presses began to appear in the 1960s in tandem with the civil rights era. A number of significant ones have established a reputation since then, including Tonatiuh Quinto-Sol, Arte Público, and Bilingual Press. Sometimes these presses have been affiliated with academic institutions but this does not turn then, at least not officially, into university presses. The budgets they depend on are external, their books are not peer-reviewed, and the board of regents of a university does not decide their fate. There are others, such as Wings and Tía Chucha, that are also relevant but release fewer titles annually. Plus, there have been a number of even smaller presses whose existence lasted for a handful of titles.

One of the oldest publishers devoted to publishing the work of Chicano writers is Tonatiuh Quinto-Sol (TQS) Publications. Originally known as Editorial Quinto Sol, the press was founded in 1967 by Herminio Ríos and Octavio I. Romano. It developed from a literary magazine, *El Grito*, a publication based in Berkeley, California, that featured the work of some of the most prominent names in Chicano literature. The name *quinto sol* (fifth sun) refers to the Aztec belief in a future cultural renaissance that would take place in a fifth age and coincide with the rise of Chicano culture.

Although not as prolific as other presses, TQS expanded on the work begun by *El Grito,* and published groundbreaking literature by young or undiscovered Chicano writers whose writing reflected a working-class or rural perspective. Its first publication, *El Espejo/The Mirror* (1968), was an anthology that included the work of Alurista, Tomás Rivera, and Miguel Méndez. The press became so influential that these writers were known as the "Quinto Sol Generation."

In 1970 the press established the Premio Quinto Sol, the first national award recognizing excellence in Chicano literature. Initially the prize included a $1,000 cash award and publication of the winning manuscript. From 1970 to 1973 the award recognized the pioneering work of three authors. In 1970 Tomás Rivera's *. . . y no se lo tragó la tierra . . . And the Earth Did Not Devour Him* received the award; in 1971 *Bless Me Ultima* by Rudolfo Anaya won the award; and in 1973 *Estampas del valle y otras obras/Sketches of the Valley and Other Works* by Rolando Hinojosa received the award.

Anaya's tale of the life of a rural Latino family, told from the perspective of a boy and the culture clash he experiences as a Latino growing up in the United States, is considered the quintessential Chi-

© RUDI VON BRIEL / PHOTOEDIT

Front window of the Lectorum Librería Hispanic bookstore in New York City.

cano tale. In 1975 Estela Portillo Trambley became the first Latina to receive the award for her short story collection *Rain of Scorpions.* TQS continues to publish today but no longer distributes the Premio Quinto Sol.

Much of Latino literature written in the United States remained unnoticed until the 1970s, when the Chicano movement began to reach its peak. There were few Latino professors in academic circles, and for those few, gaining support from their respective colleges for literary research projects proved difficult. As the civil rights movement, from which the Chicano Movement was born, improved the opportunities for people of color, groundbreaking initiatives emerged, particularly in academia.

In 1972 a young professor at the University of Indiana, Nicolás Kanellos, alarmed at the vulnerable and unexplored state of Latino literature, formed the *Revista Chicana-Riqueña,* a quarterly magazine for Latino literature, art, and thought. Coedited by Luis Dávila, it eventually evolved into *The Americas Review.*

Based on the magazine's success Kanellos founded Arte Público Press in 1979 to further the prospects of Latino authors. That year the new independent publishing house published its first work, *La Carreta Made a U-Turn* by the New York City-based Puerto Rican poet Tato Laviera. One year later, Kanellos, a New York native of Puerto Rican descent, received an offer from the University of Houston, Texas, to teach Hispanic and classical languages. He was also asked to bring his young press with him. Kanellos accepted the offer, becoming the Brown Foundation Professor of Hispanic Literature and Spanish. Kanellos has published several of his own works including *A History of Hispanic Theater in the United States: Origins to 1940* (1980), *Thirty Million Strong: Reclaiming the Hispanic Image in American Culture* (1997), and *Biographical Dictionary of Hispanic Literature in the United States* (1989).

True to its mission, Arte Público Press has provided publishing opportunities to many Latino writers, particularly in English. Some of its earliest authors include Víctor Villaseñor who wrote the groundbreaking novel *Rain of Gold.* Called the "Latino Roots" (in reference to *Roots,* the 1976 best-seller by Alex Haley that recaptured his family's history in the drama of 18th-century slave Kunta Kinte and his descendants), Villaseñor's opus related his family's history on his mother's side, beginning with his grandmother's childhood during the late 19th century in Mexico.

Arte Público published the first works of many popular Latina authors. In 1983 the press published *The House on Mango Street,* a collection of short stories by Sandra Cisneros. *The Last of the Menu Girls* by Denise Chávez, her first novel, was published in 1986; and *Women Not Roses,* a collection of poems by Ana Castillo, was published in 1984. Today, Arte Público Press publishes 20 to 30 books per year and has a catalog of more than 500 titles.

In 1992 Kanellos initiated a research project aimed at identifying, cataloguing, publishing, and archiving Hispanic writing in the United States that dates from the American colonial period through 1960. Funded initially by a grant from the Rockefeller Foundation, the U.S. Hispanic Literary Heritage Project has successfully identified some of the earliest works by Latinos, beginning with the memoirs of Cabeza de Vaca.

In 2002, the project published the first comprehensive collection of U.S. Hispanic plays, poems, journals, fictional excerpts, and articles in Spanish, *En Otra Voz: Antologia de Literatura España de los Estados Unidos / Herencia* (In Another Voice: Anthology of Spanish Literature in the United States/ Heritage). The project continues to recover, catalog, archive, and publish works by Latino authors in books and periodicals.

Located in Tempe, Arizona, and affiliated with the Hispanic Research Center at Arizona State University, Bilingual Review Press has been publishing the work of Latino authors in English since 1974. Since its founding, the press has been committed to selecting books for publication based on importance and significance by veteran and emerging writers, rather than purely commercial appeal.

The press has more than 150 titles in its backlist and publishes 8 to 10 titles a year. Most of these books are written by or about U.S. Hispanics and are written in English, although a smaller portion may be bilingual or Spanish-only. In addition to new works the Press has also conserved classic works of Chicana and Chicano fiction through its Clásicos Chicanos/Chicano Classics imprint.

The Press also publishes *The Bilingual Review,* a quarterly journal with articles on bilingualism, bilingual education, and ethnic scholarship, as well as creative pieces from Hispanic authors, and reviews of the latest works by Hispanic authors.

University Presses

The small but important role that a handful of university presses have played in disseminating English-language Latino literature cannot be ignored. Although most of the volumes released by these publishers are, by definition, academic, they also bring out fiction, literary nonfiction, and, to a limited extent, poetry. For years a number of presses maintained a list of titles. With rare exceptions the geographic locations of the presses determine their thematic content. For instance, the University of Arizona Press (Tucson) tends to focus on Chicano and southwestern authors while the University of Florida Press (Gainesville) publishes mostly Caribbean (predominantly Cuban American) writers.

Most university presses today publish Latino-oriented books but few specialize in that area. The University of California Press, the University of Wisconsin Press, and New York University Press have a more recent interest in the field. Those that do specialize in the area, including the University of New Mexico Press, the University of Arizona Press, and the University of Texas Press, focused on this area of expertise even before it became fashionable. Es-

tablished by the board of regents at the time, the University of New Mexico Press in Albuquerque began publishing in 1929. Initially, the press published pamphlets, reports, and journals that served the university community. Its first publications featured studies on archaeology, education, geology, and engineering. The press's mission crystallized in 1944 when Joseph A Brandt, director of the University of Chicago Press, suggested that it focus on furthering the understanding of New Mexico citizens and their history and economics.

As the university evolved so did the press. In the 1970s the university gained notoriety for its development of Native American and Latin American and Chicano and Chicana studies. Today, the press has become one of the largest to publish English-language and bilingual books by Latino authors. The press publishes 85–100 titles annually, ranging from poetry to children's books. Fifty to sixty percent of these titles are either written by Latino authors or focus on Latino culture.

In 1993 the press published *The Magic of Blood,* a collection of short stories by up-and-coming Chicano writer Dagoberto Gilb. The press also obtained the rights to future works by Chicano author and New Mexico native Rudolfo Anaya. The press celebrated this acquisition as well as its 75th anniversary with the reprint of Anaya's novel *Tortuga* and the printing of *Serafina's Stories,* a collection of Anaya's short stories modeled after the *Arabian Nights,* and *The Santero's Miracle,* a book for children.

The University of Texas Press (Austin) was created in 1950. It publishes about 90 books a year and has a couple of thousand in print. It is devoted, among other topics, to Latin American and Latino literature, releasing books in translation. In 1958 the press released the groundbreaking ethnographic study by Américo Paredes, *With His Pistol in His Hand: A Border Ballad and Its Hero.* It has released volumes on narcocorridos, studies on Cuban American culture by Gustavo Pérez-Firmat and others, and volumes of interviews with Isabel Allende, among other books. The University of Arizona Press, founded in 1959—the year the first novel by a Chicano published in English by a New York house (Doubleday) was released, *Pocho* by José Antonio Villareal—annually produces about 50 new titles and has some 550 in print. These include scholarly works on American Indian studies, anthropology, archaeology, environmental studies, geography, Chicano studies, history,

Latin American studies, and the space sciences. It houses the series Camino del Sol: A Chicana/o Literary Series, which includes books by such Chicanos as Juan Felipe Herrera, Demetria Martínez, and Sergio Troncoso.

Children's Books

Several publishing houses produce bilingual and English-language books for children. The three oldest presses include Cinco Puntos Press, Piñata Books, and the Children's Book Press.

Founded by Bobby and Susie Byrd in 1985, Cinco Puntos Press (CPP) is an independent literary press that specializes in publishing books for children from the U.S.-Mexico border. Based in El Paso, Texas, CPP has received the American Book Award for its work and has been inducted in the Latino Literary Hall of Fame.

In 1999, CPP received national attention when it published *The Story of Colors/La Historia de los Colores* by Subcomandante Insurgente Marcos of Mexico's Zapatista Army of National Liberation. The children's book is based on a Mayan legend about a group of gods who set out to find all the colors of the world. Controversy arose when it was reported that a National Endowment for the Arts (NEA) grant of $7,500 to publish the book was unilaterally revoked. NEA chairperson Bill Ivey explained that his decision was based on concern that the grant money would end up in the hands of the Mexican rebels. CPP promptly received a grant from the Lannan Foundation to replace the NEA grant and published *The Story of Colors*, which remains in the CPP catalog.

In 1994 Arte Público Press received a grant from the Mellon Foundation that allowed it to create Piñata Books, an imprint devoted to bilingual books for children and young adults. The press's first five books published in 1995 were *The Desert is My Mother* by Pat Mora; *Walking Stars* by Víctor Villaseñor; *Juanita Fights for the School Board* by first-time author Gloria Velásquez; *Mexican Ghost Tales of the Southwest* by Alfred Avila; and *Hispanic Female and Young,* a collection of stories, poems, and essays written by New York City teenagers. Committed to publishing ten books each year, the press has had particular success with its bilingual Spanish-English picture books for young readers.

Founded in 1975 by Harriet Rohmer, Children's Book Press (CBP) was one of the first publishers in the United States to focus on quality literature for children of Latino, African American, Asian American, and Native American heritage. The nonprofit publisher began with books taken from the oral traditions of the indigenous inhabitants of North America. Today the publisher seeks original works for elementary school–aged children that reflect contemporary life in the Latino and Chicano, African American, Asian American, Native American, multiracial, and other minority and new-immigrant communities. Folktales are no longer the focus of the publishing program.

Chicano writers such as Lucha Corpi have branched out into the children's book genre through CBP. Known as a detective novelist, Corpi wrote *Where the Fireflies Dance/Ahí donde bailan los luciérnagas,* her first children's book published in 2000 by CBP. Artists, too, have found publishing opportunities at CBP. Carmen Lomas Garza, a Texas native and Chicano artist known for her naive style of painting, has written and illustrated several books for CBP including *In My Family/En mi familia*, published in 1996 and winner of the Pura Belpré Award from the American Library Association.

Mainstream Publishing Houses

Small and midsize presses continue to devote their energy to Latino literature. However, since the late 1980s the New York publishing industry has also played an important role in printing and disseminating books in English by Hispanics in the United States. Having almost totally ignored this tradition, a shift came in 1989 when Oscar Hijuelos received the Pulitzer Prize for *The Mambo Kings Play Songs of Love,* a novel published by Farrar, Straus and Giroux, which became a best-seller and was turned into a Hollywood movie. Overnight a rush to find new Latino talent took place among Manhattan houses. In the early 1990s, represented by powerful New York literary agent Susan Bergholz, Sandra Cisneros moved from Arte Público to Random House when her collection of stories *Woman Hollering Creek* was released in hardcover along with a paperback edition of *The House on Mango Street*. With a cover review in *The New York Times Book Review,* the collection became a sensation. Other Latino authors followed suit including, among others, Julia Alvarez, Ana Castillo, and Rosario Ferré. Bergholz also catered a move for Rudolfo Anaya from small presses to Warner in New York, which brought out a pa-

At the launch of Scholastic's Lee y Serás reading initiative in San Francisco children explore a mobile learning center designed to promote reading development in Latino communities.

perback edition of *Bless Me Ultima* and hardcovers of Anaya's new work. Several more Latino authors including Richard Rodríguez, Esmeralda Santiago, Junot Díaz, Dagoberto Gilb, and Ilan Stavans are published by New York houses. This transition would have been impossible a couple of decades ago. The mainstream press woke up to the fact that Latinos are a major purchasing force in America.

By the late 1990s there was talk in the mainstream industry of finding the "Latina" Terry McMillan, a female author whose work would cross ethnic and cultural lines, being embraced by readers of all backgrounds. There were also experiments in bilingual publishing by St. Martin's Press and the launching of new imprints such as Rayo at HarperCollins, fully devoted to Latino authors and topics.

With these changes came more Latino representation in the publishing houses themselves. The increase has been slow, though. Editors with knowl-edge of the Spanish language and of Latino culture in general are still scarce but it is clear that their role is essential to successfully acquire, publish, promote, and sell books to a Latino readership that is not always responsive and that, in the eyes of many, is a treasure box still awaiting the key that will open it.

RELATED ARTICLES

Alvarez, Julia; Anaya, Rudolfo; Business; Cisneros, Sandra; Hijuelos, Oscar; Hinojosa-Smith, Rolando; Laviera, Jesús; Literature; Literature, Children's; Literature, Cuban American; Literature, Dominican American; Literature, Gay and Lesbian; Literature, Latin American; Literature, Mexican American; Literature, Puerto Rican on the Mainland; Literature of Exile; Núñez Cabeza de Vaca, Alvar; Rivera, Tomás; Ruíz de Burton, María Amparo; Williams, William Carlos.

FURTHER READING

Augenbraum, Harold, and Margarite Fernández Olmos, eds. *The Latino Reader.* Boston: Houghton Mifflin, 1997.

Gutiérrez, Ramón, and Genaro Padilla, eds. *Recovering the U.S. Hispanic Literary Heritage.* Houston, Tex.: Arte Público Press, 1993.

Kanellos, Nicolás, ed. *The Hispanic Literary Companion.* Detroit, Mich.: Visible Ink Press, 1997.

Selected Web Sites

Arte Público Press. www.arte.uh.edu/artepublico

Bilingual Review Press. www.asu.edu/brp/

Children's Book Press. www.cbookspress.org

Cinco Puntos Press. www.cincopuntos.com

Rayo. www.harpercollins.com

Tonatiuh Quinto-Sol (TQS) Publications. www.tqsbooks.com

University of New Mexico Press. www.unmpress.com

VALERIE MENARD

Publishing, Spanish-Language

The reading material of any nation is ideally reflective of the educational, cultural, spiritual, and informational needs of its inhabitants. While about one-fourth of the U.S. Latino population does not speak Spanish, Latinos share a common cultural circumstance: they are U.S. residents who can identify on some level with American and Latino culture, history, and literary expression. This segment of American society also commands $600 billion in annual consumer power. Since these figures are only expected to rise, the U.S. book publishing industry has had to respond to the unique tastes of this significant reading market.

As recently as 1990, literary and commercial fiction, nonfiction, self-help books, travel narratives, medical manuals, and religious material published in Spanish went unrepresented in U.S. retail bookstores. To find Spanish-language reading material, Latinos had to visit local libraries, purchase it from their countries of origin, or send for books by mail. Mainstream presses did not view the Spanish-language reading market as profitable, principally because Latinos were not known to be voracious readers. While this changes from generation to generation, consumer power has not traditionally been identified with the acquisition of books. In any case, Spanish was not considered an attractive publishing language. Moreover, since the primary language in the United States is English, the publishing industry operated under the fallacious belief that only first-generation U.S. residents or immigrants would be inclined to read in their native tongues. Put simply, it was assumed that native language or Spanish reading would be abandoned in favor of assimilation.

However, efforts by small publishers and presses, risk-taking ventures by larger publishing houses, and the work of publishing and educational organizations have proved that this is not the case. Bilingual education programs, launched in the early 1960s, have produced a population fully or partially fluent in two languages, English and Spanish, and sometimes Spanglish, as well. Thus, the bilingual reading market is beginning to be identified, segmented, cultivated, and even celebrated, although its marketing potential is as yet unknown.

Works by Ecuadorian, Puerto Rican, Cuban, Mexican, Spanish, and other Latino authors are being imported and sold in both Spanish and English in the United States. Conversely, books by American authors are being translated into Spanish and sold in regions with particularly high Latino populations, such as Los Angeles, San Diego, Miami, New York, Washington, D.C., San Francisco, San Antonio, Chicago, and Philadelphia. Some publishing houses that capitalize on the Spanish-language reading market in the United States do so solely for commercial purposes. Others seek to preserve Latino American, Spanish Latino, Afro-Latino, and Caribbean Latino cultures for immigrants and their American-born descendents. Whatever their motivations, these companies have begun to change the face of the U.S. publishing industry.

Spanish-Language Publishing Precursors

At the forefront of identifying the Latino reading market through bilingual English and Spanish publications was Arte Público Press. Founded in 1979 by Nicolás Kanellos and operated out of the University of Houston where Kanellos teaches Hispanic literature, Arte Público has grown into the largest and most established bilingual publishing house in the United States. In the early years of the 21st century, the house published 90 percent of its books in English and the remaining 10 percent in Spanish. It specializes in short stories, poetry, dramas, novels, and works of nonfiction that represent the cultural values, stories, and experiences of Latino culture long ignored by mainstream presses.

A chief goal of Arte Público Press is to increase the visibility of Latino authors so that they might be picked up by mainstream publishers. Some Latino authors represented by Arte Público Press include Luis Valdéz, Miguel Piñero, Rolando Hinojosa-Smith, Víctor Villaseñor, and Nocholasa Mohr. Arte

Público's aim is a cultural one that seeks to provide more Latino writing in the areas of history, mythology, religion, and the arts. Arte Público recognized the cultural implications of the lack of bilingual and Latino-themed U.S. publishing. Its efforts have proved that Latinos can write their own artistic expressions, records of experiences, and histories—for themselves and for mainstream audiences.

In 1992 Arte Público launched a four-pronged project entitled Recovering the U.S. Hispanic Literary Heritage. This ten-year initiative was a landmark in Latino publishing history and constitutes the nation's largest recovery, indexing, and publishing of lost Latino writing. Publications from this project, representing work originally written from 1542 to 1960, include Tomás Rivera's *. . . y no se lo tragó la tierra/And the Earth Did Not Devour Him.* The project culminated in an anthology, published in English and Spanish in 2003, entitled *En Otra Voz.* Divided into three historical periods, this comprehensive Spanish-language anthology boasts writing by Hispanic authors from the colonial period to the present. Arte Público also produced the Hispanic Civil Rights Series, although books in the series are published mostly in English. A series for children and young adults was created in 1994 called Piñata Books. Titles such as Ana Baca's *Chiles for Benito/Chiles para Benito,* Raquel Benatar's *Isabel Allende: Recuerdos para un cuento/Isabel Allende: Memories for a Story,* and Samuel Caraballo's *Estrellita se despide de su isla/Estrellita Says Goodbye to Her Island* support Americans of Hispanic descent who want to raise their children as bicultural individuals, fully aware that they are at once American and Latino. But the embrace of the native language is not without its challenges. These titles are always published in a bilingual format, signaling the dual cultures of their readers but also emphasizing the fact that Spanish alone might not be enough to appeal to a younger generation of Latinos.

Other publishing houses that produce works expressly for Spanish-language readers include Bilingual Press in Arizona, Latino American Literary Review Press in Pennsylvania, and Ediciones Universal in Florida. The latter specializes in Cuban culture, history, and literature. Founded by Cuban exiles Marta Or and Juan Manuel Salvat in 1965, Ediciones Universal and its Librería and Distribuidora Universal have expanded into a worldwide, full-service book publishing and distribution company. Its client base

includes U.S. and international readers, universities, and libraries. (Owing to Cuba's current censorship policy and political climate, Ediciones Universal's products cannot officially be shipped to the island from which its founders hail.) Still a family-run business, the firm's mission is to "rescue" and publish the history and the literary expression of a multifaceted culture—works that mainstream U.S. publishing houses might not option because of their specialized focus.

The company imports and distributes books from Spain, but its catalog clearly maintains a Cuban focus. Ediciones Universal carries many Spanish titles that it distributes from other publishers in Spain and Latin America in addition to publishing books on Afro-Cubano art, history, and culture, and Afro-Cubano literature through its Ébano y Canela (Ebony and Cinnamon) collection. It also publishes many Spanish-language dictionaries, reference books, and textbooks. Some Ediciones Universal titles include Eduardo G. Noguer's *Historia del cine cubano: Cien años* (History of Cuban Cinema: One Hundred Years); Guillermo Cabrera Infante's *¡Vaya Papaya!—Ramón Alejandro;* and Cristóbal Díaz Ayala's *Cuando salí de la Habana (1898–1997): Cien años de música cubana por el mundo* (When I Left Havana, 1898–1997: One Hundred Years of Cuban Music for the World).

Major commercial houses in Spain such as Santillana (which owns Alfaguara), Planeta, Vida Publications, and Unilit, have tried their luck releasing books in Spanish in the United States with mixed results. These firms publish both Latino-themed fiction and English-language literature translated into Spanish. Promoting a Latino reading presence for a long-neglected public, these small companies are also ideal for young Spanish writers seeking a forum through which to gain national and even international exposure. While maintaining their independence and individual missions and objectives, these companies have formed alliances and joint ventures with larger publishers in the United States, such as the partnership between Vintage Español and Alfaguara. In most cases the titles are written by best-selling authors in Spain and Latin America. A growing number of Spanish-language courses on college and university campuses make such titles attractive to publishing houses. Spanish reprints of such books are rarely reviewed in the mainstream media. Their appeal is based on the previously proven marketability of the author in the Spanish-speaking world.

Spanish-Language Commercial Ventures

Other companies have recognized the significant need for and market potential of Spanish-language books for children and young readers. Started over 42 years ago Lectorum Publications prides itself on being the largest Spanish-language book distributor in the United States, distributing 25,000 titles from more than 500 domestic and foreign publishing houses, as well as publishing its own line of Spanish-language children's books. Lectorum's Spanish publications have not been limited to traditional Latino themes such as love, family, friendship, dancing, music, and food. The company also publishes Spanish translations of mainstream English-language children books, such as the Dr. Seuss, Arthur, and Franklin series.

Many mainstream children's book labels have ventured into Spanish-language markets. Their motive is more commercial than cultural, since the increasing Latino population and the presence of bilingual education in American public elementary and secondary schools are sure to provide more bilingual readers in their formative years. By the end of the 1990s companies such as Scholastic and Penguin were publishing in Spanish and distributing books aimed at the primary and secondary school markets, with a particular interest in the bilingual education market. Harcourt Brace's imprint Libros Viajeros capitalized on paperback translations of children's books. Putnam/PaperStar audited its inventory for children's books in English that contained "Latino" themes or were written by Latino authors, reprinting such titles as Gary Soto's *Chato y su Cena/Chato's Kitchen* and Tomie dePaola's *La Leyenda de la Flor de Nochebuena/The Legend of the Poinsettia* as bilingual editions (English and Spanish). Other English-Spanish publishers for this market include PGW-distributed Turtle Books and smaller companies such as Star Bright Books, which released Rochelle Bunnett's *Amigos en la Escuela/Friends at School* and *¡Nosotros Sí Podemos Hacerlo!/We Can Do It!* by Laura Dwight.

Larger and better-known publishing houses in the United States had been experimenting with Spanish-language publishing for adult readers, but Spanish-language literature, novels, and commercial fiction remained scarce. This changed in October 1992, when Anchor Books/Doubleday published acclaimed Mexican author Laura Esquivel's novel *Como agua para chocolate (Like Water for Chocolate)* in English. When the Latino American publication remained on *The New York Times* best-seller list for over 66 weeks, Doubleday purchased the Spanish-language rights to the novel for a 1994 release. The enormous financial success of this unprecedented endeavor triggered other larger publishing houses to form imprints dedicated solely to Spanish-language books for adult readers in the United States. Examples of this phenomenon include HarperCollins' Rayo and Harlequin's Red Dress Ink imprints. Reader's Digest has also developed its own Spanish-language line of books. Simon and Schuster's Augilar Libros en Español focuses on medical and practical guides.

Plaza y Janés, Random House's sister company in Barcelona, Spain, has delved into the Spanish-language reading market in the United States, as has Random House's Vintage Español imprint. Random House's Knopf group has released Nobel laureate Gabriel García Márquez's autobiography, *Vivir para contarla* (Living to Tell the Tale), having published earlier paperback editions of his *El amor en los tiempos del cólera* (Love in the Time of Cholera), *Crónica de una muerte anunciada* (Chronicle of a Death Foretold), and *El general en su laberinto* (The General in his Labyrinth). Ebsco Publishing launched its Medic-Latino, a Spanish-language online medical database, which, when purchased, also features English-Language medical research archives. A Spanish-language researcher and reader in this specialized profession can now gain access to medical journals such as *Revista Cubana de Cardiología y Cirugía Cardiovascular, Revista de la Facultad de Medicina de la UNAM, Revista Médica del IMSS,* and *Revista Mexicana de Patología Clínica.*

The Spanish-Language Market

The art of identifying the Spanish-language market in the United States is still difficult. Immigrants are busy surviving in America and are known to have little spare time. As for bilingual Latinos, do they like to read in Spanish when the same title is available in English? Whether fiction or nonfiction, cultural or commercial, once the financial potential was seen in Spanish-language readers, publishing companies across the nation—by way of their Spanish-language affiliates and imprints—had to determine exactly what this market wanted and what publications would generate the greatest profits. Publishers in the United States found that best-selling English-language books were not necessarily ideal for Spanish translation and marketing. However, books by popular authors including John Grisham and Stephen King sell well in both markets.

The works of Latino America's most notable or commercially successful writers, such as Gabriela Mistral, Julio Cortázar, Jose Luis Borges, Jorge Amado, Octavio Paz, Gabriel García Márquez, and Isabel Allende, appealed to U.S. publishing houses as logical choices for Spanish-language book releases. As publishing companies and alliances were formed in the United States, it became clear that the Latino population was multifaceted. Like any large segment of American society, the Spanish reading market represents multiple regions, generations, reading levels, motivations, professions, religions, and tastes.

New York-based Lipton Communications Group was successful at defining the Spanish-language reading market. Lipton acquired publishing houses such as Simon and Schuster, Ballantine, HarperCollins, Vintage, and Doubleday as clients, providing research on the Spanish-language reading public north of the Rio Grande. The research found, for example, that a publication that appealed to a Mexican reader would not necessarily appeal to a Cuban reader, and thus would not be successful in Cuban areas. San Francisco-based Hispanic Marketing Solutions in 1994 set out to accomplish similar objectives. These business efforts developed effective marketing strategies to attract Spanish-language readers for their clients' publications and, in turn, increased consumers' reading choices. Thus a foundation was established for understanding and quantifying what had previously been viewed as a nonexistent or elusive market.

A key aspect in book publishing in any language is distribution. Once a book is published it must make its way to some venue for sale or purchase. Few major publishing houses perform this function internally. Owing to the rapid boost in U.S. Spanish-language publishing since the mid-1990s, the number of distribution companies specializing in sending Spanish-language titles directly to readers and bookstores has also increased.

Two important Spanish-language distributors who specialize in library sales and acquisitions are Linda Goodman and Michael Shapiro. Goodman's Bilingual Publications Company, headquartered in New York City, has furnished libraries across the country with thousands of books for every segment of the Spanish-language reading population. Bilingual Publications maintained that until this publishing "boom," the Spanish reading market in the United States had been grossly underserved, oversimplified, and underestimated. Her distribution program not only filled the void of Spanish language publications available in libraries, but also served as a model for this market's demographics.

Shapiro and his Spanish-language book distribution label, Libros Sin Fronteras (based in Olympia, Washington), issued a call to arms for commercial publishers across the country. Based on his company's experiences with public and school librarians who stocked bilingual publications on their shelves, he profiled the multifaceted character of this growing market and published his recommendations in a 1997 issue of *Publisher's Weekly*. Shapiro identified a great need for more Spanish-language books written in multiple genres (including pictorial or illustrative publications, nonfiction, spiritual, educational, vocational, large-print editions, and philosophical) from high to low reading levels, which addressed "Hispanic, Chicano, Latino, African American and other minority and immigrant experiences," "folklore traditions and holidays from world cultures and religions," and "examinations of parallels and interconnections between Latinos and other communities in the U.S."

Spanish-language book distribution companies are located throughout the United States, and on the Internet (such as Compulibros.com and Espanol-.com). There are many book distribution companies in southwestern, southern, and coastal U.S. territories, such as Astran Inc. (Miami, Florida), Anderson News Co. (Knoxville, Tennessee), Vientos Tropicales (Durham, North Carolina), Books from Mexico (Mount Shasta, California), Books on Wings (San Francisco, California), Cultural Legacy Books (Denver, Colorado), Gavilanes Books from Indoamerica (New Orleans, Louisiana), Hispanic Book Distributors, Inc. (Phoenix, Arizona), Forsa Editores, Inc. (San Juan, Puerto Rico), Libros Latinos (Redlands, California), and Spanish Language Book Services, Inc. (Miami, Florida). Others are based in midwestern and eastern regions of the United States, such as Adler's Foreign Books (Evanston, Illinois), Consortium Book Sales and Distribution (Saint Paul, Minnesota), Distribooks Inc. (Stokie, Illinois), and Librería del Lobo Inc. (Gaithersburg, Maryland).

Some types of distribution companies specialize in the educational market and sell to schools in English and Spanish. This is the case with New York's Ideal Foreign Books, National Educational Systems (San Antonio, Texas), Denver's Continental Book Company, and Schoenhof's Foreign Books in Cambridge, Massachusetts. The widespread presence of these companies indicates that Spanish-language readers are not a fringe group, located only in coastal cities and border towns. Indeed, Latinos are a viable and expanding national market.

Monitoring a Legitimate Market

Since the 1990s cultural and commercial Spanish-language publishers and distributors have put into place a working business model for getting Spanish-language texts to the American public. Although this model is still in its early stages (compared with the U.S. publishing, marketing, and distribution model as a whole), it is large enough to have captured the recognition of the publishing industry's main organizations and publications.

The Association of American Publishers (AAP)—the national trade association of the U.S. book publishing industry—formally named 2003 the Year of Publishing for Latinos. Valuing the need to understand the nature and preferences of the Spanish reader, the AAP assembled a Publishing Latino Voices for America Task Force. Composed of Latino writers, publishing industry executives, and distributors, bookstore owners, and translators, it sought to advance the mainstream awareness of the Latino bilingual reading market, and included a commercial campaign entitled, "¡Ajá, Leyendo!/Get Caught Reading," as well as panels and workshops centered around developing the nation's repertoire of Spanish-language books.

AAP's Publishing Latino Voices for America Task Force celebrated June 2004 as Latino Books Month, and published on their Web site a Latino Summer Reading List of bilingual adult and children's reading. Timely and diverse in subject matter and genre, this compilation speaks to the staggering evolution that Spanish-language and bilingual publishing in the United States has undergone since 1990. Representing works originally written in both English and Spanish, it includes the following selections: *¡Azúcar!: The Biography of Celia Cruz/¡Azucar! La biografía de Celia Cruz* by Eduardo Marceles; *Good Jobs Wanted/Se buscan buenos empleos,* compiled and published by the Research Department of Inter-American Development Bank; *Natural Patagonia/Patagonia Natural: Argentina and Chile* by Marcelo D. Beccaceci; *Living History/Historia viva* by Hillary Rodham Clinton; *See Jane Date/Un novio para Jane* by Melissa Senate; *Your Baby's First Year/El primer año de su bebé* by Dr. Steven P. Shelov (American Academy of Pediatrics); and Jorge Ramos' *The Latino Wave: How Hispanics Will Elect the Next American President/La ola latina: Cómo los hispanos elegirán al próximo presidente de los Estados Unidos.*

AAP's children's reading list features works including *Rooster Galo* by Jorge Lujan; *Harvesting Hope: The Story of César Chávez/Cosechando Esperanza: La historia de César Chávez* by Kathleen Krull; *Breaking Through/Senderos fronterizos* by Francisco Jiménez; and *My Island and I: The Nature of Puerto Rico/Mi isla y yo: La naturaleza de Puerto Rico* by Alfonso Silva Lee.

Finally, Spanish-language readership in the United States has prompted *Publisher's Weekly* to launch a sister publication, *Críticas,* which, ironically, is published in English. Targeted to book publishers, distributors, and retailers in the United States and published on a weekly basis, it is devoted to analyzing the Spanish-language book market. Each week the magazine brings its readers previews of coming bilingual books, interviews with writers and Latino publishing industry figures, a list of the week's top 14 best-selling Spanish books, tips for publishers by librarians and other distributors, and information concerning Spanish-language book events. These include the annual Guadalajara Book Fair, conferences and roundtables, and events hosted by the AAP's Publishing Latino Voices for America initiative. New distributors are also announced, as are any vital trends in the Spanish-language reading market in the United States. The trade publication has even published a comprehensive directory of all Spanish-language book distributors, publishers, translators, literary agents, and bookstores located in the United States.

The condition of Spanish-language publishing in the United States has progressed from nonexistence to obscurity to curiosity to a recognition that people read in different ways according to their own needs. The industry is aware of the potential of selling to Spanish readers but continues to look for ways to make the investment not only a dream but a profitable reality. The multicultural character of the United

States certainly will be well served by a more diversified reading list from publishing houses.

RELATED ARTICLES

Bilingual Education; Bilingualism; Business; Literature; Spanish in the United States.

FURTHER READING

Duffus, Robert Luther. *Books, Their Place in a Democracy.* Boston: Houghton Mifflin Company, 1930.

Esquivel, Laura. *Como agua para chocolate: Novela de entregas mensuales con recetas, amores, y remedios caseros.* New York: Anchor Bks., 1992.

Greco, Albert. *The Book Publishing Industry.* Boston: Allyn & Bacon, 1997.

Kanellos, Nicholas, ed. *The Hispanic Literary Companion.* Detroit, Mich.: Visible Ink Press, 1997.

ERIKA HERNÁNDEZ

PUENTE, TITO

Born: April 20, 1923; New York, New York
Died: June 1, 2000; New York, New York

Tito Puente is unquestionably one of the seminal figures in the history of Latin music. Born Ernest Anthony Puente, his musical legacy spans more than 60 highly productive years—from his employment in 1939 (at age 16) as a drummer, working alongside a young Cuban pianist named José Curbelo (who would later become Puente's agent), until his death.

Puente was considered a musical prodigy; he became expert not only as a *timbalero*, but also as a "trap" drummer, pianist, vibraphonist, and saxo-

© KEVORK DJANSEZIAN/ AP/WIDE WORLD PHOTOS

Tito Puente and his all-star jazz band entertain the crowd after he was honored with a star on the Hollywood Walk of Fame in 1990.

phone player. His innate musical genius, his drive, his knowledge of dancing (which came from an early minicareer as a partner with his sister Anna), along with his studies at the world-famous Juilliard School of Music, enabled him to excel not only as a multi-instrumentalist, but also as a composer and arranger—not to mention a unique on-stage show personality.

Throughout his professional career Puente made close to 120 recordings, creating a substantial body of music for the widest possible range of Latin music enthusiasts. He wrote, played, and recorded original compositions in the context of Cuban *son*-based *música tipica criolla* (down-home music for the Latin community) as well as any musician of his era. At the opposite end of the spectrum, he created a great deal of somewhat Americanized quasi-Latin music for general consumption in non-Latin venues around the world. (In doing this, Puente, like Xavier Cugat and Pérez Prado, introduced millions of people to Latin music—who would most likely never have been exposed to it otherwise.) Following deliberately in the musical footsteps of one of his idols, Mario Bauza (musical director of Machito and His Afro Cubans), Puente assembled one of the most innovative orchestras in Latin music. With this powerful ensemble Puente expressed, enhanced, and expanded the musical language of Cuban *son, guaracha, guajira,* and bolero well beyond what anyone before him had achieved. At the famous Palladium Ballroom in New York City, Puente was one of the "Big Three," a triumvirate of the very best, most popular Latin bands of the 1950s' "Mambo Era" (which also comprised the orchestras of Machito and Tito Rodriguez). Finally, Puente was a major force in Latin jazz. Like Mario Bauza, Stan Kenton, and Dizzy Gillespie, Puente was captivated by the complex musical possibilities of modern jazz. Early in his career he incorporated jazz melodies, harmonies, and orchestral arrangements into his "Palladium" big band, and later formed a smaller Latin jazz group (known as the Latin Ensemble), which recorded extensively in the "hard-bop plus Latin percussion" mode of contemporary Latin jazz.

In the 1970s Santana, then a young California Latin rock fusion band, recorded one of Puente's compositions, *Oye como va*. As a result, Puente suddenly gained additional worldwide fame among people who had never heard of Cuban-based Latin music. Thereafter, during engagements, Puente was often asked by audience members to play "that Santana song," which he did with great pleasure.

During the 1950s at the New York Palladium, Puente was crowned *el rey del mambo* (the mambo king) by his fans. Of the many accolades he received over the course of his illustrious career—including his own star on the Hollywood Walk of Fame—this title was the one he often professed to treasure most, since it placed him at the very top of his profession during its golden years in New York City and around the world.

RELATED ARTICLES

Afro-Latino Influences; Cruz, Celia; Jazz; Music, Popular; Santana, Carlos.

FURTHER READING

Chediak, Nat, *Diccionario de Jazz Latina* (Dictionary of Latin Jazz). Madrid: Fundacion Autor, 1998.
Fernández, Raúl, *Latin Jazz: The Perfect Combination.* San Francisco: Chronicle Bks. 2002.
Loza, Steven, *Tito Puente and the Making of Latin Music.* Chicago: Univ.of Ill.Press, 1999.
Puente, Tito,and Payne, Jim, *Tito Puente's Drumming with the Mambo King.* Hudson Music, 2000.
Salazar, Max, *Mambo Kingdom: Latin Music in New York.* New York: Schirmer Trade Book, 2002.

PAQUITO D'RIVERA
FRAN CHESLEIGH

PUERTO RICAN DAY PARADE

The largest ethnic-pride event in the United States, the Puerto Rican Day Parade has been held yearly in New York City since 1958. Available statistics for 1996 indicate that the parade drew close to 100,000 participants, 3 million street spectators, and the highest Nielsen ratings for any televised program in the New York–New Jersey metropolitan area. Given that there are only 3 million Puerto Ricans living in the United States as a whole, and close to 800,000 in New York City, the impressive level of on-street participation and viewership underscores the event's cultural and political importance for the community and the city itself.

In response to the increase of Puerto Rican population outside of Manhattan, the organizers changed the event's name from New York Puerto Rican Parade to the National Puerto Rican Day Parade in 1995. The change of name was intended to send a signal of inclusion to Puerto Ricans across the country, attract participants living in other parts of the country, and encourage the formation of parades in other cities. According to the organizers, the current parade's objective is to "raise the self-esteem of our people and use their pride to promote economic development, education, cultural improvement and recognition." It also seeks to "create a national consciousness and appreciation of Puerto Rican culture and its contribution to American culture and society."

Partly inspired by the popularity of the religious San Juan Bautista celebrations of 1953 and 1954, the contemporary parade was the direct offshoot of an earlier event called the Hispanic Parade or Desfile Hispano first held in 1956. The Basque Jesús de Galíndez, a professor of Spanish and political science at Columbia University, is credited with conceptualizing the parade as a pan-Latino, nonpolitical event. Organizing efforts for the inaugural parade began in 1955 by the Federación de Sociedades Hispanas, Incorporated, and the first parade took place on April 15, 1956. The stated objective of the event was to "demonstrate unity, discipline and civic strength."

Internal dissent, however, characterized the parade from its inception. Although Puerto Ricans and Puerto Rican organizations constituted the majority of the Hispanic Parade organizers and supporters, ideological differences emerged between those who felt that the parade should primarily showcase a common "Spanish" culture and those who favored a more popular event that allowed Puerto Ricans to show off the community's growing numbers and political influence. Another key axis of contention was whether the parade's main objective should be integration into U.S. culture and polity or the defense of a separate identity. Negotiations between factions finally broke down when such demands as the incorporation of the term *Puerto Rican* into the Hispanic Parade's title and that Puerto Ricans march at the head were denied by the organizers.

The breakdown of negotiations resulted in the secession of most *boricuas* from the Desfile Hispano's organizing committee after the second Hispanic parade. Even the intervention of the governor of Puerto Rico, Luis Muñoz Marín, in support of separation underscores the political importance attributed to this split. In opting to organize as Puerto Ricans and not under the more general category of Hispanics, the *boricua* political and civic leadership sought to assert itself as a distinct ethnic constituency within the city that could in turn lead other Hispanics. The fact that Puerto Ricans were not only culturally different from other Latinos but also the only ones who were born U.S. citizens shaped the parade as a stage to reiterate ethnonational specificity, make political demands on the city, and occupy socially valorized public space as colonial migrants.

Planning for the new event began on October 22, 1957, and the first Puerto Rican event took place on April 13, 1958. Victor López served as president of the organization, José Caballero as organizer, and attorney Oscar González Suárez was the grand marshal. The first parade was deemed an instant success by its organizers as New York and Puerto Rico political notables participated, 25,000 people marched, and 200,000 people attended. Originally, most of the parade's participants and support came from the hometown associations.

The relative importance of the associations declined during the 1960s, and the parade became nurtured by a broader number of social, civic, union, neighborhood, cultural, and political groups, many of which were funded by the state after the 1970s. Despite the fact that the majority of the parade's participants and spectators are Puerto Ricans, the privileged audience includes the mostly white power brokers of the city, followed by island-based officials. As Judith H. Herbstein has observed, the success of the parade is often measured by its organizers "in terms of the power and prestige of the individuals representing the American political structure or seeking its support on behalf of Puerto Ricans."

As the parade's name suggests, the participants march down the street in quasimilitary fashion, following a hierarchical order, particularly at the head of the parade where political and civic leaders share the spotlight with popular entertainers and other notables. By displaying a capacity for discipline, orderly conduct, and civic accomplishment, the parade seeks to assure other New Yorkers that Puerto Ricans are a mature community who can be politically rewarded as other ethnic groups have been before them. The mayor of New York, for instance, underscores this message by proclaiming the day of the parade as "Puerto Rican Day" and the second week in June as "Puerto Rican Week." The proclamation highlights the contributions of Puerto Ricans to the city and the state of New York.

The adoption of the same parade route used by formerly stigmatized European groups such as the Italians and the Irish—starting at 44th street and ending at 86th street along Fifth Avenue—connotes a desire to not only temporarily occupy but permanently lay claim to New York City's economic, political, and cultural centers. As former city councilman Luis A. Olmedo, grand marshal of the 1981 parade declared, "We have to show these people that the best way for them to get their rights is to get involved in politics . . . Take a lesson from the Irish." The choice of organizing a parade rather than other types of community-building events such as a *fiesta patronal,* or carnival, suggests that the Puerto Rican leadership conceived the parade as a primarily political event. In fact, for many politicians in New York courting Puerto Rican voters, the parade marks the beginning of the campaign season. The political dimensions of the parade are also evident in that many parade organizers are seen as mediators between the community and the city, are politically involved, or have political aspirations.

Yet the parade exceeds the intent of the organizers. For participants and onlookers, the parade is one of the most anticipated festivities of the year, one that allows Puerto Ricans, many of whom continue to be excluded from educational and job opportunities, to affirm their cultural, social, and community values while enjoying themselves in the center of New York's power corridor. As arguably the most significant display for Puerto Rican ethnonational affirmation in the United States, groups who are critical of the leadership or are marginalized within the community also bring their claims to bear. This constitutes the parade as a space for the negotiation of conflicting constructions of Puerto Rican identity along ethnic, national, racial, sexual, and gender axes.

The parade, for instance, has been the object of critique by proindependence and leftist nationalist groups, particularly since the early 1970s, for its alleged assimilationist bent. Despite ideological and political differences, the majority of these groups have historically used the visibility and popular appeal of the parade to promote their own causes, which have ranged from advocating the release of political prisoners to supporting the exit of the U.S. Navy from the island of Vieques. Another marginalized sector, Puerto Rican gays and lesbians, have marched with left-leaning groups during the 1970s and as a sepa-

© CALÉ/POLARIS IMAGES

Crowd waving Puerto Rican flags at the annual Puerto Rican Day Parade in New York City, 2003.

rate contingent since 1989, seeking greater acceptance and visibility across several communities.

Over time another aspect that has grown in importance is the use of the parade to advertise and market products to Puerto Ricans. Although since the parade began, small businesses have had a substantial role in financing the festivities and in participating in the event, today's parade draws an impressive number of multinational corporations as supporters, sponsors, and participants. The growing number of Puerto Rican pop stars who also make appearances at the parade, generally as grand marshals, further blurs the line between identity and commerce, ethnic pride and advertising.

Despite its five-decade tradition as a largely enjoyable event in the life of the city, the parade has often been the object of scorn by other New Yorkers. As recently as 1997, a columnist for the London-based journal *The Spectator* infuriated many Puerto Ricans by affirming that the parade only served to underscore that there will never be "a single positive contribution by a Puerto Rican outside of receiving American welfare and beating the system." Although the mayor of New York at the time, Rudolph Giuliani, demanded an apology, only a year later an episode of the popular television show *Seinfeld* reignited the tensions between the community's leadership and the media. In the show's highly rated episode titled "The Puerto Rican Day," one of the show's main characters accidentally burns and stomps on a Puerto Rican flag during the parade. The National Puerto Rican Coalition and other groups successfully pressured NBC (National Broadcasting Company) to not rerun that episode of the show.

Since the parade runs along Fifth Avenue, the route's largely affluent residents have historically complained about the noise, litter, and traffic that accompany the event. Some of the measures taken include boarding up the buildings along the route before the parade begins. These practices became even more pronounced in the aftermath of the 2000 parade in which 18 men were convicted or pleaded guilty to sexual assault and disorderly conduct. The incident involved the sexual harassment and groping of 50 women near Central Park and was described as a "wilding" by the press. A subsequent investigation revealed that several police officers had refused to diffuse the situation, underscoring the conflictive relations that persist between the city and Puerto Ricans.

Parade organizers and the Puerto Rican leadership sought distance from this incident by, among other actions, banning rap music. In doing so, the parade again became a site of debate over what constitutes Puerto Rican culture and what is the event's main goal. Yet despite a temporary withdrawal of support in the aftermath of the 2000 parade, the event's enduring popularity and growth underscores its mainstream political effectiveness, medular site for ethnonational self-definition, and the community's need for a public ritual that challenges everyday economic, social, political, and cultural hierarchies despite the discomfort of some with one of New York's most vital communities.

RELATED ARTICLES
Carnaval; Holidays; New York City; Puerto Ricans on the Mainland.

FURTHER READING
Aparicio, Frances R. "Re-Racializing the Puerto Rican Day Parade: Recent Media Representations of U.S. Puerto Ricans in the Public Space." In *None of the Above*. Ed. by Frances Negrón-Muntaner. New York: Palgrave, 2004.
Estades, Rosa. "Symbolic Unity: The Puerto Rican Parade." In *Historical Perspectives on Puerto Rican Survival in the U.S.* Ed. by Clara E. Rodríguez and Virginia Sánchez Korrol. Princeton, N.J.: Markus Wiener Pubs., 1980.
Herbstein, Judith F. *Rituals and Politics of the Puerto Rican Community in New York City.* Ph.D. Dissertation, City Univ. of N.Y., 1978.
Kasinitz, Philip, and Judith Freiderberg-Herbstein. "The Puerto Rican Parade and West Indian Carnival: Public Celebrations in New York City." In *Caribbean Life in New York City: Sociocultural Dimensions.* Ed. by Constance R. Sutton and Elsa M. Chaney. New York: Ctr. for Migration Studies, 1987.
La Fountain-Stokes, Lawrence. "Queer Puerto Ricans on Parade, T-Shirts with the Flag, etc." *The Dirty Goat* 9 (1998): 1–9.
"Taki's Tacky Attack on Puerto Ricans." *Institute for Puerto Rican Policy* (June 16, 1997).
Theodoracopulos, Taki. "Why Should We Pay?" *Spectator* (June 14, 1997): 62–63.

FRANCES NEGRÓN-MUNTANER

PUERTO RICAN LEGAL DEFENSE AND EDUCATION FUND

Founded in 1972, the Puerto Rican Legal Defense and Education Fund (PRLDEF) is a nonprofit charitable organization dedicated to securing and promoting the civil and human rights of Puerto Ricans in particular and Latinos in general. PRLDEF is modeled after the NAACP (National Association for the Advancement of Colored People) Legal Defense and

Education Fund (LDF) and the Mexican American Legal Defense and Education Fund (MALDEF). Like MALDEF, PRLDEF received early support from the Ford Foundation. Unlike MALDEF, PRLDEF has confined its activities mostly to a single state: New York. Since its inception the group has been head-quartered in New York City.

PRLDEF's founding executive director was the highly visible lawyer César A. Perales. Together with Jorge L. Batista and Victor Marrero, Perales developed plans to start a civil rights organization for Puerto Ricans while they were working for New York City mayor John V. Lindsay. After leading PRLDEF from 1972 to 1974, Perales went on to become director of human resources in the U.S. Department of Health and Human Services. He returned to lead the group again, in 1981 and 2003, on those occasions as president and general counsel. Meanwhile, in 1981 Perales joined New York governor Mario Cuomo's administration as state commissioner of social services. Other key PRLDEF leaders were Oscar García-Rivera, Lita Taracido, Jack John Olivero, and Linda Flores.

Of the group's three divisions—litigation, education, and policy—litigation has been the one most closely identified with the whole organization. The litigation division has won significant language and voting rights cases. For example, in 1976, PRLDEF obtained final judgment in *ASPIRA* v. *Board of Education,* which forced the New York City school system to recognize and address the special needs of non-English-speaking students. In 1982 PRLDEF won *Flateau* v. *Anderson,* which required immediate reapportionment of the state's senate, assembly, and congressional districts to more fairly reflect the Puerto Rican voting population. The group has also secured victories in the areas of employment, environmental justice, housing, and immigration.

The education division offers a variety of services to prospective and current law students, including preadmission counseling, low-cost preparation for the Law School Admission Test (LSAT), scholarships, and summer internships. The policy division, which is a product of the 1998 merger between PRLDEF and the 15-year-old Institute for Puerto Rican Policy, conducts research and offers information relating to policy analysis and advocacy, civic participation, and networking with allied organizations. In recent years the policy division has conducted studies in bilin-

gual education, municipal priorities, Latinos and the census, election reform, and advocacy training.

With more than ten different chief executives, PRLDEF has experienced a high rate of leadership turnover. This has been caused by both the group's tradition of short-term office holding and its recurrent funding crises; in 2003, facing a $500,000 deficit, PRLDEF imposed temporary salary cuts for staff and dismissed 6 of 23 employees. This has caused concern among the group's major supporters, including the Ford Foundation. Nevertheless, PRLDEF has remained active in pursing its agenda. In 2004, the organization helped immigrant day laborers persuade officials in Freehold, New Jersey, to halt the practice of issuing vagrancy citations to men looking for work.

RELATED ARTICLES

Activism; Mexican American Legal Defense and Education Fund; Politics, Puerto Rican.

FURTHER READING

Relano, Maruxa, and Hillary Hawkins, trans. "Puerto Rican Legal Defense and Education Fund Looks to the Future." *Hoy* (November 21, 2003).

Sánchez Korrol, Virginia E. *From Colonia to Community: The History of Puerto Ricans in New York City.* Westport, Conn.: Greenwood Press, 1983.

SELECTED WEB SITES

Centro de Estudios Puertorriqueños. *Archives: Finding Aids.* www.centropr.org/lib-arc/prldef2.html

Puerto Rican Legal Defense and Education Fund. *Litigation, Education, and Policy.* www.prldef.org.htm

CHRISTOPHER DAVID RUIZ CAMERON

PUERTO RICANS ON THE MAINLAND

The presence of Puerto Ricans in New York and other parts of the United States can be traced back to the mid-19th century, almost a half century before the U.S. invasion of Puerto Rico that ended Spanish colonial rule. In 1898 the United States declared war against Spain after the mysterious explosion of the U.S. battleship *Maine,* stationed at the time in Havana Harbor. When the United States invaded Cuba, creole rebels had been fighting the Spanish army for almost three years and had made significant progress in what was the island's second war for independence. Their first one, known as the Ten Years' War, began with the Grito de Yara uprising of October 10, 1868. In contrast, Puerto Rico's

Grito de Lares independence revolt of September 23, 1868, had been rapidly crushed by Spanish troops and, during the decades that followed, Puerto Ricans were unable to overcome the repressive political environment under Spanish rule or secure independence. Thus the occupation of Puerto Rico was one of the side effects of the war of 1898, also known as the Spanish-Cuban-American War.

Military intervention by the United States in the second Spanish-Cuban war, which had begun in 1895, and the subsequent takeover of Puerto Rico, put an end to Spanish domination in the Americas. The war ended with the Treaty of Paris in which Spain relinquished what was left of its overseas empire: Puerto Rico, Cuba, the Philippines, and Guam.

Commercial relations between the Antillean islands of Cuba and Puerto Rico and the United States had begun to develop during the early part of the 19th century while the islands were still Spanish colonies. These relations intensified over the course of the century as the islands provided the North American nation with sugar, tobacco, and other agricultural products, and the United States found new consumer markets for its manufactured goods. By the mid-1820s Spain had lost most of its colonial possessions in the New World with the exception of Puerto Rico and Cuba, and the monarchy was determined to not relinquish control of its remaining colonies. Spanish governors ruled both islands with iron fists and allowed few civil liberties. Because of the unfavorable political environment in Puerto Rico and Cuba, many Antillean creole liberals, especially those advocating reforms, a larger degree of self-government, or complete separation from Spain, were imprisoned or forced into exile.

The Migration Pioneers

Puerto Rican and Cuban political exiles found refuge in several U.S. cities, especially New York, Philadelphia, New Orleans, Tampa, and Key West; in European cities such as Paris and Madrid; as well as in several Latin American countries. These early settlements were called *colonias*. Among the Antillean expatriates to the United States were prominent political and intellectual leaders, but also students, artisans, and factory workers.

During this period Puerto Rican merchants and other businessmen involved in the sugar and tobacco trades were frequent sojourners to the United States, and the island's creole elite saw the United States as a model of democracy, progress, and modernity for the other new republics in the Americas to emulate. There was a sector of the incipient creole bourgeoisie that favored the islands' annexation to the United States. There also was a strong interest on the part of the U.S. government in achieving control of the strategically located Hispanic Caribbean islands, and some attempts were made during the decades that preceded the Spanish-Cuban-American War to purchase them from Spain. The growing manufacturing industrial sector in the United States attracted and relied on immigrant labor, especially from Western Europe and the Americas. Sugar-related exports and cigar making were major economic activities that linked Cuba and Puerto Rico with the United States, and the latter sector drew a large number of workers from the islands. Beginning in the mid-1800s numerous tobacco shops and factories were established in several U.S. cities, especially in Tampa and New York City. These provided employment for Puerto Rican, Cuban, and other immigrant *tabaqueros* (cigar makers).

The *tabaqueros* were an enlightened artisan sector of the working class. Influenced by socialist ideology they hired readers in the tobacco factories that kept them abreast of daily news and exposed them to many of the classic works in social and political thought and creative literature. These workers also started their own newspapers. There were many talented political and literary writers among the *tabaqueros,* although to a large extent their writings remained scattered throughout the many workers' publications. Women workers were also represented in this sector and were largely employed as tobacco strippers.

The influx of Antillean separatist émigrés to the United States intensified after the Grito de Lares and Grito de Yara armed rebellions. The presence of Puerto Rican and Cuban expatriates in various U.S. cities is documented by the substantial number of newspapers and organizations they founded, especially during the second half of the 19th century. As early as 1865 Antillean separatists initiated the Sociedad Republicana de Cuba y Puerto Rico (Republican Society of Cuba and Puerto Rico) in New York to garner support for the separatist cause. Among its leaders was Puerto Rican physician José Francisco Basora. That same year the newspaper *La Voz de América* (The Voice of America) was founded to promote activities aimed at ending Spanish domination in the Americas. Basora, along with Puerto

Rican expatriate separatists Ramón Emeterio Betances and Segundo Ruíz Belvis, started the Comité Revolucionario de Puerto Rico (Revolutionary Committee of Puerto Rico) in 1867. This group coordinated the activities that led to the Grito de Lares revolt a year later. Several other separatist organizations and newspapers were initiated in subsequent decades, especially in the 1880s after Cuban patriot José Martí arrived in New York City and became the main leader of the Antillean émigré independence movement.

Several other prominent Puerto Rican separatists, both from the creole propertied class and the working class, also arrived in New York during these years. Betances, the leader of the Puerto Rican expatriate movement, only stayed briefly in New York and ended up settling in Paris, where he had lived as a student and received a degree in medicine. Among those with longer stays in New York were writer and educator Eugenio María de Hostos (1839–1903), journalist typographers Sotero Figueroa (1851–1923) and Francisco "Pachín" Marín (1863–1897), the poet Lola Rodríguez de Tió (1843–1924), and her journalist husband Bonocio Tió.

Hostos arrived in New York in 1869 and became a writer for the separatist newspaper La Revolución (1869–1876). But his opposition to those Antillean separatists supporting the annexation of the islands to the United States made him unpopular and shortened his stay in the city. He left to spend many years traveling and working throughout Latin America, with long stays in Venezuela, Colombia, Chile, and the Dominican Republic. While residing in each of these countries, Hostos continued to be one of the most fervent advocates of Cuban and Puerto Rican independence, promoting his vision of an Antillean federation of free republics. His prolific writings and intellectual prominence throughout the continent gained him the appellative of "Citizen of the Americas." After the conclusion of the Spanish-Cuban-American War and the U.S. takeover of Cuba and Puerto Rico, Hostos returned to New York and established the Liga de Patriotas (Patriots' League) to persuade the U.S. government to hold a plebiscite and allow the Puerto Rican people to decide their own political future, but he died before the Liga was able to accomplish its goals.

Figueroa started his own press and closely collaborated with Martí in the publication of the separatist newspaper Patria (1898–1901), including the administration of the newspaper and the writing of editorials. Marín published the separatist newspaper El Postillón (The Conductor; 1892), which he had started in Puerto Rico and was the main cause of his exile. Lola Rodríguez de Tió wrote several memorable revolutionary poems that were published in Patria and, along with other separatist women, assisted in the movement's fund-raising efforts. Her husband also pursued his journalistic endeavors in several of the city's Spanish-language newspapers.

An Afro-Puerto Rican apprentice typographer, Arturo Alfonso Schomburg (1874–1938) arrived in New York in 1891 and also joined the separatist movement. A friend of the tabaquero artisans, he joined some of them in founding the separatist Club Dos Antillas (The Two Antilles Club), an organization aimed at procuring financial assistance and other kinds of support for the independence effort. He was the club's secretary for four years, but his involvement with the separatist movement ended with the War of 1898. In subsequent years Schomburg moved to the black section of Harlem and cultivated friendships with several African American and West Indian intellectuals and artists of the pan-Africanist movement and the Harlem Renaissance. He also engaged in the task of collecting books and other materials as a part of his broader vision to document the experience of African diasporas around the world and their contributions to the histories of many countries. His impressive collection was sold to the New York Public Library in 1927 and is now part of the Schomburg Center for Research on Black Culture.

The U.S. Takeover and the Growth of the Early *Colonias*

The Spanish-Cuban-American War was an important factor in increased migration of Puerto Ricans to the continental United States. Puerto Rican labor migration to New York began to grow after the U.S. takeover, but not in any significant numbers until the late 1910s. Shortly after the takeover, North American colonial authorities in Puerto Rico promoted policies that facilitated the migration of agricultural and industrial workers by allowing companies to recruit from among the large impoverished island population. The majority of workers went to New York City to work in manufacturing and service occupations, but they also went to other U.S. cities. There was also active recruitment of agricultural workers for migrant camps in New York and New

Jersey and the sugarcane plantations of Hawaii. Steamship travel from San Juan to New York was frequent and, although Puerto Ricans were not U.S. citizens until the 1917 Jones Act decree, their relationship with the United States and their status as colonial migrants allowed them easy access to the metropolis. After Puerto Ricans became U.S. citizens, an increased migration pattern between the island and the continent developed. This pattern continues today.

For many decades the majority of the U.S. Puerto Rican population was concentrated in New York City. Pre–World War II communities developed around the Brooklyn Navy Yard, the Chelsea area of Lower Manhattan, and East Harlem (later known as El Barrio, or Spanish Harlem). Newspapers and literary works published in the various New York Puerto Rican communities are the most valuable sources for learning about their historical development and about the major issues confronting the daily lives of migrants in their process of adapting to a culturally and linguistically different environment, as well as about the economic and cultural contributions that Puerto Ricans have made to U.S. society.

The writings of two working-class migrants, Bernardo Vega (1885–1965) and Jesús Colón (1901–1974) have been particularly useful in documenting experiences during the formative years of New York City's Puerto Rican community. Vega, a socialist *tabaquero* from the Puerto Rican mountain town of Cayey, came to the United States in 1916. His uncle Antonio Vega, however, had migrated to the city during the 1880s and Bernardo learned a great deal about the experiences of early migrants from the stories his uncle told him. Colón, another migrant from the town of Cayey, was also deeply influenced by the socialist ideology of the *tabaqueros*.

Colón arrived in New York in 1918 as a stowaway on a steamship. Vega's and Colón's stories reflect the efforts of many working-class migrants to adapt and survive in a society in which they were marginalized because of their ethnic and racial backgrounds. Both men were actively involved in the establishment of several organizations that served the cultural, social, and political needs of New York Puerto Ricans. They also wrote frequently for newspapers and gave a voice to the concerns of a primarily working-class community. In 1927 Bernardo Vega bought the workers' newspaper *Gráfico* (The Illustra-

tor; 1926–1931) and Colón wrote a weekly column for this publication.

Vega lived in New York for about 40 years. He wrote his memoirs in the 1940s, but they were not published until 1977, almost a decade after his death in Puerto Rico. In his memoirs he goes as far back as his uncle Antonio's arrival in New York and to the stories he learned from him. He provides meticulous details about individuals, events, names of newspapers and community organizations, and offers a working-class perspective of the experiences and survival struggles of pre–World War II Puerto Rican migrants. In recognition of its importance for documenting the history of the New York Puerto Rican community, the book *Memorias de Bernardo Vega* (Memoirs of Bernardo Vega; 1983) was translated into English and published in the United States.

Colón published the book *A Puerto Rican in New York and Other Sketches* (1961), and many of his other journalistic writings from the 1920s to the 1970s were

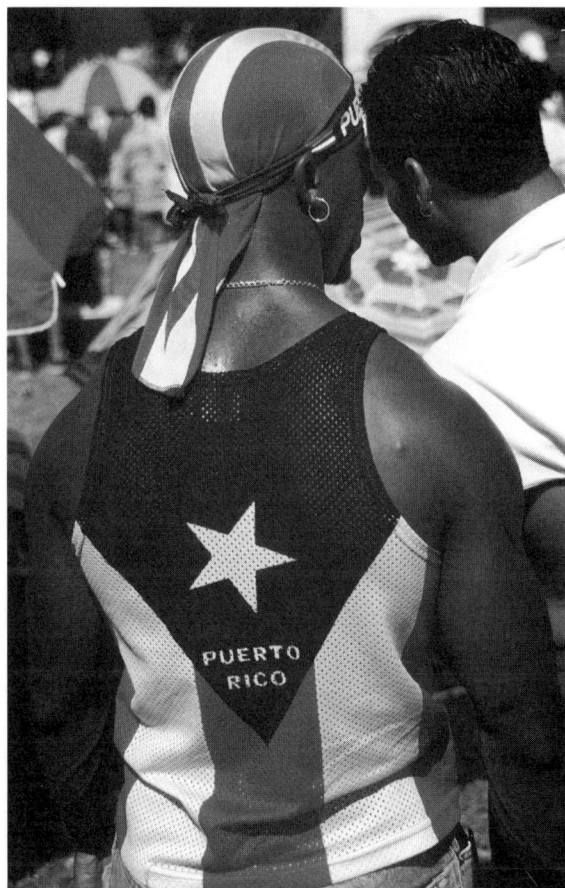

© JEFF GREENBERG / PHOTOEDIT

Puerto Rican man at a concert in Dade County, Florida.

425 ☀

collected in the volume *The Way It Was and Other Writings by Jesús Colón* (Acosta-Belén and Sánchez Korrol, 1993). He died in New York after living there for more than a half century. The writings of both Colón and Vega contain a wealth of information about the evolution of the New York Puerto Rican community and the early experiences and struggles of Puerto Rican migrants in the process of adapting to a new, culturally different racist environment. They also confirm the role of Puerto Ricans as productive workers and involved citizens.

Two feminist tobacco-stripper union activists, Luisa Capetillo and Franca de Armiño, also came to the United States during the early decades of the 20th century. Known for their participation in labor struggles in Puerto Rico, they continued these activities in the metropolis and wrote for workers' newspapers, in addition to doing their own creative writing. Capetillo arrived in the United States in 1912 and moved between the tobacco factories of New York City and Ybor City, Florida, for a couple of years. This experience shaped some of the writings in her book *Influencias de las ideas modernas* (Influence of Modern Ideas; 1916), a series of texts that reflect her anarcho-feminist ideals and a revolutionary utopian vision that defies social norms and uneven power relations between the sexes and classes. She returned to New York City in 1919 and continued writing for workers' newspapers, worked as a reader in a tobacco factory, and ran a boardinghouse. Before going to New York, Franca de Armiño had been the leader of a workers' suffragist organization and of a tobacco-stripper union in Puerto Rico. There is some evidence of her presence in New York City during the late 1920s and 1930s. She wrote a few articles in *Gráfico* and published the revolutionary play *Los Hipócritas* (The Hypocrites; 1937).

Another important intellectual figure during those years was Josefina "Pepiña" Silva de Cintrón, founder of the *Revista de Artes y Letras* (Review of Arts and Letters; 1933–1945). For over a decade this publication paid a great deal of attention to women's concerns and feminist issues, but it had more of a middle-class, professional orientation. The review had a wide circulation and engaged the collaboration of many prominent intellectuals from the New York community, Puerto Rico, and other Spanish-speaking countries.

Post–World War II Great Migration to the Present

The massive growth of the Puerto Rican population in New York City and other major cities such as Chicago and Philadelphia is a post–World War II phenomenon. This first major migratory influx of Puerto Ricans to the United States by airplane is frequently referred to as the Great Migration. Between 1940 and 1950 the U.S. Puerto Rican population increased 330.7 percent, and between 1950 and 1960, by 194.5 percent (see Table). Although most Puerto Ricans settled in the New York City area during those years, they also became a more visible presence in Chicago, Philadelphia, Newark, and smaller cities such as Lorain, Ohio.

The main catalyst for the Great Migration was the U.S.-led industrialization of Puerto Rico that began with the implementation of Operation Bootstrap, known in Spanish as Operación Manos a la Obra, meaning put your hands to work, economic development program. Industrialization created a major displacement of the island's large agricultural workforce. Once again, U.S. and Puerto Rican government officials promoted migration to the United States as an escape valve to reduce island unemployment and poverty and, at the same time, satisfy the needs for low-wage labor of mainland agricultural and manufacturing industries. Many U.S. industries actively recruited Puerto Rican workers, and migration was also facilitated by inexpensive airfares between San Juan, New York, and other major U.S. cities. Thus a large number of Puerto Rican migrants were and continue to be from the working class.

During the years after the Great Migration, other Puerto Rican settlements grew in the Lower East Side of Manhattan, the Williamsburg section of Brooklyn, the South Bronx, and in Brentwood, Long Island. For many decades New York City has remained the locality with the largest number of Puerto Ricans. Another significant demographic increase in the total U.S. Puerto Rican population occurred in the 1990s. By the year 2000 the population had increased to 3.4 million, 46.2 percent more than what it was in 1990 (see Table). In addition to population increases, a new demographic dispersion pattern began in the 1980s when Puerto Ricans started to move out of New York City and establish residence in midsize U.S. cities in the northeastern states. Of the 3.4 million Puerto Ricans recorded in the 2000 U.S. Census, fewer than 1 million now live in New York City, still the largest concentration compared to all other Latino nationalities living there. The remaining 2.4 million Puerto Ricans live in other parts of the United States, particularly in other New York State localities, and in New Jersey, Connecticut, Massachusetts, Pennsylvania, Illinois, and Florida. This geographic settlement change was mostly influenced by a decline in New York's manufacturing sector. The population of Puerto Rico stood at 3.8 million in the year 2000, suggesting that in a few years there might be as many Puerto Ricans residing in the United States as there are on the island.

The Table illustrates the growth of the U.S. Puerto Rican population from 1910–2000. Puerto Rican migration is a continuing process, with recent figures comparable to those of the Great Migration years. These increases have occurred since the 1970s because of the significant reduction in manufacturing jobs in New York City, and especially during periods of economic recession, which forced workers to search for employment opportunities outside the city in both blue- and white-collar occupations. Another factor that has influenced Puerto Rican families moving out of large urban areas such as New York City into midsize or smaller urban and semiurban localities is the possibility of a better quality of life and education for their offspring in environments less plagued with inner-city problems, such as high crime rates, overcrowded schools, and a lack of quality affordable housing. In a recent census,

Hartford, Connecticut, was the U.S. city with the largest percentage of Puerto Ricans, constituting about a fourth of that city's total population. About 42 percent of all Puerto Ricans residing in the United States were born in Puerto Rico.

Migration to the United States has been and still is a continuing process for the Puerto Rican population. Different from many prior groups of immigrants, they maintain a commuting relationship with their country of origin. The transnational contact between Puerto Ricans on the island and in the diaspora contributes to particular sociocultural dynamics in which both communities are reciprocally influenced. The dramatic growth of the U.S. Latino population, and the increased representation and participation of Latinos in the U.S. political process have been beneficial for island Puerto Ricans, who are U.S. citizens by birth, but lack any voting representation in Congress. A good example of this support was evident in the movement to get the U.S. Navy to stop its bombing training exercises on the Puerto Rican island of Vieques. Thus the lives of Puerto Ricans on both shores are expected to continue to be collectively intertwined.

Puerto Ricans, along with other U.S. Latinos, still have a low socioeconomic status when compared to the non-Latino white population. About one-fourth of all U.S. Puerto Ricans live below the poverty line but, according to census data for the year 2000, they place second to Cubans in the percentage of workers with annual earnings of $35,000 or more. The rate was 34.4 percent for Cubans, 29.6 percent for Puerto Ricans, and 23.3 percent for the total U.S. Latino population. Puerto Ricans also fare well in educational attainment when compared with other Latino nationalities. Their slow socioeconomic progress in U.S. society has not precluded them from struggling for their civil rights, combating racism and discrimination, and working toward the improvement of their overall status. Organizations such as ASPIRA (Aspire), founded in New York in 1961, and the Puerto Rican Legal Defense and Education Fund (PRLDEF), founded in 1972, have been at the forefront of educational and civil rights issues. Increased political participation has resulted in the election of two Puerto Ricans from New York City districts to the U.S. Congress, and one from a Chicago district, and there are numerous elected officials in the state legislatures and city halls of various states.

GROWTH OF THE PUERTO RICAN POPULATION IN THE UNITED STATES, 1910–1990

Year	Total Population	% of Increase
1910	1,513	------
1920	11,811	680.6
1930	52,774	346.8
1940	69,967	32.6
1950	301,375	330.7
1960	887,662	194.5
1970	1,429,396	61.0
1980	1,983,000	38.7
1990	2,330,000	17.5
2000	3,406,178	46.2

Source: U.S. Census Bureau, Census 2000, Summary File 1; U.S. Dept. of Commerce, Bureau of the Census, *The Hispanic Population in the United States*, CPS for March 1989 and March 1997; *Statistical Handbook on U.S. Hispanics* (Oryx Press, 1991); *A Survey of Puerto Ricans on the U.S. Mainland in the 1970s* (Praeger, 1975).

One important organization that has taken root across the country is the National Conference of Puerto Rican Women, founded in January 1972 in Washington, D.C., by a group of Puerto Rican women committed to the participation of Puerto Rican and other Hispanic women in economics, politics, and social life of the United States. The group works to connect Puerto Rican and Latina women nationwide in order to shape public policy based on consensus; to promote awareness and attention to Latino concerns, specifically among policy makers and civic community leaders; and to increase Latino visibility and activities in the public eye.

The founding of hometown clubs, mutual aid societies and other service, labor, educational, and political organizations, and newspapers and magazines are important components of U.S. Puerto Rican cultural, social, and political life. In 1959 the New York Puerto Rican community initiated the celebration of El Desfile Puertorriqueño (The Puerto Rican Day Parade), which is now an annual summer tradition that promotes unity and cultural affirmation. The event has been replicated in other Puerto Rican communities and has inspired other Caribbean groups in the city to organize similar events. Chicago's Paseo Boricua is another example of how Puerto Ricans maintain and revitalize their cultural heritage in their various U.S. communities.

In the late 1960s the process of documenting the history and contributions of Puerto Ricans and other U.S. ethnoracial minorities was favored by the emergence of Puerto Rican studies programs at colleges and universities within the City University of New York (CUNY), the State University of New York (SUNY), and the Rutgers University of New Jersey systems. As a result, the Center for Puerto Rican Studies (Centro) was established in 1973 under the leadership of prominent scholar Frank Bonilla. The Centro led the way in creating a valuable library and archives currently located at Hunter College. In 1969 the Museo del Barrio was founded in New York City to promote the artistic work of Puerto Ricans and other Latinos and to bring art-related programming to the community.

There is a substantial body of creative literature about the migrant experience written by U.S. Puerto Rican authors. These authors write in English, Spanish, or bilingually. Most notable are prose fiction writers who relate many of their personal experiences growing up Puerto Rican in U.S. society, and

those associated with New York's Nuyorican Poets' Café. The first group includes leading authors such as Piri Thomas, Nicholasa Mohr, Judith Ortiz Cofer, and Esmeralda Santiago. Among those in the second group receiving critical acclaim are Miguel Piñero, Miguel Algarín, Pedro Pietri, Tato Laviera, and Sandra María Estéves. There are many other writers giving expression to the realities of Puerto Rican life in the United States.

The visual arts are enriched by the many artists affiliated with New York's Taller Boricua, Philadelphia's Taller Puertorriqueño, and Chicago's Institute for Puerto Rican Arts and Culture. One of the artists who has been quite successful in capturing the images, traditions, and dilemmas of Puerto Rican barrio life with his powerful murals and collages is Juan Sánchez.

Contributions to the film and television industries are represented by the acting achievements of Oscar-winners José Ferrer, Rita Moreno, and Benicio del Toro, and the successful careers of Raúl Juliá, Jimmy Smits, and Jennifer Lopez, to name only a few. The popular-music charts include several well-recognized Puerto Rican performers; from creators of Latin jazz, such as Tito Puente to interpreters of salsa music, such as Willie Colón, to pop rock idols such as Ricky Martin and Marc Anthony.

Many of the aforementioned efforts, along with the work of scholars, activists, writers, and other artists, are reflections of a vital community. These efforts and works contribute to dispelling some of the myths and stereotypes about Puerto Ricans that still prevail in U.S. society, particularly in much of the conventional scholarship and the media.

RELATED ARTICLES

Art, Puerto Rican on the Mainland; Colón, Willie; Cuisine, Puerto Rican; Hostos, Eugenio Maria de; Literature, Puerto Rican on the Mainland; Martí, José; Moreno, Rita; Muñoz Marín, Luis; Nuyorican Poets Café; Operation Bootstrap; Politics, Puerto Rican; Puente, Tito; Puerto Rican Day Parade; Puerto Rican Legal Defense and Education Fund; Puerto Rican Studies; Puerto Rican Young Lords; Schomburg, Arthur; Thomas, Piri; Vega, Bernardo.

FURTHER READING

Acosta-Belén, Edna, et al. *Adiós, Borinquen querida: La diáspora puertorriqueña, su historia y sus aportaciones (The Puerto Rican Diaspora, Its History and Contributions)*. Albany, N.Y.: CELAC and Comisión, 2000.

Labor Migration Under Capitalism: The Puerto Rican Experience. New York: Monthly Review Press, 1979 [City Univ. of N.Y.'s Center for Puerto Rican Studies, History Task Force].

Sources for the Study of Puerto Rican Migration, 1879–1930. New York: Centro, 1982 [City Univ. of N.Y.'s Center for Puerto Rican Studies, History Task Force].

Rivera-Batiz, Francisco, and Carlos E. Santiago. *The Changing Reality of Puerto Ricans in the United States.* Washington, D.C.: National Puerto Rican Coalition, 1994.

Rodríguez, Clara. *Puerto Ricans Born in the USA.* Boston: Unwyn Hyman, 1989.

Sánchez Korrol, Virginia. *From Colonia to Community: The History of Puerto Ricans in New York City, 1917–1948.* 1983; Berkeley: Univ. of Calif. Press, 1994.

EDNA ACOSTA-BELÉN

PUERTO RICAN STUDIES

On July 9, 1969, the Board of Higher Education of the City University of New York (CUNY) announced the institution of programs in Puerto Rican studies throughout the CUNY system. This act responded to protests by Puerto Rican students about the absence within academia of serious and accurate study of their reality. During the 1970s the field was circumscribed to New York. Eventually, academic departments and programs examined the Puerto Rican problem nationally. Also, their curriculum incorporated the experience of other Latino groups. On the eve of the 21st century, for both intellectual and pragmatic reasons, many departments examined Puerto Ricans under the Latino studies umbrella and some included African Americans on their instructional and research agenda.

Puerto Rican studies programs began as an experiment in critical thinking, innovative scholarship, and democracy. Advocates proposed a collaborative, oppositional, and empowering mode of knowledge production. Individualistic modes of operation and achievement in scholarly work were discouraged. New knowledge was supposed to be critical of society and of the concept of the university as an "ivory tower." Applied research was favored, especially if it helped working-class people examine and change their lives. During the 1980s this vision was seen by many as utopian, at best, and dysfunctional, at worst. And by the end of the 20th century it had all but succumbed to traditional ideas about knowledge production and publication. By then the viability of the field depended on the sympathy of administrators, the availability of resources, and robust enrollments.

The structure of Puerto Rican studies is threefold, consisting of degree-granting academic departments and programs, such as the Department of Puerto Rican and Latino Studies at Brooklyn College and the Program in Latin American and Hispanic Caribbean Studies at City College; research centers, such as the Center for Puerto Rican Studies at Hunter College and the Center for Latino, Latin American, and Caribbean Studies at the State University of New York (SUNY)-Albany; and public policy and advocacy organizations, such as the Institute for Puerto Rican Policy and the National Puerto Rican Coalition. The field also includes organizations that focus on Puerto Rican culture, such as the Segundo Ruiz Belvis Cultural Center in Chicago; two book series, at Temple University Press and at the University Press of Florida; a major Web site, Puerto Rico and the American Dream (www.prdream.com), as well as a trade group, the Puerto Rican Studies Association, founded in 1992.

Courses cover the social, economic, cultural, and political experience of Puerto Ricans and other minorities from a comparative and interdisciplinary perspective. Research focuses on the causes of the diasporic experience, with an emphasis on migration and settlement patterns, socioeconomic characteristics, and cultural and political behavior. More than the study of one ethnic group in the North American context, Puerto Rican studies promote the analysis of historical, social, economic, and political linkages between the United States, Latin America, and the Caribbean. A major challenge facing Puerto Rican studies in the 21st century is how to negotiate the preservation of their autonomy and integrity amid fiscal and intellectual pressures to subsume their field under the rubrics of race and ethnicity, Latin American, Latino, or American studies.

RELATED ARTICLES

Education, Higher; Latino Studies; Puerto Ricans on the Mainland.

FURTHER READING

Bonilla, Frank, and Emilio González, eds. "New Knowing, New Practice: Puerto Rican Studies." In *Structures of Dependency.* Stanford, Calif.: Stanford Univ. Press, 1973.

Sánchez, María E., and Antonio M. Stevens-Arroyo, eds. *Toward a Renaissance of Puerto Rican Studies: Ethnic and Area Studies in University Education.* Highland Lakes, N.J.: Atlantic Res. and Pubs., 1987.

Vázquez, Jesse M. "Embattled Scholars in the Academy, A Shared Odyssey." *Callaloo* 15, no. 4 (Fall 1992): 1039–1051.

Vázquez, Jesse M. "Puerto Rican Studies in the 1990s: Taking the Next Turn in the Road." *Centro Journal* 2, no. 6 (Summer 1989): 8–19.

JOSÉ E. CRUZ

PUERTO RICAN YOUNG LORDS

The Young Lords were a multicity organization that fought for the self-determination and civil rights of Puerto Ricans throughout the United States and Puerto Rico. Originally a Chicago street gang, the group, under the leadership of José "Cha Cha" Jiménez, would later evolve into an activist organization mounting "offensives" (actions) and establishing chapters that eventually made the Young Lords Organization a nationally recognized social movement.

Established in 1969, the Young Lords' New York chapter, known as the Young Lords Party, became the most notable chapter of the organization. Established by David Pérez, Felipe Luciano, Pablo "Yoruba" Guzmán, Denise Oliver, and others, the Young Lords Party arranged free breakfast programs, testing for tuberculosis, free clothing drives, and workshops on Puerto Rican history. Their first "offensive," which took place on July 27, 1969, involved blocking Second and Third avenues in New York City with loads of collected garbage to protest neglected sanitation in Puerto Rican communities. Later that year the Young Lords took over the First Spanish Methodist Church after church officials refused the group the use of available space. For 11 days the Young Lords occupied the church, renaming it "The People's Church," providing day care and free breakfast for the community.

The Young Lords Party also organized several offensives at Lincoln Hospital, located in New York City's South Bronx, to bring attention to the high rates of tuberculosis and lead poisoning within the Puerto Rican community. The occupation of the hospital resulted in the establishment of a drug rehabilitation program as well as the construction of a new Lincoln Hospital. In addition, the Young Lords are recognized for their efforts to persuade the New York City board of education to include Puerto Rican and Latino and Latina history courses in their public school curricula.

AP/WIDE WORLD PHOTOS

A member of the Puerto Rican Young Lords stands guard near the casket of a comrade, who was found hanged in his cell in the Tombs prison in New York City, 1970.

In 1972, however, as a result of both government infiltration and internal problems, The Young Lords Organization collapsed. Although the organization ceased to exist, the principles it stood for remained strong among its constituency. In a 1977 offensive five years after the organization's demise, former members of the Young Lords Party took over the Statue of Liberty, hanging the Puerto Rican flag over its crown as a declaration of independence for the island of Puerto Rico.

The Young Lords had a tremendous impact on the conditions of Puerto Rican and Latino communities throughout the United States. During its peak, roughly between 1969 and 1972, the Young Lords developed branches in Philadelphia, Newark, Boston, Connecticut, New York, Chicago, and Puerto Rico. The organization published and distributed a community-based newspaper called *Pa'lante* (Forward), and produced a weekly radio show of the same name. As members of the Rainbow Coalition, the Young Lords addressed issues concerning Latino and Latina rights, the working poor, police brutality, and Eurocentric education, offering a sense of pride and belonging to Puerto Ricans as cultural citizens of the United States. The political goals of the Young Lords Organization have been memorialized in their 13-point program. Among their objectives were the liberation of Puerto Rico from U.S. colonial rule and the self-determination for all Latinos and Latinas, issues that continue to affect the Puerto Rican community in the 21st century.

RELATED ARTICLES

Activism; Civil Rights; New York City; Politics, Puerto Rican.

FURTHER READING

Abramson, Michael. *Pa'lante: Young Lords Party.* New York: McGraw-Hill, 1971.
Oboler, Suzanne. *Ethnic Labels, Latino Lives: Identity and the Politics of (Re)Presentation in the United States.* Minneapolis: Univ. of Minn. Press, 1995.
Torres, Andres, and José E. Velázquez. *The Puerto Rican Movement: Voices from the Diaspora.* Philadelphia, Penn.: Temple Univ. Press, 1998.

BRIAN MONTES

PUERTO RICO

The history of Puerto Rico is plagued by conquest and colonization. When Christopher Columbus reached its shores during his second trip in 1493, he immediately took possession of the island for the Spanish crown and named it San Juan Bautista, after Prince Juan, heir to the Spanish throne. Yet initially the Spanish did not make great efforts to occupy the island. This changed in 1508, when Ponce de León came to the island from the neighboring Hispaniola (later Dominican Republic). The Tainos resisted at first and staged rebellions, but could not ultimately match the Spanish weapons. By 1565, the recorded date of the last Taino rebellion, the native population was decimated, close to extinction.

Puerto Rico remained a Spanish colony until 1898 and the Spanish-American War. Prior to this time some Puerto Ricans had shown their displeasure about the colonial status of the island. This unhappiness culminated in "El Grito de Lares," an insurrection of 600 to 1,000 men led by Ramón Emeterio Betances on September 23, 1868. The Spanish government soon quashed the rebellion, during which eight of the insurgents died. Ironically, the relationship between the Spanish government and Puerto Rico improved after this tragedy, with the Spanish government showing a clear willingness to loosen its hold on Puerto Rico. For example, three decades later, under laws and decrees highlighted by the Autonomic Charter of 1897, Puerto Rico had its own parliament, with an elective House of Representatives and a Council of Administration, with a majority of its membership also elected to office.

This progress ended soon after December 10, 1898, and the conclusion of the war (the treaty was ratified by the U.S. Senate on February 6, 1899; signed by the queen regent of Spain, María Cristina, on March 19; and proclaimed on April 11, 1899). Under Article III of the Treaty of Paris, Spain ceded to the United States "the island of Puerto Rico and the other islands now under Spanish sovereignty in the West Indies, and the island of Guam in the Marianas or Ladrones." (Spain also ceded the Philippines, under Article III of the Treaty). The United States had a very different vision for the island.

Beyond the Foraker Act

Soon after the United States took control of the island, it instituted a military government. This was followed by the Foraker Act, signed into law by President McKinley on April 12, 1900. Under the Act, the President of the United States would appoint a governor for the island, with the advice and consent of the U.S. Senate. The governor would

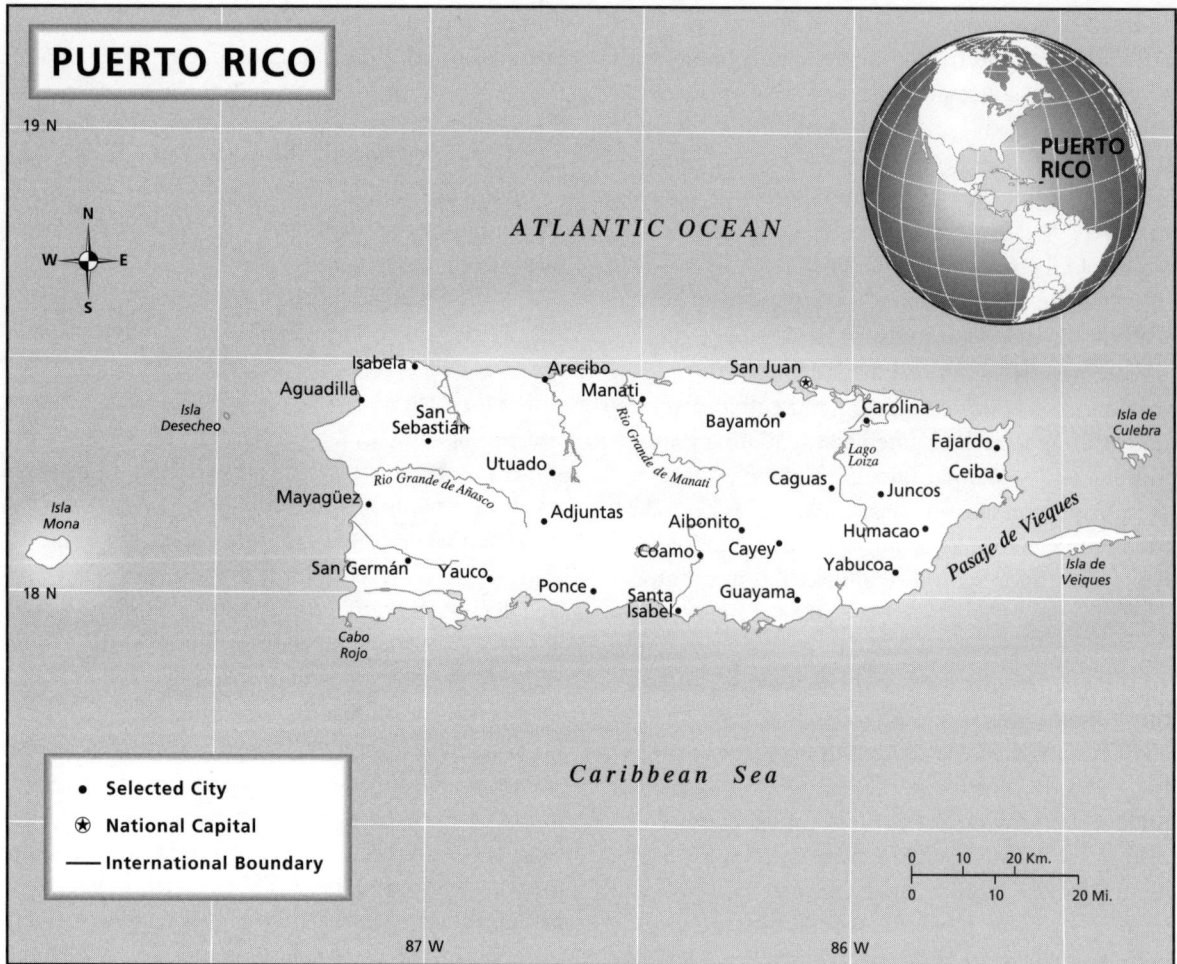

PUERTO RICO

19 N

ATLANTIC OCEAN

N
W E
S

Isla
Desecheo

Isla
Mona

18 N

Cabo
Rojo

Isabela
Aguadilla
San
Sebastián
Mayagüez
Utuado
Adjuntas
San Germán Yauco
Ponce
Santa
Isabel

Arecibo
Manati
Río Grande de Añasco
Río Grande de Manati
Coamo
Cayey
Guayama

San Juan
Bayamón
Carolina
Lago
Loiza
Caguas
Aibonito
Humacao
Yabucoa

Fajardo
Ceiba
Juncos

Pasaje de Vieques

Isla de
Culebra

Isla de
Veiques

Caribbean Sea

• Selected City
✪ National Capital
— International Boundary

0   10   20 Km.
0   10   20 Mi.

87 W   86 W

serve for a term of four years, although the president could remove the governor at will. The Act also established two legislative chambers, the Executive Council and the Legislative Assembly. The members of the Council were appointed by the president, with the advice and consent of the Senate, while members of the Assembly were elected for two-year terms. Finally, the Act created a Supreme Court of Puerto Rico, its members appointed by the president with the advice and consent of the Senate.

The Foraker Act was also quite telling in what it did not do. For example, and in spite of the efforts of Senator Foraker, U.S. citizenship was not extended to the people of Puerto Rico. Also, Puerto Rico would not have representation in Congress. Instead, the Act created the office of commissioner resident, elected for a term of two years. Finally, it did not offer Puerto Rico full rights to self-government, since Congress held plenary powers over the island and could annul at will laws enacted by the Puerto Rican legislature.

Issues of market control and strategic positioning vis-à-vis the imperial powers of the day played a prominent policy-making role in the United States. More specifically, public opinion at the turn of the century wished for land, for property, for imperial expansion. It did not wish for the responsibilities that were necessarily inherent in these acquisitions. Rather, it wished for colonialism.

These issues translated into real and difficult constitutional questions. Namely, what was the constitutional status of the island from the time of U.S. occupation, on July 25, 1898, to the signing of the Treaty of Paris on December 10 of that same year? Second, what was the island's status between the time of the signing of the Treaty to the passage of the Foraker Act? Finally, how did the Foraker Act affect the constitutional status of the island and its inhabitants? This final question has two components. One, what are Congress's powers concerning the territories? And two, what rights must be accorded to territorial residents?

In a series of cases known collectively as the "Insular Cases," the U.S. Supreme Court answered these questions. The status of Puerto Rico under the tariff laws was that of a foreign nation, as it was "exclusively within the sovereignty of a foreign nation, and without the sovereignty of the United States." Puerto Rico ceased to be a foreign country after the Treaty of Paris. At this time, the island had become a territory of the United States, "although not an organized territory in the technical sense." In specific reference to the question at issue, a territory could not be simultaneously foreign and domestic, so tariff laws applicable to foreign countries cannot be applied to Puerto Rico.

Finally, and in the leading case of *Downes* v. *Bidwell* (1901) the Court offered conflicting answers to the question of congressional powers. Writing for himself, Justice Henry Brown argued that Congress has plenary authority over any and all acquired territories and the Constitution applies to them at the discretion of Congress. This view comes with a ready exception: the Constitution does extend to the territories, even against congressional wishes, when dealing with "those fundamental limitations in favor of personal rights which were formulated in the Constitution and its amendments." The Court never followed this position. In concurrence, Justice Edward White developed the "incorporation theory," which soon became the leading view in this area. The initial concern, he explained, was over the congressional disposition of the territory at issue. This question had a simple answer: the Constitution generally applies to incorporated territories. Yet, in the case of Puerto Rico, an unincorporated territory, only those fundamental principles "which are the basis of all free governments" would affect congressional actions. For all other matters, Congress is free to legislate at will.

The Jones Act

In 1917 Congress enacted the second Organic Act, the Jones Act. Under the Act, Puerto Rico could have an elective Senate, thus providing Puerto Ricans for the first time with a fully elected legislature. Legislation was still subject to the governor's veto, at which time the president would hold final say about the fate of the legislation. Puerto Rico also remained subject to Congress's plenary power. Of note, the Act conferred U.S. citizenship on the people of Puerto Rico by way of a process of collective naturalization, yet this was a hollow conferral. Puerto Rico still had no representation within the federal government, since the Act did not extend the right to vote in the Electoral College, nor did Puerto Rico gain any representation in Congress. This was second-class citizenship at best.

For many years the people of Puerto Rico asked for an elective governor. Their request was finally granted in 1947, with the Elective Governor Act. In the subsequent election of 1948, Luis Muñoz Marín became the first governor elected by the people of Puerto Rico.

Two years later, on July 3, 1950, President Harry Truman signed Public Law 600. The first section of the law provided that "[f]ully recognizing the principle of government by consent, this Act is now adopted in the nature of a compact so that the people of Puerto Rico may organize a government pursuant to a constitution of their own adoption." The second section required submission of the Act to a referendum, conducted on June 4, 1951, and approved by 76.5 percent of the vote. A constitutional convention was then convened, with its work submitted to the people of Puerto Rico for approval. The proposed Constitution received 80 percent of the vote. Congress then offered its stamp of approval as well, subject to some modifications. Finally, on July 25, 1952, the new Constitution established the Commonwealth of Puerto Rico (or Estado Libre Asociado de Puerto Rico).

Public Law 600 refers to the language of "compact." Similarly, Article I of the Constitution of Puerto Rico states that the political power of the Commonwealth of Puerto Rico "shall be exercised . . . within the terms of the compact agreed upon between the people of Puerto Rico and the United States of America." These words have led some scholars and commentators to view the relationship between the United States and Puerto Rico as a compact based on mutual consent. Of note, the United States Supreme Court has accepted this view. Yet this position also finds many detractors. Some respected critics contend that Puerto Rico has been a colony since 1898, a fact that remained unaltered by the adoption of the 1952 Constitution. According to federal judge José Cabranes, the status of

Puerto Rico must be described as "colonialism with the consent of the governed." On this account the fact that Congress retains plenary power over the island and its affairs is determinative, even if Congress has never acted to annul a law passed by the legislature of Puerto Rico.

Calls for Change

The status of Puerto Rico under U.S. rule has been the subject of heated discussion and disagreement, a controversy that continues to this day. The issues are clear yet complex. The leading parties in Puerto Rico reflect this complexity. One party, the Partido Nuevo Progresista (New Progressive Party), established in 1968 by Luis A. Ferré, advocates statehood for the island. The Partido Popular Democratico (Popular Democratic Party), founded in 1938 by Muñoz Marín, advocates commonwealth status. The Partido Independentista Puertorriqueño (Puerto Rican Independence Party), founded in 1946 by Gilberto Concepción de Gracia, advocates independence from the United States. All three parties continue to work toward their professed goals.

One aspect of the parties' work is reflected in the various plebiscites held through the years about the status of the island. The first such plebiscite was held on July 23, 1967. Sixty percent of the votes sided with continuing the commonwealth status, while only 39 percent sided with the statehood option. One percent voted for independent status. These results are exemplary of other plebiscites, even if the numbers are different. In 1993 a plebiscite resulted in 48 percent of the vote for the status quo, commonwealth status; 46 percent sided with the statehood option; and 4 percent sided with independence.

Another plebiscite in 1998 reached similar results. The voting public was offered five choices this time: "Territorial" commonwealth; free association; statehood; independence; or "None of the above." The Commonwealth Party campaigned for the "None of the Above" option in protest, because it disagreed with the wording of the various options, which it deemed unfairly worded to benefit the statehood option. In the end the statehood option received 46.5 percent of the vote, while the independence option received 2.5 percent. "None of the Above" received 50.3 percent of the vote.

Other groups have also tried to influence the debate over the status of the island, although their means have been far more violent. In 1950 a Puerto Rican nationalist, Oscar Collazo, failed in his attempt to assassinate President Truman. On March 1, 1954, four Puerto Rican nationalists, Lolita Lebron, Rafael Cancel Miranda, Andrés Figueroa Cordero, and Irving Flores Rodríguez walked into the U.S. House of Representatives and opened fire, injuring five congressmen. They were arrested and sentenced to 50 years in prison. President Jimmy Carter granted them executive clemency in 1979.

The Fuerzas Armadas de Liberación Nacional (FALN; or Armed Forces of National Liberation) and the Macheteros have also carried out terrorist acts in the name of Puerto Rican independence. On January 24, 1975, FALN claimed responsibility for setting off a bomb in Fraunces Tavern in New York City that killed four people and injured more than 50. Various other bombings have been attributed to the group. The Macheteros are responsible for the 1983 robbery of a Wells Fargo facility in West Hartford, Connecticut, as well hundreds of other attacks. On August 8, 1999, President Bill Clinton offered clemency to 16 Puerto Rican nationalists. A month later, on September 11, members of FALN accepted the president's offer and were released from federal prison.

Migration

While the debate over the status of Puerto Rico continued, Puerto Rican citizens began to migrate to the United States. Travel from the island was slow at first, beginning with negligible levels of migration during the late 19th century. College students from affluent families and political exiles plotting against the Spanish government were among the few who came to the United States during this time. The annexation of Puerto Rico by the United States changed the migratory flow. The period from 1900 to 1940 witnessed a slow yet growing migration from Puerto Rico to the United States. By 1910 the Puerto Rican population in the United States was 1,513. This figure rose to almost 12,000 by 1920, and surpassed 50,000 by the 1930s. By 1940 almost 70,000 Puerto Ricans lived in the United States.

The causes of this migratory flow are many. For one, the grant of U.S. citizenship to the people of Puerto Rico in 1917 allowed for easier entry into the United States, unaffected by the regulatory scheme established under the immigration laws. Economic hardship on the island and the hope of a better life abroad were contributing factors. These factors played a key role during the 1930s, a period of reverse migration back to the island, owing largely to the economic hardship borne by the Great Depression.

The migratory flow from the island increased exponentially in the post–World War II period. The mass migration was fueled by the loss of agricultural jobs to the industrial sector on the island, and the concomitant availability of low-wage jobs in the United States, and particularly New York City. The low rates for air travel also helped fuel the migration. The numbers tell a clear story. By 1950 the number of Puerto Ricans in the United States reached 300,000. This figure grew to 850,000 by 1960, and to 1.4 million in 1970. According to the 2000 Census, close to 3.5 million persons of Puerto Rican origin now live on the United States mainland.

In the early stages of the migration, a vast majority of those who came to the United States settled in New York City, increasingly being described under the rubric of "Nuyoricans." The figures grew steadily through the decades, to a high of 896,763 after the 1990 Census. The number of Puerto Ricans living in New York City decreased after the 2000 Census, to just under 800,000. This decline was the result of many factors, including return migration by older, retired persons, movement to the suburbs, and the rise of alternate locations. Among these, Florida, and particularly the city of Orlando, have witnessed a boom in their Puerto Rican population. Other cities where Puerto Ricans have settled include Chicago, Illinois; New Haven and Hartford, Connecticut; Boston, Massachusetts; Jersey City, New Jersey; and Philadelphia, Pennsylvania.

An important effect of the Puerto Rican migration to the U.S. mainland is seen in the many contributions made by the people of Puerto Rico, as well as persons of Puerto Rican descent, in U.S. culture and society. These contributions are seen and felt across a number of different sectors of society. In sports, the best example of this contribution is seen in Major League Baseball. The first Puerto Rican to play in the major leagues was Hiram Bithorn, for the Chicago Cubs, in 1942. Many others followed in his footsteps. The leading figure is that of Roberto Clemente, a right fielder for the Pittsburgh Pirates who died tragically in an airplane crash on December 31, 1972, while attempting to deliver goods to the people of Nicaragua in the aftermath of a devastating earthquake. The following year, the Baseball Writer's Association of America waived its five-year

rule and immediately inducted Clemente into the National Baseball Hall of Fame on August 8, 1973; he was the first Latino inducted into the Hall. During the ceremony baseball commissioner Bowie Kuhn established the Roberto Clemente Award in his honor, which is given every year to the baseball player who best exemplifies the values of sportsmanship and community activism.

Many other Puerto Ricans have left a mark in baseball. In 1993 Orlando Cepeda became the second player from Puerto Rico elected into the Hall of Fame. Five Puerto Ricans, Iván (Pudge) Rodríguez, Roberto Alomar, Benito Santiago, Sandy Alomar, and Bernie Williams, have won Gold Gloves. Five Puerto Ricans have also won the Most Valuable Player Award: Roberto Clemente in 1966; Orlando Cepeda in 1967; Guillermo Hernández in 1984; Juan González, both in 1996 and 1998; and Pudge Rodríguez in 1999.

Puerto Ricans have also distinguished themselves in various other professional sports. In professional golf, for example, the charismatic Chi-Chi Rodríguez won 8 Professional Golf Association (PGA) tournaments and 22 Senior PGA tour tournaments during his career. In tennis, Gigi Fernández won 14 Grand Slam doubles titles, as well as 2 Olympic Tennis Gold Medals, at Atlanta and Barcelona. And in boxing, Wilfredo Benítez became the youngest boxer in the history of the sport to win a world title, accomplishing this feat at the age of 17. He was inducted into the Boxing Hall of Fame at 37, becoming in the process the youngest boxer inducted in the history of the Hall. The list of boxers to win world titles is long, and it includes Félix Trinidad, John Ruíz, Sixto Escobar, Wilfredo Gómez, Edwin "Chapo" Rosario, José "Chegüii" Torres, Carlos Ortíz, Macho Camacho, Wilfredo Vázquez, John John Molina, and Esteban de Jesús.

Puerto Ricans have also left an indelible mark on the arts. The Puerto Rican actress Rita Moreno won an Oscar in 1962 for Best Supporting Actress for her work in the film version of the musical *West Side Story* (which had starred Chita Rivera on Broadway), the first Latina actress to win an Academy Award. She was also the first actress to win an Oscar, an Emmy, a Grammy, and a Tony throughout her career. Other Puerto Rican actors and actresses include José Ferrer, Benicio del Toro, Raúl Julia, Jimmy Smits, Jennifer Lopez, and Miriam Colón.

The music industry has also seen its share of Puerto Rican success. A list of notable performers must include Grammy winners Tito Puente, José Feliciano, Ricky Martin, Olga Tañón, and Marc Anthony, as well as the opera baritones Carlos Conde, Justino Díaz, Pablo Elvira, and Jorge Ocasio.

The idiosyncratic, hybrid parlance of Puerto Ricans in New York City, a mixing of English and Spanish that depends on code-switching, the coining of new terms, and simultaneous translation, is known as Nuyorican. There are novels, collections of poetry, theater, and a solid number of musical genres that have used it to express the plight of its users. Nuyorican has been studied by sociolinguists. Its syntactical rules share much with Dominicanish, Cubonics, and Chicano Spanglish, but also have unique qualities. Among the important works in which Nuyorican is found are Tato Laviera's *AmeRícan,* Giannina Braschi's *Yo-Yo Boing,* and those of Miguel Piñero, Pedro Pietri, and Victor Hernández Cruz.

The people of Puerto Rico have also had their share of influence on American politics. Three have served as members of the United States Congress: Luis Gutiérrez, Representative from Chicago; José Serrano, Representative from the Bronx, New York; and Nydia Velázquez, Representative from Brooklyn, New York. Many other Puerto Ricans have also been elected to state and local offices.

Within the executive branch, Antonia Novello was the first woman and the first Latina to serve as Surgeon General of the United States. Similarly, Aída Alvarez was the first Latina member of a president's Cabinet when she was appointed as administrator of the Small Business Administration in 1997.

Political Status

On April 19, 1999, a security guard working on the Puerto Rican island of Vieques, David Sanes Rodríguez, was killed by a stray bomb released by one of two U.S. Navy jets flying off course while conducting war games in the Vieques passage. The incident led to many protests and arrests, and shone the bright lights of the world's public opinion on the relationship between the United States and Puerto Rico. The U.S. Navy had controlled large parts of Vieques for military practice for many decades. After the death of Sanes Rodríguez, public opinion on the island galvanized against the navy and its presence there. Yet short of showing its displeasure through polling and acts of civil disobedience, Puerto Rico

could do very little else. As a commonwealth, the island is represented in Congress by a nonvoting commissioner resident. The island does not have a vote in the Senate, nor does it have the right to choose electors for the Electoral College. Its representation in the national legislature is minimal.

Ultimately, presidents Clinton and George W. Bush agreed to pull the navy out of Vieques, which finally occurred on May 1, 2003. The reasons for this acquiescence to the will of the people of Puerto Rico are interesting and worthy of further study. More important, however, is the fact that Puerto Ricans could not show their displeasure at the polls, but instead had to rely on indirect pressure from Latinos in the United States. It also emphasized Puerto Rico's dependent status on the United States. The debate over the status of the island vis-à-vis the United States focuses on retaining the current political situation, becoming a state, or breaking all ties and becoming an independent nation. Most scholars believe, however, that in order for the relationship between the United States and Puerto Rico to develop and its people to have full political participation in their own governance, the island's status as either a U.S. state or independent country will have to be decided.

RELATED ARTICLES

Art, Puerto Rican on the Mainland; Baseball; Cuisine, Puerto Rican; Immigration, Latino; Jones Act; Literature, Puerto Rican on the Mainland; Politics, Puerto Rican; Puerto Ricans on the Mainland; Puerto Rican Studies; Vieques; Supreme Court, United States.

FURTHER READING

Aleinikoff, T. Alexander. "Puerto Rico and the Constitution: Conundrums and Prospects." *Constitutional Commentary* 11 (1994): 15.

Burnett, Christina Duffy, and Burke Marshall, eds. *Foreign in a Domestic Sense: Puerto Rico, American Expansion, and the Constitution.* Durham, N.C.: Duke Univ. Press, 2001.

Cabranes, José A. *Citizenship and the American Empire.* New Haven, Conn.: Yale Univ. Press, 1979.

Cabranes, José A. "Puerto Rico and the Constitution." *Federal Rules Decisions* 110 (1986): 475.

Malavet, Pedro A. "Puerto Rico: Cultural Nation, American Colony." *Michigan Journal of Race and Law* 6 (2000): 1.

Montalvo-Barbot, Alfredo. *Political Conflict and Constitutional Change in Puerto Rico 1989–1952.* Lanham, Md.: Univ. Press of America, 1997.

Ramos, Efren Rivera. "The Legal Construction of American Colonialism: The Insular Cases (1901–1922)." *Revista Jurídica de la Universidad de Puerto Rico* 65 (1996): 225.

Torruella, Juan. *Puerto Rico and the Constitution: The Doctrine of Separate and Unequal.* Río Piedras: Univ. of Puerto Rico Press, 1985.

Trías Monge, José. "Plenary Power and the Principle of Liberty: An Alternative View of the Political Condition of Puerto Rico." *Revista Jurídica de la Universidad de Puerto Rico* 68 (1999): 1.

Trías Monge, José. *Puerto Rico: The Trials of the Oldest Colony in the World.* New Haven, Conn.: Yale Univ. Press, 1997.

LUIS FUENTES-ROHWER

Q

QUETZALCÓATL

A complex, ancient Mesoamerican deity, Quetzalcóatl, known by many names and guises, is probably the most widely recognized god of any ancient American pantheon. Quetzalcóatl is a Nahuatl name usually translated as plumed or feathered serpent, but the deity is also known by or associated with the names Nine Wind; Ehécatl or Wind; Yohualli Ehécatl or Night and Wind; Cuculcan, Cocolcan, Kukulcan, or Gucumatz—all Maya names meaning plumed or bird serpent; and Nácxit or Four Feet. While he may have been honored as early as 300 B.C. at the round temple of Cuicuilco, the iconography of the Plumed Serpent emerges powerfully in the murals at the Temple of the Feathered Serpent in Teotihuacan (100–200 A.D.), perhaps as a sign of the cosmic power and legitimacy of the city's ruler-priest. In the Postclassic period (900 A.D.) he became strongly associated with the planet Venus, particularly in its morning star phase, and with warfare. This iconography, especially the spiral Venus-sign known as *ehecacozcatl* (wind necklace, from the cross section of the conch shell), is evident in the splendid murals of Cacaxtla and at Chichen Itzá. As Nine Wind, a god born of a flint knife, he was revered especially by the Mixtecs. As Ehecatl, or Wind, he wore a distinct conical hat and large buccal (trumpetlike mask) and was honored by the Huastecs of the Gulf Coast. By the time of the Aztec Empire, all of these had contributed to the god Quetzalcóatl, whose round temple stood directly in front of the great temple of Huitzilopochtli-Tlaloc at the ritual center of Tenochtitlan's Templo Mayor. When the Spanish arrived, his greatest temple was at Cholollan (modern Cholula), a pilgrimage city for Quetzalcóatl's worshippers, where the great pyramid is still the largest by volume in the world.

By one account he was the third son of the first divine pair, Lord and Lady of Our Sustenance, and one of the original creator gods who, with Huitzilopochtli, created other gods, the oceans, the earth itself from a great reptile, and the first man and woman. Quetzalcóatl and Tezcatlipoca became successive suns. After a great deluge brought down the heavens and destroyed the earth, they raised the sky again, created new men, and became lords of the stars and the Milky Way, "where they were found and still are."

This god is often confused with the semidivine culture hero and priest-king of the legendary Toltecs, Ce Acatl Topiltzin Quetzalcóatl (Our Beloved Lord One Reed Quetzalcóatl), whose paradigmatic and tragic life is told by the informants of Sahagún, by Fray Diego Durán, and most powerfully and poetically in the anonymous *Annals of Cuauhtitlan*. His historical reality was believed by the Aztecs and remains in dispute to this day; Fray Durán suggested he may have been the apostle Thomas, an idea that resurfaced powerfully in the late 18th century. Ce Acatl was a devoted and pious ruler in his glorious city, Tollan, where cotton grew in many colors; where he taught the people artistry in featherwork, earthenware, precious metals, and stones; and where human sacrifice was refused. He was betrayed and disgraced by a trio of sorcerers led by Tezcatlipoca in the guise of a farmer who brought a mirror to show Ce Acatl his body, which he had never seen. Horrified by the sight, Ce Acatl isolated himself in his palace until another sorcerer brought him pulque, an alcoholic drink that he had never touched before, to relieve his depression. After becoming drunk he called for his pious sister, Quetzalpetlatl, and they may have committed incest. Another account describes many deadly deceits by which the sorcerers killed and oppressed the Toltecs. Utterly disgraced, Ce Acatl left the city with his disciples, after burning or burying its treasures, and wandered about the land, leaving marks and footprints in many places until arriving at the seacoast where he built a pyre and immolated himself, his heart rising up as a jade or a quetzal bird to become the planet Venus. Informants of Sahagún report he built a raft of serpents and disappeared into the east. It was Ce Acatl who Moteuc-zoma reportedly thought Cortéz might be when he welcomed him "back" to his kingdom "where I have been in charge for you."

The images and stories of Quetzalcóatl have persisted, frequently associated with nativist aspirations to power or an enlightened leader embodying justice and prosperity. Quetzacóatl is second only to the Virgin of Guadalupe as an indigenous figure in Mexican ideology and popular consciousness. The anonymous author of the *Annals of Cuauhtitlán* puts him forward as a pre-Christian model of American spirituality. The Dominican friar Servando Teresa de Mier, born in Nuevo León, was imprisoned and exiled in the late 18th century by Spanish authorities for his vigorous preaching that Quetzalcóatl was the apostle Thomas who brought Christianity to the Americas long before the Spanish and their apostle James; New Spain, said Mier, therefore had claim to a Christian autonomy and political independence from Spain.

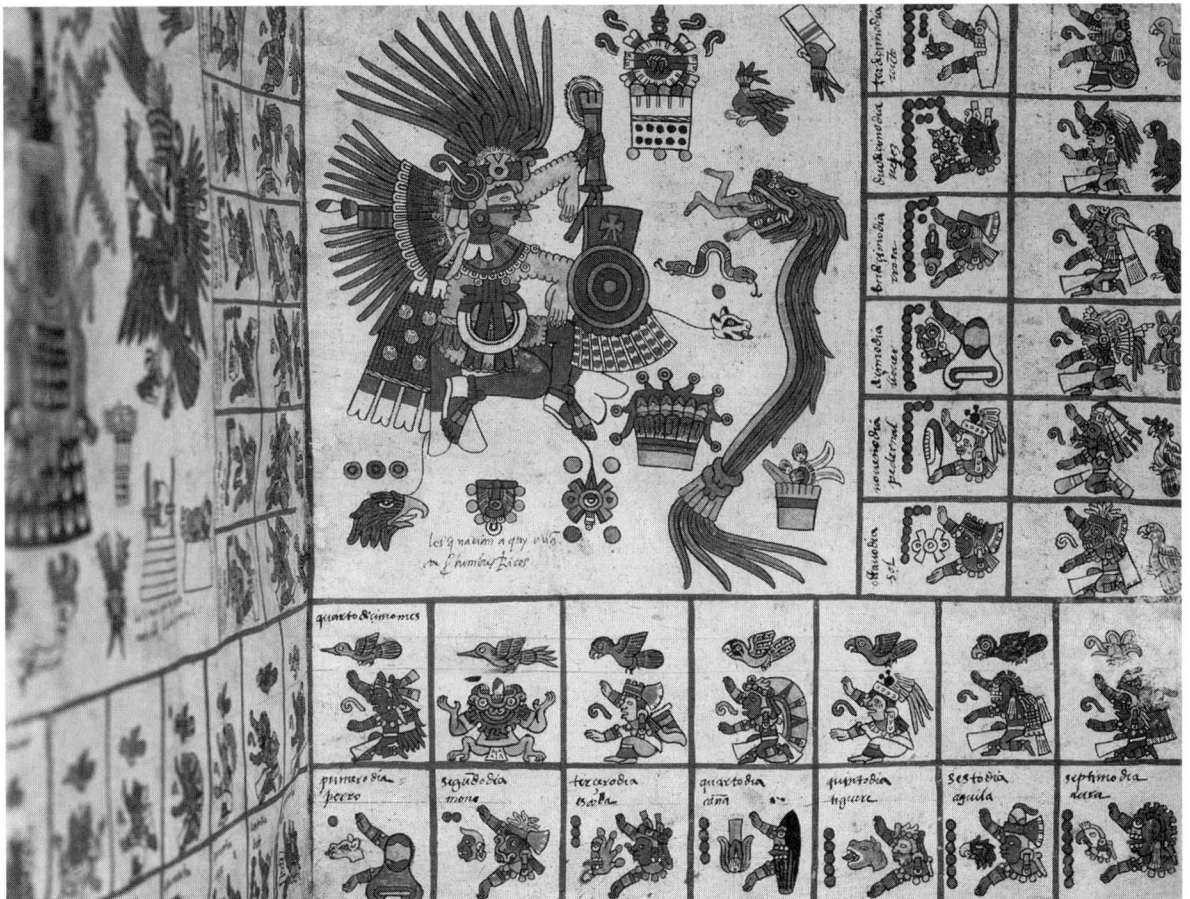

Detail of the Aztec *Codex Borbonicus* "Tonalamatl," depicting Quetzalcóatl and Tezcatlipoca.

In Chicano and Chicana culture and iconography, images of the plumed serpent abound. The first mural collectively painted in 1973 by the Congreso de Artistas Chicanos en Aztlán in San Diego's Chicano Park, after the park had been forcibly claimed by the residents of Barrio Logan, is called Quetzalcóatl and features a large, plumed serpent. Other murals in the park refer to the story of Quetzalcóatl's descent into Mictlan to retrieve the bones from which mankind was created. The plumed serpent icon appears in numerous other murals, among them the enormous *Wall that Talks* in Highland Park, Texas, and the famous Orozco murals at Dartmouth College, *The Epic of American Civilization,* which feature several portraits of a fierce and bearded Quetzalcóatl, including one on a raft of serpents pointing east toward the coming Europeans. Rudolfo Anaya has published a retelling of the Quetzalcóatl myths in *Lord of the Dawn*; Luís Valdez, founder of Teatro Campesino, has referred to César Chávez as a reincarnation of Quetzalcóatl; and D. H. Lawrence, in his 1926 novel set in Mexico, *The Plumed Serpent,* described an uprising centered on a revival of the cult of Quetzalcóatl. An order of Masons called the Order of Quetzalcóatl, with numerous "Teocallis" throughout North America, claims to be the "only Order of American origin."

RELATED ARTICLES

Huitzilopochtli; Mesoamerica; Nahuas; Religion.

FURTHER READING

Anaya, Rudolfo. *Lord of the Dawn: The Legend of Quetzalcóatl.* Albuquerque: Univ. of N.Mex. Press, 1987.

Anonymous. *History and Mythology of the Aztecs: The Codex Chimalpopoca.* Tr. by John Bierhorst. Tucson: Univ. of Ariz. Press, 1992.

Durán, Diego. *Book of the Gods and Rites and The Ancient Calendar.* Tr. and ed. by Fernando Horcasitas and Doris Heyden. Norman: Univ. of Okla. Press, 1971.

Florescano, Enrique. *El mito de Quetzalcóatl. (The Myth of Quetzalcóatl).* 2d ed. Mexico City: Fondo de Cultura Económica, 1995.

Gingerich, Willard. "Quetzalcóatl and the Agon of Time: A Literary Reading of the *Anales de Cuauhtitlan.*" *New Scholar* 10 (1986): 41–60.

Lafaye, Jacques. *Quetzalcóatl and Guadalupe: The Formation of Mexican National Consciousness, 1531–1813.* Tr. by B. Keen. Chicago: Univ. of Chicago Press, 1976.

Nicholson, Henry B. *Topiltzin Quetzalcóatl: The Once and Future Lord of the Toltecs.* Boulder: Univ. Press of Colo., 2001.

Sahagún, Bernardino de, ed. *Florentine Codex: General History of the Things of New Spain.* 12 vols. Tr. and ed. by Arthur J. O. Anderson and Charles E. Dibble. Salt Lake City: Univ. of Utah Press, 1950–1982.

WILLARD GINGERICH

QUINCEAÑERA

Quinceañera is the celebration of the 15th birthday of a Latino girl; the word can also refer to the young woman having the birthday. The celebration is unique; a rite of passage from childhood to adulthood performed by girls of Latino background, it signifies the reaffirmation of the girl's baptismal and confirmation vows, an affirmation of the importance of Christian faith in her life, and the celebration of her entrance into womanhood. For many Latino communities in the United States it is also a cultural symbol, a festivity of heritage rooted in the history of Hispanic and indigenous ancestors. The origins of the rite itself remain obscure. Some scholars suggest they can be traced back to the time of the Aztecs, the Toltecs, the Quechua, and the Mayas; while others claim an origin in Jewish tradition. The elaborate style of the celebration, with its waltz music, has been viewed as a legacy from the Austrian emperor Maximilian and his wife, empress Carlota, who introduced an opulent style for celebrations into Mexico.

The commemoration of *quinceañeras* has been an important tradition in Mexico, Cuba, Puerto Rico, and many Latin American countries where, despite some variations in the rite's form and scope, the essential elements have been preserved. Traditionally a *quinceañera* has both religious and a secular components. Although the ritual was not originally a Catholic tradition and is not a sacrament, the celebration usually begins with a Roman Catholic Mass of thanksgiving, *misa de acción de gracias,* and is followed by a fiesta consisting of dinner and dance. In the Mass, during the liturgy, the parents thank God for giving them their daughter, and the girl and her parents thank God for allowing the young woman to reach the age of 15. The girl thanks her parents for their love and guidance throughout her childhood and during her transition into a mature young adult. *Quinceañeras* are expected to prove their newly acquired maturity and motivation by meditation about their responsibilities and roles as adults as well as active service as committed members of their families, their communities, the church, and society.

Although generally accepted, *quinceañeras* have critics among church officials, educators, and feminists. The Catholic Church has viewed the event as a popular rite of passage as well as offering an opportunity to bring together life and faith and, thus, as a chance to evangelize and to bring the young women, their families, and the community closer to the sacramental and liturgical aspects of the Catholic faith. In their desire to institutionalize the rite, however, church officials dispute whether the religious service should be performed at all since they argue that the spiritual essence and solemnity of the celebration has been lost in the commercialization and excitement of an often sumptuous fiesta. Some churches discourage the exaggerated expense of fiestas, which are sometimes a means to show off wealth and status, arguing that the money could be better spent on the young woman's education or other practical needs she might have. Other officials and some educators disapprove of a rite that, owing to the *quinceañera* dress's resemblance to a wedding dress, tends to look like a wedding without a male partner. They view it as a ceremony that seems to stress the young woman's sexual maturity, encouraging sexual activity at a time when many adolescents face unwanted pregnancies. For these reasons not all Catholic priests agree to celebrate a liturgy for the event, and some dioceses have issued guidelines that may include a compulsory period of religious instruction for the girl with her mother or the whole family as preparation for the rite; sometimes community work has been incorporated.

Some feminist critics have viewed this intervention of the church as an attempt to control the sexual education of the girl and to inculcate and reinforce Catholic views on womanhood, family, dignity, purity, sacrifice, and service to the family. Chicano feminist scholars have suggested that *quinceañeras,* rather than being a Latino cultural tradition, are part of nostalgic discursive practices that reinforce gender roles and culture. They feel that the celebration plays an important role in the construction of the young woman's identity as a female and as a *mexicana.* From a feminist perspective, a traditional celebration in which the church and the community place high expectations on the young woman has become a way of keeping tradition and culture alive to the detriment of the girl's potential, since the rite prescribes the choices in her life and discourages her self-determination.

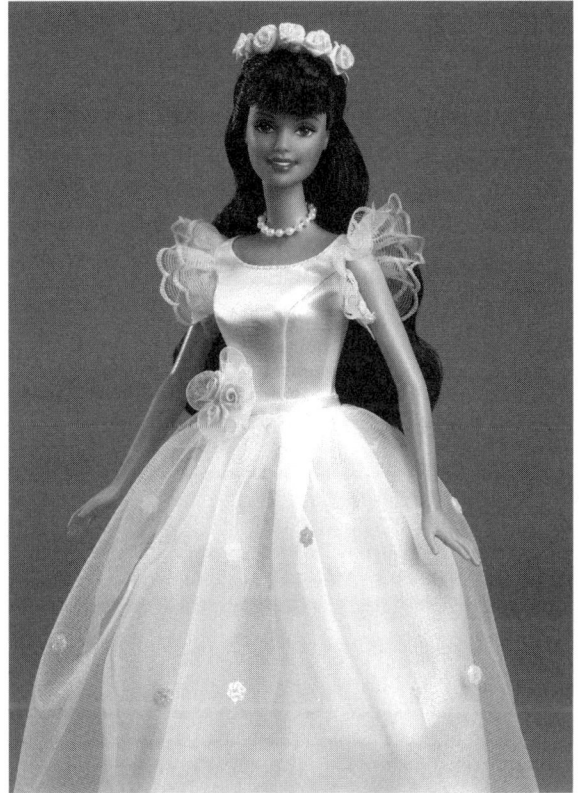

MATTEL, INC.

Mattel's Quinceañera Barbie.

In a *quinceañera,* the preparation is as important as the fiesta itself. The complexity of the event is dictated by the financial standing of the girl's parents, and its organization may take many months and sometimes more than a year. Although the event is organized to celebrate a girl's 15th birthday, the celebration is sometimes held weeks or months after the actual birthday to allow out-of-town friends and relatives to join the fiesta, strengthening the bond among family members and the community. Because the number of guests invited to the celebration can number in the hundreds, the costs of a *quinceañera* can be very high, sometimes reaching five figures. For this reason, its organization often becomes a community effort where extended family members, relatives, and close friends offer themselves as sponsors to share the expense of the celebration and to assist in the planning. The joining of forces in the community signifies its promise to support the young woman and to welcome her as a new adult.

A *quinceañera,* to a certain extent, can be considered the Latino version of the American "Sweet Sixteen." Although in the United States many Latinos and Catholic officials view the *quinceañera* as a means to signify self-affirmation and defense of their cultural traditions and ethnic identity in the face of discrimination, the American celebration has been having an effect on the Latino rite, and many Latinas are postponing their *quinceañera* for a year and calling it "Sweet Sixteen" instead.

RELATED ARTICLES

Childhood and Adolescence; Feminism; Holidays; Religion.

FURTHER READING

Cantú, Norma Elia, ed. "Chicana Life-Cycle Rituals." In *Chicana Traditions. Continuity and Change.* Ed. by Norma E. Cantú and Olga Nájera-Ramírez. Urbana: Univ. of Ill. Press, 2002.

Chávez, Thomas, Jr. *Quinceañera: A Liturgy in the Reformed Tradition.* San Angelo, Tex.: Presbytery of Tres Rios, 1983.

Davalos, Karen Mary. "*La Quinceañera:* Making Gender and Ethnic Identities." In *Perspectives on Las Américas. A Reader in Culture, History, and Representation.* Ed. by Matthew C. Gutmann, et al. Malden, Mass.: Maxwell Pub., 2003.

Erevia, Angela. *Quince Años: Celebrating a Tradition.* San Antonio, Tex.: Missionary Catechists of Divine Providence, St. Andrew's Convent, 1985.

Hoyt-Goldsmith, Diane. *Celebrating a Quinceañera. A Latina's 15th Birthday Celebration.* New York: Holiday House, 2002.

LUZ ANGÉLICA KIRSCHNER

QUINN, ANTHONY

Born: April 21, 1915; Chihuahua, Mexico
Died: June 3, 2001; Boston, Massachusetts

Actor Anthony Quinn was born to an Irish father and a Mexican mother. When he was nine years old, he took up painting and continued it throughout his life, although he did not show his work in public for many years. As a young man with little formal education, he took up boxing, but decided early on that he would never be good enough to turn professional. He turned to acting.

Before he could become an actor, Quinn had to deal with a speech impediment. He was literally "tongue-tied," a mild birth defect that gave his speech a strangled sound. Although he managed to have the operation that corrected the problem, his stage career never took off. Nonetheless, he set off for Hollywood, determined to be an actor.

By dint of tenacity and belief in himself, Quinn found small roles in B pictures. His ethnic appearance along with a somewhat rough mien enabled him to play Mexicans, Native Americans, and any variety of villain. Despite Quinn's marriage to Katherine DeMille, the adopted daughter of Cecil B. DeMille, he found his career stalled. His father-in-law did not approve of the marriage, so he saw to it that Quinn was not given important parts. Quinn kept working, although he was mired in a series of minor parts in second-rate movies.

Quinn decided to try the stage again; at least it would get him away from his father-in-law's disapproving gaze. After several unmemorable roles, he was chosen to replace Marlon Brando in *A Streetcar Named Desire.* This was the breakthrough he needed. He received excellent reviews and went on tour with the play for three years. His marriage, however, ended during this period.

The part got Quinn noticed again in Hollywood, but he made up his mind to return only if he could get substantial roles. He was no longer interested in playing heavies, as he had in *City for Conquest* in 1940, *Blood and Sand* in 1941, and *The Oxbow Incident* in 1943, among others.

In 1951 Quinn's role in Robert Rossen's *Brave Bulls* was a step closer to the kind of parts Quinn wanted. This was followed by *Viva Zapata,* in which he played Marlon Brando's brother. *Lust For Life*

PHOTOFEST

Anthony Quinn and Marlon Brando in the film *Viva Zapata!,* 1952.

found Quinn somewhat appropriately playing the painter Paul Gaugin. Both roles brought him Academy Awards for best supporting actor. He was finally taken seriously as an actor, and his persona as a earthy, lusty man was emerging.

Partly out of curiosity, Quinn went to Italy for a few years. He was an admirer of the neorealism of Italian films. His most notable role was in Fellini's masterpiece, *La Strada,* in which he played a circus strong man.

Back in Hollywood, the 1960s brought him *Zorba the Greek, Lawrence of Arabia,* and *Requiem for a Heavyweight.* He was finally established as a star in his own right. Other prestigious films followed: *The Guns of Navarone, Behold a Pale Horse,* and *The Secret of Santa Vittoria.* Quinn continued to make theatrical films until the late 1970s and made several appearances on television. Although his career was flourishing, his private life was stormy. He married a series of volatile women, with all of whom he had children. His last two were born when Quinn was in his 80s.

Quinn had matured as a painter and sculptor, and his work was good enough to be shown in reputable galleries, attracting healthy sales and favorable reviews. Quinn continued to make movies through the 1990s, most of them forgettable. His autobiographies, *The Original Sin* (1972) and *One Man Tango* (1995), appeared and were, for the most part, well received.

RELATED ARTICLES
Film; Theater.

FURTHER READING
Marill, Alvin H. *The Films of Anthony Quinn.* New York: Lyle Stuart, 1975.

SYLVIA SHORRIS

QUIRARTE, JACINTO

Born: August 17, 1931; Jerome, Arizona

A specialist in the history and criticism of pre-Columbian, Latin American, and Hispanic American arts, Jacinto Quirarte has been an influential intellectual presence in the discussion, dissemination, and consolidation of major traditions in the Americas.

A professor emeritus in the department of art and art history at the University of Texas at San Antonio since 1999, he received his bachelor's degree in 1954

and his master's in 1958 in art history from San Francisco State University. His deep interest in the Maya led him to Mexico, where he received his doctorate in 1964 from the National Autonomous University of Mexico for a dissertation on Maya mural painting.

Quirarte has published extensively on Mexican (pre-Columbian, colonial, and modern), Chicano, and Hispanic American art. As a Chicano who experienced life as an outsider, he is interested in "otherness" and in points of cultural contact. Eschewing superlatives, he writes in a clear, concise style. *Izapan Style Art: A Study of its Form and Meaning* (1973) examined a transitional (post-Olmec, pre-Maya) site on the Pacific slope of Mexico. The stylistic analyses he made in the 1970s that linked Teotihuacan and the Maya have subsequently been confirmed by the decipherment of Maya glyphs.

Quirate's seminal work, *Mexican-American Artists,* published in 1973, was the first monograph devoted to Mexican American and Chicano art. It brought attention to a number of important artists, such as Chelo González Amézcua, Octavio Medellín, Mel

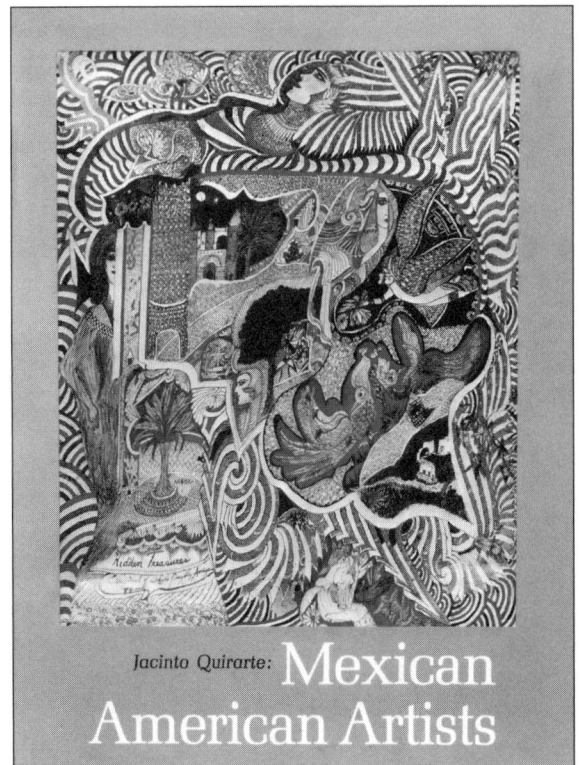

Cover of *Mexican American Artists* by Jacinto Quirarte (1973).

Casas, Luis Jiménez, and Amado Peña. This important work was followed by monographs that consolidated Quirarte's reputation. Throughout his career he has been a crucial figure in the understanding of pre-Columbian, Latin American, and Chicano art in the larger context. His views have served to contextualize the iconography of Hispanic artists and to understand their role at the larger national and international levels. He has taught at a number of institutions, including the University of Texas at Austin, Yale, and the University of California at Santa Barbara, and has also held administrative positions.

Quirarte is best known for his popular treatise *How to Look at a Masterpiece: Europe and the Americas*, reprinted numerous times. In the Hispanic field he is recognized for his contribution to *A History and Appreciation of Chicano Art*. Released in 1984 this volume offered a panoramic view of Mexican American art and its relationship with politics. It was accompanied by an edited volume, *Chicano Art History: A Book of Selected Readings*, published the same year. His next two books look southward, returning to Mesoamerican topics: *Maya Vase and Mural Painting* (1989) and *The Art and Architecture of Ancient Guatemala: A Selection of Masterpieces* (1997). In his later scholarly period, the art critic has returned to his roots. His volume *The Art and Architecture of the Texas Missions*, published in 2002, filled a scholarly lacunae. It won awards from the San Antonio Conservation Society, the Texas State Historical Association, and the Sons of the Republic of Texas.

RELATED ARTICLES

Art Criticism; Art, Mexican American and Chicano.

FURTHER READING

Quirarte, Jacinto. *Izapan Style Art: A Study of its Form and Meaning*. Washington, D.C.: Dumbarton Oaks, 1973.

Quirarte, Jacinto. *Mexican-American Artists*. Austin: Univ. of Tex. Press, 1973.

Quirarte, Jacinto. "Izapan and Mayan Traits in Teotihuacan III Pottery." *Contributions of the University of California Archaeological Research Facility*. Special Issue 18 (1973):11–29.

Quirarte, Jacinto. "Maya and Teotihuacan Traits in Classic Maya Vase Painting of the Peten." *Cultural Continuity in Mesoamerica*. Washington, D.C.: Dumbarton Oaks, 1978:289–302.

Quirarte, Jacinto. *The Art and Architecture of the Texas Missions*. Austin: Univ. of Tex. Press, 2002.

Quirarte, Jacinto. *How to Look at a Masterpiece: Europe and the Americas*. 6th ed. New York: McGraw-Hill, 2003.

RUBÉN CORDOVA

QUISQUEYA HEIGHTS. *See*

WASHINGTON HEIGHTS.

R

RACE

Although the popular understanding of the history of race relations in America has generally been marked by bipolar racial conflicts between whites and blacks, race as a political construct in the United States has been complicated by the immigration of peoples from around the world, whose varied physical and cultural characteristics often result in a politics of difference, in which difference creates hierarchy. Because the racial divide has mostly focused on white versus black, darker-skinned Latinos in the United States have confronted racial barriers consistent with similar groups whose skin color marked them for racial discrimination.

Race is especially complex among U.S. Latinos. Arguably, a common language is what most distinguishes Latinos. Within that linguistic group, or at least the heritage of that language, Latino ancestry derives from Africa—especially in the Caribbean—Mexico, the Middle East, and Asia, with physical characteristics from many of these areas present in a single person.

Adding to the difficulties regarding the diverse ancestral lines of Latinos is the problem of how to define the term *race*. Scholars have debated this concept, and the argument has centered on biological, sociological, or legal interpretations. The biological definition of race at times has posited that the genetic makeup of an individual can determine attributes such as human intelligence. Employing a biological definition of race has limitations, how-

ever—a major one being that many human biologists consider race invalid from a genetic standpoint. There are not enough genetic differences among the so-called races to justify racial groupings. Moreover, even if one allowed the validity of racial categories, the fact is that humans have interbred, resulting in different human physical types; therefore, attempting to place a group into one assigned racial category is problematic. The very idea of racial "purity" is considered unrealistic and not probable given the amount of racial mixing. Since the 1960s, there have been few if any supporters of the biological definition of the term *race*.

The sociological definition argues that race is a socially constructed concept. In other words, individuals and their racial background are largely determined by the history of race relations. In the United States, racial groups, particularly those with dark skin, have experienced historically systematic discrimination. According to sociologists Michael Omi and Howard Winant, the "social meaning of race is constantly subject to change through political struggle." In short, the definition of race should be based on a socially determined meaning, given the history of conflict and the different meanings applied to race at various periods in the United States.

The supporters of the legal definition present a different way to define race. Legal scholar Kevin R. Johnson has pointed out how racial differences have been used to legally define and restrict people of color when biological or sociological definitions were not sufficient:

Mixed race people put the proverbial final nail in the coffin of the view that race is a biological reality. The changing, fluid boundaries exemplified by racial mixture demonstrate how society constructs people differently based on physical appearance and cultural, class, religious, and other traits. For example, even if the fundamental biological makeup of siblings is virtually identical, they may be treated as of different races in certain social contexts if they do not look alike physically. Society constructs each person in different ways. Moreover, different societies may construct the same person differently. The laws surrounding mixed race people—indeed, the "one drop" rule itself—demonstrate that race is a construction, something that people make up, a figment of collective imagination. The law otherwise would be largely unnecessary to enforce racial boundaries. Nevertheless, the rigid racial classifications embedded in law often bear little resemblance to the real, fluid racial boundaries in everyday social life. As in other areas, the law finds it difficult to keep up with the changing racial constructions and modern social realities.

Historically, Latinos can trace their "racial" heritage back to Latin America. With the colonization of Latin America beginning in the 16th century, the Spaniards entered into relations with the indigenous population, as was the case when Spanish conquistadors conquered Mexico in 1621. The indigenous tribes of Mexico mixed with their lighter-skinned colonizers; throughout Latin America, indigenous women interbred with the Spanish conquerors, resulting in progeny who were labeled with a new racial category: the mestizo. Later, with the introduction of the slave trade to Latin America and the willingness of slave owners to use their slaves for sexual purposes, it was not long before there were Latinos of African descent in Mexico and other parts of Latin America. Thus the historical events of colonization and the slave trade led to the reconfiguration of racial groups in Latin America. As sociologist Martin Marger has pointed out, "Over the past centuries, [Latin America's] population has been transformed into one dominated by mestizos, a physical type combining European and Indian traits."

According to sociologists Clara Rodríguez and Héctor Cordero-Guzmán, "[In] Latin America, race may have had blood lines as a referent, but there were also other dimensions brought into racial classification," for example, class, physical type, and ethnic background. For Latinos who have recently arrived in the United States, the knowledge of how race is defined becomes quite a new experience.

Once in the United States, Latinos are subject to the struggles of each group's incorporation into the nation. From light-skinned to dark-skinned, Mexicans, Puerto Ricans, and Cubans have run the gamut regarding their "racial" differences. There is an old *dicho* (Latin American saying) regarding the rainbow of races: *Somos café con leche, unos con más café, otros con más leche* (We are coffee with milk, some with more coffee, some with more milk). There are few scholars who would argue against the significance of how Latinos' bloodlines affect their "life chances" in the United States. A person's life chances can determine such things as job opportunities, health status, educational achievement, and other related aspects of life.

Mexicans

Part of Mexican history is the relationship between Spanish conquistador Hernán Cortés and a Mexican woman of apparently high standing, La Malinche, also known as Doña Marina and as Malintzin. Besides serving as a language translator for Cortés, La Malinche bore the children produced by her relationship with the man who would overthrow the Mexican empire. According to Marger, the relationship between Cortés and La Malinche would "fix further along the social relations of indigenous natives and the invading Spaniards, producing the 'mestizo race' which is the most prominent throughout various parts of the Latin America today."

The racial mixing of Mexican Americans has been ongoing since their incorporation into the United States. Although there were small communities of Mexicans in what is now the U.S. Southwest following the end of the Mexican-American War in 1848, it had long been established that Mexicans and Anglos interbred. Racial intermarriages, however, were largely confined to upper-class Mexicans and Anglos. Sociologist Tomás Almaguer's analysis of racial divisions in the Southwest points out that upper-class Mexican women were sometimes seen marrying Anglos newly arrived from the east. The lighter skin color among these upper-class Mexican women made them favorable to race-conscious Anglos. In addition, the marriages gave Anglos opportunities for land acquisition. Mexican women's economic fortunes were tied to the large haciendas found throughout states such as California, where former Spanish landowners had once prevailed, and historians who examine the mid- to late 19th century in the Southwest have consistently noted how vast amounts of land once owned by Spanish *hacendados* (landowners) were later in the hands of Anglos. However, the misfortunes of former Mexican owners who lost their lands throughout the Southwest were only partially explained by intermarriages entered into by upper-class Mexican women and Anglo men.

In the 1920s, following the Mexican Revolution, José Vasconcelos, the minister of education, wrote a book about *mestizaje* in which he developed the notion of *la raza cósmica* (the cosmic race) to address the racial divide that existed in Mexico between those who were *más indio* (more Indian) and those who were *más europeo* (more European). The idea of the cosmic race, in which all Hispanic people would eventually be blended into one mixed, unified race, was an interesting but problematic one, which has reappeared throughout the 20th century, as in the contemporary use of the term *raza* as a catchall phrase for all Latinos, even though a substantial portion of the Latino community—those from the Caribbean Basin in particular—would not fit into this rubric.

As migration from Mexico increased during the 20th century, the racial hierarchy between Mexican Americans and Anglos throughout the Southwest became more pronounced. Anglos determined that Mexican Americans were just as "racially inferior" to them as they had perceived African Americans and Native Americans to be. The effects of race on the "life chances" of Chicanos could be determined, therefore, by the dominant group's (in this case, Anglos) perception of them.

In one study researchers found that life chances for darker-skinned Chicanos who tended toward the Native American phenotype were more likely to be found at lower socioeconomic levels than those of Chicanos whose phenotype more resembled that of a lighter-skinned European. Drawing on data from the 1979 Chicano survey conducted by the Survey Research Center at the University of Michigan, Carlos Arce and associates found evidence to suggest that dark-skinned Chicanos were more likely to experience discrimination. Their investigation showed that the dark (Indian) group earned less than the light (European) group. The earning disparity was only one of the conclusions of the analysis of the effects of phenotype differences on Chicano life chances. Dark-skinned Chicanos had fewer socioeconomic benefits attributed to them; indeed, light-skinned

Chicanos were by all accounts able to out-achieve their dark-skinned counterparts.

A study by sociologist John Logan of U.S. Census data determined that "black" Latinos experienced lower incomes, less education, and fewer opportunities when compared with those who defined themselves as "white" Hispanics. Logan's examination of the 939,000 Hispanics who identified themselves as black suggested that black Hispanics endured similar socioeconomic disparities as those experienced by African Americans. In short, black Hispanics seemed to be more affected by the issue of race than light-skinned Hispanics. Black Latinos were mostly found among Dominican Americans, Puerto Rican Americans, and some Mexican Americans.

Puerto Ricans

Since race is seen as part of one's "social marker" in a society such as that of the United States, issues of race become quite complex for Latinos who vary from light skinned to dark skinned. One example of racial diversity among Latinos can be understood from observing Puerto Ricans. As sociologist Clara E. Rodriguez reports, Puerto Ricans have been labeled the "rainbow" people, since a broad array of racial "colors" are found in Puerto Rico: "*blancos,* the equivalent of Whites in this country; *indios,* similar to the U.S. conception of (Asian) Indians, that is, dark skinned and straight haired; *morenos,* dark skinned and with a variety of Negroid or Caucasian features; and *negros,* equivalent to very dark-skinned Black people in the United States." Given the previous narrow paradigm for classifying racial groups in the United States, such as the one-drop rule to classify African Americans, Puerto Ricans challenge the former black and white classification.

The history of Puerto Ricans raised on the island homeland has had a significant impact on their settlement on the mainland, where they are made conscious of their dark-skinned features. In the United States the general social taboo against interracial marriage is not found among Puerto Ricans. Dark-skinned Puerto Ricans and light-skinned Puerto Ricans have consistently intermarried. Once on the mainland, where the racial divide has been biologically, sociologically, and legally demarcated, Puerto Ricans have to adjust to their new surroundings.

Just as many cities in the U.S. Southwest can be labeled as Mexican American settling areas—such as San Antonio, Texas, and Los Angeles—New York

City has been a primary settling region for Puerto Ricans. There have been three different waves of Puerto Rican migration to the mainland. In each of those periods Puerto Ricans have been made aware of their racial background. Many dark-skinned Puerto Ricans have had to endure the same racism experienced by blacks in the United States. A study of the effects of race on the life chances of Puerto Ricans in New York City, similar to the one that Arce and associates conducted on Chicanos, found results supporting fewer opportunities for dark-skinned Puerto Ricans. Employing data from the 1980 census, sociologist Clara Rodríguez's research led to some important findings. Using the categories of "White," "Black, "and "Other," Rodríguez was able to see the effects race had on Puerto Ricans. Some Puerto Ricans elected to identify themselves as racially white; the black category was used to identify Puerto Ricans who considered themselves black or Spanish; in the "other" category Puerto Rican respondents wrote in *Puerto Rican, Boricua,* or some other Spanish descriptor. Within the statistical analysis race was examined from a number of different independent variables (for example, education, labor force participation, age, sex, and so forth). Among the significant results Rodríguez found was that in most cases it was the category of "Other" that was most affected by racial background. For example, lower incomes were associated more often with the category of "Other" than with that of "Black" or "White." Additional findings in Rodríguez's analysis of racial differences for New York Puerto Ricans continued to demonstrate the disadvantages of those who categorized themselves as "Other." Among men who picked the "Other" category, the disadvantages were in the areas of poverty, education, jobs, and incomes.

An examination of Latinos in the Northeast with respect to the effects of skin color on Puerto Ricans and Dominican men and women also produced interesting results. Employing data from the Boston Social Survey Data of Urban Inequality, Christina Gómez examined the correlation of skin-color to differences in employment, education, and other social rewards. Gomez found that light-skinned Latino males, especially Puerto Ricans and Dominicans, had positive results: "Lighter skinned Latinos had more education, owned more homes at higher rates, were more likely to be married, and used Spanish more often as language for communication than their darker skinned counterparts." Puerto Rican and Do-

minican Latinas, according to Gomez's results, had fewer problems associated with their skin color. Indeed, Gomez suggested the following results: "For Latinas, in this sample, only union membership and industry [occupation] variables are significant, whereas skin color, marriage, and union membership are significant for Latinos."

Racial divisions continue to be a source of social inequality, affecting the opportunities afforded to Latinos in the United States. Race ultimately has an impact on housing ownership, job discrimination, educational opportunities, and racial intermixing among Latinos and non-Latinos. Black Latinos, a new racial category created by the U.S. Census as of 2000, was employed to account for the growing number of Latinos who identified as black. The census count for the number of Latinos who chose the "Black" category was significantly higher than that previously predicted by researchers.

Cubans

Since the Cuban Revolution there have been two significant migrations to the United States from Cuba. The first occurred shortly after Fidel Castro came into power, the second in the late 1970s. There were different reasons for the sudden migrations of Cubans, and different racial backgrounds of Cubans characterized each of the two waves.

The first wave, beginning in the early 1960s, when the U.S. government labeled immigrants from Cuba as political refugees fleeing a repressive Communist regime, was marked by the large number of middle- and upper-middle-class Cubans. Not only were these immigrants educated persons from business-class backgrounds, many of them were also light skinned. Just as in other areas of Latin America, light-skinned Cubans could be seen holding the prestigious jobs prior to the revolution, and they more or less reflected the pattern of racial stratification found in various parts of Latin America. Light-skinned Latin Americans can often be seen in the best-paying jobs and holding leadership positions, and are seen more often in the popular media. In contrast, dark-skinned Latin Americans are less fortunate. Indian-looking Latin Americans are more prone to discrimination; within Mexico and various other regions of Latin America, the racial stratification between light-skinned Hispanics and Indian-looking Hispanics is well known. Those who are Indian-looking are less likely to have access to higher paying jobs; they are not often seen

holding leadership positions; and if seen in the media, they are likely to be secondary figures in the popular "telenovellas" of Univisión and Telemundo.

In the late 1970s Fidel Castro, in an attempt to embarrass the United States, allowed Cubans to emigrate. Unknown to U.S. officials, many of them in this second wave of migration were former criminals. These new arrivals had more problems adjusting to life in the United States, not just because they were immigrants but also because of their darker features. While the first wave of Cubans who immigrated following the Cuban Revolution had a somewhat easier time adjusting to life in the United States, the second wave of dark-skinned Cubans confronted the black-white paradigm of racial strife in the United States.

Conclusion

The topic of race continued into the 21st century. Racial diversity in the United States is increasing in several ways. First, with the passage of the 1965 Immigration Act, the growing number of immigrant groups from Latin American countries and also from Asian countries has changed the racial makeup of the United States. Second, high fertility rates among Latinos and Asians have helped to transform states such as California, where Latinos have become the majority population, replacing the Anglo majority of just a few decades earlier.

Nationally, with the recent ascent of Latinos to the largest minority group in America, the topic of race takes on a significantly different perspective. The discussion of race for most of the 20th century was examined through a black and white lens. Today Latinos complicate the racial discussion, not simply because of the size of their population, but also because they identify across the racial spectrum. Employing the old, broad racial categories of Caucasoid (white), Negroid (black), and Mongoloid (yellow)—no longer considered biologically valid—Latinos arguably fit into all three. The "re-emerging" Latino population has become crucial in redefining race relations in America. According to Lisa Navarrete, the spokesperson for the National Council of La Raza, "We need to formulate a new paradigm for race and ethnicity in the country." She further states, "It's not a black-white paradigm in this country anymore, if it ever was." Lacking a significant Latino population presence during the 1960s, race relations in America were largely determined by differences between Af-

rican Americans and whites. The broadening of race relations in order to include Latinos suggests that social scientists must consider new ways of thinking about race relations.

In recent years Mexican American intellectuals such as Richard Rodriguez, the author of *Brown: The Last Discovery of America,* have delved into the debate on race as a way to understand where Latinos stand in the racial divide of the United States and how the country has changed in demographic and cultural terms. But while this discussion is allowing the general public to go beyond the discussion of blackness versus whiteness, its impact is still limited. No doubt the effect of the racial issue on the Latino community will have a tremendous impact on the continued settlement of Latinos in the United States.

It will remain to be seen how white people will react when they become a minority population in various regions in the United States. If the past is any indication of what can occur, there is a possibility that as whites feel their access to good-paying jobs, quality education, and segregated neighborhoods is threatened, the response would be increased nativism toward Latinos. In fact, anti-immigrant movements such as "Operation Gate Keeper" along the U.S.-Mexico border does not bode well for better cooperation between whites and Latinos. Additionally, the history of discrimination against persons with dark-skinned features is likely to persist as both Latinos and African American communities continue to find limited access to societal resources.

Racism will remain an issue for persons of color in the United States. Because Latinos fit into various categories from light skin to dark skin, the compromised life chances of dark-skinned Latinos are readily acknowledged by the various studies, which suggest their lower socioeconomic status. The United States, since its founding, has placed a premium on light skin color. By contrast, those with dark features have had to endure less advantage. It is quite likely that despite their increasing numbers, Latinos will continue to endure the affects of race on their opportunities in the United States.

RELATED ARTICLES

Affirmative Action; African Americans, Influence and Relations; Brownness; Civil Rights; Discrimination; Mestizaje; Nativism; Passing; Stereotypes and Stereotyping.

FURTHER READING

Almaguer, Tomás. *Racial Fault Lines: The History of White Supremacy in California.* Berkeley: Univ. of Calif. Press, 1994.

Arce, Carlos, H., et al. "Phenotype and Life Chances among Chicanos." *Hispanic Journal of Behavioral Sciences* 9, no. 1 (1987).

Gómez, Christina. "The Continual Significance of Skin Color: An Exploratory Study of Latinos in the Northeast." *Hispanic Journal of Behavioral Science* 22, no. 1 (2000).

Johnson, Kevin R., ed. *Mixed Race and the Law: A Reader.* New York: N.Y. Univ. Press, 2003.

Logan, John. *How Race Counts for Hispanic Americans.* Albany, N.Y.: Lewis Mumford Ctr., Univ. of Albany, 2003.

Marger, Martin N. *Race and Ethnic Relations: American and Global Perspectives.* 6th ed. Belmont, Calif.: Wadsworth, 2003.

Omi, Michael, and Howard Winant. *Racial Formation in the United States: From the 1960s to the 1980s.* New York: Routledge, 1986.

Rodríguez, Clara E. *Puerto Ricans Born in the U.S.A.* Boulder, Colo.: Westview Press, 1989.

Rodríguez, Clara E., and Héctor Cordero-Guzmán. "Placing Race in Context." *Ethnic and Racial Studies* 14, no. 4 (1992).

Rodriguez, Richard. *Brown: The Last Discovery of America.* New York: Viking, 2002.

PAUL LÓPEZ